W9-BIK-408

T Volume 19

The World Book Encyclopedia

World Book, Inc.
a Scott Fetzer company
Chicago

The World Book Encyclopedia

World Book, Inc.
233 North Michigan Avenue
Chicago, IL 60601

www.worldbook.com

Library of Congress Cataloging-in-Publication Data

The World Book encyclopedia.—2006 ed.
p. cm.
Includes bibliographical references and index.
ISBN 0-7166-0106-0
1. Encyclopedias and dictionaries. I. World Book, Inc.

AE5 .W55 2006
031—dc22

2005016631

Printed in the United States of America

06 5 4 3 2 1

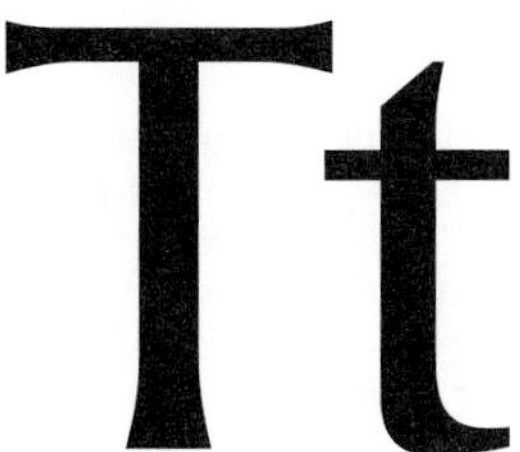

T is the 20th letter of our alphabet. It was also a letter in the alphabet of the Semites, who once lived in Syria and Palestine. They called the letter *taw,* their word for *mark.* They used a cross-shaped mark they may have borrowed from an Egyptian *hieroglyphic* (picture symbol) used as a check mark. The Greeks borrowed the letter from the Phoenicians. However, when the Greeks adopted the letter, they moved the crossbar to the top of the vertical stroke. The Greeks called their letter *tau.* See **Alphabet.**

Uses. *T* or *t* is about the second most frequently used letter in books, newspapers, and other printed material in English. As an abbreviation in geographic names, it may stand for *territory* or *township.* As a musical abbreviation, *t* may indicate *tenor, tempo,* or *time.* In grammars and dictionaries, it means *tense* or *transitive.* It may also stand for *ton, temperature,* or *Testament,* as in *O.T.,* or *Old Testament.*

Pronunciation. A person pronounces *t* by placing the point of the tongue on the upper teethridge, with the lips and vocal cords open, and expelling the breath between the teeth and tongue. In such words as *fasten* or *castle,* the *t* is silent. In the combination *tion, t* may be pronounced *sh* as in *nation,* or *ch* as in *question.* In the combination *th,* as in *thin,* a person pronounces *t* by placing the tongue blade below the points of the upper teeth and expelling the breath between the tongue and teeth, with the vocal cords relaxed. In words like *thine,* the process is the same, but the vocal cords vibrate. See **Pronunciation.** Marianne Cooley

Development of the letter T

The ancient Egyptians used this check mark about 3000 B.C.

The Semites, about 1500 B.C., used a cross-shaped letter that they called *taw,* their word for *mark.*

The Phoenicians had a cross-shaped letter in their alphabet about 1000 B.C.

The Greeks, about 600 B.C., put the crossbar at the top of the vertical stroke. They called the letter *tau.*

The Romans gave the letter T its capital form about A.D. 114.

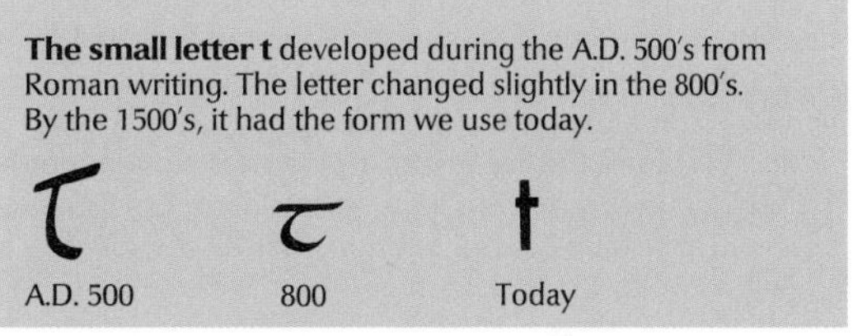

The small letter t developed during the A.D. 500's from Roman writing. The letter changed slightly in the 800's. By the 1500's, it had the form we use today.

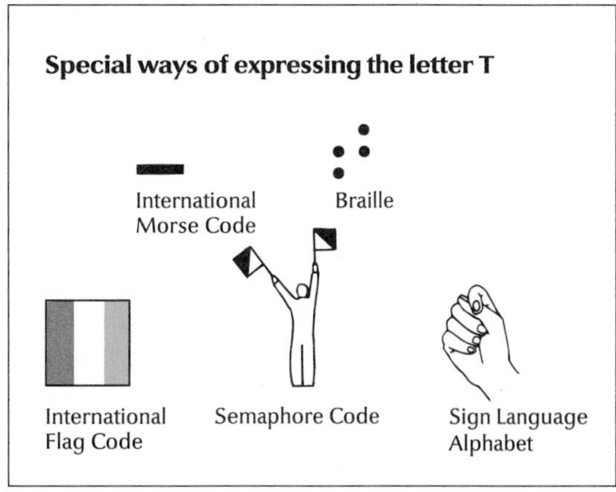

Special ways of expressing the letter T

Common forms of the letter T

Handwritten letters vary from person to person. *Manuscript* (printed) letters have straight lines, *left,* and simple curves. Cursive letters, *right,* have flowing lines.

Tt *Tt*

Roman letters have small finishing strokes called *serifs* that extend from the main strokes. The type face shown above is Baskerville. The italic form appears at the right.

Tt *Tt*

Sans-serif letters are also called *gothic letters.* They have no serifs. The type face shown above is called Futura. The italic form of Futura appears at the right.

T

Computer letters have special shapes. Computers can "read" these letters either optically or by means of the magnetic ink with which the letters may be printed.

T cell. See Thymus.

Tabasco, *tuh BAS koh* or *tah VAHS koh,* is a state of southeastern Mexico along the Bay of Campeche (see **Mexico** [political map]). Tabasco has a population of 1,889,367 and an area of 9,756 square miles (25,267 square kilometers). It lies on a low, tropical plain, much of which is marshy. Tabasco is the largest source of petroleum in Mexico. Its chief farm products include bananas, coconuts, cacao, and sugar cane. The large forests produce hardwoods, rubber, resins, and dyes. Tabasco was crossed by Hernando Cortés in 1524. It is one of the original states of Mexico. Villahermosa is its capital. James D. Riley

See also **Olmec Indians**.

Tabernacle, also called the Tent of Meeting, was the center of worship of the Israelites during early Biblical times. According to the Book of Exodus, the Hebrews built the Tabernacle during their wanderings in the desert. Its purpose was to provide a symbolic dwelling place for God in the midst of the Israelite camp or settlement. Other places of worship are sometimes called tabernacles.

While on Mount Sinai, Moses received instructions for building the Tabernacle. The materials were provided by the free offerings of the people. The Tabernacle was dedicated on the first day of the second year after the Israelites fled from Egypt on their way to the Promised Land (modern Israel).

According to the Bible, the place of worship was 45 feet (14 meters) long and had a height and width of 15 feet (4.6 meters). Its framework of acacia wood was overlaid with fine gold. The ceiling was of white linen with figures of blue, purple, and scarlet angels woven into it. The structure was covered with a curtain of goat's hair and a layer of skins. A veil of linen divided the inside into the Holy of Holies and the Holy Place. The Holy of Holies contained the Ark of the Covenant, which held the Tables of the Law—the Ten Commandments.

The Ark was called the Ark of the Covenant because it was a symbol of the Jews' *covenant* (agreement) with God. Above the Ark was a cover of gold with a figure called a cherub at each end. In the Holy Place were the table of the *shewbread* (bread made without yeast), the altar of incense, and a candlestick, all made of gold.

The Tabernacle stood within a court, enclosed by rich curtains and brass pillars. It opened toward the east and faced the altar where the people brought their sacrifices to be offered by the priests. The court also contained a *laver* (basin), where the priests washed their hands and feet before entering the Holy Place.

The Tabernacle could be carried from place to place. The Bible reports that it was moved from the desert to Gilgal, then to Shiloh after the Israelites conquered Canaan. Later, it was moved to Jerusalem, where its relics were preserved in Solomon's Temple. B. Barry Levy

See also **Ark of the Covenant; Temple.**

Tabernacles, Feast of. See Sukkot.

Tabes, *TAY beez,* is a medical term that refers to the wasting away of the body. Today, physicians use the term almost exclusively to describe a wasting of the nervous system caused by advanced, untreated syphilis, a sexually transmitted disease (see **Syphilis**). If the syphilis infection is located in the spinal cord, the *dorsal* (back) portion of the spinal cord may begin to waste away. This condition is is referred to as *tabes dorsalis.* The condition is characterized by *lightning pains* (sudden, sharp pains), a loss of coordination, and abnormalities of the eye and pupil. Early treatment of syphilis with penicillin or other antibiotics can prevent the development of tabes. Marc B. Garnick

Illustration from the *First Leningrad Bible;* Leningrad Public Library

The Tabernacle was an ornate portable place of worship that the Israelites built during their wanderings in the desert. This fragment from a Bible dating from A.D. 929 shows the Tabernacle and its implements. A fence with a triple gate encloses the Tabernacle. In the center, a sacred candlestick called a *menorah* appears in the court, beneath the Ark of the Covenant.

David R. Frazier

Table tennis, also called *ping-pong,* provides indoor recreation for people of all ages. Many schools and youth clubs have table tennis tables, which can be used by two or four players.

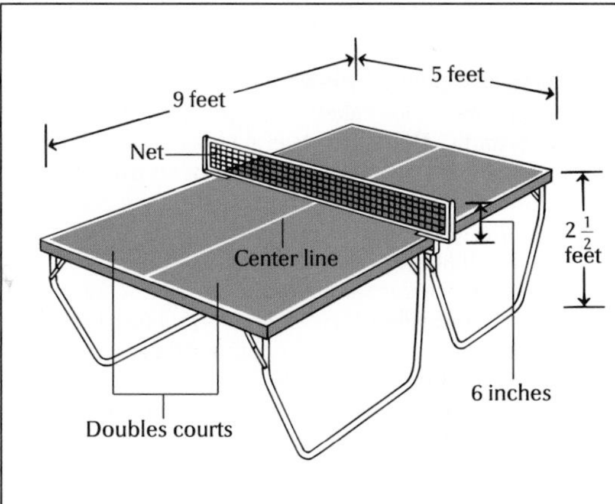

A table tennis table is divided into halves by a low net. A white center line further divides the surface of the table into four courts, which are used when playing doubles.

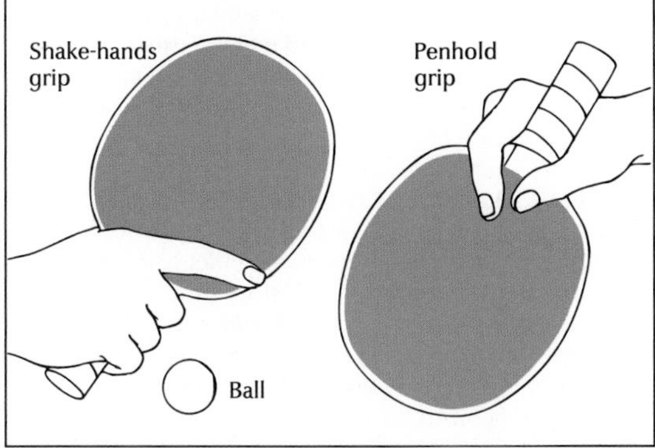

WORLD BOOK illustrations by Richard Fickle

Two ways to hold a table tennis racket are shown here. The *shake-hands grip* is used by most players in the United States and other Western countries.

Table tennis, or ping-pong, is a lively indoor game that resembles a miniature version of tennis. The players use rackets, which are often called *paddles,* to hit a ball back and forth over a net that stretches across a table. They score points by hitting the ball so their opponent or opponents cannot return it. Table tennis may be played by two or four persons. If two persons play, the game is called *singles.* If four play, the game is called *doubles.*

Table tennis developed in Britain during the late 1800's. Today, it is a popular form of recreation and an international sport. Players from about 140 countries belong to the International Table Tennis Federation (ITTF). The ITTF holds a world championship tournament every two years. USA Table Tennis sponsors national tournaments, including the U.S. National Championships and the U.S. Open.

Equipment for table tennis consists of a table, net, rackets, and ball. The table measures 9 feet (274 centimeters) long, 5 feet (152.5 centimeters) wide, and 30 inches (76 centimeters) high. Most tables are dark green with a white line along the edges. A white center line runs the length of the table. The center line divides the table into *courts* that are used for doubles. The net, which is suspended between two posts, extends across the width of the table at its center. The net measures 6 inches (15.25 centimeters) high.

The rackets may be any shape, size, or weight. All are made of wood and are covered with pimpled or smooth sponge. Each side must be of a uniform dark color, though the sides may be different colors. The covering material cannot be more than $\frac{1}{6}$ inch (4 millimeters) thick on either side of the racket.

The ball is round and hollow and made of Celluloid. It measures 38 millimeters ($1\frac{1}{2}$ inches) in diameter and weighs 2.5 grams ($\frac{1}{11}$ ounce).

How the game is played. Table tennis players toss a coin to determine who serves first. The server places the ball on the palm of the hand, throws it up vertically, and hits it with the racket. When throwing the ball, the server must keep the fingers straight and together, and the thumb extended. The hand must be behind the end of the table when the server hits the ball. The ball must bounce on the server's side of the net, clear the net, and bounce on the opponent's side.

For a good return, a player must hit the ball after one bounce so that it clears the net and bounces on the opponent's court. *Volleying* (hitting the ball before it bounces) is not allowed. Play continues until one person misses the ball, hits it off the table, or hits it into the net. When a player fails to make a good serve or a good return, the opponent scores a point. After every five points, the other player serves.

The player who first scores 21 points wins the game. However, the winner must have at least a two-point lead. If both players score 20 points, they alternate serving after each point until one person leads by 2 points. A match consists of either two out of three games or three out of five games.

When playing doubles, the player who is serving must do so from his or her right-hand court into the opponents' right-hand court. The teammates must alternate in hitting the ball on the returns.

Critically reviewed by USA Table Tennis

Taboo is an action, object, person, or place forbidden by law or culture. The word *taboo* comes from the Polynesian word *tapu,* or *tabu,* which means *something sacred, special, dangerous,* or *unclean.* Many societies believe that people who go to a taboo place or touch a taboo object will suffer serious injury. Society may also punish the offenders or may consider them to be taboo.

Sacred objects or people are taboo because they supposedly have a mysterious force that enables them to injure or kill a person. Unclean objects are taboo because they supposedly bring evil to a person or group.

People in many parts of the world avoid taboos. Until the 1900's, for example, Fiji Islanders could not touch any article that belonged to the tribal chief or priest. Australian Aborigines must not say the name of a dead person aloud. Muslims and Orthodox Jews must not eat pork or shellfish. All societies consider *incest* taboo. They forbid marriage or sexual relations between closely related people, such as a brother and sister. See also **Magic** (The magician; Homeopathic magic); **Mythology** (Mythology of the Pacific Islands). Alan Dundes

Tabriz, *tuh BREEZ* (pop. 1,191,043), is one of the largest cities in Iran. It is the capital of East Azerbaijan province, in the northwestern corner of Iran. It lies about 35 miles (56 kilometers) from Lake Urmia and is almost surrounded by mountains. For location, see **Iran** (map). Earthquakes have nearly destroyed the city several times.

Tabriz is famous for its fine Persian rugs, and it has a large trade in dried fruits and leather goods. The city also produces flour, matches, and textiles.

Historians do not know exactly when the city was founded, but it was probably before the A.D. 300's. It was Iran's capital briefly in the early 1500's. Russian troops occupied Tabriz in 1827 and during World War I (1914-1918) and World War II (1939-1945). In 1990, a major earthquake struck Tabriz, causing thousands of deaths and extensive property damage. Michel Le Gall

Taché, *ta SHAY,* **Sir Étienne-Paschal,** *ay TYEHN PAS kuhl* (1795-1865), a Canadian statesman, served as prime minister of the Province of Canada twice. He presided over the 1864 Quebec Conference, paving the way for federation of the British North American colonies.

Taché was born on Sept. 5, 1795, in St.-Thomas, Lower Canada (part of present-day Quebec). In 1841, he was elected to the Legislative Assembly of the Province of Canada as a moderate reformer. He later served as commissioner of public works, speaker of the legislative council, and receiver-general. Taché worked hard to develop an alliance between French-Canadian moderates and English-Canadian Conservatives in the province.

In 1856 and again in 1864, Taché became a coleader of the province's government with John A. Macdonald, a statesman from Upper Canada (part of present-day Ontario). The two men were associate prime ministers. Macdonald dominated both ministries, but Taché had influence. Taché was knighted in 1858. J. M. Bumsted

See also **Macdonald, Sir John A.**

Tachometer, *tuh KAHM uh tuhr,* is a device that measures how fast an object spins. The spinning object may be an engine shaft, an automobile wheel, or a computer disk. Tachometers typically measure the speed of rotation by counting the number of complete turns the object makes in one minute, called *revolutions per minute* or *rpm.*

A simple kind of tachometer employs a device called a *sensor* attached to the spinning object. This type of tachometer counts one revolution each time the sensor spins one complete turn. A computer records the number of turns over a certain period. To calculate the speed in rpm, the computer divides the number of turns by the number of minutes that have passed. Some tachometers use many sensors placed around the spinning object to record rotation speed more precisely.

Many tachometers use magnets to measure the speed of rotation. A magnet attached to a spinning object produces an *electric field,* a region around the object in which electric force can be felt. The voltage of the field is *proportional* to the speed of the spinning object—that is, the faster the object spins, the higher the voltage will be. Such a tachometer measures the voltage of the electric field to determine the rotation speed.

In automobiles and other vehicles, tachometers measure the engine speed to control the flow of fuel to the engine and to signal the transmission to shift gears. In a vehicle with manual transmission, a tachometer gauge helps the driver decide when to shift gears. A compact disc (CD) player or disk drive must spin at precisely the correct speed to read a CD or computer disk. These devices use a tachometer to measure and control the speed of rotation. Greg R. Luecke

Tachycardia, *tak uh KAHR dee uh,* is an unusually fast heartbeat sometimes called *palpitation.* The disorder is usually organic. There are several types of tachycardia, depending upon the chamber of the heart from which the palpitations originate and how often they occur. For example, *paroxysmal atrial tachycardia* (*PAT*) is a rapid heart action that originates in the heart's *atria* (upper chambers) and occurs at intervals. Bruce A. Reitz

See also **Defibrillator; Heart** (Abnormal heart rhythms).

Tachyon, *TAK ee ahn,* is a hypothetical elementary particle. An elementary particle is a subatomic particle that has no known smaller parts. If tachyons exist in nature, they never stand still but always move at speeds greater than the speed of light. Light travels 186,282 miles (299,792 kilometers) per second. The faster a tachyon travels, the lower its energy. The name *tachyon* comes from a Greek word meaning *swift.*

According to the special theory of relativity, ordinary matter can move only at speeds less than the speed of light. The German American physicist Albert Einstein published the special theory of relativity in 1905. But in 1962, several physicists realized that the existence of particles that travel faster than light is not necessarily incompatible with Einstein's theory. No convincing experimental evidence has been found for the existence of tachyons. Joel R. Primack

Tacitus, *TAS ih tuhs,* **Cornelius,** *kawr NEE lee uhs* (about A.D. 55-about 120), was one of the world's greatest historians. His most important works were the *Annals,* which described Roman history from Augustus's death to Nero's death, and the *Histories,* which covered the emperors from Galba to Domitian. Part of the *Annals* and all but the first few books of *Histories* have been lost. Tacitus favored the republican form of government. His *Histories* and *Annals* strongly criticized the Roman emperors. He condemned them in sharp, unforgettable phrases and ignored any merits of the imperial system. The *Histories* and *Annals* cover periods for which other sources are scanty. Another work, *Germania,* is important because it contains one of the first written accounts of the customs and habits of the Germanic peoples, who later spread over most of western Europe. Tacitus also wrote *Life of Agricola* and *Dialogue on Orators.*

Tacitus was probably born in northern Italy. He led an active public life and was *consul* (chief magistrate) in A.D. 97. He served as governor of the Roman province of Asia in 112 and 113. D. Brendan Nagle

Tackle. See **Block and tackle.**

Tacoma, *tuh KOH muh* (pop. 193,556; met. area pop. 700,820), is one of the largest cities in Washington. This seaport is also an industrial and commercial center, and the heart of a major military complex. The city lies on Commencement Bay, an inlet of Puget Sound, between Seattle and Olympia (see **Washington** [political map]).

Tacoma is located between the Olympic Mountains on the west and the Cascade Mountains on the east. The city rises steeply from the bay to more than 400 feet (120 meters) above sea level. The Puyallup River flows through the city from Mount Rainier, which lies about 40 miles (65 kilometers) to the southeast. The name *Tacoma* is the Indian word for Mount Rainier, which is the state's highest peak at 14,410 feet (4,392 meters).

Seattle-Tacoma International Airport, several smaller airports, railroads, and steamship lines serve the Tacoma area. The Tacoma Narrows Bridge, one of the world's longest suspension bridges, crosses Puget Sound and connects Tacoma with the Kitsap Peninsula.

Tacoma is one of the nation's chief gateways of trade. Major imports include automobiles, automobile parts, clothing, and ore. Exports include grain, logs, wood and paper products, and synthetic resins. Tacoma was a shipbuilding center for many years, but that industry had declined greatly by the 1980's. The city is a center for chemical processing and metal processing. It is also the home of a large forest products industry, including milling, woodworking, furniture making, and pulp and papermaking. The city operates hydroelectric dams on rivers draining the Cascade and Olympic mountains.

Several military bases and military medical facilities operate in the area. Near the outskirts of the city are Fort Lewis, McChord Air Force Base, and Madigan Army Medical Center. Tacoma is the home of the University of Puget Sound, Pacific Lutheran University, and campuses of the University of Washington and Evergreen State College. The glass-walled Greater Tacoma Convention and Trade Center is one of the state's largest meeting and convention facilities. The Tacoma Dome, a large domed arena, hosts many concerts and sporting events.

Puyallup Indians occupied what is now Tacoma before the first white settlers arrived. The Puyallup now have a reservation in the city and an adjoining area. White people settled the region when a sawmill was built near the bay in 1852. In 1868, two settlements developed, called Tacoma and Tacoma City. In 1873, the Northern Pacific Railroad chose a site called New Tacoma for the western end of its transcontinental railroad. Service to the eastern United States began in 1883. The villages merged into a single city in 1884. Tacoma has a council-manager form of government. It is the seat of Pierce County. Glenn Storbeck

See also **Washington** (picture).

© Jim Richardson, Corbis

Tacoma is one of the largest cities in Washington state and an important U.S. port. It lies on an inlet of Puget Sound. Mount Rainier, *background,* rises southeast of Tacoma.

Taconite, *TAK uh nyt,* is an extremely hard rock that serves as an important source of iron metal. It consists mainly of a flintlike form of quartz called *chert.* The chert contains small flecks or thin bands rich in the iron oxide minerals *magnetite* and *hematite.* Taconite mined for iron ore typically contains 17 to 35 percent iron.

Taconite often forms deposits called *banded iron formations.* These formations consist of bands of chert containing varying amounts of iron oxide. Millions of years ago, water deposited the chert and iron oxide as layers of tiny particles called *sediments.* Over time, the layers of sediment hardened into rock. Large banded iron formations are found in Australia, Brazil, Canada, China, India, Russia, southern and western Africa, and the United States. The name *taconite* comes from the Taconic Mountains of Massachusetts, New York, and Vermont, where small amounts of the rock are found. The Mesabi Range of northern Minnesota contains enormous quantities of taconite. The range includes a belt of relatively iron-rich taconite that is more than 100 miles (160 kilometers) long and several miles or kilometers wide.

For hundreds of years, people have known that the world's taconite formations contain large amounts of iron ore. Until the 1950's, however, companies did not mine taconite because the rock was too hard and contained too little iron to be produced at a profit. In the mid-1950's, scientists developed new techniques and equipment to profitably mine taconite and extract the iron ore. Taconite mining greatly increased the world's available supply of iron.

Most taconite is mined using a device called a *jet*

E. R. Degginger

Taconite is a hard rock that contains iron.

piercing machine. The machine shoots alternating streams of burning kerosene and cold water at the rock. The flame heats the taconite to about 4700 °F (2600 °C). The water then cools the rock suddenly, causing it to break apart. By repeating this process, the jet piercing machine bores holes in the rock. Workers then insert explosives in the holes to blast the taconite into chunks that can be removed.

After mining, taconite is processed to increase its iron content. First, machines crush the chunks of taconite into smaller pieces. Workers mix these pieces with water and feed the mixture into machines that grind the taconite into sand-sized particles. Magnets extract the particles that contain much iron. The iron-poor residue, called *tailings,* is discarded as waste material. The wet, iron-rich powder, called the *concentrate,* is mixed with clay in rotating steel cylinders. The sticky mixture forms marble-sized balls that contain 60 to 65 percent iron. The balls are then baked to harden them into pellets for shipping. The pellets have a more uniform size and iron content than unprocessed ore, enabling iron and steel manufacturers to process them into metal more efficiently. Mark Cloos

See also **Iron and steel** (Taconite); **Minnesota** (The mid-1900's).

Tadpole, also called *polliwog,* is an immature frog or toad. A tadpole is a *larva,* which is an early stage of an animal. Tadpoles live in water. When a tadpole hatches from its egg, it looks like a small fish. The tadpole grows larger and eventually develops the physical characteristics of the mature animal. The process of changing from a larva to an adult is called *metamorphosis.* The tadpole stage may last from 10 days to more than 2 years, depending on the species of frog or toad.

Tadpoles live in shallow waters wherever frogs and toads are found. Most tadpoles inhabit ponds, lakes, or slow-moving rivers. The greatest variety of tadpoles live in the tropics. Most tadpoles hatch from a jellylike mass of eggs laid in the water. A tadpole has a large, rounded head and a long, flat tail. It uses the tail to propel itself through the water. Tadpoles breathe by means of gills. Most tadpoles eat algae and plant material.

Most tadpoles are dark-colored, varying from solid black in common toads to olive-green in some frogs. Tadpoles usually grow less than 1 inch (2.5 centimeters) long. But bullfrog tadpoles are over 4 inches (10 centimeters) long. Tadpoles of the paradoxical frog of South America grow over 10 inches (25 centimeters) in length.

A tadpole has no legs when it hatches, but it begins to grow hind legs during the first stages of metamorphosis. Gradually, its head flattens and the tail becomes shorter. The digestive system changes, enabling the tadpole to eat insects and other animals. During the final stages of metamorphosis, the tadpole's front legs appear. The gills disappear as lungs develop, forcing the tadpole to gulp air at the water's surface. The animal absorbs the remaining part of the tail after emerging from the water to become a land-living adult. See also **Frog** (with pictures); **Toad.** J. Whitfield Gibbons

Tadzhikistan. See Tajikistan.

Tae kwon do, *TY kwahn DOH,* is a Korean martial art that resembles the Japanese technique called *karate.* Tae kwon do is famous for its wide range of kicks. In Korean, *tae* means *kick, kwon* means punch, and *do* means *art* or *way.* Tae kwon do also emphasizes breaking power, such as splitting wood, smashing bricks, or destroying tiles with the bare hands and feet. Training consists of a variety of punching, kicking, dodging, jumping, parrying, and blocking techniques. It also includes sparring and learning formalized pattern of movements called *hyung.*

The beginnings of tae kwon do are obscure. Historians believe it originated in a martial arts form called t'aekyon over 1,000 years ago. Beginning about 1910, the introduction of Chinese and Japanese techniques transformed the older art. Like most martial arts, tae kwon do changed in the late 1900's, when it was practiced increasingly as a combat sport. Paul Crompton

See also **Martial arts.**

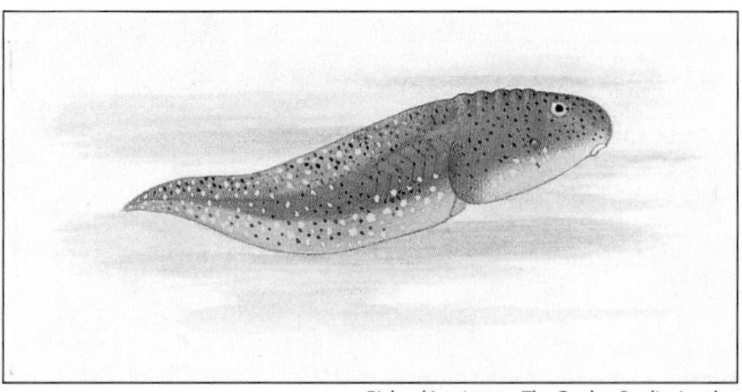

Richard Lewington, The Garden Studio, London

A newly hatched tadpole resembles a small fish. Eventually, the animal develops the physical traits of a mature frog or toad. The tadpole stage may last only 10 days or as long as 2 years.

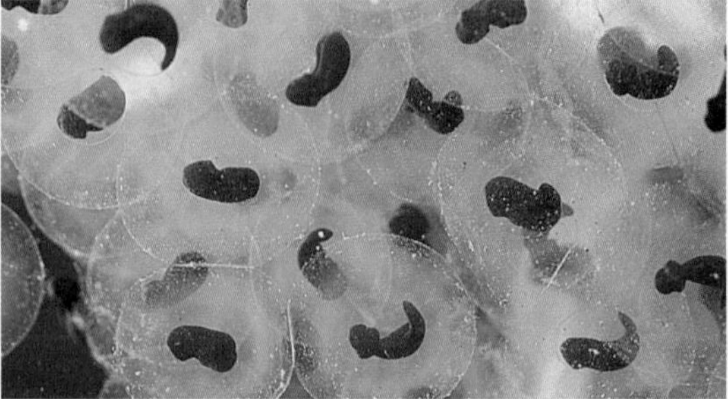

Jane Burton, Bruce Coleman Inc.

Eggs of the common European frog are jellylike and transparent. Inside each egg is an unborn tadpole. The rounded head and long tail of some of them have already formed.

Taegu, *ty goo* (pop. 2,473,990), is South Korea's third largest city. Seoul and Pusan have more people. Taegu lies in southern South Korea (see **Korea, South** [political map]). It is a commercial and educational center.

Taegu stands on a fertile plain and is surrounded by huge mountains on the north and south. Its landmarks include the Talsong fortress, which dates from the A.D. 200's, and many Confucian shrines. The city has two universities, a women's college, and several technical schools. Buddhist monasteries lie in the mountains around Taegu. The city ranks as South Korea's largest producer of textiles, and it is a market for farm products and minerals of its area.

Korean people had established a settlement on the site of what is now Taegu by A.D. 366. Taegu became a major commercial center during the 1400's.

Chong-Sik Lee

Tafari, Ras. See **Haile Selassie I.**

Taft, Lorado (1860-1936), was an American sculptor, teacher, and writer. He is best remembered for *The History of American Sculpture* (1903), the first book on the subject. Taft also wrote *Modern Tendencies in Sculpture* (1921), which attacked abstract sculpture and defended the conservative academic tradition.

Taft's best-known sculptures include *Fountain of Columbus* (1912) in Washington, D.C., *Fountain of the Great Lakes* (1913) and *Fountain of Time* (1922) in Chicago, *Thatcher Memorial Fountain* (1917) in Denver, and *Young Lincoln* (1917) and *Alma Mater* (1929) in Urbana, Illinois. In 1911, Taft completed a giant outdoor statue of the Indian chief Black Hawk near Oregon, Illinois.

Lorenzo Zadoc Taft was born on April 29, 1860, in Elmwood, Illinois. He graduated from what is now the University of Illinois in 1879. He studied sculpture in Paris from 1880 to 1883 and from 1884 to 1886. He established a studio in Chicago and taught at the Art Institute of Chicago and the University of Illinois from 1886 to 1929. He died on Oct. 30, 1936. George Gurney

Taft, Robert Alphonso (1889-1953), was an American statesman. He was called Mr. Republican because of his influence as a policymaker in his party.

Taft was born on Sept. 8, 1889, in Cincinnati, Ohio. His father, William Howard Taft, became the nation's 27th president. The younger Taft attended Yale University and Harvard Law School. He practiced law in Cincinnati and served in the Ohio legislature. Taft won election to the U.S. Senate in 1938 and was reelected in 1944 and 1950. He argued for a balanced budget and opposed most of President Franklin D. Roosevelt's proposals for domestic spending. He coauthored the Taft-Hartley Act of 1947, which set up controls over labor unions. Taft supported federal aid for housing and education.

Before World War II (1939-1945), Taft opposed major U.S. involvement in foreign affairs. But he later accepted U.S. policies aimed at blocking attempts by the Soviet Union and China to spread Communism to other lands.

Taft was a candidate for the Republican nomination for president in 1940, 1948, and 1952. He was the leading opponent of Dwight D. Eisenhower for the presidential nomination in 1952. After Eisenhower's election to the presidency, Taft became Senate majority leader and one of the president's most trusted advisers. He died on July 31, 1953. From 1971 to 1977, his son Robert A. Taft, Jr., served as a U.S. senator from Ohio. James T. Patterson

Artstreet

A Lorado Taft sculpture called *Fountain of the Great Lakes* (1913) stands outside the Art Institute of Chicago. Taft became known for creating large outdoor sculpture groups.

27th president of the United States 1909-1913

T. Roosevelt
26th president
1901-1909
Republican

Taft
27th president
1909-1913
Republican

Wilson
28th president
1913-1921
Democrat

James S. Sherman
Vice president
1909-1913

Oil painting by Anders L. Zorn (1911), © White House Historical Association (National Geographic Society)

Taft, William Howard (1857-1930), was president of the United States from 1909 to 1913. In 1921, he was named chief justice of the United States. He was the only person in U.S. history who served first as president, then as chief justice. Taft did not want to be president. At heart, he was a judge and had little taste for politics. Above all, he wanted to be a justice of the Supreme Court of the United States.

Before becoming president, Taft, a Republican, served as governor of the Philippines and as U.S. secretary of war under President Theodore Roosevelt. However, Taft spent most of the first 20 years of his career as a lawyer and judge. His mother recognized his distaste for politics. "I do not want my son to be president," she said. "His is a judicial mind and he loves the law." But Taft's wife opposed his career as a judge because she felt it was a "fixed groove."

In the end, Taft's mother proved to be right. Hardly any other president has been so unhappy in office. When Taft left the White House in 1913, he told incoming President Woodrow Wilson: "I'm glad to be going. This is the lonesomest place in the world." When he was appointed chief justice of the United States eight years later, Taft said it was the highest honor he ever received. He wrote: "The truth is that in my present life I don't remember that I ever was president."

Taft was the largest person ever to serve as president. He stood 6 feet (183 centimeters) tall and weighed more than 300 pounds (136 kilograms). A newspaperman wrote that he looked "like an American bison—a gentle, kind one." Taft had a mild, pleasant personality, but he clung firmly to what he considered the rugged virtues. He did not smoke or drink. He was honest by nature, plain of speech, and straightforward in action. He was completely, and sometimes blindly, loyal to his friends and to his political party.

The modest Taft felt he was not fully qualified for the presidency. He had no gift of showmanship like his predecessor, Theodore Roosevelt. Taft gave the public an adequate administration, but he failed to capture popular imagination. Many people called him a failure as president.

Early life

William Howard Taft was born in Cincinnati, Ohio, on Sept. 15, 1857. He was the second son of Alphonso Taft and Alphonso's second wife, Louise Maria Torrey Taft.

Alphonso Taft's ancestors had lived in Massachusetts and Vermont since emigrating from England in the 1600's. His wife was descended from an English family that helped settle Weymouth, Massachusetts, in 1640. Alphonso Taft, whose father was a Vermont judge, moved to Cincinnati about 1838. He became a successful lawyer and a nationally prominent figure in the Republican Party.

Will Taft was a large, fair, and attractive youth. He was brought up in the Unitarian faith. Two older half brothers, two younger brothers, and a younger sister were his playmates. They called Taft "Big Lub" because of his size. During the summers, the five Taft boys visited their Grandfather Torrey in Millbury, Massachusetts. He made them cut wood in his wood lot to pay for their vacations and also to teach them the value of money.

When Taft was 13 years old, he entered Woodward High School in Cincinnati. At 17, he enrolled in Yale College. In 1878, Taft graduated second in his class. He then studied law at the Cincinnati Law School. He received a law degree in 1880 and was admitted to the Ohio bar.

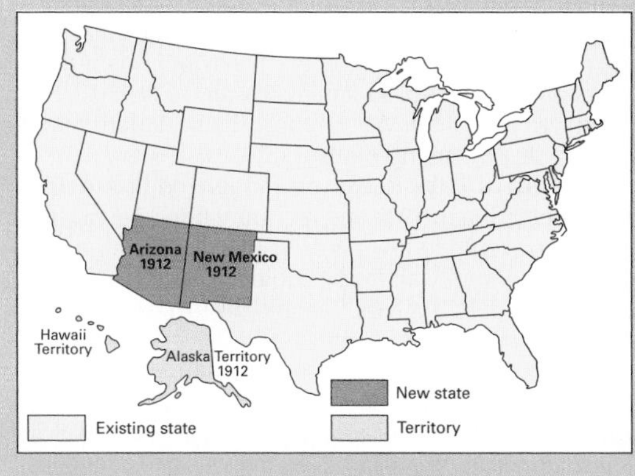

New Mexico and Arizona joined the Union during Taft's term. They became the 47th and 48th states in 1912. Congress established Alaska as a U.S. territory in 1912.

The United States flag had 46 stars when Taft took office. Two more stars—for New Mexico and Arizona—were added during his presidency.

The world of President Taft

The National Association for the Advancement of Colored People (NAACP) was founded in 1909 to promote racial equality.
The invention of Bakelite, the first completely synthetic resin, was a milestone in the plastics industry. New York chemist Leo Baekeland patented the substance in 1909.
Polar explorers gained world attention. In 1909, Robert Peary of the United States became the first person credited with reaching the North Pole. Norwegian explorer Roald Amundsen led the first successful expedition to the South Pole in 1911.
Revolution erupted in Mexico in 1910 and led to the overthrow of dictator Porfirio Díaz.
Youth organizations developed in the United States. Boy Scouts and Camp Fire Girls were founded in 1910. Girl Scouts was established in 1912.
Hollywood became the nation's movie capital after the first motion-picture studio was built there in 1911.
Ragtime music became popular and led to such new dance crazes as the "turkey trot."
The Republic of China was founded in 1912, with Sun Yat-sen as provisional president.
The electric starter, a major improvement in automobiles, was introduced by General Motors in its 1912 Cadillac.
The passenger ship *Titanic* sank after hitting an iceberg in the Atlantic Ocean on the night of April 14-15, 1912. About 1,500 passengers drowned, and 705 were rescued.
Amendment 16 to the Constitution took effect in 1913, giving Congress authority to levy a national income tax.

WORLD BOOK map

Political and public career

First offices. During 1881 and 1882, Taft served as assistant prosecuting attorney of Hamilton County, Ohio. In March 1882, President Chester A. Arthur appointed him collector of internal revenue for the first district, with headquarters at Cincinnati. Taft resigned a year later because he did not want to discharge good workers just to make jobs for deserving Republicans. He then formed a successful law partnership.

Taft's family. On June 19, 1886, Taft married Helen "Nellie" Herron (June 2, 1861-May 22, 1943), the daughter of John W. Herron of Cincinnati. Herron had been a law partner of President Rutherford B. Hayes. Taft wrote that his wife was "a woman who is willing to take me as I am, for better or for worse." Mrs. Taft was both intelligent and ambitious. Throughout her husband's career, she encouraged him to seek public office.

The Tafts had three children. Robert Alphonso Taft (1889-1953) became a famous U.S. senator from Ohio and a leader of the Republican Party (see **Taft, Robert Alphonso**). Helen Herron Taft Manning (1891-1987) served as professor of history and dean of Bryn Mawr College in Bryn Mawr, Pennsylvania. Charles Phelps Taft II (1897-1983), a lawyer, was mayor of Cincinnati from 1955 to 1957.

State judge. Taft was happy as a lawyer, but his father's importance in the Republican Party kept pushing him toward political life. Early in 1885, Taft was named assistant county solicitor for Hamilton County. In March 1887, Governor J. B. Foraker of Ohio appointed him to a vacancy on the Cincinnati Superior Court. The next year, the voters elected Taft to the court for a five-year term. This was the only office except the presidency that Taft won by popular vote.

Solicitor general. Taft resigned from the Cincinnati

Important dates in Taft's life

1857	(Sept. 15) Born in Cincinnati, Ohio.
1886	(June 19) Married Helen Herron.
1892	Appointed judge of U.S. Circuit Court of Appeals.
1901	Appointed governor of the Philippines.
1904	Appointed secretary of war.
1908	Elected president of the United States.
1912	Defeated for reelection by Woodrow Wilson.
1921	Appointed chief justice of the United States.
1930	(March 8) Died in Washington, D.C.

William Howard Taft National Historic Site

Taft's birthplace was this comfortable house in the Mt. Auburn section of Cincinnati, Ohio. Taft spent his entire boyhood there, with two half brothers, two brothers, and a sister.

Library of Congress

Helen Herron Taft was an intelligent, ambitious woman who urged her husband to seek the presidency. She was a gracious hostess but limited her activities after suffering a stroke in 1909.

Superior Court in 1890 to accept an appointment by President Benjamin Harrison as solicitor general of the United States. During his first year, he won 15 of the 18 government cases that he argued before the Supreme Court.

Federal judge. In March 1892, President Harrison appointed Taft a judge of the sixth circuit of the newly established United States Circuit Court of Appeals (now the United States Court of Appeals). Taft spent the next eight years as a circuit judge. From 1896 to 1900, he also was dean of the University of Cincinnati Law School.

Governor of the Philippines. In 1900, President William McKinley appointed Taft chairman of a civil commission to govern the newly acquired Philippines. The next year Taft was named the first civil governor of the islands.

Taft's career in the Philippines was an example of the best in colonial government. He established new systems of courts, land records, vital and social statistics, and sanitary regulations. He built roads and harbors, worked toward the establishment of limited self-government, and led a movement for land reform. Taft also established schools in many areas and worked steadily to improve the economic status of the people.

Taft ardently desired to be a justice of the Supreme Court. But in 1902, he turned down his first chance for appointment to the court because he felt he had not finished his work in the Philippines.

Secretary of war. Secretary of War Elihu Root resigned in February 1904. Taft returned to Washington to assume this post in President Theodore Roosevelt's Cabinet. Taft's appointment was good politics. The 1904 presidential campaign was approaching, and Taft had won great popularity for his work in the Philippines.

The president soon began using Taft as his unofficial troubleshooter, both at home and abroad. Roosevelt continued to do so after winning the 1904 election. Taft's department supervised the construction of the Panama Canal and set up the government in the Canal Zone. Taft himself advanced Roosevelt's tariff policy and assisted the president in negotiating the Treaty of Portsmouth, which ended the Russo-Japanese War (1904-1905). Everything was all right in Washington, the president said, because Taft was "sitting on the lid."

Election of 1908. Roosevelt announced he would not seek reelection in 1908 and recommended Taft as the man who would follow his policies. At first, Taft objected, preferring to wait for possible appointment to the Supreme Court. But Mrs. Taft and his brothers helped change his mind.

With Roosevelt's support, Taft won the nomination on the first ballot at the Republican National Convention, which was held in Chicago. Representative James S. Sherman of New York received the vice presidential nomination. In the election, the voters gave Taft a plurality of more than a million votes over William Jennings Bryan, who suffered his third loss as Democratic nominee for president. Bryan shared the Democratic ticket with John W. Kern, a Democratic Party leader of Indiana.

Taft's administration (1909-1913)

"Even the elements do protest," said Taft unhappily when a blizzard swept Washington on the morning of his inauguration in March 1909. From the start, Taft was filled with doubt about being president. He knew he could not be another Roosevelt. "There is no use trying to be William Howard Taft with Roosevelt's ways," he remarked. "Our ways are different." Taft decided to "complete and perfect the machinery" with which Roosevelt had tried to solve the problems of the United States.

Legislative defeats. Taft began his term with a divided party, although the Republicans controlled both houses of Congress. On the advice of Roosevelt, Taft refused to support the liberal Republicans in their fight to curb the almost unrestricted powers of the Speaker of the House, Joseph "Uncle Joe" Cannon of Illinois. But these Republicans, led by Representative George W. Norris of Nebraska, overthrew "Cannonism" (see **Norris, George William**). Because of his political inexperience

Library of Congress

As governor of the Philippines, Taft earned a reputation for fair and effective leadership. Appointed by President William McKinley, Taft served as governor from 1901 to 1904.

Collection of Edmund Sullivan

A campaign plate for the 1908 election featured Taft and his running mate, Representative James S. Sherman of New York.

Taft's election

Place of nominating convention	Chicago
Ballot on which nominated	1st
Democratic opponent	William Jennings Bryan
Electoral vote*	321 (Taft) to 162 (Bryan)
Popular vote	7,676,258 (Taft) to 6,406,801 (Bryan)
Age at inauguration	51

*For votes by states, see **Electoral College** (table).

in this and other matters, Taft soon lost the support of most liberal Republicans.

Like many other Americans, Taft believed in tariff protection. But he also felt that somewhat lower tariffs would help control trusts. He called Congress into special session to pass a tariff-reduction law but was reluctant to impose his ideas on Congress. The House passed a bill with big reductions. But in the Senate, Nelson W. Aldrich of Rhode Island, one of Taft's chief advisers, led the campaign to keep high tariffs. The resulting law, the Payne-Aldrich Tariff, lowered some tariff rates slightly but left the general level of rates as high as they had been. Taft said he knew he "could make a lot of cheap popularity by vetoing the bill." Instead, he accepted it as better than nothing, defended it in public, and suffered from the great unpopularity that the bill received.

Taft further antagonized the liberal Republicans by his stand in the Pinchot case. In late 1909, Chief Forester Gifford Pinchot made sensational charges that the Department of the Interior, and especially Secretary of the Interior Richard A. Ballinger, had abandoned the conservation policies of Theodore Roosevelt. Pinchot also accused the department of selling land concessions to water and power companies too cheaply and of illegal transactions in the sale of Alaska coal lands. Taft upheld Ballinger, who was later cleared by a congressional investigating committee. Taft then dismissed Pinchot. Liberal Republicans became convinced that some of Pinchot's charges were true, and they began to turn to Roosevelt as their true leader.

Vice president and Cabinet

Vice president	*James S. Sherman
Secretary of state	Philander C. Knox
Secretary of the treasury	Franklin MacVeagh
Secretary of war	Jacob M. Dickinson Henry L. Stimson (1911)
Attorney general	George W. Wickersham
Postmaster general	Frank H. Hitchcock
Secretary of the navy	George von Lengerke Meyer
Secretary of the interior	Richard A. Ballinger Walter L. Fisher (1911)
Secretary of agriculture	James Wilson
Secretary of commerce and labor	Charles Nagel

*Has a separate biography in *World Book*.

Legislative achievements of the Taft administration included the first scientific investigation of tariff rates, for which the president established the Tariff Board. Taft took the first steps toward establishing a federal budget by asking his Cabinet members and their staffs to submit detailed reports of their financial needs. Congress created the Postal Savings System in 1910 and parcel post in 1913. At Taft's request, Congress also organized a commerce court and enlarged the powers of the Interstate Commerce Commission. The president pushed a bill through Congress requiring that campaign expenses in federal elections be made public. During Taft's administration, Alaska received full territorial government, and the Federal Children's Bureau was established. The president took action against many trusts. Nearly twice as many "trust-busting" prosecutions for violation of the Sherman Antitrust Act took place during Taft's four years in office as had occurred during Roosevelt's administration of almost eight years.

Foreign affairs. The Taft administration had an uneven record in international relations. During the late 1800's, nations customarily used diplomacy to expand their commercial interests. "Dollar diplomacy," as promoted by Secretary of State Philander C. Knox, had just the opposite purpose. To Knox, it meant the use of trade and commerce to increase a nation's diplomatic influence (see **Dollar diplomacy**). The United States made loans to China, Nicaragua, Honduras, and other countries in order to encourage investments by bankers in loans to these nations. Taft ended the second American occupation of Cuba in 1909 and negotiated treaties of arbitration with the United Kingdom and France. These treaties ranked as landmarks in the effort of nations to settle their differences peacefully, but the Senate rejected them.

Life in the White House. Mrs. Taft, a skillful hostess, enjoyed presiding at state functions and entertaining friends at small teas. She hired a woman to replace the traditional male steward because she thought the service would be improved. At Mrs. Taft's request, the mayor of Tokyo presented about 3,000 cherry trees to the American people. The trees were planted along the banks of the Potomac River.

Mrs. Taft suffered a stroke in the winter of 1909.

Bettmann Archive

A presidential tradition began when President Taft threw out the first ball to open the 1910 major league baseball season.

Thereafter, her daughter, Helen, or her sister, Mrs. Louis More, often acted as Taft's official hostess. Mrs. Taft had a better head for politics than did her husband. Taft relied on his wife's judgment and missed her help after she became ill.

On summer evenings, the Tafts often sat on the south portico of the White House and listened to favorite phonograph recordings. Taft was an excellent dancer, and Mrs. Taft organized a small dancing class for his diversion. He played tennis and golf well and often rode horseback.

Election of 1912. Theodore Roosevelt had returned in 1910 from an African hunting trip. He denied an interest in running for the presidency again but began making speeches advocating a "New Nationalism." Under this slogan, Roosevelt included his old policies of honest government, checks on big business, and conservation, as well as demands for social justice, including old-age and unemployment insurance. Conservative Republicans lined up with Taft against Roosevelt.

Although Roosevelt won most of the primary elections, a majority of the delegates to the nominating convention were pledged to Taft. The president was renominated on the first ballot, and James S. Sherman was renominated as vice president.

Roosevelt and the progressive Republicans accused Taft of "stealing" the convention by recognizing the votes of pro-Taft delegations. They organized the Progressive Party with Roosevelt as their nominee and chose Senator Hiram W. Johnson of California as his running mate. The Democrats nominated Governor Woodrow Wilson of New Jersey for president and Governor Thomas R. Marshall of Indiana for vice president.

Taft faced inevitable defeat. He received only 8 electoral votes, against 88 for Roosevelt and 435 for Wilson.

Later years

Law professor. After Taft left the White House in March 1913, he became professor of constitutional law at Yale University. That same year, he was elected president of the American Bar Association. During World War I (1914-1918), President Wilson appointed Taft joint chairman of the National War Labor Board.

During the war, Taft also headed the League to Enforce Peace. The organization recommended the formation of a league of nations that could work to prevent future wars. Taft became the leading Republican to support such a league, and he cooperated with President Wilson in promoting the idea. Wilson became the chief planner of the League of Nations. See **League of Nations.**

Chief justice. In 1921, President Warren G. Harding appointed Taft chief justice of the United States. Taft regarded this appointment as the greatest honor of his life. His accomplishments as administrator of the nation's highest court were more important than his decisions. The Supreme Court had fallen far behind in its work. In 1925, Taft achieved passage of the Judiciary Act. This law gave the court greater control over the number and kinds of cases it would consider and made it possible for the court to function effectively and get its work done. Taft was also instrumental in obtaining congressional approval for a new court building. See **Supreme Court of the United States.**

Taft performed more than his share of the court's great workload and often advised President Calvin Coolidge. He watched his health and held his weight to about 300 pounds (136 kilograms). Taft became a familiar figure in Washington as he walked the 3 miles (5 kilometers) between his home and the court almost every morning and evening. But finally the strain of overwork became too great. Bad health, chiefly due to heart trouble, forced his retirement on Feb. 3, 1930. Taft died on March 8 and was buried in Arlington National Cemetery. Taft and President John F. Kennedy are the only presidents buried there. David H. Burton

Related articles in *World Book* include:

Dollar diplomacy
President of the United States
Roosevelt, Theodore
Tariff
Wilson, Woodrow

Outline

I. Early life

II. Political and public career
A. First offices
B. Taft's family
C. State judge
D. Solicitor general
E. Federal judge
F. Governor of the Philippines
G. Secretary of war
H. Election of 1908

III. Taft's administration (1909-1913)
A. Legislative defeats
B. Legislative achievements
C. Foreign affairs
D. Life in the White House
E. Election of 1912

IV. Later years
A. Law professor
B. Chief justice

Questions

What were Taft's chief personal virtues?
What were the main legislative achievements of his administration?
When did Taft achieve his lifelong ambition?
What was the Pinchot case? The Payne-Aldrich Tariff?
How did Taft lose the confidence of liberal Republicans during his term?
Where is Taft buried?
What was the only public office except the presidency to which Taft was elected?
What were Taft's main achievements as governor of the Philippines?
Who helped change Taft's mind about running for president?
What were some of Taft's accomplishments as secretary of war?

Additional resources

Burton, David H. *The Learned Presidency: Theodore Roosevelt, William Howard Taft, Woodrow Wilson.* Fairleigh Dickinson, 1988. *Taft, Holmes, and the 1920s Court.* 1998.

Casey, Jane C. *William Howard Taft.* Children's Pr., 1989. Younger readers.

Taft-Hartley Act is the popular name for the federal Labor-Management Relations Act of 1947. The act was named for its main sponsors, Senator Robert A. Taft and Representative Fred Hartley. It was an amendment to the Wagner Act (National Labor Relations Act of 1935). It continued the Wagner Act's basic guarantees of workers' rights, outlawed certain union tactics, and expanded the act's concept of *unfair labor practices* to include practices of labor organizations. The Taft-Hartley Act provided that the start of strikes which might cause a national emergency can be delayed for 80 days.

The act forbids unions to use force or discrimination against individuals during organizing campaigns. It also prohibits unions from using dues collected from members for political contributions in national elections. The act prohibits use of the *secondary boycott, sympathy strike,* and *jurisdictional strike.* A secondary boycott occurs when striking employees bring pressure on a party not involved in the dispute in hopes that the party will stop doing business with their employer. A sympathy strike is called by one union in support of another union that is striking against its employer. A jurisdictional strike is called by rival unions over which union has the right to work on a job.

The Taft-Hartley Act bans the *closed shop,* the practice of hiring only union members. The act also gives the states power to restrict the *union shop,* in which employees have to join the union after being hired. The act requires unions to file such information as constitutions and financial statements with the federal government.

Taft-Hartley supporters said the act equalized power between union and management. Unions called it a "slave labor law," and tried to repeal or amend it.

James G. Scoville

See also **Closed shop; Open shop; Union shop.**

Additional resources

Aaseng, Nathan. *You Are the Senator.* Oliver Pr., 1997. Discusses the Taft-Hartley Act. Younger readers.

Lee, R. Alton. *Truman and Taft-Hartley.* 1966. Reprint. Greenwood, 1980.

Taglioni, *tah LYOH nee,* **Marie** (1804-1884), was one of the most famous ballerinas of the early 1800's. She was one of the first ballerinas to make toe-dancing beautiful. Her leaps are described as slow flights through the air. To audiences, the grace of her movements made her appear weightless. Her dancing and her acting looked effortless and cool.

Taglioni was born on April 23, 1804, in Stockholm, Sweden. She was rigorously trained by her father, Filippo Taglioni, an Italian dancer and *choreographer* (dance creator). Her dancing in his ballets, particularly in *La Sylphide* (1832), helped to bring about the romantic period in ballet that lasted until the 1850's. Audiences in Europe idolized her. She retired in 1847. Katy Matheson

See also **Ballet** (Romantic ballet; picture).

Tagore, *tuh GAWR,* **Rabindranath,** *ruh BIHN druh naht* (1861-1941), was one of the most influential cultural and political figures in the history of modern India. In 1913, Tagore won the Nobel Prize in literature, the first Asian writer to receive the award. Tagore produced a massive amount of literature in the Bengali language of India. Perhaps his best-known work is the poetry collection *Gitanjali* (1910). He also wrote plays, essays, novels, stories, and social commentary, along with founding a university. Tagore's writings show his sympathy for India's downtrodden, and he supported India's independence movement from British colonial rule. Tagore was an internationalist in spirit, stressing the need for a dialogue between the world's diverse cultures.

Tagore was born on May 7, 1861, in Calcutta (now Kolkata) and studied law in England. He was knighted in 1915 but returned the title in 1919 to protest British policies in India. Tagore died on Aug. 7, 1941. Vinay Lal

Tagus River, *TAY guhs,* also called *Tajo,* is the longest river of the Iberian Peninsula of southwest Europe. It rises in central Spain and flows west across Portugal to the Atlantic Ocean. The river is 626 miles (1,007 kilometers) long and drains an area of about 31,000 square miles (80,300 square kilometers). The mouth of the Tagus, at Lisbon, Portugal, forms one of Europe's most important harbors. Douglas L. Wheeler

Tahiti, *tuh HEE tee,* an island in the South Pacific Ocean, is known for its beauty and tropical climate. It is the largest island in French Polynesia, a French possession made up of five main island groups. Tahiti is one of the 14 Society Islands. For the location of Tahiti, see **Pacific Islands** (map). Papeete is the largest city and chief port of Tahiti. The city is also the capital of French Polynesia.

Tahiti gained worldwide fame as a tropical paradise through the works of many artists and writers who visited the island or lived there. The French artist Paul Gauguin portrayed Tahiti's lush beauty and peaceful atmosphere in many paintings. Many authors, including Herman Melville and James Michener of the United States and Robert Louis Stevenson of Scotland, wrote glowing descriptions of the island. Such works have helped make Tahiti popular with tourists.

Tahiti covers 402 square miles (1,041 square kilometers). A broken coral reef surrounds the island. Most of the population lives on a strip of flat, fertile land that lies along the coast. The interior of the island is mountainous, and the land is so steep that it is almost entirely uninhabited. Heavy rainfall helps create many fast-flowing streams and spectacular waterfalls. The island is covered with tropical vegetation, including coconut palms and banana, orange, and papaya trees.

About 170,000 people live on Tahiti. About 80 percent of them are Polynesians or have mixed Polynesian and European ancestry. Most of the rest of the population is made up of Chinese and Europeans.

Many Tahitians live in or near Papeete and work in the tourist industry, the base of the island's economy. Tahiti's Chinese population is involved in much of the retail and shipping trade on the island. People in rural areas farm the land or work in the fishing industry. The farmers grow breadfruit, taro, and yams for their own use and produce small quantities of copra and vanilla for export.

The earliest inhabitants of Tahiti were Polynesians who came there from Asia hundreds of years ago. The first European to visit the island was the British sea cap-

© Bruce Berg

Tahiti is an island in the South Pacific Ocean. The island is famous as a tropical paradise. Papenoo Beach, *shown here,* lies on the northern coast of Tahiti.

tain Samuel Wallis in 1767. He claimed Tahiti for Britain. The next year, a French navigator named Louis-Antoine de Bougainville landed on Tahiti and claimed it for France. Tahiti became a French protectorate in 1842 and a colony of France in 1880. In 1946, France declared Tahiti and the other islands of French Polynesia to be a French overseas territory. Several independence movements began in French Polynesia during the mid-1900's, but most of the people have wanted to remain under French rule. In 2004, French Polynesia became a French *overseas country.* The new status gave French Polynesia more power over local matters. Nancy Davis Lewis

See also **Gauguin, Paul; Society Islands.**

Tahoe, Lake. See Lake Tahoe.

T'ai chi ch'uan, *ty jee chwahn,* is a form of Chinese martial art. The name, also spelled *taijiquan,* means *supreme* or *grand ultimate fist.* The art is characterized by slow, continuous movements that harmonize with breathing to help circulate the individual's *chi.* According to Chinese medical and philosophical theory, *chi* is internal energy that runs through all living things. Although t'ai chi ch'uan may be used for combat, it is chiefly used as a method of mental and physical relaxation.

Students first learn to relax and find good posture. Then they practice a *form,* an unbroken sequence of postures and movements that is the heart of the system. A form may consist of more than 100 movements and postures. Later, students learn Pushing Hands, an exercise in which two partners gently push and yield with their hands against each other's arms. The beginnings of t'ai chi ch'uan are obscure. Historians believe it has been practiced for about 1,000 years. Paul Crompton

See also **Asian Americans** (picture: Ancient Chinese exercises); **Martial arts.**

Tail is the part of the body of a vertebrate animal that extends backward beyond the pelvis. In animals without limbs, the tail is the part of the body that extends beyond the anus. The term *tail* includes the fleshy part and the outgrowths it may have, such as fins and feathers.

Animals use their tails in many ways. The tails of most water animals serve to move them and to steer them. Squirrels use their tails to keep their balance when they are leaping and climbing. Woodpeckers and kangaroos prop themselves up with their tails. Spider monkeys and opossums grasp things with their tails.

Jerry F. Downhower

Tailorbird is a songbird found in tropical regions of China, India, Malaysia, and the Philippines. Its name comes from the way it builds its nest in a large folded leaf. It sews the edges of the leaf together with strips of silk or wool thread, or vegetable fiber, using its bill as a needle. The nest inside the leaves is made from plant down, fine grass, and hair. The female lays three or four eggs. They vary in color from reddish-white to bluish-green and are marked with brownish-red. Tailorbirds are 4 to $5\frac{1}{2}$ inches (10 to 14 centimeters) long. There are nine species. Fred J. Alsop III

WORLD BOOK illustration by Trevor Boyer, Linden Artists Ltd.

The ashy tailorbird uses its long bill as a needle.

Scientific classification. Tailorbirds belong to the family Sylviidae. The scientific name of the ashy tailorbird, a well-known species, is *Orthotomus ruficeps.*

See also **Bird** (picture: Kinds of bird nests).

Taine, *tayn* or *tehn,* **Hippolyte Adolphe,** *ee paw LEET a DAWLF* (1828-1893), was a French intellectual and critic. His application of the philosophy of *determinism* to art and literature did much to shape French intellectual attitudes in the 1800's.

To understand the origin and development of an artist's or writer's work, Taine said we must discover all the significant facts about the person's *race* (heredity), *milieu* (environment), and *moment* (state of the artistic tradition in which the person worked). Through this theory and through his emphasis on documentation, Taine greatly influenced the Naturalist movement in literature (see **Naturalism**). Taine's *History of English Literature* (1863) and *Philosophy of Art* (1865-1869) illustrate his deterministic philosophy. His *Origins of Contemporary France* (1875-1893) blames the French Revolution for the decline he saw in France's greatness.

Taine was born on April 21, 1828, in Vouziers. He was a professor at the École des Beaux-Arts in Paris almost continuously from 1864 to 1883. Thomas H. Goetz

Taipei, *ty pay* or *ty bay* (pop. 2,637,100; met. area pop. 6,603,000), is the capital and largest city of the island country of Taiwan. It lies on the Hsintien, Keelung, and Tanshui rivers at the island's north end. For location, see **Taiwan** (map). The name *Taipei* means *north Taiwan.*

Taipei and its surrounding area make up the commercial, cultural, and tourist center of Taiwan. Taipei's landmarks include Chiang Kai-shek Memorial Hall; the Lungshan Temple, believed to be the oldest Buddhist temple in the city; and the Grand Hotel, which resembles an ancient Chinese palace. Taipei 101, in the city's business district, is the world's tallest building. The city's National Palace Museum houses an outstanding collection of Chinese art. Taipei has large department stores and exotic bazaars. It is the home of several universities, including National Taiwan University, National Taiwan Normal University, and National Chengchi University.

In 1967, Taipei annexed the towns of Chingmei, Mucha, Nankang, Neihu, Shihlin, and Peitou. As a result, the city grew from 26 to 105 square miles (67 to 272 square kilometers).

Taipei is one of the most densely populated cities in the world. Overcrowded housing is a problem in the city. Many high-rise buildings have been erected in Taipei with little concern for zoning laws. Heavy traffic is another problem. Air pollution has resulted from motor vehicles and the factories in and near the city.

Products made in Taipei include textiles, electrical machinery and appliances, wires and cables, refrigerators, motorcycles, rubber goods, and various handicrafts. More than a dozen airlines serve the nearby Chiang Kai-shek International Airport. Railways and bus lines connect the city to all parts of Taiwan.

The Chinese began making large settlements in Taiwan during the 1600's. The Chinese founded Taipei in 1708. Japan took control of Taipei and the rest of Taiwan from China in 1895. The Japanese made Taipei the administrative and economic center of the island and greatly expanded the city's area.

After World War II ended in 1945, Japan returned Taiwan to China. In 1949, the army of the Chinese Communist Party overthrew the Nationalist government of China. The Nationalist Chinese, led by Chiang Kai-shek, retreated from the mainland to Taiwan and established their own government in Taipei. Since then, Taipei and its suburbs have expanded greatly. Frederic Wakeman, Jr.

See also **Transportation** (picture: An electric railroad).

Taiwan, *ty wahn,* is a mountainous island in the South China Sea, about 90 miles (140 kilometers) off the Chinese coast. In Chinese, *Taiwan* means *terraced bay.* The island's wild, forested beauty led Portuguese sailors in 1590 to name it *Ilha Formosa,* meaning *beautiful island.*

After the Chinese Communists conquered mainland China in 1949, the Chinese Nationalists moved to Taiwan. Nationalist leader Chiang Kai-shek declared Taipei the capital of the Republic of China and refused to recognize China's Communist government. The Nationalist government also controls several islands in the Taiwan Strait, which separates Taiwan and China. These islands include the Quemoy, Matsu, and Pescadores groups.

Government. The Chinese Nationalist government is based on a Constitution adopted in 1946 on the mainland. It provides for five branches of government—executive, legislative, judicial, control, and examination. Each branch is headed by a *yuan* (council).

The president is Taiwan's most powerful government official. The president is elected by the people to a four-year term. The president appoints a prime minister to head the Executive Yuan, which carries out the operations of the government. The Legislative Yuan makes most of Taiwan's laws.

© Cai Yumao, IMAGINECHINA

Taipei is Taiwan's capital. A skyscraper called Taipei 101 towers above the business district and dominates the city's skyline. The 101-story structure is the tallest building in the world.

Taiwan

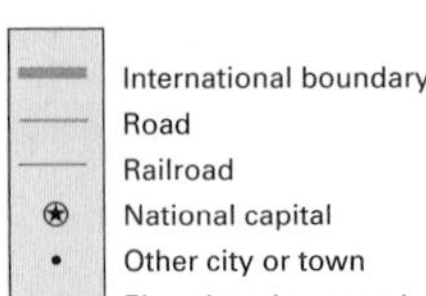

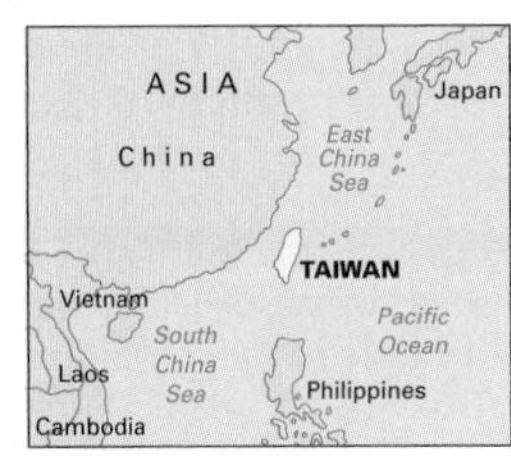

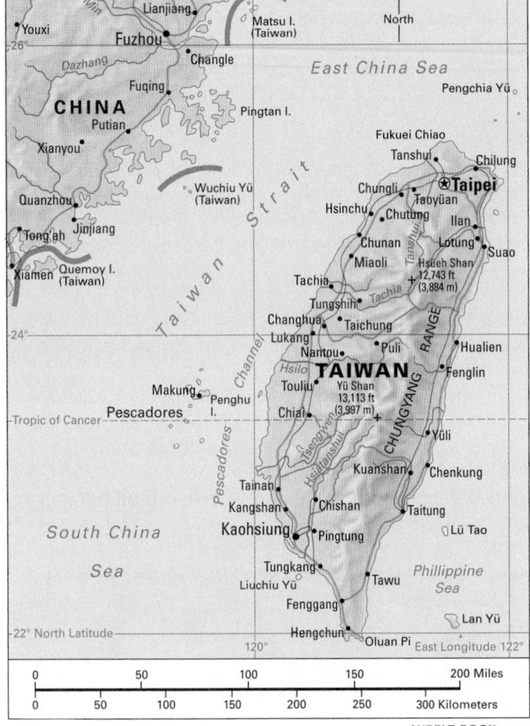

WORLD BOOK maps

After moving to Taiwan in 1949, the Nationalist legislative bodies were made up of members who had been elected on the mainland in 1947 and 1948. The members were allowed to keep their seats indefinitely and became known as "life-term" members. Beginning in the 1960's, some elections were held for new members. A 1990 judicial decision declared the system of "life-term" members unconstitutional. All remaining "life-term" members retired at the end of 1991.

The Legislative Yuan has 225 members. Beginning with the Legislative Yuan elected in 2007, the number of members will be reduced to 113. They will serve four-year terms. Voters will directly elect about two-thirds of the members. The remaining one-third will be chosen by *proportional representation.* Under this system, voters will cast a ballot for a political party, and legislative seats will be assigned to each party according to its share of the vote.

The Judicial Yuan is Taiwan's highest court. The Control Yuan reviews activities of government officials and has power of impeachment. The Examination Yuan gives tests for hiring and promoting government workers.

Although Taiwan is the seat of the Chinese Nationalist government, it is administered as a province of China. The president appoints a provincial governor who serves an indefinite term. The people elect the members of a provincial assembly to four-year terms. The people also elect county and city government officials.

Taiwan's leading political parties are the Nationalist Party, or Kuomintang (KMT), and the Democratic Progressive Party (DPP). The KMT was Taiwan's only legal party until 1989.

People. Most Taiwanese are Chinese whose ancestors came to the island from Fujian (also spelled Fukien) and Guangdong (Kwangtung) provinces on the mainland. More than 1 ½ million more people fled to Taiwan from the mainland after the Communist take-over in 1949. A small percentage of the population are non-Chinese native peoples, sometimes called *aborigines,* related to Indonesians and Filipinos.

Almost all the people of Taiwan live on the coastal plain that makes up the western third of the island. Rapid industrial development in this region has led to problems with air and water pollution. Most of the native peoples live on reservations in the mountains.

About 80 percent of Taiwan's people live and work in urban areas. Most city people wear clothing similar to that worn by North Americans and Europeans. About 10 percent of Taiwan's people farm the land. Farms on the island average only 2 or 3 acres (0.8 to 1.2 hectares) in size. Most of the farmhouses are made of brick, with tile roofs and central courtyards of packed earth or cement. A typical Taiwanese meal includes rice, served with vegetables and chopped meat or fish. Farmers and others who work in the hot sun wear cone-shaped straw hats.

The Taiwanese people speak various Chinese dialects. However, almost all the people also use Northern Chinese (Mandarin), which is the official Chinese dialect. Most adults can read and write. The law requires children to have six years of elementary school and three years of high school.

About half the people practice a local traditional religion that involves the worship of special gods and god-

Facts in brief

Capital: Taipei.

Official language: Northern Chinese (Mandarin, or putonghua).

Area: 13,902 mi² (36,006 km²), including the Pescadores islands, but excluding Matsu and Quemoy. Greatest distances—north-south, 235 mi (378 km); east-west, 90 mi (145 km). *Coastline*—555 mi (893 km).

Elevation: *Highest*—Yü Shan (Mount Morrison), 13,113 ft (3,997 m) above sea level. *Lowest*—sea level.

Population: *Estimated 2006 population*—22,781,000; population density, 1,639 per mi² (633 per km²); distribution, 78 percent urban, 22 percent rural. *2000 census*—22,167,159.

Chief products: *Agriculture*—asparagus, bananas, chickens and ducks, citrus fruits, hogs, mushrooms, pineapples, rice, sugar cane, sweet potatoes, tea, vegetables. *Fishing*—shrimp, snapper, tuna. *Forestry*—cedar, hemlock, oak. *Manufacturing*—calculators, clothing and textiles, iron and steel, paper, plastics, plywood, processed foods, radios, ships, sporting goods, sugar, television sets, toys.

Flag: The flag has a red field. A white sun appears on a blue canton in the upper left-hand corner. Red stands for liberty and sacrifice, and white for fraternity and honesty. Adopted in 1928. See **Flag** (picture: Flags of Asia and the Pacific).

Money: *Basic unit*—new Taiwan dollar (also called yuan). See **Yuan**.

A fertile valley near Taipei includes a farming community. About 10 percent of Taiwan's people farm the land. Most of the country is too mountainous for farming.

Photri from Marilyn Gartman

desses. Buddhism and Taoism are also popular. A small fraction of the people follow Christianity or I-Kuan Tao, another traditional religion.

Land and climate. Taiwan, including the Pescadores islands, covers about 13,900 square miles (36,000 square kilometers). This area does not include the Quemoy and Matsu island groups, which are part of Fujian province. Thickly forested mountains run from north to south and cover about half of Taiwan. The highest peak, Yü Shan (Mount Morrison), rises 13,113 feet (3,997 meters) above sea level. On the eastern coast, the mountains often drop sharply to the sea. Short, swift rivers have cut gorges through the mountains. In the west, the mountains slope to gently rolling hills and level land.

Taiwan has a subtropical climate, with hot, humid summers and an average annual rainfall of more than 100 inches (250 centimeters). Temperatures average about 80 °F (27 °C) in summer and 65 °F (18 °C) in winter. Summer monsoons bring strong winds and rain to Taiwan. In winter, monsoons bring rain and cooler weather to the north. Typhoons occur almost every year.

Economy. Taiwan has few natural resources except its forests. Cedars, hemlocks, and oaks are the most valuable timber trees. Other forest products include bamboo, camphor, paper, and plywood. Taiwan's economy relies heavily on manufacturing and foreign trade. Factories produce cement, clothing and textiles, computer equipment, furniture, iron and steel, plastic goods, processed foods, ships, shoes, sports equipment, sugar, televisions, radios, and toys. Many manufactured goods are exported, especially clothing and textiles, electronics, plastic goods, plywood, and toys. Taiwan's main trading partners include Germany, Japan, and the United States. Taiwan also trades with Hong Kong, a special administrative region of China.

Only about a fourth of Taiwan's land can be farmed. The farmers have terraced many hills to provide more fields for growing rice. By using fertilizers, farmers are able to harvest two or three crops a year from the same field. The chief crops include asparagus, bananas, citrus fruits, corn, mushrooms, peanuts, pineapples, rice, sugar, sweet potatoes, tea, and vegetables. Farmers also raise hogs, chickens, and ducks. The fishing industry

© Michael K. Nichols, Magnum

Manufacturing plays a major role in Taiwan's economy. This worker is assembling a television set. Taiwan exports TV sets, computer equipment, and many other manufactured products.

catches such ocean fish as shrimp, snapper, and tuna. Carp, eels, and other fish are caught in inland ponds.

Coal is Taiwan's most important mined product, but the island has only small deposits. Copper, limestone, natural gas, petroleum, salt, and sulfur are also mined.

Taiwan has good roads, including an expressway that links Taipei and Kaohsiung. Bus service is excellent. The government operates several rail lines. Kaohsiung and Chilung are the chief seaports. Taiwan has two international airports, one near Taipei, another in Kaohsiung.

About 30 daily newspapers are published in Taiwan. Most families own a TV set and one or more radios.

History. Aborigines were the first inhabitants of Taiwan. Some Chinese came to the island as early as the 500's, but large settlements did not begin until the 1600's. Dutch traders occupied a Taiwanese port from 1624 until 1661. Koxinga, a Chinese Ming dynasty official, drove them out. Manchu conquerors had overthrown the Ming dynasty in mainland China, and Koxinga wanted Taiwan as a base from which to attack the Manchus. However, the Manchus conquered Taiwan in 1683.

Japan gained control of Taiwan as a result of the Sino-Japanese War of 1894-1895. The Japanese developed Taiwan's agriculture and industry and expanded its transportation networks. Chinese Nationalists took control of the island after World War II ended in 1945. Their harsh rule led to violent resistance by native Taiwanese. Troops arrived from the mainland and put down the revolt in what came to be known as the White Terror.

In 1949, the Chinese Communists defeated Chiang Kai-shek's Nationalist forces and took control of the mainland. Chiang moved his government to Taiwan on Dec. 8, 1949. After the Korean War began in 1950, the United States said it would protect Taiwan against possible attack from mainland China. The U.S. and Chinese Nationalist governments signed a mutual defense treaty in 1954. The Chinese Communists repeatedly shelled Matsu and Quemoy during the 1950's. Taiwan received about $1 ½ billion in U.S. economic and technical aid up to 1965. That year, Taiwan said its economy could stand on its own. But it continued to receive U.S. military aid.

In 1971, the United Nations (UN) expelled Nationalist China from its UN seat and admitted Communist China. In the 1970's, a number of nations ended their diplomatic relations with Taiwan and established ties with Communist China. The United States ended diplomatic ties with Taiwan in late 1978 and established diplomatic relations with Communist China early in 1979. The mutual defense treaty between the two countries was ended on Dec. 31, 1979. But the United States agreed to continue to give Taiwan military aid and to carry on unofficial relations through nongovernmental agencies.

President Chiang Kai-shek died in 1975. Chiang's son Chiang Ching-kuo had become prime minister in 1972. He became the country's most powerful leader after his father died. He was elected president of Taiwan in 1978 and was reelected in 1984. Chiang died in 1988. Vice President Lee Teng-hui succeeded him as president.

Also in the 1980's, the government began political reforms that increased democracy in the country. In 1987, it ended *martial law,* which had been in effect since 1949. Under martial law, the military had some legal and political powers. Opposition parties were legalized in 1989. The Nationalist Party had been Taiwan's only legal political party. Multiparty elections were held in 1991 for the National Assembly and in 1992 for the Legislative Yuan. The Nationalist Party won a majority of seats in both elections and retained control of the government.

In 1995 elections for the Legislative Yuan, the Nationalists won a slim majority. In 1996, for the first time, Taiwanese voters directly elected their president. The National Assembly had elected the president. Voters elected President Lee Teng-hui to a four-year term.

In 2000, Chen Shui-bian of the Democratic Progressive Party (DPP) was elected president, ending 50 years of Nationalist Party rule. Chen had always advocated Taiwanese independence, and Chinese officials warned that any moves toward independence would provoke war. But as president, Chen said he would not declare independence as long as China did not try to invade Taiwan. In elections in 2001 for the Legislative Yuan, the DPP won more seats than any other party. In 2004, Chen was reelected president by a slim margin after surviving an apparent assassination attempt the day before the election. Supporters of the Nationalist candidate, Lien Chan, held protests and filed two lawsuits seeking to overturn Chen's victory. However, Taiwan's High Court threw out both lawsuits. Also in 2004, elections for the Legislative Yuan were held, and an alliance led by the Nationalists won a majority of seats. Murray A. Rubinstein

Related articles in ***World Book*** include:

Chiang Ching-kuo	Lee Teng-hui	Quemoy
Chiang Kai-shek	Pescadores	Taipei

Additional resources

Copper, John F. *Historical Dictionary of Taiwan.* 2nd ed. Scarecrow, 2000. *Taiwan: Nation-State or Province?* 4th ed. Westview, 2003.

Insight Guide: Taiwan. 4th ed. APA Pubns., 2001.

Roy, Denny. *Taiwan: A Political History.* Cornell Univ. Pr., 2003.

Ryan, Micheala. *Taiwan.* Gareth Stevens, 2003.

Taj Mahal, *TAHJ muh HAHL,* is one of the most beautiful and costly tombs in the world. The Indian ruler Shah Jahan ordered it built in memory of his favorite wife, Mumtaz Mahal, who died in 1629. The tomb stands at Agra in northern India. About 20,000 workers built it between about 1630 and 1650.

According to tradition, the Taj Mahal was designed by a Turkish architect. It is made of white marble and rests on a platform of red sandstone. At each corner of the platform stands a slender *minaret* (prayer tower). Each tower is 133 feet (40.5 meters) high. The building itself is 186 feet (56.7 meters) square. A dome covers the center of the building. It is 70 feet (21.3 meters) in diameter and 120 feet (36.6 meters) high. Passages from the Muslim holy book, the Qur'ān, decorate the outside along with inlaid floral patterns. A central room contains two *cenotaphs* (monuments). Visitors can see the monuments through a carved alabaster screen. The bodies of Shah Jahan and his wife lie in a vault below. The tomb stands in a garden. William J. Hennessey

See also **Asia** (picture); **India** (picture).

Tajikistan, *tuh JIHK uh STAN,* also spelled *Tadzhikistan,* is a mountainous country in central Asia. Its name in the Tajik language is Jumhurii Tojikiston (Republic of Tajikistan). Its capital and largest city is Dushanbe. Tajikistan became independent in 1991, after more than 60 years as a republic of the Soviet Union. In 1992, civil war broke out. A peace agreement was signed in 1997.

Government. Tajikistan is a republic. The head of state is the president, who is elected by the people.

The president appoints a prime minister, who heads a cabinet called the Council of Ministers. The cabinet helps carry out the functions of the government. The president also appoints council members. A parliament elected by the people makes Tajikistan's laws. The main units of local government are regions and cities.

Tajikistan's highest court is the Supreme Court. There are also regional courts and local courts.

People. About 62 percent of Tajikistan's people are ethnic Tajiks. Uzbeks make up about 24 percent of the population. Russians make up about 7 percent. Other ethnic groups include Tatars, Kyrgyz, Kazakhs, and Turkmen.

Most Tajiks are Sunni Muslims. Groups of Shiite Muslims live in remote mountain areas. Small communities of a sect called the Ismaili Khoja Muslims live in the Pamirs, a mountain range in southeastern Tajikistan.

The most heavily settled regions of Tajikistan are valleys in the southwest. Most people live in rural villages that are made up of sun-dried earthen houses surrounded by earthen walls. City dwellers live in single-story houses and multistory apartment buildings.

Most families in Tajikistan are large. Many members of an extended family may live together in one household, including parents, married children and their offspring, and other relatives. Because of marriage patterns, it is common for all people in a village to be related. Some Tajiks follow a Muslim custom that permits a man to have as many as four wives.

Tajiks wear both Western-style and traditional clothing. Traditional garments include loose cotton trousers and a dark or multicolored robe for men and colorful, embroidered silk dresses for women. Both men and women wear embroidered skullcaps.

Traditional Tajik foods include a rice dish called *pilaf* and *shashlik* (lamb or beef broiled on skewers). Green tea is the most popular drink.

Tajik is an Iranian language. It is much like Farsi, the chief language of Iran.

The government requires children to attend school from the ages of 6 to 17. Tajikistan has one university

Facts in brief

Capital: Dushanbe.
Official language: Tajik.
Area: 54,865 mi² (142,100 km²). *Greatest distances*—north-south, 300 mi (485 km); east-west, 425 mi (685 km).
Elevation: *Highest*—Pik Imeni Ismail Samani, 24,590 ft (7,495 m). *Lowest*—Syr Darya river at northwestern border, 980 ft (300 m).
Population: *Estimated 2006 population*—6,574,000; population density, 120 per mi² (46 per km²); distribution, 73 percent rural, 27 percent urban. *2000 census*—6,127,000.
Chief products: *Agriculture*—cotton, fruit, grain, livestock, vegetables. *Manufacturing*—food processing, textiles, wine. *Mining*—antimony, coal, fluorite, lead, molybdenum, natural gas, petroleum, salt, tungsten, uranium, zinc.
Flag: The flag has horizontal stripes of reddish orange, white, and green. An emblem lies in the center of the middle white stripe. It consists of an arc of seven yellow, five-pointed stars over a yellow figure resembling a crown. See **Flag** (picture: Flags of Asia and the Pacific).
Money: *Basic unit*—somoni. One hundred dirams equal one somoni.

Tajikistan

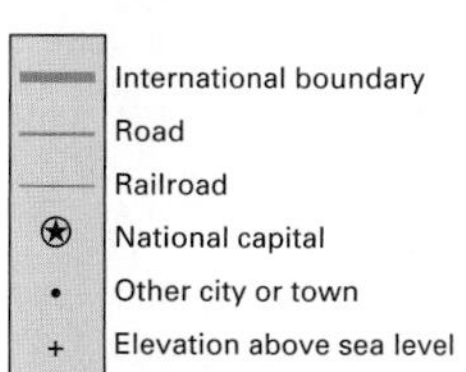

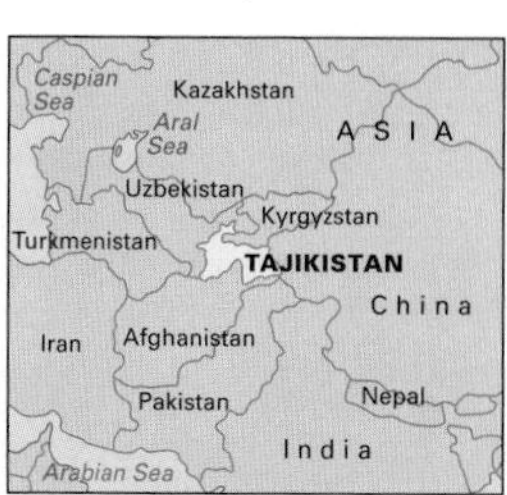

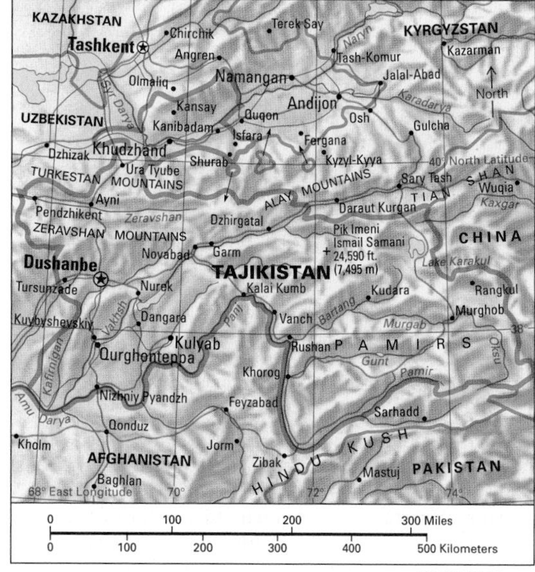

WORLD BOOK maps

and several other schools of higher education.

Land and climate. Over 90 percent of Tajikistan is mountainous, and over half lies above 10,000 feet (3,050 meters). The highest peaks are snow-covered all year. The towering Pamirs rise in the southeast. The Alay and Tian Shan mountain ranges stretch across much of the rest of the country. Fedchenko Glacier, one of the world's longest glaciers, extends 48 miles (77 kilometers) in the Pamirs. The Amu Darya, a major river of central Asia, flows along part of Tajikistan's southern border. Another major river, the Syr Darya, flows across part of northeastern Tajikistan. Other rivers include the Vakhsh, Kafirnigan, and Zeravshan. Earthquakes often occur throughout the region.

Summers in the valleys are typically long, hot, and dry. Winters in the highlands are long and cold. Temperatures in the valleys average 36 °F (2 °C) in January and 86 °F (30 °C) in July. Temperatures in the highlands average −4 °F (−20 °C) in January and 72 °F (22 °C) in July. In parts of the eastern Pamirs, temperatures can drop to −58 °F (−50 °C). Tajikistan receives annual rainfall of less than 8 inches (20 centimeters).

Economy. Agriculture accounts for almost two-fifths of the value of Tajikistan's economic production. Cotton is Tajikistan's chief agricultural product. Other crops include various fruits, grains, and vegetables. Farmers also raise a variety of livestock, including cattle, chickens, horses, Karakul sheep, and yaks. Chief agricultural areas lie in the country's southwest and north.

© Naomi Duguid, Asia Access

A mountain village in Tajikistan lies nestled in a narrow valley. Mountains cover more than 90 percent of Tajikistan. Most Tajiks live in valleys in the southwestern part of the country.

Tajikistan's industries, which include food processing, hydroelectric power generation, mining, and textile manufacturing, account for about a third of the value of the country's economic production. Dushanbe and Khudzhand are the chief industrial centers. The mines of the region yield a variety of minerals, including antimony, coal, fluorite, lead, molybdenum, salt, tungsten, uranium, and zinc. The huge Nurek Dam on the Vakhsh River provides hydroelectric power for industries and water for irrigation projects.

Tajikistan has a limited highway and railroad system. Heavy snows close roads in the Pamirs at least half of the year. The airport in Dushanbe handles all flights.

A radio and a television station broadcast from Dushanbe in several languages. The country also publishes newspapers and magazines in several languages. However, the government controls the means of communication in Tajikistan.

History. People have inhabited the area that is now Tajikistan for thousands of years. Persians of the Achaemenid Empire settled in the region as early as the 500's B.C. These Persians became the ancestors of the Tajiks. They ruled the region until Alexander the Great gained control of their empire in 331 B.C.

After Alexander's death in 323 B.C., the region split into a number of independent states. Part of Tajikistan was absorbed by the Seleucids, who ruled until about 250 B.C. Another part came under the control of the Bactrian State, which ruled until about 130 B.C. At that time, nomadic tribes from western China invaded the region. These tribes were overthrown by the Kushans by the A.D. 100's. Sassanians from Persia and White Huns from central Asia defeated the Kushans by the 400's.

Arab armies swept into the region in the mid-600's and introduced Islam. Turkic tribes began moving into the region in about the 700's. Various Turkic peoples from eastern Persia and central Asia ruled what is now Tajikistan from about 900 to 1200. Mongols led by Genghis Khan conquered the region in the 1200's. Turkic tribes called Uzbeks ruled from the 1500's to the 1800's.

Soviet rule. In the late 1800's, czarist Russian forces conquered part of the region. In 1917, revolutionaries known as Bolsheviks (later called Communists) took control of Russia. By 1921, Russians controlled all of what is now Tajikistan. In 1922, the Soviet Union was formed under Russia's leadership. A rebel group of nationalist Muslim Tajiks known as the *Basmachis* resisted Soviet control into the mid-1920's. In 1924, the Tajik Autonomous Soviet Socialist Republic was formed within the Uzbek Soviet Socialist Republic. In 1929, it acquired additional territory inhabited mostly by Uzbeks and became the Tajik Soviet Socialist Republic.

The Soviets made many changes in Tajikistan. The Soviet government built roads, railroads, schools, and modern housing. It also developed industries, especially agriculture and mining. In addition, the Soviets *collectivized* agriculture—that is, they transferred control of farms and livestock to the government. They also tried to reduce the influence of Islam and prohibited the Tajiks from practicing many of their traditions.

Independence. In the 1980's, opposition groups began to protest against the Communist-controlled government, demanding better housing and more control over their own affairs. In 1989, Tajik replaced Russian as the official language of the republic. In 1990, Tajikistan declared that its laws overruled Soviet laws. In September 1991, Tajikistan declared its independence. In December, it joined other republics in a loose association called the Commonwealth of Independent States. The Soviet Union was formally dissolved on December 25.

Recent developments. In September 1992, anti-Communist and Islamic opposition groups forced the resignation of President Rakhman Nabiyev, a former Soviet Communist Party chief. In November, the opposition groups were forced out of power by supporters of the former government, most of whose leaders were former Communist officials. The parliament eliminated the office of president and made the chairman of parliament the head of state. These events triggered violence and led to a civil war. Tens of thousands of people died in the fighting, and hundreds of thousands fled their homes. The war also disrupted the country's economy.

In November 1994, a new constitution abolished the office of chairman and reestablished the office of president. Emomali Rahmonov was elected president. In 1997, the government and opposition leaders signed a peace agreement to end the civil war. Rahmonov was reelected in 1999. Nancy Lubin

See also **Commonwealth of Independent States; Dushanbe.**

Tajo River. See Tagus River.

Takakkaw Falls, *TAK uh kaw,* consist of a series of waterfalls in the Canadian Rockies. The main falls drop 833 feet (254 meters). The Takakkaw Falls are near the eastern border of British Columbia, near the village of Field. They are on the Yoho River in Canada's Yoho National Park. See also **Waterfall** (chart). Graeme Wynn

Takin, *TAH kihn,* is a large hoofed mammal closely related to goats, sheep, and musk oxen. Takins live in central, western, and southwestern China, in Myanmar, and in the Himalaya. They inhabit dense bamboo forests and thickets of rhododendrons on steep, rugged slopes.

Takins resemble musk oxen, with stout forelegs, a large head, and a thick neck. They have shaggy fur that varies from blackish-brown to golden or yellowish-white. A stripe runs along the middle of the back. Both males and females grow horns, but the females' horns are smaller. Takins measure up to 3 $\frac{1}{2}$ feet (107 centimeters) tall at the shoulder and weigh up to 770 pounds (350 kilograms). Males are heavier than females.

Takins are active mostly at dusk and dawn, but they may be active throughout the day in foggy or cloudy weather. Normally, they spend the daylight hours hidden in dense vegetation. During the warm months, takins feed primarily on young trees, grass, and tender herbs. In winter, they eat mostly the tips of bamboo stems and willow branches.

During the summer, takins gather in large herds led by an old *bull* (male). In winter, the herds are smaller and move to valleys at lower elevations. Takins mate in July or August. The *cow* (female) gives birth to a single young, called a *kid,* in March or April. Duane A. Schlitter

Scientific classification. Takins belong to the bovid family, Bovidae. They are *Budorcas taxicolor.*

Zoological Society of San Diego

The takin is a large hoofed mammal that resembles a musk ox. The animal lives in Myanmar, the Himalaya, and parts of China.

Talbotype, *TAL buh typ* or *TAWL buh typ,* was one of the first two photographic processes that marked the beginning of photography. Talbotype and the other process, daguerreotype, were introduced in 1839 (see **Daguerreotype**). The name talbotype honors its inventor, William H. Fox Talbot, an English classical archaeologist and translator. *Calotype* is another word for the talbotype process and the prints made by the process.

Fox Talbot made sheets of paper sensitive to light by bathing them in solutions of common salt and silver nitrate. He then exposed the paper to light from images projected by a lens within a device known as a camera obscura (see **Camera obscura**). Since silver salts turn dark where light falls upon them, he created negatives when he exposed the paper to the images. Further chemical treatment made the negatives permanent. Fox Talbot used the negatives to print positives onto other sensitized sheets. The negative-positive concept of photography used today is based on this process. Fox Talbot's *The Pencil of Nature* (1844) was the first photographically illustrated book. David F. Silver

See also **Photography** (History).

Talc is an extremely soft mineral that may be white, light green, or gray. Manufacturers use ground talc in the making of ceramics, rubber, plastics, and lubricants. Talc serves as a dusting agent to prevent molded products from sticking to the mold and as a coating on finished products. It is also used as a filler in paint, paper, and soap. Cosmetics manufacturers grind pure talc into fine talcum powder. The talc-rich rock steatite, also known as *soapstone,* serves as an electric insulator, as a liner for furnaces and stoves, and as an acid-proof covering for tables, sinks, and containers.

Talc is so soft that it can be scratched with a fingernail. It defines the softest rating, 1, on the Mohs hardness scale, a ranking of mineral hardness used by geologists. Talc has a distinct greasy or soapy feel. Its chemical formula is $Mg_3Si_4O_{10}(OH)_2$. It often forms when the minerals olivine, pyroxene, or dolomite react with water under heat and pressure. Mark Cloos

See also **Mineral** (picture); **Soapstone.**

Talent is a famous old unit of weight and value. The Hebrews, Babylonians, Greeks, and Romans used it. No coin of this denomination was ever *struck* (made), because such a coin would be too large. Instead, a certain number of other coins equaled a talent. The Hebrew silver talent equaled 3,000 shekels in silver. The gold talent had different weights and values in different places. The present use of the word *talent,* meaning *special ability,* may come symbolically from a Bible story (Matthew 25: 14-30). Burton H. Hobson

Taliban are a group of conservative Muslims that controlled most of Afghanistan from the mid-1990's to 2001. *Taliban* (also spelled *Taleban*) means *seekers after knowledge* and refers to the group's origin in Islamic schools. In 2001, the United States and its allies helped Afghan rebels drive the Taliban from power.

The Taliban strictly enforced their interpretation of Islamic laws. For example, the Taliban prohibited most modern forms of entertainment and made women cover themselves from head to toe. Those who violated these laws were punished severely.

The Taliban formed in the early 1990's. They sought to end the lawlessness that had resulted from years of war in Afghanistan. The Taliban captured Afghanistan's second largest city, Kandahar, in November 1994. Throughout 1995, they gained more territory. In 1996, they seized the capital city, Kabul.

In 1998, the United States accused Osama bin Laden, the Saudi-born head of the al-Qa'ida terrorist network, of organizing the bombing of U.S. embassies in Africa. Bin Laden was living in Afghanistan, where he had set up terrorist training camps. The United States asked the Taliban to turn in bin Laden, but they refused. In 2001, the United States accused bin Laden of organizing the September 11 terrorist attacks on the World Trade Center in New York City and the Pentagon Building near Washington, D.C. The United States demanded that the Taliban hand over bin Laden. The Taliban refused, and the United States and its allies launched a military campaign against them. The campaign enabled Afghanistan's Northern Alliance and other rebel groups to drive the Taliban from power. Abraham Marcus

See also **Afghanistan** (History); **Bin Laden, Osama; Qa`ida, Al-; September 11 terrorist attacks.**

Talipes. See **Clubfoot.**

Tallahassee, *TAL uh HAS ee* (pop. 150,624; met. area pop. 284,539), is the capital of Florida. It lies in the northwest part of the state, near the Georgia border. For location, see **Florida** (political map). The name Tallahassee comes from an Indian word meaning *old town.*

The economy of Tallahassee is based on government activities. The city's industries include printing, publishing, seafood processing, and the production of computers and wood products. Tallahassee is the home of Florida Agricultural and Mechanical University, Florida State University, and Tallahassee Community College.

Tallahassee has been the capital since 1824, two years after Florida became a United States territory. A new, high-rise State Capitol and other new state government office buildings were built in the late 1900's. Tallahassee has a commission-manager government and is the seat of Leon County. Peter O. Muller

See also **Florida** (pictures; Climate).

Tallchief, Maria (1925-), became the first American-trained ballerina of international importance. She was known especially for her technical brilliance. Tallchief danced with the Ballet Russe de Monte Carlo from 1942 to 1947, but her career was chiefly associated with the New York City Ballet. She danced with this company from 1947 to 1965.

Tallchief was born on Jan. 24, 1925, in Fairfax, Oklahoma, the daughter of an Osage Indian father and a Scottish-Irish-Dutch mother. She was married to New York City Ballet director George Balanchine from 1946 to 1951. She created roles in many of his ballets, including *Orpheus* (1948) and *Scotch Symphony* (1952). Her dancing in Balanchine's version of *The Firebird* (1949) established her international reputation. Tallchief founded the Chicago City Ballet in 1980 and served as its artistic director from 1980 to 1987. Katy Matheson

© Martha Swope

Maria Tallchief danced the title role in *The Firebird, shown here,* with American ballet dancer Francisco Moncion.

Talleyrand, *TAL ih rand* (1754-1838), was a French statesman famous for his diplomatic achievements under Emperor Napoleon I and at the Congress of Vienna. His full name was Charles Maurice de Talleyrand-Périgord, Prince de Bénévent. He was born on Feb. 2, 1754, in Paris. He became a priest in 1775. In 1789, he was named bishop of Autun, a high Roman Catholic post.

Supports state above church. Talleyrand was elected in 1789 to the Estates-General, the French parliament. He became a moderate leader of the French Revolution. He favored constitutional monarchy and signed the Declaration of the Rights of Man and of the Citizen. He was elected president of the National Assembly (part of the Estates-General) in 1790. Talleyrand won popularity for proposing that the government take church property to pay its debts. The pope *excommunicated* him (expelled him from the church) in 1791 for his part in giving control of the French Catholic Church to the state and for taking an oath to the Constitution.

Talleyrand was in England on a political mission when the revolution took a radical turn in 1792. The new French government accused him of supporting the monarchy and forbade his return to France. After two years in England, he fled to the United States.

Joins Napoleon. Talleyrand was allowed to return to France in 1796. Through the influence of his friend Madame de Staël, Talleyrand was made minister of foreign affairs in the new French government called the Directory. He decided to rebuild his fortune. In the famous XYZ Affair in 1797, he was accused of demanding bribes of the U.S. representatives (see **XYZ Affair**).

Talleyrand also decided to build his political future by attaching himself to Napoleon. He helped Napoleon replace the Directory, first with the Consulate in 1799, and then with the Empire in 1804. As Napoleon's adviser and foreign minister, he led delicate negotiations, such as those producing the Peace of Tilsit with Russia in 1807.

Deserts Napoleon. Napoleon depended on Talleyrand but distrusted him. Talleyrand came to oppose Napoleon's conquests as harmful to France and to European peace. After 1807, Talleyrand was dismissed by Napoleon and became the center of the growing opposition to the emperor. In 1814, he helped remove Napoleon from power and put Louis XVIII, of the Bourbon royal family, on the French throne. Talleyrand's diplomatic skill at the Congress of Vienna of 1814 and 1815 gave defeated France an acceptable peace settlement (see **Vienna, Congress of**).

His last years. After 1815, the Bourbon court excluded Talleyrand from public affairs. But in 1830, when the Bourbons lost public confidence, he helped steer a revolution toward constitutional monarchy under Louis Philippe. Talleyrand became ambassador to the United Kingdom, where he guided negotiations that made Belgium independent, and brought France and the United Kingdom into alliance. He died on May 17, 1838.

Eric A. Arnold, Jr.

Tallinn, *TAHL lihn* (pop. 500,000), is the capital and largest city of Estonia. It lies on the northern coast of Estonia, along the Gulf of Finland (see **Estonia** [map]).

Tallinn is an important industrial and cultural center and seaport. Its industries include food processing and the manufacture of industrial machinery, paper, and textiles. The city is best known for its many beautiful churches, castles, and other buildings that were erected from the 1200's to the 1500's.

Tallinn was founded in 1219 by Danish forces that conquered the Estonians settled in the area. The city was the capital of the independent nation of Estonia from 1918 to 1940. In 1940, the Soviets seized Estonia and forced it to become part of the Soviet Union. In September 1991, Estonia became an independent nation again.

Jaroslaw Bilocerkowycz

Tallis, *TAL ihs,* **Thomas** (1505?-1585), was an English composer of religious vocal music during the Renaissance period. Tallis's earlier music was written for the Roman Catholic Church. It was complicated, with many interweaving voices known as *counterpoint,* and used Latin words. Later, under Protestant Queen Elizabeth I, Tallis composed *anthems* (choral pieces with English words). His late music is less elaborate and more expressive. *Spem in alium,* a spectacular unaccompanied choral work called a *motet,* is often performed by choruses today. With his younger colleague William Byrd, Tallis shared the post of organist at the Chapel Royal, the queen's private chapel. In 1575, the two composers published a famous collection called *Cantiones sacrae (Sacred Music).* Tallis's birthplace is unknown.

Jocelyn Godwin

Tallow is a fatty substance used in many products. It is obtained by *rendering* (melting) and refining the fat of cattle, goats, or sheep. Tallow is classified as either *edible* or *inedible.* Edible tallow is used primarily as an ingredient in shortening for cooking. Most inedible tallow produced in the United States is used to make animal feed, such as cattle feed and pet food. Inedible tallow is also chemically treated to make soaps and detergents (see **Detergent and soap** [How detergents are made]). Edible tallow is white and almost tasteless. Inedible tallow may be white, yellow, or brown.

Tallow is an important source of certain fatty acids. About half the fatty acid molecules in tallow are *saturated*—that is, they contain as many hydrogen atoms as possible (see **Fat**). Fatty acids obtained from tallow are used to make hundreds of everyday products, including automobile tires, cosmetics, detergents, lubricants, and plastics. These acids can do the job of many of the chemicals ordinarily manufactured from petroleum. Therefore, tallow can help conserve the limited supply of petroleum in the world. Paul Bradley Addis

Tallowtree is the name of several trees that produce a waxy substance that can be used like tallow for making candles. Today, mineral waxes usually are used instead of tallow in candle making. In the past, the tree most often used for its tallow was the *Chinese tallowtree.* The seeds of this tree hang on waxlike threads among the leaves. Workers crushed and boiled the capsules and seeds and skimmed off the tallow as it rose to the surface. The tallow was then melted and refined.

The Chinese tallowtree has been planted as a shade tree and along streets in the Southeastern United States for over 100 years. It now grows wild in areas along the Atlantic and Gulf coasts. Its leaves flutter in the slightest breeze and give it the appearance of a poplar. The leaves turn brilliant red in autumn. Paul Bradley Addis

Scientific classification. Tallowtrees belong to the spurge family, Euphorbiaceae. The scientific name for the Chinese tallowtree is *Sapium sebiferum.*

Talmud *TAL muhd,* is a collection of Jewish religious and civil laws, together with scholarly interpretations of their meaning. The Talmud ranks second to the Bible as the most sacred and influential written work of the Jewish religion. Judaism considers the full-time study of the Talmud to be one of the most honorable occupations.

The Talmud consists of two parts, the *Mishnah* and the *Gemara.* The Mishnah is the written version of traditional Jewish oral law. Short passages of the Mishnah are followed by extremely thorough explanations, which make up the Gemara. The scholars who wrote the Gemara did not always agree in their interpretations of the Mishnah. As a result, the Gemara includes many debates on small details of Jewish law. It also discusses history and Jewish customs and includes Jewish folk tales.

The Talmud consists of 63 sections called *tractates,* which are divided into six *orders.* Each order deals with a different subject. For example, the order *Nashim* (Women) discusses marriage, divorce, and other matters that concern relationships between a man and a woman. The other orders cover agriculture, festivals, civil and criminal law, purity, and sacrificial worship.

According to Jewish tradition, the Mishnah and Gemara are based on the Oral Law, consisting of interpretations of the Bible that originated in the time of Moses, about 1250 B.C. These interpretations were memorized and handed down orally. The Mishnah's contents were collected from about A.D. 70 to 200. The Gemara, which has two versions, was written between about 200 and 500. The *Palestinian Gemara* was completed about 425 and the *Babylonian Gemara* about 500. The Talmud laid the groundwork for all future Jewish observance. Lawrence H. Schiffman

See also **Akiva ben Joseph.**

Additional resources

Abrams, Judith Z. *A Beginner's Guide to the Steinsaltz Talmud.* Jason Aronson, 1999.

Cohen, Abraham. *Everyman's Talmud.* 1949. Reprint. Schocken, 1995.

Strack, Hermann L., and Stemberger, Gunter. *Introduction to the Talmud and Midrash.* Rev. ed. Augsburg, 1992.

Talon *tah LOHN,* **Jean Baptiste,** *zhahn bah TEEST* (1625-1694), a French official, served from 1665 to 1672 as *intendant* (administrative head) of justice and finance in Canada, then called New France. Talon set up royal administration in the French colony. He oversaw the settlement of some 2,000 colonists, mainly soldiers and Frenchwomen. Talon conducted the first Canadian census in 1666. He put the economy on a sound basis and established a royal shipyard in Quebec City. Talon was born on Jan. 8, 1625, in Chalons-sur-Marne, France.

John A. Dickinson

Tamarack. See **Larch.**

Tamarin, *TAM uhr ihn,* is a type of small monkey that lives in tropical rain forests in Central and South America. It is closely related to, but slightly larger than, the marmoset (see **Marmoset**). Tamarins grow up to 12

San Diego Zoo

Lion tamarins have long, golden-orange hair. These small monkeys are found in tropical rain forests of eastern Brazil.

inches (31 centimeters) long, not including the tail, which may be up to 17 inches (44 centimeters) long. The animals weigh up to 2 pounds.

There are 14 species of tamarins. Most are multicolored, with red, white, and brown the most common color patterns. Some species have long hair on the top of the head and showy mustaches. The *lion tamarins* of eastern Brazil have a mane of long, silky hair on the head and a bright golden-orange coloring. Lion tamarins are in danger of extinction. The growth of urban areas has destroyed much of their habitat.

Tamarins eat fruit, insects, frogs, and tree gums. They live in groups of up to 40 members and communicate with each other by using a wide variety of high-pitched calls. Infant tamarins cling to the backs of their parents or other family members. Roderic B. Mast

Scientific classification. Tamarins belong to the tamarin and marmoset family, Callitrichidae. Lion tamarins are genus *Leontopithecus.* Other tamarins are genus *Saguinus.*

Tamarind, *TAM uhr ihnd,* is a large evergreen tree that grows in the tropics. It is native to Asia and, probably, to Africa. The tree may grow 75 feet (23 meters) tall. It has leaves that consist of 10 to 18 pairs of leaflets and small, pale yellow flowers. The tamarind tree produces brown pods that are 2 to 6 inches (5 to 15 centimeters) long. The pods of the tamarind contain an acidic pulp that may be eaten fresh or used to make jams, sauces, syrups, and drinks. The seeds of the tamarind may be roasted and eaten. The tamarind is grown as a shade tree in southern Florida. J. Massey

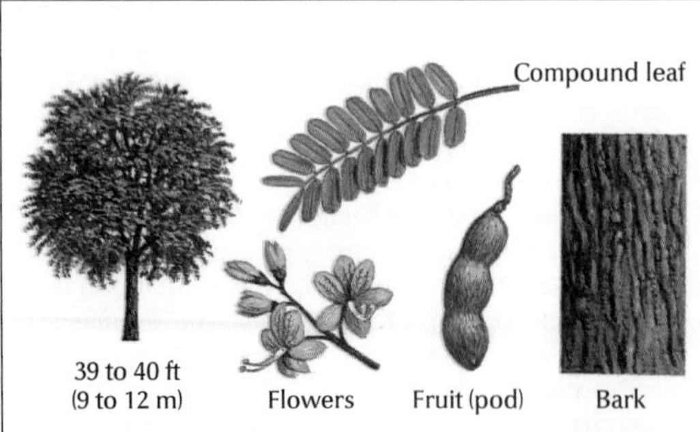

WORLD BOOK illustration by John D. Dawson

The tamarind has compound leaves and small flowers. The pods contain an acidic pulp used to make jams and tart drinks.

Scientific classification. The tamarind belongs to the pea family, Leguminosae or Fabaceae. Its scientific name is *Tamarindus indica.*

Tamayo, *tah MAH yoh,* **Rufino,** *roo FEE noh* (1899-1991), was an important Mexican painter. He became noted for his bold, brightly colored paintings of human figures, animals, and still lifes. Tamayo painted in a semiabstract style, in which he distorted forms to make them more expressive. His paintings reflect the influence of the folklore, history, and landscape of Mexico. However, unlike other major Mexican artists of his day, Tamayo seldom emphasized nationalism or political ideology.

Tamayo was born on Aug. 29, 1899, in Oaxaca. In the early 1920's, he worked sketching ancient Indian sculpture for the National Museum of Anthropology in Mexico City. In the 1930's and early 1940's, his style was affected by his exposure to the works of the modern European painters Georges Braque, Joan Miró, and Pablo Picasso. Beginning about 1970, Tamayo's paintings became more abstract and philosophical, often exploring the individual's relation to the universe.

Judith Berg Sobré

Tambourine, *TAM buh REEN,* is a percussion instrument that consists of a narrow wooden or metal hoop with a thin sheet of plastic or animal skin stretched across one side. All tambourines have small metal disks attached to the hoop. Performers hold the tambourine in one hand. They play it by striking it with the other hand, by hitting it against the knee or upper leg, and by shaking it. The tambourine was made popular by Turkish soldiers called Janissaries, who played the instrument in military bands from the 1400's to the early 1800's. Western musicians began using the tambourine during the 1700's. John H. Beck

WORLD BOOK photo

A tambourine

Tamerlane. See Timur.

Tammany, Society of, also called the Columbian Order, was founded in New York City in 1789 by William Mooney. The organization took its name from the Sons of Saint Tammany. This colonial society was named after an early Delaware Indian chief known for his wisdom. Tammany began as a "fraternity of patriots solemnly consecrated to the independence, the popular liberty, and the federal union of the country."

But Tammany soon came to have a political purpose. For many years, it wielded vast powers as a Democratic political machine in New York and New York City. Its popular name, Tammany Hall, came from the name of its headquarters building, located at 331 Madison Avenue, New York City. Many scandals have darkened the organization's history. The most famous one was exposed in 1871, when Tammany boss William M. Tweed and others were arrested and charged with defrauding New York City of several million dollars. The organization soon regained its power and dominated much of the city's politics until 1933. Donald R. McCoy

See also **Bucktails; Cleveland, Grover** (Governor of New York); **Nast, Thomas; Tilden, Samuel Jones; Tweed, William M.**

Tamoxifen is a drug widely prescribed throughout the world for treatment of breast cancer. In breast tissue, tamoxifen blocks the action of the hormone *estrogen.* Estrogen stimulates some breast cancer cells to grow and divide by attaching to proteins inside the cells called *estrogen receptors.* Tamoxifen also binds to these receptors and prevents attachment of estrogen, depriving cancer cells of growth signals.

Not all breast cancer cells have estrogen receptors, and tamoxifen is most useful for patients whose cancers do have them. The drug helps prevent reappearance of cancer in women whose tumors have been removed surgically. In patients whose cancer has already reappeared, tamoxifen can slow the growth of tumors and prolong life. Some women with cancer in one breast have an increased risk that a new cancer will develop in their other breast. Tamoxifen lowers the risk that these new cancers will form. Studies show that tamoxifen is even more effective when given with another estrogen-suppressing drug called *letrozole.* Some studies suggest that tamoxifen also significantly reduces the likelihood that breast cancer will develop in healthy women who have an increased risk for the disease.

The main side effects of tamoxifen are nausea, vomiting, and *hot flashes* (sudden, intense sensations of body heat). In some tissues, tamoxifen behaves like estrogen rather than blocking its action. Like estrogen, tamoxifen increases the risk of developing cancer of the uterus. But the risk is still small, and most experts agree that the benefits of tamoxifen far outweigh this risk for women with breast cancer. Some studies suggest that tamoxifen can help prevent *osteoporosis (AHS tee oh puh ROH sihs),* a loss of bone tissue as people age. Tamoxifen may also help lower cholesterol levels. V. Craig Jordan

See also **Breast cancer.**

Tampa, Florida (pop. 303,447), is a major United States seaport and an important commercial and industrial center of the state. Tampa, one of the largest cities in Florida, lies on the northeast shore of Tampa Bay (see **Florida** [political map]). St. Petersburg, Tampa's "twin city," lies about 15 miles (25 kilometers) southwest across the bay from Tampa. The metropolitan area of Tampa, St. Petersburg, and Clearwater has a population of 2,395,997. The area has grown rapidly since the 1970's.

In 1823, Robert J. Hackley, a pioneer from New York City, became the first United States citizen to settle in the area that is now Tampa. The U.S. Army built Fort Brooke there the next year. White settlers soon established a village near the fort. They named the village Tampa for the bay. The bay was named for an Indian village that once stood in the area.

Description. Tampa, the county seat of Hillsborough County, covers about 170 square miles (440 square kilometers). This area includes about 65 square miles (168 square kilometers) of inland water. Part of the city lies on islands and peninsulas. Tampa's downtown area lies at the mouth of the Hillsborough River, near the point where the river empties into Hillsborough Bay. Hillsborough Bay is the northeast arm of Tampa Bay.

Hispanic Americans make up about 20 percent of Tampa's population. Most of the city's Hispanics live in a neighborhood known as Ybor City that is located just northeast of downtown. Blacks make up about a fourth of Tampa's population. Most blacks live in neighborhoods west and north of Ybor City.

Tampa is the home of the University of Tampa. The University of South Florida is just north of the city. The city's public schools form part of the Hillsborough County school system. The Tampa Public Library operates about 15 branch libraries.

Cultural attractions in Tampa include the Tampa Museum, the Hillsborough County Museum of Science and Industry, and the Henry B. Plant Museum on the campus of the University of Tampa. The Florida Orchestra, the Tampa Ballet, and various dramas are staged at the Tampa Bay Performing Arts Center, a three-theater complex completed in 1987. The Dark Continent/Busch Gardens, a famous theme park and zoo, attracts millions of visitors annually. Every February, the Gasparilla Festival is held in Tampa. The festival features a "pirate attack" on the city. The Florida State Fair is also held in Tampa every February. Three professional sports teams play in the Tampa area: the Tampa Bay Buccaneers of the National Football League, the Tampa Bay Devil Rays of baseball's American League, and the Tampa Bay Lightning of the National Hockey League.

Economy of Tampa is based mainly on service industries. The most important service industries include banking, wholesale trade, and tourism. The tourist-related activities include the operation of hotels, motels, car rental agencies, and cruise ship lines. Data processing and health care are also important service industries in Tampa. Food processing is the city's most important manufacturing activity. Tampa's leading food products are fish and soft drinks.

The Port of Tampa handles more cargo than any other Florida port. Its exports include phosphate ore from nearby mines. Fishing fleets based in Tampa catch large amounts of shrimp and other seafood. Nearby MacDill Air Force Base employs many residents of the Tampa area. Major airlines use Tampa International Airport.

Government. Tampa has a mayor-council form of government. The voters elect the mayor and the seven council members, all to four-year terms.

History. Calusa and Timucuan Indians lived near what is now Tampa Bay when white people first arrived. Several groups of Spanish explorers visited the area during the 1500's. One of these expeditions, led by Hernando de Soto, landed near the bay in 1539.

Robert J. Hackley, a pioneer from New York City, came to the area in 1823 and built a plantation. In 1824, the U.S. government moved many Seminole Indians to a reservation near Tampa Bay. The Indians had fought to keep their hunting grounds in northern Florida but the Army defeated them. The Army built Fort Brooke on Tampa Bay to supervise the Seminole. Tampa grew up around the fort. The city was incorporated in 1855 and had a population of 885 in 1860. Union troops occupied Tampa during the American Civil War (1861-1865).

Henry B. Plant, an industrialist from Atlanta, Georgia, spent millions of dollars in the late 1800's to develop Tampa. Plant built a railroad that connected Tampa with the North and established the city's tourist industry. In

1886, a Florida tobacco processor, Vicente Martinez Ybor, founded a cigar industry in what is now Ybor City. Phosphate mining began near Tampa in 1888. The city served as a military base during the Spanish-American War (1898) and as a shipbuilding center during World War I (1914-1918). By 1920, 51,608 people lived in Tampa.

Real estate speculation in Florida attracted thousands of people to Tampa during the 1920's. The city had 101,161 people by 1930. For an account of the real estate boom, see **Florida** (History [The early 1900's]). Shipbuilding thrived in Tampa in the first half of the 1940's, during World War II, and the Army Air Forces operated three bases nearby. The 1950's brought industrial growth to the city. By 1960, Tampa had 274,970 people.

In the 1960's and 1970's, Tampa undertook several urban renewal projects. One project eliminated some slums near the Hillsborough River. New construction on the site included apartment buildings, a convention hall, a new city library, and office towers.

Tampa and its suburbs have grown rapidly since the 1970's. The growth included a boom in the construction of new buildings. Over a dozen new office towers were constructed downtown in the late 1970's and early 1980's. A major new office complex named Westshore was completed near Tampa International Airport in the mid-1980's. The airport itself was expanded in the late 1980's to accommodate more passengers and freight. The Tampa Bay Performing Arts Center opened in 1987.

Tampa's rapid growth has caused problems. Some public services and facilities have been unable to keep pace with the growth. For example, roads and highways have become overcrowded. Peter O. Muller

Tampere, *TAHM puh RAY* (pop. 195,468; met. area pop. 270,753) is one of Finland's largest cities and industrial centers. Only Helsinki has more industry. The city lies in southern Finland between Lakes Näsijärvi and Pyhäjärvi (see **Finland** [political map]).

Tampere's chief industries are food and metal processing and paper and textile production. The Tammerkoski River and waterfalls run through the city. Tampere has abundant parks and other recreational areas. It is the home of the University of Tampere. Most of the city's people live in apartments. Some of its suburbs stand on beautiful ridges overlooking the lakes.

During the Middle Ages, the site of what is now Tampere was an important market and milling center. King Gustav III of Sweden and Finland established Tampere as a city in 1779. The city began its industrial growth in the mid-1800's. Pekka Kalevi Hamalainen

Tampico, *tam PEE koh* (pop. 294,789), is Mexico's second most important port, after Veracruz. It stands 7 miles (11 kilometers) west of the Gulf of Mexico on the Pánuco River (see **Mexico** [political map]). It is a refining center for Mexico's petroleum industry and is the chief outlet for oil exports. A mild winter climate and good hunting and fishing make it a favorite resort center. Spaniards settled Tampico in the 1500's. James D. Riley

Tana, Lake. See Lake Tana.

Tanager, *TAN uh juhr,* is the common name given a subfamily of American birds, many of which have brilliant red, blue, or green feathers. Tanagers are from 6 to 8 inches (15 to 20 centimeters) long and are usually found in the forests, where they feed on insects, fruits, and flowers. There are more than 200 species of tanagers, most of which live in Central and South America. Only a few species of tanagers live in the United States.

Ron Austing

The summer tanager nests in the southern United States. The male, *shown here,* is also called the *summer redbird.*

The well-known *scarlet tanager* has a loud, cheery song somewhat like that of the robin. Scarlet tanagers nest in the eastern United States and as far north as eastern Canada. They are sometimes called *firebirds.* The male has bright red feathers, with velvety black wings and tail. The female is dull yellow below and olive-green above, with darker wings and tail. The tanager builds its frail, saucer-shaped nest near the end of a horizontal limb. The female lays three to five bluish-green eggs with reddish-brown markings.

In the Southern States, the *summer tanager* is a familiar bird. It has rosy-red feathers. Its nesting habits are much like those of the scarlet tanager. The *western tanager,* or *Louisiana tanager,* lives in summer from the Rockies to the Pacific Coast. The male has a black back, tail, and wings, red head, and yellow underparts.

The tanagers eat many types of insects, including some insect pests. The western tanager has a great fondness for cherries and may harm cherry orchards.

Bertin W. Anderson

Scientific classification. Tanagers form the tanager subfamily, Thraupinae. The scarlet tanager is *Piranga olivacea.* The summer tanager is *P. rubra.* The western tanager is *P. ludoviciana.*

See also **Bird** (picture: Birds of forests and woodlands).

Tananarive. See Antananarivo.

Taney, *TAW nee,* **Roger Brooke** (1777-1864), served as chief justice of the United States from 1836 to 1864. The merit of his work is clouded by his decision in the Dred Scott case of 1857, which helped bring about the American Civil War (1861-1865). In the Dred Scott case, Taney held that Congress did not have power to abolish slavery in the territories.

Brown Bros.

Roger B. Taney

Taney was born on March 17, 1777, in Calvert County, Maryland. He attended Dickinson College, and he began practicing law in Annapolis, Maryland, in 1799.

Taney served several years in the Maryland state Senate. He also won a high reputation as a lawyer. In 1831, President Andrew Jackson appointed Taney the attorney general of the United States and made him an adviser.

Jackson was opposed to the United States Bank and decided to end its influence by withdrawing the government deposits over the opposition of Congress (see **Bank of the United States**). In 1833, he appointed Taney secretary of the treasury to have him withdraw the funds. The Senate was so angered that it refused to confirm Taney's appointment, and he retired to private life.

In 1835, Jackson appointed Taney an associate justice of the Supreme Court, but the Senate refused to confirm the appointment. In 1836, the Senate majority changed. Jackson named Taney as chief justice, and the Senate approved. Taney favored states' rights and a greater role for the judicial branch of the federal government. He died on Oct. 12, 1864. Bruce Allen Murphy

See also **Dred Scott Decision.**

Tang dynasty, *tahng,* was a series of rulers who governed China from A.D. 618 to 907. Many historians consider the Tang period the golden age of Chinese civilization. The dynasty's capital city, Chang'an (now Xi'an), became one of the great cultural centers of the world. Artists, poets, scholars, merchants, and government and religious leaders from many countries visited Chang'an and the Chinese coastal trading centers.

The Tang rulers united China and established a strong central government. They carefully hand-picked their chief officials. The Tang emperors also set up a council of ministers to act as advisers. In addition, the emperors sent inspectors into the provinces of China to check on the activities of local governors.

The Tang rulers also promoted trade, which became the basis of the empire's great prosperity. Jade, porcelain, rice, silks, spices, tea, and other Chinese products flowed to India, the Middle East, and Europe along trade routes opened by the Tang emperors.

During the Tang period, the Chinese invented block printing, which soon replaced the handwritten scriptures of the Chinese Buddhists. In 868, the Chinese produced the *Diamond Sutra,* the world's first block-printed book.

The rise of the dynasty. The Tang dynasty followed the Sui dynasty, which had ruled China from A.D. 581 to 618. Li Yuan, an aristocrat, overthrew the Sui emperor and became the first Tang ruler (see **Li Yuan**). He set up his capital at Chang'an in northwestern China. *Chang'an* meant *long peace,* but China was soon torn by civil war. In addition, a struggle for power developed among the nobility. In 626, Li Yuan turned the control of China over to his son Li Shimin, who took the name Tang Taizong (also spelled *T'ang T'ai-tsung*). Taizong ruled for 23 years and became one of the greatest emperors in Chinese history.

Taizong was a powerful leader. He destroyed his competitors for the throne, began an alliance with the Korean state of Silla, and forced Turkish nomads out of Northern China. His armies conquered parts of Tibet and Turkestan, opening overland trade routes from China to India and central Asia. The trade routes not only brought great wealth to the empire, but they also promoted religious and cultural exchange. The routes gave Christian and other foreign missionaries an overland entrance into China and allowed Chinese Buddhist pilgrims to visit India.

Taizong reorganized the administration of the empire. He built colleges to help select and train officials for government work. Although Buddhism was the country's main religion, Taizong knew that many Chinese who could help him carry out his programs followed Confucianism. As a result, he named many Confucians to high government posts.

In 649, Tang Gaozong (also spelled *T'ang Gao-tsung*) became emperor. But his wife, Empress Wu, soon took

The Tang Empire about A.D. 750

This map shows the land ruled by the Tang emperors from their capital at Chang'an. The Tang Empire reached its greatest size under Emperor Xuanzong. It controlled territory from eastern China to Persia. Arabs defeated Chinese armies at Talas in A.D. 751. This battle marked the end of Tang power in Turkestan and the closing of overland trade routes to the west.

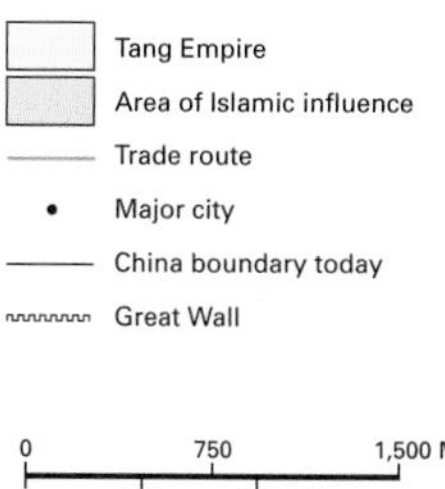

WORLD BOOK map

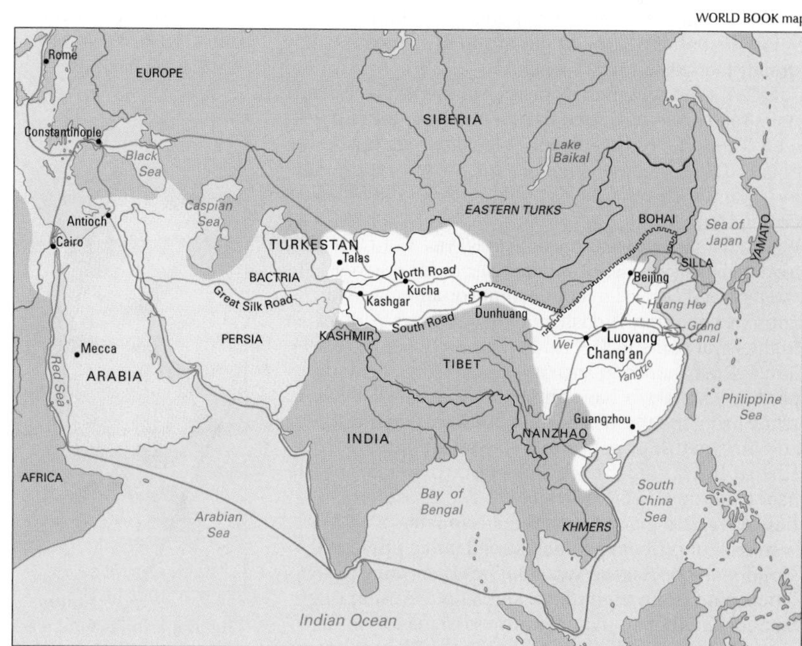

The Snite Museum of Art, University of Notre Dame, Gift of Mr. and Mrs. Lester Wolfe

Figures of four female musicians illustrate the simple charm of pottery figures of the Tang dynasty. The figures were created to be placed in a tomb when a person was buried.

control of the government. Gaozong died in 683, and his son became emperor—but Empress Wu continued to control the government. She eventually proclaimed herself emperor, becoming the only woman in Chinese history to rule as emperor.

Empress Wu governed China with a great amount of skill. She appointed able ministers to major government posts and had the loyalty of her advisers and officials. Empress Wu maintained the high reputation of the Tang dynasty abroad because of her political brilliance. The empress also showed great favoritism to Buddhism and promoted art and literature. During the late 600's, Tibet forced the Chinese out of Turkestan. To protect China's trade routes there, Empress Wu sent her armies into the region and recovered the Tang territory.

The middle years. Tang Xuanzong, the grandson of Empress Wu, became emperor in 712. Xuanzong, also known as Ming Huang (Brilliant Emperor), was the last of the three great Tang rulers. During his reign, China produced some of its best artists and such great poets as Li Bo (also spelled *Li Po)* and Du Fu (also spelled *Tu Fu).* Xuanzong's economic programs, including the development of new farming regions in the Yangtze Valley, greatly increased China's wealth.

In 747, China reached its peak of influence in western Asia. Tang armies invaded Bactria and Kashmir and defeated an Arab-Tibetan alliance that had been formed against China's allies in central Asia. But in 751, a revolt in Turkestan closed China's trade routes to the Middle East.

When Xuanzong was more than 60 years old, he fell in love with his son's wife and took her as his mistress. She soon gained control over the emperor and made him appoint a cunning Turkish military governor, An Lushan, to the royal court. In 755, An Lushan organized a rebellion against Xuanzong and captured and briefly occupied the capital of Chang'an. In 756, Xuanzong gave his son, Suzon, the throne. In 763, a combination of Chinese and foreign troops defeated the rebel armies of An Lushan. But during the rebellion, army generals and military governors in the provinces had increased their power, weakening the central government.

In addition, Tibet had been united into a powerful kingdom while Suzong was fighting An Lushan. In 763, Tibetan forces invaded China. Forces of the Tang rulers battled the Tibetans in northwestern China for about 80 years. This conflict further weakened the Tang dynasty.

The fall of the dynasty. Border wars and rebellions in the provinces troubled China from 763 to 874. Yet the Tang dynasty remained prosperous, largely because of a new tax system. The Chinese had been required to pay their taxes with labor and goods. Under the new system, they could also pay with cash. This new system was more efficient than the older one and provided increased income. In 874, Huang Chao led a peasant uprising, and in 881 the rebels captured the capital of Chang'an. They were defeated in 884. But afterward, the weakened central government could no longer control its generals or provincial governors.

In 907, the Tang dynasty finally came to an end. Until the Song dynasty gained control of China in 960, the country was governed by a series of short-lived military dynasties. Grant Hardy

See also **China** (The Tang dynasty; picture: Multicolor ceramics).

Tanganyika. See **Tanzania.**

Tanganyika, Lake. See **Lake Tanganyika.**

Tangelo, *TAN juh loh,* is a mandarin citrus fruit that results from cross-pollination between a tangerine and a grapefruit. The word tangelo comes from *tang*erine and pom*elo,* another name for grapefruit. Tangelos have thin peels and a delicious flavor. Important American varieties include the Minneola and the Orlando. The Ugli is a Jamaican tangelo that is widely grown in the West Indies. Wilfred F. Wardowski

See also **Tangerine; Tangor.**

Tangerine, *TAN juh REEN,* is the popular name for a citrus fruit of the mandarin group. These fruits look like oranges, but are smaller and flatter, peel more easily, and the sections separate more readily. The tangerine is an orange-red mandarin fruit which originated in Southeast Asia. It has a thin, fragrant peel. The fruit of the tangerine is delicate, but the tree is more resistant to cold than is the orange tree. Varieties of tangerines include Clementine, Dancy, Ponkan, and hybrid varieties such as Kinnow, Robinson, Sunburst, and Wilking. In the United States, tangerines are grown in Arizona, California, and Florida. Tangerines are also grown in Brazil, China, Italy,

WORLD BOOK illustration by Kate Lloyd-Jones, Linden Artists Ltd.

The tangerine is a popular citrus fruit. Tangerines are smaller than oranges, peel more easily, and have a delicate taste.

Japan, and Spain. Wilfred F. Wardowski

See also **Tangelo; Tangor.**

Scientific classification. The tangerine belongs to the rue family, Rutaceae. The scientific name for the tangerine is *Citrus reticulata.*

Tangier, *tan JEER* (pop. 497,147), also spelled *Tanger,* is a city on the northern coast of Morocco. It lies along the Strait of Gibraltar, which connects the Atlantic Ocean and the Mediterranean Sea. For Tangier's location, see **Morocco** (map). Tangier is the capital of the province of Tangier. It ranks second only to Casablanca among Morocco's seaports and is the country's main port for passenger vessels. From the sea, the city looks like an amphitheater, with rows of white houses lining its hills.

Most of the people of Tangier are Arabs or Berbers. But Spanish and French—as well as Arabic and Berber—are widely spoken there. Tangier is a center of shipping and tourism. It has few manufacturing industries.

In ancient times, Phoenicians and Romans built settlements near what is now Tangier. The city came under Arab control in the 700's. Portugal, Spain, and England held Tangier at different times from the 1400's until the late 1600's, when the sultan of Morocco gained control. In 1912, Morocco fell under the control of France and Spain. But Tangier remained free from control by any one European nation, though the sultan granted special privileges to several European countries. In 1923, the major European powers placed the city under international control.

Tangier came back under full control of Morocco after the country gained its independence from France and Spain in 1956. During that year, the sultan of Morocco called a conference of the nations that controlled Tangier. The nations voted to end the city's international status, and to give up most of their former rights in the area. Kenneth J. Perkins

Tango, *TANG goh,* was the first Latin American dance to gain great international popularity. The tango is a ballroom dance in slow $\frac{2}{4}$ or $\frac{4}{4}$ time. The dancers alternate long, slow steps with short, quick steps, sometimes making sudden turns and striking dramatic poses.

The tango was danced in the United States about 1912 by Vernon and Irene Castle, a famous ballroom dancing team. It also became popular in Paris and London. Today's tango is related to an Argentine dance called the *milonga,* a Cuban dance called the *habañera,* and a tango from Spain's Andalusian region. Patricia W. Rader

See also **Ballroom dancing.**

Tangor, *TAN jawr,* is a citrus fruit that belongs to the mandarin family (see **Mandarin**). It is produced by cross-pollination between a tangerine and an orange. The parents of tangors are seldom known for certain, except when the fruits result from carefully controlled plant breeding programs. The *Temple* and the *Honey Tangerine* are among the most important tangors cultivated today. Wilfred F. Wardowski

Tank is an armored combat vehicle. Most tanks travel on continuous tracks. They carry such weapons as cannons, machine guns, and grenade launchers. In most tanks, these weapons are mounted in a revolving structure called a *turret.* Some tanks carry smoke generators that can help conceal their positions from an enemy. A tank has a crew of three or four members. It may have metal or ceramic armor.

Tanks are used to attack other armored vehicles, infantry, and ground targets; and to fire on aircraft. Armies throughout the world have many thousands of tanks available for active service. Tanks are classified as *main battle tanks* or as *armored reconnaissance vehicles.* Main battle tanks weigh from 35 to 70 tons (32 to 64 metric tons). Armored reconnaissance vehicles weigh from 10 to 25 tons (9 to 23 metric tons).

Performance. Tanks travel as fast as 50 miles (80 kilometers) per hour on level ground. They average 10 to 20 miles (16 to 32 kilometers) per hour on rough terrain. Tanks can climb and descend slopes as steep as 30 degrees. They can turn around within their own length.

Modern tanks have 120- or 125-millimeter guns and computer fire control systems. These guns can hit small targets 1 mile (1.6 kilometers) away, even while the tank is moving. Modern tanks have heavy frontal armor that can withstand attack by weapons usually capable of penetrating 20 to 40 inches (51 to 102 centimeters) of steel. These tanks can also withstand the blast, heat, and most of the radiation from a nuclear explosion.

History. Tanks got their name from the British, who developed them during World War I (1914-1918). While they were being built, the British called them water tanks to conceal their purpose. The British first used tanks against the Germans in the Battle of the Somme in 1916. The early tanks were slow and clumsy, but they were used successfully in the Battle of Cambrai in 1917.

During World War II (1939-1945), all the warring nations used tanks. German tank units won important vic-

WORLD BOOK illustration by Kim Downing

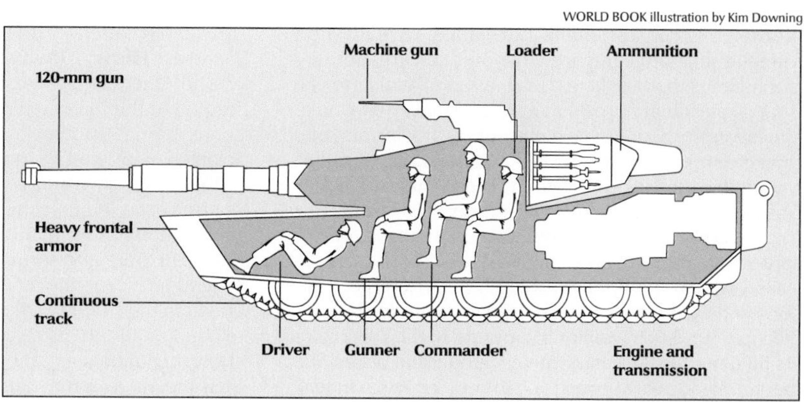

The crew and basic parts of a tank

This diagram of a U.S. Army M1A1 main battle tank shows the position of the crew members, plus some parts of the vehicle. The crew consists of a commander and three other people. One crew member drives the tank, one loads the guns, and the other two fire the guns.

E. R. Degginger

Tankers transport chiefly liquid cargo. Oil tankers like this one are divided into compartments by bulkheads. The bulkheads strengthen the ship's hull, keep liquid cargo from sloshing, and allow the ship to carry more than one product at the same time.

tories over Poland, France, and the Soviet Union. In 1943, the Soviets defeated the Germans at Kursk, in the Soviet Union, in the greatest tank battle in history. In 1944, Allied tanks swept into Germany, helping to assure victory in Europe.

Tanks have taken part in many regional wars, especially in the Middle East. Over 6,000 tanks were used in the Arab-Israeli War of 1973. Nearly half were destroyed in only 18 days of combat. Precision-guided weapons were first used against tanks during this war. During the Persian Gulf War of 1991, the United States used over 2,000 tanks but suffered few losses. Iraq, however, lost more than 3,500 tanks in combat. The United States and its allies also used tanks in taking control of Iraq in the Iraq War, which began in 2003. Robert Powell Smith

See also **Army, U.S.** (Armor); **Michigan** (picture); **Periscope; World War I** (picture); **World War II** (picture).

Tanker is a ship designed to carry liquid cargo. Most tankers transport petroleum products, but they may also carry such cargoes as molasses, wine, chemicals, and even coal, grain, and iron ore.

A tanker has as many as 25 tanks, the walls of which are formed in part by the hull. A crew of 25 to 40 people lives in the deckhouse, which usually stands above the engines at the stern. On most tankers, the deckhouse has five or six stories, with the bridge on top. Cargo pumps and piping line the main deck.

Kinds of tankers. There are three chief kinds of tankers: (1) oil tankers, (2) combination carriers, and (3) liquefied natural gas carriers.

Oil tankers carry crude oil and refined petroleum products. A hull forms the outside of the tanks. *Bulkheads* (walls) run the length and width of the ship and divide the ship into compartments. This construction strengthens the hull. It also enables an oil tanker to carry several petroleum products at once. The larger a tanker, the lower the carrying cost per pound or kilogram of oil.

Extra large oil tankers, called *supertankers,* were developed in the 1960's and 1970's. These ships are also known as *very large crude carriers* (VLCC's) or *ultra large crude carriers* (ULCC's), depending on their size. The largest supertanker ever built was *Seawise Giant.* Now called *Jahre Viking,* it measures 1,504 feet (458 meters) long and 225 feet (69 meters) wide. It can hold about 1.2 billion pounds (550 million kilograms) of oil. When filled, its hull extends 80 feet (24 meters) under the water. Supertankers cruise at speeds of about 15 *knots* (nautical miles per hour) and are extremely difficult to maneuver. A VLCC making an emergency stop may travel over 3 miles (5 kilometers) before stopping completely.

Most supertankers transport oil from the Middle East to Europe and Japan. In those areas, supertankers load and unload cargo through underwater pipelines provided by offshore ports. If a port is not deep enough for a supertanker, the oil is transferred to smaller tankers and brought ashore. The supertanker may deliver some of the oil itself after being made lighter by such a transfer.

Combination carriers carry such cargoes as grain and ore, as well as oil. These ships are divided into two groups, *ore/oil carriers* and *ore/bulk/oil carriers* (OBO's). They have tanks and pumps for storing and unloading liquids. They also have large hatches on the main deck for loading and unloading dry cargo.

Liquefied natural gas (LNG) carriers were developed in the 1960's. When natural gas is chilled to −260 °F (−162 °C), it shrinks to about $\frac{1}{600}$ of its volume and becomes liquid. Plants on shore liquefy natural gas and pump it into specially insulated tanks on the tankers.

Oil spills. Tankers spill about 2 $\frac{1}{2}$ billion pounds (1.1 billion kilograms) of oil into the oceans annually due to accidents and normal ship operations. Many nations are cooperating to reduce this pollution. Most tankers built since the early 1990's have double hulls to minimize oil loss in accidents. Shipping companies have developed methods to help prevent spilled oil from spreading over the water's surface and to help remove spills. Crews also try to prevent discharge of the oily seawater carried in deep holds to stabilize the ships. A. Thayamballi

See also **Petroleum** (Environmental problems); **Ship** (Tankers; pictures).

Tanner, Henry Ossawa, *AHS uh wuh* (1859-1937), was an American painter. During the early 1880's, he studied under the noted artist Thomas Eakins at the Pennsylvania Academy of the Fine Arts in Philadelphia. Eakins encouraged Tanner to paint professionally.

Tanner's early works reflect the influence of Eakins's realistic style. Tanner, an African American, first won recognition for his pictures of black life on plantations.

In 1891, Tanner moved to Europe to continue his studies and to escape the racial prejudice he had experienced in the United States. He settled in Paris and began to paint pictures with religious themes. These works show the influence of the Dutch artist Rembrandt in their glowing, warm colors and dramatic contrasts be-

Oil painting on canvas (1893); Collis P. Huntington Memorial Library, Hampton Institute, Hampton, Virginia

Tanner's *The Banjo Lesson* shows the painter's sympathetic treatment of life among Southern blacks during the late 1800's.

tween light and dark areas. Tanner was born on June 21, 1859, in Pittsburgh and died in Paris on May 25, 1937.

Sarah Burns

See also **Painting** (picture: *The Thankful Poor*).

Tannhäuser, *TAHN hoy zuhr* or *TAN hoy zuhr,* was a German *minnesinger* (minstrel) of the 1200's. He led a restless life and even went to the Holy Land on a crusade. A ballad of the 1500's tells the story that one evening, as he was riding by the Hörselberg in Thuringia, a beautiful woman appeared before him. He recognized her as the goddess Venus. He followed her to a palace inside the mountain and spent seven years there.

Finally, Tannhäuser left Venus and went on a pilgrimage to Rome to seek forgiveness for his sins. The pope said that just as the staff he held in his hand could never blossom, so would Tannhäuser's sins never be forgiven. Tannhäuser went sorrowfully back to Germany. Three days later, the pope's staff miraculously bore flowers. Messengers hurried to seek out Tannhäuser, but he had gone back to Venus. Richard Wagner's opera *Tannhäuser* is based on this legend. James F. Poag

Tannic acid, also called *tannin,* is a group of chemical substances found in the bark, leaves, fruit, roots, and other parts of many trees. Tannin is obtained from oaks, mangroves, wattles, chestnuts, hemlocks, and quebrachos. Tannins are used to tan animal hides. The hides contain gelatin that combines with the tannin, converting the hides to leather. Tannins are also used as *mordants* (dye fixatives) and in manufacturing inks.

Tannins from different sources have different chemical formulas. Most of the tannin used in the United States comes from quebracho trees in Argentina and Paraguay. This tannin is a thick, reddish-brown liquid that may be dried to form a hard cake. Roger D. Barry

See also **Leather** (Tanning).

Tanning. See **Leather; Tannic acid.**

Tansy, *TAN zee,* is a plant related to the daisy. The tansy first grew in Europe, but is now found throughout North America. It is usually grown in gardens, but also grows wild. The leaves and flowers of the tansy have a bitter taste and a strong odor. The leaves were once used in flavoring. These dark green leaves give off an oil which is known as *oil of tansy.* This oil is poisonous, but it is used to some extent in medicines. The flowers of the tansy are yellow. Margaret R. Bolick

Scientific classification. Tansies make up the genus *Tanacetum* in the family Compositae.

Tantalum, *TAN tuh luhm,* is a hard shiny, silver-colored metallic element. Its chemical symbol is Ta. Pure tantalum metal is *ductile* (easily shaped). It serves as an important element in many strong *alloys* (combinations of two or more metals). Engineers use tantalum alloys to make aircraft and missile parts and to build devices called *nuclear reactors* that produce energy. Doctors and dentists use tantalum in surgical instruments and other medical devices because the metal does not react with body fluids.

At normal temperatures, a film of tantalum oxide (Ta_2O_5) forms on the surface of tantalum, protecting the metal from *corrosion* (chemical breakdown). Tantalum oxide serves as a good *insulator*—that is, it does not conduct electric current well. For this reason, electronics manufacturers use tantalum in devices called *capacitors* that store an electric charge. Camera manufacturers add tantalum oxide to glass to increase the *refracting* (light-bending) power of camera lenses.

Tantalum is a relatively rare element in nature. Significant concentrations of the element appear in the minerals columbite and tantalite. These minerals contain both tantalum and niobium, which are chemically similar and therefore difficult to separate from each other. Manufacturers obtain tantalum for commercial use as a by-product in the production of tin. Leading tantalum-producing countries include Australia, Brazil, Canada, Congo (Kinshasa), Ethiopia, and Rwanda.

Tantalum's *atomic number* (number of protons in its nucleus) is 73. Its *relative atomic mass* is 180.9479. An element's relative atomic mass equals its *mass* (amount of matter) divided by $\frac{1}{12}$ of the mass of carbon 12, the most stable isotope of carbon. Tantalum has high melting and boiling points. It melts at 3017 °C and boils at around 5458 °C. Its density is 16.4 grams per cubic centimeter. Tantalum was discovered in 1802 by the Swedish chemist Anders G. Ekeberg. Kenton H. Whitmire

See also **Columbite; Niobium.**

Tantalus, *TAN tuh luhs,* was a king of Lydia in Greek mythology. He was the son of Zeus and the nymph Pluto. Tantalus was punished because he killed his son Pelops and served him to the gods as food. Later, Pelops was restored to life. In Hades, the land of the dead, Tantalus was forced to stand under threat of a hanging rock and up to his chin in water. When he tried to drink, the water always vanished. Fruit hung above him. When he tried to eat the fruit, the winds whirled the branches out of reach. The word *tantalize,* which means to tease or torment by keeping something out of reach, is taken from his name. Justin M. Glenn

Honkanen, H. Armstrong Roberts from Zefa

Dar es Salaam, Tanzania's largest city, has modern buildings and large parks. The city's harbor, *background,* has helped it become an important trading center.

Tanzania

Tanzania, *TAN zuh NEE uh* or *tan ZAN ee uh,* is a large country in eastern Africa that borders the Indian Ocean. Most of Tanzania lies on the mainland of Africa. Several nearby islands make up the rest of the country. Dar es Salaam is Tanzania's largest city, and Dodoma is the capital. The country's official name is the United Republic of Tanzania.

Tanzania's population consists mainly of black Africans. The rest are people of Asian or European descent. Tanzania is one of the world's poorest countries. Most of its people live in rural areas and farm for a living. The government has tried to develop industries, but the economy still depends heavily on agricultural production and imported goods.

Tanzania's fascinating wildlife and spectacular scenery are world famous. Elephants, giraffes, lions, zebras, and many other wild animals roam across the vast Serengeti National Park, Selous Game Reserve, and other areas where hunting is banned or limited. Africa's highest mountain, the majestic, snow-capped Kilimanjaro, rises 19,340 feet (5,895 meters) in northern Tanzania. Lake Tanganyika, the world's longest freshwater lake, extends 420 miles (680 kilometers) along the country's western border. Part of Lake Victoria, which is the largest lake in Africa, lies within northern Tanzania. Lake Victoria covers an area of 26,828 square miles (69,484 square kilometers).

In the 1800's, Germany founded a colony on the mainland of what is now Tanzania. The United Kingdom ruled Zanzibar, a group of nearby islands. In the early 1900's, the mainland became the British colony of Tanganyika. Both Tanganyika and Zanzibar gained independence in the early 1960's. In 1964, they united to form Tanzania.

Government

From 1964 to 1992, Tanzania was a one-party state. The Chama Cha Mapinduzi (CCM) or Revolutionary Party established government policies. In 1992, Tanzania legalized opposition parties. The country's first national multiparty elections were held in late 1995.

National government. Voters throughout Tanzania elect a president, who heads the national government. Voters in Zanzibar also elect their own president. Both presidents serve five-year terms. The president of Tanzania is assisted by a Cabinet, which includes the vice president, a prime minister, and other ministers appointed by the president, as well as the president of Zanzibar.

The National Assembly is the nation's lawmaking body. It has 296 members. In addition, Zanzibar has a 60-member House of Representatives. This body makes laws for Zanzibar, though the national government controls Zanzibar's finances. Voters elect most members of both legislatures. Some members are appointed. Mem-

Facts in brief

Capital: Dodoma.
Official languages: English and Swahili (also called Kiswahili).
Area: 341,217 mi² (883,749 km²).
Population: *Estimated 2006 population*—36,962,000; density, 101 per mi² (39 per km²); distribution, 78 percent rural, 22 percent urban. *2002 census*—34,443,603.
Chief products: *Agriculture*—bananas, beef, cashews, cassava, cloves, coconuts, coffee, corn, cotton, milk, millet, rice, sisal, sorghum, sugar cane, tea, tobacco, wheat. *Manufacturing*—fertilizer, food products, textiles.
National anthem: "Mungu ibariki Afrika" ("God Bless Africa").
Money: *Basic unit*—Tanzanian shilling. One hundred cents equal one shilling.

bers of both bodies serve five-year terms.

Regional and local government. Tanzania is divided into 25 regions for administrative purposes. Local government has special responsibility in the areas of agriculture, education, and health care.

Politics. The Chama Cha Mapinduzi is Tanzania's largest political party. Other parties include the Civic United Front (CUF) and the National Convention for Construction and Reform-Mageuzi Party (NCCR-Mageuzi).

Courts. The Tanzania Court of Appeals is the country's highest court. Lower courts include district courts and local primary courts.

Armed forces. Tanzania has an army of about 45,000 members. The country also has a small navy and air force. Military service is voluntary.

People

Population and ancestry. More than half of Tanzania's people live in the northern third of the country. Areas near mountains in the north and lakes in the west have especially dense populations. Most of the country's people live in rural areas.

About 98 percent of Tanzania's people are black Africans. Most of the rest are people descended from Arabs, Europeans, and Asians from India and Pakistan.

The black Africans belong to about 120 ethnic groups, including the Sukuma, Chagga, Makonde, and Nyamwezi peoples. No single group is large enough to control the country, and Tanzania has not suffered the ethnic violence that has troubled other African nations. Tanzania's ethnic balance has helped the government develop a sense of national unity.

Way of life. Most rural Tanzanians farm for a living. Some raise livestock, such as chickens, goats, and sheep. Raising cattle is the chief activity of the Masai and other peoples in the interior of Tanzania. Fishing is an important activity for people who live along the Indian Ocean coast, on the nearby islands, and near inland lakes.

Many city dwellers work for the national government. Many others work in trade, tourism, and other service industries.

Under Tanzanian law, women have the same rights as men. In practice, however, women still have lesser rights in such areas as education, marriage, and ownership of property. Women are largely responsible for homemaking and raising children. In rural areas, they often perform more farm work than men.

Languages. Swahili (also known as Kiswahili) and English are the official languages of Tanzania. Swahili, a blend of Arab and African languages, is more commonly used in everyday speech and serves as the national language. Many of Tanzania's black ethnic groups have their own languages. Almost all of these languages are in the Bantu language family.

© Bernard Pierre Wolff, Photo Researchers

Farmers transplant rice near a lake in central Tanzania. Rice ranks among the country's chief food crops. Agriculture employs about 80 percent of Tanzania's workers.

Tanzania's flag was adopted in 1964. The green represents agriculture; the black, the nation's people; the blue, the Indian Ocean; and the gold, mineral resources.

The coat of arms was adopted in 1964. The flaming torch represents freedom and knowledge, and the ax and the hoe stand for agricultural development.

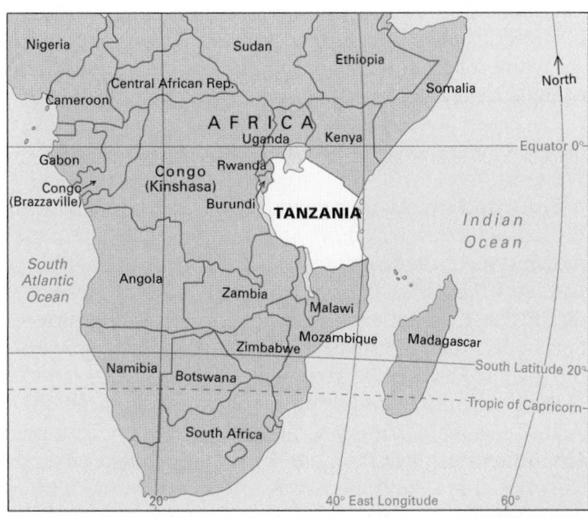

WORLD BOOK map

Tanzania is a large country in eastern Africa. It includes several islands in the Indian Ocean near the mainland.

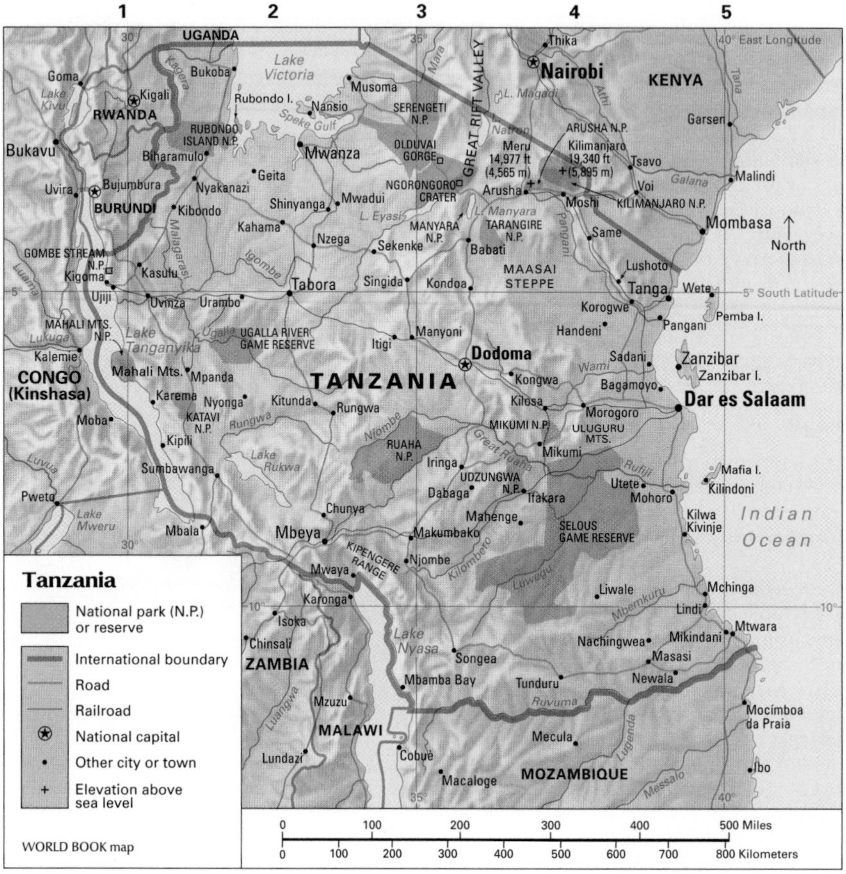

Tanzania

National park (N.P.) or reserve
International boundary
Road
Railroad
National capital
Other city or town
Elevation above sea level

WORLD BOOK map

Tanzania map index

Cities and towns

City	Population	Map key	
Arusha	134,708	B	4
Dar es Salaam	1,360,850	C	5
Dodoma	203,833	C	3
Iringa*	57,182	C	3
Kigoma*	50,044	B	1
Mbeya	152,844	D	2
Morogoro	117,760	C	4
Moshi*	52,000	B	4
Mtwara*	48,510	D	5
Mwanza	223,013	A	2
Shinyanga	100,724	B	2
Tabora*	67,392	B	2
Tanga	187,455	B	5
Zanzibar	157,634	C	5

Source: 1988 United Nations estimates, except for *(1978 census).

Physical features

Feature	Map key	
Arusha Natl. Park	A	4
Gombe Stream Natl. Park	B	1
Great Ruaha River	C	4
Indian Ocean	D	5
Katavi Natl. Park	C	1
Kilimanjaro (mtn.)	A	4
Kipengere Range	D	3
Lake Eyasi	B	3
Lake Manyara	B	3
Lake Natron	A	3
Lake Nyasa	D	3
Lake Rukwa	C	2
Lake Tanganyika	C	1
Lake Victoria	A	2
Mahali Mts.	C	1
Mahali Mts. Natl. Park	C	1
Manyara Natl. Park	B	3
Maasai Steppe	B	4
Mikumi Natl. Park	C	4
Mount Meru	A	4
Olduvai Gorge	A	3
Pangani River	B	4
Pemba Island	B	5
Ruaha Natl. Park	C	3
Rubondo I. Natl. Park	A	2
Rufiji River	C	4
Ruvuma River	E	4
Selous Game Reserve	D	4
Serengeti Natl. Park	A	3
Tarangire Natl. Park	B	4
Ugalla River Game Reserve	C	2
Uluguru Mts.	C	4
Wami River	C	4
Zanzibar Island	C	5

Housing. Most homes are made of wooden frames plastered with mud and include a garden area nearby. Some homes are round with thatched roofs. Others are rectangular with flat mud roofs. Some homes have metal roofs. In urban areas, some homes are made of cement blocks or baked clay bricks.

Clothing in Tanzania is similar to that worn in other parts of eastern Africa. Traditional clothing among the black Africans includes a colorful, wrap-style garment for women called the *kanga,* and the *kikoi wrap* for men. Many Muslim men wear a flowing white robe called the *kanzu.* Since about 1960, Western-style pants and shirts have become increasingly popular among the men of Tanzania.

Food and drink. Tanzanians prepare a variety of dishes with corn, sorghum, and other grains. One of the most popular meals, called *ugali,* is a porridge made with corn. Fish is an important part of the diet of Tanzanians who live on the islands and along the coast. Bottled beers and soft drinks are popular. The Chagga people produce a well-known beer called *mbege.*

Recreation. The most common forms of recreation in Tanzania include dancing and singing. Many Tanzanians also enjoy playing soccer or watching soccer matches. A number of Tanzanians have become world-class long-distance runners.

Religion. About 35 percent of the population are *Muslims* (followers of Islam). Many of Tanzania's Muslims live on Zanzibar and along the country's coast. Christians make up about 30 percent of Tanzania's population. Most other Tanzanians practice traditional African religions.

Education. Most of the adult population of Tanzania can read and write. For the country's literacy rate, see **Literacy** (table: Literacy rates for selected countries). Although Tanzanian law requires seven years of elementary education, only about half of the children go to elementary school. Very few attend high school. Many children who do not attend school come from poor families and are needed to work on family farm plots. Due to economic problems, schools have a shortage of basic school supplies.

The University of Dar es Salaam is Tanzania's chief university. It has about 3,500 students. Many adults attend technical and vocational schools.

The arts. Tanzania's most common artistic expressions include traditional African music and dance. These art forms often tell stories of tribal heroes and local gods. Other notable art forms are associated with various ethnic groups, such as carved figures and masks of the Makonde, carved animal figures of the Zaramo, and leather shields of the Maasai.

Land and climate

Lake Nyasa, Lake Tanganyika, and many mountains of Tanzania are part of the Great Rift Valley. This long valley, which runs north and south through eastern Africa, consists of a series of cracks in the earth that form deep, steep-sided valleys. Branches of the valley extend through central Tanzania and along the country's western border. Tanzania's land regions include the (1) coastal lowlands and islands, (2) plateaus, and (3) highlands.

The coastal lowlands and islands. The mainland borders the Indian Ocean along a 500-mile (800-kilometer) coast. The coastal strip has many mangrove swamps and coconut palm groves. The northern and southern lowlands extend inland from 10 to 40 miles (16 to 64 kilometers). The central lowlands extend farther into the country.

Zanzibar Island, the largest coral island off the African coast, covers 640 square miles (1,658 square kilometers). Another Tanzanian island, Pemba Island, lies 25 miles (40 kilometers) northeast of Zanzibar Island. Pemba covers 380 square miles (984 square kilometers). Zanzibar Island, Pemba Island, and a few other islands make up the Zanzibar island group.

The coastal lowlands and islands are the hottest and wettest part of Tanzania. High temperatures average 85 °F (29 °C) year round. Annual rainfall is between about 31 and 55 inches (80 and 140 centimeters) on the lowlands and exceeds 40 inches (100 centimeters) on the islands.

The plateaus rise gradually from the coastal lowlands. They include a vast grassland in northeastern Tanzania, called the Masai Steppe, and a grassy central plateau that covers more than a third of the country. The Masai Steppe rises to about 3,500 feet (1,100 meters) above sea level. It is home to the Maasai people, who graze cattle there. West of the steppe, the central plateau reaches about 4,000 feet (1,200 meters) above sea level. The central section is usually drier than the coastal lowlands or highlands. It is mostly covered by grasses or barren land, with patches of trees and shrubs. Parts of this region receive less than 20 inches (50 centimeters) of rain annually. The plateaus have average daytime highs of 84 °F (29 °C) and cool nights.

The highlands. Northern Tanzania has some of the country's highest mountain ranges, which include Kilimanjaro. Several other highlands rise in the central and southern regions. Temperatures in the highlands average about 75 °F (24 °C). Highland regions often receive more than 40 inches (100 centimeters) of rain each year.

Rivers and lakes. The Rufiji is Tanzania's chief river. It flows from the southern highlands and drains much of southern Tanzania. Other major rivers include the Pangani, the Ruvuma, and the Wami. Lake Victoria lies in northern Tanzania and forms part of its border with Kenya and Uganda. Lakes Tanganyika and Nyasa lie along the country's western border.

Animal life. Tanzania is famous for its millions of large, wild animals that thrive in vast parklands. In northern Tanzania, Serengeti National Park covers about 5,600 square miles (14,500 square kilometers) and is noted for its lions and huge herds of antelopes and zebras. In the south, the Selous Game Reserve—the world's largest animal reserve—covers about 21,000 square miles (54,000 square kilometers). It has about 50,000 elephants—one of the largest populations in Africa. Other animals common to Tanzania include baboons, buffaloes, hippopotamuses, giraffes, monkeys, and rhinoceroses. The government allows limited hunting in some areas. But *poachers* (people who hunt illegally) remain a problem.

Economy

Tanzania has a developing economy based on agriculture. The country follows a socialist economic system, under which the government controls the nation's banks, major industries, and large farms. Some small businesses are privately owned. Although the government has encouraged industrial development, most industries are small and unprofitable. Tanzania depends

E. R. Degginger

Zebras and gnus roam across Tarangire National Park, *shown here,* in northern Tanzania. These animals and other wildlife are protected in Tanzania's many national parks. The country also has many game reserves, where hunting is limited. These parklands cover large areas of Tanzania and include Serengeti National Park, Ngorongoro Crater, and Selous Game Reserve.

on hydroelectric plants and imported petroleum to generate electric power.

Agriculture. Although only about 5 percent of Tanzania's land area is used for farming, agriculture accounts for more than a third of the country's economic production. The richest soil lies in the northern and southern highlands and around Lake Victoria.

Most farming is done by hand. Many farmers can grow only enough food to feed themselves and their families. Chief food crops include bananas, cassava, corn, millet, rice, sorghum, wheat, and vegetables. The Maasai and some other peoples raise cattle.

Large, government-operated farms produce many of the crops that Tanzania exports. Most of these farms were private plantations under British rule. The major export crops include coffee, cotton, tea, and tobacco. About two-thirds of Tanzania's export earnings come from these crops. Other important crops produced for foreign trade include cashew nuts, cloves, coconuts, *sisal* (a plant used in making rope), and sugar cane.

Service industries account for about half the total value of Tanzania's economic production. Government and trade are the leading service industries. Other service industries include banking, education, health care, insurance, and tourism. The government administers many service industries. Most of Tanzania's wholesale and retail trade involves the sale of farm products. Tourism benefits many types of establishments. The chief tourist attractions are the wildlife in national parks. Tourists also enjoy the palm-shaded coastal beaches.

Manufacturing contributes about 5 percent of the country's economic production. Food processing is Tanzania's chief industry. Other important industries produce fertilizer, textiles, and petroleum products. Tanzania also has factories that produce aluminum, cement, paper, sugar, and steel.

Mining accounts for less than 1 percent of the economic production of Tanzania. Mining operations produce diamonds and other gemstones, coal, and gold.

Kim Naylor, Aspect Picture Library Ltd.

Tanzanians sell bananas at an open-air market on the island of Zanzibar, *shown here.* Selling farm products is an important economic activity in Tanzania's cities and towns.

Foreign trade. Coffee, cotton, tea, and tobacco are Tanzania's main exports. Zanzibar's primary export is cloves. The leading imports include chemicals, construction materials, food, machinery, petroleum and petroleum products, and transportation equipment. Tanzania's main trading partners are Germany, Italy, Japan, and the United Kingdom.

Transportation and communication. Tanzania's large area and poor economic conditions have made development of transportation and communication services difficult. The country has about 50,000 miles (80,000 kilometers) of roads. But few roads are paved, and most are poorly maintained. Less than 1 percent of all Tanzanians own a car. Tanzania's main railway links Dar es Salaam with Zambia on the west. Dar es Salaam, which has a fine harbor, is Tanzania's chief port. It handles trade from Burundi, Congo (Kinshasa), Malawi, Rwanda, Uganda, and Zambia. International airports operate at Dar es Salaam, near Arusha, and on Zanzibar Island.

Three daily newspapers are published in Tanzania—two in Swahili and one in English. The country has two radio stations and an average of 1 radio for every 40 people. Television service is available only on Zanzibar.

History

In Tanzania, scientists have found remains of some of the earliest known human settlements. Anthropologist Louis Leakey and other members of the Leakey family discovered bones, tools, and other signs of early human life in the Olduvai Gorge area of northern Tanzania. Some remains date back more than 1 million years.

The prehistoric human beings who lived in what is now Tanzania were hunters and gatherers. They lived in small groups, catching animals and collecting wild plants for food. By about A.D. 500, people who spoke Bantu languages migrated from the north and from central Africa to eastern Africa.

The development of trade. Arab traders from the Middle East began to settle along the coast of eastern Africa during the 1100's. These traders often married African women. These Arab-African families and their settlements produced the Swahili culture. Major trading centers developed on Zanzibar and other islands.

In the early 1500's, Portuguese traders gained control of Africa's east coast. Local rebellions helped push out the Portuguese in the late 1600's. In 1698, Arabs from Oman, a country on the Arabian Peninsula, took control of Zanzibar and developed trade on the mainland. By this time, the Nyamwezi and Yao ethnic groups had become active in long-distance trade. Their caravans brought gold, ivory, and slaves from the interior to the coast, where they exchanged them for such items as cloth, glassware, and ceramics from Asia.

The Arabs also developed the slave trade. From the mid-1700's to the late 1800's, the Arabs sold thousands of black Africans from the mainland into slavery. Zanzibar was a major slave market. The slave trade caused much conflict and broke up many African communities.

German and British rule. In the 1800's, explorers and Christian missionaries from Europe traveled deep into the mainland of what is now Tanzania. European nations increasingly competed for control of African territory. During the 1880's, Germany took control of the

Kim Naylor, Aspect Picture Library Ltd.

The Palace of Wonders on Zanzibar, *shown here,* was home to many Arab *sultans* (rulers). The Arabs developed Zanzibar into a trading center during their rule in the 1700's and 1800's.

present-day mainland of Tanzania. The Germans forced many Africans to work on plantations. This action contributed to a major uprising in 1905 called the Maji Maji rebellion. German forces killed many thousands of Africans before putting down the revolt.

The United Kingdom made Zanzibar and Pemba islands a British protectorate in 1890. The British gradually took over the powers of the Omani sultans in local affairs. After Germany's defeat in World War I (1914-1918), the United Kingdom gained control over the mainland and named it Tanganyika. During this period, people from other parts of the British Empire and Europe began to settle in Tanganyika. These immigrants included thousands of Indians who worked as merchants and traders.

Independence. In 1946, Tanganyika became a United Nations trust territory. The United Kingdom had the responsibility of preparing it for independence.

In Tanganyika, the United Kingdom sought to create a political system equally representing Europeans, Asians, and Africans. The Africans argued that such a system denied them their rights as the vast majority. In 1954, they formed the Tanganyika African National Union (TANU). Led by Julius Nyerere and others, TANU won independence with majority rule for Tanganyika in 1961. The next year, Nyerere was elected president. The United Kingdom granted Zanzibar—the island group containing Zanzibar and Pemba islands—independence in 1963.

The united republic. Tanganyika and Zanzibar joined together in April 1964 and adopted the name of the United Republic of Tanzania in October. Nyerere became the country's first president. Under his direction, Tanzania adopted a socialist economic system. Nyerere based the system on *ujamaa,* a Swahili word for traditional African cooperation and self-reliance. The government took control of many privately owned businesses. It also encouraged farmers to move from small, widely scattered village sites to larger *ujamaa villages.* These villages were supposed to increase agricultural production and make it easier for the government to provide health and educational services.

At first, families moved voluntarily to ujamaa villages. But during the mid-1970's, police and military forces forced about 5 million others to move. Many farmers disliked the ujamaa villages, which were far from the farmers' plots of land in their former villages.

In foreign affairs, Nyerere worked to increase regional cooperation. In 1967, Tanzania, Kenya, and Uganda formed the East African Community. This organization promoted trade and coordinated economic development among its members. In 1977, however, the community fell apart, largely because of Kenya's emphasis on private enterprise and Tanzania's commitment to socialism. In addition, Uganda was ruled by a brutal dictator, Idi Amin Dada. In 1978, Ugandan troops invaded Tanzania. Tanzanian forces beat back the invaders and helped Ugandan rebels overthrow Amin. The war was a moral and military triumph for Tanzania. But it cost over $500 million at a time when the country's economy was suffering from the high price of imported oil.

Recent developments. During the 1980's, growing trade deficits and debt contributed to an economic collapse. The economic hard times forced Tanzania to alter its socialist system. The government decreased its control of the economy and opened more areas for private businesses. Some improvements occurred, but the economy still faced serious difficulties.

Nyerere retired as president in 1985 and as CCM chairman in 1990. But he remained a major influence in Tanzania until his death in 1999. Ali Hassan Mwinyi succeeded Nyerere as president and as CCM chairman. Mwinyi continued to work for less state control of the economy. Opposition parties were legalized in 1992, and the country's first multiparty elections were held in 1995. Benjamin Mkapa of the CCM was elected president. He was reelected in 2000.

In 1999, Tanzania, Kenya, and Uganda signed a treaty to reestablish the East African Community. The community, which aims to promote economic and political cooperation, was launched in 2001. Stephen K. Commins

Related articles in *World Book* include:

Dar es Salaam
Dodoma
Kilimanjaro
Lake Tanganyika
Lake Victoria
Leakey, Louis S. B.
Leakey, Mary D.
Nyerere, Julius K.
Zanzibar

Outline

I. Government
- A. National government
- B. Regional and local government
- C. Politics
- D. Courts
- E. Armed forces

II. People
- A. Population and ancestry
- B. Way of life
- C. Languages
- D. Housing
- E. Clothing
- F. Food and drink
- G. Recreation
- H. Religion
- I. Education
- J. The arts

III. Land and climate
- A. The coastal lowlands and islands
- B. The plateaus
- C. The highlands
- D. Rivers and lakes
- E. Animal life

IV. Economy
- A. Agriculture
- B. Service industries
- C. Manufacturing
- D. Mining
- E. Foreign trade
- F. Transportation and communication

V. History

Questions

What two former British colonies united in 1964 to form Tanzania?
When did Tanzania hold its first multiparty elections?
What are Tanzania's chief exports?
What led to the collapse of the East African Community in 1977?
Who was the first president of Tanzania?
What are Tanzania's *ujamaa villages*?
Where is most of Tanzania's fertile land?
Which European countries ruled what is now Tanzania during the late 1800's and early 1900's?
How did the slave trade affect Tanzanian communities?
What is the national language of Tanzania?

Tanzanite, *TAN zuh nyt,* is a semiprecious gemstone. It is a variety of a mineral called *zoisite.* Tanzanite crystals are *trichroic* (three-colored). As the gemstone is turned, its color changes from deep blue to purple to yellowish-green. When heat is applied to the crystals, they become uniformly blue. The blue color is most popular, so the majority of tanzanite is heat-treated.

Tanzanite is cut into gemstones with numerous *facets* (flat, polished surfaces), which emphasize its light-reflecting quality. The gemstones are used in such jewelry as rings, earrings, and pendants.

Tanzanite was discovered in 1967 in Tanzania, for which it was named. Tanzania is the only known source of tanzanite. Because the supply is limited, the gemstones are expensive. Pansy D. Kraus

Tao Te Ching. See **Taoism; Laozi.**

Taoism, *TOW ihz uhm* or *DOW ihz uhm,* is a philosophy that began in China, probably during the 300's B.C. Taoism is also the name of a religion that began in about the 100's B.C. Through the centuries, the philosophy has influenced artists and writers in the East and West. The word *tao* (also spelled *dao)* originally meant *road* or *way.* The Tao (Way) represents the characteristics or behavior that makes each thing in the universe what it is. The word is also used to mean reality as a whole, which consists of all the individual "ways."

A symbol of Taoism stands for what Taoists believe are the two basic forces in the universe—*yin* (female) and *yang* (male). The black shape in the center and the broken lines represent yin. The center red shape and the solid lines symbolize yang.

Taoism as a philosophy. The beliefs of Taoism as a philosophy appear in two books, the *Lao-tzu* (later renamed the *Tao Te Ching, The Classic of the Way and the Virtue)* and the *Chuang-tzu.* The *Lao-tzu* is a collection from several sources, and its authors and editors are unknown. The ideas were partly a reaction against *Confucianism,* a philosophy that developed in China beginning in about 500 B.C.

According to Confucianism, people can live a good life only in a well-disciplined society that stresses attention to ceremony, duty, morality, and public service. The Taoist ideal, on the other hand, is a person who avoids conventional social obligations and leads a simple, spontaneous, and meditative life close to nature.

Taoist philosophy had a great influence on Chinese literature and art. For example, the poetry of Tao Qian (T'ao Ch'ien) (A.D. 365?-472?) expresses a distaste for worldly affairs and a yearning for a life in harmony with nature. During the early 1200's, Xia Gui (Hsia Kuei) painted landscapes that reflect the Taoist sensitivity to nature (see **Painting** [Asian painting]).

Taoism as a religion was influenced by Chinese folk religion. In folk religion, most of the gods are human beings who displayed exceptional powers during their lifetimes. For example, Guan Di, who is the protector of business people, lived as a general during the A.D. 200's.

Taoism has a hereditary priesthood. The priests conduct public rituals, during which they submit the people's prayers to the gods of folk religion. The chief priest, who is in a trance, prays to other divinities on behalf of the worshipers. These divinities are not former human beings but represent aspects of the Tao.

The members of some Taoist groups have sought to attain immortality through magic, meditation, special diets, breath control, or the recitation of scriptures. The Taoist search for knowledge of nature has led many believers to pursue various sciences, such as alchemy, astronomy, and medicine. N. Sivin

See also **Confucianism; Laozi; Religion** (Taoism; picture: Taoist deities); **Zhuangzi.**

Additional resources

Cleary, Thomas. *The Essential Tao.* 1992. Reprint. Harper San Francisco, 1993.
Hartz, Paula R. *Taoism.* Facts on File, 1992.
Pas, Julian F. *Historical Dictionary of Taoism.* Scarecrow, 1998.
Robinet, Isabelle. *Taoism: Growth of a Religion.* Stanford, 1997.

Taos, *tows* or *TAH ohs* (pop. 4,700), is a historic city in north-central New Mexico, just north of Santa Fe (see **New Mexico** [political map]). Taos is three communities in one. Taos proper, which was originally founded as Don Fernando de Taos during the 1790's, serves as a center of trade for the nearby farm and ranch region. The ancient Pueblo Indian village of San Geronimo de Taos lies north of the town. To the south is the old Spanish farming center, Ranchos de Taos, established by Spaniards in the early 1700's. All three communities lie at an elevation of about 7,000 feet (2,100 meters) at the base of the Sangre de Cristo Mountains in the Southern Rockies.

Sights of interest to visitors include the Plaza, the center of community life during the 1800's; the "Kit" Carson House, a home of the famous frontiersman; the Charles Bent House, where Territorial Governor Bent was murdered during a revolt against American rule in 1847; the Millicent Rogers Museum, which displays the art of northern New Mexico; and Taos Pueblo, which stood on its present site in 1540 when Francisco Vásquez de Coronado led the first Europeans to the area.

In 1898, artists attracted by the local light and scenery established a Taos "art colony." Taos has continued to draw artists and remains an important art center.

Taos has a mayor-council form of government. It is the seat of Taos County. Jon Hunner

Tap-dancing. See **Dance** (Other forms of theatrical dance).

Tape recorder is a device for recording sound, pictures, and various other kinds of data on magnetic tape. It can also play back tape recordings. Tape recorders are widely used by the recording industry and in radio and television broadcasting. Millions of people enjoy listening to music or recorded books on tape recorders in their homes and automobiles or on portable tape recorders.

Tape recordings can be edited by cutting out the unwanted sections and then joining the ends of the tape. But tapes are less durable than compact discs (CD's).

This article deals with audiotape recorders, which record only sound. For information on tape recorders that record visual images as well as sound, see **Videotape recorder.**

Audio recording tape is a thin plastic ribbon coated on one side with particles of a substance that can be easily magnetized, such as iron oxide or chromium dioxide. A tape recorder receives sounds in the form of electric signals, which it converts into a changing magnetic field. During recording, the field arranges the particles on the tape into magnetic patterns. When the tape is played back, the magnetic patterns generate electric signals that the recorder uses to reproduce the original sound. Tape recording can be accomplished by two different processes: *analog recording* and *digital recording.*

In analog recording, the patterns of the electric signals are *analogous* (similar) to those of the magnetic signals. Analog tape recordings store a signal in a form that looks like the wave form of the original sound. In a digital recording, the electric signals are converted to a *digital* (numeric) code for storage on the tape. This code represents the sound. Digital recording produces better sound quality with less background noise and distortion than analog recording does.

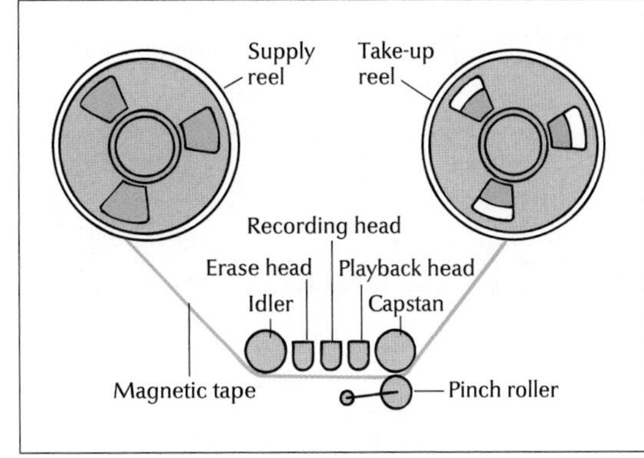

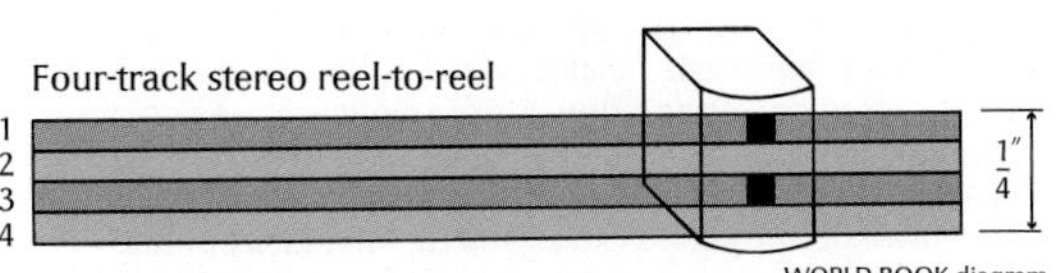

WORLD BOOK diagram

In an analog tape recorder, *shown here,* the tape travels from the supply reel to the take-up reel past various stationary heads. Each side of the tape holds two tracks that run the length of the tape. Some digital recorders also have stationary heads.

How tape recorders work

Most audiotape recorders operate in a similar way, whether they are analog or digital. Magnetic tape unrolls from a *supply reel* and is wound onto a *take-up reel.* Between the two reels, a soft rubber pinch roller presses the tape tightly against a metal rod called a *capstan.* During recording and playback, a motor turns the capstan. The turning capstan pulls tape from the supply reel. At the same time, the take-up reel pulls gently on the tape to wind it up.

Before the tape reaches the capstan, it passes the *heads* of the tape recorder. The heads are small electromagnets that erase, record, and play back. The speed at which the tape moves past the heads depends on the type of tape recorder. The speeds are measured in inch-

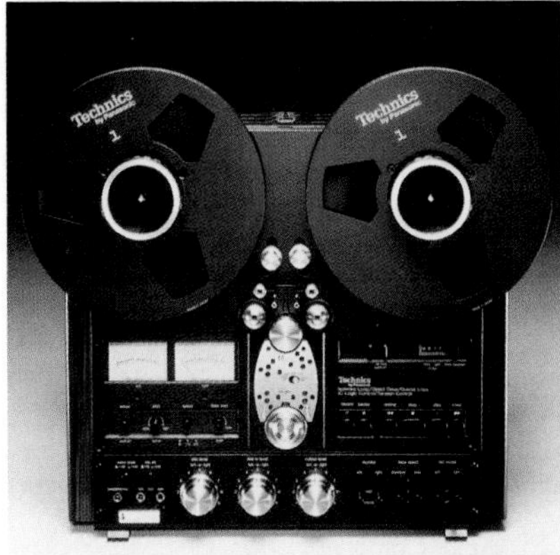

Panasonic

An open-reel tape recorder produces better-quality sound than a cassette recorder. Open-reel recorders are used by recording studios and broadcasting stations.

WORLD BOOK photo by Jeff Guerrant

A cassette recorder is more compact and easier to operate than an open-reel recorder. A plastic cassette, which encloses audiotape and miniature reels, simply snaps into the recorder and is ready to play.

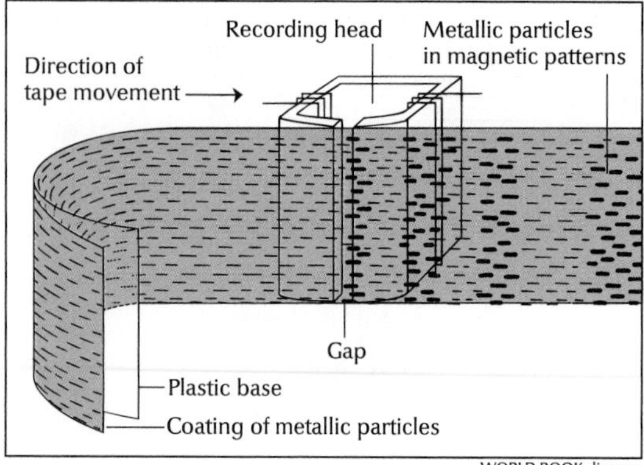

The analog recording process. Recording tape consists of a plastic base coated with metallic particles that are easily magnetized. In recording, electric signals from a microphone create a magnetic field around a gap in the recording head. The field places the particles on the tape into a magnetic pattern. This pattern represents the sound waves entering the microphone.

es per second (ips). The most commonly used speeds are 1 $\frac{7}{8}$, 3 $\frac{3}{4}$, 7 $\frac{1}{2}$, and 15 ips (4.8, 9.5, 19, and 38 centimeters per second). The higher speeds produce recordings of the best quality, but recording at slower speeds increases the playing time of the tape.

Erasing and recording. When an analog tape recording is made, the tape first comes into contact with the *erase head.* The erase head, which is automatically activated during recording, produces a strong magnetic field that removes any previous recording from the tape. The blank tape then moves past the *recording head.*

A microphone translates the sounds to be recorded on the tape into a varying electric current. An *amplifier* strengthens the current, which is then fed into the recording head. As the current flows through the head, it sets up a changing magnetic field around a small gap in the electromagnet of the head. When the analog tape passes the gap, the magnetic field arranges the magnetic particles on the tape into a pattern that represents the sound waves entering the microphone.

Unlike analog recorders, most digital recorders have no erase head. Instead of erasing the tape first, they use a process called *overwriting* to record new sound. Recording and playback heads may be either stationary or rotating. Stationary heads are like the heads on an analog tape recorder. In a rotating system, two heads are mounted opposite each other on a rotating cylinder called a *drum.* During recording and playback, the tape moves past the spinning drum.

A digital audiotape recorder converts the original electric signals to digital information in several steps. First, the signal is filtered to prevent interference from unwanted high frequencies. Next, each second of sound is broken into thousands of segments called *samples.* Each sample corresponds to a specific numeric code, which is recorded on the tape as a magnetic pattern.

Different kinds of tape recorders use different widths of magnetic tape. Most tape recorders can record more than one *track* (separate recording) on a tape. To produce stereophonic sound, a tape recorder must record at least two tracks at the same time, each track from a different channel of sound.

Playing back. Before a tape recording can be played, it must be rewound on the supply reel. The tape is then sent through the recorder again. This time, the playback head is switched on, and neither the erase head nor the recording head is activated. As the tape passes the playback head, the magnetic patterns on the tape generate a weak electric current in the electromagnet. An amplifier strengthens the current before it reaches a speaker, which reproduces the recorded sound.

During playback, the pattern of the current generated by an analog tape corresponds to the pattern of the recorded sound waves. Playing a digital tape produces electric pulses that represent a numeric code. The recorder translates the code into a varying current, which an amplifier strengthens and sends to the speakers.

Kinds of tape recorders

There are two main kinds of audiotape recorders: open-reel and cassette.

Open-reel tape recorders are used by recording studios and broadcasting stations. They produce better-quality sound than do cassette recorders. To use an open-reel recorder, the operator places a supply reel and a take-up reel on spindles on the outside of the recorder. The tape is threaded by hand past the heads of the recorder and through the capstan and pinch roller.

Recording studios usually record at 15 or 30 ips (38 or 76 centimeters per second). Many professional analog recorders use 2-inch (5-centimeter) tape, which carries 24 tracks. Professional digital recorders often use $\frac{1}{2}$-inch (1.3-centimeter) tape, which carries up to 48 tracks. Such analog and digital recorders are called *multitrack tape recorders.*

Cassette tape recorders are designed for use by consumers rather than recording industry professionals. They are easier to operate than open-reel recorders because the tape does not have to be threaded through them. A cassette recorder uses a small plastic case, called a *cassette,* which encloses a miniature supply reel and take-up reel. The cassette is snapped into the recorder. Many cassette recorders have electronic *noise reduction systems,* which reduce the faint hissing sound made by the tape. Cassette tape measures only 0.15 inch (3.81 millimeters) wide. Analog cassette tape carries four tracks, two on each side. It operates at 1 $\frac{7}{8}$ ips (4.8 centimeters per second).

A cassette deck, also called a *tape deck,* is a tape recorder that usually operates as a *component* (part) of a stereophonic sound system. Deck features called *synchronized start* and *dubbing* allow recordings to be made from CD's or cassette tapes. An *auto reverse* feature switches the direction of tape movement so that both sides of the tape can be recorded or played back without removing and reinserting the cassette.

DAT (*d*igital *a*udio *t*ape) cassettes produce far better sound quality than do analog cassettes. A DAT cassette is smaller than an analog cassette but has a longer playing time. It uses two tracks and is played on only one side. A DAT cassette operates at 0.321 ips (8.15 millimeters per second), using a rotating head.

History

In 1898, Valdemar Poulsen, a Danish engineer, invented the first machine for recording sound magnetically.

He called his invention the telegraphone. It used an electromagnet to make a magnetic recording on steel wire. However, phonograph recordings were more popular at that time, and little use was made of magnetic recording for a number of years.

A small number of audio recorders began to be produced commercially in the early 1930's. Initially, steel wire and steel ribbon were the only recording materials used. But they were awkward to handle and store and nearly impossible to edit. During World War II (1939-1945), German engineers perfected the *magnetophon,* the first recorder to use plastic magnetic tape.

By 1950, tape recorders were being widely used in the radio and recording industries. Manufacturers began to produce stereo tape recorders for use in the home in the mid-1950's. Cartridge tape systems were introduced in 1958. Such systems, which are often called *8-track,* used an endless loop of tape in a cartridge to play four stereo music programs. Eight-track systems were especially popular for use in automobiles.

In the mid-1960's, cassettes revolutionized the tape recorder market. They gained even greater popularity when noise reduction was added, and they began to compete with phonograph records.

Manufacturers introduced digital recording systems in the 1970's. The market for prerecorded music became even more competitive in 1983 with the introduction of audio compact discs. CD's gradually became more popular than audiotapes. Digital audiotape recorders became available in the 1990's, but they had little success with consumers. In the late 1990's, digital music recordings, which can be played on computers and digital music players, became available over the Internet. Since that time, cassette tapes have declined further in popularity. Ken C. Pohlmann

Related articles in *World Book* include:

Electromagnet
Headphones
Phonograph
Recording industry
Speaker
Stereophonic sound system
Videotape recorder

Additional resources

Jorgensen, Finn. *The Complete Handbook of Magnetic Recording.* 4th ed. TAB, 1996.
Morton, David L. *Off the Record: The Technology and Culture of Sound Recording in America.* Rutgers, 2000.
Rumsey, Francis, and McCormick, Tim. *Sound and Recording.* 3rd ed. Focal Pr., 1997.

Tapestry is a woven fabric made from threads of different colors to form a picture or design. Most tapestries serve as indoor wallhangings.

How tapestries are made. Tapestries are woven on a loom. Like other woven fabrics, tapestries consist of vertical threads, which make up the *warp,* and horizontal threads, which form the *weft.* A weaver winds the threads of the weft over and under the threads of the warp, which are attached to the loom. In ordinary woven cloth, the warp and the weft can both be seen. But in tapestry cloth, the weft completely covers the warp.

A tapestry weaver works from the back of the tapestry and follows a pattern called the *cartoon,* which indicates

The Metropolitan Museum of Art, New York City, Gift of John D. Rockefeller, Jr., The Cloisters Collection, 1937

A French tapestry woven during the late 1400's, *left,* has a *millefleurs* design in the background. Such a design consists of numerous flowers and leaves. A detail from the design appears above. This tapestry, called *The Unicorn at the Fountain,* is part of a famous series known as *The Hunt of the Unicorn.*

the design and thread colors. When the tapestry is finished, its design is the reverse of the cartoon. Linen and wool have been the most common materials, along with gold and silver thread.

History. Tapestry is one of the oldest techniques in textile art. It probably originated in prehistoric times, but the oldest surviving cloth fragments and written accounts date from about 1500 B.C. They come from many parts of the ancient world, including Egypt, Babylonia, China, and Peru.

Tapestry flourished in Europe in the Middle Ages, especially from the 1300's to the 1500's. Professional workshops produced sets for castles and churches. Most weavers worked from a full-scale cartoon painted by another artist. Because most tapestries were wool, they helped insulate rooms as well as decorate them. Kings and nobles took tapestries with them when they traveled to create attractive and familiar surroundings, and sometimes hung them in their tents on the battlefield.

Paris became the first major tapestry-making center in Europe. The *Apocalypse of Angers,* one of the oldest sets of tapestries in existence, was produced there during the 1370's or 1380's. During the 1400's, Arras in France, and Brussels and Tournai in Belgium, became famous tapestry-making centers.

Most tapestries from the Middle Ages depict scenes from history, mythology, the Bible, or daily life. Many have a *millefleurs* design as background. Millefleurs is a French word that means *a thousand flowers.* The design consists of flowers and leaves in realistic detail scattered over a background, making the picture seem flat like the wall it decorates. One famous set is called *The Lady with the Unicorn.* See **Unicorn** (picture).

In the early 1500's, the Italian painter Raphael designed cartoons for a set of tapestries called the *Acts of the Apostles.* They looked like paintings with figures standing in a three-dimensional space. Their realistic compositions greatly influenced tapestry design.

Tapestry weaving continued to thrive in Europe during the 1600's and 1700's. The Gobelin factory in Paris was one of the most famous centers. Such famous artists as Peter Paul Rubens, François Boucher, and Francisco Goya designed cartoons for various factories.

The popularity of tapestry declined during the 1800's, when wallpaper became widely used in homes. The Industrial Revolution also contributed to its disappearance. In the late 1800's, the Englishman William Morris founded the Arts and Crafts movement to revive the handicrafts displaced by the machine. He also rediscovered handweaving and dyeing techniques of the Middle Ages. Morris greatly influenced artists of the 1900's.

In the early 1900's, French artist Jean Lurçat introduced the use of modern artists' designs at Aubusson, France, a tapestry center important since the Middle Ages. A modern crafts revival occurred after the end of World War II in 1945. Since the 1950's, artists have experimented with materials and weaving to create many new forms of wall tapestry. Nancy A. Corwin

See also **Hannibal** (picture); **Jesus Christ** (picture: Jesus was brought before Pilate).

Additional resources

Nemati, Parviz. *The Splendor of Antique Rugs and Tapestries.* Rizzoli, 2001.

Phillips, Barty. *Tapestry.* Phaidon, 1994.

Tapeworm is any of a group of tapelike flatworms that live as parasites. Adult tapeworms inhabit the intestines of human beings or other animals. They have a headlike organ called a scolex and a series of blocklike segments in a flat body. A tapeworm has no mouth or intestine. It absorbs food through its body wall. Some tapeworms measure less than 1 inch (2.5 centimeters) long and have only a few segments. Others grow as long as 60 feet (18 meters) and have thousands of segments.

A tapeworm's scolex has suckers or hooks or both. The worm uses the scolex to attach itself to the intestine of the *host*—that is, the animal in which the worm lives. The rest of the worm's body grows from a necklike region behind the scolex. Segments develop as the worm grows. Each segment contains male and female reproductive organs and produces many eggs. Segments filled with eggs may drop off the end of the body. The segments then may pass out of the host with body wastes and release the eggs outside the host.

Almost all tapeworms have one or more *larval* (immature) stages and develop in two or three hosts. A newly hatched tapeworm is called an *oncosphere.* It is round and has small hooks. An oncosphere develops in a host that eats it or the egg from which it hatches. The oncosphere burrows through its host's intestine and travels to other organs or to muscles. If another animal eats this host, the oncosphere may develop into another larval stage or into an adult tapeworm. A person may become infected by a tapeworm after eating improperly cooked fish, pork, or beef that contains tapeworm larvae.

Most adult tapeworms produce no bad effects in people. Sometimes they cause loss of appetite, abdominal discomfort, diarrhea, nausea, weakness, or anemia. Tapeworm larvae are much more dangerous to people. A person who accidentally eats eggs of the pork tapeworm may have young worms develop in almost every organ of the body, including the eyes, brain, and heart.

Seth Tyler

Scientific classification. Tapeworms belong to the class Cestoda of the phylum Platyhelminthes.

See also **Flatworm.**

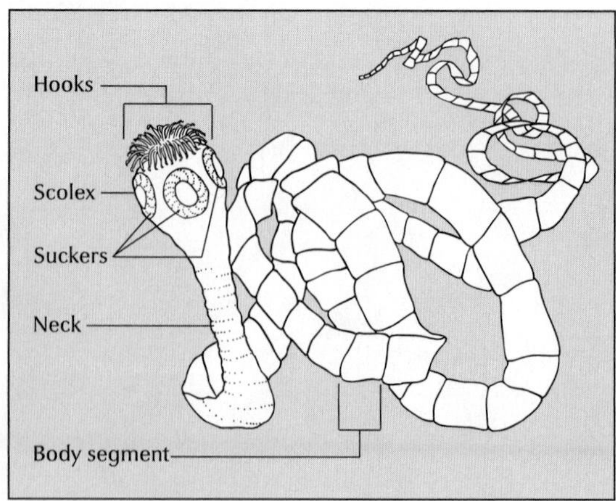

WORLD BOOK illustration by Zorica Dabich

A pork tapeworm has a flat, ribbonlike body. Its headlike scolex has both hooks and suckers, which the worm uses to attach itself to the intestines of people and other animals.

Tapioca, *TAP ih OH kuh,* is a food starch that is widely used in making puddings. It is taken from the root of the cassava, a tropical plant of the same family as the castor bean. Tapioca pudding is healthful and easily digested.

Commercial tapioca comes chiefly from Brazil, Java, and the Malay Peninsula. A single plant may yield up to 10 pounds (5 kilograms) of starch. The roots are 2 to 8 inches (5 to 20 centimeters) thick, and 1 to 4 feet (30 to 120 centimeters) long. They are washed to remove the prussic acid they contain, and then reduced to a pulp. The pulp is strained until all the starchy particles are separated from the root fibers. The starchy pellets are then set on hot iron plates to dry. The starch pellets form the small, uneven white balls known as *pearl tapioca.* Pearl tapioca must be soaked in water for an hour before it can be cooked. A finer granular form, called *quick-cooking tapioca,* does not require soaking.

Tapioca swells and thickens the liquid in which it is cooked. A flour made from cassava root is also used as a thickening. This flour is one of the starches called *arrowroot.* Kay Franzen Jamieson

See also **Cassava.**

Tapiola, *tap ee OH luh,* a community in the city of Espoo, Finland, became world famous as a model for city planning. It lies in southern Finland. For the location of Espoo, see **Finland** (political map).

A private organization and its sponsors founded Tapiola as a new community, or *new town,* in the 1950's. The founders tried to create a community that blends completely with its natural surroundings. They also wanted Tapiola to offer its inhabitants many types of employment, housing, and services so the community would be self-sufficient. Tapiola features a wide variety of architectural styles, and many walking paths. Some of Finland's best-known architects helped plan the community. Today, Tapiola is the largest business center of Espoo. However, it does not yet provide jobs for all its inhabitants. Many of its approximately 35,000 people work nearby, especially in Helsinki.

Pekka Kalevi Hamalainen

Tapir, *TAY puhr,* is related to the horse and rhinoceros, though it looks more like a pig. The tapir has a short, heavy body and a thick neck. Its nose is drawn out to form a movable, short trunk. Its front feet have four toes, and the hind feet have three toes. The tail is short. Tapirs are wary creatures. They live in the depths of the forests, and near water, in which they love to swim. Tapirs feed on the twigs and foliage of trees and shrubs, and on fruit and other vegetable food.

Warren Garst, Tom Stack & Assoc.

The tapir resembles a pig but actually is related to the horse and rhinoceros. Tapirs have a sturdy body and a movable, short trunk. They eat fruits, vegetables, and foliage.

There are two kinds of tapirs that live in South America. The most common one is found in the forest regions east of the Andes. The other makes its home high in these mountains. The two species of tapirs that live in Central America are the smallest of the family. All full-grown American tapirs are dark brown in color. Young American tapirs are marked with yellowish streaks.

The Malayan tapir is found in Sumatra and the Malay Peninsula. It stands 3 to $3\frac{1}{2}$ feet (91 to 107 centimeters) high at the shoulder. The back, rump, and sides are white while the rest of the thinly haired body is glossy black or dark brown.

People hunt tapirs for their flesh and thick hides. As a result of both hunting and the cutting of forests, tapirs have become rare in many areas. C. Richard Taylor

Scientific classification. Tapirs form the tapir family, Tapiridae. The South American tapir is *Tapirus terrestris.* The mountain tapir is *T. pinchaque.* The Central American tapir is *T. bairdi.* The Malayan tapir is *T. indicus.*

See also **Animal** (picture: Animals of the tropical forests); **South America** (Animals).

Tar is any of a group of thick, oily, dark brown or black liquids. Most tars are by-products of the conversion of such organic matter as coal, petroleum, or wood into useful industrial products.

Coal tar is condensed from vapors given off during the manufacture of coke from soft coal (see **Coke**). A type of coal tar called *high-temperature coke-oven tar* is the most important industrial tar. This tar is used as a raw material for such products as disinfectants, dyes, perfumes, plastics, roofing and water-proofing materials, and synthetic drugs. See **Coal tar.**

Coal gasifier tar is a by-product of certain manufacturing processes that convert coal into a high-energy gas. This gas can be used as a substitute for natural gas. Coal gasifier tar is a source of organic chemicals.

Petroleum tar is generally a by-product of processes that convert heavier parts of crude oil into gasoline and other fuels. Chemical processes used to prepare *ethylene* (an organic gas) are another source of petroleum tar. This tar is used to produce asphalt, coke, and pitch.

Wood tar is a by-product of the *destructive distillation* of wood in the production of charcoal (see **Distillation** [Destructive distillation]). The tar is condensed from vapors given off during the process. It is an important source of acetic acid, methyl alcohol, pine oil, and turpentine. Walter W. Turner

See also **Pitch.**

Tar sands. See **Bituminous sands.**

Tarabulus. See **Tripoli.**

Tarantella, *TAR uhn TEHL uh,* is a regional folk dance of southern Italy, including Sardinia and Sicily. It is named for the city of Taranto. The tarantella is usually performed by a couple, often surrounded by a circle of onlookers, to a brisk 6/8 time. The dancers typically accompany themselves on tambourines and castanets. The steps of the dance can be performed in many sequences. In some steps, the dancer moves forward and backward while hopping on one foot. Other steps feature heel-toe movements across the standing foot. The steps are linked by runs, skips, and movements with a partner.

The tarantella probably dates from at least the early 1600's, and may have been influenced by Spanish dance. Elements of the tarantella were first adopted into classical ballet in the early 1800's. Patricia W. Rader

Tarantula, *tuh RAN chuh luh,* is a common name for a variety of mostly large spiders. Tarantulas inhabit warm climates around the world, especially tropical regions. Some types live for more than 20 years. Tarantulas get their name from a distantly related wolf spider that lives around Taranto in Italy. People once believed this spider's bite caused a disease called *tarantism.* The victims supposedly leaped in the air and ran about making strange noises. According to superstition, the best cure was a lively Italian folk dance that became known as the *tarantella.*

One of the world's largest spiders, the *Goliath birdeater tarantula,* lives in South America. Its body often measures from 3 to 3 ½ inches (7.6 to 8.9 centimeters) long. It can spread its legs more than 7 inches (18 centimeters). Like other large tarantulas, the Goliath birdeater may eat small rodents, reptiles, amphibians, and birds.

WORLD BOOK illustration by Oxford Illustrators Limited

A tarantula looks fierce. But its bite usually is no more dangerous than that of other spiders. Tarantulas have eight legs and two *pedipalpi,* or leglike parts that form the sides of the mouth.

Many tarantulas live in burrows, and a few inhabit trees. Some types have a poisonous bite that can prove harmful to people. Most tarantulas, however, are not particularly poisonous. Their chief means of defense consists of thousands of tiny, irritating, hairlike body parts that can be flung into the air by rubbing motions of the hind legs.

One common group of spiders, the *trap-door spiders,* often are referred to as tarantulas. They grow about 1 inch (2.5 centimeters) long (see **Trap-door spider**).

Edwin W. Minch

Scientific classification. The Goliath birdeater tarantula belongs to the family Theraphosidae. Its scientific name is *Theraphosa blondi.* Trap-door spiders make up the family Ctenizidae.

See also **Insect** (pictures: A fierce battle); **Spider** (Tarantulas).

Tarascan Indians, *tuh RAS kuhn,* live on the high plateaus of west-central Mexico, in what is now the state of Michoacán. They ruled a powerful empire in the area from the late 1300's to the early 1500's. The Tarascan empire bordered the larger Aztec empire to the east.

The Tarascan empire was highly organized. It included several major settlements near Lake Pátzcuaro, including the empire's capital, Tzintzuntzan (pronounced *TSEENT soont SAHN).* The Tarascan fished in the numerous marshy lakes in the region. They also hunted deer and smaller animals and raised turkeys and such crops as corn, beans, squash, and chili peppers. The Spanish conquered the Tarascan empire in the 1520's.

Today, many Tarascan still follow their traditional ways of life. These people farm and fish in the rugged areas of Michoacán. They also carve wooden objects and weave nets, mats, and baskets. In their local communities, many Tarascan still speak Tarascan dialects instead of Spanish, the language most widely spoken in Mexico. William O. Autry

Tarawa, *tah RAH wah* (pop. 24,598), is the capital of Kiribati, a country of 33 small islands in the central Pacific Ocean. Tarawa is an *atoll* (ring-shaped reef) composed of many coral islets that cover a total of 9 square miles (23 square kilometers).

The commercial and shipping center of Kiribati is Betio, a densely populated islet in the southwest area of Tarawa. Bairiki, east of Betio, is the government center. Bonriki, in the southeast, has an international airport.

In 1788, the British explorer Captain Thomas Gilbert became the first European to sight Tarawa. The British took control of Tarawa in 1892. In 1942, during World War II, Japanese troops seized the atoll. American forces captured Tarawa from the Japanese in 1943 in one of the bloodiest battles of the war. After the war, the United Kingdom continued to govern Tarawa until 1979, when it became the government center of the independent nation of Kiribati. Michael R. Ogden

See also **Kiribati; World War II** (Island hopping in the Central Pacific).

Tarbela Dam, *tahr BEHL uh,* in Pakistan, is one of the largest dams in the world. It contains 138,600,000 cubic yards (106,000,000 cubic meters) of rocks and earth packed firmly in layers over a watertight core. The dam is located on the Indus River near Rawalpindi (see **Pakistan** [terrain map]). The Tarbela Dam was built primarily to provide irrigation water and hydroelectric power. The dam's enormous reservoir stores water during the rainy summer months. The water is released through an extensive irrigation system in the dry winter months. The reservoir has a capacity of about 11 million acre-feet (14 billion cubic meters). The dam's hydroelectric power plant generates 1,750 megawatts of electricity. The dam was completed in 1976. Arthur H. Walz, Jr.

Tarbell, Ida Minerva (1857-1944), an American author, led in the muckraking movement of the early 1900's which attacked dishonesty in politics and business. Her *History of the Standard Oil Company* (1904) exposed the practices of some corporations and strengthened the movement for outlawing monopolies. She also wrote biographies of Napoleon I and Abraham Lin-

Drake Well Museum, Titusville, Pa.

Ida M. Tarbell

coln and an autobiography, *All in the Day's Work* (1929).

Ida Tarbell was born in Erie County, Pennsylvania. She was graduated from Allegheny College, and studied in Paris. Between 1883 and 1915, she was successively associate editor of *The Chautauquan, McClure's Magazine,* and *American Magazine.* Michael Emery

Targum. See **Bible** (The first translations).

Tariff, *TAR ihf,* is a tax placed on goods that one nation imports from another. Many nations use tariffs to protect their industries from foreign competition. Tariffs provide protection by acting to raise the price of imported goods. Thus, tariffs encourage domestic firms to increase their production, and consumers are forced to pay higher prices for the protected goods. Tariffs on exports from the United States are prohibited by the U.S. Constitution. But such tariffs are sometimes used in other countries to raise revenue. A nation may also use tariffs to influence, or protest against, political or economic policies of other countries.

Nations set their tariff rates in various ways. They may have commercial treaties that include a *most-favored-nation* (MFN) clause, sometimes called a *normal trading relations* clause. Under an MFN clause, each nation's lowest regular tariff rates apply to all countries that sign the treaty. *Preferential tariffs,* which are lower than MFN tariffs, may be applied to favor imports from less developed countries. Nations that form a *customs union* eliminate tariffs on trade among themselves. These nations also have a common set of tariffs that cover their trade with nonmember countries. A *common market* has the same tariff policies as a customs union but provides for greater economic cooperation among its members. Nations that form a *free trade area* have no tariffs among themselves, but each member may set its own tariffs on goods produced by nonmembers.

Main kinds of tariffs

Tariffs may be classified according to their purpose. Tariffs levied to restrict imports are called *protective tariffs.* Those levied to increase government revenue are known as *revenue tariffs.* Many governments used revenue tariffs in the past. But today, income taxes and sales taxes are the main sources of government revenue, and revenue tariffs are seldom used. Protective tariffs are used more often. But protective tariffs have also been reduced substantially in the United States and many other major countries since World War II ended in 1945.

Tariffs may also be classified according to the way in which they are levied. *Specific tariffs* are levied as a certain sum of money per unit of the product imported. For example, a government may levy a specific tariff on a product at a rate of 10 cents per pound or 25 cents per liter. Many specific tariffs are levied against such raw materials as iron ore and rubber and such food products as sugar, wheat, and wine. *Ad valorem tariffs* are levied as a percentage of the value of a product. For example, a rate of 5 percent may apply to imports of such manufactured products as automobiles.

Why tariffs are levied

Tariffs are often levied (1) to protect domestic jobs, (2) to protect new industries, (3) to offset unfair trade practices of other countries, or (4) to prevent dependence on foreign products.

Protecting domestic jobs. Firms and workers sometimes have difficulty competing with imports when foreign firms and workers are more efficient. The affected groups may promote tariffs to increase or maintain company profits and keep wages high.

Protecting new industries. In some instances, a new industry cannot compete successfully with established industries in other countries. A protective tariff may shield the new industry from foreign competition until its workers and firms become more productive.

Offsetting unfair trade practices. Some governments use tariffs to protect their industries from the effects of *export subsidies* and *dumping.* Export subsidies are support payments paid by a government to its export industries. Such payments are designed to allow the industries to sell their goods for less overseas. Dumping involves pricing items below their production cost to drive competitors out of an import market. For example, radio manufacturers in one country may sell their products so cheaply in another country that radio firms in the importing nation cannot compete successfully. As a result, those firms may go out of business. The importing nation would then have to depend on foreign manufacturers for radios. The foreign firms could then raise prices far above their original levels.

In some cases, export subsidies or dumping may not harm an importing country's industries. In such cases, if no tariff is imposed, consumers may benefit from the lower prices that result from these practices.

Preventing dependence on foreign products. Many nations do not want to depend on other countries for such essential products as petroleum, steel, or food. Supplies of these products from foreign sources may be cut off or disrupted in time of war or international tension. Thus, some nations use tariffs to protect industries that produce these goods.

Arguments against tariffs

Arguments against tariffs include the belief that they result in (1) higher prices, (2) industrial inefficiency, and (3) unfair support for some industries. Tariffs may reduce trade, and so many economists believe they lower the standard of living in trading nations.

Higher prices. Many people believe tariffs waste a nation's supply of labor and natural resources and thus raise prices. A country wastes money if it tries to produce everything it needs. Therefore, it should produce chiefly what it makes best and most economically. If a country has excellent factories but poor farmland, for example, it should export manufactured products and import most of its food. If such a nation tries to expand its farming by placing a tariff on imported food, its people will have to pay higher prices for food. In addition, many people who believe that certain industries must be protected think that it is better to support them with direct subsidies than with tariffs. Unlike tariffs, subsidies do not raise consumer prices.

Industrial inefficiency. Tariffs may encourage inefficiency by protecting industries from competition. Without competition, an industry has little need to become more efficient. If a nation's tariff policy encourages inefficiency, its industries will lose business to the industries of more efficient countries. Many economists claim that tariffs themselves cannot make—or keep—a nation prosperous by protecting inefficient industries.

Unfair support for some industries. Tariffs may help some industries—but only at the expense of others. If a high tariff protects a nation's aluminum industry, for example, aluminum might cost more in that country than it would without a tariff. All domestic industries that use aluminum would save money if they could buy the imported product at a lower price.

History

Tariff policies reflect the economic and political conditions within various countries. Throughout history, nations have changed their tariff policies to keep in step with their economic and political goals.

The first tariffs. In early times, nations did not have formal tariffs—but they did collect such taxes. Most tariff collectors simply charged merchants the highest duties they thought they could get.

From about 1100 to 1300, the Christian military campaigns called the Crusades brought increased trade between Europe and the Middle East. The rise in trade led to formal tariffs during this period. The first tariff agreements were made by Italian trading cities, such as Genoa and Venice, with various commercial partners in Africa and Asia. England levied a revenue tariff in 1303 that included an ad valorem duty on imported and exported goods. Collectors based this duty, called *poundage,* on the value in pounds of the goods.

Beginning in the 1490's, the explorations of Christopher Columbus, Vasco da Gama, and other Europeans resulted in a great increase in foreign trade. European trading nations began to follow an economic policy called *mercantilism.* This policy involved the use of high tariffs to limit imports, so that exports would exceed imports. An excess of exports over imports produced a *favorable balance of trade*—and boosted the size of a nation's treasury. Mercantilism flourished until the 1700's.

The changing role of tariffs. During the late 1700's, the beginning of industrialization in Europe led to a major change in the role of tariffs. The production of goods increased in the industrial nations, such as Belgium and Britain. As a result, these nations wanted to sell more products to other countries. To increase trade, many industrial nations sought lower tariffs with their trade partners. But nations that were just beginning to industrialize kept tariffs high to protect their new industries. Efforts to reduce tariffs increased as industrialization progressed during the 1800's and 1900's.

Modern tariff policies. By the 1950's, three major trading groups had developed. These groups were (1) the chief Western industrialized countries, (2) the less developed countries, and (3) the Communist nations. The major Western industrialized countries began negotiations to increase their trade by reducing tariffs on manufactured and agricultural goods. These negotiations took place under a treaty called the General Agreement on Tariffs and Trade (GATT). In 1995, the countries that had formed the GATT helped create the World Trade Organization. This organization administers the GATT and works to reduce barriers to trade in services and in other areas not covered by the GATT. Since the late 1950's, Western European countries have eliminated almost all tariffs on one another's goods. They have done so as members of the European Free Trade Association and the European Economic Community, which was incorporated into the European Union in 1993. Many developing countries in Africa, Asia, and Latin America continue to use high tariffs to protect their industries.

Traditionally, imports and exports of Communist nations were controlled by centralized economic planning, and tariffs did not play an important role. But after 1980, some Communist governments relaxed strict control of their economies. They expanded their countries' international trading and became concerned with winning favorable tariff treatment from Western industrialized nations. In the late 1980's and early 1990's, the Communist trading group largely disintegrated after Communists lost control of the governments of many Eastern European countries and the Soviet Union. In 1991, most of the Soviet republics declared their independence, and the Soviet Union was dissolved. The new Eastern European governments and the former Soviet republics continued to seek favorable tariff treatment.

United States tariffs have played a major role in the nation's history. The U.S. government has changed its tariff policies many times through the years.

The revolutionary period. Many people in the American Colonies resented the tariffs that Britain put on goods that they imported. They sought independence partly to free themselves from British tariffs.

Soon after the Revolutionary War ended in 1783, many Americans demanded that the government establish a tariff. They argued that a tariff would (1) protect the nation's industries, (2) raise government revenue, and (3) encourage other nations to grant fair tariffs to the United States. The first Congress passed the Tariff Act of 1789, which set up U.S. tariffs.

The 1800's. The nation's first tariffs were low, but most of them rose during the early 1800's. People in various parts of the country called for different tariff policies. For example, people in the New England and Middle Atlantic states sought high tariffs to protect their manufacturing industries. But Southerners, whose income came chiefly from agriculture, demanded low tariffs. They wished to buy European products, which were better and cheaper than those made in the United States. Westerners, whose income also came mostly from agriculture, at first opposed high tariffs. But they came to accept a plan called the "American System" proposed by Representative Henry Clay of Kentucky. This plan included a protective tariff. In 1824, Congress boosted most tariffs as a result of Clay's proposals.

Many people, especially Southerners, protested the rising tariffs, particularly what they called the "Tariff of Abominations" of 1828. This tariff again increased the cost of foreign products needed by farmers. To satisfy those who wanted to eliminate all tariffs, Clay helped work out the Compromise Tariff of 1833. This law maintained some high duties but included a plan to reduce tariffs gradually until 1842. However, poor economic conditions resulted in a new and higher tariff in 1842. In 1846, after the economy had improved, Congress lowered tariffs with the Walker Tariff Act. Further reductions were made in 1857, but the Morrill Tariff Act of 1861 once again raised tariffs.

The tariff disagreement between the North and South helped cause the Civil War, which began in 1861. Southerners felt betrayed when the Westerners and Northerners joined in support of high tariffs.

During the Civil War, the government raised tariffs to new highs. Most tariffs remained high throughout the 1800's. Several attempts to lower them failed. For example, the Mills bill of 1888 included President Grover Cleveland's proposal to lower tariffs. The House of Representatives passed the bill, but the Senate never voted on it. The McKinley Tariff Act of 1890 raised the average level of tariffs to a new high.

The 1900's. In the early 1900's, many people in the United States wanted to increase U.S. trade by lowering tariffs. The Payne-Aldrich Tariff of 1909 changed many tariff rates, but it failed to lower the average level of tariffs. In 1913, the Underwood Tariff Act generally reduced tariffs. But a decline in shipping during World War I (1914-1918) cut trade and limited the effects of the lower tariffs. In 1922, the Fordney-McCumber Tariff Act raised tariff rates sharply. United States tariffs reached an all-time high under the Smoot-Hawley Tariff Act of 1930.

In 1934, during the Great Depression, Congress passed the Reciprocal Trade Agreements Act to increase trade. This law authorized the president to cut tariffs for certain nations by as much as half. It also enabled him to make agreements setting the tariff rate for each product. Formerly, Congress had set the rates.

In 1947, the United States and 22 other nations signed the General Agreement on Tariffs and Trade. This treaty reduced tariffs and provided for the settlement of trade disputes. It also sought to limit the situations in which its signers restricted imports from one another.

Beginning in the 1950's, Congress passed a series of laws that enabled the United States to participate in negotiations under the GATT. The negotiations were designed to further reduce tariffs and other trade barriers. Since then, several major rounds of GATT negotiations have taken place. As a result of these talks, the tariff rates of the United States and other major industrialized countries have been reduced substantially. By the mid-1990's, about 120 nations had signed the GATT.

Many industrialized countries, including the United States, have had difficulty adjusting to competition from imports. This difficulty has resulted in an increase in attempts to protect domestic industries by means of nontariff measures that are not clearly illegal under the GATT. These measures include special import quotas and voluntary export restraints. Such measures have been used to restrict the importation of automobiles, raw materials, textiles and clothing, footwear, steel products, electronic goods, and some food products. For many products, nontariff restrictions have become more important than tariffs in the United States and other major industrialized countries.

In GATT negotiations, efforts have been made to design acceptable rules governing conditions for the use of nontariff trade barriers. But it has proven difficult to define the circumstances in which protection should be used. In 1995, the United States became a founding member of the World Trade Organization. The organization was designed, in part, to deal more effectively with nontariff trade barriers. Robert M. Stern

Related articles in ***World Book*** include:

Asia-Pacific Economic Cooperation
Balance of payments
Customs union
European Free Trade Association
European Union
Exports and imports
Foreign trade zone
Free trade
General Agreement on Tariffs and Trade
Globalization
International trade
Mercantilism
Mercosur
North American Free Trade Agreement
Reciprocal trade agreement
Sanctions, Economic
World Trade Organization

Tariff Commission, United States. See International Trade Commission, United States.

Tariff of abominations. See Adams, John Quincy (The "tariff of abominations").

Tarkenton, Fran (1940-), became one of the greatest quarterbacks in National Football League (NFL) history. He was noted for his passing and his ability to scramble—that is, to avoid tacklers. Tarkenton played 18 years for the Minnesota Vikings and the New York Giants. He set career records for most passes attempted (6,467) and most yards rushing for a quarterback (3,674). He also completed 3,686 passes for 47,003 yards and 342 touchdowns, all NFL career records until Dan Marino of the Miami Dolphins broke them in 1995.

Francis Asbury Tarkenton was born on Feb. 3, 1940, in Richmond, Virginia. From 1958 to 1960, he played for the University of Georgia. Tarkenton played for the Vikings from 1961 to 1966. He was traded to the Giants in 1967 but returned to the Vikings in 1972. Tarkenton helped lead Minnesota to National Football Conference titles in the 1973, 1974, and 1976 seasons. He retired from football after the 1978-1979 season. In 1986, he was voted into the Pro Football Hall of Fame. Carlton Stowers

See also **Football** (picture).

Tarkington, Booth (1869-1946), was an American novelist and dramatist. His writings are considered one of the best mirrors of the wholesome aspects of life in the Middle West. Tarkington's works range from the sentimentally romantic *Monsieur Beaucaire* (1900) to the humor of *Penrod* (1914) and the realism of *Alice Adams* (1921). A trilogy of novels called *Growth* (1927) presents a cross section of city life such as it was in his hometown, Indianapolis. The trilogy consists of *The Turmoil* (1915), *The Magnificent Ambersons* (1918), and *The Midlander* (1923). *Penrod, Penrod and Sam* (1916), and *Seventeen* (1916) portray the joys and problems of young people.

Tarkington also published plays, short stories, and essays. He was amiable, optimistic, and somewhat passive in emphasizing the smiling aspects of life and the joys of boyhood. Tarkington was awarded two Pulitzer Prizes for literature, in 1919 and 1922, for *The Magnificent Ambersons* and *Alice Adams*.

Tarkington was born on July 29, 1869, in Indianapolis. He was elected to the Indiana House of Representatives for the 1902-1903 term. He was a neighbor and admirer of the poet James Whitcomb Riley, and a devotee of William Dean Howells and Mark Twain. Tarkington also wrote some of the verses that were sung in the *Ziegfeld Follies* in the early 1900's. Several of Tarkington's short stories dealing with political life were collected into one work entitled *In the Arena*. He also wrote *The Gentleman from Indiana* (1899), *The Beautiful Lady* (1905), *Beauty and the Jacobin, an Interlude of the French Revolution* (1912), and *The Plutocrat* (1927). Bert Hitchcock

Tarnish. When a metal rusts, or combines with oxygen, it is tarnished. When a metallic or mineral surface loses its luster, it is also tarnished. The word *tarnish* is used for rust formed on metals other than iron, or *nonferrous* metals. See also **Rust**.

Taro, *TAH roh* or *TA roh,* is a tropical plant used as food. The edible portion of the plant consists of one or more large, starchy underground stems. The taro is grown in many tropical regions, especially in Hawaii and on other Pacific Islands. Several different forms of the plant are cultivated. In the southern United States, the taro is called *dasheen.* In other countries, it is sometimes known by such names as *eddo, malanga,* and *yautia.* The taro is closely related to the ornamental plants called *elephant's-ear* and *caladium.* Alwyn H. Gentry

See also **Caladium** (with picture); **Elephant's-ear** (with picture); **Hawaii** (Food).

Scientific classification. The taro belongs to the arum family, Araceae. It is classified as *Colocasia esculenta.*

Tarot cards. See **Magic** (History; picture).

Tarpan. See also **Horse** (Wild horses).

Tarpon, *TAHR pahn,* is a large game fish that resembles a herring. It lives in the Atlantic Ocean from Long Island to Brazil, in the Gulf of Mexico, and in West Indian waters. It is abundant off the southern Atlantic Coast of the United States. It also is found off the coasts of Spain, Portugal, and the Azore Islands. The tarpon grows to a length of 8 feet (2.4 meters) and sometimes weighs 200 pounds (91 kilograms). Its flesh is coarse and not desirable for food. The large, tough, silvery scales are used in decorative designs. The tarpon is a popular sport fish in the United States because it is a strong, skillful fighter. Most fishing for tarpon is done off the south Atlantic Coast. Tarpon enter fresh waters and may be seen rolling, giving off bubbles of air as they dive. Sometimes they leap out of the water. Tarpon spawning sites are unknown. John D. McEachran

Scientific classification. Tarpons are in the tarpon family, Elopidae. The tarpon found near Florida is *Megalops atlanticus.*

See also **Fish** (picture: Fish of coastal waters).

Tarragon, *TAR uh gahn,* is an aromatic herb closely related to American sagebrushes. Tarragon is widely cultivated for its leaves and young shoots, which are used as a flavoring for vinegar. Tarragon vinegar is used in preparing pickles and as a flavoring for mayonnaise, tartar sauce, and Dijon mustard.

The tarragon plant grows 2 to 5 feet (61 to 150 centimeters) high. Its narrow leaves have sharp tips. The plant bears numerous small, drooping flowers.

Tarragon thrives in prairies, plains, and rocky, barren regions. It grows wild in the western and midwestern parts of the United States, in Russia, in western Asia, and in parts of Canada and Mexico. Donna M. Eggers Ware

Scientific classification. Tarragon belongs to the family Asteraceae or Compositae. It is *Artemisia dracunculus.*

Tarsier, *TAHR see uhr,* is a type of small mammal with a round head and unusually large eyes. Tarsiers live in the tropical rain forests of Brunei, Indonesia, Malaysia, and the Philippines. They sleep in trees during the day and move about at night. Like human beings and apes, tarsiers belong to the order Primates (see **Primate**).

Tarsiers have big ears and a long, thin tail with tufts of hair on the end. Their long hind legs make them strong jumpers, and they can leap as far as 20 feet (6 meters). They use pads on their long fingers and toes to cling to branches. Tarsiers can rotate their head like an owl and thus see in any direction, though they cannot move their eyes. Most tarsiers measure from $3\frac{1}{4}$ to 6 inches (8.5 to 16 centimeters) long. The tail usually is from $5\frac{1}{4}$ to $10\frac{3}{4}$ inches (13.5 to 27 centimeters) long. They weigh only about 4 ounces (113 grams). Tarsiers feed chiefly on birds, insects, and small lizards.

Roderic B. Mast and Russell A. Mittermeier

Scientific classification. Tarsiers belong to the tarsier family, Tarsiidae. They make up the genus *Tarsius.*

See also **Eye** (picture: Some animal eyes).

M. P. L. Fogden, Bruce Coleman Ltd.

The tarsier is a small Southwest Pacific animal with large eyes. Pads on its fingers and toes help it to grip branches.

Tarsus, *TAHR suhs* (pop. 187,500), a city in south-central Turkey, is an agricultural center. Tarsus was the birthplace of Saint Paul. Ancient Tarsus was an important trading center, surrounded by fertile land. The Cydnus (now called the Tarsus) River linked the city with a good harbor on the Mediterranean Sea, and an important trade road ran through Tarsus. For location, see **Turkey** (political map).

Tarsus was first mentioned in the records of the Assyrians, a group of people from western Asia. The Assyrians probably seized control of the city about 850 B.C. from Greek colonists. After 67 B.C., the Romans took control of Tarsus. The city was ruled by the Roman Empire, and later by the Byzantine Empire, for several hundred years. After the A.D. 600's, many different groups ruled Tarsus. In the 1500's, the Ottomans made Tarsus part of their empire. F. Muge Gocek

Tartan, *TAHR tuhn,* is a plaid cloth pattern that developed chiefly in Scotland. The design consists of stripes of various widths and colors. The stripes cross at right angles against a solid color background. The principal *clans* (tribes) in Scotland, especially those in the Highlands, have their own tartans. Scottish regiments have also adopted tartans. In the United States, the word *tartan* also means a cloth or a garment with a tartan design.

The cloth that is used to make tartan is usually wool. A tartan design is called a *sett.* The sett may be made in any size, depending on the intended use of the cloth.

But the proportions of the stripes must remain the same. The colors of a sett may vary in shade.

A Scottish Highlander wears a tartan *kilt* (a knee-length pleated skirt) and may carry a *plaid* over the left shoulder. A plaid is a blanketlike mantle fastened at the shoulder with a brooch. The costume also includes a *sporran* (pouch) hanging in front of the kilt, a *doublet* (jacket), and a *bonnet* (cap). The stockings may be of tartan pattern, and the *brogues* (shoes) are low-cut. Tartan *trews* (trousers) are sometimes worn as an alternative to the kilt, especially by the Lowland Scottish regiments.

The use of checkered garments dates back to ancient times. The Irish, the Britons, the Caledonians of Scotland, and the Celts in Europe wore them. Scottish literature first referred to tartan in the 1200's. Originally, tartans in Scotland were associated with districts. Later, they were used to identify the chief clan or family of an area. Extra lines were added to some setts to show rank.

Originally, the kilt and the plaid were a single large piece of tartan cloth. Wearers folded the tartan lengthwise and held it at the waist with a belt. They threw the rest over the shoulder and pinned it. In bad weather, they wore it over the head and shoulders. When sleeping outside, they used it as a blanket. Today, a smaller kilt called a *filibeg* and the plaid are worn separately.

After the Jacobite Rebellion in 1745, the British Parliament banned tartan and the use of Highland dress until 1782. Some old setts were lost, but many new ones were invented, especially about 1820, when the works

The tartan of the British royal family is called the Royal Stewart. The Stuarts, the royal family of Scotland from 1371 to 1714 and of England from 1603 to 1714, regarded it as their tartan. The name of the family was originally *Stewart,* but it later came to be spelled *Stuart.*

Stewart, Royal

Stewart, Dress

Stewart, Hunting

Exclusive WORLD BOOK photos by Sidney H. Siegel; tartans courtesy Kinloch Anderson, Ltd., Edinburgh, Scotland

Colorful Scottish tartans developed chiefly in the Highlands of Scotland, where each clan and family designed its own pattern. Some Scottish clans wear a bright tartan on formal occasions, and a more restrained hunting tartan for everyday wear. Some of the best-known clan tartans are shown on this page. Because of the problem of matching dyes, the colors of different samples of the same tartan may vary in shade.

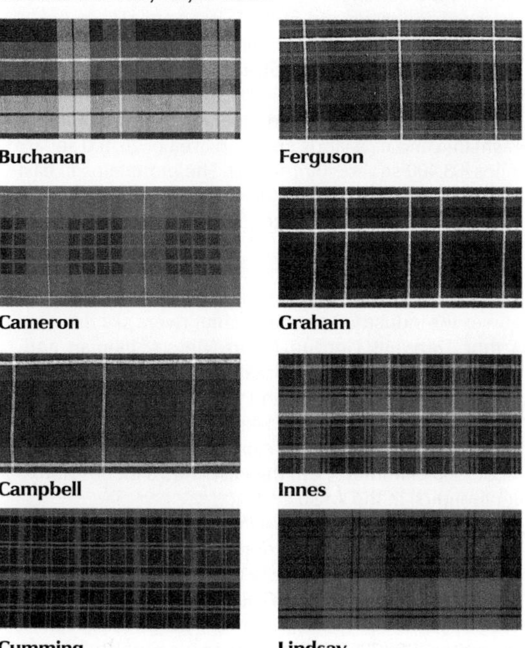

Buchanan **Ferguson**

Cameron **Graham**

Campbell **Innes**

Cumming **Lindsay**

MacDuff **MacTavish**

MacGregor **Menzies, Dress**

MacLeod of Lewis **Murray of Tullibardine**

MacMillan, Ancient **Robertson**

Macpherson, Dress **Sinclair**

of Scottish writer Sir Walter Scott awakened interest in Highlands traditions. Today, the tartan is popular throughout the world, particularly in countries where many people have Scottish ancestors. People often wear tartans associated with their name or ancestry.

Critically reviewed by the Royal Celtic Society

See also **Clan; Scotland** (picture: Bagpipes and kilts).

Tartaric acid, *tahr TAR ihk,* is an organic chemical that occurs naturally in grapes and several other fruits. It is commonly used in the production of jellies and carbonated grape beverages. Most commercial tartaric acid is obtained as a by-product of the wine industry. The acid's colorless crystals are derived from potassium hydrogen tartrate, or *argol,* which collects on the walls of wine vats during the fermentation of grapes.

Three salts of tartaric acid—cream of tartar, tartar emetic, and Rochelle salt—are used by the food industry and other industries. Cream of tartar is an ingredient of some baking powders and is also used in making hard candies and taffy. Tartar emetic and Rochelle salt are used in some medicines. Crystals of Rochelle salt, which are *piezoelectric,* are also an important part of some microphones (see **Piezoelectricity**). In addition, tartaric acid and some of its salts are used in cleaning and polishing metals and in dyeing fabrics.

Tartaric acid was first isolated by Carl W. Scheele, a Swedish chemist, in 1770. The acid has a chemical formula of $C_4H_6O_6$. Robert J. Ouellette

Tartars. See Tatars.

Tartarus, *TAHR tuhr uhs,* was a deep pit below the surface of the earth in early Greek mythology. It was as far below the surface as heaven was above the earth. High walls and a river of fire called Phlegethon (or Pyriphlegethon) encircled Tartarus. Zeus, the ruler of the gods, imprisoned the rebellious gods called Titans there. Any god who swore a false oath by the River Styx in the Underworld was held for nine years (see **Styx**).

In later Greek and Roman belief, Tartarus was a place of punishment for the most wicked sinners and was part of Hades, the kingdom of the dead (see **Hades**). In some ways, Tartarus resembled the Christian idea of hell.

Justin M. Glenn

Tartini, *tahr TEE nee,* **Giuseppe,** *joo ZEHP peh* (1692-1770), was a great Italian violinist, composer, and teacher. He influenced violin playing by introducing a system of violin bowing and fingering. He also started the use of thicker strings and lighter bows. In 1728, he founded a school of violin playing at Padua. His best-known composition for violin is the *Devil's Trill Sonata.* He also composed about 140 concertos, 40 trios, 150 violin sonatas, and wrote essays on violin playing methods and the theory of acoustics. Tartini was born on April 8, 1692, in Pirano, Italy (now Piran, Slovenia). He died on Feb. 26, 1770. Stephen Clapp

Tarzan. See **Burroughs, Edgar Rice.**

Tashkent, *tahsh KEHNT* (pop. 1,986,000), also spelled Toshkent, is the capital of Uzbekistan, a country in central Asia. The city lies in the valley of the Chirchik River (see **Uzbekistan** [map]). Tashkent used to be divided into two sections, an old city and a new city. Today, there is little difference between the two. Many structures of the old city were destroyed during a powerful earthquake in 1966. They were replaced by multistory apartment buildings, stores, and office buildings. Tashkent has machinery plants and a cotton-textile mill. It is the regional center for cotton fabric production. William Fierman

Tasman, *TAZ muhn,* **Abel Janszoon,** *AH buhl YAHN sohn* (1603?-1659), a Dutch navigator employed by the Dutch East India Company, explored the South Pacific. In 1642, he sailed southeast from Batavia, Java—now Jakarta, Indonesia—and became the first European to reach the island now called Tasmania and to sight New Zealand (see **Tasmania** [History]).

On the voyage, Tasman also explored the Tonga and Fiji island groups. In addition, he sailed completely around Australia without sighting it. Thus, the question of whether Australia or New Zealand were parts of a great southern continent remained unanswered until the voyages of Captain James Cook (see **Cook, James**). On a voyage in 1644, Tasman entered the Gulf of Carpentaria along northern Australia. Historians believe he was born at Lutjegast, the Netherlands, near Groningen. He died in October 1659. Barry M. Gough

Tasman Sea, *TAZ muhn,* is that part of the Pacific Ocean which lies between southeastern Australia, Tasmania, and New Zealand. It covers about 900,000 square miles (2,300,000 square kilometers). A communications cable on the seabed links Australia and New Zealand. The Dutch navigator Abel Janszoon Tasman reached the sea in the mid-1600's. Nicole F. Morcom

Tasmania, *taz MAY nee uh,* is the island state of Australia. It is the smallest Australian state and one of the most beautiful. Many Australians vacation there.

Two animals are native only to Tasmania—the Tasmanian thylacine (commonly known as the *Tasmanian tiger)* and the Tasmanian devil. The thylacine became extinct in 1936, but Tasmanian devils are plentiful. These badger-sized, bearlike animals get their name from the shrill screams they make at night.

Land and climate. Tasmania once formed the southeastern corner of the Australian mainland. But it was cut off from the continent by rising waters more than 8,000 years ago, after the end of the last ice age. The rough waters of Bass Strait now separate Tasmania from the state of Victoria. See **Bass Strait.**

Tasmania administers several small islands, including Bruny, Flinders, King, Macquarie, and Maria islands. Tasmania and its islands cover an area of 26,400 square miles (68,400 square kilometers). The mountains in eastern Tasmania form part of the Great Dividing Range that runs down the eastern edge of the Australian mainland. Mount Ossa (5,305 feet or 1,617 meters) in western Tasmania is the highest point on the island.

Tasmania's lakes and rivers are the source of electric power for industry. The state's chief rivers are the Arthur, Derwent, Gordon, Huon, Mersey, Pieman, and Tamar. The lakes include Great Lake and Lakes Echo, Gordon, Pedder, St. Clair, and Sorell.

Tasmania's temperature averages 70 °F (21 °C) in January and 52 °F (11 °C) in July. Annual rainfall averages 23 inches (60 centimeters) in the east and 78 inches (198 centimeters) in the west.

Natural resources. Tasmania has many mineral deposits. They include coal, copper, gold, iron, lead, magnesite, nickel, silver, tin, and zinc. Large forests cover parts of the island. Some of the seeds that produced California's first eucalyptus trees came from Tasmania.

People. The 2001 Australian census reported that Tas-

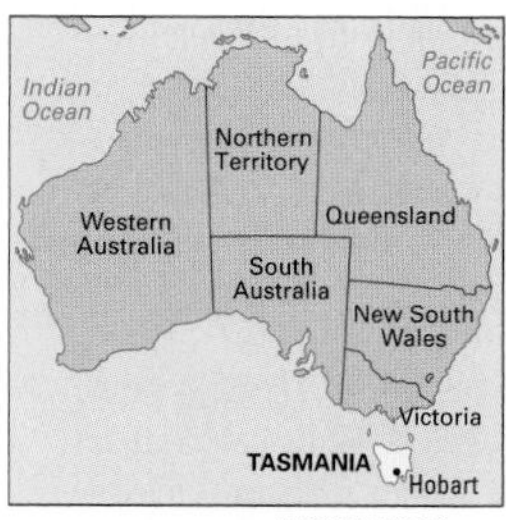

WORLD BOOK map

Tasmania is Australia's island state. Most of the state's trade and shipping goes through Hobart, Tasmania's capital and largest city, *shown here.*

© Australian Picture Library from Corbis

mania had 456,652 people. Most of the state's people were born in Australia and are of British descent. The major cities and towns of Tasmania lie near the coast. Hobart is Tasmania's capital and largest city, and Launceston ranks as the second largest city. Other important towns in Tasmania include Burnie and Devonport.

Education is free and required until the age of 16. The University of Tasmania is based in Hobart and has campuses in Launceston and Burnie.

Economy. Farmers use a narrow strip of land near the northwest, north, and eastern coasts, where the soil is rich. Produce includes potatoes, onions, and other vegetables; apples; and cereal crops. Sheep, cotton, milk, and wool are also important products. Specialized produce includes lavender; pyrethrum, used to make insecticide; and opium poppies. Tasmania produces more than 40 percent of the world's *opiate* (made from opium) products used by the pharmaceutical industry to make codeine, morphine, and other medicines. Atlantic salmon farming is a fast-growing industry concentrated in the state's southeast region.

Important minerals taken from Tasmania include copper, iron, lead, silver, and zinc. Hobart has one of Australia's largest zinc-processing factories. Bell Bay is the site of an aluminum-processing plant. Other industries include fruit and vegetable processing, dairy products, and wool. Wood chips are a major export. Paper is made near Burnie, and newsprint is produced at Boyer.

Tasmania has about 540 miles (870 kilometers) of railroads for hauling freight. The state has no passenger railroads, except for small tourist railways. The island has 15,000 miles (24,000 kilometers) of roads. It is served by Australian airlines and national and international shipping companies.

Government. The British Crown appoints the governor of Tasmania. The voters elect a 15-member Legislative Council for six years and a 25-member House of Assembly for four years. Tasmania sends 12 senators and 5 representatives to the Australian Parliament.

History. The first Aborigines reached Tasmania more than 20,000 years ago. In 1642, the Dutch navigator Abel Janszoon Tasman became the first European to reach Tasmania (see **Tasman, Abel Janszoon**). He called the island Van Diemen's Land, in honor of the governor of the Dutch East Indies (later Netherlands Indies). British convicts settled on the island in 1803. After the Europeans' arrival, most of the Tasmanian Aborigines died from starvation, disease, or attacks by European settlers. Officials moved the few remaining Aborigines to Flinders Island in Bass Strait. See **Aborigines, Australian.**

The United Kingdom granted some self-government to the island in 1855, and its name was changed to Tasmania the following year. In 1901, it became part of the Commonwealth of Australia. Ian McCausland

See also **Hobart; Tasmanian devil; Tasmanian tiger.**

Tasmanian devil, *taz MAY nee uhn,* is a fierce animal that lives on the Australian island of Tasmania. It feeds on any dead animals it can find and also hunts small animals. It is active mainly at night and spends the day in a cave, a hollow log, or some other shelter.

Tasmanian devils measure from 3 to 4 feet (0.9 to 1.2 meters) long, including a tail of about 1 foot (30 centimeters). Most have black fur with white markings, but some are entirely black.

Tasmanian devils are *marsupials.* Female marsupials bear tiny, poorly developed offspring that are carried in a pouch on the mother's belly until they develop more fully. Female Tasmanian devils usually give birth to four young. The young spend about 15 weeks in the pouch, feeding on the mother's milk. Michael L. Augee

Scientific classification. The Tasmanian devil belongs to the family Dasyuridae. Its scientific name is *Sacrophilus harrisii.*

Fritz Prenzel

The Tasmanian devil is a fierce animal of the Australian island of Tasmania. It often feeds on the remains of dead animals.

Tasmanian tiger, *taz MAY nee uhn,* also called *Tasmanian wolf,* was a large animal of Australia. Most sci-

David Fleay

The Tasmanian tiger, which most scientists believe is extinct, had stripes along its back like those of a tiger. This photo, taken in 1933, shows the last Tasmanian tiger in captivity.

entists believe it is extinct. Fossils indicate that this animal was once common throughout Australia. But it lived only on the island of Tasmania when Europeans began settling the region in the late 1700's. The Europeans hunted the animal because they thought it preyed on sheep and poultry. The last known Tasmanian tiger died in captivity in 1936. Australians often call Tasmanian tigers *thylacines.* The Tasmanian tiger measured about 5 feet (1.5 meters) long, including a tail of about 20 inches (51 centimeters). It had short gray or yellowish-brown fur and dark stripes across the rear of its back.

The Tasmanian tiger was a *marsupial.* Like other marsupials, the female Tasmanian tiger carried its young in a pouch on its belly until they developed more fully. The pouch of the Tasmanian tiger was unusual because it opened to the rear of the body. In most other marsupials, the pouch opens to the front. Michael L. Augee

Scientific classification. Tasmanian tigers are the only members of the family Thylacinidae. They are *Thylacinus cynocephalus.*

Tasso, *TAS oh,* **Torquato,** *tawr KWAH taw* (1544-1595), was an Italian poet of the late Renaissance period. The musicality of his language and his mournful moods are considered unsurpassed.

Tasso's masterpiece is *Jerusalem Delivered* (completed 1575, published 1581), an epic poem about the First Crusade (1096-1099). Tasso departed from literary tradition by showing strong concern for historical truth in his epic. However, he still filled the poem with magic and miracles, as well as love and sensuality. The poem is written in eight-line stanzas common to Italian Renaissance poetry. Later, Tasso was bothered by criticisms of his work, and by worries that the Roman Catholic Church might censor his poem because of its mythical and sensual elements. These concerns, along with his respect for historical truth, led him to write a restrained version of his epic, *Jerusalem Conquered* (1593).

Besides his many lyrics, Tasso wrote philosophical dialogues, plays, and essays on literary theory. One of his greatest works is the pastoral drama *Aminta* (1573).

Tasso was born on March 11, 1544, in Sorrento. He spent a number of years at the court of Alfonso II d'Este, Duke of Ferrara. Tasso was hospitalized for mental illness in 1577 and from 1579 to 1586. He died on April 25, 1595. Paolo Cherchi

Taste is an important sense by which human beings and animals detect many chemicals in their environment. In the body, specialized skin cells that detect taste are grouped into clusters called *taste buds.* They are found primarily on the tongue, contained within small mounds called *papillae.* Taste buds also are present on the *soft palate* (back of the roof of the mouth) and other parts of the mouth and throat. The word *taste* refers to the quality of a substance that is detected by the taste buds. Taste is a component of *flavor,* which also includes smell, touch, and temperature sensations.

Chemicals associated with the taste qualities of sour, salty, bitter, and sweet stimulate *receptor cells* of the taste buds. Some scientists think a fifth distinct taste, called *umami,* can be detected. This taste, initially described by Japanese scientists, is usually described as "savory" or "meaty." The sensation of umami is caused by a chemical called *glutamate,* which is found in many protein-rich foods. However, not all scientists agree that umami constitutes a fifth category of taste.

The taste receptor cells in taste buds are connected to branches of three *cranial nerves,* which connect directly to the brain. Taste sensation begins when these cells are stimulated by chemicals from food or other substances dissolved in saliva. When taste cells are stimulated, they

How taste works

The sense of taste is sent to the brain through taste buds in the tongue. These drawings show the structures in the mouth and nose that are involved in the sense of taste.

WORLD BOOK diagrams by Barbara Cousins

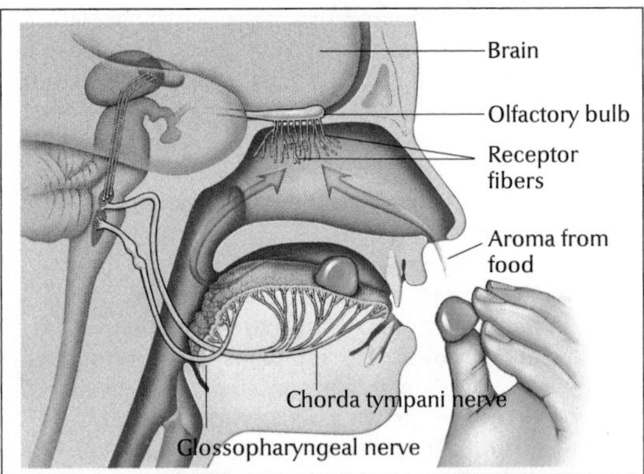

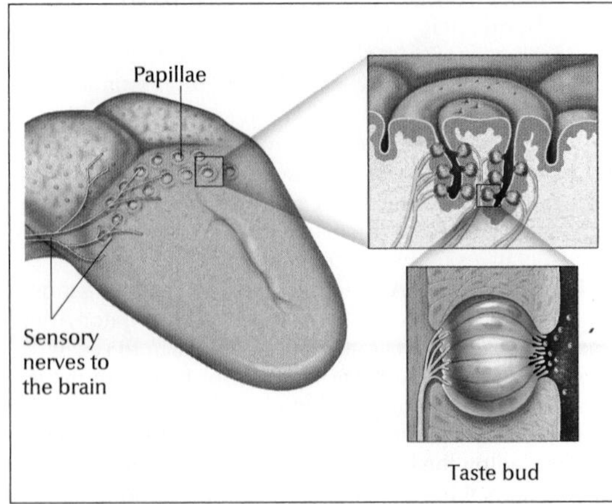

transmit sensory signals to the *medulla,* the lower part of the brain stem. Here, some taste signals are separated and travel to the front of the brain stem to the area called the *thalamus.* From the thalamus, the signals move to the *cerebral cortex,* the part of the brain that controls higher brain functions. At the cerebral cortex, the brain interprets the nerve signals it has received, and we become aware of taste.

Most cells in the taste buds are sensitive to two or more taste qualities. The sensation of distinct tastes comes from responses by nerve cells creating a pattern of activity within the brain. The nerve cells themselves cannot distinguish different tastes, although the cells usually respond most strongly to one type of taste. Scientists have discovered genes that control the action of receptor cells, including those responsible for sweet and bitter taste.

Taste plays a major role in monitoring food intake and avoiding foods that may be harmful. Many carbohydrates taste sweet, and poisonous substances are often bitter. Most animals, including human beings, will readily accept sweet foods and reject bitter foods. Illness associated with the consumption of a well-defined taste often results in a long-lasting dislike of that taste. This dislike can occur after a single instance of a particular taste associated with illness. It may develop even if the illness begins two or more hours after the food is eaten.

Taste also affects how the body regulates metabolism, nutritional balance, and even mood. In human infants and other animals, experiments have shown that sweet tastes have a general calming effect and cause an increased tolerance to pain. David V. Smith

See also **Smell** (Taste and smell).

Tatars, *TAH tuhrz,* also called Tartars (pronounced *TAHR tuhrz),* are a Turkic-speaking people of Europe and Asia. Most of the 6 million Tatars in the world today live in Russia, Ukraine, and Uzbekistan. Kazan, the capital of the Russian republic of Tatarstan, is a center of Tatar culture (see **Kazan**). Sizable Tatar communities are also found in Bulgaria, China, Kazakhstan, Romania, and Turkey. Most Tatars belong to the Sunni branch of Islam.

In the 1200's, Tatars joined the Mongols and other nomadic peoples to invade eastern Europe. In 1944, during World War II, the Soviet Union deported thousands of Tatars from the Soviet republic of Crimea to central Asia. The Tatars were falsely accused of helping the Nazis. Tatars began returning to Crimea in 1989. But many Crimean Tatars remain in exile. Ali Eminov

Tate, Allen (1899-1979), was an American poet, critic, novelist, and biographer. Tate's writing stresses links between the present and the past. A major theme in his work is a yearning for the rural, aristocratic way of life common in the South before the American Civil War (1861-1865). Many of Tate's writings express dislike for what he regarded as the crowded, dehumanizing way of life in modern industrial society.

Tate is best known for his poetry, much of which is powerful and written in violent language. Tate's conversion to Roman Catholicism in 1950 led to an increased concern with religion and ethics in his work. His *Collected Poems: 1919-1976* was published in 1977.

As a literary critic, Tate became noted for his essays on the nature of the imagination and the value of literature. He became known for his essays about literary figures and for detailed analyses of poems. Many of his critical works were published in *Essays of Four Decades* (1969). Tate included both critical and autobiographical essays in *Memoirs and Opinions* (1975).

John Orley Allen Tate was born on Nov. 19, 1899, in Winchester, Kentucky. As a student at Vanderbilt University, he was invited by his teacher, John Crowe Ransom, to join the Fugitives along with Tate's roommate Robert Penn Warren. This group of Southern writers hoped to preserve the cultural heritage of the South. Tate's ties with the South can be seen in his novel *The Fathers* (1938) and in his biographies *Stonewall Jackson: The Good Soldier* (1928) and *Jefferson Davis: His Rise and Fall* (1929). Tate died on Feb. 9, 1979. Bonnie Costello

Tattooing is the practice of dying the skin with permanent designs. Tattoos are created by pricking the skin with needles that inject small amounts of ink or other pigments to the underlayers of the skin. Tattooing is an art form in many cultures. People have also used tattoos to label cattle, brand prisoners and slaves, confer magical powers, cure illness, declare religious conviction or romantic devotion, and express opinions.

The practice of tattooing is ancient. Cave paintings that are more than 8,000 years old show human figures who appear to have tattoos. Tattooing has been practiced by many peoples, including American Indians, peoples of Indonesia and India, and some African peoples. The most elaborate traditions of tattooing, however, are found in Japan and Polynesia. Japanese tattooing is known for colorful designs that may cover the entire body. Polynesians traditionally used tattoos to protect an individual from attacks by unseen forces and to project the person's own sacred power.

Until the 1900's, Western cultures generally disapproved of tattooing, and Jewish and Christian tradition banned such skin decoration. In Western society, generally the only people who had tattoos were sailors who had visited other parts of the world, prisoners, gang members, and prostitutes. However, decorative tattooing became more common in the 1900's, particularly among men in military service. Since the 1990's, tattooing has become popular and fashionable among young people in the United States and Europe. Peter W. Wood

See also **Body art.**

© Bob Krist, Corbis

This Samoan man has traditional Polynesian tattoos.

Tatum, Art (1909-1956), ranks among the greatest piano soloists of jazz improvisation. Tatum's delicate touch and swinging beat were perhaps unequaled among pianists of his time. His brilliant keyboard technique earned him the praise of many classical pianists.

Arthur Tatum was born on Oct. 13, 1909, in Toledo, Ohio. He was blind in one eye from birth and had only slight vision in the other eye. He arrived in New York City in 1932 as an accompanist for a singer. In the late 1930's, he first became a favorite soloist in the small nightclubs along Manhattan's West 52nd Street, a hotbed of jazz during the 1930's and 1940's. Tatum led a trio for many years. However, he was one of the rare jazz pianists who needed no support from a rhythm section.

Frank Tirro

Taurus, *TAWR uhs,* is the second sign of the zodiac. Taurus, an earth sign, is symbolized by a bull. Astrologers believe that the planet Venus, named for the ancient Roman goddess of love and beauty, rules Taurus.

According to astrologers, people born under the sign of Taurus, from April 20 to May 20, are loyal, patient, practical, and trustworthy. They appreciate beauty, comfort, and the countryside. Taureans move slowly and can be lazy, but they are determined to finish any task they begin. They have a down-to-earth personality and rely on their common sense.

Taurus—The Bull

Birth dates: April 20-May 20.
Group: Earth.
Characteristics: Affectionate, conservative, loyal, sensible, possessive, stubborn.

Signs of the Zodiac
Aries
March 21-April 19
Taurus
April 20-May 20
Gemini
May 21-June 20
Cancer
June 21-July 22
Leo
July 23-Aug. 22
Virgo
Aug. 23-Sept. 22
Libra
Sept. 23-Oct. 22
Scorpio
Oct. 23-Nov. 21
Sagittarius
Nov. 22-Dec. 21
Capricorn
Dec. 22-Jan. 19
Aquarius
Jan. 20-Feb. 18
Pisces
Feb. 19-March 20

Taureans, though not talkative, are affectionate, friendly, and warm-hearted. They are even-tempered but can become fierce when angered. They are stubborn, and tend to keep grudges. Christopher McIntosh

See also **Astrology; Horoscope; Zodiac.**

Taussig, *TOW sihg,* **Helen Brooke** (1898-1986), was an American physician who specialized in children's heart diseases. She discovered the major defects that cause the bluish tinge in the skin of *blue babies* (see **Blue baby**).

From 1930 to 1963, Taussig served as chief of the Cardiac Clinic of the Harriet Lane Home, the children's section of the Johns Hopkins Hospital in Baltimore. She found that at birth most blue babies have an abnormal opening in the *septum* (wall between the chambers of the heart) and a partial blockage of the pulmonary artery. The heart pumps blood through this artery to the lungs, where oxygen enters the blood. A lack of oxygen in the blood gives the skin a bluish color. From 1941 to 1944, Taussig and a surgeon, Alfred Blalock, developed an operation that enables the blood to bypass the faulty artery.

Taussig was born on May 24, 1898, in Cambridge, Massachusetts. She graduated from the University of California at Berkeley in 1921 and received her M.D. degree from the Johns Hopkins University School of Medicine in 1927. Miriam Schneir

Tautog. See **Blackfish.**

Tax Court, United States, is a federal court that handles disputes involving income, estate, gift, and other taxes. Taxpayers who cannot reach an agreement with the Internal Revenue Service may file a petition with the U.S. Tax Court. The court has offices in Washington, D.C., but it holds sessions at locations throughout the country for the convenience of taxpayers.

Taxpayers may choose to take a case involving $10,000 or less to the court's Small Tax Division. This division provides simplified procedures for handling cases, and its decisions are final. All other Tax Court rulings may be appealed to the U.S. Court of Appeals and then to the Supreme Court of the United States.

The Tax Court was established in 1924 as the U.S. Board of Tax Appeals. It received its present name in 1969. Critically reviewed by the United States Tax Court

Taxation is a system of raising money to finance government services and activities. Governments at all levels—local, state, and national—require people and businesses to pay taxes. Governments use the tax revenue to pay the cost of police and fire protection, health programs, schools, roads, national defense, and many other public services.

Taxes are as old as government. The general level of taxes has varied through the years, depending on the role of the government. In modern times, many governments—especially in advanced industrial countries—have rapidly expanded their roles and taken on new responsibilities. As a result, their need for tax revenue has become great.

Through the years, people have frequently protested against tax increases. In these situations, taxpayers have favored keeping services at current levels or reducing them. Voters have defeated many proposals for tax increases by state and local governments.

Kinds of taxes

Governments levy many kinds of taxes. The most important kinds include *property taxes, income taxes,* and *taxes on transactions.*

Property taxes are levied on the value of such property as farms, houses, stores, factories, and business equipment. The property tax first became important in ancient times. Today, it ranks as the chief source of income for local governments in the United States and Canada. Most states of the United States and provinces of Canada also levy property taxes. Property taxes are called *direct taxes* because they are levied directly on the people expected to pay them.

Income taxes are levied on income from such sources as wages and salaries, dividends, interest, rent, and earnings of corporations. There are two main types of income taxes—*individual income taxes* and *corporate income taxes.* Individual income taxes, also called *personal income taxes,* are applied to the income of individuals and families. Corporate income taxes are levied on corporate earnings. Income taxes may also be levied on the earnings of estates and trusts. Income taxes generally are considered to be direct taxes.

Most nations in the world levy income taxes. In the United States, income taxes are levied by the federal government, most state governments, and some local governments. Many people and businesses in the United States also pay special income taxes that help fund Social Security programs. These taxes are known as *Social Security contributions* or *payroll taxes.* In Canada, income taxes are levied by the federal government and by the country's 10 provincial governments.

Taxes on transactions are levied on sales of goods and services and on privileges. There are three main types—*general sales taxes, excise taxes,* and *tariffs.*

General sales taxes apply one rate to the sales of many different items. Such taxes include state sales taxes in the United States and the federal sales tax in Canada. The *value-added tax* is a general sales tax levied in many countries in Europe, Latin America, and elsewhere throughout the world. It is applied to the increase in value of a product at each stage in its manufacture and distribution.

Excise taxes are levied on the sales of specific products and on privileges. They include taxes on the sales of such items as gasoline, tobacco, and alcoholic beverages. Other excise taxes are the *license tax,* the *franchise tax,* and the *severance tax.* The license tax is levied on the right to participate in an activity, such as selling liquor, getting married, or going hunting or fishing. The franchise tax is a payment for the right to carry on a certain kind of business, such as operating a bus line or a public utility. The severance tax is levied on the processing of natural resources, such as timber, natural gas, or petroleum.

Tariffs are taxes on imported goods. Countries can use tariffs to protect their own industries from foreign competition. Tariffs provide protection by raising the price of imported goods, making the imported goods more expensive than domestic products.

General sales taxes and taxes on gasoline and other products are called *indirect taxes* because they tax a service or privilege instead of a person. Manufacturers and business owners pay these taxes, then add the cost to the prices they charge. These taxes may be called *shifted taxes* because manufacturers and business owners shift the cost of the tax to their customers.

Other taxes include *estate taxes, inheritance taxes,* and *gift taxes.* An estate tax is applied to the value of property before it has been given to heirs. An inheritance tax is levied on the value of property after it has been given to heirs. A gift tax is applied to the value of property that is given away during a donor's lifetime. The donor pays the tax.

In the United States, the federal government and some state governments levy estate and gift taxes. Only

Taxes in the United States

This graph shows how much of the United States *gross domestic product* (GDP) goes toward paying taxes. The GDP is the total value of all goods and services produced in a country in a year. The table shows taxes collected in the United States for selected years.

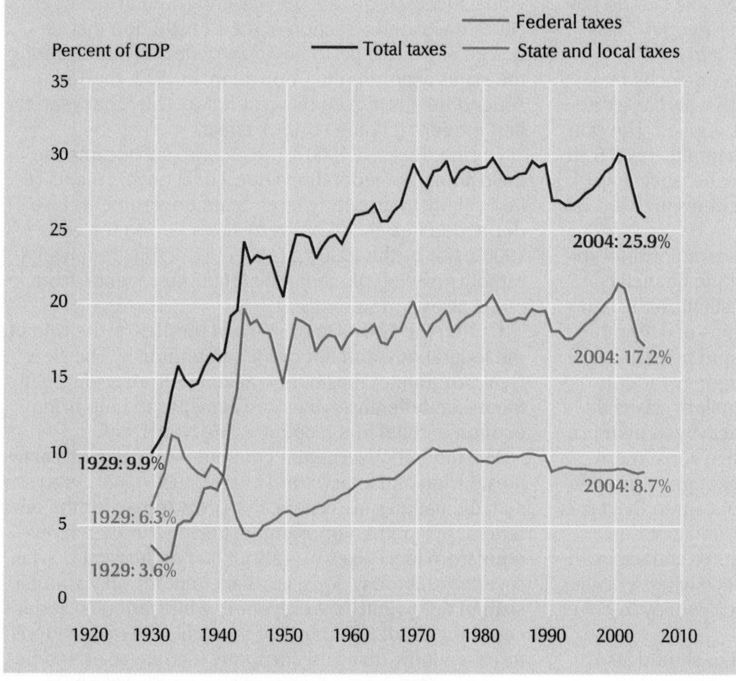

Year	Total tax (millions)	Total tax per person
1900	$ 1,332	$ 17.53
1905	1,561	18.59
1910	2,021	21.97
1915	2,781	28.14
1920	9,599	90.80
1925	8,359	73.17
1930	9,700	79.01
1935	10,500	82.53
1940	16,900	128.35
1945	52,100	369.02
1950	67,800	449.91
1955	99,200	601.17
1960	136,900	763.43
1965	183,900	961.42
1970	294,700	1,450.04
1975	460,300	2,142.02
1980	816,400	3,603.69
1985	1,205,600	5,063.65
1990	1,564,000	6,288.63
1995	2,036,300	7,682.27
1998	2,543,400	9,252.68
1999	2,719,500	9,777.05
2000	2,969,300	10,522.15
2001	3,023,100	10,603.49
2002	2,920,300	10,142.06
2003	2,895,700	9,957.62
2004	3,033,900	10,331.33

Source: *World Book* estimates based on data from the U.S. Department of Commerce.

The U.S. federal government dollar

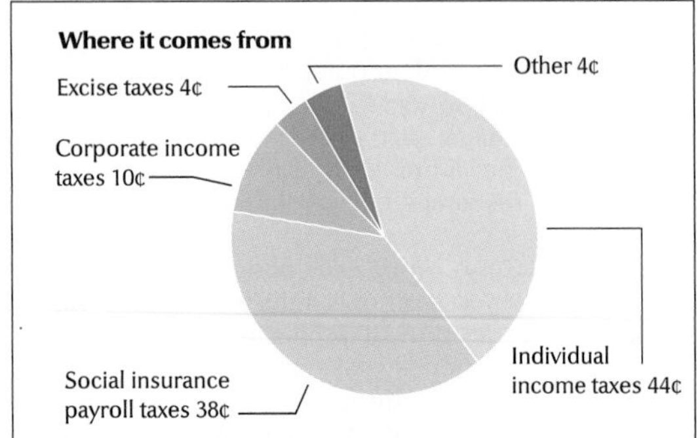

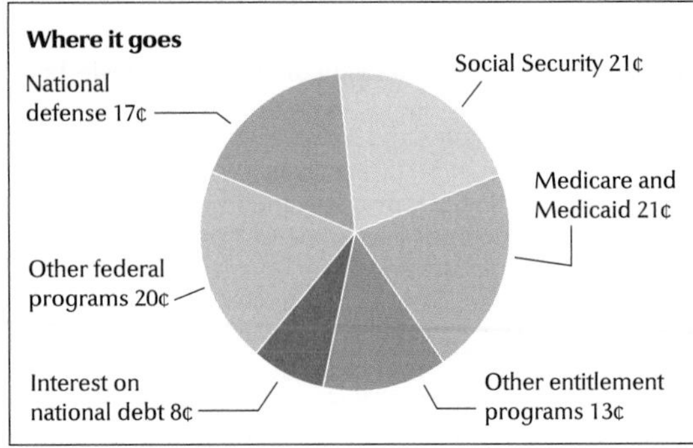

Proposals made by President Bush in February 2005 for fiscal year Oct. 1, 2005-Sept. 30, 2006.

state governments levy inheritance taxes. In Canada, only the province of Quebec levies gift and inheritance taxes. Canada has no estate taxes.

Principles of taxation

A good tax system must satisfy several general principles of taxation. The main principles include *productivity, equity,* and *elasticity.*

Productivity. The chief goal of a tax system is to generate the revenue a government needs to pay its expenses. When a tax system produces such revenue, it satisfies the principle of productivity. If a tax system fails to produce the needed revenue, the government may have to add to its debt by borrowing money.

Equity. Most people agree that a tax system should be *equitable* (fair) to the taxpayers. Economists refer to two kinds of equity—*horizontal* and *vertical.* Horizontal equity means that taxpayers who have the same amounts of income should be taxed at the same rate. Vertical equity implies that wealthier people should pay proportionately more taxes than poorer people. This is sometimes called the principle of *ability to pay.*

Governments often try to achieve tax equity by making their taxes *progressive.* A progressive tax has a rate that depends on the sum to which it is applied. The rate increases as that sum increases. For example, the U.S. individual income tax is a progressive tax because it applies a higher rate to larger taxable incomes than it does to smaller ones.

Elasticity. A tax system should be *elastic* (flexible) so that it can satisfy a government's changing financial needs. In an elastic system, taxes help stabilize the economy. For example, taxes increase in times of economic growth and thus help limit *inflation* (rapid price increases). Increasing taxes would leave less money for consumers to spend to send prices up. Similarly, taxes decrease during a decline in economic activity to help prevent a recession. This action would leave consumers more money to spend and thus spur economic growth.

Other principles of taxation. People agree that taxes should be convenient and easy to pay, and that they should be inexpensive for governments to collect. In addition, taxpayers should know in advance when a tax has to be paid, so that they can save enough money to cover the payment.

Some economists believe a tax system should also satisfy the principle of *neutrality.* According to this principle, tax laws should not affect taxpayers' economic decisions, such as how to spend, save, or invest their money. But other economists believe a tax system must defy the principle of neutrality to achieve tax equity or to stabilize economic growth. Still other economists believe a tax system should play an active role in redistributing wealth. They support taxing the wealthy at highly progressive rates and using the collected revenue to finance services for the poor.

Taxation in the United States

The Constitution of the United States gives Congress the sole right to levy federal taxes. Congress first used its tax powers in 1789, when it began to levy a tariff. Tariffs were the chief sources of federal revenue until the outbreak of the American Civil War in 1861. Then the cost of the war prompted the government to levy a series of excise taxes and other new taxes.

In 1894, the federal government levied a tax on individual incomes. But the tax was abolished in 1895 because it violated a section of the Constitution that required any direct tax to be *apportioned* (divided) among the states according to population. In 1913, the 16th Amendment removed this restriction. Later that year, the first modern income tax took effect.

During the early 1900's, the income tax became the main source of federal revenue. Local governments relied chiefly on property taxes. State governments also depended heavily on property taxes during the early 1900's. But by the 1930's, state governments received a rapidly growing percentage of their tax revenue from income taxes and sales taxes.

During the Great Depression of the 1930's, the role of the federal government grew tremendously. The New Deal program of President Franklin D. Roosevelt greatly increased federal services and activities to help bring economic relief to the country (see **New Deal**).

The federal government continued to expand its activities during and after World War II (1939-1945). As a result, the nation's tax system also grew to pay for the new federal programs. For example, during the 1920's, revenue from local taxes was about half of the total U.S. tax revenue. But today, local taxes account for only about a sixth of the country's tax revenue, while federal taxes account for about two-thirds of the total. The main federal taxes are individual and corporate income taxes and Social Security contributions. Some revenue from these taxes goes to state and local governments to finance such projects as roadbuilding and public housing.

Taxation in Canada

The individual income tax ranks as Canada's chief source of federal revenue. The federal government also levies corporate income taxes, a general sales tax, tariffs, and excise taxes on such items as gasoline, alcohol, and tobacco. Canada's 10 provincial governments also rely most heavily on individual and corporate income taxes. The provinces also levy property taxes, sales taxes, and excise taxes on gasoline, tobacco, and motor vehicle licenses. Some provinces tax gifts, logging, and health-care programs. Local governments get most of their revenue from property taxes. Vito Tanzi

Related articles in *World Book* include:

Assessment
Capital gains tax
Congressional Budget Office
Excise
Flat tax
Franchise
Gasoline tax
Income tax
Inheritance tax
Inland revenue
Internal revenue
License
Poll tax
Property tax
Revenue sharing
Road (How roads and highways are paid for)
Sales tax
Single tax
Social security (Financing social security)
Stamp
Stamp Act
Tariff
Tithe
Turnpike
Value-added tax

Additional resources

Adams, Charles. *For Good and Evil: The Impact of Taxes on the Course of Civilization.* 2nd ed. Madison Bks., 1999.
Slemrod, Joel, and Bakija, J. M. *Taxing Ourselves.* MIT Pr., 2000.

Taxco, *TAHS koh* (pop. 99,907), is a historic silver-mining town 70 miles (113 kilometers) southwest of Mexico City. Its official name is Taxco de Alarcón *(day AH lahr KOHN).* Taxco looks like an old Spanish town. Narrow cobblestone streets climb its steep hills. To preserve the town's appearance, Taxco was made a national monument. It is illegal to erect buildings in the contemporary style. Taxco's charm, crafts, and mild climate attract tourists, artists, and writers. It has been a mining center since Hernán Cortés founded it in 1529. It is the center of Mexico's silverware industry. See also **Cortés, Hernán; Mexico** (political map). James D. Riley

Taxidermy, *TAK suh DUR mee,* is a technique for preserving animals and showing them as they looked when they were alive. The word taxidermy comes from Greek words meaning *arrangement* and *skin.* Museums of natural history often exhibit birds, fish, antelope, tigers,

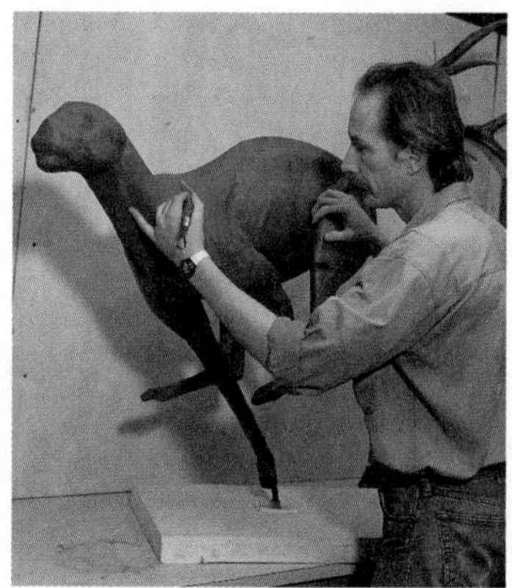

A taxidermist proceeds through several steps to create a lifelike model of a running cheetah. First, the skin is removed from the animal and tanned, *left.* A clay model of the animal is then sculpted, *center.* Next, a casting is made from a mold of the sculpture, *right.*

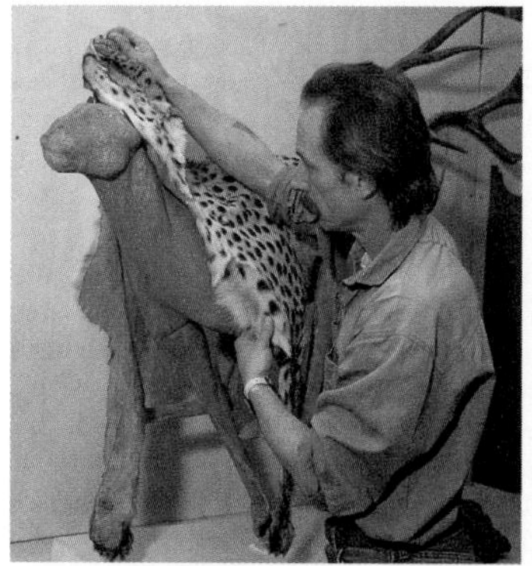

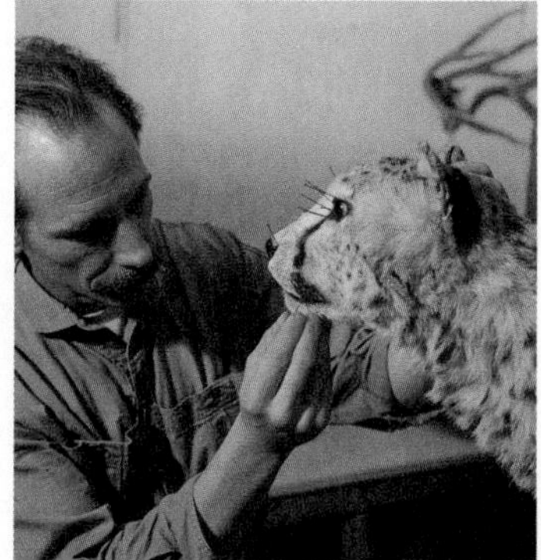

Field Museum, Chicago (Taxidermy by Paul O. Brunsvold; photography by Ron Testa and Diane Alexander White)

The taxidermist then places the tanned skin on the casting, *left.* Finally, the taxidermist sews, glues, and pins the skin into place, *center.* After other body features—such as eyes, ears, and a tongue—are added, the model is complete, *right.*

bears, and other wild animals in their natural settings.

Process of mounting. The taxidermist first takes accurate measurements of the dead animal's anatomy. The animal's skin is carefully removed and treated with a preservative, such as arsenical soap. The taxidermist then makes a drawing of the animal's body structure, including the muscles, bones, and depressions. This copy becomes a guide. Next, the taxidermist makes a framework out of wood and metal. The animal's skeleton also may be used. The taxidermist adds clay to the framework and sculpts the animal's anatomy. The clay model is used to make a thin, hollow casting of plaster, papier-mâché, burlap, and sometimes mesh wire. This casting must correspond accurately with the animal's figure. Finally, the taxidermist places the skin on the casting and sews and glues it together. Skins of large, heavy animals must be tanned before being mounted on the casting.

Taxidermists must add many other body features and use special materials to make the eyes and tongue. Taxidermists may use painted hollow globes instead of glass eyes to give the preserved animal a natural expression. They must also shape the ears.

Some museums use a *freeze-drying* technique to preserve specimens. This method is used mainly for small animals, such as songbirds and squirrels.

Careers in taxidermy. Taxidermy is a complicated art. It requires a knowledge of anatomy, natural history, drawing, sculpture, mechanics, tanning, and dyeing. Many museums have taxidermists on their staffs. Some museums hire commercial studios to mount their specimens. Most taxidermists learn their skills at a technical institute or by training under an experienced taxidermist. Further information about careers in taxidermy can be obtained from the National Taxidermists Association in Cleveland, Ohio. Francis M. Greenwell

Additional resources

Moyer, John W. *Practical Taxidermy.* 2nd ed. 1979. Reprint. Krieger, 1992.

Williamson, Bob, and Edwards, Ken. *Serious Sportsman Taxidermy for Beginners.* WASCO Mfg., 1991. Seven pamphlets.

Taxol, *TAK sawl,* is a drug used to treat advanced cancers of the breast and ovaries. It is the Bristol-Myers Squibb Company's trade name for its anticancer drug *paclitaxel.*

Taxol was originally obtained from the bark of the Pacific yew, a slow-growing tree found in the Pacific Northwest. However, harvesting the bark destroyed the trees, and great numbers were needed to produce even small amounts of Taxol. Environmentalists feared that increasing use of the drug would endanger the survival of the species. Today, Taxol is prepared from clippings of new growth from another species, the English yew. Scientists can also collect small amounts of Taxol from yew cells grown in the laboratory.

Taxol belongs to a class of drugs known as *taxoids,* which have shown promise in treating various types of cancer. Scientists believe taxoids will work well when used in combination with other drugs. Another taxoid that is used for treating advanced breast cancer is *docetaxel,* known by the trade name Taxotere. Researchers continue to search for other new taxoids and to test their effectiveness. Thomas H. Maugh II

See also **Breast cancer.**

Taxonomy. See **Classification, Scientific.**

Tay-Sachs disease is a hereditary disorder of the nervous system. It occurs chiefly among Jewish children of eastern European ancestry. Tay-Sachs disease causes severe brain damage, enlargement of the head, convulsions, blindness, deafness, lack of energy, and eventually death. Victims develop a reddish spot on the retina of the eye. They begin to have symptoms when they are about 6 months old. There is no treatment for Tay-Sachs disease. Most victims live for only three or four years.

Tay-Sachs disease occurs in children who have too little of the enzyme *hexosaminidase A.* This enzyme controls the amount of *ganglioside* that accumulates in nerve cells. Ganglioside is a fat produced by normal cell growth. Nerve cells that store too much ganglioside become swollen and eventually die. A large number of damaged or dead nerve cells causes brain damage.

Tay-Sachs symptoms were first reported during the 1880's by two physicians, Waren Tay of Britain and Bernard Sachs of the United States. In 1969, researchers discovered that the lack of hexosaminidase A caused the disease. Today, scientists use a variety of tests to determine the activity of hexosaminidase A in samples of blood and various tissues. These tests can reveal if unborn babies have the disease. They also show whether adults are carriers. Carriers do not have the disease themselves. But if two carriers marry, their children may inherit the disease from them. Reuben Matalon

See also **Races, Human** (The founder effect).

Tay-Sachs disease

Tay-Sachs disease is a hereditary brain disorder that occurs chiefly among Jews of eastern European ancestry. People who inherit the Tay-Sachs gene from both parents have the disorder.

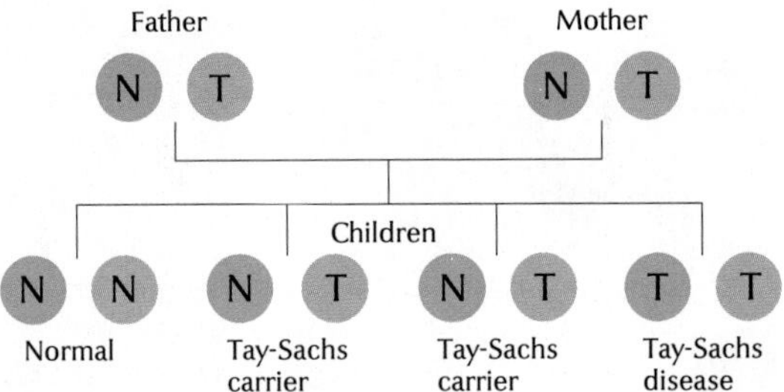

WORLD BOOK diagram

In this chart, each parent carries one normal gene and one Tay-Sachs gene. Such people are called *carriers.* A child of such parents has one chance in four of inheriting the Tay-Sachs gene from both parents—and thus having Tay-Sachs disease. People who inherit the Tay-Sachs gene from only one parent do not get the disease, but they may transmit the one abnormal gene to their children.

Taylor, Edward (1642?-1729), was the finest poet in colonial American literature. Taylor was born in Leicestershire, England. Unwilling to sign a loyalty oath to the Church of England, he sailed to New England in 1668. In 1671, he became a pastor in Westfield, Massachusetts, a post he held the rest of his life. His best poetry appears in *Preparatory Meditations,* a collection. In *God's Determination,* he used a debate between good and evil to emphasize God's mercy for people caught in the battle between Jesus Christ and Satan. Taylor achieved his complex thought in a few words. His work shows the influence of the intricate style of the English metaphysical poets of the 1600's. Although his language is complicated, Taylor's use of examples from everyday life makes his poetry understandable. Edward W. Clark

Taylor, Elizabeth (1932-), is an American motion-picture actress. She became as famous for her beauty and turbulent personal life as for her film work.

Taylor has appeared in about 50 films. She made her film debut in *There's One Born Every Minute* (1942) and became a child star in *Lassie Come Home* (1943). Taylor won Academy Awards for best actress in *Butterfield 8* (1960) and *Who's Afraid of Virginia Woolf?* (1966). Her other films include *National Velvet* (1944), *A Place in the Sun* (1951), *Raintree County* (1957), *Cat on a Hot Tin Roof* (1958), and *Suddenly Last Summer* (1959).

Elizabeth Rosemond Taylor was born on Feb. 27, 1932, in London to American parents. Her eight marriages have included two marriages to British actor Richard Burton. Her other husbands have included American film producer Michael Todd and American singer Eddie Fisher. Taylor has been active in charity work. In 2000, Queen Elizabeth II made Taylor a Dame Commander in the Order of the British Empire. Louis Giannetti

Culver

Elizabeth Taylor won an Academy Award for her performance in *Who's Afraid of Virginia Woolf?* (1966). The film also starred her husband, Richard Burton, *center,* and George Segal, *right.*

Taylor, Frederick Winslow (1856-1915), was an American engineer and efficiency expert. He joined Midvale Steel Works in Philadelphia in 1878 as a laborer, and left the company in 1890 as chief engineer. During this time, he conducted experiments to determine the maximum possible efficiency of people and machines. Taylor later expanded his ideas into a detailed system for organizing and systematizing factory work. The best-known part of his system is the *time and motion study.* In this study an efficiency expert clocks each step in a job and looks for ways to reduce the time and manpower needed to do the job. Taylor's system was only one of many proposed in the early 1900's. However, after the publication of his book *The Principles of Scientific Management* in 1911, the entire efficiency movement was often called *Taylorism.* Taylor was born on March 20, 1856, in Germantown, Pennsylvania. George H. Daniels

Taylor, George (1716-1781), was a Pennsylvania signer of the Declaration of Independence. He served in Pennsylvania's provincial assembly from 1764 to 1770 and in 1775. He became a colonel in the Pennsylvania militia in 1775. He also served as a member of the Continental Congress. Elected a member of the First Supreme Executive Council of Pennsylvania in 1777, he soon retired because of illness. Taylor was born in Ireland. He came to Pennsylvania about 1736 and became a successful iron manufacturer. Gary D. Hermalyn

Taylor, Maxwell Davenport (1901-1987), gained fame as a United States general in World War II (1939-1945) and the Korean War (1950-1953). He later helped shape U.S. strategy in the Vietnam War (1957-1975).

Taylor was born on Aug. 26, 1901, in Keytesville, Missouri. He graduated from the U.S. Military Academy in 1922. In World War II, Taylor helped organize the Army's first airborne divisions and later served as artillery commander of the 82nd Airborne Division in Sicily and Italy. He was the first U.S. general to land in Normandy, France, during the Allied invasion on D-Day, June 6, 1944. Taylor commanded the 101st Airborne Division in 1944 and 1945. Taylor commanded the U.S. Eighth Army in the Korean War in 1953. From 1955 to 1959, he served as U.S. Army chief of staff. Taylor became chairman of the Joint Chiefs of Staff in 1962 and ambassador to South Vietnam in 1964, during the Vietnam War. Taylor served there about a year and then became a special consultant to President Lyndon Johnson. D. Clayton James

Taylor, Mildred D. (1943-), is one of America's leading authors of children's books. Her fiction reflects stories she heard growing up in an African American family, and her own childhood experiences. Taylor's books explore themes of family unity, love of the land, black pride, bigotry, and racism.

Taylor has published six novels about the Logans, a black family living in rural Mississippi. Many are set in the 1930's during the Great Depression. Her *Roll of Thunder, Hear My Cry* (1976) won the 1977 Newbery Medal and was immediately recognized as a classic. The other Logan novels are *Song of the Trees* (1975), *Let the Circle Be Unbroken* (1981), *The Road to Memphis* (1990), *The Well: David's Story* (1998), and *The Land* (2001). Taylor's other novels are *The Friendship* (1987), *The Gold Cadillac* (1987), and *Mississippi Bridge* (1990). Mildred Delois Taylor was born on Sept. 13, 1943, in Jackson, Mississippi. Nellie Y. McKay

Taylor, Paul (1930-), is an American *choreographer* (dance creator). Since founding the Paul Taylor Dance Company in 1955, he has created more than 100 dances. In his earliest works, Taylor used ordinary gestures and postures. In 1956, he originated a new style of dance movement for his ballet *4 Epitaphs* (later shortened and renamed *3 Epitaphs*). In this work, figures dressed in black shrugged and slumped across the stage to the music of a New Orleans band. Some later works, such as *Aureole* (1962), *Orbs* (1966), *Esplanade* (1975), *Promethean Fire* (2002), *Dream Girls* (2003), and *Le Grand Puppetier* (2004), were high-spirited celebrations of movement in Taylor's athletic, often humorous style. Other works, such as *Churchyard* (1969) and *Last Look* (1985), dealt with themes of darkness and corruption.

Paul Bellville Taylor was born July 29, 1930, in Allegheny County, Pennsylvania. He began his career as a dancer in the companies of Merce Cunningham (1953-1954) and Martha Graham (1955-1962). Selma Landen Odom

12th president of the United States 1849-1850

Polk	Taylor	Fillmore
11th president	12th president	13th president
1845-1849	1849-1850	1850-1853
Democrat	Whig	Whig

Millard Fillmore
vice president
1849-1850

Oil painting by John Vanderlyn, Corcoran Gallery of Art, Washington, D.C.

Taylor, Zachary (1784-1850), served his country for 40 years as a soldier and for 16 months as president. His courage and ability during the Mexican War made him a national hero. Taylor showed the same courage while he was president, but he died before he could prove his full abilities as a statesman. He was succeeded by Vice President Millard Fillmore.

President Taylor was one of the large slaveowners of the South. But he did not oppose admitting California and New Mexico to the Union as free states. The South demanded that other slavery problems be settled before those territories became states, and threatened to secede. Taylor replied that he was ready to take his place at the head of the army to put down any such action. He died at the height of this argument. President Fillmore's policies delayed the Civil War for 10 years.

Taylor made his greatest contribution to his country as a soldier. This quiet, friendly man was not a military genius but was a good leader. He never lost a battle. His troops nicknamed him "Old Rough and Ready."

Early life

Childhood. Zachary Taylor was born near Barboursville, Virginia, on Nov. 24, 1784. He was the third son in a family of six boys and three girls. His parents, Richard and Sarah Strother Taylor, came from leading families of the Virginia plantation region. Richard Taylor served as an officer in the Revolutionary War. In 1783, he received a war bonus of 6,000 acres (2,400 hectares) of land near Louisville, Kentucky. He settled there in 1785.

There were no schools on the Kentucky frontier, but Zachary studied for a while under tutors, and gained practical knowledge by working on his father's farm.

Perhaps it was natural that Zachary should turn to a military career. He grew up in the midst of Indian warfare, and heard tales of the Revolutionary War from his father. In 1808, he was appointed a first lieutenant in the U.S. Army. In 1810, he was promoted to captain.

Taylor's family. Early in 1810, Taylor met Margaret Mackall Smith (Sept. 21, 1788-Aug. 14, 1852). She was the orphaned daughter of a Maryland planter. Taylor and Smith were married on June 21, 1810. They had a son and five daughters, two of whom died as infants. Their daughter Sarah married Jefferson Davis, the future president of the Confederacy. She died three months after her wedding. The Taylors' son, Richard, served as a general in the Confederate Army.

Military career

Indian campaigns. During the War of 1812, Taylor won promotion to major for his defense of Fort Harrison in the Indiana Territory. In 1819, he became a lieutenant colonel. He served in Wisconsin during the Black Hawk War, and received the surrender of Chief Black Hawk in 1832 (see **Black Hawk**).

Taylor was sent to Florida in 1837. There he defeated the Seminole Indians at Lake Okeechobee on Dec. 25, 1837. This victory brought him the honorary rank of brigadier general. In 1841, Taylor became commander of the second department of the western division of the U.S. Army, with headquarters at Fort Smith, Arkansas.

Mexican War. In 1846, Mexico threatened war with the United States over the annexation of Texas. Taylor was ordered to the Rio Grande with about 4,000 troops. Mexico considered this advance an invasion, and Mexican forces crossed the river to drive off the Americans. Taylor defeated them in battles at Palo Alto and Resaca de la Palma. The United States declared war on May 13,

Revolutions swept Europe in the late 1840's. The uprisings led to increased immigration to the United States.

The California gold rush brought thousands of treasure seekers, called "Forty-Niners," to the West Coast in 1849.

The world of President Taylor

The Department of the Interior was established by Congress in 1849. The department took over duties in such areas as Indian affairs, public lands, and mining.
Amelia Jenks Bloomer began publishing a journal called the *Lily* in 1849 to promote temperance and women's rights. She became famous for wearing long, gathered pants called "bloomers" under her skirts.
Charles Dickens enjoyed a reputation as the most popular English writer of his time. He published *David Copperfield,* a semiautobiographical novel, in 1849-1850.
Overland mail service by wagon began in 1850, when a stagecoach route opened between Independence, Missouri, and Santa Fe, New Mexico. It took about 30 days for mail to be delivered from one end of the route to the other.
The slavery issue led to some of the most memorable debates in the history of the United States Senate. Senator Henry Clay of Kentucky proposed a series of resolutions that became the basis for the Compromise of 1850. Such noted orators as Daniel Webster of Massachusetts, Stephen Douglas of Illinois, and John Calhoun of South Carolina led the historic debates.
The Scarlet Letter, published in 1850, brought international fame to American author Nathaniel Hawthorne. The novel dealt with sin and morality in Puritan Boston.
Popular uprisings against undemocratic governments in Europe won American sympathy. Hungarian revolutionary leader Lajos Kossuth toured the United States in 1849 and was hailed as the "Hungarian George Washington."

Bibliothèque Nationale, Paris; California Historical Society

1846. Taylor then advanced into Mexico and captured Matamoros and Monterrey.

After these victories, Taylor seemed the obvious choice to lead an invading army into the central valley of Mexico. But President James K. Polk, a Democrat, knew that Taylor favored the rival Whig Party. Because Polk feared the growth of a popular Whig leader, he named General Winfield Scott to lead the campaign.

On Feb. 22-23, 1847, before Scott's army departed, Taylor's army of about 5,000 men was attacked by between 16,000 and 20,000 Mexican troops in the Battle of Buena Vista. Taylor's troops won a stunning victory over the forces of General Santa Anna. The triumph was due more to the skill and vigor of Taylor's officers than to his generalship, but the victory made Taylor a national hero. See **Mexican War; Santa Anna, Antonio López de.**

Nomination for President

Many Whig leaders, especially in the South, believed Taylor could easily win the presidency because of his military fame. Taylor hesitated to enter politics, but the Whigs nominated him anyway. They chose Millard Fillmore, comptroller of New York, for vice president. The Democrats nominated Senator Lewis Cass of Michigan and General William O. Butler of Kentucky.

Important dates in Taylor's life

1784	(Nov. 24) Born near Barboursville, Virginia.
1810	(June 21) Married Margaret Mackall Smith.
1812	Defended Fort Harrison against Tecumseh.
1832	Received surrender of Black Hawk.
1847	Defeated Santa Anna in Battle of Buena Vista.
1848	Elected president of the United States.
1850	(July 9) Died in the White House.

During the campaign, both Whigs and Democrats took a two-sided stand on the divisive issue of slavery, seeming to favor it at one time and oppose it at other

Taylor's election

Place of nominating convention	Philadelphia
Ballot on which nominated	4th
Democratic opponent	Lewis Cass
Electoral vote*	163 (Taylor) to 127 (Cass)
Popular vote	1,361,393 (Taylor) to 1,223,460 (Cass) and 291,501 (Van Buren)
Age at inauguration	64

*For votes by states, see **Electoral College** (table).

The Granger Collection

The Battle of Buena Vista established Taylor as a hero of the Mexican War. Taylor, shown here on the white horse, led his outnumbered troops to a decisive victory over the Mexicans.

White House Historical Association

Mary Elizabeth Bliss, the Taylors' youngest daughter, served as White House hostess. Her mother, Margaret Smith Taylor, took little part in Washington social life. Most historians believe that no likeness of Taylor's wife exists.

times. Only the Free Soil Party, led by former President Martin Van Buren, campaigned to ban slavery in the newly acquired Mexican territories (see **Free Soil Party**). Van Buren did not carry a single state, but he drew many votes from Cass. Taylor and Fillmore won by 36 electoral votes. The presidential election of 1848 was the first held at the same time in all the states.

Taylor's administration (1849-1850)

Taylor was inaugurated on March 5, 1849. He would normally have taken office on March 4, but declined to be inaugurated on Sunday. Some historians claim that David R. Atchison, president pro tempore of the Senate, served as acting president on March 4 because the presidency was vacant on that day.

Taylor relied on the advice of other people because he knew that he lacked political experience. However, no one could influence him to act against his conscience.

Life in the White House. Mrs. Taylor had not favored the idea of her husband running for president. She viewed it as a plot to deprive her of his company. Mrs. Taylor, a semi-invalid, took little part in the White House social life. Hostess duties passed to her daughter Mary Elizabeth, known as Betty. Betty's husband, Colonel William W. S. Bliss, served as Taylor's secretary.

The Nicaragua Canal. The acquisition of territory on the Pacific Coast during President James K. Polk's administration revived the dream of a water route across Central America. American businessmen tried to obtain rights to build a canal across Nicaragua. The British were also interested in such a canal. In 1850, the United States and Britain signed the Clayton-Bulwer Treaty, which guaranteed the neutrality of any such canal. See **Clayton-Bulwer Treaty**.

Sectional quarrels. Controversy over the extension of slavery in new territories reached a new high in 1849 as California prepared to apply for admission to the Union as a free state. Taylor urged Congress to admit California and New Mexico immediately as states rather than make them territories first. In this manner, he hoped to avoid the dispute over slavery in the territories. But Southerners angrily demanded the adjustment of other slavery problems before new states were admitted to the Union. During the next months, Congress had one of its greatest debates. Southerners threatened secession, and Northerners promised war in order to preserve the Union. Though he owned many slaves, Taylor sided with the North. He pledged to use force to uphold the Union.

Numerous congressional leaders, including Senator Henry Clay of Kentucky, urged compromise. However, Taylor scorned any compromise, and insisted that California be admitted to the Union. Supporters of compromise eventually won, but not until Fillmore had succeeded to the presidency. Congress then adopted laws referred to as the Compromise of 1850. See **Compromise of 1850**.

Death. Before the slavery issue could be settled, Taylor became ill and died on July 9, 1850. He was buried in the family cemetery near Louisville, Kentucky. Mrs. Taylor died on Aug. 14, 1852, and was buried beside her husband.

In 1991, a team of experts examined President Taylor's body to determine whether he had been assassinated by poisoning. They concluded that he died of natural causes. Michael F. Holt

Vice president and Cabinet

Vice president	*Millard Fillmore
Secretary of state	*John M. Clayton
Secretary of the treasury	William M. Meredith
Secretary of war	George W. Crawford
Attorney general	Reverdy Johnson
Postmaster general	Jacob Collamer
Secretary of the Navy	William B. Preston
Secretary of the interior	Thomas Ewing

*Has a separate biography in *World Book.*

Related articles in *World Book* include:

Davis, Jefferson
Fillmore, Millard
Gold rush
President of the United States
War of 1812
Whig party

Outline

I. **Early life**
   A. Childhood
   B. Taylor's family
II. **Military career**
   A. Indian campaigns
   B. Mexican War
III. **Nomination for president**
IV. **Taylor's administration (1849-1850)**
   A. Life in the White House
   B. The Nicaragua Canal
   C. Sectional quarrels
   D. Death

Questions

How did Taylor become a national hero?
What was one reason that President Polk did not choose Taylor to lead the invasion of Mexico's central valley?
How may Taylor have become interested in the army?
How did President Taylor reply to a Southern threat to secede from the Union?

Why do some historians claim that an acting president served the first day of Taylor's term?
Who performed the duties of White House hostess during Taylor's administration?

Additional resources

Bauer, K. Jack. *Zachary Taylor.* 1985. Reprint. La. State Univ. Pr., 1993.
Joseph, Paul. *Zachary Taylor.* Abdo, 1999. Younger readers.
Smith, Elbert B. *The Presidencies of Zachary Taylor & Millard Fillmore.* Univ. Pr. of Kans., 1988.

Tayra, *TY ruh,* is a large member of the weasel family. It lives in tropical forests from Mexico to Argentina. Most tayras have black or dark brown fur, with a white or yellow patch on the chest. The fur on the head gradually turns brown or gray as the animal grows older. An adult tayra weighs about 10 pounds (5 kilograms) and measures about $3\frac{1}{2}$ feet (107 centimeters) long, including a tail 16 inches (41 centimeters) long.

© Fulvio Eccardi, Bruce Coleman Inc.
The tayra lives in tropical forests of the Americas.

Tayras wander the forests and are active both day and night. They travel alone or in family groups. These graceful animals climb well and can run swiftly.

Tayras eat birds, small mammals, and fruits. The female tayra gives birth to two to four young in a nest she has built in a tree or on the ground. Bruce A. Brewer

Scientific classification. The tayra belongs to the weasel family, Mustelidae. It is *Eira barbara.*

TB. See **Tuberculosis.**

Tbilisi, *tuh BIHL uh see* (pop. 1,081,679), is the capital and largest city of the country of Georgia. It lies on the Kur River (see **Georgia** [map]). *Tbili* means *warm* in the Georgian language, and the city is named for its warm mineral springs. The city's name in Russian is Tiflis.

People have lived in the area for over 2,000 years. Part of Tbilisi is modern, while the older section has medieval buildings, courtyards, and narrow streets. The city is home to Tbilisi State University and the Georgian Academy of Sciences. Tbilisi is the country's main economic and transportation center. Jaroslaw Bilocerkowycz

See also **Georgia** (picture).

Tchaikovsky, Peter Ilich, *chy KAWF skee, PYAW tuhr IHL yihch* (1840-1893), was the first Russian composer whose music became part of the standard concert program in western Europe. Tchaikovsky had a gift for creating memorable lyric melodies and for contrasting instrumental sounds, particularly those of wind instruments, in his orchestrations.

Brown Bros.
Peter Tchaikovsky

Tchaikovsky combined native Russian materials with western European influences. His scores contain quotations and transformations of Russian folk melodies. Tchaikovsky's music contains varied and contrasting moods. The last movement of Symphony No. 6 (1893) projects a dark and melancholy atmosphere. This symphony is also known as the *Pathétique* (Pathetic). However, his *Slavonic March* (1876) and the *1812 Overture* (1882) are spirited and colorful examples of nationalism in Russian music. Some of Tchaikovsky's most original orchestral textures and appealing melodies appear in his ballet scores, from which he arranged concert suites.

His life. Tchaikovsky was born on May 7, 1840, in Votkinsk, Russia. From 1862 through 1865, he studied music at the St. Petersburg Conservatory with Anton Rubinstein, a Russian pianist and composer. At the conservatory, Tchaikovsky became the first Russian composer to receive systematic Western-style academic training in the fundamentals of music.

In 1866, Tchaikovsky began teaching at the Moscow Conservatory of Music. During the next several years, his early emotional sensitivity developed into long periods of depression. But he wrote some of his most optimistic music during this time. Tchaikovsky was married briefly in 1877. However, he and his wife separated after a few weeks, and he left Russia to travel in Switzerland and Italy.

In 1876, Tchaikovsky began his correspondence with Nadezhda von Meck, a wealthy widow who admired his music. She offered financial support so he could devote himself to composition. She insisted that they never meet, but for years they exchanged letters. Assured of a steady income, Tchaikovsky left the Moscow Conservatory in 1877 to concentrate on composition. He also began to travel widely and in 1891 conducted some of his works in concerts in Baltimore, Philadelphia, and New York City. He died on Nov. 6, 1893.

His music. Tchaikovsky's six numbered symphonies and his *Manfred Symphony* (1886) are landmarks in his artistic development. His first three symphonies (written 1866, revised 1874; written 1872, revised 1880; and 1875) are performed less often than the last three. His Symphony No. 4 (1878) is his first success in the symphonic form, and Symphony No. 5 (1888) is excellent from the standpoint of formal construction. Symphony No. 6 departed from tradition through its tragic final movement. Other important orchestral works include *Italian Capriccio* (1880), the fantasy-overture *Romeo and Juliet* (3rd version, 1886), the symphony fantasy *Francesca da Rimini* (1877), and four orchestral suites (1879, 1884, 1885, and 1887).

Tchaikovsky is remembered today outside Russia primarily for his orchestra works. However, he devoted equal attention throughout his career to opera.

Of his nine completed operas, only *Eugene Onegin* (1879) and *The Queen of Spades* (1890) have gained popularity in the West. Both are based on works by Alexander Pushkin, a Russian writer who died in 1837. Tchaikovsky's other music for the stage includes three ballets: *Swan Lake* (1877), *The Sleeping Beauty* (1890), and *The Nutcracker* (1892).

Tchaikovsky's Piano Concerto No. 1 in B-flat minor (1875) and his Violin Concerto in D major (1881) are fine examples of the late romantic concerto. He also wrote *Variations on a Rococo Theme* (1877) for violoncello and orchestra. Tchaikovsky's many piano works and songs are seldom performed outside Russia. More popular in the West are three string quartets (1872, 1876, and 1877), the Piano Trio in A minor (1882), and a string sextet, *Souvenir de Florence* (written 1890, revised 1892).

Edward V. Williams

Additional resources

Brown, David. *Tchaikovsky.* 4 vols. Norton, 1979-1992.
Kearney, Leslie, ed. *Tchaikovsky and His World.* Princeton, 1998.
Nice, David. *Peter Ilyich Tchaikovsky.* Pavilion Bks., Ltd., 1997.
Poznansky, Alexander. *Tchaikovsky.* 1991. Reprint. Music Sales Corp., 1995. *Tchaikovsky Through Others' Eyes.* Ind. Univ. Pr., 1999.

Te Kanawa, *teh KAH nah wah,* **Kiri,** *KIHR ee* (1944-), a New Zealand opera singer, is one of the most praised sopranos in the world. She has sung the major roles in operas of such composers as Wolfgang Amadeus Mozart, Giacomo Puccini, Giuseppe Verdi, Georges Bizet, and Richard Strauss. Her voice is rich and lyric, and impresses with its freshness and warmth.

Te Kanawa was born on March 6, 1944, in Gisborne, New Zealand. Te Kanawa's first major operatic success came in 1971 in the role of Countess Almaviva in Mozart's *The Marriage of Figaro* at Covent Garden in London. In 1974, she made her debut with the Metropolitan Opera in New York City. This appearance came on about three hours' notice, when she substituted for an ailing performer as Desdemona in Verdi's *Otello.* Her performance helped make her an international star. In 1982, Queen Elizabeth II made her a Dame Commander in the Order of the British Empire; she became known as Dame Kiri Te Kanawa. Charles H. Webb

Lyric Opera of Chicago

Kiri Te Kanawa

Tea is a beverage prepared by pouring boiling water over dry processed tea leaves. It ranks as the world's most popular refreshing drink.

The annual worldwide production of dried tea leaves totals almost 3.3 million tons (3 million metric tons). India produces more tea leaves than any other nation. Other major tea-growing countries include China, Kenya, and Sri Lanka.

Tea production

Growing tea. The tea plant is an evergreen that grows in tropical and subtropical regions. The finest tea comes from elevations of 4,000 to 7,000 feet (1,200 to 2,100 meters). The plant grows more slowly in the cool air at such elevations, adding to its flavor.

Tea plants have small, white, sweet-smelling flowers. Each flower produces one to three seeds that look like hazelnuts. Traditionally, tea growers would cultivate new plants from the seeds.

Today, the best method of cultivating tea involves planting cuttings from tea plants with desirable qualities, such as high yield or special flavor, in a nursery bed. From six months to a year later, when the plants are about 8 inches (20 centimeters) high, they are transplanted to the field.

Wild tea plants grow as high as 30 feet (9 meters) or more. But a commercial tea plant is pruned to keep it from 3 to 4 feet (91 to 120 centimeters) high. The plant matures in three to five years and produces a *flush* (growth of new shoots). Each shoot consists of several leaves and a bud. At lower altitudes and warmer climates, tea plants may grow several flushes throughout the year. At higher altitudes and cooler climates, a plant grows flushes only in warmer periods.

Workers called tea pluckers pick two leaves and a bud from each shoot by hand. A plucker can harvest about 40 pounds (18 kilograms) of tea leaves a day, enough to make about 10 pounds (4.5 kilograms) of processed tea. Mechanical pluckers are common on large tea estates. Each of these devices can harvest as much tea leaf as up to 100 manual pluckers. However, tea of higher quality is generally hand-plucked.

Processing tea. There are three main kinds of tea: (1) black, (2) green, and (3) oolong. They differ in the method used to process the leaves. Processing takes place in a factory on or near the tea plantation.

Black tea. To make black tea, workers first spread the leaves on shelves called *withering racks.* Air is blown over the leaves to remove excess moisture, leaving them soft and flexible.

After the withering stage, the tea leaves are rolled and broken into pieces to release their flavor. They may be broken up by the *orthodox* or the *cut, tear, and curl* (CTC) method. In the orthodox method, a machine crushes the leaves under rollers, giving the leaves a rolled appearance. In the CTC method, leaves pass between *serrated* (toothed) rollers running at different speeds. The serrations cut the tea leaves into pieces, and the different speeds of the rollers give the pieces a curled shape. Leaves processed by the orthodox method yield fewer cups per pound or kilogram but have a smoother flavor than leaves processed by the CTC method.

Workers next put the broken leaves into a *fermenting* room, where they turn coppery in color. Finally, the leaves are dried in ovens and become brownish-black.

Some of the best-known black teas come from India. *Darjiling tea* ranks among the world's finest and most expensive teas, while *Assam tea* is one of India's most common. Other popular teas include *Dimbula tea* of Sri Lanka, used in many English teas, and *Keemun tea* from China. Popular flavored teas include black currant, Earl Grey, lemon, and mint.

Green and oolong tea. Most of the green and oolong tea comes from China, Japan, and Taiwan. *Green tea* is made by steaming the leaves to soften them. Green tea manufacturers use the orthodox method to break up the

Tea Council of the U.S.A., Inc.

Shostal

Tea pluckers near Kandy, Sri Lanka, pick leaves from mature tea plants, *left.* The tea plants produce shoots called *flushes,* which consist of several leaves and a bud, *above.* After being picked, the flushes are processed into tea in a nearby factory.

leaves, or they roll whole leaves by hand. They then dry the leaves with hot air. Because green tea leaves are not fermented, they retain a greenish color. *Oolong tea* is made by partially fermenting whole leaves. These leaves are lighter in color than those of black teas.

Grades of tea generally vary only according to the size and appearance of the leaves. Except for oolong teas, the grade of a tea leaf has nothing to do with the quality of the tea.

Manufacturers use three different categories of grades for black and green teas: (1) *leaf grades* for whole and large leaf pieces, (2) *broken grades* for smaller pieces, and (3) *fannings* and dusts for leaves that have been reduced to the finest particles or to powder. Leaf grades include *golden flowery orange pekoe* (*PECK oh*) and *gunpowder.* Broken grades include *broken pekoe* and *flowery broken orange pekoe. Fannings* and *dusts* go into tea bags. Oolong teas are graded according to the quality of the leaves instead of size or appearance.

Instant tea is made by brewing large quantities of tea and then removing the water by a drying process until only a powder remains. People make instant tea by simply adding water to the powder.

Brewing tea. Black tea is brewed by pouring boiling water over a teaspoon of loose tea, or one tea bag, per cup. Green and oolong teas require lower water temperatures. To obtain the best flavor, black tea should *steep* (soak) for three to five minutes before being served. Steeping times for green and oolong teas vary from one to seven minutes, depending on the tea.

Iced tea is prepared by first brewing a strong hot tea. For each two glasses, three teaspoons of loose tea or three tea bags should be used. After steeping for five minutes, the tea is cooled and served over ice.

Leading tea-growing countries

Country	Amount of tea produced in a year
India	922,000 tons (836,400 metric tons)
China	802,900 tons (728,300 metric tons)
Sri Lanka	334,700 tons (303,600 metric tons)
Kenya	271,900 tons (246,700 metric tons)
Indonesia	179,600 tons (163,000 metric tons)
Turkey	158,600 tons (143,900 metric tons)
Japan	93,700 tons (85,000 metric tons)
Vietnam	86,400 tons (78,400 metric tons)
Argentina	65,600 tons (59,600 metric tons)

Figures are for a three-year average, 2000-2002.
Source: Food and Agriculture Organization of United Nations.

Tea and health

For centuries, people believed that tea possessed healing qualities and used it in folk medicines. Scientists now know that tea contains chemical substances called *antioxidants,* which may prevent some types of cell damage. Researchers are studying the possibility that teas help prevent heart disease and certain kinds of cancer.

Most teas contain a substance called *caffeine,* which occurs naturally in the tea leaves. Caffeine is a *stimulant*—that is, it helps increase the activity of the circulatory and nervous systems. However, some people claim caffeine causes sleeplessness or other problems. Manufacturers make teas without caffeine, called *decaffeinated teas,* for people who do not consume caffeine.

History

According to legend, the use of tea was discovered by Emperor Shen Nong of China about 2737 B.C. The earliest known mention of tea appeared in Chinese literature of about A.D. 350. The custom of tea drinking spread to Japan around A.D. 600. The first known shipment of tea to Europe was made about 1610 by Dutch traders who imported it from China and Japan. Portuguese traders began shipping tea to Europe about the same time. By 1650, the Dutch were importing tea into the American Colonies.

In 1657, the beverage was sold for the first time in coffee houses in England. Tea went on to become the national drink of the United Kingdom. In 1767, the United Kingdom placed a tax on tea used by American colonists. Colonial resistance to the tax brought about the Boston Tea Party in 1773 and contributed to the American independence movement.

The use of iced tea and tea bags began in the United States. Richard Blechynden, an Englishman trying to increase the use of tea in the United States, first served iced tea in 1904 at the Louisiana Purchase Exposition in St. Louis. That same year, Thomas Sullivan, a New York City coffee and tea merchant, sent his customers samples of tea leaves in small silk bags instead of the usual tin containers. People found that they could brew tea more easily in bags. Instant tea was developed in the United States and first marketed in 1948. Savi Lamba

Scientific classification. The tea plant is a member of the tea family, Theaceae. Its scientific name is *Camellia sinensis.*

See also **Boston Tea Party; Caffeine; Kenya** (picture: Kenya's highland); **Labrador tea; Maté.**

Additional resources

Chow, Kit, and Kramer, Ione. *A Pocket Guide to All the Tea in China.* China Bks., 1998.
Stella, Alain, and others. *The Book of Tea.* Flammarion, 1992.

Tea tax. See **Revolutionary War in America** (The Tea Act).

Teach, Edward. See Blackbeard.

Teacher. See Teaching; Education.

Teachers, American Federation of. See American Federation of Teachers.

Teachers College, Columbia University, is the graduate school of education at Columbia University in New York City. It prepares men and women for professional service at every level of education.

Through its 19 departments, Teachers College offers programs in all phases of teaching, curricular planning, computing technology, and administration for the training of educational personnel. It provides advanced work in psychology, counseling, and guidance. The university also prepares students for careers in nursing, health, and nutrition education. It conducts research in all these areas and provides field service to schools throughout the United States and abroad. Teachers College also sponsors numerous international activities in education.

Organization. Teachers College is financially independent, with its own charter, board of trustees, and president. It forms a division of Columbia University by formal agreement between the trustees of the college and the trustees of the university. Under this agreement, faculty members at Teachers College are also members of the Columbia University faculty, and university courses are open to students of Teachers College. The university grants degrees earned at Teachers College.

Many research and service activities at Teachers College are conducted through various institutes and special projects. These activities concern such areas as the needs of disabled children, higher education, the philosophy and politics of education, and the education of gifted students. The activities also deal with psychological services, motor learning, urban and minority education, health promotion, and curriculum development.

History. Teachers College was founded in 1887 as the New York College for the Training of Teachers. Sponsored by the Industrial Education Association, it prepared teachers in various fields, particularly family and consumer sciences and industrial arts. The college greatly expanded its curriculum under the leadership of Nicholas Murray Butler, who served as president from 1887 to 1891, and Walter L. Hervey, the president from 1891 to 1897. In 1892, the New York State Regents granted the college a permanent charter. In 1898, Teachers College became part of Columbia University.

The college became a world leader in educational research and experimentation during the administrations of James E. Russell, its dean from 1897 to 1927, and William F. Russell, the dean from 1927 to 1949 and president from 1949 to 1954. These men—father and son—emphasized research and experimentation to advance knowledge about educational goals and processes and to improve teaching practices in academic institutions. As a result of their efforts, many important educational developments were pioneered at Teachers College.

Critically reviewed by Teachers College

© Lee Snider

Teachers College offers graduate-level courses and is part of Columbia University in New York City. The college's campus, *shown here,* includes buildings that date from the late 1800's.

©Jose Pelaez, The Stock Market

© Lawrence Migdale

Teaching involves guiding students in many different learning experiences. The high school teacher on the left shows students how individual computers link to a vast network called the Internet. The kindergarten teacher above helps youngsters recognize how letters of the alphabet look and sound.

Teaching

Teaching is helping other people learn. It is one of the most important ways that people relate to one another. Teaching helps people acquire the knowledge they need to become responsible citizens, to earn a living, and to lead useful, rewarding lives. Teaching also transfers knowledge from one generation to the next.

Much teaching takes place outside school. In homes, for example, parents communicate values and teach their children many types of skills and habits. Businesses and industries teach their employees necessary job skills. Children eagerly share new abilities and information with one another. But when most people speak of teaching, they mean the instruction provided in schools by professional teachers. More people engage in teaching than in any other profession. About 58 million men and women throughout the world are teachers.

Teaching developed into a profession after the early 1800's, when the first teacher-training schools were founded in Europe. Before that time, schoolteachers received little or no special training. Today, most countries require teachers to complete a specialized training program and to meet professional standards of skill, performance, and conduct. For detailed information about the history of teaching, see **Education** (History).

Stephen M. Fain, the contributor of this article, is Professor of Education at Florida International University.

Teaching as a profession

Teachers' skills and attitudes influence everything that happens in their classrooms. During the years that young people spend in school, teachers are among the most important people in their lives. Good teachers know their subjects and understand the material that they are teaching. They present lessons in creative ways that help students of different ability levels and learning styles master the material.

Teachers often help students as much by personal example as they do by offering instruction. Students who see their teachers demonstrate patience, trustworthiness, attention to work, and love of learning may be encouraged to develop similar qualities in themselves. Students may also accept assistance more readily from a teacher whom they respect and admire.

For most schoolteachers, practical day-to-day aspects of their jobs include (1) preparing to teach classes; (2) guiding and assisting student learning; (3) checking student progress; and (4) duties outside the classroom.

Preparing to teach classes. Elementary and high-school teachers have guidelines to help them plan their teaching. One of the most important guidelines is the *curriculum,* a broad educational plan that outlines subjects that should be taught and other learning activities. In some states, local school boards decide the curriculum. But in many cases, they follow standards estab-

Teachers help students master computers and other technologies. Here, a teacher explains the features of a *desktop publishing program.* These popular programs enable people to use personal computers to write and illustrate publications ranging from simple newsletters to full-length books.

WORLD BOOK photo by Steven Spicer (Lane Technical High School)

lished by state governments. Many school boards also involve teachers in planning the curriculum. Teachers are often evaluated according to student performance on tests based on curriculum objectives.

Many teachers develop a strategy called a *daily lesson plan* to break the curriculum into units for each class session. To develop the lesson plan, a teacher must review subject matter, prepare learning activities, and plan special projects.

Guiding and assisting student learning. At times, teachers guide the learning of individual students. In other learning situations, teachers offer guidance to small or large groups. Even when dealing with students as a group, a good teacher remains concerned with the individual progress of each student.

Teachers have long depended on textbooks and other printed materials to assist learning. Teachers also use teaching aids called *audio-visual materials,* such as tape recordings and videotapes. Since the 1950's, many new devices and techniques have been adapted for classroom use. These advanced learning aids include computers, educational television, and language laboratories. School systems now expect teachers to have sufficient computer skills to guide students in the use of computers and other technologies in their classrooms.

Computer *software,* also called a *program,* provides many types of learning assistance that students can use at their own pace. For example, *drill-and-practice programs* imitate flashcards. Programs called *simulations* create computer representations of such realistic situations as dissecting a frog. *Word-processing programs* enable students to use computers for writing and editing. With computers connected to telephone lines, students can communicate by e-mail and do research over the vast electronic network called the Internet.

Teachers generally select teaching methods and materials that are suited to the different abilities, ages, and needs of their classes. Preschool teachers, for example, use educational toys and games to attract and hold the interest of young children. Many teachers try to choose instructional materials that reflect students' personal concerns and experiences. For example, a teacher of reading in a city school might select textbooks that relate to urban life.

One challenge facing teachers is discovering the best way that each individual student learns. The theory of *multiple intelligences,* put forth by the American psychologist Howard Gardner, has influenced many teachers. This theory suggests that there are a number of types of intelligence, such as linguistic intelligence, spatial intelligence, and musical intelligence, and therefore a number of ways to learn. Building on Gardner's theory, many teachers have developed a wide variety of methods to present information to their students. Such methods include the use of music, art activities, multimedia presentations, and field trips.

Teachers must also take into account the differing needs and abilities of individual students. Teachers may use special materials to help students who lack basic communication and study skills or those who have other exceptional needs. For more information on how teachers assist student learning, see **Education** (The study of learning and teaching).

Checking student progress. Most teachers give formal and informal written or oral tests to help evaluate the progress of their students. By comparing test results among individuals, teachers can discover which students need special help and decide what kind of help they need. By evaluating the performance of an entire group, teachers can judge the effectiveness of their teaching methods and materials.

Most schools group students in grades according to age. In these schools, teachers use test results to give students specific marks in their courses. *Nongraded schools* do not group students according to age. Instead, students advance in each subject at their own pace. They attend classes with other students of any age who work at the same level. In most of these schools, teachers give general evaluations rather than specific marks. The evaluations may be written, or a teacher may meet with students and their parents to discuss each student's progress. For more information about school tests and how they are used, see the article **Testing.**

Duties outside the classroom. Many teachers have a variety of duties in addition to their teaching responsibilities. They may be required to supervise lunchrooms, playgrounds, or study sessions. Teachers advise, sponsor, or coach such student groups as hobby clubs or sports teams. Many teachers serve as official or unofficial student counselors after school hours.

Most teachers also take part in professional activities outside school. Conferences provide an opportunity to meet with other teachers and explore issues of mutual interest. Many teachers further their education by taking advanced courses in college or study trips.

Becoming a teacher

A person who wants to become a teacher should like people and get satisfaction from helping them succeed. Good teachers have a thorough knowledge of the subjects they teach and know how to make these subjects interesting. They speak and write effectively and enjoy communicating. The best teachers make learning enjoyable for all their students. They realize that some students find learning difficult and that such students require extra patience and steady encouragement.

Most countries also require teachers to have certain types of education and professional certification. The requirements vary from country to country. This section deals chiefly with the United States and Canada, but many other countries follow similar procedures.

Teacher-training programs. Almost all teacher-training programs in the United States and Canada are offered at general colleges or universities. Most U.S. teacher-training programs include three main types of courses: (1) general education courses, also called *liberal arts courses;* (2) professional teaching courses; and (3) advanced courses in a particular area of study, such as English or mathematics. Many U.S. programs are accredited by the National Council for Accreditation of Teacher Education. Canada's teacher-training programs are similar to those in the United States.

During the first two years in college, teachers-in-training take general education courses in many areas of study. General education requirements might include courses in history, foreign languages, mathematics, sciences, and computer science. These courses provide basic familiarity with many subjects. General courses also develop intellectual curiosity, critical thinking, and the ability to express ideas effectively.

© Lawrence Migdale

Teaching science involves experiments that reveal the basic laws and principles of how the universe works. Here, a teacher helps students discover how changing conditions affect the flight of model rockets.

During their second two years, teaching students begin to take professional training courses in such subjects as child development, instructional methods, and instructional technology. Also during their second two years, most teaching students specialize in a particular subject called the *major subject.* Many students choose the area in which they plan to teach—for example, history, mathematics, or biology—as their major subject.

At one time, many teaching students majored in education and had no specialized area of study except for their professional training courses. But school districts now prefer to hire teachers who have majored in a particular subject.

During their final year of training, aspiring teachers perform *student teaching.* In student teaching, a trainee teaches classes under the guidance of an experienced teacher. Some programs require education majors to complete a student internship during their final year.

Certification of teachers. Every state requires public elementary and high-school teachers to obtain a teaching certificate before they may teach in that state. The certificate provides official recognition that teachers meet the state's basic requirements for professional education and certain other conditions. Some states also require certification to teach in a preschool, private school, or public junior college. Teachers in four-year colleges and universities do not need a certificate. Instead, they must obtain an advanced degree and demonstrate their teaching ability through satisfactory on-the-job performance.

Almost all states issue separate certificates for elementary and high-school teachers. Every state requires beginning teachers to be college graduates. Teachers must also have completed a professional training program that prepares them to teach in either elementary or high school. In addition, high-school teachers must be qualified to teach a particular subject. Many states also require such qualification for elementary-school teachers. Some teachers in special fields earn certificates that enable them to teach at both the elementary and high school levels. These fields include art, music, and the education of children with exceptional needs.

Most states issue special certificates for such positions as school principal, school librarian, and guidance counselor. People in these careers must meet the basic requirements for a teaching certificate and have special training for each particular position. Classroom assistants called *teacher aides,* also known as *paraprofessional teachers,* may not need a professional teaching certificate. Teacher aides work under the supervision of a professional teacher to assist with classroom activities and give students individual attention.

Most states issue an initial certificate, also called a provisional certificate, to new teachers who meet the basic professional requirements. Teachers may apply for an advanced certificate after they have taught a certain number of years. Many states also require additional college courses or a master's degree for advanced certification. A few states issue advanced certificates to new teachers who meet a higher level of requirements than those for basic certification. Some states issue advanced certificates on a permanent basis. Other states require teachers to renew their certificate every few years. About half the states recognize certification from other states. The rest require teachers from out of state to take certain courses or to pass a special examination.

A national certification movement has arisen to improve teaching by creating high standards of training and performance for teachers throughout the United States. The nonprofit National Board for Professional Teaching Standards was founded in 1987 to develop these standards and grant national certification.

Public elementary and high-school teachers in Canada must also have a teaching certificate. Each province sets the requirements for its own certificates. Most provinces require elementary and high-school teachers to have a three- or four-year college degree and a year or more of teacher-training courses.

Job opportunities. Schools in the United States and Canada hire new teachers each year. Some openings occur because experienced teachers retire or leave to pursue other careers. Growth or decline in local population affects the number of teachers needed in particular communities. Some changes in population affect the teacher needs of entire nations. For example, from 1946 to 1964, the United States experienced a sharp rise in birth rate called the *baby boom.* The baby boom led to rising school enrollments and a teacher shortage in the 1950's and 1960's. Most states offer alternative certification programs in times of shortages.

The demand for teachers in the United States and Canada varies somewhat by subject area, grade level, and location. For example, there is generally a demand for teachers of mathematics and the sciences. Many communities need teachers of *vocational education,* which prepares students for jobs in such skilled areas as carpentry and automobile repair. Demand generally exists for preschool teachers, school administrators, guidance counselors, librarians, and psychologists. Many rural areas and poor neighborhoods in large cities experience chronic shortages of teachers in all subjects.

At one time, almost all elementary school teachers in the United States and Canada were women, and almost all college and university teachers were men. But this situation has slowly changed. Men now make up a significant percentage of elementary school teachers. Women also hold a growing number of teaching posts at colleges and universities. Teaching jobs in high schools are divided fairly equally between the sexes.

Employment practices. In most public school districts, the local school board hires teachers. Most boards sign a contract with every teacher they hire. In the contract, the board agrees to pay a certain salary for the teacher's services. The contract covers a specified period, after which a new contract must be signed. In many school districts, a teachers union or other professional organization also signs a master contract with the school board. This contract covers not only the teachers who belong to the organization but also all other teachers in the district, including any new teachers the school board hires. Before signing the contract, the organization tries to obtain from the board the highest possible salaries and other benefits for the teachers. The master contract is good for only a certain period. A new contract must then be signed after the teachers organization and the board have again agreed to its terms.

Most colleges and universities in the United States and Canada grant teachers *tenure.* Tenure means that after a certain period of service, teachers cannot be dismissed except for certain limited reasons that are specified in their contracts. Most school districts in the two countries also grant tenure to public-school teachers.

Rewards of teaching. For many teachers, the greatest reward of teaching is the opportunity to work with and influence young people. Teachers enjoy seeing students succeed at their studies and develop into productive, responsible citizens.

In most U.S. school districts, teachers receive pay raises according to a set salary schedule. The schedule grants salary increases for each additional year or other period of service and for additional professional training. Teachers organizations generally seek to raise scheduled salaries when they work out a new master contract with a school board. Some U.S. school districts use a *merit pay system* or a *differentiated staffing system* to grant pay increases. The merit pay system bases pay increases on student performance rather than teacher experience and additional training. The differentiated staffing system divides the teaching positions in a school into various levels according to the amount of responsibility they involve. Teachers receive raises mainly by being promoted to a higher level.

Many colleges and universities, and some school districts, grant teachers a period of professional leave called a *sabbatical* after a certain number of years of service. Many sabbaticals consist of a semester's leave of absence with full pay. Teachers are expected to use a sabbatical to further their professional growth.

Continuing professional development. All teachers are expected to continue their professional growth throughout their careers. Many teachers use their vacation time to take advanced college courses or to attend meetings for teachers in their field. Many school districts provide *in-service training,* which helps experienced, working teachers improve their teaching. Such training for teachers may include conferences, workshops, or special reading materials. A variety of journals and other publications help teachers keep informed about developments in their field.

Teachers organizations. In the United States, teachers may join a number of professional organizations. The National Education Association of the United States (NEA) has more teachers as members than any other U.S. educational organization. It has branches in every state and in many cities and towns. The NEA works chiefly to raise educational standards and to improve the pay and working conditions of teachers. The American Federation of Teachers (AFT) is a national teachers union that works to improve teachers' salaries and working conditions and to increase student achievement. Hundreds of local teachers unions throughout the United States are associated with the AFT.

Many U.S. teachers organizations concentrate on a particular field, such as English, mathematics, or special education. For example, the National Council of Teachers of English is an organization for English instructors at all school levels. The National Catholic Educational Association offers membership to educators and administrators in Roman Catholic schools. The Association of Teacher Educators works to promote quality programs for teacher education.

Canada has a number of large provincial and local teachers organizations and unions with goals similar to those of the NEA and AFT. The Canadian Education Association is a national organization that works to improve the quality of education throughout Canada. The Association for Supervision and Curriculum Development (ASCD) brings together all levels of professional educators from the United States, Canada, and other countries to improve education.

Current issues in teaching

In many countries, a period of intense social change began in the 1960's and continued for several decades. One such change was a growing expectation that authorities and institutions should respect and respond to the needs of individuals. In schools, this expectation led to reduced emphasis on group instruction and increased focus on individual development. Parents began to feel that schools should appreciate and encourage different learning styles. Classrooms should offer good experiences for children of all races, cultures, and physical and intellectual ability levels.

Family structures and child care arrangements also changed during this time. Many women began to work outside the home, and many children began living in single-parent homes. Stress on families put pressure on teachers to provide increased support and services for students. Curriculums expanded to cover many new subjects, including such areas as sex education, drug abuse awareness, and multicultural appreciation.

This focus on individual students and expanded curriculums increased work for teachers. Some teachers responded to the growing demands of their jobs by going on strike for higher pay and better working conditions. Communities have reacted in various ways to requests by teachers for more pay and recognition. Some people question the right of teachers to strike for any reason. Some communities have turned down tax increases for education because voters feel unable to pay the added taxes. Other districts have approved tax increases for educational funding.

The debate about the changing role of schools and teachers ranges over many issues. Two of the most important issues relate to (1) the effectiveness of teaching and (2) the effectiveness of teacher training.

The effectiveness of teaching. Many people have urged that teachers be required to prove that they teach well before they are granted pay raises. One means of determining teacher effectiveness is called an *accountability system.* In education, accountability systems assume that the quality of teaching has a direct effect on how well students learn. These systems hold teachers *accountable*—that is, responsible—for their students' level of achievement.

A number of states and local school districts have established accountability systems. The systems differ, but most require a method of teacher evaluation. Some evaluations rely on tests to see if students have achieved desired learning goals. Other systems require evaluation of teachers by administrators or supervisors. In most accountability systems, a teacher who continually receives poor evaluations faces dismissal.

Many teachers oppose accountability. They feel that many factors in addition to the quality of teaching affect how well students learn. Such factors include home and social environments, size of classes, and the availability of equipment and supplies.

The effectiveness of teacher training. Ideas about how to train teachers to help other people learn have changed over the years. The first professional teacher-training programs in the United States were established in the mid-1800's at institutions called *normal schools.* Normal schools offered two-year courses of study that emphasized practical skills needed by teachers.

By the 1970's, most teacher-training programs had become part of colleges and universities. Many people felt that extending teacher training had created too much emphasis on educational theory. As a result, an approach to teacher training called *competency-based education* gained popularity in the 1970's. This approach emphasized teachers' ability to function effectively in the classroom. Before graduating, teachers-in-training had to show that they could teach, that they knew their subject areas thoroughly, and that they could maintain discipline.

By the late 1900's, many teacher-training programs had begun to place equal emphasis on theoretical knowledge and practical skills. The content of training programs had also expanded to include the growing number of subjects teachers must cover. Most training curriculums now include such topics as use of computers, respect for different cultures, and education for exceptional children.

Teaching around the world

Schools around the world teach children to read, write, and work with numbers. Students also usually learn their country's customs and their duties as citizens. In many countries, children also study such subjects as geography, history, and science. Many countries expect teachers to instruct students in the use of computer technology in classrooms.

Brazil, France, Germany, Italy, Japan, and many other countries expect teachers to teach a national curriculum. These countries usually require students to take standardized examinations to determine how well they have learned certain information and skills. National guidelines generally ask teachers to cover specific topics and values that are important to the country in which they are teaching. For example, the Czech Republic, which established a democratic government in 1993, has instituted national standards for the teaching of civics and government. Many countries, including Australia, the Netherlands, and the United Kingdom, ask teachers to actively promote tolerance and acceptance of cultural differences.

In many developing countries, teachers work in settings without computers and other materials usually found in classrooms in developed countries. These teachers usually emphasize basic literacy skills and often teach adults as well as children. In many cases, teachers are expected to focus on health and disease prevention in addition to other studies. Stephen M. Fain

Related articles in *World Book.* See **Education** and its list of *Related articles.* See also the following articles:

Organizations

American Federation of Teachers
Canadian Education Association
Childhood Education International, Association for
National Catholic Educational Association
National Congress of Parents and Teachers
National Education Association
Parent-teacher organizations

Other related articles

Academic freedom
Audio-visual materials
Bilingual education
Computerized instruction
Curriculum
Educational psychology
Elementary school
Fulbright Scholarship
Grading
Guidance
High school
Junior high school
Kindergarten
Learning
Middle school
Multiculturalism
National Defense Education Act
Nursery school
Reading (The teaching of reading)
School
Special education
Study
Testing
Universities and colleges

Outline

I. Teaching as a profession
A. Preparing to teach classes
B. Guiding and assisting student learning
C. Checking student progress
D. Duties outside the classroom

II. Becoming a teacher
A. Teacher-training programs
B. Certification of teachers
C. Job opportunities
D. Employment practices
E. Rewards of teaching
F. Continuing professional development
G. Teachers organizations

III. Current issues in teaching
A. The effectiveness of teaching
B. The effectiveness of teacher training

IV. Teaching around the world

Questions

What are four important duties of teachers?
What is a *teaching certificate?* Who must have one?
Why do teachers give tests?
What is a *sabbatical leave?*
What are some characteristics of a good teacher?
How do teachers continue their professional growth throughout their careers?
What factors affect the availability of teaching jobs?
What two national organizations work to improve the pay and working conditions of U.S. teachers?
What is *tenure?*
What is an *accountability system* in education?

Additional resources

Banner, James M., Jr., and Cannon, H. C. *The Elements of Teaching.* Yale, 1997.
Bromfield, Richard. *Handle with Care: Understanding Children and Teachers.* Teachers Coll. Pr., 2000.
Fine, Janet. *Opportunities in Teaching Careers.* Rev. ed. NTC/Contemporary Pub. Co., 2000.
Grant, Gerald, and Murray, C. E. *Teaching in America.* Harvard Univ. Pr., 1999.

Teaching machine. See Computerized instruction.

Teagarden, Jack (1905-1964), was an American trombone player and blues singer. His intense, warm, blues-rooted trombone style was widely imitated. Teagarden was also the first successful nonblack blues singer. His most famous records are "I've Got a Right to Sing the Blues" and "Basin Street Blues." They illustrate his rich, deeply moving vocal style.

Teagarden was born Aug. 20, 1905, in Vernon, Texas. He was partly American Indian in ancestry. His full name was Leo Weldon John Teagarden. Mainly a self-taught musician, Teagarden went to New York City in 1927 and toured with Ben Pollack's band from 1928 to 1933. In this time, he recorded outstanding performances with Louis

Armstrong and Red Nichols. He later performed with Paul Whiteman's band and recorded with Benny Goodman. He led his own band from 1939 to 1947, and worked four years with Louis Armstrong. He led small groups after 1951. Frank Tirro

Teak is a forest tree native to southeastern Asia. Its wood is highly valued for shipbuilding and for making furniture, cabinets, and trim. Teakwood is strong and durable and resists water. It takes a high polish and has an oil that helps it resist insects and decay. The tree sometimes grows to a height of 150 feet (46 meters). The leaves often grow 2 feet (61 centimeters) long and 1 $\frac{1}{2}$ feet (46 centimeters) wide. They yield a purple dye and are also used for thatch and for wrapping material.

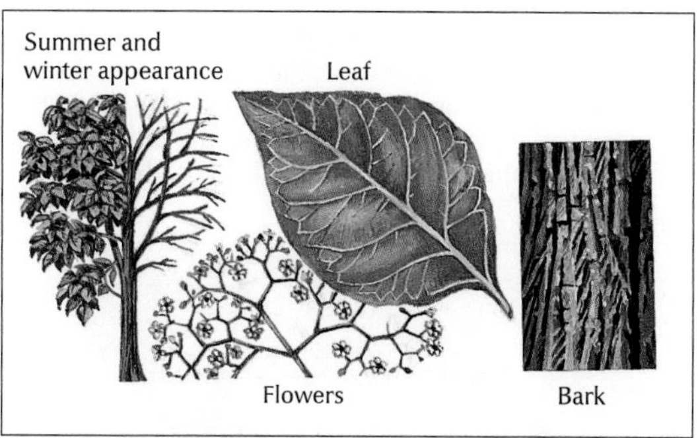

WORLD BOOK illustration by Chris Skilton

The teak tree grows in forests of southeastern Asia.

Chester B. Stem, Inc. (WORLD BOOK photo)

Teakwood is used in making ships, furniture, and other products. A panel of teakwood, *shown here,* has beautiful grain patterns.

Teakwood is produced commercially throughout most of the teak tree's natural range—in India, Indonesia, and Myanmar. Because of its commercial value, the tree has been widely planted throughout the world. Today, teak trees are also commercially harvested in tropical Africa and Latin America. Jim L. Bowyer

Scientific classification. The teak tree is in the family Verbenaceae. Its scientific name is *Tectona grandis.*

Teal is a name given to several species of small ducks that live throughout the world. Three species of teals—*blue-winged, cinnamon,* and *green-winged*—are common in North America. These teals nest near shallow lakes, ponds, and marshes in Canada and the northern United States. They usually eat the seeds of water plants, but blue-winged teals also eat some insects. Cinnamon teals migrate to Mexico and Central America to spend the winter. Most blue-winged teals migrate to northern South America, but some winter in Louisiana.

The blue-winged teal measures 15 to 16 inches (38 to 41 centimeters) long. It is mostly brown with large gray-blue patches on its wings. The male has a crescent-shaped white mark in front of each eye. The cinnamon teal is about 16 inches (41 centimeters) long. The male has red eyes, cinnamon-red feathers, and blue wing patches. The female is light brown and looks almost exactly like the female blue-winged teal.

Peter Arnold

The cinnamon teal is a small North American duck. The male, *shown here,* has dark cinnamon-red plumage and blue patches on its wings. Teals live near ponds, streams, and marshes.

The green-winged teal measures 13 to 15 inches (33 to 38 centimeters) long. The male has gray feathers with a speckled breast and a reddish-brown head with a green patch. The female is brown. Both the male and the female have a green patch along the edge of each wing.

Eric G. Bolen

Scientific classification. Teals belong to the genus *Anas* in the family Anatidae. The blue-winged teal is *Anas discors.* The cinnamon teal is *A. cyanoptera.* The green-winged teal is*A. crecca.*

Team handball is a fast and exciting sport for men and women in which players try to score goals by throwing a ball into their opponents' goal. Team handball can be played indoors or outdoors. Modern team handball at the international level is an indoor game. This article describes the indoor version that has been an event in the Summer Olympic Games since 1972.

Teams consist of seven players—six court players and a goalkeeper. A team handball court is 40 meters (131 feet) long and 20 meters (65 $\frac{1}{2}$ feet) wide. A goal line runs the width of the field at each end. Side lines enclose the playing area lengthwise. A goal is centered lengthwise on each goal line. It consists of two posts 2 meters (6 $\frac{1}{2}$ feet) high and 3 meters (9 $\frac{3}{4}$ feet) apart. The posts are connected by a horizontal bar. A net is attached to the posts and bar. The ball consists of a leather-covered rubber bladder. The ball in men's competition is 58 to 60 centimeters (23 to 23 $\frac{1}{2}$ inches) in circumference. The ball in women's games is slightly smaller.

Games are divided into two 30-minute periods. Many of the rules resemble soccer rules except that players can use their hands but cannot use their feet to pass and dribble the ball. Two referees supervise play.

Critically reviewed by the United States Team Handball Federation

Teamsters Union is one of the largest labor unions in the United States. Its official name is International Brotherhood of Teamsters, Chauffeurs, Warehousemen, and Helpers of America. The Teamsters also has local unions in Canada and Puerto Rico. Its membership includes truckdrivers, chauffeurs, warehouse employees, and helpers; people who work with automotive vehicles, including salespeople; garage and service-station employees; dairy, brewery, food-processing, and soft-drink plant employees; and industrial workers and airline and public service employees.

The Teamsters has about 1 $\frac{1}{2}$ million members. It is organized primarily through its nearly 800 local unions in the United States, Canada, and Puerto Rico. In addition, the Teamsters Union has joint councils and an international convention. Major duties of the joint councils include adjusting jurisdictional disputes between local unions, approving or disapproving strikes or boycotts planned by locals, and evaluating wage scales that the locals plan to submit to employers. The convention is the supreme governing body of the union. It meets every five years. Each local's representation is based on the size of its membership.

The Teamsters Union was chartered by the American Federation of Labor (AFL) in 1899 as the Team Drivers' Union. The group split into two unions, which reunited at Niagara Falls, New York, in 1903, the official date of the founding of the Teamsters Union. The union grew rapidly under presidents David Beck and James R. Hoffa in the 1950's and early 1960's. It was expelled from the AFL-CIO in 1957, after its leaders were accused of unethical practices. The union was readmitted to the AFL-CIO in 1987.

In 1989, the Teamsters Union and the U.S. Department of Justice reached an out-of-court settlement of a federal racketeering lawsuit filed against the union. Some Teamsters officials had long been suspected of having ties to organized crime. The terms of the agreement included creation of a three-member board to oversee union activities. One board member is appointed by the U.S. attorney general, the second by the union, and the third by mutual consent of the union and the attorney general. The board was set up in 1992. Union headquarters are in Washington, D.C. James G. Scoville

See also **Fitzsimmons, Frank E.; Hoffa, James Phillip; Hoffa, James Riddle.**

Teapot Dome was one of the most notorious government scandals in United States history. It occurred during the administration of President Warren G. Harding and contributed to his low standing among U.S. presidents.

Committees of the U.S. Senate and a special commission investigated the scandal from 1922 to 1928. The investigators found that Secretary of the Interior Albert B. Fall had persuaded Harding to transfer control of three naval oil reserves from the Navy Department to the Department of the Interior in 1921. Fall leased the reserves, at Elk Hills, California, and Teapot Dome, Wyoming, mostly without competitive bidding, to the private oil companies of Edward L. Doheny and Harry F. Sinclair in 1922.

For helping to arrange the Elk Hills transfer, Fall received a "loan" of $100,000 from Doheny. For the Teapot Dome transfer, Fall received over $300,000 in cash, bonds, and valuable livestock from Sinclair. Fall resigned in 1923 and joined Sinclair's oil business.

In 1927, the government successfully sued to cancel the leases. In 1929, Fall was convicted of accepting a bribe, fined $100,000, and sentenced to a year in prison. He was the first Cabinet member ever to go to jail for crimes committed while in office. Robert D. Parmet

See also **Fall, Albert Bacon.**

Tears are the secretion of the lacrimal glands. The tears continually bathe the *cornea,* the tough outer layer of the eyeball. They help to clear it of foreign particles, such as dust and hairs, and keep it from drying out, which would result in blindness.

Two lacrimal glands, one over each eye, lie behind the eyelid. They pour out their fluid through several small ducts in the underside of the lid. Each time the eyelid blinks, it sucks a little fluid from the glands. When a person feels some emotion, such as grief or anger, very strongly, the muscles around the lacrimal glands may tighten up and squeeze out the tear fluid. The same thing happens if a person laughs very heartily.

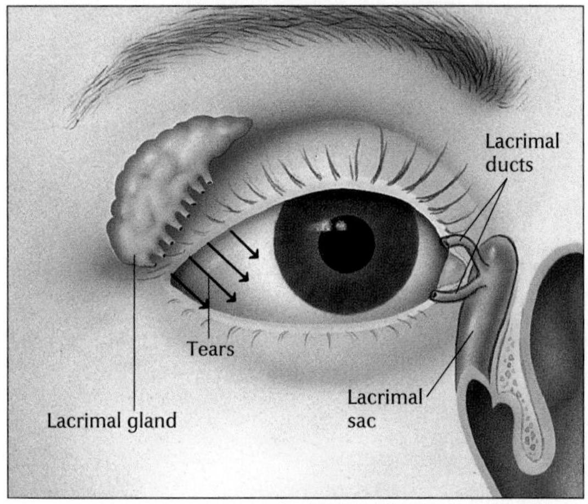

WORLD BOOK illustration by Charles Wellek

Tears are produced by the *lacrimal glands,* one of which lies above each eyeball. The tears wash across the eye and empty into the *lacrimal ducts,* which lead to the *lacrimal sac.* From there, they drain through a passage into the nose.

After the tears pass across the eyeball, they flow out through two lacrimal ducts that open at the inner corner of each eye. They lead to a lacrimal sac and then to the nasal duct. This duct runs the length of the nose and finally opens into it. Tears flowing through this opening make the nose run when a person cries.

Mostly a salt solution, lacrimal fluid also contains substances that fight bacteria and proteins that help make the eye immune to infection. Nandalal Bagchi

Tears, Trail of. See Trail of Tears.

Teasdale, Sara (1884-1933), was an American lyric poet. Some of her work anticipates modern feminist verse and the intimate, autobiographical style known as *confessional poetry.* A large number of Teasdale's poems deal with love and death. Many of the speakers in her lyrics are women who face the death or desertion of a loved one. They also face the fact of their own mortality with disillusionment, but not as cynics. Teasdale associated moral and spiritual beauty with the harmonies of the natural world.

Teasdale was born on Aug. 8, 1884, in St. Louis, Missouri. Besides writing her own poetry, she edited an anthology of love lyrics by women called *The Answering Voice* (1917, rev. ed. 1928). She also edited *Rainbow Gold* (1922), a collection of poetry for young people. Her *Collected Poems* was published in 1937. William Harmon

Teasel, *TEE zuhl,* is the name of a group of herbs with prickly stems. The only commercially valuable species of teasel is the *fuller's teasel,* also called *clothier's teasel* and *clothier's brush.* The dried flower heads of this plant are used to raise the *nap* (threads) on cloth. The dried flowers or fruits of several species of teasel are also used in arrangements of dried flowers.

The fuller's teasel is native to Europe, northern Africa, and parts of Asia. It also is grown in the United States. The plant has long, stemless leaves; pale lilac or white flowers; and stiff *bracts* (modified leaves) surrounding the flower heads. The dried heads are cut in two and attached to a cylinder that revolves against the cloth. The best heads are used for raising the nap on garments. The largest heads are used on blankets. Small heads are used for fine fabrics. Howard L. Needles

Scientific classification. Teasels belong to the teasel family, Dipsacaceae. The scientific name for the fuller's teasel is *Dipsacus sativus.*

Tebaldi, *tuh BAHL dee,* **Renata,** *ruh NAH tuh,* (1922-2004), an Italian singer, was one of the great operatic sopranos of her time. Her voice was noted for its evenness and velvety quality. Tebaldi performed almost exclusively in Italian operas. Her early lyric roles included Desdemona in *Otello* and Mimi in *La Bohème.* She progressed to more dramatic roles, including the title roles in *Aida* and *Tosca.* Tebaldi was born on Feb. 1, 1922, in Pesaro. She made her debut in Rovigo, Italy, in 1944 as Elena in *Mefistofele.* She first sang in the United States in 1950 in San Francisco and made her debut at the Metropolitan Opera in New York City in 1955 as Desdemona. She sang there regularly until 1973. She died on Dec. 19, 2004. Charles H. Webb

Technetium, *tehk NEE shee uhm,* was the first artificially created chemical element. The Italian physicists Carlo Perrier and Emilio Segrè first isolated it in 1937. The element appears as a silvery metal or gray powder. Its chemical symbol is Tc. Its *atomic number* (number of protons in its nucleus) is 43. Technetium resists *oxidation* (chemically reacting with oxygen) but can be oxidized by nitric or sulfuric acid.

Technetium has many different *isotopes.* Isotopes are forms of an element with the same number of protons but different numbers of neutrons. The most stable isotope of technetium has an *atomic mass number* (total number of protons and neutrons) of 98. Technetium 98 has a *half-life* of 4.2 million years—that is, due to radioactive decay, only half the atoms in a sample of technetium 98 would still be atoms of that isotope after 4.2 million years. Physicians sometimes inject patients with an isotope called *technetium 99m* to produce images of body tissues. That isotope has a half-life of around 6 hours, so it does not remain in the body for long after tests.

Perrier and Segrè obtained the first technetium from a sample of molybdenum that had been bombarded with *deuterons* (particles consisting of one proton and one neutron). The scientists proved that the bombardment resulted in the addition of a proton to the nucleus of the molybdenum atom, forming technetium. They thought the new element, which they called *masurium,* would be easy to find in nature. However, they discovered that natural processes produce only tiny amounts of the element. The name was then changed to technetium, which comes from the Greek word for *artificial.* Technetium is now obtained in large quantities as a by-product of *atomic fission* (the splitting of atoms to produce energy).

Technetium melts at 2172 °C and boils at 4877 °C. It has a density of 11.5 grams per cubic centimeter at 25 °C. Kenton H. Whitmire

Technical assistance is a form of foreign aid. Through technical assistance programs, people in developing countries learn skills that help increase production and raise living standards.

There are various forms of technical assistance. Experts from more prosperous countries may set up demonstrations or provide on-the-job training in developing countries. Workers, executives, and engineers from developing countries may go to prosperous countries for training. Technical assistance may be as simple as teaching a farmer to use a plow instead of a forked stick. It may be as involved as showing a government how to keep statistics on its economy.

President Harry S. Truman's Point Four Program of 1949 was an early technical assistance plan (see **Point Four Program**). Some private and public agencies gave such aid before 1949. The United Nations and its agencies also offer technical assistance. The United States Agency for International Development has a major technical assistance program. Its aid ranges from short-term assistance to three-year projects.

Technical assistance may be used by a larger country to coerce a smaller country. The smaller, receiving country may be expected to support the larger country in world affairs in return for the aid. Michael P. Sullivan

See also **Foreign aid; United Nations** (Economic and technical aid); **Colombo Plan; Agency for International Development; Developing country.**

Technical drawing. See **Mechanical drawing.**

Technicolor is a patented process for making motion pictures in color. It involves producing three separate black-and-white negatives of the scene being filmed. Each negative is exposed to one of the *primary colors* of light—red, blue, or green—from the scene. The negative images are then printed on film to produce positive images. Technicians dye the positives to reproduce the red, blue, and green areas recorded on the negatives. Next, the dyed positive images are transferred onto blank film to make the final print. The transferred colors blend to produce all the original colors of the filmed scene. Technicolor results in color reproduction of high quality. But the process is difficult and costly to produce.

Herbert T. Kalmus, an American chemical engineer, developed Technicolor in the early 1900's. The first full-length film made with the process, *The Gulf Between,* appeared in theaters in 1917. Originally, Technicolor was a two-color system. The improved three-color process was introduced in 1932. Many Technicolor films were made in the 1930's and 1940's. Since then, however, Technicolor has largely been replaced by simpler and less expensive color film processes. Peter J. Eaves

Timken Company, Canton, Ohio

An automated steel mill produces huge steel bars at the touch of a button. The computer-controlled machines that roll the glowing bars are products of modern technology. Other machines and methods will turn the bars into a variety of industrial and household products.

Technology

Technology refers to the inventions—including tools, techniques, and processes—that people make and use to survive and prosper. Technology has made it much easier for people to satisfy their needs and desires. It has also helped make people more productive and freed individuals to explore such endeavors as art and science without having to worry about simple survival.

Technology and science are closely related, and each contributes to the other. Science attempts to gain knowledge about natural occurrences by making observations and collecting facts. Technology sometimes uses scientific methods and knowledge. But much of technology is not based on science, nor is understanding science necessary to all of technology. For example, people made bronze by mixing copper and tin long before they learned how the metals actually combine to form it.

This article describes some of the ways in which technology has influenced the development of society. It also discusses challenges people face in using technology effectively. The history of technology largely parallels the history of invention, traced in the article on **Invention.** Information on the development of specific technologies can be found in the History sections of such articles as **Agriculture, Communication,** and **Medicine.**

History of technology

The term *technology* includes primitive tools and methods of work as well as highly advanced ones. For example, a person using a sharpened stick to dig up roots to eat is using a primitive form of technology. Therefore, we could say that human beings have lived in a technological society since prehistoric times. When people speak of technology today, however, they usually mean *high technology*—the most advanced and sophisticated kinds of electronics and other modern technology that currently exist.

Primitive technology. Toolmaking was probably the first kind of technology. Humanlike creatures who lived before the first human beings used simple tools that they made from wood, stone, or animal bones. About 600,000 years ago, prehistoric people discovered how to make fire.

Agriculture and civilization. By 8000 B.C., people in many areas of the world had begun to master the skills of raising crops and tending animals. This meant that they no longer had to go in search of food, so many began to settle down in small groups. Then, partly because farming produced larger food supplies, these groups began to grow larger. In time, towns and cities developed. Some people became free to do other jobs besides producing food. Classes of warriors, priests, craftworkers, and merchants developed. This development is known as *division of labor.*

Human and animal labor was then the chief source of mechanical power. But people began to realize that wind, water, gravity, and other natural sources of power could be used to do physical work. By the 2000's B.C., people had begun to construct irrigation canals to bring water where it was needed and to build ships with sails to harness wind power. At the start of the Iron Age, about 1500 B.C., people learned to make more durable and precise tools, weapons, and other items out of iron.

Technological advances were carried throughout the world by traders and other travelers. For example, the traders who brought silk and spices to Europe from China also brought technological ideas, such as gunpowder. The Chinese invented gunpowder before A.D. 900, and it was brought to Europe around 1250 by travelers who saw it being used in the East.

The Chinese began using block printing to produce printed documents about the A.D. 600's. This technique was introduced to Europe in the 1300's. But books were not published in great numbers until the introduction of printing presses that used movable type. These presses were developed in Europe in the mid-1400's. Over the next 200 years, books became widely available and affordable throughout most of Europe. More and more people learned to read. In the 1500's, books from around the world began to be translated into different languages. People were then able to read opinions and ideas from other countries and continents.

The Industrial Revolution was a period of rapid technological innovation that began in Britain in the 1700's and spread to some other parts of the world in the middle to late 1800's. It brought tremendous change to the way people lived and worked. This period featured the extensive use of water power, the development of steam-powered machinery, the growth of factories, and the mass production of goods. Later in the period, inventors and engineers developed machines that ran on gasoline or other fossil fuels. See **Industrial Revolution.**

The first factories were built by textile manufacturers. Before factories, individuals worked at home to spin thread and weave it into cloth. Beginning in the 1700's, several new kinds of spinning and weaving machines appeared. Textile producers realized that several of these machines could be powered by a single source by connecting them all to a water wheel or steam engine.

The development of interchangeable parts led to mass production. Beginning about 1800, Eli Whitney attempted, with limited success, to produce muskets from identical parts created using *machine tools.* The idea was slowly developed in the 1800's. Beginning in the early 1900's, the automaker Henry Ford used interchangeable parts with a moving assembly line to produce such complex goods as automobiles. Mass-production made it possible for many items to be made more quickly and cheaply. It also made it possible to repair many products by replacing broken parts with identical replacements.

By the mid-1800's, the Industrial Revolution had caused the people of some parts of the world to abandon ways of life that had persisted for thousands of years. Many people moved away from rural areas to the cities, where they hoped to find work in factories. Cities grew and became more crowded. New roads, waterways, and railroads were developed to make transportation of goods easier and to handle the huge increase in the number of people traveling from place to place.

The development of electronics. Beginning in the late 1800's and early 1900's, scientific discoveries about the nature of electricity and electromagnetic waves led to a series of technological advances. Electric motors, which create a magnetic field that can turn mechanical parts, were one major result. But the most dramatic advances were in communications.

Just as the printing press had done centuries before, the invention of the telegraph and the telephone brought about major social changes. For the first time, people could communicate with one another almost instantly across great distances. Later, the broadcasting of radio and television signals revolutionized mass communication by making it possible for people almost anywhere in the world to receive sound and pictures.

The computer age. In the 1940's, the first electronic computers were built to solve complex mathematical problems for scientists and for the governments of the United States and the United Kingdom. These early machines could perform a few thousand calculations per second. They were so big that it took a large room to house each of them.

In the late 1940's, engineers and scientists developed the transistor, a tiny device that controls the flow of electric current in electronic equipment. In the 1960's, the development of the integrated circuit enabled manufacturers to put thousands of tiny transistors and other parts on a small computer chip made of silicon or other material. Integrated circuits could also be built to operate as tiny computers called *microprocessors.* These and other innovations have helped to make computers ever smaller, lighter, faster, and less expensive.

In the 1960's, the development of the integrated circuit was partly responsible for the start of what people began to call the *space age.* Rockets lifted satellites into orbit to help with communications, scientific study, and military tasks. Spacecraft carried people to the moon, and remotely controlled probes explored other planets in the solar system. As computers became less expensive, businesses and universities began to use them more. Linking computers so that people could transfer information between them soon became important.

Toward the end of the 1960's, the U.S. government linked its computers using existing telephone lines. In the 1970's and 1980's, some universities and businesses worked together to establish their own computer networks. Soon there were thousands of such networks. In the late 1980's, computer scientists developed ways to link these networks into one large network, the Internet.

Computers eventually became so inexpensive that families and individuals could afford them. Today, millions of people use them at work and at home. Many use the World Wide Web, a system of computer files linked together on the Internet. These files include text, pictures, sounds, and moving images.

Many things that people use in everyday life have simple computers that help them function. For example, many automobiles are built with an *antilock braking system,* in which a microprocessor adjusts the individual braking force of each wheel to prevent skidding.

Emerging technologies today include not only electronics, but also *biotechnology* and nuclear energy. Biotechnology involves both the use of technology to solve medical problems and the use of biological science to aid in industrial processes. Recent advances in genetic research have changed the ways in which people fight disease and hunger. The manipulation of the chemical

© Stuart Cohen, Comstock

Harmful effects of technology include air pollution and noise pollution caused by motor vehicles. The large number of automobiles, buses, and motorcycles in urban areas can expose people to carbon monoxide gas and unhealthy levels of noise.

information contained in cells has resulted in the creation of cells that make insulin and plastics, and plants that are more resistant to disease and yield larger amounts of food.

Scientific research into the structure of atoms has led to the creation of nuclear power plants. In the field of medicine, such research has led to the use of radiation to fight cancer. It has also resulted in the development of X rays and other methods of examining structures inside the body without surgery.

Technology and society

People develop particular technologies to fit their needs and desires. People also influence how technologies evolve once they are developed. For example, the inventors and businessmen who designed the early telephone systems intended the telephone, like the earlier telegraph, to be used for business messages, not personal conversation. But people liked using the telephone to talk to friends and relatives. Telephone systems were eventually modified to reflect what people wanted.

Just as people influence how technology develops, it influences the way people live. Most technologies have benefits, but technologies also create new problems.

Benefits of technology. The control over nature brought by technology has benefited many people, especially those living in industrial nations. The use of tractors, chemical fertilizers, pesticides, and new plant breeds has increased food production all over the world. Transportation systems and refrigeration technology enable people in industrial countries to enjoy a variety of foods, ranging from fruit grown in the tropics to fish caught near the Arctic Circle.

It was once unusual for people to travel more than a few miles from where they were born. The development of trains, automobiles, and airplanes has given many people the ability to travel far from their place of birth for both business and pleasure. New communication technologies, such as satellites, television, and the World Wide Web, allow people to see things thousands of miles away without ever leaving their homes.

Once, people had few personal possessions. Mass production technologies permit manufacturers to produce items far more than cheaply than they could by hand. As a result, people in many industrial countries today own many manufactured things.

People who lived in cities before 1900 frequently became sick because they did not have ways to get clean water or dispose of their wastes. Today, in the industrial world, water supply systems provide clean, germ-free water to every home, and sewerage systems collect and purify wastes. Technology has made city life freer from disease and more comfortable.

Challenges of technology. Many technological developments that benefit society are accompanied by harmful effects. Such products of technology as motor vehicle emissions, industrial waste, and insecticides have some damaging effects on people, animals, and plants. The majority of industrial countries face problems of air, water, soil, and noise pollution.

Many people welcomed the automobile as a machine that would be quieter and cleaner than the horses it would replace. But eventually, millions of people began

John C. Evans, Chemical Manufacturers Association

One technology cleans up after another when a filter press squeezes solid particles out of wastewater in a chemical plant.

E. R. Degginger

Recycling recovers raw materials from wastes and so helps to conserve resources used by technology. The iron and steel in this discarded material is being separated for recycling.

to drive automobiles. In some large cities, traffic noise, automobile exhaust gases, and severe traffic congestion became common problems.

The atomic bomb, developed by U.S. scientists during World War II (1939-1945), helped to end the war quickly. Today, several nations possess nuclear weapons thousands of times more powerful than those used in World War II. A war involving these weapons would cause severe large-scale damage to the earth. New chemical and biological weapons that have become part of the world's arsenals could pose severe environmental damage.

The use of electrically powered machinery in industrial countries has greatly increased factory production. But at the same time, it has reduced the world's supply of oil and other fossil fuels, which are burned to produce most of the world's electric power. These fuels cannot be replaced after they are used.

New technologies are constantly changing the way people do their jobs. Advances in technology, such as *mechanization* (the use of machines to do physical work) or *automation* (the use of machines to perform tasks without human supervision), often result in the elimination of jobs. But new technologies also create new jobs, such as those in the electronics industry.

Using technology safely. Industries can help control environmental pollution by developing substitute technologies to replace those that produce harmful effects. For example, energy producers can improve efficiency so that power plants will burn less fossil fuel. They can also make greater use of renewable energy sources, such as solar, wind, and water power. Manufacturers can help conserve mineral and timber supplies by recycling materials left over from production processes, such as paper and metal scrap.

Developing a substitute technology can be costly. An industry may need to hire technology experts or invest in expensive new equipment. Most industries pay for these added costs by raising prices, which may hurt their business or affect consumers. For this reason, profit-seeking industries may decide not to use a substitute technology. Sometimes the decision affects the health and well-being of an entire community, state, or nation. In such cases, government agencies may require industries to develop or use substitute technologies. For example, many state and local governments require factories to use pollution-control devices.

In spite of their benefits, substitute technologies can also have undesirable effects. For example, nuclear power plants can produce tremendous amounts of electric power using only small amounts of uranium. And they do not pollute the air as do fuel-burning plants. Nuclear plants, however, leave behind dangerous radioactive waste that must be disposed of carefully.

Some experts believe that most harmful effects of technology can be prevented. They urge that any proposed large-scale technology be thoroughly tested and then evaluated before it is put into use. Such an evaluation is called a *technology assessment.* Its purpose is to discover in advance the possible effects that a new technology may have so that governments can make laws to reduce or prevent the harmful effects and encourage the beneficial effects. An assessment might show that the benefits of a new technology outweigh its costs. Or it might show that the costs exceed any benefits.

Sharing the benefits of technology is one of today's major challenges. Technology's benefits are limited largely to the industrially developed nations of Europe, Asia, and the Americas. But even in these nations, the benefits of technology are not evenly distributed. Many families lack all but the basic necessities of life.

The less developed nations of the world enjoy few benefits of modern technology. But people living in these countries want many of the goods and services that technology has made available to industrial nations.

Helping poorer nations develop industrial technology

will pose special problems. Many such countries do not have the wealth required to buy or build large technological systems. Even if they do, people of these countries need to learn new job skills.

Installing technology effectively requires an understanding of the ways in which it will affect a country's economic, political, and social values. Without such awareness, the introduction of technology may create social problems and even endanger the quality of life.

By itself, technology is neither good nor bad. It can be either, or both, depending on how people use it. In the future, as in the past, people must use intelligence, imagination, and skill to apply technology wisely and to deal with the problems it creates. Terry S. Reynolds

Related articles in *World Book.* See **Engineering, Industry, Invention,** and **Manufacturing** with their lists of *Related articles.* See also the following articles:

Assembly line	Energy supply	Internet
Automation	Environmental pollution (Local efforts)	Machine
Careers	Factory	Machine tool
Computer	Industrial Revolution	Mass production
Digital technology		Materials
Electronics		Mining

Additional resources

Bell, Trudy E., and Dooling, David. *Engineering Tomorrow: Today's Technology Experts Envision the Next Century.* IEEE Pr., 2000.

Cone, Robert J. *How the New Technology Works.* 2nd ed. Oryx, 1998.

Marcus, Alan I., and Segal, H. P. *Technology in America.* 2nd ed. Harcourt, 1999.

Stix, Gary, and Lacob, Miriam. *Who Gives a Gigabyte? A Survival Guide for the Technologically Perplexed.* Wiley, 1999.

Wright, Michael, and Patel, M. N., eds. *Scientific American: How Things Work Today.* Crown, 2000.

Technology Assessment, Office of, or OTA, was an advisory agency of the United States Congress. It operated from 1972 to 1995. The agency gave congressional committees analyses of the potential of new technologies and their possible economic, environmental, and social effects. The OTA also pointed out areas that might have required legislative action. It published numerous documents each year to keep Congress and the public informed about the consequences of technological change. Topics studied by the OTA included biotechnology, communications, defense, education, energy, food, health, industrial competitiveness, natural resources, transportation, and world trade.

A congressional board established the agency's policies and approved new studies. It consisted of six senators, six members of the House of Representatives, and the OTA director. The OTA relied on many experts outside the government for advice and information.

Technology education. See **Industrial arts.**

Tectonic plate. See **Plate tectonics.**

Tecumseh, *tih KUHM suh* (1768?-1813), was an outstanding leader of the eastern American Indian tribes in the late 1700's and early 1800's. He worked to unite all the tribes into a single alliance that would defend Indian lands against invasion by white people. Tecumseh means *shooting star* or *meteor.*

Tecumseh, the son of a Shawnee war chief, is believed to have been born at Old Piqua, a Shawnee village on the Mad River, northeast of present-day Dayton, Ohio. His father and two brothers were killed in battles

Lithograph (1841) by Nathaniel Currier (Granger Collection)

Tecumseh was an Indian leader who fought to defend Indian lands against invasion by white people. He allied his Indian forces with the British Army against the Americans during the War of 1812 and died at the Battle of the Thames, depicted here.

with the American colonists.

White settlers were rapidly taking Indian lands, and Tecumseh and his brother Tenskwatawa began a crusade to keep Indian lands for the Indians. Tenskwatawa, known as the Shawnee Prophet, led a religious revival. Tecumseh, a strong warrior and gifted orator, led in politics and war. He traveled frequently from his home in Ohio to visit other tribes east of the Mississippi River. The two men did much to restore the culture of the Indians of the Ohio River Valley region.

Tecumseh condemned a treaty that William Henry Harrison, then governor of the Indiana Territory, made with the Indians. His action led to the Battle of Tippecanoe in November 1811. Tecumseh joined the British to fight the Americans in the War of 1812 and commanded the Indian allies. He was killed on Oct. 5, 1813, leading his forces in Canada. Michael D. Green

See also **Indian wars** (Conflicts in the Midwest); **Shawnee Prophet; War of 1812** (Thames River).

Tedder, Arthur William (1890-1967), Baron Tedder of Glenguin, became a marshal of the Royal Air Force of the United Kingdom in 1945. Tedder was deputy supreme commander to General Dwight D. Eisenhower, the supreme Allied commander, in World War II (1939-1945). He later became deputy supreme commander of the North Atlantic Treaty Organization (NATO) forces in Europe.

Tedder was born on July 11, 1890, in Stirlingshire (now Central Region), Scotland. He died on June 3, 1967. Ian F. W. Beckett

Teen-age. See **Adolescent.**

Teeth

Teeth are hard, bonelike structures in the upper and lower jaws of human beings and many kinds of animals. They are the hardest parts of the body.

People use their teeth chiefly to chew food. Chewing is the first step in the process of *digestion.* Digestion begins as the teeth chop and grind chunks of food into smaller pieces. As the teeth chew the food, it is mixed with *saliva,* a liquid produced in the mouth. The food becomes a moist pulp, which is easy to swallow. The food is further broken down in the stomach and the small intestine, where it is absorbed by the blood. The blood carries the digested food to all parts of the body. Without teeth, people could not eat foods that must be chewed. They could only swallow soft foods and liquids.

Teeth also play an important part in speech. The teeth and tongue are used together to form many sounds that make up words. To produce the *th* sound, for example, the tip of the tongue is placed against the upper front teeth. A person who lacks these teeth may be unable to make the sound. Teeth also help support the muscles around the mouth and so contribute to a person's appearance. People who have lost their teeth lack this support. Unless they wear artificial teeth, they may have deep, saggy lines around the mouth.

Like human beings, most animals use their teeth to chew food. They also use their teeth to obtain food. Many animals that eat plants tear off the leaves or stalks of the plants with their teeth. Most meat-eating animals use their teeth to seize and kill prey.

This article chiefly discusses human teeth. The last section of the article describes the differences in the teeth of various kinds of animals.

Kinds of teeth

Human beings grow two sets of teeth: (1) deciduous teeth and (2) permanent teeth. The individual deciduous teeth appear and fall out gradually early in life. They are replaced, one by one, by the permanent teeth. See the table *Ages at which teeth appear* for the times deciduous and permanent teeth generally appear.

Deciduous and permanent teeth have the same basic structure. Each tooth has a *crown* and one or more *roots.* The crown is the part of the tooth that can be seen in the mouth. Bone and gums cover the root or roots. The roots hold the tooth in a socket in the jawbone.

Deciduous teeth are also called *baby teeth, milk teeth,* or *primary teeth.* They start to form about 7 $\frac{1}{2}$ months before a baby is born. They begin as oval or round swellings called *buds,* which gradually develop into teeth. When a baby is born, parts of all the deciduous teeth are present deep within the jaws. As the teeth grow, they push through the gums. This process is called *eruption* or *teething.* Babies begin to teethe at about 6 to 9 months of age. Most children have all their deciduous teeth by about 2 years of age.

There are 20 deciduous teeth, 10 of them in each jaw. They consist of three kinds of teeth: (1) incisors, (2) canines, and (3) molars. Each jaw has 4 incisors, 2 canines, and 4 molars. The incisors and canines are used to bite into food, and the molars are used to grind food. The positions of all the deciduous teeth in the mouth are shown in the illustration *Kinds of teeth.*

The deciduous teeth help the permanent teeth erupt in their normal positions. Most of the permanent teeth form near the roots of the deciduous teeth. When a child is about 3 years old, the roots of various deciduous teeth begin to dissolve slowly. By the time a permanent tooth is ready to erupt, the root of the deciduous tooth has completely dissolved. The crown of the tooth then becomes loose and falls out.

Permanent teeth, like deciduous teeth, begin to develop before birth. But most of their growth occurs after birth. The permanent teeth begin to erupt after the deciduous teeth start to fall out. The first permanent teeth appear when a child is about 6 or 7 years old. Between the ages of 6 and 12, a child has some permanent and some deciduous teeth in the mouth. The last permanent teeth erupt when a person is 17 to 21 years old.

There are 32 permanent teeth, 16 in each jaw. They are larger than the deciduous teeth and consist of four kinds of teeth. The four kinds are (1) incisors, (2) canines, (3) premolars, and (4) molars. Each jaw has 4 incisors, 2 canines, 4 premolars, and 6 molars. The following discussion describes the four kinds of permanent teeth. Their positions in the mouth are shown in the illustration *Kinds of teeth.*

Incisors are the chief biting teeth. They have a sharp, straight cutting edge. In most cases, incisors have one root. The central incisors of the lower jaw are the smallest permanent teeth.

Canines are used with the incisors to bite into food. They are also used to tear off pieces of food. The name *canines* comes from *canis,* the Latin word for *dog,* because they resemble some of a dog's teeth. They have a sharp, pointed edge and one root. Canines are also

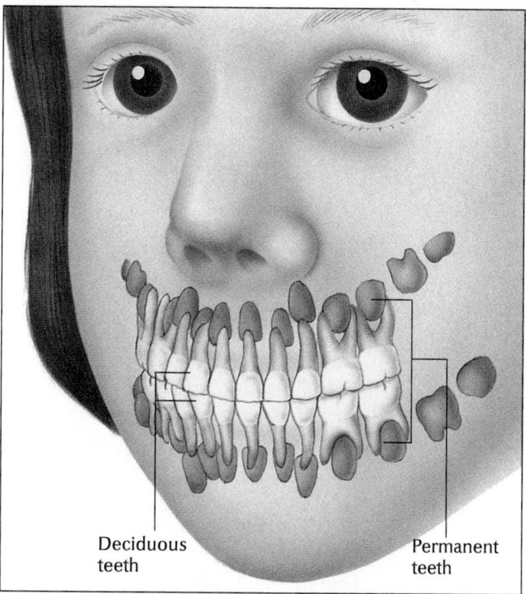

WORLD BOOK diagram by Charles Wellek

The teeth of a child. By the time a child is about 4 years old, most of the permanent teeth have formed within the jaws near the roots of the deciduous teeth. The deciduous teeth, all of which have erupted by about age 2, will gradually fall out and be replaced, one by one, by the permanent teeth.

Kinds of teeth

These illustrations show the kinds of deciduous and permanent teeth and their positions in the mouth.

WORLD BOOK diagrams by Charles Wellek

Deciduous teeth

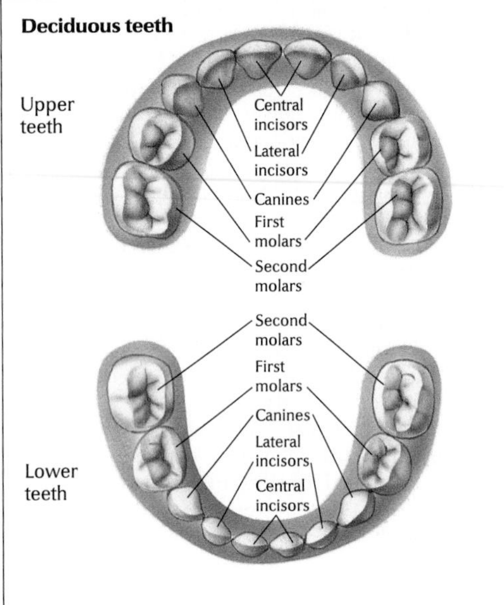

Permanent teeth

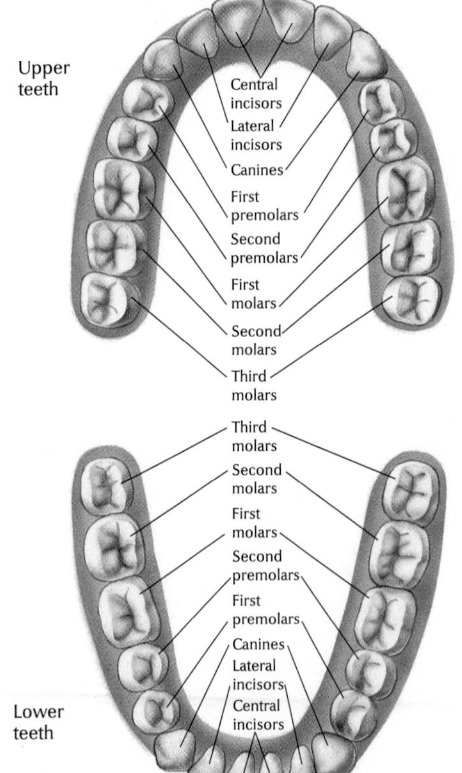

Ages at which teeth appear*

Deciduous teeth:	Lower teeth	Upper teeth
Central incisors	6 months	7 months
Lateral incisors	7 months	9 months
Canines	16 months	18 months
First molars	12 months	14 months
Second molars	20 months	24 months
Permanent teeth:	**Lower teeth**	**Upper teeth**
Central incisors	6-7 years	7-8 years
Lateral incisors	7-8 years	8-9 years
Canines	9-10 years	11-12 years
First premolars	10-12 years	10-11 years
Second premolars	11-12 years	10-12 years
First molars	6-7 years	6-7 years
Second molars	11-13 years	12-13 years
Third molars	17-21 years	17-21 years

*The ages given are approximate. In many cases, individual teeth may erupt at an earlier or later age.

called *cuspids* or *dogteeth.* The upper canines are sometimes known as *eyeteeth.*

Premolars are used to crush and grind food. They have a broad, lumpy top instead of a sharp biting edge. The small surface lumps are called *cusps.* The cusps enable the teeth to mash pieces of food.

Premolars are sometimes called *bicuspids* because, in most cases, they have two cusps. The prefix *bi* means *two.* The first upper premolars normally have two roots. The other premolars have one root. The premolars erupt in the place of the deciduous molars.

Molars, like premolars, are used to grind food. They are shaped much like premolars but are larger. The various molars normally have three to five cusps and two or three roots.

The permanent molars do not form beneath any of the deciduous teeth. They develop as the jaws grow, which makes space for them. Some adults lack one or more of the third molars, which are commonly called *wisdom teeth.* In many cases, the jaws do not grow large enough to provide space for the wisdom teeth. As a result, the wisdom teeth may become *impacted*—that is, wedged between the jawbone and another tooth. The wisdom teeth must then be removed.

Parts of a tooth

A tooth consists of four kinds of tissues. They are (1) pulp, (2) dentin, (3) enamel, and (4) cementum. Connective tissue surrounds the root of the tooth. This tissue, called the *periodontal ligament,* holds the root in the socket in the jaw.

Pulp is the innermost layer of a tooth. It consists of connective tissue, blood vessels, and nerves. The blood vessels nourish the tooth. The nerves transmit sensations of pain to the brain.

The pulp has two parts, the *pulp chamber* and the *root canal.* The pulp chamber lies in the crown of the tooth. The root canal lies in the root of the tooth. Blood vessels and nerves enter the root canal through a small hole at the tip of the root. They extend through the root canal and into the pulp chamber.

Dentin is a hard, yellow substance that surrounds the pulp. It makes up most of a tooth. Dentin is harder than bone. It consists mainly of mineral salts and water but also has some living cells.

Parts of a tooth

The *crown,* or visible part of a molar tooth, includes projections called *cusps.* The *root* extends into the bone of the jaw. A tissue called *dentin* makes up most of the tooth. A layer of *enamel* covers the dentin of the crown, and *cementum* overlies the dentin of the root. Within the dentin lies the *pulp,* including the *pulp chamber* and the *root canal,* through which blood vessels and nerves enter the tooth. The *periodontal ligament* surrounds the root and holds the tooth in its socket.

WORLD BOOK diagram by Charles Wellek

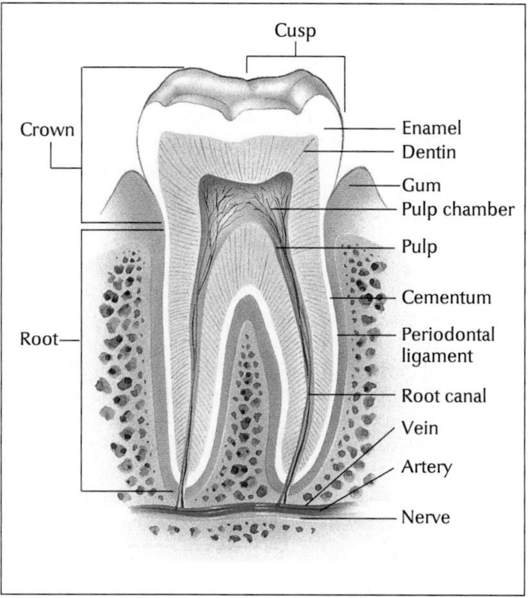

Enamel overlies the dentin in the crown of the tooth. It forms the outermost covering of the crown. Enamel is the hardest tissue in the body. It enables a tooth to withstand the pressure placed on it during chewing. Enamel consists of mineral salts and a small amount of water. Enamel is white but transparent. The yellow color of the dentin shows through the enamel, and so most teeth appear slightly yellowish.

As a person grows older, small amounts of enamel begin to wear away. This process, called *attrition,* results from the use of the teeth over a long period. As the enamel wears away, the dentin becomes exposed.

Cementum overlies the dentin in the root of the tooth. In most cases, the cementum and enamel meet where the root ends and the crown begins. As the surface of the tooth wears away, the tooth grows farther out of its socket, exposing the root. These areas may then become more sensitive to hot and cold liquids. Cementum is about as hard as bone. Like dentin and enamel, it consists mainly of mineral salts and water.

Periodontal ligament consists of small fibers. These fibers extend through the cementum and into the bony socket, which is called the *alveolus.* Besides anchoring the tooth in the alveolus, the periodontal ligament serves as a shock absorber during chewing.

Care of the teeth and gums

Most cases of tooth decay and gum disease could be prevented if people took proper care of their teeth and gums. Proper care requires (1) a good diet, (2) cleaning the teeth after eating, and (3) dental checkups.

A good diet. Dentists advise people to eat well-balanced meals. Such meals include a variety of foods and provide the *nutrients* (nourishing substances) needed by the teeth and gums. Nutrition experts divide foods into groups to help people plan well-balanced meals. The article **Nutrition** describes the Food Pyramid, developed by the U. S. Department of Agriculture (USDA). The pyramid shows the recommended number of daily servings of the major food groups in a healthful diet.

Dentists also urge people to eat fewer sugary foods because these foods contribute to tooth decay. Bacteria in the mouth digest sugar and produce an acid as a result. The acid dissolves tooth enamel, forming a cavity.

Foods that have a large amount of sugar include candies, pastries, most breakfast cereals, and sweetened canned fruits. Many people eat sugary foods as snacks. In place of sugary foods, dentists advise people to snack on such foods as fresh fruits and vegetables, cheeses, and nuts. They also recommend that people drink skim milk or unsweetened fruit and vegetable juices instead of soft drinks and other sugar-sweetened beverages.

Dentists further recommend that children drink water with chemical compounds called *fluorides.* Fluorides are absorbed by the enamel as the teeth grow. They help the teeth resist acid that forms cavities. Some communities have a water supply that naturally contains fluorides. Many other communities add fluorides to the water supply. But some people oppose *fluoridation* (the addition of fluorides to water supplies). For information on the arguments, see **Fluoridation**.

Fluorides may be applied directly to a child's teeth during a dental checkup. In some cases, dentists prescribe a fluoride substance that children can apply at home. Most dentists also advise children to brush their teeth with a toothpaste that contains fluorides.

Cleaning the teeth. Dentists advise people to clean their teeth by brushing after every meal and by using *dental floss* once a day. Dental floss is a thin thread that comes in a roll. It is used to clean the areas between teeth and under the gum line. Brushing and flossing remove trapped food particles and *plaque* from the teeth. Plaque is a sticky film that consists of saliva, food particles, and bacteria. The bacteria digest certain foods, particularly sugars, and form an enamel-dissolving acid.

To brush the teeth, you should use a small, soft toothbrush and a toothpaste that contains fluorides. There are several methods of brushing. You should use the one recommended by your dentist. One commonly recommended method is to place the brush against the teeth at a slight angle, with the bristles pointed toward the gums. Brush the upper teeth with a downward, sweeping motion. Brush the lower teeth with an upward, sweeping motion. Clean both the outside and the inside surfaces of the teeth in this way. Use a scrubbing motion to clean the biting surfaces of the premolars and molars. Lastly, brush the tongue to remove food particles and bacteria, which contribute to bad mouth odors. Then rinse the mouth thoroughly with water or mouthwash.

To floss the teeth, cut a piece of floss about 18 inches (46 centimeters) long from the roll. Wrap one end of the floss around each middle finger. Using the index fingers and thumbs, gently guide the floss between two teeth.

Then pull the floss up and down, cleaning the sides of both teeth and the areas around the gum line. Repeat this procedure on all the teeth.

Some people use *disclosing tablets* to see if any areas of the teeth remain unclean after brushing and flossing. Disclosing tablets contain a red or purple dye. When you chew a tablet, the dye sticks to unclean areas of the teeth. You can then rebrush and refloss these spots.

Dental checkups. Dentists advise people to have a dental checkup at least once a year. Children should start going to a dentist after all their deciduous teeth have erupted. Dentists can recognize and treat diseases of the teeth and gums at an early stage, before the diseases cause serious damage. Dentists also provide services that help prevent diseases of the teeth and gums. Many dentists employ a licensed *dental hygienist* to help them in their work.

During a checkup, the dentist looks at the teeth, gums, and other tissues inside the mouth for signs of diseases. The dentist—or the dental hygienist—also may X-ray the teeth. X rays can show the location of dental decay that cannot be seen. They also show any abnormal conditions of the jawbones and other tissues that support the teeth. Based on the examination, the dentist may decide to fill cavities or plan other treatment. The dentist or hygienist then cleans the teeth to remove plaque and *calculus,* a hard, yellowish substance formed by the buildup of plaque. Calculus is also called *tartar.* After the teeth have been cleaned, a fluoride substance is applied to help the teeth resist decay. Generally, only children and teen-agers receive applications of fluorides. Lastly, the dentist or hygienist may instruct the patient on how to brush and floss the teeth properly.

Diseases and defects of the teeth

Dental decay, also called *caries,* is the most common disease of the teeth. Most people under the age of 35 who lose their teeth do so because of dental decay. A defect in the position of the teeth, called *malocclusion,* is also a common problem among young people. Diseases of the gums and alveolus, called *periodontal diseases,* are the chief dental problem of people over the age of 35. A less common but very severe disease is *oral cancer,* which kills about 8,000 people in the United States each year. The following discussion describes the causes and treatment of (1) dental decay, (2) malocclusion, (3) periodontal diseases, and (4) oral cancer.

Dental decay is a complex process that involves plaque, bacteria, and food. Saliva produces an invisible film on the teeth. Bacteria and food particles stick to this film, forming plaque. The bacteria digest the *carbohydrates* (sugars and starches) in food and produce an acid. The acid dissolves enamel, causing a cavity. If the cavity is not treated, the decay will progress through the enamel and into the dentin. When the decay reaches the pulp, a toothache results.

The *occlusal* (biting) surfaces of the premolars and molars tend to decay easily because they have many small pits, which trap food. This type of decay may be prevented in deep pits by applying a *surface sealant.*

How to brush your teeth Use a small, soft toothbrush and a toothpaste that contains fluorides. Place the brush against the teeth at a slight angle, with the bristles pointed toward the gums. These illustrations show one of the brushing methods commonly recommended by dentists.

WORLD BOOK diagrams by Charles Wellek

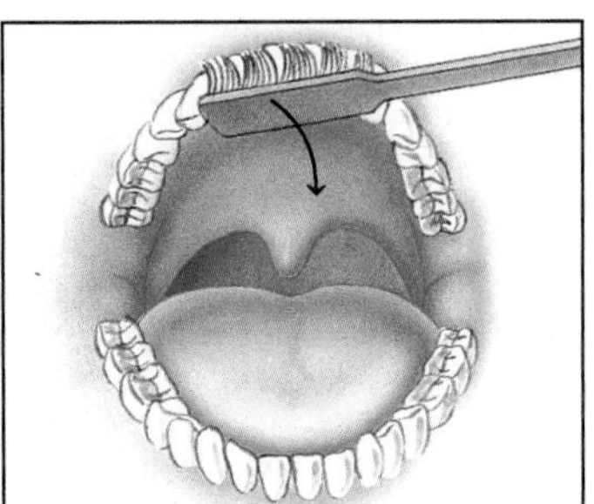

Outside surfaces of upper teeth. Use a downward, sweeping motion.

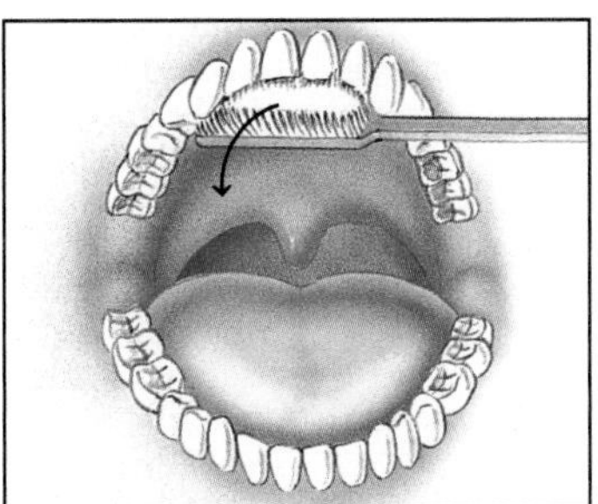

Inside surfaces of upper teeth. Use a downward, sweeping motion.

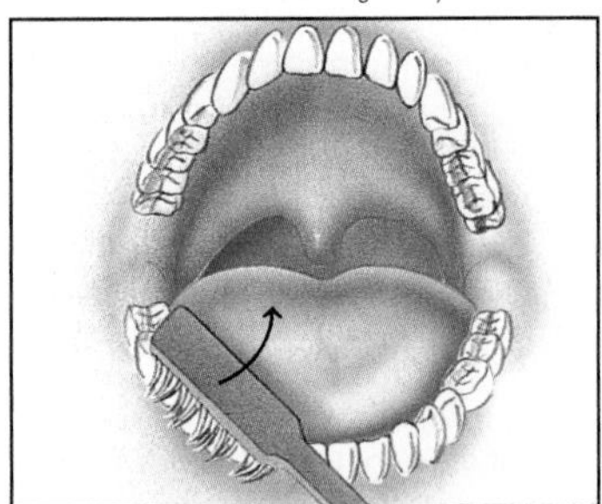

Outside surfaces of lower teeth. Use an upward, sweeping motion.

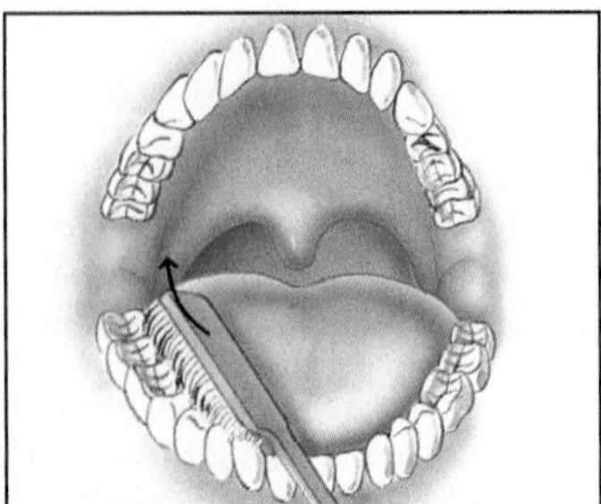

Inside surfaces of lower teeth. Use an upward, sweeping motion.

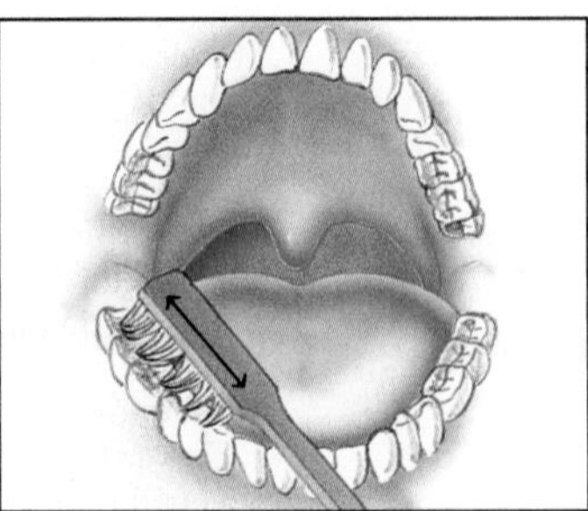

Biting surfaces of premolars and molars. Scrub back and forth.

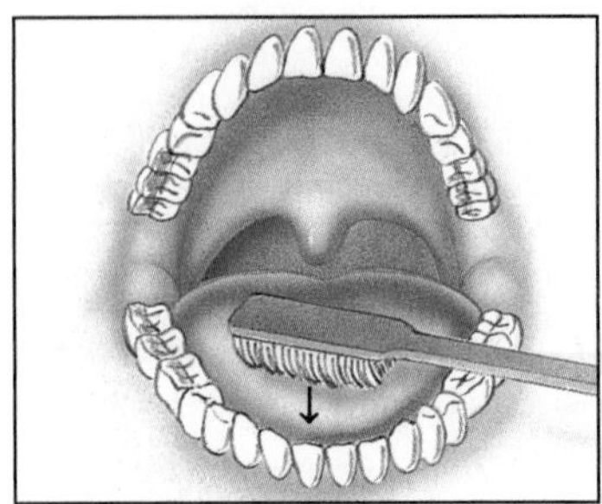

The tongue. Brush to remove food particles and bacteria.

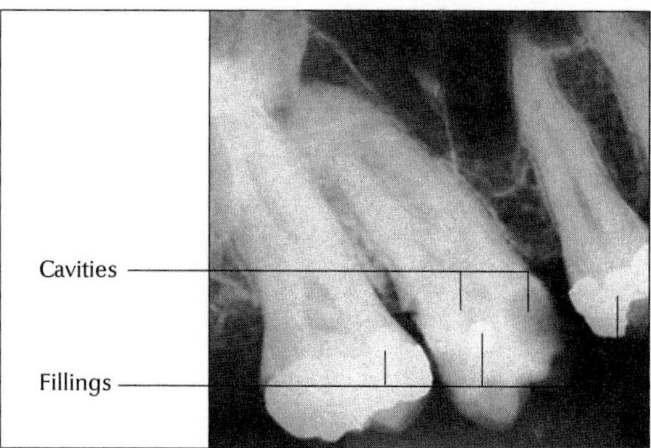

Patrick D. Toto

An X ray of the teeth shows cavities and fillings. Cavities appear as dark spots. Fillings show up as distinct white areas.

The sealant is a plasticlike material and is bonded to the occlusal surface.

Dentists have several methods of treating dental decay, depending on the severity. The most common methods include (1) filling a cavity, (2) performing root canal therapy, (3) crowning a tooth, and (4) removing and replacing teeth. Before beginning any of these procedures, the dentist usually injects an *anesthetic* (painkilling drug) into the gums near the nerves of the tooth. In some procedures, *electronic anesthesia* may be used. This technique sends gentle electronic impulses to the brain through *electrodes* (conductors) positioned in the mouth. These impulses block pain signals. The patient uses a handheld remote control unit to increase or decrease the amount of anesthesia.

Filling a cavity. To fill a cavity, the dentist first removes the decayed and soft parts of the tooth, using small hand instruments, a laser, or an air-powered or electric drill. The dentist then makes tiny undercuts or ledges in the hole. These undercuts help hold the filling, which is not adhesive. The filling is packed into the hole and allowed to harden slightly. The dentist then carves the filling to restore the original shape of the tooth. In most cases, dentists fill cavities with *silver amalgam* or gold. Silver amalgam consists of a mixture of silver and mercury and a small amount of copper and tin. Another method of filling cavities uses a plasticlike *resin* that is shaded to match the tooth color. This method is particularly useful in repairing decay or breaks in the front teeth. After any decay has been removed, a small amount of dilute acid is applied to the area to be filled. The acid etches or grooves the surrounding enamel surface and is left in place for about one minute. The acid is then rinsed off with water and the area is dried. The resin is then applied to the etched area and formed into the shape of the cavity or break. After hardening, the resin is shaped and polished with a drill.

Performing root canal therapy. Root canal therapy is the removal of the pulp of a tooth. It is performed if the pulp has become infected. When decay extends into the pulp, a small sac of pus, called an *abscess,* may form. An abscess can be extremely painful. If it is not treated, infection may spread to other parts of the body.

To perform root canal therapy, the dentist first anesthetizes the area and then drills a hole into the crown of the tooth. The dentist uses small files to reach through the hole and clean out the pulp. After removing the pulp, the dentist fills the empty space, usually with a rubberlike substance called *gutta-percha.* Sometimes, the hole in the crown of the tooth is then filled. But in the majority of cases, the tooth must be fitted with an artificial crown.

Crowning a tooth. Crowns are toothlike caps that may be made of metal, porcelain, or plastic. They are used when the natural crown is so badly damaged that it does not have enough healthy tissue to hold a filling.

To crown a tooth, the dentist first anesthetizes the area and then prepares the natural crown by grinding it down slightly. Next, the dentist covers the prepared tooth and the teeth next to it with a jellylike material. After this material hardens, it is removed from the patient's mouth and serves as an *impression* (mold). The dentist also makes an impression of the teeth in the opposite jaw that press against the prepared tooth and the teeth next to it. The impressions are used to make a plaster reproduction of the prepared tooth and other teeth. Dental technicians then produce a crown, using the plaster reproduction as a model. They must make sure that the crown not only fits the prepared tooth but also fits in place with the other teeth.

Meanwhile, a temporary crown is placed on the tooth. When the permanent crown is ready, the dentist

Filling a cavity

These illustrations show how a dentist fills a cavity. The dentist usually begins by injecting a drug called an *anesthetic* into the gums near the tooth. The anesthetic prevents the patient from feeling the pain that drilling might produce.

WORLD BOOK diagrams by Charles Wellek

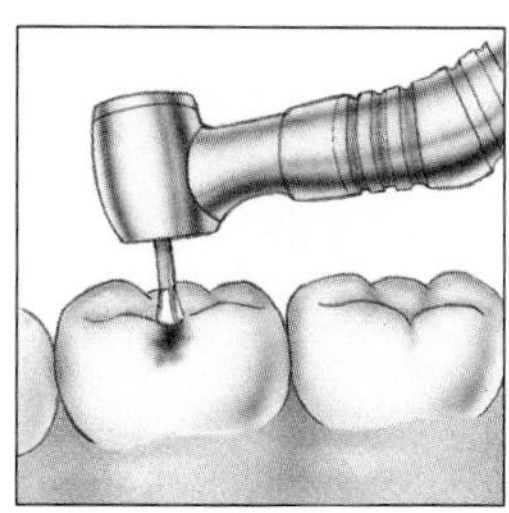

Drilling. The dentist uses a drill to remove decayed and soft parts of the tooth and to form undercuts or ledges that will help hold the filling.

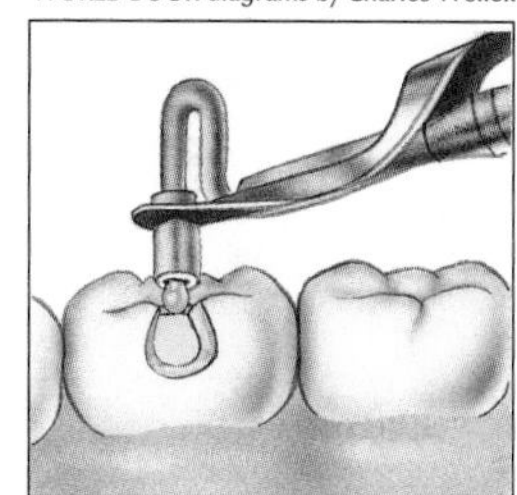

Filling. An instrument is used to place filling material into the hole. Silver amalgam, made from silver, copper, and tin, is a commonly used filling.

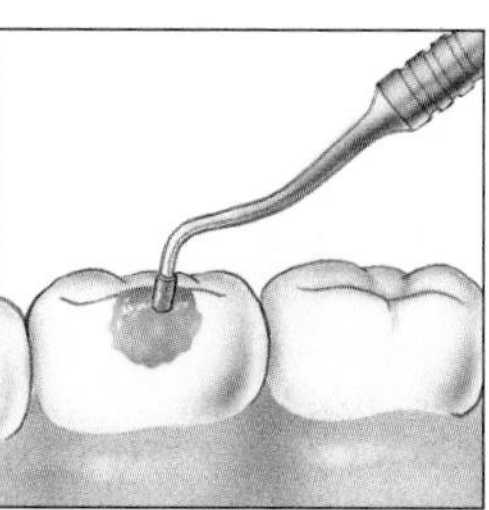

Packing. Using another instrument, the dentist firmly packs the filling into the hole. The filling is then allowed to harden slightly.

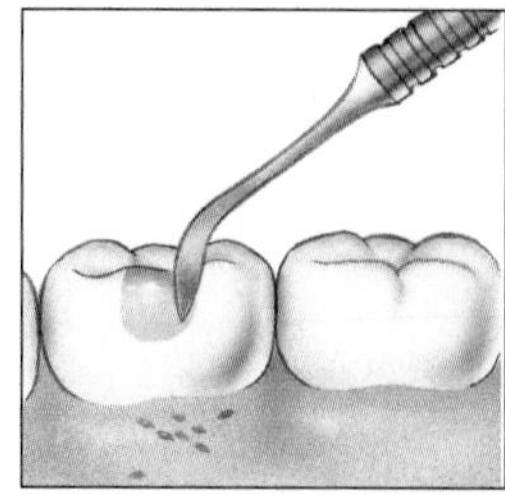

Shaping. The dentist carefully carves the filling to restore the original shape of the tooth. Finally, any rough edges are smoothed down.

removes the temporary crown and cements the permanent one onto the tooth.

Crowns can also be made by a computerized method that eliminates the need for impressions and plaster models. This method is called *computer-aided design and computer-aided manufacturing* (CAD/CAM). The dentist uses an optical probe system to record electronic images of the tooth. This information is entered into a computer, which designs an electronic model of the tooth. The design is then transferred through the computer to the head of a cutting tool, which prepares the crown to exactly fit the tooth.

If a tooth is only slightly damaged, a dentist may cover the tooth with thin porcelain sheets called *veneers.* The veneers are made to match the shape and color of a tooth and are bonded to the tooth using a cementlike material. They are used primarily to improve the appearance of front teeth.

Removing and replacing teeth. In severe cases of dental decay, a dentist may remove one or more teeth and replace them with artificial ones. But artificial teeth do not function as well as natural teeth. Dentists therefore remove teeth only if no other method of treatment is considered possible. To remove a tooth, a dentist first anesthetizes the area. The dentist uses an instrument that resembles a pliers to grip the crown of the tooth and loosen the root from the socket. Both the crown and the root are then removed. After the gums heal, the patient can be fitted with an artificial tooth.

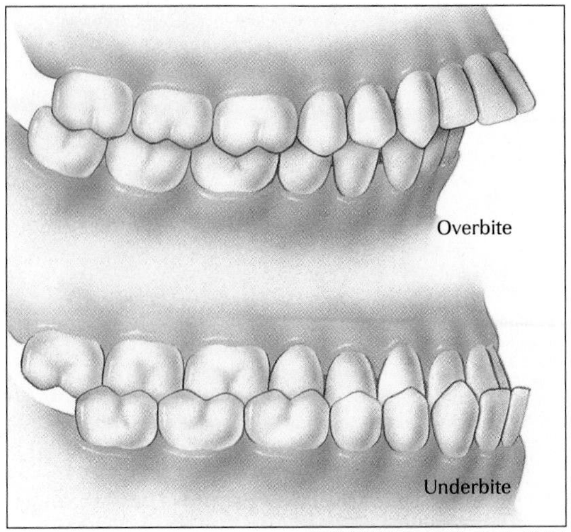

WORLD BOOK diagrams by Charles Wellek

Malocclusion is the failure of the upper and lower teeth to meet properly when a person bites. Two kinds of malocclusions are *overbite* and *underbite.* In overbite, the upper front teeth stick out farther than normal over the lower ones. In underbite, the lower front teeth extend in front of the upper ones.

Crowning a tooth

A crown is a toothlike cap made of metal, porcelain, or plastic, which is cemented onto a damaged tooth. It is used when a tooth does not have enough healthy tissue to hold a filling.

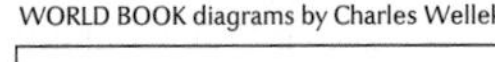

WORLD BOOK diagrams by Charles Wellek

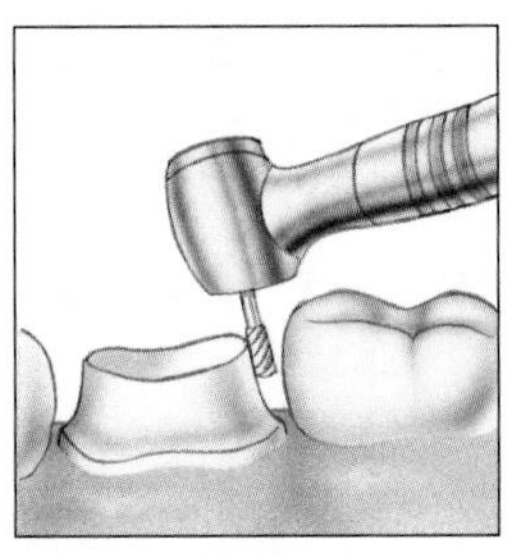

Preparing the tooth. The dentist uses a drill to remove damaged parts of the tooth and to shape the tooth so that a crown will fit over it.

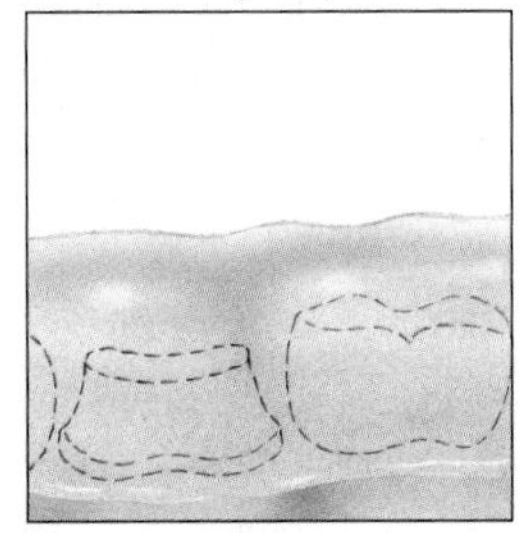

Making a mold. The teeth are covered with a gel that forms a mold. Plaster teeth made in this mold serve as models for making the crown.

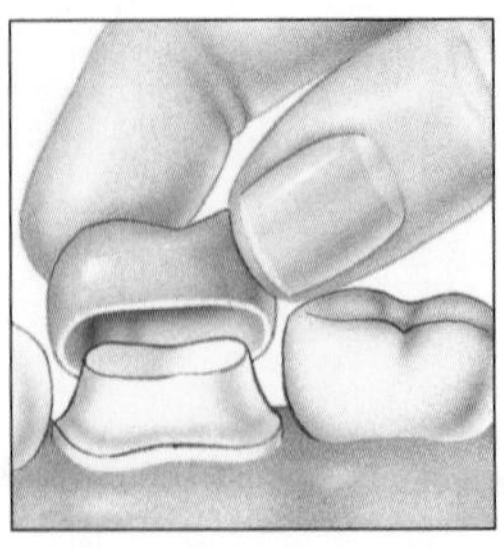

Cementing the crown. The crown must fit the prepared tooth and also fit in place with the teeth next to it and those in the opposite jaw.

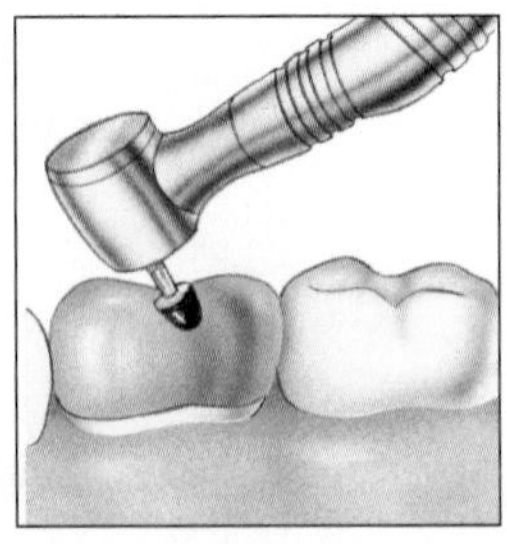

Final fitting. The dentist may use a small grinding stone to make minor adjustments in the crown so that it will fit properly.

Artificial teeth are made from impressions taken of the patient's mouth. In most cases, the teeth are made of plastic. The most common types of artificial teeth are *bridges, partial dentures,* and *full dentures.* Bridges are permanently fixed in the mouth, but partial dentures and full dentures are removable. Bridges are used when only a few teeth are missing. They consist of one or more artificial teeth with a metal or porcelain crown on each side. The crowns fit over the adjoining natural teeth, which must be prepared to hold the crowns. Partial dentures are also used to replace only a few missing teeth. A partial denture has metal clasps that hook around nearby teeth and hold the denture in place. Full dentures are used when all the teeth of one or both jaws are missing. In a full denture, the artificial teeth are attached to a plastic base that fits over the ridge left after the teeth have been removed. In the upper jaw, the plastic base also covers the roof of the mouth.

Another method of replacing one or more missing teeth involves the use of *dental implants.* In the most common implant procedure, metal or ceramiclike cylinders, called *fixtures* or *root forms,* are surgically implanted in the area of the jaw where the teeth are missing. After the area has healed, artificial teeth are permanently attached to the root forms. Implants cannot be used if the jaw area is severely damaged.

Malocclusion is the failure of the teeth in the upper and lower jaws to meet properly when a person bites. Normally, the upper front teeth should slightly overlap the lower front teeth. There are three main types of malocclusions, *overbite, underbite,* and *crowding.* In overbite, the upper front teeth stick out too far over the lower front teeth. This defect is commonly called *buck teeth.* In underbite, the lower front teeth extend in front

How braces work Braces consist of a system of metal brackets and wires. The brackets are bonded to the front surface of each tooth and connected by wires, *left.* A spring wire is tightened periodically, forcing the irregularly positioned tooth to move. In time, the tooth moves into its correct position, *right.*

WORLD BOOK diagrams by Charles Wellek

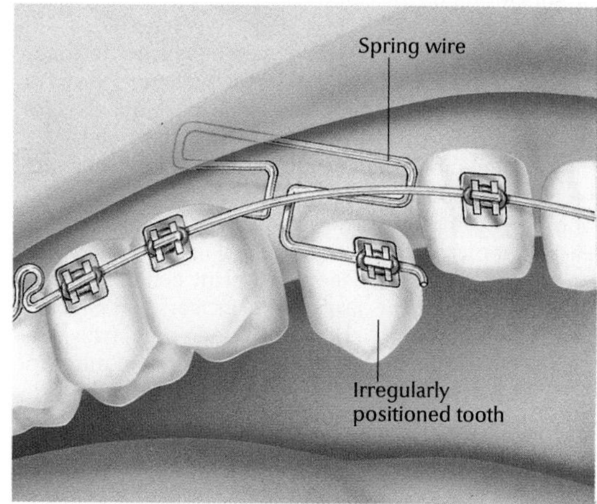

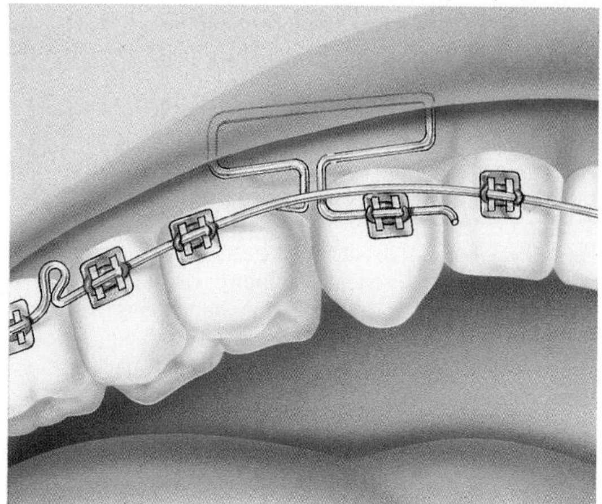

of the upper ones. Many people have the correct *occlusion* (bite), but their teeth are crowded. Crowding is the most common malocclusion.

Malocclusion has various causes. In some cases, a deciduous tooth falls out before a permanent tooth is ready to erupt. The nearby teeth then gradually move into the open space and prevent the permanent tooth from erupting in the correct position. In other cases, the permanent teeth are too large for the jaw and crowd one another. The edges of some teeth may then overlap, or one tooth may grow above another. In still other cases, the jaws do not grow properly.

Malocclusion prevents the teeth from functioning normally when a person chews food. It also may affect the way a person speaks. In addition, malocclusion contributes to the development of dental decay and periodontal diseases, partly because irregularly positioned teeth are hard to clean.

Most cases of malocclusion can be corrected with *braces.* Braces consist of metal or clear ceramic brackets that are bonded on the front surface of each tooth and connected by wires. The wires are tightened periodically to force the teeth to move into the correct position. But the teeth must be moved slowly, and so the treatment may take a year or more. In some cases, one or more teeth must be removed to allow enough space for the others to move into a normal position.

Periodontal diseases are caused chiefly by the build-up of plaque and calculus between the gums and teeth. The plaque and calculus irritate the gums, causing them to become inflamed. In time, the jawbones may become infected. The best way to prevent plaque from building up under the gum line is by flossing daily. The gums can also become irritated by habitually breathing through the mouth, smoking or chewing tobacco, brushing improperly, or wearing ill-fitting dentures. Irregularly positioned teeth can also irritate the gums.

There are three main kinds of periodontal diseases. They are (1) gingivitis, (2) periodontitis, and (3) Vincent's infection.

Gingivitis is an inflammation of the *gingivae* (gums). The gingivae become red and swollen and bleed easily when brushed or prodded. Dentists treat gingivitis by cleaning the teeth and gums to remove plaque and calculus. They also instruct patients on how to brush and floss the teeth and on how to massage the gums. If gingivitis is not treated, it can lead to periodontitis.

Periodontitis, also called *pyorrhea,* is a severe infection of the gingivae, alveolus, and other tissues that support the teeth. The infection gradually destroys the bony walls of the sockets, and the teeth become loose. Periodontitis is difficult to cure, but it can be effectively controlled. Treatment involves surgical or nonsurgical removal of the damaged tissues and repair of the remaining healthy tissues. Some dentists use the heat of a beam from a laser to remove infected tissue. The laser process may quicken healing because it does little

Periodontal diseases

These illustrations show two kinds of periodontal diseases. In *gingivitis,* calculus builds up between gums and teeth, causing the gums to become inflamed. Gingivitis may lead to *periodontitis,* an infection that gradually destroys the bony socket.

WORLD BOOK diagrams by Charles Wellek

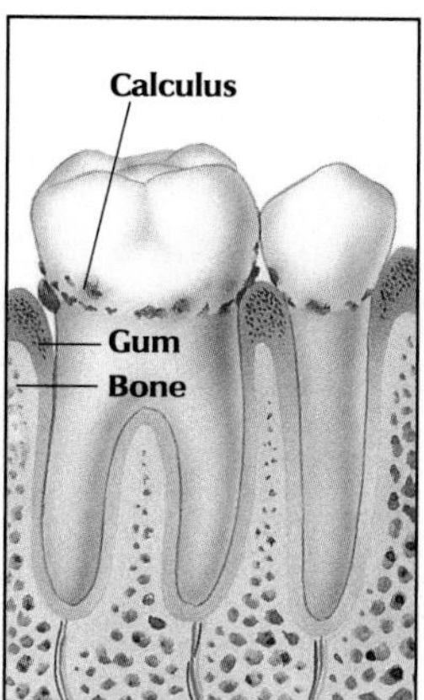

Gingivitis

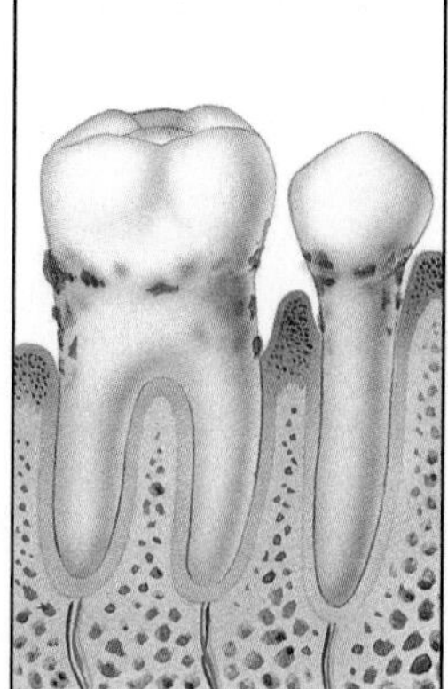

Periodontitis

damage to the surrounding healthy area. Sometimes, loose teeth can be *splinted* (attached) to nearby teeth that are still firm. But in many cases, the loose teeth must be removed and replaced by artificial ones.

Vincent's infection, also called *trench mouth,* is a painful infection of the gingivae. The gums become red and swollen and bleed easily. The mouth has an extremely bad odor, and the victim may develop a fever. To treat Vincent's infection, a dentist cleans the teeth and gums thoroughly and instructs the patient on mouth care. In most cases, the dentist also prescribes antibiotics to combat the infection.

Oral cancer is a disease that destroys the tissues of the mouth and may spread to other parts of the body. Scientists do not know for certain what causes oral cancer. But many factors can contribute to its development. For example, people who smoke or chew tobacco or drink excessive amounts of alcoholic beverages increase the risk of developing oral cancer.

Oral cancer may be painless and unnoticeable in its early stages. The first symptom may be a small sore in the mouth that does not heal. To test for cancer, a dentist removes some tissue from the sore. The tissue is examined under a microscope to determine if it is cancerous. Oral cancer may be treated with drugs, radiation, or surgery.

Teeth of animals

Many kinds of animals have teeth. However, birds, toads, turtles, and some types of insects and whales do not have teeth.

Cats, dogs, and most other mammals have *heterodont teeth*—that is, they have at least two types of teeth, which have different uses. For example, they may have incisors for biting into food and molars for crushing or grinding food.

The teeth of various kinds of mammals differ in shape and size, depending chiefly on what the animals eat. For example, plant-eating mammals, such as elephants, giraffes, and sheep, have unusually broad, flat molars. They use the molars to chew and mash plants. Meat-eating mammals, such as lions, tigers, and wolves, have long, pointed canines. They use the canines to rip and tear the bodies of their prey.

Some mammals have teeth that grow continuously. The tusks of elephants are actually incisors that have become very long. The tusks have an open pulp, which enables them to keep growing. Beavers, rats, and other rodents also have teeth that grow continuously. But most of the growth is worn down by continual use of the teeth, and so the teeth of these animals do not lengthen greatly.

Unlike most mammals, many fish and most reptiles have *homodont teeth*—that is, all their teeth are about the same size and shape and have only one use. In general, animals that have homodont teeth use their teeth to catch prey. Fish and reptiles lose and replace their teeth continuously.

Snakes have teeth that curve back toward the throat. Snakes swallow their prey whole and use their teeth to pull the prey back into the throat. In poisonous snakes, certain teeth have a canal or a groove, through which

Some animal teeth Animal teeth vary in size and shape. Most mammals have *heterodont teeth,* which consist of two or more types: incisors and canines for biting and tearing food, and molars for crushing it. Most reptiles and many fish have *homodont teeth,* a single type that generally is used to catch prey.

WORLD BOOK diagrams by Patricia J. Wynne

Heterodont teeth

Incisors
Lion
Molars
Canines
Molars
Incisors
Elephant
Bison
Molars
Incisors

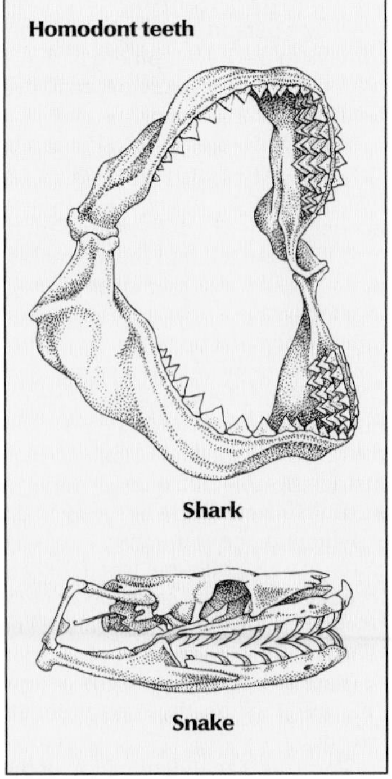

poison can be ejected. The poison comes from glands in the roof of the mouth. John P. Wortel

Related articles in *World Book* include:

Human teeth

Abscess	Mouth
Dental hygiene	Orthodontics
Dentistry	Periodontitis
Fluoridation	Saliva
Fluorine	Toothpaste and toothpowder
Mastication	Trench mouth

Animal teeth

Animal (Teeth and jaws)	Hog (Teeth)
Beaver (Teeth)	Horse (Teeth)
Cat (The body of a cat)	Insect (Mouthparts)
Cattle (Teeth)	Lion (The body of a lion)
Dog (Body structure)	Mammal (What mammals eat)
Elephant (Tusks and teeth)	Rodent
Evolution (picture: The evolution of mammals from reptiles)	Ruminant
	Shark (Teeth and scales)
	Snake (Skeleton)
Hippopotamus (The body of a river hippopotamus)	Whale (picture)

Outline

I. Kinds of teeth
- A. Deciduous teeth
- B. Permanent teeth

II. Parts of a tooth
- A. Pulp
- B. Dentin
- C. Enamel
- D. Cementum
- E. Periodontal ligament

III. Care of the teeth and gums
- A. A good diet
- B. Cleaning the teeth
- C. Dental checkups

IV. Diseases and defects of the teeth
- A. Dental decay
- B. Malocclusion
- C. Periodontal diseases
- D. Oral cancer

V. Teeth of animals

Questions

How often should the teeth be brushed?
What are the incisors and canines used for?
What are the four kinds of tissues that make up a tooth?
When should children start going to a dentist?
What are some of the causes of malocclusion?
When does dental decay result in a toothache?
How does eating foods that have a large amount of sugar contribute to dental decay?
What is dental floss used for?
What is the chief cause of periodontal diseases?
Why do most teeth appear slightly yellowish?

Additional resources

Level I

McGinty, Alice B. *Staying Healthy: Dental Care.* Rosen Pub., 1997.
Royston, Angela. *Healthy Teeth.* Heinemann Lib., 2003.
Silverstein, Alvin, and others. *Tooth Decay and Cavities.* Watts, 1999.

Level II

Diamond, Richard. *Dental First Aid for Families.* Idyll Arbor, 2000.
Serio, Francis G. *Understanding Dental Health.* Univ. Pr. of Miss., 1998.
Siegel, Dorothy S. *Dental Health.* Chelsea Hse., 1993.

Teflon is a trade name for *polytetrafluoroethylene,* a type of *synthetic* (artificially made) material that is used in cookware, insulation, and many other products. It is manufactured by the DuPont Company, and the name *Teflon* is a registered trademark of DuPont. Roy J. Plunkett, an American chemist, invented this material in 1938.

Teflon is a *polymer,* a substance consisting of long, chainlike molecules. Each molecule is made up of a chain of tens of thousands of carbon atoms, with each carbon atom also connected to two fluorine atoms. Teflon is *inert*—that is, it does not react with most other chemicals. It also resists moisture and remains stable in extreme heat and cold. It feels slippery to the touch, and adhesive materials will not stick to it. Dorothy M. Feigl

Tegucigalpa, *teh GOO see GAHL pah* or *tuh GOO sih GAL puh* (pop. 624,542), is the capital and largest city of Honduras. It lies along the Choluteca River in the south-central part of the country (see **Honduras** [map]).

The oldest parts of Tegucigalpa lie on the slopes of Mount Picacho, north of the Choluteca River. Neighborhoods in this area are characterized by narrow brick streets and buildings that date from the 1800's. Since the mid-1900's, many office buildings, banks, and hotels have been built near the Plaza Morazán, also called Parque Central. Important downtown buildings include the National Cathedral and the Presidential Palace. The National University lies outside of Tegucigalpa.

Manufacturing plants and government agencies employ many of Tegucigalpa's people. Chief products include textiles and processed foods and beverages.

Tegucigalpa was founded by Spaniards in 1578. In 1880, it replaced Comayagua as the capital. In 1938, Comayaguela, a city south of the Choluteca River, merged with Tegucigalpa. In 1998, sections of Tegucigalpa were heavily damaged by floods and landslides caused by Hurricane Mitch. Neale J. Pearson

See also **Honduras** (picture).

Teheran. See Tehran.

Tehran, *teh RAHN* (pop. 6,758,845), also spelled *Teheran,* is the capital of Iran and the second largest city in the Middle East. Only Cairo, the capital of Egypt, has more people. Tehran is Iran's cultural, economic, and political center. It lies in northern Iran, at the foot of the Elburz Mountains. For location, see **Iran** (map).

The city. Tehran has many wide boulevards lined with tall, modern buildings of Western-style architecture. The major business and government buildings are near the center of the city. In the same area is an old business section where merchants sell fabrics, jewelry, and other handmade products at a bazaar that is hundreds of years old.

Most of Tehran's middle-class residents live in apartment buildings. Large numbers of poor people live in run-down apartments and houses in the southern part of Tehran.

Tehran has many parks and theaters. Its museums include the Archaeological and Ethnological museums and the Golestan Palace, which feature many treasures from Iran's past. The city has several universities, the largest of which is the University of Tehran.

Economy. The Iranian government employs many of Tehran's people. The city's industries include banking, construction, and petroleum processing. Its factories make bricks, cigarettes, textiles, and other products.

Buses and taxis provide public transportation in Tehran. An international airport lies west of the city.

History. People probably lived on the site of what is now Tehran at least 3,000 years ago. Tehran was a small town until the 1200's, when it began to grow. The city became the capital of Iran in 1788.

During the 1920's, many of Tehran's old buildings were torn down and replaced by new ones. Between 1960 and 1980, the population increased by about 4 mil-

© Michael Coyne

A bazaar in Tehran attracts many people. It lies in the old business section, near the center of the city. Tehran is the capital of Iran and the second largest city in the Middle East.

lion. This rapid growth caused a number of problems, including a housing shortage, pollution, and traffic jams. Since the 1970's, a number of residential and office buildings have been built in the city. Since the 1980's, however, tough economic conditions in Iran have resulted in a dramatic decline in the standard of living of many of Tehran's people. Michel Le Gall

See also **Iran** (picture: A boulevard in Tehran).

Tehran Conference was the first meeting of the main Allied leaders during World War II. These leaders, called the Big Three, were Prime Minister Winston Churchill of the United Kingdom, President Franklin Delano Roosevelt of the United States, and Premier Joseph Stalin of the Soviet Union. The meeting was also the first summit conference involving the heads of the Soviet Union and the United States. It took place from Nov. 28 to Dec. 1, 1943, in Tehran, Iran's capital.

The two main military decisions made at the conference were that the United States and the United Kingdom would launch an invasion of France in 1944 and that the Soviet Union would enter the war against Japan after Germany's defeat. The leaders also discussed plans for creating a United Nations organization, for dividing and disarming Germany, and for moving Poland's borders westward after the war. The Polish-Soviet border would be redrawn to add territory to the Soviet Union that had been part of Russia before World War I began in 1914. The cooperative spirit of the conference paved the way for later agreements among the Allied war leaders at the Yalta Conference in 1945. Diane Shaver Clemens

Teilhard de Chardin, *TAY YAR duh SHAR DAN,* **Pierre** (1881-1955), was a French *paleontologist* (expert on prehistoric life). He helped discover the Peking fossils, the remains of an early type of human being. But his greatest fame rests on his attempt to integrate evolutionary theory and Christian revelation. According to Teilhard, the universe evolves toward the fullness of Christ, who is the *Omega,* or end point of the cosmic process.

Teilhard entered the Jesuit order in 1899 and was ordained a priest in 1911. He lectured at the Catholic Institute in Paris. His view of the Roman Catholic doctrine of original sin in light of evolution was not considered to be sufficiently orthodox. Thus, church authorities forbade him to continue teaching in Paris. Teilhard lived in China from 1923 to 1946, where he was a consultant to the National Geological Survey. He began his fossil research in 1923. He wrote extensively in China. Since most of his writings were controversial, they were not published until after his death.

Teilhard's thought influenced some of those who attended Vatican Council II. He insisted on dialogue between the Catholic tradition and modern science and culture. This view is reflected in the council's *Pastoral Constitution on the Church in the Modern World.* Since his death, Teilhard's views have been criticized by scientists and theologians for being too speculative and optimistic. His best-known works, both published after his death, are *The Phenomenon of Man* (1955) and *The Divine Milieu* (1957). Robert P. Imbelli

Tektite, *TEHK tyt,* is a rounded, glassy stone that may resemble a ball, disk, rod, button, dumbbell, or teardrop. Tektites have smooth, grooved, or pitted surfaces and range in color from jet-black to greenish or yellowish. Most tektites are peanut-sized and weigh about 0.1 ounce (3 grams). The largest known tektite weighs about 28 pounds (13 kilograms). The youngest tektites known, which formed about 750,000 years ago, are found scattered across Australia and Southeast Asia. Other major tektite fields occur in the southern and eastern United States and Cuba; the Czech Republic, Slovakia, and Austria; Côte d'Ivoire; and Libya.

Tektites' shapes suggest that they formed from molten rock flying through the air. But, their composition differs from that of volcanic glass. People once thought tektites were meteorites or volcanic material from the moon. Most scientists now believe tektites formed from globs of molten rock blasted from Earth by meteorite or comet impacts. Many tektite fields appear near impact craters, but scientists have had difficulty matching them with impact craters through precise dating. Mark Cloos

Tel Aviv, *TEHL uh VEEV* (pop. 357,400), is Israel's second largest city and chief commercial, financial, and industrial center. Only Jerusalem has more people. Tel Aviv is one of the most modern cities in the Middle East. It lies on the eastern shore of the Mediterranean Sea (see **Israel** [political map]).

The heart of Tel Aviv is a major downtown intersection called Dizengoff Circle. Fashionable shops and sidewalk cafes line the nearby streets. The 37-story Shalom Tower, Israel's tallest building, stands in the city's financial district, several blocks south of Dizengoff Circle. The southwestern section of the city was formerly a separate town called *Jaffa (Yafo* in Hebrew). Jaffa, an ancient port area that dates back to Biblical times, has many historic sites that have been restored by archaeologists. It also has many art galleries, cafes, restaurants, and nightclubs. Most of Tel Aviv's people live in apartment buildings.

Cultural attractions in Tel Aviv include the Museum Haaretz and the Tel Aviv Museum. Tel Aviv University is one of the city's several institutions of higher learning. Bar Ilan University is in Ramat Gan, a suburb of the city.

Tel Aviv is the center of Israel's chief manufacturing district. About half the nation's business companies are in the area. Their products include building materials, chemicals, clothing, electronic equipment, machine tools, and processed foods. The city is also the nation's leading center for banking, publishing, and trade.

In 1909, Jewish immigrants from Europe founded Tel

© Richard Dunoff, The Stock Market

Tel Aviv, Israel's chief commercial, financial, and industrial center, lies on the eastern shore of the Mediterranean Sea. Pleasure boats dock near modern buildings of the city.

Aviv northeast of Jaffa. Tel Aviv was administered as part of Jaffa at first, but it became a separate town in 1921. Tel Aviv grew rapidly as Jewish immigrants poured in, mainly from Europe. It became Israel's first capital when the nation was established in 1948. The capital was moved to Jerusalem in 1949, but the Israeli Ministry of Defense and many foreign embassies remained in Tel Aviv. Most government departments maintain offices in Tel Aviv. In 1950, Tel Aviv and Jaffa merged to form the city of Tel Aviv-Yafo. Tel Aviv-Yafo remains the official name, but the city is almost always called Tel Aviv.

Tel Aviv continued to grow rapidly in the 1950's and early 1960's. Its population reached about 392,100 in 1965 and then began to decline, but the suburban population continued to rise. The rapid growth of the Tel Aviv area resulted in such problems as air pollution, slums, and traffic jams. During the Persian Gulf War of 1991, Iraq fired about 25 missiles toward Tel Aviv. Several missiles and some falling debris struck residential areas in or around Tel Aviv. Two people were killed, and about 7,500 apartments were damaged. Bernard Reich

See also **Israel** (picture); **Jaffa.**

Telecommunications refers to communication across a distance by means of various types of equipment. Visual signaling with flags, lamps, or smoke was the earliest form of telecommunication. Today, the term most often refers to a wide variety of electrical and electronic communication systems that transmit information throughout the world. This information may include sound, images, or text, or any combination of these elements. It may be in either *analog* or *digital* format. Analog information uses signals that are exact reproductions of the sound or picture being sent. It is transmitted in the form of a wave. Digital information is a numeric code that represents sound, images, or text.

Most telecommunication systems transmit information through a wire or through the air. The earliest systems, beginning with the telegraph in the mid-1800's, sent messages over a wire. The coming of the telephone resulted in the creation of a vast network of telephone lines and cables. Use of the telephone network has expanded to applications beyond the transmission of sound. For example, a fax machine uses the telephone network to send copies of documents.

Modern telecommunication technologies have caused the world's telephone network to evolve into a vast computer network as well. Many smaller computer networks, such as those operated by businesses, are part of this global network. The network, called the Internet, carries information from millions of computer users in much the same way as a modern highway system carries automobile traffic. A device called a *modem* enables computer users to send digital information to one another over the telephone lines (see **Modem**).

Types of information sent through the air include television and radio broadcasts, both transmitted as radio waves. Cellular telephone communications use the same technology. Radio waves called *microwaves* transmit television signals and telephone communication signals over long distances. Communications satellites use microwaves to transmit telephone, television, and other communication signals worldwide. Don M. Gruenbacher

Related articles in *World Book* include:

Broadband communication
Cable
Cellular telephone
Coaxial cable
Communication (The development of electronics; The digital age)
Communications satellite
Computer
Digital technology
Electromagnetic waves
Electronics
Fax machine
Fiber optics
International Telecommunication Union
Internet
Microwave
Modem
Pager
Sony Corporation
Telegraph
Telemetry
Telephone
Television
Wireless communications
World Wide Web

Telegram. See Telegraph.

Telegraph was an important means of communication from the mid-1800's to the mid-1900's. The telegraph was the first instrument used to send messages by means of wires and electric current. Telegraph operators sent signals using a device that interrupted the flow of electric current along a wire. They used shorter and longer bursts of current, with spaces in between, to represent the letters of the message in what became known as *Morse code.* A device at the receiving end converted the signals to a series of clicks that a telegraph operator or a mechanical printer translated into words. The message was called a *telegram* if it was sent over wires stretched across land and a *cablegram,* or simply a *cable,* if it was sent through cables laid underwater.

Today, the original telegraph technology is rarely used. The telephone took the place of the telegraph for many uses. Other modern forms of communication, such as *e-mail* (electronic mail) and fax, can transmit more information more quickly than the telegraph could. Certain telegraph services still survive, however, though the means of sending messages differ from the original technology. Messages now begin and end in computers, and they travel great distances by fiber-optic cable, radio, satellites, and other means of transmission.

Development of the telegraph

Before the telegraph, most long-distance messages traveled no faster than the fastest horse. An exception was the *semaphore* method, in which a sequence of lights or other markers signaled from point to point. However, semaphore systems did not work well at night or in bad weather. Even in good weather, they could transmit only a small amount of information.

Early discoveries. The path to the telegraph began with discoveries that showed how electric current could be produced. In the 1780's, the Italian physician Luigi Galvani conducted experiments in animal physiology in which he unknowingly discovered *galvanism*—that is, the production of an electric current from two metals in contact with a moist environment. In the late 1790's, the Italian scientist Alessandro Volta used galvanism to create the first practical battery.

In 1820, Hans Christian Oersted, a Danish physicist, discovered that an electric current will cause a magnetized needle to move. This discovery about the relationship between electric currents and magnetism made possible the invention of the telegraph. An operator could send a message through a wire by varying the electric current. The movement of magnetized needles or of devices called *electromagnets* would show the variations in the current. Thus, an operator at the other end could receive and decode the message. In the decade following Oersted's discovery, a number of primitive telegraphic devices were created by inventors in the United Kingdom and other countries.

The English inventor William Sturgeon developed an early electromagnet in 1825. A few years later, the American physicist Joseph Henry greatly improved on Sturgeon's design. In 1830, Henry set up a crude telegraph using electromagnets that sent signals over more than 1 mile (1.6 kilometers) of wire. In 1837, he invented a device to boost the electrical signal along a wire when the signal became weak.

The most notable early device using electromagnets and needles was the one invented in England by William F. Cooke, an inventor, and Charles Wheatstone, a physicist. Cooke and Wheatstone created a telegraph that used five needles, each of which was connected to a separate wire, to transmit messages. Pulses of electric current caused two needles at a time to move and point to individual letters. Cook and Wheatstone patented their telegraph in England in 1837. They continued to develop their telegraph, eventually creating a version that used two wires and two needles. A later version used only one wire and one needle.

The Morse telegraph. The American inventor and painter Samuel F. B. Morse is credited with making the first practical telegraph in 1837. He received a U.S. patent for his telegraph in 1840. However, Morse's invention came after several decades of research by many people. He did not accomplish his feat alone.

Morse became interested in the telegraph in 1832. In November of that year he built his first model, which used a device called a *portrule* to turn the flow of electric current on and off at intervals. Morse also began work on a code for the telegraph, though not the code for which he is best known. His original code was based on the idea that a certain sequence of numbers would represent a word.

In 1835, Morse built a larger model that used an electromagnet to deflect a pencil suspended from a small picture frame. The pencil made short marks, called dots, or longer marks, called dashes, on a paper tape. The length of the marks was determined by the amount of electric current sent over a wire.

In 1836, Morse began to work with a chemistry professor named Leonard Gale. Gale helped Morse to improve the battery and the electromagnet in the telegraph so that electric current could be sent greater distances. Morse demonstrated this improved version of the telegraph on Sept. 2, 1837, sending a message over 1,700 feet (520 meters) of wire.

At that demonstration, Morse met machinist Alfred Vail, whose father agreed to help pay for further development of the telegraph. Later that year, Vail suggested that the dots and dashes represent letters rather than numbers. Vail assigned the simplest codes, such as one dot or one dash, to the most commonly used letters. Less frequently used letters have more complicated codes. For example, in Morse code the letter *e* is one dot, but the much more rarely used letter *x* is a dot, a dash, and two dots.

Vail also developed a sending and receiving device called a *key.* The key had a lever that the operator moved up and down to send signals. It also had a receiving device called a *sounder.* In the sounder, each burst of electric current caused an electromagnet to attract an iron bar called an *armature.* The armature struck the electromagnet and made a clicking noise that represented either a dot or a dash in Morse code. With each click, a pointed instrument attached to the armature marked the code on a strip of paper.

Construction and growth. In 1843, the U.S. Congress approved $30,000 for Morse to build a telegraph line from the Capitol in Washington, D.C., to Baltimore. The first demonstration of the line occurred on May 1, 1844, when the Whig Party met in Baltimore to nominate candidates for president and vice president. Vail, who

© Bradley Smith

Granger Collection

Radio Times Hulton Picture Library

The first telegraphs. Samuel Morse's first telegraph, *left,* patented in 1840, produced V-shaped marks on paper. Later, Morse developed a telegraph with a sounder to click out coded messages, *center.* Cooke and Wheatstone of England produced a telegraph in 1836 in which needles pointed to letters to spell out messages. A later version of their machine appears at the right.

was waiting at the end of the telegraph line near Baltimore, found out from the passengers on a train traveling from Baltimore to Washington that the Whig Party had nominated Henry Clay for president and Theodore Frelinghuysen for vice president. He telegraphed the message to Morse in Washington. The train later arrived, and its passengers confirmed the news. On May 24, 1844, Morse sat at a sending device in the Supreme Court chamber of the Capitol and sent the first official telegraph message, "What hath God wrought!"

A year after the demonstration of the Washington-to-Baltimore telegraph line, Morse formed the Magnetic Telegraph Company. The company controlled his telegraph patents. Morse licensed the patents to others, setting off a great wave of telegraph line construction.

The telegraph quickly became an important means of transmitting news. Six New York City newspapers founded the Associated Press in 1848 to share the expense of gathering news by telegraph. In 1849, a German businessman named Paul Julius Reuter began a service that used homing pigeons to carry stock-market quotations between the terminal points of the telegraph lines in Belgium and Germany. In 1851, he founded the news service Reuters in London to relay European financial news.

By 1851, the United States had more than 50 telegraph companies. Each one had short telegraph lines, and many lines were poorly built. As a result of faulty construction, lawsuits, and fierce competition, several companies went bankrupt. The public came to view the telegraph as unreliable. Delivery was unpredictable, many messages did not arrive, and rates were high.

Uses for the telegraph. Despite poor service and high rates, many new uses for the telegraph developed during this period of early growth. For example, telegraph companies soon began to offer financial services. The first money order was sent on June 1, 1845.

Newspaper reporters used the telegraph to send stories to their newspapers. From the start of the construction of telegraph lines, telegraph companies advertised for business from newspapers. Many operators offered the newspapers special rates.

The telegraph became a vital tool during the American Civil War (1861-1865), not only for the press, but also for the armies on both sides. Telegraph operators felt so overworked during the war that they formed the National Telegraphic Union in 1863.

Brokers on Wall Street used the telegraph to gain quick access to important information, such as the current price of gold. In 1867, the New York Stock Exchange introduced *stock tickers,* telegraph devices that reported the purchase and sale of stocks.

Railroads used the telegraph to create a more efficient transportation network. In agreements between railroads and telegraph companies, railroads agreed to string telegraph lines along railroad rights of way. In return, telegraph companies agreed to transmit messages relating to railroad business free of charge and to give priority to messages concerning the movement of trains.

Western Union. During the 1850's, the U.S. telegraph industry worked to overcome the problems caused by the existence of more than 50 telegraph companies. The industry rebuilt short, disconnected, broken-down lines and combined them into extensive networks.

In 1851, Hiram Sibley and a group of businessmen from Rochester, New York, started the New York and Mississippi Valley Printing Telegraph Company. They hoped to combine all the western telegraph lines into a single network. They bought and leased telegraph lines, railroad rights of way, and patent rights from other companies. In 1856, the company's name became Western Union Telegraph Company. By 1866, Western Union had gained control of its major competitors and become the most successful of the telegraph companies.

Service expansion and improvement. Telegraphy continued to spread around the world. In 1847, the German inventor Ernst Werner von Siemens helped found a company (now Siemens AG) that set up telegraph lines in Germany, Russia, and other nations. In 1850, the first underwater telegraph cable was laid between France and the United Kingdom. After several failed attempts, a permanent transatlantic link was achieved in 1866. The British scientist William Thompson, later Lord Kelvin, supervised the Atlantic cable project. See **Cable** (Telegraph cables).

By the 1860's, central telegraph offices existed in most major cities in the United States and Europe. Western Union completed the first transcontinental telegraph line in North America in 1861. In 1865, the International Telegraph Union, the forerunner of the International Telecommunications Union, was formed. This organization established standards for international telegraph communications. In 1869, a telegraph went into operation between Tokyo and Yokohama, Japan. By 1870, several lines connected India and the United Kingdom.

Western Union sent out weather reports from its major cities and began providing weather maps in 1868. The company established the first time service in 1877, relaying signals from the official government timekeeper, the U.S. Naval Observatory in Washington, D.C. Through these and other services, the telegraph connected communities and companies across North America and Europe. The government of the United Kingdom took over the British telegraph industry in 1870 and made it part of the British Post Office.

Improvements in telegraphy increased the message capacity of single wires and the speed of message handling and transmission. The duplex system, which could send two messages over one wire at the same time, one in each direction, had been developed in 1853 by the Austrian inventor Wilhelm Julius Gintl. But Gintl's system failed to compensate for electrostatic interference in the wire, and so was impractical. The American inventor Joseph B. Stearns improved on this system. The system Stearns devised began operating in the United States in 1872. Two years later, American inventor Thomas A. Edison developed a quadruplex system, which handled four messages at the same time. In 1875, Émile Baudot, a French telegrapher, developed a multiplex system that could handle five at once.

Decline. By the late 1800's, the telegraph was a vital part of commerce, government, and the military. The introduction of the telephone in the 1870's took away most of the telegraph's short-distance communication business. By the late 1890's, long-distance telephone communication threatened much of the remaining telegraph business. But the telegraph continued to be used in the 1900's, and the development of faster automated sending and receiving devices helped improve telegraph service. About 1900, the British inventor Donald Murray devised a telegraph system using a keyboard to send text and a printer to receive it. He developed the system for the British Post Office. United States telegraph companies purchased Murray's patent rights in 1912, and had developed their own printing telegraph systems by the 1920's. The number of telegrams sent reached its peak in 1929, when over 200 million were transmitted.

In 1931, the American Telephone and Telegraph Company (now AT&T Corp.) introduced *TWX,* a telegraph service that sent messages directly from one unit equipped with a telephone line, printer, and typewriter to another. In 1958, Western Union introduced *Telex,* an advanced version of TWX, to the United States.

Telegraph service today

Despite the advances made in the 1900's, the traditional telegraph could not compete with such communications equipment as computers and communications satellites. These machines, which operate much faster than the telegraph and can process many kinds of information, have largely replaced the telegraph.

Western Union Financial Services, Inc., still offers telegram service in the United States. But this service has little in common with original telegraph services. The sender contacts a Western Union operator by telephone and dictates a message. The operator types the message on a computer, storing it as an electronic file. This file is then sent along telephone lines to the office

WORLD BOOK illustrations by Eileen Mueller Neill

Making a simple telegraph set

Two-way communication can be achieved with two telegraph sets. Each set includes a key, a sounder, and a battery. The key of one set is connected to the sounder of the other. Directions for making a set are given below.

1. The base of the set is a flat piece of wood that holds the sounder. First, nail together the wood base, one of the smaller wood blocks, and the T-shaped piece of flexible steel, as shown.

2. The sounder. Hammer two steel nails into one end of the base. Wind a piece of insulated wire around the nails—about 30 turns for each—to form coils. Connect the coils to the battery with one end of the wire. Leave the other end loose to connect the coils to the key. Hammer a bent aluminum nail next to, but not touching, the T-shaped piece of metal.

3. The key is the thin metal strip mounted on one of the small blocks. Push two thumbtacks halfway through the key. Scrape the insulation from one end of the wire attached to the sounder coils. Wrap the bare wire around the tacks and press down.

4. Bend the key upward about half an inch from the block. Press the third thumbtack under the raised end. Take a piece of wire and scrape the insulating material from each end. Connect the tack to the battery with the wire. The key should touch the tack when pressed and spring up when released.

5. Touching the key to the tack causes electric current to flow through the circuit. Electromagnets pull the metal T down, making a clicking sound. When the key is released, the T springs up and strikes the bent nail, making another clicking sound. These sounds form the dots and dashes of the telegraph code.

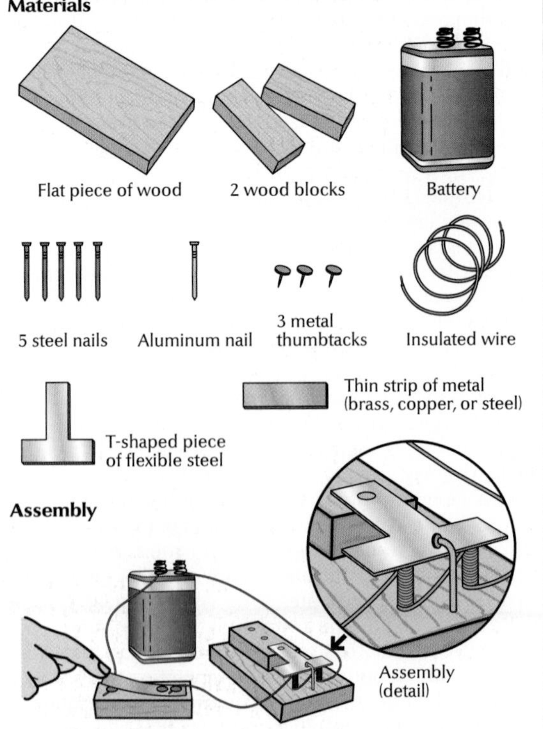

nearest the receiver. In most cases, an operator at that office calls the receiver and reads the message or sends the message to the receiver by fax. Arthur R. Brodsky

Related articles in *World Book* include:

Biographies

Cornell, Ezra	Morse, Samuel Finley Breese	Wheatstone, Sir Charles
Edison, Thomas A.	Siemens, Ernst Werner von	Woods, Granville T.
Field, Cyrus West		
Henry, Joseph		
Kelvin, Lord		

Other related articles

Associated Press	Morse code	Stock ticker
Cable	News service	Western Union
Communication		

Additional resources

Coe, Lewis. *The Telegraph: A History of Morse's Invention and Its Predecessors in the United States.* McFarland, 1993.

Jepsen, Thomas C. *My Sisters Telegraphic: Women in the Telegraph Office, 1846-1950.* Ohio Univ. Pr., 2000.

Solymar, Laszlo. *Getting the Message: A History of Communications.* Oxford, 1999. Includes the history of the telegraph.

Standage, Tom. *The Victorian Internet: The Remarkable Story of the Telegraph and the Nineteenth Century's On-Line Pioneers.* 1998. Reprint. Berkley Pub., 1999.

Telegraph plant is an herb about 4 feet (1.2 meters) high. It is native to tropical Asia. If the plant, or especially its leaves, is touched, the leaves quickly droop downward, like the arms of a railroad semaphore signal. The plant bears small purple flowers. The seed pods are jointed and can be separated easily. See also **Sensitive plant.** Daniel F. Austin

Scientific classification. The telegraph plant is in the pea family, Fabaceae or Leguminosae. It is *Desmodium motorium.*

Telemann, *TAY luh MAHN,* **Georg Philipp,** *gay AWRK FEE lihp* (1681-1767), was perhaps the most famous German composer of his day. He wrote thousands of compositions in the popular forms of the 1700's. He wrote more than 1,000 cantatas as well as operas, concertos, oratorios, and chamber music. His music forms an important link between the Baroque style of George Frideric Handel and the Classical style of Joseph Haydn.

Telemann's works show an understanding of the national styles of his time, including folk music. He was also concerned with writing music suitable for performance by amateurs. His best-known works include the comic opera *Pimpinone* (1725), the religious cantata cycle *Harmonischer Gottes-Dienst* (1725-1726), and instrumental pieces called *Musique de Table* (1733). His music for the recorder is especially popular today.

Telemann was born on March 14, 1681, in Magdeburg and studied in Leipzig. In 1721, he became the music director for the five main churches in Hamburg, where he spent the rest of his life. From 1722 to 1738, he was director of the Hamburg Opera. He died on June 25, 1767. Joscelyn Godwin

Telemarketing is the selling of goods or services by telephone. In some cases, a salesperson calls a potential customer, or *prospect,* to present a sales message. In other cases, the prospect calls the seller, usually in response to an advertisement or a catalog display. During the conversation, the salesperson can respond to questions or comments by adapting the sales message.

In another form of telemarketing using online computer services, the prospect views a sales message on a computer screen. The message—which usually resembles a magazine advertisement or a catalog page—travels to the computer over telephone lines. The prospect can respond by typing on the computer keyboard.

Telemarketing is effective because it enables sellers to contact many people at minimum expense. It became widespread in the 1980's, mostly because of improvements in telephone technology, the availability of lists of prospects, and a growing acceptance of credit cards.

Some businesses that use telemarketing hire firms that specialize in telephone sales. In some countries, individuals can register to prevent telemarketers from calling them. In 2003, the United States government introduced a program enabling individuals to add their names to a national "do-not-call" list. William H. Bolen

Telemetry, *tuh LEHM uh tree,* means *measuring at a distance.* Scientists and engineers use telemetry in many ways. Scientists send weather balloons as high as 20 or 30 miles (32 or 48 kilometers) above Earth to measure air temperature, pressure, and humidity. Radios attached to the balloons relay this information back to Earth.

Telemetry also helps people explore outer space. Rockets and spacecraft send information about their own performance and conditions in outer space to scientists and engineers on Earth. On human space flights, telemetry systems provide data on astronauts' physical condition by reporting their pulse rate, blood pressure, and temperature. To save space and weight, special miniature equipment is used in spacecraft.

A telemetry system consists of a measuring instrument, a transmitter, and a receiving station. For example, a telemetry system that records temperatures at remote locations uses an electrical thermometer as the measuring instrument. Signals produced by the thermometer are transmitted by radio or by wire to a receiving station. Instruments at the receiving station record the signals on magnetic tape and convert them into meter readings and graphs. Arthur C. Aikin

Teleology. See **Ethics** (Modern ethics).

Telepathy, *tuh LEHP uh thee,* is the communication of thoughts, feelings, or knowledge from one person to another without the use of the senses of hearing, sight, smell, taste, or touch. It is sometimes called *mind reading* or *thought transference.* An example of telepathy would be if a person thought of something specific and another person stated or wrote the thought correctly. But to be telepathic, the performance would have to be repeated and could not be explainable in any other way.

Telepathy is part of the subject matter of parapsychology and is studied by scientists called *parapsychologists.* Parapsychologists believe that neither distance nor time affects telepathy. Thus, a person's thoughts might be received by another person who is far away. Parapsychologists also believe that a person may know in advance the thoughts, feelings, or knowledge that another person will have at a later time. If true, this would be an example of *precognitive telepathy.*

Telepathy is considered a major form of *extrasensory perception* (ESP), which is an awareness of something without the use of the known senses. Telepathy is under scientific investigation. Its existence is still in question, but many scientists doubt its reality. James E. Alcock

See also **Clairvoyance; Extrasensory perception; Parapsychology; Psychical research.**

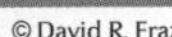

© David R. Frazier

© PhotoDisc, Inc. from Getty Images

AT&T

The telephone is a valuable means of communication. An automatic telephone answering device, *above left,* records messages from callers. A cellular telephone, *top right,* uses radio waves to send and receive telephone calls. A fax machine, *left,* lets people send written words and pictures over telephone lines.

Telephone

Telephone is an instrument that sends and receives voice messages, usually by means of electric current. It is one of our most valuable means of communication. In just a few seconds, you can telephone a person across the street, in another part of the country, or on another continent. Alexander Graham Bell, a Scottish-born teacher of the deaf, patented the telephone in 1876. The word *telephone* comes from two Greek words meaning *far* and *sound.*

In its most basic form, a telephone enables people to talk with each other at distances beyond the range of the human voice. More sophisticated telephones and telephonelike devices can send and receive not only voice messages but also written words, drawings, photographs, and even video images.

Telephones are connected through a vast, complex telephone network. The network includes large computers, tremendous lengths of copper wire and hair-thin strands of glass, cables buried in the ground and laid along the bottom of the oceans, radio transmitters and receivers, and artificial satellites orbiting far above Earth.

Most telephones connect with the telephone network by means of wires that run through the walls of houses and other buildings. A small clip connects each telephone to the wiring. Other phones, called *wireless telephones,* are not wired to the telephone network but rather are linked to it via radio signals.

How a telephone works

A telephone has four main parts: (1) a dialing mechanism, (2) a transmitter, (3) a ringer, and (4) a receiver.

The dialing mechanism enables a caller to enter telephone numbers. The mechanism may be built into the *handset,* the part of a telephone that a person picks up to make a phone call. Or it may be part of a separate base unit that connects by cord to the handset. Before making a call, the person listens in the earpiece for a *dial tone.* This sound indicates that a telephone line is available to handle the call.

In most telephones manufactured since the 1960's, the dialing mechanism consists of a set of buttons or keys called a *keypad.* A standard keypad has 12 keys—10 keys with the digits 0 through 9, a key with the symbol * called a *star key,* and a key with the symbol # called a *pound key.* The keys numbered 1 through 9 each include groupings of 3 letters of the alphabet. The key numbered 0 sometimes includes the letters "Q" and "Z".

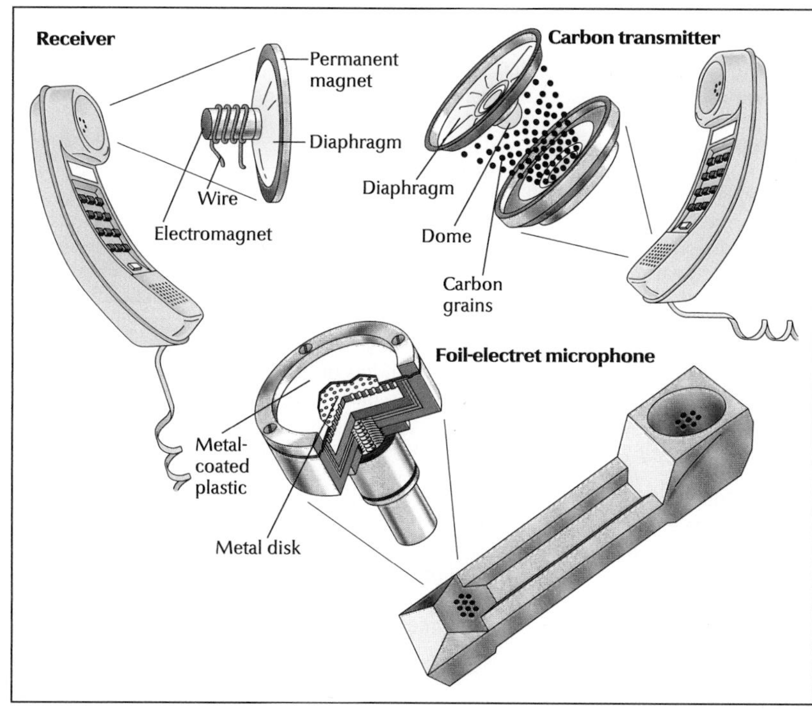

WORLD BOOK diagrams by J. Harlan Hunt, Koralik Associates

A telephone handset includes a transmitter or microphone, which produces an electric "copy" of the user's voice, and a receiver, which duplicates the voice of the person on the other end of the line. In a carbon transmitter, the sound wave of the user's voice makes a diaphragm vibrate. The vibrations cause a metal dome to exert pressure on carbon grains. Electric current flows through the grains with a strength related to this pressure, "copying" the voice. In a foil-electret microphone, the sound waves cause a sheet of metal-coated plastic to vibrate next to a metal disk. This leads to variations in the strength of a current in the microphone, "copying" the voice. In a receiver, the electric "copy" of the caller's voice flows through a wire, producing variations in the magnetic field of an electromagnet. As a result, a permanent magnet vibrates a diaphragm, generating sounds like those of the voice.

A business may incorporate letters or words into its telephone number in advertisements to help people remember the number more easily. Most telephones with keypads use *tone dialing.* In tone dialing, each key generates a pair of accurately controlled tones when pressed. Computers in the telephone network recognize the sequence of tones as the telephone number and direct the call accordingly.

The dialing mechanism on some older telephones consists of a disk called a *rotary dial.* The dial has finger holes that correspond to the digits 0 through 9. Rotary telephones use *pulse dialing.* A caller enters a telephone number by rotating and releasing the dial. This action generates electric pulses that are used to direct the call.

The transmitter, also called the *microphone,* converts the sound waves of a person's voice into an electric current and sends this current farther into the telephone network. The transmitter is built into the handset, behind the mouthpiece.

Modern telephones use a *foil-electret condenser microphone* to transmit sound. This device has a circular *diaphragm* consisting of a thin sheet of electrically charged plastic with a metal coating on one side. This diaphragm, called a *foil electret,* is stretched over a hollow metal disk called a *backplate.* The metal coating on the diaphragm faces away from the backplate.

The diaphragm touches the backplate only in certain areas. In other areas, the two pieces are separated by air pockets. The diaphragm can vibrate in these pockets when hit by sound waves.

The electric charge carried by the diaphragm sets up an electric field between the diaphragm and the backplate. The distance between the diaphragm and the backplate influences the strength of this field.

When a person speaks into the mouthpiece, sound waves hit the diaphragm. The resulting vibrations change the distance between the diaphragm and the backplate—and thus the strength of the electric field. These variations in field strength trigger corresponding variations in an electric current. The current variations are an electric "copy" of the speaker's voice.

Older telephones use a *carbon transmitter.* This device has an aluminum diaphragm that vibrates when a person speaks into the handset. The vibration causes a small metal dome behind the diaphragm to exert pressure on carbon grains in a small compartment called a *carbon chamber.* Electric current flows through the grains with a strength related to this pressure, "copying" the speaker's voice.

The ringer signals an incoming call. A small bell inside early telephones rang when a call came in. As electronic parts replaced mechanical ones, the bell disappeared from most telephones. In its place is a computer chip that generates a chirp or some other sound, or even part of a song.

The receiver converts the electric current coming through the telephone line into sound. It is located behind the earpiece in the handset.

The receiver consists of a small speaker that uses a coil of wire, a magnet, and a thin diaphragm attached to the magnet. When pulses of electric current run through the coil, a magnetic force is created around it. According to the strength and direction of the current, the coil either attracts or repels the magnet, moving the magnet back and forth. The motion of the magnet causes the diaphragm to vibrate, creating sound waves that duplicate the voice of the person speaking on the other end of the line.

How a telephone call travels

Two basic processes enable a call to reach its intended destination. They are (1) routing the call and (2) transmitting the telephone signals.

Routing the call. At one time, telephone operators *switched* (routed) telephone calls manually by plugging electric cords into a switchboard. Today, electronic switches—actually computers—route most calls.

After a telephone number has been dialed, pairs of copper wires carry the resulting electric signals to a *central office,* a facility of the local telephone company, also known as a *local exchange carrier.* A switch sends the call on its way, using the telephone number as the routing "address."

If the call is local, the switch routes the signals to another switch that is usually owned by the same company. If the call is long-distance, the signals travel into the network of a long-distance company, or *interexchange carrier.* They may pass through several more switches in this network, but eventually they reach the central office of the local exchange carrier that serves the telephone being called. A switch in that office then routes the signals to this telephone. All the routing and switching occurs in seconds.

Transmitting the telephone signals. Once a connection is established, the signals that make up the message must be carried between the two telephones. A majority of telephone calls today are sent through a system of *digital switches.* A digital switch takes the continuous electric current that corresponds to a telephone message and transforms it into a series of electrical impulses. These electrical impulses represent the digits 0 and 1—the same digits used by computers. The sequence of 0's and 1's, which corresponds to the telephone message, moves through the telephone network. A digital switching system duplicates the sequence as the signal moves through each switch. This duplication maintains the impulses' strength and accuracy over long distances.

An older type of switching system uses *analog switches.* An analog switch directs the current signal through the network without translating it into 0's and 1's. Such a signal fades over distance, so it requires continuous *amplification* (strengthening). Amplification often lessens the quality of the sound being transmitted. Digital switches have replaced most analog switches.

Switches, whether digital or analog, may be connected by cables consisting of many twisted pairs of copper wires or by bundles of *optical fibers.* In these *fiber-optic cables,* hair-thin glass fibers carry telephone signals as impulses of light. A laser at one end of a fiber transforms electric signals corresponding to a telephone message into an on-and-off light sequence in which "off" represents 0 and "on" represents 1. At the other end of the fiber, a special device transforms the emerging impulses back into electric signals.

Fiber-optic cables can carry tremendous amounts of information. A strand of optical fiber can carry thousands of times as much information as a pair of copper wires. Both wire cables and fiber-optic cables may be buried in the ground or laid on the ocean floor.

Some telephone messages are transmitted through the air on short radio waves called *microwaves.* The telephone network uses a series of relay stations to direct microwave signals over vast distances. A dish antenna at a relay station receives a signal, and another dish antenna retransmits the signal to the next station. To direct microwave signals across oceans, the telephone network uses communications satellites.

WORLD BOOK diagram by Rolin Graphics

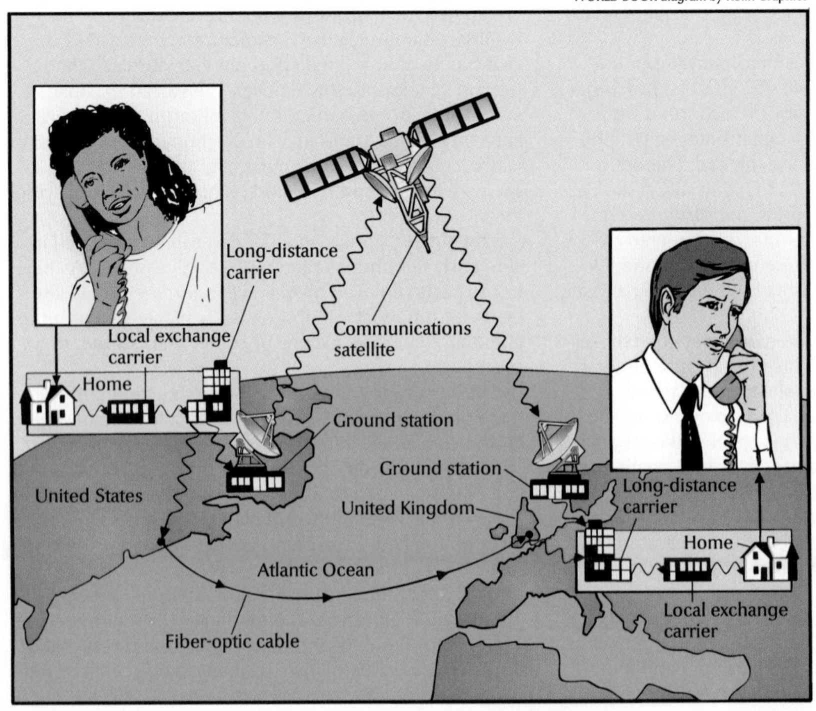

An intercontinental call from the United States to the United Kingdom travels through the sky or under the ocean. Telephone signals pass from the caller's home phone to one or more local telephone offices called *local exchange carriers,* which pass the signals to a *long-distance carrier.* This office directs the call in one of two ways. In one method, the signals go to a *ground station,* which beams them to a communications satellite. The satellite relays the signals to a British ground station. In the other transmission method, the long-distance carrier routes the signals to a fiber-optic cable that runs beneath the Atlantic Ocean. With both methods, the signals reach a British long-distance carrier. The call then passes through one or more local exchange carriers and finally reaches its intended destination.

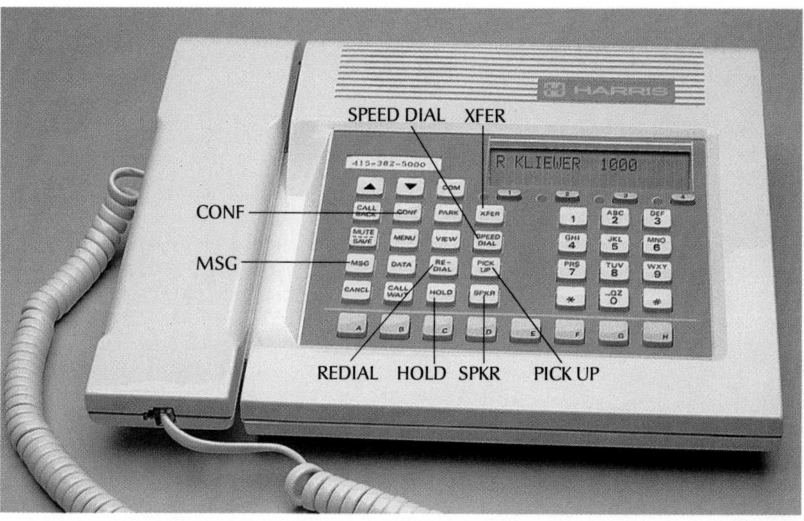

Harris Co.

A modern office telephone has special keys that enable the user to perform a wide variety of functions. The box to the right of the photograph describes some of these functions.

What special keys enable the telephone user to do
CONF: Talk with people on more than one line at the same time.
XFER: Transfer a call to another phone.
SPEED DIAL: Dial programmed phone numbers by pressing only one or two number keys.
MSG: Play messages in voice mail.
REDIAL: Retry the last number dialed.
PICK UP: Use this phone to answer another phone that is ringing.
HOLD: Temporarily take another person off the line.
SPKR: Talk over a speaker system instead of the handset.

Telephones that use radio

Regular telephones send and receive sound messages as electric signals. Special telephones and related devices, however, transmit messages with radio signals. These include cordless telephones and wireless telephone equipment.

Cordless telephones have no cord connecting the handset to the base. The handset creates radio signals corresponding to spoken messages and broadcasts the signals through the air. The base picks up the radio signals, translates them into electric signals, and transmits them through wires to the network. Similarly, the base translates incoming electric signals into radio signals and transmits them to the handset. The base is connected to the telephone network like a regular telephone. A person can take the handset of a cordless telephone from room to room or even outdoors—within a limited range—while talking on the telephone.

Wireless telephone equipment communicates with the regular telephone network via radio waves rather than wires. Such equipment includes cellular telephones, telephones in certain remote areas, and pagers.

Cellular telephones are mobile devices that transmit and receive radio signals. A cellular telephone communicates with an antenna transmitter that serves a small geographical area called a *cell.* The antenna transmitter in each cell communicates with the regular telephone network through a mobile telephone switching office. When a person using a cellular phone moves from one cell to another, the mobile telephone network passes the signals to the next cell without interrupting the call.

Most cellular phones are small enough to be carried in a pocket or bag, or on a belt clip. The earliest models were big and bulky and were mounted in cars.

Telephones in remote areas. In some sparsely populated regions, people live so far apart that it would be too expensive to use wires or optical fibers to connect their homes with the telephone network. In these areas, *Basic Exchange Telephone Radio Service* (BETRS) bridges the gap. Each house has a transmitter that sends radio signals to the regular telephone network, in many cases by way of other transmitting stations.

Pagers. A *pager,* or *beeper,* is a small radio receiver that responds with a tone or vibration when activated by a signal. Most pagers have their own telephone number. When this number is dialed from a telephone, the resulting signals travel to a special network. A transmitter in this network sends a radio signal to the pager. Pagers display the phone number of the caller or other information. The person being paged can then return the call using a nearby telephone. Pagers themselves cannot make or receive telephone calls. However, many modern paging devices can receive and send text messages.

Transmitting data

With special equipment, people can send computer data, written words, photographs and drawings, and even video images through the regular telephone network. This special equipment includes (1) modems, (2) fax machines, and (3) videophones.

Modems, along with special software, enable computer users to send and receive data in electronic form over the telephone network. Many people use personal computers to contact other computer users or to connect to the Internet. A modem translates outgoing computer signals into signals the telephone network can use, and it translates incoming telephone signals into computer signals. Special modems can connect portable computers with the cellular network.

Telephone services called ISDN (integrated services digital network) and DSL (digital subscriber line) can increase the information-carrying capacity of traditional copper phone lines. These services use a modemlike *adapter* to connect a computer to the telephone network. They enable the transmission of data between the network and the computer at speeds far higher than can be achieved using a true modem. Data services supplied

AT&T

A videophone has a TV screen and, in a round hole above the screen, a TV camera, so users can see images of each other. Ordinary telephone lines transmit the sound and picture signals.

by cable television companies use devices called *cable modems* to connect computers to a cable network that is, in turn, linked to the telephone network.

A computer equipped with a modem, DSL or ISDN adapter, or cable modem can use the telephone network to connect to the Internet. While connected, a computer user can browse the World Wide Web, a system of computer files linked to one another on the Internet. The user may also contact computerized information services called *online services*. Some online services offer current news bulletins, shopping services, encyclopedias, or games. Others feature back issues of newspapers, magazines, or other research materials. A popular online service is *e-mail,* also called *electronic mail,* through which individual users send messages to each other. See also **E-mail; Internet; Online service.**

Fax machines, or *facsimile machines,* send images of documents over telephone lines. A fax machine resembles a computer printer but is equipped with a telephone or connected to one. To send a document, the user inserts it into the machine and dials the telephone number of the fax machine that is to produce a copy of the document. After the connection has been made, an electronic scanner on the transmitting machine generates electric signals that correspond to the image on the page. The telephone network uses these signals to instruct the receiving machine to print a copy of the document. Portable fax machines connect with cellular telephone networks. Some computers can send and receive faxes.

Videophones. Ordinary telephone lines can transmit video signals to a *videophone,* a telephone combined with a television camera and screen. Users can see pictures of each other during a call. Special cameras that connect to personal computers enable computer users to place video calls over the Internet to other users whose computers are similarly equipped. Video calls transmit pictures that change only a few times per second, so the movements appear jerky.

Telephone services

The telephone network supports a variety of services, including operator, business, and residential services. Telephone companies provide these services.

Operator services use human operators or computers that imitate the human voice to provide various kinds of assistance. For example, a person who needs help to complete a call can dial 0 to reach an operator. A service called *directory assistance* provides callers with the telephone numbers of parties they wish to call, and can connect calls as well. Some countries have short numbers that can be dialed to reach emergency police, fire, or ambulance service. In the United States and Canada, the standard emergency number is 911. In the United States, cellular telephone emergency numbers vary from state to state, but the country is working toward a 911 standard.

Business services. Most businesses have more than one telephone. A business may set up its telephone system in either of two ways. In one arrangement, which is provided by the local telephone company, each telephone has its own telephone number. One name for this service is *Centrex service.* In the other arrangement, known as a *private branch exchange* (PBX), several lines owned by the telephone company are connected to a switching system owned by the business. In this system, the business usually has one telephone number, and each phone has a separate extension number. Such a system enables employees to call each other merely by dialing the proper extension number.

Private line service, or *dedicated service,* is designed for businesses that have branch offices with which they communicate frequently. The phone company sets up a line or group of lines that run only between those offices. Private line service eliminates the need to send each of these calls over the public telephone network. Private lines may be equipped to handle large amounts of computer data or fax transmissions.

In many businesses, a system called *voice mail* answers incoming calls. A voice recording stored on a computer chip gives callers instructions to help them reach the desired party. If that party is not available, the caller can leave a recorded message.

Another common business service is *toll-free service.* A subscriber to the service is issued a *toll-free number,* and pays the charges for all calls received by that number. Many companies that sell goods or services by mail or by telephone use toll-free service. The service is also commonly called *800 service,* because the first three digits of toll-free numbers—which in an ordinary telephone number would be the area code—were all originally 800. Today, some toll-free numbers begin with the prefixes 877 or 888.

Residential services. Many home telephone users have access to a wide variety of services. For example, the telephone company can provide voice-mail service similar to that used by businesses. Some long-distance companies offer toll-free numbers to home users.

Another service provides for different-sounding rings, depending on the caller. *Call waiting* lets a person put one telephone call on hold in order to speak with another caller. *Call forwarding* automatically sends all calls to a designated telephone number. *Call blocking* automatically rejects calls from telephones whose numbers are designated by the subscriber. A service called *automatic caller identification,* or *caller I.D.,* enables a person with a special device attached to the telephone to see the caller's telephone number or name before answering. *Automatic callback* service notifies a caller when a busy number he or she has been dialing becomes free.

Other services. Many hotels, restaurants, and other public places have *pay telephones.* These phones require callers to pay for calls with coins, credit cards, or *calling cards,* special cards issued by local or long-distance telephone companies. Owners of pay telephones include local telephone companies and firms that provide long-distance service or operator services.

Other telephone services supply information or advice, or enable callers to participate in informal polls or to enter contests. The most popular of these is called *900 service* or *pay-per-call service.* Such services originally used numbers whose first three digits—in place of the area code—were 900. Calling a 900 number can be expensive. Providers of 900 services are required by law to give callers the price before providing a service. Today, some numbers for pay-per-call services begin with 976 instead of 900.

The telephone industry

In the United States. The United States has about 1,400 local telephone companies. Some have only a few hundred lines, and others have millions of lines.

Four firms provide the vast majority of local telephone service. These firms are: (1) BellSouth; (2) Qwest Communications International Inc.; (3) SBC Communications Inc.; and (4) Verizon Communications. In many major cities, two or more of these firms offer local service. The firms also operate cellular telephone networks, some of which cover nearly the entire country.

There are about 500 long-distance companies in the United States. Some own all of their telephone lines and switches. Others—mostly the smaller companies—buy service from large firms and resell it to their customers. The largest U.S. long-distance carriers include AT&T Corp., MCI, Sprint, and Verizon.

A third type of U.S. telephone company is the *competitive local exchange carrier* (CLEC). It provides telephone services in competition with established local telephone companies, most often to businesses.

State government agencies set prices for local service and other telephone services within states. The Federal Communications Commission (FCC), a U.S. government agency, has authority over phone services between states, such as long-distance and toll-free services.

In other countries. For many years, the government provided telephone service in most countries. But since the 1980's, many nations have sold part ownership—or, in some cases, a whole telephone company—to private citizens. In some countries, a government body regulates the telecommunications industry.

In general, Africa's telephone system is poor. South Africa has the continent's only extensive telephone networks. Telephone equipment is concentrated in the larger towns, and people in rural areas usually have no telephone access at all. It is expensive to develop ground-based telephone networks, especially in sparsely populated areas. Thus, some rural regions operate public telephones that transmit messages via satellite.

Some Asian countries, such as Japan and South Korea, have extensive telephone systems. But in many parts of Asia, telephone networks are restricted mainly to cities. As in Africa, many regions use wireless equipment to link to the global communication system. In many parts of Asia, few families have telephones, but public phones are widely available in cities and towns.

Telephone services link South America's cities. But telephone service has not reached many remote areas.

Australia, Europe, and parts of North America have modern telephone systems that link almost all regions with each other and with the other continents. The developing countries in the southern part of North America have less extensive telephone systems.

Telephone service continues to improve as the result of new technology. For example, many developing countries, such as those in eastern Europe, have developed advanced cellular services to replace poor ground-based telephone networks.

History

Bell's invention. Alexander Graham Bell, a Scotsman who came to the United States in 1871, invented the telephone. Bell was a teacher of the deaf in Boston. At night, he experimented with a *harmonic telegraph,* a device for sending several telegraph messages at once over one wire. Bell developed the idea of the telephone in 1874 but continued experiments with the harmonic telegraph.

On June 2, 1875, one of the metal reeds of the harmonic telegraph stuck. Bell's assistant, Thomas A. Watson, plucked the reed to loosen it. Bell, who was in another room, heard the sound in his receiver. He realized that the vibrations of the reed had caused variations of electric current. In turn, the electric current had reproduced the same variations in the receiver he was using.

On March 10, 1876, Bell finally succeeded in speaking words over a telephone. He was about to test a new transmitter. In another room, Watson waited for the test message. Suddenly, Bell spilled some acid from a bat-

Historical Pictures Service

Telephone operators connected almost all calls manually by switchboard until the early 1900's. This photograph shows the central telephone exchange of New York City about 1900.

Popular telephone models of the past

The first telephone was this device, patented in 1876 by Alexander Graham Bell.

An 1882 wall phone had a handheld receiver and a crank to signal the operator.

A 1919 dial telephone required complex switching equipment.

The 1928 desk telephone combined receiver and transmitter in a handset unit.

The "300" model desk phone, introduced in 1937, contained a bell in its base.

The colored telephone of 1954 gained widespread popularity as a decorative item.

The Princess phone of 1959 featured a compact design and an illuminated rotary dial.

AT&T

The "trimline" telephone of 1968 featured push buttons on the handset.

tery on his clothes. He cried out, "Mr. Watson, come here. I want you!" Watson heard every word clearly and rushed into the room. In June 1876, Bell exhibited his telephone at the Centennial Exposition in Philadelphia.

Early telephones. In August 1876, Bell received the first one-way long-distance call. This call came over an 8-mile (13-kilometer) telegraph line between Brantford, Ontario, and Paris, Ontario. In October 1876, Bell and Watson held the first two-way long-distance telephone conversation. They spoke between Boston and Cambridgeport, a part of Cambridge, Massachusetts, a distance of about 2 miles (3 kilometers). In 1877, Charles Williams, an electrical workshop owner, installed the first line intended exclusively for telephone use. It extended 3 miles (5 kilometers) between Williams's home in Somerville, Massachusetts, and his shop in Boston.

The first telephones used no switchboards. A pair of iron wires connected each pair of phones. As more telephones came into use, each was connected to all the others. Over 1,000 connections were required to link only 50 phones. Switchboards solved this problem by bringing together the wires from all phones in an area. The first switchboard began operating in 1877 in Boston.

Telephone services soon began operating in other parts of the world. Service began in Australia in 1878 and in the United Kingdom in 1879.

Almon B. Strowger, an American inventor, patented an automatic switching system in 1891. The first commercial switchboard based on his patent opened in La-Porte, Indiana, in 1892. The caller pressed buttons to get the number, then turned a crank to ring the phone.

In 1891, the first international telephone connection was established between London and Paris. In 1892, phone service began between New York City and Chicago. In 1896, the first dial telephones began operating in Milwaukee.

The Bell System. Bell, Watson, Gardiner G. Hubbard, and Thomas Sanders formed the Bell Telephone Company in 1877. Hubbard was Bell's father-in-law, and Sanders was the father of one of Bell's pupils. They had helped pay for Bell's experiments. The Western Union Telegraph Company also entered the telephone business in 1877. Western Union used transmitters developed by Thomas A. Edison, the great American inventor. Elisha Gray, another American inventor, developed their receivers. The Bell company met the competition by using the improved transmitters of Emile Berliner, a German immigrant, and Francis J. Blake, an American.

In 1878, the Bell company sued Western Union to protect Bell's patents. Western Union claimed that Gray, not Bell, had invented the telephone. Gray had notified the U.S. Patent Office that he was working on a device to transmit speech on the same day Bell had applied for his first patent, Feb. 14, 1876. However, Gray gave his notification after Bell submitted his application. Bell's patent was issued on March 7, 1876. In 1879, Western Union recognized Bell's patents and sold its telephone business to the Bell company. This case was the first of about 600 lawsuits over Bell's patents. The Supreme Court of the United States upheld Bell's patents in 1888.

In 1878, the first telephone exchange opened in New Haven, Connecticut. It had 21 customers. Exchanges soon opened throughout the United States and Canada.

In 1878, two companies were formed as successors to the Bell Telephone Company: the New England Telephone Company and a new Bell Telephone Company.

The New England Telephone Company licensed telephone service in New England, and the Bell Telephone Company licensed phone service in the rest of the United States. In 1879, the two companies combined to form the National Bell Telephone Company. The American Bell Telephone Company was founded as the successor to National Bell in 1880. In 1885, the American Telephone and Telegraph Company (AT&T) was established to operate the long-distance network. AT&T took over American Bell in 1899 and became the parent company of the Bell System.

Improvements in telephone technology. Transcontinental phone service began between New York City and San Francisco in 1915. Transatlantic radiotelephone service between New York City and London began in 1927. The first long-distance coaxial cable linked New York City and Philadelphia in 1936. Undersea telephone cables between North America and Europe began operating in 1956. A cable joined the U.S. mainland to Hawaii in 1957. The first commercial communications satellite, Early Bird, was launched in 1965.

In 1970, International Direct Distance Dialing (IDDD) began operating between New York City and London. IDDD, which now serves many of the world's cities, enables people to dial overseas directly.

In 1980, a fiber-optic system for transmitting local calls was installed in Atlanta, Georgia. A fiber-optic system between New York City and Washington, D.C., began operating in 1983. Fiber-optic cables began carrying messages across the Atlantic Ocean in 1988 and across the Pacific in 1989.

The FCC issued the first license for commercial cellular systems in the United States in 1983. Cellular service was available in most of the nation by the late 1980's. The service began in parts of Europe in the early 1980's.

Competition in the U.S. telephone industry. In the early 1900's, AT&T began buying small telephone companies. In 1913, the U.S. attorney general warned AT&T that some of its planned purchases could violate antitrust laws designed to protect competition. AT&T promised not to buy any more competing telephone companies and to allow all local phone companies to connect to its long-distance network.

The FCC ruled in 1968 that telephone users could buy their own telephones and other equipment to connect to the telephone network. Previously, AT&T and its local companies leased all phone equipment to users. In 1969, the FCC cleared the way for MCI Telecommunications to offer long-distance service. MCI thus became the first long-distance carrier to compete with AT&T.

In 1974, the U.S. government filed a lawsuit against AT&T, charging it with anticompetitive practices. The case was settled in 1982, and AT&T agreed to give up its local telephone companies on Jan. 1, 1984. On that day, the local companies were grouped into seven regional holding companies (RHC's), each of which provided local service in a particular U.S. region. The settlement allowed AT&T to keep its equipment-manufacturing plants, its long-distance business, and its research facilities. In 1994, the American Telephone and Telegraph Company changed its name to AT&T Corp.

The Telecommunications Act of 1996 loosened many restrictions that had limited competition in the U.S. telephone industry. It allowed local telephone companies, long-distance companies, and cable-television companies to enter each other's businesses. The act also allowed the RHC's to compete in local markets outside their own regions. Beginning in the late 1990's, many telephone companies and other communication firms merged to form large national or international communication corporations. Most of the RHC's became parts of large telecommunication corporations through mergers, often with other RHC's. In 2005, SBC Communications Inc., which traces its roots to several of the local telephone companies separated from AT&T in 1984, announced plans to buy AT&T Corp. Arthur R. Brodsky

Related articles in *World Book* include:

Biographies

Bell, Alexander Graham
Berliner, Emile
De Forest, Lee
Edison, Thomas Alva
Gray, Elisha
Pupin, Michael I.

Other related articles

AT&T Corp.
Cable
Cellular telephone
Communication
Communications satellite
Communications Satellite Corporation
Computer
Electromagnet
Etiquette (Telephone etiquette)
Fax machine
Federal Communications Commission
Fiber optics
Headphones
Intercom
Modem
Pager
Radio
Telecommunications

Outline

I. How a telephone works
A. The dialing mechanism
B. The transmitter
C. The ringer
D. The receiver
II. How a telephone call travels
A. Routing the call
B. Transmitting the telephone signals
III. Telephones that use radio
A. Cordless telephones
B. Wireless telephone equipment
IV. Transmitting data
A. Modems
B. Fax machines
C. Videophones
V. Telephone services
A. Operator services
B. Business services
C. Residential services
D. Other services
VI. The telephone industry
A. In the United States
B. In other countries
VII. History

Questions

What processes enable a call to reach its destination?
How do fiber-optic cables carry telephone signals?
How does a digital switch work?
What happens when a person uses a cellular telephone?
What is *caller identification?*
When a person speaks into the mouthpiece of a telephone, what happens to a foil-electret condenser microphone?
What were the first words spoken over a telephone?
What is *voice mail?*
When was the first local fiber-optic system installed?
How does a cordless telephone work?

Additional resources

Gearhart, Sarah. *The Telephone.* Atheneum, 1999. Younger readers.
Nobleman, Marc T. *The Telephone.* Capstone Pr., 2004. Younger readers.
Noll, A. Michael. *Introduction to Telephones and Telephone Systems.* 3rd ed. Artech Hse., 1998.
Stern, Ellen S., and Gwathmey, E. M., eds. *Once upon a Telephone: An Illustrated Social History.* Harcourt, 1994.

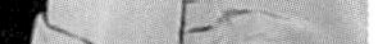

© John Bova, Photo Researchers

© Roger Ressmeyer, Starlight

NASA

Telescopes enable us to view distant objects and study the universe far beyond earth. Telescopes vary greatly in size from small units used by amateur astronomers to huge instruments in observatories. Some telescopes orbit the earth in satellites.

Telescope

Telescope is an instrument that magnifies distant objects. A telescope can also produce images of objects that are too faint to see with the unaided eye. Astronomers use telescopes to study the planets, stars, and other heavenly bodies.

Telescopes vary in shape and size from binoculars that can be held in the hands to bowl-shaped reflectors that measure up to 1,000 feet (305 meters) across. A pair of binoculars is actually two telescopes joined side by side. There are telescopes in large, dome-shaped buildings on the surface of the earth and telescopes in artificial satellites in orbit around the earth. Space probes that journey to other planets also carry telescopes.

The most familiar telescopes are *optical telescopes.* These instruments, like our eyes, work with visible light. In an optical telescope, a mirror or lens collects the light and uses it to form an image. Small telescopes used by amateur astronomers also have an *eyepiece* containing small lenses for viewing the image. But professional astronomers rarely look through the large optical telescopes they use. Instead, they record the image with an electronic sensor called a *charge-coupled device* (CCD) or, less often, with photographic film. A CCD in a large telescope is a more powerful version of the device that takes the pictures in an ordinary digital camera.

Objects in space also *emit* (give off) many kinds of radiation that people cannot see, such as radio waves, ultraviolet rays, and even X rays. Astronomers use other kinds of telescopes equipped with electronic detectors to form images with this radiation.

The Dutch optician Hans Lippershey probably made the first telescope—an optical telescope—in 1608. Lippershey mounted two glass lenses in a narrow tube. Within a year, Italian astronomer and physicist Galileo Galilei built a similar device and became the first person to use a telescope to study the sky. In 1668, English scientist, astronomer, and mathematician Isaac Newton built a telescope that used a mirror instead of lenses. Today, most large optical telescopes use mirrors.

J. Roger P. Angel and W. Thomas Roberts, Jr., the contributors of this article, are astronomers at the University of Arizona's Steward Observatory. Angel is Director of the Mirror Laboratory, and Roberts is a Research Associate.

What telescopes do

Telescopes detect visible light and other forms of *electromagnetic radiation* that move through space in waves. The various forms of radiation differ in *wavelength,* the distance between the crest of one wave and the crest of the next. The forms of electromagnetic radiation are—from the longest to the shortest wavelength—radio waves, infrared rays, visible light, ultraviolet rays, X rays, and gamma rays. These different forms of radiation also carry different amounts of energy in small units called *photons.* The shorter a photon's wavelength, the higher its energy.

Telescopes perform three main tasks: (1) they produce images of distant objects in fine detail; (2) they detect objects that are too faint to see with the unaided eye; and (3) they gather light for *spectrographs,* devices that analyze the light.

Producing detailed images. Astronomers call a telescope's ability to produce images in fine detail its *resolution* or *resolving power.* Resolution is a measure of the ability to show that objects which appear to be together are clearly separate. A telescope does this by magnifying the image of the objects, enabling astronomers to get a "closer view."

High magnification is relatively easy to achieve, but it is less important than high resolution. There is no value in magnifying an image more than necessary to see the smallest detail. A high magnification of an image formed by a telescope with a low resolution would produce a large picture, but the picture would be blurry.

Telescopes used by amateur astronomers have about 100 times the resolution of the unaided eye. The following example may help you understand this comparison: Suppose you go outdoors without a telescope and look at a group of what seem to be single stars. Then you concentrate on one of the brighter stars, and you realize that this "star" is actually two stars. You have *resolved* the stars. But suppose you were to use an optical telescope with 100 times the resolution of the unaided eye. You could then as easily resolve two stars that are 100 times closer together than the first pair of stars.

The resolution that a telescope can achieve in perfect viewing conditions depends mainly on the diameter of its mirror or lens and the wavelength of the radiation collected. The larger the mirror or lens and the shorter the wavelength, the higher the resolution. But viewing conditions for ground-based optical telescopes are far from perfect. Wind and daily heating and cooling of the atmosphere produce pockets and swirls of warm and cool air. The differences in air temperature affect the speed and direction of light through the air. Light waves become distorted, so the telescope produces a blurred image.

To achieve high resolution in spite of atmospheric blurring, astronomers are beginning to install special equipment called *adaptive optics* on ground-based telescopes. In the mid-1990's, astronomers began to install adaptive optics on large telescopes that collect visible light and infrared rays.

Orbiting observatories avoid atmospheric blurring by operating in space, above almost all the air. The Hubble Space Telescope has produced thousands of images that are 10 times sharper than images made by ground-based telescopes without adaptive optics.

Detecting faint objects. A telescope's ability to detect faint objects depends, like the telescope's resolution, on the diameter of the main mirror or lens. Huge optical telescopes can gather about 1 million times more light than the unaided eye. These telescopes therefore can detect objects about 1 million times fainter than objects that are visible with the unaided eye.

The use of photographic film and CCD's further increases the advantage of optical telescopes over the unaided eye. If film is exposed to a dim object for a long time, a bright picture results. Thus, photographs of the sky taken through a telescope reveal many details that could not be seen through an eyepiece attached to the telescope. In the mid-1970's, astronomers began to use CCD's instead of film because the CCD's are about 50 times more sensitive to light than film is. A CCD translates the light that strikes it into electric charges, which produce signals used to form images on a computer screen. Electronic sensors that detect invisible forms of electromagnetic radiation work similarly.

Gathering light for spectrographs. Most research telescopes also reflect light to devices called spectrographs. A spectrograph breaks up the light, spreads it out into its different colors, and records it for analysis. The band of spread-out light is known as a *spectrum* (plural *spectra*). The most familiar spectrum is the band of colored light in a rainbow, produced when raindrops break up and spread out sunlight. Astronomers analyze spectra to determine the chemical composition and temperature of stars, planets, and gas clouds, and to calculate how fast an object is approaching or moving away from the earth.

Optical telescopes

There are three main types of optical telescopes: (1) refracting telescopes, (2) reflecting telescopes, and (3) refracting-reflecting telescopes. All three types operate according to the same principles.

Light waves from distant objects in the universe arrive at the earth with their crests a succession of almost perfectly flat planes. These planes are parallel to one another but strike the ground at an angle—unless the object being viewed is directly overhead. Each crest is known as a *wave front.* The main mirror or lens gathers a wide section of a wave front and brings the waves together at a point called the *focus.*

Wave fronts from stars in different parts of the sky concentrate at different points. All these points, however, lie an equal distance from the mirror or lens in an area called the *focal plane.* The distance from a mirror or lens to its focal plane is called the *focal length.* If you were to place a sheet of paper at the focal plane, you would see an image of the part of the sky "viewed" by the mirror or lens. To record an image, astronomers place a CCD or photographic film at the focal plane. For direct observation, an eyepiece would replace the CCD or film. The eyepiece magnifies the image. The magnifying power of the telescope equals the focal length of the mirror or lens divided by the focal length of the eyepiece.

Refracting telescopes, also called *refractors,* have a large lens called an *objective lens*—or simply an *objective*—at one end of a long, narrow tube. The objective is *convex* (curved outward) on both sides so that the middle of the lens is thicker than the edges. The glass slows down the light waves as they pass through the lens. A wave slows down the most in the middle of the lens,

How optical telescopes work

Optical telescopes concentrate light to produce images of objects that are too faint to see with the unaided eye. Telescopes may have eyepieces as shown or may be equipped with electronic devices or film mountings for photographing the images.

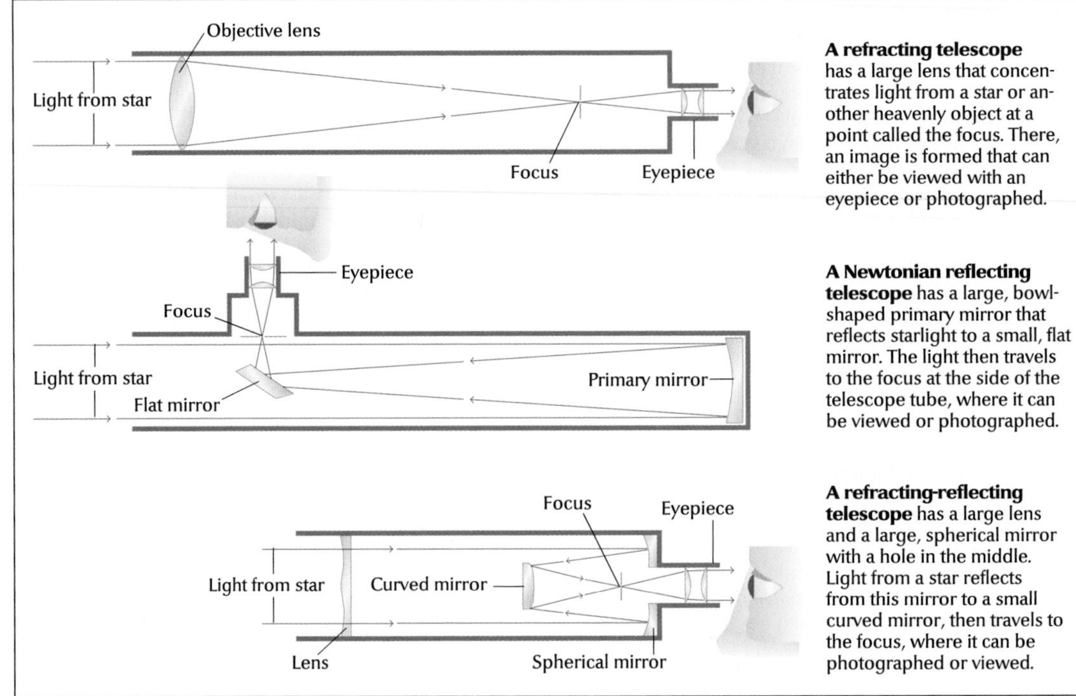

A refracting telescope has a large lens that concentrates light from a star or another heavenly object at a point called the focus. There, an image is formed that can either be viewed with an eyepiece or photographed.

A Newtonian reflecting telescope has a large, bowl-shaped primary mirror that reflects starlight to a small, flat mirror. The light then travels to the focus at the side of the telescope tube, where it can be viewed or photographed.

A refracting-reflecting telescope has a large lens and a large, spherical mirror with a hole in the middle. Light from a star reflects from this mirror to a small curved mirror, then travels to the focus, where it can be photographed or viewed.

WORLD BOOK illustrations

where the glass is thickest. At the ends of the lens, where the glass is thinnest, the wave slows down the least. The speed differences cause the wave crests to curve so that they arrive at the same place—the focus—at the same time.

Galileo made all his discoveries using refracting telescopes. Galileo's instruments and other early refractors, however, produced images with rainbow coloring around the edges called *chromatic aberration.* This coloring appeared because a convex lens slows down different colors of light passing through it by different amounts. For example, the lens slows down violet light more than red. As a result of this difference in speed, a wave front of violet light curves to a shorter focus than does a wave front of red light. Wave fronts whose focal lengths were significantly shorter or longer than that of the image produced the rainbow coloring.

Astronomers found that less-curved lenses produced less chromatic aberration. But these lenses had long focal lengths and therefore required extremely long tubes. Some early telescopes were more than 200 feet (60 meters) long. In the early 1800's, however, German optician Joseph von Fraunhofer found a way to avoid building such long telescopes. He fitted together two lenses made of different types of glass. The resulting *compound lens* had a short focal length and produced almost no chromatic aberration.

Reflecting telescopes, also called *reflectors,* use bowl-shaped mirrors instead of lenses. The bowl-shaped mirror, called the *primary mirror,* has a surface shaped so that any line across its center is a *parabola,* a curve like the path of a ball batted high in the air. A mirror with this shape reflects light rays to a sharp focus. A secondary mirror reflects the rays to a CCD, a piece of photographic film, or an eyepiece.

Astronomers generally prefer reflecting telescopes to refracting telescopes because mirrors have some advantages over lenses. The weight of a large lens can cause it to bend and warp. But a large, heavy mirror can be supported from behind. As a result, mirrors can be made much larger than lenses and, thus, can gather more light. In addition, mirrors are useful because they can also collect infrared rays and ultraviolet rays, which are absorbed by glass lenses. Finally, because they do not refract light, mirrors do not produce chromatic aberration.

Isaac Newton's first reflecting telescope used a small, flat mirror to reflect light from the primary mirror to an eyepiece at the side of the telescope tube. In 1672, a French telescope maker known as Cassegrain designed a telescope using a small convex mirror in front of the primary mirror. The small mirror reflected the light through a hole in the primary mirror to an eyepiece behind it. Astronomers now use this design for most optical and infrared telescopes.

The mirrors of early reflecting telescopes were shaped like a section of a sphere rather than a parabola. The main reason for using spherical mirrors was that they are much easier to grind and polish to the proper shape. However, spherical mirrors produce another form of aberration, a blurring called *spherical aberration.*

To avoid both chromatic and spherical aberration, scientists developed ways to make parabolic mirrors in the early 1700's. They made early mirrors of *speculum metal,* a mixture of copper and tin. But this mixture tarnishes easily, so the mirrors required repeated polishing. In the mid-1800's, German chemist Justus von Liebig learned how to deposit a thin coating of silver on glass to produce a brilliantly reflecting surface. When the surface tarnished or dulled, he could recoat it without having to polish it. Today, almost all reflecting telescopes have glass mirrors, most of them coated with aluminum.

The first telescope to use a large glass mirror was built in 1908 on Mount Wilson, near Pasadena, California. It is a Cassegrain telescope with a mirror 60 inches (1.5 meters) in diameter. Telescope designers still use the Mount Wilson telescope as a model for most large telescopes. For many years, the largest was the Hale Telescope, an instrument with a 200-inch (5-meter) mirror. This telescope, located on Palomar Mountain in southwestern California, began operating in 1948.

In the 1980's, astronomers began to work on a new generation of telescopes whose mirrors are larger and smoother than any built before. Like a large lens, an extremely large mirror of ordinary design would bend or warp under its own weight. Several new designs, including segmented mirrors, thin-disk mirrors, and honeycomb mirrors, overcame this limitation on mirror size. Many of the new telescope mirrors were made by an advanced technique called *spin-casting,* which replaces much of the costly, laborious process of grinding. In spin-casting, a huge rotating oven spins melted glass at a carefully controlled speed. The liquid glass flows into a shape that is nearly perfect for a telescope mirror.

Segmented mirrors consist of several small mirrors designed to do the job of one large mirror. Two identical telescopes called Keck I and Keck II have segmented mirrors. Each consists of 36 *hexagonal* (six-sided) mirrors mounted close together. These mirrors form a reflecting surface 33 feet (10 meters) in diameter. An electronic sensing system helps hold the segments in place. If a segment gets out of position, sensors on its edges activate pistons in the support structure that move the segment. The two Keck telescopes are on Mauna Kea, a mountain on the island of Hawaii.

Thin-disk mirrors use computer-controlled pistonlike devices called *actuators* to maintain the shape of a thin disk of glass. Four identical telescopes known together as the Very Large Telescope (VLT) use this design. Each individual telescope has a mirror 27 feet (8.2 meters) in diameter, but only 7 inches (18 centimeters) thick. When all four telescopes are focused on the same object, they will have the light-gathering power of a single telescope with a mirror 52 feet (16 meters) in diameter. The European Southern Observatory (ESO), led by astronomers from several European nations, built the VLT on Paranal Mountain in Chile. All four telescopes were making observations by September 2000.

Honeycomb mirrors are made from a mold filled with hundreds of hexagonal blocks. Melted glass covers the blocks and fills the spaces between them. Workers remove the blocks after the glass cools, leaving a stiff structure that is so light it could float on water.

Astronomers at the University of Arizona's Steward Observatory used this design to make the world's largest single telescope mirror. This mirror, completed in 1998, is $27\frac{1}{2}$ feet (8.4 meters) in diameter. It is the first of twin mirrors planned for the Large Binocular Telescope (LBT), which is being built on Mount Graham in southeastern Arizona. The mirrors will be mounted side by side, like the lenses of a gigantic pair of binoculars. Observatories in the United States, Italy, and Germany are building the LBT.

Refracting-reflecting telescopes, also called *catadioptric* telescopes, have a large lens at the front end of the tube and a large spherical mirror at the rear. The lens refracts light rays slightly to correct the spherical aberration produced by the mirror.

Bernhard Schmidt, an Estonian optician, invented the catadioptric telescope in 1930. This telescope forms images of a larger region of the sky than is possible with any other telescope design. Astronomers have used large Schmidt telescopes to photograph the entire sky.

Controlling a telescope. To collect as much light as possible from a faint object, astronomers often focus a telescope on the object for several hours. Because the rotation of the earth causes the stars to appear to move overhead throughout the night, the telescope must move to remain focused on the object.

In older telescopes, a structure called an *equatorial mount* makes it easy to keep the telescope pointed at the object. A part of this structure called the *yoke* holds the telescope tube near the center of the tube. The tube pivots relative to the yoke, swinging up or down. The yoke rotates on a circular support whose axis is inclined at an angle parallel to the rotational axis of the earth. Once the tube is fixed on the object, there is no need to move the tube relative to the yoke. All that is necessary is to rotate the yoke at a rate equal and opposite to the earth's spin. Thus, the equatorial mount is simple to use. However, it is large and expensive to build.

The development of modern computers has made it practical to use a smaller, less expensive mount called an *azimuthal (az uh MYOOTH uhl) mount.* In this mount, the yoke rotates on a circular support that is vertical, rather than inclined. To keep the tube sighted on the object, both the yoke and the tube must move at variable speeds. A computer calculates the speeds and controls the movements.

Analyzing spectra. Telescopes use spectrographs with CCD's or photographic film to produce images of spectra and measure the brightness of each of their colors. Astronomers find much information in dark and bright *spectral lines.* When a spectrum of visible light is spread out horizontally, spectral lines appear as thin, vertical lines in various locations across the spectrum. The entire spectrum, considered as a whole, also contains information about the object that emitted the light.

Light is a form of energy, and the dark lines, known as *absorption lines,* arise when light energy passes through a group of atoms. The atoms absorb fixed units of energy—that is, photons. Because this energy is removed from the passing light, absorption lines appear in the spectrum. Each chemical substance has its own pattern of lines. Thus, the spectrum indicates the composition of the object through which the light passes. Astronomers have analyzed the absorption lines of sunlight, for example, to determine what elements are present in the sun's surface layer, the *photosphere.*

The bright spectral lines, called *emission lines,* occur when hot atoms emit photons. Emission lines in the

E-Systems

The Very Large Array radio interferometer, located near Socorro, New Mexico, is one of the world's most powerful radio telescopes. It consists of 27 radio telescope reflectors, each measuring 82 feet (25 meters) in diameter.

spectrum of the *corona,* the outer edge of the sun's atmosphere, indicate the presence of iron atoms heated to millions of degrees.

An analysis of the entire band of radiation can also reveal an object's temperature. The various colors of light spread out across the spectrum according to their energy. In the visible spectrum, for example, the lowest-energy color, red, is at one end. At the other end is violet, the highest-energy color—but scientists refer to this end of the spectrum as the *blue end,* named after the color next to violet. The spectrum of a relatively cool star is more intense at the red end, while the spectrum of a relatively hot star is more intense at the blue end.

Spectral analysis can reveal an object's speed due to a phenomenon known as *redshift.* In the spectrum of any object moving toward or away from the earth, the spectral lines are shifted from where they would appear in the spectrum of a stationary object. If the object is approaching the earth, the lines shift toward the blue end of the spectrum. If the object is moving away, the lines shift toward the red end.

Adaptive optical systems are coming into use to correct atmospheric blurring in ground-based telescopes. The heating and cooling of the atmosphere produces blurring by distorting the wave front of light from an astronomical object. Some segments of the wave front get ahead of the main wave front and other segments lag behind. Adaptive optical systems correct a wave front before it reaches the focus of the telescope.

The first task in correcting a wave front is to make an electronic map of it as it comes into the telescope. A device called a *wave front sensor* provides the data for the map. In a *natural guide-star system,* the sensor uses a bright star whose position in the sky is close to the object being observed by the telescope. The atmosphere distorts a wave front coming from the guide star in almost exactly the same way in which it distorts a wave front coming from the object being observed.

Inside the sensor, tiny lenses focus different parts of a wave front from the guide star onto a CCD. Electronic signals representing this wave front travel to a computer, which "draws" the map.

As a wave front from the object being observed travels through the telescope, it reflects off a special mirror called a *deformable mirror.* Actuators controlled by the computer can change the shape of this mirror several hundred times each second. When the map indicates that one segment of the wave front is too far ahead, the computer moves the corresponding area of the deformable mirror back. The wave front segment must now travel farther. The main part of the wave front therefore can catch up with it. Similarly, a wave front segment that lags behind can catch up by reflecting from an area of the mirror that has been moved forward. In this way, the system can remove the wave front distortion.

If there is no bright star close enough to the object being observed, astronomers shoot a laser beam into the sky close to the object. The beam scatters off atoms at the top of the atmosphere and returns to the system, appearing as an artificial "star."

Radio telescopes

Radio telescopes collect and measure faint radio waves given off by objects in space. American engineer Karl G. Jansky discovered radio waves from space in 1931. In the late 1930's, Grote Reber, another American engineer, built the first bowl-shaped radio telescope and operated it in his backyard. Early radio telescopes found that the sun and the center of our galaxy were strong sources of radio waves. They also detected strong radio waves coming from dark areas of space. These sources were discovered to be the remains of exploded stars and a rare type of distant galaxy.

Since then, astronomers using radio telescopes have discovered objects that had been missed by optical telescopes. These discoveries include giant clouds of gas molecules; *pulsars,* collapsed stars that send out radio waves that arrive at the earth as regular pulses; and *quasars,* extremely distant starlike objects that produce enormous amounts of radiation.

How radio telescopes work. Most radio telescopes collect radio waves with a large reflector, often called a *dish antenna* or simply a *dish.* The dish has the same shape as the parabolic mirror of a reflecting telescope. Radio waves, however, are much longer than light waves. As a result, a radio telescope's dish need not be polished or shaped as accurately as the mirror of a reflecting telescope. But it must be much larger in diameter to collect the radio waves.

The reflector focuses the waves onto an antenna that translates them into electric signals. The signals contain information on the intensity of waves of different frequencies. A radio receiver amplifies the signals and sends them to a computer. The computer analyzes the radio spectrum of the wave source or produces an image of the source.

Types of radio telescopes. In most radio telescopes, motors turn the dish toward an object in the sky. The largest moving-dish telescopes measure 330 feet (100 meters) across. One such telescope is in Effelsberg, Ger-

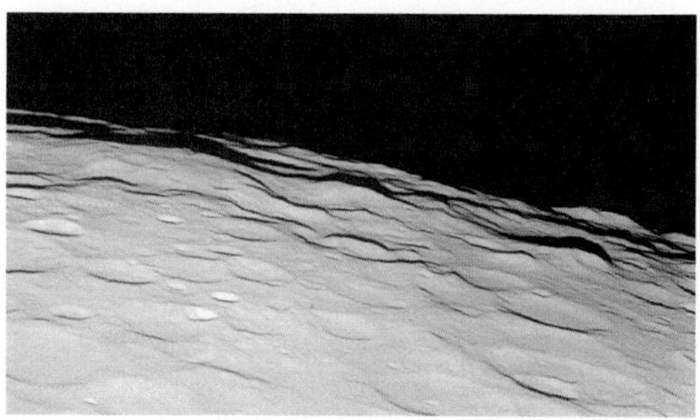

Steward Observatory, University of Arizona

An infrared image of the moon shows the warmest parts of the moon's surface as bright areas. The dark areas are partially or completely hidden from sunlight and are cooler.

many, near Bonn, and the other is in Green Bank, West Virginia.

Astronomers use fixed-dish telescopes to study objects that are faint in the radio spectrum. The world's largest radio telescope is a fixed dish built into a bowl-shaped valley near Arecibo, Puerto Rico. The dish is 1,000 feet (305 meters) in diameter. Scientists often use it to locate pulsars and measure their radiation.

Because the wavelength of radio waves is much longer than that of visible light, the resolution of a radio telescope is much lower than that of an optical telescope of the same diameter. However, a technique known as *radio interferometry* can produce extremely sharp images. This technique works best with many dishes spread out over long distances. The telescopes, considered as a unit, are called a *radio interferometer,* and the longest distance between dishes is the *baseline.*

In radio interferometry, computers at a central station combine data from the various dishes. First, however, the computers must introduce time delays into the data. The delays are necessary because each wave front comes in at an angle and therefore strikes the dishes at different times. The delays make up for the time differences. The combined data are equivalent to what would be received from a single dish that was much larger than any individual dish in the interferometer. The longer the interferometer's baseline is, the better is the resolution of the interferometer.

The most sensitive radio interferometer is the Very Large Array (VLA), which stands on a high plain near Socorro, New Mexico. The VLA has 27 movable dishes, each 82 feet (25 meters) in diameter. The sharpest radio images come from the Very Long Baseline Array (VLBA), a system of 10 reflectors spread across one side of the earth. Their locations range from the Virgin Islands north to New Hampshire and west to Hawaii. As an in-

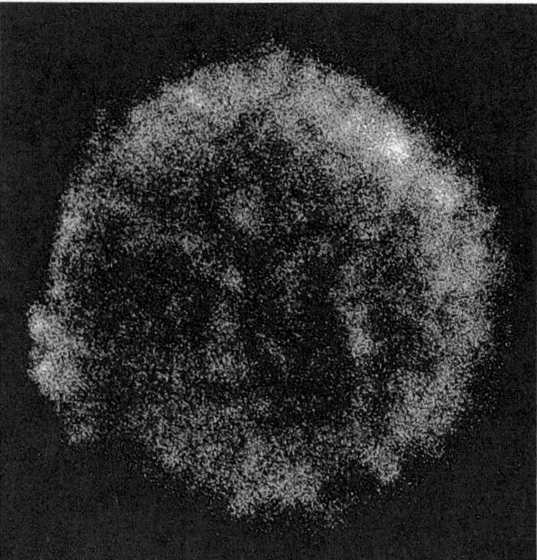

NASA

An X-ray image taken by the Rosat satellite in 1992 shows the remains of a star that exploded in 1572. The explosion was so violent that it was clearly visible to the unaided eye.

An X-ray telescope reflects X rays off curved mirrors at a slight angle called a *grazing incidence.* The nested-mirror design was used in the Rosat satellite shown here, and is also used in today's X-ray satellites.

WORLD BOOK illustrations by Oxford Illustrators Limited

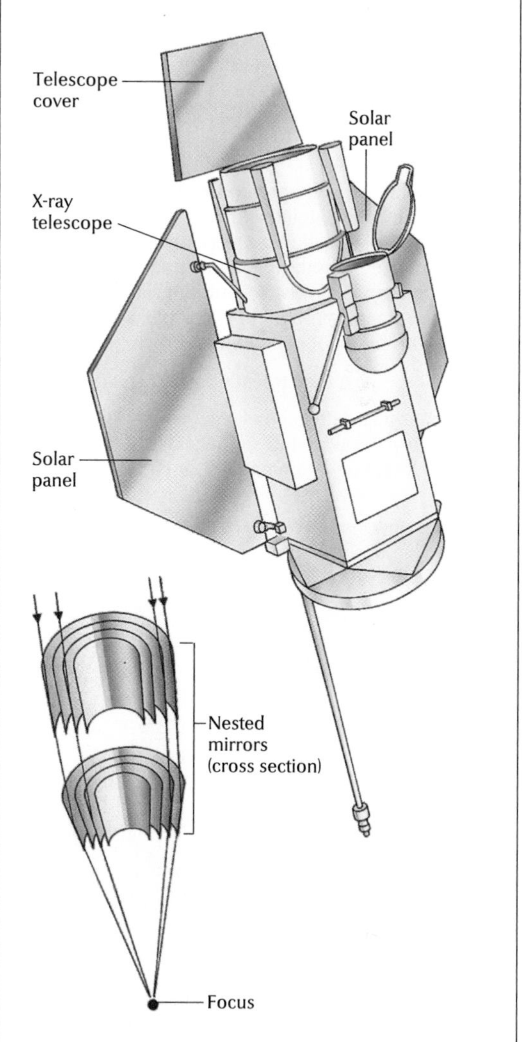

terferometer, the VLBA is equivalent to a single dish with a diameter roughly equal to the diameter of the earth.

Infrared telescopes

An infrared telescope collects *infrared* (heat) rays from objects in space. Most infrared telescopes are reflecting optical telescopes equipped with an electronic device called an *infrared array detector* instead of a CCD. But infrared telescopes have two special requirements: (1) parts of them must be kept cold while they operate, and (2) the telescopes must be located at high altitudes.

The cooling is necessary because any object that is at room temperature gives off tremendous amounts of infrared rays. Even heat from the telescope itself could interfere with the radiation from space.

High altitudes are necessary because water vapor and carbon dioxide in the atmosphere block infrared rays of many wavelengths. Astronomers build infrared telescopes on mountaintops where the air is thin and dry. They also send infrared telescopes into space aboard satellites.

In 1961, American physicist Frank J. Low built the first infrared detector that was sensitive enough for general use in astronomy. The device, called a *bolometer,* was an electronic thermometer housed in a vacuum and cooled to an extremely low temperature. When infrared rays hit the bolometer, it warmed up and emitted an electric signal.

An infrared telescope operated in orbit aboard the Infrared Astronomical Satellite (IRAS) from January to November 1983. Liquid helium cooled the telescope to only a few degrees above absolute zero (−273.15 °C). IRAS detected rings of dust around the star Vega and other nearby stars that might be solar systems in the process of forming.

Other telescopes

Telescopes that detect the electromagnetic radiation with the shortest wavelengths—the shortest ultraviolet rays and all X rays and gamma rays—look different from other telescopes. These rays have so much energy that a normal parabolic mirror cannot reflect them. As a result, the telescopes have unusual mirrors or no mirror at all.

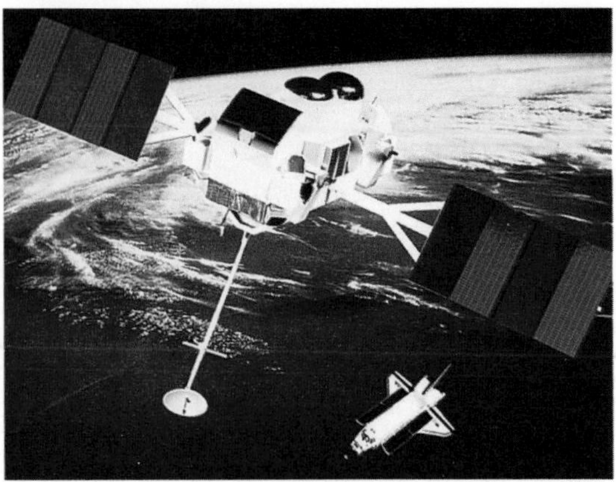

NASA

The Compton Gamma Ray Observatory, a satellite launched in 1991, carried instruments called *scintillators* to detect gamma rays, measure their intensity, and locate their sources.

In addition, the atmosphere absorbs all gamma rays and X rays and all but the longest ultraviolet rays. To detect these rays, astronomers therefore send telescopes into space on satellites.

Ultraviolet telescopes. A parabolic mirror can reflect all ultraviolet rays but those with the shortest wavelengths almost as well as it can reflect visible light. Astronomers therefore use reflecting telescopes in space to detect the longer-wavelength rays.

However, *extreme ultraviolet rays,* those with the shortest wavelengths, can reflect off a mirror at only a small angle called a *grazing incidence.* The reflection of a ray at a grazing incidence is like the skipping of a stone off the surface of a pond. Telescopes that detect extreme ultraviolet rays have mirrors that resemble a group of short tubes nested within one another. The rays reflect off the inner surfaces of the individual

John Florence, University of Arizona

A huge telescope mirror was made by University of Arizona astronomers without costly grinding to give the surface the correct shape. First, the telescope makers filled a mold with hundreds of hexagonal blocks. Next, they poured melted glass over the blocks and into the spaces between them. A circular oven then spun the the mold while keeping the glass melted. The liquid glass flowed into the correct shape, with the outer edge higher than the center. The mirror is 27 $\frac{1}{2}$ feet (8.4 meters) across.

© Roger Ressmeyer, Starlight

The Keck I Telescope, on Mauna Kea on the island of Hawaii, has a huge segmented mirror measuring 33 feet (10 meters) across. The mirror consists of 36 smaller mirrors.

mirrors and then proceed to the focal plane.

Astronomers use ultraviolet telescopes to study extremely hot objects, such as quasars and stars called *white dwarfs.* Other uses include investigations of how stars form and the study of the gas between the stars.

X-ray telescopes. The X rays that have the shortest wavelengths can pass straight through the materials that make up most telescope mirrors. But the longer-wavelength X rays, like extreme ultraviolet rays, will reflect at a grazing incidence. Some X-ray telescopes therefore resemble telescopes that detect extreme ultraviolet rays.

The simplest X-ray telescopes, however, have no mirror. Instead, they have an arrangement of iron or lead slats. The slats block all X rays except those from one line across the sky. The rays that enter the telescope go to a detector filled with a gas that absorbs X rays. An electronic device inside the detector counts the number of times the X rays interact with the gas. By scanning the sky, these telescopes can locate sources of X rays.

Many of the brightest X-ray sources are pairs of stars that orbit each other. In these pairs, one of the stars has collapsed to become a small, dense star called a *neutron star* or a *black hole*—an invisible object with such powerful gravitational force that not even light can escape its surface. The collapsed star pulls gas off the other star. When gas falls into the collapsed star, the gas emits the X rays.

Gamma-ray telescopes. Gamma rays have the highest energy of any electromagnetic radiation. When a gamma ray passes through a group of atoms, it can produce a shower of subatomic particles and low-energy radiation. The shower travels in the same direction as the original gamma ray and is detected with devices called *scintillators.*

Gamma-ray telescopes on the Compton Gamma Ray Observatory, which was in orbit from 1991 to 2000, enabled scientists to learn more about pulsars and quasars. The High Energy Transient Explorer-2 (HETE-2), a satellite launched in 2000, detects gamma-ray bursts and computes the locations of their sources. The satellite immediately sends this information to a ground-based communication system. Within seconds of the detection of a source, optical telescopes on the ground can begin to study the source.

A satellite known as Integral (*Inte*rnational *G*amma-*R*ay *A*strophysics *L*aboratory) carries devices that can detect an object's gamma rays, X rays, and visible light at the same time. Integral was launched in 2002.

J. Roger P. Angel and W. Thomas Roberts, Jr.

Related articles. See **Observatory**, with its list of *Related articles.* See also:

Aberration
Astronomy (Modern astronomy)
Binoculars
Bolometer
Charge-coupled device
Galileo
Green Bank Telescope
Hubble Space Telescope
Jansky, Karl G.
Lens
Light (How light behaves)
Lovell, Sir Bernard
Newton, Sir Isaac (Light and color)
Satellite (Telescopes)
Spectrometer
Sun (History of modern solar studies; pictures)
World, History of the (picture: New scientific devices)

Outline

I. What telescopes do
- A. Producing detailed images
- B. Detecting faint objects
- C. Gathering light for spectrographs

II. Optical telescopes
- A. Refracting telescopes
- B. Reflecting telescopes
- C. Refracting-reflecting telescopes
- D. Controlling a telescope
- E. Analyzing spectra
- F. Adaptive optical systems

III. Radio telescopes
- A. How radio telescopes work
- B. Types of radio telescopes

IV. Infrared telescopes

V. Other telescopes
- A. Ultraviolet telescopes
- B. X-ray telescopes
- C. Gamma-ray telescopes

Questions

What is a charge-coupled device?
Why are parts of infrared telescopes cooled to low temperatures?
How does an optical telescope focus light?
Why must astronomers make radio telescopes larger than optical telescopes?
What is a grazing incidence telescope?
Why do astronomers build infrared telescopes on mountaintops?
What is a radio interferometer?
Who first used a telescope to observe objects in space?
Why do astronomers usually prefer reflecting telescopes to refracting telescopes?
What causes star images to blur? How do astronomers correct blurring in telescopes?

Additional resources

Dickinson, Terence, and Dyer, Alan. *The Backyard Astronomer's Guide.* Rev. ed. Firefly Bks., 2002.
Matloff, Gregory L. *More Telescope Power: All New Activities and Projects for Young Astronomers.* Wiley, 2002. Younger readers.
Panek, Richard. *Seeing and Believing: How the Telescope Opened Our Eyes and Minds to the Heavens.* 1998. Reprint. Penguin, 1999.
Scagell, Robin. *Cambridge Guide to Stargazing with Your Telescope.* Cambridge, 2000.

Television

Television, also called TV, is one of our most important means of communication. It brings moving pictures and sounds from around the world into millions of homes. People with a television set can sit at home and watch the leader of a nation make a speech or visit a foreign country. They can see a war being fought, and they can watch government leaders try to bring about peace. Through television, viewers can see and learn about people, places, and things in distant lands. Television can take viewers into the depths of the ocean, out into space, and into strange worlds that can be seen only beneath a microscope.

In addition to all these things, television brings its viewers a steady stream of programs designed to entertain and inform. Entertainment programs include dramas, comedies, game shows, sports events, cartoons, variety shows, and motion pictures. Informational programs include documentaries, news, political coverage, talk shows, and financial information.

Most homes in industrialized nations have at least one television set. In the United States, for example, a TV set is in use in each home for an average of seven hours a day. Because of its widespread popularity, television has an important influence on today's culture, including how people spend their time and money, and what they see and learn.

The name *television* comes from a Greek word meaning *far* and a Latin word meaning *to see.* Thus, *television* means *to see far.* Television systems change the light and sound waves from a scene into electronic signals called *electromagnetic waves.* A television set receives these signals and turns them back into pictures and sounds.

Experiments leading to the invention of TV began in the 1800's, but progress was slow. Television as we know it today was not developed until the 1920's. It had little importance in communication until the late 1940's. During that time television stations began local *over-the-air broadcasting,* using electromagnetic waves to send programs from a transmitter to antennas in homes.

What television offers

Today, most people watch television programs that are broadcast over the air by commercial or public television stations. But over-the-air broadcasting is only one of several methods for delivering TV programs. In many countries, people who own television sets may subscribe to *cable television services,* which use cables to bring programs to the home. Other households subscribe to *direct-broadcast satellite* (DBS) services, which enable viewers to receive signals directly from satellites. Viewers pay a fee for these services.

Schools, businesses, hospitals, and many other organizations use *closed-circuit television.* In closed-circuit TV, signals are sent—by way of wires—to only certain television sets rather than to all sets within the area that broadcast signals could reach.

Gerald I. Isenberg is Professor in the School of Cinema-Television at the University of Southern California. Arun N. Netravali is Executive Vice President of Research at the Bell Laboratories division of Lucent Technologies.

Astronaut Edwin Aldrin reaches the moon (NASA)

News events

Television is sometimes called "the device that brings the world into the home." TV provides millions of home viewers with a wide variety of entertainment, information, and special events. The pictures on this and the following page show some examples of television's far-reaching coverage.

Since the late 1970's, new types of electronic equipment have changed the way people use television in their homes. For example, many homes have videocassette recorders (VCR's) and other devices that enable people to watch prerecorded entertainment. In addition, people can use a TV set with a video game system to play electronic games. Or they can subscribe to a televised information service. New technologies are bringing the abilities of a computer to television and providing new ways to use television for information and entertainment.

Commercial television is broadcast by stations that sell advertising time to pay for their operating costs and to make a profit. Most commercial television stations broadcast many more entertainment programs than any other kind. These shows include light dramas called *situation comedies;* action-packed dramas about detectives, doctors, lawyers, and police officers; and movies, including some made expressly for television. Entertainment programs also include game shows, *soap operas* (melodramatic plays), and children's shows.

Another kind of commercial television program is the *documentary.* A documentary is a dramatic, but nonfic-

Opening ceremonies of Winter Olympic Games at Nagano, Japan; © Cary M. Prior, Allsport

Sports events

"Mobil Masterpiece Theater"; Granada TV from Shooting Star

Literary dramas

"ER"; AP/Wide World

Medical dramas

"The Simpsons"; 20th Century Fox from Shooting Star

Comedy shows

tional, presentation of information. Some TV documentaries entertain as well as inform. These include travel programs about faraway places. Television also presents documentaries about such serious social issues as alcoholism, drug abuse, poverty, and racial prejudice. The *newsmagazine show* is a popular format for the presentation of these documentaries.

Some commercial television stations broadcast many talk shows, also called *discussion shows.* On these shows, a host interviews people from many walks of life—including athletes, authors, motion-picture and TV stars, politicians, and groups of people who share a common problem or experience.

Commercial television stations may also cover sports events—from baseball and football to table tennis and skiing. Every two years, TV brings its viewers the colorful Olympic Games—often from halfway around the world.

Most commercial stations broadcast brief summaries of local, national, and international news every day. Also, stations often interrupt their regular program schedules to present extended coverage of special events, such as political conventions and royal weddings or funerals.

Public television is broadcast by stations that are nonprofit organizations. Methods of funding these stations vary from country to country. Under one arrangement, public television stations rely on business, government, and public contributions to pay for their operating costs. Such stations usually make their own decisions about program content. Some of these stations also broadcast brief commercial messages. Another way public television may be financed is from license fees paid by owners of television sets. In some countries, stations are almost entirely paid for and run by the government, which makes, or influences, decisions about program content.

Public television usually provides more educational and cultural programming than does commercial television. Because public television stations are less dependent on advertising, they do not need to attract huge audiences.

Some public stations broadcast educational programs on a wide range of subjects—from literature and physics to cooking and yoga. In some cases, viewers can earn school credit by passing tests based on what the programs teach. Some educational programs on public TV take much the same form as classroom instruction. But others use a more entertaining approach. One such program is "Sesame Street," a lively, yet educational, children's show. "Sesame Street" first appeared in the United

States but now has local versions produced in many countries.

Public television stations offer many programs that combine entertainment and cultural enrichment. They telecast such offerings as plays by leading dramatists, performances of ballets and symphonies, and surveys of art and history. Such television shows may draw audiences that are small by commercial TV standards, but which are much larger than the number that could attend a performance in a theater or concert hall.

News and current affairs programs make up an important portion of programming for most public television stations. Many stations provide news bulletins throughout the day, with a main national news program in the evening. In addition, there may be programs dealing specifically with local and regional news. Some public television stations also have programs in which journalists and others concerned with current events discuss topics in the news. Politicians may be interviewed about important matters of the day. In some programs, members of the studio audience are invited to join in discussion of a particular topic or topics.

Cable television delivers signals to home TV sets through cables. It has two important advantages over commercial and public television. First, it offers improved reception of network and local station programs. Second, it provides a greater variety of programming.

Cable television was first used in the late 1940's. Its original purpose was to bring network and local programs to places that either cannot receive TV signals through the air, or can receive them only with much interference. Such places include isolated communities, mountain valleys, extremely hilly regions, and areas with many tall buildings.

Improved reception of regular television programs still ranks as an important purpose of cable television. But since the 1960's, people have begun to use it for other purposes. Some cable systems carry more than 100 channels—far more than can be broadcast over the airwaves even in the largest urban areas. This increase in the number of channels available has made *narrowcasting* possible. Unlike broadcasting, which tries to appeal to the largest possible audience, narrowcasting offers programs that appeal to a particular age, ethnic, or interest group. For example, cable channels may specialize in movies, news, sports, music, comedy, health, religion, weather, or Spanish-language programs. Such channels focus on attracting viewers with particular interests. Some cable services offer channels that present adult education classes. Many communities also require cable operators to reserve channels for programs of local interest, such as city council meetings or local school graduation ceremonies. Thus, cable television offers a wide variety of programming to its viewers.

Certain channels, such as premium movie channels, charge a fee that a customer pays in addition to the monthly fee for basic cable service. In addition, most cable services offer one or more channels that present movies or events that viewers can subscribe to on a *pay-per-view* basis. A consumer orders the programming by telephone or through an *addressable set-top box,* a device that receives cable signals and also allows communication with a cable company. The charge is applied to the next month's cable service bill.

Satellite television offers an even greater number of channels to its subscribers than does cable TV. It does not carry local programming, however. Millions of homes in many countries receive signals from *direct-broadcast satellites* (DBS). Satellite transmissions cover a wide reception area. A satellite operating over western Europe, for example, can beam programs to viewers in France, Germany, the Netherlands, the United Kingdom, and several other countries. Subscribers use dish-shaped antennas to receive DBS signals. Most DBS programming is provided by the same services that supply programs to cable television.

Closed-circuit television has a number of specialized uses. Many schoolrooms have TV sets that receive special lessons by closed-circuit television. Also, a lesson in one class can be shown simultaneously to stu-

Closed-circuit television enables security personnel to monitor many locations in a jail at the same time.

dents in other parts of the school through closed-circuit TV. Businesses use videotaped television programs extensively to train their employees. Many large corporations operate their own private TV studios.

Closed-circuit TV in banks, stores, and prisons enables guards to observe many people at once. Hospitals use closed-circuit TV to *monitor* (keep track of) patients. Television cameras are placed in operating rooms to give medical students close-up views of actual surgical procedures. Some companies conduct long-distance meetings and conferences via live TV. This procedure, called *videoconferencing,* saves the time and expense of travel.

Video entertainment systems include videocassette recorders (VCR's), video compact disc players, CD-i players, DVD players, and video game systems. Each of these devices sends video and audio signals to a viewer's television set, usually via cables that connect the device to the TV. Many people also connect video entertainment devices to a stereophonic sound system to provide sound similar to that in a movie theater.

Videocassette recorders enable people to tape television programs on videocassettes and play them back later. People also may buy or rent prerecorded videotapes. Many of these are tapes of such entertainments as movies, concerts, or sports events. Others include exercise programs or other instructional information. See **Videotape recorder.**

Many people like to capture vacations, parties, and other family events on videotape. A videocassette recorder serves as the recording mechanism in many *camcorders,* devices that combine a camera and a recording mechanism in one unit. Many camcorders use a tape that cannot be played in a standard VCR. In such cases, cables connect the camcorder to a television set for playback, or the camcorder sends an infrared signal to a receiver attached to the television set.

Video compact disc players play video compact discs (VCD's), a type of *optical disc* that carries both sound and picture information. Compact discs store information in *digital* (numeric) code. The information on a compact disc, as on other optical discs, is played back by a device called a *laser* inside the player. VCD players can also play audio CD's, which contain no video information. VCD players are most widely used in China and other Asian countries. See **Compact disc.**

CD-i players play special *interactive* compact discs. These players and discs enable a viewer to use a remote control to react to certain prerecorded programs by means of words and symbols shown on the TV screen. CD-i's have uses in education, entertainment, and other fields. Some CD-i players can also play VCD's.

DVD players work with DVD's, optical discs that are the same size as a compact disc but store much digital information. One side of a standard DVD can hold an entire full-length movie. For even greater capacity, each side of a disc may contain two layers of data, one embedded beneath the other. Such a disc can hold as many as four movies, or one movie plus such added features as scenes cut from the picture's theatrical release or comments from the movie's director.

Some DVD players can also play VCD's. *DVD recorders* can record television programs on special DVD's. Some camcorders store video images on recordable DVD's. These discs may then be played back using a DVD player. See **DVD.**

Video game systems often use a television screen as a game board. Video games are played on a computer-controlled unit connected to a TV set. Each game has its own program on a cartridge, compact disc, or DVD that is inserted into the unit. Players operate controls that move electronic characters and other images that appear on the TV screen. See **Video game.**

Televised information services provide viewers with news stories, stock market listings, and other kinds of information. One type of service, called *teletext,* is broadcast as part of ordinary television signals. A device attached to the television set enables a viewer to access any of a few hundred "pages" of information per TV channel. Another type of service, called *videotext, videotex,* or *viewdata,* is brought into the home over cables or telephone lines. Like teletext, the service may be used to display information. But unlike teletext, videotext enables a user to conduct two-way transactions. Some users shop, perform banking transactions, and pay their bills using videotext. Televised information services were developed in the United Kingdom during the late 1960's and in Canada and France during the 1970's.

Producing television programs

The *production* (putting together) of a television program is an extremely complicated process. A program requires careful planning, much preparation, and the combined efforts of many skilled workers.

Most television productions take place in television studios. But production companies also create TV shows in movie studios, on city streets, in stadiums, in deserts and jungles, and even underwater. Broadcasters telecast some programs *live* (as they happen). Live telecasts include coverage of political conventions, speeches by world leaders, awards presentation shows, and sports events. The parts of newscasts in which the announcers speak are also live. But most of the news stories shown on these programs come from videotape recordings.

Most TV programs—including almost all entertainment shows—are prerecorded and then telecast later. The recording may be done on videotape or on film. Many prerecorded programs are produced from beginning to end, in the manner of a stage play. Television production companies also use the *piecemeal* approach of the motion-picture industry. In the piecemeal approach, each scene is recorded separately and *spliced* (connected together) later.

The first two parts of this section—*Planning and preparation* and *Putting a show on the air*—trace the production of a program in a television studio. But much of the information under these headings applies to all TV productions. The last part of this section describes other production methods.

Planning and preparation. The planning of television shows begins in the programming department of the networks and stations that broadcast them. Members of these departments decide what programs their companies will telecast. Networks and stations produce many programs themselves. Independent producers create other programs and sell them to networks and stations. In either case, once a programming depart-

A television production requires the combined efforts of many professionals. Newscasters must appear natural on camera as they read news stories from a TelePrompTer and take directions from the stage manager.

NBC (WORLD BOOK photo by Ralph Brunke)

ment approves an idea for a program, a *producer* takes responsibility for its production.

The producer usually begins by obtaining a script and choosing a director. Sometimes—especially for uncomplicated shows—producers write their own script. They may also serve as their own director—in which case they become a *producer-director.* But more often, the producer assigns the scriptwriting to a professional writer or team of writers, and the directing to a professional director. The producer and director select the *talent* (actors and other people who will appear on the show). The producer also chooses the production specialists needed to produce the show. These people may include an art director, a costume designer, and a composer. In addition, the producer works closely with the director throughout the production process. The producer of a news program decides which of the day's events to include in the newscast and in what order to present them.

Writers prepare the scripts for television programs. A television script is a written account of what is to be said and done during the program.

The amount of detail a script contains varies, depending on the program. A talk show script, for example, may include only the host's opening remarks and some of the key questions to ask the guests. During most of the show, the host and the guests carry on *ad-libbed* (unplanned) conversations. A script for a television drama, on the other hand, includes every word to be spoken by the cast members. It also describes the actions they are to perform. For a newscast, writers prepare the script that the announcers read. Reporters usually prepare questions and comments for news stories they cover outside the studio.

The director. After the writers finish the script, the director reads it and decides how to translate it into an actual television program. Directors develop opinions about how the characters should speak, move, and generally behave. They decide what camera shots will be needed to create the effects they visualize. Sometimes, the director has an artist prepare a *storyboard* (series of drawings) that shows how key parts of the program will look.

Production specialists. The producer and director call on many production specialists to help prepare for the program. An *art director* and artists and craftspeople who work with the art director design and build the show's scenery. A *costume designer* creates or obtains costumes needed for the production. A *property manager* gets special items called *props* for the show. These items include furniture, vases of flowers, and guns. Specialists in technical work also play a key role in the production process. They advise the producer and director on what kinds of cameras, microphones, and lights will be needed. A *production manager,* also called a *production coordinator,* sees to it that all the required equipment is available when needed.

Talent is a technical term for all the people who appear on television programs. Talent may appear on television as themselves, as do newscasters, sports announcers, and talk show hosts. Or a talent may play someone else, as does an actor or actress in a TV drama or situation comedy.

Selection of talent ranks among the key steps in the planning of a television program. The producer and director do this important job. If the talent are big stars, they may get television roles because of their fame and proven ability. But usually, the talent must *audition* (try out) for the parts they want to play. During an audition, the director and producer may ask the talent to take a *screen test* (perform in front of a camera).

The talent who earn a job get a script so they can study their lines. An actor or actress may have less than a week to learn the lines for a one-hour drama. Those

NBC (WORLD BOOK photo by Ralph Brunke)

NBC (WORLD BOOK photo by Ralph Brunke)

Production preparations include reporting news stories and videotaping the coverage for playback during the newscast, *left.* At the studio, a videotape editor and a reporter work to cut a story so that it presents only the most important information, *right.*

who perform on TV's daily soap operas have only a few hours each day to memorize their lines.

Some television productions make use of *cue cards* to help the talent with their lines. A cue card is a large piece of cardboard or similar material with writing on it. The writing may be a key word or phrase, or an entire passage from a script. An off-camera stagehand holds the card up so the talent can see it.

Television performers who deliver commercials, speeches, and news stories often use an aid called a *TelePrompTer* or *Autocue.* Such devices display the words from a script. The display moves continuously, giving the talent a line-by-line view of the script. The TelePrompTer or Autocue is located so that a person reading from it appears to be looking directly at the camera.

Composers and musicians. Most entertainment programs include music. A producer and director may decide they need an original musical composition for their show. If so, the producer hires a composer. The composer meets with the producer and director to discuss the theme, mood, and *climaxes* (dramatic high points) of the program. Composers base their compositions on what they learn about the show. Often, producers and directors use existing music for their programs. To do so, they must get permission from the holders of the copyright on the music, and pay them a fee.

The producer hires musicians and a conductor to perform the music. For prerecorded shows, the musicians often record the music after the actual program is produced. Then, technicians combine the music with the rest of the program.

Rehearsals are practice sessions for TV shows. Most TV productions require at least one rehearsal. Complicated productions often require many more.

During a rehearsal, the talent—under the director's guidance—practice their lines and their actions. The director also directs the actions of the camera operator and other off-camera workers.

Rehearsal for a dramatic production may begin with a *script reading.* Then, the director may call for a *dry run* (rehearsal without equipment or costumes). Many dry runs take place in a *rehearsal room.* This room has lines on the floor that indicate where such things as doors, chairs, and tables will be during the actual production. A director may watch a dry run through a *director's viewfinder.* This device resembles the viewfinder on a still camera. It enables the director to get an idea of how scenes will appear on television.

Finally, the director calls for a *dress rehearsal,* also known as a *camera rehearsal,* in the studio. The goal of a dress rehearsal is to achieve a performance that is the same as the final production will be. In fact, directors sometimes record both the dress rehearsal and the actual production. In reviewing both recordings, directors may decide that parts of the dress rehearsal came out better than the actual production. They may then substitute the parts of the dress rehearsal they like for the corresponding parts of the actual production.

Television rehearsals aim for split-second timing. A TV show cannot run even a few seconds past its planned time, because that time is set aside for the next program.

Putting a show on the air. When the time comes to tape a program, everything needed for the process is brought together in a television studio. Workers put the scenery and props in place. Other workers set up floodlights and spotlights. Technicians turn these lights off and on and brighten and dim them during the production to achieve the desired effect for various scenes. Often, a single televised scene requires as many as 20 different lighting instruments. One or more microphones are set up. Workers bring television cameras—usually at least two and sometimes four or five—into the studio.

NBC (WORLD BOOK photo by Ralph Brunke)

NBC (WORLD BOOK photo by Ralph Brunke)

Putting a show on the air requires the skills of many workers. Control-room monitors show scenes shot by studio cameras and scenes taped earlier. The producers work with the director in deciding which scenes go on the air, *left.* An audio engineer controls the sound, *right.*

The people responsible for the technical parts of the show's production get ready in the *control room.* This room is located near the site of the telecast.

Some studios have rows of seats, very much like a theater. Visitors can come to these *audience areas* and watch shows being produced.

Before the show begins, makeup artists apply makeup to the talent who will appear on the show. Makeup helps people look natural on camera. The talent put on special costumes, if the show calls for such costumes. Finally, they come into the studio and perform the production before the cameras.

The cameras used for *shooting* (making pictures of) the production are big instruments. They are mounted on wheels so the camera operators can move them around the studio to change the direction of their shots. Some cameras are operated by remote control from the control room instead of by an operator in the studio. Cameras can tilt up and down to change the vertical angles and turn left and right to follow action. In addition, cameras can adjust from a close-up to a long-range view of a scene by means of a device called a *zoom lens.* The zoom lens enables the camera to vary televised scenes without moving. *Zooming* (moving in and out on scenes) is a widely used production technique.

Microphones. Most studio TV productions involve the use of one or more *boom microphones.* A boom microphone is attached to a *boom* (long metal arm). A worker called the *boom operator* uses mechanical devices to move the microphone above and in front of the person speaking. For dramatic productions, it is essential that the microphone stay out of camera view. Imagine a dramatic scene in which an actor lies exhausted in a hot desert, crying for help. If suddenly the boom microphone that hangs above him dropped into camera view, the scene would look ridiculous. Sometimes, television makes use of *hidden microphones*—either in addition to, or in place of, boom microphones. They may be hidden in or behind scenery or props or in a talent's clothing.

Talk shows and other nondramatic productions may use boom microphones. But they also use microphones that viewers can see. These include *desk microphones,* which stand on desks or tables in front of performers; and *hand microphones,* which performers hold. Another kind of microphone, the *lavalier,* is hung around a performer's neck or attached to a performer's clothing. It may be in camera view or hidden in the clothing.

The control room. During a television program, scenes from each of the studio's cameras appear one at a time. Pictures from other video sources, including filmed commercials, taped news stories, and images bearing titles, also appear on the screen. The job of determining which scene appears at a given time is performed in the control room. A program may also include sounds from several sources. Technicians in the *audio control* section of the control room regulate the sounds. Engineers in the control room operate equipment that maintains the quality of the pictures and sounds.

The control room has several *monitors* (television sets). Each monitor shows the scenes from one camera or other video source. The director watches the monitors when choosing which scenes to put on the air. The picture that is on the air at any given time appears on a monitor called the *program monitor, line monitor,* or *master monitor.*

An important piece of equipment in the control room is the *switcher* or *vision mixer.* This instrument has many buttons, including buttons for selecting any of the studio cameras and any other picture source. On command from the director, a technician called the *technical director* (TD) or *vision engineer* presses buttons to change the televised scene. The switcher also enables television broadcasters to *cut* (switch instantly) from the program to commercials, and back again.

The switcher also has levers. By moving levers in various ways, the TD can combine scenes from two or more cameras or other video sources. The TD can also make other changes. These combinations and changes are called *special effects.* They include the *dissolve,* the *super,* the *wipe, keying,* and *digital video effects.*

The *dissolve* is a gradual change from one picture to another in which the two pictures overlap briefly. Directors use the dissolve to move smoothly from scene to scene and, sometimes, to indicate a passage of time.

The *super,* also known as *superimposition,* is the blending together of two scenes. Television often uses this device to show dream scenes. One camera shows a close-up of the face of the sleeping person, and the other shows the scene about which the person is dreaming.

A *wipe* is a special effect in which one picture seems to push another picture off the screen. A wipe stopped halfway is called a *split screen.* TV productions use the split-screen technique to show scenes from two different places at the same time. Other wipes include the *circle* and the *diamond,* in which the second picture appears on the screen as an expanding circle or diamond.

Keying (sometimes called *matting*) is a technique that is used to show text over a scene. It may also be used to change the background in a scene. A camera shoots a person against a bright blue or green background, which is then replaced by another picture so that the person seems to stand in front of the new background. TV productions use this technique to place weather reporters in front of maps.

Digital video effects systems may be part of the switcher or separate devices. The TD can use them to perform a variety of special effects, including shrinking pictures and changing colors in a scene.

The sound inputs of a television program are controlled by an instrument called an *audio console.* An *audio engineer* operates this instrument. The audio engineer pushes buttons and moves levers to choose and mix together various audio inputs. For example, a scene of two people sitting in an automobile might require the audio engineer to mix the sounds of the people's conversation with recorded sounds of the automobile engine, outside traffic, and background music. The audio engineer also controls the volume of sounds.

Taping the program. Broadcasters usually record live programs on videotape at the same time as they telecast them. This allows the broadcasters to rerun all or parts of a show later. For example, videotaped highlights of live telecasts of speeches by world leaders are often shown later on newscasts. Videotapes of live sports events allow sportscasters to rerun and analyze key plays immediately after they happen. This process is called *instant replay.*

Master control is the electronic nerve center of a television station. Much of the electronic equipment that helps create television pictures is there. A program goes from master control by cable, satellite, or microwave to the transmitter. Then, the transmitter sends it on its way to the viewers. Master control also has equipment for switching from program to program. The programs include those that originate at the station, at network headquarters, and at remote locations.

Other production methods. A television production can differ from the method just described in four chief ways. (1) Television producers put some programs together piecemeal rather than straight through. (2) They shoot many programs on film or videotape rather than with TV cameras. (3) They record many programs for broadcast later instead of telecasting them live. (4) They create programs away from studios. Such programs are called *remote telecasts.*

The piecemeal approach involves recording a program on videotape or film scene-by-scene with *stopdowns* (pauses) between scenes. Each recorded scene is called a *take.* If tape is used, the director can play back the tape and judge its merits. If the director likes the take, the crew goes on to another one. If the director does not like it, he or she can call for a *retake* (shooting the scene over again). The piecemeal approach also allows directors to shoot scenes out of order. If, for example, the first and last scenes of a TV play happen in the same location, the director may shoot them one right after the other. Upon completion, film or tape editors splice all the scenes together in their proper order to create a continuous story.

Filming and taping programs. Many TV producers use film or video cameras to create programs that take place at several locations. For example, television news programs, which report on widely scattered events, use film or videotape. In addition, motion-picture studios create many entertainment programs with film cameras. For more information on such filming, see **Motion picture** (How motion pictures are made).

After camera operators film a program, broadcasters telecast it from a *telecine* (pronounced *TEHL uh SIHN ee*) unit, a device that converts film images to TV signals. For technical information, see *Telecine* later in this article.

Prerecorded telecasts include nearly all entertainment programs. These programs are produced straight through in the television studio and recorded on videotape for later broadcast. The director reviews the finished tape, and tape editors correct any major errors in it. Then, the tape is played when the program is scheduled for broadcasting. For technical information on videotape, see *Videotape recording* later in this article.

Remote telecasts. Almost all remote telecasts are broadcast live. They include telecasts of sports events and political conventions. Producers of these programs use regular-sized television cameras. But they also use *minicams,* handheld cameras that are small enough to be carried around. Such cameras help TV crews provide live coverage from such huge areas as sports fields and convention halls. Broadcasters park a *remote truck* or other *control vehicle* near the place of the telecast. This vehicle contains control room and master control equipment needed to create TV signals. The signals travel by microwave, wire, or satellite from the vehicle to the transmitter.

In addition, television crews may use *camcorders,* cameras that contain a videocassette recorder that immediately captures sound and images on videotape. The videotape can be edited later for use in newscasts or other programming.

The U.S. television industry

The popularity of TV programs in the United States created a huge television industry in a short time. In 1946, there were only six television stations in the United

States. Today, the country has more than 1,500 stations. About three-fourths are commercial stations, and the rest are public stations.

The number of TV stations accounts for only part of television's impact on the American economy. The manufacture and sales of television sets and broadcasting equipment became big businesses because of the rise of television. In addition, broadcasting, manufacturing, and sales created thousands of new jobs.

The national networks. About three-fourths of all commercial television stations in the United States are *affiliates* of one of the four major national networks—ABC, CBS, FOX, and NBC. An affiliate agrees to carry programs provided by a network. The ABC television network is owned by the Walt Disney Company; CBS by Viacom Inc.; FOX by News Corporation; and NBC by NBC Universal, Inc. Three smaller networks, the United Paramount Network (UPN), the Warner Brothers (WB) Television Network, and PAX TV, each broadcast several hours of programming per week. Two Spanish-language networks, Univision and Telemundo, supply programming to stations in a number of cities.

The networks create some of their programs and buy others from independent producers. A network pays its affiliates for carrying the programs. Sponsors, in turn, pay the networks for showing their commercials on the stations.

The success of cable television has reduced the size of the broadcast networks' average audience to about two-thirds the audience they attracted in the 1980's. But, sparked by laws of supply and demand, advertising revenue has grown enough to more than offset the loss of viewers. Still, a network's success depends on its ability to select programs that attract large audiences. The bigger a program's audience, the more money sponsors will pay for the right to show commercials on it.

Choosing new programs. The TV executives who choose network programs know that famous entertainers and championship sports contests usually attract large audiences. But these executives cannot be certain

Television access in selected countries

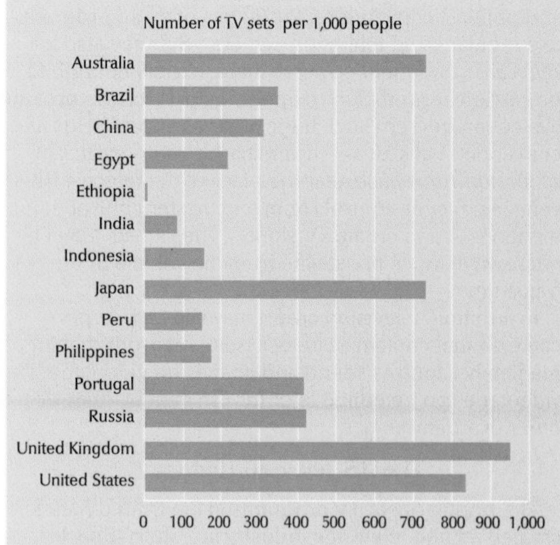

Figures are for 2001. Source: World Bank.

how many viewers other shows will draw. They may be helped in choosing programs by specialists in *audience research.* Such specialists collect data about people's interests and the kinds of programs they like. These specialists also gather the responses of audiences invited to view special "pilot" episodes of new programs. Such research has limited success in predicting a program's popularity for various reasons. For example, an audience's response to a single exposure to a program might differ from its response to a series. As a result, network executives must ultimately rely on their own intuition in choosing programs.

Measuring a program's success. The success of a program is measured in *ratings* and *share.* Ratings measure the percentage of all households equipped with television that are tuned to a particular program. Share measures the percentage of TV homes with a set switched on that are tuned to a particular program.

Nielsen Media Research ranks as the most important national audience measurement service. It provides television stations and advertisers with information about ratings and share and with *demographic data* about audiences. Demographic data describe the makeup of an audience in terms of gender, age, income, education, race, place of residence, and other features. The Arbitron Ratings Company is the leading American audience measurement service at the local level. Advertisers are often willing to pay more for certain selected types of viewers, such as women 18-49 years old. Therefore, network programmers choose offerings that will appeal to the advertiser's most desired demographic.

A national audience survey typically consists of about 5,000 households that are paid a small fee. The viewing habits in these households supposedly reflect the habits of the entire nation. Networks usually cancel a series that receives low ratings, often after only a few shows. The most advanced device to measure a TV audience is the People Meter, which resembles a TV remote-control unit. Family members each press an assigned key on the meter to indicate who is watching TV. In this way, the People Meter registers the age and gender of a program's viewers for advertisers.

Commercial stations. About 1,200 local commercial stations operate in the United States. About 75 percent of them are affiliates of the four major networks. The rest operate independently or as affiliates of the two smaller networks.

An affiliate carries many hours of network programs daily. In 1971, however, the Federal Communications Commission (FCC)—which regulates broadcasting in the United States—limited the amount of network programming affiliates can carry during *prime time.* Prime time refers to the evening hours, when TV draws the most viewers. The FCC ruled that local stations in the nation's 50 largest TV markets cannot broadcast more than three hours of network programs during prime time (or four hours on Sunday). This ruling was designed to force the stations to offer a wider variety of programs—especially programs of local interest—during prime time.

Syndicated programming. In spite of the FCC ruling, most non-network programs are old movies, talk shows, game shows, and reruns of old network shows. These programs are *syndicated*—that is, sold to the stations individually by independent organizations called *syndica-*

tors. Affiliates or independent stations buy syndicated programs rather than produce new ones because it is far less expensive. In addition, syndicated programs are generally well known. Local stations fill some time with shows they produce themselves, especially newscasts.

Production companies may create television series for original distribution through a system known as *first-run syndication.* Examples of such series include "Star Trek: The Next Generation," "Baywatch," and "Xena, Warrior Princess." First-run syndication most often uses an arrangement called *barter sales.* Under this arrangement, individual stations acquire programs by splitting the available advertising time with the syndicator. The syndicator recovers the cost of production by selling national advertising time. By eliminating the network, a syndicator can make a greater profit from a popular program. A greater risk of failure falls on the producer and syndicator, however. The addition of UPN and WB in the 1990's reduced the market for original syndicated programming by filling much of the available station time.

Advertising. Both affiliates and independent stations sell time to advertisers to cover the costs of their programs. Television commercials appear between and during most programs. The vast majority urge viewers to buy a product, such as dog food, shampoo, cars, or insurance policies. At election time, many political candidates buy advertising time on television to try to convince people to vote for them.

A small percentage of TV advertising provides a *public service announcement* (PSA). PSA's may include messages urging people to drive carefully, to avoid drugs, or to stay in school. They also include announcements about local community activities.

Infomercials. Many commercial stations fill time slots not suitable for original or syndicated programming by selling broadcast time to companies with products to sell. These companies may promote a product in a program called an *infomercial.* On a typical infomercial, which usually lasts 30 minutes, a celebrity or other spokesperson demonstrates and endorses a product. Direct appeals to purchase the product over the telephone or through the mail are often part of the program.

Criticism of commercial television. Commercial television attracts huge audiences. Often, more than 50 million people tune in to a top entertainment show or sports event. On a typical day, more than 25 million homes have a TV set tuned to one of the major-network evening news programs. Thus, it can be assumed that large numbers of people like what commercial television offers. Even so, many people criticize its coverage. They say that commercial TV provides too many programs designed only to entertain, and not enough shows that inform, educate, or furnish cultural enrichment. The critics also claim that much of the entertainment is of poor quality because it aims at the largest possible audience. They express concern that much commercial programming has an excess of violence and sexual content. They also criticize newscasts for being too brief to provide thorough coverage of the news.

The people responsible for deciding what appears on commercial television respond to such criticisms by pointing out that commercial TV must sell advertising at high prices. To do so, the programs must attract large numbers of viewers. Many more people watch popular shows and brief news reports than watch culturally enriching shows and in-depth news analysis.

The Home Shopping Network

Home shopping services display items that television viewers can purchase by calling a number on the screen.

Public stations. More than 350 public TV stations operate in the United States. These stations create many of the programs they show and buy programs from independent producers. Often, a program created by one public station is carried by many others. An agency called the Public Broadcasting System (PBS) serves as a distributor of locally produced public programs.

Public stations are nonprofit organizations, but they need money to cover their production and operating costs. The largest part of a station's funds come from viewer contributions. Businesses and foundations also help support public television. Local and state taxes help pay for many public stations. Stations also get funds from the Corporation for Public Broadcasting.

The Corporation for Public Broadcasting, created by Congress in 1967, gets most of its funds from the federal government. The corporation helps public stations serve their communities through grants for programming and technical facilities. It also finances the production of programs distributed by PBS and sets policies for a national public broadcasting service.

Cable and satellite systems bring television to the home by means of cables or through the air to a satellite receiving dish. These services make up a fast-growing part of the television industry.

Most programming for cable and satellite television is provided by national program suppliers called *programming services.* Each service tries to appeal to a particular demographic group or specializes in a particular type of programming. Lifetime, a network for women, and BET (Black Entertainment Television) are examples of services that try to appeal to a certain demographic group. CNN (Cable News Network) and Comedy Central are services that supply a particular form of programming.

For picking up a programming service, the cable or satellite supplier pays a charge per subscriber. The supplier passes on this cost to the consumer. Subscribers pay a monthly fee for the basic service plus additional fees for special services. Most basic programming services sell advertising to help support their costs. Many channels also run infomercials in program-length time slots. Some cable services syndicate programs to over-the-air broadcast stations. Nonprofit cable channels offer public affairs programming without advertising.

Special services include *premium channels* that a subscriber can choose to pay for individually. These channels usually do not carry advertising. The programming features recent motion pictures, and may include specials, such as live sports events, music concerts, and documentaries. The main premium channels, including HBO (Home Box Office) and Showtime, also produce original movies and series. This programming does not face the same limitations on violence, nudity, and language that are imposed on network programming. Some channels offer movies and sports events to the subscriber on a *pay-per-view* basis. A consumer transmits a special order for the programming, and the charge is applied to the next month's service bill.

New digital technologies promise to make hundreds of additional channels available to the consumer. Programming services hope to use the additional channels to introduce new categories of programming and to grant consumers greater convenience. One feature, *near-video-on-demand,* involves broadcasting the same movie on several channels at the same time, but staggering the start by an interval of time, for example, 15 minutes. A viewer would thus never be more than 15 minutes away from the beginning of the next viewing. And if a person's viewing was interrupted, he or she could, upon returning to the television, simply change channels and return to approximately the same place in the movie.

Television awards are presented each year by a number of organizations. The best-known awards, the Emmys, are given by the Academy of Television Arts and Sciences and by the National Academy of Television Arts and Sciences. The two academies recognize achievements of the preceding year in various fields of the TV industry. Some local chapters of the National Academy also present Emmys for local achievements.

Television throughout the world

The popularity of television has created a huge television industry, particularly in such industrial countries as Australia, Germany, Japan, and the United Kingdom. In such countries, television broadcasting plays a major part in the lives of nearly all the people. Television programs produced in the United States are sold all over the world, and in many countries such programs fill a substantial amount of viewing time.

In Africa. On average, the countries of Africa have fewer television stations than those of other regions of the world. Most of the stations are government-owned. Several countries licensed their first independent stations during the 1990's. Because the people of many African countries do not share a common language, some stations broadcast programs in several languages. Many stations broadcast only a few hours of programming a day. Some parts of Africa receive no broadcasts at all.

Most countries of Africa provide or receive satellite television programming. An Arab satellite, ARABSAT, transmits programming throughout Africa, the Middle East, and Europe. Gabon transmits programming to other African countries via satellite. The United States, India, and several European countries also supply Africa with satellite television programming.

In Asia. The television stations in a majority of Asian countries are operated exclusively by the government. Some countries have only one television network. Centrally located areas in some rural regions of Asia display public television sets for public viewing. Several of the former Soviet republics receive relayed transmissions of Russian television programming.

In Japan, almost every household has at least one television set. A public corporation operates two noncommercial networks in Japan, and the country has many privately owned stations as well. In India, a network of transmitters is linked through the Indian National Satellite system (INSAT). The country's broadcast operations include educational programs that provide classroom education at all levels. All of China's television networks are operated by the Chinese government.

In Australia and New Zealand. The largest Australian network, the Australian Broadcasting Corporation (ABC), provides national, noncommercial television service. In addition, commercial television is carried in all states. Closed-circuit television is used as part of a long-distance instructional program called *schools of the air.* These schools transmit lessons directly into the homes of children who live in isolated areas, far from any town.

Television broadcasting in New Zealand is dominated by the state-owned Television New Zealand Limited. In addition, several private networks offer a variety of programs.

In Europe. Most European countries have at least one public broadcasting company and at least one privately owned company. In some countries, a government organization or a private organization oversees the whole of television broadcasting. The Western European countries generally have more stations than the Eastern European nations, and a greater percentage of those stations are independent. Several countries began to move away from complete government control of television operations in the late 1980's. Many European countries, including Germany, Poland, Sweden, and the United Kingdom, license television receivers for use. People pay a fee to use the receivers that supports the cost of programming. Cable and satellite television service are available throughout Europe.

In Russia, the government operates two public television stations and one educational station. The country also has an independent television network and several local stations. In the United Kingdom, almost all broadcasting is controlled by the British Broadcasting Corporation (BBC) or by the Independent Television Commission (ITC). The BBC operates two programming channels and the ITC operates three. Radio Telefis Éireann (RTE) is responsible for most television broadcasting in the Republic of Ireland.

In Latin America. Most Latin American countries have a mix of state-owned and privately owned televi-

© Lulzim Lika, Reuters/Archive Photos

Dish-shaped antennas for satellite television reception dot the side of this apartment building in Albania. Satellite television service is available throughout Europe and North America.

sion stations. In a few countries, the government either controls or supervises all television operations. Satellite and cable services are available in several countries.

In Canada. About 300 television stations operate in Canada. Nearly all homes in the country have television sets. About three-fourths of all Canadian households subscribe to cable television services.

The Canadian Broadcasting Corporation (CBC), a publicly owned corporation, operates two national television networks. One network broadcasts in English, and the other in French. The CBC delivers programs by satellite to people in northern Canada. Some of these programs are in American Indian and Inuit (Eskimo) languages. See **Canadian Broadcasting Corporation.**

Canada's other national networks are the CTV Television Network and the Global Television Network. Smaller networks operate in several provinces. Privately owned stations depend heavily on programs produced in other countries, especially the United States. Canadian homes receive nearly all U.S. network programs.

International television awards include Italy's Prix Italia and Switzerland's Golden Rose of Montreux. Television producers from many countries submit programs for judging for these awards.

Effects of television

In many countries, television ranks as a major influence on life. It affects the way people spend their time and what and how they learn. TV also affects politics, the other media, and sports. Some authorities believe TV has a greater influence on young people than on adults.

Effects on leisure time. Throughout the industrialized world, watching television is one of the most time-consuming leisure activities among adults. It frequently takes time away from other activities, such as reading, conversation, social gatherings, and exercise.

Effects on learning. Television can contribute greatly to what home viewers learn. It may benefit people by widening their experience. On the other hand, TV also may contribute to harmful impressions of the world.

Enriched experience. No communication system has ever provided so many people with as wide a range of new experiences as television has. Without leaving their homes, TV viewers can watch government officials perform important functions and see how people in far-off lands look and live. Television takes viewers to deserts, jungles, and the ocean floor. A TV viewer can see how a famous actor performs the role of Hamlet, and how top comedians draw laughter. Television gives its viewers a glimpse of real-life tragedy, such as when it covers the victims of war, natural disasters, and poverty. It also captures moments of great triumph, such as when astronauts first set foot on the moon. Some authorities, however, question how much specific information viewers remember from watching television.

Harmful impressions. Many social scientists believe that people will likely form false impressions from watching a lot of television. One of these impressions is that many people are better off than they are. Another is that the world is an unfriendly place, filled with untrustworthy people and risky circumstances.

Television programs often show people leading more glamorous lives and owning more material goods than most viewers. In addition, TV commercials constantly urge viewers to buy things. Many sociologists believe that as a result, the material expectations of TV viewers are raised, sometimes to an unrealistic level. One harmful effect results when people fail to achieve the success they see on TV and become dissatisfied or bitter.

The violent, crime-filled world shown on TV may contribute to an impression of an evil world. Studies indicate that people who watch a great deal of television are more likely to hold fearful or pessimistic views of the world than those who watch less TV. Some researchers argue, however, that people who watch a lot of television already hold such views.

Effects on society. Television has brought about major changes in several parts of society, including politics, motion pictures and radio, and sports.

Politics. Every election year, thousands of political candidates use television in their campaigns. They buy commercial time to urge voters to support them. They also appear in debates with other candidates and answer interviewers' questions about their views. Television plays a great role in national elections. Before TV, candidates for president, prime minister, or other high office tried to make as many personal appearances and speeches as possible. Today, candidates reach more voters through a single TV appearance than through all the in-person campaigning they do.

In some countries, including the United States, candidates can buy TV time for a spot announcement. Spot announcements are political messages that generally last 30 seconds. In some other countries, such advertisements are illegal. Instead, broadcasting authorities allow the main political parties some free television time to present their policies and points of view.

Television does much to promote interest in politics and political issues. But political advertising and news coverage on TV also draw criticism. In countries where political advertising is allowed, critics say spot announcements are too short to allow candidates to discuss issues. Instead, candidates use the time to present oversimplified statements. Critics also claim that, because television time is so expensive, TV campaigning gives unfair advantage to the candidates with the most money. Critics are also concerned that news programs often televise only a sentence or two, called a *sound bite,* from a candidate's remarks. These contrast sharply with the long political speeches that are typical of traditional in-person campaigning.

Other forms of entertainment. From the 1920's through the 1940's, films and radio were the chief forms of entertainment for millions of people. Many families went to the movies at least once a week. They listened to comedies, dramas, and other entertainment programs on the radio almost every night. The rise of TV in the 1950's caused a sharp drop in movie attendance. Since then, the movie industry has frequently faced economic problems. Radio entertainment changed completely after TV became a part of everyday life. Almost every radio entertainment show went off the air. Recorded music became the chief kind of radio programming.

National magazines also suffered after the arrival of television. Some popular magazines that had circulations of many millions went out of business when advertisers shifted large amounts of money to television.

Professional sports have long attracted millions of spectators yearly. But many more millions now watch the events on television. Television networks and stations pay team owners huge amounts of money for the right to televise games. These funds, in turn, help owners pay the huge salaries of today's professional athletes. Television also helps increase the popularity of sports. For example, the popularity of American football has soared largely because of television. On the other hand, minor league baseball lost much of its audience after television brought major league games into the home.

Effects on young people. There is little agreement about how television affects young people. Parents have long been concerned about the amount of time young people spend watching TV. Studies have linked watching a lot of television with poor performance in school. However, these studies do not prove that TV viewing actually causes students to perform poorly. Watching television may simply be an activity preferred by young people who do poorly in school. Other studies suggest that televised violence encourages aggressive behavior.

Regulating U.S. television

The Federal Communications Commission (FCC) regulates television—and also radio—broadcasting in the United States. An agency of the federal government, the FCC issues broadcasting licenses to stations and assigns frequencies on which the stations must broadcast. These regulations are needed to maintain order in the airwaves. If anyone who wanted to were allowed to broadcast and use any frequency, signals would interfere with each other and make broadcasting impossible.

The FCC also sets standards for broadcasters. The agency cannot censor programs, but it has the power to take away, or refuse to renew, a station's license if the station violates the standards too much. The FCC expects stations to avoid obscenity and pornography in their programs. The agency requires stations to provide public services and programs designed to meet the needs of their local communities. Another FCC standard requires television broadcasters to give equal time to all legally qualified candidates for public office. In addition, the FCC, along with the Federal Trade Commission (FTC), evaluates truthfulness in television advertising.

Congress can also regulate broadcasting. For example, it passed a law prohibiting cigarette advertising on television. The law was based on the government's conclusion that cigarette smoking is harmful to health. In 1996, Congress passed the Telecommunications Act, which required that, by 1998, all new TV sets contain a computer chip that would enable parents to block programs they considered inappropriate for their children. The television industry would rate programs on their explicitly violent or sexual content. The chip, popularly known as the *V-chip* (for *violence*), would block out programs as instructed according to the rating.

Broadcasters and regulations. Broadcasters generally oppose government regulations. They say regulations affecting programming interfere with their rights to freedom of expression. Most members of Congress disagree, as do many citizens' groups. They claim that because the airwaves are public property, the government must create regulations that serve the public's interest.

Program ratings. In 1997, under pressure from the public as well as from legislators, most television and cable networks adopted a voluntary ratings system. The system received FCC approval in 1998. Its purpose is to inform viewers of the appropriate audience for a specific program based upon its content. The ratings identify the program in six possible categories, including TVG (suitable for all audiences), TVY7 (inappropriate for children under age 7), and TVMA (for mature audiences only). The rating may have one or more additional letters attached indicating the nature of the questionable content, such as *V* for *violence* or *L* for *indecent language.*

Under the FCC-approved system, each network evaluates its own programs and attaches a rating to them that is displayed at the start of the program and in all program schedules and promotions. A television with a V-chip can block viewing of programs with a certain rating. The FCC-approved ratings system is still voluntary, however, and a few television networks have instituted a different ratings system. The V-chip cannot block programs on channels not using the FCC-approved system.

History of U.S. television broadcasting

The start of broadcasting. Many experimental telecasts took place in the late 1920's and the 1930's. In the

United States, CBS and NBC in were leaders in experimental telecasts. The British Broadcasting Corporation (BBC) performed experimental telecasts in the United Kingdom. But World War II (1939-1945) and economic problems afterward caused the BBC to abandon TV experiments. The United States moved far ahead of the rest of the world in TV broadcasting.

In 1936, the Radio Corporation of America (later RCA Corporation), which owned NBC, installed television receivers in 150 homes in the New York City area. NBC's New York station began experimental telecasts to these homes. A cartoon of Felix the Cat was its first program. NBC established the first regular TV broadcasts in the United States in 1939. The United States entered World War II in 1941. Television broadcasting was suspended until after the war ended in 1945.

The television boom. The national networks—all based in New York City—resumed broadcasting shortly after the war. At first, their telecasts reached only the Eastern Seaboard between Boston and Washington, D.C. But by 1951, they extended coast-to-coast. TV stations sprang up throughout the country. Entertainment, news, special events, and sports contests replaced the simple, largely experimental, prewar shows.

The American people became fascinated with the idea of having so wide a range of visual events available in their homes. The demand for TV sets became enormous. In 1945, there were probably fewer than 10,000 sets in the country. This figure soared to about 6 million in 1950, and to almost 60 million by 1960. In TV's early days, people who had no set often visited friends who had one just to watch television. Also, many stores placed television sets in windows, and crowds gathered on the sidewalk to watch programs.

Early programs. Milton Berle became the first television entertainer to attract a huge, nationwide audience. His show, "The Texaco Star Theater," was filled with zany comedy routines. It ran from 1948 to 1956, and often attracted 80 percent of the TV audience. "I Love Lucy," starring Lucille Ball, went on the air in 1951. This early situation comedy also attracted a huge following. Westerns, such as "Gunsmoke" and "Have Gun Will Travel," became popular in the mid-1950's. Other popular early entertainment programs included Ed Sullivan's variety show, "The Toast of the Town"; the comedy-variety program "Your Show of Shows," starring Sid Caesar; professional wrestling matches; and quiz shows offering prizes of thousands of dollars. A major scandal hit TV in 1959, when it was learned that quiz show producers had helped some contestants answer questions.

Coverage of special events did much to widen TV's appeal. In 1951, TV broadcast the Kefauver hearings, in which U.S. Senator Estes Kefauver and his Senate committee questioned alleged mobsters about organized crime. In 1954, TV covered the Army-McCarthy hearings. Viewers watched spellbound as Senator Joseph R. McCarthy accused the U.S. Army of "coddling Communists," and the Army charged McCarthy's staff with "improper conduct." The hearings reached a dramatic climax when Joseph Welch, a soft-spoken lawyer for the Army, and the outspoken McCarthy clashed in an emotion-filled argument (see **McCarthy, Joseph R.**).

The 1960's opened with a milestone of television broadcasting. During the fall of 1960, presidential candidates John F. Kennedy and Richard M. Nixon faced each other and the nation in a series of TV debates. It marked the first time presidential candidates debated on TV. Many people believe the debates made an important contribution to Kennedy's victory in the 1960 election.

Hank Walker, *Life* Magazine, © Time, Inc.

TV coverage of the Army-McCarthy hearings of 1954 brought a major historical event into millions of homes. The dramatic hearings included charges by U.S. Senator Joseph R. McCarthy, *right,* that the Army was "coddling Communists."

Popular entertainment remained the major part of television's coverage during the 1960's. But TV also reflected the turmoil that marked American life. President Kennedy was assassinated on Nov. 22, 1963. Two days later, millions of viewers witnessed one of the most startling scenes ever shown on television. In full view of TV cameras, Jack Ruby shot and killed accused Kennedy assassin Lee Harvey Oswald as the police were taking Oswald from one jail to another.

From the mid-1960's on, television regularly brought viewers battle scenes from the Vietnam War. The conflict was sometimes called "the first war to be fought on television." Television viewers also watched war protesters demonstrate—sometimes violently—and witnessed bitter debates over the war policy of the United States. Civil rights protests by African Americans and other minority groups also became part of TV coverage.

Originally, broadcasters avoided controversial themes, such as abortion, alcoholism, divorce, drug abuse, political satire, prejudice, and sex. They feared such themes would result in a loss of viewers. But in the late 1960's, broadcasters found that they could deal with controversial themes and still draw big audiences. The comedy show "Rowan and Martin's Laugh-In" included many jokes about sex and much political satire, and it became the top-rated show of the late 1960's.

The 1970's established television entertainment as a reflector, and often a leader, of public opinion and social customs. Such programs as "All in the Family" and "The Mary Tyler Moore Show" and many movies made for television continued to examine controversial social issues. Public television proved that TV can be an entertaining form of education when the children's program "Sesame Street" gained widespread popularity. Investigative news shows—such as "60 Minutes" and "20/20" —provided a means for network news departments to increase their scope. These news departments expanded from simply reporting the news to investigating and originating newsworthy information.

In the late 1970's, broadcasters began to present an increasing number of made-for-TV movies, serialized dramas called *miniseries,* and other special programs. The most popular such presentation was *Roots,* an eight-part drama tracing the history of an African American family from slavery to freedom.

The 1980's and 1990's saw network entertainment adjust for changes in national taste and the competition provided by the new networks and by cable. Comedy programs used more sexual humor. Such shows were led by "Married . . . with Children," which featured a family whose members often openly expressed dislike for each other. This show was intended as a reaction to the model family represented by "The Cosby Show," the most successful comedy of the mid-1980's.

Television producers transformed the hourlong drama in the 1980's. Such dramas previously told single stories always featuring the same lead characters. The new form featured multiple characters and storylines in which the lead characters changed from week to week. These shows also depicted more graphic violence, sexual situations, and coarse language. Notable dramas of this type included the groundbreaking police show "Hill Street Blues" and the medical drama "St. Elsewhere."

Many people believed, however, that television had gone too far in presenting controversial themes. In particular, the amount of violence and sex on TV drew criticism (see the section *Television ratings* in this article).

As more of the viewing audience became attracted to cable and to the smaller networks, the major networks struggled to find hit shows. Hits had become crucial to a network's entire economic structure. This situation resulted in tremendous salaries and fees for the talent and studios associated with a hit show. In the late 1990's, producers of the dramatic series "ER" commanded the highest price ever per episode. Jerry Seinfeld, the star and producer of the popular comedy "Seinfeld," was paid $1 million per episode for his show's final year of production in 1997-1998.

In the 1980's and 1990's, viewer erosion, along with the cost of keeping hits on the air, forced networks to develop less expensive forms of programming to maintain profits. The networks increasingly turned to news and other "reality-based" programs instead of costlier situation comedies, dramas, or television movies. For example, the networks added more prime-time news magazine shows, such as "Dateline NBC" and "PrimeTime Live," to their schedules. Another reality-based program was "Cops," in which camera crews followed real police officers through their day. Still another was "America's Funniest Home Videos," which featured amusing home movies submitted by ordinary people.

Also in the 1990's, the great number of channels available on cable and satellite television gave birth to *narrowcasting.* This practice targeted specific interest groups rather than trying to capture large audiences.

Creating television signals

The first step in sending pictures and sound is changing the light and sound waves from a scene into a television signal. This signal begins when light from the scene enters a television camera. The camera changes the light into electronic signals. At the same time, a microphone picks up the sounds and changes them into electronic signals. Television engineers call the signals from a camera *video* and the signals from a microphone *audio.*

This section describes how a TV camera creates video signals. It also explains how video signals are produced by telecine and videotape. TV audio signals are created in the same way as radio signals. For information on this process, see **Radio.**

To capture motion, the television camera shoots many pictures every second, just as a motion picture film camera does. A TV camera divides a picture into several hundred thousand tiny parts by a process called *scan-*

RCA

An experimental telecast of the late 1920's showed a statue of the comic strip character Felix the Cat.

Culver

Milton Berle became the first big TV star. His zany comedy show drew a huge audience during the early 1950's.

CBS

"The $64,000 Question" was one of several television quiz shows of the 1950's that offered valuable prizes to contestants.

ning. As the camera scans the picture, it creates electronic signals from each tiny part of the picture.

TV stations in most countries broadcast *composite color video signals.* These video signals produce a color picture when received on a color television set, and they produce a black-and-white picture on a black-and-white TV set.

Color TV uses the three primary colors in light—red, blue, and green—to produce full-color pictures. The proper mixture of these three colors can produce any color of light. For example, a mixture of red and green light produces yellow light. Equal amounts of red, blue, and green light produce white light.

The television camera. In producing a composite color video signal, the TV camera must (1) capture the image of the scene being telecast; (2) create video signals from the image; and (3) encode the color signals for transmission. To perform these tasks, a television camera uses a lens, a system of mirrors and filters, image sensors, and complex electronic circuits.

Capturing the image. The lens gathers the *image* (picture) of the scene in front of the camera. Like the lenses in other cameras and the human eye, the TV lens *focuses* (collects and bends) the light from the scene to form a sharp image. This image contains all the colors of the scene. To produce color signals, however, the camera must split the full-color image into three separate images—one for each primary color.

Most TV cameras use two *dichroic mirrors* to split the image into the primary colors. These mirrors, like the color filters used in photography, reflect light of only one color and let other colors through. The first mirror reflects the blue image and allows red and green light to pass through. The second mirror reflects the red image, leaving only the green image. Other mirrors reflect each image to a separate image sensor. In many cameras, this color separation is done by color filters and prisms contained in a small compartment called the *prism block.*

Creating the video signals. An image sensor changes the light image into electronic signals. A black-and-white camera has only one sensor. Most high-quality color cameras have three sensors. These sensors create a separate electronic signal for each of the three primary colors. Many small, lower-quality, portable cameras are equipped with a single sensor. This sensor has many thin red, blue, and green *filter stripes* on its surface. The stripes divide the light into the three primary colors, and the sensor then converts each of the colors into a separate signal.

Two types of image sensors may be used in television cameras. *Tube cameras* contain improved versions of a vacuum tube called a *vidicon. Solid-state cameras* contain electronic sensing mechanisms called *charge-coupled devices* (CCD's). Solid-state cameras are smaller, lighter, and more reliable than tube cameras. Tube cameras, however, produce more accurate colors and sharper pictures. This section describes the working of one sensor in cameras that have three.

A vidicon tube has a glass *faceplate* at its front end. In back of the faceplate is a transparent coating called the *signal plate.* A second plate, known as the *target,* lies behind the signal plate. The target consists of a layer of *photoconductive material,* which conducts electric current when exposed to light. At the rear of the tube is a device called an *electron gun.*

Light from the image reaches the target after passing through the faceplate and signal plate. The light causes negatively charged particles called *electrons* in the photoconductive material to move toward the signal plate. This movement leaves the back of the target with a positive electric charge. The strength of the positive charge on any area of the target corresponds to the brightness of the light shining on that area. The camera tube thus changes the light image gathered by the lens into an identical electric image of positive charges on the back of the target.

The electron gun shoots a beam of electrons across the back of the target. The beam moves across the target in an orderly sequence called a *scanning pattern.* As the beam moves across the target, it strikes areas with different amounts of positive charge. Areas of the target that have the strongest charge attract the most electrons from the beam. This occurs because particles of unlike

UPI/Bettmann Newsphotos

Vietnam War scenes first came on TV in the 1960's. They brought the horrors of war into millions of homes.

© 1979 Tandem Lisc. Corp. All Rights Reserved

"All in the Family" became a hit show during the 1970's. The program combined comedy with the treatment of controversial topics.

© D. Fineman, Sygma

Music videos, which became popular in the 1980's, featured such performers as singer Michael Jackson.

electric charge attract each other. Other areas of the target attract fewer electrons. The electrons from the beam move through the target and cause an electric current to flow in the signal plate. The voltage of this current changes from moment to moment, depending on whether the beam is striking a bright or dim part of the image. This changing voltage is the video signal from that camera tube.

A charge-coupled device is a silicon chip with tiny, square photoconductive *elements* (parts) arranged on its surface. Light falling on an element (also called a *pixel)* causes electrons to flow into the element's *capacitor,* a device that stores an electrical charge. As more light falls on the element, more electrical charge accumulates in the capacitor. The CCD thus changes the light coming through the camera lens into an identical electric image. The CCD then reads out the image by releasing the charge stored in each capacitor to cause an electric current to flow. This current is the video signal from that CCD. The CCD releases the capacitor charges according to the scanning pattern.

Most television systems use *interlaced scanning.* A scanning beam scans every other line of the picture, beginning at the top left corner of the screen as seen by a viewer. After it reaches the bottom right corner, the beam returns to the starting point and scans the remaining lines, again from top left to bottom right.

The scanning pattern of TV cameras in North America, most of South America, and Japan and several other Asian countries was developed in the United States as the NTSC (National Television System Committee) system. It is made up of 525 lines (262 1/2 odd-numbered and 262 1/2 even-numbered lines). The camera completes one field each time it scans 262 1/2 lines. Two fields make up a complete television picture, called a *frame.* The camera scans so quickly that it produces 30 complete frames in a second. This speed is fast enough so the picture shows moving images smoothly. The scanning patterns of TV cameras throughout the rest of the world use one of two other systems: PAL (*p*hase *al*ternating *l*ines), which originated in Germany, and SECAM (*se*quence *é*lectronique *c*ouleur *a*vec *m*émoir), which originated in France. Both systems display 625 lines per frame at 25 frames per second.

In all three systems, each of the three image sensors converts one of the three primary colors to an electronic signal by means of the scanning process. Wires carry the signals to electronic circuits in the camera that *amplify* (strengthen) them. The three signals then go to the *encoder.*

Encoding the color signals. At the encoder, the three electronic signals are combined with other signals to produce a composite color video signal. The first step in this process involves combining the three electronic signals into two color-coded signals and a black-and-white signal. The two color-coded signals are called *chrominance signals,* and the black-and-white signal is known as a *luminance signal.* A circuit in the encoder, called the *matrix,* performs this function.

The encoder then combines the chrominance and luminance signals and adds a *color burst* and *synchronizing signals.* The color burst enables a color TV set to separate the color information in the chrominance signals. This information, along with the luminance signal, produces a full-color picture on the TV screen. A black-and-white set uses only the luminance signal. The synchronizing signals enable the TV set to repeatedly return to the beginning of each scan line and field without interruption.

Telecine is equipment that transfers motion pictures or slides into TV signals. The name comes from the word *television* and the word *cinema,* which refers to film. Telecine uses a combination of film and slide projectors and a single television camera to create such signals. A typical telecine unit, often called a *film chain,* consists of two motion-picture projectors, a slide projector, a *multiplexer,* and a telecine camera. The multiplexer is a system of mirrors that directs the images from film or slides into the telecine camera. The camera then converts these images into video signals.

Videotape recording stores television pictures and sound as magnetic impulses on tape. The video signals are usually recorded as diagonal tracks in the center of the tape, and sound and control signals are recorded along the tape's edge. Unlike film, which must be developed before showing, a videotape can be played back immediately.

Computer-generated video. *Character generators* and *video paint boxes* are electronic devices that can generate letters or pictures. TV productions use these graphics devices to create a variety of materials, including advertisements and weather maps.

Computers have been used to produce animated cartoons for many years. Other television shows have used computer-generated images for special effects. Today, fast computers and clever computer programs can be used to create video that is more realistic than ever before. Computer functions enable TV crews to mix such video with natural video captured by television cameras.

Transmitting television signals

Television signals must be transmitted to the television receiver. Some signals are broadcast through the air. Engineers at a television station use a device called a transmitter to produce a TV signal from separate audio and video signals. The signal is then carried by wire to an antenna and broadcast. The signal is called an *electromagnetic wave.* Such waves travel through the air at the speed of light, about 186,282 miles (299,792 kilometers) per second. But the strength of the signal decreases the farther it travels. The signal can be received clearly only up to a distance of about 150 miles (240 kilometers). To send TV signals farther, other means of transmitting must be used. These include coaxial cable and fiber-optic cable, microwaves, and satellites.

Broadcasting. Before a TV signal is broadcast, the transmitter boosts its *frequency* (rate of vibration) to the proper *broadcast band,* the region allocated for TV transmission on a particular channel. A TV signal needs a high frequency to carry the picture information through the air, and it must be transmitted within a certain frequency so that it does not interfere with other signals in the air. The transmitter amplifies the signal so it has enough power to reach a large area. The signals can then be received by TV antennas in the area.

The transmitter increases the frequency of both the video and audio signals by a process called *modulation.* High-frequency electromagnetic waves, called *carrier waves,* are first generated by the transmitter. The transmitter uses the video signal to vary the *amplitude* (strength) of the carrier waves to produce the video part of the TV signal. This process is called *amplitude modulation* (AM).

The transmitter uses the audio signals to modulate another carrier wave, which becomes the audio part of the TV signal. This process, called *frequency modulation* (FM), shifts the frequency of this carrier wave slightly. The transmitter then combines the modulated video and audio carrier waves to form the TV signal. This signal is then amplified to a power of 1,000 to 100,000 watts.

A wire called the *transmission line* carries the signal to the transmitting antenna. This antenna releases the signal into the air. Television stations erect their antennas on high buildings or towers so that the signal can reach as far as possible. The maximum range of most television signals is from 75 to 150 miles (120 to 240 kilometers).

Television stations in the same area transmit on different frequencies so their signals do not interfere with one another. The group of frequencies over which one station broadcasts is known as a *channel.*

Throughout the world, television stations broadcast in the VHF (very high frequency) and UHF (ultrahigh frequency) bands. VHF refers to signals with a frequency from 30 to 300 *megahertz* (million vibrations per second). UHF signals have a frequency from 300 to 3,000 megahertz.

In North America, 82 channels are available for over-the-air broadcasting. Channels numbered 2 through 13 operate on the VHF band, and channels numbered 14 through 83 are on the UHF band. Broadcasts on the UHF band are less susceptible to electromagnetic interference than VHF broadcasts are.

Coaxial cable and fiber-optic cable carry television signals for long distances or to areas that have difficulty receiving signals. In some countries, television networks send programs to their affiliated stations through coaxial cables. The affiliates then broadcast the programs to their viewers. Cable television systems use coaxial or fiber-optic cables to carry signals to the homes of subscribers. See **Coaxial cable; Fiber optics.**

Microwaves are electromagnetic waves similar to television signals. In some countries, relay towers spaced about 30 miles (50 kilometers) apart across the country carry programs from the networks to affiliate stations on these waves. Equipment in a tower automatically receives, amplifies, and then retransmits the microwave signal to the next tower. The affiliate stations change the microwave signals back into TV signals.

Satellites carry television signals between stations where cables or microwave towers cannot be built. For example, satellites relay signals across oceans. Satellites work like relay towers in space. They receive coded TV signals from a special earth station, amplify them, and send them on to another earth station. The two stations may be thousands of miles or kilometers apart. News correspondents working in remote locations sometimes use portable satellite links with dish-shaped antennas to transmit live reports via satellite to their broadcasting companies.

Satellite television systems use *direct-broadcast satellites* (DBS) to carry signals directly to the homes of subscribers. Such signals are received by dish-shaped antennas. Many older antennas measure about 10 feet (3 meters) across. Some newer home antennas measure only 18 inches (45 centimeters) across.

Receiving television signals

The television signals from a transmitter are fed into a home TV set through a *receiving antenna* (also called an *aerial),* a cable, or a satellite dish. A television receiver decodes the signals and changes them back into copies of the light and sound waves that came from the original scene.

The scanning process used in a TV set rapidly puts the tiny parts of the picture back together piece by piece. The process works so seamlessly that the viewer seems to see only a complete picture. In reproducing the television program, a TV set uses a tuner, amplifiers and separators, and a picture tube or projection system.

Receiving equipment includes antennas and satellite dishes. A good antenna collects a strong enough television signal for the receiver to produce a picture. A simple indoor antenna, commonly called *rabbit ears,* picks up a strong enough signal within a few miles or kilometers of the transmitter. At greater distances, a more elaborate antenna mounted on the roof may be needed. The best reception results when the antenna is pointed toward the desired station. Some antennas can be rotated by remote control to align them with widely separated stations.

Cable television signals are transmitted from a station that uses satellite dishes to receive special programming signals from transmission satellites. Satellite dishes for DBS reception are installed so that they aim at a specific point in the sky, from which a satellite in a fixed orbit sends out signals.

Tuner. Signals from an antenna are fed into the set's tuner. The tuner selects only the signal from the station the viewer wants to receive, rejecting all others. On some TV sets, especially older ones, the viewer first selects the VHF or UHF function, then turns a dial or knob on the set to select a channel. With most newer models, the viewer uses a remote control device with buttons that can select channels in any frequency.

Most TV sets also have a *cable-ready tuner,* which can receive from about 70 to well over 100 channels. By switching the TV set to this tuner, most cable-TV subscribers can view basic cable programming. Signals for premium and pay-per-view channels are scrambled by the cable supplier so that people cannot view the programming without paying for it. A device commonly called a *set-top box, cable box,* or *descrambler* unscrambles the signal so that such programs may be viewed. A set-top box may be rented from a cable company, or it may be purchased. People who purchase their own box are expected to inform their cable company. An *addressable* set-top box enables the viewer to key in a request for a pay-per view event. The cable supplier then turns the descrambler on when the program begins and off when it ends.

Satellite television reception also requires the use of a set-top box. The box decodes the signals received by the satellite dish, and allows access to premium and pay-per-view programming.

Amplifiers and separators. From the tuner, the television signal goes to a group of complicated electronic

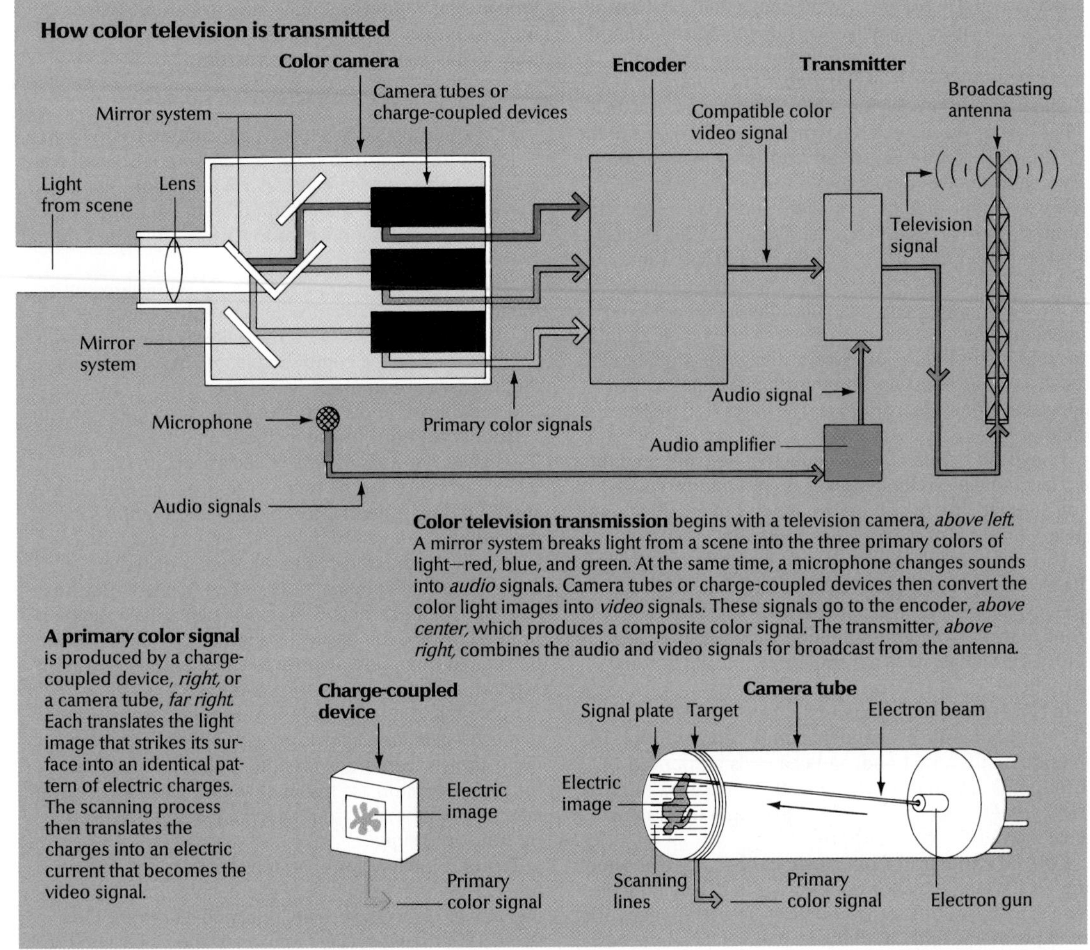

How color television is transmitted

Color television transmission begins with a television camera, *above left.* A mirror system breaks light from a scene into the three primary colors of light—red, blue, and green. At the same time, a microphone changes sounds into *audio* signals. Camera tubes or charge-coupled devices then convert the color light images into *video* signals. These signals go to the encoder, *above center,* which produces a composite color signal. The transmitter, *above right,* combines the audio and video signals for broadcast from the antenna.

A primary color signal is produced by a charge-coupled device, *right,* or a camera tube, *far right.* Each translates the light image that strikes its surface into an identical pattern of electric charges. The scanning process then translates the charges into an electric current that becomes the video signal.

WORLD BOOK diagram by Mas Nakagawa

circuits in the set. These circuits amplify the signal and separate the audio and video portions of it. The audio signals are changed into sound waves by the speaker. The video signals go to the *picture tube,* also called the *kinescope,* where they re-create the picture.

A color set has circuits that use the color burst to separate the video signal into the two chrominance signals and the luminance signal. Another group of circuits, called the *decoder* or *matrix,* transforms these signals into red, blue, and green signals that duplicate the signals from the three camera tubes.

The picture tube transforms the video signals into patterns of light that duplicate the scene in front of the camera. One end of the picture tube is rectangular and nearly flat. This end forms the screen of the television set. Inside the set, the picture tube tapers to a narrow neck. The neck of a color picture tube holds three electron guns—one each for the red, blue, and green signals. A black-and-white tube has only one electron gun.

Each electron gun in a color picture tube shoots a separate beam of electrons at the screen. Each beam scans the screen just as the beam in each camera tube scanned its target. The synchronizing signal, which is a part of the video signal, ensures that the picture tube's scanning pattern follows exactly the pattern used by the camera. The beams must be in step with each other to produce a steady, undistorted picture.

The screen of a color tube is coated with dots or stripes of red, green, and blue chemicals called *phosphors.* These chemicals glow with their respective color when struck by an electron beam. A metal plate perforated with thousands of tiny holes lies about $\frac{1}{2}$ inch (13 millimeters) behind the screen. This plate is called the *shadow mask.* Its holes keep the beams from hitting any color phosphors but their own.

The amount of light given off by the phosphors depends on the beam's strength at the instant it strikes them. Because the beam's strength is controlled by the video signal from the camera, the phosphors are bright where the scene is bright and dark where the scene is dark. When the TV set shows a color program, the three colored phosphors seem to blend together to produce the colors in the original scene. The phosphors appear to produce only differing amounts of white light when showing a black-and-white program.

Projection television systems use three small, high-density cathode ray tubes to project the television picture onto a screen. A front-projection system projects a

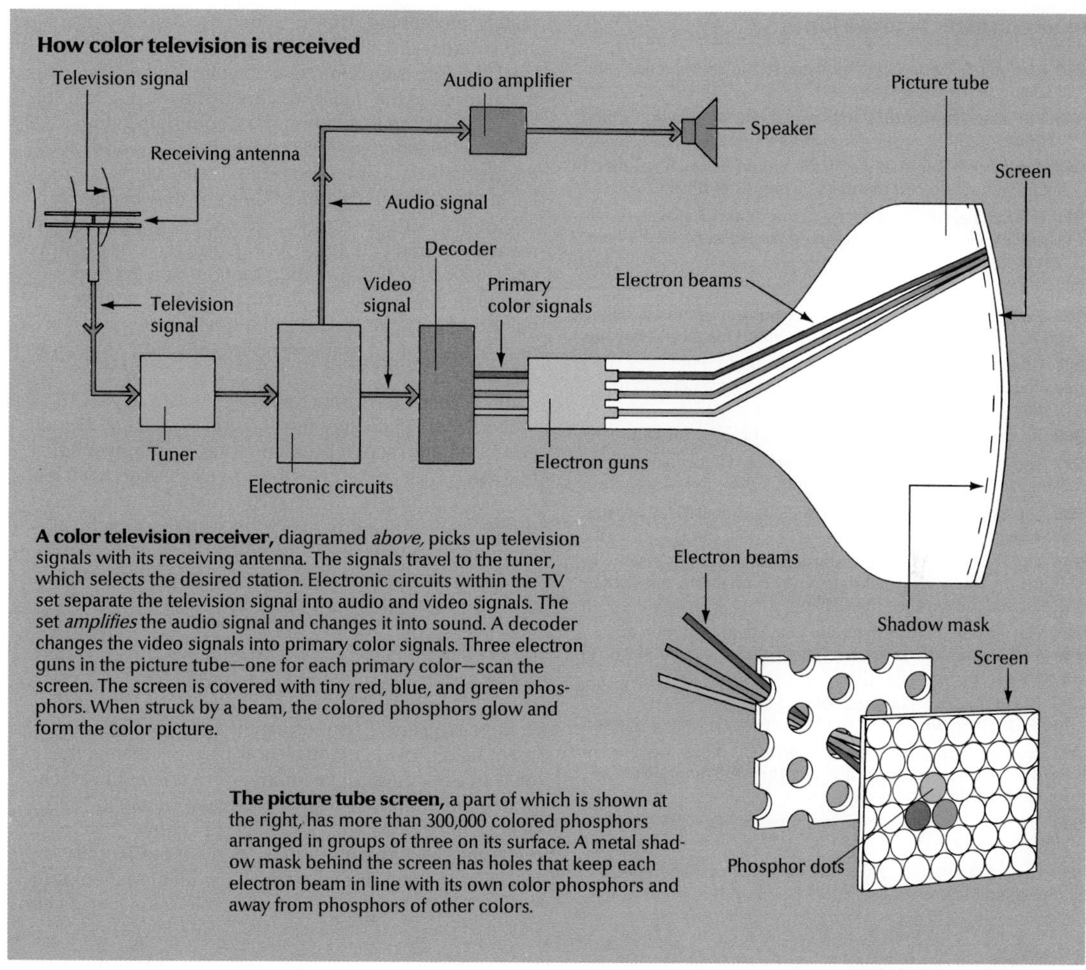

A color television receiver, diagramed *above,* picks up television signals with its receiving antenna. The signals travel to the tuner, which selects the desired station. Electronic circuits within the TV set separate the television signal into audio and video signals. The set *amplifies* the audio signal and changes it into sound. A decoder changes the video signals into primary color signals. Three electron guns in the picture tube—one for each primary color—scan the screen. The screen is covered with tiny red, blue, and green phosphors. When struck by a beam, the colored phosphors glow and form the color picture.

The picture tube screen, a part of which is shown at the right, has more than 300,000 colored phosphors arranged in groups of three on its surface. A metal shadow mask behind the screen has holes that keep each electron beam in line with its own color phosphors and away from phosphors of other colors.

WORLD BOOK diagram by Mas Nakagawa

picture from in front of the screen. In a rear-projection system, the tubes project images onto the back of a screen. Rear-projection sets typically employ mirrors to reflect the image toward the screen. A rear-projection TV set takes less space than a front-projection system.

Front-projection displays produce a lower light output, and so viewing is best in a dark room. Rear-projection displays are direct-view monitors that can be watched in a variety of lighting conditions. Projection televisions can provide a better viewing experience for a large group of people. Large screen displays are also useful for business applications, such as videoconferencing.

The development of television technology

Early development. Many scientists contributed to the development of television, and no one person can be called its inventor. Television became possible in the 1800's, when people learned how to send communication signals through the air as electromagnetic waves. This process is called *radio communication.* For details on its development, see **Radio** (History).

The first radio operators sent code signals through the air. By the early 1900's, operators could transmit words. Meanwhile, many scientists had done experiments involving the transmission of pictures. As early as 1884, Paul Gottlieb Nipkow of Germany had invented a scanning device that sent pictures over short distances. His system worked mechanically, rather than electronically as television does. In 1922, Philo T. Farnsworth of the United States developed an electronic scanning system. In 1925, John Logie Baird, a Scottish engineer, gave the first public demonstration of a mechanical television system. Vladimir K. Zworykin, a Russian-born American scientist, invented the iconoscope and the kinescope in 1923. The iconoscope was the first television camera tube suitable for broadcasting. The kinescope is the picture tube used in TV receivers. Zworykin demonstrated the first completely electronic, practical television system in 1929.

Technological advances made during the 1950's and 1960's helped improve the physical quality of telecasts. At first, most telecasts were live productions or programs made from film. The film took time to develop. Also, the equipment and techniques used yielded pictures and sounds of poor quality. Videotaping of programs began in the mid-1950's and became a major production method. Videotapes can be played back imme-

Important dates in television

1929 Vladimir K. Zworykin demonstrated the first practical, all-electronic television system.

1936 BBC made the world's first regular telecasts, in the United Kingdom.

1948 A television boom began in the United States. It resulted in making television part of most U.S. homes by 1960.

1951 The first nationwide telecast in the United States showed President Harry S. Truman opening the Japanese Peace Treaty Conference in San Francisco.

1953 Regular color telecasts began.

1965 Early Bird, the first commercial communications satellite, relayed TV programs between the United States and Europe.

1967 Congress established the Corporation for Public Broadcasting to help direct and finance public TV stations in the United States.

1969 TV viewers saw the first moon landing by astronauts.

1977 The miniseries became a popular U.S. TV format with the broadcast of *Roots* over eight nights.

1989 The world's first high-definition television (HDTV) broadcasts began in Japan.

1993 The Fox network began to broadcast programs seven nights per week, becoming the first new national network in the United States since the 1950's.

1993 The International Organization for Standardization approved a standard for data compression for digital television systems.

1996 The FCC adopted a group of standards for digital and high-definition television broadcasting in the United States.

1997 A worldwide audience estimated at $2\frac{1}{2}$ billion people—the largest audience in TV history—watched the funeral services for Diana, Princess of Wales.

1998 The FCC adopted a voluntary rating system for U.S. television programming.

1998 High-definition television (HDTV) broadcasting began in the United States.

diately after taping. They produce good quality pictures and sounds, and allow flexibility in program scheduling. Later, scientists developed equipment and techniques that improved the quality of filmed shows.

Early Bird, the first commercial communications satellite, was launched in 1965. Satellites made worldwide television broadcasting possible. Today, viewers can see such events as the Olympic Games as they happen.

Videocassette recorders skyrocketed in popularity in many industrial countries during the 1980's. Many viewers enjoyed renting pretaped motion pictures and watching them at home. Also in the 1980's, satellites gained importance in distributing television programs to cable systems, broadcasting stations, and home subscribers.

In TV's early days, most screens measured 7 or 10 inches (18 or 25 centimeters) diagonally. Today, 27-inch (69-centimeter) screens are common, and conventional televisions are available with screens as large as 40 inches (100 centimeters). In the 1970's, manufacturers introduced front-projection television systems, which beamed programs onto a screen as large as 7 feet (2 meters) measured diagonally. Today, rear-projection televisions are more popular, and the screens of these TV sets commonly measure from 48 inches to 60 inches (122 centimeters to 180 centimeters) diagonally. Other TV sets, small enough to fit in a pocket, have screens measuring about 3 inches (7.6 centimeters) diagonally.

Improvements in broadcasting and receiving equipment help provide much clearer pictures than in the past. In early days, all programs were telecast in black and white. Color television broadcasts began in 1953. Today, most programs are telecast in color.

Digital television represents one of the biggest changes in television since the introduction of color in the 1950's. Digital systems convert television signals into

A projection television set has a larger screen than a conventional television. In this rear-projection set, cathode ray tubes project the image onto the back of a screen.

© Zenith Electronics Corporation

High-definition television (HDTV) produces a super-sharp image, as shown on the left side of the photograph. The image on the right side was produced by a standard television set.

sequences of 1's and 0's—that is, the same numerical code used by computers. Each of the 1's and 0's is called a *bit,* which is short for *binary digit.* Digital systems provide stronger and more reliable signals. Such signals are less likely to be disrupted by electrical interference from appliances and thunderstorms or by reflections from tall buildings and aircraft.

Digital systems also improve TV pictures by making it possible for television signals to carry more information. Digital systems use a technique called *data compression* that removes unnecessary information from the signal. For example, a frame of a TV signal usually resembles the one before it. Digital systems take advantage of *digital memory* in the receiver to avoid retransmitting the parts of the picture that remain the same. The system thus can fit more information into existing channels.

In 1993, the International Organization for Standardization (ISO) approved a standard for data compression of the audio and video portions of digital television signals. The ISO, based in Geneva, Switzerland, tries to establish uniform sizes and other specifications to ease the worldwide exchange of goods and services. The flexibility of the international compression standard allows it to be adapted to a number of applications. These applications include videoconferencing over telephone networks, desktop video for video-telephone applications, DBS communications, and high-definition television.

In 1996, the FCC adopted a new standard for over-the-air broadcasting of digital television in the United States. This standard delivers approximately 20 million bits of information per second to a local broadcaster's coverage area. This capacity can be used to deliver a mixture of video, audio, and data services. An FCC policy established in 2002 requires television manufacturers to include a digital tuner in every television with a 13-inch (33-centimeter) or larger screen by 2007.

High-definition television (HDTV) is a type of digital television that produces very sharp images. It employs from 720 to over 1,000 scanning lines, each of which carries a greater amount of detail than an ordinary line. HDTV provides a picture about four times as sharp as standard TV does. HDTV's scanning pattern, called *progressive scanning,* offers greater clarity than interlaced scanning because it scans all the lines at one time in every frame. The screen of an HDTV set is wider in relation to its height than that of a traditional set.

Major U.S. broadcasters began broadcasting digital television signals incorporating HDTV in 1998. HDTV began in some parts of Europe in the late 1990's. Limited HDTV transmissions began in Japan in 1989.

Web television. The growth of the World Wide Web has given people access to a variety of information using personal computers. The World Wide Web is a system of computer files linked together on the Internet. These files include sounds, pictures, moving images, and text. Sports scores, travel information, and encyclopedia articles are among the information available online. A number of people, however, consider personal

United Airlines

Flat-panel television sets aboard an airplane, *shown here,* are stowed between seats when not in use and allow passengers to choose from a number of programs for individual viewing.

computers unfriendly, difficult to use, and expensive. Some of the functions of personal computers can be merged with television to create Web television. This application enables a person to browse the Internet as easily as watching television.

Interactive television is a form of digital television that can give viewers some control over the content of a program and of related information referenced in the program. This capability is especially useful with such applications as video-on-demand, Internet browsing, home shopping and banking, and multiplayer games.

Flat-panel, large-screen television became available in the late 1990's. These television sets hang on a wall as a picture does. Flat-panel systems use a variety of technologies. One system, called *plasma displays,* uses a layer of gas between two glass panels. An electric current passed through the gas ionizes it, producing ultraviolet light that excites red, blue, and green phosphors. Another system is called *thin-film transistor active-matrix liquid-crystal displays,* in which thousands of tiny transistors on the inner surface of a glass screen control electric signals that activate a liquid crystal. In a *field-emission display,* microscopic *cathodes* release electrons that jump across a small distance to an *anode.* The electrons strike a phosphor on the anode, producing light. The principle of this display is similar to the cathode ray tube of a conventional television set. There is a much greater number of cathodes, however, and the distance traveled by the electrons is much shorter.

Careers in television

The television industry has thousands of job opportunities. It needs such workers as writers, producers, directors, camera operators, engineers, electronics technicians, stagehands, lighting specialists, graphic artists, and set designers to help produce TV shows. Actors, actresses, and other talent are needed to appear in them. TV news departments provide various jobs for journalists. TV broadcasting also creates many jobs for specialists in management, market research, and advertising.

The television industry also employs workers in technical fields outside of broadcasting. Scientists and engineers are needed to design television equipment. Factory workers manufacture television sets and other TV equipment. Technicians service home receivers.

Almost all careers in television require special training. Many colleges and universities have departments that train students in nontechnical broadcasting careers. Journalism schools teach courses in broadcast journalism. Technological institutes and engineering departments of colleges offer training in technical areas of television. The National Association of Broadcasters in Washington, D.C., provides information on TV careers in the United States. Gerald I. Isenberg and Arun N. Netravali

Related articles in *World Book* include:

Biographies

Baird, John L.
Ball, Lucille
Carson, Johnny
Cleese, John
Cosby, Bill
Cronkite, Walter
De Forest, Lee
Farnsworth, Philo T.
Henson, Jim
Hertz, Heinrich Rudolf
Koppel, Ted
McLuhan, Marshall
Murrow, Edward R.
Turner, Ted
Winfrey, Oprah
Zworykin, Vladimir K.

Equipment and physical principles

Antenna
Audio-visual materials
Camcorder
Closed captioning
Coaxial cable
Communications satellite
Data compression
Electromagnetism
Electronics
Frequency modulation
Image orthicon
Microphone
Microwave
Radio
Speaker
Static
Tape recorder
Transistor
Videotape recorder

Other related articles

Advertising
British Broadcasting Corporation
Canadian Broadcasting Corporation
Copyright
Corporation for Public Broadcasting
Federal Communications Commission
Journalism
Multimedia
Science fiction (Growing popularity)
Soap opera
Telemarketing
Viacom Inc.

Outline

I. What television offers
- A. Commercial television
- B. Public television
- C. Cable television
- D. Satellite television
- E. Closed-circuit television
- F. Video entertainment systems
- G. Televised information services

II. Producing television programs
- A. Planning and preparation
- B. Putting a show on the air
- C. Other production methods

III. The U.S. television industry
- A. The national networks
- B. Commercial stations
- C. Public stations
- D. Cable and satellite television systems
- E. Television awards

IV. Television throughout the world
- A. In Africa
- B. In Asia
- C. In Australia and New Zealand
- D. In Europe
- E. In Latin America
- F. In Canada
- G. International television awards

V. Effects of television
- A. Effects on leisure time
- B. Effects on learning
- C. Effects on society
- D. Effects on young people

VI. Regulating U.S. television
- A. The Federal Communications Commission
- B. Congress
- C. Broadcasters and regulations
- D. Program ratings

VII. History of U.S. television broadcasting

VIII. Creating television signals
- A. The television camera
- B. Telecine
- C. Videotape recording
- D. Computer-generated video

IX. Transmitting television signals
- A. Broadcasting
- B. Coaxial cable and fiber-optic cable
- C. Microwaves
- D. Satellites

X. Receiving television signals
- A. Receiving equipment
- B. Tuner
- C. Amplifiers and separators
- D. The picture tube
- E. Projection television systems

XI. The development of television technology
- A. Early development
- B. Technological advances
- C. Digital television

D. Flat-panel, large screen television

XII. Careers in television

Questions

What is the role of electromagnetic waves in television?
What is a *dissolve?* A *super?* A *wipe?*
How did Vladimir K. Zworykin help develop TV?
Who was the first major U.S. television entertainer?
What are some career opportunities in television?
What are the methods of transmitting TV programs?
What are some false impressions that people may form from watching a lot of television?
On what does the quality of a television picture depend?
Who regulates television broadcasting in the United States?
What are some specialized uses of television?

Additional resources

Level I

Calabro, Marian. *Zap! A Brief History of Television.* Four Winds, 1992.

Merbreier, W. Carter. *Television: What's Behind What You See.* Farrar, 1995.

Riehecky, Janet. *Television.* Cavendish, 1996.

Level II

Newcomb, Horace, ed. *Encyclopedia of Television.* 3 vols. Fitzroy Dearborn, 1997.

Reed, Maxine K. and Robert M. *Career Opportunities in Television, Cable, Video, and Multimedia.* 4th ed. Checkmark, 1999. *The Facts on File Dictionary of Television, Cable, and Video.* Facts on File, 1994.

Smith, Anthony, and Paterson, Richard, eds. *Television: An International History.* 2nd ed. Oxford, 1998.

Watkinson, John. *An Introduction to Digital Video.* 2nd ed. Focal Pr., 2001.

Telford, Thomas (1757-1834), a Scottish civil engineer, was the greatest of the early builders of iron bridges. Telford's cast-iron arch bridges were built as part of canals and roads that he engineered. In 1826, Telford completed work on a suspension bridge over the Menai Straits in Wales. The bridge spanned 579 feet (176 meters), the longest of any bridge until 1834. It is still in use today. In addition, Telford devised improved methods for road construction. The *Telford method*—the use of large, flat stones for road foundations—is named after him. Telford was born on Aug. 9, 1757, in Eskdale, Scotland. He died on Sept. 2, 1834.

Terry S. Reynolds

Tell, William, was a legendary hero of Switzerland. His story, though not verified by history, represents the spirit of the Swiss movement for independence from the Austrian Habsburgs in the 1300's.

According to legend, Tell was a man of great strength and the most skilled marksman in the whole *canton* (state) of Uri. The Austrian bailiff, Gessler, had ordered all Swiss to bow to a hat he had set up on a pole in the main square of Altdorf. When Tell refused to bow, he was arrested. Gessler knew of Tell's skill with the crossbow and promised to let him go free if Tell could shoot an apple off his own son's head. Tell hit the apple and then said if he had hurt his son, he would have killed Gessler. Gessler then had him seized and put in chains.

While Tell was being taken across a lake in a boat, a storm broke. Gessler ordered Tell untied to help steer the boat. Tell escaped and shot an arrow through the tyrant's heart. This act led to a Swiss revolt, in which Tell played a leading role. This tale is the basis of Johann Friedrich Schiller's drama *William Tell* (1804). Gioacchino Rossini composed the opera *William Tell* (1829).

Ellen J. Stekert

Teller, Edward (1908-2003), an American physicist, became known as the father of the hydrogen bomb. His work in nuclear physics helped lead to the development of the H-bomb in 1952.

Teller was born on Jan. 15, 1908, in Budapest, Hungary. He earned a doctor's degree from the University of Leipzig. Teller went to the United States in 1935. During World War II (1939-1945), he joined the effort to develop a nuclear weapon. He worked at the laboratory at Los Alamos, New Mexico, where the first atomic bomb was built. In 1952, he helped found what is now the Lawrence Livermore National Laboratory, a facility at Livermore, California, dedicated to designing nuclear weapons. Teller was associate director from 1954 to 1958 and from 1960 to 1975 and director from 1958 to 1960. He taught at the University of California at Berkeley from 1953 to 1975. Teller died on Sept. 9, 2003.

Daniel J. Kevles

Tellurium, *teh LUR ee uhm,* is a rare semimetallic chemical element. Pure tellurium often appears as shiny, silvery-white crystals. In nature, the element most often occurs in combination with such metals as copper, gold, lead, mercury, and silver. Pure tellurium is usually obtained as a by-product of copper refining. Tellurium is used in the production of iron, steel, and certain *alloys* (combinations of two or more metals). Manufacturers use tellurium in the making of semiconductors and blasting caps. Tellurium helps *cure* (harden) rubber and *catalyzes* (stimulates) chemical reactions in petroleum refining. It is also used to color glass and ceramics.

Tellurium's chemical symbol is Te. Its *atomic number* (number of protons in its nucleus) is 52. Its *relative atomic mass* is 127.60. An element's relative atomic mass equals its *mass* (amount of matter) divided by $\frac{1}{12}$ of the mass of carbon 12, the most abundant form of carbon. Tellurium melts at 449.5 °C and boils at 989.8 °C. The Austrian chemist Franz Müller von Reichenstein discovered tellurium in 1782.

Marianna A. Busch

Detail of a woodcut (Granger Collection)

William Tell was a legendary Swiss patriot. The character is known for shooting an apple off his son's head with a crossbow.

Tempera. See Painting (Tempera; pictures).

Temperance Union, Woman's Christian. See Woman's Christian Temperance Union.

Temperature is a measure of how easily an object gives up or receives heat. Heat will always flow naturally from an object with a higher temperature to an object with a lower temperature.

Thermometers measure temperature in various units. A metric unit known as the *degree Celsius* (°C) is in general use throughout the world. Another metric unit, the *kelvin* (K), is used in some scientific work. In the United States, people use the nonmetric *degree Fahrenheit* (°F) for most commercial and everyday purposes.

The unit 1 °F equals $\frac{5}{9}$ of the unit 1 °C, and a temperature measurement of 32 °F equals a measurement of 0 °C. So you can use the following equation to convert a temperature measured in degrees Fahrenheit to one measured in degrees Celsius: $°C = (°F - 32) \times \frac{5}{9}$.

The unit 1 K is exactly the same as the unit 1 °C, and a measurement of 273.15 K equals a measurement of 0 °C. Thus, you can use the following equation to convert a temperature measured in kelvins to one measured in degrees Celsius: $°C = K - 273.15$. The International System of Units (SI), the modern metric system, uses this equation to define the Celsius scale in terms of the kelvin scale.

SI defines the kelvin scale in terms of two points: (1) *absolute zero* and (2) the *triple point temperature* of water. Absolute zero is the lowest possible temperature. It is assigned a value of 0 K. The triple point of a substance is the one temperature and pressure at which *its solid, liquid, and gas phases can coexist in equilibrium.* This means that, at water's triple point, a quantity of water can be partly ice, partly liquid, and partly vapor; and the proportions of ice, liquid, and vapor will remain the same. The triple point of water occurs at 0.06 *atmosphere* of pressure and at a temperature that is defined as 0.01 °C or 273.16 K. One atmosphere equals 14.696 pounds per square inch (101.325 kilopascals).

Temperature is different from heat, or *thermal energy.* Heat is the total amount of *kinetic energy* (energy of motion) associated with the random movement of molecules in an object. Thus, a cold lake, with many slowly moving molecules, has more thermal energy than a hot cup of tea, with fewer, faster molecules. Kieran Mullen

Related articles in *World Book* include:

Absolute zero	Freezing point	Melting point
Boiling point	Heat	Thermometer

Temperature, Body. Body temperature is a measurement of the heat in an animal's body. The body of an animal generates heat by burning food. But the animal also loses heat to—or gains heat from—its environment.

Birds and mammals, including human beings, are *warm-blooded animals.* Their body temperature almost always stays fairly constant, regardless of the temperature of their environment. The body of a warm-blooded animal balances the amount of heat it exchanges with the environment with the amount it produces by burning food. Nearly all other animals are *cold-blooded animals.* Their body cannot balance this heat exchange so accurately. As a result, their body temperature tends to vary with the temperature of their environment.

When taken orally, the average body temperature of a healthy, resting adult human being is 98.6 °F (37.0 °C). Physicians consider a temperature within 1 °F (0.5 °C) of this figure normal. A higher temperature may indicate a fever (see Fever). A lower temperature may be a sign of old age or of certain illnesses.

Warm-blooded animals make various physical and behavioral adjustments to regulate their heat exchange with the environment. In cold surroundings, they increase the production of body heat and decrease the amount of heat lost to the environment. In hot surroundings, they do just the opposite. A part of the brain called the *hypothalamus* controls these adjustments. Certain nerves in the skin and deep within the body send messages to the hypothalamus. The hypothalamus compares the temperatures of these areas with that of the brain. It triggers the necessary responses by nerves and glands to keep a normal body temperature.

Even with the various controls, the body temperature of a warm-blooded animal does not remain entirely constant. It changes slightly throughout the day. In a healthy human being, for example, the body temperature is lowest in the morning and then rises until late afternoon. It falls again during sleep. Strenuous activity can raise the body temperature. In cold surroundings, the temperature of the skin and limbs may drop far below the temperature deep within the body.

Each species of warm-blooded animal has its own normal body temperature. Each species also functions best when the temperature of its surroundings stays in a certain range. This range varies greatly from species to species, depending on such factors as the thickness of fur and the rate at which its body burns food. Some warm-blooded animals hibernate. During hibernation, their body temperature drops below normal. In fact, the body temperature of most hibernators drops almost to the temperature of their environment. See **Hibernation.**

Cold-blooded animals lack the precise temperature regulation abilities that characterize warm-blooded creatures. However, many cold-blooded animals can exercise some physical and behavioral control over body temperature. Reptiles, for example, can alter the amount of heat their body absorbs from the sun by changing their skin color. Moreover, many reptiles alternately warm themselves in the sun and cool themselves in the shade, thereby maintaining a fairly constant body temperature throughout the day. James Edward Heath

See also **Warm-blooded animal; Cold-blooded animal; Hyperthermia; Hypothermia.**

Temperature-humidity index. See Heat index.

Tempering is a process of hardening glass and metals, especially steel. First, the steel is heated to a high temperature. Next, it is *quenched* (cooled rapidly) by plunging it into water, oil, or other liquid. Then, it is heated again to a temperature lower than that used before quenching it, and is allowed to cool slowly.

Tempering changes the internal structure of the steel. Different uses of steel require different properties, such as varying degrees of hardness, strength, and toughness. To obtain those properties, the structure of steel is changed by tempering it in different gases at various temperatures and for various lengths of time.

Glass is tempered in a somewhat similar way. It is heated until it becomes almost soft, then chilled by blasts of air or by plunging it into oil or other liquids. Glass which has been tempered may be up to five times as hard as ordinary glass. It may be used to hammer nails into wood. Joel S. Hirschhorn

See also **Annealing**.

Temple is a house of worship. The word *temple* usually refers to Buddhist, Confucian, Hindu, Taoist, and ancient Near Eastern and European places of worship. In Christianity, it is generally used only for certain Mormon buildings. In Judaism, Reform houses of worship are commonly called temples, but Conservative or Orthodox ones are usually called synagogues.

Most temples are built to honor God, a god, or many gods. Many of these buildings are considered the homes of gods. Worship at temples often involves traditional ceremonies and may include sacrifices. Many people visit temples as individuals or in small groups, rather than as members of large congregations.

Temples range from small, simple huts to huge, elaborately decorated buildings. Many contain a picture or statue of the honored god. In a typical temple, the holiest image or object of worship is in a central room. To reach this area, worshipers may have to pass through a series of gates or doors that symbolize a spiritual journey. In many temples, only the clergy may enter the room. An altar stands inside or in front of many temples.

Certain temples stand on sacred sites. For example, some were built where people believed that miracles or divine revelations occurred. King Solomon of ancient Israel erected a temple in Jerusalem at the place where God was believed to have stopped a plague. This temple, which served as the center of the Hebrew religion, is considered the most important one in the history of Western religion. Temples also have been built where people thought sacred forces flowed together in the most favorable way. Hindus and Taoists use an elaborate procedure involving the interpretation of divine signs to choose the most favorable location for a temple.

The design of numerous temples is symbolic. In Eastern Asia, for example, a number of Buddhist temples are towerlike buildings called *pagodas,* which have many stories. The stories represent the levels of the earth and heaven, or the various spiritual goals that a Buddhist must achieve to gain salvation. Robert S. Ellwood, Jr.

Milt and Joan Mann

The Hall of the Great Buddha, part of the Todaiji Temple in Nara, Japan, is the world's largest wooden building. A bronze statue of Buddha more than 50 feet (15 meters) high stands inside the temple.

Related articles in *World Book* include:

Abu Simbel, Temples of	Indonesia (picture)	Pantheon
Architecture (pictures)	Japan (pictures)	Parthenon
Greece, Ancient (pictures)	Mormons (picture: The Mormon Temple)	Sculpture (pictures)
	Pagoda	World, History of the (pictures)

Temple, Henry John. See Palmerston, Viscount.

Temple, Shirley (1928-), was the most popular child motion-picture star of the 1930's. She made her movie debut at the age of 3 and became a star in the 1934 film musical *Stand Up and Cheer.* Shirley Temple made about 25 movies during the 1930's, including *Little Miss Marker* (1934), *The Little Colonel* (1935), *The Littlest Rebel* (1935), and *Dimples* (1936). She played teen-age roles in many movies during the 1940's.

Shirley Temple retired from motion pictures in 1949. She married Charles A. Black in 1950. In 1969, President Richard M. Nixon appointed her a U.S. representative to the United Nations General Assembly. In 1974, President Gerald R. Ford named her the U.S. ambassador to Ghana. In 1976 and 1977, she was chief of protocol in the Department of State, the first woman to hold that post. In 1989, President George H. W. Bush appointed her ambassador to Czechoslovakia. She held that post until 1992. She was born on April 23, 1928, in Santa Monica, California. Gerald Bordman

Scene from *Just Around the Corner* (1938); Bettmann Archive

Shirley Temple, a child motion-picture star of the 1930's, appeared in several films with dancer Bill Robinson, *shown here.*

Temple of Zeus. See Olympia.

Temples of Abu Simbel. See Abu Simbel, Temples of.

Ten Commandments is a list of rules for living and for worship that, according to the Bible, God wrote and gave to Moses on Mount Sinai. The Ten Commandments are also called the *Decalogue,* from two Greek words that mean *ten words.*

The Ten Commandments appear twice in the Bible, in Exodus, chapter 20, and in Deuteronomy, chapter 5. The verse numbers vary in different editions of the Bible, and the wording is not exactly the same in the two passages. The idea that there are exactly 10 commandments appears in Exodus 34:28.

The list below reflects one common numbering of the Commandments. The wording is taken from Exodus in the King James Version of the Bible. The verse numbers follow each Commandment in parentheses:

1. I am the Lord thy God. (2) Thou shalt have no other gods before me. (3)
2. Thou shalt not make unto thee any graven image, or any likeness of any thing that is in heaven above, or that is in the earth beneath, or that is in the water under the earth. ... (4-6)
3. Thou shalt not take the name of the Lord thy God in vain. ... (7)
4. Remember the sabbath day, to keep it holy. ... (8-11)
5. Honor thy father and thy mother. (12)
6. Thou shalt not kill. (13)
7. Thou shalt not commit adultery. (14)
8. Thou shalt not steal. (15)
9. Thou shalt not bear false witness against thy neighbor. (16)
10. Thou shalt not covet thy neighbor's house, thou shalt not covet thy neighbor's wife, nor his manservant, nor his maidservant, nor his ox, nor his ass, nor any thing that is thy neighbor's. (17)

This list indicates there may actually be more than 10 commandments in the passage, though there are, perhaps, 10 prohibitions. Scholars have offered several suggestions on how to divide them into 10. Most people see the Ten Commandments as two natural groups. It is often stated that the first group deals with the relationships between people and God, while the second group deals with relationships among people.

The similarity in the form of the last short commandments (verses 13-16 and part of 17) suggests that they be grouped together as the last five. This requires fitting verses 2-12 or 3-12 into the first five. Some people do not count verse 2 as a commandment.

The Ten Commandments became very important for both Judaism and Christianity, but in somewhat different ways. Judaism believes that God gave 613 commandments in the *Torah* (the first five books of the Bible), of which these 10 are an essential part. Some interpreters tried to show that all 613 are hinted at in the 10. Other writers felt that all 613 were of equal importance. Christianity sees the Ten Commandments as the basic principles that should govern human conduct. B. Barry Levy

See also **Moses** (The covenant with God); **Shavuot; Ark of the Covenant; Law** (Early developments in the East).

Tenant, in law, is a person who holds or possesses lands or buildings by any kind of title. In popular speech, a tenant is a person who has the right to occupy and use lands or buildings that belong to another person, known as the landlord. Usually, a written agreement called a *lease* states the terms and conditions of a tenancy. The lease is signed by both the *lessor* (landlord) and the *lessee* (tenant). But leases may also be oral.

There are many types of tenancies. The most common are (1) periodic tenancies, (2) tenancies for years, and (3) tenancies at will. A periodic tenancy runs for a recurring period of time, generally month to month, until either the landlord or the tenant gives advance notice to end it. A tenancy for years runs for a definite period of time, such as a year or a month, and then ends. In a tenancy at will, the landlord or the tenant can end the tenancy at any time by giving notice in advance.

The relation of landlord and tenant had its origin in the feudal system of the Middle Ages. Some of the feudal obligations still survive in the present laws. For example, the landlord's duty not to interfere with the tenant's quiet enjoyment of the leased premises dates back to feudal times. James E. Krier

See also **Eviction; Joint tenancy; Lease.**

Tenant farming is a common farming practice that involves raising crops and livestock on rented land. Farmers who rent the land they farm are called *tenants.* People who own the land are called *landlords.*

There are two basic types of leases used in tenant farming—(1) cash leases and (2) share leases. Under a cash lease, the tenant pays a fixed amount of rent. The landlord provides land and buildings, and the tenant pays all other production costs.

Under a share lease, the tenant and landlord agree to share both the crop and the cost of producing it. For example, in a 50-50 share lease, the landlord may supply land and buildings and pay for half the necessary seed, fertilizer, and chemicals. The tenant furnishes labor, machinery, and the rest of the seed, fertilizer, and chemicals. The tenant and landlord each receive half the crop.

Warren F. Lee

See also **Asia** (Farm organization); **United States, History of the** (1870-1916 [The war-torn South]).

Tendon, *TEHN duhn,* also called *sinew, SIHN yoo,* is a strong white cord that attaches muscles to bones. Muscles move bones by pulling on tendons. A tendon is a bundle of many tough fibers. Some tendons are round, others long or flat. One end of a tendon arises from the end of a muscle. The other end is woven into the substance of a bone. The tendon may slide up and down inside a sheath of fibrous tissue, as an arm moves in a coat sleeve. The tendon and sheath are held in place by con-

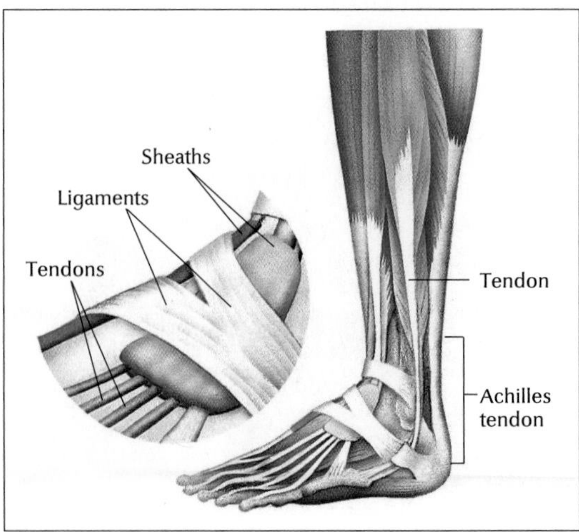

WORLD BOOK illustration by Leonard Morgan

Tendons connect bones and muscles, thus allowing the muscles to move the bones. Leg tendons include the Achilles tendon at the heel. Foot tendons are covered by protective sheaths.

nective tissue called *ligaments.* A cut tendon can be *sutured* (sewed) together. Healing may take six weeks or more. Bruce Reider

See also **Achilles tendon; Hand; Human body** (picture: Ligaments and tendons); **Muscle** (Skeletal muscles); **Repetitive strain injury.**

Tenement is a term usually used to describe a crowded, decaying apartment building. But a tenement may refer to any dwelling that is rented to two or more families or tenants. A tenement can be an old residential building that has been divided to house low-income families at low standards. It can also be a new structure built for many low-income families—each in its own small apartment. An urban district that houses numerous tenements is often called a *slum.*

Tenements are strong income-producing properties. Each family may pay a low rent, but many people are crowded in small, poorly maintained areas. Thus, the rent per unit of area in a tenement is often greater than that paid by middle-income people in larger and better apartments.

Historians believe tenements have existed since ancient times, when the Romans built them to house the poor and the slaves. Most tenements in the United States were built to house poor immigrants. Today, housing standards prevent construction of new tenements. But such standards do not prevent old buildings from being converted into tenements. Oscar Newman

Teng Hsiao-p'ing. See **Deng Xiaoping.**

Teniers, *tuh NEERZ* or *TEHN yurz,* **David, the Younger** (1610-1690), was a Flemish painter. He painted peasants, alchemists, witches, soldiers, and the middle class, often showing these people working or enjoying festivals. Teniers's landscapes celebrate the virtues of idealized rural life. Teniers also painted religious subjects, especially the temptations of Saint Anthony. In addition, he created paintings that functioned as inventories of the rooms used as art galleries in wealthy homes.

Most of Teniers's paintings present detailed, brightly colored small figures, often in crowded compositions. Many of Teniers's scenes include a large group of objects arranged in a still life at one side in the foreground. The objects usually contribute to a moral that is expressed in the painting. For example, a broken jug might refer to unacceptable behavior taking place within the painting.

David Teniers the Younger was born on Dec. 15, 1610, in Antwerp in Flanders, now part of Belgium. David Teniers the Elder, his father, was also a noted painter. In 1651, David the Younger moved to Brussels, where he was court painter to the governor who represented the Spanish king. In the early 1660's, Teniers helped establish the important Academy of Fine Arts in Antwerp to train painters and elevate their status in society. Teniers had a large workshop of assistants who produced copies of his paintings to satisfy the demand for his work. Linda Stone-Ferrier

Tennent, Gilbert (1703-1764), was a colonial American religious leader. During the early 1700's, Tennent played a major role in the Protestant religious movement called the Great Awakening. An important aspect of the Great Awakening was *revivalism,* an emotional approach to religion that emphasized individual religious experience rather than church doctrines.

As a Presbyterian minister in New Jersey from 1726 to 1743, Tennent became active in the Great Awakening. In 1739, he gave a sermon, "The Danger of an Unconverted Ministry," in which he attacked ministers who favored established church doctrines and opposed revivalism. The publication of this sermon in 1740 contributed to a split in the Presbyterian Church in America in 1741. Tennent eventually became more willing to compromise with his critics. Tennent helped reunite the church in 1758.

Tennent was born on Feb. 5, 1703, in County Armagh, now a district in Northern Ireland. He came to America when he was about 15. His father, William Tennent, was also a well-known minister. Charles H. Lippy

See also **Great Awakening; Tennent, William.**

Tennent, William (1673-1746), was an important Presbyterian minister in colonial America. In 1726, he became pastor of a church in Neshaminy, Pennsylvania, near Philadelphia. There Tennent founded the Log College to train Presbyterian ministers according to the principles of *revivalism* (see **Revivalism**). Some church leaders' disapproval of revivalist training at the college contributed to a split in 1741 within the Presbyterian Church of America. Tennent ran the college until his death. The college closed, but its supporters later founded the College of New Jersey (now Princeton University).

Tennent was probably born in Ireland. He immigrated to America about 1718. His four sons—Gilbert, William, Jr., John, and Charles—also became Presbyterian ministers. Charles H. Lippy

See also **Tennent, Gilbert.**

The Guardhouse (about 1640-1650), an oil painting on canvas by David Teniers the Younger;

A Teniers painting is an example of *genre* painting, which was popular in northern Europe in the 1600's. Genre paintings portray scenes from everyday life, such as this guardhouse interior.

Tennessee Tourist Development

The Great Smoky Mountains stretch across eastern Tennessee in the state's Blue Ridge region. The thickly forested mountains create a dense, humid atmosphere that looks like a smoky mist.

Tennessee *The Volunteer State*

Tennessee is one of the states that link the North and the South of the United States. Life in West and Middle Tennessee resembles life in the Deep South. East Tennessee is similar to parts of the North. Even during the American Civil War (1861-1865), Tennessee loyalties were divided between the North and the South. Tennessee was the last Confederate state to leave the Union, and the first to return.

Nashville is the capital of Tennessee and the center of the state's largest metropolitan area. Memphis is the state's largest city. It is the center of Tennessee' s second largest metropolitan area.

Tennessee stretches from North Carolina, one of the easternmost states, to Arkansas, one of the westernmost states in the South. At its eastern boundaries, Tennessee starts high in the Blue Ridge Mountains. The land becomes lower toward the west until it reaches the banks of the Mississippi River.

A pioneer wearing a coonskin cap and carrying a rifle is a symbol of Tennessee's great past. But a better symbol of the present and future is the nuclear physicist working in an Oak Ridge laboratory or the technician who controls the robots on the assembly line of a motor vehicle manufacturing plant. Most people in the state are employed by business offices, stores, and factories.

Trade, restaurants, and hotels and other service industries play a leading role in Tennessee's economy. The state is a popular tourist destination, and spending by visitors contributes to the economy. Manufacturing is an important source of income and jobs. Tennessee's fertile soil and abundant mineral deposits make it an important agricultural and mining state.

Indians once roamed Tennessee's mountains and forests. Early explorers passed through the region, and people from Europe fought to decide who would own it. Pioneers crossed the mountains to settle in the wilderness. The pioneers brought with them the spirit of independence and daring that has become a part of Tennessee's history. In 1796, Tennessee became the 16th state in the Union. Such Tennesseans as John Sevier in the Revolutionary War in America (1775-1783), Andrew Jackson in the War of 1812, and Alvin C. York in World War I (1914-1918) established a Tennessee military tradition of honor and bravery.

More battles of the American Civil War were fought in Tennessee than in any other state except Virginia. Three men who were later elected president of the United States—Andrew Jackson, James K. Polk, and Andrew Johnson—all distinguished themselves in Tennessee. In 1920, the state became the final state needed to ratify the 19th Amendment to the U.S. Constitution, giving women the right to vote.

The name *Tennessee* comes from *Tanasie,* the name of a Cherokee village in the region. Tennessee is usually called the *Volunteer State* because of its great military traditions.

The contributors of this article are Charles S. Aiken, Professor of Geography, and Stephen V. Ash, Associate Professor of History, both at the University of Tennessee at Knoxville.

Bob Mooty, Shostal

Douglas Dam, on the French Broad River near Sevierville, is part of the Tennessee Valley Authority (TVA) system. It provides electric power and flood control and forms Douglas Lake.

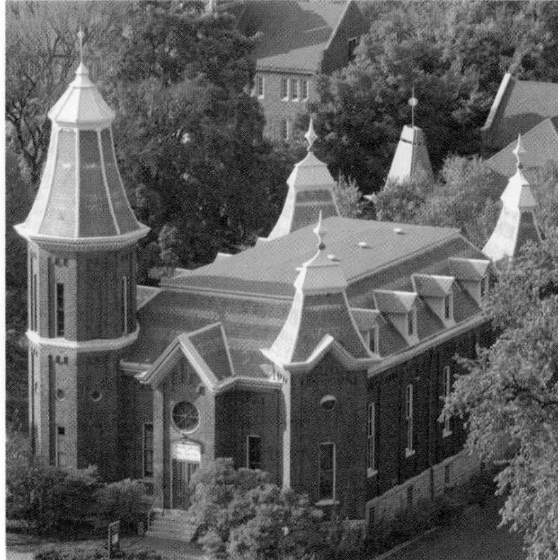

Vanderbilt University News Service

The Fine Arts Building at Vanderbilt University, in Nashville, is a campus landmark. It was built in 1880 and originally served as the school gymnasium. Today, it houses the Fine Arts Gallery.

Interesting facts about Tennessee

WORLD BOOK illustrations by Kevin Chadwick

The first guide dog for the blind in the United States was "Buddy," a female German shepherd who lived in Nashville with her owner, Morris Frank. Buddy was trained in Switzerland in 1928 by The Seeing Eye, the first organization to train guide dogs.

First guide dog

The State of Franklin existed from 1784 to 1788 in what is now East Tennessee. It had broken away from North Carolina. Franklin was named for American statesman Benjamin Franklin. It had its own constitution and governor beginning in 1785. A movement to make it a state of the Union failed. The area was part of the land that became Tennessee in 1796.

Two brothers competed in a gubernatorial election for the first time on Nov. 2, 1886, in Tennessee. Robert Love Taylor, the Democratic candidate, defeated his brother Alfred Alexander Taylor, the Republican candidate, in the event known to Tennesseans as the "War of the Roses."

Kingston was the capital of Tennessee for one day. In 1807, the state legislature voted to meet in Kingston on September 21. Its business, to discuss a treaty with the Cherokee Indians, was completed that day.

The first publications wholly devoted to abolishing slavery were written by Elihu Embree, a slaveholder living in Tennessee, a slave state. Embree called for the abolition of slavery in a weekly newspaper published in 1819 in Jonesborough, and later in the monthly magazine *The Emancipator,* which was published from April 30 to Oct. 31, 1820.

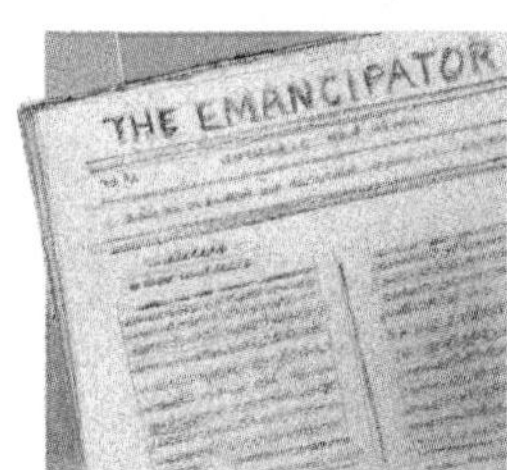
THE EMANCIPATOR

The Emancipator

Memphis Convention & Visitors Bureau

Downtown Memphis stands along the Mississippi River. Memphis is Tennessee's largest city and its chief center of commerce, industry, and transportation. Visitors may enjoy a cruise on a Mississippi riverboat, *in foreground.*

Tennessee in brief

Symbols of Tennessee

The state flag, adopted in 1905, has three stars representing East, Middle, and West Tennessee. On the state seal, a plow, a sheaf of wheat, and a cotton plant symbolize the importance of agriculture. The riverboat represents commerce. The date 1796 is the year the first state Constitution was approved. The current state seal came into use during the term of Governor William G. Brownlow (1865-1869) and was officially adopted in 1987.

State flag

State seal

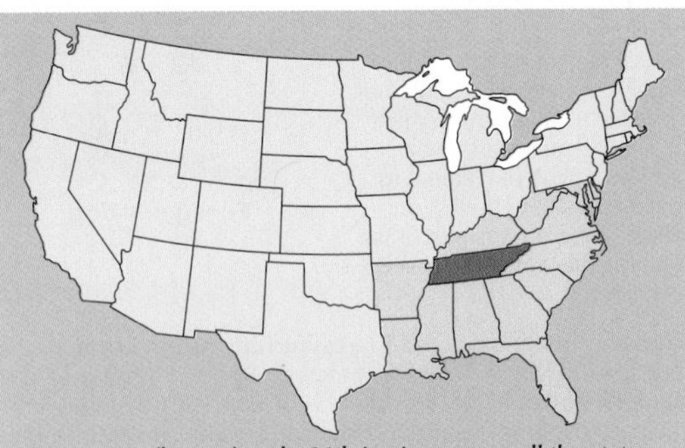

Tennessee (brown) ranks 34th in size among all the states and 8th in size among the Southern States (yellow).

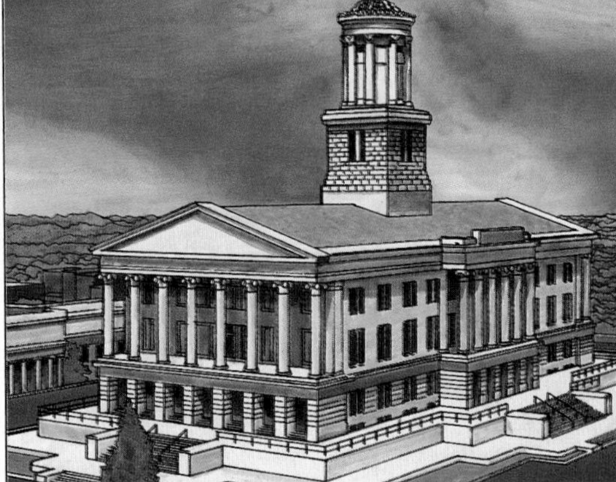

The State Capitol is in Nashville, the capital since 1826. Earlier capitals were Knoxville (1792-1812, 1817), Kingston (1807, for one day), Nashville (1812-1817), and Murfreesboro (1818-1826).

General information

Statehood: June 1, 1796, the 16th state.
State abbreviations: Tenn. (traditional); TN (postal).
State motto: *Agriculture and Commerce.*
State songs: "Rocky Top." Words and music by Boudleaux and Felice Bryant. "The Tennessee Waltz." Words by Pee Wee King; music by Redd Stewart (two of five state songs).

Land and climate

Area: 42,146 mi² (109,158 km²), including 926 mi² (2,400 km²) of inland water.
Elevation: *Highest*—Clingmans Dome, 6,643 ft (2,025 m) above sea level. Lowest—182 ft (55 m) above sea level in Shelby County.
Record high temperature: 113 °F (45 °C) at Perryville on July 29 and Aug. 9, 1930.
Record low temperature: −32 °F (−36 °C) at Mountain City on Dec. 30, 1917.
Average July temperature: 78 °F (26 °C).
Average January temperature: 38 °F (3 °C).
Average yearly precipitation: 52 in (132 cm).

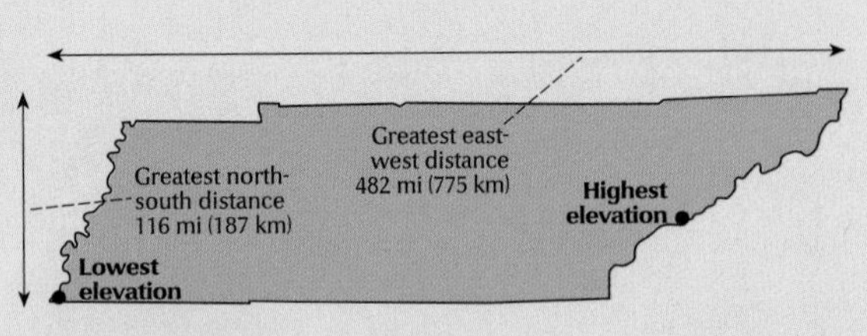

Important dates

1540 Hernando de Soto of Spain led the first European expedition into the Tennessee region.

1714 Charles Charleville set up a French trading post near the present site of Nashville.

1780 Nashville settlers signed the Cumberland Compact.

1796 Tennessee became the 16th state on June 1.

State bird
Mockingbird

State flower
Iris

State tree
Tulip-poplar (yellow-poplar)

People

Population: 5,689,283
Rank among the states: 16th
Density: 135 per mi² (52 per km²), U.S. average 78 per mi² (30 per km²)
Distribution: 64 percent urban, 36 percent rural

Largest cities in Tennessee

City	Population
Memphis	650,100
Nashville	569,891
Knoxville	173,890
Chattanooga	155,554
Clarksville	103,455
Murfreesboro	68,816

Source: 2000 census.

Population trend

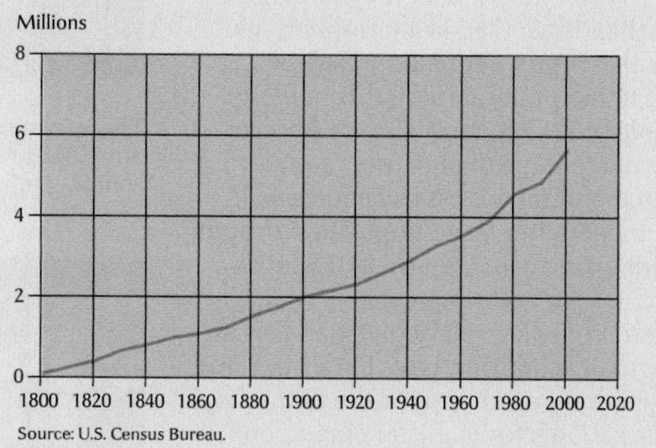

Source: U.S. Census Bureau.

Year	Population
2000	5,689,283
1990	4,877,185
1980	4,591,120
1970	3,926,018
1960	3,567,089
1950	3,291,718
1940	2,915,841
1930	2,616,556
1920	2,337,885
1910	2,184,789
1900	2,020,616
1890	1,767,518
1880	1,542,359
1870	1,258,520
1860	1,109,801
1850	1,002,717
1840	829,210
1830	681,904
1820	422,823
1810	261,727
1800	105,602
1790	35,691

Economy

Chief products

Agriculture: beef cattle, broilers, greenhouse and nursery products, tobacco, cotton, soybeans, corn.
Manufacturing: processed foods and beverages, chemicals, transportation equipment, machinery, metal products, plastics and rubber products.
Mining: crushed stone, coal, cement.

Gross state product

Value of goods and services produced in 2002: $190,122,000,000. *Services* include community, business, and personal services; finance; government; trade; and transportation and communication. *Industry* includes construction, manufacturing, mining, and utilities. *Agriculture* includes agriculture, fishing, and forestry.

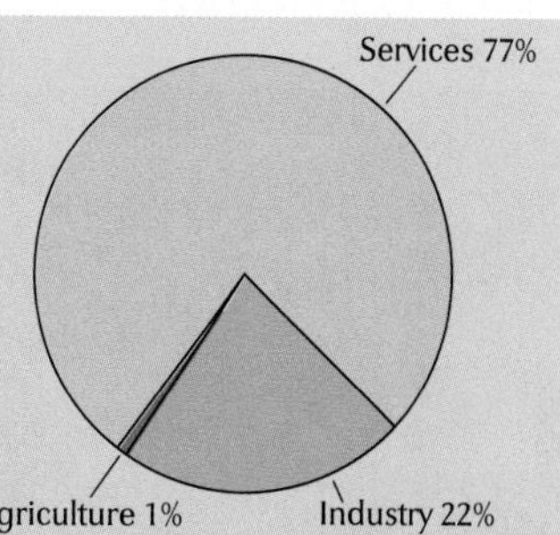

Source: U.S. Bureau of Economic Analysis.

Government

State government

Governor: 4-year term
State senators: 33; 4-year terms
State representatives: 99; 2-year terms
Counties: 95

Federal government

United States senators: 2
United States representatives: 9
Electoral votes: 11

Sources of information

For information about tourism, write to: Department of Tourist Development, 312 8th Avenue North, 25th Floor, Nashville, TN 37243. The Web site at http://www.tnvacation.com/ also provides information.
For information on the economy, write to: Department of Economic and Community Development, 312 Eighth Avenue North, 11th Floor, Nashville, TN 37243-0405.
The state's official Web site at http://www.state.tn.us also provides a gateway to much information on Tennessee's economy, government, and history.

1878 A yellow fever epidemic killed about 5,200 of the 19,600 people in Memphis.

1933 The U.S. Congress created the Tennessee Valley Authority.

1942 The federal government began building the atomic energy center at Oak Ridge.

1982 A world's fair was held in Knoxville.

1996 Tennessee marked the bicentennial of its statehood.

People

Population. The 2000 United States census reported that Tennessee had 5,689,283 people. The population had increased about 17 percent over the 1990 census figure, 4,877,185. According to the 2000 census, Tennessee ranks 16th in population among the 50 states.

Memphis is the state's largest city, followed by Nashville, Knoxville, Chattanooga, and Clarksville. Each of these cities has over 100,000 people. The sixth largest city is Murfreesboro with about 69,000 people. Ten other cities in Tennessee have populations of 25,000 or more. About a third of Tennesseans live in rural areas.

About two-thirds of the state's people live in one of the state's metropolitan areas (see **Metropolitan area**). These metropolitan areas are, in order of population, Nashville; Memphis; Knoxville; Johnson City-Kingsport-Bristol, Virginia; Chattanooga; Clarksville-Hopkinsville, Kentucky; and Jackson. For the population of these areas, see the *Index* to the political map of Tennessee.

About 16 out of every 100 Tennesseans are African Americans, a lower percentage than in most southern states. About 43 percent of the blacks in Tennessee live in Memphis. Tennessee's other large population groups include people of Irish, German, English, and Scotch-Irish descent.

Schools. Education in Tennessee began with privately owned schools, usually controlled by churches. Samuel Doak, a Presbyterian minister, started the first school in about 1780. Public schools for children of the poor were established during the early 1800's. In 1873, free education was made available to all children.

Walking Horse Owners Association

The International Grand Championship Walking Horse Show features walking horses bred in Middle Tennessee. This annual autumn event is held in Murfreesboro.

Tennessee Tourist Development

The National Storytelling Festival takes place each October in Jonesborough. Master storytellers from the United States and many other countries spin tales before fascinated listeners.

David R. Frazier

The Adventure Science Center in Nashville has a planetarium and interactive exhibits. The motion of the pendulum, *shown here,* proves that the earth rotates.

Population density

West Tennessee, Middle Tennessee, and East Tennessee each have densely populated areas. Thinly populated areas separate the three regions.

Persons per sq. mi.	Persons per km²
More than 100	More than 40
50 to 100	20 to 40
25 to 50	10 to 20
Less than 25	Less than 10

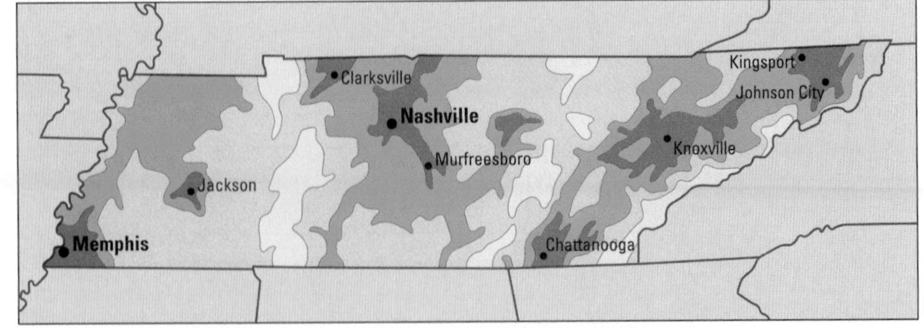

WORLD BOOK map; based on U.S. Census Bureau data.

The governor appoints a commissioner of education to a four-year term. The commissioner heads the State Department of Education and makes recommendations to the State Board of Education. The board is composed of 10 members appointed by the governor and confirmed by the General Assembly. Nine of the members represent the state's nine congressional districts and are appointed to nine-year terms. The remaining member is a student, who is appointed to a one-year term.

Children in Tennessee must attend school from age 6 to age 18. For the number of students and teachers in Tennessee, see **Education** (table).

Libraries. Tennessee has about 300 public libraries and 12 regional libraries. In addition, most of the state's public and private schools have library media centers. The largest library collections are at Vanderbilt University in Nashville and the University of Tennessee in Knoxville, as well as the metropolitan public libraries in Chattanooga, Knoxville, Nashville, and Memphis. Most libraries in Tennessee provide Internet access and online information services in addition to books and magazines.

Museums. The Tennessee State Museum in Nashville has exhibits on Tennessee history. The Adventure Science Center in Nashville has a planetarium and interactive exhibits. The Museum of Appalachia in Norris features exhibits on early American life. The Knoxville Museum of Art and the Memphis Brooks Museum of Art both have large collections of artwork. The National Civil Rights Museum in Memphis is in the motel where civil rights leader Martin Luther King, Jr., was shot and killed in 1968. The Memphis Pink Palace Museum has exhibits on the history of the mid-South. Other museums include the American Museum of Science and Energy in Oak Ridge, the Casey Jones Home and Railroad Museum in Jackson, and the Country Music Hall of Fame and Museum in Nashville. The Mississippi River Museum at Mud Island River Park in Memphis features a riverboat steam engine and a paddle wheel.

University of Tennessee

The University of Tennessee's Neyland Stadium is one of the largest college stadiums in the United States. It stands near the Tennessee River on the university's Knoxville campus.

Universities and colleges

This table lists the universities and colleges in Tennessee that grant bachelor's or advanced degrees and are accredited by the Southern Association of Colleges and Schools.

Name	Mailing address
Aquinas College	Nashville
Austin Peay State University	Clarksville
Baptist Memorial College of Health Science	Memphis
Belmont University	Nashville
Bethel College	McKenzie
Bryan College	Dayton
Carson-Newman College	Jefferson City
Christian Brothers University	Memphis
Church of God Theological Seminary	Cleveland
Crichton College	Memphis
Cumberland University	Lebanon
East Tennessee State University	Johnson City
Emmanuel School of Religion	Johnson City
Fisk University	Nashville
Free Will Baptist Bible College	Nashville
Freed-Hardeman University	Henderson
Harding University Graduate School of Religion	Memphis
Johnson Bible College	Knoxville
King College	Bristol
Lambuth University	Jackson
Lane College	Jackson
Lee University	Cleveland
LeMoyne-Owen College	Memphis
Lincoln Memorial University	Harrogate
Lipscomb University	Nashville
Martin Methodist College	Pulaski
Maryville College	Maryville
Meharry Medical College	Nashville
Memphis, University of	Memphis
Memphis College of Art	Memphis
Memphis Theological Seminary	Memphis
Mid-America Baptist Theological Seminary	Germantown
Middle Tennessee School of Anesthesia	Madison
Middle Tennessee State University	Murfreesboro
Milligan College	Milligan College
Rhodes College	Memphis
South, University of the	Sewanee
South College	Knoxville
Southern Adventist University	Collegedale
Southern College of Optometry	Memphis
Tennessee, University of	*
Tennessee State University	Nashville
Tennessee Technological University	Cookeville
Tennessee Wesleyan College	Athens
Trevecca Nazarene University	Nashville
Tusculum College	Greeneville
Union University	Jackson
Vanderbilt University	Nashville

*For campuses, see Tennessee, University of.

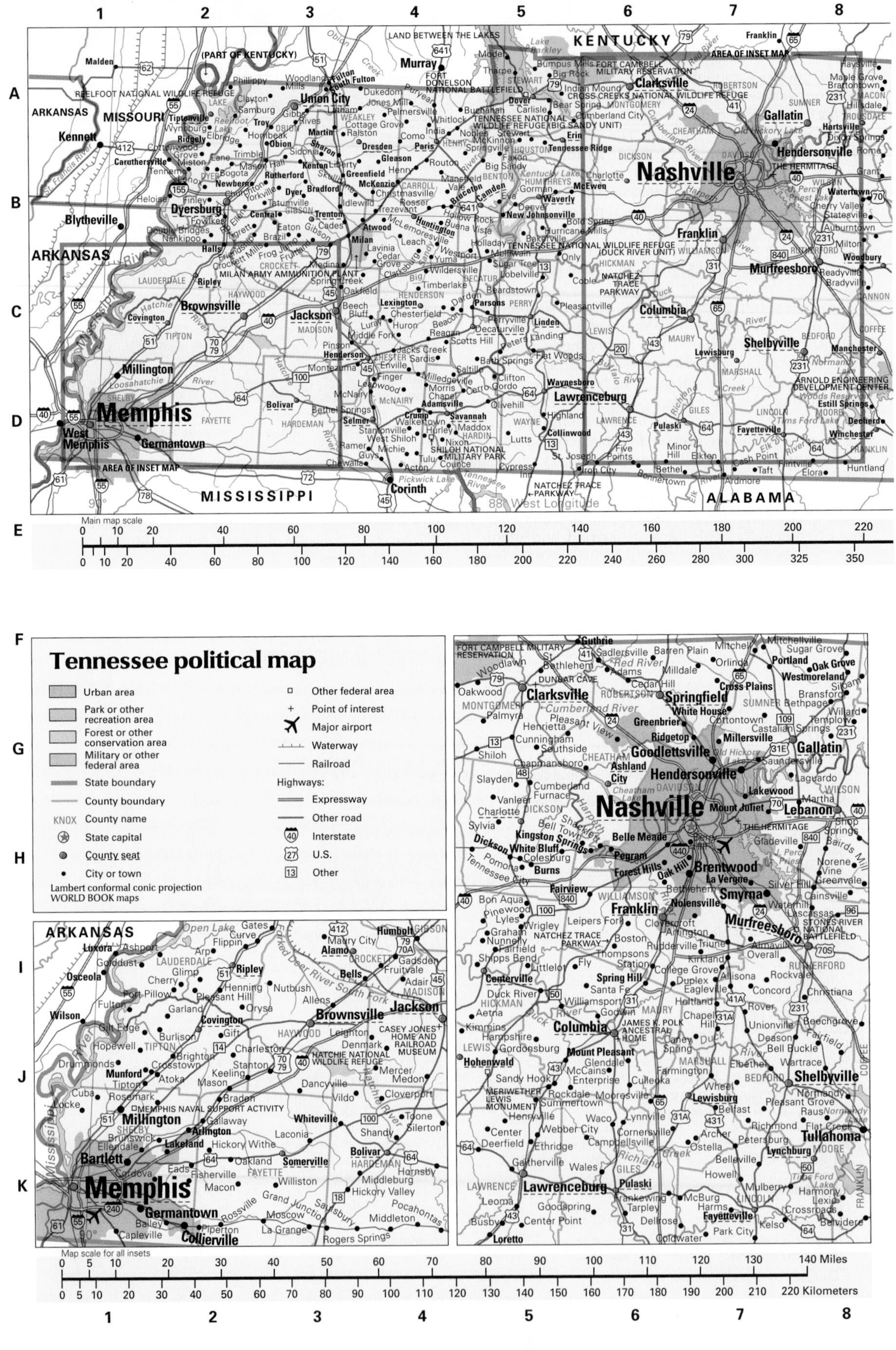

Tennessee political map

- Urban area
- Park or other recreation area
- Forest or other conservation area
- Military or other federal area
- State boundary
- County boundary
- KNOX County name
- State capital
- County seat
- City or town
- Other federal area
- Point of interest
- Major airport
- Waterway
- Railroad

Highways:

- Expressway
- Other road
- Interstate
- U.S.
- Other

Lambert conformal conic projection
WORLD BOOK maps

Main map scale

Map scale for all insets

Miles

Kilometers

AREA OF INSET MAP

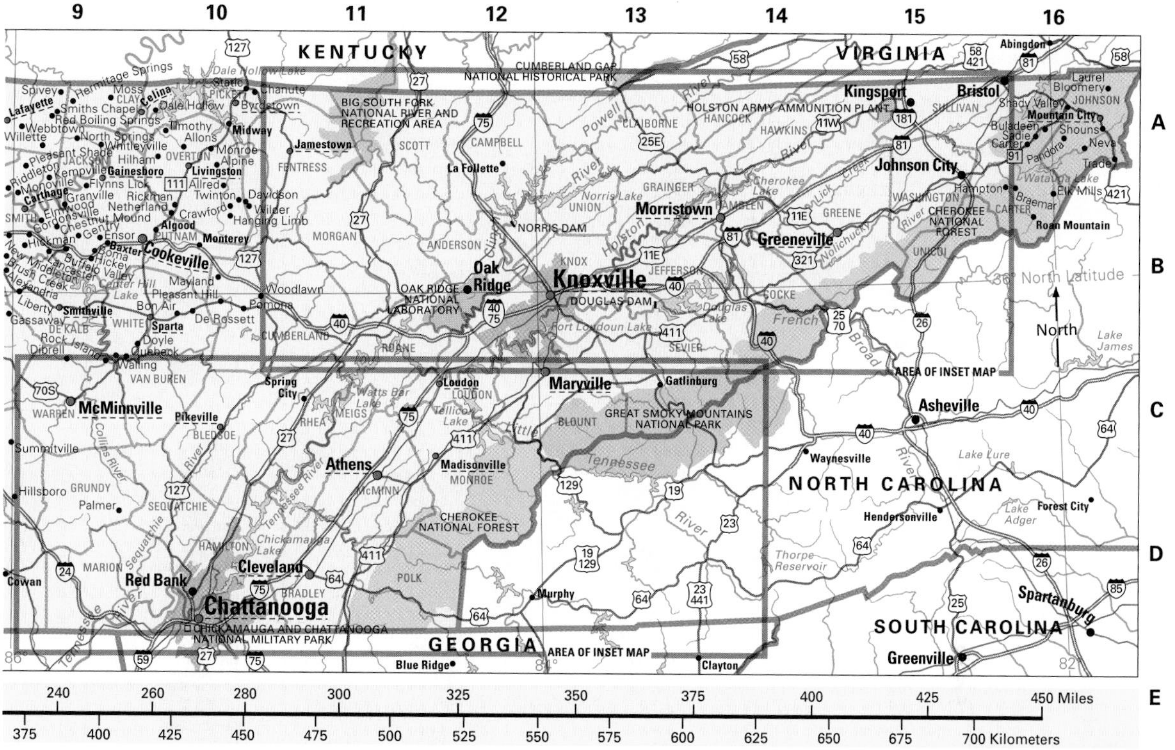

9 10 11 12 13 14 15 16

A B C D E

KENTUCKY
VIRGINIA
NORTH CAROLINA
SOUTH CAROLINA
GEORGIA

CUMBERLAND GAP NATIONAL HISTORICAL PARK
BIG SOUTH FORK NATIONAL RIVER AND RECREATION AREA
HOLSTON ARMY AMMUNITION PLANT
NORRIS DAM
OAK RIDGE NATIONAL LABORATORY
DOUGLAS DAM
GREAT SMOKY MOUNTAINS NATIONAL PARK
CHEROKEE NATIONAL FOREST
CHICKAMAUGA AND CHATTANOOGA NATIONAL MILITARY PARK
AREA OF INSET MAP

Lafayette
Celina
Livingston
Gainesboro
Carthage
Cookeville
Algood
Monterey
Smithville
Sparta
McMinnville
Pikeville
Jamestown
La Follette
Kingsport
Bristol
Johnson City
Morristown
Greeneville
Oak Ridge
Knoxville
Maryville
Gatlinburg
Spring City
Athens
Madisonville
Cleveland
Red Bank
Chattanooga
Murphy
Blue Ridge
Clayton
Asheville
Waynesville
Hendersonville
Forest City
Spartanburg
Greenville
Abingdon
Mountain City
Roan Mountain
Elk Mills
Hampton
Cowan

36° North Latitude
North

240 260 280 300 325 350 375 400 425 450 Miles
375 400 425 450 475 500 525 550 575 600 625 650 675 700 Kilometers

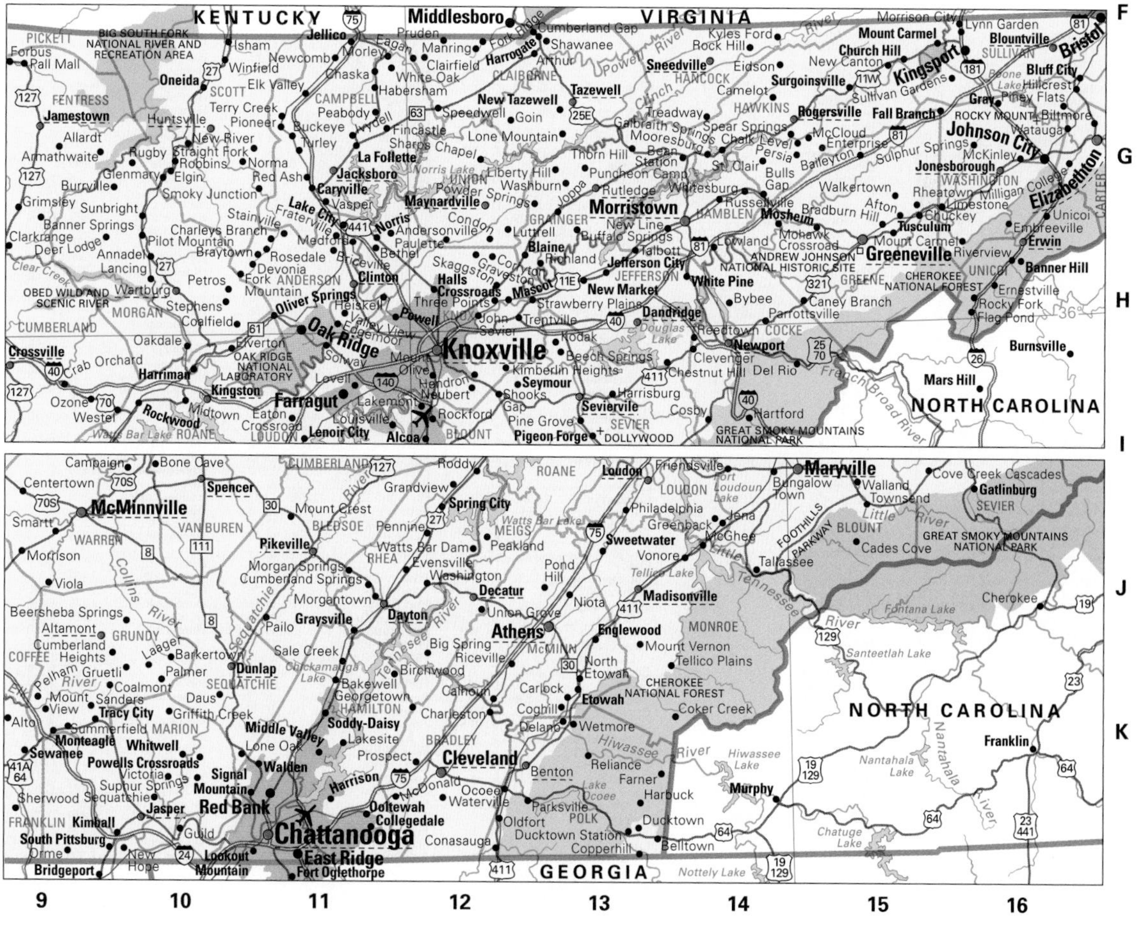

F G H I J K

KENTUCKY
VIRGINIA
NORTH CAROLINA
GEORGIA

Middlesboro
Jellico
Harrogate
Cumberland Gap
Sneedville
Tazewell
New Tazewell
Mount Carmel
Church Hill
Kingsport
Bristol
Bluff City
Rogersville
Surgoinsville
Blountville
Johnson City
Jonesborough
Elizabethton
Erwin
Unicoi
Greeneville
Tusculum
Mosheim
Morristown
White Pine
Dandridge
Newport
Jefferson City
Maynardville
Jacksboro
Caryville
La Follette
Lake City
Norris
Clinton
Oliver Springs
Oak Ridge
Knoxville
Farragut
Kingston
Harriman
Rockwood
Lenoir City
Alcoa
Seymour
Sevierville
Pigeon Forge
Oneida
Jamestown
Crossville
Burnsville
Mars Hill
Banner Hill

McMinnville
Spencer
Pikeville
Spring City
Dayton
Decatur
Athens
Madisonville
Sweetwater
Loudon
Maryville
Gatlinburg
Tellico Plains
Etowah
Englewood
Cleveland
Graysville
Dunlap
Soddy-Daisy
Middle Valley
Signal Mountain
Red Bank
Chattanooga
East Ridge
Fort Oglethorpe
Collegedale
Ooltewah
Jasper
Kimball
South Pittsburg
Bridgeport
Monteagle
Sewanee
Whitwell
Tracy City
Murphy
Franklin
Cherokee
Ducktown
Benton
Walden
Lookout Mountain

9 10 11 12 13 14 15 16

Tennessee map index

Metropolitan areas

Chattanooga 424,347
(310,396 in Tenn.;
113,951 in Ga.)
Clarksville-
Hopkinsville 207,033
(134,768 in Tenn.;
72,265 in Ky.)
Jackson 107,377
Johnson City-
Kingsport-
Bristol (Va.) 480,091
(388,218 in Tenn.;
91,873 in Va.)
Knoxville 687,249
Memphis 1,135,614
(977,549 in Tenn.;
50,866 in Ark.;
107,199 in Miss.)
Nashville 1,231,311

Counties

Anderson ....71,330 ..B 12
Bedford ....37,586 ..C 8
Benton ....16,537 ..B 5
Bledsoe ....12,367 ..C 10
Blount ....105,823 ..C 13
Bradley ....87,965 ..D 11
Campbell ....39,854 ..A 12
Cannon ....12,826 ..C 8
Carroll ....29,475 ..B 4
Carter ....56,742 ..B 16
Cheatham ....35,912 ..A 7
Chester ....15,540 ..C 4
Claiborne ....29,862 ..A 13
Clay ....7,976 ..A 9
Cocke ....33,565 ..B 14
Coffee ....48,014 ..C 8
Crockett ....14,532 ..C 3
Cumberland ....46,802 ..B 11
Davidson ......569,891 ..B 7
Decatur ....11,731 ..C 5
De Kalb ....17,423 ..C 9
Dickson ....43,156 ..B 6
Dyer ....37,279 ..B 2
Fayette ....28,806 ..D 2
Fentress ....16,625 ..A 11
Franklin ....39,270 ..D 8
Gibson ....48,152 ..B 3
Giles ....29,447 ..D 7
Grainger ....20,659 ..A 13
Greene ....62,909 ..B 14
Grundy ....14,332 ..D 9
Hamblen ....58,128 ..B 14
Hamilton ......307,896 ..D 10
Hancock ....6,786 ..A 14
Hardeman ......28,105 ..D 3
Hardin ....25,578 ..D 5
Hawkins ....53,563 ..A 14
Haywood ....19,797 ..C 2
Henderson .....25,522 ..C 4
Henry ....31,115 ..A 4
Hickman ....22,295 ..C 6
Houston ....8,088 ..B 5
Humphreys .....17,929 ..B 5
Jackson ....10,984 ..A 9
Jefferson ....44,294 ..B 13
Johnson ....17,499 ..A 16
Knox ....382,032 ..B 13
Lake ....7,954 ..A 2
Lauderdale .....27,101 ..C 2
Lawrence ....39,926 ..D 6
Lewis ....11,367 ..C 6
Lincoln ....31,340 ..D 7
Loudon ....39,086 ..C 12
Macon ....20,386 ..A 8
Madison ....91,837 ..C 3
Marion ....27,776 ..D 9
Marshall ....26,767 ..D 7
Maury ....69,498 ..C 7
McMinn ....49,015 ..D 11
McNairy ....24,653 ..D 4
Meigs ....11,086 ..C 11
Monroe ....38,961 ..D 12
Montgomery ..134,768 ..A 6
Moore ....5,740 ..D 8
Morgan ....19,757 ..B 11
Obion ....32,450 ..A 3
Overton ....20,118 ..A 10
Perry ....7,631 ..C 5
Pickett ....4,945 ..A 10
Polk ....16,050 ..D 11
Putnam ....62,315 ..B 10
Rhea ....28,400 ..C 11
Roane ....51,910 ..C 11
Robertson ......54,433 ..A 7
Rutherford ....182,023 ..B 8
Scott ....21,127 ..A 11
Sequatchie .....11,370 ..D 10
Sevier ....71,170 ..C 13
Shelby ....897,472 ..D 1
Smith ....17,712 ..B 9
Stewart ....12,370 ..A 5
Sullivan ....153,048 ..A 15
Sumner ....130,449 ..A 8
Tipton ....51,271 ..C 2
Trousdale ....7,259 ..A 8
Unicoi ....17,667 ..B 15
Union ....17,808 ..B 13
Van Buren ....5,508 ..C 10
Warren ....38,276 ..C 9
Washington ...107,198 ..A 15
Wayne ....16,842 ..D 5
Weakley ....34,895 ..A 3
White ....23,102 ..B 9
Williamson ....126,638 ..B 7
Wilson ....88,809 ..B 8

Cities and towns

Adams ....566 ..F 6
Adamsville ....1,983 ..D 4
Alamo° ....2,392 ..I 3
Alcoa ....7,734 ..I 12
Alexandria ....814 ..B 9
Algood ....2,942 ..B 10
Allardt ....642 ..G 9
Allons ....A 10
Allred ....A 10
Almaville ....I 7
Alpine ....A 10
Altamont° ....1,136 ..J 9
Alto ....K 9
Andersonville ....H 11
Antioch ....K 10
Archer ....K 7
Ardmore ....1,082 ..D 7
Arlington ....2,569 ..J 2
Armathwaite ....G 9
Arp ....I 2
Arrington ....I 7
Arthur ....F 13
Ashland City° ....3,641 ..G 6
Ashport ....I 2
Athens° ....13,220 ..D 11
Atoka ....3,235 ..J 2
Atwood ....1,000 ..B 4
Auburntown ....252 ..B 8
Baileyton ....504 ..G 15
Bakewell ....K 11
Banner Hill† .....1,053 ..H 16
Banner
Springs ....G 9
Barkertown ....K 10
Barren Plain ....F 6
Bartlett ....40,543 ..K 1
Bath Springs ....C 5
Baxter ....1,279 ..B 9
Beacon ....C 5
Bean Station ....G 14
Bear Spring ....A 5
Beardstown ....C 5
Beech Bluff ....C 4
Beech Springs ....H 13
Beechgrove ....J 8
Beersheba
Springs ....553 ..J 10
Belfast ....J 7
Bell Buckle ....391 ..J 8
Belle Meade .....2,943 ..H 6
Belleville ....K 7
Bells ....2,171 ..I 4
Belvidere ....K 8
Benton° ....1,138 ..K 13
Berry Hill ....674 ..H 7
Berry's Chapel* ....B 7
Bethel ....D 7
Bethel ....H 11
Bethel Springs .....763 ..D 4
Bethlehem ....H 6
Bethpage ....G 8
Big Rock ....A 5
Big Sandy ....518 ..B 5
Big Spring ....J 12
Biltmore ....G 16
Birchwood ....K 12
Blaine ....1,585 ..H 12
Blooming-
dale*†° ....10,350 ..A 15
Blountville†° ....2,959 ..F 16
Bluff City ....1,559 ..F 16
Bogota ....B 2
Bold Spring ....B 6
Bolivar° ....5,802 ..D 3
Boma ....B 9
Bon Air ....B 10
Bon Aqua ....H 5
Bone Cave ....I 10
Bonnertown ....D 6
Boones
Creek* ....A 15
Boston ....I 6
Bradburn Hill ....G 15
Braden ....271 ..J 2
Bradford ....1,113 ..B 3
Bradyville ....C 8
Braemar ....A 16
Bransford ....G 8
Brattontown ....A 8
Braytown ....H 11
Brazil ....B 3
Brentwood .....23,445 ..H 7
Briceville ....H 11
Bridwell
Heights* ....A 15
Brighton ....1,719 ..J 2
Bristol ....24,821 ..A 16
Brownington ....K 8
Brownsville° ....10,748 ..I 3
Bruceton ....1,554 ..B 4
Brunswick ....K 2
Brush Creek ....B 9
Buchanan ....A 5
Buckeye ....G 11
Buena Vista ....B 4
Buffalo Springs ....H 13
Buffalo Valley ....B 9
Buladeen ....A 16
Bulls Gap ....714 ..G 14
Bumpus Mills ....A 5
Bungalow
Town ....I 14
Burlison ....453 ..J 2
Burns ....1,366 ..H 5
Burrville ....G 9
Busby ....K 5
Bybee ....H 14
Byrdstown° ....903 ..A 10
Cades ....B 3
Cades Cove ....J 15
Cainsville ....H 8
Calhoun ....496 ..K 12
Camden° ....3,828 ..B 5
Campaign ....I 10
Campbells-
ville ....K 6
Caney Branch ....H 14
Caney Spring ....J 7
Capleville ....K 1
Carlisle ....A 5
Carlock ....K 13
Carter ....A 16
Carthage° ....2,251 ..B 9
Caryville ....2,243 ..G 11
Cash Point ....D 7
Castalian
Springs ....G 8
Cedar Bluff* ....B 13
Cedar Grove ....C 4
Cedar Hill ....298 ..F 6
Celina° ....1,379 ..A 10
Center ....K 5
Center Point ....K 5
Centertown ....257 ..I 9
Centerville° ......3,793 ..I 5
Central† ....2,717 ..B 3
Chalk Level ....G 14
Chanute ....A 10
Chapel Hill ....943 ..J 7
Chapmans-
boro ....G 6
Charleston ....J 2
Charleston ....630 ..K 12
Charleys
Branch ....H 11
Charlotte° ....1,153 ..H 5
Chaska ....F 11
Chatta-
nooga° ......155,554 ..D 10
Cherokee* ....A 15
Cherry ....I 2
Cherry Valley ....B 8
Chesterfield ....C 4
Chestnut Hill ....H 13
Chestnut
Mound ....B 9
Chewalla ....D 4
Christiana ....I 8
Christmasville ....B 4
Chuckey ....G 15
Church Hill ....5,916 ..F 15
Churchton ....B 3
Clairfield ....F 12
Clarkrange ....H 9
Clarksburg ....285 ..B 4
Clarksville° ....103,455 ..F 5
Clayton ....A 3
Cleveland° .....37,192 ..D 11
Clevenger ....H 14
Clifton ....2,699 ..D 5
Clinton° ....9,409 ..H 11
Clovercroft ....I 7
Cloverport ....J 4
Coalfield ....H 10
Coalmont ....948 ..K 10
Coble ....C 6
Coghill ....K 13
Coker Creek ....K 14
Coldwater ....K 7
Colesburg ....H 5
College Grove ....I 7
Collegedale ......6,514 ..K 11
Collierville ......31,872 ..K 2
Collinwood ......1,024 ..D 5
Colonial
Heights*† ......7,067 ..A 15
Columbia° ......33,055 ..J 6
Como ....A 4
Conasauga ....K 12
Concord ....I 7
Condon ....H 12
Cookeville° .....23,923 ..B 10
Copperhill ....511 ..K 13
Cordova ....K 2
Cornersville ....962 ..K 6
Corryton ....H 12
Cosby ....I 14
Cottage Grove ......97 ..A 4
Cottontown ....G 7
Cottonwood
Grove ....B 2
Counce ....D 4
Cove Creek
Cascades ....I 15
Covington° ......8,463 ..C 2
Cowan ....1,770 ..D 9
Crab Orchard ......838 ..I 9
Crawford ....B 10
Crockett Mills ....B 3
Cross Plains ......1,381 ..F 7
Crosstown ....J 2
Crossville° ....8,981 ..H 9
Crump ....1,521 ..D 4
Cuba ....J 1
Culleoka ....J 6
Cumberland
City ....316 ..A 6
Cumberland
Furnace ....G 5
Cumberland
Gap ....204 ..F 13
Cunningham ....G 5
Curve ....I 2
Cypress Inn ....D 5
Dancyville ....J 3
Dandridge° ......2,078 ..H 13
Darden ....C 4
Daus ....K 10
Davidson ....B 10
Dayton° ....6,180 ..J 11
Decatur° ....1,395 ..J 12
Decaturville° ......859 ..C 5
Decherd ....2,246 ..D 8
Deer Lodge ....H 9
Deerfield ....K 5
Del Rio ....H 14
Delano ....K 13
Dellrose ....K 7
Denmark ....J 4
Denver ....B 5
De Rossett ....B 10
Devonia ....H 11
Dibrell ....C 9
Dickson ....12,244 ..H 5
Dixon Springs ....A 8
Double
Bridges ....B 2
Dover° ....1,442 ..A 5
Dowelltown* ....302 ..B 9
Doyle ....525 ..C 9
Dresden° ....2,855 ..A 4
Drummonds ....J 1
Duck River ....I 5
Ducktown ....427 ..K 13
Ducktown
Station ....K 13
Dukedom ....A 4
Dunlap° ....4,173 ..K 10
Duplex ....I 7
Dyer ....2,406 ..B 3
Dyersburg° .....17,452 ..B 2
Eads ....K 2
Eagan ....F 12
Eagleton
Village*† ....4,883 ..C 12
Eagleville ....464 ..I 7
East
Brainerd*† ...14,132 ..D 10
East
Cleveland*† ...1,729 ..D 11
East Ridge ......20,640 ..K 11
Eastview* ....618 ..D 4
Eaton ....B 3
Eaton
Crossroad ....I 11
Edgemoor ....H 11
Eidson ....F 14
Elbethel ....J 7
Elbridge ....A 2
Elgin ....G 10
Elizabethton° ...13,372 ..G 16
Elk Mills ....A 16
Elk Valley ....G 11
Elkton ....510 ..D 7
Ellendale ....K 1
Elmwood ....B 9
Elora ....D 8
Elverton ....H 10
Englewood ....1,590 ..J 13
Ensor ....B 9
Enterprise ....J 6
Enterprise ....G 15
Enville ....230 ..C 4
Erin° ....1,490 ..A 5
Ernestville ....H 16
Erwin° ....5,610 ..H 16
Estill Springs .....2,152 ..D 8
Ethridge ....536 ..K 5
Etowah ....3,663 ..K 13
Eva ....B 5
Evensville ....J 12
Fairfield
Glade*† ....4,885 ..H 9
Fairmount*† .....2,600 ..K 11
Fairview ....5,800 ..H 6
Fall Branch† .....1,313 ..G 15
Farmington ....J 7
Farner ....K 13
Farragut ....17,720 ..I 11
Faxon ....B 5
Fayetteville° .....6,994 ..D 7
Fincastle ....G 11
Finger ....350 ..D 4
Finley ....B 2
Fisherville ....K 2
Five Points ....D 6
Flag Pond ....H 16
Flat Creek ....J 8
Flat Woods ....C 5
Flintville ....D 8
Flippin ....I 2
Flynns Lick ....A 9
Forbus ....F 9
Fordtown* ....A 15
Forest Hills ......4,710 ..H 6
Fork
Mountain ....H 10
Fork Ridge ....F 12
Fort Pillow ....I 2
Fowlkes ....B 2
Frankewing ....K 6
Franklin° ....41,842 ..B 7
Fraterville ....H 11
Friendship ....608 ..B 3
Friendsville ....890 ..I 14
Fruitland ....B 3
Fruitvale ....I 4
Fulton ....I 1
Gadsden ....553 ..I 4
Gainesboro° ....879 ..A 9
Gaitherville ....K 5
Gallatin° ....23,230 ..A 8
Gallaway ....666 ..J 2
Garland ....309 ..I 2
Gassaway ....B 9
Gates ....901 ..I 3
Gatlinburg ....3,382 ..C 13
Gentry ....B 9
Georgetown ....K 12
Germantown ...37,348 ..K 1
Gibbs ....A 3
Gibson ....305 ..B 3
Gift ....J 2
Gilt Edge ....489 ..J 1
Gladeville ....H 8
Gleason ....1,463 ..B 4
Glendale ....J 6
Glenmary ....G 10
Glimp ....I 2
Godwin ....I 6
Goin ....G 12
Golddust ....I 1
Goodlettsville ...13,780 ..G 7
Goodspring ....K 6
Gordonsburg ....I 5
Gordonsville .....1,066 ..B 9
Gorman ....B 5
Graham ....I 5
Grand Junction ....301 ..K 3
Grandview ....I 12
Grant ....B 8
Granville ....B 9
Graveston ....H 12
Gray† ....1,273 ..G 16
Graysville ....1,411 ..J 11
Greenback ....954 ..I 14
Greenbrier ......4,940 ..G 7
Greeneville° ....15,198 ..H 15
Greenfield ....2,208 ..B 3
Greenvale ....H 8
Griffith Creek ....K 10
Grimsley ....G 9
Guild ....K 10
Guys ....483 ..D 4
Habersham ....G 11
Halls ....2,311 ..B 2
Halls Cross-
roads ....H 12
Hampshire ....J 5
Hampton ....A 16
Hanging Limb ....B 10
Harbuck ....K 13
Harmony ....K 8
Harms ....K 7
Harriman ....6,744 ..I 10
Harrisburg ....I 13
Harrison† ....7,630 ..K 11
Harrogate
(-Shawnee)† ...2,865 ..F 12
Hartford ....I 14
Hartsville° ......2,395 ..A 8
Haysville ....A 8
Heiskell ....H 11
Heloise ....B 2
Henderson° .....5,670 ..C 4
Henderson-
ville ....40,620 ..G 7
Hendron ....I 12
Henning ....970 ..I 2
Henrietta ....G 6
Henry ....520 ..B 4
Henryville ....J 5
Hermitage
Springs ....A 9
Hickey ....B 9
Hickman ....B 9
Hickory Valley .....136 ..K 3
Hickory Withe ...2,574 ..K 2
Highland ....D 5
Hilham ....A 10
Hillcrest ....G 16
Hillsboro ....D 9
Hillsdale ....A 8
Hohenwald° .....3,754 ..J 5
Holladay ....B 5
Hollow Rock ....963 ..B 4
Holtland ....I 7
Hopewell ....J 1
Hornbeak ....435 ..A 3
Hornsby ....306 ..K 4
Howell ....K 7
Humboldt ....9,467 ..I 4
Hunter*† ....1,566 ..B 16
Huntingdon° .....4,349 ..B 4
Huntland ....916 ..D 8
Huntsville° ....981 ..G 10
Hurley ....D 4
Huron ....C 4
Idlewild ....B 3
India ....A 4
Indian Mound ....A 5
Indian
Springs* ....A 15
Iron City ....368 ..D 6
Isham ....F 10
Ivydell ....G 11
Jacks Creek ....C 4
Jacksboro° ....1,887 ..G 11
Jackson° ....59,643 ..I 4
Jamestown° ......1,839 ..A 11
Jasper° ....3,214 ..K 10
Jefferson
City ....7,760 ..H 13

Jellico 2,448 F 11
Jena J 14
John Sevier H 12
Johnson City 55,469 A 16
Jones Mill A 4
Jonesborough° 4,168 G 16
Joppa G 13
Karns* B 12
Keeling J 2
Kelso K 8
Kempville A 9
Kenton 1,306 B 3
Kimball 1,312 K 10
Kimberlin Heights I 12
Kimmins J 4
Kingsport 44,905 A 15
Kingston° 5,264 I 10
Kingston Springs 2,773 H 6
Kirkland I 7
Knoxville° 173,890 B 12
Kodak H 13
Kyles Ford F 14
Laconia K 3
Ladds K 10
Lafayette° 3,885 A 9
La Follette 7,926 A 12
La Grange 136 K 3
Lake City 1,888 G 11
Lakeland 6,862 K 2
Lakemont I 12
Lakesite 1,845 K 11
Lakewood 2,341 G 7
Lancaster B 9
Lancing H 10
Lane B 2
Lascassas I 8
Latham A 4
Laurel Bloomery A 16
La Vergne 18,687 H 7
Lavinia B 4
Lawrenceburg° 10,796 D 6
Leach B 4
Leapwood D 4
Lebanon° 20,235 H 8
Leighton J 4
Leipers Fork I 6
Lenoir City 6,819 I 11
Lenox B 2
Leoma K 5
Lewisburg° 10,413 C 7
Lexie Crossroads K 8
Lexington° 7,393 C 4
Liberty B 4
Liberty 367 B 9
Liberty Hill G 13
Limestone G 15
Linden° 1,015 C 5
Littlelot I 5
Livingston° 3,498 A 10
Lobelville 915 C 5
Locke J 1
Lone Mountain G 13
Lone Oak K 10
Lookout Mountain 2,000 K 11
Loretto 1,665 K 5
Loudon° 4,476 C 12
Louisville 2,001 I 11
Lovell I 11
Lowland H 14
Luray C 4
Luttrell 915 H 12
Lutts D 5
Lyles I 5
Lynchburg° 5,740 K 8
Lynn Garden F 16
Lynnville 345 J 6
Macon K 2
Maddox D 4
Madisonville° 3,939 C 12
Manchester° 8,294 C 8
Manring F 12
Mansfield B 4
Maple Grove A 8
Martha H 8
Martin 10,515 A 3
Maryville° 23,120 C 12
Mascot† 2,119 H 12
Mason 1,089 J 2
Mason Hall B 3
Maury City 704 I 3
Mayland B 10
Maynardville° 1,782 G 12
McBurg K 7
McCains J 6
McCloud G 14
McDonald K 12
McEwen 1,702 B 6
McGhee J 14
McIllwain B 5
McKenzie 5,295 B 4
McKinley G 16
McKinnon A 5
McLemoresville 259 B 4
McMinnville° 12,749 I 9
McNairy D 4
Medford H 11
Medina 969 C 3
Medon 191 J 4
Memphis° 650,100 D 1
Mercer J 4
Michie 647 D 4
Middle Fork C 4
Middle Valley† 11,854 K 11
Middleburg K 4
Middleton 602 K 4
Midtown 1,306 I 10
Midway† 2,491 A 10
Milan 7,664 B 3
Milldale F 7
Milledgeville 287 D 4
Millersville 5,308 G 7
Milligan College G 16
Millington 10,433 J 1
Milton B 8
Minor Hill 437 D 6
Miston B 2
Mitchell F 7
Mitchellville 207 F 7
Model A 5
Mohawk Crossroad G 14
Monoville B 9
Monroe A 10
Monteagle 1,238 K 9
Monterey 2,717 B 10
Montezuma C 4
Mooresburg G 14
Mooresville J 6
Morgan Springs J 11
Morgantown J 11
Morley F 11
Morris Chapel D 4
Morrison 684 J 9
Morrison City F 15
Morristown 24,965 B 14
Moscow 422 K 3
Mosheim 1,749 G 14
Moss A 9
Mount Carmel 4,795 F 15
Mount Carmel H 16
Mount Crest J 11
Mount Juliet 12,366 H 7
Mount Olive I 12
Mount Pleasant 4,491 J 6
Mount Vernon J 13
Mount View K 9
Mountain City° 2,383 A 16
Mulberry K 8
Munford 4,708 J 1
Murfreesboro° 68,816 B 8
Nankipoo B 2
Nashville° 569,891 H 7
Netherland B 10
Neubert I 12
Neva A 16
New Canton F 15
New Hope 1,043 K 10
New Johnsonville 1,905 B 5
New Line G 13
New Market 1,234 H 13
New Middleton B 9
New River G 10
New Tazewell 2,871 G 13
Newbern 2,988 B 3
Newcomb F 11
Newport° 7,242 H 14
Niota 781 J 13
Nixon D 4
Nobles A 5
Nolensville† 2,099 H 7
Norene H 8
Norma G 10
Normandy 141 J 8
Norris 1,446 H 11
North Etowah K 13
North Springs A 9
Nunnelly I 5
Nutbush I 3
Oak Grove† 4,072 F 8
Oak Hill 4,493 H 7
Oak Ridge 27,387 B 12
Oakdale 244 H 10
Oakfield C 3
Oakland 1,279 K 2
Oakwood F 5
Obion 1,134 A 3
Ocoee K 12
Oldfort K 12
Olivehill D 5
Oliver Springs 3,303 H 11
Oneida 3,615 G 10
Only B 5
Ooltewah† 5,681 K 11
Orebank* A 15
Orlinda 594 F 7
Orme 124 K 9
Orysa I 2
Ostella K 7
Overall I 8
Ozone I 9
Pailo J 11
Pall Mall F 9
Palmer 726 K 10
Palmersville A 4
Palmyra G 5
Pandora A 16
Paris° 9,763 A 4
Park City K 7
Parksville K 13
Parrottsville 207 H 14
Parsons 2,452 C 5
Paulette H 12
Peabody G 11
Peakland J 12
Pegram 2,146 H 6
Pelham K 9
Pennine J 12
Perryville C 5
Persia G 14
Peters Landing C 5
Petersburg 580 K 7
Petros H 10
Philadelphia 533 I 13
Philippy A 2
Pigeon Forge 5,083 I 13
Pikeville° 1,781 C 10
Pilot Mountain H 10
Pine Crest*† 2,872 B 16
Pine Grove I 13
Pinewood I 5
Piney Flats G 16
Pinson C 3
Pioneer G 11
Piperton 589 K 2
Pittman Center* 477 C 13
Pleasant Grove J 7
Pleasant Hill 544 I 2
Pleasant Hill B 10
Pleasant Shade A 9
Pleasant View G 6
Pleasantville C 5
Pocahontas K 4
Pomona H 5
Pomona B 10
Portland 8,458 F 7
Powder Springs G 12
Powell H 12
Powells Crossroads 1,286 K 10
Prospect K 12
Pruden F 12
Pulaski° 7,871 D 7
Puncheon Camp G 13
Puryear 667 A 4
Quebeck C 9
Ralston A 3
Ramer 354 D 4
Raus J 8
Readyville C 8
Reagan C 4
Red Ash G 11
Red Bank 12,418 D 10
Red Boiling Springs 1,023 A 9
Reedtown H 14
Reliance K 13
Rheatown G 15
Riceville K 12
Richland H 13
Richmond J 7
Rickman B 10
Riddleton A 9
Ridgely 1,667 A 2
Ridgeside* 389 D 10
Ridgetop 1,083 G 7
Ripley° 7,844 C 2
Riverview H 16
Rives 331 A 3
Roan Mountain† 1,160 B 16
Robbins G 10
Rock Hill F 14
Rock Island C 9
Rockdale J 5
Rockford 798 I 12
Rockvale I 7
Rockwood 5,774 I 10
Rocky Fork H 16
Roddy I 12
Ro Ellen B 2
Rogers Springs K 4
Rogersville° 4,240 G 14
Rome B 8
Rosedale H 11
Rosemark J 1
Rosser B 4
Rossville 380 K 2
Routon B 4
Rover I 7
Rudderville I 7
Rugby G 10
Russellville G 14
Rutherford 1,272 B 3
Rutledge° 1,187 G 13
Sadie A 16
Sadlersville F 6
St. Bethlehem F 5
St. Clair G 14
St. Joseph 829 D 6
Sale Creek K 11
Saltillo 342 D 4
Samburg 260 A 2
Sanders K 9
Sandy Hook J 5
Santa Fe I 6
Sardis 445 C 4
Saulsbury 99 K 3
Saundersville G 7
Savannah° 6,917 D 4
Scotts Hill 894 C 4
Selmer° 4,541 D 4
Sequatchie K 10
Sevierville° 11,757 I 13
Sewanee† 2,361 K 9
Seymour† 8,850 I 12
Shacklett H 6
Shady Valley A 16
Sharon 988 B 3
Sharps Chapel G 12
Shawanee, see Harrogate [-Shawnee]
Shelbyville° 16,105 C 8
Sherwood K 9
Shiloh G 5
Shipps Bend I 5
Shooks Gap I 12
Shop Springs H 8
Shouns A 16
Sidonia B 3
Signal Mountain 7,429 K 10
Silerton 60 J 4
Siloam F 8
Silver Hill H 8
Skaggston H 12
Skullbone B 3
Slayden 185 G 5
Smartt J 9
Smiths Chapel A 9
Smithville° 3,994 B 9
Smoky Junction G 11
Smyrna 25,569 H 7
Sneedville° 1,257 F 14
Soddy-Daisy 11,530 K 11
Solway H 11
Somerville° 2,519 K 3
South Carthage* 1,302 B 9
South Cleveland*† 6,216 D 11
South Fulton 2,517 A 3
South Pittsburg 3,295 K 9
Southside G 5
Sparta° 4,599 B 10
Spear Springs G 14
Speedwell G 12
Spencer° 1,713 I 10
Spivey A 9
Spring City 2,025 C 11
Spring Creek C 4
Spring Hill 7,715 I 6
Springfield° 14,329 G 6
Springville B 5
Spurgeon*† 3,460 A 15
Stainville H 11
Stanton 615 J 3
Stantonville 312 D 4
Statesville B 8
Stephens H 10
Stewart A 5
Strawberry Plains H 13
Sugar Grove F 8
Sugar Tree C 5
Sullivan Gardens G 15
Sulphur Springs K 10
Sulphur Springs G 16
Summerfield K 9
Summertown J 5
Summit* D 10
Summitville C 9
Sunbright 577 G 10
Surgoinsville 1,484 G 15
Sweetwater 5,586 J 13
Sylvia H 5
Taft D 7
Talbott H 13
Tallassee J 14
Tarpley K 6
Tatumville B 3
Tazewell° 2,165 G 13
Tellico Plains 859 K 14
Templow G 8
Tennemo B 2
Tennessee City H 5
Tennessee Ridge 1,334 A 5
Terry Creek G 11
Tharpe A 5
Thompsons Station 1,283 I 6
Thorn Hill G 13
Three Points H 12
Tigrett B 3
Timberlake C 4
Timothy A 10
Tipton J 1
Tiptonville° 2,439 A 2
Toone 330 J 4
Townsend 244 I 15
Tracy City 1,679 K 9
Trade A 16
Treadway G 14
Trenton° 4,683 B 3
Trentville H 12
Trezevant 901 B 4
Trimble 728 B 3
Triune I 7
Troy 1,273 A 3
Tullahoma 17,994 K 8
Tulu D 4
Turley G 11
Tusculum 2,004 H 15
Twinton B 10
Unicoi 3,519 G 16
Union City° 10,876 A 3
Union Grove J 12
Unionville J 7
Vale B 4
Valley Forge* B 16
Valley View H 11
Vanleer 310 G 5
Vasper G 11
Victoria K 10
Vildo J 3
Vine H 8
Viola 129 J 9
Vonore 1,162 J 14
Waco J 6
Walden 1,960 K 11
Wales K 6
Walkertown D 4
Walkertown G 15
Walland I 15
Walling C 9
Walnut Hill*† 2,756 A 15
Wartburg° 890 H 10
Wartrace 548 J 8
Washburn G 13
Washington J 12
Watauga 403 G 16
Waterhill H 8
Watertown 1,358 B 8
Waterville K 12
Watts Bar Dam J 12
Waverly° 4,028 B 5
Waynesboro° 2,228 D 5
Webber City K 5
Webbtown A 9
West Shiloh D 4
Westel I 10
Westmoreland 2,093 F 8
Westport B 4
Wetmore K 13
Wheel J 7
White Bluff 2,142 H 5
White House 7,220 G 7
White Oak F 11
White Pine 1,997 H 14
Whitesburg G 14
Whiteville 3,148 J 3
Whitleyville A 9
Whitlock A 4
Whitwell 1,660 K 10
Wilder B 10
Wildersville C 4
Wildwood Lake*† 3,050 D 11
Willard G 8
Willette A 9
Williamsport I 6
Williston 341 K 3
Winchester° 7,329 D 8
Winfield 911 F 10
Woodbury° 2,428 C 8
Woodland Mills 296 A 3
Woodlawn F 5
Woodlawn B 10
Wrigley I 5
Wynnburg A 2
Yorkville 293 B 3
Yuma B 4

°County seat.
*Does not appear on map; key shows general location.
†Census designated place—unincorporated, but recognized as a significant settled community by the U.S. Census Bureau.

Places without population figures are unincorporated areas.
Source: 2000 census.

Visitor's guide

Tennessee's rugged mountains, thick forests, and beautiful lakes and rivers are ideal for outdoor sports, camping, and sightseeing. The majestic beauty of Great Smoky Mountains National Park attracts millions of visitors a year. Students of American history delight in the state's many sites of historic interest. Music lovers travel to Tennessee in order to hear outstanding performances by bluegrass, blues, and country artists. The Memphis in May International Festival is one of the largest annual events in the United States. This month-long celebration honors a different nation each year and includes five major weekend festivals. The unique cultural heritage of Memphis is also featured during this popular celebration.

The Grand Ole Opry

"The Grand Ole Opry" at the Grand Ole Opry House in Nashville

Places to visit

American Museum of Science and Energy, at Oak Ridge, features exhibits on energy and energy production.

Casey Jones Home and Railroad Museum, in Jackson, is the restored home of the famous railroad hero. The home is maintained as a railroad museum.

Country Music Hall of Fame and Museum, in Nashville, presents exhibits on the history of country music. Its collection includes many video clips and recordings.

Dollywood, in Pigeon Forge, is named for the entertainer Dolly Parton. Live music shows and other attractions bring to life the fun and folklore of the Smoky Mountains.

Graceland, in Memphis, is the former home of famous rock music star Elvis Presley. The estate features Presley's mansion and grave site and exhibits of his film and stage costumes and other mementos of his life.

Grand Ole Opry House in Nashville features performances of "The Grand Ole Opry," a live country music radio show.

James K. Polk Ancestral Home, in Columbia, is the only Tennessee home still standing of the former U.S. president. Built in 1816, it contains furniture used by the Polks.

Lookout Mountain rises 2,146 feet (654 meters) above sea level at the Moccasin Bend of the Tennessee River near Chattanooga. There, in November 1863, during the American Civil War, Union forces won an important victory in the "Battle Above the Clouds."

Rocky Mount, a log house near Johnson City, was the first capitol of The Territory of the United States South of the River Ohio.

Tennessee Aquarium, in Chattanooga, is the world's largest freshwater aquarium, with over 9,000 fish and other animals.

The Hermitage, near Nashville, was the home of President Andrew Jackson. Jackson and his wife are buried on the grounds.

National parklands. Almost half of Great Smoky Mountains National Park lies in Tennessee, and the rest is in North Carolina. Cherokee National Forest lies along the eastern border of Tennessee. Andrew Johnson National Historic Site is in Greeneville. Tennessee has two national military parks. They are Chickamauga and Chattanooga, which Tennessee shares with Georgia; and Shiloh, near Savannah. Stones River National Battlefield is in Murfreesboro. Fort Donelson National Battlefield lies near Dover. Cumberland Gap National Historical Park lies in the area where Kentucky, Virginia, and Tennessee meet. Big South Fork National River and Recreation Area lies in Tennessee and Kentucky.

State parklands. For information on state parks, write to Director of State Parks, Department of Conservation, 7th Floor, L and C Tower, 401 Church Street, Nashville, TN 37243.

Tennessee Tourist Development

View from Lookout Mountain near Chattanooga

Memphis Chamber of Commerce

Hall of Gold Records at Graceland

David R. Frazier

Great Smoky Mountains National Park

Annual events

January-March

Eagle watch tours at Reelfoot Lake near Tiptonville (January-March); National Field Trial Championships for bird dogs in Grand Junction (February).

April-June

Dogwood Arts Festival in Knoxville (April); Mule Day in Columbia (April); Spring Wildflower Pilgrimage in Gatlinburg (April); World's Largest Fish Fry in Paris (April); East Tennessee Strawberry Festival in Dayton (May); Iroquois Steeplechase in Nashville (May); Festival of British and Appalachian Culture in Rugby (May); West Tennessee Strawberry Festival in Humboldt (May); International Country Music Fan Fair in Nashville (June); Riverbend Festival in Chattanooga (June); Rhododendron Festival in Roan Mountain (June).

July-September

Old Time Fiddlers' Jamboree and Crafts Festival in Smithville (July); Historic Rugby Pilgrimage of Homes in Rugby (August); International Grand Championship Walking Horse Show in Murfreesboro (August); Elvis International Tribute Week in Memphis (August); Tennessee Walking Horse National Celebration in Shelbyville (August); Tennessee Valley Agriculture and Industrial Fair in Knoxville (September); Tennessee State Fair in Nashville (September); Mid-South Fair in Memphis (September).

October-December

National Storytelling Festival in Jonesborough (October); Autumn Gold Festival in Coker Creek (October); Oktoberfest in Memphis (October); Fall Color Cruise and Folk Festival in Chattanooga (October); Museum of Appalachia Tennessee Fall Homecoming in Norris (October).

Main Event, Inc.

Iroquois Steeplechase in Nashville

Land and climate

Land regions. Tennessee has six main land regions. These are, from east to west: (1) the Blue Ridge, (2) the Appalachian Ridge and Valley Region, (3) the Appalachian Plateau, (4) the Highland Rim, (5) the Nashville Basin, and (6) the Gulf Coastal Plain.

The Blue Ridge region skirts the entire eastern edge of Tennessee. The region's elevation averages 5,000 feet (1,500 meters), the highest in the state. Clingmans Dome, the state's tallest peak, rises to 6,643 feet (2,025 meters). Several mountain ranges make up the region. They include the Chilhowee, Great Smoky, and Snowbird mountains. Valleys and sheltered hollows called *coves* lie within the mountains. The region has a great deal of timber and some minerals.

The Appalachian Ridge and Valley Region stretches westward from the mountainous Blue Ridge for about 55 miles (89 kilometers). This region has fertile farm country in valleys that lie between parallel wooded ridges. The broad valleys and low narrow ridges in the eastern part of the region make up an area called the *Great Valley.*

The Appalachian Plateau, or *Cumberland Plateau,* lies west of the Ridge and Valley Region. There, the land rises in rocky cliffs that range from 1,500 to 1,800 feet (457 to 549 meters) high. The plateau region consists of flat-topped mountains and V-shaped valleys. Tennessee's coal comes from this region. The area also has deposits of petroleum and natural gas. From Lookout Mountain, in the southern part of the region, visitors can see seven states.

Tennessee Tourist Development

Cane Creek Falls, near Pikeville, is in the Appalachian Plateau region of Tennessee. Rocky cliffs in this area rise from 1,500 to 1,800 feet (457 to 549 meters) high.

The Highland Rim is an elevated plain that surrounds the Nashville Basin. Steep slopes reach from the rim to the basin below. Underground streams and caves lie beneath the surface of the region. The area of the Highland Rim north of the Nashville Basin is sometimes called the Pennyroyal Region.

The Nashville Basin lies within the Highland Rim. Most of the basin drains toward the northwest. The basin has rich farming areas where cattle graze in fertile pastures, and farms produce bumper crops. In addition, the region has phosphate deposits.

The Gulf Coastal Plain is part of an important land region that begins at the Gulf of Mexico and extends northward as far as southern Illinois. In Tennessee, the Plain has three parts. A hilly strip of land about 10 miles (16 kilometers) wide runs along the west bank of the Tennessee River. The second part is a wide area of low rolling hills and wide stream valleys called *bottoms.* At Memphis, this area ends in steep bluffs that overlook the Mississippi River. The Mississippi Alluvial Plain, the third part of the region, lies along the western edge of the state north of Memphis. This flat strip along the Mississippi River averages less than 300 feet (91 meters) above sea level. It is the lowest part of the state and is sometimes called *The Delta.* Farmers raise soybeans and other crops on the Alluvial Plain.

Land regions of Tennessee

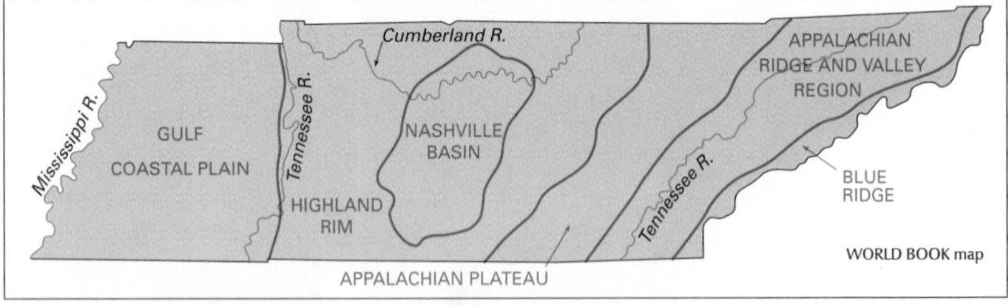

Map index

- Appalachian Mountains ... C 7
- Bald Mountains ... C 9
- Bays Mountains ... C 8
- Big Bald (mountain) ... C 9
- Big Frog Mountain ... E 7
- Black Oak Ridge ... D 7
- Boone Lake ... C 9
- Buffalo River ... D 3
- Center Hill Lake ... C 6
- Cheatham Lake ... C 4
- Cherokee Lake ... C 8
- Chickamauga Lake ... D 6
- Clinch River ... C 8
- Clingmans Dome (mountain) (highest point in Tennessee) ... D 8
- Crab Orchard Mountains ... D 6
- Cross Mountain ... C 7
- Cumberland Gap Natl. Hist. Park ... B 8
- Cumberland Mountains ... C 7
- Cumberland Plateau ... D 6
- Cumberland River ... C 3
- Dale Hollow Lake ... C 6
- Douglas Lake ... C 8
- Duck River ... D 4
- Eastern Highland Rim ... D 5
- Elk River ... E 4
- Forked Deer River ... D 1
- Fort Loudoun Lake ... D 7
- Fort Patrick Henry Lake ... C 9
- French Broad River ... C 8
- Great Smoky Mountains Natl. Park ... D 8
- Great Valley ... D 7
- Harpeth River ... D 4
- Hatchie River ... D 2
- Haw Knob ... D 7
- Hiwassee River ... D 7
- Holston River ... C 8
- Iron Mountains ... B 9
- J. Percy Priest Lake ... C 5
- Kentucky Lake ... C 3
- Lake Barkley ... B 3
- Little Tennessee River ... D 7
- Lookout Mountain ... E 6
- Melton Hill Lake ... C 7
- Mississippi River ... C 1
- Nashville Basin ... D 4
- Norris Dam ... C 7
- Norris Lake ... C 7
- Obion River ... C 1
- Old Hickory Lake ... C 5
- Pennyroyal Plateau ... C 4
- Pickwick Lake ... E 3
- Pine Mountain ... C 7
- Reelfoot Lake ... C 1
- Sequatchie River ... D 6
- South Holston Lake ... C 9
- Stones River ... C 5
- Tellico Lake ... D 7
- Tennessee River ... D 3, D 6
- Walden Ridge ... D 6
- Watauga Lake ... C 9
- Watts Bar Lake ... D 7
- Western Highland Rim ... C 4
- Woods Reservoir ... D 5

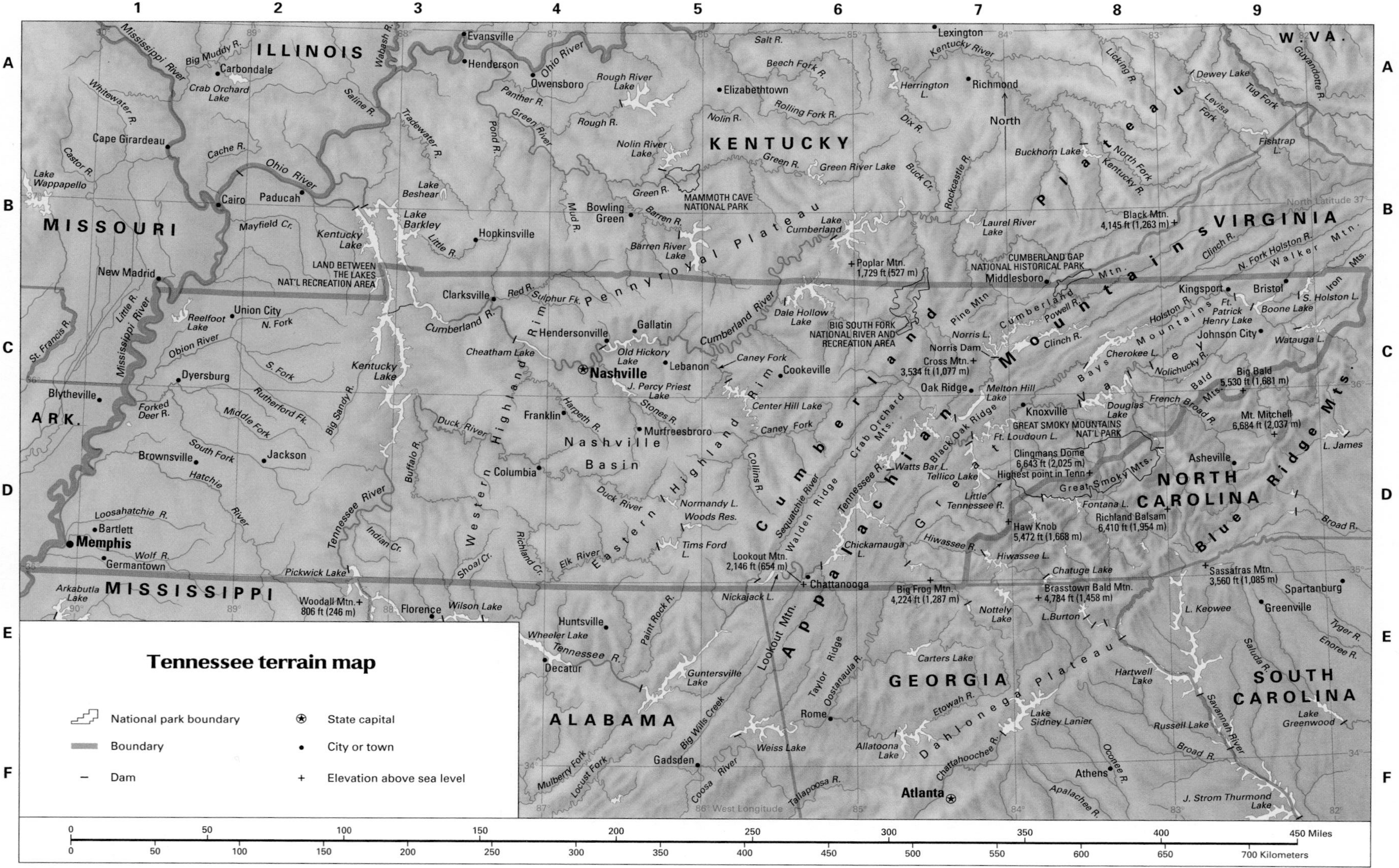

Tennessee terrain map
National park boundary
Boundary
Dam
State capital
City or town
Elevation above sea level
0 50 100 150 200 250 300 350 400 450 Miles
0 50 100 150 200 250 300 350 400 450 500 550 600 650 700 Kilometers
North
ILLINOIS
MISSOURI
KENTUCKY
VIRGINIA
W. VA.
ARK.
MISSISSIPPI
ALABAMA
GEORGIA
NORTH CAROLINA
SOUTH CAROLINA
Pennyroyal Plateau
Cumberland Plateau
Appalachian Mountains
Great Appalachian Valley
Highland Rim
Eastern Highland Rim
Western Highland Rim
Nashville Basin
Blue Ridge Mts.
Great Smoky Mts.
Dahlonega Plateau
Nashville
Memphis
Atlanta
Knoxville
Chattanooga
Clarksville
Jackson
Murfreesboro
Johnson City
Kingsport
Bristol
Oak Ridge
Franklin
Columbia
Cookeville
Lebanon
Gallatin
Hendersonville
Dyersburg
Union City
Brownsville
Bartlett
Germantown
Middlesboro
Bowling Green
Hopkinsville
Paducah
Cairo
Evansville
Henderson
Owensboro
Elizabethtown
Lexington
Richmond
Carbondale
Cape Girardeau
New Madrid
Blytheville
Florence
Huntsville
Decatur
Gadsden
Rome
Athens
Asheville
Greenville
Spartanburg
Mississippi River
Ohio River
Tennessee River
Cumberland River
Duck River
Kentucky Lake
Lake Barkley
Reelfoot Lake
Pickwick Lake
Norris Dam
Norris L.
Clingmans Dome 6,643 ft (2,025 m)
Highest point in Tenn.
Woodall Mtn. 806 ft (246 m)
Lookout Mtn. 2,146 ft (654 m)
Big Frog Mtn. 4,224 ft (1,287 m)
Cross Mtn. 3,534 ft (1,077 m)
Poplar Mtn. 1,729 ft (527 m)
Black Mtn. 4,145 ft (1,263 m)
Big Bald 5,530 ft (1,681 m)
Mt. Mitchell 6,684 ft (2,037 m)
Haw Knob 5,472 ft (1,668 m)
Richland Balsam 6,410 ft (1,954 m)
Brasstown Bald Mtn. 4,784 ft (1,458 m)
Sassafras Mtn. 3,560 ft (1,085 m)
GREAT SMOKY MOUNTAINS NAT'L PARK
MAMMOTH CAVE NATIONAL PARK
CUMBERLAND GAP NATIONAL HISTORICAL PARK
BIG SOUTH FORK NATIONAL RIVER AND RECREATION AREA
LAND BETWEEN THE LAKES NAT'L RECREATION AREA
North Latitude 37°
West Longitude
WORLD BOOK map

Rivers and lakes. Three large river systems—the Mississippi, Cumberland, and Tennessee—drain the state. The Mississippi drains most of West Tennessee. Its largest tributaries in Tennessee include the Forked Deer, Hatchie, Loosahatchie, Obion, and Wolf rivers. The Cumberland and Tennessee drain most of the rest of the state. They rise in the Appalachian Plateau and join the Ohio River. Branches of the Tennessee include the Big Sandy, Buffalo, Clinch, Duck, Elk, French Broad, Hiwassee, Holston, Little Tennessee, Powell, and Sequatchie rivers. Tributaries of the Cumberland in Tennessee include the Caney Fork, Harpeth, and Stones rivers.

Since 1933, the Tennessee Valley Authority (TVA) and the U.S. Army Corps of Engineers have built many dams along the Cumberland and Tennessee rivers and their tributaries. Artificial lakes formed by these dams have more than doubled the inland water area of Tennessee. The largest of these artificial lakes is Kentucky Lake. Others include Boone, Cherokee, Chickamauga, Douglas, Fort Loudoun, Fort Patrick Henry, Norris, Pickwick, Tellico, Watauga, and Watts Bar reservoirs. These lakes are often called the *Great Lakes of the South.*

Plant and animal life. Forests cover more than half the state. Tennessee's most important trees include the hickory, red and white oaks, shortleaf pine, and yellow-poplar. Other common trees include ash, cherry, elm, maple, sycamore, and walnut. Azaleas, mountain laurel, rhododendron, and other shrubs cover the mountain slopes. The iris and passion-flower grow throughout the state. Common wildflowers include the dragonroot, hop clover, spring-beauty, and yellow jasmine.

Tennessee's mountains, forests, and waters abound with wild game. Hunters seek deer, ducks, wild turkeys, and other game. Black bears and wild hogs roam remote parts of the mountains. Beavers, muskrats, rabbits, raccoons, skunks, and squirrels live in the fields and forests. Common songbirds include the mockingbird, robin, and wood thrush. Bass, crappie, trout, and walleyed pike are found in the lakes and streams.

Climate. Most of Tennessee has a humid, subtropical climate. Temperatures rarely go above 100 °F (38 °C) or below 10 °F (−12 °C). The lowlands and plains in West Tennessee generally are warmer than the mountainous eastern regions. Average temperatures in the west range from 40 °F (4 °C) in January to 79 °F (26 °C) in July. The east averages 37 °F (3 °C) in January and 71 °F (22 °C) in July.

Tennessee's lowest recorded temperature, −32 °F (−36 °C), occurred on Dec. 30, 1917, at Mountain City in the northeast. Its highest recorded temperature, 113 °F (45 °C), occurred on July 29 and Aug. 9, 1930, at Perryville in the west.

Eastern Tennessee averages about 10 inches (25 centimeters) of snow a year, while the west averages 4 to 6 inches (10 to 15 centimeters). Most of the state averages about 52 inches (132 centimeters) of *precipitation* (rain, melted snow, and other forms of moisture) a year.

Average monthly weather

Knoxville

	Temperatures °F High	°F Low	°C High	°C Low	Days of rain or snow
Jan.	50	31	10	−1	13
Feb.	53	32	12	0	12
Mar.	61	38	16	3	13
Apr.	71	47	22	8	11
May	79	56	26	13	12
June	87	65	31	18	12
July	89	68	32	20	12
Aug.	88	66	31	19	11
Sept.	84	61	29	16	8
Oct.	73	48	23	9	7
Nov.	59	38	15	3	9
Dec.	50	32	10	0	12

Nashville

	Temperatures °F High	°F Low	°C High	°C Low	Days of rain or snow
Jan.	49	31	9	−1	12
Feb.	52	33	11	1	11
Mar.	60	40	16	4	12
Apr.	71	49	22	9	11
May	79	57	14	14	10
June	88	66	31	19	10
July	91	69	33	21	10
Aug.	89	68	32	20	9
Sept.	85	62	29	17	8
Oct.	74	50	23	10	7
Nov.	59	39	15	4	9
Dec.	50	33	10	1	11

Average yearly precipitation
Tennessee has a humid climate with the greatest amount of precipitation falling in the central and southeastern sections.

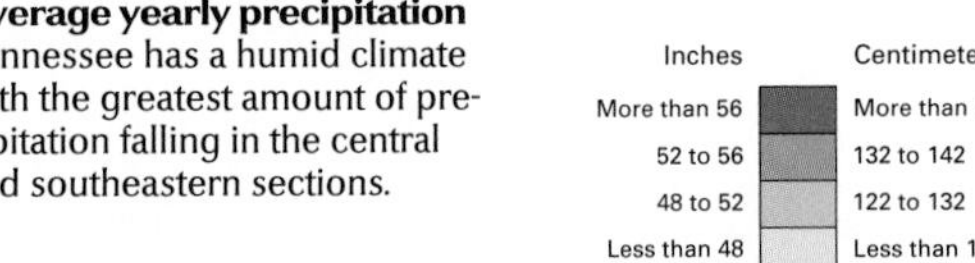

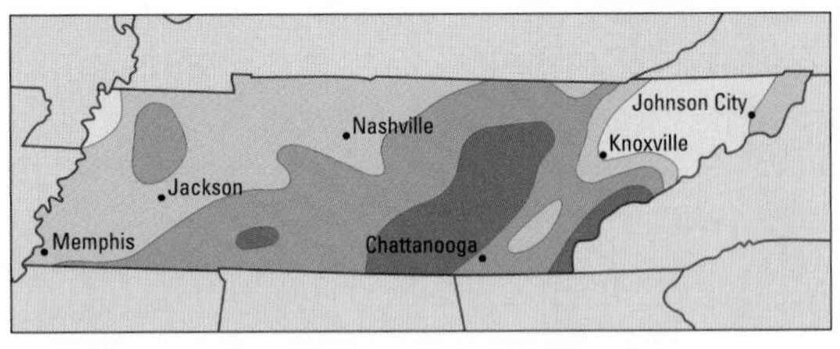

Average January temperatures
Tennessee has moderate winters. Temperatures throughout the state generally average well above freezing.

Degrees Fahrenheit	Degrees Celsius
Above 40	Above 4
38 to 40	3 to 4
36 to 38	2 to 3
Below 36	Below 2

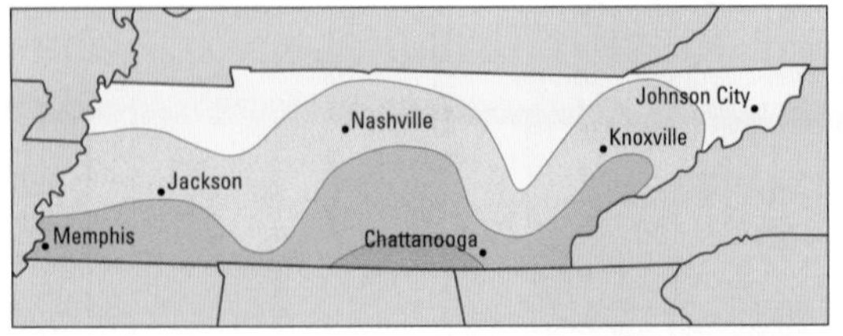

Average July temperatures
The lowlands and plains of the west usually remain warmer in the summertime than the mountainous eastern regions.

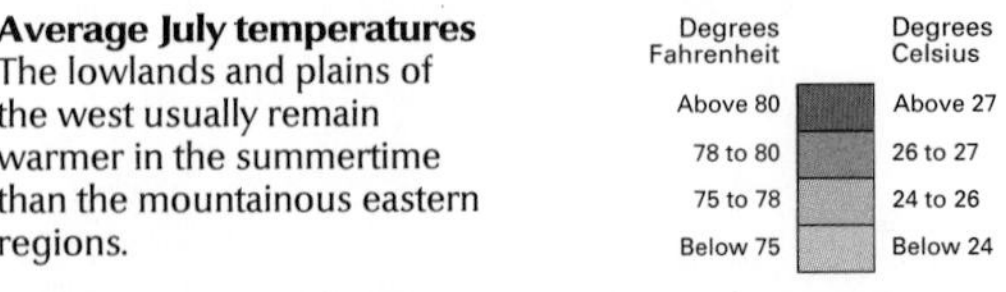

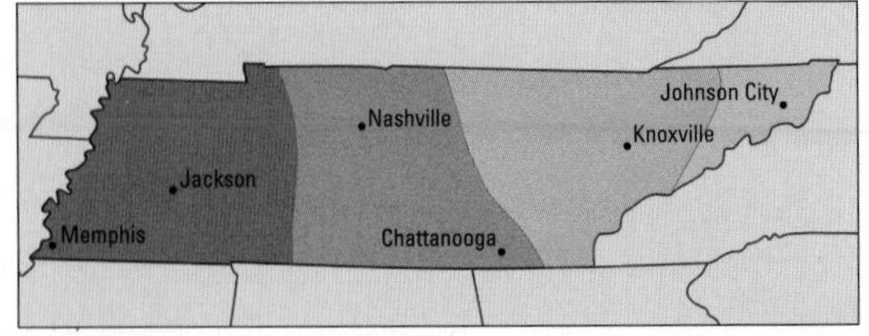

WORLD BOOK maps

Tennessee has a diverse economy. A variety of service industries, from health care to retail stores, employ most of the state's workers. But manufacturing is also important in Tennessee. Processed foods and beverages, transportation equipment, and chemicals are the state's leading products.

Natural resources. Tennessee's fertile soil, temperate climate, vast water supply, and abundant minerals make the state rich in natural resources.

Soil. The most fertile and productive soils lie in the Appalachian Ridge and Valley Region, the Nashville Basin, and the Gulf Coastal Plain. A limestone-based soil covers the mountain coves in the Blue Ridge region. A clay loam formed from weathered limestone covers the valley floors in the Ridge and Valley Region. The Appalachian Plateau and much of the Highland Rim have poor soils. The best agricultural area of the Highland Rim is the Pennyroyal Region along the Tennessee-Kentucky border. A loam soil, formed from rich soluble limestone, covers the Nashville Basin. The Gulf Coastal Plain has light soils that produce well. Fertile sand, silt, and clay soils cover the Mississippi Alluvial Plain.

Minerals. Tennessee mines produce a wide variety of materials. East Tennessee has large deposits of fluorite, marble, pyrite, and zinc. Middle Tennessee contains rich stores of limestone, phosphate rock, and zinc. The Appalachian Plateau has major deposits of coal, and small amounts of petroleum and natural gas. Ball clay, lignite, and sand and gravel are found in West Tennessee. The state also mines barite and other materials.

Service industries account for the greatest portion of Tennessee's *gross state product*—the total value of all goods and services produced in a state in a year. Most of the service industries are concentrated in the state's seven metropolitan areas.

Community, business, and personal services forms Tennessee's most important service industry. This group employs more people than any other industry group in the state. Community, business, and personal services include such economic activities as business services, law firms, and private health care. Johnson City, Knoxville, Memphis, and Nashville are important regional health centers with colleges of medicine and large hospitals. FedEx Corporation, one of the world's largest delivery services, has its headquarters in Memphis and is one of the state's largest employers. Business services play an important role in the Knoxville area's economy.

Trade, restaurants, and hotels forms the second most important service industry. Memphis, one of the nation's leading distribution centers, is Tennessee's leading area for wholesale trade. It has direct connections to many of the country's largest cities by means of highways, railroads, and the Mississippi River. The wholesale trade of cotton is important in Memphis. The chief retail establishments in the state include car dealerships and grocery stores. Auto-Zone, a leading auto parts retailer, is based in Memphis. Many restaurants and hotels are lo-

Production and workers by economic activities

Economic activities	Percent of GSP* produced	Employed workers: Number of people	Employed workers: Percent of total
Community, business, & personal services	22	1,026,700	30
Trade, restaurants, & hotels	19	761,600	22
Manufacturing	18	440,000	13
Finance, insurance, & real estate	17	244,800	7
Government	11	427,900	12
Transportation & communication	8	221,300	6
Construction	4	202,600	6
Agriculture	1	116,800	3
Mining	†	5,700	†
Utilities	†	3,800	†
Total‡	100	3,451,200	100

*GSP = gross state product, the total value of goods and services produced in a year.
†Less than one-half of 1 percent.
‡Figures may not add up to 100 percent due to rounding.
Figures are for 2002; employment figures include full- and part-time workers.
Source: *World Book* estimates based on data from U.S. Bureau of Economic Analysis.

Eastman Chemical Company

A chemical factory in Tennessee produces rolls of transparent plastics, a kind of chemical product. Tennessee ranks among the leading states in the manufacture of chemical products.

cated in Knoxville, Memphis, and Nashville.

Finance, insurance, and real estate ranks third among Tennessee's service industries in terms of the gross state product. Memphis and Nashville are the state's leading banking centers. The First Tennessee Bank, based in Memphis, is the largest bank.

Government is Tennessee's fourth-ranking service industry. Government services include public schools and hospitals, and military activities. Nashville, the state capital, is a hub for government activities. The Tennessee Valley Authority, a federal government corporation, is one of the nation's largest electric power companies. Its headquarters are in Knoxville.

Transportation and communication forms the fifth-ranking service industry. Many airlines and trucking firms operate in Memphis, an important U.S. transportation center. More information about transportation and communication appears later in this section.

Manufacturing. Tennessee's manufactured goods have a *value added by manufacture* of about $46 billion a year. This figure represents the increase in value of raw materials after they become finished products.

As a group, processed foods and beverages rank first among Tennessee's products in terms of value added by manufacture. Grain products, including bread, breakfast cereals, and flour, are a leading processed food group. Memphis is the state's leading producer of bread and cereals. Beverages produced in the state include beer, whiskey, and soft drinks. Moore County and Coffee County have two of the largest whiskey distilleries in the United States. The state's other important food products include candy, dairy products, meats, and vegetable oil.

Chemicals ranks second among Tennessee's manufactured goods. The state is among the leading producers of chemicals. Plants in Tennessee produce industrial chemicals, paints, pharmaceuticals, plastics resins, and soaps. Eastman Chemical, a leading maker of a variety of chemical products, is headquartered in Kingsport.

Transportation equipment ranks third among Tennessee's manufactured products. Saturn, a division of General Motors, operates a major automobile plant in Spring Hill, and Nissan has a large plant in Smyrna. Many manufacturers of automobile parts operate near these plants. Nashville factories produce boats and aircraft equipment.

Machinery ranks fourth among the state's manufactured products in terms of value added. The most important type of machinery made in the state is heating and refrigeration equipment. Other types of machinery made in Tennessee include construction equipment, engines, farm and garden equipment, machine parts, and metalworking machinery.

Other products made in the state include metal products and plastic and rubber products. Nashville is the center of metal products manufacturing. Aluminum is the leading part of the primary metals sector. Large tire plants operate in La Vergne, Morrison, and Union City.

Agriculture. Farmland covers nearly half of Tennessee's land area. The state has about 91,000 farms.

Beef cattle are the leading source of farm income in Tennessee. Cattle farms are scattered throughout the state. *Broilers* (young, tender chickens) rank next among the state's farm products. Dairy products are also an important source of farm income. Tennessee also has many hog and horse farms. Hogs are mainly raised in northwest Tennessee. The famous Tennessee walking horse breed was developed in Middle Tennessee.

Soybeans rank as Tennessee's leading field crop. Soybeans are mainly grown in western Tennessee. Cotton ranks next, followed by corn. These crops are grown in the western part of the state. Tennessee is one of the leading tobacco producers. Tobacco is grown in northeastern and Middle Tennessee. Hay, which is used chiefly for livestock feed, is grown throughout the state.

Greenhouse and nursery products are an important part of Tennessee agriculture. These products include flowers, fruit trees, and ornamental shrubs. Many of the fruit trees planted in the southeastern United States come from nurseries in Tennessee.

Fruits and vegetables provide a small part of Tennessee's farm income. Snap beans and tomatoes are the most important vegetables grown in the state. Apples and peaches are the leading fruits.

Mining. Crushed stone is Tennessee's most valuable

Economy of Tennessee

This map shows the economic uses of land in Tennessee and where the state's leading farm and mineral products are produced. Major manufacturing centers are shown in red.

WORLD BOOK map

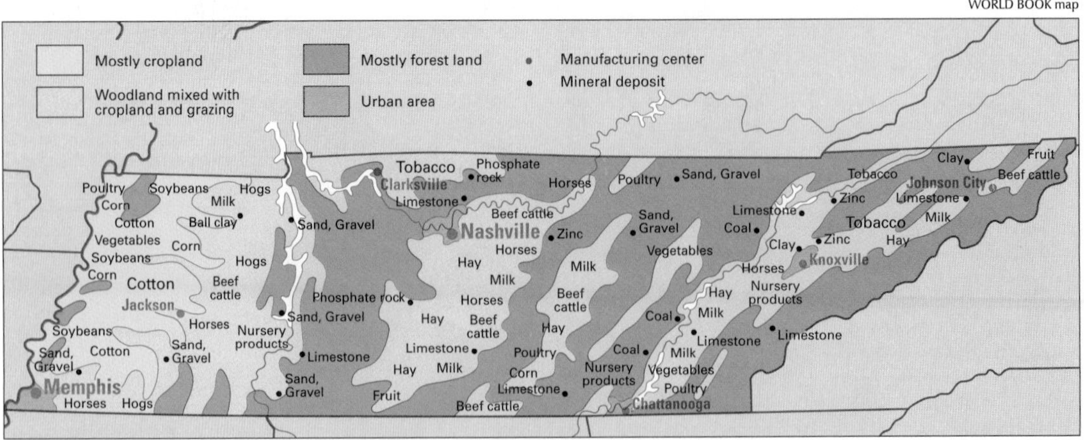

mined product. Coal ranks next in value among the state's mined products, followed by cement.

Limestone deposits are the source of almost all of the crushed stone produced in Tennessee. The largest limestone deposits lie in the eastern half of the state. The primary uses of crushed stone are for the construction of roadbeds and the production of concrete.

Tennessee's coal is mined on the Appalachian Plateau. About 70 percent of the coal comes from surface mines, and about 30 percent comes from underground mines.

Tennessee ranks among the leading zinc-producing states. Most of Tennessee's zinc comes from deposits near Knoxville. Other products mined in Tennessee include clays, gemstones, limestone, phosphate rock, and sand and gravel.

Electric power and utilities. Tennessee's utilities provide electric, gas, and water service. The Tennessee Valley Authority (TVA) generates almost all the state's electric power. The TVA produces more power than any other system in the country and distributes it to local electric power systems (see **Tennessee Valley Authority**). About 60 percent of the state's power comes from steam-generating plants that burn coal. About 30 percent comes from nuclear plants, and hydroelectric plants provide about 8 percent. Plants that burn natural gas and plants that burn petroleum each produce less than 1 percent of the state's electric power.

Transportation. Tennessee faced many problems in building its transportation systems. Many bridges and tunnels had to be built through hilly and mountainous areas. This raised the costs of railroad and highway construction. From about 1800 to 1860, private companies built turnpikes and collected tolls to maintain them. In 1913, the legislature authorized counties to issue bonds for highway construction. Tennessee has about 89,000 miles (143,000 kilometers) of highways and roads.

Tennessee's busiest airports are at Memphis and Nashville. Memphis International Airport serves as a hub for passenger airlines. Knoxville and Chattanooga also have important air terminals. Six major rail lines provide freight services, and passenger trains link Memphis with Chicago and New Orleans. Barges float along the Cumberland, Mississippi, and Tennessee rivers. Memphis ranks as one of the busiest ports on the Mississippi River. The Tennessee-Tombigbee Waterway connects the Tennessee River to the Gulf of Mexico and so links Tennessee cities with ports on the gulf.

Communication. Tennessee has about 140 newspapers, about 20 of which are dailies. Newspapers with the largest daily circulations include the *Chattanooga Times Free Press, The Knoxville News-Sentinel, The* (Memphis) *Commercial Appeal,* and *The* (Nashville) *Tennessean.*

Tennessee's first radio station, WNAV, began broadcasting at Knoxville in 1922. The first television station, WMCT-TV (now WMC-TV), started operations at Memphis in 1948. Today, Tennessee has about 400 radio stations and 35 television stations. Cable television systems and Internet providers serve communities statewide.

Government

Constitution. Tennessee's Constitution was adopted in 1870. The state had two earlier constitutions. The first was adopted in 1796, the year Tennessee achieved statehood, and the second was adopted in 1835.

Either the state legislature or a constitutional convention can propose amendments to the Constitution. In the legislature, a proposed amendment first needs the approval of a majority of both houses. Then, during the next regular legislative session, it must be approved by two-thirds of the members of each house. Finally, a majority of people voting in an election for governor must approve the amendment.

Constitutional conventions cannot be held more often than once every six years. They may be called by a majority of the legislators with the approval of a majority of voters. Amendments proposed by a constitutional convention must be approved by a majority of voters.

Executive. Tennessee's governor holds office for a four-year term and may serve any number of terms, but not more than two in a row. The speaker of the state Senate has the title of lieutenant governor.

The governor appoints the heads of Tennessee's 21 chief administrative departments. But the governor does not have the power to appoint the state's four top administrative officers. The legislature chooses the secretary of state, who serves a four-year term, and both the state treasurer and the state comptroller of the treasury, who serve for two years. The state Supreme Court selects the attorney general to serve an eight-year term.

Legislature, called the General Assembly, consists of a 33-member Senate and a 99-member House of Representatives. Senators serve four-year terms, and House members serve two-year terms. They are elected from legislative districts.

The General Assembly meets in odd-numbered years on the second Tuesday in January for an organizational session lasting no longer than 15 days. The regular session begins on the Tuesday following the end of the organizational session. Regular sessions are limited to 90 legislative days. Special sessions may be called by the governor or by two-thirds of the members of each house.

Courts. The highest court is the state Supreme Court. It has a chief justice and four associate justices, elected by the voters for eight-year terms. The Court of Appeals has 12 judges. It hears civil cases that have been transferred from lower courts. The Court of Appeals may serve as a complete body or in as many as three separate divisions. The Court of Criminal Appeals also has 12 judges. It hears appeals from criminal trial courts.

Tennessee has 31 judicial districts for its circuit courts, 26 for its chancery courts, and 13 for its criminal courts. Circuit courts have *jurisdiction* (authority) over any matters where jurisdiction is not given to another court. Other trial courts are general sessions courts, probate courts, juvenile and domestic relations courts, and city or municipal courts. All judges in Tennessee are elected to eight-year terms.

Local government. County commissions govern almost all of Tennessee's 95 counties. Each commission consists of from 9 to 25 county commissioners. Either a county executive or the chairman of the commission presides over commission meetings. The commission must meet at least four times a year to perform such duties as setting the property tax rate, approving the county's budget, and authorizing bond issues. All counties have such officials as a sheriff, assessor of property, trustee, register of deeds, and county clerk.

Any of Tennessee's approximately 335 incorporated cities and towns may, by popular vote, adopt *home rule.* That is, a city may vote to frame and operate its own charter instead of remaining under the control of the state legislature. But only 13 cities have adopted home rule since a constitutional amendment made it available in 1953. About 200 cities have a mayor-council government. Other cities use either the council-manager or commissioner system. Three cities in Tennessee, including Nashville, have combined their city and county governments into a single unit.

Revenue. Taxes account for nearly half of the state government's *general revenue* (income). Federal grants and other U.S. government programs make up most of the rest. Sources of tax revenue include a general sales tax and taxes on motor fuels, corporate income, insurance premiums, motor vehicle licenses, interest and dividend income, tobacco products, and alcoholic beverages.

Politics. Tennessee was a Democratic stronghold for most of its history, though parts of East Tennessee were Republican. During the 1960's, though, Republicans made strong gains in the state legislature. In 1966, Howard H. Baker, Jr., became the first Republican elected to the U.S. Senate from Tennessee since the 1860's. In 1970, Winfield Dunn became the first Republican in 50 years to be elected governor of Tennessee. By the end of the 1970's, Tennessee had become a two-party state.

Tennessee State Legislature

The Tennessee state legislature, called the *General Assembly,* is made up of a Senate and a House of Representatives. The Senate chambers are shown here.

Democrats carried Tennessee in most presidential elections in the late 1800's and the first half of the 1900's. But Republicans have won the state in most presidential elections after 1948. For a record of the state's electoral votes, see **Electoral College** (table).

The governors of Tennessee

	Party	Term		Party	Term
John Sevier	* Dem.-Rep.	1796-1801	**Peter Turney**	Democratic	1893-1897
Archibald Roane	Dem.-Rep.	1801-1803	**Robert Love Taylor**	Democratic	1897-1899
John Sevier	Dem.-Rep.	1803-1809	**Benton McMillin**	Democratic	1899-1903
Willie Blount	Dem.-Rep.	1809-1815	**James B. Frazier**	Democratic	1903-1905
Joseph McMinn	Dem.-Rep.	1815-1821	**John I. Cox**	Democratic	1905-1907
William Carroll	Dem.-Rep.	1821-1827	**Malcolm R. Patterson**	Democratic	1907-1911
Sam Houston	Dem.-Rep.	1827-1829	**Ben W. Hooper**	Republican	1911-1915
William Hall	Democratic	1829	**Tom C. Rye**	Democratic	1915-1919
William Carroll	Democratic	1829-1835	**A. H. Roberts**	Democratic	1919-1921
Newton Cannon	Whig	1835-1839	**Alfred A. Taylor**	Republican	1921-1923
James K. Polk	Democratic	1839-1841	**Austin Peay**	Democratic	1923-1927
James C. Jones	Whig	1841-1845	**Henry H. Horton**	Democratic	1927-1933
Aaron V. Brown	Democratic	1845-1847	**Hill McAlister**	Democratic	1933-1937
Neill S. Brown	Whig	1847-1849	**Gordon Browning**	Democratic	1937-1939
William Trousdale	Democratic	1849-1851	**Prentice Cooper**	Democratic	1939-1945
William B. Campbell	Whig	1851-1853	**Jim McCord**	Democratic	1945-1949
Andrew Johnson	Democratic	1853-1857	**Gordon Browning**	Democratic	1949-1953
Isham G. Harris	Democratic	1857-1862	**Frank G. Clement**	Democratic	1953-1959
Andrew Johnson			**Buford Ellington**	Democratic	1959-1963
(Military governor)	Democratic	1862-1865	**Frank G. Clement**	Democratic	1963-1967
William G. Brownlow	Republican	1865-1869	**Buford Ellington**	Democratic	1967-1971
DeWitt Clinton Senter	Republican	1869-1871	**Winfield Dunn**	Republican	1971-1975
John C. Brown	Democratic	1871-1875	**Leonard Ray Blanton**	Democratic	1975-1979
James D. Porter	Democratic	1875-1879	**Lamar Alexander**	Republican	1979-1987
Albert S. Marks	Democratic	1879-1881	**Ned McWherter**	Democratic	1987-1995
Alvin Hawkins	Republican	1881-1883	**Don Sundquist**	Republican	1995-2003
William B. Bate	Democratic	1883-1887	**Phil Bredesen**	Democratic	2003-
Robert Love Taylor	Democratic	1887-1891			
John P. Buchanan	Democratic	1891-1893			

*Democratic-Republican

Early days. Indians probably lived in what is now Tennessee at least 8,000 years ago. The earliest known groups of Indians settled the area more than 1,000 years ago. They built mounds to support their temples and chiefs' houses. See **Mound Builders**.

When the first Europeans arrived in the area, the Cherokee Indians lived in what is now Middle Tennessee. The Chickamauga, a branch of the Cherokee, lived near the present site of Chattanooga, in East Tennessee. The Chickasaw occupied West Tennessee.

Exploration. In 1540, a party of Spanish explorers led by Hernando de Soto raided some Indian villages in the valley of the Tennessee River. Moving westward, de Soto became the first European to reach the Mississippi River. He came upon it in 1541.

No other explorers entered the region until 1673, when James Needham and Gabriel Arthur of England explored the Tennessee River Valley. That same year, Louis Jolliet of Canada and Father Jacques Marquette of France sailed down the Mississippi River. In 1682, René-Robert Cavelier, Sieur de La Salle, claimed the entire Mississippi Valley for France. He built Fort Prud'homme on the Chickasaw Bluffs, near what is now Memphis. But the post was so isolated that the French soon had to abandon it. In 1714, Charles Charleville set up a French trading post at French Lick, near what is now Nashville.

France, Spain, and Britain all claimed the Tennessee region and competed for the trade and the friendship of the Indians. The dispute eventually became a contest between the British and the French. In 1754, the French and Indian War broke out between British and French settlers. The French were outnumbered by about 20 to 1 but won decisive victories in the early years of the war. But after nine years of fighting, the British won out. In 1763, by the Treaty of Paris, the French surrendered to the British all claim to lands east of the Mississippi.

Early settlement. By 1769, permanent settlers lived in the eastern Tennessee region. New settlers began to come into the area from Virginia and North Carolina.

The Tennessee region belonged to the British colony of North Carolina. But vast, rugged mountains separated settlers in Tennessee from the protection of the mother colony. In 1772, a group of settlers established law and order in the wilderness by forming their own government, the Watauga Association. They drew up one of the first written constitutions in North America. See **Watauga Association.**

A group called the Transylvania Company bought a large area of present-day Tennessee and Kentucky from the Cherokee in 1775. Pioneer Daniel Boone, working for the company, blazed a trail from the Holston River in eastern Tennessee across the mountains at Cumberland Gap to open this land to settlement. Boone's trail, the Wilderness Road, became the main route to the new settlements.

Territorial years. In 1779, two groups of pioneers, led by James Robertson and John Donelson, pushed far into the wilds and settled around the Big Salt Lick on the Cumberland River. They built Fort Nashborough (later Nashville), which formed the center of the Middle Tennessee settlements. These pioneers drew up an agreement called the Cumberland Compact. It established representative government for all settlers and created a court system to enforce its provisions.

In 1780, during the Revolutionary War in America, John Sevier led a group of pioneers from the Tennessee region across the Great Smoky Mountains into South Carolina. These men helped American forces defeat the British at the Battle of Kings Mountain on October 7.

Meanwhile, the settlers and Indians were trying to drive each other out of the Tennessee region. The settlers appealed for help to North Carolina. But help did not come. In 1784, three counties in East Tennessee revolted against North Carolina and formed the independent State of Franklin. They made John Sevier, the hero of Kings Mountain, their governor. North Carolina regained control of the area in 1788 (see **Franklin, State of**). In 1789, North Carolina gave the Tennessee region to the United States. The federal government made it into a new territory, and called it The Territory of the United States South of the River Ohio. William Blount became its first and only governor.

The Chickasaw owned nearly all West Tennessee until 1818, when they ceded their land to the federal government. But the Cherokee still held a large area in Middle Tennessee and a smaller tract south of the Little Tennessee and Sequatchie rivers in the east.

Statehood. On Feb. 6, 1796, Tennessee adopted a constitution in preparation for statehood. It became the 16th state in the Union on June 1. Tennesseans elected John Sevier as their first governor. The new state had a population of about 77,000 and was the first state to be created out of government territory.

Black slaves toiled on many West and Middle Tennessee farms before the American Civil War. But few farmers in the eastern part of the state owned slaves. Free blacks could vote in Tennessee until a new constitution, adopted in 1835, took that right away from them.

Building the state. Three men who were later elected president of the United States played key roles in the development of Tennessee. They were Andrew Jackson, James K. Polk, and Andrew Johnson.

Andrew Jackson helped draw up Tennessee's first constitution in 1796. He served as the state's first United States representative and later as a U.S. senator from Tennessee. He also served as a justice of the Tennessee Supreme Court. During the War of 1812, Jackson led his Tennessee troops to victory against the Creek Indians. He became a national hero by leading U.S. forces in an overwhelming defeat of the British Army at the Battle of New Orleans. Tennessee supported Jackson when he ran unsuccessfully for the presidency in 1824 and when he was elected in 1828.

As president, Jackson urged that the Cherokee be moved to western lands. Congress approved the Indian Removal Act of 1830. The act called for the removal of all Indian tribes east of the Mississippi River and their relocation on land west of the river. Thousands of Cherokee died during the forced migration that took place in the winter of 1838-1839, after Jackson had left office.

James K. Polk was a close friend and supporter of Andrew Jackson. Polk served Tennessee for two years in the state legislature, for 14 years in the U.S. House of Representatives, and for a two-year term as governor. Polk was elected president in 1844 on a platform of expansionism. During his presidency, he led the country to victory in the Mexican War and nearly doubled the territory of the United States.

As a state senator, Andrew Johnson tried to reduce the voting power of the powerful slave owners. Johnson served as a U.S. representative, as governor of Tennessee, and as a U.S. senator. Although he did not oppose slavery, he believed strongly in the Union. Johnson pleaded with the people of Tennessee to remain in the Union.

Many Tennesseans were in favor of staying in the Union. But when Confederate troops fired on Fort Sumter and war appeared inevitable, feelings in favor of seceding grew stronger. On June 8, 1861, about two months after the American Civil War broke out, over two-thirds of the people voted to join the Confederacy. Tennessee was the last state to secede. Andrew Johnson was the only senator who did not secede with his state.

The American Civil War. The people of Tennessee were divided in their sympathies between the North and the South. Most Union sympathy came from the eastern part of the state. Confederate forces moved into that region and held it captive for a good part of the war.

In 1862, the war spread across the state's middle and western regions. Union forces under General Ulysses S. Grant invaded Tennessee in February of that year and quickly captured Fort Henry and Fort Donelson, strong points on the Tennessee and Cumberland rivers. Grant then proceeded along the Tennessee River to Pittsburg Landing. There, one of the bloodiest battles of the war took place. It was called the Battle of Shiloh, after a church that stood on the battlefield. Despite enormous losses, Union troops won an important victory at Shiloh. Federal control of Middle and West Tennessee was established in 1862. President Abraham Lincoln appointed Andrew Johnson the military governor of Tennessee. Johnson required Tennesseans to accept *emancipation* (freedom of the slaves). As a result, slaves in Tennessee gained their freedom earlier than in most other Confederate states.

Union forces captured Chattanooga in September 1863, but Confederate troops soon regained the area outside the city. In November, Grant attacked the Confederate positions. In the first day of fighting, Union General Joseph Hooker drove the Confederate forces from Lookout Mountain in the "Battle Above the Clouds." The Union troops won control of Chattanooga after two more days of fighting.

In 1864, General William T. Sherman's troops marched from Chattanooga into Georgia and captured Atlanta. In Tennessee, Confederate forces under General John B. Hood tried to draw Sherman back by attacking Franklin and Nashville. But General George H. Thomas defeated Hood's army at Nashville.

The Union Party, consisting of Republicans and War Democrats, nominated Andrew Johnson to run for vice president under President Lincoln in the 1864 election. They won the election. But on April 14, 1865, President Lincoln was assassinated. Andrew Johnson was inaugurated as president on April 15, 1865. He declared the rebellion in Tennessee at an end on June 13. But a strong group in Congress tried to block Tennessee's readmission to the Union. On July 24, 1866, after considerable debate, Tennessee became the first Confederate state to be readmitted.

Reconstruction. The years following the American Civil War also were difficult ones for the people of Tennessee. The war had left much of the state in ruin and had left thousands of people homeless.

Bettmann Archive

Yellow fever swept through Tennessee during the 1870's. The epidemic hit especially hard in Memphis, where about 5,200 of the city's 19,600 residents died from the disease in 1878.

A group of Union sympathizers, called *Radicals,* gained control of the state's government after the war. This group included the governor and most of the state legislature. They gave black men the right to vote, but they took voting privileges away from a number of Confederate sympathizers. Most of these Radicals were voted out of office in 1869. Tennessee adopted a new Constitution in 1870. This Constitution reduced the power of the governor, set limits on legislative salaries, and extended the right to vote to all male citizens 21 or older.

Plantations in Middle and West Tennessee were divided into smaller farms that were operated by tenants. Many of the tenant farmers were former slaves. During the years after the war, the manufacturing and mining industries began to grow. But the state's economy continued to depend mainly on agriculture.

Disease swept across the state during the 1870's. One of the worst yellow fever epidemics in U.S. history hit Memphis in 1878, killing about 5,200 of its 19,600 residents. Many people fled the city. Memphis faced severe financial difficulties because of its population loss and other factors. It declared bankruptcy and lost its city charter in 1879. It did not regain the charter until 1893.

Poor management of state funds in Tennessee banks left the state deeply in debt after the American Civil War. In 1890, the Tennessee Banking Association began a campaign to reform the banking system. In 1913, a state banking department was set up to protect the public against bank mismanagement, fraud, and harmful speculation.

The early 1900's brought much change to the state.

Historic Tennessee

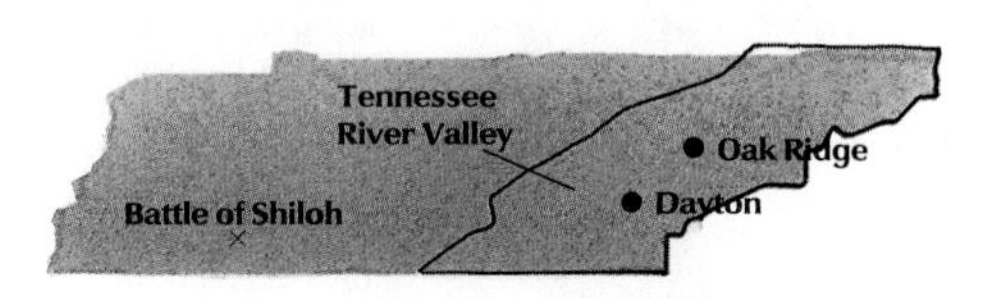

The earliest known groups of Indians in what is now Tennessee settled the area more than 1,000 years ago. They were mound builders. They built large monuments of earth to support their temples and chiefs' houses.

The Battle of Shiloh in 1862 ended in a victory for the North when Confederate troops tried to stop a Union advance on Corinth, Mississippi. Over 10,000 Confederates and over 13,000 Union soldiers were lost.

Oak Ridge, begun in 1942, had the world's first nuclear reactor. The device was used to produce materials for the first atomic bomb.

The Tennessee Valley Authority, created in 1933, built a network of dams to furnish electric power and control floods.

The Scopes trial in Dayton in 1925 centered on a Tennessee law that made the teaching of the theory of evolution illegal in state schools.

WORLD BOOK illustrations by Kevin Chadwick

Important dates in Tennessee

1540 Hernando de Soto of Spain led the first European expedition into the Tennessee region.

1673 James Needham and Gabriel Arthur of England, and Louis Jolliet of Canada and Father Jacques Marquette of France explored the region.

1682 Robert Cavelier, Sieur de La Salle, claimed the Mississippi River Valley for France.

1714 Charles Charleville set up a French trading post near the present site of Nashville.

1763 France surrendered to Britain all claim to lands east of the Mississippi River.

1772 The Watauga Association drew up one of the first written constitutions in North America.

1784 Three counties established the State of Franklin.

1796 Tennessee became the 16th state on June 1.

1818 The Chickasaw Indians sold all their land east of the Mississippi River to the U.S. government.

1838 The Cherokee were forced out of Tennessee.

1861 Tennessee became the last state to secede from the Union, on June 8.

1866 Tennessee became the first state to be readmitted to the Union, on July 24.

1870 A new constitution gave all male citizens 21 or older the right to vote.

1878 One of the worst yellow fever epidemics in U.S. history killed about 5,200 of the 19,600 people in Memphis.

1925 John Scopes was convicted of teaching evolution in a Tennessee public school.

1933 Congress created the Tennessee Valley Authority.

1942 The federal government began building the atomic energy center at Oak Ridge.

1962 The U.S. Supreme Court ruled, in a Tennessee case, that federal courts could challenge legislative apportionment.

1970 Winfield Dunn became the first Republican in 50 years to be elected governor of Tennessee.

1982 A world's fair was held in Knoxville.

1996 Tennessee celebrated the bicentennial of its statehood.

Estes Kefauver waves to onlookers in Memphis in 1948 during his successful campaign for U.S. senator. In 1950, Kefauver won recognition for his role as head of the U.S. Senate committee for investigating organized crime. Kefauver was the Democratic candidate for vice president in 1956 but was not elected.

AP/Wide World

New and better highways and railroads spread across Tennessee. People began to move away from the farms and into the cities. By the mid-1930's, manufacturing was beginning to overtake farming as the leading industry.

In 1920, the state legislature narrowly approved the 19th Amendment, which gives women the right to vote. Tennessee became the 36th—and final—state needed to ratify the amendment.

In 1925, John T. Scopes, a high school teacher in Dayton, Tennessee, was charged with teaching British naturalist Charles Darwin's theory of evolution, contrary to state law. The state brought Scopes to trial. The noted orator and American statesman William Jennings Bryan aided the prosecution. Clarence Darrow, the most famous American lawyer of the time, defended Scopes. The trial aroused enormous controversy. Scopes lost and was fined $100, but the conviction was reversed because of a minor legal error. Over 40 years later, Tennessee repealed the law under which Scopes had been convicted.

In 1933, the federal government established the Tennessee Valley Authority (TVA) to conserve and develop the resources of the Tennessee River Valley.

The mid-1900's. In 1942, the federal government began to build an atomic energy plant in Oak Ridge. Scientists there worked on the development of the atomic bomb during World War II (1939-1945).

After the war, Tennessee continued to shift from an agricultural to an industrial economy. The TVA built more dams and steam plants to control floods, provide plentiful water supplies, and furnish cheap electric power. These facilities and the state's large labor force attracted new industries. Recreational areas built near scenic sites drew many tourists. A multimillion-dollar music industry grew up in Nashville, which became one of the nation's largest recording centers. The industry had its beginning in "The Grand Ole Opry," a radio program featuring country and western music.

Tennessee's political life changed after the war, as many veterans became active in politics. This helped cause a revolt in the 1948 state elections against control by Memphis political boss E. H. Crump. In the elections, Crump began to lose power for the first time in over 20 years as Estes Kefauver won a seat in the U.S. Senate. Kefauver, who represented Tennessee in the U.S. House of Representatives, had run an anti-Crump campaign.

A constitutional convention was held in 1953, the state's first since 1870. Voters approved all eight of the convention's proposed amendments, which included extending the governor's term from two to four years. Also during the 1950's, the Republican Party began to grow in the state. In 1966, Republicans won their first statewide office in Tennessee since 1920 with the election of Howard H. Baker, Jr., to the Senate. In 1970, the voters elected their first Republican governor in 50 years, Winfield Dunn.

Political control in Tennessee shifted from rural to urban areas. The shift resulted from an increase in city populations and from a ruling by the Supreme Court of the United States. In 1962, the Supreme Court ruled in *Baker v. Carr,* a Tennessee case, that federal courts have legal power over state legislative apportionment. In

A world's fair was held in Knoxville in 1982. The Sunsphere, a 266-foot (81-meter) tower, symbolized the fair's theme, "Energy Turns the World."

Jim Ayres, Black Star

1964, a federal court ordered Tennessee to redraw its legislative districts. The state did so in 1965, giving equal representation according to population.

Much social change in the state concerned desegregation. Tennessee's Constitution made it illegal for black children and white children to attend the same schools. But in 1954, the U.S. Supreme Court ruled that compulsory segregation in public schools was illegal. Desegregation of state-supported schools began in 1956 in Clinton. State officials sent the National Guard to enforce the order.

On April 4, 1968, civil rights leader Martin Luther King, Jr., was murdered in Memphis. He had gone there to lead protests for striking garbage workers. James Earl Ray, an escaped convict, pleaded guilty to the crime and was sentenced to 99 years in prison.

The late 1900's. In 1974, the state legislature passed a *sunshine law* that allows the public to attend local and state government meetings. In 1978, voters approved an amendment to the state Constitution that limits spending by the state government. Another amendment adopted in 1978 made governors eligible for reelection.

In 1982, a world's fair held in Knoxville helped promote tourism in Tennessee. Knoxville renovated 70 acres (28 hectares) of its downtown area for the event.

Despite economic progress since the mid-1900's, the living standard of many Tennesseans remained low. To increase its job opportunities, Tennessee worked to attract new industry. In 1983, Nissan opened a new truck assembly plant at Smyrna. In 1985, the Tennessee River was connected to the Gulf of Mexico by the $2-billion Tennessee-Tombigbee Waterway project. The new water passage soon began to stimulate economic growth. In 1990, General Motors opened a new automobile plant in Spring Hill.

The early 2000's. In 2004, Tennessee became the first state to enact a law against *outsourcing.* A number of U.S. companies had come under criticism for having data-entry and call-center jobs performed outside the country. The Tennessee law asks state officials to give preference for state projects to companies with U.S.-based workers.

Charles S. Aiken and Stephen V. Ash

Study aids

Related articles in *World Book* include:

Biographies

Acuff, Roy
Agee, James
Arnold, Eddy
Atkins, Chet
Baker, Howard Henry, Jr.
Bell, John
Blount, William
Crockett, Davy
Davis, Samuel
Forrest, Nathan B.
Frist, Bill
Gore, Al
Handy, W. C.
Houston, Sam
Hull, Cordell
Jackson, Andrew
Johnson, Andrew
Kefauver, Estes
Parton, Dolly
Polk, James K.
Presley, Elvis
Ross, John
Sequoyah
Sevier, John
White, Hugh L.
York, Alvin C.

Cities

Chattanooga
Knoxville
Memphis
Nashville

History

Civil War, American
Franklin, State of
Natchez Trace
Scopes trial
Tennessee Valley Authority
Watauga Association
Westward movement in America

Physical features

Blue Ridge Mountains
Clingmans Dome
Cumberland Gap
Cumberland Mountains
Cumberland River
Great Smoky Mountains
Mississippi River
Tennessee River

Other related articles

Graceland
Great Smoky Mountains National Park
Oak Ridge National Laboratory

Outline

I. People
- A. Population
- B. Schools
- C. Libraries
- D. Museums

II. Visitor's guide
- A. Places to visit
- B. Annual events

III. Land and climate
- A. Land regions
- B. Rivers and lakes
- C. Plant and animal life
- D. Climate

IV. Economy
- A. Natural resources
- B. Service industries
- C. Manufacturing
- D. Agriculture
- E. Mining
- F. Electric power
- G. Transportation
- H. Communication

V. Government
- A. Constitution
- B. Executive
- C. Legislature
- D. Courts
- E. Local government
- F. Revenue
- G. Politics

VI. History

Questions

Which Tennessee land region includes the lowest part of the state?
Why did Memphis lose its city charter in the 1870's?
Who started the first school in Tennessee?
How is most electric power in Tennessee generated?
When did a group of people called *Radicals* gain control of Tennessee's government?
How can Tennessee's Constitution be amended?
What is the leading source of farm income in Tennessee?
Where does the name *Tennessee* come from?
How did the decision in *Baker v. Carr* affect Tennessee?
What was the Watauga Association? The Cumberland Compact?

Additional resources

Level I

Aylesworth, Thomas G. and Virginia L. *The Southeast: Georgia, Kentucky, Tennessee.* Rev. ed. Chelsea Hse., 1995.
Barrett, Tracy. *Tennessee.* Benchmark Bks., 1997.
Kent, Deborah. *Tennessee.* Children's Pr., 2001.
Kummer, Patricia K. *Tennessee.* Capstone Pr., 1998.
Thompson, Kathleen. *Tennessee.* Raintree Steck-Vaughn, 1996.

Level II

Corlew, Robert E. *Tennessee: A Short History.* 2nd ed. 1981. Reprint. Univ. of Tenn. Pr., 1990.
Dykeman, Wilma. *Haunting Memories: Echoes and Images of Tennessee's Past.* Univ. of Tenn. Pr., 1996. Tennessee: A History. Rev. ed. 1984. Reprint. Wakestone Bks., 1993.
Goodstein, Anita S. *Nashville, 1780-1860.* Univ. Pr. of Fla., 1989.
Groom, Winston. *Shrouds of Glory: From Atlanta to Nashville—The Last Great Campaign of the Civil War.* 1995. Reprint. Pocket Bks., 1996.
O'Brien, Tim. *Tennessee: Off the Beaten Path.* 5th ed. Globe Pequot, 2001. A travel guide.
Vile, John R., and Byrnes, Mark, eds. *Tennessee Government and Politics.* Vanderbilt Univ. Pr., 1998.

Tennessee, University of, is a coeducational, state-assisted institution. Its largest campus is in Knoxville. It also has campuses in Chattanooga, Martin, and Memphis. The university grants bachelor's, master's, and doctor's degrees.

The Knoxville campus includes colleges of agriculture, architecture, business administration, communications, education, engineering, human ecology, law, liberal arts, nursing, social work, and veterinary medicine; and a graduate school. The campus is the headquarters for the university's statewide programs of agricultural research and extension, continuing education, and public service.

The Chattanooga and Martin campuses also offer a wide variety of programs, including business administration, education, engineering, and liberal arts. The Memphis campus has colleges of basic medical sciences, allied health sciences, dentistry, medicine, nursing, and pharmacy; and a graduate school of medical sciences.

The University of Tennessee also operates research facilities. The main agricultural experiment station is in Knoxville. Other facilities at the university conduct studies in business and economics, engineering, the environment, health sciences, transportation, and water resources.

The university was founded in 1794 as Blount College. It received its present name in 1879.

Critically reviewed by the University of Tennessee

Tennessee River is the largest tributary of the Ohio River. It begins at Knoxville, Tennessee, where the Holston and French Broad rivers meet, and flows southwest through Tennessee and Alabama. Then the river curves north. It flows back through Tennessee and northwest across Kentucky. At Paducah, Kentucky, it empties into the Ohio River. The Tennessee River drains an area of about 41,000 square miles (106,000 square kilometers).

Development of the Tennessee River's water power to generate electricity began in 1913 with the construction of Hales Bar Dam, near Chattanooga, Tennessee. Nickajack Dam replaced Hales Bar Dam in 1968. Wilson Dam, near Muscle Shoals, Alabama, began generating electricity in 1925.

In 1933, the Tennessee Valley Authority began building a series of dams that converted the Tennessee River into a chain of lakes. The river's 650-mile (1,046-kilometer) course is navigable by barges. In 1985, the completion of the Tennessee-Tombigbee Waterway connected the Tennessee River with the Tombigbee River of Mississippi and Alabama (see **Tombigbee River**). The waterway provides a route to the Gulf of Mexico.

Charles S. Aiken

Tennessee Valley Authority (TVA) is a federal corporation that works to develop the natural resources of the Tennessee Valley. Congress created the TVA in 1933 and gave it the overall goal of conserving the resources of the valley region. Congress also directed the TVA to speed the region's economic development and, in case of war, to use the Tennessee Valley's resources for national defense.

Beginning in colonial times, the valley's forests had been cut down for lumber or to clear the land for farming and mining. The roots of trees and shrubs had held the soil in place and absorbed moisture. But when the forests were removed, the water ran off the land, carrying the topsoil with it. Farming became decreasingly productive, and flooding rivers caused loss of life and property.

Through the years, the TVA has built dams to control floods, create electric power, and deepen rivers for shipping. The TVA has also planted new forests and preserved existing ones, and it has developed highly effective fertilizers.

The valley. The Tennessee Valley covers 40,910 square miles (105,956 square kilometers). The valley includes parts of Tennessee, Kentucky, Virginia, North Carolina, Georgia, Alabama, and Mississippi. The land varies from peaks 1 mile (1.6 kilometers) high in the Great Smoky Mountains to the low, muddy plains near the mouth of the Tennessee River. The valley has rich deposits of coal, copper, gravel, iron, limestone, manganese, marble, sand, and zinc.

The achievements of the TVA program have been spread far outside the valley. Power from TVA dams and steam plants reaches homes, farms, factories, stores, and mines in an area of about 80,000 square miles (210,000 square kilometers). In addition, phosphate fertilizers developed and improved under the TVA program have been tested and demonstrated throughout the United States.

The dams. Thirty-nine dams on the Tennessee River and its branches work as a single system, making this one of the most effectively controlled waterways in the world. The TVA built most of the dams. The agency also directs the storage and release of water and the genera-

© Gene Ahrens

TVA's Norris Dam on the Clinch River is 265 feet (81 meters) high and 1,860 feet (567 meters) long. Its reservoir stores over 2 $\frac{1}{2}$ million acre-feet (3.1 billion cubic meters) of water.

tion of power at four dams owned by Alcoa Inc. TVA also buys power from eight dams of the Cumberland River system, run by the U.S. Army Corps of Engineers.

The dams are of two general types. On the main stream of the Tennessee River, long dams were built, making a continuous chain of lakes from Paducah, Kentucky, to Knoxville, Tennessee. Each of these dams has a lock by which towboats and barges may be raised or lowered from one lake level to another. On the branches of the Tennessee River, high dams were constructed to create great water reservoirs between the hills and mountains. The highest of these dams is Fontana Dam, 480 feet (146 meters) high, on the Little Tennessee River.

TVA dams on the Tennessee River itself are Chickamauga, Fort Loudoun, Guntersville, Kentucky, Nickajack, Pickwick Landing, Watts Bar, Wheeler, and Wilson. Kentucky Dam, the largest, measures 8,422 feet (2,567 meters) long and 206 feet (63 meters) high. It creates a lake about 185 miles (298 kilometers) long.

Electric power. In 1933, the TVA region used only 16,000 kilowatt-hours of electricity a year. Today, the region uses about 160 billion kilowatt-hours each year. During TVA's early years, dams generated much of its power. But as the demand for electric power increased, the agency had to find other power sources. By the early 2000's, water power supplied less than 10 percent of the electric power generated in the TVA system. The rest came from nuclear power plants and from large steam plants that generated power from coal.

TVA has worked to control environmental damage related to producing electric power. In the past, for example, much of the coal used by TVA to generate electric power came from *strip mining*. Strip mining, a method of surface mining, usually scars the landscape, pollutes rivers, and destroys valuable timber. TVA was criticized for buying coal from strip mines. As a result, TVA has since 1965 required operators of the strip mines supplying coal to its power plants to reclaim any damaged land. TVA also manages one of the largest programs for controlling air pollution from coal-burning plants. Its engineers and scientists work to develop ways of burning coal that will be less harmful to the atmosphere.

In addition, TVA provides practical assistance and low-interest loans to homes and businesses to encourage them to conserve energy and to install solar-energy devices. This program aims to help cut overall energy costs and reduce the need for new power plants.

TVA was designed to provide abundant power for the region at the lowest possible rates. Household users of TVA power pay about a third less per kilowatt-hour than do consumers on the average in the United States. About 160 local nonprofit electric power distributors furnish TVA power for consumers.

River shipping. The Tennessee River provides a 650-mile (1,046-kilometer) route for boats of 9-foot (2.7-meter) draft. It links to an inland waterway system. During the early 2000's, barges on this system carried about 50 million tons (45 million metric tons) of freight yearly.

Tennessee Valley Authority (TVA)

TVA provides electric power, flood control, water recreation, and navigable waterways in Tennessee and the surrounding states. It builds and operates power plants and dams and directs the operation of several Alcoa and Corps of Engineers dams.

WORLD BOOK map

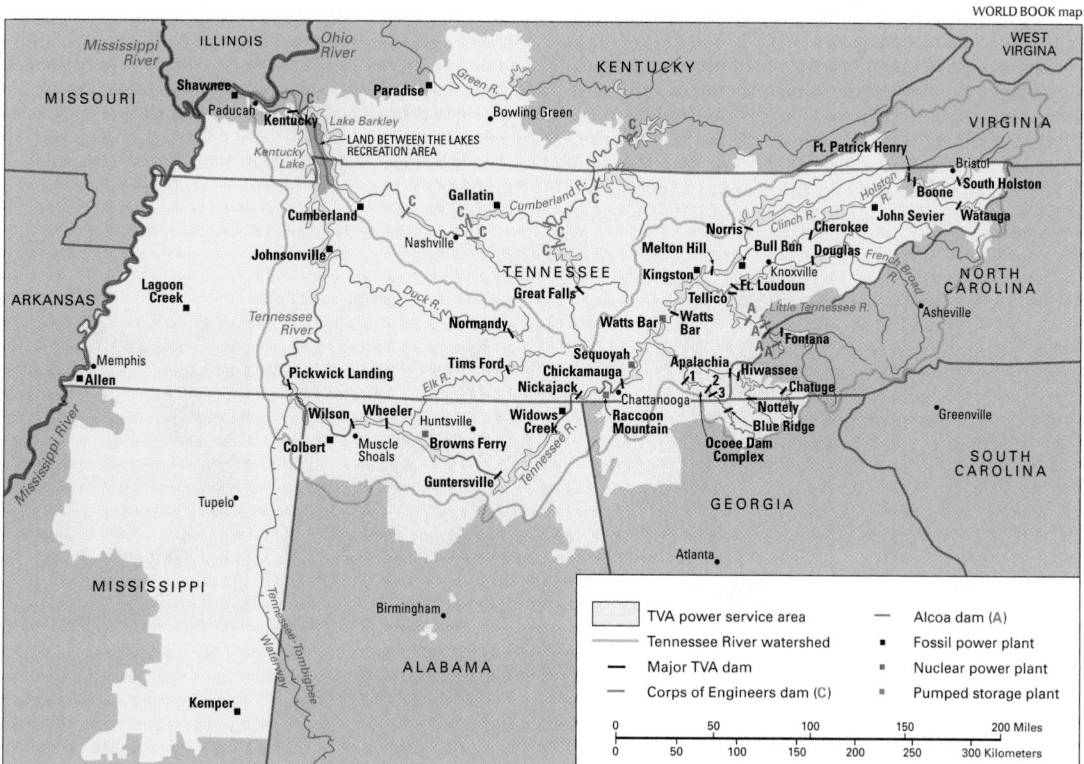

Flood control. Most floods on the Tennessee River occur in late winter and early spring. TVA lowers the lakes in the region during fall and early winter to create space for the expected floodwaters. As the flood season passes in late spring, TVA allows the lakes to fill gradually to high levels for the summer.

Other activities. TVA operates the National Fertilizer Development Center at Muscle Shoals, Alabama. Scientists and engineers at the center seek to develop fertilizers and improve methods of producing them. TVA tests the products from the centers on farms nationwide and encourages the private fertilizer industry to mass produce the most successful ones.

In the Tennessee Valley, TVA helps sponsor demonstrations of farming devices and techniques designed to control soil erosion, increase crop yields, and improve farm management and income levels. TVA also works to promote better management of the region's forests. It encourages greater use of them as sources of lumber, furniture, paper, and other wood products.

The lakes created by damming the Tennessee River and its branches add to the beauty of the region. They also provide many recreational opportunities. States, counties, cities, and private organizations have developed many parks and other facilities. TVA itself developed the huge Land Between the Lakes recreational area between Kentucky Lake and Lake Barkley in Kentucky and Tennessee.

History. Congress established the Tennessee Valley Authority after about 15 years of debate on how to use the government's two nitrate plants and Wilson Dam at Muscle Shoals. These projects, built under the National Defense Act of 1916, had not been finished in time for use during World War I. The TVA Act transferred them from the War Department to TVA.

The new corporation represented a great change in United States policy. Responsibility for various projects in the Tennessee Valley had been divided among the Departments of Agriculture, the Army, and the Interior. The TVA Act recognized that all conservation problems were related to one another. The act gave one agency the responsibility of improving all types of conservation and development of resources.

The creation of TVA became a highly controversial issue and remained so for many years. Private power companies strongly opposed government production of electric power. State and local agencies in the Tennessee Valley feared that TVA would take over their functions. Political opponents of President Franklin D. Roosevelt's New Deal used the issue of the TVA's creation to embarrass him.

TVA pays no federal income taxes, but it pays more than $100 million a year in dividends and repayments to the U.S. Treasury. It also makes payments to states and counties in place of taxes.

A board of three members directs TVA. The president of the United States appoints them to nine-year terms with the consent of the Senate, and they report to the president. Critically reviewed by the Tennessee Valley Authority

Related articles in *World Book* include:

Kentucky Lake
Muscle Shoals
Norris, George W.
Tennessee River
Willkie, Wendell L.

Additional resources

Colignon, Richard A. *Power Plays: Critical Events in the Institutionalization of the Tennessee Valley Authority.* State Univ. of N.Y. Pr., 1996.
Creese, Walter L. *TVA's Public Planning.* Univ. of Tenn. Pr., 1990.
Van Fleet, Alanson A. *The Tennessee Valley Authority.* Chelsea Hse., 1987.

Tenniel, *TEHN yuhl,* **Sir John** (1820-1914), an English cartoonist and book illustrator, illustrated Lewis Carroll's *Alice's Adventures in Wonderland* (1865) and *Through the Looking-Glass* (1871). He also became famous for his political cartoons in *Punch,* a magazine for which he worked for about 50 years after 1850. His work was admired for its originality, dignity, and excellent technique. Tenniel and other artists of his time helped the United Kingdom keep leadership in the field of book illustration. He was born on Feb. 28, 1820, in London.

Elizabeth Broun

See also **Carroll, Lewis** (The *Alice* books); **Literature for children** (The rise of illustration; picture: *Through the Looking-Glass*).

Macmillan & Co., Ltd.; Radio Times Hulton Picture Library

Sir John Tenniel became famous as the illustrator of Lewis Carroll's *Alice's Adventures in Wonderland.* His drawing of the mad tea party expressed comic dignity.

Russ Adams Productions

Important tennis tournaments attract thousands of fans who come to watch the world's finest players compete against each other. The tournament held each summer in Wimbledon, England, *shown here,* ranks as the unofficial world championship for men and women players.

Tennis

Tennis is a game in which opposing players—one or two on each side—use rackets to hit a ball back and forth over a net. The game is played on a flat surface called a *court.* Each player tries to score points by hitting the ball so that the opposing player or players cannot return it over the net and inside the court.

Tennis may be played indoors or outdoors. If two people play, the game is called *singles.* If four people play, it is called *doubles.* In most singles and doubles matches, men play men and women play women. In *mixed doubles,* a man and a woman play on each side.

Millions of people play tennis for exercise and recreation. They play on courts in public parks and in private tennis clubs. Players of almost any age can enjoy the sport. The United States Tennis Association (USTA), which governs American tennis, sponsors national tournaments for players as young as 12 and as old as 75.

Professional tennis players travel throughout the world to compete in tournaments that offer thousands of dollars in prize money. Many countries enter men's and women's teams that compete for international trophies. The most famous trophy is the Davis Cup, which represents the world's men's team championship.

Tennis ranks as one of the world's most popular spectator sports as well as a favorite participant sport. Thousands of fans attend the many tournaments held each year. Millions more watch important matches on TV.

Tennis as it is played today developed in Britain during the late 1800's. The game quickly spread to the United States and other countries. By 1900, tennis had become a major international sport.

Chris Evert, the contributor of this article, won 18 women's singles titles in major tennis championships during her career.

The court and equipment

The court is a rectangle divided into halves by a net stretched across the middle. The net measures 3 feet (91 centimeters) high at the center and $3\frac{1}{2}$ feet (107 centimeters) high at the side posts that support it. The court is 78 feet (23.7 meters) long. Almost all courts are marked off so that both singles and doubles games can be played on them. The singles court measures 27 feet (8.2 meters) wide. The doubles court is $4\frac{1}{2}$ feet (1.37 meters) wider on each side. Various lines divide the singles and doubles court into sections. For the names of these lines and the sizes and names of the sections, see the diagram of a court in this article.

For many years, major tennis tournaments were played on grass courts. In fact, the early name for tennis was lawn tennis. Grass courts are the most comfortable for players, but require daily maintenance and a rest period after heavy play. Therefore, they are limited to private clubs and residences that can afford the expense.

The most popular surfaces for outdoor courts are hard courts, with an asphalt or concrete base and an acrylic color surface or a cushioned surface. Clay courts are more comfortable than hard courts but need daily maintenance. Indoor tennis can be played on either hard surfaces or clay courts.

Tennis balls are hollow and are made of rubber covered with a felt fabric woven of Dacron, nylon, and wool. They must have a diameter of more than $2\frac{1}{2}$ inches (6.35 centimeters) but less than $2\frac{5}{8}$ inches (6.67 centimeters). They must weigh more than 2 ounces (56.7 grams) but less than $2\frac{1}{16}$ ounces (58.6 grams). Balls used in tournaments may be either white or yellow. Manufacturers also make balls in other colors.

Tennis rackets. Rules allow the use of tennis rackets that are up to 29 inches (74 centimeters) long and up to 12 $\frac{1}{2}$ inches (32 centimeters) wide. No rules govern racket weight. Most men and women players use a racket that weighs 10 to 11 ounces (283 to 312 grams). In general, young players use a racket that weighs about 9 ounces (255 grams). A typical racket frame is made of fiberglass and graphite. The most common striking surface is a net of tightly strung nylon or other synthetic material.

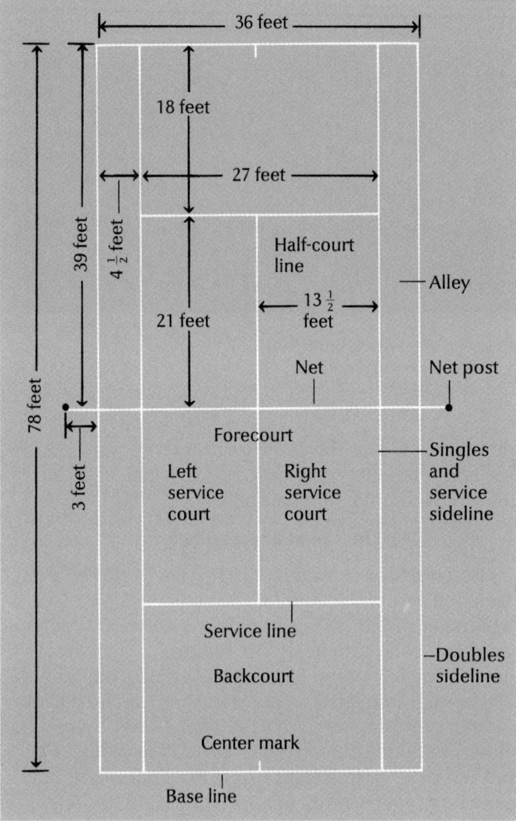

A tennis court is a rectangle divided into halves by a net. Various white lines further divide the court into sections.

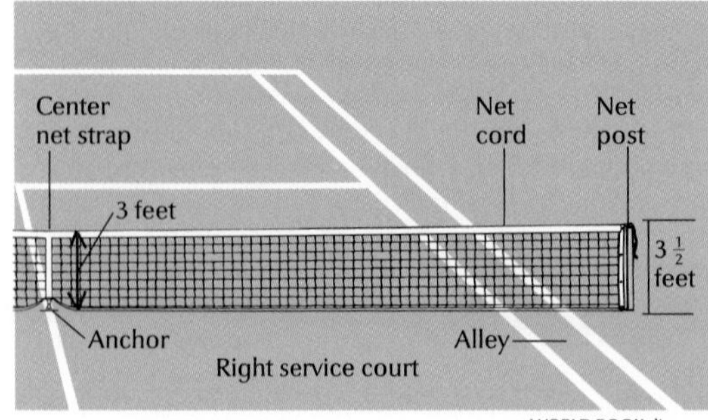

The net is suspended across the court by a cable or cord. Two posts, one outside each doubles sideline, support the net. A narrow strap in the middle holds the net tight.

Tennis clothes should fit comfortably so that a player can move freely. During the late 1800's and early 1900's, men players wore long-sleeved shirts and trousers, and women wore ankle-length dresses. Such bulky clothing limited a player's movements. Today, men wear short-sleeved shirts and shorts. Women wear minidresses or blouses and short skirts.

Shoes are perhaps the most important item in a player's wardrobe. Tennis shoes are designed specially for the sport. They are made of cloth and have rubber soles and no heels. The shoes help keep players from slipping and do not damage the court.

How tennis is played

Before they begin to play tennis, the players must decide who serves first and which end of the court each player or team will defend. Most players make these decisions by means of a racket "toss." For example, they may use the manufacturer's markings on one side of a racket handle as "heads" and on the other side as "tails." One player stands the racket upright on the frame and spins it. The opposing player or team calls which side will land faceup. If the call is correct, the player or team may either (1) choose to serve or receive first or (2) decide which end of the court to defend.

The court diagram in this article locates the various lines and playing areas discussed in this section.

Scoring. Tennis is scored in terms of points, games, and sets. A player or doubles team scores a *point* when the opposing side fails to return the ball properly or commits an error. To win a *game,* one side must score four points and lead by at least two points. The first

Terms used in tennis

Ace, or *service ace,* is a point scored by a server when the receiver is unable to touch a legal serve.
Deuce is a tie score after 6 points in a game or 10 games in a set.
Fault is called when a player serves into the net or outside the receiver's service court. A server commits a *foot fault* by stepping over the base line or changing position by walking or running before hitting the ball during a service. A server who makes two faults in a row commits a *double fault* and loses a point.
Game is the next highest unit of scoring after a point. To win a game, a player must score at least four points and lead by at least two points.
Ground stroke is any shot that a player uses after the ball bounces once on the court.
Let is a serve that hits the net and drops into the proper service court. A let does not count and is replayed.
Lob is a shot hit high into the air. It is intended to land behind an opponent, forcing the player to retreat from the net.
Love is the scoring term for zero.
Overhead smash is a hard swing at an opponent's shot from above the head.
Set is the highest unit of scoring in a match. To win a set, a player or team must win at least six games and lead by at least two games unless a tie breaker is played.
Tie breaker is a play-off of a certain number of points to decide the winner of a set. Many tie breakers are played after the game score reaches 6-6.
Volley is any shot made by hitting the ball before it bounces on the court.

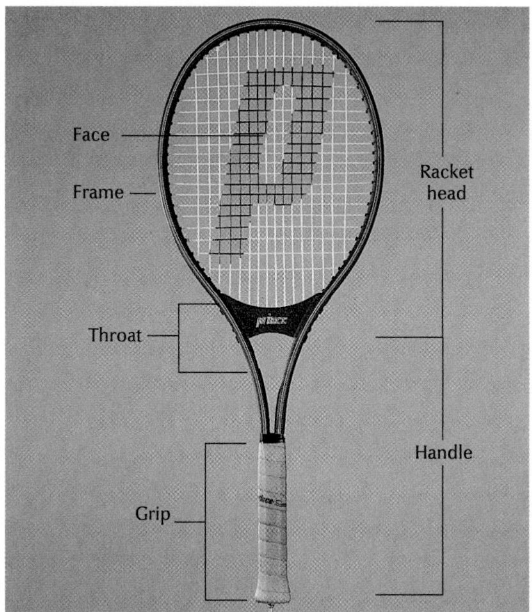

WORLD BOOK photo

A typical tennis racket has a frame made of 85 percent fiberglass and 15 percent graphite. The racket's face is a net of nylon or other synthetic material. Leather covers the grip.

point is called *15;* the second, *30;* the third, *40;* and the fourth, *game point.* A score of zero is called *love.* Historians are not certain how this scoring system began.

The server's score is always given first. For example, if the serving side leads three points to one, the score is *40-15.* If the receiving side wins the first two points, the score is *love-30.* If both sides win three points, the score is *40-40,* which is called *deuce.* To win a deuce game, one side must lead by two points. The first point scored after deuce is called the *advantage* or *ad.* If the server wins the first point after deuce, the point is often announced as *ad in.* If the receiving side wins the point, it may be announced as *ad out.* If the side with the advantage loses the next point, the game returns to deuce.

To win a *set,* one side must win six games and lead by at least two games. If the game score is 5-5—a deuce set—play continues until one side has a two-game margin. In some tournaments, if the score reaches 6-6, a *tie breaker* is played. It consists of a play-off of a certain number of points. The side that wins the tie breaker wins the set by a score of 7-6.

In most competitions, the first side to win two sets wins the tennis *match.* In some tournaments, the first side to win three sets takes the match.

The serve, or *service,* puts the ball into play at the start of each game and after each point is scored. The server must toss the ball into the air and hit it before it strikes the ground. The ball must then travel into the service court diagonally opposite. The server begins each game by serving from the right side of the court. The serve then alternates between the left and right sides following each point. The server must serve from behind the base line and within the imaginary continuation of the center mark and the singles sideline.

In a singles match, a player serves until a game is completed. Then the receiver serves. The players continue to alternate serves after each game. In a doubles match, the serve also changes sides after each game. In addition, the members of each team alternate serves. If a team serves odd-numbered games, for example, one member would serve the first game, the other the third game, and so on. In both singles and doubles matches, the opposing players change ends of the court after the first, third, and all following odd-numbered games.

If a serve lands in the net or outside the receiver's service court, the server has committed a *fault.* A server commits a *foot fault* by stepping on or over the base line or changing position by running or walking before hitting the ball. A player who commits a fault or foot fault gets a second serve. But if this serve fails through a fault or foot fault, the player has committed a *double fault* and loses the point. If the ball hits the top of the net and drops into the proper service court, the serve is called a *let* and is replayed. A let is also called if a player serves before the receiver is ready.

A powerful, accurate serve can help a player win easy points. A player can serve an *ace,* which is a legal serve that the receiver is unable to touch. Even if the receiver manages to return a serve, the return may be so weak the server can easily hit a winning shot.

Receivers may stand anywhere on their end of the court during the service. A receiver often takes a position based on knowledge of an opponent's serve. If the server has a very fast serve, for example, the receiver will stand far back to allow enough time to sight the ball for the return shot.

The ball in play. After the serve, the receiver must hit the ball on the first bounce and return it over the net. The ball must land in the area bounded by the base line and the singles sidelines or, in team play, the doubles sidelines. A shot that lands on a sideline or base line is in play. A shot that hits the net and drops into the opposing court is also in play. After the ball has been served and returned, it may be hit either on the fly, which is called a *volley,* or after the first bounce, which is called a *ground stroke.* The players *rally* (hit the ball back and forth) until one side scores a point. During play, a player or team wins a point if the opposing side (1) hits the ball into the net, (2) hits the ball outside the court, (3) allows a ball to bounce twice, or (4) touches the ball.

Players may use a variety of ground strokes and volleys. The basic shots are the *forehand drive* and the *backhand drive.* Right-handed players hit a forehand drive on the right, or racket, side of the body. They hit a backhand drive by reaching across the body to the left side. Left-handed players hit a forehand drive on the left side and a backhand drive on the right.

To force an opponent away from the net, a player may hit a *lob*—a high shot deep into the opponent's court. The opponent must retreat from the net to reach the ball. If the lob is not hit deep enough, however, the opponent may reply with an *overhead smash.* This shot is made by hitting the ball from above the head. A smash often is so powerful that it cannot be returned.

By hitting the ball in a certain way, a player can give a shot *topspin* or *underspin.* Spin causes the ball to react in such a way that it is difficult to return. A lob hit with topspin accelerates. A shot hit with underspin decelerates.

The grip is the way in which a player holds the racket. Most players use a grip called the *Continental grip* to serve and a form of the *Eastern grip* to hit forehand and backhand drives. In each grip, the player places the palm and fingers on the handle as shown at the right.

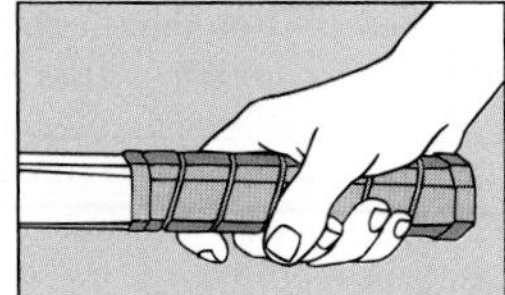

Continental serve

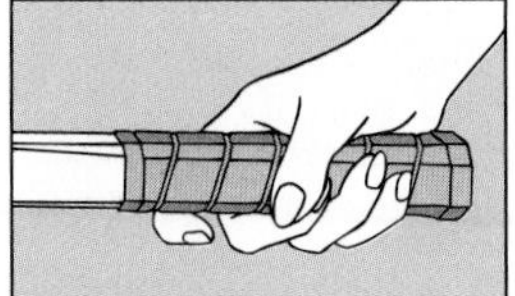

Eastern forehand

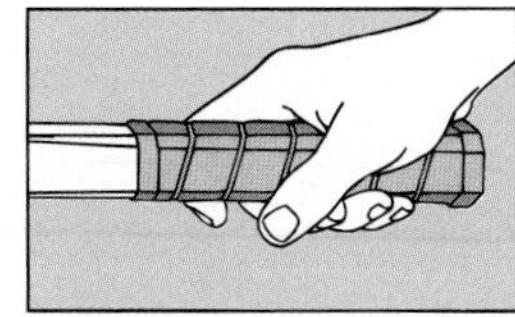

Eastern backhand

WORLD BOOK illustrations by James Curran

The serve. (1) The player points his racket toward the net and places one foot comfortably behind the other. (2 and 3) He then tosses the ball into the air with his thumb and first two fingers and starts his backswing. (4) He next moves the racket back until it is behind him and pointing toward the ground. (5) The player then hits the ball with his arm fully extended and the ball slightly in front of him. (6) He ends the stroke with a strong follow-through.

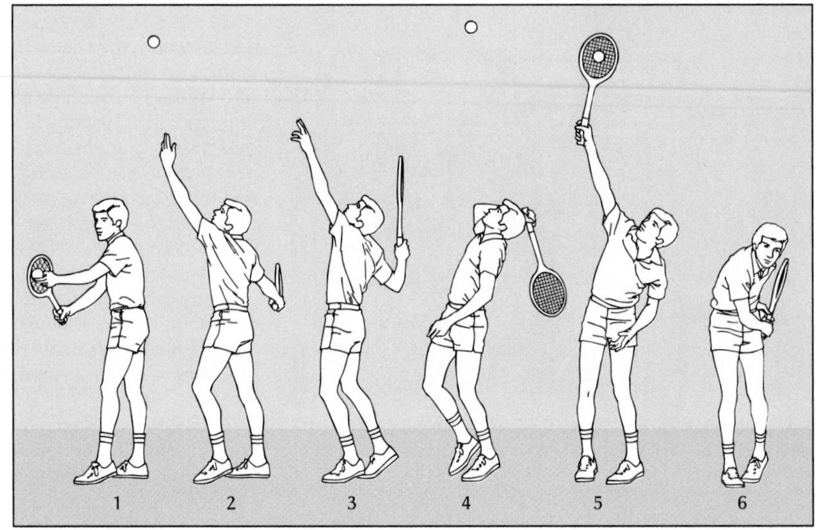

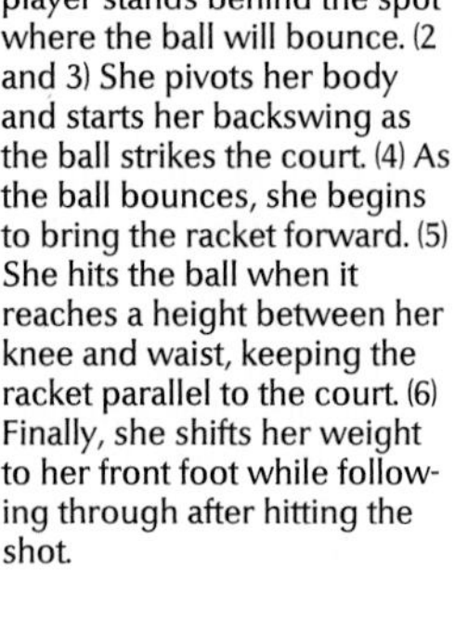

The forehand drive. (1) The player stands behind the spot where the ball will bounce. (2 and 3) She pivots her body and starts her backswing as the ball strikes the court. (4) As the ball bounces, she begins to bring the racket forward. (5) She hits the ball when it reaches a height between her knee and waist, keeping the racket parallel to the court. (6) Finally, she shifts her weight to her front foot while following through after hitting the shot.

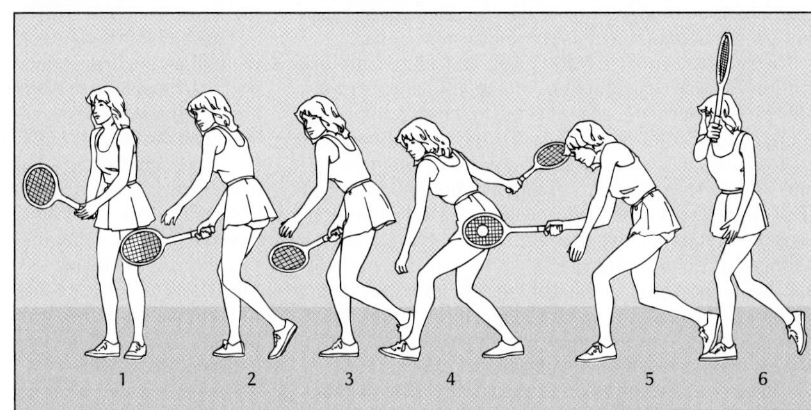

The backhand drive. (1) The player holds the grip with one hand and lightly grasps the throat of the racket with the other hand. (2) As he sights the ball, he turns his shoulder toward the net, pivots, and begins his backswing. (3) He ends the backswing with the racket behind him. (4 and 5) He then swings the racket forward, hip high and parallel to the court, and strikes the ball while it is still rising. (6) He follows through to complete the stroke.

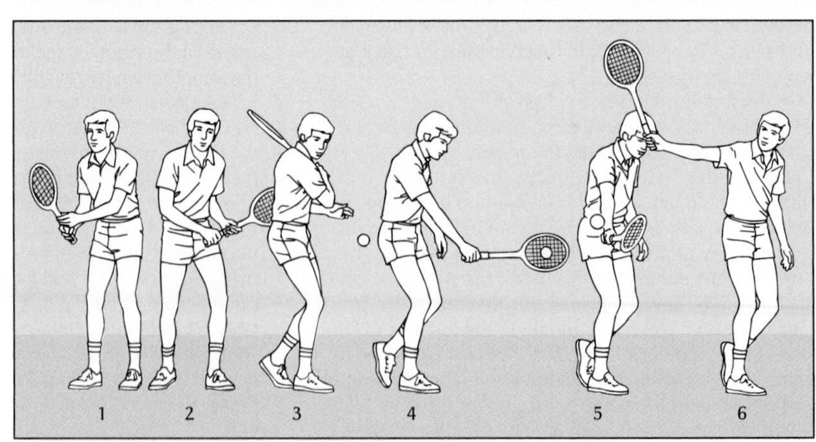

Officials. In most tennis matches, the players themselves act as officials and keep their own score. But in an important tournament, many officials may be used. The chief official is the tournament referee, who has charge of the entire tournament. On the court, the top official is the chair umpire. The chair umpire sits on a high chair alongside center court and announces the score to the crowd. The chair umpire also supervises as many as 13 linespersons. These officials are positioned along the lines around the court. They determine whether a ball has been served legally and whether shots are *good* (inside the court) or *out* (outside the court).

Organized tennis

Amateur tennis. Most of the world's tennis players are amateurs. They play for enjoyment and exercise and receive no pay. Many of them play in small organized interclub competitions, chiefly on weekends. High schools and colleges also sponsor tennis teams as part of their athletics programs.

The International Tennis Federation (ITF) governs tennis worldwide. It consists of the national tennis associations of about 100 countries. These associations include the U.S. Tennis Association, the Canadian Lawn Tennis Association, the Lawn Tennis Association of Australia, and the United Kingdom's Lawn Tennis Association.

Professional tennis. For many years, nearly all the world's leading tournament players were amateurs. Professional tennis first became widely accepted in the late 1960's, and today all the top players are professionals. Professionals play tennis for money, or they are paid for coaching or teaching the game.

Both men and women professionals have formed organizations to represent them and supervise their tournaments. Men professionals established the Association of Tennis Professionals in 1972. The same year, women professionals formed the Women's Tennis Association.

Tennis tournaments. Only amateurs could play in major tournaments before 1968. That year, the member countries of the ITF voted to allow amateurs and professionals to compete in the same tournaments. These events became known as *open* tournaments. Today, almost all major tournaments are open.

The most important tournaments for individual players are the national championships of Great Britain, the United States, Australia, and France. The British meet, popularly called the Wimbledon, is the most highly regarded of the world's major championships. Together, the four championships make up the *grand slam.* Only two men have won all four in the same year. Don Budge of the United States won the grand slam in 1938. Rod Laver of Australia is the only player to win it twice, in 1962 and 1969. Three women have won the grand slam—Maureen Connolly of the United States in 1953, Margaret Smith Court of Australia in 1970, and Steffi Graf of West Germany in 1988.

Three organizations are in charge of professional tournaments. The ITF supervises the major international events, including the grand slam tournaments. The ITF also organizes international junior tournaments in which young players compete for international rankings. The Association of Tennis Professionals (ATP) organizes the men's professional tennis tour. The Women's Tennis Association (WTA) supervises the women's professional tour. Both the ATP and WTA set schedules for the tours and award dates to the sponsors.

Most amateur and professional tournaments use a system called *seeding* to prevent top players from meeting each other in an early round. The best player would be seeded number one; the next best, number two; and so on. Players are seeded according to their records and reputations. One player is normally seeded for every four in the tournament. Matches are arranged so that seeded players do not face each other until the quarterfinal round, unless unseeded players defeat them.

Several tournaments are held for international team trophies. The best-known trophy is the Davis Cup, donated in 1900 by Dwight Davis, an American player. Competition for the cup takes place every year for teams of men players from 16 eligible nations. The teams meet in a series, called a *tie,* consisting of one doubles and four singles matches. The ITF supervises the tournament. For the annual results of the final round of cup competition, see **Davis Cup.**

In 1963, the International Tennis Federation established the Federation Cup for teams of women representing member nations. Each round in this elimination tournament consists of two singles and one doubles.

History

Beginnings. Most historians agree that the French originated tennis during the 1100's or 1200's. The French called it *jeu de paume,* meaning *game of the palm.* The players batted the ball back and forth over a net with the palm of their hand.

Major Walter Clopton Wingfield of England is generally considered the father of modern tennis. In 1873, he introduced a version of the game closely resembling the modern sport. In 1874, he patented tennis equipment and rules for playing on grass courts. Wingfield called the game *sphairistike,* the Greek word for *playing ball.* But the name was soon replaced by *lawn tennis.* Some historians feel that Major Harry Gem of England should share credit as the sport's founder. Gem played a form of tennis in the 1860's.

Tennis soon replaced croquet as England's most popular outdoor sport. In 1877, the All England Croquet Club changed its name to the All England Lawn Tennis and Croquet Club. Also in 1877, the club sponsored the first major tennis tournament at its headquarters in Wimbledon, a suburb of London. This tournament has become the unofficial world championship for men's and women's singles and doubles.

The spread of tennis. Mary Ewing Outerbridge, an American sportswoman, introduced tennis into the United States. In 1874, she purchased tennis equipment from British army officers in Bermuda. Outerbridge used the equipment to set up the first U.S. tennis court. The court was on the grounds of the Staten Island Cricket and Baseball Club in New York City.

The United States National Lawn Tennis Association (now the United States Tennis Association) was established in 1881. That same year, the association sponsored the first U.S. men's championship tournament in Newport, Rhode Island.

In 1900, the American player Dwight Davis donated the Davis Cup to be awarded annually to the country that wins the world's men's championship. The trophy

All-England (Wimbledon) Championships

The All-England Championships are held annually in the London suburb of Wimbledon. Men's competition began in 1877, and women's competition in 1884. This table lists the Wimbledon singles champions since 1920.

Men's singles

Year	Winner	Country
1920	Bill Tilden	United States
1921	Bill Tilden	United States
1922	Gerald Patterson	Australia
1923	Bill Johnston	United States
1924	Jean Borotra	France
1925	René Lacoste	France
1926	Jean Borotra	France
1927	Henri Cochet	France
1928	René Lacoste	France
1929	Henri Cochet	France
1930	Bill Tilden	United States
1931	Sid Wood	United States
1932	Ellsworth Vines	United States
1933	Jack Crawford	Australia
1934	Fred Perry	United Kingdom
1935	Fred Perry	United Kingdom
1936	Fred Perry	United Kingdom
1937	Don Budge	United States
1938	Don Budge	United States
1939	Bobby Riggs	United States
1940-45		No competition
1946	Yvon Petra	France
1947	Jack Kramer	United States
1948	Bob Falkenburg	United States
1949	Ted Schroeder	United States
1950	Budge Patty	United States
1951	Dick Savitt	United States
1952	Frank Sedgman	Australia
1953	Vic Seixas	United States
1954	Jaroslav Drobny	Egypt
1955	Tony Trabert	United States
1956	Lew Hoad	Australia
1957	Lew Hoad	Australia
1958	Ashley Cooper	Australia
1959	Alex Olmedo	United States
1960	Neale Fraser	Australia
1961	Rod Laver	Australia
1962	Rod Laver	Australia
1963	Chuck McKinley	United States
1964	Roy Emerson	Australia
1965	Roy Emerson	Australia
1966	Manuel Santana	Spain
1967	John Newcombe	Australia
1968	Rod Laver	Australia
1969	Rod Laver	Australia
1970	John Newcombe	Australia
1971	John Newcombe	Australia
1972	Stan Smith	United States
1973	Jan Kodes	Czechoslovakia
1974	Jimmy Connors	United States
1975	Arthur Ashe	United States
1976	Björn Borg	Sweden
1977	Björn Borg	Sweden
1978	Björn Borg	Sweden
1979	Björn Borg	Sweden
1980	Björn Borg	Sweden
1981	John McEnroe	United States
1982	Jimmy Connors	United States
1983	John McEnroe	United States
1984	John McEnroe	United States
1985	Boris Becker	West Germany
1986	Boris Becker	West Germany
1987	Pat Cash	Australia
1988	Stefan Edberg	Sweden
1989	Boris Becker	West Germany
1990	Stefan Edberg	Sweden
1991	Michael Stich	Germany
1992	Andre Agassi	United States
1993	Pete Sampras	United States
1994	Pete Sampras	United States
1995	Pete Sampras	United States
1996	Richard Krajicek	Netherlands
1997	Pete Sampras	United States
1998	Pete Sampras	United States
1999	Pete Sampras	United States
2000	Pete Sampras	United States
2001	Goran Ivanisevic	Croatia
2002	Lleyton Hewitt	Australia
2003	Roger Federer	Switzerland
2004	Roger Federer	Switzerland
2005	Roger Federer	Switzerland

Women's singles

Year	Winner	Country
1920	Suzanne Lenglen	France
1921	Suzanne Lenglen	France
1922	Suzanne Lenglen	France
1923	Suzanne Lenglen	France
1924	Kitty McKane	United Kingdom
1925	Suzanne Lenglen	France
1926	Kitty McKane Godfree	United Kingdom
1927	Helen Wills	United States
1928	Helen Wills	United States
1929	Helen Wills	United States
1930	Helen Wills Moody	United States
1931	Cilly Aussem	Germany
1932	Helen Wills Moody	United States
1933	Helen Wills Moody	United States
1934	Dorothy Round	United Kingdom
1935	Helen Wills Moody	United States
1936	Helen Hull Jacobs	United States
1937	Dorothy Round	United Kingdom
1938	Helen Wills Moody	United States
1939	Alice Marble	United States
1940-45		No competition
1946	Pauline Betz	United States
1947	Margaret Osborne	United States
1948	Louise Brough	United States
1949	Louise Brough	United States
1950	Louise Brough	United States
1951	Doris Hart	United States
1952	Maureen Connolly	United States
1953	Maureen Connolly	United States
1954	Maureen Connolly	United States
1955	Louise Brough	United States
1956	Shirley Fry	United States
1957	Althea Gibson	United States
1958	Althea Gibson	United States
1959	Maria Bueno	Brazil
1960	Maria Bueno	Brazil
1961	Angela Mortimer	United Kingdom
1962	Karen Hantze Susman	United States
1963	Margaret Smith	Australia
1964	Maria Bueno	Brazil
1965	Margaret Smith	Australia
1966	Billie Jean King	United States
1967	Billie Jean King	United States
1968	Billie Jean King	United States
1969	Ann Haydon Jones	United Kingdom
1970	Margaret Smith Court	Australia
1971	Evonne Goolagong	Australia
1972	Billie Jean King	United States
1973	Billie Jean King	United States
1974	Chris Evert	United States
1975	Billie Jean King	United States
1976	Chris Evert	United States
1977	Virginia Wade	United Kingdom
1978	Martina Navratilova	United States
1979	Martina Navratilova	United States
1980	Evonne Goolagong	Australia
1981	Chris Evert Lloyd	United States
1982	Martina Navratilova	United States
1983	Martina Navratilova	United States
1984	Martina Navratilova	United States
1985	Martina Navratilova	United States
1986	Martina Navratilova	United States
1987	Martina Navratilova	United States
1988	Steffi Graf	West Germany
1989	Steffi Graf	West Germany
1990	Martina Navratilova	United States
1991	Steffi Graf	Germany
1992	Steffi Graf	Germany
1993	Steffi Graf	Germany
1994	Conchita Martinez	Spain
1995	Steffi Graf	Germany
1996	Steffi Graf	Germany
1997	Martina Hingis	Switzerland
1998	Jana Novotna	Czech Republic
1999	Lindsay Davenport	United States
2000	Venus Williams	United States
2001	Venus Williams	United States
2002	Serena Williams	United States
2003	Serena Williams	United States
2004	Maria Sharapova	Russia
2005	Venus Williams	United States

United States Open

The United States Open is held in Flushing Meadow in New York City. This table lists winners since competition was opened to professionals in 1968. The champions listed before 1968 won amateur competitions called the United States National Championships. Men's competition began in 1881, and women's in 1887. This table lists U.S. singles champions since 1920.

Men's singles

Year	Winner	Country
1920	Bill Tilden	United States
1921	Bill Tilden	United States
1922	Bill Tilden	United States
1923	Bill Tilden	United States
1924	Bill Tilden	United States
1925	Bill Tilden	United States
1926	René Lacoste	France
1927	René Lacoste	France
1928	Henri Cochet	France
1929	Bill Tilden	United States
1930	John Doeg	United States
1931	Ellsworth Vines	United States
1932	Ellsworth Vines	United States
1933	Fred Perry	United Kingdom
1934	Fred Perry	United Kingdom
1935	Wilmer Allison	United States
1936	Fred Perry	United Kingdom
1937	Don Budge	United States
1938	Don Budge	United States
1939	Bobby Riggs	United States
1940	Don McNeill	United States
1941	Bobby Riggs	United States
1942	Ted Schroeder	United States
1943	Joe Hunt	United States
1944	Frank Parker	United States
1945	Frank Parker	United States
1946	Jack Kramer	United States
1947	Jack Kramer	United States
1948	Pancho Gonzalez	United States
1949	Pancho Gonzalez	United States
1950	Art Larsen	United States
1951	Frank Sedgman	Australia
1952	Frank Sedgman	Australia
1953	Tony Trabert	United States
1954	Vic Seixas	United States
1955	Tony Trabert	United States
1956	Ken Rosewall	Australia
1957	Mal Anderson	Australia
1958	Ashley Cooper	Australia
1959	Neale Fraser	Australia
1960	Neale Fraser	Australia
1961	Roy Emerson	Australia
1962	Rod Laver	Australia
1963	Rafael Osuna	Mexico
1964	Roy Emerson	Australia
1965	Manuel Santana	Spain
1966	Fred Stolle	Australia
1967	John Newcombe	Australia
1968	Arthur Ashe	United States
1969	Rod Laver	Australia
1970	Ken Rosewall	Australia
1971	Stan Smith	United States
1972	Ilie Nastase	Romania
1973	John Newcombe	Australia
1974	Jimmy Connors	United States
1975	Manuel Orantes	Spain
1976	Jimmy Connors	United States
1977	Guillermo Vilas	Argentina
1978	Jimmy Connors	United States
1979	John McEnroe	United States
1980	John McEnroe	United States
1981	John McEnroe	United States
1982	Jimmy Connors	United States
1983	Jimmy Connors	United States
1984	John McEnroe	United States
1985	Ivan Lendl	Czechoslovakia
1986	Ivan Lendl	Czechoslovakia
1987	Ivan Lendl	Czechoslovakia
1988	Mats Wilander	Sweden
1989	Boris Becker	West Germany
1990	Pete Sampras	United States
1991	Stefan Edberg	Sweden
1992	Stefan Edberg	Sweden
1993	Pete Sampras	United States
1994	Andre Agassi	United States
1995	Pete Sampras	United States
1996	Pete Sampras	United States
1997	Patrick Rafter	Australia
1998	Patrick Rafter	Australia
1999	Andre Agassi	United States
2000	Marat Safin	Russia
2001	Lleyton Hewitt	Australia
2002	Pete Sampras	United States
2003	Andy Roddick	United States
2004	Roger Federer	Switzerland
2005	Roger Federer	Switzerland

Women's singles

Year	Winner	Country
1920	Molla Bjurstedt Mallory	United States
1921	Molla Bjurstedt Mallory	United States
1922	Molla Bjurstedt Mallory	United States
1923	Helen Wills	United States
1924	Helen Wills	United States
1925	Helen Wills	United States
1926	Molla Bjurstedt Mallory	United States
1927	Helen Wills	United States
1928	Helen Wills	United States
1929	Helen Wills	United States
1930	Betty Nuthall	United Kingdom
1931	Helen Wills Moody	United States
1932	Helen Hull Jacobs	United States
1933	Helen Hull Jacobs	United States
1934	Helen Hull Jacobs	United States
1935	Helen Hull Jacobs	United States
1936	Alice Marble	United States
1937	Anita Lizana	Chile
1938	Alice Marble	United States
1939	Alice Marble	United States
1940	Alice Marble	United States
1941	Sarah Palfrey Cooke	United States
1942	Pauline Betz	United States
1943	Pauline Betz	United States
1944	Pauline Betz	United States
1945	Sarah Palfrey Cooke	United States
1946	Pauline Betz	United States
1947	Louise Brough	United States
1948	Margaret Osborne duPont	United States
1949	Margaret Osborne duPont	United States
1950	Margaret Osborne duPont	United States
1951	Maureen Connolly	United States
1952	Maureen Connolly	United States
1953	Maureen Connolly	United States
1954	Doris Hart	United States
1955	Doris Hart	United States
1956	Shirley Fry	United States
1957	Althea Gibson	United States
1958	Althea Gibson	United States
1959	Maria Bueno	Brazil
1960	Darlene Hard	United States
1961	Darlene Hard	United States
1962	Margaret Smith	Australia
1963	Maria Bueno	Brazil
1964	Maria Bueno	Brazil
1965	Margaret Smith	Australia
1966	Maria Bueno	Brazil
1967	Billie Jean King	United States
1968	Virginia Wade	United Kingdom
1969	Margaret Smith Court	Australia
1970	Margaret Smith Court	Australia
1971	Billie Jean King	United States
1972	Billie Jean King	United States
1973	Margaret Smith Court	Australia
1974	Billie Jean King	United States
1975	Chris Evert	United States
1976	Chris Evert	United States
1977	Chris Evert	United States
1978	Chris Evert	United States
1979	Tracy Austin	United States
1980	Chris Evert Lloyd	United States
1981	Tracy Austin	United States
1982	Chris Evert Lloyd	United States
1983	Martina Navratilova	United States
1984	Martina Navratilova	United States
1985	Hana Mandlikova	Czechoslovakia
1986	Martina Navratilova	United States
1987	Martina Navratilova	United States
1988	Steffi Graf	West Germany
1989	Steffi Graf	West Germany
1990	Gabriela Sabatini	Argentina
1991	Monica Seles	Yugoslavia
1992	Monica Seles	Yugoslavia
1993	Steffi Graf	Germany
1994	Arantxa Sanchez Vicario	Spain
1995	Steffi Graf	Germany
1996	Steffi Graf	Germany
1997	Martina Hingis	Switzerland
1998	Lindsay Davenport	United States
1999	Serena Williams	United States
2000	Venus Williams	United States
2001	Venus Williams	United States
2002	Serena Williams	United States
2003	Justine Henin-Hardenne	Belgium
2004	Svetlana Kuznetsova	Russia
2005	Kim Clijsters	Belgium

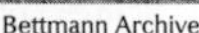

Bettmann Archive

United Press Int.

Great women players include Hazel Hotchkiss Wightman, *left,* and Helen Wills Moody, *right,* of the United States. Wightman starred in the early 1900's, and Moody during the 1920's and 1930's.

became recognized as the top prize in team tennis.

Many of the greatest stars in tennis history played during the 1920's. But the period was dominated by Bill Tilden, an American who is generally considered the sport's finest male player. Tilden won the United States singles title every year from 1920 through 1925 and again in 1929. He also won the Wimbledon championship three times.

The top women players in the 1920's were Suzanne Lenglen of France and Helen Wills (later Helen Wills Moody) of the United States. Lenglen won six Wimbledon and six French championships. Moody won eight Wimbledon and seven U.S. championships.

Perhaps the outstanding individual player of the 1930's was Don Budge of the United States. In 1938, Budge became the first player to win the grand slam.

The mid-1900's. Until the 1950's, France, the United Kingdom, and the United States produced almost all of the world's major players. Then Australia became the leader in men's competition. From 1950 through 1967, Australian teams won the Davis Cup 15 times. Such players as Roy Emerson, Lew Hoad, Rod Laver, John Newcombe, Ken Rosewall, Frank Sedgman, and Fred Stolle helped Australia maintain its top international position.

During the 1940's and 1950's, several American players achieved worldwide success. The most notable included Pancho Gonzalez, Jack Kramer, Art Larsen, Frank Parker, Ted Schroeder, Vic Seixas, and Tony Trabert.

The United States provided most of the top women players from the mid-1940's through the mid-1960's. Its stars included Louise Brough, Maureen Connolly, Margaret Osborne duPont, and Doris Hart. Connolly was probably this period's greatest woman player. In 1953, she became the first woman to win the grand slam.

Althea Gibson of the United States became the first important black tennis player. She won the U.S. and Wimbledon titles in 1957 and 1958. In the late 1960's, Arthur Ashe of the United States became the first black male tennis star. In 1968, he won the U.S. singles title.

Laver ranked as the top male star of the 1960's. The Australian became the only player to win the grand slam twice, in 1962 as an amateur and in 1969 as a professional. Other leading male players of the 1960's included Manuel Santana of Spain and Stan Smith of the United States. In the 1960's, Margaret Smith (later Margaret Smith Court) became the first Australian woman to win the U.S. and Wimbledon singles titles. She won the grand slam in 1970. Maria Bueno of Brazil and Billie Jean King of the United States also ranked as important players of the period.

Tennis today. International tennis has largely been a professional sport since 1968. Professionals compete for

United Press Int.

United Press Int.

Great men players include, *from left to right,* Bill Tilden of the United States and Rod Laver of Australia. Tilden dominated international competition throughout the 1920's. Laver was the world's leading player during the 1960's.

Focus on Sports

Focus on Sports

© Bob Martin, Allsport

Modern women tennis stars include, *from left to right,* Chris Evert and Martina Navratilova of the United States and Steffi Graf of Germany. Evert and Navratilova dominated the sport from the mid-1970's to the late 1980's, when Graf became the leading player.

millions of dollars in prize money annually. Television played an important role in increasing the popularity of tennis during the 1970's and 1980's. Major tournaments are televised to many countries.

Several highly publicized matches were arranged largely for television audiences. In 1973, Bobby Riggs, a top-ranked American player of the late 1930's and 1940's, defeated Margaret Smith Court in a televised "battle of the sexes." Later that year, Riggs played Billie Jean King in the Houston Astrodome before 30,472 spectators, the largest crowd ever to watch a tennis match. Millions more people watched on television as King defeated Riggs.

The Davis Cup became a center of political dispute in the 1970's. In 1974, South Africa won the cup by forfeit from India. The Indian government refused to allow its team to play because of South Africa's *apartheid* (racial separation) policies. The Davis Cup had already lost some of its importance because many players refused to participate. They claimed that the many weeks of cup play-offs would force them to miss too many tournaments. In 1981, cup competition was compressed into a shorter time period and the prize money was increased.

By the mid-1970's, a new generation of players had begun to dominate tennis. The most successful men players of the 1970's and early 1980's included Jimmy Connors, Arthur Ashe, and John McEnroe of the United States; Björn Borg of Sweden; Guillermo Vilas of Argentina; and John Newcombe of Australia. Leading women players included Tracy Austin, Chris Evert, Andrea Jaeger, and Martina Navratilova of the United States; and Evonne Goolagong of Australia.

In 1990, Navratilova won her ninth women's singles title at Wimbledon, more than any other woman in the history of modern tennis. In 1992, Navratilova set a career record by winning her 158th singles championship.

By the mid-1990's, a new group of young players began to dominate the sport. The leading men players included Boris Becker of Germany; Thomas Muster of Austria; Marcelo Rios of Chile; and Andre Agassi,

Focus on Sports

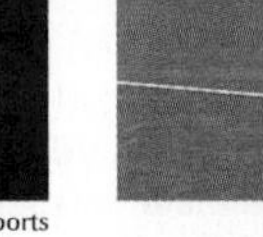

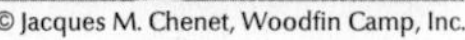

© Jacques M. Chenet, Woodfin Camp, Inc.

AP/Wide World

Modern men tennis stars include, *from left to right,* Björn Borg of Sweden and John McEnroe and Pete Sampras of the United States. Borg was the world's top player in the 1970's. McEnroe was a dominant player in the 1980's, and Sampras ranked among the top players of the 1990's.

The Williams sisters dominated women's tennis during the early 2000's. Serena Williams, *left,* and Venus Williams, *right,* both won several Grand Slam singles championships. The American sisters also won several titles as a doubles team.

© Adam Pretty, Getty Images

Michael Chang, Jim Courier, and Pete Sampras of the United States. Women stars included Conchita Martinez and Arantxa Sanchez Vicario of Spain; Steffi Graf of Germany; and Lindsay Davenport and Monica Seles of the United States. In the early 2000's, Martina Hingis of Switzerland and Jennifer Capriati and the sisters Serena and Venus Williams of the United States dominated women's tennis. Men's stars of the early 2000's included Lleyton Hewitt of Australia, Marat Safin of Russia, and Andy Roddick of the United States. Chris Evert

Related articles in *World Book* include:

Agassi, Andre
Ashe, Arthur
Badminton
Becker, Boris
Borg, Björn
Budge, Don
Connors, Jimmy
Court, Margaret Smith
Davis Cup
Evert, Chris
Gibson, Althea
Gonzalez, Pancho
Graf, Steffi
Hingis, Martina
King, Billie Jean
Laver, Rod
Lendl, Ivan
McEnroe, John
Moody, Helen Wills
Navratilova, Martina
Platform tennis
Roddick, Andy
Sampras, Pete
Seles, Monica
Table tennis
Tilden, Bill
Williams, Serena
Williams, Venus

Outline

I. The court and equipment
A. The court
B. Tennis balls
C. Tennis rackets
D. Tennis clothes

II. How tennis is played
A. Scoring
B. The serve
C. The ball in play
D. Officials

III. Organized tennis
A. Amateur tennis
B. Professional tennis
C. Tennis tournaments

IV. History

Questions

What is an open tournament?
How does a player hit a backhand drive?
What is a *tie breaker?*
Why have most grass courts been replaced by other surfaces?
What is a *fault?* A *double fault?*
When would a player hit a smash?
What is the Davis Cup?
What is the Wightman Cup?
Where is the All-England Championship held?
Who is considered the father of modern tennis?

Additional resources

Blackall, Bernie. *Tennis.* Heinemann Lib., 1999. Younger readers.
Gillmeister, Heiner. *Tennis.* 1997. Reprint. N. Y. Univ. Pr., 1998.
Perlstein, Scott. *Winning Tennis.* Lyons Pr., 1999.
World of Tennis. International Tennis Fed. Published annually.

Tennyson, Lord (1809-1892), was one of the most important English poets of the 1800's. He succeeded William Wordsworth as poet laureate of the United Kingdom in 1850. Tennyson earned his position in literature because of the remarkable range of his talents and his dedication throughout his long career to perfecting his art. Tennyson stands both as a great national poet and as one of the supreme craftsmen in the English language.

His life. Alfred Tennyson was born on Aug. 6, 1809, in Somersby, Lincolnshire. His father was *rector* (clergyman in charge) of the parish there. Tennyson entered Cambridge University in 1828 but never got a degree. At Cambridge, he joined "The Apostles," a society of undergraduates that included several men who later became intellectual leaders of the age. Tennyson's closest friend in this circle was Arthur Henry Hallam. Hallam's sudden death in 1833 was a crucial event in the poet's life. Tennyson wrote his great *elegy* (poem mourning a death) *In Memoriam* (1850) in memory of Hallam.

Tennyson was the most popular British poet of the Victorian era, but he avoided public life. He married in 1850 and lived quietly in his country homes at Farringford on the Isle of Wight and Aldworth in Surrey. Tennyson's long list of works showed his consistent inspiration and creative vitality, beginning with *Poems, Chiefly Lyrical* (1830) and extending to *The Death of Oenone and Other Poems,* published after Tennyson's death on Oct. 6, 1892. He was awarded the title of Baron Tennyson in 1883. His full title was Baron of Aldworth and Farringford.

His poems. Tennyson's influential place in the intellectual life of his age comes largely from his concern with the vital issues confronting Victorian England. He reveals his sense of political responsibility in such patriotic verses as "Ode on the Death of the Duke of Wellington" and his famous "The Charge of the Light Brigade," which was inspired by an incident in the Crimean War (see **Balaklava, Battle of**). *Maud,* which is a narrative in the form of separate lyrics, describes the withering effect of the materialistic spirit of his day on a sensitive young lover.

Tennyson's accurate and concrete descriptions of nature reflect his informed interest in science. The stars, for example, suggest to the unhappy speaker in *Maud:*

> A sad astrology, the boundless plan
> That makes you tyrants in your iron skies,
> Innumerable, pitiless, passionless eyes,
> Cold fires, yet with power to burn and brand
> His nothingness into man.

Tennyson's masterpiece, *In Memoriam,* consists of 133 individual poems composed between his friend Arthur Hallam's death in 1833 and their publication in 1850. The work ranks as one of the greatest examples of the elegy in English poetry. *In Memoriam* is personal and specific in its focus on Tennyson's struggles as artist and thinker. The poem frequently offers general consolation to a troubled age:

> I stretch lame hands of faith and grope,
> And gather dust and chaff, and call
> To what I feel is Lord of all,
> And faintly trust the larger hope.

Perhaps no English poet had a more acute ear for fine shades of poetic expression or a greater range of verse style than Tennyson. His exquisite lyrics perfectly express emotions and experiences shared by all people. Among the most moving of these are many of the sections from *In Memoriam,* as well as "Break, Break, Break" and "Tears, Idle Tears." Following the author's wishes, "Crossing the Bar," the noble address to death, always ends collections of his poems.

Tennyson's most characteristic form of poetry was the idyl, a poem about country life developed by the ancient Greeks. These poems often take the form of dramatic *reveries* (daydreams) spoken by mythical figures. They tell a story, but depend primarily on the creation of mood through the power of richly described settings, as in "The Lotos-Eaters." Many of these stories indirectly urge Victorians to act heroically. The speakers commonly fall into two groups: the lovelorn maidens of "Mariana," "The Lady of Shalott," and "Oenone"; and the aged heroes and prophets of "Ulysses," "Tithonus," "Tiresias," and "Merlin and the Gleam."

Tennyson's lifelong fascination with King Arthur and his knights led to his *Idylls of the King,* a series of 12 narrative poems that he constantly revised between 1842 and 1885. The work has an *allegorical* (symbolic) side, suggested by the many implied comparisons between Arthur and Queen Victoria's husband, Prince Albert, who had died in 1861. It also ends with an allegorical *epilogue* (closing) to the queen with its invitation to:

> accept this old imperfect tale
> New-old, and shadowing Sense at war with Soul,
> Ideal manhood closed in real man ...

Nevertheless, the poem is most likely to move a modern audience as the story of King Arthur's vision of the perfect state. This vision was tragically betrayed by the inability of the king's followers to live up to his heroic ideals. Richard J. Dunn

See also **Galahad, Sir; January** (Quotations); **Poetry** (Introduction).

Additional resources

Levi, Peter. *Tennyson.* Scribner, 1994.
Martin, Robert B. *Tennyson.* Oxford, 1980.
Page, Norman. *Tennyson.* New Amsterdam, 1993.
Ricks, Christopher. *Tennyson.* 2nd ed. Univ. of Calif. Pr., 1989.

Tenochtitlan, *tay nohch TEE tlahn,* was the capital of the Aztec empire. It stood at the site of present-day Mexico City. The Aztec established Tenochtitlan between about 1325 and 1350 on an island in what was then Lake Texcoco. From the city, the Aztec ruled most of central and southern Mexico and parts of Guatemala in the 1400's and early 1500's. By 1520, Tenochtitlan was one of the world's largest cities in population. It had about 200,000 to 300,000 people and covered about 8 square miles (20 square kilometers). Spain controlled the city briefly in 1519 and 1520 and conquered and destroyed it in 1521. The Spaniards built Mexico City over the ruins. Lake Texcoco was drained in the 1600's.

Tenochtitlan contained plazas, palaces, and pyramids topped with temples, as well as ball courts and a zoo. The Great Temple, a pyramid that stood about 130 feet (40 meters) tall, dominated the center of the city. The people grew much of their food on small islands they made by scooping up mud from the bottom of Lake Texcoco. Canals crisscrossed the city, and raised earthen roads linked it to the mainland. Parts of Tenochtitlan's buildings can be seen in Mexico City. Payson Sheets

See also **Aztec** (History); **Indian, American** (Indians of Middle America [picture: The Aztec capital]).

Tenrec is the name of about 30 species of small mammals that live primarily in Madagascar. There are two main types, *shrew tenrecs* and *hedgehog tenrecs.* They vary widely in appearance and habitat. Shrew tenrecs have a long tail and soft fur. Hedgehog tenrecs have a short tail or no tail at all, and stiff, needlelike spines on the back. Some tenrecs live in trees, some live underground, and others are aquatic.

Tenrecs range in size from about 1 ½ to 15 inches (4 to 38 centimeters) long. They have small eyes, small ears, and a long nose with long whiskers. Tenrecs eat small animals, especially insects and earthworms. Some species also eat fruits and other plant material. Most tenrecs move about at night and sleep during the day. Tenrecs may hibernate during periods of dry or cool weather for up to six months. Duane A. Schlitter

Scientific classification. Tenrecs belong to the tenrec family, Tenrecidae.

© H. Uible, Photo Researchers

The greater hedgehog tenrec has needlelike, white-tipped spines on its back. It lives in Madagascar.

Tense is a feature of verbs that indicates the time of an action. There are three divisions of time—present, past, and future. Within these divisions, English has six tenses—present, past, future, present perfect, past perfect, and future perfect.

Simple past and present tense are the only forms of English verbs that can express time by themselves. All other forms include *helping verbs,* also called *auxiliaries.* These forms combine such helping verbs as *has, had, will,* or *shall* with the simple present *(see),* the present participle *(seeing),* or the past participle *(seen).* The following list shows examples of all six tenses:

Present	She sees.
Past	She saw.
Future	She will see.
Present perfect	She has seen.
Past perfect	She had seen.
Future perfect	She will have seen.

These tenses are written in the *active voice,* in which the subject performs the action. For a complete list of the tenses for all forms of a verb, see **Conjugation.**

The *progressive* forms of a verb indicate that an action is in progress at a particular time—for example, *She is seeing the picture for the first time.* The *emphatic* forms provide emphasis, as in *She does see.* However, this form is more commonly used to ask questions, such as *Does she see?* It is also used to make negative statements, such as *She does not see.*

The perfect tenses express time relationships other than simple present, past, and future. The present perfect expresses an action that belongs to the past but touches the present: *Until now, we have seen Paris three times.* The past perfect expresses an action completed at some past time: *In 1945, we had seen Paris only once.* The future perfect expresses an action to be completed at some future time: *By next year, we will have seen Paris for the fourth time.* Patricia A. Moody

See also **Verb.**

Tenskwatawa. See **Shawnee Prophet.**

Tent is a portable shelter that many campers use for protection against the weather and insects. Most tents consist of a wooden, fiberglass, or metal frame with a covering and floor made of nylon, canvas, or cotton.

Tents range from small models for one person to large cabin tents for as many as six adults. Extremely large tents are used for such activities as circuses and church meetings. This article discusses camping tents.

Kinds of tents. There are over half a million styles and sizes of camping tents. Most of them are variations of one of four types: (1) A-frame tents, (2) dome and hoop tents, (3) umbrella tents, and (4) wall tents.

A-frame tents rise to a point at the top and resemble the letter *A.* One or two people can sleep in these small, lightweight tents, which are ideal for backpack trips. These tents are easy to pitch and relatively inexpensive.

Dome and hoop tents use arches in their design. They are lightweight but provide maximum space. Most mountaineering tents made for year-round use have a dome or hoop design. Because of their shape, these tents are stable and shed rain, snow, and wind well. Most of them are free-standing. Two to four people can sleep in them.

Umbrella tents are larger and heavier than A-frame tents. An umbrella tent has slightly slanted walls and a pyramid-shaped top. Some models have a center pole that decreases the space inside the tent, but newer ones lack this pole. Umbrella tents have sleeping space for four to six people. They are sturdy shelters that can withstand high winds.

Wall tents resemble small houses. They have vertical walls and an A-frame roof. They provide more sleeping and standing room than A-frame or umbrella tents but are harder to pitch. One kind of wall tent, the *cabin tent,* offers the highest degree of camping comfort. Its spacious interior and high walls allow more room for standing, walking, and sleeping than any other kind of tent. Wall tents and most umbrella tents are too large and heavy to carry in a backpack. They are used mainly by campers who drive to campsites.

Most tents are made of canvas or nylon. Canvas tents weigh much more but are less likely to leak. Some nylon tents are specially treated to prevent leakage. However, this treatment also seals moisture inside the tent and may cause the interior to become damp. Some nylon tents have a canvas roof that lets moisture escape. Most have a roof with an untreated nylon layer through which moisture can pass, plus a treated nylon covering, called a rain fly, which keeps rain out.

All tents provide some type of ventilation and protection against rain and insects. Cabin tents have large windows and a door, and smaller tents have vents and a door flap. In most tents, these openings are covered with netting that keeps insects out. Many tents have flaps to close over the windows during a storm. Some have a storm flap to put over the entire tent.

Caring for a tent. A tent properly cared for will last for years. It must be kept as clean and dry as possible. Insects and debris should be wiped off the tent each time it is taken down. If the tent is wet, it should be pitched and dried as soon as possible to avoid mildew and discoloration. After a camping trip, a tent should be cleaned and dried before storage. Canvas and nylon tents can be washed in mild detergent. Poles and stakes should not be packed with the tent fabric because they could puncture it. David VanDerWege

See also **Camping.**

Tent caterpillar is the *larva* (second stage in the life cycle) of certain moths that damage trees. Tent caterpillars get their name because most species spin loose, white, tentlike webs in the forks of trees. The caterpillars crawl from this tent to feed on leaves.

In midsummer, the female tent caterpillar moth lays masses of from 150 to 350 shiny brown eggs. The larvae hatch the following spring. After four to six weeks, the larvae migrate from the tree to find a protected place, such as beneath fallen leaves or branches. There, they spin silky white cocoons and enter the *pupa stage.* After 10 days to 2 weeks, pale brown moths emerge.

Tent caterpillars damage trees because they eat the leaves. A nest of these caterpillars can eat all the leaves on a small tree and kill it. The *eastern tent caterpillar* feeds on fruit and shade trees. It has a yellowish-white stripe edged by two orangish lines along its back.

The *forest tent caterpillar* is the only species that does not build a tent. It has two thin orange lines and a central line of white diamonds along its back. Both species are black with blue spots and whitish hair. They live in eastern and central North America. Tent caterpillars can be controlled by collecting their egg masses or by burning the larvae in their tents. Charles V. Covell, Jr.

Scientific classification. Tent caterpillars are larvae of moths in the tent caterpillar moth family, Lasiocampidae. They are in the genus *Malacosoma.*

Tentacle, *TEHN tuh kuhl,* is a slender and flexible growth on the head of certain animals. Tentacles are ordinarily used for protection or as feelers. Sea anemones and squids use tentacles to capture food. See also **Cnidarian; Jellyfish** (pictures); **Mollusk** (Gastropods; Octopuses and squids).

Tenure of Office Act. See **Johnson, Andrew** (Increased tension); **Reconstruction** (The impeachment of Johnson).

Tenzing Norgay (1914-1986), a Sherpa guide from Nepal, became one of the first two people to reach the top of Mount Everest and return. On May 29, 1953, Tenzing and Sir Edmund Hillary of New Zealand reached the 29,035-foot (8,850-meter) top of the mountain. Their expedition had spent more than two months moving supplies and equipment up the mountain. The men spent 15 minutes at the summit. Tenzing had tried six times previously to reach the top of Everest.

Tenzing was born in May 1914 in Thamey, a village in the Solo Khumbu, a district inhabited by Sherpa people in Nepal near the base of Mount Everest. The Sherpas had migrated to Tibet from Mongolia many years previously and then left Tibet to settle in the Solo Khumbu district. The Sherpas were known for their skill in mountain climbing. After his ascent with Hillary, Tenzing became internationally famous and a hero to the Sherpa and Nepalese people. He devoted the rest of his life to improving the way of life of the Sherpas. He died on May 9, 1986. Dennis R. Jackson

See also **Hillary, Sir Edmund P.; Mount Everest.**

Teotihuacán, *tay oh tee wah KAHN,* was one of the largest cities of ancient Mexico. Its population probably reached a peak of between 150,000 and 200,000 during the A.D. 500's. The city's ruins lie about 30 miles (50 kilometers) northeast of Mexico City.

Teotihuacán covered about 8 square miles (20 square kilometers). The city contained palaces, apartment buildings, a marketplace, and huge pyramids topped with temples. The streets were laid out in a grid pattern. The merchants traded with central and southern Mexico and what are now Belize and Guatemala.

Teotihuacán began as a small farming village. It stood near a cave used for religious ceremonies. By 100 B.C., Teotihuacán's population had begun to grow rapidly. This growth was due to an increasing number of worshipers at the cave and to the area's rich deposits of *obsidian* (volcanic glass), which was used in making tools. About 750, much of the city was burned, possibly during an invasion or a rebellion. After that, the population decreased. The Aztec Indians, who ruled much of Mexico in the 1400's and early 1500's, honored Teotihuacán as a religious center. Payson Sheets

See also **Monte Albán; Pyramid** (picture: The Pyramid of the Sun).

Tepee, also spelled *tipi,* was the type of tent most commonly used by the Plains tribes of North American Indians. A tepee was made by stretching a buffalo-skin covering over poles. The poles were arranged in the shape of a cone. At the top, the ends of the poles crossed and stuck out of the covering. Two flap "ears" were opened at the top to let out smoke from the campfire. The tent was pegged to the ground all around the bottom. The front had a slit partly closed with wooden pins to form an entrance. W. Roger Buffalohead

See also **Indian, American** (pictures); **Tent; Wigwam.**

Terbium, *TUR bee uhm* (chemical symbol, Tb), is a chemical element and one of the rare-earth metals. Terbium resembles silver in appearance. Many terbium compounds glow with a green color and are used in *phosphors,* dots on television picture tubes.

Terbium's *atomic number* (number of protons in its nucleus) is 65. Its *relative atomic mass* is 158.92534. A chemical element's relative atomic mass equals its *mass* (amount of matter) divided by $\frac{1}{12}$ of the mass of carbon 12, the most abundant form of carbon. Terbium has a density of 8.23 grams per cubic centimeter at 24 °C. It melts at about 1356 °C and boils at around 3230 °C.

The Swedish chemist Carl Mosander first discovered terbium in 1843. Another chemist, Georges Urbain of France, first isolated it in an almost pure form in 1905. Julia Y. Chan

See also **Element, Chemical; Rare earth.**

Terence, *TEHR uhns* (190?-159? B.C.), was a Roman comic playwright. His plays are essentially Latin versions of Greek plots, more refined than those of Plautus and marked by pure style, careful construction, and fine characterization. Six of his comedies survive. They are *The Woman of Andros, The Self-Tormentor, The Eunuch, Phormio, The Mother-in-Law,* and *The Brothers. The Brothers* is a thoughtful comedy about two brothers, a country man and a city man. Each brings up one of the sons of the country brother. The country man is strict, and the city man is permissive. The resulting idea, that education must pay attention to human nature, perhaps reflects Terence's own experience.

Terence was born Publius Terentius Afer in Carthage. He came to Rome as a slave in the household of a senator who educated and freed him. Anthony A. Barrett

Teresa, *tuh RAY suh,* **Mother** (1910-1997), was a Roman Catholic nun who received the 1979 Nobel Peace Prize for her work with the poor. She became known as the *saint of the gutters.* In 1950, Mother Teresa founded a religious order in Calcutta (now Kolkata), India, called the Missionaries of Charity. The order provides food for the needy and operates hospitals, schools, orphanages, youth centers, and shelters for lepers and the dying poor. It has branches in about 50 Indian cities and about 30 other countries.

Mother Teresa, whose original name was Agnes Gonxha Bojaxhiu, was born on Aug. 27, 1910, in what is now Skopje, Macedonia. In 1928, she joined a religious order, which sent her to India. She took the name *Teresa* after joining the order. A few years later, she began teaching in Calcutta. In 1948, the Catholic Church granted her permission to leave her convent and work among the city's poor people. She became an Indian citizen that year.

Wide World
Mother Teresa

Mother Teresa received

many awards for her work with the needy. These awards include the Pope John XXIII Peace Prize, which she received in 1971; India's Jawaharlal Nehru Award for International Understanding, given to her in 1972; and honorary U.S. citizenship, given to her in 1996. Mother Teresa died on Sept. 5, 1997. In 2003, Pope John Paul II *beatified* Mother Teresa. Beatification is an important step toward declaring a person a saint in the Roman Catholic Church. James McGovern

Teresa, *tuh REE suh* or *tay RAY sah,* **Saint** (1515-1582), also spelled *Theresa,* is a saint of the Roman Catholic Church. She was a Spanish nun, and is one of the patron saints of Spain.

Saint Teresa was born on March 28, 1515, at Avila in Old Castile. Her study at an Augustinian monastery and her reading of the tales of ancient martyrs inspired her to seek martyrdom for herself. In 1533, she entered a Carmelite convent. The lack of severity and *asceticism* (self-denial) displeased her, but for many years she made no attempt to bring about reforms.

A reading of the *Confessions* of Saint Augustine, combined with the death of her father and certain supernatural visitations, wakened in her a strong spirituality. She began to feel that it was her duty to restore the Carmelite order to the original austerity of its rule. Accordingly, she withdrew in 1562 and set up a new convent to put her ideas into effect. Opposition to her plan was strong, but the pope approved of the idea. At last, the general of the order asked her to introduce her reforms into other convents. She opened many new convents in Castile and even beyond its boundaries, and accomplished much in her efforts to reform existing Carmelite houses.

Several cities contended for her body after her death on Oct. 4, 1582, at Alba de Tormes, near Salamanca. The power of working miracles was believed to be in her relics, which were carried to various places. Pope Gregory canonized her in 1622. Saint Teresa wrote an autobiography and several treatises and letters, all published in 1587. Her feast day is October 15. Anne E. Carr

Tereshkova, *teh rehsh KAW vah,* **Valentina Vladimirovna,** *VAH lehn TEE nah vlah DEE mih RAWV nuh* (1937-), a Soviet cosmonaut, became the first woman to travel in space. In the spacecraft Vostok 6, Tereshkova made 48 revolutions around Earth in a 70-hour 50-minute space flight from June 16 to June 19, 1963. Tereshkova orbited Earth once every 88 minutes during her historic journey. She operated her spacecraft by manual controls.

Tereshkova parachuted from the Vostok 6 after reentering Earth's atmosphere. She landed about 380 miles (612 kilometers) northeast of Qaraghandy (or Karaganda), Kazakhstan, in central Asia.

Tereshkova, the first space traveler with no experience as a test pilot, became interested in parachuting as a hobby. She made more than 125 jumps before volunteering for space-flight training school. Tereshkova also received training as an airplane pilot.

Tereshkova was born on March 6, 1937, in Maslennikovo, in western Russia, near Yaroslavl. She went to work in a textile mill when she was 18 years old. Tereshkova became an active member of the Young Communist League while at the mill. In 1963, she married cosmonaut Andrian G. Nikolayev. Cathleen S. Lewis

See also **Astronaut** (The cosmonauts; picture).

Term limits prevent elected officials from serving more than a specified number of terms, and therefore years, in office. Some term limits prohibit all service in an office after the limit is reached. Other term limits only require a break in service.

Term limits are typically specified in a constitution. For example, the 22nd Amendment to the Constitution of the United States says that the nation's president cannot be elected to more than two four-year terms. The constitutions of many U.S. states set similar limits on the terms of the states' governors.

People disagree on whether term limits are needed. Supporters of such limits maintain that an *incumbent* (person who holds office) has an unfair advantage in an election. They claim incumbents can use their power as elected officials to promote themselves politically and thus ensure their reelection. Supporters of term limits believe there are many people who could do a good job in office, and that special experience is not needed.

Opponents of term limits believe the limits are undemocratic because they restrict voter choice. They argue that elections themselves allow sufficient control over the time officials stay in office. In addition, they claim that term limits remove expert people from office and shift power away from elected officials and toward bureaucrats and other nonelected staff members.

In the early 1990's, a widespread movement emerged in the United States to set term limits for members of the U.S. Congress and for state and local legislators. In 1995, the Supreme Court of the United States ruled that it was unconstitutional for states to set term limits for members of Congress. By the early 2000's, courts in many states had overturned their states' term-limits laws, and some state legislatures had repealed the laws. Gerald Benjamin

Term paper. See the section *A Student Guide to Better Writing, Speaking, and Research Skills* in the Research Guide/Index, Volume 22.

Termite is the common name for certain groups of small insects that live in large colonies. Termites feed primarily on *cellulose* and *lignin,* substances found in the cell walls of plants. These substances make up the key ingredients in all wood and wood products. Termites inhabit many parts of the world, especially in warm, humid regions.

Termites somewhat resemble ants. But ants have narrow waists and elbowed antennae, while termites have thick waists and antennae that resemble strings of beads. Termites cannot digest cellulose directly, so many rely on bacteria and protozoa living in their intestines. These microscopic organisms supply most of the *enzymes* needed for cellulose digestion. Enzymes are substances that speed up chemical reactions.

Termites play important roles in the environment. For example, they help break down and recycle dead wood and other plant tissues. They also provide food for such animals as ants, anteaters, and slender blind snakes. Yet termites rank among the most damaging pests for human beings. They attack wood in homes, fences, and other valuable structures. They also damage such agricultural crops as potatoes and sugar cane.

The termite colony forms a large extended family. Within the family, various *castes* (groups) have different functions.

© Giuseppe Mazza

Termites live in colonies where each *caste* (group) has a certain job. The queen, *shown at top,* mates and reproduces. This queen's abdomen has become swollen with eggs. The reddish soldier, *upper left,* defends the colony against attack. The brownish worker, *lower left,* has duties that include gathering food and caring for other termites in the colony. Termites attack wood and wood products, and they cause great damage to buildings in many parts of the world.

The *worker caste* makes up the largest group. It consists of small, blind, wingless individuals with soft bodies. Depending on the colony, the worker caste can number in the hundreds, thousands, or even millions. Workers perform all of the hard labor in the colony. They clean, maintain, and repair the nest; gather food and water; care for the young; and construct new tunnels and chambers in the nest as the colony grows.

Members of the *soldier caste* grow larger than do the workers, but they are fewer in number. These blind, wingless insects have large heads and often powerful jaws. They guard the nest site and protect it from attacks by ants or other invaders. Soldiers of some species lack jaws. Instead, they have a large head gland that shoots chemicals through a nozzle at the front of the head. Most such chemicals form a sticky substance that can slow down smaller enemies. The worker termites care for the soldiers by feeding and grooming them.

The *reproductive caste* includes a *king* and *queen,* the parents of the colony. A queen can lay large numbers of eggs. Once the king and queen have produced worker offspring, the workers then feed the parent couple. Some termite colonies have a few other reproductives that share egg laying duties. Each year, every mature colony develops a group of young winged reproductives that swarm from the nest for a short mating flight. After the flight, their delicate wings break off, and the new kings and queens set out to start new colonies. Reproductives are the only fully developed adult termites.

Termite colonies typically produce both males and females in every caste. In other insect colonies, such as those of ants or bees, males serve only to mate.

Kinds of termites. Hundreds of different termite species exist. Scientists may divide them into two main groups: (1) those that live within wood and (2) those that tunnel and nest in soil. Wood-dwelling types often nest only in rotten wood, damp wood, or dry wood. Their colonies remain rather small and persist only as long as the food source lasts. All wood-dwelling termites produce distinctive waste pellets. For people, these pellets often act as an early warning sign of termite activity.

Soil-dwelling termites construct underground nests. If a particular source of food runs out, these species can tunnel through the soil to find new food sources. Such colonies usually live much longer than do wood-dwelling colonies. Some may survive well over 70 years. Underground colonies also grow much larger, often containing several million individuals.

Soil-dwelling termites of North America and Europe commonly invade wooden structures above the ground. They do this by building earthen tubes that serve as protective tunnels between the nest and their food source. Such tubes warn people of a termite invasion.

In various warm regions, especially in Africa and Australia, other soil-dwelling species build nest mounds up to 20 feet (6 meters) tall. These complex mounds have thick outer walls and numerous inner chambers and tunnels. The king and queen live in a chamber deep inside the mound. When reproducing, the queen's abdomen grows large enough to hold many thousands of eggs. She then lays these eggs at the rate of several thousand a day. Worker termites carry the eggs away to specially constructed cells in the nest. There the workers care for the young as they hatch from the eggs.

Certain mound-building termites do not have bacteria or protozoa in their intestines to help digest cellulose. Instead, these insects rely for digestion on a fungus that they cultivate in underground fungus gardens. To create these gardens, workers first collect plant material and mix it with saliva and their own waste products to form a paste. They then inject the paste with fungus *spores* (reproductive cells) and place it in certain chambers in the nest. As the fungus gardens grow, the termites feed on digestible structures produced by the fungi.

Termite control. To protect buildings from termite damage, people should use brick, stone, or concrete foundations. All wood less than 18 inches (46 centimeters) from the ground should receive extensive treatment with wood preservatives. Such preservatives create an environment poisonous to termites. People also may use pesticides and other chemicals to fight these insects. One method for controlling soil-dwelling termites involves planting underground baits. The baits typically dispense slow-acting chemicals that disrupt the insects' growth and development. John R. Meyer

Scientific classification. Termites make up the order Isoptera in the class Insecta. This order contains seven families.

See also **Insect** (pictures; table: The orders of insects).

Tern is a subfamily of sea birds related to gulls. Terns are famous for their powers of flight. About 35 or more kinds of terns are found in different parts of the world. Fourteen kinds are native to North America. Most of them live along seacoasts, rivers, and lakes, rather than in the open sea. The *sooty tern* and some others often range far from land.

Terns have long, pointed bills and webbed feet. Their pointed wings can carry them through the air swiftly and for long distances. Their swift, graceful flight has given them the name *sea swallow.* Terns feed mainly on small fish. They seize the fish by darting quickly into the water from the air, with the bill pointing down.

Great colonies of terns inhabit islands during the nesting season. Usually, the nests are slightly hollowed-out places in the ground. Sometimes, the terns lay eggs on bare rock or sand. Some make nests of seaweed. The *fairy tern* lays its single egg on a hollow place on a small branch, or on a rock ledge with no nest. The parents incubate the egg by sitting on it until it hatches.

One of the largest kinds is the *Caspian tern,* a handsome bird 21 inches (53 centimeters) long. It has a shining black crest, and pearl-gray back and wings. The smallest is the *least tern,* 9 inches (23 centimeters) long. Large numbers of the beautiful *common tern* live on the Atlantic Coast of North America. Once hunters almost killed off this species in seeking its eggs and plumes. All types of terns are now protected by law. The common tern has light, pearl-gray feathers and a white tail and throat. It is about 15 inches (38 centimeters) long. The common tern lays three or four eggs, which vary in color from whitish to brownish and are thickly spotted with brown and lavender. A tern usually seen on inland marshes and lakes is the *black tern.* Other types include *gull-billed, royal,* and *Arctic terns.* The Arctic tern flies farther in its migration than any other bird known. Some Arctic terns travel 22,000 miles (35,400 kilometers) in a year, from the Arctic Circle to the Antarctic Circle and back. See **Arctic tern.** George L. Hunt, Jr.

Scientific classification. Terns are in the gull family, Laridae, and make up the subfamily Sterninae. Most of them are genus *Sterna,* including the common tern, *S. hirundo;* the sooty tern, *S. fuscata;* and the Arctic tern, *S. paradisaea.* The Caspian tern is *Hydroprogne caspia;* the royal tern, *Thalasseus maximus;* the gull-billed tern *Gelochelidon nilotica;* and the fairy tern, *Gygis alba.* The black tern is *Chlidonias niger.*

Terpsichore. See **Muses.**

Terra cotta, *TEHR uh KAHT uh,* is a hard, durable kind of earthenware. Like other kinds of earthenware, terra cotta is a type of baked clay. It ranges in color from buff to brown to various shades of red and is usually unglazed. Terra cotta is widely used to make flowerpots, fountains, tiles, architectural ornaments, and decorative garden sculptures. Because terra cotta can be molded easily, many sculptors have used the material to make preliminary models of their works.

Terra cotta was developed during prehistoric times. The ancient Greeks and Romans used it to make decorative objects. They also used terra cotta to make gutters, pipes, and other construction materials. The term *terra cotta* is Italian for *cooked earth.* John W. Keefe

See also **Della Robbia, Luca** (picture).

Terrapin, *TEHR uh pihn,* is the common name of certain freshwater or salt-marsh turtles. Terrapins eat crabs, clams, snails, and other water animals, as well as green plants. The female, which is larger than the male, has an upper shell that measures 6 to 9 inches (15 to 23 centimeters) long. The common United States terrapins are the *diamondback terrapins,* of which there are several subspecies. They live along the Gulf and Atlantic coasts as far north as Massachusetts. D. Bruce Means

© Laura Riley, Bruce Coleman, Inc.

The diamondback terrapin gets its name from the shape of the pattern on its shell. This small turtle makes its home in fresh waters and salt marshes of North America.

Scientific classification. Terrapins belong to the common turtle family, Emydidae. The scientific name for the diamondback terrapin is *Malaclemys terrapin.*

Terrarium, *tuh RAIR ee uhm,* is the name for a transparent container in which small plants or small land animals are kept. Terrariums reproduce as closely as possible a natural setting or habitat. People set up terrariums in glass or plastic containers. The containers are usually covered to prevent the loss of moisture. The word *terrarium* comes from a Latin word that means *earth.*

To prepare a terrarium, place a layer of small pebbles on the bottom of the container for drainage. A layer of broken charcoal should be added to absorb odors and to provide additional drainage. Then add commercial potting soil or a mixture made up of garden loam, fresh-water sand, and either peat moss or *leaf mold* (decomposed leaves). This mixture should be heated in an oven at 200 °F (93 °C) for one hour to kill harmful bacteria and other soil pests. When it is cool, put it into the container.

Plants that grow well together under the same conditions are best suited for a terrarium. Each plant should be carefully placed in the soil leaving enough space between plants to allow for growth. The soil should be moistened thoroughly, but not so much that it becomes soggy. Animals often kept in terrariums include lizards, small snakes, toads, and salamanders.

The completed terrarium should be placed in an area that is well-lit but out of direct sunlight. When covered, a balanced terrarium preserves temperature and moisture inside to provide excellent growing conditions. If the container clouds with moisture, the lid may be opened to decrease humidity. William H. Carlson

Terrell, *TEHR uhl,* **Mary Church** (1863-1954), joined the struggle to gain equal rights for African Americans in the 1890's. Terrell remained active in this equal rights movement until she died at age 90 on July 24, 1954.

Mary Church Terrell was born in Memphis on Sept. 23, 1863. Her father was a former slave who became a millionaire through real estate and other business transactions. Mary graduated from Oberlin College in 1884, and then settled in Washington, D.C. She became a member of the Washington school board in 1895, and she helped found the National Association of Colored Women in 1896. Through most of her career, Mary advised government leaders on racial problems. In 1953, she led a committee that won a suit to end discrimination in Washington hotels, restaurants, buses, and other public facilities. Robert A. Pratt

Terrier is the name of a group of breeds of dogs. The name comes from the Latin *terra,* meaning *earth,* because terriers were once used to drive game out of holes, or burrows. Most terriers originated in England. The American Kennel Club recognizes 26 terrier breeds: *Airedale terrier, American Staffordshire terrier, Australian terrier, Bedlington terrier, border terrier, bull terrier, cairn terrier, Dandie Dinmont terrier, Irish terrier, Kerry blue terrier, lakeland terrier, Manchester terrier, miniature bull terrier, miniature schnauzer, Norfolk terrier,*

Norwich terrier, Parson Russell terrier, Scottish terrier, Sealyham terrier, Skye terrier, smooth fox terrier, soft-coated wheaten terrier, Staffordshire bull terrier, Welsh terrier, West Highland white terrier, and *wire fox terrier.*

Four other breeds are called terriers. But they are not members of the terrier group. The *Boston terrier* and *Tibetan terrier* are classed as nonsporting dogs. The *Silky terrier* and *Yorkshire terrier* are toy dogs. Each breed has an article in *World Book.*

Critically reviewed by the American Kennel Club

See also **Dog** (table; pictures: Terriers).

Territorial waters are areas of the ocean where a nation has *sovereign rights.* These rights include control of fishing, navigation, and shipping, as well as the use of the ocean's natural resources.

A nation's territorial waters include its *internal waters* and its *territorial sea.* Internal waters include lakes, rivers, and the waters within such coastal areas as bays and gulfs. A country's territorial sea lies beyond its coast or the boundary of its internal waters. Nations have more authority over their internal waters than over their territorial seas. The main difference is that ships of other nations can freely cross territorial seas in peacetime.

Various nations have set different outer limits for their territorial sea. A United Nations-sponsored treaty called the Law of the Sea Convention, which took effect in 1994, provides for a territorial sea of 12 nautical miles. A nautical mile equals about 1.2 statute miles or 1.9 kilometers. Most of the approximately 120 coastal nations, including the United States, observe the 12-mile limit. A few nations claim as much as 200 nautical miles.

Many countries prohibit foreigners from fishing in their territorial sea. Many nations also claim exclusive fishing and other rights in an exclusive economic zone, which extends 200 nautical miles from shore.

George P. Smith II

See also **High seas; Law of the Sea Convention.**

Territoriality is a form of animal behavior in which an individual animal or a group defends an area against other members of the same species or against members of other species. The defended area is called a *territory.* An individual usually wins encounters with intruders while on its own territory, but it usually loses encounters when intruding onto another territory. A territory contains resources that the animal needs to survive and reproduce. These resources may include shelter, food, and water; places where mates can be found; and places where animals can escape from their enemies.

Territoriality is common in *vertebrates* (animals with a backbone), including fish, amphibians, reptiles, birds, and mammals. It is less common among insects and other *invertebrates* (animals without a backbone).

The size of a territory varies, depending on the effort required to defend the area and the resources available. Animals may establish small territories in the immediate vicinity of nesting sites or in areas of abundant food. They may claim large territories when resources are widely scattered. The period a territory is held may vary from less than a day to many years or a lifetime.

Animals may defend a territory by being openly aggressive, such as by chasing and fighting intruders. They also may defend the territory through signals of potential aggression. For example, a wolf marks out its territory by urinating on bushes, rocks, and other objects. The scent of urine warns intruders of the wolf's presence and the risk of an encounter. The more aggressive forms of defense generally are used when the intruder is especially persistent. Larry L. Wolf

See also **Dominance.**

Territory is a type of region that belongs to or is controlled by a country or other independent political unit. In countries with a federal government, such as Australia, Canada, Mexico, and the United States, territories rank below states or provinces. In these countries, the national government establishes separate governments for the individual territories. In most cases, the territories have no representation in the national government. The territories have varying degrees of self-rule.

In the United States

The United States has four main territories: American Samoa, Guam, the Virgin Islands, and various Pacific islands. For many years, the United States had many more outlying territories. Two of them, Alaska and Hawaii, became states. One, the Philippines, became an independent country. Two others, Puerto Rico and the Northern Mariana Islands, became U.S. commonwealths. See **Philippines** (History); **Puerto Rico** (Government); **Northern Mariana Islands, Commonwealth of the.**

From 1947 to 1994, the United States administered the Trust Territory of the Pacific Islands under an agreement with the United Nations. The trust territory originally consisted of the Marshall Islands, the Caroline Islands, and all the Mariana Islands except Guam. The trust territory ceased to exist when Palau, the last remaining member, became independent in 1994. See **Pacific Islands, Trust Territory of the.**

In the United States, territorial government is an older institution than the U.S. Constitution. In 1787, under the Articles of Confederation, Congress passed the Northwest Ordinance. This law set up the first American territory, the Northwest Territory (see **Northwest Territory**). The Northwest Ordinance also set the pattern for congressional action in governing territories and providing for their eventual statehood. The United States Constitution, also written in 1787, provides that "new States may be admitted by the Congress into this Union." Accordingly, Congress has full control over the admission of territories. During the 1800's, Congress in many cases admitted territories on the basis of U.S. domestic politics. All but 19 states—the original 13 and 6 others—were once territories.

Up to 1867, Congress always set up territories in mainland areas on the frontiers of the United States. Alaska, bought in 1867, was the first area not directly connected with the rest of the states. Gradually, the United States gained other distant territories, most of them after the Spanish-American War of 1898. These new territories presented special problems. For example, the new territories were far away, and their peoples had little or no experience of democratic self-government. In addition, the territories contained large nonwhite populations. For these reasons, Congress was unwilling to consider the territories for statehood and was reluctant to extend to their residents all the protections provided by the Constitution.

As a result, in the Insular Cases of 1901, the Supreme Court of the United States drew a distinction between *incorporated* and *unincorporated* territories. It held that all rights guaranteed by the Constitution applied in incorporated territories. In unincorporated ones, only fundamental rights applied—as distinguished from formal or procedural rights, such as the right to negotiate or to petition. Congress has the power to decide whether a territory has incorporated or unincorporated status. Incorporated territories may become states. Unincorporated territories may not. A third class of territories includes *wholly unorganized and unincorporated* territories. These territories are controlled by executive-branch officials, not by Congress.

The territories of American Samoa, Guam, and the Virgin Islands each elect one delegate to the U.S. House of Representatives. However, the delegates may vote only in House committees.

American territorial government

Alaska and Hawaii were the last fully incorporated U.S. territories. Unincorporated territories include the Virgin Islands and Guam. Unorganized and unincorporated territories include American Samoa, Wake Island, and other Pacific islands.

The Virgin Islands were purchased from Denmark in 1917. The people elect their own governor and legislature. But Congress can disallow acts passed in the Virgin Islands. See **Virgin Islands, United States.**

Guam was acquired from Spain in 1898. With authorization from Congress, Guam drew up a constitution in 1969. Since 1970, its people have elected their own governor and legislature. See **Guam.**

American Samoa consists of a group of islands ceded to the United States between 1900 and 1925. The territory is controlled by the Department of the Interior. The people are *nationals,* but not citizens, of the United States. See **American Samoa.**

Pacific Islands. Most of these islands, including Midway Island, are governed by the Department of the Interior. Wake Island and a few other islands are governed by the Department of Defense. See **Pacific Islands.**

Territories in Canada

Canada has three territories: the Northwest Territories, Nunavut, and Yukon. Each has a commissioner appointed by the federal government and a government leader elected by the people. The commissioner's office is largely honorary. The government leader is the actual head of the government.

Northwest Territories has an executive council and a 24-member Legislative Assembly. The people elect Assembly members and two representatives to the House of Commons. See **Northwest Territories.**

Nunavut has an executive council and a 19-member Assembly. The people elect the Assembly members. They also elect one representative to the Canadian House of Commons. Nunavut was created in 1999 from land that had been part of the Northwest Territories. See **Nunavut.**

Yukon has an executive council and a 17-member Assembly. The people elect the Assembly members. They also elect one representative to the House. See **Yukon.**

Kinley J. Brauer

See also **Australia** (Government); **Canada, Government of; Enclave; Trust territory.**

AP/Wide World

The worst terrorist attack in United States history destroyed the towers of the World Trade Center in New York City on Sept. 11, 2001. Terrorists crashed hijacked planes into the buildings.

Terrorism is the use or threat of violence to create fear and alarm, usually to promote a movement or cause. Terrorists may set off bombs, murder and kidnap individuals, hijack airplanes, release harmful chemical and biological substances, or take other violent or threatening actions. Terrorists typically have political, religious, or other *ideological* goals—that is, goals having to do with beliefs and ideas. They hope to achieve their goals through violence and the creation of fear. Many terrorists represent revolutionary movements seeking a change in government or liberation from a governing power. Some hope to attract attention and support for particular political philosophies or religious beliefs. Others have unclear goals or simply oppose all forms of authority.

Individuals may commit terrorist acts, but terrorism is usually the work of organized networks or groups. Many groups operate within a single nation or region. Others have branches and operations in many countries. Because terrorists generally cannot match the strength of conventional military forces, they often rely on *guerrilla warfare.* Guerrilla warfare involves attacks by roving bands of fighters who torment the enemy with ambushes, bombings, sudden raids, and other hit-and-run tactics. The fighters blend in with ordinary citizens, strike suddenly, and try to avoid capture.

In addition to the death and destruction caused by the attacks, terrorists seek to create panic and fear throughout the general population. They may try to cripple the economy by destroying bridges, dams, telephone networks, or other essential structures or services.

Tom Mockaitis, the contributor of this article, is Professor of History at DePaul University.

Many terrorists hope that people who observe the attacks will lose their sense of security and their confidence in the existing government or political system.

All terrorist acts are crimes under international law. Many countries fight terrorism by gathering *intelligence* (information); by increasing security at airports, government buildings, and other likely targets; and by working together with international organizations and with other nations facing terrorist threats. Some countries train special military and law enforcement units to confront terrorist situations. Efforts to prevent terrorism are called *counterterrorism.*

Features of terrorism

Terrorist groups and individuals generally attack people who oppose their causes, or buildings and places that symbolize such opposition. Common victims of kidnappings and assassinations include business executives, diplomats, judges, police, and political leaders. Some terrorists attack churches, mosques, synagogues, and other places of worship. Others target airplanes, buses, trains, and nightclubs. Terrorists often choose targets certain to attract media coverage. Such targets include government buildings, national monuments and landmarks, and skyscrapers.

Terrorist methods. Terrorists seek to create instability and alarm through a number of methods. Traditional methods include bombings, assassinations, kidnappings, and hijackings. Newer threats include computer-based terrorism and *weapons of mass destruction*—that is, biological, chemical, and nuclear weapons.

Bombings make up about half of all terrorist acts. Bombs may be placed in automobiles, backpacks, garbage cans, suitcases, or elsewhere. Many bombings involve cars or trucks packed with explosives and parked next to a building or other target. Terrorists may also try to smuggle concealed bombs onto airplanes or into crowded sports arenas or concert halls. In some cases, a bomber may strap explosives to his or her own body and detonate them on a bus or in a crowded area. Such bombings are commonly called *suicide bombings,* because the terrorist takes his or her own life while conducting the attack.

Assassinations and kidnappings. Terrorists may seek to create alarm by assassinating government officials or other prominent individuals. Terrorists may also kidnap individuals and hold them hostage until certain demands are met. In some cases, terrorists target travelers from other countries in an attempt to discourage others from visiting.

Hijackings. Some terrorists *hijack,* or seize control of, airplanes, buses, or other vehicles. They typically use weapons or bomb threats to gain control. Once in control, hijackers may take passengers as hostages and threaten to kill the passengers if their demands are not met. In some cases, hijackers may threaten to blow up an airplane, or they may intentionally crash a plane into a target. Such hijackings are especially dangerous because planes loaded with fuel can become "flying bombs" capable of causing great destruction.

Biological attacks involve the intentional spreading of harmful bacteria, viruses, and *toxins* (poisons). The use of biological *agents* (substances) to inflict harm is sometimes called *germ warfare* or *bioterrorism.* Bioterrorists may seek to contaminate food or water supplies; to distribute toxins, such as ricin; or to spread dangerous diseases, such as anthrax or smallpox. They may put harmful bacteria in restaurant salad bars or send contaminated items through the mail. However, many biological weapons are difficult for terrorists to prepare and use effectively.

Chemical attacks involve the intentional release of toxic chemicals. Some chemical agents affect the central nervous system and can cause paralysis or death. Others can burn or damage the skin, eyes, nose, throat, or lungs. Dangerous chemical agents include mustard gas, a blistering agent that causes burns and blindness; hydrogen cyanide, a poisonous gas sometimes used to execute condemned criminals; and sarin, a deadly nerve gas. Terrorists may attempt to buy, steal, or manufacture chemical weapons and then disperse them in crowded areas. However, many chemical weapons are difficult for terrorists to prepare and use.

Nuclear attacks. Governments have long sought to keep nuclear materials out of the hands of terrorist organizations. As a result, no nuclear terrorist attack has yet occurred. However, counterterrorism experts have studied how terrorists might potentially use nuclear weapons or radioactive materials to conduct attacks.

Terrorist groups might seek to acquire nuclear devices from an underground weapons supplier or from a government that has such devices. Alternatively, terrorists might try to obtain radioactive materials—such as weapons-grade plutonium or uranium—and manufacture their own weapons. If terrorists are unable to acquire or build nuclear weapons, they might instead try to cause explosions at existing nuclear facilities. Terrorists might also bundle radioactive materials with conventional explosives to create *radiological dispersion devices.* Such devices—sometimes called "dirty bombs"—could give off invisible radiation capable of causing sickness or death. The radioactive contamination could keep people out of a vital area, such as a downtown business section, for months or even years.

Computer-based terrorism, also called *cyberterrorism,* involves the sabotage of computer information systems. Cyberterrorists may design and circulate *computer viruses,* which can disrupt computer operations and destroy data. Cyberterrorists may also seek to steal or alter sensitive or valuable information, or to attack systems that provide important services.

Other forms of terrorism. Terrorists may use any other form of violence or threats of violence to create fear and alarm. Some governments use terrorist methods—such as torture and murder—to intimidate their opposition and increase their power. The use of such methods by oppressive governments is called *state terrorism* or *state-conducted terrorism.* War crimes, genocide, and other international violations may also be considered acts of terror.

Terrorist organizations. Individuals may carry out terrorist acts—such as bombings or the distribution of computer viruses—without assistance from others. However, most terrorists are associated with specific movements or organized groups. Terrorist organizations vary greatly in terms of size and structure. Most groups are small and focus on activities within their own nation or region. Other groups, however, have international net-

© Tokyo Shimbun, Corbis/Sygma

Chemical terrorism involves the intentional release of toxic chemicals. In 1995, members of a Japanese religious cult spread the nerve gas sarin in the Tokyo subway system, *shown here.*

works that carry out attacks throughout the world. One of the largest global terror groups is al-Qa'ida, which seeks to promote the goals of Islamic extremists.

Most terrorist organizations have a leader or group of leaders who develop strategies and direct operations. Active terrorists within the organization then carry out the plans. Many terrorist organizations consist of small groups called *cells.* Terrorist cells may receive specific instructions from leaders, or they may plan their own activities based on the organization's central goals. Terrorist groups generally take great efforts to hide the identities of group members, the locations of cells, and their channels of communication. Typically, only one member of each cell knows how to contact the larger organization. As a result, the larger group may remain safe even if a cell is discovered and destroyed. The secrecy and complexity of the cell structure makes it difficult for governments to gather information about terrorist groups.

Sources of funding for terrorist groups are usually carefully concealed. Some governments secretly support or sponsor terrorist groups by providing weapons, training, and money. Some terrorist groups raise money through criminal activities such as theft or the sale of illegal drugs. In some cases, a group posing as a social service organization may secretly direct donations, without the donors' knowledge, toward terrorist causes.

Fighting terrorism

Counterterrorism efforts involve numerous activities. Governments gather and evaluate information about suspected terrorists and terrorist groups. They identify potential terrorist threats and develop a wide variety of security measures and emergency procedures. Many governments refuse to negotiate with terrorists or with nations that support terrorists. National security services, such as the United States Department of Homeland Security and the United Kingdom's Security Service (MI5), lead advanced counterterrorism efforts. They receive assistance from intelligence services, such as Israel's Mossad, the United Kingdom's Secret Intelligence Service (MI6), and the U.S. Central Intelligence Agency (CIA). International organizations, such as the United Nations (UN) and Interpol, help nations work together for the prevention of terrorism.

Intelligence efforts. National governments, international organizations, police departments, and specialized intelligence services collect, share, and analyze information relating to terrorism. Such efforts can help prevent attacks by identifying terrorist suspects and by detecting terrorist plots while they are being planned.

Many intelligence and law enforcement agencies use *electronic surveillance* to monitor suspected terrorists and to intercept their communication. *Wiretapping* is the interception of telephone conversations by a listening device connected to a telephone wire or placed nearby. Other forms of surveillance include special aircraft and artificial satellites that can produce detailed images of suspected terrorist bases or camps.

Governments may work with agents from foreign countries or send undercover agents to obtain information from within a terrorist group. Governments may also receive valuable information by questioning detained terrorists and by searching areas where terrorists have lived or gathered.

In some cases, governments can examine financial records and trace the funding of terrorist organizations. They may order banks to *freeze* (make unusable) the assets of terrorists or of individuals or groups believed to be contributing to terrorist activity.

Security measures. Most governments work to protect, or "harden," potential terrorist targets, such as airports and airplanes, large public gatherings, and government buildings. Target-hardening efforts typically involve careful security systems and procedures and the work of trained security personnel.

Thorough security at airports and on airplanes can decrease the likelihood of hijackings and other attacks. People who travel on airplanes must pass through multiple airport checkpoints. Guards scan or search checked baggage and carry-on items, and they may *frisk* (search) passengers before letting them board the plane. Security measures on the airplane itself may include reinforced cockpit doors and armed air marshals.

Many structures, especially skyscrapers and government buildings, have physical barriers to keep car or truck bombs from getting near. Also, many buildings have metal detectors or other security checkpoints to search for dangerous items and to prevent unauthorized people from entering. Police officers may be assigned to guard bridges, tunnels, or monuments believed to be at risk. At some crowded events, cameras scan people's faces and attempt to match them with photos of suspected terrorists in a computer database.

The risk of cyberterrorism can be reduced by computer security measures, such as antivirus programs and electronic barriers called *firewalls.* As technology improves, new target-hardening methods will continue to emerge.

The protection of key sites is an essential part of counterterrorism. However, in many cases, target hardening

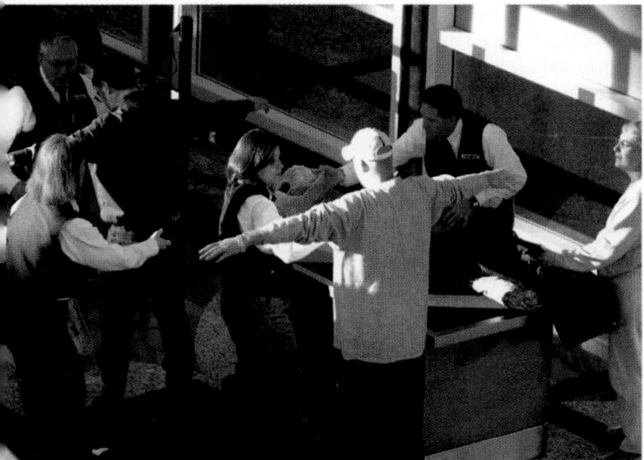

AP/Wide World

Airport security procedures aim to prevent terrorist attacks involving airplanes. Trained security personnel check passengers and baggage for dangerous items and materials.

may lead to *target displacement*—that is, it may cause terrorists to shift their plans to different sites that are not as well protected. No system of protection can fully safeguard every building, bridge, and tunnel. A site with relatively little protection is sometimes called a "soft" target.

Diplomatic, economic, and military pressure. Because of the global reach of terrorist activity, the cooperation of organizations and governments from various countries is an essential element of counterterrorism. The UN and other international bodies help promote this cooperation. Numerous treaties and international agreements have sought to address terrorist activity. For example, *extradition treaties* allow people linked to terrorism in one country to be arrested in a different country and deported for trial in the country where an attack took place. Such treaties make it difficult for terrorists to escape criminal charges.

The international community may isolate or punish nations that support terrorism. Governments may impose *economic sanctions* on nations that support terrorism. In other words, they may limit or end economic relations with the country until it changes its policies. If sanctions and diplomatic pressure fail, countries may launch military strikes against terrorist bases and camps or against countries that sponsor terrorism.

Counterterrorism and civil rights. A government's ability to fight terrorism depends largely on its ability to intercept communication to and from suspected terrorists, to search individuals for weapons and dangerous materials, and to investigate and detain suspects. However, many of these actions may conflict with the basic rights and freedoms associated with democracy. A major challenge facing governments today is the need to provide effective counterterrorism while still respecting individuals' privacy and civil rights. Government officials, legal scholars, and civil rights activists often disagree over how best to balance the two interests.

History of terrorism

The beginnings of terrorist violence closely followed the spread of early civilization. From ancient times to the present, individuals, rebel groups, and governments have used cruelty and force to eliminate enemies, to spread fear and panic, and to achieve political, religious, and other ideological goals.

Early terrorism. The empire builders of ancient times often maintained control over conquered peoples through brutality and fear. In 71 B.C., for instance, the Roman general Crassus crushed a revolt led by the gladiator Spartacus. Crassus then publicly crucified the captured rebels to warn others of the consequences of revolt. Some rebel groups used terrorist methods to resist their rulers. For instance, a Jewish group called the Sicarii waged violent campaigns against the Romans from about A.D. 6 to 73.

Starting in the 800's, Japanese *ninja,* members of a secret organization of peasant families, spread terror through sabotage, assassination, and kidnapping. Ninja were masters at various forms of armed and unarmed combat, including the use of disguises and poisons. In the 1100's, a secret society called *assassins* or *hashshashin* (hemp-eaters) carried out violent campaigns in

Granger Collection

The Reign of Terror was a period of the French Revolution (1789-1799) in which thousands of suspected opponents of the revolution were beheaded by guillotine. The word *terrorism* originated during the Reign of Terror.

AP/Wide World

The Ku Klux Klan, an American group, used terrorism to keep African Americans from voting and to deny other rights to African Americans, Jews, and other minority groups. Klan members are shown here on horseback in Tulsa, Oklahoma, in 1923.

Persia (now Iran) and Asia Minor (now part of Turkey). They smoked a drug called *hashish,* made from the hemp plant, and killed their enemies while under its influence. In the 1300's and 1400's, peasant uprisings in Europe produced widespread violence, much of which would now be considered terrorist in nature.

The beginnings of modern terrorism. The word *terrorism* first appeared during the French Revolution (1789-1799). Some of the revolutionaries who seized power adopted a policy of violence against people they considered enemies of the revolution. The revolutionary government executed around 40,000 people. Because of the number of executions and the fear that they produced, the period of rule by the revolutionaries became known as the Reign of Terror. By the early 1800's, terrorism had become a fixture of rebellion and conflict throughout the world.

In the 1930's, the dictators Adolf Hitler of Germany, Benito Mussolini of Italy, and Joseph Stalin of the Soviet Union used terrorist tactics to discourage opposition to their governments. From 1973 to 1990, General Augusto Pinochet Ugarte controlled Chile as a military dictator. During his rule, more than 3,000 Chileans disappeared or were murdered, and many more were tortured. Many authoritarian governments continue to use state terrorism today to frighten and control the population.

Terrorist groups and movements have long used violence to pursue their goals. An American group, the Ku Klux Klan, has used terrorism to oppose the advancement of African Americans, Jews, and other minority groups since the late 1800's. In Northern Ireland, Roman Catholic extremists have used terrorism in efforts to end British rule and to unite Northern Ireland with the Republic of Ireland. At the same time, Protestant extremists have used similar methods to demand the continuation of British rule.

In Spain's Basque region, a group called Euskadi ta Askatasuna (Basque Homeland and Freedom), abbreviated ETA, has used violence to push for the creation of an independent Basque state. In Chechnya, rebel groups have used terrorism in an attempt to win independence from Russia. Chechen groups have taken hostages and conducted suicide bombings against Russian targets.

Before the independence of Israel in 1948, a Jewish group called Irgun Zvai Leumi (National Military Organization) used terror to speed the end of British rule in Palestine and create a Jewish homeland. Since 1960, Palestinian groups, including Hamas and Islamic Jihad of Palestine, have carried out campaigns of terrorism aimed at establishing an independent Palestinian state. Such groups have conducted numerous attacks—including a wave of suicide bombings in the early 2000's—against Israel. Israel has responded with military strikes that have taken civilian lives.

During the 1960's and 1970's, several terrorist groups sought the destruction of the political and economic systems in their home countries and the development of new systems. These groups included the Red Brigades in Italy, the Red Army Faction (also known as the Baader-Meinhof Gang) in West Germany, and the Weather Underground in the United States. Since the 1980's, Peru has faced attacks by leftist terrorist groups called Shining Path and the Tupac Amaru Revolutionary Movement.

Many terrorists have had religious motives rather than political ones. In 1995, members of a Japanese religious cult released the nerve gas sarin into the Tokyo subway system, killing 12 people and injuring thousands. In the United States and other countries, extremists opposed to abortion have bombed and burned down clinics and murdered doctors who performed abortions. People who strongly oppose abortion generally do so because of religious beliefs.

Some groups in the United States and other countries have used terrorism to promote animal rights and other causes relating to nature and the environment. Such groups—including the Earth Liberation Front and the Animal Liberation Front—have attacked lumber companies and laboratories that conduct research on animals. Terrorism for nature-related causes is often called *ecoterrorism.*

Individuals with unusual or unclear agendas have also committed acts of terror. From 1978 to 1995, an American known as the Unabomber sent bombs through the mail. Because he disliked modern industrial civilization, he targeted scientists and engineers in the computer industry and other high-technology fields. The Unabomber, identified as Theodore J. Kaczynski, was convicted in 1998. In 1995, two Americans, Timothy J. McVeigh and Terry L. Nichols, were convicted of bombing the Murrah Federal Building in Oklahoma City. They believed that actions of the U.S. government had deprived citizens of their freedom.

The changing face of terrorism. In the late 1900's, many terrorist groups began forming networks and operating on an increasingly global scale. Some of these groups, particularly in the Middle East, held a deep hatred for the United States and for Western countries in general. Concerns that terrorists might obtain weapons of mass destruction increased dramatically.

In 1993, a bomb exploded in the parking garage of the World Trade Center in New York City. A federal court convicted four men, including two Palestinians and an Egyptian cleric, of planning the bombing. In 1998, terrorists bombed U.S. embassies in Kenya and Tanzania. American officials linked the bombings to Osama bin Laden, a Saudi-born millionaire and Islamic extremist.

Bin Laden's group, al-Qa'ida, has been suspected in numerous other attacks, including the bombing of the U.S. Navy warship *Cole* at a port in Yemen in 2000. Terrorists who claimed links to al-Qa'ida conducted a series of train bombings in Madrid, Spain, in 2004.

The September 11 terrorist attacks. On Sept. 11, 2001, about 3,000 people died as a result of the worst terrorist attack in U.S. history. Qa'ida hijackers seized two commercial airplanes and deliberately crashed them into the two 110-story towers of the World Trade Center in New York City. Less than an hour later, another hijacked plane crashed into the Pentagon Building just outside Washington, D.C. Shortly after that, a fourth hijacked airplane crashed into a rural area in Somerset County, Pennsylvania.

In response to the September 11 attacks—commonly known as 9/11—U.S. President George W. Bush called for a worldwide campaign against international terrorist networks. He declared that he would target terrorist organizations and any governments that supported them. Bush's antiterrorism effort is commonly called the "war on terrorism" or the "war on terror."

At the time of the attacks, bin Laden and al-Qa'ida were being protected by the Taliban, a militant Islamic group that controlled the government of Afghanistan. Military strikes led by the United States caused the Taliban to fall from power in Afghanistan in December 2001. Numerous Qa'ida members and officers were captured or killed. However, bin Laden was not found.

Since the September 11 attacks, counterterrorism has become a top priority for governments throughout the world. In October 2001, the U.S. Congress passed the USA Patriot Act, which granted government authorities greater power to conduct searches, use wiretaps, and detain and question suspects. Other nations, including India and the United Kingdom, introduced similar antiterrorism measures.

In 2002, the U.S. Congress established the Department of Homeland Security, a new executive department devoted primarily to fighting terrorism. In 2004, Congress passed the Intelligence Reform and Terrorist Prevention Act. The act reorganized the government's intelligence community and introduced additional measures to detect, investigate, and prevent terrorist activity.

The Iraq War. In March 2003, the United States led a military campaign against the Iraqi government of Saddam Hussein. The U.S. government claimed that Hussein supported terrorist organizations and could potentially supply such organizations with weapons of mass destruction. The invasion caused the fall of Hussein's government in early April.

In the following months, a number of terrorist attacks occurred in Iraq. United States government officials suspected that the attacks were the work of Iraqi groups opposed to the U.S.-led invasion, of Hussein's supporters and allies, or of al-Qa'ida and other terrorist groups.

Recent developments. On July 7, 2005, a series of suicide bombings in London killed more than 50 people and injured hundreds of others. Bombs exploded on three subway trains and one bus. Four additional bombings were attempted in London on July 21, but none of the bombs exploded. Authorities arrested a number of suspects in connection with the July 21 plot.

Tom Mockaitis

Related articles in *World Book* include:

Anarchism
Arab-Israeli conflict
Assassination
Bin Laden, Osama
Bomb
Central Intelligence Agency
Chemical-biological-radiological warfare
Civil defense
Crime (Political crime)
Fatah
Federal Bureau of Investigation
French Revolution (Terror and equality)
Guerrilla warfare
Hamas
Hezbollah
Hijacking
Homeland Security, Department of
Hostage
Intelligence service
Iraq War
Islamic Jihad of Palestine
Jihad
Kidnapping
Ku Klux Klan
New York City (Recent developments)
Nuclear weapon
Oklahoma City bombing
Olympic Games (Terrorism in Munich)
Patriot Act
Police
Qa'ida, Al-
Sanctions, Economic
September 11 terrorist attacks
Taliban
United Nations (Working for peace and security)
United States, History of the (Recent events)

Outline

I. Features of terrorism
A. Terrorist methods
B. Terrorist organizations

II. Fighting terrorism
A. Intelligence efforts
B. Security measures
C. Diplomatic, economic, and military pressure
D. Counterterrorism and civil rights

III. History of terrorism

Questions

What are some of the main elements of counterterrorism?
When did the word *terrorism* first appear?
What are some common goals of terrorist attacks?
How was state-conducted terrorism used in the 1900's?
What is a terrorist cell?
What are some common methods of gathering intelligence?
How did the United States respond to the September 11 attacks?
What is computer-based terrorism?
What are weapons of mass destruction?
Describe the relation between counterterrorism and civil rights.

Additional resources

Barker, Jonathan. *The No-Nonsense Guide to Terrorism.* Verso, 2003.
Kushner, Harvey W. *Encyclopedia of Terrorism.* Sage, 2003.
Shanty, Frank G., and others, eds. *Encyclopedia of World Terrorism.* 2 vols. Sharpe Reference, 2003.
Talbott, Strobe, and Chanda, Nayan, eds. *The Age of Terror.* 2001. Reprint. Basic Bks., 2002.

Terry, Ellen (1847-1928), was a leading English actress noted for her performances in the plays of William Shakespeare. Terry appeared in many plays with the English actor and theater manager Sir Henry Irving.

Ellen Alice Terry was born in Coventry on Feb. 27, 1847. She made her first stage appearance at the age of 9 in *The Winter's Tale.* She lived with the British architect Edward Godwin. They had two children who had notable theatrical careers—Edith Craig, an actress, and Edward Gordon Craig, a scenic designer. King George V made Terry a Dame Grand Cross in the Order of the British Empire in 1925, and she became Dame Ellen Terry. She died on July 21, 1928. J. P. Wearing

Tertiary Period was a time in Earth's history that lasted from about 65 million to 2 million years ago. During this period, mammals and birds flourished. The Tertiary Period marked the beginning of the Cenozoic Era, often called the *Age of Mammals.*

The Tertiary Period followed a mass extinction in which the dinosaurs and many other species died off. Many scientists believe a meteor impact or global climate change killed off much life during this time. The extinction marked the end of the Mesozoic Era, often called the *Age of Reptiles.* Many reptiles survived into the Tertiary Period, but they never regained their previous dominance. Mammals and birds became the dominant forms of life on land. Broad-leafed flowering plants spread. Plentiful grasses made it possible for grazing mammals, such as deer, antelope, and horses, to evolve.

During the Tertiary Period, the continents approached their present locations. Early in the period, India, Africa, and South America were island continents. India moved north and collided with Asia, raising up the Himalaya. Africa joined the land mass that is Europe and Asia, which some geographers call Eurasia, allowing species from the continents to mingle. Many creatures traditionally considered African, such as antelopes and large cats, actually migrated into Africa from Eurasia during the Tertiary Period. Elephants, on the other hand, evolved in Africa and spread into Eurasia.

In the Western Hemisphere, the Rocky Mountains rose in North America and the Andes rose in South America. The Isthmus of Panama rose from the sea, forming a land bridge that connected the two continents. Until that time, South America, like modern-day Australia, was home to a unique range of *marsupials* (mammals that usually carry their young in pouches). After the continents joined, most of the South American marsupials became extinct. The one exception, the opossum, survived and spread into North America.

Early in the Tertiary, Antarctica separated from Australia and drifted toward the South Pole. By about 38 million years ago, glaciers had begun forming in Antarctica.

Global climate in the early Tertiary Period was among the warmest in Earth's history, but the planet's surface gradually grew cooler. By about 2 million years ago, cooling resulted in a widespread advance of ice that marked the end of the Tertiary Period and the beginning of the Quaternary Period. Steven I. Dutch

See also **Earth** (The Cenozoic Era); **Prehistoric animal** (The Age of Mammals).

Tesla, Nikola (1856-1943), was a pioneer in electrical technology. He received over 100 patents for inventions. But he is best known for his development of systems that produce and use *alternating current* (AC)—that is, electric current that reverses direction regularly, many times a second. Systems developed by Tesla remain the heart of electric power operations in most of the world.

Early life. Tesla was born on July 9 or 10, 1856, in Smiljan, Austria-Hungary (now in Croatia), to Serbian parents. He studied engineering at two institutions in Austria-Hungary—Graz Technical University (now in Austria) and the University of Prague (now in the Czech Republic). Tesla left the University of Prague in 1880, without a degree, after his father died. He then worked for a short time for Austria-Hungary's telephone system in Budapest (now in Hungary). In 1882, Tesla moved to Paris, where he worked for the Continental Edison Company.

The alternating-current system. While at Graz Technical University, Tesla had seen a demonstration of a generator run as a *direct current* (DC) motor. Direct current is electric current that flows in only one direction. During the demonstration, the *brushes* and the *commutator* of the motor sparked violently. The brushes are devices that conduct the current in a DC motor. The commutator continually reverses the current so that the motor continues to rotate in one direction. Tesla believed a motor without a commutator could be devised. In 1883, while on assignment for Continental Edison in Strasbourg, France, Tesla used his spare time to build his first *polyphase* (out-of-step) AC motor. In such a motor, coils are arranged so that when out-of-step alternating currents energize them, the resulting magnetic field rotates at a predetermined speed. See **Electric motor.**

In 1884, Tesla left Europe for the United States and went to work for the inventor Thomas Edison. Edison respected the young engineer. But the American inventor was a strong supporter of DC, and so he had little interest in Tesla's AC generation, transmission, and motor system. Tesla quit Edison after one year.

In 1887, Tesla started the Tesla Electric Company in New York City. There, he produced three complete systems of AC machinery. For each system, Tesla designed generators to supply the current, motors that use the current, transformers to raise and lower voltages, and a variety of devices to automatically control the machinery. Tesla received patents for his polyphase system of AC generators, transformers, and motors in 1888. That same year, he sold his patents to the U.S. industrialist George Westinghouse. Tesla then worked at the Westinghouse Electric Company in Pittsburgh for a year to help develop commercial uses of the AC system. Tesla became a U.S. citizen in 1889.

In 1893, Westinghouse used Tesla's AC system to light the World's Columbian Exposition in Chicago. In 1895, Westinghouse's Niagara Falls Power Project used Tesla's generators and motors to harness the waterfall's power. The project produced AC power and delivered it to Buffalo, New York, 22 miles (35 kilometers) from the falls.

Other inventions. In 1891, Tesla invented the *Tesla coil,* a type of high-frequency transformer that is still used in radio and television transmission. He experimented with wireless control, and, in 1898, he demonstrated a radio-controlled boat he had invented. In 1899, Tesla created artificial lightning in one of his laboratories. Tesla's other achievements include early experiments with X rays and radar, aircraft design, and the invention of neon and fluorescent lighting.

Tesla died on Jan. 7, 1943. Later that year, the Supreme Court of the United States invalidated most of the patents held by the Italian inventor Guglielmo Marconi for radio communications equipment. It gave Tesla credit for the invention of the radio based on various patents in his name that predated Marconi's. In 1956, the scientific community named a unit of magnetic field strength the *tesla.* Robert B. Prigo

Test Acts were statutes passed by the English Parliament in 1673 and 1678. These laws restricted the political activities of people who were not members of the Church of England. The name *Test Acts* comes from the law's requirement that all people who wished to hold civilian or military office or positions of public trust fulfill certain conditions, or tests. These tests included swearing allegiance to the English Crown, declaring that one did not believe in the doctrine of transubstantiation, and receiving Communion in the Church of England.

The laws were aimed at Protestant nonconformists and Roman Catholics. The acts were repealed in a series of laws passed between 1828 and 1871. Richard L. Greaves

Test pilot is a person who flies new aircraft to test them for safety. There are two kinds of test pilots—experimental test pilots and production test pilots.

Experimental test pilots test the performance capabilities of newly designed aircraft. They become the first people to fly such aircraft. These pilots test the performance limits, called the *flight envelope,* of an aircraft by subjecting it to greater-than-normal flight stresses. Most experimental test pilots have at least a bachelor's degree in engineering, mathematics, or one of the physical sciences. Most have also attended a military test-pilot school. The majority of these pilots have several thousand hours of flying time and can react calmly and quickly to unexpected situations.

Many astronauts and cosmonauts formerly served as experimental test pilots. Charles E. Yeager, an American experimental test pilot, became the first person to fly faster than the speed of sound.

Production test pilots test factory-produced aircraft before the aircraft are delivered to customers. These pilots make sure that the aircraft's engines, flight controls, and mechanical systems are functioning properly. Production test pilots typically have a strong understanding of aircraft mechanics. James P. Johnson

See also **Airplane** (Design and testing).

Testes. See **Testicle.**

Testicle is either of a pair of small oval glands in the male reproductive system. The testicles, also called *testes* (singular, *testis),* hang behind the penis in a sack called the *scrotum.* Their two main functions are (1) producing sperm, and (2) secreting male sex hormones, particularly *testosterone.*

In an adult, each testicle measures approximately 1 ½ inches (4 centimeters) long and about 1 ¼ inches (3 centimeters) wide, and each weighs about ⅔ ounce (20 grams). The testicle is covered by a dense fibrous material. This material enters the rear of the gland and separates into sheets that divide the testicle into about 250 sections. Each section contains one to four twisting tubes called *seminiferous tubules,* in which sperm are produced. All of the tubules combine to form 12 to 15 larger tubes called *efferent ducts,* which transport the sperm to the *epididymis,* a highly coiled tube at the rear of each testicle. In the epididymis, the sperm develop further before being released from the body during sexual climax.

Testosterone is produced in the tissue between the seminiferous tubules by specialized cells called *Leydig cells.* Testosterone controls the development during puberty of such male characteristics as a beard, enlarged muscle mass, a deep voice, and increased size of the sex organs. This hormone also stimulates male sexual behavior. Earl F. Wendel

See also **Penis; Prostate gland; Reproduction, Human; Testicular cancer; Testosterone.**

Testicular cancer is an uncontrolled division of cells in the testicles, a pair of oval glands of the male reproductive system. The testicles, also called *testes,* hang behind the penis in a sack called the *scrotum.* Testicular cancer is a relatively rare type of cancer. But unlike many other cancers, it occurs primarily in men under 35 years of age. Research shows that the incidence of this type of cancer may be slowly rising.

A painless lump or area of hardness in one testicle is the most common symptom of testicular cancer. Other signs may sometimes include back pain or tenderness of the breasts. Doctors advise young men to conduct a testicular self-examination every month to detect lumps or abnormal growths. A doctor may examine a lump using *ultrasound* (high frequency sound waves). Physicians also perform blood tests to detect certain chemicals that testicular cancer cells release. These chemicals, which include *human chorionic gonadotropin* (hCG) and *alpha fetoprotein* (AFP), can be measured in tiny amounts.

Doctors usually begin treatment of testicular cancer by surgically removing the affected testicle. A *pathologist* (expert on tissue changes) examines the tissue under a microscope to confirm that cancer is present and to determine certain properties that affect treatment choices. Surgery may also include removal of lymph nodes to check if cancer has spread. Testicular cancer rarely spreads to other parts of the body, and surgery usually results in a complete cure. A patient is considered completely cured if blood tests after surgery find no trace of hCG or AFP. The removal of one testicle does not usually interfere with a man's ability to have sexual relations, and many patients can still have children. If the cancer has spread beyond the testicle, surgery may be followed with radiation or *chemotherapy* (drugs that kill cancer cells). One type of testicular cancer, called *seminoma,* is treatable with radiation. Another type, called *nonseminoma,* is best treated with chemotherapy. Even patients whose cancer has spread have an excellent chance of being cured. Marc B. Garnick

Testing, in education and psychology, is an attempt to measure a person's knowledge, intelligence, or other characteristics in a systematic way. There are many types of tests. Teachers give tests to identify the abilities of students and to see how well students have learned a subject. Some tests help people choose a career. Others help people understand their personality traits or other psychological characteristics.

Most printed tests taken by students and others are *standardized.* A test has been standardized after it has been used, revised, and used again until it shows consistent results. Firms that prepare standardized tests provide information on how to administer and score each test. A standardized test score can be used to compare one person's performance with the performances of other people who took the same test. Governments in many countries fund and operate standardized testing programs to monitor student progress and ability.

Kinds of tests

Most tests are designed to measure one of several characteristics. The most common of these characteristics are (1) learning achievement, (2) learning ability, (3) aptitude and interest, and (4) personality.

Tests of learning achievement try to measure how much an individual has learned about a particular subject. Schools use achievement tests more than any other kind of test. Throughout elementary school, high school, and college, teachers rely on such tests when rating a student's progress. Teachers may use both standardized tests and tests that they develop themselves. *Nonstand-*

ardized tests usually follow the teacher's own method of instruction.

Many governments and school systems use standardized achievement testing programs to monitor the effectiveness of teachers and schools. In many countries, special achievement tests are used to license people in such professions as law, medicine, and accounting.

Tests of learning ability attempt to predict how well an individual will perform in a situation requiring intellectual ability. These tests are sometimes called *intelligence tests, mental ability tests, academic aptitude tests,* or *scholastic aptitude tests.*

An *intelligence quotient,* which is also called an *IQ,* is a number that is used to indicate a person's level of intelligence compared with other people. Intelligence quotients are determined from tests that measure learning, memory, judgment, reasoning, and problem-solving skills. See **Intelligence; Intelligence quotient.**

Tests of aptitude and interest reveal an individual's talents or preferences for certain activities. On tests called *interest inventories,* a person indicates preferences among groups of activities, ideas, and circumstances. For instance, an interest inventory might ask, "Would you rather fix a broken clock, keep a set of accounts, or paint a picture?" A person's answer indicates the strength of his or her interest in various fields.

Personality tests attempt to scientifically measure an individual's personal traits. Some personality tests consist of lists of questions requiring yes or no answers. The answers can be analyzed for various characteristics. For example, a person might score high in *social introversion,* which would indicate a strong preference for being alone. Personality tests are usually less reliable than other kinds of tests.

Current issues in testing

Testing can help teachers and schools identify what students know, what students seem able to learn, and what methods of teaching are most effective. However, testing systems also have flaws and limitations.

Many educators and social scientists advise against placing a heavy emphasis on a single test score. A test score reflects only a sample of a person's skill or knowledge. It can tell only how well the individual performed on one particular test on one particular day. Test scores should be viewed as estimates, not as precise measurements. For this reason, some scores are reported as bands rather than as single numbers. The bands show the range in which a person's actual ability probably lies.

The general effects of testing on education have also caused concern. Standardized tests sometimes lag behind educational thought and practice. If tests do not include the content of new programs, they may fail to encourage educational progress. Also, some educators believe multiple-choice tests penalize students who have expert knowledge of a subject. Such a student may see flaws in the answer generally accepted as correct.

Some experts argue that standardized tests discriminate against certain cultural groups. For instance, some students may be unfamiliar with words, terms, and concepts used in the tests. To give these students an equal chance, some educators have tried to prepare *culture-fair* or *culture-free* tests. Such tests seek to reduce the influence of cultural background on performance.

The shortcomings of testing programs have led some educators to pursue *alternative assessment* techniques—that is, nontraditional methods of evaluating student performance. Such methods often require students to show their knowledge by completing a project or by giving a demonstration, rather than by taking a test.

Laurence Parker

Related articles in *World Book* include:

College entrance examination
Competency-based education
Education (How can student performance be improved?)
Grading
National Assessment of Educational Progress
No Child Left Behind Act
Personality
Study

Additional resources

Gregory, Robert J. *Psychological Testing.* 3rd ed. Allyn & Bacon, 2000.

Lyman, Howard B. *Test Scores & What They Mean.* 6th ed. Allyn & Bacon, 1998.

McCullough, Virginia E. *Testing and Your Child.* 1992. Reprint. NAL, 1998.

Wodrich, David L. *Children's Psychological Testing: A Guide for Nonpsychologists.* 3rd ed. Brookes, 1997.

Testing, Drug. See **Drug testing.**

Testing, Genetic. See **Genetic testing.**

Testosterone, *tehs TAHS tuh rohn,* is a hormone that stimulates sexual development in male human beings. It belongs to a family of hormones called *androgens.* Androgens are produced primarily by the *testicles,* a pair of male sex glands (see **Testicle**). The ovaries in females and the adrenal glands in both sexes also yield small amounts of testosterone and other androgens.

In a boy's early teen-age years, a hormone from the pituitary gland stimulates his testicles to secrete increasing amounts of testosterone, particularly during sleep. Testosterone enters the blood and acts on certain body tissues to cause many physical changes. These include growth of hair on the face and in the genital area, muscle development, deepening of the voice, and maturation of the sex organs. Testosterone also helps in the production of sperm by the testicles. After a man reaches old age, the testicles produce less testosterone. In adult females, testosterone contributes to the formation of *estrogens* by the ovaries. Estrogens are hormones necessary for female sexual development. See **Estrogen.**

In many kinds of animals, testosterone influences male sexual behavior. For example, some deer breed in the fall. At this time, the testicles of male deer secrete large amounts of testosterone. As a result, the males spend much time pursuing females.

Drugs called *anabolic steroids* are made from testosterone. They are used by some athletes who feel such drugs increase strength and endurance. Most doctors agree that anabolic steroids can have dangerous side effects and should not be used. See **Steroid** (The sex steroids). P. Landis Keyes

Tet offensive. See **Vietnam war** (The Tet offensive).

Tetanus, *TEHT uh nuhs,* is a serious disease that affects muscles. It is also called *lockjaw* because severe *spasms* (violent muscle contractions) of the jaw muscles make it hard for victims to open their mouths.

Tetanus is caused by *toxins* (poisons) produced by a bacterium called *Clostridium tetani.* These germs thrive in dust and dirt, and need no air to live. They get into the body through breaks in the skin. Any dirt in a wound may contain tetanus germs. The germs grow quickly if no air gets to the wound.

Symptoms of tetanus usually start within several weeks after infection. The victim feels depressed, has headaches, and soon has trouble opening the mouth or swallowing. After a while, all of the body muscles tighten, and spasms may interfere with breathing. If not treated, the victim may die from exhaustion.

Tetanus can be prevented. All wounds should be cleaned thoroughly. People may be immunized against infection with injections of *tetanus toxoid,* a substance made from specially treated toxins of the bacillus. But if tetanus develops, doctors treat the disease with antitoxin injections. People with severe tetanus may need to undergo a *tracheotomy.* In this operation, surgeons make an artificial opening in the *trachea* (windpipe) to help the patient breathe. Thomas J. Gill III

Tetany, *TEHT uh nee,* is a disorder associated with overexcitability and spontaneous activity of the nervous system. It is characterized by periodic muscle spasms and small, fluttering tremors. Affected body parts may tingle or feel numb. The hands are usually affected first, but spasms may later spread to the face, body, and throat. The spasms are only painful in severe cases. Tetany results from a deficiency of calcium salts or a chemical imbalance in the body. William J. Weiner

Teton, Grand. See **Grand Teton National Park.**

Teton Range, *TEE tahn,* is a rugged group of Rocky Mountain peaks south of Yellowstone National Park in western Wyoming. The highest peak is Grand Teton (13,770 feet, or 4,197 meters). The range is 40 miles (64 kilometers) long and 10 to 15 miles (16 to 24 kilometers) wide. It forms part of Grand Teton National Park. See also **Wyoming** (pictures). Ronald E. Beiswenger

Tetra, *TEHT ruh,* is a type of small tropical fish that lives in rivers of South America and Africa. Tetras are also called *characins.* There are nearly 1,500 species of these fish. Tetras are popular aquarium fish because they can be raised in captivity and have beautiful colors. Most tetras grow 2 to 3 inches (5 to 8 centimeters) long and live 3 to 4 years.

Popular species for home aquariums include neon tetras, bleeding-heart tetras, cardinal tetras, and diamond tetras. The neon tetra has a brilliant blue stripe along the side of its body. The bleeding-heart tetra has a red splotch on the middle of its side. The cardinal tetra is deep red on the sides and the belly. The diamond tetra has a bright silver color. John E. McCosker

Scientific classification. Tetras belong to the family Characidae.

Tetracycline, *TEHT ruh SY kleen* or *TEHT ruh SY klihn,* is any of a family of antibiotics used to treat infections. The tetracyclines affect many kinds of bacteria and other microorganisms, including *rickettsias* (see **Rickettsia**). Doctors use tetracyclines to treat such serious diseases as typhus and Rocky Mountain spotted fever. They also use tetracyclines in the treatment of acne.

The first tetracycline became available in 1948. Since then, tetracyclines have been widely—and often inappropriately—used to treat a great variety of diseases. This widespread use caused many microorganisms to become resistant to the effects of these antibiotics.

All the tetracyclines fight most of the same microorganisms. They differ chiefly in how well they are absorbed by the body and in how long their effects last. Tetracyclines act by blocking the process by which bacteria make proteins. Although generally safe, tetracyclines can cause many side effects. For example, large doses of these antibiotics can seriously damage the liver and kidneys. In addition, tetracyclines can permanently discolor developing teeth. For this reason, doctors do not prescribe tetracyclines in treating children and pregnant women. Eugene M. Johnson, Jr.

See also **Antibiotic.**

Tetzel, *TEHT suhl,* **Johann,** *YOH hahn* (1465?-1519), was a Dominican friar who sold papal indulgences in Germany. He declared that anyone who bought an indulgence was freed from punishment for confessed sins and even could choose a soul to be freed from purgatory. Tetzel's claim led Martin Luther in 1517 to draw up his Ninety-Five Theses in protest. Tetzel's action thus helped start the Protestant Reformation. Many Roman Catholics criticized Tetzel for his exaggerated claims for indulgences. He defended himself vigorously but clumsily. Tetzel was born in Pirna, Germany. In 1504, Tetzel started his long career of selling indulgences. He died on Aug. 11, 1519. M. U. Edwards

See also **Luther, Martin** (The Ninety-Five Theses); **Reformation** (picture: The sale of indulgences).

Teutonic Knights, *too TAHN ihk,* was the name of an organization of German crusaders that arose in Europe during the 1100's. The Teutonic Knights were organized for service in the Holy Land. They modeled their organization after two earlier crusading orders, the Knights Templars and the Knights Hospitallers (see **Knights Templars; Knights Hospitallers**).

In the 1200's, the Teutonic Knights shifted their activities to central Europe, where they tried to convert and control the people of what became Prussia, Lithuania, Latvia, and Estonia. Their power and influence spread throughout central and eastern Europe.

In the 1300's, the Teutonic Knights lost much of their power, and finally the Poles and Lithuanians overthrew them. In 1525, the Grand Master, Albert of Hohenzollern, embraced Protestantism, and changed the Order from a religious to a civil organization. In 1618, the Order's territory passed to the Hohenzollern Elector of Brandenburg.

Bryce Lyon

See also **Latvia** (History); **Lithuania** (History).

Teutons, *TOO tuhnz,* is a name sometimes given to the Germanic peoples. The term comes from the *Teutones,* or *Teutoni,* who, with the Cimbri, were the first Germanic peoples to threaten ancient Rome's power. With their neighbors, the Ambrones, the Teutones left their homeland around the mouth of the Elbe River in the 100's B.C. In Gaul (mainly present-day France), they allied themselves with the Cimbri. The Roman general Gaius Marius defeated the Teutones at Aquae Sextiae (now Aix-en-Provence, France) in 102 B.C. He defeated the Cimbri in Italy the following year.

Later, the remnants of the Teutones mixed with other early groups that wandered through Europe. They eventually gave their name to a whole group of *Teutonic,* or *Germanic, languages.* These languages include Dutch, English, German, and the Scandinavian tongues.

Arthur M. Eckstein

Tom Algire

Big Bend National Park lies within the great bend of the Rio Grande River in western Texas. The Chisos Mountains rise in the background. Texas, the second largest state in area, has vast regions of fertile lowlands, dry plains, and mountain ranges.

Texas *The Lone Star State*

Texas has a larger area than any other state in the United States except Alaska. It is bigger than Illinois, Indiana, Iowa, Michigan, and Wisconsin combined. According to the 2000 census, Texas ranked second among the states in population, after California. Five cities in Texas rank among the nation's top 25 in population. These cities include Houston, Dallas, San Antonio, Austin, and El Paso.

Frontier cowboys with their 10-gallon hats have long been a symbol of Texas. Cowboys still ride across the plains driving great herds of cattle. And cowboy boots and hats still make up part of the everyday dress of many rural Texans. However, the Texans of today are just as likely to be workers in an oil field or scientists in a laboratory as they are to be cowboys. Or they might be engineers in a chemical plant, computer operators in a bank, or musicians in a symphony orchestra. Thousands of Texans are also employed in the aerospace industry. The Lyndon B. Johnson Space Center, located in Houston, serves as the headquarters for all manned spacecraft projects of the National Aeronautics and Space Administration (NASA).

The land of Texas has helped make the state rich. Many industries, such as trade and finance, benefit from the state's huge agricultural and mining production. Today, the state's leading economic activities include community, business, and personal services; trade; and manufacturing. Vast plains and rolling hills provide fertile soil and rich grasslands. Texas has more farms and farmland than any other state. It leads the country in the production of cattle, sheep, and wool. It also leads all other states in the production and refining of petroleum.

Many colorful people have played important roles in Texas history. Spanish adventurers began exploring the region about 450 years ago. Texas received its name

The contributors of this article are William E. Doolittle, Associate Professor and Chair, Department of Geography at the University of Texas at Austin; and Clifford L. Egan, Professor of History at the University of Houston.

Interesting facts about Texas

WORLD BOOK illustrations by Kevin Chadwick

The Comal River, the shortest river in Texas, is only $2\frac{1}{2}$ miles (4 kilometers) long. The Comal originates in a spring at one end of New Braunfels and ends at the Guadalupe River, still within the city's limits.

Marshall, Texas, served as the capital of Missouri during the Civil War from 1863 to 1865. Thomas C. Reynolds, Missouri's governor, fled to Texas when Union forces took his state. He rented two buildings, one of which served as the Missouri state capitol, the other as the Missouri governor's mansion.

Santa Gertrudis cattle, the first recognized beef breed in the Western Hemisphere, were developed between 1910 and 1940 at the King Ranch in southern Texas.

Texas has the right to divide into as many as five states under the terms of the 1845 annexation treaty that made the Republic of Texas one of the United States.

Santa Gertrudis cattle

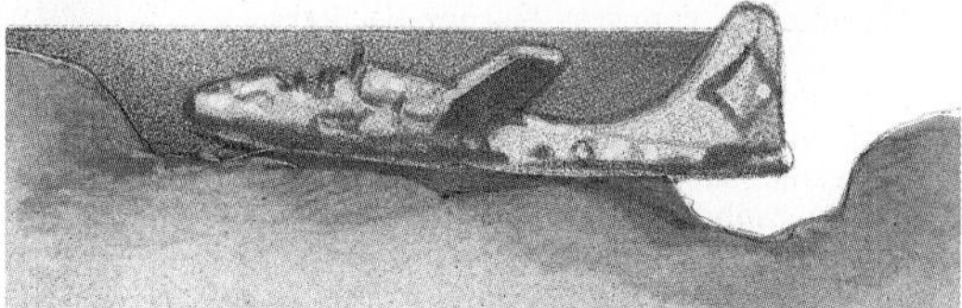

Lucky Lady II

The first round-the-world nonstop airplane flight originated from the former Carswell Air Force Base in Fort Worth. It began on February 26 and ended March 2, 1949. Captain James G. Gallagher, Lieutenant Arthur Neal, and Captain James Morris piloted the B-50 Superfortress *Lucky Lady II* on the flight, which took 94 hours, 1 minute. The airplane was refueled four times in the air by B-29 tanker planes.

The first play-by-play radio broadcast of a football game took place in College Station in November 1919. The game was played between the University of Texas and the Agricultural and Mechanical College of Texas, located at College Station.

© Walter Frerck, Odyssey Productions

Downtown Houston has many modern skyscrapers. Houston is the largest city in Texas and a major industrial center. Buffalo Bayou winds through Houston's Sabine Park in the foreground.

from their pronunciation of the Indian word *Tejas* (friends or allies). The Tejas formed a group of united Indian tribes that lived in what is now the northeastern part of the state.

Texas was part of Mexico when the first settlers from the United States arrived there in 1821. In 1836, Davy Crockett, Jim Bowie, and other famous heroes died at the Alamo fighting for independence from Mexico. Sam Houston led the Texans to their final victory against the Mexicans. One of his battle cries was "Remember the Alamo!" For nearly 10 years after the war with Mexico, Texas was an independent republic. After Texas became a state in 1845, the settlers fought Indians for many years to protect their families and homes.

Texas is called the *Lone Star State* because of the single star on its flag. Through the years, the flags of six nations have flown over Texas. Besides the United States, these nations were Spain, France, Mexico, the Republic of Texas, and the Confederate States of America. Austin is the capital of Texas, and Houston is the largest city.

Paul Conklin

Paseo del Rio (River Walk), a popular dining and shopping area, stretches along the San Antonio River in San Antonio.

Texas in brief

Symbols of Texas

The state flag, known as the Lone Star Flag, was adopted in 1839. The red stands for bravery, the white represents purity, and the blue is for loyalty. The front of the state seal also has a lone star. The oak branch to the left of the star symbolizes strength, and the olive branch to the right of the star stands for peace. The reverse side of the seal includes a display of the six flags that have flown over Texas.

State flag

State seal

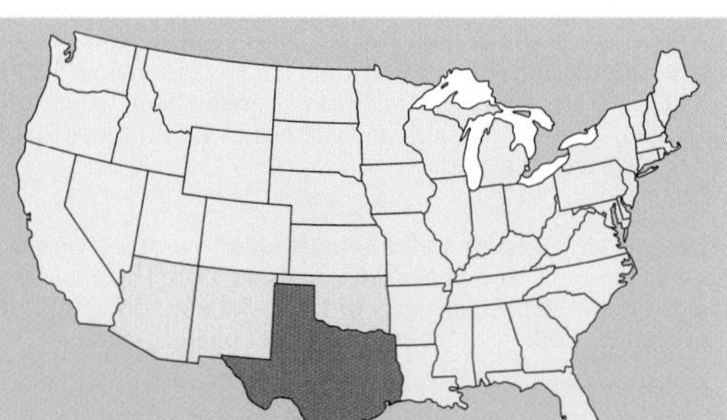
Texas (brown) ranks second in size among all the states and is the largest of the Southwestern States (yellow).

The State Capitol is in Austin, Texas's capital since 1845. Other capitals were Houston (1837-1840), Austin (1840-1842), and Washington-on-the-Brazos (1842-1845).

General information

Statehood: Dec. 29, 1845, the 28th state.
State abbreviations: Tex. (traditional); TX (postal).
State motto: *Friendship.*
State song: "Texas, Our Texas." Words by Gladys Yoakum Wright and William J. Marsh; music by William J. Marsh.

Land and climate

Area: 266,874 mi² (691,201 km²), including 4,959 mi² (12,843 km²) of inland water but excluding 404 mi² (1,047 km²) of coastal water.
Elevation: *Highest*—Guadalupe Peak, 8,749 ft (2,667 m) above sea level. *Lowest*—sea level, along the Gulf of Mexico.
Coastline: 367 mi (591 km).
Record high temperature: 120 °F (49 °C) at Seymour on Aug. 12, 1936, and Monahans on June 28, 1994.
Record low temperature: −23 °F (−31 °C) at Tulia on Feb. 12, 1899, and at Seminole on Feb. 8, 1933.
Average July temperature: 83 °F (28 °C).
Average January temperature: 46 °F (8 °C).
Average yearly precipitation: 27 in (67 cm).

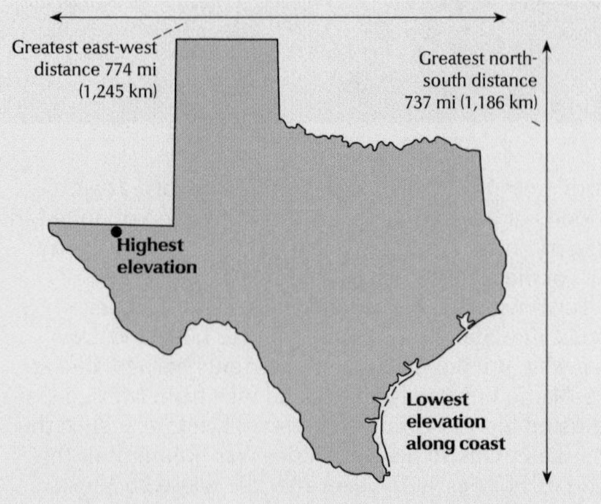

Important dates

1519 Alonso Álvarez de Piñeda of Spain mapped the Texas coast.

1682 Spanish missionaries built the first two missions in Texas, near present-day El Paso.

1835 The Texas Revolution against Mexico began.

State bird
Mockingbird

State flower
Bluebonnet

State tree
Pecan

People

Population: 20,851,820
Rank among the states: 2nd
Population density: 78 per mi² (30 per km²), U.S. average 78 per mi² (30 per km²)
Distribution: 83 percent urban, 17 percent rural

Largest cities in Texas

Houston	1,953,631
Dallas	1,188,580
San Antonio	1,144,646
Austin	656,562
El Paso	563,662
Fort Worth	534,694

Source: 2000 census.

Population trend

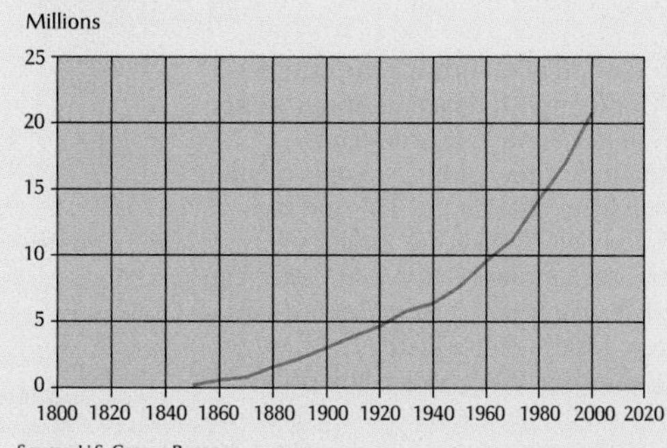

Year	Population
2000	20,851,820
1990	16,986,510
1980	14,227,574
1970	11,198,655
1960	9,579,677
1950	7,711,194
1940	6,414,824
1930	5,824,715
1920	4,663,228
1910	3,896,542
1900	3,048,710
1890	2,235,527
1880	1,591,749
1870	818,579
1860	604,215
1850	212,592

Source: U.S. Census Bureau.

Economy

Chief products

Agriculture: beef cattle, greenhouse and nursery products, sheep, cotton, milk, corn, hay.
Manufacturing: computer and electronic equipment, chemicals, food products, petroleum products, machinery, fabricated metal products, transportation equipment.
Mining: petroleum, natural gas, cement, crushed stone, salt.

Gross state product

Value of goods and services produced in 2002: $773,455,000,000. *Services* include community, business, and personal services; finance; government; trade; and transportation and communication. *Industry* includes construction, manufacturing, mining, and utilities. *Agriculture* includes agriculture, fishing, and forestry.

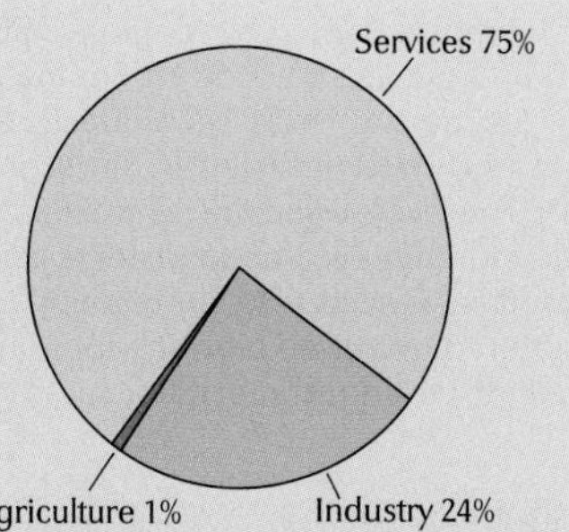

Source: U.S. Bureau of Economic Analysis.

Government

State government

Governor: 4-year term
State senators: 31; 4-year terms
State representatives: 150; 2-year terms
Counties: 254

Federal government

United States senators: 2
United States representatives: 32
Electoral votes: 34

Sources of information

For information about tourism, write to: Texas Department of Transportation, 125 E. 11th Street, Austin, TX 78701-2483. The Web site at www.traveltex.com also provides information.
For information on the economy, write to: Department of Economic Development, P.O. Box 12728, Austin, TX 78711-2728.
The state's official Web site at www.state.tx.us also provides a gateway to much information on Texas's economy, government, and history.

1836 Texas became the independent Republic of Texas.
1845 Texas became the 28th state on December 29.
1901 The great Spindletop oil field was discovered.
1963 President John F. Kennedy was assassinated in Dallas.
1964 The Manned Spacecraft Center in Houston (now the Lyndon B. Johnson Space Center) became headquarters for U.S. astronauts.
1994 The Census Bureau reported that Texas had become the second most populous state.

People

Population. The 2000 United States census reported that Texas had 20,851,820 people. The population had increased 23 percent over the 1990 figure, 16,986,510.

About 85 percent of Texans live in metropolitan areas (see **Metropolitan area**). Nearly 60 percent live in the metropolitan areas of Austin-San Marcos, Dallas, Fort Worth-Arlington, Houston, and San Antonio. In all, Texas has 27 metropolitan areas. For their populations, see the *Index* to the political map. Texas has 24 cities with more than 100,000 people. Houston is the state's largest city, followed by Dallas, San Antonio, Austin, El Paso, and Fort Worth.

About 32 percent of the people of Texas are of Hispanic origin. This is a higher percentage than in any other state except for New Mexico and California. Mexican Americans make up a majority of the state's Hispanic residents. Other large population groups include people of German, Irish, and English descent. About 12 percent of the state's people are African Americans.

Schools. Texas had only a few public schools when it gained independence from Mexico in 1836, and they held classes only in Spanish. The lack of English-language instruction was a major reason why American settlers objected to Mexican rule. In 1854, Texas established a school system for the entire state.

The Texas Education Agency supervises the public school system. It consists of the commissioner of education and the State Board of Education. The governor appoints the commissioner, who is then confirmed by the state Senate. The State Board of Education has 15 elected members. Texas law requires children to attend school from age 6 to age 18. For the number of students and teachers in Texas, see **Education** (table).

In 1984, Texas enacted public school reform legislation. The law revised the school finance system to provide more equity among districts. In addition, it imposed basic skills tests for certified teachers and administrators. It required high school seniors to pass a test in reading, writing, and mathematics before they could graduate. Also, beginning in 1985, high school students who failed a class could not participate in extracurricular activities until they improved their mark to a passing grade.

Population density

Texas has a number of large urban areas. About 85 percent of the people live in metropolitan areas. Most of the largest cities in Texas lie in the eastern part of the state.

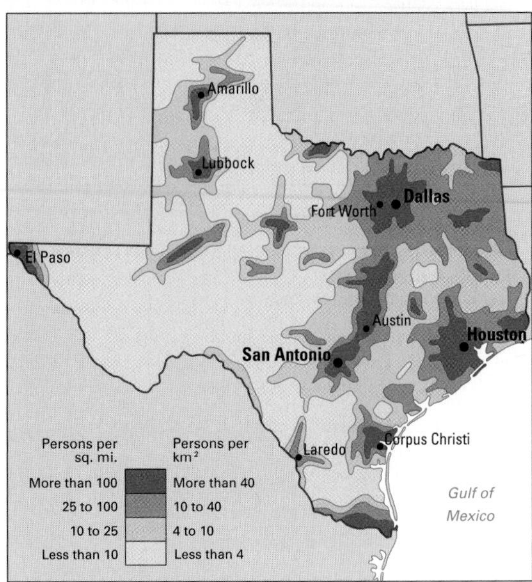

WORLD BOOK map; based on U.S. Census Bureau data.

Libraries. The Texas State Library, established in Austin in 1839 by the Republic of Texas, is Texas's oldest library. Texas has more than 150 college and university libraries and over 500 public libraries. The Houston Public Library and Dallas Public Library have the state's largest public library collections. The Lyndon Baines

© Joe Viesti

Schoolchildren listen to a lesson at the Alamo school in Galveston. Texas law requires children to attend school from age 6 to age 18.

Johnson Library and Museum, which houses the papers and mementos of the 36th president of the United States, is on the campus of the University of Texas in Austin. The George Bush Presidential Library and Museum is on the campus of Texas A&M University in College Station. It houses the official and personal papers of George H. W. Bush, the 41st U.S. president.

Museums. Collections at the Museum of Fine Art, Houston, include Italian Renaissance paintings, French Impressionist works, and African and pre-Columbian gold. The Amon Carter Museum in Fort Worth features painting and sculpture of the Old West by American artist Frederic Remington. The Dallas Museum of Art has a collection of American paintings. The Kimbell Art Museum in Fort Worth displays paintings by European masters.

The Houston Museum of Natural Science includes exhibits on astronomy, chemistry, and minerals. The Witte Museum in San Antonio has exhibits on Texas wildlife and ecology, American Indians, dinosaurs, mummies, and paintings and furniture of early Texas and America. Other museums include the Texas Hall of State in Dallas, the Sam Houston Memorial Museum in Huntsville, and the San Antonio Museum of Art.

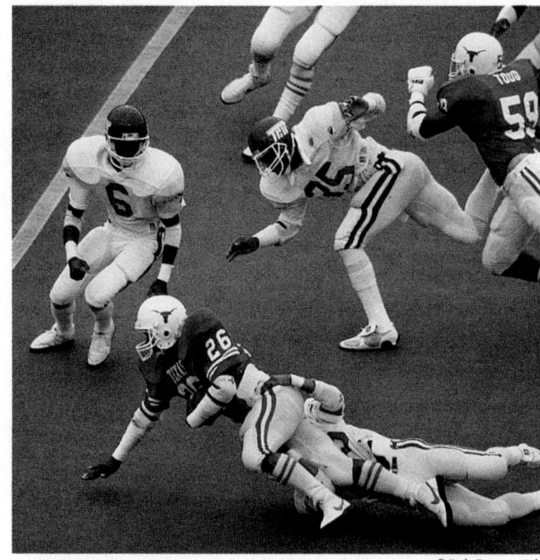

© Bob Daemmrich

The University of Texas Longhorns play their home football games at Memorial Stadium in Austin.

Universities and colleges

This table lists the universities and colleges in Texas that grant bachelor's or advanced degrees and are accredited by the Southern Association of Colleges and Schools.

Name	Mailing address
Abilene Christian University	Abilene
Amberton University	Garland
American InterContinental University	Houston
Angelo State University	San Angelo
Argosy University	Dallas
Art Institute of Dallas	Dallas
Art Institute of Houston	Houston
Austin College	Sherman
Austin Graduate School of Theology	Austin
Austin Presbyterian Theological Seminary	Austin
Baptist Missionary Association Theological Seminary	Jacksonville
Baylor College of Medicine	Houston
Baylor University	Waco
Concordia University at Austin	Austin
Criswell College	Dallas
Dallas, University of	Irving
Dallas Baptist University	Dallas
Dallas Theological Seminary	Dallas
Del Mar College	Corpus Christi
DeVry University	*
East Texas Baptist University	Marshall
Episcopal Theological Seminary of the Southwest	Austin
Hardin-Simmons University	Abilene
Houston, University of	†
Houston Baptist University	Houston
Howard Payne University	Brownwood
Huston-Tillotson College	Austin
Incarnate Word, University of the	San Antonio
Jarvis Christian College	Hawkins
Lamar University	Beaumont
LeTourneau University	Longview
Lubbock Christian University	Lubbock
Mary Hardin-Baylor, University of	Belton
McMurry University	Abilene
Midwestern State University	Wichita Falls
North Texas, University of	‡
Oblate School of Theology	San Antonio
Our Lady of the Lake University	San Antonio
Parker College of Chiropractic	Dallas
Paul Quinn College	Dallas
Prairie View A&M University	Prairie View
Rice University	Houston
St. Edward's University	Austin
St. Mary's University	San Antonio
St. Thomas, University of	Houston
St. Thomas More, College of	Fort Worth
Sam Houston State University	Huntsville
Schreiner University	Kerrville
Southern Methodist University	Dallas
Southwestern Adventist University	Keene
Southwestern Assemblies of God University	Waxahachie
Southwestern Baptist Theological Seminary	Fort Worth
Southwestern Christian College	Terrell
Southwestern University	Georgetown
Stephen F. Austin State University	Nacogdoches
Sul Ross State University	Alpine
Tarleton State University	Stephenville
Texas, University of	§
Texas A&M International University	Laredo
Texas A&M University	#
Texas Chiropractic College	Pasadena
Texas Christian University	Fort Worth
Texas College	Tyler
Texas Lutheran University	Seguin
Texas Southern University	Houston
Texas Southmost College	Brownsville
Texas State University	San Marcos
Texas Tech University	Lubbock
Texas Wesleyan University	Fort Worth
Texas Woman's University	Denton
Trinity University	San Antonio
Wayland Baptist University	Plainview
West Texas A&M University	Canyon
Wiley College	Marshall

*Campuses at Houston and Irving.
†Campuses at Houston and Victoria.
‡Campuses at Denton and Fort Worth.
§For campuses, see **Texas, University of.**
#For campuses, see **Texas A&M University.**

Texas political map
Urban area
Park or other recreation area
Forest or other conservation area
Military or other federal area
International boundary
State boundary
County boundary
BELL County name
State capital
County seat
City or town
Park or other recreation area
Point of interest
Major airport
Waterway
Railroad
Highways:
Expressway
Other road
Interstate
U.S.
Other
Lambert conformal conic projection
WORLD BOOK maps
Main map scale
0 25 50
0 25 50 100
San Antonio inset map scale
0 5 10 20 30 40 50 60 Miles 70
0 5 10 20 30 40 50 60 70 80 Kilometers 110
1 2 3 4 5 6 7 8
A B C D E F G H I J K
NEW MEXICO
CHIHUAHUA
COAHUILA
NUEVO LEÓN
TAMAULIPAS
U.S.
MEXICO
Amarillo
Lubbock
Midland
Odessa
Abilene
San Angelo
Wichita Falls
Austin
San Antonio
Laredo
El Paso
Juárez
Chihuahua
Ciudad Acuña
Piedras Negras
Nuevo Laredo
Reynosa
McAllen
Lawton
Killeen
Del Rio
Eagle Pass
CARLSBAD CAVERNS NATIONAL PARK
GUADALUPE MOUNTAINS NATIONAL PARK
BIG BEND NATIONAL PARK
FORT DAVIS NATIONAL HISTORICAL SITE
RIO GRANDE WILD AND SCENIC RIVER
AMISTAD NATIONAL RECREATION AREA
LAKE MEREDITH NAT'L. REC. AREA
ALIBATES FLINT QUARRIES NAT'L. MONUMENT
RITA BLANCA NATIONAL GRASSLAND
CHAMIZAL NATIONAL MEMORIAL
AREA OF INSET MAP
New Braunfels
Schertz
Seguin
Live Oak
Universal City
RANDOLPH AIR FORCE BASE
FORT SAM HOUSTON
LACKLAND AIR FORCE BASE
KELLY AIR FORCE BASE
BROOKS AIR FORCE BASE
SAN ANTONIO MISSIONS NATIONAL HISTORICAL PARK

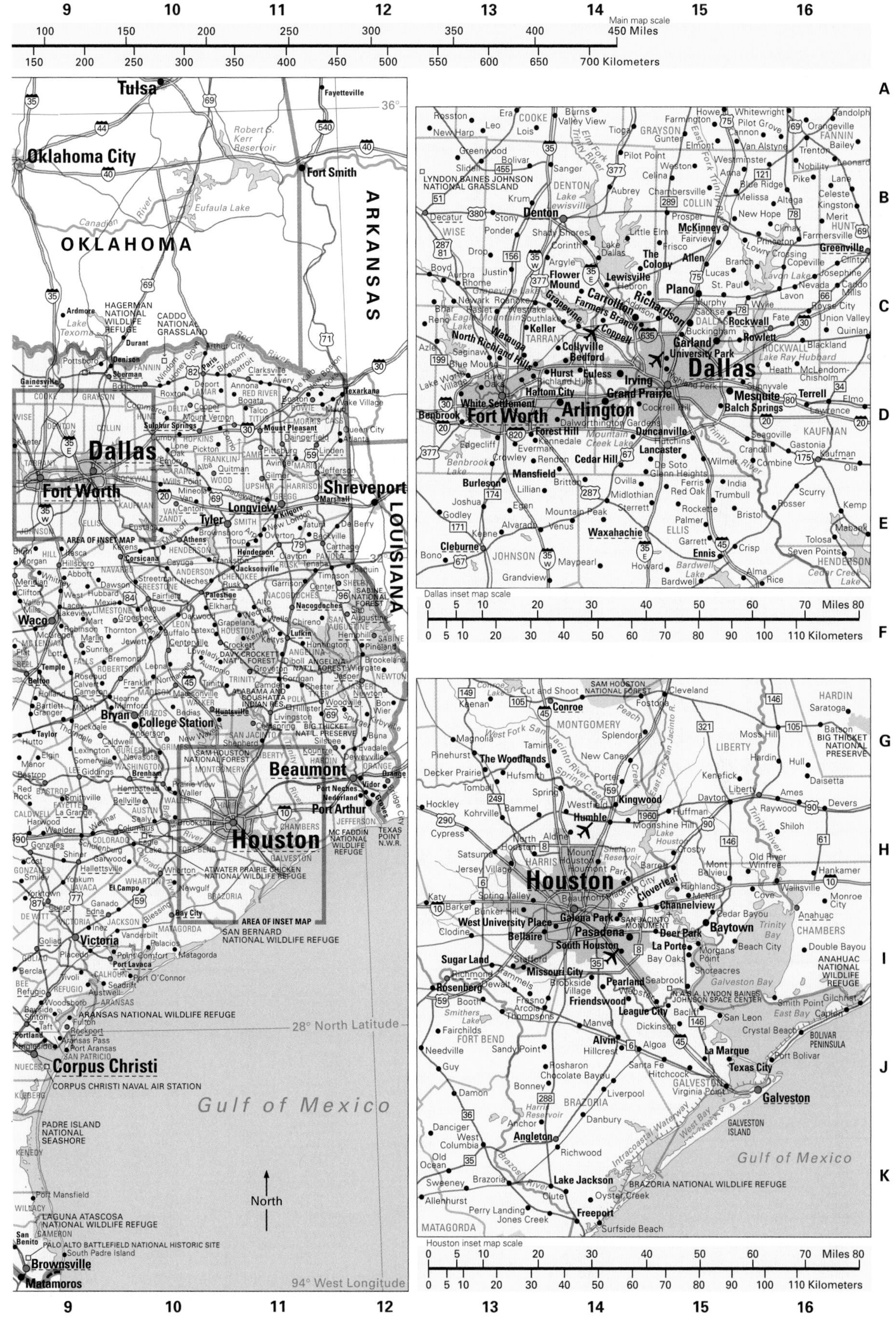

9 10 11 12 13 14 15 16
Main map scale
100 150 200 250 300 350 400 450 Miles
150 200 250 300 350 400 450 500 550 600 650 700 Kilometers
A
B
C
D
E
F
G
H
I
J
K
Tulsa
Oklahoma City
Fort Smith
OKLAHOMA
ARKANSAS
LOUISIANA
Eufaula Lake
Robert S. Kerr Reservoir
HAGERMAN NATIONAL WILDLIFE REFUGE
CADDO NATIONAL GRASSLAND
Dallas
Fort Worth
Shreveport
Tyler
Longview
Texarkana
Waco
Bryan
College Station
Huntsville
Beaumont
Port Arthur
Houston
Victoria
Corpus Christi
CORPUS CHRISTI NAVAL AIR STATION
PADRE ISLAND NATIONAL SEASHORE
LAGUNA ATASCOSA NATIONAL WILDLIFE REFUGE
PALO ALTO BATTLEFIELD NATIONAL HISTORIC SITE
Brownsville
Matamoros
ARANSAS NATIONAL WILDLIFE REFUGE
SAN BERNARD NATIONAL WILDLIFE REFUGE
ATWATER PRAIRIE CHICKEN NATIONAL WILDLIFE REFUGE
MC FADDIN NATIONAL WILDLIFE REFUGE
TEXAS POINT N.W.R.
SAM HOUSTON NATIONAL FOREST
DAVY CROCKETT NAT'L FOREST
ANGELINA NAT'L FOREST
SABINE NATIONAL FOREST
BIG THICKET NAT'L PRESERVE
ALABAMA AND COUSHATTA INDIAN RES.
AREA OF INSET MAP
Gulf of Mexico
28° North Latitude
94° West Longitude
36°
32°
North
Denton
McKinney
Plano
Richardson
Garland
Irving
Grand Prairie
Arlington
Mesquite
Lewisville
Carrollton
Denison
Sherman
Paris
Cleburne
Waxahachie
Ennis
LYNDON BAINES JOHNSON NATIONAL GRASSLAND
Dallas inset map scale
0 5 10 20 30 40 50 60 70 Miles 80
0 5 10 20 30 40 50 60 70 80 90 100 110 Kilometers
Conroe
The Woodlands
Kingwood
Humble
Baytown
Pasadena
Sugar Land
Missouri City
Pearland
League City
Texas City
Galveston
La Marque
Angleton
Lake Jackson
Freeport
Galveston Bay
BOLIVAR PENINSULA
GALVESTON ISLAND
ANAHUAC NATIONAL WILDLIFE REFUGE
BRAZORIA NATIONAL WILDLIFE REFUGE
N.A.S.A. LYNDON BAINES JOHNSON SPACE CENTER
SAN JACINTO MONUMENT
Houston inset map scale
0 5 10 20 30 40 50 60 70 Miles 80
0 5 10 20 30 40 50 60 70 80 90 100 110 Kilometers

Texas map index

Metropolitan areas

Abilene ... 126,555
Amarillo ... 217,858
Austin-San Marcos ... 1,249,763
Beaumont-Port Arthur ... 385,090
Brazoria ... 241,767
Brownsville-Harlingen-San Benito ... 335,227
Bryan-College Station ... 152,415
Corpus Christi ... 380,783
Dallas ... 3,519,176
El Paso ... 679,622
Fort Worth-Arlington ... 1,702,625
Galveston-Texas City ... 250,158
Houston ... 4,177,646
Killeen-Temple ... 312,952
Laredo ... 193,117
Longview-Marshall ... 208,780
Lubbock ... 242,628
McAllen-Edinburg-Mission ... 569,463
Odessa-Midland ... 237,132
San Angelo ... 104,010
San Antonio ... 1,592,383
Sherman- Denison ... 110,595
Texarkana-Texarkana (Ark.) ... 129,749 (89,306 in Tex.; 40,443 in Ark.)
Tyler ... 174,706
Victoria ... 84,088
Waco ... 213,517
Wichita Falls ... 140,518

Counties

Anderson ... 55,109 .. F 10
Andrews ... 13,004 .. E 4
Angelina ... 80,130 .. F 11
Aransas ... 22,497 .. I 9
Archer ... 8,854 .. D 8
Armstrong ... 2,148 .. B 5
Atascosa ... 38,628 .. I 8
Austin ... 23,590 .. H 10
Bailey ... 6,594 .. C 4
Bandera ... 17,645 .. H 7
Bastrop ... 57,733 .. G 9
Baylor ... 4,093 .. D 7
Bee ... 32,359 .. I 8
Bell ... 237,974 .. F 9
Bexar ... 1,392,931 .. H 8
Blanco ... 8,418 .. G 8
Borden ... 729 .. E 5
Bosque ... 17,204 .. F 8
Bowie ... 89,306 .. D 11
Brazoria ... 241,767 .. H 11
Brazos ... 152,415 .. G 10
Brewster ... 8,866 .. G 3
Briscoe ... 1,790 .. C 5
Brooks ... 7,976 .. K 8
Brown ... 37,674 .. F 7
Burleson ... 16,470 .. G 9
Burnet ... 34,147 .. G 8
Caldwell ... 32,194 .. H 9
Calhoun ... 20,647 .. I 9
Callahan ... 12,905 .. E 7
Cameron ... 335,227 .. K 9
Camp ... 11,549 .. D 11
Carson ... 6,516 .. B 5
Cass ... 30,438 .. D 11
Castro ... 8,285 .. C 4
Chambers ... 26,031 .. H 11
Cherokee ... 46,659 .. F 11
Childress ... 7,688 .. C 6
Clay ... 11,006 .. D 8
Cochran ... 3,730 .. D 4
Coke ... 3,864 .. F 6
Coleman ... 9,235 .. F 7
Collin ... 491,675 .. D 9
Collingsworth ... 3,206 .. B 6
Colorado ... 20,390 .. H 10
Comal ... 78,021 .. H 8
Comanche ... 14,026 .. E 7
Concho ... 3,966 .. F 6
Cooke ... 36,363 .. D 9
Coryell ... 74,978 .. F 8
Cottle ... 1,904 .. C 6
Crane ... 3,996 .. F 4
Crockett ... 4,099 .. G 5
Crosby ... 7,072 .. D 5
Culberson ... 2,975 .. F 2
Dallam ... 6,222 .. A 4
Dallas ... 2,218,899 .. E 9
Dawson ... 14,985 .. E 5
Deaf Smith ... 18,561 .. B 4
Delta ... 5,327 .. D 10
Denton ... 432,976 .. D 9
De Witt ... 20,013 .. I 9
Dickens ... 2,762 .. D 6
Dimmit ... 10,248 .. I 6
Donley ... 3,828 .. B 6
Duval ... 13,120 .. J 8
Eastland ... 18,297 .. E 7
Ector ... 121,123 .. E 4
Edwards ... 2,162 .. H 6
Ellis ... 111,360 .. E 9
El Paso ... 679,622 .. E 1
Erath ... 33,001 .. E 8
Falls ... 18,576 .. F 9
Fannin ... 31,242 .. D 10
Fayette ... 21,804 .. H 9
Fisher ... 4,344 .. E 6
Floyd ... 7,771 .. C 5
Foard ... 1,622 .. C 7
Fort Bend ... 354,452 .. H 10
Franklin ... 9,458 .. D 11
Freestone ... 17,867 .. F 10
Frio ... 16,252 .. I 7
Gaines ... 14,467 .. E 4
Galveston ... 250,158 .. H 11
Garza ... 4,872 .. D 5
Gillespie ... 20,814 .. G 7
Glasscock ... 1,406 .. F 5
Goliad ... 6,928 .. I 9
Gonzales ... 18,628 .. H 9
Gray ... 22,744 .. B 6
Grayson ... 110,595 .. D 9
Gregg ... 111,379 .. E 11
Grimes ... 23,552 .. G 10
Guadalupe ... 89,023 .. H 8
Hale ... 36,602 .. C 5
Hall ... 3,782 .. C 6
Hamilton ... 8,229 .. F 8
Hansford ... 5,369 .. A 5
Hardeman ... 4,724 .. C 7
Hardin ... 48,073 .. G 11
Harris ... 3,400,578 .. H 11
Harrison ... 62,110 .. E 11
Hartley ... 5,537 .. A 4
Haskell ... 6,093 .. D 7
Hays ... 97,589 .. G 8
Hemphill ... 3,351 .. A 6
Henderson ... 73,277 .. E 10
Hidalgo ... 569,463 .. K 8
Hill ... 32,321 .. E 9
Hockley ... 22,716 .. D 4
Hood ... 41,100 .. E 8
Hopkins ... 31,960 .. D 10
Houston ... 23,185 .. F 11
Howard ... 33,627 .. E 5
Hudspeth ... 3,344 .. F 1
Hunt ... 76,596 .. D 10
Hutchinson ... 23,857 .. A 5
Irion ... 1,771 .. F 5
Jack ... 8,763 .. D 8
Jackson ... 14,391 .. I 10
Jasper ... 35,604 .. G 12
Jeff Davis ... 2,207 .. G 2
Jefferson ... 252,051 .. H 12
Jim Hogg ... 5,281 .. K 7
Jim Wells ... 39,326 .. J 8
Johnson ... 126,811 .. E 9
Jones ... 20,785 .. E 6
Karnes ... 15,446 .. I 8
Kaufman ... 71,313 .. E 10
Kendall ... 23,743 .. H 7
Kenedy ... 414 .. K 9
Kent ... 859 .. D 6
Kerr ... 43,653 .. G 7
Kimble ... 4,468 .. G 7
King ... 356 .. D 6
Kinney ... 3,379 .. H 6
Kleberg ... 31,549 .. J 9
Knox ... 4,253 .. D 7
Lamar ... 48,499 .. D 10
Lamb ... 14,709 .. C 4
Lampasas ... 17,762 .. F 8
La Salle ... 5,866 .. I 7
Lavaca ... 19,210 .. H 9
Lee ... 15,657 .. G 9
Leon ... 15,335 .. F 10
Liberty ... 70,154 .. G 11
Limestone ... 22,051 .. F 9
Lipscomb ... 3,057 .. A 6
Live Oak ... 12,309 .. I 8
Llano ... 17,044 .. G 8
Loving ... 67 .. E 3
Lubbock ... 242,628 .. D 5
Lynn ... 6,550 .. D 5
Madison ... 12,940 .. G 10
Marion ... 10,941 .. E 11
Martin ... 4,746 .. E 5
Mason ... 3,738 .. G 7
Matagorda ... 37,957 .. I 10
Maverick ... 47,297 .. I 6
McCulloch ... 8,205 .. F 7
McLennan ... 213,517 .. F 9
McMullen ... 851 .. I 8
Medina ... 39,304 .. H 7
Menard ... 2,360 .. G 6
Midland ... 116,009 .. F 4
Milam ... 24,238 .. F 9
Mills ... 5,151 .. F 8
Mitchell ... 9,698 .. E 6
Montague ... 19,117 .. D 8
Montgomery ... 293,768 .. G 10
Moore ... 20,121 .. A 5
Morris ... 13,048 .. D 11
Motley ... 1,426 .. C 6
Nacogdoches ... 59,203 .. F 11
Navarro ... 45,124 .. E 10
Newton ... 15,072 .. G 12
Nolan ... 15,802 .. E 6
Nueces ... 313,645 .. J 9
Ochiltree ... 9,006 .. A 6
Oldham ... 2,185 .. B 4
Orange ... 84,966 .. G 12
Palo Pinto ... 27,026 .. E 8
Panola ... 22,756 .. E 11
Parker ... 88,495 .. E 8
Parmer ... 10,016 .. C 4
Pecos ... 16,809 .. G 4
Polk ... 41,133 .. G 11
Potter ... 113,546 .. B 5
Presidio ... 7,304 .. G 2
Rains ... 9,139 .. D 10
Randall ... 104,312 .. B 5
Reagan ... 3,326 .. F 5
Real ... 3,047 .. H 6
Red River ... 14,314 .. D 11
Reeves ... 13,137 .. F 3
Refugio ... 7,828 .. I 9
Roberts ... 887 .. A 6
Robertson ... 16,000 .. F 9
Rockwall ... 43,080 .. D 10
Runnels ... 11,495 .. F 6
Rusk ... 47,372 .. E 11
Sabine ... 10,469 .. F 12
San Augustine ... 8,946 .. F 12
San Jacinto ... 22,246 .. G 11
San Patricio ... 67,138 .. J 9
San Saba ... 6,186 .. F 7
Schleicher ... 2,935 .. G 6
Scurry ... 16,361 .. E 6
Shackelford ... 3,302 .. E 7
Shelby ... 25,224 .. F 12
Sherman ... 3,186 .. A 5
Smith ... 174,706 .. E 11
Somervell ... 6,809 .. E 8
Starr ... 53,597 .. K 7
Stephens ... 9,674 .. E 7
Sterling ... 1,393 .. E 5
Stonewall ... 1,693 .. D 6
Sutton ... 4,077 .. G 6
Swisher ... 8,378 .. C 5
Tarrant ... 1,446,219 .. E 9
Taylor ... 126,555 .. E 6
Terrell ... 1,081 .. G 4
Terry ... 12,761 .. D 4
Throckmorton ... 1,850 .. D 7
Titus ... 28,118 .. D 11
Tom Green ... 104,010 .. F 6
Travis ... 812,280 .. G 8
Trinity ... 13,779 .. F 11
Tyler ... 20,871 .. F 11
Upshur ... 35,291 .. D 10
Upton ... 3,404 .. F 4
Uvalde ... 25,926 .. H 7
Val Verde ... 44,856 .. H 5
Van Zandt ... 48,140 .. E 10
Victoria ... 84,088 .. I 9
Walker ... 61,758 .. G 10
Waller ... 32,663 .. H 10
Ward ... 10,909 .. F 3
Washington ... 30,373 .. G 10
Webb ... 193,117 .. J 7
Wharton ... 41,188 .. H 10
Wheeler ... 5,284 .. B 6
Wichita ... 131,664 .. C 8
Wilbarger ... 14,676 .. C 7
Willacy ... 20,082 .. K 9
Williamson ... 249,967 .. G 8
Wilson ... 32,408 .. H 8
Winkler ... 7,173 .. E 3
Wise ... 48,793 .. D 9
Wood ... 36,752 .. E 10
Yoakum ... 7,322 .. D 4
Young ... 17,943 .. D 8
Zapata ... 12,182 .. K 7
Zavala ... 11,600 .. I 6

Cities, towns, and villages

Abernathy ... 2,839 .. C 5
Abilene° ... 115,930 .. E 7
Addison ... 14,166 .. C 15
Agua Dulce† ... 738 .. J 8
Alabama and Coushatta Indian Reservation ... 480 .. G 11
Alamo* ... 14,760 .. K 8
Alamo Heights ... 7,319 .. J 2
Albany° ... 1,921 .. E 7
Aldine† ... 13,979 .. H 14
Aledo* ... 1,726 .. E 8
Alice° ... 19,010 .. J 8
Allen ... 43,554 .. C 15
Alpine° ... 5,786 .. G 3
Alto ... 1,190 .. F 11
Alton* ... 4,384 .. K 8
Alvarado ... 3,288 .. E 13
Alvin ... 21,413 .. J 14
Alvord ... 1,007 .. D 8
Amarillo° ... 173,627 .. B 5
Ames ... 1,079 .. H 16
Amherst ... 791 .. C 4
Anahuac° ... 2,210 .. I 16
Anderson° ... 257 .. G 10
Andrews° ... 9,652 .. E 4
Angleton° ... 18,130 .. K 14
Anna ... 1,225 .. B 15
Anson° ... 2,556 .. E 6
Anthony ... 3,850 .. E 1
Anton ... 1,200 .. C 4
Aransas Pass ... 8,138 .. J 9
Archer City° ... 1,848 .. D 8
Argyle ... 3,265 .. C 14
Arlington ... 332,969 .. D 14
Arp ... 901 .. E 11
Asherton ... 1,342 .. I 6
Aspermont° ... 1,021 .. D 6
Athens° ... 11,297 .. E 10
Atlanta ... 5,745 .. D 12
Aubrey ... 1,500 .. B 14
Austin° ... 656,562 .. G 8
Azle ... 9,600 .. C 13
Bacliff† ... 6,962 .. I 15
Baird° ... 1,623 .. E 7
Balch Springs ... 19,375 .. D 15
Balcones Heights ... 3,016 .. J 1
Ballinger° ... 4,243 .. F 6
Bandera° ... 957 .. H 7
Bangs ... 1,620 .. F 7
Barrett† ... 2,872 .. H 15
Bartlett ... 1,675 .. G 9
Bastrop° ... 5,340 .. G 9
Bay City° ... 18,667 .. I 10
Baytown ... 66,430 .. I 15
Beach City ... 1,645 .. I 15
Beaumont° ... 113,866 .. G 12
Beckville ... 752 .. E 11
Bedford ... 47,152 .. D 14
Beeville° ... 13,129 .. I 8
Bellaire ... 15,642 .. I 14
Bellmead* ... 9,214 .. F 9
Bellville° ... 3,794 .. H 10
Belton° ... 14,623 .. F 9
Benavides ... 1,686 .. J 8
Benbrook ... 20,208 .. D 13
Benjamin° ... 264 .. D 7
Bertram ... 1,122 .. G 8
Beverly Hills* ... 2,113 .. F 9
Bevil Oaks* ... 1,346 .. G 12
Big Lake° ... 2,885 .. F 5
Big Sandy* ... 1,288 .. E 11
Big Spring° ... 25,233 .. E 5
Big Wells ... 704 .. I 7
Bishop ... 3,305 .. J 8
Blanco ... 1,505 .. G 8
Blossom ... 1,439 .. D 10
Blue Mound ... 2,388 .. D 13
Boerne° ... 6,178 .. H 7
Bogata ... 1,396 .. D 11
Bonham° ... 9,990 .. D 10
Booker ... 1,315 .. A 6
Borger ... 14,302 .. A 5
Boston° ... D 11
Bovina ... 1,874 .. C 4
Bowie ... 5,219 .. D 8
Boyd ... 1,099 .. C 13
Brackettville° ... 1,876 .. H 6
Brady° ... 5,523 .. F 7
Brazoria ... 2,787 .. K 13
Breckenridge° ... 5,868 .. E 7
Bremond ... 876 .. F 9
Brenham° ... 13,507 .. G 10
Briar† ... 5,350 .. C 13
Bridge City ... 8,651 .. G 12
Bridgeport ... 4,309 .. D 8
Bronte ... 1,076 .. E 6
Brookshire ... 3,450 .. H 10
Brookside Village ... 1,960 .. I 14
Brownfield° ... 9,488 .. D 4
Brownsville° ... 139,722 .. K 9
Brownwood° ... 18,813 .. F 7
Bruceville-Eddy* ... 1,490 .. F 9
Bryan° ... 65,660 .. G 10
Buffalo ... 1,804 .. F 10
Bunker Hill ... I 13
Burkburnett ... 10,927 .. C 8
Burleson ... 20,976 .. E 13
Burnet° ... 4,735 .. G 8
Cactus ... 2,538 .. A 5
Caddo Mills ... 1,149 .. C 16
Caldwell° ... 3,449 .. G 9
Calvert ... 1,426 .. F 9
Cameron° ... 5,634 .. G 9
Canadian° ... 2,233 .. A 6
Canton° ... 3,292 .. E 10
Canyon° ... 12,875 .. B 5
Carrizo Springs° ... 5,655 .. I 6
Carrollton ... 109,576 .. C 14
Carthage° ... 6,664 .. E 11
Castle Hills ... 4,202 .. J 2
Castroville ... 2,664 .. K 1
Cedar Hill ... 32,093 .. D 14
Cedar Park* ... 26,049 .. G 8
Celina ... 1,861 .. B 15
Center° ... 5,678 .. F 12
Centerville° ... 903 .. F 10
Chandler* ... 2,099 .. E 10
Channelview† ... 29,685 .. I 15
Channing° ... 356 .. A 4
Charlotte ... 1,637 .. I 7
Chico ... 947 .. D 8
Childress° ... 6,778 .. C 6
Chillicothe ... 798 .. C 7
China* ... 1,112 .. G 12
Cisco ... 3,851 .. E 7
Clarendon° ... 1,974 .. B 6
Clarksville° ... 3,883 .. D 11
Claude° ... 1,313 .. B 5
Clear Lake Shores* ... 1,205 .. H 11
Cleburne° ... 26,005 .. E 13
Cleveland ... 7,605 .. F 14
Clifton ... 3,542 .. E 8
Clint* ... 980 .. E 1
Cloverleaf† ... 23,508 .. I 14
Clute ... 10,424 .. K 14
Clyde ... 3,345 .. E 7
Coahoma ... 932 .. E 5
Cockrell Hill ... 4,443 .. D 14
Coldspring° ... 691 .. G 11
Coleman° ... 5,127 .. F 7
College Station ... 67,890 .. G 10
Colleyville ... 19,636 .. C 14
Colorado City° ... 4,281 .. E 6
Columbus° ... 3,916 .. H 9
Comanche° ... 4,482 .. E 8
Combes* ... 2,553 .. K 8
Comfort† ... 2,358 .. H 7
Commerce ... 7,669 .. D 10
Conroe° ... 36,811 .. G 14
Converse ... 11,508 .. J 2
Cooper° ... 2,150 .. D 10
Coppell ... 35,958 .. C 14
Copperas Cove ... 29,592 .. F 8
Corinth ... 11,325 .. B 14
Corpus Christi° ... 277,454 .. J 9
Corrigan ... 1,721 .. F 11
Corsicana° ... 24,485 .. E 10
Cotulla° ... 3,614 .. I 7
Cove ... 323 .. H 16
Crandall ... 2,774 .. D 16
Crane° ... 3,191 .. F 4
Crockett° ... 7,141 .. F 11
Crosbyton° ... 1,874 .. D 5
Cross Plains ... 1,068 .. E 7
Crowell° ... 1,141 .. C 7
Crowley ... 7,467 .. D 13
Crystal Beach ... J 16
Crystal City° ... 7,190 .. I 7
Cuero° ... 6,571 .. I 9
Cut and Shoot ... 1,158 .. G 14
Daingerfield° ... 2,517 .. D 11
Daisetta ... 1,034 .. G 16
Dalhart° ... 7,237 .. A 4
Dallas° ... 1,188,580 .. D 10
Dalworthington Gardens ... 2,186 .. D 14
Danbury* ... 1,611 .. J 14
Dawson ... 852 .. F 9
Dayton ... 5,709 .. H 15
Decatur° ... 5,201 .. B 13
Deer Park ... 28,520 .. I 15
De Kalb ... 1,769 .. D 11
De Leon ... 2,433 .. E 7
Del Rio° ... 33,867 .. H 6
Denison ... 22,773 .. D 9
Denton° ... 80,537 .. B 14
Denver City ... 3,985 .. D 4
De Soto ... 37,646 .. D 15
Detroit ... 776 .. D 11
Devine ... 4,140 .. K 1
Diboll ... 5,470 .. F 11
Dickens° ... 332 .. D 5
Dickinson ... 17,093 .. J 15
Dilley ... 3,674 .. I 7
Dimmitt° ... 4,375 .. C 4
Donna ... 14,768 .. K 8
Dublin ... 3,754 .. E 8
Dumas° ... 13,747 .. A 5
Duncanville ... 36,081 .. D 15
Eagle Lake ... 3,664 .. H 10
Eagle Pass° ... 22,413 .. I 6
Early ... 2,588 .. F 7
Earth ... 1,109 .. C 4
Eastland° ... 3,769 .. E 8
Edcouch* ... 3,342 .. K 8
Eden ... 2,561 .. F 6
Edgecliff ... 2,550 .. D 13
Edgewood* ... 1,348 .. E 10
Edinburg° ... 48,465 .. K 8
Edna° ... 5,899 .. I 9
El Campo ... 10,945 .. H 10
Eldorado° ... 1,951 .. G 6
Electra ... 3,168 .. C 7
Elgin ... 5,700 .. G 9
Elkhart ... 1,215 .. F 10
El Lago* ... 3,075 .. I 15
El Paso° ... 563,662 .. E 1
Elsa* ... 5,549 .. K 8
Emory° ... 1,021 .. D 10
Ennis ... 16,045 .. E 15
Euless ... 46,005 .. D 14
Everman ... 5,836 .. D 13
Fabens† ... 8,043 .. F 1
Fairfield° ... 3,094 .. F 10
Fairview ... 2,644 .. B 15
Falfurrias° ... 5,297 .. K 8
Farmers Branch ... 27,508 .. C 14
Farmersville ... 3,118 .. B 16
Farwell° ... 1,364 .. C 4
Ferris ... 2,175 .. E 15
Flatonia* ... 1,377 .. H 9
Florence* ... 1,054 .. G 8
Floresville° ... 5,868 .. K 3
Flower Mound ... 50,702 .. C 14
Floydada° ... 3,676 .. C 5
Forest Hill ... 12,949 .. D 14
Forney* ... 5,588 .. D 16
Fort Bliss† ... 8,264 .. E 1
Fort Davis† ... 1,050 .. G 3
Fort Hood† ... 33,711 .. F 8
Fort Stockton° ... 7,846 .. F 4
Fort Worth° ... 534,694 .. E 9
Franklin° ... 1,470 .. F 10
Frankston ... 1,209 .. E 11
Fredericksburg° ... 8,911 .. G 7
Freeport ... 12,708 .. K 14
Freer ... 3,241 .. J 7
Friendswood ... 29,037 .. I 14
Friona ... 3,854 .. C 4
Frisco ... 33,714 .. B 15
Fritch ... 2,235 .. A 5
Fuller Springs* ... F 11
Gail° ... D 5
Gainesville° ... 15,538 .. D 9
Galena Park ... 10,592 .. I 14
Galveston° ... 57,247 .. J 16
Ganado ... 1,915 .. I 9
Garden City° ... E 5
Garland ... 215,768 .. C 15
Garrison ... 844 .. F 11
Gatesville° ... 15,591 .. F 8
George West° ... 2,524 .. I 8
Georgetown° ... 28,339 .. G 8
Giddings° ... 5,105 .. G 9
Gilmer° ... 4,799 .. E 11
Gladewater ... 6,078 .. E 11

Place	Population	Key
Glenn Heights	7,224	E 15
Glen Rose○	2,122	E 8
Goldthwaite○	1,802	F 7
Goliad○	1,975	I 9
Gonzales○	7,202	H 9
Gorman	1,236	E 7
Graham○	8,716	D 7
Granbury○	5,718	E 8
Grand Prairie	127,427	D 14
Grand Saline*	3,028	E 10
Grandview	1,358	F 13
Granger	1,299	G 9
Grapeland	1,451	F 11
Grapevine	42,059	C 14
Greenville○	23,960	B 16
Gregory*	2,318	J 9
Grey Forest	418	J 1
Groesbeck○	4,291	F 10
Groom	587	B 5
Groves	15,733	H 12
Groveton○	1,107	F 11
Grulla		K 8
Gruver	1,162	A 5
Gun Barrel City*	5,145	E 16
Gunter	1,230	A 15
Guthrie○		D 6
Hale Center	2,263	C 5
Hallettsville○	2,345	H 9
Hallsville*	2,772	E 11
Haltom City	39,018	D 14
Hamilton○	2,977	F 8
Hamlin	2,248	D 6
Hardin	755	G 16
Harker Heights	17,308	G 8
Harlingen	57,564	K 8
Hart	1,198	C 4
Haskell○	3,106	D 7
Hawkins*	1,331	E 11
Hearne	4,690	G 10
Heath	4,149	D 16
Hebbronville○†	4,498	J 7
Hedwig Village*	2,334	I 13
Hemphill○	1,106	F 12
Hempstead○	4,691	G 10
Henderson○	11,273	E 11
Henrietta○	3,264	C 8
Hereford○	14,597	B 4
Hewitt*	11,085	F 9
Hickory Creek*	2,078	C 14
Hico	1,341	E 8
Hidalgo*	7,322	K 8
Highland Park	8,842	D 15
Highland Village*	12,173	C 14
Highlands†	7,089	H 15
Hill Country Village*	1,028	J 2
Hillcrest	722	J 14
Hillsboro○	8,232	E 9
Hitchcock	6,386	J 15
Holland	1,102	G 8
Holliday	1,632	C 7
Hollywood Park*	2,983	J 2
Hondo○	7,897	H 7
Honey Grove	1,746	D 10
Hooks	2,973	D 11
Houston○	1,953,631	H 11
Howe	2,478	A 15
Hubbard	1,586	F 9
Hudson*	3,792	F 11
Hughes Springs*	1,856	D 11
Humble	14,579	H 14
Hunters Creek Village*	4,374	I 13
Huntington	2,068	F 11
Huntsville○	35,078	G 11
Hurst	36,273	D 14
Hutchins	2,805	D 15
Idalou	2,157	D 5
Ingleside	9,388	J 9
Iowa Park	6,431	C 7
Iraan	1,238	F 5
Irving	191,615	D 14
Italy*	1,993	E 9
Itasca	1,503	E 9
Jacinto City	10,302	H 14
Jacksboro○	4,533	D 8
Jacksonville	13,868	E 11
Jasper○	8,247	F 12
Jayton○	513	D 6
Jefferson○	2,024	D 12
Jersey Village	6,880	H 13
Joaquin	925	E 12
Johnson City○	1,191	G 8
Jones Creek	2,130	K 13
Joshua	4,528	E 13
Jourdanton○	3,732	I 8
Junction○	2,618	G 7
Justin	1,891	C 13
Karnes City○	3,457	I 8
Katy	11,775	H 13
Kaufman○	6,490	D 16
Keene	5,003	E 13
Keller	27,345	C 14
Kemah*	2,330	I 15
Kemp	1,133	E 16
Kenedy	3,487	I 8
Kenefick	667	G 15
Kennedale	5,850	D 14
Kerens	1,681	E 10
Kermit○	5,714	E 3
Kerrville○	20,425	H 7
Kilgore	11,301	E 11
Killeen	86,911	G 8
Kingsland†	4,584	G 8
Kingsville○	25,575	J 8
Kingwood		H 14
Kirby	8,673	J 2
Kirbyville	2,085	G 12
Knox City	1,219	D 6
Kountze○	2,115	G 11
Kress	826	C 5
Krum	1,979	B 13
Kyle	5,314	H 8
Lackland Air Force Base†	7,123	K 1
Lacey-Lakeview	5,764	F 9
La Coste	1,255	K 1
La Feria*	6,115	K 8
La Grange○	4,478	H 9
La Joya*	3,303	K 8
Lake Dallas	6,166	C 14
Lake Jackson	26,386	K 14
Lake Worth Village		D 13
Lakeport*	861	E 11
Lakeside*	1,040	D 8
Lakeway*	8,002	G 8
La Marque	13,682	J 15
Lamesa○	9,952	D 4
Lampasas○	6,786	F 8
Lancaster	25,894	D 15
La Porte	31,880	I 15
La Pryor†	1,491	I 6
Laredo○	176,576	J 7
Las Milpas*		K 8
Laughlin Air Force Base†	2,225	H 5
La Villa*	1,305	K 8
League City	45,444	I 15
Leakey○	387	H 7
Leander*	7,596	G 8
Lefors	559	B 6
Leon Valley	9,239	J 1
Leonard	1,846	A 16
Levelland○	12,866	D 4
Lewisville	77,737	C 14
Lexington	1,178	G 9
Liberty○	8,033	G 15
Liberty City*†	1,935	E 11
Lindale*	2,954	E 10
Linden○	2,256	D 12
Lipscomb†○	44	A 6
Little Elm	3,646	B 14
Little River-Academy*	1,645	F 9
Littlefield○	6,507	C 4
Live Oak	9,156	J 2
Livingston○	5,433	G 11
Llano○	3,325	G 7
Lockhart○	11,615	H 8
Lockney	2,056	C 5
Lone Star*	1,631	D 11
Longview○	73,344	E 11
Loraine	656	E 6
Lorenzo	1,372	C 5
Los Fresnos*	4,512	K 9
Lott	724	F 9
Lowry Crossing	1,229	C 16
Lubbock○	199,564	D 5
Lucas	2,890	C 15
Lufkin○	32,709	F 11
Luling	5,080	H 8
Lumberton*	8,731	G 12
Lyford	1,973	K 8
Lytle	2,383	K 1
Mabank	2,151	E 16
Madisonville○	4,159	G 10
Magnolia	1,111	G 13
Malakoff	2,257	E 10
Manor	1,204	G 9
Mansfield	28,031	E 13
Manvel	3,046	J 14
Marble Falls	4,959	G 8
Marfa○	2,121	G 2
Marlin○	6,628	F 9
Marshall○	23,935	E 12
Mart	2,273	F 9
Mason○	2,134	G 7
Matador○	740	C 6
Mathis	5,034	I 8
Maud	1,028	D 12
McAllen	106,414	K 8
McCamey	1,805	F 4
McGregor	4,727	F 9
McKinney○	54,369	B 15
McLean	830	B 6
McLendom-Chisholm	914	D 16
McQueeney†	2,527	J 3
Memphis○	2,479	B 6
Menard○	1,653	G 6
Mentone○		F 3
Mercedes	13,649	K 8
Meridian○	1,491	F 9
Merkel	2,637	E 7
Mertzon○	839	F 5
Mesquite	124,523	D 16
Mexia	6,563	F 9
Miami○	588	A 6
Midland○	94,996	E 4
Midlothian	7,480	E 14
Mineola	4,550	E 10
Mineral Wells	16,946	D 8
Mission	45,408	K 8
Missouri City	52,913	I 13
Monahans○	6,821	F 4
Mont Belvieu	2,324	H 15
Montague○		D 8
Moody*	1,400	F 9
Morgan's Point Resort*	2,989	F 9
Morton○	2,249	C 4
Moulton*	944	H 9
Mount Pleasant○	13,935	D 11
Mount Vernon○	2,286	D 11
Muenster*	1,556	D 9
Muleshoe○	4,530	C 4
Munday	1,527	D 7
Murphy	3,099	C 15
Nacogdoches○	29,914	F 11
Naples*	1,410	D 11
Nash*	2,169	D 12
Nassau Bay*	4,170	I 15
Natalia	1,663	K 1
Navasota	6,789	G 10
Nederland	17,422	H 11
Needville	2,609	J 12
New Boston	4,808	D 11
New Braunfels○	36,494	I 3
New London	987	E 11
New Waverly	950	G 10
Newton○	2,459	G 12
Nixon	2,186	K 4
Nocona	3,198	D 8
Nolanville*	2,150	F 9
North Richland Hills	55,635	D 13
North San Pedro*†	920	J 8
Northcrest*		F 9
Oak Ridge North*	2,991	G 14
Odem*	2,499	J 9
Odessa○	90,943	E 4
O'Donnell	1,011	D 5
Old River-Winfree	1,364	H 15
Olmos Park	2,343	J 2
Olney	3,396	D 7
Olton	2,288	C 4
Orange○	18,643	G 12
Orange Grove	1,288	J 8
Ore City*	1,106	E 11
Overton	2,350	E 11
Ovilla	3,405	E 14
Oyster Creek	1,192	K 14
Ozona○†	3,436	G 5
Paducah○	1,498	C 6
Paint Rock○	320	F 6
Palacios	5,153	I 10
Palestine○	17,598	F 10
Palmer	1,774	E 15
Palo Pinto○		E 8
Pampa○	17,887	B 6
Panhandle○	2,589	B 5
Panorama Village*	1,965	G 11
Pantego*	2,318	D 14
Paris○	25,898	D 10
Parker*	1,379	C 15
Pasadena	141,674	I 14
Patton*		G 14
Pearland	37,640	I 14
Pearsall○	7,157	I 7
Pecos○	9,501	F 3
Perryton○	7,774	A 6
Petersburg	1,262	C 5
Petrolia	782	C 8
Pharr	46,660	K 8
Phillips		A 5
Pilot Point	3,538	B 14
Pinehurst	2,274	G 13
Pineland	980	F 12
Piney Point Village*	3,380	I 13
Pittsburg○	4,347	D 11
Plains○	1,450	D 4
Plainview○	22,336	C 5
Plano	222,030	C 15
Pleasanton	8,266	I 8
Point Comfort	781	I 9
Port Aransas	3,370	J 9
Port Arthur	57,755	H 12
Port Isabel*	4,865	K 9
Port Lavaca○	12,035	I 9
Port Mansfield†	415	K 9
Port Neches	13,601	G 12
Port O'Connor		I 10
Portland	14,827	I 9
Post○	3,708	D 5
Post Oak Bend City*	404	D 16
Poteet	3,305	I 8
Poth	1,850	I 8
Pottsboro	1,579	D 9
Prairie View	4,410	G 10
Premont	2,772	J 8
Presidio	4,167	H 2
Primera*	2,723	K 8
Princeton	3,477	B 16
Quanah○	3,022	C 7
Queen City	1,613	D 12
Quinlan	1,370	C 16
Quitman○	2,030	D 10
Ralls	2,252	D 5
Ranger	2,584	E 7
Rankin○	800	F 5
Raymondville○	9,733	K 8
Red Oak	4,301	E 15
Refugio○	2,941	I 9
Reno*	2,767	D 10
Reno	2,441	C 12
Richardson	91,802	C 15
Richland Hills	8,132	D 13
Richmond○	11,081	I 13
Richwood	3,012	K 14
Rio Grande City○†	11,923	K 7
Rio Hondo*	1,942	K 9
Rising Star	835	E 7
River Oaks	6,985	D 13
Roanoke	2,810	C 13
Robert Lee○	1,171	E 6
Robinson	7,845	F 9
Robstown	12,727	J 8
Roby○	673	E 6
Rockdale	5,439	G 9
Rockport○	7,385	J 9
Rocksprings○	1,285	G 6
Rockwall○	17,976	C 16
Rogers*	1,117	F 9
Rollingwood*	1,403	G 8
Roma-Los Saenz		K 7
Roman Forest*	1,279	G 14
Roscoe*	1,378	E 6
Rosebud	1,493	F 9
Rosenberg	24,043	I 13
Rotan	1,611	D 6
Round Rock	61,136	G 8
Rowlett	44,503	C 15
Royse City	2,957	C 16
Rule	698	D 6
Runge	1,080	I 8
Rusk○	5,085	F 11
Sabinal	1,586	H 7
Sachse	9,751	C 15
Saginaw	12,374	C 13
St. Jo*	977	D 9
San Angelo○	88,439	F 6
San Antonio○	1,144,646	H 8
San Augustine○	2,475	F 12
San Benito	23,444	K 9
San Diego○	4,753	J 8
San Elizario†	11,046	E 1
San Juan	26,229	K 8
San Leon†	4,365	I 15
San Marcos○	34,733	H 8
San Saba○	2,637	F 7
Sanderson○†	861	G 4
Sanger	4,534	B 14
Sansom Park*	4,181	D 13
Santa Anna	1,081	F 7
Santa Fe	9,548	J 15
Santa Rosa*	2,833	K 8
Sarita○		K 8
Savoy*	850	D 10
Schertz	18,694	J 2
Schulenburg	2,699	H 9
Seabrook	9,443	I 15
Seadrift	1,352	I 9
Seagoville	10,823	D 15
Seagraves	2,334	D 4
Sealy	5,248	H 10
Seguin○	22,011	J 3
Seminole○	5,910	D 4
Seth Ward†	1,926	C 5
Seven Points	1,145	E 16
Seymour○	2,908	D 7
Shady Shores	1,461	B 14
Shallowater	2,086	D 5
Shamrock	2,029	B 6
Shavano Park	1,754	J 2
Shenandoah*	1,503	G 14
Shepherd	2,029	G 11
Sherman○	35,082	D 9
Shiner	2,070	H 9
Shoreacres	1,488	I 15
Sierra Blanca○†	533	F 1
Silsbee	6,393	G 12
Silverton○	771	C 5
Sinton○	5,676	I 9
Skellytown	610	B 5
Slaton	6,109	D 5
Smithville	3,901	H 9
Snyder○	10,783	E 5
Somerset	1,550	K 1
Somerville	1,704	G 9
Sonora○	2,924	G 6
Sour Lake*	1,667	G 11
South Houston	15,833	I 14
South Padre Island	2,422	K 9
Southlake	21,519	C 14
Southside Place*	1,546	I 14
Spearman○	3,021	A 5
Spring Valley	3,611	H 13
Springtown*	2,062	D 8
Spur	1,088	D 6
Stafford	15,681	I 13
Stamford	3,636	D 6
Stanton○	2,556	E 5
Stephenville○	14,921	E 8
Sterling City○	1,081	F 5
Stinnett○	1,936	A 5
Stockdale	1,398	K 3
Stratford○	1,991	A 5
Sudan	1,039	C 4
Sugar Land	63,328	I 13
Sulphur Springs○	14,551	D 10
Sundown	1,505	D 4
Sunnyvale	2,693	D 15
Sunray	1,950	A 5
Sunset Valley*	365	G 8
Surfside Beach	763	K 14
Sweeny	3,624	K 13
Sweetwater○	11,415	E 6
Taft	3,396	J 9
Tahoka○	2,910	D 5
Talco	570	D 11
Tatum	1,175	E 11
Taylor	13,575	G 9
Taylor Lake Village*	3,694	I 15
Teague	4,557	F 10
Temple	54,514	F 9
Tenaha	1,046	E 11
Terrell	13,606	D 16
Terrell Hills	5,019	J 2
Texarkana	34,782	D 12
Texas City	41,521	J 15
The Colony	26,531	C 15
The Woodlands†	55,649	G 14
Thorndale	1,278	G 9
Three Rivers	1,878	I 8
Throckmorton○	905	D 7
Tilden○		I 8
Timpson	1,094	F 12
Tomball	9,089	G 13
Tool*	2,275	E 16
Trinidad*	1,091	E 10
Trinity	2,721	F 11
Troup	1,949	E 11
Troy*	1,378	F 9
Tulia○	5,117	C 5
Tye*	1,158	E 6
Tyler	83,650	E 11
Universal City	14,849	J 2
University Park	23,324	C 15
Uvalde○	14,929	H 6
Valley Mills	1,123	F 9
Van	2,362	E 10
Van Alstyne	2,502	A 15
Van Horn○	2,435	F 2
Vega○	936	B 4
Vernon○	11,660	C 7
Victoria○	60,603	I 9
Vidor	11,440	G 12
Waco○	113,726	F 9
Waelder	947	H 9
Wake Village	5,129	D 12
Waller	2,092	G 10
Wallis*	1,172	H 10
Waskom*	2,068	E 12
Watauga	21,908	C 13
Waxahachie○	21,426	E 14
Weatherford○	19,000	E 8
Webster	9,083	I 15
Weches		F 11
Weimar	1,981	H 9
Wellington○	2,275	B 6
Wells	769	F 11
Weslaco	26,935	K 8
West	2,692	F 9
West Columbia	4,255	K 13
West Lake Hills*	3,116	G 8
West Orange*	4,111	G 12
West University Place	14,211	I 14
Westworth*	2,124	D 13
Wharton○	9,237	H 10
Wheeler○	1,378	B 6
White Deer	1,060	B 5
White Oak*	5,624	E 11
White Settlement	14,831	D 13
Whitehouse*	5,346	E 11
Whitesboro*	3,760	D 9
Whitewright	1,740	A 16
Whitney	1,833	E 9
Wichita Falls○	104,197	C 8
Willis*	3,985	G 11
Willow Park*	2,849	E 8
Wills Point	3,496	E 10
Wilmer	3,393	D 15
Windcrest*	5,105	J 2
Wink	919	F 3
Winnsboro*	3,584	D 11
Winters	2,880	E 6
Wolfe City*	1,566	D 10
Wolfforth*	2,554	D 5
Woodsboro	1,685	J 9
Woodville○	2,415	G 11
Woodway*	8,733	F 9
Wortham*	1,082	F 10
Wylie	15,132	C 15
Yoakum	5,731	H 9
Yorktown	2,271	H 9
Zapata○†	4,856	K 7

*Does not appear on map; key shows general location.
†Census designated place—unincorporated, but recognized as a significant settled community by the U.S. Census Bureau.

○County seat.
Places without population figures are unincorporated areas.
Source: 2000 census.

Some of the most popular resort centers in Texas are on the Gulf Coast. Sandy beaches stretch along most of the coast. Many deep-sea fishing enthusiasts sail from the coastal cities of Aransas Pass, Corpus Christi, and Galveston. They catch marlin, red snapper, sailfish, and tarpon in the Gulf of Mexico.

In northeast Texas, rolling timberlands provide many recreational areas. The region's rivers and lakes offer fine fishing. Central and west Texas are popular deer-hunting sites.

Texas has more than 500 fairs, festivals, and expositions each year—more than any other state. The greatest event is probably the State Fair of Texas, held in Dallas for 24 days in late September and early October. About 3 million people visit this fair yearly, making it the largest annual fair held in the United States.

Kent and Donna Dannen

Malaquite Beach at Padre Island National Seashore

Places to visit

Following are brief descriptions of some of the many interesting places to visit in Texas.

The Alamo, a chapel of an old Spanish mission, stands in downtown San Antonio. A famous battle was fought there in 1836 during the Texas Revolution.

Aquarena Springs, at Spring Lake in San Marcos, features large springs that form the beginning of the San Marcos River. The attractions include glass-bottom boats, a re-created frontier village, and mission ruins.

East Texas Oil Museum, in Kilgore, re-creates an oil boom town of the 1930's. Exhibits include mementos of the area's early oil industry and a study of oil formations within Earth.

Fair Park, in Dallas, covers about 200 acres (81 hectares) and is the home of the State Fair of Texas. The park includes the Cotton Bowl stadium, the Science Place Museum, the Music Hall, an amusement park, recreational areas, livestock exhibition buildings, an aquarium, the Hall of State, the Museum of Natural History, the Museum of Natural Resources, and the Dallas Garden Center.

La Villita, in San Antonio, is a restoration and reconstruction of an early Texas city. The city shows the influence of Spanish culture and has a museum and arts-and-crafts shops.

Lyndon B. Johnson Space Center, at Houston, is the headquarters for all astronaut flights of the National Aeronautics and Space Administration (NASA). A visitors' center called Space Center Houston includes spacecraft from past missions and exhibits and films dealing with the U.S. space program. See **Johnson Space Center**.

Mission San Jose, in San Antonio, is the largest Texas mission. Established in 1720, the church is a marvel of Spanish architecture. The mission is part of a national historic park and is a state historic site.

Padre Island National Seashore extends about 110 miles (177 kilometers) along the Texas coast on Padre Island. It includes dunes and beaches. Congress established the seashore in 1962.

San Jacinto Monument, near Channelview, honors the Texans who fought in the Battle of San Jacinto. In this battle, Texas won independence from Mexico. The monument, one of the tallest in the world, rises 570 feet (174 meters).

Sea World, in San Antonio, features dolphin, killer whale, and sea lion shows. The marine center also has large collections of sharks and penguins, and a colorful water-skiing show.

Six Flags Theme Parks offer amusement rides and shows. Six Flags over Texas, in Arlington, features the history of the state under the six flags of Spain, France, Mexico, the Republic of Texas, the Confederacy, and the United States. Six Flags Hurricane Harbor, in Arlington, and Six Flags Splashtown, in Houston, are waterparks. Six Flags Fiesta Texas, in San Antonio, and Six Flags AstroWorld, in Houston, offer traditional thrill rides plus waterparks.

Texas Memorial Museum, in Austin, has displays featuring Texas botany, geology, history, and zoology. The museum also exhibits many historical records and documents.

Texas Ranger Hall of Fame, in Waco, honors the Texas Rangers, a group of Texas law enforcers that has existed for more than 150 years. On the site is a museum that is a replica of an early Rangers outpost.

National Park Service facilities. Texas has two national parks. Big Bend National Park lies within the great bend of the Rio Grande. Guadalupe Mountains National Park lies in Culberson and Hudspeth counties. The state's four national forests are in east Texas. Sabine National Forest is the largest. The other national forests in Texas are Angelina, Davy Crockett, and Sam Houston. For general information on the state's national parklands, see **National Park System**. See also **Big Bend National Park; Guadalupe Mountains National Park.**

State parks. Texas began its state park system during the 1920's and now has about 100 state parks. For information on the parks, write to Park Operations Division, Texas State Parks and Wildlife Department, 4200 Smith School Road, Austin, TX 78744.

© Bob Daemmrich

Cinco de Mayo celebration in Austin

Annual events

January-March

Texas Citrus Festival in Mission (January or February); Southwestern Exposition and Fat Stock Show and Rodeo in Fort Worth (January or February); Charro Days Festival in Brownsville (February); San Antonio Stock Show and Rodeo (February); Houston Livestock Show and Rodeo Exposition (February-March); Texas Independence Day (March 2).

April-June

Fiesta San Antonio in San Antonio (April); Texas Sand Sculpture Festival in Port Aransas (April); Jefferson Historical Pilgrimage in Jefferson (April or May); Buccaneer Days in Corpus Christi (April or May); Cinco de Mayo Celebration in Austin and elsewhere (May 5); Kerrville Folk Festival (late May and early June); Watermelon Thump in Luling (June).

July-September

Texas Cowboy Reunion and Rodeo in Stamford (July); Texas Folklife Festival in San Antonio (August); Rice Festival in Winnie, near Port Arthur (September or October); State Fair of Texas in Dallas (late September and early October).

October-December

East Texas Yamboree in Gilmer (October); Texas Rose Festival in Tyler (October); AIRSHO in Midland (October); Wurstfest in New Braunfels (November); Fiesta de las Luminarias, or Festival of the Lights, in San Antonio (December).

Paul Conklin

Lyndon B. Johnson Space Center in Houston

© Bob Daemmrich

Memorial service at the Alamo in San Antonio

Francis M. Martin, Houston Livestock Show and Rodeo

Houston Livestock Show and Rodeo Exposition

Land and climate

Land regions. Texas has five main land regions. These are, from east to west: (1) the Gulf Coastal Plains, (2) the Prairie Plains, (3) the Rolling Plains, (4) the Great Plains, and (5) the Basin and Range Region.

The Gulf Coastal Plains of Texas are part of the fertile lowland that lies along the entire Gulf Coast of the United States. They range in elevation from sea level to about 300 feet (91 meters) above sea level. A subtropical region extends along a large part of the coast.

The southernmost part of the coastal plains consists of the fertile Rio Grande Valley. Just north of this valley lies the Middle Nueces Valley, part of the Nueces Plains. The two valleys are famous for their winter vegetables and fruits. The region along the coast from the Rio Grande Valley to Louisiana has rich soils. Cotton and several types of grain thrive in this region.

The northeastern part of the plain is a timberland with thick forests of oak, pine, sweet gum, and other trees. This area is often called the Piney Woods. Major lumber and paper companies own most of the land. Farmers in this area raise beef and dairy cattle and poultry. The region has many large mineral deposits.

The Prairie Plains lie west of the forest belt of the Coastal Plains. The Prairie Plains feature alternating belts of rugged hills and rolling hills. The rugged hills are covered with oak and hickory forests. The region includes the fertile Black Waxy Prairie. The prairie has rich soils for farming.

The Rolling Plains are a hilly area west of the Prairie Plains. The area's elevation increases as it approaches the Great Plains to the west. The region has scattered belts of fertile farmland and rich petroleum deposits.

The Great Plains reach westward from the Prairie Plains and Rolling Plains into New Mexico. They form part of the series of treeless plains that extends northward through the western United States into Canada. The Great Plains of Texas rise from an altitude of about 700 feet (213 meters) above sea level in the east to over 4,000 feet (1,200 meters) above sea level in the west.

A large part of the Great Plains region lies within the *Texas Panhandle,* the part of the state that juts northward alongside New Mexico and Oklahoma. The western part of the Panhandle is called the *Llano Estacado* (Staked Plains) or the High Plains. This treeless grassland is a high plateau. The Llano Estacado has many irrigated cotton, grain sorghum, and wheat farms. The southern part of this area lies above an underground region called the Permian Basin. The state's largest petroleum and natural gas deposits are in the Permian Basin.

The Edwards Plateau forms the southern part of the Great Plains. Its surface is mainly bare limestone bedrock, but it is dotted with shrubs and sparse grasses. Thick grasses grow in the plateau's river valleys and basins. In the eastern part of the plateau, the land becomes irregular, forming what is called the Texas Hill Country. More sheep and goats are raised in the Edwards Plateau than in any other part of the United States.

The Basin and Range Region, commonly called the *Trans-Pecos Region,* makes up the westernmost part of Texas. It includes high, partly dry plains that are crossed by *spurs* (extensions) of the Rocky Mountains. These spurs include, from north to south, the Guadalupe, Davis, and Chisos mountains. The peaks that do not form continuous ranges are called *lost mountains.* Farmers use the level sections mainly for raising cattle, with some irrigated agriculture on the plains along the Rio Grande. Many beautiful mountain gorges are along the upper Rio Grande, which forms the region's western border. Santa Elena Canyon, in Big Bend National Park, is one of the most spectacular gorges.

Coastline. A series of narrow sand bars, enclosing shallow lagoons, lies along the Texas coast. These sand bars help protect the coast from ocean storms and huge, destructive waves called *tsunamis.* Padre Island, the largest sand bar, is about 100 miles (160 kilometers) long. Other large sand bars include the islands of Galveston, Matagorda, and San Jose.

The Texas coast has 27 artificially created ports. They were once filled by *silt* (particles of earth) left by the many streams emptying into the Gulf of Mexico. Only small vessels could use them. By removing the silt and deepening the harbors, engineers built 12 deepwater ports and 15 ports for barges and small ships.

The general coastline of Texas is 367 miles (591 kilometers) long along the Gulf. The tidal shoreline, including bays, offshore islands, and river mouths, is 3,359 miles (5,406 kilometers) long.

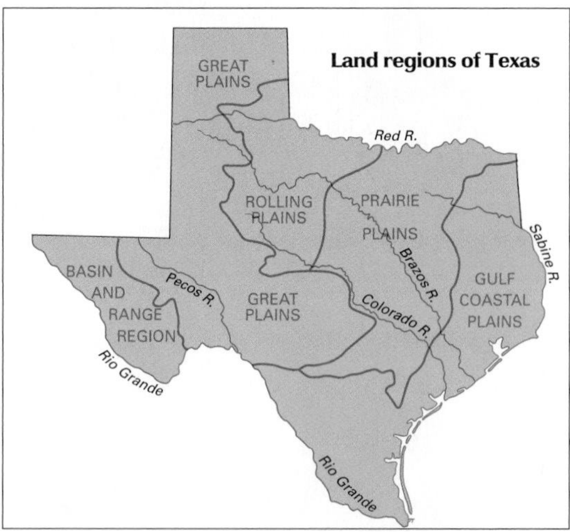

WORLD BOOK map

Map index

Place	Grid	
Alibates Flint Quarries Natl. Monument	A	4
Aransas Bay	E	7
Baffin Bay	F	7
Belton Lake	C	7
Big Bend Natl. Park	D	3
Big Thicket Natl. Preserve	D	8
Black Waxy Prairie	C	7
Blue Mts.	D	6
Brady Mts.	D	5
Brazos R.	D	7
Canadian R.	A	5
Cedar Creek Lake	C	7
Chinati Peak	D	3
Chisos Mts.	E	4
Colorado R.	C	6
Davis Mts.	D	3
Devils R.	D	5
Sierra Diablo	C	3
Edwards Plateau	D	5
Frio R.	E	6
Galveston Bay	D	8
Galveston I.	E	8
Glass Mts.	D	4
Guadalupe Peak (highest point in Texas)	C	3
Guadalupe R.	E	7
Gulf of Mexico	F	9
Hubbard Creek Lake	C	6
Hueco Mts.	C	2
Laguna Madre (lagoon)	F	7
Lake Kemp	B	6
Lake Lewisville	B	7
Lake O' the Pines	C	8
Lake Tawakoni	C	7
Lake Texoma	B	7
Lake Whitney	C	6
Llano Estacado (plain)	C	4
Matagorda Bay	E	7
Matagorda I.	E	7
Matagorda Peninsula	E	8
Mount Livermore	D	3
Neches R.	C	8
Nueces Plains	E	6
Nueces R.	E	6
Padre Island Natl. Seashore	F	7
Palo Duro Canyon	A	4
Pecos R.	C	4
Pedernales R	D	6
Red R. North Fork	A	5
Rio Grande	D	4
Sabine R.	D	8
Sam Rayburn Reservoir	C	8
San Antonio Bay	E	7
San Jose I.	E	7
Santa Elena Canyon	E	3
Santiago Mts.	D	4
Stockton Plateau	D	4
Sulphur R.	B	8
Sierra Vieja Mts.	D	3
Toledo Bend Reservoir	C	8
Trinity R.	C	7
Waco Lake	C	7
White R.	B	4

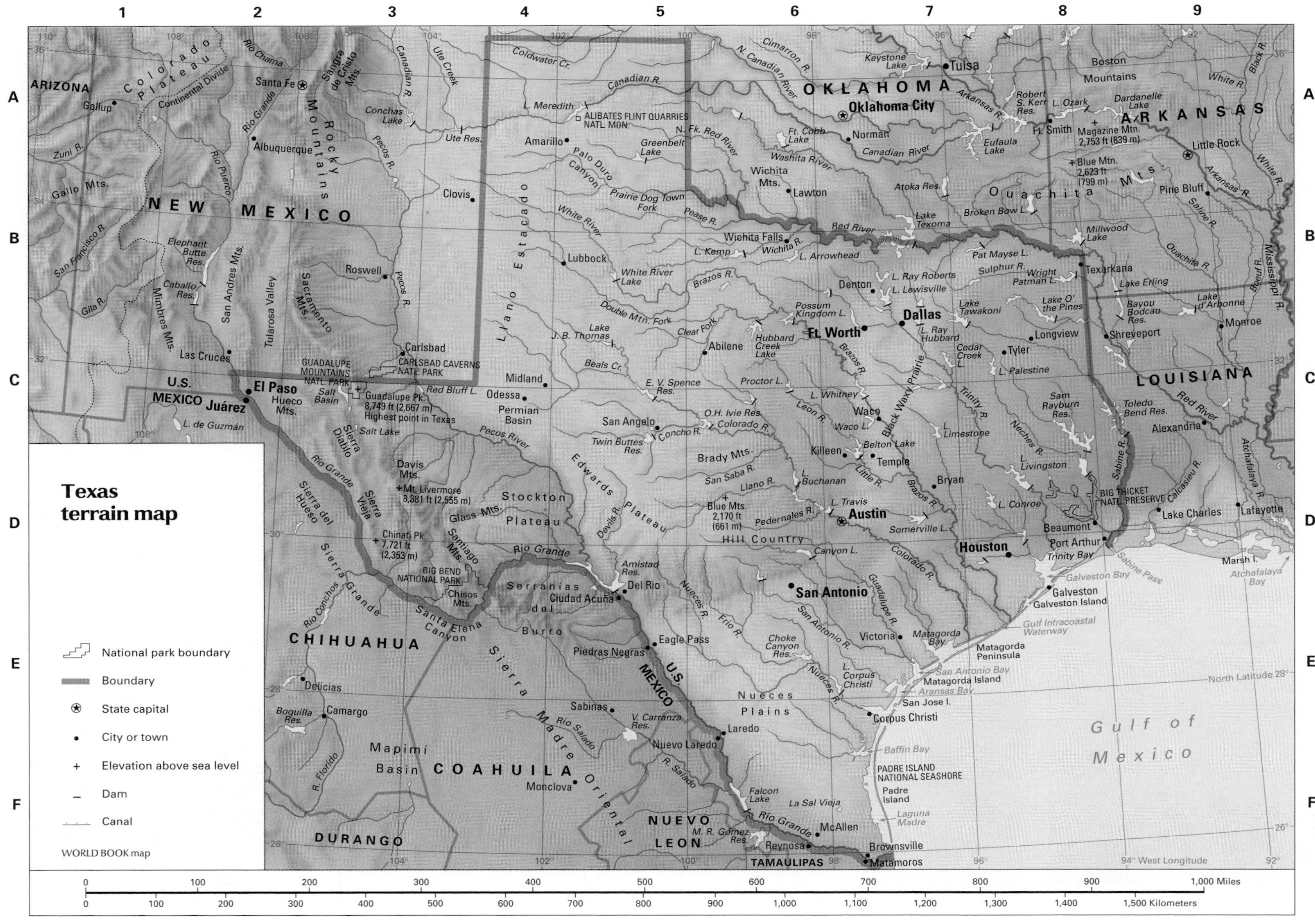
Texas
terrain map
National park boundary
Boundary
State capital
City or town
Elevation above sea level
Dam
Canal
WORLD BOOK map
0 100 200 300 400 500 600 700 800 900 1,000 Miles
0 100 200 300 400 500 600 700 800 900 1,000 1,100 1,200 1,300 1,400 1,500 Kilometers
1
2
3
4
5
6
7
8
9
A
B
C
D
E
F
ARIZONA
NEW MEXICO
OKLAHOMA
ARKANSAS
LOUISIANA
CHIHUAHUA
COAHUILA
DURANGO
NUEVO LEON
TAMAULIPAS
U.S.
MEXICO
Gulf of Mexico
Colorado Plateau
Continental Divide
Rocky Mountains
Sangre de Cristo Mts.
Llano Estacado
Edwards Plateau
Stockton Plateau
Hill Country
Nueces Plains
Ouachita Mts.
Boston Mountains
Sierra Madre Oriental
Serranías del Burro
Mapimí Basin
Santa Elena Canyon
BIG BEND NATIONAL PARK
GUADALUPE MOUNTAINS NATL. PARK
CARLSBAD CAVERNS NATL. PARK
ALIBATES FLINT QUARRIES NATL. MON.
BIG THICKET NATL. PRESERVE
PADRE ISLAND NATIONAL SEASHORE
Guadalupe Pk. 8,749 ft (2,667 m) Highest point in Texas
Mt. Livermore 8,381 ft (2,555 m)
Chinati Pk. 7,721 ft (2,353 m)
Blue Mts. 2,170 ft (661 m)
Magazine Mtn. 2,753 ft (839 m)
Blue Mtn. 2,623 ft (799 m)
Austin
Oklahoma City
Little Rock
Santa Fe
Dallas
Ft. Worth
Houston
San Antonio
El Paso
Juárez
Amarillo
Lubbock
Midland
Odessa
Abilene
San Angelo
Wichita Falls
Waco
Killeen
Temple
Bryan
Denton
Tyler
Longview
Texarkana
Beaumont
Port Arthur
Galveston
Victoria
Corpus Christi
Laredo
Nuevo Laredo
McAllen
Reynosa
Brownsville
Matamoros
Del Rio
Ciudad Acuña
Eagle Pass
Piedras Negras
Tulsa
Lawton
Norman
Shreveport
Alexandria
Lake Charles
Lafayette
Monroe
Pine Bluff
Ft. Smith
Albuquerque
Las Cruces
Roswell
Carlsbad
Clovis
Gallup
Delicias
Camargo
Monclova
Sabinas
Rio Grande
Pecos River
Red River
Brazos R.
Colorado R.
Canadian R.
Trinity R.
Sabine R.
Neches R.
Nueces R.
Guadalupe R.
San Antonio R.
Gulf Intracoastal Waterway
Galveston Bay
Matagorda Bay
Baffin Bay
Laguna Madre
North Latitude 28°
94° West Longitude

© Don Klumpp

Big Thicket National Preserve, located north of Beaumont, was set aside to protect a variety of rare plant life. The preserve has 84,550 acres (34,220 hectares) of bayous and forests.

Mountains. Texas's highest mountains rise in the Basin and Range Region. The chief ranges include the Chisos, Davis, and Guadalupe mountains. The main peak of the Guadalupe Mountains is Guadalupe Peak. It rises 8,749 feet (2,667 meters) above sea level and is the highest point in Texas.

Rivers and lakes. The Rio Grande, Texas's largest river, is one of the longest and most historic rivers in North America. For 1,241 miles (1,997 kilometers), it forms the boundary between the United States and Mexico (see **Rio Grande**). Other Texas rivers include the Brazos, Canadian, Colorado, Guadalupe, Neches, Nueces, Pecos, Red, Sabine, San Antonio, and Trinity.

Most of the state's rivers flow in a southeastward direction into the Gulf of Mexico. But the Canadian River drains into the Arkansas River, and the Pecos River flows into the Rio Grande. The Red River and its branches empty into the Mississippi River. In the dry western parts of Texas, many streams have water only after a rainstorm.

Texas has thousands of lakes that have been made or enlarged by human effort. Most of these lakes were created as part of the state's many programs for generating hydroelectric power, irrigating farmland, and storing water. The largest artificially created lake is Toledo Bend, which extends into Louisiana. The reservoir was created by Toledo Bend Dam, which crosses the Sabine River. Other artificially created lakes include Amistad, Buchanan, Falcon, Sam Rayburn, and Texoma.

Many saltwater lakes and ponds lie in the High

Average monthly weather

	Corpus Christi					Dallas					
	Temperatures °F High	°F Low	°C High	°C Low	Days of rain or snow		Temperatures °F High	°F Low	°C High	°C Low	Days of rain or snow
Jan.	66	47	19	8	8	Jan.	55	36	13	2	8
Feb.	70	51	21	11	7	Feb.	60	40	16	4	8
Mar.	75	56	24	13	6	Mar.	68	47	20	8	7
Apr.	80	63	27	17	5	Apr.	77	56	25	13	9
May	86	69	30	21	6	May	84	64	29	18	9
June	90	74	32	23	5	June	92	72	33	22	6
July	93	75	34	24	4	July	95	76	35	24	5
Aug.	93	75	34	24	5	Aug.	96	76	36	24	6
Sept.	89	72	32	22	8	Sept.	89	69	32	21	5
Oct.	84	65	29	18	6	Oct.	80	58	27	14	6
Nov.	75	55	24	13	6	Nov.	66	45	19	7	7
Dec.	68	49	20	9	6	Dec.	58	39	14	4	6

Average January temperatures

Texas temperatures vary widely in winter. The south is the warmest and temperatures decline steadily to the north.

Degrees Fahrenheit / Degrees Celsius
Above 56 / Above 13
50 to 56 / 10 to 13
44 to 50 / 7 to 10
38 to 44 / 3 to 7
Below 38 / Below 3

Amarillo
Lubbock
Dallas
El Paso
Austin
Houston
San Antonio
Corpus Christi

Average July temperatures

Summers are hot in Texas with little variation in temperature. The northwest and southwest have the mildest summers.

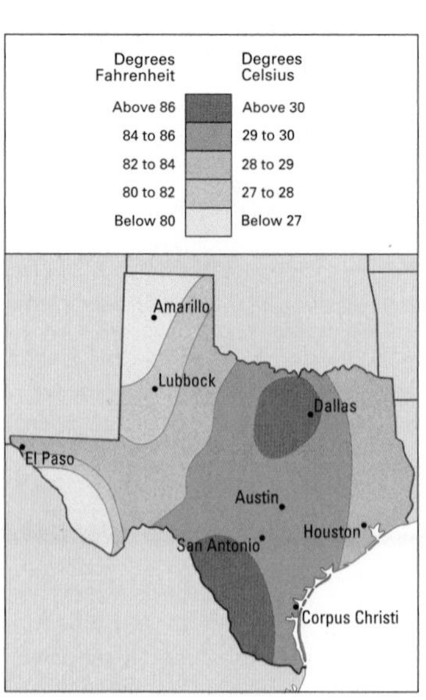

Average yearly precipitation

The western half of Texas is dry. However, the far eastern area receives more than 48 inches (122 centimeters) of rain.

WORLD BOOK maps

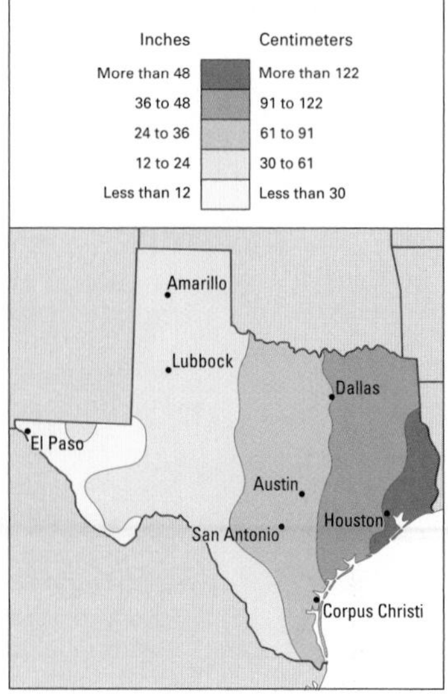

Plains, in the Basin and Range Region, and near the mouth of the Rio Grande. The largest include La Sal Vieja, Sal del Rey, and Salt Lake.

Plant and animal life. Forests cover about 15 percent of the state. The trees that are most valuable commercially are sweet gums, oaks, and pines. Other common trees in Texas include cat's-claw, bald cypress, elm, juniper, magnolia, mesquite, native pecan, and tupelo.

More than 500 kinds of grasses grow in Texas. They include bluestem, buffalo grass, curly mesquite, grama, and side oats. More than 4,000 kinds of wildflowers grow in the state. They include daisies, goldenrod, primroses, and sunflowers. The bluebonnet is the state flower. Many varieties of cactuses grow in the dry Basin and Range Region.

Much wildlife is found in the eastern forests and on the western plains. Deer, pronghorn, and wild turkeys are the chief game animals of Texas. Other animals include armadillos, bears, coyotes, mountain lions, and wild pigs. The state's large reptile population includes alligators, snakes, and lizards. The most common freshwater fish include bass, catfish, and sunfish. Crabs, menhaden, oysters, and shrimp thrive in the Gulf of Mexico.

Climate of Texas ranges from subtropical in the lower Rio Grande Valley to moderately temperate in the northwest. The lower Rio Grande Valley is the warmest region of the state. It has an average January temperature of 60 °F (16 °C), and an average July temperature of 85 °F (29 °C). The coldest area is the Panhandle, in the northwest. The Panhandle has an average January temperature of 35 °F (2 °C) and an average July temperature of 79 °F (26 °C). The lowest temperature in Texas, −23 °F (−31 °C), was recorded at Tulia on Feb. 12, 1899, and at Seminole on Feb. 8, 1933. The record high in the state was 120 °F (49 °C), at Seymour on Aug. 12, 1936, and Monahans on June 28, 1994.

Along the Gulf of Mexico, the coast has a warm, damp climate. There, winds from the Gulf reduce the heat of summer and the cold of winter. Central Texas has a mild climate that makes it a popular resort area the year around. In the northeast, the weather is damp and cool. The northwest sometimes has long, cold winters. The west has a dry, cool climate.

Rainfall in Texas decreases from east to west. East Texas averages 46 inches (117 centimeters) of *precipitation* (rain, snow, sleet, and other forms of moisture) a year. Parts of west Texas average only 12 inches (30 centimeters) a year. Port Arthur, in the southeastern part of the state, gets about 45 more inches (114 centimeters) of rain a year than El Paso, in the far west. Along the coast, most of the rain falls in autumn.

Sleet, winds, and heavy rain from the north occasionally sweep across the state in the winter. Strong winds often blow throughout the High Plains. During periods of drought, these winds carry away the soil. Snow seldom falls in the south-central and central regions. But the High Plains have an average of more than 24 inches (61 centimeters) of snow a year.

Economy

As one might expect from a state so large and populous, Texas has one of the nation's largest and most diverse economies. Service industries provide the largest part of Texas's *gross state product*—the total value of all goods and services produced in a state in a year.

For many years, the petroleum and natural gas industries dominated the Texas economy. The condition of these industries still has a strong effect on the state's overall economic health. But this effect has been moderated by the development of large aircraft, chemical, electronics, food-processing, and machinery production industries. The growth of finance, trade, and other service industries has also helped to diversify the economy. The Dallas-Fort Worth and Houston areas host the headquarters of many of the nation's largest companies.

Natural resources. The great natural wealth of Texas includes large mineral deposits, especially petroleum and natural gas. In addition, the state has fertile soils and rich grasslands.

Minerals. Texas is one of the world's great petroleum storehouses. The state's known petroleum deposits account for a third of the country's known supply. Most of the state's petroleum reserves lie near the Odessa-Midland area in the west-central part of the state. Natural gas deposits also lie in this area, as well as in the Panhandle and the far southern part of the state.

Other mined resources of Texas include large sulfur deposits in the Gulf Coastal Plains and the Basin and Range Region. Underground salt deposits occur in the Gulf Coastal Plains and in western Texas. Surface deposits of salt are found in northwestern, southern, and western Texas. Layers of rock containing beds of lignite cover about 75,000 square miles (194,000 square kilometers), extending from Laredo to Texarkana. Iron ore occurs in the eastern part of the state.

Limestone occurs in a broad belt extending from the Red River to the Rio Grande. Gypsum deposits lie at several sites in the state. Gravel and silica sand are plentiful

Production and workers by economic activities

Economic activities	Percent of GSP* produced	Employed workers: Number of people	Employed workers: Percent of total
Community, business, & personal services	20	3,665,200	30
Trade, restaurants, & hotels	18	2,696,700	22
Finance, insurance, & real estate	17	1,032,200	8
Government	12	1,768,400	14
Manufacturing	12	994,500	8
Transportation & communication	8	720,400	6
Construction	5	834,500	7
Mining	5	218,900	2
Utilities	3	52,900	†
Agriculture	1	363,100	3
Total‡	100	12,346,800	100

*GSP = gross state product, the total value of goods and services produced in a year.
†Less than one-half of 1 percent. ‡Figures may not add up to 100 percent due to rounding.
Figures are for 2002; employment figures include full- and part-time workers.
Source: *World Book* estimates based on data from U.S. Bureau of Economic Analysis.

in many areas. The largest asphalt deposits are near Uvalde. Potash occurs in the Basin and Range Region. Molybdenum, titanium, and uranium are found in the southern and western parts of the state. Texas also has deposits of basalt, fluorite, fuller's earth and other clays, granite, helium, iron ore, lead, marble, and talc.

Soil. Texas has more than 1,200 types of soil. This variety enables farmers to grow many kinds of crops. A narrow belt along the state's Gulf Coast has marshy soils, mixed with clays. Rich soils lie along the banks of rivers throughout the state. Large sections of the interior of the Gulf Coastal Plains have soils composed of sands and clays. Rich, heavy, blackland clays make up a belt in the interior of the plains. The Prairie Plains Region has soils of clays, limestone, and sands. The High Plains and the Rolling Plains include clays, clay loam, and sandy loam soils. The Basin and Range Region has rough, stony mountain soils.

Service industries account for the largest portion of the gross state product of Texas. Most of the service industries are concentrated in the metropolitan areas.

The leading service industry in Texas is community, business, and personal services. This industry group contributes more to the gross state product than any other economic activity. It is also the state's leading employer. Community, business, and personal services includes private health care, law firms, engineering companies, and repair shops. Engineering companies that service oil and gas companies are an important part of this industry group.

Trade, restaurants, and hotels form the second most important service industry. The wholesale trade of food products, motor vehicles, and petroleum products is important in the state. Many of the nation's largest wholesale petroleum distributors are headquartered in Texas. Retail businesses include department stores, grocery stores, and service stations. The Dallas-Fort Worth area is the home of several major retailers, including the companies that own J. C. Penney, 7-Eleven, and RadioShack stores. About three-fourths of the state's hotel and motel income comes from the Austin, Dallas-Fort Worth, Houston, and San Antonio metropolitan areas.

Finance, insurance, and real estate rank next among the service industries of Texas in terms of the gross state product. Real estate is the largest part of this industry. The buying and selling of buildings and other property is a major part of the economy in most areas of Texas. Houston and Dallas are the chief financial centers in the state. Dallas serves as the headquarters of many insurance companies.

Ranking next among the service industry groups of Texas are government services. This group includes the operation of public schools, public hospitals, and military bases. The public school system is one of the state's major employers. Fort Sam Houston and several United States Air Force bases are in the San Antonio area. In addition, the federal government operates the Johnson Space Center in the Houston area. State government offices are based in Austin, the state capital.

Ranking fifth is transportation and communication. Airlines and trucking companies generate most of the income for the transportation sector. Pipeline companies are also important. Pipelines transport much of the state's oil and natural gas. Many shipping companies operate along the Gulf Coast. American Airlines, Continental Airlines, and Southwest Airlines have headquarters in the state. Telecommunications and broadcasting companies are the lead the communications sector.

Manufacturing. Goods made in Texas have a *value added by manufacture* of about $120 billion a year. This figure represents the increase in value of raw materials after they become finished products. Texas is one of the leading manufacturing states. It employs more manufacturing workers than any state but California.

Computer and electronic equipment are the state's leading type of manufactured products in terms of value added by manufacture. Dallas-based Texas Instruments, a major producer of electronic components and military

The Houston Ship Channel stretches 51 miles (82 kilometers) from the Gulf of Mexico to the Port of Houston. Ocean vessels use the channel to reach the port, which is one of the leading seaports in the United States. Houston's downtown skyscrapers rise in the distance.

© Robert Mitchell

Petroleum is one of Texas's most valuable mined products. The state produces about a fifth of the nation's crude oil and ranks first among the states in oil refining.

communication systems, has plants in several Texas cities. Dell Inc., a leading computer manufacturer, is based in Round Rock, near Austin.

Chemicals rank second among Texas's manufactured products. Texas leads the United States in chemical manufacturing. Important chemical products include benzene, ethylene, fertilizers, propylene, and sulfuric acid. The Texas chemical industry is located chiefly in cities along the Gulf Coast.

Food processing is third in value added among manufacturing activities in Texas. Beverages provide the greatest income for this industry. Fort Worth, Houston, and San Antonio have large breweries and soft-drink bottling plants. Baked goods, preserved fruits and vegetables, snack foods, and meat products are also important to the state. The Dallas-Fort Worth and Houston areas have many bakeries. Amarillo, El Paso, San Antonio, and many other places have meat-packing plants.

Petroleum products rank fourth. Texas ranks first among the states in oil refining. About 25 petroleum refineries operate throughout the state. The largest refineries are located along the Gulf Coast in Baytown, Beaumont, Houston, Port Arthur, Texas City, and other port cities. Exxon Mobil, one of the largest petroleum companies in the world, has its headquarters in Irving.

Other goods produced in Texas include fabricated metal products, machinery, and transportation equipment. Industrial valves and sheet metal are the leading fabricated metal products made in the state. The leading types of machinery made in Texas include refrigeration and heating equipment, farm equipment, and machinery for the oil and gas industry. The Houston, Dallas, and Austin areas are centers for machinery manufacturing. Important types of transportation equipment include aircraft and aircraft parts. Dallas and Fort Worth are the leading manufacturing centers for transportation equipment. The state's other manufactured products include cement and concrete, paper, plastics, and printed items.

Mining. Texas leads the states in value of mined products, largely due to oil and gas. About a fifth of the oil produced in the United States is from Texas. The state's leading oil-producing area is a belt that runs from Hockley County to Pecos County in west Texas. This area lies above an underground region called the Permian Basin. The Permian Basin contains vast deposits of oil and gas.

Economy of Texas

This map shows the economic uses of land in Texas and where the state's leading farm and mineral products are produced. Major manufacturing centers are shown in red.

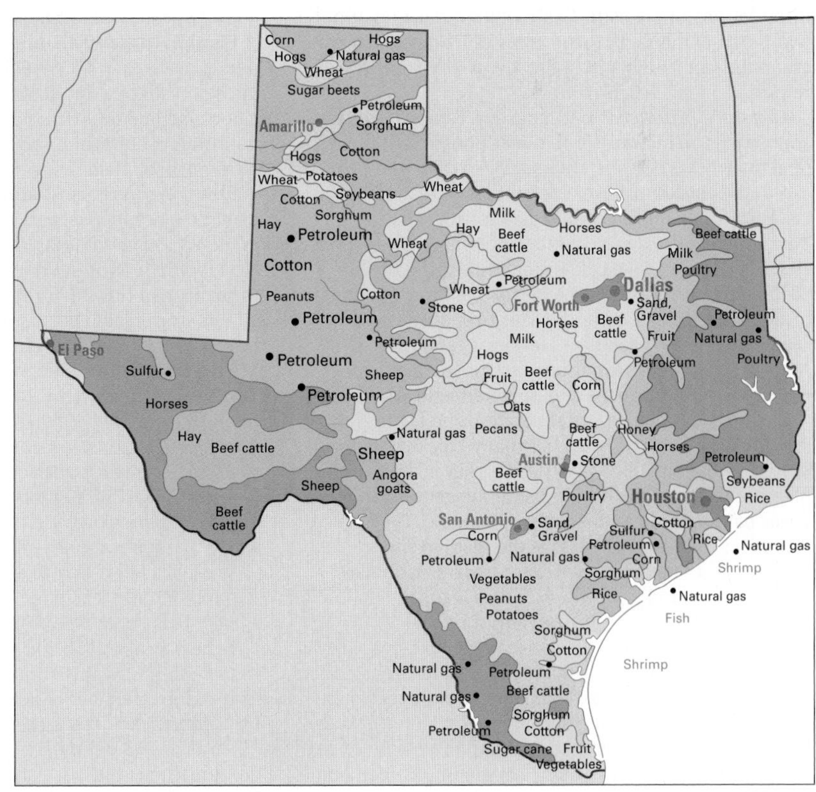

WORLD BOOK map

Drillers first discovered oil in Texas near Nacogdoches in 1866. Large-scale production began with the opening of the Spindletop field near Beaumont in 1901. For several years, the Spindletop and other Gulf Coast fields formed the center of the Texas oil industry. Later, large fields were opened in the Panhandle, the Pecos Valley, and east, north, and south Texas. Drillers made the state's greatest petroleum discovery in 1930, when they found the famous East Texas oil field near Kilgore.

Texas leads the states in natural gas production. About one-fourth of the natural gas produced in the United States comes from Texas. Webb and Zapata counties in south Texas lead the state in natural gas production. Large gas fields also lie in Panola and Wise counties, and in the Panhandle. Some of the state's gas is obtained as a by-product of petroleum mining. Pipelines carry Texas's natural gas to such major urban areas as New York and Chicago.

Among other mined products of Texas, cement, coal, crushed stone, lime, salt, and sand and gravel provide the most income. Texas is among the leading states in the production of all of these mined products. Limestone quarries provide most of Texas's cement, crushed stone, and lime. The largest limestone quarries lie near the major cities. Limestone and sand and gravel are used in manufacturing concrete and constructing roads. Sand and gravel are dredged from riverbeds and dug from pits. Coal comes from surface mines in southern and eastern parts of the state. Most of the salt production in Texas comes from the Houston area.

Agriculture. Texas has about 229,000 farms, far more than any other state. Ranches and farms cover about three-fourths of the state. Cattle ranches take up about two-thirds of this land. Large areas of irrigated cropland are in the Panhandle and in the lower Rio Grande Valley region.

Livestock products. Beef cattle are Texas's largest source of farm income, providing about half of the annual total. Texas winters are usually so mild that cattle can graze outdoors all year around. As a result, Texans can raise cattle more cheaply than northern farmers. Texas leads the states in number of beef cattle. Almost all parts of Texas have cattle ranches. During the late 1800's, ranchers raised large herds of a breed of beef cattle called *Texas longhorns.* This breed was gradually replaced by such breeds as Herefords and Aberdeen-Angus. Today, Texas longhorns are used mainly for crossbreeding purposes and to produce low-fat beef.

The northeastern part of the state is the leading dairy farming area. Eastern Texas has many chicken and egg farms. Farmers in Texas also raise turkeys. The central plains and Panhandle have most of the state's hog farms. Texas has more sheep than any other state. The Edwards Plateau of west-central Texas is the leading sheep-raising area in the country. Texas farmers also raise goats, horses, and honey bees. Texas leads the nation in the production of mohair from angora goats.

Field crops. Cotton is Texas's leading field crop. Texas produces more cotton than any other state. Texas cotton thrives best on the coastal plain and in the Great Plains region. Irrigated cotton grows in the Rio Grande Valley. Jared Groce, who is sometimes called the *Father of Texas Agriculture,* and other early settlers introduced commercial cotton growing. They planted cotton in the fertile valley of the Brazos River during the early 1820's.

Corn, grain sorghum, hay, rice, and wheat are also major sources of farm income in Texas. Corn is grown mainly in the Prairie Plains region. Only Kansas grows more grain sorghum than Texas. Most of Texas's grain sorghum is grown in the Panhandle and in South Texas. Most cattle ranchers also raise hay. Grain sorghum and hay are used mainly as cattle feed. Texas is one of the few states that grows large amounts of rice. Rice is grown along the eastern Gulf Coast. Northern Texas has most of the large wheat farms. The state's other field crops include oats, peanuts, potatoes, soybeans, sugar beets, and sugar cane.

Greenhouse and nursery products are the leading source of agricultural income in the state's urban areas. These products include flowers, ornamental shrubs, and young trees. Texas ranks among the top states in annual income from greenhouse and nursery products.

Fruits, vegetables, and nuts. The lower Rio Grande Valley is one of the leading areas of the United States for growing fruits and vegetables. This region helps supply many northern states with produce during winter. Temperatures in the valley usually remain warm during winter, so crops can be grown year around. The production of citrus fruits, such as grapefruits and oranges, and melons, such as cantaloupes and honeydews, is especially important in the lower Rio Grande Valley. Fruit and vegetable farms also lie near the major cities of Texas.

Texas is among the leading states in the production of nuts. Pecans are the most important nuts harvested in the state. Pecan trees grow along rivers and streams throughout most of the state, except in the High Plains and the Basin and Range Region.

Fishing industry. Texas has an annual fish catch valued at more than $150 million. It ranks among the leading states in the production of shrimp. The state's fish catch also includes Atlantic croaker, black drum, crabs, flounder, oysters, and red snapper. Texas also produces farm-raised catfish.

Electric power and utilities. Texas utility companies provide electric, gas, and water service. Texas ranks first in the nation in electric power production. About half of the electric power generated in Texas comes from power plants that burn natural gas. More than one-third comes from plants that burn coal. Most of the remaining power is generated by nuclear plants.

Transportation. Several famous trails crossed the Texas wilderness in the early days. During the period of Spanish rule, many of these trails served as transportation routes for missionaries and explorers. The first railroad in Texas was built between Harrisburg (now part of Houston) and Richmond in 1852 and 1853. Today, about 40 railroad lines provide freight service in Texas, and intercity passenger trains serve about 30 cities.

The Dallas-Fort Worth and Houston areas each have two major airports. Other large airports in Texas are in Austin, El Paso, and San Antonio.

Texas has about 300,000 miles (483,000 kilometers) of roads and highways. About 3,200 miles (5,200 kilometers) of the interstate highway system cross Texas. Eight U.S. highways in Texas connect with roads in Mexico.

Texas has 13 deepwater ports along the Gulf of Mexico. Houston is the busiest port. Much cargo shipped to Houston is then transported by truck to Mexico. The state's other deepwater ports are Beaumont, Brownsville, Corpus Christi, Freeport, Galveston, Orange, Port Aransas, Port Arthur, Port Isabel, Port Lavaca, Port Mansfield, Sabine Pass, and Texas City. Fifteen shallow ports also lie along the coast and handle barges, fishing vessels, and other shallow-draft vessels.

The Gulf Intracoastal Waterway runs the length of the Texas coast from Brownsville to Orange. This waterway is used by boats from the state's 15 shallow ports. The Gulf Intracoastal Waterway connects with the Mississippi River at New Orleans.

Communication. José Álvarez de Toledo, a Mexican, printed Texas's first newspaper, *Gaceta de Texas,* in Nacogdoches in 1813. Today, Texas publishers issue more than 500 newspapers, about 85 of which are dailies. Texas newspapers with the largest circulations include the *Austin American-Statesman, The Dallas Morning News,* the *El Paso Times,* the *Fort Worth Star-Telegram,* the *Houston Chronicle,* and the *San Antonio Express-News.*

The first radio station in Texas, WRR, began broadcasting in Dallas in 1920. The state's first television station, WBAP-TV (now KXAS-TV), started in Fort Worth in 1948. Texas now has more than 800 radio stations and 110 television stations. Cable television systems and Internet providers serve communities statewide.

Government

Constitution of Texas was adopted in 1876. The state had four earlier constitutions—those adopted in 1845, 1861, 1866, and 1869. An amendment to the Constitution must first be approved by two-thirds of the members of each house of the state Legislature. Then, the amendment must get the approval of a majority of the voters in a statewide election.

Executive. The governor of Texas holds office for a four-year term and can serve an unlimited number of terms. The governor has the power to appoint two of the top state officials—the secretary of state and the adjutant general. All other state officials are elected, most to four-year terms. They include the lieutenant governor, attorney general, commissioner of agriculture, commissioner of the general land office, and comptroller.

The voters also elect the three members of the Texas Railroad Commission. This group controls the state's petroleum production by deciding how much oil the Texas petroleum industry can pump each year.

Legislature consists of a Senate of 31 members and a House of Representatives of 150 members. Voters in each of the 31 senatorial districts elect one senator to a four-year term. Voters in each of the 150 representative districts elect one member of the House of Representatives to a two-year term. Both houses meet in odd-numbered years on the second Tuesday in January. By law, regular sessions are limited to 140 calendar days. Special legislative sessions can last only 30 days.

© Bob Daemmrich

The Texas House of Representatives meets in the State Capitol in Austin. The Texas Legislature consists of the House, which has 150 members, and the Senate, which has 31 members.

Courts. The highest civil court in Texas is the Supreme Court. It has a chief justice and eight justices.

The governors of Texas

	Party	Term
J. Pinckney Henderson	Democratic	1846-1847
George T. Wood	Democratic	1847-1849
P. Hansborough Bell	Democratic	1849-1853
Elisha M. Pease	Democratic	1853-1857
Hardin R. Runnels	Democratic	1857-1859
Sam Houston	Independent	1859-1861
Francis R. Lubbock	Democratic	1861-1863
Pendleton Murrah	Democratic	1863-1865
Under federal military rule		1865
Andrew J. Hamilton	Conservative	1865-1866
James W. Throckmorton	Conservative	1866-1867
Elisha M. Pease	Republican	1867-1869
Under federal military rule		1869-1870
Edmund J. Davis	Republican	1870-1874
Richard Coke	Democratic	1874-1876
Richard B. Hubbard	Democratic	1876-1879
Oran M. Roberts	Democratic	1879-1883
John Ireland	Democratic	1883-1887
Lawrence S. Ross	Democratic	1887-1891
James S. Hogg	Democratic	1891-1895
Charles A. Culberson	Democratic	1895-1899
Joseph D. Sayers	Democratic	1899-1903
S. W. T. Lanham	Democratic	1903-1907
Thomas M. Campbell	Democratic	1907-1911
Oscar B. Colquitt	Democratic	1911-1915
James E. Ferguson	Democratic	1915-1917
William P. Hobby	Democratic	1917-1921
Pat M. Neff	Democratic	1921-1925
Miriam A. Ferguson	Democratic	1925-1927
Dan Moody	Democratic	1927-1931
Ross Sterling	Democratic	1931-1933
Miriam A. Ferguson	Democratic	1933-1935
James V. Allred	Democratic	1935-1939
W. Lee O'Daniel	Democratic	1939-1941
Coke R. Stevenson	Democratic	1941-1947
Beauford H. Jester	Democratic	1947-1949
Allan Shivers	Democratic	1949-1957
Price Daniel	Democratic	1957-1963
John B. Connally	Democratic	1963-1969
Preston Smith	Democratic	1969-1973
Dolph Briscoe	Democratic	1973-1979
Bill Clements	Republican	1979-1983
Mark White	Democratic	1983-1987
Bill Clements	Republican	1987-1991
Ann W. Richards	Democratic	1991-1995
George W. Bush	Republican	1995-2000
Rick Perry	Republican	2000-

The highest criminal court is the Court of Criminal Appeals. It has nine judges, including a presiding judge. Members of both courts are elected to six-year terms.

Each of the 14 supreme judicial districts in Texas has a court of appeals. Each of these courts has a chief justice and a number of justices. The number of associate justices varies from 2 to 12. All justices for the courts of appeals are elected for six-year terms.

The chief trial courts are the district courts. The voters of each judicial district elect a district judge to a four-year term. Other trial courts include the county, municipal, justice of the peace, and criminal district courts. The voters elect judges of all these courts, except municipal courts, to four-year terms. Most municipal court judges are appointed to two-year terms.

Local government. Texas has 254 counties—more than any other state. Each one is governed by a county commissioners court made up of the county judge and four commissioners. This court performs such administrative duties as adopting the county budget and setting the county tax rate. County judges are elected to four-year terms. The commissioners are elected to four-year terms from each of four commissioner precincts in a county. Other county officials include the assessor-collector of taxes, the county attorney, the sheriff, and the treasurer.

Texas has more than 1,100 incorporated cities, towns, and villages. More than 200 cities have *home rule.* That is, they have adopted their own city charters. The Texas Constitution permits all cities with populations of more than 5,000 to adopt home rule. About 180 home-rule cities use either the council-manager or the commission-manager form of government. All other home-rule cities use the mayor-council system of government. Towns with populations of 5,000 or fewer are incorporated under general law.

Revenue. Taxes bring in about half of the state's *general revenue* (income). Most of the remaining revenue comes from federal grants and other U.S. government programs, and from charges for government services. A retail sales tax on all items except food and medicine is the largest source of tax revenue. The second largest source of tax revenue is a motor-fuel use tax. Other sources include a corporation-franchise tax and a tax on petroleum and natural gas production. Texas does not collect individual or corporate income taxes.

Politics. The Democratic Party controlled Texas politics throughout most of the state's history. But in the 1970's, the Republican Party began gaining strength. In 1978, Bill Clements became the first Republican to be elected governor since 1869. In 1998, George W. Bush, son of former President George H. W. Bush, became the first Republican governor to be elected to a second term. George W. Bush was elected president of the United States in 2000. Although Bush was not born in Texas, two other U.S. presidents were born in the state. Dwight D. Eisenhower was born in Denison, and Lyndon B. Johnson was born near Stonewall.

In every presidential election since 1980, Texas's electoral votes have gone to the Republican candidate. For Texas's electoral votes and voting record in presidential elections, see **Electoral College** (table).

History

Indian days. When the first Europeans arrived, about 30,000 Indians lived in what is now Texas. The largest group was the Caddo Indians, in the eastern part of the region. These Indians lived in permanent homes and were farmers. Some of the Caddo tribes, including the Nacogdoches, Nasoni, and Neche, formed a league called the *Hasinai Confederacy.* The Arkokisa, Attacapa, Karankawa, and other smaller tribes lived along the coast. The Coahuiltecan Indians occupied south Texas. Warlike Lipan Apache lived on the Edwards Plateau in the west. Comanche and Tonkawa Indians roamed the Rolling Plains and the Prairie Plains.

Spanish exploration. Spanish adventurers, for "glory, God, and gold," began exploring Texas during the early 1500's. In 1519, the Spanish governor of Jamaica sent Alonso Álvarez de Piñeda to explore the Gulf Coast from Florida to Mexico. Piñeda mapped the coastline. Most historians believe he and his followers were the first white men in Texas. In 1528, members of a Spanish expedition that planned to explore the southern United States reached the Texas coast. Álvar Núñez Cabeza de Vaca, a leader of the expedition, and three companions traveled among the Indians. For eight years, they gradually made their way westward. They finally reached a Spanish settlement in Mexico near the Pacific Coast. The men brought to Mexico City stories of cities of great wealth that supposedly lay north of their westward route.

The Spaniards sent many expeditions to look for these golden cities, called the *Seven Cities of Cíbola.* In 1540, Francisco Vásquez de Coronado led a party north from Mexico. He passed through Texas in 1541. But Coronado found only the grass-house villages of the Plains Indians and the adobe huts of the Pueblo Indians. In 1542, some members of an expedition originally led by Hernando de Soto entered northeast Texas after their leader died. They reached the vicinity of present-day Texarkana. Spain based its claims to Texas on these and other explorations, and on missions that Spanish friars built later. Franciscan missionaries built Texas's first two missions in 1682. These missions were located near the present site of El Paso.

French exploration in Texas began in 1685. That year, René-Robert Cavelier, Sieur de La Salle, landed at Matagorda Bay. He had intended to establish a colony at the mouth of the Mississippi River. Perhaps a storm on the Gulf of Mexico drove him to Texas. La Salle established a colony, Fort St. Louis, inland, and made expeditions westward in search of gold and silver. One of La Salle's men killed him in a quarrel in 1687. Disease and Indians killed off the rest, and Fort St. Louis was destroyed by the Indians.

La Salle's explorations in Texas alarmed the Spaniards. In 1689, an expedition led by Alonso de León set out from Mexico to destroy Fort St. Louis. The party found the ruins of the fort and then traveled eastward as far as the Neches River. In 1690, a Franciscan friar with De León's expedition established the first mission in east

Historic Texas

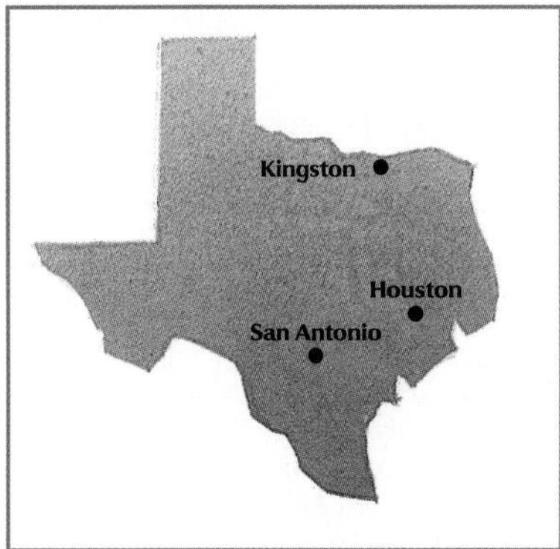

Texas longhorns were driven northward on the Chisholm Trail from 1867 to about 1885.

NASA established its headquarters for the U.S. piloted spacecraft program in Houston in 1964.

"Remember the Alamo" became the battle cry for Texans in their war for independence after they were defeated by Mexican forces at the famous San Antonio mission in 1836.

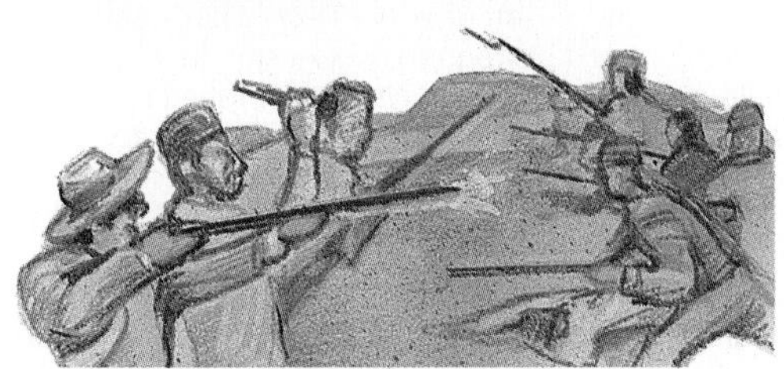

The last battle of the Civil War was fought at Palmito Hill on May 13, 1865. The soldiers had not heard that the war had ended on April 9.

WORLD BOOK illustrations by Kevin Chadwick

Important dates in Texas

1519 Alonso Álvarez de Piñeda of Spain mapped the Texas coast.

1528 Álvar Núñez Cabeza de Vaca and three other survivors of a shipwrecked Spanish expedition landed on the Texas coast and later explored parts of the region.

1541 Francisco Vásquez de Coronado traveled across part of west Texas.

1542 Hernando de Soto's expedition explored part of northeast Texas.

1682 Spanish missionaries built the first two missions in Texas, near present-day El Paso.

1685 René-Robert Cavelier, Sieur de La Salle, founded Fort Saint Louis, a French settlement, on the Texas coast.

1690 A Franciscan friar established the first mission in east Texas.

1718 The Spaniards established a mission and a fort on the site of present-day San Antonio.

1821 Texas became part of the new Empire of Mexico. The first colony of Americans settled in Texas under the sponsorship of Stephen F. Austin.

1835 The Texas Revolution began.

1836 Texas declared its independence from Mexico. The Alamo fell to Mexican forces. Sam Houston defeated the Mexicans in the Battle of San Jacinto. Texas became the independent Republic of Texas.

1845 Texas became the 28th state on December 29.

1861 Texas seceded from the Union and joined the Confederate States of America.

1870 Congress readmitted Texas to the Union.

1900 A hurricane struck Galveston resulting in about 6,000 deaths.

1901 Oilmen discovered the great Spindletop field.

1925 Texas became the second state to have a woman governor—Miriam A. Ferguson.

1947 A ship explosion in Texas City harbor killed about 500 persons and injured about 3,000.

1953 Congress restored Texas tidelands to the state.

1963 President John F. Kennedy was assassinated in Dallas. Lyndon B. Johnson of Texas was sworn in as the 36th president at Dallas Love Field Airport.

1964 The Manned Spacecraft Center (now the Lyndon B. Johnson Space Center) at Houston became the permanent headquarters of the U.S. astronauts.

1994 The Census Bureau reported that Texas had risen from third to second in state population, passing New York.

2001 Texas Governor George W. Bush became the 43rd president of the United States.

Texas, San Francisco de los Tejas. It stood near the present-day community of Weches.

The mission period. By 1731, Spain had sent more than 90 expeditions into what is now Texas. Spain also had established missions throughout central, east, and southwest Texas. The Spaniards built forts near some missions to protect them from Indians. In 1718, they built a fort, later called San Antonio de Bexar, to guard the mission of San Antonio de Valero. The mission (which was later called the Alamo) and the fort stood on the site of present-day San Antonio, where other missions were also built. In 1772, San Antonio became the seat of Spanish government in Texas. Spanish colonization of Texas proceeded slowly. The region had only about 7,000 white settlers in 1793, after more than a hundred years of missionary effort.

President Thomas Jefferson of the United States purchased the Louisiana Territory from France in 1803. The United States then claimed all territory as far south as the Rio Grande on the basis of earlier French claims. In 1819, a treaty fixed the southwestern boundaries of the Louisiana Territory at the Sabine and Red rivers.

Mexico broke away from Spain in 1821, and Texas became part of the new Empire of Mexico. Mexico became a republic in 1824.

American settlement. In 1820, Moses Austin, a Missouri banker, asked Spanish officials in Mexico to let him establish a colony of Americans in Texas. The Spanish government granted his request, but Austin died before he could organize the colony. His son, Stephen F. Austin, carried out the plan and brought 300 families to Texas. In 1821, Austin's group made its first settlements at Washington-on-the-Brazos and Columbus in southeast Texas. Austin arrived later and officially established the colony in 1822. It grew rapidly. In 1823, Austin laid out San Felipe de Austin in present-day Austin County as the colony's seat of government. Mexico soon issued new land grants to Austin, and he extended the boundaries of his colony.

Other Americans also received land grants from Mexico to establish colonies. The Mexicans called these American colonizers *empresarios.* The empresarios founded many colonies in Texas during the 1820's. From 1821 to 1836, the number of settlers grew to between 25,000 and 30,000. Almost all were Americans.

Mexican officials became alarmed by the increasing number of settlers from the United States. In 1830, they halted American immigration to Texas. From then on, relations between the American settlers and Mexican officials grew steadily worse. In 1834, General Antonio López de Santa Anna, a Mexican politician and soldier, overthrew Mexico's constitutional government and made himself dictator. The next year, the American colonists in Texas revolted against Mexico.

The Texas revolution. After a few battles with Mexican soldiers, Texas leaders met at San Felipe de Austin on Nov. 3, 1835. They organized a temporary government. Texas troops, led by Colonel Benjamin Milam, attacked San Antonio. The Mexicans there surrendered on December 11. The fall of San Antonio alarmed Santa Anna. He assembled a large army and marched on San Antonio. Texan rebels in the city withdrew behind the walls of the Alamo, the Spanish mission that had originally been called San Antonio de Valero. Santa Anna's forces attacked the Alamo from Feb. 23 to March 6, 1836, when it finally fell. Some historians believe that all its defenders, including Jim Bowie, Davy Crockett, and William B. Travis, were killed in the battle. Other historians believe that a few men, perhaps including Crockett, survived the battle but were then executed by the Mexicans. Texas leaders met at Washington-on-the-Brazos on March 2. They issued a declaration of independence from Mexico and chose David G. Burnet as temporary president and Sam Houston as commander of the army. See **Alamo**.

After the fall of the Alamo, Santa Anna moved swiftly to put down the revolution. He ordered more than 330 Texas prisoners shot to death at Goliad after they had surrendered on March 27. But the Texans continued to fight, inspired by the battle cries of "Remember the Alamo" and "Remember Goliad." In April, after a long retreat, the smaller army of Sam Houston camped near Santa Anna's forces. On April 21, the Texans took the overconfident Mexicans by surprise. They captured

Oil painting (1886) by William Henry Huddle in the South Foyer of the Capitol in Austin *(Texas Highways Magazine)*

General Santa Anna surrendered to General Sam Houston and his army on April 22, 1836, ending the Texas Revolution against Mexico. Santa Anna, *standing center,* signed a treaty granting Texas its independence the day after Houston's forces won the Battle of San Jacinto. Houston, shown lying beneath the tree, was shot in the ankle during the battle.

Santa Anna and crushed his army in the Battle of San Jacinto. The victory ended the war, and guaranteed Texas independence. See **San Jacinto, Battle of.**

The Republic of Texas faced serious problems. It had no money, and raiding Indians and Mexicans threatened its people. In the new republic's first national election, Texans chose Sam Houston as president. They also voted to join the United States. But the great powers of Europe, especially France and Britain, wanted Texas to remain independent. They feared the United States would gain control of the Southwest. The South wanted Texas to join the Union. But the North objected because Texas allowed slavery.

During the nearly 10 years when Texas was an independent republic, its population increased rapidly. Most of the people farmed for a living. In 1839, Texans passed the first homestead exemption act, which many states later adopted. This law prevented farms from being seized for payment of debts.

Statehood and early progress. In 1844, the U.S. Senate defeated a treaty to annex Texas to the United States. The treaty failed to win the approval of two-thirds of the senators voting. Texas finally joined the Union on Dec. 29, 1845. It became the 28th state by a joint resolution of both houses of Congress. Passage of the resolution required the votes of only a majority of the members present in each house.

The statehood agreement provided that Texas could keep its public lands and that it would pay its own public debts. The federal government would settle all boundary disputes with other countries.

After Texas joined the Union, Mexico ended diplomatic relations with the United States. Disputes arose over the boundary between Texas and Mexico. The Mexican War between the United States and Mexico began in 1846. Mexico surrendered in 1848. In the Treaty of Guadalupe Hidalgo, Mexico gave up all claims to Texas and other southwestern lands. See **Guadalupe Hidalgo, Treaty of; Mexican War.**

Texas claimed much of the southwestern region that Mexico turned over to the United States. In 1850, the federal government agreed to pay the state $10 million

Archives Division, Texas State Library

The Texas Rangers roamed the frontier during the 1800's tracking murderers, train robbers, and other outlaws. They were organized in 1835 to protect settlers from the Indians.

for its claims. The agreement also called for Texas to give up other claims against the federal government. Texas used part of this money to pay its public debts. Settlers continued to flock to the state. During the 1850's, Texas organized 89 new counties. Northeast Texas and the region east of Waco and Fort Worth attracted the largest number of settlers.

The Civil War and Reconstruction. Texas *seceded* (withdrew) from the Union in February 1861. The state seceded in spite of strong Union feeling in some sections of Texas. Governor Sam Houston refused to take an oath to support the constitution of the Confederate States. As a result, he was put out of office. In March 1861, Texas joined the Confederate States of America. More than 50,000 Texans fought for the Confederacy during the Civil War (1861-1865). Texas also furnished the Confederacy with great amounts of supplies. The Union navy blockaded the Texas coast and occupied Galveston for a short time. The last battle of the Civil War was fought at Palmito Hill, near the mouth of the Rio Grande, on May 13, 1865. The soldiers had not heard that the war ended on April 9.

After the war, Northern sympathizers called *Radicals* rose to power in Texas state politics. Lawlessness gripped the state as racial violence broke out and the Ku Klux Klan became powerful (see **Ku Klux Klan**). During the Reconstruction period, Texas was ruled by a military government, an appointed governor, and three governors elected by the Radicals. Congress readmitted Texas to the Union on March 30, 1870. Reconstruction ended in the state when Democrat Richard Coke became governor in 1874. See **Reconstruction.**

Conquering the frontier. In the mid-1860's, Texans began driving cattle along trails to railroad centers in Kansas and Missouri. These trail drives continued during the 1870's and 1880's. Indian raids slowed the settlement of the western part of the state. The tribes were subdued by 1880, and cattle ranchers began to occupy the Panhandle and the western plains. Railroads crossed Texas in the 1880's, ending the cattle drives and aiding settlement. Pioneers followed the railroads west and began farming the western regions of the state. The Texas Rangers, organized in 1835, helped protect the far western settlers from bandits such as Sam Bass. During the 1890's, the state legislature passed various business-reform laws, preventing some price and trade abuses by the railroads and other large corporations.

The early 1900's. Between 1900 and 1920, Texas increased its railroad mileage and built a road system. The state also developed irrigation and farming on land previously used for raising livestock. A major disaster occurred in Texas in 1900, when a hurricane struck Galveston resulting in about 6,000 deaths.

The state's great oil and gas industries began in 1901 with the discovery of the Spindletop oil field near Beaumont. To develop the mineral resources, Texans built great refineries and other manufacturing plants. They deepened coastal harbors to help ship their oil and other products. The annual value of manufactured goods more than doubled between 1900 and 1910. Between 1900 and 1920, many Texans became city workers, and the number of cities and towns doubled. By 1920, a third of the people in Texas lived in cities. After the United States entered World War I in 1917, the

Spindletop oil field, near Beaumont, was the first gusher in Texas. It sprayed more than 800,000 barrels of oil into the air in 1901 before it was first brought under control.

federal government set up many military training camps in Texas.

In the early 1920's, Governor Pat M. Neff improved education and prisons. He also led the push for a state park system. In 1925, Texas became the second state, after Wyoming, to have a woman governor. She was Miriam A. "Ma" Ferguson. Her husband, James E. Ferguson, had previously been governor.

Great highway construction took place in Texas during the 1920's and 1930's. New legislation helped ease hardships caused by the Great Depression and the droughts of the 1930's. The new legislation included the establishment of old-age pensions and special relief programs. In 1936, the Texas Centennial Exposition at Dallas celebrated a hundred years of independence. In 1937, the Greater Texas and Pan American Exposition in Dallas promoted trade among nations of the Western Hemisphere.

The mid-1900's. During World War II (1939-1945), over a million servicemen trained in Texas. Lieutenant Audie Murphy, who was born in Kingston, was the most decorated U.S. soldier of the war.

After the war, manufacturing expanded rapidly in Texas. The aerospace, chemical, and electronics industries built many facilities in the state. Thousands of Texans moved from rural areas to cities to find jobs in new factories, and the state began to shift from a rural, farm economy to an urban, industrial economy.

Texas suffered one of its greatest disasters on April 16, 1947, when a French ship loaded with chemicals blew up in the harbor at Texas City. The explosion of the ship killed about 500 people.

In 1950, the Supreme Court of the United States ruled that Texas had lost ownership of its oil-rich *tidelands* (submerged offshore lands) when it entered the Union in 1845. The ruling meant that the U.S. government owned the oil beneath the tidewaters. But in 1953, the U.S. government restored ownership of the tidelands to Texas.

Like many other states, Texas faced racial problems in the 1950's and 1960's. The state maintained separate public schools for blacks and whites. In 1954, the U.S. Supreme Court ruled that compulsory segregation in public schools was unconstitutional. By the late 1960's, most of the public school districts in Texas had been integrated.

Texas took a leading role in the U.S. space program during the 1960's. In 1962, the National Aeronautics and Space Administration (NASA) began building a Manned Spacecraft Center near Houston. The center became the headquarters of the U.S. piloted spacecraft program in 1964. In 1969, scientists and engineers at the center directed the Apollo 11 flight, in which astronauts made the first landing on the moon.

Texas also gained in national political importance in the mid-1900's. Sam Rayburn of Texas became one of the nation's most influential leaders. He was speaker of the U.S. House of Representatives for almost 17 years between 1940 and 1961.

In 1963, Lyndon B. Johnson of Texas became the first Southern U.S. president since the Civil War. Johnson became president on Nov. 22, 1963, after an assassin had killed President John F. Kennedy and wounded Texas Governor John B. Connally in Dallas. Vice President Johnson was sworn in as the 36th president aboard the presidential plane at Love Field in Dallas. Lee Harvey Oswald was accused of shooting President Kennedy. Two days after Kennedy's death, Jack Ruby, a Dallas nightclub owner, killed Oswald.

The late 1900's. The Manned Spacecraft Center was renamed the Lyndon B. Johnson Space Center in 1973. It made southeastern Texas a major center for space research. Besides NASA, several corporations design and test space equipment there. Universities conduct research in space medicine and other fields. In 1977, Houston annexed the area next to the space center.

Texas continued the industrial expansion and urban growth that began after World War II. More Texans now work in manufacturing than in farming and mining combined. About four-fifths of the people in Texas live in urban areas.

During the mid-1980's, however, the state's economy was deeply hurt by a sharp decline in oil and natural gas prices. This decline emphasized the need to attract new types of industries to the state and to find new sources of tax revenue. In 1986, lawmakers agreed to raise the state sales tax and to cut the budgets for health, welfare, and higher education. Economic improvements in the late 1980's and into the 1990's led to a recovery from the sharp decline of the state's economy.

Recent developments. In 2001, Texas Governor George W. Bush became the 43rd president of the United States. Bush resigned as governor after being elected president, and Lieutenant Governor Rick Perry became Texas's new governor.

William E. Doolittle and Clifford L. Egan

Related articles in *World Book* include:

Biographies

Armey, Dick
Austin, Stephen F.
Baker, James A., III
Bass, Sam
Bean, Judge Roy
Bentsen, Lloyd M., Jr.
Bowie, James
Bush, George H. W.
Bush, George Walker
Connally, John B.
Cortina, Juan Nepomuceno
Crockett, Davy
DeLay, Tom
Dobie, J. Frank
Eisenhower, Dwight D.
Garner, John N.
Gramm, Phil
Gutiérrez, José Angel
Hobby, Oveta C.
House, Edward M.
Houston, Sam
Johnson, Lyndon B.
Jordan, Barbara C.
Long, Jane
Maverick, Samuel A.
Murphy, Audie
Rayburn, Sam
Travis, William B.
Tyler, John
Wright, James Claude, Jr.

Cities

Amarillo
Austin
Beaumont
Corpus Christi
Dallas
El Paso
Fort Worth
Galveston
Houston
Laredo
Lubbock
San Antonio
Waco
Wichita Falls

History

Alamo
Flag (pictures: Flags in American history [Texas flags])
Guadalupe Hidalgo, Treaty of
Hispanic Americans (In the Southwest)
Jefferson, State of
Mexican War (Background of the war)
Mission life in America
San Jacinto, Battle of
Texas Rangers
Western frontier life in America
Westward movement in America (Texas)

Physical features

Big Bend National Park
Colorado River
Dust Bowl
Guadalupe Mountains National Park
Gulf of Mexico
Lake Texoma
Padre Island
Pecos River
Red River
Rio Grande

Other related articles

Alibates Flint Quarries National Monument
Fort Bliss
Fort Hood
Fort Sam Houston
Gulf Intracoastal Waterway
Gulf of Mexico
Johnson Space Center
King Ranch
Lackland Air Force Base

Outline

I. People
A. Population
B. Schools
C. Libraries
D. Museums

II. Visitor's guide
A. Places to visit
B. Annual events

III. Land and climate
A. Land regions
B. Coastline
C. Mountains
D. Rivers and lakes
E. Plant and animal life
F. Climate

IV. Economy
A. Natural resources
B. Service industries
C. Manufacturing
D. Mining
E. Agriculture
F. Fishing industry
G. Electric power
H. Transportation
I. Communication

V. Government
A. Constitution
B. Executive
C. Legislature
D. Courts
E. Local government
F. Revenue
G. Politics

VI. History

Questions

How did Texas win independence from Mexico?
What urban area of Texas has the corporate headquarters of many of the nation's largest companies?
What is Texas's most valuable crop?
Who established the first colony of Americans in Texas? When was it established?
Which six nations have flown flags over Texas?
Why was Governor Sam Houston put out of office during the American Civil War?
What was the source of the name *Texas*?
What role does Texas play in the United States space program?
Which two minerals have contributed to making Texas a wealthy state?
Which political party has controlled Texas politics throughout most of the state's history?

Additional resources

Level I

Bredeson, Carmen. *Texas.* Benchmark Bks., 1997.
Heinrichs, Ann. *Texas.* Children's Pr., 1999.
McComb, David G. *Texas: An Illustrated History.* Oxford, 1995.
Sorrels, Roy. *The Alamo in American History.* Enslow, 1996.
Turner, Robyn M. *Texas Traditions.* Little, Brown, 1996.
Wills, Charles A. *A Historical Album of Texas.* Millbrook, 1995.

Level II

Chipman, Donald E. *Spanish Texas, 1519-1821.* Univ. of Tex. Pr., 1992.
The Encyclopedia of Texas. 2 vols. Somerset, published biennially.
Hatch, Thom. *Encyclopedia of the Alamo and the Texas Revolution.* McFarland, 1999.
Hendrickson, Kenneth E., Jr. *The Chief Executives of Texas: From Stephen F. Austin to John B. Connally, Jr.* Tex. A&M Univ. Pr., 1995.
James, Gary. *The Texas Guide.* Fulcrum, 2000. A travel guide.
La Vere, David. *Life Among the Texas Indians: The WPA Narratives.* Tex. A&M Univ. Pr., 1998.
Lack, Paul D. *The Texas Revolutionary Experience.* 1992. Reprint. Tex. A&M Univ. Pr., 1996.
May, Janice C. *The Texas State Constitution: A Reference Guide.* Greenwood, 1996.
McComb, David G. *Texas: A Modern History.* Univ. of Tex. Pr., 1989.
Moneyhon, Carl, and Roberts, Bobby. *Portraits of Conflict: A Photographic History of Texas in the Civil War.* Univ. of Ark. Pr., 1998.
Parent, Laurence E. *Official Guide to Texas State Parks.* Tex. Parks and Wildlife Pr., 1997.
Richardson, Rupert N., and others. *Texas.* 8th ed. Prentice Hall, 2001.
Tijerina, Andres. *Tejanos and Texas Under the Mexican Flag, 1821-1836.* Tex. A&M Univ. Pr., 1994.

Texas, University of, is a coeducational, state-supported system of higher education. Its official name is the University of Texas System. The system consists of nine academic institutions and six health-related institutions. The system's administrative offices are in Austin.

University of Texas at Arlington has colleges of business administration, engineering, liberal arts, and science; schools of nursing, social work, and architecture; and graduate schools. It also has a school of urban studies and public affairs and a center for professional teacher education. The university grants bachelor's, master's, and doctor's degrees. The campus opened in 1895 as a private college. It became part of the University of Texas System in 1965.

University of Texas at Austin grants bachelor's, master's, and doctor's degrees. It has colleges of business administration, communication, education, engineering, fine arts, liberal arts, natural sciences, and pharmacy; and schools of architecture, nursing, and social work. Its graduate schools include business, law, library and information science, and public affairs. The Lyndon Baines Johnson Library is on the Austin campus. Major research facilities include the McDonald Observatory at Mount Locke and the Marine Science Institute at Port Aransas. The university was founded in 1883.

University of Texas at Brownsville is open to graduate and upper-level undergraduate students. It grants bachelor's and master's degrees in arts and sciences, business, and education. The school was originally a study center of Pan American University, which was based in Edinburg, Texas. It became a university in 1977 and joined the University of Texas System in 1989.

University of Texas at Dallas is located in the Dallas suburb of Richardson. The university offers programs that lead to bachelor's, master's, and doctor's degrees. Formerly a private research institution, the University of Texas at Dallas was created in 1969.

University of Texas at El Paso grants bachelor's, master's, and doctor's degrees. It has colleges of business administration, education, engineering, liberal arts, nursing and allied health, and science. It opened in 1913 as the Texas School of Mines and Metallurgy. It became part of the University of Texas System in 1919.

University of Texas-Pan American in Edinburg grants bachelor's and master's degrees. It has schools of business administration and education, a college of arts and sciences, and a division of health-related professions. The school was established in 1927 as a community college and later became Pan American University. It became part of the University of Texas System in 1989.

University of Texas of the Permian Basin, in Odessa, offers courses at the junior, senior, and graduate levels. It grants bachelor's and master's degrees. The university was established in 1969.

University of Texas at San Antonio grants bachelor's and master's degrees. It has colleges of business, fine arts and humanities, sciences and mathematics, and social and behavioral sciences. The university was established in 1969.

University of Texas at Tyler offers upper-level programs that lead to the bachelor's degree, and graduate programs that lead to the master's degree. It has schools of business administration, education and psychology, liberal arts, and sciences and mathematics. It opened in 1971 as Texas Eastern University and became part of the University of Texas System in 1979.

Health-related institutions in the system are the Southwestern Medical Center at Dallas; the Health Science Centers at Houston and San Antonio; a health center at Tyler; the Medical Branch at Galveston; and the University of Texas System Cancer Center, which has facilities located both in Houston and near Smithville.

Critically reviewed by the University of Texas System

Texas A&M University is the flagship institution in a large network of public universities and state agencies in Texas. The official name of this network is the Texas A&M University System. Agencies in the system conduct research and provide services in a number of areas, including agriculture, forestry, and veterinary medicine. The system has 11 universities.

Texas A&M University, in College Station, is the oldest public university in Texas. It was established in 1876 as the Agricultural and Mechanical College of Texas. Students at Texas A&M can earn bachelor's, master's, and doctor's degrees in over 100 fields of study. The George Bush Presidential Library in College Station is affiliated with the university.

Prairie View A&M University, in Prairie View, provides numerous areas of major study, including nursing, electrical engineering, and biology.

Tarleton State University, in Stephenville, offers bachelor's and advanced degrees in arts and science, agriculture and technology, business, education, and fine arts.

Texas A&M International University, in Laredo, has colleges of arts and humanities, business, education, and science and technology. It has graduate programs in international trade and business administration.

Texas A&M University System Health Science Center-Baylor College of Dentistry, in Dallas, offers bachelor's, master's, and doctor's degrees in dental fields and other biomedical sciences.

Texas A&M University-Commerce has colleges of arts and sciences, business and technology, and education. The campus also offers graduate programs.

Texas A&M University-Corpus Christi offers undergraduate and graduate studies. Special programs focus on environmental issues affecting the Gulf of Mexico.

Texas A&M University at Galveston, located on Galveston Bay, focuses on ocean-related studies. Subjects include business, biological and physical sciences, engineering, and transportation.

Texas A&M University-Kingsville has programs in agriculture and human sciences, arts and sciences, business, education, engineering, and graduate studies.

Texas A&M University-Texarkana provides nonresidential, career-oriented programs for junior, senior, and graduate-level students.

West Texas A&M University, in Canyon, offers a career-oriented curriculum, including programs in teacher education, music, and nursing.

Critically reviewed by the Texas A&M University System

Texas Christian University is an independent coeducational teaching and research institution in Fort Worth, Texas. It is related to the Christian Church (Disciples of Christ). The university has divisions of arts and sciences, business, divinity, education, fine arts and communication, and nursing. Courses lead to bachelor's, master's, and doctor's degrees. The university offers an honors program, a ranch management program, and study programs in Washington, D.C.; New Mexico; and 13 foreign countries. It also operates a bilingual speech and hearing clinic and a school for children with learning disabilities. Texas Christian University was founded in 1873.

Critically reviewed by Texas Christian University

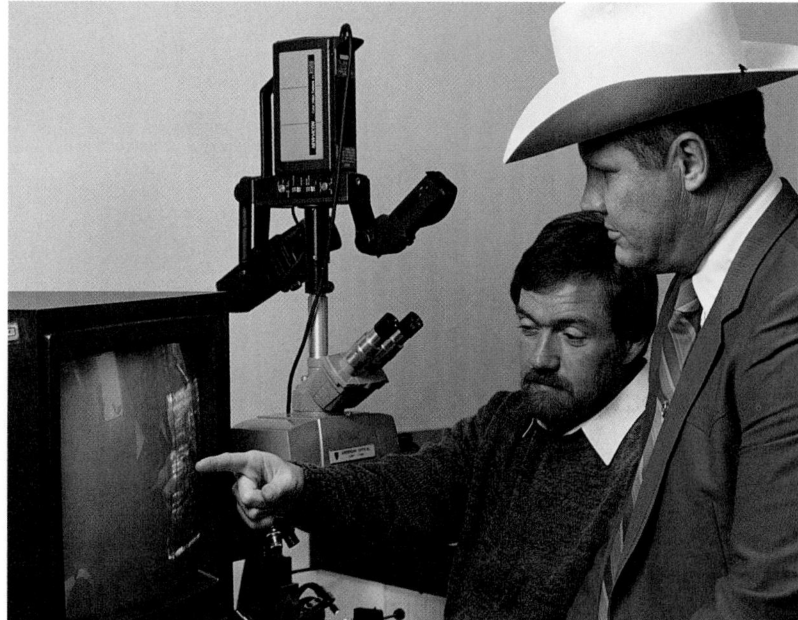

Susan Hoermann, Texas Department of Public Safety

Texas Rangers are part of the state police of Texas. In their crime laboratory, *shown here,* specially trained Rangers use modern equipment to analyze bloodstains, fingerprints, and other evidence connected with the crimes they investigate.

Texas Rangers are special police officers of the state of Texas. They serve under the authority of the State Department of Public Safety. One noted Ranger summarized their qualities in these words: "The Texas Rangers can ride like a Mexican, trail like an Indian, shoot like a Tennessean, and fight like a very devil." The Rangers have a tradition of individualism, resourcefulness, and self-reliance. They wear no official uniforms and furnish their own clothing. The state provides weapons and transportation. But Rangers may carry their own weapons, and they ride their own horses.

Early days. The Rangers were originally a band of mounted riflemen. As early as 1826, Stephen F. Austin formed bands of "rangers" to protect American settlers along the Brazos River from Indian warriors and Mexican bandits.

In 1835, the Texas Consultation, an unofficial government of Texas, formally organized the Rangers and assigned them the task of defending the frontier against Indians. One company of 25 men patrolled east of the Trinity River. Later, other companies worked in the areas between the Trinity and the Brazos, and between the Brazos and Colorado rivers.

The Rangers adopted the practices of their enemies. The Comanche Indians, with their speed and courage, set the pattern of Plains warfare. The Rangers learned the Indian skills of horsemanship, woodcraft, and direction finding. They were excellent marksmen, and adopted the revolving six-shooter as their standard weapon.

After Texas gained its independence in 1836, it faced a Mexican and Indian danger on a 1,000-mile (1,600-kilometer) frontier. With a population of about 400,000, it could not afford a standing army. Texas required a fighting force that was small and inexpensive, available in time of need but inactive when not needed. The Texas Rangers, without uniforms, drill, or regular pay, met these requirements. The Rangers served as a mobile and efficient frontier defense organization.

After Texas joined the Union in 1845, the Rangers continued to play a major role in the defense of the frontier. During the Mexican War (1846-1848), a group of Rangers performed valuable services as scouts and guerrilla fighters with the American armies in Mexico. When the federal government established forts along the Texas frontier and garrisoned them with regular troops, Texans still placed their faith in the Rangers. Sam Houston once said in the United States Senate: "Give us 1,000 Rangers, and we will be responsible for the defense of our frontier. ... We ask no regular troops; withdraw them if you please. I ask this not through any unkindness to them, but because they have not the efficiency for frontier service."

Later history. During the Reconstruction period that followed the American Civil War, Texas suffered from lawlessness, murder, and Indian raids. In 1874, 450 Texas Rangers received commissions as peace officers. They continued to fight the Comanche along the northern border and Mexican cattle thieves along the Rio Grande. They also tracked down murderers, smugglers, bank and train robbers, and mine bandits. Within 10 years, they restored peace and quiet to the interior of Texas. In 1917 and 1918, they succeeded in clearing the rocky Big Bend region of outlaws.

Today, the Rangers use modern methods to investigate crimes. But they still ride horses in pursuit of lawbreakers in rugged areas. Joseph A. Stout, Jr.

Additional resources

Davis, John L. *The Texas Rangers.* Rev. ed. Univ. of Tex. Inst. of Texan Cultures, 2000.

Knowles, Thomas W. *They Rode for the Lone Star.* Taylor Pub. Co., 1998.

Webb, Walter P. *The Texas Rangers: A Century of Frontier Defense.* 2nd ed. 1965. Reprint. Univ. of Tx. Pr., 1990.

Texoma, Lake. See Lake Texoma.

WORLD BOOK photo by Jeff Guerrant

A wide variety of textile products—from bedding, carpeting, and clothing to umbrellas, furnace filters, painters' canvases, and bookbindings—helps meet the needs of people throughout the world.

Textile

Textile has traditionally meant a woven fabric. The term comes from the Latin word *texere,* meaning *to weave.* Today, *textile* refers to any product that is woven, knitted, braided, or otherwise constructed of fibers. The textile industry also uses the term *textiles* to refer to the fibers themselves. The term *fabric* is closely related to *textile,* and it generally refers to textiles that are eventually made into consumer products, especially clothing and home furnishings. In popular usage, however, *fabric* is often used to mean any textile.

Textile manufacturing plants produce an incredible variety of textiles made from such fibers as acetate, cotton, flax, nylon, polyester, rayon, silk, and wool. These textiles come in every color imaginable and in countless patterns.

Textiles are used in thousands of products, including basketball nets, boat sails, bookbindings, fire hoses, flags, insulation materials, mailbags, parachutes, and umbrellas. Automobile manufacturers use textiles to make air bags, brake linings, carpeting, seat belts, tires, and upholstery. Hospitals use such textile products as adhesive tape, bandages, and surgical gowns.

Most textiles are produced by twisting fibers into yarns and then knitting or weaving the yarns into a fabric. This method of making cloth has been used for thousands of years. But for most of that time, workers did the twisting, knitting, or weaving largely by hand. With today's modern machinery, textile manufacturing plants can produce as much fabric in a few seconds as workers could make in weeks by hand.

In the United States, clothing and accessories make up the largest share of textile production. The second largest share is used in industrial products, such as conveyor belts and filters. The third largest share goes to rug and carpet manufacturers. The rest is used to make such household products as draperies, blankets, sheets, and towels.

Sources of textile fibers

Fibers are the raw materials for all textiles. Some fibers occur in nature as fine strands that can be twisted into yarns. These *natural fibers* come from plants, animals, and minerals. Most natural fibers used for textile production measure $\frac{1}{2}$ to 8 inches (1.3 to 20 centimeters) or longer. Such short fibers are called *staple fibers.*

For most of history, people had only natural fibers to use in making cloth. But textile scientists have learned how to produce fibers by chemical and technical means. Unlike most natural fibers, the majority of manufactured fibers are produced in long, continuous lengths called *filaments.* Many manufactured fibers are designed to have certain qualities superior to those of natural fibers. For example, they may be stronger or more elastic.

Natural fibers. Plants provide more textile fibers than do animals or minerals. In fact, one plant, cotton, accounts for the vast majority of the natural fibers used in textiles. Cotton fibers produce soft, absorbent fabrics that are used for clothing, sheets, and towels. Fibers of the flax plant are made into linen. The strength and beauty of linen have made it a popular fabric for fine tablecloths, napkins, handkerchiefs, and clothing. Fibers of the jute plant can be woven into burlap, a coarse, heavy cloth used for sacks and as backing for rugs and carpets. Ramie and kenaf are plant fibers that can be used for clothing.

The main animal fiber used for textiles is wool. Sheep supply most of the wool, but members of the camel family and some goats also furnish wool. Wool provides warm, comfortable fabrics for dresses, pants, suits, and sweaters. Another animal fiber, silk, produces one of the most luxurious fabrics. Silk comes from cocoons spun by silkworms. Workers unwind the cocoons to obtain long, natural filaments. Silk fabrics are soft and lustrous, and they can be dyed brilliant colors. Silk is especially popular for scarves and neckties.

The only natural mineral fiber used for textiles is asbestos, which comes from rocks. It will not burn, but it melts at high temperatures. The use of asbestos to make textiles was discontinued in many countries after scientists determined that inhalation of the mineral can result in serious lung disease. But manufacturers in a few countries still use asbestos in automobile brake linings and other products.

Manufactured fibers. Most manufactured fibers are made from *wood pulp,* cotton *linters,* or *petrochemicals.* Wood pulp comes from trees and the waste products of the lumber industry. Linters are the short fibers remaining on cottonseeds after the longer fibers have been removed by a cotton gin. Petrochemicals are chemicals made from crude oil and natural gas.

The fibers made from wood pulp and linters are rayon and acetate. These fibers are called *cellulosics* because they are made from the cellulose in wood pulp and cotton. Rayon and acetate are widely used for clothing, draperies, and upholstery. The properties of rayon resemble those of cotton. Rayon produces absorbent fabrics that dye easily. Fabrics of acetate are silkier than those of rayon. Acetate resists shrinking and stretching.

The chief fibers manufactured from petrochemicals include nylon, polyester, acrylic, olefin, and elastomeric fibers. Nylon has exceptional strength, wears well, and is easy to launder. It is popular for hosiery and other clothing and for carpeting and upholstery. Such products as conveyor belts and fire hoses are also made of nylon. Polyester resists wrinkling and is widely used in clothing. Acrylic fibers produce soft, bulky, lightweight fabrics for blankets, carpeting, and cold-weather clothing. Olefin cleans easily, dries quickly, and resists mildew. It is widely used for indoor-outdoor carpeting. Elastomer-

Textile terms

Broadcloth is a tightly woven fabric of cotton, silk, or soft wool, used for coats, suits, shirts, and dresses.

Brocade is a fabric with raised designs of colored or metallic yarns woven into it. Brocade may be cotton, linen, rayon, silk, wool, or synthetic fiber. It is used for bedspreads, draperies, upholstery, and evening dresses.

Canvas is a strong, coarse plain-weave cloth, usually cotton. It is used for shoes, sails, tents, and the surfaces on which artists paint.

Challis is a soft plain-weave fabric made from wool, rayon, or cotton, used for dresses, blouses, and sleepwear.

Chambray is a lightweight plain-weave fabric with colored *warp* (lengthwise) threads, usually a solid color, and white *filling* (crosswise) threads. Chambray is used for shirts, dresses, and children's clothes.

Chenille is a fuzzy yarn made of cotton, silk, wool, or rayon, used to make bedspreads, sweaters, bathrobes, and fringes.

Corduroy is a cotton or cotton-blend fabric with *napped* (fuzzy) *ribs* (ridges), used for jackets, slacks, draperies, and upholstery.

Damask is a firm, lustrous fabric with a flat, woven design on both sides, used for tablecloths, napkins, and draperies. It may be woven from various fibers. The design is satin weave on one side, and the background is in satin weave on the other side.

Denim is a sturdy twill-weave fabric made from cotton or cotton-synthetic blends. Usually, the *warp* (lengthwise) threads are colored and the *filling* (crosswise) threads are white. Denim is used for jeans, sportswear, and work clothes.

Felt is a fabric made of wool fibers or animal hair matted together by heat, moisture, and pressure, used to make hats, slippers, chalkboard erasers, and padding for saddles.

Flannel is a soft cotton, wool, or wool-blend fabric with a brushed surface, used for coats and suits. It may be plain weave or twill weave.

Fleece is a bulky fabric with a deep, soft *nap* (fuzz) or pile, used for cold-weather clothing. Fleece is usually made of synthetic fiber and may be knitted or woven.

Gabardine is a twill-weave fabric made from wool, cotton, rayon, or synthetic blends. It is used for shirts, dresses, raincoats, slacks, suits, and uniforms.

Jersey is a plain knit used for dresses, sweaters, lingerie, and sportswear. Jersey may be smooth or napped.

Lace is a decorative fabric that consists of an open, netlike pattern of threads. The thread is traditionally linen but may be cotton, silk, wool, or synthetic fiber. Flowers or leaves are a common design. Lace is used for tablecloths, to decorate clothing, and to make ornamental items.

Muslin is a closely woven plain-weave fabric made from white or unbleached cotton cord. Sheer muslin is used for curtains, heavier muslin for shirts and sheets.

Net is an open fabric produced by knotting or looping together yarns to leave spaces between the knots or loops. Net is usually made of cotton, nylon, or polyester, and it is used to make bridal and evening gowns, curtains, hammocks, and tablecloths. Light, fine net called *tulle* is used in veils and ballet costumes.

Percale is a closely woven plain-weave fabric, usually a print, made from combed cotton yarn. It is used for dresses, pajamas, shirts, and sheets.

Satin is a weave with long raised threads called *floats* along the *warp* (lengthwise) or *filling* (crosswise) direction on one side. Satin weave produces a smooth fabric with one shiny side. The term *satin* also refers to satin-weave fabrics made from rayon, silk, or synthetic fiber, used for bridal and evening gowns, draperies, and bed linens. Satin-weave cotton is called *sateen.*

Terry cloth, also called *toweling,* is an absorbent fabric with a pile consisting of loops, usually on both sides of the fabric. Terry cloth is used for towels, washcloths, and bathrobes.

Tweed is a rough, heavy, hairy, woolen or wool-blend fabric used for suits, coats, and sportswear. Tweed may be plain weave or twill and usually has two or more colors.

Twill is a weave with raised diagonal lines where the *warp* (lengthwise) threads and *filling* (crosswise) threads interlace. It is used for coats, suits, and slacks.

Velour is a soft fabric with a short, dense pile that lies flat. It is used for draperies, upholstery, bathrobes, and coats. Velour is usually made of cotton, polyester, or rayon, and may be woven or knitted.

Velvet is a plush, lustrous fabric with a short, thick pile, used to make dressy clothing, upholstery, and draperies. Velvet is commonly made of cotton, rayon, or silk.

Voile is a sheer plain-weave fabric used for curtains and summer clothing.

ic fibers, such as *spandex,* are often blended with other fibers to provide stretch and comfort in sportswear and other clothing.

Other manufactured fibers include those made from glass and metals. Glass fibers are used for insulation and to make flame-resistant textiles. Metallic fibers are made chiefly by bonding aluminum, gold, and silver foils to plastics. These fibers provide decorative yarns for bedspreads, evening gowns, and tablecloths.

Kinds of textiles

To make textiles, manufacturing plants may use yarns finer than sewing thread or as heavy as rug yarn. The majority of textiles are made by weaving or knitting.

Woven fabrics are made of two sets of yarns—a lengthwise set called the *warp* and a crosswise set called the *filling* or *weft.* The warp yarns are threaded into a loom through a series of frames called *harnesses.* During weaving, the harnesses raise some warp yarns and lower others. This action creates a space, called a *shed,* between the yarns. In traditional looms, a device called a *shuttle* carries the filling through the shed and so forms the crosswise yarns of the fabric. In modern weaving machines, called *shuttleless looms,* the filling yarn is carried from one side to the other by other means, such as jets of air or water. The pattern in which the harnesses are raised and lowered for each insertion of the filling yarn determines the kind of weave. There are three basic patterns: (1) plain weave, (2) twill weave, and (3) satin weave.

Plain weave is the simplest and most common pattern. In this weave, the crosswise filling passes over one warp yarn and under the next alternately across the width of the fabric. The weave produces long-lasting, flat-textured fabric used for such products as sheets, dresses, and upholstery. Plain-weave fabrics include gingham, percale, and taffeta.

Twill weave has a pattern of raised diagonal lines. The filling crosses over and then under two, three, or four warp yarns at a time, with each row following the same pattern. However, each row's pattern begins slightly to the right or left of the pattern in the previous row. This technique creates the diagonal lines. Twill weave produces strong, tightly woven fabric used in coats, sportswear, and work clothes. Popular twill fabrics include denim and gabardine.

Satin weave is the least common pattern. The filling may span as many as 12 warp yarns. The weave produces soft, luxurious fabric, but it may snag easily. Satin-weave fabrics are made into such products as draperies and formal clothing. Common satin weaves include damask and satin fabrics.

Knitted fabrics are made from a single yarn or a set of yarns. In making fabric, a knitting machine forms loops in the yarn and links them to one another by means of needles. The finished fabric consists of crosswise rows of loops, called *courses,* and lengthwise rows of loops, called *wales.* This looped structure makes knitted fabrics more elastic than woven ones. Garment manufacturers use knitted fabrics to produce comfortable, lightweight clothing that resists wrinkling. Textile mills manufacture knit goods by two basic methods: (1) weft knitting and (2) warp knitting.

Weft knitting is done with single lengths of yarn, which a knitting machine forms into the crosswise courses one row at a time. The loops of each course are pulled through the loops of the previous course. This process forms the wales at the same time as the courses. Weft knits can be made in the shape of a tube or as flat pieces of fabric.

Most weft-knitted fabrics are used in making T-shirts, hosiery, sweaters, and underwear. These fabrics are knitted in three basic constructions, known as *jersey fabric, rib fabric,* and *purl fabric.* All of them are based on a simple loop. In jersey fabric, which is sometimes called *plain knit* or *single knit,* the long part of the loop forms a V shape over the face of the fabric. The curved, or bottom, part of the loop forms the reverse side. In rib fabrics, the V part of the loop makes up long, vertical raised wales that alternate with wales consisting only of the curved part of the loop. A kind of rib fabric commonly called *double knit* is made with smaller, tighter stitches. Double knits are used for sportswear. Lightweight cotton double knits are usually sold as *interlock knits.* A purl fabric consists of rows in which the V shape alternates with the curved part of the loop.

Warp knitting requires hundreds of yarns fed as a sheet to a knitting machine. A separate needle for each

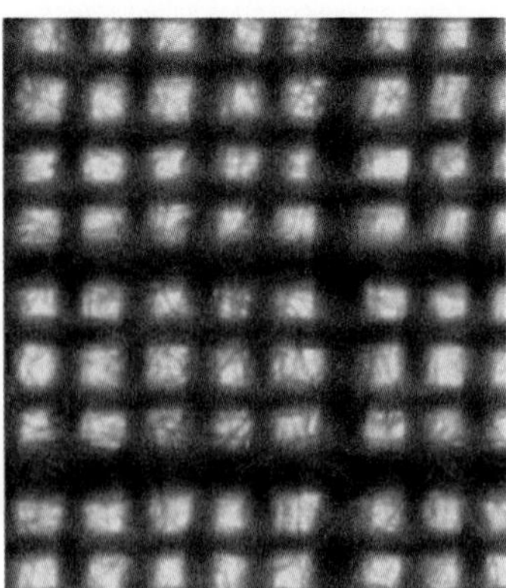

WORLD BOOK photo by Steven Spicer

A woven fabric consists of two sets of yarns. The yarns are crossed over and under each other to form cloth.

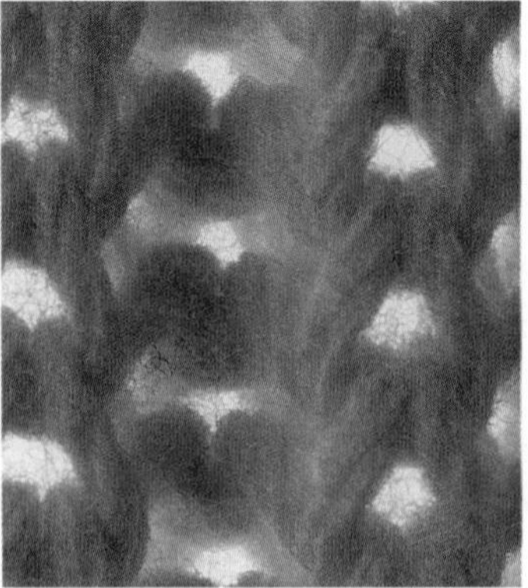

WORLD BOOK photo by Steven Spicer

A knitted fabric has a single yarn or a set of yarns. Loops are made in the yarn and linked together, forming cloth.

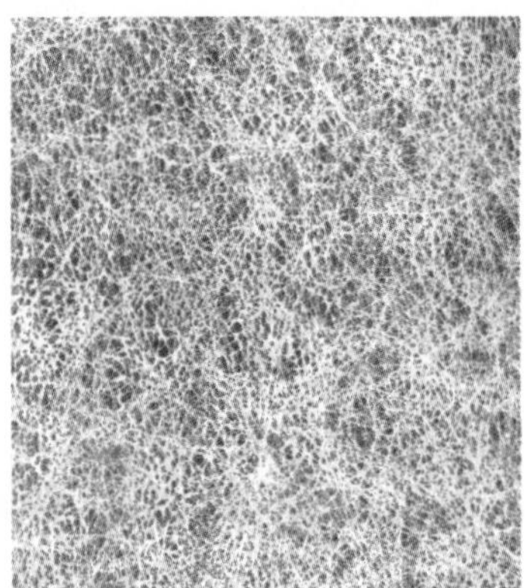

WORLD BOOK photo

A nonwoven fabric consists of one or more sheets of fibers joined together by any of several bonding processes.

yarn forms the wales of the fabric. At the same time, the needles interloop the wales crosswise and so form the yarns into a fabric. Almost all warp knits are produced in flat pieces.

Warp-knitted fabrics may be tightly constructed and thus may not stretch as much as weft knits. In warp knits, the loops stand out on the face of the fabric, and the connecting yarns stand out on the back. Common warp-knitted fabrics include tricot and raschel. Tricot knits are lightweight fabrics that are widely used in making sheets, blouses, dresses, and women's underwear. Raschel knits can be either finely knitted, lacelike fabrics or heavier, bulkier fabrics. They are used for a variety of products, including blankets, swimwear, and *thermal* (cold-weather) underwear.

Other textiles include tufted fabrics, nets and laces, braids, felt, and a category of textiles called nonwovens. None of these textiles are woven or knitted.

Tufted textiles consist of cut or uncut loops of yarn that have been punched through a backing material. Such textiles make up the vast majority of carpeting.

Nets and laces, which are called *open-mesh fabrics,* have wide spaces between the yarns. These fabrics can be produced on certain kinds of knitting machines. Netting is used for curtains, fishing nets, hammocks, and tennis nets. Laces have delicate designs and are popular as trim for clothing.

Braids consist of three or more interlaced yarns. Braided textiles are used for shoelaces, drawstrings, and similar items.

Felt is produced chiefly from fibers of wool, fur, or animal hair. The fibers are matted together by moisture, heat, and pressure. Felt is used in making such items as slippers, hats, and padding.

Nonwovens consist of one or more sheets of fibers bonded together by any of several methods. The fibers are generally produced in a *web* (continuous sheet). One bonding method, *chemical bonding,* involves the addition of an adhesive or solvent. In *thermal bonding,* heat softens some of the fibers so that they fuse to other fibers. A form of *mechanical bonding* called *needle-punching* uses hooked needles to create physical tangles among the fibers. Webs may also be stitched together.

Nonwovens are sometimes classified as either *disposable* or *durable.* Disposables are used only once, such as disposable diapers and surgical gowns. Durable nonwovens are more versatile than wovens and knits. Typical durable nonwovens include window shades and many blankets and carpets.

Certain nonwovens known as *geotextiles* help reinforce soil and protect against erosion. These nonwovens may be durable textiles that last for many years. Or they may be *biodegradable* mats that hold grass or flower seeds in place, then gradually break down when the seedlings begin to grow.

How textiles are produced

Designing a fabric. Most fabric designers work for companies that manufacture fabrics for clothing or other consumer products. Designers create new patterns and decide what fibers and methods of construction to use in various fabrics. Fabrics must be designed so that manufacturers can produce them economically on standard textile machinery, such as looms, knitting machines, and tufting machines. In addition, a design must appeal to consumers for the fabric to be profitable.

Burlington Industries

Designing a fabric requires not only artistic ability but also knowledge of fibers and textile machinery. Textile designers can quickly prepare elaborate fabric patterns using computers.

Making the yarn. Yarn can be manufactured in various ways. Fiber companies may take filaments and draw 15 to 100 of them together to make *multifilament* yarn. Or they may use a single filament to make *monofilament* yarn. Some filament yarns, including those made from nylon and polyester, can be *heat-set* to form *stretch yarns.* In one method of heat-setting, manufacturers tightly twist the yarn and heat it. After the yarn is untwisted, it tends to snap back like a spring. Such yarn is used in double-knit and stretch-woven fabrics. Other treatments can be applied to filament yarns to give them a bulky texture.

Filaments may also be cut into staple lengths measuring 1 to 3 inches (2.5 to 7.6 centimeters) long. Staple fibers cut from filaments produce yarn that is softer and less lustrous than filament yarn. Yarn producers can also mix together natural fibers and manufactured fibers of staple length to form *blended yarns.* These yarns have the characteristics of each of the fibers used in their construction. For example, yarn produced from cotton and polyester is absorbent because it contains cotton and wrinkle resistant because it contains polyester.

Yarn made from natural fibers or manufactured fibers of staple length is called *staple yarn* or *spun yarn.* All staple yarns are manufactured in much the same way, whether they are blended or consist of only one kind of fiber. The fibers arrive at the mill in bales, which workers feed into a series of *opening machines.* These machines break up the large masses of fibers, remove some of the impurities, and mix the fibers together. A *carding machine* then removes smaller impurities and some of the exceptionally short fibers and arranges the remaining fibers into a loose rope called a *sliver* (pronounced *SLY vuhr).* Next, as many as eight slivers at a time are drawn together into another sliver. This sliver is then formed into a thin strand called a *roving.* The roving is twisted on a *spinning frame* to form yarn. Some

Society for Visual Education Inc. (Burt Munk Productions)

Making yarn involves processing fibers through various machines. A carding machine, *above,* arranges the fibers into a loose rope called a *sliver.* The slivers are coiled into cans and fed into a spinning frame, *right,* which twists them into yarn.

Burlington Industries, Inc.

spinning frames produce yarn directly from slivers. Different kinds of fibers may be blended when the bales are opened, when the slivers are drawn together, or when the roving is spun.

After the yarn has been manufactured, it is wound onto large spools. Sometimes, two or more strands of yarn are twisted together for added strength. Each strand of such yarn is referred to as a *ply.* Three-ply yarn, for example, consists of three strands. After the yarn has been spooled, it is ready to be made into fabric.

Making the fabric begins when workers place the spools of yarn on a rack called a *creel.* The creel feeds the yarns onto a *beam* (roller) that is placed on a loom or a knitting machine. For a discussion of how looms and knitting machines make fabric, see the previous section, *Kinds of textiles.*

Manufacturers produce fabrics in various lengths and widths. For example, woven fabrics made for clothing manufacturers are usually produced in widths of 36 to 60 inches (91 to 152 centimeters). Most woven *narrow goods,* used for such products as clothing labels and gauze bandages, measure $\frac{1}{2}$ to 3 inches (1.3 to 7.6 centimeters) wide.

A knitting mill usually specializes in one of four kinds of products—piece goods (uncut fabric on the bolt); hosiery; underwear; or such outerwear as dresses,

Burlington Industries

Weaving on a loom can produce fabrics with complex patterns for such items as towels and upholstery. A computerized system controls the machinery that guides the yarn.

J. P. Stevens & Co., Inc.

Knitting on a circular knitting machine, *right,* produces fabric for hosiery, underwear, and many other garments. A device at the bottom of the machine rolls up the fabric as it is knitted.

shirts, slacks, and sweaters. Most fabric in widths of 80 to 168 inches (203 to 427 centimeters) is sold to clothing manufacturers. Fabrics made in the shape of tubes are used for the bodies of sport shirts and T-shirts. Such fabric can also be cut and sewed together like flat-knitted fabrics to make garments.

Finishing the fabric. Fabrics that come directly from a loom or knitting machine are called *greige* (pronounced *gray) goods.* This term means that the fabric has not received any finishing treatments and so is unsuitable for most purposes.

Almost all greige goods are washed to remove dirt, grease, and other unwanted substances. Many fabrics are also bleached to whiten them or to prepare them for dyeing or printing. Cotton fabrics may be treated with a chemical called *caustic soda* before dyeing. This process, called *mercerization,* increases the luster of the fabric, makes it stronger, and enhances its ability to hold dye.

Some greige goods are made from dyed yarn. Such fabric may have brilliant colors and highly detailed designs. But most textiles are dyed a single color after the yarn has been made into fabric. Dyeing machines pull the fabric through a dyebath or force the dye into the fabric by means of pressure.

Designs are printed on fabrics by any of several methods. *Roller printing* uses rollers that have designs deeply engraved on their surface. Dye is applied to the rollers and then wiped off the surface. The dye that remains in the engraved design is then transferred onto the fabric by the rollers. *Screen printing* is similar to using a stencil to form a design. Dye is pressed onto the fabric through a pattern on a screen. In one common method, called *rotary screen printing,* porous rollers hold the dye. The rollers are covered with cylindrical screens and force the dye into the fabric through patterns on the screens. In another process, called *heat transfer printing,* the design is printed on paper with special ink and then ironed onto the fabric. When the paper is peeled off, it leaves the design on the fabric. Some fabrics are dyed and then printed. In *digital inkjet printing,* a computer directs tiny nozzles to spray intricate patterns of ink directly on fabrics or onto heat transfers.

After the fabric has been dyed or printed, it may be dried and stretched on a machine called a *tenter frame.* Fabrics made from heat-set fibers may also be treated by this device to help the fabric resist shrinking. A patented process called *Sanforizing* preshrinks fabric to prevent it from shrinking or stretching more than 1 percent in home laundering. Other finishing treatments help fabrics resist wrinkling, fading, flames, water, stains, static electricity, bacteria, mildew, and moths. Other special finishes include ones that increase absorbency, reflect heat or light, or enable a fabric to change thickness in response to temperature changes.

The final step in manufacturing fabric is ironing it between heavy rollers in a process called *calendering.* The fabrics are then rolled onto bolts for shipment to clothing makers and other customers.

The textile industry

Textile manufacturers worldwide produce more than 100 billion pounds (45 billion kilograms) of textile fiber

Burlington Industries, Inc.

Dyeing processes may be used either to color fibers and yarns before they are made into cloth or to color the fabric itself. In *package dyeing,* tubes of yarn are dyed in large vats.

Burlington Industries, Inc.

Printing produces fabrics with beautiful designs and a variety of colors. In *rotary screen printing,* the dye is forced through patterns on cylindrical screens that fit around rollers.

Ferenc Berko, DPI

Weaving with a hand loom is still a major way of making cloth in many developing countries. This woman in Guatemala weaves a colorful fabric by an age-old method.

annually. About 30 million people are employed in the production of textiles throughout the world. In some developing nations, millions of workers weave fabrics of natural fibers by hand. In industrial nations, manufacturers work with both natural and manufactured fibers. They apply modern technology to produce high-quality products quickly and inexpensively. Textiles are important as both imports and exports in many countries.

In the United States and Canada. The United States textile industry is concentrated in the southern states, especially Georgia, North Carolina, and South Carolina. The U.S. government requires the textile industry to observe certain federal laws designed to protect consumers and give them information about the textiles they buy. The Wool Products Labeling Act of 1939 provides that all garments made of wool have a label telling the amount and kind of wool used. The Flammable Fabrics Act of 1953 prohibits the sale of fabrics that burn rapidly. The Textile Fiber Products Identification Act of 1960 requires that all textile items have a label listing the names of the fibers from which they are made. The Federal Trade Commission (FTC) requires that most finished textile products have a permanently affixed label giving instructions for the care of the item.

Canada's Textile Labelling Act requires a label on all clothing to show the fiber content by percentage. The Competition Bureau enforces the law.

In Africa, several nations have modern textile manufacturing plants. But many people also weave textiles by hand. In some countries, including Egypt, Ethiopia, Mali, and Nigeria, textile production ranks among the leading manufacturing activities. Textiles are a chief export of Botswana and Mauritius. Some of the peoples of Ghana and Togo weave a ceremonial fabric called *Kente cloth* for use in important social and religious activities. In Northern Africa, many people weave fabric by hand as a form of Islamic art (see **Islamic art**).

In Asia, manufacturers operate many large, modern textile plants. China produces about four-fifths of the world's textiles. India produces nearly a third of the world's cotton fabrics. The textile industry is important to the economies of Bangladesh, Indonesia, Japan, the Philippines, Sri Lanka, Thailand, Turkey, Vietnam, and other Asian countries.

In Australia and New Zealand, textile production is modern and highly mechanized. Most textile factories are controlled by a few large firms. Australia's government protects the textile and clothing industries against cheap imports.

In Europe, textile production is highly mechanized. Germany, Italy, and Switzerland are leading exporters of textile machinery. European textile manufacturers have long been major innovators in the textile industry, and they have developed many new fabrics and processes.

In Latin America, textile production is important to the economies of most countries. Brazil is one of the leading producers of cotton fabrics. Textiles are a chief manufactured product of Colombia, Costa Rica, El Salvador, Honduras, and Mexico. Colombia, Costa Rica, and El Salvador count textiles among their most valuable exports.

History

Prehistoric and ancient times. No one knows when people first made textiles. Impressions of cloth on pottery, as well as prehistoric weaving tools, indicate that people knew how to weave at least 27,000 years ago. The oldest known textile is a fragment of linen found in what is now southern Turkey, dated between 8000 and 7000 B.C. Evidence of woolen textiles comes from the same area and dates from about 6000 B.C. In Egypt, people wove flax into linen wrappings about 5000 B.C. Archaeologists have found Egyptian mummies from the 2500's B.C. wrapped in linen as well made as that produced today.

Cotton was grown in the Indus River Valley in what are now Pakistan and western India by about 3000 B.C. Cotton may also have been used for textiles in the Americas by this time. The Chinese began to cultivate silkworms about 2700 B.C. They developed special looms for silk filaments.

The ancient Greeks used chiefly woolen textiles. They also used some linen. In the 300's B.C., the army of Alexander the Great brought cotton goods from what is now Pakistan to Europe. The ancient Romans developed an enormous trade in textiles. They imported woolens from Britain, Gaul, and Spain; linen from Egypt; cottons from India; and silks from China and Persia.

During the Middle Ages, from about the A.D. 400's through the 1400's, the textile industry gradually developed in Europe. As the textile industry expanded, production techniques improved, stimulating further growth. The spinning wheel came into use by the 1200's. The production of woolens centered in England; northern Italy; and Flanders, a region that covered parts of present-day Belgium, France, and the Netherlands. Italy became the silk center of Europe. The invention of a machine to unwind silk from cocoons led to further expansion of Italy's silk industry.

In the large towns of Europe, associations of weavers and other craftworkers regulated textile production. These associations, called *guilds,* established prices and standards of quality for all products made by their members. But the *cottage industry,* also called the *domestic system,* produced most textiles during the Middle Ages. Under this system, merchants delivered raw materials to workers in their homes in rural areas. The merchants later collected the work, paying the workers by the piece.

The Industrial Revolution. Important developments in textile production continued after the Middle Ages. For example, an English clergyman named William Lee invented a machine for knitting hosiery in 1589. During the 1600's, textile workers in the Netherlands developed improved methods of dyeing and finishing fabric. But the greatest advances in the textile industry occurred during the Industrial Revolution, a period of rapid industrialization that began in England in the 1700's. In fact, the Industrial Revolution was largely a "textile revolution" created by a flood of English inventions that greatly increased the production of yarns and fabrics.

In 1733, John Kay, an engineer, invented the *fly shuttle* (also called the *flying shuttle*). This device enabled weavers to pass the filling through the warp yarns mechanically instead of by hand. About 1764, a weaver named James Hargreaves invented the *spinning jenny,* the first machine that could spin more than one yarn at a time. In 1769, Richard Arkwright, a former barber, patented the water frame, a spinning machine that ran on water power. A weaver named Samuel Crompton introduced the *spinning mule* in 1779. This machine combined the features of the spinning jenny and the water frame and gradually replaced them both. Edmund Cartwright, an Anglican clergyman, patented the first power loom in 1785.

In the United States, the New England region became the center of the textile industry. In 1790, an English textile worker named Samuel Slater built the first successful water-powered machines for spinning cotton in the United States. The machines were installed in a mill in Pawtucket, Rhode Island.

The production of cotton textiles in New England grew rapidly after the American inventor Eli Whitney developed his cotton gin in 1793. Before Whitney's invention, workers had to remove cotton fibers from the seed by hand. This slow process could not meet the textile mills' demand for cotton. Whitney's gin separated the fibers far faster than workers could by hand. As a result, mills received ever-increasing supplies of cotton. During the 1920's and 1930's, most of these mills moved to the Southern States, nearer to the supply of cotton.

The age of modern textiles began in 1884, when Hilaire Chardonnet, a French chemist, developed the first practical manufactured fiber. This fiber, now known as rayon, was first produced in the United States in 1910 under the name *artificial silk.* Wallace H. Carothers, an American chemist, developed nylon in the mid-1930's. During the 1940's and 1950's, polyester, acrylic, and other manufactured fibers were introduced.

In the 1960's, textile companies began making double-knit fabrics of textured polyester yarns. These fabrics were lighter in weight and more comfortable than double knits made of other materials. As a result, the popularity of knits greatly increased.

Today the textile industry is among the most modern and diversified of all industries. Computerized equipment can produce fabrics with highly complex patterns at tremendous speeds. Continued research and development has resulted in new processing methods that enable manufacturers to maintain reasonable production costs. Helen H. Epps

Related articles in ***World Book*** include:

Biographies

Arkwright, Sir Richard
Crompton, Samuel
Hargreaves, James
Jacquard, Joseph Marie
Slater, Samuel

Culver

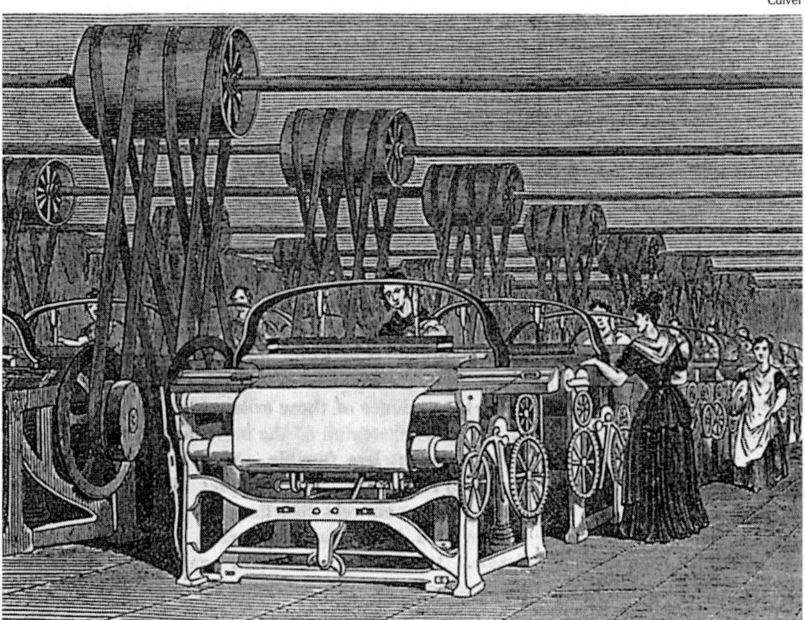

New textile machinery of the 1800's greatly increased fabric production. In textile mills like the one shown here, women operated looms powered by steam engines or water wheels.

Textiles

See the articles on clothing materials that are listed in the **Related articles section** of the **Clothing** article. See also:

Acetate	Burlap	Tapestry
Aramid	Fiber	Twill
Braiding	Oilcloth	Velcro

Treatments and processes

Batik	Knitting	Teasel
Bleach	Knitting machine	Tie dyeing
Dye	Spinning	Waterproofing
Embroidery	Spinning jenny	Weaving

Other related articles

Brown lung	Guild
Clothing	Industrial Revolution
Cottage industry	Rugs and carpets
Engineering (Textile engineering)	UNITE HERE

Outline

I. **Sources of textile fibers**
   A. Natural fibers
   B. Manufactured fibers
II. **Kinds of textiles**
   A. Woven fabrics
   B. Knitted fabrics
   C. Other fabrics
III. **How textiles are produced**
   A. Designing a fabric
   B. Making the yarn
   C. Making the fabric
   D. Finishing the fabric
IV. **The textile industry**
   A. In North America
   B. In Africa
   C. In Asia
   D. In Australia and New Zealand
   E. In Europe
   F. In Latin America
V. **History**

Questions

What was the first practical manufactured fiber?
What product makes up the largest share of all textile production?
What was the domestic system?
How are most carpeting fabrics made in the United States?
What are *greige goods?*
What is the most important natural fiber?
What is the earliest evidence of textiles?
From what substances are most manufactured fibers produced?
What are some laws the U.S. textile industry must observe?
What is *blended yarn? Staple yarn?*

Thackeray, William Makepeace (1811-1863), was one of the great novelists of the English Victorian Age. His *Vanity Fair* is one of the finest and best-known novels in English literature. Thackeray wrote in a colorful, lively style, with a simple vocabulary and clearly structured sentences. These qualities, combined with his honest view of life, give him an important place in the history of realistic literature.

Early career. Thackeray was born on July 18, 1811, in Calcutta (now Kolkata), India. At age five, he was sent to England to live with relatives and begin his education. He was lonely and unhappy during his school years. "I have the same recollection of Greek in youth that I have of castor oil," Thackeray once said. He entered Trinity College, Cambridge University, in 1829. No great scholar, he left after a year and a half to travel abroad.

Thackeray had trouble finding a career. He studied law for a short time, and went to art school in Paris. Meanwhile, he had spent his inheritance, losing part of it to professional gamblers. To make a modest living, he turned to writing book reviews, stories, and satirical sketches for magazines.

In 1836, Thackeray married Isabella Shawe. She became incurably insane following the birth of their third daughter in 1840. This tragedy darkened Thackeray's natural good humor. But he needed money more than ever, and he continued turning out articles and stories.

Most of Thackeray's early writings were humorous, and were published under such ridiculous pen names as Michael Angelo Titmarsh. In 1848, he published *The Book of Snobs,* a collection of his magazine writings in which he poked fun at social pretentiousness.

Later career. Thackeray ensured his fame with *Vanity Fair* (1847-1848), probably his best novel. Like most of his books, it was first published in monthly parts. A gifted caricaturist, Thackeray did his own illustrations for this novel, which traces the fortunes of a group of young Londoners of the early 1800's.

Thackeray called *Vanity Fair* "a novel without a hero," in keeping with his belief that most people are a mixture of the heroic and the ridiculous. He knew that men and women are complex, and he avoided oversimplifying them. He wrote with affection about kind and gentle Amelia Sedley. But he also called Amelia "a silly little thing." Becky Sharp, low born but more clearly the "heroine," is selfish, cunning, and cynical. Becky is never bitter, however, and readers admire her ability to survive by her wits in a society based mainly on privilege and wealth.

The novel *Pendennis* (1848-1850) is partly autobiographical. It has the mellow, reflective quality that colors much of Thackeray's writing.

Henry Esmond (1852) is set in England in the early 1700's, a period that Thackeray loved. The book describes the loves and adventures of Esmond, who narrates the book. Henry is also only "part hero." Although a virtuous man, he is also complex and often gloomy.

The Newcomes (1853-1855) is the complex story of three generations of the Newcome family. Ethel Newcome is one of Thackeray's finest characters. She has gentleness and sympathy, but also intelligence and spirit.

Thackeray's view of life. Thackeray disliked people who were unduly impressed by birth and rank. His skillful ridicule of snobs and hypocrites is even evident amid the broad humor of his early works. His realistic temperament enabled him to see and satirize inconsistencies in life. He once said of one of his characters that he "failed somehow in spite of a mediocrity which ought to have ensured any man a success." Thackeray knew that rogues sometimes do well while the innocent suffer, and that virtuous people can be dull and rascals can be lively. Such ironic twists in his books were misunderstood by some people, who accused Thackeray of being cynical.

Others complained that Thackeray's writings were sentimental. For example, he seemed to admire womanhood as an abstract ideal. When he wrote about young ladies who were gentle and affectionate but perhaps not very bright, he sometimes fell into a style of adoration. But his deep honesty made him show, at the same time, how these sentimental people were often stupid and occasionally harmful. His critics often fail to see that Thackeray really hated cruelty and greed, and admired goodness and warm-heartedness. Thackeray died in London on Dec. 24, 1863. K. K. Collins

Robert Frerck, Odyssey Productions

Bangkok, a booming metropolis on the Chao Phraya River, is Thailand's capital and largest city. Its landmarks include the ornate towers of the Grand Palace, shown here.

Thailand

Thailand, *TY land,* is a country in tropical Southeast Asia. The people of Thailand are called Thai. In the past, Thailand was primarily an agricultural country. Even today, a majority of Thai live in rural areas. However, Thailand has a rapidly developing economy, and its urban centers have expanded at a fast pace. More than 6 million people live in the city limits of Bangkok, Thailand's capital and largest city.

Thailand is the only nation in Southeast Asia that has never been ruled by a Western power. For most of its history, the country was called Siam. In 1939, it officially adopted the name Thailand.

Government

National government. Thailand is a constitutional monarchy, a government in which the constitution limits the power of the king or queen. The nation's Constitution provides for a monarch, a prime minister, and a National Assembly. The monarch has an advisory role as head of state. The prime minister heads the government.

The National Assembly consists of a 500-member House of Representatives and a 200-member Senate. The people of Thailand directly elect 400 House members. The remaining 100 members are elected through *proportional representation.* This system grants political parties a share of seats in proportion to their share of the total vote cast in the election. House members serve four-year terms. The senators are directly elected by the people of Thailand to six-year terms. The House selects the prime minister from among its members. The prime minister is then formally appointed by the monarch. The prime minister selects a Cabinet.

Local government. Thailand is divided into 76 provinces. The provinces are subdivided into 876 districts, 7,255 local units called *tambons,* and about 70,000 villages. Each province has a governor, and every district has a district officer. These officials are appointed by the minister of the interior. Thai villages range in size from a few hundred to a few thousand people. Each village

The contributors of this article are Pasuk Phongpaichit, Professor of Economics at Chulalongkorn University in Bangkok, Thailand, and Chris Baker, an independent researcher based in Bangkok.

Facts in brief

Capital: Bangkok.
Official language: Thai (Central dialect).
Official name: Pratet Thai.
Area: 198,115 mi² (513,115 km²). *Greatest distances*—north-south, 1,100 mi (1,770 km); east-west, 480 mi (772 km). *Coastline*—1,625 mi (2,615 km).
Elevation: *Highest*—Inthanon Mountain, 8,514 ft (2,595 m). *Lowest*—sea level.
Population: *Estimated 2006 population*—64,645,000; population density, 326 per mi² (126 per km²); distribution, 69 percent rural, 31 percent urban. *2000 census*—60,606,947.
Chief products: *Agriculture*—cassava, coconut, corn, oil palm, pineapples and other fruits, poultry, rice, rubber, soybeans, sugar cane. *Manufacturing*—automobiles, cement, electronic and electrical goods, food products, textiles. *Fishing*—anchovies, herring, mackerel, shrimp and other shellfish, tuna. *Mining*—barite, feldspar, gypsum, kaolin, lead, lignite, limestone, natural gas, precious stones, rock salt, tin, zinc.
Money: *Basic unit*—baht. One hundred satang equal one baht.

Thailand's flag was adopted in 1917. The red represents the nation; the white, purity; and the blue, the monarchy.

The national emblem, adopted in 1910, shows the *garuda,* a birdlike creature of Southeast Asian mythology.

WORLD BOOK map

Thailand is a country that lies mostly in mainland Southeast Asia. Southern Thailand extends down the Malay Peninsula.

elects a *headman* to be its leader. The people in each tambon then select from among the village headmen a *kamnan,* or chief administrator, for their tambon. The people in each tambon also elect the members of a Tambon Administrative Organization.

Politics. Thai citizens 18 years old or older have the right to vote. Thai political parties often have been organized around leaders rather than common political philosophies, and few parties have had lasting strength.

Courts. The Supreme Court, the highest court, consists of a chief justice and 21 judges. The entire court meets only for special cases. The Court of Appeals, the second highest court, reviews decisions of lower courts. A panel called the Judicial Commission chooses all Thai judges. The judges are formally appointed by the king.

Armed forces of Thailand consist of an army, a navy, and an air force. The forces have a total membership of about 300,000. Men from 21 to 30 years old may be drafted for at least two years of military duty. Women may serve on a voluntary basis.

People

Ancestry. Most of Thailand's people belong to the Thai ethnic group. The Thai's ancestors migrated from southern China over a period of several centuries beginning over 1,000 years ago. At various times, other peoples also came to the area as migrants, war prisoners, or refugees. These peoples included Mons, Khmers, Indians, Vietnamese, and Malays. Most descendants of

Tourism Authority of Thailand

Wat Phrathat Doi Suthep is a Buddhist temple near Chiang Mai. Its gilded tower dates from the 1300's.

these groups now consider themselves Thai.

During the 1800's and 1900's, many Chinese came to Bangkok and other cities and towns. They often intermarried with the Thai and adopted local customs. Many of them now think of themselves as Thai of Chinese descent. Small, isolated groups, such as the Hmong, Karen, and Lua, live in the hills of the north and northwest.

Way of life. About two-thirds of Thailand's people live in rural areas, mainly in small villages. Each Thai village has a *wat* (Buddhist temple-monastery) that is the religious and social center of the community. Village life in Thailand traditionally has been organized around religious and agricultural rituals and festivals. But now radio and television also have a strong influence.

Since the early 1960's, large numbers of Thai—especially young adults—have moved from rural areas to cities in search of jobs and educational opportunities. A middle class has emerged in the cities and their suburbs. Many middle-class Thai work in modern office jobs. However, others who have come to the cities work in low-paying factory jobs. Many lower-class Thai live in slums. The rapid city growth has created problems, including crowded living conditions, traffic jams, pollution, the growth of prostitution, and the spread of AIDS.

In the past, Thai people wore simple, light clothing suitable for a tropical climate. Today, most Thai wear the same clothing styles worn in Europe and North America. Some people wear clothing made of Thai silk or of *batik* (a cloth dyed using a special process). Some people wear clothing decorated with traditional Hmong or Karen embroidery.

Housing. Many villagers live in wood houses that are on stilts. The houses are built 7 to 10 feet (2 to 3 meters) above the ground mainly for protection against floods. In towns, some shop owners, especially Chinese, live in rows of two-story brick buildings. They work in shops on the first floor and live on the second. Middle-class Thai, especially in Bangkok and its suburbs, live in apartments or large developments of single-family homes.

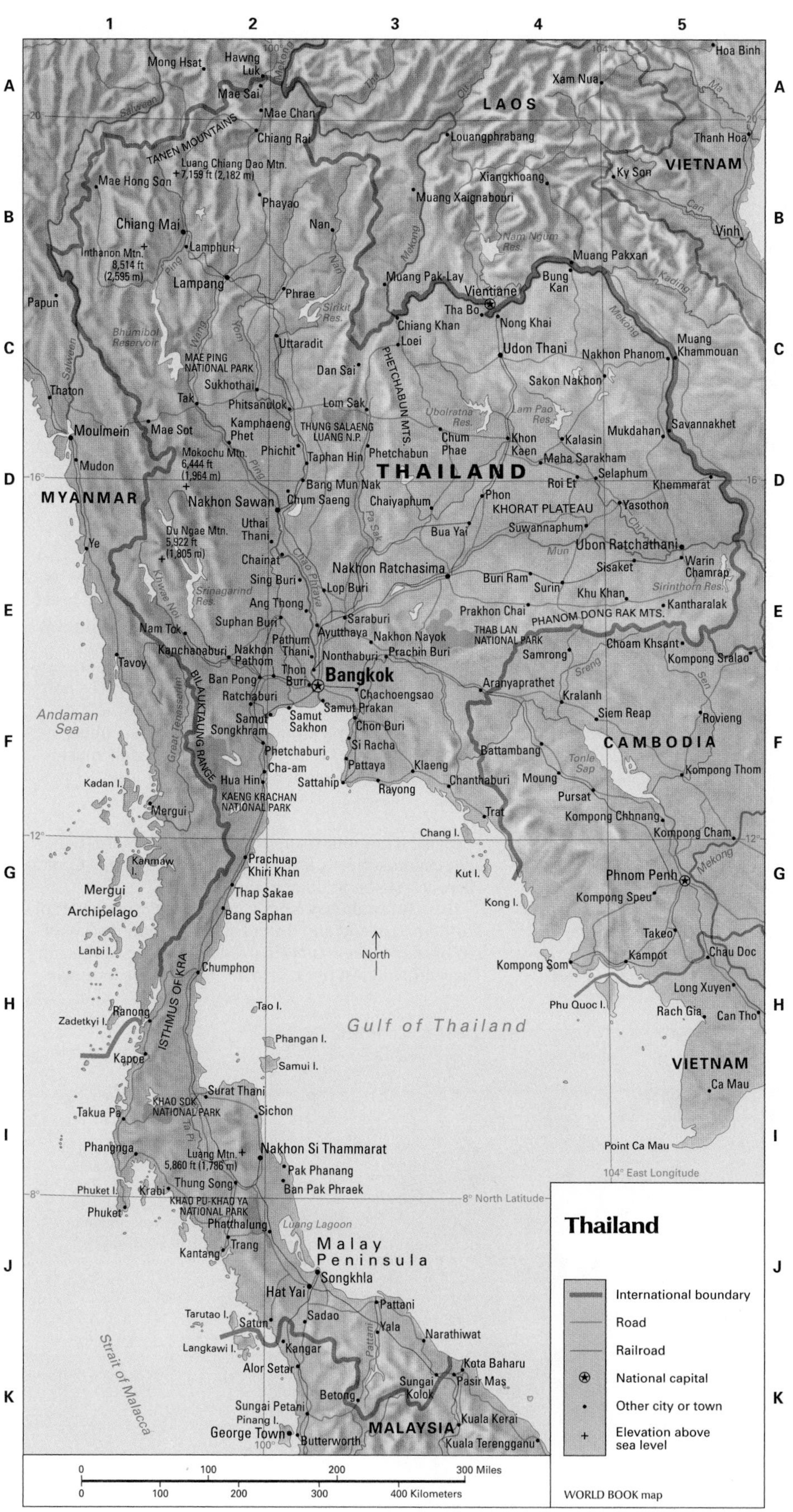

Thailand map index

Cities and towns

City	Population	Key	
Ayutthaya	75,916	E	2
Ban Pong	51,708	E	2
Bangkok	6,320,174	E	2
Buri Ram	29,170	E	4
Chachoengsao	47,076	F	3
Chaiyaphum	53,873	D	3
Chanthaburi	86,461	F	3
Chiang Mai	174,438	B	1
Chiang Rai	61,188	A	2
Chon Buri	183,317	F	3
Chumphon	48,571	H	2
Hat Yai	187,920	J	2
Hua Hin	41,953	F	2
Kalasin	46,773	D	4
Kamphaeng Phet	43,648	D	2
Kanchanaburi	52,369	E	2
Khon Kaen	141,202	D	4
Lampang	148,199	B	2
Lop Buri	54,373	E	3
Mae Sot	41,158	D	1
Maha Sarakham	52,012	D	4
Mukdahan	33,330	D	5
Nakhon Pathom	120,818	F	2
Nakhon Phanom	30,785	C	5
Nakhon Ratchasima	204,641	E	3
Nakhon Sawan	91,802	D	2
Nakhon Si Thammarat	118,729	I	2
Nan	21,628	B	3
Narathiwat	42,010	K	3
Nong Khai	59,776	C	4
Nonthaburi	291,555	E	2
Pak Kret*	142,225	E	2
Pattani	43,690	J	3
Pattaya		F	3
Phatthalung	42,193	J	2
Thanyaburi*	113,825	E	3
Phetchabun	42,208	D	3
Phetchaburi	40,259	F	2
Phichit	33,370	D	2
Phitsanulok	84,311	C	2
Phrae	40,059	B	2
Phra Pradaeng*	171,544	F	2
Phuket	52,796	J	1
Prachin Buri	25,157	E	3
Ratchaburi	82,803	F	2
Rayong	106,737	F	3
Roi Et	35,159	D	4
Sadao	44,833	J	2
Sakon Nakhon	65,638	C	4
Samut Prakan	378,741	F	3
Samut Sakhon	68,391	F	2
Samut Songkhram	34,985	F	2
Saraburi	67,763	E	3
Si Racha	141,410	F	3
Sisaket	41,102	E	5
Songkhla	84,264	J	2
Sukhothai	35,713	C	2
Sungai Kolok	37,671	K	3
Suphan Buri	52,666	E	2
Surat Thani	111,340	I	2
Surin	41,582	E	4
Tak	21,662	C	2
Trang	64,666	J	2
Ubon Ratchathani	106,602	D	5
Udon Thani	222,425	C	4
Uttaradit	52,878	C	2
Warin Chamrap	37,701	D	5
Yala	74,139	J	3
Yasothon	22,221	D	5

Physical features

Feature	Key	
Bhumibol Reservoir	C	1
Bilauktaung Range	F	2
Chang Island	G	3
Chao Phraya (river)	E	2
Chi (river)	D	5
Du Ngae Mountain	E	1
Gulf of Thailand	H	3
Inthanon Mountain	B	1
Isthmus of Kra	H	1
Khorat Plateau	D	4
Khwae Noi (river)	E	1
Kut Island	G	4
Luang Mountain	I	2
Luang Chiang Dao Mountain	B	1
Luang Lagoon	J	2
Malay Peninsula	J	2
Mekong (river)	C	5
Mokochu Mountain	D	2
Mun (river)	D	4
Nan (river)	B	3
Pa Sak (river)	D	3
Phangan Island	H	2
Phanom Dong Rak Mts.	E	4
Phetchabun Mts.	C	3
Phuket Island	I	1
Ping (river)	B	1
Samui Island	H	2
Srinagarind Res.	E	2
Ta Pi (river)	I	2
Tanen Mts.	A	2
Wang (river)	C	2
Yom (river)	C	2

*Does not appear on map; key shows general location.
Source: 2000 census.

Food. Thai people eat rice with almost every meal. Favorite foods to accompany the rice include hot, spicy stews called curries; salads of meat, fish, and vegetables; stir-fry dishes; and broiled or fried fish with sauces. Noodles are also popular, especially for lunches.

Recreation. Thai people prize the art of *sanuk,* or having fun. The national sport is *Muay Thai* (Thai boxing), also known as *kickboxing,* in which opponents fight with their feet as well as their hands. In another popular sport, called *takraw,* the players try to keep a ball made of *rattan* (woven palm stems) in the air by using their head, legs, and feet. Soccer is also popular.

Languages. Thai, the language spoken by almost all people in Thailand, has four main dialects. The Central Thai dialect is the official language and is taught in the schools. Many people speak this dialect in addition to their own regional or ethnic dialect. Many people also speak Malay or Chinese. English is taught in many schools and is often used in business and government.

Religion. About 95 percent of the Thai people are Buddhists. Most Thai follow the *Theravada* (Way of the Elders) tradition, a form of Buddhism that emphasizes the virtues of monastic life. According to custom, many Thai men become monks for at least a short time, from about one week to several months. They wear yellow robes and lead lives of simplicity, meditation, and study.

Most Chinese in Thailand follow Confucianism in addition to practicing other religions. About 5 percent of Thailand's people are Muslims. Most of the Muslims are Malays living in the south or in Bangkok.

Education. Thai law requires children to attend school from age 6 to 14. The government provides free public elementary and secondary education, but some students attend private schools. Thailand has more than 20 public universities and more than 40 private universities. Almost all of Thailand's adult population can read and write. For the country's literacy rate, see **Literacy** (table: Literacy rates for selected countries).

The arts in Thailand are greatly influenced by Buddhism. Buddhist temples display some of the finest Thai architecture. The image of Buddha appears in many Thai paintings and sculptures. Modern Thai painting features traditional religious themes and international styles.

© Horst Gossler, The Stock House

Thai boxing, known as *Muay Thai* or *kickboxing,* is the national sport. Opponents fight with their feet as well as their hands.

Most traditional Thai literature was written as poetry or as drama and performed for the royal court. Some dramas were *shadow plays* performed with puppets (see **Puppet** [Shadow plays]). Other dramas were performed by classical dancers wearing masks and spectacular costumes. The stories came from such legends as the *Ramakian,* the Thai version of the *Ramayana,* a great epic poem of India. Today, Thailand's people enjoy motion pictures and television shows.

Early Thai folk musicians traveled to villages and festivals and performed songs and ballads. Today, Thai folk music remains popular. Traditional musicians in the northeast still play a mouth organ made of bamboo pipes known as a *khaen.* In addition, some folk music has been adapted into modern Thai pop music.

The land

Thailand has four main land regions. They are (1) the Mountainous North, (2) the Khorat Plateau, (3) the Central Plain, and (4) the Southern Peninsula.

The Mountainous North. Mountains occupy part of northern Thailand and extend along the country's western border to the Malay Peninsula. Inthanon Mountain, Thailand's highest peak, is in this region. The mountain

Saul Lockhardt, Advertasia Co., Ltd.

Middle-class housing in Thailand consists mainly of small, single-family dwellings. These houses belong to a housing development in a suburb of Bangkok.

Saul Lockhardt, Advertasia Co., Ltd.

Thai classical dancers act out traditional stories with religious themes. Jewels and embroidery decorate their costumes.

rises 8,514 feet (2,595 meters) above sea level. Forests of evergreen trees and some broadleaf trees, such as teak, cover most of the region. The mountains are broken by rivers running south. These rivers form narrow, fertile valleys where farmers grow rice and other crops.

The Khorat Plateau, also known as Isan, lies in northeastern Thailand and makes up about one-third of the country's land area. Mountains separate the plateau from central Thailand to the west and Cambodia to the south. The Mekong River forms the region's northern and eastern boundaries. Two other rivers, the Chi and the Mun, also run through the region. But generally, the area is dry with sandy soil that makes poor farmland.

The Central Plain extends from the foothills of the north to the Gulf of Thailand. Its soil is so fertile that farmers raise more rice there than anywhere else in the country. Thailand's main river, the Chao Phraya (pronounced *chow PRY uh* or *chow prah YAH),* runs through the region and provides irrigation and transportation.

Edward S. Ross

The Mountainous North region includes Thailand's highest peak, 8,514-foot (2,595-meter) Inthanon Mountain, *background.* In the foreground is a dwelling of the region's Hmong people.

The Southern Peninsula shares its northwestern border with Myanmar and extends south to Malaysia. The center of the peninsula consists mainly of jungle and mountains. Narrow plains run along the coast. Fishing, rubber production, and tin mining in the region contribute much to the Thai economy.

Animal life. Thailand's forests once abounded with elephants, tigers, wild pigs, deer, crocodiles, king cobras and other snakes, and many varieties of birds. But since the mid-1900's, many species of wildlife have become endangered. Thousands were hunted and killed for profit before the practice was made illegal. Also, agriculture, logging, and industry have destroyed more than half of Thailand's forest area since the mid-1900's.

Climate

Thailand has a tropical climate. Most of the country has three seasons—a hot, dry season from March to May; a hot, wet period from June to October; and a cool, dry season from November to February. Bangkok has an average temperature of 77 °F (25 °C) in December and 86 °F (30 °C) in April. The mountain areas are cooler.

From late May to October, winds called *monsoons* cause heavy rains throughout Thailand. The Southern Peninsula region may receive more than 100 inches (254 centimeters) of rain in one year. Bangkok has an average annual rainfall of 55 inches (140 centimeters).

Economy

The Thai economy is based on free enterprise, in which businesses operate largely free of government control. In the past, the main economic activities were agriculture and forestry, especially the harvesting of teak. But the economy is changing rapidly. Today, about 40 percent of the nation's workers make their living by farming or fishing. But agriculture and fishing make up only about 10 percent of the country's *gross domestic product* (GDP)—the value of all goods and services produced in the country in a year. Manufacturing makes up about 35 percent of the GDP and employs about 15 percent of the nation's workers. Government, education, trade, transportation, and other service industries employ many people in Thailand. Other people work in construction and mining. The gap between the rich and the poor in Thailand is among the largest in the world.

Agriculture. Farmland makes up about 40 percent of the nation's land. The chief crop is rice. Thailand is one of the world's largest producers and exporters of rice. Other farm products include *cassava* (a potatolike plant used to make tapioca), coconut, corn, oil palm, pineapples and other fruits, poultry, rubber, soybeans, and sugar cane. Farms in Thailand average about 10 acres (4 hectares). The majority of farmers own their land.

Manufacturing, particularly textile production, first gained importance in Thailand in the 1970's. Since the mid-1980's, many foreign companies have built factories in Thailand to make products for export. These products include computer parts, other electronic and electrical goods, and automobiles. Food processing is another important manufacturing activity in Thailand.

Fishing has always been a mainstay of the Thai economy. Throughout the country, people catch fish for local consumption and sale. Commercial fisheries in the south and southeast fish by *trawling,* pulling a funnel-shaped net through the sea. Some farmers convert their land into ponds to raise fish and shrimp.

Mining. Zinc is Thailand's most valuable mineral. Thailand also has barite, feldspar, gypsum, kaolin, lead, lignite, limestone, rock salt, and tin. Large amounts of natural gas lie under the Gulf of Thailand. Rubies and sapphires are mined in central Thailand. Other precious stones are brought in from Cambodia and Myanmar.

Tourism contributes greatly to Thailand's national income. Millions of tourists visit each year to see the country's magnificent temples, interesting historical sites, beaches, and exciting night life.

International trade. Thailand's chief exports are industrial products, especially automobiles, clothing and textiles, and electrical and electronic goods. Agricultural goods, fish, and shellfish are also important exports. The major imports include chemicals, fuels, iron and steel, and machinery. Much of Thailand's trade is with China and with other countries in Southeast Asia. Japan and the United States are also important trading partners.

Transportation. Most people in Thailand travel by road. Major highways link the nation's cities. Almost all villages can be reached on a paved road. Small motorcycles are popular. There is a railroad system, but it is less developed than the road system.

Bangkok has become famous for traffic jams. Because of poor planning, not enough space is devoted to roads. The city has an elevated railroad and a subway system. Bangkok is Thailand's largest and busiest port. The city's international airport is the nation's main airport.

Communication. Thailand has dozens of daily newspapers. Most of them are published in the Thai language. Several are in Chinese, and a few are in English. The newspapers are privately owned. However, the government runs nearly all television and radio stations.

History

Early years. People have lived in what is now Thailand for tens of thousands of years. The Mon and the Khmer peoples had settlements throughout Southeast Asia more than 2,000 years ago. Some scholars believe they originally migrated there from southern China. Before A.D. 1000, many small states were scattered throughout the region. Little is known about them other than their names. One, named Dvaravati (pronounced *duh VAHR uh VAH tee),* was a Mon state based in the delta of the Chao Phraya River. Foreign traders brought Buddhism and Hinduism to the region from India. The ancestors of today's Thai migrated to the region from southern China over a period of many centuries, beginning between about the A.D. 400's and 700's.

Early kingdoms. From 1200 to 1400, several kingdoms arose in the region. The capitals of the main kingdoms were Chiang Mai, Sukhothai, and Ayutthaya.

Chiang Mai *(chee AHNG my* or *jee AHNG my)* was in the hills of the north. Its great king, Mangrai *(mehng ry),* founded the city in 1296 as the capital of the Lan Na kingdom. Chiang Mai became an important religious, cultural, political, and commercial center.

Sukhothai *(soo KOH ty)* was founded in 1238 between the hills and the central plain. The city was a Buddhist center with many skilled craftworkers. A ceramic industry based in and near Sukhothai exported products to many parts of eastern Asia. Sukhothai's famous ruler, King Ramkhamhaeng *(rahm kahm HANG),* reigned from about 1279 to 1317. Many historians believe he may have developed a writing system for the Thai language.

Ayutthaya *(ah YOOT tah yah),* sometimes spelled Ayudhya, was established in 1351 on an island in the Chao Phraya River, an ideal place for trade and defense. U Thong founded the city and became its first king, taking the name Ramathibodi *(RAHM uh tee BOH dee).* Ayutthaya was the most important of a group of trading cities around the Gulf of Thailand. The city's early population probably included not only Thai but also Khmer, Chinese, and other groups.

The rise of Ayutthaya. In the late 1300's and early 1400's, Ayutthaya gained control over much nearby territory, including the lands of the Sukhothai kingdom. Between 1400 and 1600, Ayutthaya became the region's leading power, mainly because of its trading wealth. At the same time, its population gradually became main-

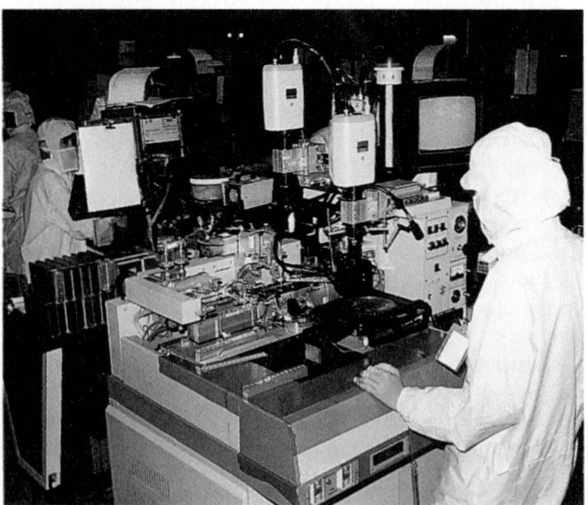

Chinteik Electronic Industries Co., Ltd.

Electronic equipment is manufactured in Thailand. Here, a worker operates machinery that produces integrated circuits—devices used in such equipment as computers and televisions.

Jeffrey Alford, Asia Access

Fishing has always been an important part of the Thai economy. This fisherman is loading traps for catching shellfish in the Andaman Sea, off the Southern Peninsula of Thailand.

ly Thai. Most of Ayutthaya's people were forced to serve in the armies and work for the kings and nobles.

By 1500, Ayutthaya was one of Asia's great trading centers. Many foreign traders settled there. The Chinese came first, followed by people from Arabia, Iran (at that time, also called Persia), India, and Japan. In 1511, Portuguese merchants became the first Europeans to establish trade relations there. Other Europeans followed. About the 1630's, the Dutch became the main European community in Ayutthaya. The foreigners included not only traders but also missionaries, *mercenaries* (soldiers for hire), engineers, and doctors. King Narai, who led Ayutthaya from 1656 to 1688, sent representatives to China, France, Iran, the Netherlands, and other countries.

Ayutthaya fought frequent wars with its neighbors—the Khmer to the east and the Burmese to the west. In 1767, the Burmese destroyed the city of Ayutthaya.

The Bangkok era. For a few years, there was famine and disorder. Several men competed for power. The victor was a military leader named Taksin. He moved the capital to Thon Buri, close to Bangkok on the west bank of the Chao Phraya. He brought in Chinese traders and migrants to help rebuild the economy, and he expelled the Burmese. He reunited the lands that had been part of the Ayutthaya kingdom and gained control of Chiang Mai. In 1782, a group of old Ayutthaya nobles overthrew Taksin. Their leader, Chaophraya Chakri *(chow PRY uh CHAHK ree* or *chow prah YAH CHAHK ree),* became King Rama I and began the Chakri *dynasty* (line of rulers), which still reigns today. Chakri moved the capital across the Chao Phraya to Bangkok. He ruled until 1809.

In the late 1700's and the 1800's, the economy grew. Many Chinese moved to Siam—the name Europeans used for the Bangkok kingdom—because of famine and revolts in China. The Chinese set up sugar processing facilities and other businesses. More Thai became independent farmers. They turned additional land into rice farms. Siam began to export rice and sugar. British, American, and other Western traders came to Bangkok. The Western powers began to seize lands in Southeast Asia as colonies. The British seized portions of Malaya (now part of Malaysia) and Burma (now Myanmar). The French seized parts of Vietnam, Cambodia, and Laos.

Modernization. Siam's kings and nobles feared becoming a Western colony. They also were impressed by some Western ideas and by Western technology, such as steam-powered ships. They decided to cooperate with Western powers and adopt Western practices that they thought would be useful. Reforms began under King Mongkut *(mawng KOOT),* also called Rama IV, who ruled from 1851 to 1868. He studied Western languages and science. His government signed treaties with Western powers that expanded trade. He also hired Western advisers who helped modernize the government.

King Chulalongkorn *(chu lah LAWNG kawn),* also called Rama V, reigned from 1868 to 1910. He is regarded as one of Siam's greatest kings. He reorganized Siam's government, introduced a modern school system, and built railroads and telegraphs. He abolished old systems of controlling people, allowing them to become independent farmers or enter other occupations. Rice exports increased greatly. Western firms were allowed to set up tin mines and timber companies.

The United Kingdom and France both threatened to colonize Siam. But neither country would let the other establish control, and so Siam was never colonized.

Changes in government. In 1932, a group of Thai, many of whom had been educated in Europe, staged a revolution. They forced the king to change the government from an absolute monarchy to a constitutional monarchy. Pridi Phanomyong *(pree dee pah nawm yawng),* a lawyer, and Phibun Songkhram *(pee boon sawng krahm),* an artillery officer, led the revolt. A parliament was established. The king was still head of state, but a prime minister now headed the government.

After the coup, a civilian government initially ruled Siam. But from 1933 to 1938, the military increased its power. Phibun became prime minister in 1938 and ran a military government. The country's name was changed to Thailand in 1939.

In World War II (1939-1945), Germany, Japan, and other Axis powers fought the Allies, which included China, the Soviet Union, the United Kingdom, and the United States. Japan invaded Thailand in 1941. Japan planned to use Thailand as a base to attack Burma, Malaya, and Singapore, three countries then under British rule. At first, Thailand resisted. But Phibun decided to cooperate, and Japan took over Thailand's harbors, airports, and railroads. As the war progressed, many Thai began to resent Japanese control. The Thai economy suffered. In 1942, some Thai officials began a Free Thai Movement to work against Japan. The Free Thai gained influence in the Thai government. The National Assembly forced Phibun out of office in 1944. From 1944 to 1947, Thailand had civilian governments led by Pridi and people from the Free Thai. But the military remained strong.

In 1946, Bhumibol Adulyadej *(POO mee PAWN ah DOON yah deht),* also called Rama IX, became king. Bhumibol's name is also spelled Phumiphon Adunyadet.

Military rule. In 1947, some military officers staged a coup. They soon established a military dictatorship in Thailand. Phibun and a series of other military leaders then ruled the country until 1973. Worldwide, this period marked the height of the Cold War, an intense rivalry between Communist and non-Communist nations. Thailand allied itself with the non-Communists, led by the United States. The United States provided Thailand with much economic and military aid, and Thailand allowed the United States to use military bases on Thai territory. The United States used these bases to attack Communist forces in North Vietnam, Cambodia, and Laos during the Vietnam War (1957-1975). Also during this war, Thailand sent troops to fight on the side of the United States.

Democracy gains strength. In 1973, university students in Thailand led a successful revolt against the military government. They demanded democratic rights and an end to dictatorship. For the next three years, Thailand experimented with parliamentary democracy. However, in October 1976, the military again seized power. Numerous student protesters were killed, and many others fled to the jungle, where they joined Communist forces.

From 1976 to 1988, the military maintained control of Thailand but gradually allowed a parliament to have more power. General Prem Tinsulanonda *(praym TIHN soo lah nawn)* became prime minister in 1980. His government enacted policies to reduce poverty and stimulate economic growth.

Beginning in the mid-1980's, Thai government policies

encouraged the building of factories for the production of export goods. Firms from Japan, South Korea, and Taiwan built many factories. For the next 10 years, Thailand had one of the world's fastest growing economies.

In 1988, Prem retired, and an elected government took control of the nation. In 1991, some military officers again seized power. But in May 1992, hundreds of thousands of people demonstrated in the streets of Bangkok against the military government. Later that year, National Assembly elections were held, and a group of civilian parties won the elections. Since then, elected civilian leaders have controlled the government.

Recent developments. In 1997, Thailand adopted a new constitution. That same year, Thailand's economy suffered a severe slump. Many businesses went bankrupt. Millions of Thai lost their jobs and fell into poverty.

In 2001, the Thai Rak Thai (Thai Love Thai) party had won National Assembly elections. Thaksin Shinawatra *(TAHK sihn shih nah WAHT),* also spelled Chinnawat, became prime minister. He worked to revive the economy, which began to improve. In 2005, Thai Rak Thai again won elections, and Thaksin remained prime minister.

In 2004, a powerful undersea earthquake in the Indian Ocean generated a series of large ocean waves called a *tsunami.* In Thailand, the tsunami killed more than 5,000 people along the southwestern coast.

Pasuk Phongpaichit and Chris Baker

Related articles in ***World Book*** include:

Asia-Pacific Economic Cooperation	Buddhism
Association of Southeast Asian Nations	Hmong
Bangkok	Kickboxing
	Mekong River
	Southeast Asia

Outline

I. Government
- A. National government
- B. Local government
- C. Politics
- D. Courts
- E. Armed forces

II. The people
- A. Ancestry
- B. Way of life
- C. Housing
- D. Food
- E. Recreation
- F. Languages
- G. Religion
- H. Education
- I. The arts

III. The land
- A. The Mountainous North
- B. The Khorat Plateau
- C. The Central Plain
- D. The Southern Peninsula
- E. Animal life

IV. Climate

V. Economy
- A. Agriculture
- B. Manufacturing
- C. Fishing
- D. Mining
- E. Tourism
- F. International trade
- G. Transportation
- H. Communication

VI. History

Questions

How does Buddhism influence the arts in Thailand?
What are some popular Thai dishes?
How did Mongkut and Chulalongkorn change the country?
What types of problems have Thai cities faced?
How has Thailand's economy changed since the 1980's?
What role has the military played in Thailand's government?
What is a *wat?* What is *batik? Muay Thai? Sanuk?*
What is Thailand's major rice-producing area?
What are Thailand's chief minerals? Manufactured products?
What was Thailand's former name?

Additional resources

Goodman, Jim. *Thailand.* 2nd ed. Cavendish, 2002. Younger readers.

Phongpaichit, Pasuk, and Baker, C. J. *Thailand, Economy and Politics.* 2nd ed. Oxford, 2002.

Thalassemia, *THAL us SEE mee uh,* is an inherited blood disease that causes anemia. It chiefly affects children whose ancestors came from near the Mediterranean Sea. Thalassemia also afflicts African Americans and some Asian and Middle Eastern peoples. Children with thalassemia do not produce enough *hemoglobin,* a pigment that gives red blood cells their color and carries oxygen. A shortage of the substance deprives the body's tissues of oxygen. Symptoms of thalassemia are present at birth or appear about six months later. They include pale skin, irritability, poor appetite, and slow growth. If untreated, thalassemia may cause an enlarged heart, liver, or spleen. The untreated disease also deforms and weakens certain bones, especially in the face.

Thalassemia is caused by abnormalities in the *genes* (units of heredity) that control production of hemoglobin. When these abnormalities affect the parts of hemoglobin called the *beta chains,* the disease is called *beta thalassemia.* The severest beta type is called *beta thalassemia major,* also known as *Cooley's anemia.* It occurs in children who inherit defective beta hemoglobin genes from both parents. Without treatment, children with beta thalassemia major may die in infancy. Some children who inherit defective beta genes from both parents develop a milder disease called *beta thalassemia intermedia.* People who inherit a defective gene from one parent have *beta thalassemia minor,* also called *beta thalassemia trait.* These people are rarely ill but can pass the faulty gene on to their children. However, if this trait is inherited with the *sickle cell trait,* a disease known as *sickle beta thalassemia* results. This disease has symptoms that closely resemble those of sickle cell anemia (see **Sickle cell anemia**).

In some cases, thalassemia can be cured with a *bone marrow transplant.* This procedure destroys a patient's blood-forming tissue and replaces it with donor tissue that produces normal amounts of hemoglobin. Many patients receive repeated blood transfusions, which keep hemoglobin near normal levels. Because hemoglobin contains iron, transfusions also supply excess iron that can damage the heart or other organs. *Iron chelation therapy* removes this excess iron. Patients who tolerate chelation therapy well can live for many years. Another promising treatment uses drugs to stimulate *fetal hemoglobin,* a form active in unborn babies that becomes much less active after birth. Alan S. Levine

See also **Bone marrow transplant; Chelation therapy.**

Thales, *THAY leez* (625?-546? B.C.), was the earliest known Greek philosopher. He was born in Miletus in Asia Minor. All that is known about Thales and his thought came from brief and scattered reports by later historians and philosophers.

According to the Greek philosopher Aristotle, Thales was the first philosopher to attempt to discover the underlying material source of all things. Aristotle wrote that Thales believed that this substance was water. He also reported that Thales believed that magnets have souls because of their ability to move iron.

Thales was perhaps the first individual to bring a philosophic and scientific approach to subjects that had previously been given mythological and supernatural explanations. He was the first to use reasoning and observation in attempting to answer questions about human beings and the universe. Thales may therefore be considered the founder of the philosophical and scientific tradition in the Western world. S. Marc Cohen

See also **Pre-Socratic philosophy.**

Thalia. See **Graces; Muses.**

Thalidomide, *tha LIHD oh myd,* is a drug that caused serious birth defects in babies born in the 1950's and early 1960's. In the most severe instances, babies were born missing arms and legs. Some babies were born with flipperlike arms and legs, a condition called *phocomelia* (pronounced *foh coh MEEL yah*). Other birth defects included missing or deformed ears, and abnormalities of the spinal cord, heart, and other organs. More than 12,000 babies were born with birth defects in 46 countries because of thalidomide.

Beginning in 1957, thalidomide was widely used throughout Germany, Canada, Japan, and other countries. Physicians prescribed the drug as a sedative and also gave it to pregnant women to relieve morning sickness. In the United States, the drug was not approved by the Food and Drug Administration (FDA) and was not sold. By 1960, physicians in several countries were shocked by a sudden increase in the number of babies born with severe birth defects. Researchers soon traced the birth defects to thalidomide. Scientists found that birth defects resulted if women had taken even a single dose of the drug during the first few months of pregnancy. The drug was banned worldwide in 1962.

Thalidomide causes birth defects by blocking *angiogenesis* (pronounced *an jee oh JEHN uh sihs*), the growth of new blood vessels in the body. New blood vessels are necessary for the development of arms and legs during the growth of a fetus. Scientists, however, think that thalidomide may be used for treating cancer tumors, which also require new blood vessels to grow. Thalidomide also blocks the action of *tumor necrosis factor (TNF) alpha,* a protein that causes inflammation, fever, weight loss, and other problems. Many diseases, such as leprosy (Hansen's disease), tuberculosis, lupus, and AIDS, increase the level of TNF alpha in the body. Researchers have found thalidomide to be effective in treating symptoms of these diseases.

In 1998, the FDA approved thalidomide as a treatment for leprosy. The FDA established a special distribution system to ensure thalidomide is not taken by pregnant women. In this system, physicians must educate patients about the dangers of the drug. Pharmacists keep detailed records of how much thalidomide is dispensed. Patients must sign an agreement that they understand the risks of thalidomide and will not share the drug with other people. Women of childbearing age must prove that they are using birth control and have frequent pregnancy tests while taking the drug. With this system, scientists hope that thalidomide can be made available safely to the people who need it. Melanie Johns Cupp

See also **Angiogenesis.**

Thallium, *THAL ee uhm,* is a soft, bluish-gray metallic element that looks like lead. Most thallium comes from iron pyrites, in which traces of thallium occur as an impurity. The element also occurs in the minerals crookesite, hutchinsonite, and lorandite. Sir William Crookes, an English scientist, discovered thallium in 1861.

Thallium has an *atomic number* (number of protons in its nucleus) of 81. Its *relative atomic mass* is 204.3833. An element's relative atomic mass equals its *mass* (amount of matter) divided by $\frac{1}{12}$ of the mass of carbon 12, the most abundant *isotope* (form) of carbon. The chemical symbol of thallium is Tl. Thallium melts at 303.5 °C and boils at 1457 (±10) °C. At 20 °C, it has a density of 11.85 grams per cubic centimeter (see **Density**). Thallium is quite toxic to human beings. Its toxic effects are *cumulative*—that is, they build up over an extended period of time. Too much exposure to it may cause nerve damage, emotional change, cramps and convulsions, and eventually coma and death due to respiratory paralysis.

Thallium and its compounds have various uses. However, these uses are limited because of the chemical's highly toxic nature. A radioactive isotope of the element, Tl-201, is useful for diagnosing certain types of heart disease. The compound thallium sulfate is widely used in ant and rat poisons. Thallium bromide, thallium iodide, and thallium sulfide undergo changes when they are exposed to infrared radiation. As a result, they are used in devices for detecting and measuring such radiant energy. Andrew R. Barron

Thames, *tehmz,* **River,** is the most famous and most important river in England. The Thames is also one of the longest rivers in England. The Severn, partly in England and partly in Wales, is about the same length. The Thames flows 210 miles (340 kilometers) from the Cotswold Hills in south-central England to southeastern England, where it empties into the North Sea. Part of the river serves as a major English trade route.

A number of towns and cities lie along the River Thames, including Oxford, Reading, Windsor, London, Tilbury, and Southend-on-Sea. The River Thames winds through the center of London. It measures about 5 miles (8 kilometers) wide at its mouth on the North Sea (see **United Kingdom** [terrain map]). The sea's tides affect the lower part of the Thames. The Thames Barrier, built across the river in East London, provides protection against floods.

London owes its origin and much of its importance to the Thames River. In London, industries were established on the banks of the river, and the city became England's most important trading port. The London docks were built on the river during the 1800's. However, in the 1900's, most of the shipping activity was moved from London to Tilbury. Most of the old docks have closed. A number of them have been converted into residential areas and commercial building sites. Oil refineries stand at the mouth of the river. M. Trevor Wild

Thane, also spelled *thegn,* is an Anglo-Saxon title that was used for many years in early England and Scotland. The word *thane* had many meanings. At various times it meant servant, attendant, or official. Early England had a system of thanehood that was like the later system of knighthood. *Freemen* (men who were not slaves or serfs) had to fulfill one of the following conditions to become a thane: gain control of a certain amount of land, make three sea voyages, or do military service.

A thane of ordinary standing received a manor from the lord he served. In time, a successful thane might become an *earl* (member of the higher nobility). In wartime, royal thanes formed the king's personal bodyguard. The title has not been used since the reign of William the Conqueror. Paul Brand

Oil painting on canvas (1935); The Art Institute of Chicago, Mr. and Mrs. Frank G. Logan Purchase Prize

Thanksgiving, a painting by the American artist Doris E. Lee, shows women preparing Thanksgiving dinner.

Thanksgiving Day is a day set aside each year for giving thanks to God for blessings received during the year. On this day, people give thanks with feasting and prayer. It is celebrated in the United States and Canada.

The first Thanksgiving Days in New England were harvest festivals, or days for thanking God for plentiful crops. For this reason, the holiday still takes place late in fall, after the crops have been gathered. For thousands of years, people in many parts of the world have held harvest festivals. The American Thanksgiving Day probably grew out of England's harvest-home celebrations.

In the United States, Thanksgiving is usually a family day, celebrated with big dinners and joyous reunions. The very mention of Thanksgiving often calls up memories of kitchens and pantries crowded with good things to eat. Thanksgiving is also a time for serious religious thinking, church services, and prayer.

The first Thanksgiving observance in America was entirely religious and did not involve feasting. On Dec. 4, 1619, 38 English settlers arrived at Berkeley Plantation, on the James River near what is now Charles City, Virginia. The group's charter required that the day of arrival be observed yearly as a day of thanksgiving to God.

The first Thanksgiving in New England was celebrated in Plymouth less than a year after the Plymouth colonists had settled in America. The first dreadful winter in Massachusetts had killed about half the colony. But new hope arose in the summer of 1621. The settlers expected a good corn harvest, despite poor crops of peas, wheat, and barley. Thus, in early autumn, Governor William Bradford arranged a harvest festival to give thanks to God for the progress the colony had made.

The festival lasted three days. The men of Plymouth had shot ducks, geese, and turkeys. The menu also included clams, eel and other fish, wild plums and leeks, corn bread, and watercress. The women of the settlement supervised cooking over outdoor fires. About 90 Indians also attended the festival. They brought five deer to add to the feast. Everyone ate outdoors at large tables and enjoyed games and a military review. Similar harvest Thanksgivings were held in Plymouth during the next several years, but no traditional date was set.

Later Thanksgiving Days in the United States. The custom of Thanksgiving Day spread from Plymouth to other New England colonies. During the Revolutionary War, eight special days of thanks were observed for victories and for being saved from dangers. In 1789, President George Washington issued a general proclamation naming November 26 a day of national thanksgiving. In the same year, the Protestant Episcopal Church announced that the first Thursday in November would be a regular yearly day for giving thanks.

For many years, the country had no regular national Thanksgiving Day. But some states had a yearly Thanksgiving holiday. By 1830, New York had an official state Thanksgiving Day, and other Northern states soon followed its example. In 1855, Virginia became the nation's first Southern state to adopt the custom.

Sarah Josepha Hale, the editor of *Godey's Lady's Book,* worked many years to promote the idea of a national Thanksgiving Day (see **Hale, Sarah Josepha**). Then President Abraham Lincoln proclaimed the last Thursday in November 1863 as "a day of thanksgiving and praise to our beneficent Father." Each year afterward, for 75 years, the president formally proclaimed that Thanksgiving Day should be celebrated on the last Thursday of November. But in 1939, President Franklin D. Roosevelt set it one week earlier. He wanted to help business by lengthening the shopping period before Christmas. Congress ruled that after 1941 the fourth Thursday of November would be observed as Thanksgiving Day and would be a legal federal holiday.

Thanksgiving Day in Canada is celebrated in much the same way as in the United States. It was formerly celebrated on the last Monday in October. But in 1957, the Canadian government proclaimed the second Monday in October to be the holiday. Joan R. Gundersen

Additional resources

Flanagan, Alice K. *Thanksgiving.* Compass Point, 2001. Younger readers.

Grace, Catherine O. *1621: A New Look at Thanksgiving.* National Geographic Soc., 2001. Younger readers.

Thant, *thahnt,* **U,** *oo* (1909-1974), a Burmese diplomat, served as secretary-general of the United Nations (UN) from 1962 to 1971. He had become acting secretary-general in 1961, filling the term of the late Dag Hammarskjöld. U Thant had only one name, as do many people from Myanmar, formerly called Burma. *U,* a title of respect, has a meaning similar to *Mister.*

U Thant was born on Jan. 22, 1909, in Pantanaw, Burma. He attended University College in Yangon, also spelled *Rangoon.* From 1928 to 1947, he taught school and was a journalist. U Thant strongly opposed colonialism. He became Burma's press director in 1947 and director of broadcasting in 1948. In 1957, U Thant became chairman of Burma's delegation to the United Nations.

Robert H. Taylor

See also **United Nations** (picture).

Thar Desert, *tuhr* or *tahr,* stretches northwest of the Aravalli Range in India across Rajasthan to the Indus River plain in Pakistan. It is also called the Indian Desert. The Punjab region forms its northern limits. For location, see **India** (physical map).

The Thar Desert covers 74,000 square miles (192,000 square kilometers). Less than 10 inches (25 centimeters) of rain falls there annually. Formerly, few people lived in the Thar Desert. They raised sheep where there was enough water for grass. But in 1986, the Indira Gandhi Canal was completed and irrigation projects were begun. The projects have attracted farmers to the area.

The Thar is rich in various types of precious minerals and stones. Pokharan, in the desert, is the site of India's nuclear test facilities. One of India's major nuclear power plants is located in the Thar at Kota. P. P. Karan

Tharp, Twyla (1941-), is an American dancer and *choreographer* (creator of dances). Her work features movements from many types of dance, including ballet, social dances, and tap dancing. Tharp uses these familiar movements in original ways to create works filled with clever gestures and abrupt, unexpected changes in motion and mood. The energy in the dances makes them seem spontaneous, but her works are carefully structured with mathematical precision.

© Martha Swope

A Twyla Tharp dance, *Deuce Coupe,* presents dancers performing to the rock music of the Beach Boys. Tharp has choreographed works to classical music and jazz as well as rock.

Tharp has used many kinds of music, including classical, pop, rock, jazz, and ragtime. In the 1960's, she even created dances to be performed in silence. After she established her own company in 1965, she created such important works as *Re-Moves* (1966), *Medley* (1969), and *Eight Jelly Rolls* (1971).

Tharp choreographed *Deuce Coupe* (1973) and *As Time Goes By* (1973) for the City Center Joffrey Ballet, *Push Comes to Shove* (1976) for the American Ballet Theatre, and *Brahms/Handel* (with Jerome Robbins, 1984) for the New York City Ballet. From 1988 to 1990, she was resident choreographer and artistic associate for the American Ballet Theatre. Tharp has choreographed for films, stage and TV shows, and ice dancing. She choreographed the hit musical *Movin' Out* (2002), based on the music of Billy Joel. She was born on July 1, 1941, in Portland, Indiana. Katy Matheson

Thatcher, Margaret (1925-), served as prime minister of the United Kingdom from 1979 to 1990. She was the first woman ever to hold the office. Thatcher became known as the "Iron Lady" for her strong opposition to socialist policies and her handling of foreign affairs.

Margaret Hilda Roberts was born on Oct. 13, 1925, in Grantham, Lincolnshire, England. She received a chemistry degree from Oxford University and later studied law. She married Denis Thatcher, a wealthy business executive, in 1951. In 1953, she became an attorney.

Reuters/Bettmann

Margaret Thatcher

Thatcher was elected to the House of Commons in 1959. She served as secretary of state for education and science from 1970 to 1974. In 1975, she became the first woman to head a British political party when she was elected leader of the Conservative Party.

Thatcher became prime minister after the Conservative Party won control of parliament in elections in 1979. In 1982, she ordered a military attack to stop Argentina from claiming the Falkland Islands, a territory of the United Kingdom. She remained in office after her party again won parliamentary elections in 1983 and 1987. Thatcher fought trade unions and worked to reduce inflation and government spending. Her government sold some public industries to private citizens and businesses. Thatcher resigned as prime minister and Conservative Party leader in 1990, after losing the support of many party members. She remained in the House of Commons until 1992. That same year, Thatcher was made a baroness and a member of the House of Lords. Brendan O'Leary

Thayer, Sylvanus, *sihl VAY nuhs* (1785-1872), was a United States Army engineer and educator who became known as the father of West Point. From 1817 to 1833, Thayer was superintendent of the U.S. Military Academy at West Point. His long service allowed him to impress his professional standards and ideas of duty, honor, and loyalty on generations of cadets. He was born on June 9, 1785, in Braintree, Massachusetts. Joel D. Meyerson

A scene from *Macbeth* by William Shakespeare; Robert C. Ragsdale

The Stratford Festival in Canada annually presents classics of world theater.

Theater

Theater, also spelled *theatre,* is a live performance before an audience. It includes every form of entertainment from the circus to plays. In more traditional terms, theater is an art form in which a script is acted out by performers. The performers, usually with the assistance of a director, interpret the characters and situations created by a playwright. The performance takes place before an audience in a space designated for the performance.

A successful theatrical event is an exciting and stimulating experience, whether it occurs in a Broadway playhouse, a high school auditorium, or a space only temporarily being used for theatrical purposes. Spectators as well as those involved in the production feel this excitement.

The word *theater* comes from a Greek word meaning *a place for seeing.* In this sense, the word refers to the space where performances are staged. However, theater in a broad sense includes everything that is involved in a production, such as the script, the stage, the performing company, and the audience. In addition, theater refers to a part of human culture that began during primitive times.

Theater is not the same as *drama,* though the words are frequently used interchangeably. Drama refers to the literary part of a performance—that is, the play. Some critics believe that a play is not really a play until it has been performed before an audience. Other critics argue that the script is only a blueprint that the director and other interpretative artists use as the basis for performance.

The theater is one of the most complex of the arts, requiring many kinds of artists. These specialists include the playwright, performers, director, scene designer, costumer, lighting designer, sound designer, and various technicians. For many productions, composers, musicians, and a *choreographer* (creator of dances) are needed. The theater is sometimes called a *mixed art* be-

The contributor of this article is Don B. Wilmeth, Professor of Theatre Arts and English at Brown University.

cause it combines the script of the playwright, the environment created by the scene designer, and the speech and movement of the performers.

In the earliest theatrical performances, the dramatist performed all artistic functions, including acting. Gradually, specialists developed and the various theater arts emerged. The actor and the playwright gained recognition first, partly because they needed each other in order to bring their arts to life.

In the modern theater, a director is used to integrate all aspects of production, including scenery, costumes, lighting, sound effects, music, and dancing. Perhaps the most important job of the director is to guide the performers in their creative process and to aid them in their interpretation of their roles.

This article describes how the theater arts are used to create a theatrical production. For a discussion of the history of written drama and theater practices, see **Drama**.

Modern theater architecture

Most theater buildings have three basic parts: (1) the auditorium, (2) the stage, and (3) the behind-the-scenes spaces.

The auditorium is where the audience sits. In the broadest sense, it also includes such facilities as the box office, lobby, entrances and exits, rest rooms, exhibition areas, and refreshment stands.

A well-designed auditorium allows every person in the audience to see and hear a performance without strain. It also permits the spectators to reach and leave their seats easily. The interior is decorated in a pleasing fashion that does not distract attention from the stage. Auditoriums may be large or small, and they vary in their basic characteristics. The seats are either all on the main floor, or on the main floor and in one or more balconies. In some older auditoriums, box seats are available on one or more levels close to the stage. The audience normally watches the action of the play from one, two, three, or all four sides. However, in some modern theaters, the audience and the performers actually share the same space. In the United States, the mixing of audience and performance spaces is often called *environmental theater.*

In a number of theaters, the seating arrangement for the audience and the location of the performing space change from production to production. In some cases, the audience is required actually to shift location during the performance, moving from one area to another as the action of the performance progresses. In England, presentations that require the audience to shift location are called *promenade* productions.

The stage. Four basic types of stage are used in today's theater: (1) the proscenium stage, (2) the open stage, also called a thrust stage or a platform stage, (3) the theater-in-the-round or arena stage, and (4) the flexible stage space. Each of these types creates a different relationship between the performers and the audience, and each requires certain adjustments in play production.

The *proscenium stage* is the most common type of stage. It is designed to be viewed only from the front. It is sometimes called a "picture frame" stage, because the opening through which the audience sees the action forms a frame for the performers and scenery. This frame is called a *proscenium arch.* An orchestra pit or a forestage area may separate the seats from the area behind the proscenium arch. Normally, the plays are per-

WORLD BOOK photo by Lisa Ebright

A proscenium stage permits the audience to see a play only from the front. Plays are usually performed behind a frame called the *proscenium arch,* which encloses the stage area.

formed behind the arch, but action may take place on the forestage as well.

A proscenium stage often has a curtain that may be used to conceal or reveal the stage. The curtain may be closed to permit changes in scenery, to indicate the passage of time, or to mark the act or scene divisions of a play. Today, the dimming of lights often takes the place of closing the curtain. Elaborate, three-dimensional scenery can be used effectively on a proscenium stage. Performers enter or leave the stage by way of openings in the scenery or by way of the *wings* at the sides of the stage.

A modern adaptation of a proscenium stage is the *end stage.* The end stage has no proscenium arch or conventional curtain.

Most *open stages* have seats arranged around three sides of a raised platform that extends into the auditorium. The shape and size of the platform may differ considerably from auditorium to auditorium. Productions presented on open stages must be carefully staged so that all elements can be seen from three sides at the same time. Large units of scenery should be used only at the back of the stage so they do not block the audience's view.

In a *theater-in-the-round,* spectators sit on four sides of the stage or completely surround it. Most stages of this type are found in small theaters with limited seating capacity. The scenery used in a theater-in-the-round must be low enough to allow the performance area to be seen from every angle. Often it is placed at the end

The Stratford Festival Thrust Stage, Ontario, Canada

An open stage extends into the auditorium on three sides. This stage permits a close relationship between audience and performers, but limits large set pieces to the rear of the stage.

WORLD BOOK photo by Lisa Ebright

A theater-in-the-round is an open area with the audience sitting on all four sides. The actors and actresses must adjust their performances so the entire audience can see and hear. Scenery must be low enough not to obstruct the view of anyone in the audience.

of an aisle or behind the audience. Scene changes are made in darkness or in view of the audience. The performers in a theater-in-the-round have to make their entrances and exits through the auditorium. They must perform to all sides and must learn to be expressive with the back as well as the front of the body.

In a *flexible theater*, the performance and audience spaces can be rearranged for each production. This adaptability allows a director the freedom of selecting the kind of audience-stage relationship most appropriate to the production. Most flexible theaters accommodate small audiences, and it is not uncommon for the stage area of such theaters to be larger than the space for the audience.

A great deal of theater today, as in primitive times, takes place in *found spaces*—that is, in areas not originally intended for theater. Audiences may sit or stand in such performance spaces, as they do in some flexible theater spaces. One of the exciting aspects of today's theater is the variety of its spaces for performers and audiences.

The behind-the-scenes spaces in a fully equipped theater may include workshops to make costumes and scenery; rehearsal and dressing rooms; lighting and sound booths; storage space for costumes, scenery, properties, and lighting instruments; office space for theater staff; and a *green room* (lounge) for performers. Many professional theaters, including those on Broadway, do not have equipment to build scenery. Many nonprofessional groups work in limited space. Only such large organizations as the Metropolitan Opera Association have all these behind-the-scenes spaces within one structure. Many groups, such as Actors Theatre of Louisville, Kentucky, house most work spaces in a building separate from the theater structure.

The producer

The process of staging a theatrical production begins with the producer. The producer may be an individual, a group of individuals, or a theater company. The producer has overall responsibility for the entire show. The producer's main duties include one or more of the following: (1) acquiring a script, (2) raising money to finance the show, (3) obtaining a theater, (4) assembling a creative team to stage the production, and (5) keeping financial records.

Acquiring a script. The starting point for most theatrical productions, professional or nonprofessional, is the playwright's script. A producer who is interested in a new script may take an *option* on it. This gives the producer exclusive production rights to the play for a certain period of time. If the producer decides to present the play, a contract is drawn up specifying the amount of the author's *royalty* (share of the profits). The contract also states the extent of the producer's control over the play. For example, the contract may require the playwright to be available for consultation and possible rewriting during the rehearsal period.

Raising money to stage a play or musical is often the producer's most difficult job. The cost of putting on a theatrical production has become increasingly high. On Broadway in New York City, a set and a small cast may cost as much as $1 million. Musicals can cost several million dollars. Few individuals can invest this much money, and so most producers seek funds from many people, groups, or corporations.

Obtaining a theater. The producer may be a theater company that has its own theater. If not, it is up to the producer to find a suitable space for performances and rehearsals.

In the past, Broadway plays often presented performances in another city before the official opening night in New York City. The producer made arrangements for the theater as well as for transportation and hotel accommodations. The purpose of most out-of-town performances was to sample audience reaction as a guide to improving the play and the production. Out-of-town performances are rare today because of the enormous expense involved. Instead, most productions present a series of preview performances in the theater where the regular performances will be held. Preview tickets are normally sold at reduced prices.

Assembling a creative team may begin even before the money is raised. The producer will try to get commitments from a certain director or performer in order to attract investors. After raising the money to finance the production, the producer is involved in selecting and negotiating contracts with all the people involved in the production.

In the Broadway theater, a producer must deal with about 15 major unions representing various employees. These employees include not only the director, actors, actresses, and designers, but also stagehands, musicians, dancers, and box-office personnel. Theater companies normally use their own directors, designers, and performers, but they may supplement their creative team with outside individuals.

Keeping financial records. The producer oversees all expenditures and income for a production. The producer is responsible for seeing that the bills are paid, from salaries and costs of sets and costumes to advertising expenses. The producer also keeps track of the income from ticket sales. Periodically, the producer's financial records must be submitted to the investors for inspection.

The director

In the modern theater, the director is responsible for the artistic effectiveness of the production as a whole. The director usually decides how the script is interpreted and coordinates the efforts of all the other artists. The director has so much control that theater in the Western world is often called a director's theater. However, the best directors are tolerant of the ideas of the other artists throughout the production process.

In traditional theater production, the director ordinarily has five major duties: (1) analyzing the text of the play and determining the interpretation that will shape the production; (2) working with the playwright, technicians, and designers of scenery, lighting, and costumes in planning the production; (3) casting the performers; (4) supervising rehearsals; and (5) coordinating each element of the final production.

Interpreting the script. The director must be thoroughly familiar with the play in order to cast and rehearse the performers intelligently and guide the various designers. He or she studies the play's structure and examines the devices the playwright uses to tell the story and to build suspense. If traditional structure is not used, as is often the case in modern theater, the director seeks to discover how the playwright creates a mood and draws responses from the audience. The director often divides the play into sections. He or she then analyzes the characters' behavior and the mood in each section, and determines how each section relates to those before and after it.

The director must understand each character's function in the play and what is demanded of the performer who will play the role. During the rehearsal process, the director will want to allow input from the actors and actresses performing the roles. But it is helpful for the director to have an initial sense of each character's personality, physical characteristics, emotional range, and vocal qualities.

The director must have an ability to visualize the scenic, costume, and lighting requirements of a production. He or she will accept ideas from the other partners in the production process, but it is usually the director's responsibility to determine the style and placement of scenery and the appropriateness of the final designs.

The amount of preparation the director must make depends on the play and the production situation. Work on a new play presents problems very different from the demands of reviving a classic. In directing a new play, for example, the director often works directly with the playwright, suggesting changes and cuts. Ideally, this process continues throughout the rehearsal period.

For an older play, the director might wish to make changes in the text so that a modern audience can better understand the language and action. This could involve cutting or changing obscure words or eliminating speeches or entire scenes. Today, such revisions are often made with the help of a *dramaturge.* A dramaturge is usually a historian or literary scholar who advises the director on matters of style or historical detail. Many directors believe that they must try to make a play more meaningful to modern audiences by changing its time and place, or by drastically reinterpreting the play. There is much controversy about how powerful a director should be in shaping the interpretation of a play.

Working with the designers. Before beginning rehearsals, the director discusses the interpretation of the play with the scenic, costume, sound, and lighting designers. These experts make suggestions about design, and the director may make specific requests. For example, doors and other openings may be needed at particular places on the stage. The director makes sure that the proposed settings and costumes reflect the action, mood, theme, characters, and period of the play. The settings and costumes also must be functional in terms of the performers' movements.

Casting. One of the director's first tasks is to select the performers for all the roles in the play. At this point, a *casting director* is often hired to select finalists for roles. An open tryout may be held to which anyone may come. In New York City, open tryouts must be held for all professional productions. Invitational tryouts also may be held. Invitational tryouts are those to which only certain performers are invited.

Actors and actresses trying out for a role may be given the play to read before the tryout. Some directors ask performers to memorize and act scenes from various

WORLD BOOK photo by Lisa Ebright

Casting is the process of filling the play's roles. Performers normally present a short selection for the director, who selects the cast, sometimes in consultation with the playwright.

plays or to present audition scenes prepared by the performer. Other directors require that a performer use pantomime, or they ask the performer to do an *improvisation*—that is, make up a scene on the spur of the moment based on suggestions given by the director.

Many factors determine the final casting. Some roles have specific physical or vocal demands. The emotional range of a role also must be considered. The director tries to cast a role with the other roles in mind in order to create a balanced and varied cast.

Rehearsing. The rehearsal process varies greatly from director to director and play to play. For most traditional directors, there are three major concerns: (1) stage picture; (2) movements, gestures, and facial expressions; and (3) voice and speech. Other directors believe the main concern is to draw the most effective performances possible from the cast by working closely with the performers as a creative partner and by guiding them toward a unified presentation.

Traditional directors believe that each moment of a play should be a *stage picture* in which an image communicates without dialogue with the audience. Each stage picture should have a center of interest and

The Goodman Theatre production of *The Winter's Tale* (WORLD BOOK photo by Lisa Ebright)

Rehearsing a play includes *blocking,* which establishes the movements of the performers. Most early rehearsals are held in a rehearsal room. Final rehearsals take place on the actual stage.

should express the dominant emotional tone and the relationships among the characters. According to this approach, the director's chief task is to focus the audience's attention on the important elements—usually one or two characters who are most important at the moment. This is done by manipulating the positions of the performers in relation to the audience and to each other. Today, most directors believe it is a mistake to place too much emphasis on stage pictures—the most mechanical part of directing—while giving too little attention to other aspects of staging.

For example, *movement* is often more vital than stage pictures alone. Movement is essential to blend one stage picture into another and to create a sense of flow and development. Movement must always be appropriate for the character, situation, mood, and type of play. *Gestures* and *facial expressions* supplement the effects of movement. Most problems of *voice* and *speech* are worked out by the performers. But the director serves as a sounding board and makes sure the performers speak clearly and with appropriate expressiveness.

Most early rehearsals take place in a rehearsal room rather than on a stage. Chalk lines or tape indicate the stage floor plan. Only basic furniture and props are used.

A rehearsal schedule for a traditional play normally includes several phases. First, the director and performers read and study the play. Then the director *blocks* action. That is, he or she arranges the broad pattern of the performers' movements, though some of these movements may be changed during later stages of rehearsal. Then detailed work begins on characterization, line readings, stage action, changes in mood, and blending the performers into a unit. Next, in technical rehearsals, problems of lighting, scenery changes, costuming, and other mechanical concerns are resolved. Some directors prefer to rehearse lighting and scenery changes without performers. Finally, in dress rehearsals, the director combines all the elements of theatrical production and presents the final product as it will be seen by an audience.

The director's assistants include a stage manager and, depending on the budget, one or more assistant stage managers, an assistant director, and a rehearsal secretary. Often, one person serves as both assistant director and rehearsal secretary.

The rehearsal secretary sits near the director during rehearsals and takes notes. An assistant director may rehearse certain scenes, coach performers, or act as a go-between for the director and designers. In the professional theater, the stage manager organizes tryouts. He or she attends all rehearsals, and records changes in dialogue and blocking on a master copy of the script. Later, during performances, the stage manager is in charge backstage. The stage manager is often called upon to direct or rehearse replacement cast members or even a complete cast for a second production of a successful show.

The performers

Performers are among the few artists who cannot separate their means of expression from themselves. They are their own instrument. They create with their own body and voice and their own psychological and mental qualities. It is often difficult to separate talent and creativity from the performer's personality. But acting is an art and, as with any art, natural ability, study, and practice are essential.

Body and voice. Performers need a flexible, disciplined, and expressive body. They must be able to use their body to represent a wide range of attitudes and reactions. They may be aided by courses in stage movement, dancing, or fencing, or by participating in sports that demand physical control and coordination. Dancing and fencing are particularly useful because they provide grace and body control. These skills also assure more job opportunities for performers. A performer who can dance as well as act is especially in demand.

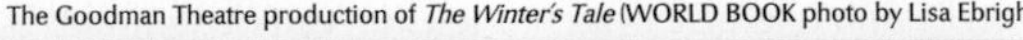
The Goodman Theatre production of *The Winter's Tale* (WORLD BOOK photo by Lisa Ebright)

Expressing emotion requires a blend of facial expression and body movement. The grouping and experience of the performers in this scene produce a strong sense of shock and grief. The sharp contrasts in lighting intensify the mood of tragedy.

The same requirements of flexibility, control, and expressiveness apply to the voice as to the body. Performers learn how to breathe properly, to achieve variety in vocal rhythm and tone, and to make themselves heard and understood. They also learn dialects. Training in oral reading, relaxation, and singing is important. However, most performers require years of practice to change their voices significantly so they can speak higher, lower, louder, or softer—and still be understood. For professional performers, therefore, work on vocal improvement, as well as on physical flexibility, should continue throughout their career.

Observation and imagination. To portray a role well, performers should know about human emotions, attitudes, and *motivations* (reasons for behavior). They must be able to express these elements so they can be understood by an audience. A good performer develops the habit of observing others and remembering how they behave. If an actor takes the role of an old man, for example, he may prepare in part by observing how old men walk, stand, and sit. He may then adapt these movements to suit the character. A performer also learns how different people react to such emotions as happiness, grief, and fear.

Performers may try to develop *emotional memory,* so that in portraying a role they can recall a situation from their past that caused a similar emotional response in them. This is a complex acting technique, however, and should be used only after developing a thorough understanding of how one should best approach this process. Performers learn to know others through knowing themselves and their emotional capacities as thoroughly as possible. They portray others partly by using their knowledge of themselves and by developing a sensitivity to their own emotions.

Concentration is particularly important for performers. They must be able to involve themselves in an imagined situation and shut out all distractions. Their goal is to give a performance that creates the illusion of something happening for the first time. Part of making this happen involves concentrating on listening to other performers in the play and responding appropriately. It also involves focusing on each moment as it happens rather than anticipating what is to come.

Systems of acting. No matter how talented or even well-trained performers are, they cannot use their skills to full effectiveness without some consistent working method. Performers should try as many approaches to acting as possible, and choose the one, or a combination of several, they consider to be most successful for them.

The differences among systems of acting are often described in terms of two extremes: *mechanical-external* and *psychological-internal.* The two differ on the question of whether a performer must be emotionally moved to act convincingly. Extreme supporters of the external system argue that emotion may interfere with good acting. They believe the performer should merely try to create the external signs of emotions. Strong advocates of the internal system claim that only through feeling can performers project themselves into a character and situation. This approach is sometimes called the *Stanislavski* system, for the Russian director Konstantin Stanislavski. The version used in the United States is known as the *Method.* For most performers, however, neither extreme provides the best approach to the art of acting or leads to the truthfulness on stage that is most believable to an audience.

Creating a role. Performers must solve several specific problems every time they play a new role, especially in conventional plays. These problems normally include (1) analyzing the role, (2) movement and gesture, (3) vocal characterization, (4) conservation and build, and (5) ensemble playing.

Analyzing the role starts with a study of the play as a whole. Then performers concentrate on their own parts. First they analyze the various aspects of characterization—a character's appearance, occupation, social and economic status, and general personality. They then examine the character's goal and behavior, both in the play as a whole and in individual scenes. Finally, they study how their role is related to the other characters and to the structure of the play. If the play takes place during an earlier time, performers may study the period and setting. They not only analyze their role independently, but also develop their interpretation in partnership with the director and the rest of the cast.

Movement and gesture are the ways in which the performer portrays the character's walk, posture, gestures, and bodily attitudes. The director plans the broad pattern of movement or works this out in rehearsal with the actors. The performer fills in the details. The performer works to understand the purpose or emotional reason behind each movement so he or she can perform every action "in character."

Vocal characterization refers to the character's general vocal qualities. Performers decide what qualities are desirable, and adjust their voices accordingly. One character may require a high-pitched voice. Another may have a soft, soothing voice. The performer also notes the demands of each scene. Some scenes may be more relaxed than others, and some may be emotionally high-keyed. A change within a scene can often be enhanced by appropriate vocal patterns. For example, growing tension can be denoted by raised pitch, greater volume, and faster tempo.

Conservation and build include the ways performers conserve their powers and heighten the role to a climax. In many modern plays there is no conventional build or climax. However, the performer must still be able to sustain a role and alter its *dynamics* (forces) as needed from beginning to end. Most characters change or show growth during the course of a play, and the performer must reflect these developments. The need to sustain and build a part is most important in highly emotional roles. If performers begin at too high an emotional pitch, they soon may not be able to build the intensity any further. The rest of the performance may seem monotonous. Performers must pace themselves so the performance grows in strength and interest as dictated by the demands of the text and the decisions made with the director.

Ensemble playing is the sense of artistic unity and cohesion that results from the cooperative efforts of the entire cast. No acting performance is fully effective unless it is integrated with all the other performances—unless the text deliberately calls for a lack of completeness. Ensemble playing results when every performer adjusts to the needs of the play, and remains aware of the methods, strengths, and weaknesses of the other performers.

Scene design

Scene design has two basic purposes—to aid the audience's understanding, and to express the distinctive qualities of a play. To aid understanding, for example, the stage setting may define the time and place of the action. The set creates an appropriate mood and expresses the play's dominant elements through composition and color.

The scene designer begins a job by studying the play as a whole. He or she then analyzes its scenic demands. Consideration must be given to the number, size, and kinds of settings needed; their physical arrangement; and the play's period, place, and social and economic background. The designer also may do research to learn about typical manners and customs, decorative details, architectural forms, furnishings, and building materials of the period. The designer meets with the director to discuss the kind of stage most appropriate for the production—if choices are available—and the budget for scenery. Also discussed are the requirements of the sets, the locations of entrances and exits, and the arrangement of furnishings.

Next, the designer makes preliminary sketches of the set and discusses them with the director. Before the designs receive final approval, the designer draws them in perspective and in color. These drawings are called *set renderings.* The designer makes floor plans of each set and may build three-dimensional scale models to show how each set will look and how scene changes can be made. The designer also makes a series of working drawings that show how each set will be built. In the professional theater, where scenery may be built by a scenic studio, every detail of construction, assembly, and painting must be indicated. In the nonprofessional theater, where the designer often supervises construction, fewer drawings are needed.

Kinds of scenery. The designer uses several basic scenic units when building sets. Most of these units may be classified as *standing* or *hanging.*

The basic standing unit is the *flat.* A flat is a rectangular wooden frame over which canvas or muslin is stretched or some other light material is attached, providing a lightweight structure. Flats can be made in any size needed, but extremely large flats are awkward to handle and move. Most flats are from 12 to 16 feet (360 to 490 centimeters) high and 1 to 6 feet (30 to 180 centimeters) wide. A plain flat has no openings. A door flat, window flat, fireplace flat, and arch flat all have appropriate openings. Other standing units include door and window frames, fireplaces, platforms, steps and staircases, rocks and built-up ground, tree trunks, and columns. A *ground row* is a low flat with a shaped edge that may give the appearance of distant hills, rows of buildings, or even an abstract shape.

Hanging units include *ceilings, borders, drops, drapes, curtains, scrims,* and *cycloramas.* Most ceilings are made from two large rectangular flats hinged together. They are suspended above the set, and lowered to rest on the tops of flats representing walls. In modern design, the ceiling often is not used at all. In most exterior settings, borders are substituted for ceilings. Borders are short curtains of black cloth or painted canvas hung parallel to the front of the stage in order to hide

The Goodman Theatre production of *The Winter's Tale* (WORLD BOOK photo by Lisa Ebright)

Set construction may be handled in the theater's own shop or by an outside studio. Generally, each piece of the set is designed so that stagehands can move it easily during the performance.

The Goodman Theatre production of *The Winter's Tale* (WORLD BOOK photo by Lisa Ebright)

The set designer, *right,* uses a scale model to demonstrate to the director, *left,* how the set will look and work. After the two agree on the designs, set construction begins.

A technical rehearsal allows the director and designers to see how the sets, costumes, and lighting look under conditions of an actual performance. Last-minute adjustments may also be made in the play's blocking.

The Goodman Theatre production of *The Winter's Tale* (WORLD BOOK photo by Lisa Ebright)

the area above the setting from the audience. Borders, like flats, can be shaped and painted to resemble any object or form.

Large pieces of canvas called drops usually extend the width of the stage. They can be painted to represent any scene. Most drapes or curtains are hung in a series parallel to the proscenium on each side of the stage to conceal offstage space. A scrim is a gauze curtain that is used for special effects. It appears transparent when lighted from the back, but opaque when lighted from the front. A cyclorama is a continuous stretched curtain suspended on a U-shaped *batten* (pipe). The cyclorama usually extends along the sides and back of the stage. Most cycloramas are neutral in color, but they can be made any color by lighting. They are often used to represent the sky.

Changing scenery. After scenery has been built, it is assembled on stage. A one-set show can be assembled permanently. A multiple-set production, however, requires careful planning so that each unit can be set up and taken down quickly and quietly during the show.

When scenery is changed by hand, each part is moved by one or more stagehands to a prearranged place offstage. New settings are then assembled or moved on stage. Another common method of changing scenery is called *flying.* Suspended units overhead are raised and lowered as needed on the stage.

Rolling platforms called *wagons* are often used to change scenery. Scenery is placed on the wagons, which can be rolled on or off the stage. One kind of wagon is called a *jackknife.* This kind of wagon is attached to the stage floor at a fixed point and moves much as a pocket jackknife opens and closes. A jackknife wagon can be of any size, and it is sometimes as wide as the proscenium opening itself. The most common wagon is a *straight-run wagon* that rolls on stage in a straight line and is pulled back out of sight of the audience for storage.

Scenery can also be changed by means of *revolving stages* or *elevator stages.* A revolving stage has a large circle of the stage floor mounted on a central supporting pivot that can be rotated. Several settings can be erected at one time and moved into view as needed by turning the stage. An elevator stage has sections of the stage floor that can be lowered to the basement of the theater. There, scenery can be changed while another set is being used.

Properties and set dressing are added to the set after the scenery has been assembled. Properties are often divided into two categories. *Set props,* such as sofas, tables, and bookshelves, function as part of the design or are a necessary part of the setting. *Hand props,* such as fans and guns, are props used by the performers. *Set dressing* includes such items as pictures, drapes, books in a bookshelf, and decorative objects on a mantel.

Lighting and sound

Lighting methods. The lighting designer analyzes a play for its dramatic values and then for its lighting needs. The designer notes everything in the script concerning light. There might be such changes in intensity as a sunrise or lamps being lit. Variations in light might be needed for various parts of the setting. The script may note the direction from which light enters the set, such as moonlight through a window.

The designer pays particular attention to the mood of the play because lighting is effective in establishing stage atmosphere. The designer must understand the style of the play. For realistic drama, for example, the designer will probably make the light appear to come from a specific source, such as a lamp or sunshine through a window.

The lighting designer confers with the scene designer and the director. In the professional theater, the lighting designer makes sketches showing how the stage will look when lighted. In most nonprofessional productions, the lighting designer and the director reach general agreement about lighting. The focus and placement of the lights cannot be finally determined until the scenery is in place.

Lighting for the stage is divided into (1) specific illumination, (2) general illumination, and (3) special effects. *Specific illumination* concentrates on a limited area. It is used principally for lighting the acting areas, which require strong emphasis. *General illumination* is used to light the sets and background elements and to blend the lighting of acting areas. It is also used to provide a gradual change between brilliantly lighted acting areas and less intense lighting on the background. *Special effects* refers to a variety of lighting techniques and instruments. Examples of special effects include projections of clouds, fires, or stars, and the creation of patterns on the stage floor suggesting light through tree branches.

In planning the lighting, the designer draws a *lighting plot* on a floor plan showing the entire stage, including the setting. A separate lighting plot is sometimes drawn for each set, as well as a plot showing the lighting for all the sets at the same time.

An *instrument schedule* provides a summary of all the technical information needed to set up the lights for a play. This schedule lists lighting instruments, mounting positions, areas to be lighted, color filters, and other technical data.

There are several types of lighting instruments. A *spotlight* illuminates a limited portion of the stage with a concentrated beam of light. They have reflectors to increase their brightness, and lenses to give light a specific type of edge, either sharp or soft. Frames enable the lighting designer to insert a transparent colored sheet in front of the lens. This sheet, called a *gelatin* or *gel,* changes the color of the light.

A *striplight* consists of a series of lamps set in a narrow, roughly rectangular trough. Striplights vary in length, wattage, and use. One type, called *borderlights,* is hung overhead to spread light to the set or background. Other striplights may be placed on the floor or elsewhere on the stage, often behind a ground row, to light a cyclorama or scenic units.

The Goodman Theatre production of *The Winter's Tale* (WORLD BOOK photo by Lisa Ebright)

A lighting control board enables one technician to control all lighting changes from a booth in the theater. Many of the most complex lighting cues are programmed in advance by computer.

Many instruments are used to create special effects. Projectors for front or rear projection are among the most useful. An entire scenic background can be projected on a screen or on a cyclorama. Some projectors have rotating disks to create the effect of movement, as in clouds.

Lighting on the stage is changed by the use of a number of *dimmers* on a control board. Dimmers allow the designer to vary the intensity of each light, ranging from full brightness to black. The level of intensity for the lights in each light change, or *light cue,* can be preset during the technical rehearsal. Today, it is common for large numbers of dimmers to be electronically controlled. A complex lighting cue can be accomplished by pushing one key on a computer. The direction or focus of specific lighting instruments can also be altered by remote control.

The Goodman Theatre production of *The Winter's Tale* (WORLD BOOK photo by Lisa Ebright)

Lighting plays a crucial part in establishing a play's atmosphere. Lighting can be used to focus an audience's attention on a certain character or part of the stage. The lighting in this scene helps to create a mood of mystery on stage.

Sound production. Sound makes its greatest contribution when it is designed as a unit and carefully integrated into the production as a whole. Sound includes music, abstract noises, and such realistic effects as thunder.

Sound performs two basic functions: (1) to establish mood and style and (2) to help tell the story. Music and abstract sound help indicate the proper atmosphere for each scene. Such realistic sounds as rainfall or a distant foghorn also contribute to mood. Sound helps tell the story through gunshots, ringing doorbells, and other realistic noises that either prepare the audience for onstage action or indicate action supposedly occurring offstage.

Sound is classified as *live* or *recorded.* Live sound is created fresh for each performance and includes doorbells and telephones. Recorded sound includes noises made by an approaching car and the sounds of a crowd offstage.

Most musicals and some nonmusical plays use microphones to increase or reinforce sound intensity. Technicians wire the microphones across the front of the stage, or the performers wear small hidden microphones that have wireless transmitters to the amplifiers.

Costumes and makeup

Costume design shares the same broad purposes as scene design. It aids the audience's understanding and expresses the play's distinctive qualities. Costumes help identify the period and country in which the action takes place and establish the specific location of a scene. They

Costume design begins with a sketch of the proposed costume, *above.* Samples of the material are usually attached. The costume must be fitted correctly, *below left,* so the performer can move freely and comfortably. The costume shown in these pictures is worn by a fortuneteller, *below right,* in George Farquhar's *The Recruiting Officer,* an English comedy written in 1706.

WORLD BOOK photos by Vories Fisher

can suggest time of day, season, occasion, and information about the characters—ages, occupations, personalities, and social and economic status.

Costumes can also clarify the relationships among characters. For example, the warring sides in many Shakespearean history plays are identified by contrasting color schemes. Costumes also express the overall mood of the play, its style, and the emotional tone of individual scenes.

Like other members of the creative team responsible for a production, the costume designer studies the script thoroughly. The costumer confers with the director, scenic designer, lighting designer, and principal performers to make sure his or her ideas fit the interpretation of the play. The costumer uses line, mass, color, texture, and ornaments to create a visual statement. Like the scene designer, the costumer records ideas in color sketches. The sketches, called *renderings,* are usually accompanied by samples of material. They are given to the director for approval. The costumer also makes a chart indicating what each character wears in each scene of the play.

Costumes may be made new, assembled from an existing wardrobe, borrowed, or rented. In the professional theater, professional costume houses make costumes to order. Nonprofessional theaters often borrow costumes or rent them from a costume rental agency. Many permanent theater organizations, both professional and nonprofessional, make their own costumes. Most maintain a wardrobe of items from past productions.

The director and designers evaluate the costumes at a *dress parade,* which shows the performers under lights similar to those used in performances. If there is no dress parade, the evaluation is done during a dress rehearsal. Any necessary changes to costumes are made during the final rehearsal period. After performances begin, a wardrobe attendant works backstage and supervises costume changes, repairs, and adjustments.

Makeup techniques. Makeup is important in establishing characterization. The appearance of the face indicates the character's age, health, and ethnicity. The face can also suggest a general occupation and basic personality. Makeup serves the additional purpose of restoring or emphasizing the face's color and form, which may be affected by the lighting or distance from the audience.

For a *straight makeup,* the performer's appearance is not changed significantly. In a *character makeup,* it is changed greatly. The makeup may age the face; make it fat, thin, smooth, or wrinkled; or emphasize some peculiar facial characteristic. For a character makeup, the performer often must alter the hands, the neck, and other portions of the body as well as the face.

Makeup effects can be achieved in two basic ways: (1) by painting or (2) by using plastic or three-dimensional pieces. Painting involves applying color, shadows, and highlights to the performer's face or body. All makeup has some painted effects. Plastic makeup devices include beards, wigs, false noses, scars, or distorted portions of the face.

Traditionally, makeup has been considered the performer's responsibility, though it also concerns the costumer. In the professional theater, performers are responsible for their own makeup, but they consult

Makeup can be used to alter a performer's appearance. Actor Robert Morse, *right,* and a makeup artist skillfully used makeup, a wig, a hat, and glasses to create a convincing likeness of the American author Truman Capote, *bottom,* for a Broadway show.

Martha Swope

Broadway musical comedy has been called the major contribution of the United States to modern theater. *A Chorus Line, shown here,* was one of the longest-running shows in Broadway history. The musical opened in 1975 and closed in 1990, playing a total of 6,137 performances.

specialists for help with problems. In many nonprofessional theaters, makeup is considered part of the costumer's duties. Sometimes the director is responsible for makeup.

Theater in the United States

Professional theater. The best-known center of professional theater in the United States is New York City, though Chicago, Seattle, and Los Angeles have become major centers as well. In addition, resident professional companies exist in many cities.

New York City. The theaters on and near Broadway have long been the most important force in theater in the United States. But the increasing expense of staging a Broadway production has narrowed the range of plays offered. Producers limit themselves almost entirely to

© Joan Marcus

The Arena Stage in Washington, D.C., is one of the leading regional theaters in the eastern United States. The theater was founded in 1950 and presents both new plays and revivals of such classics as *The Cherry Orchard, shown here,* by the Russian dramatist Anton Chekhov.

shows that indicate promise of success or that have been successful elsewhere. As a result, Broadway drama has less richness and variety than it might have.

The theater reviews, particularly those of the New York newspapers, greatly influence the commercial success of a play. If all or most of the reviews criticize a play severely, the producer normally will close the show. If the play is the work of a well-known playwright, or has a major star, the advance sale of tickets may save it despite poor reviews. However, a play must be a big box-office hit to survive long on Broadway. Many productions close after only a few performances with great losses. On the other hand, some run for years, especially large, spectacular musicals. The "hit" or "flop" pattern has created a situation in which a play must be a great success financially, or it is considered a failure.

In the 1950's, *off-Broadway theater* developed in New York City from dissatisfaction with conditions on Broadway. Its purpose was to offer an alternative, more experimental theater and to present plays of greater artistic quality than those produced on Broadway. Most off-Broadway theaters were originally located in low-rent areas. Most had poorly equipped stages, limited seating, and few conveniences for the audience. The originality of the script, the creativeness of the performers, and the low cost of production made up for such disadvantages. By the 1960's, however, costs began to increase, and off-Broadway theater was too often being used to test commercial possibilities.

With the decline of off-Broadway, unknown artists began to present productions in storefront theaters and lofts. In these spaces, inventive plays and staging are still possible. This movement became known as *off-off-Broadway.* Since the mid-1960's, these theaters have become a major force in experimental drama. However, off-off-Broadway also is beginning to reflect commercial theater values and standards.

Theater outside New York City. Starting in the 1950's, resident acting companies were established in cities

Troy Mellott and Jay Thompson, Mark Taper Forum

The Mark Taper Forum in Los Angeles became noted for its productions of new works. *Stand-Up Tragedy, shown here,* deals with poor minority boys in a private New York City school.

© Lisa Ebright

The Steppenwolf Theatre led an explosion of regional theater activity in Chicago beginning in the 1970's. The Steppenwolf company gained recognition for its powerful productions of such modern dramas as *Orphans, shown here.*

The Alley Theatre in Houston became one of the first major regional theaters to emerge after World War II. It began in 1947 as an amateur theater and started using professional actors two years later. The theater emphasizes modern plays, such as *Who's Afraid of Virginia Woolf?, shown here,* by Edward Albee.

Alley Theatre

throughout the United States. In the 1960's, with the financial aid of the Ford Foundation and other organizations, these companies increased in number and reputation. Today, there are about 350 nonprofit professional theaters. During the late 1900's, many theaters closed because of economic pressures.

Most resident theaters perform in their own facilities. Many of them try to vary their programs with plays of different periods and styles. Some are dedicated to producing new plays. Usually, directors and performers are hired for a single production. Occasionally, they are employed for the entire season. Most resident theaters have a permanent administration, often including an artistic director and a managing director.

Most resident theaters operate *subscription seasons.* The theater offers prospective patrons a discount on ticket prices if they purchase seats for every play before the season begins. The subscription plan assures audiences of seats for every show at reduced prices. Subscription sales allow theaters to get a considerable amount of money before the season begins. This protects the institutions from severe financial loss if one or more of the season's shows is a failure. But even with a healthy subscription sale, the financial stability of many theaters remains a major concern. They still must rely heavily on financial support from government, which declined in the 1990's, and private sources, as well as individual patrons of the arts.

Nonprofessional theater groups exist throughout the United States. They include college and high school groups and community theaters.

College and high school theater. Many colleges and universities have theater and drama departments. They produce plays as part of the education of their students and as a service to the community. The best college theaters are organized administratively like resident professional companies. Because their purpose is educational, such theaters usually present standard works from earlier periods as well as more recent plays. Many theaters also produce original plays. Occasionally, a professional performer may appear in a production, but all-student casts are customary.

Almost all U.S. high schools have some kind of theater production program. The production of plays may be assigned to people untrained in the theater, with poor results. But a number of high schools have developed theater programs of excellent quality, supervised by qualified staffs. Many of these schools have superb facilities and offer courses in play production, dramatic literature, and related areas.

Community theater developed between 1900 and 1920. Today, there are more than 5,000 community theaters in the United States. The community theater not only provides entertainment for local audiences, but also furnishes an outlet for the creative talents of its members. Many community theaters employ a full-time director who supervises all productions. Many of these theaters are run exclusively by volunteers. Others pay the director of each production and also provide fees for the designer and chief technician. Most plays staged by community theaters are comedies and musicals.

Theater in other countries

Nearly all major cities have theater districts similar to Broadway in organization and appeal. Many productions are commercial enterprises supported by private investment. However, the theaters with the highest reputations are permanent organizations.

Canada, most European countries, and some Asian and African nations have several government-supported theaters. These theaters employ staffs of directors, performers, designers, and other creative people. Many state-supported theaters also hire performers, directors, and designers for single productions.

National Theatre production of *The Secret Rapture* (© Donald Cooper, Photostage)

Britain's Royal National Theatre is one of the leading theater companies in the world. The National stages classics of world drama as well as premieres of new works, such as the drama shown here by the modern English playwright David Hare.

A number of theaters operate in government-owned buildings and pay no rent. The government gives them an annual sum of money called a *subsidy.* A subsidy usually does not cover all production costs, but it supplements the income from ticket sales. The subsidy enables a theater to charge lower admission prices and provides protection against financial loss. Most subsidized companies produce a season of plays annually. Each play is performed for a limited time or in rotation with other plays. Some plays are presented at regular intervals through the years.

Canada has two strong theater traditions—French and English. The French-Canadian tradition began in 1606. The English theater in Canada developed in the mid-1700's. Among the prominent French-Canadian institutions are Le Théâtre du Nouveau Monde in Montreal and several companies in Manitoba, Toronto, and Quebec City. English-speaking Canada has several internationally known theater organizations. The Stratford Festival in Stratford, Ontario, began in 1953. It revolutionized theater in Canada and created a standard for professional theater in that country. The Shaw Festival in Niagara-on-the-Lake, Ontario, was founded in 1962. It emphasizes the production of plays by George Bernard Shaw and his contemporaries. There are also alternative theater festivals in many cities across the country devoted to experimentation or special interest groups.

Britain. The British government started to give subsi-

National Theatre of Norway

Theater in Scandinavia features the works of the major playwrights of Denmark, Sweden, and Norway. The National Theatre of Norway has presented revivals of plays by Henrik Ibsen, Norway's greatest dramatist and a founder of modern drama in the Western world. This scene is from Ibsen's early fantasy, *Peer Gynt.*

dies to the theater in the 1940's. In the late 1900's, however, subsidies were reduced. Many smaller theaters, especially outside London, lost most of their support. However, in the 1990's, money from a national lottery was used to renovate numerous theaters. The Royal National Theatre, which is still highly subsidized, is one of the world's outstanding companies. It was created in 1962 as an outgrowth of the Old Vic company. The Old Vic was formed in 1914 and gave its last performances in 1963. In 1976, the National Theatre moved into a new theater center in London built especially for it.

Another subsidized theater, the Royal Shakespeare Company, was created from the organization that produced the Stratford-upon-Avon Shakespeare Festival. It divides its company between London's Barbican Arts Centre and the Royal Shakespeare Theatre in Stratford. Of the smaller subsidized theaters in London, the English Stage Company at the Royal Court Theatre is the best known. Since 1956, it has introduced the works of many new dramatists. Several resident theaters in cities outside London receive subsidies from the local governments. One of the most prominent of these is the Royal Exchange Theatre in Manchester.

France. The world's oldest operating state theater is the Comédie-Française in Paris. It was founded in 1680. The Théâtre Nationale Populaire, the Odéon, and several other notable French theaters also receive government support. The state supports dramatic centers in such cities as Lyon, Marseille, Nice, Rennes, St.-Étienne, Strasbourg, Toulouse, and Tourcoing. The theatrical companies of many of these cities tour nearby communities. The state also subsidizes touring companies and summer drama festivals. But some of the most exciting work in French theater since the early 1980's has occurred at nonsubsidized theaters, such as Théâtre du Soleil.

Germany has the most extensive system of state-supported theaters in the world. It has several hundred theaters that are state-owned or city-owned. Many of its state-supported theaters date back to the late 1700's.

Almost every large German city has drama, opera, and ballet companies. All subsidized companies in a city generally operate under one manager appointed by the city or state. All the companies share a staff of directors and designers. Outstanding organizations include the Theater am Kurfürstendamm in Berlin. Since reunification in 1990, German theater has suffered economic difficulties for the first time since World War II ended in 1945.

Italy. The Italian theater operates differently than that of most European countries in that the most important Italian drama companies tour the larger cities of Italy. In addition, a small number of resident theaters are subsidized by city or provincial governments. The leading resident theaters are in Genoa, Milan, Rome, and Turin.

Scandinavia. There are major subsidized theaters in each of the Scandinavian countries. In Sweden, the most notable are the Royal Dramatic Theater in Stockholm and the city theater of Malmö. However, nonsubsidized groups called *free groups* have grown in number since 1970. Major subsidized theaters in Norway include the Norske Teatret. In the 1970's, five regional subsidized theaters opened. Most major theaters in Denmark are subsidized, including the Kongelige Teater and Folketeater in Copenhagen and provincial theaters in Århus, Alborg, and Odense. But an influential theater in Denmark is Odin Teatret, an international theatrical community founded in 1964 by Eugenio Barba, an expatriate Italian. Since 1966, Odin Teatret has been based in Holstebro.

Russia was part of the Soviet Union from 1922 to 1991. Before World War II (1939-1945), theater was generously subsidized by the Soviet government. Theater suffered a blow in 1946 when many subsidies were withdrawn and tight censorship was imposed. After Premier Joseph Stalin died in 1953, the government relaxed

Novosti from Sovfoto

The Maly Theatre is the oldest theater in Moscow. It features traditional Russian plays and classics. *Serfs, shown here,* by Pyotr Gnedich, explores the lives of the Russian aristocracy during the 1800's.

Scene from *You Never Can Tell* by George Bernard Shaw (David Cooper)

Theater in Canada has gained international recognition through the productions of the Stratford Festival and the Shaw Festival, both in Ontario. The Shaw Festival, *shown here,* features the works of British dramatist George Bernard Shaw and other playwrights of the late 1800's and early 1900's.

its censorship, and the variety of plays increased greatly.

Moscow and St. Petersburg are the two major theater centers in Russia. The Moscow Art Theater, founded in 1898, is perhaps the most respected theater in Russia. The Maly Theatre, founded in 1824, is the city's oldest theater. The Theater of the Revolution was founded in 1922 and renamed the Mayakovsky Theater in 1954 in honor of Vladimir Mayakovsky, a Russian writer. Newer theaters in Moscow include the Taganka, founded in 1946, and the Sovremennik, founded in 1958. In St. Petersburg, the Alexandrinsky Theater was opened in 1824 and was renamed the Pushkin Theater in honor of Alexander Pushkin, Russia's greatest poet. The other major St. Petersburg theater is the Gorky, founded in 1919 and named for Maxim Gorky, a modern Russian dramatist.

Training for the theater

There is much dispute over the proper way to train theater artists. Some argue that a general liberal arts education is preferable, with no theater training or with only basic theater courses included. Concentrated work in the theater arts would then follow at a more advanced level. Those who favor this method believe that liberal arts training is especially valuable for the study of theater and drama, which deal with all aspects of human experience. Others believe a general education is unnecessary, and that professional training should be taken from the start. Still others think liberal arts courses and professional training should be combined.

In certain areas, such as acting training, some argue that classes should begin at a very young age. Others believe that classes should begin after the student is of high school age.

Colleges and universities. Many colleges and universities provide some training in the theater arts. The majority of these institutions offer courses in dramatic literature and theory and theater history. But many educators believe that performance training, other than that at the most basic level, should take place in specialized graduate schools or professional training programs.

Other colleges and universities give academic credit for a wide range of theater courses, such as playwriting; acting; directing; pantomime; scene, costume, and lighting design; technical production; dance; stage movement; and even mask-making and theater management. The student may be expected to follow a course of study that provides a broad liberal arts education. Depending on the program, however, one-fourth to one-third or more of the course work may be devoted to the theater arts. Graduate programs may offer one to three additional years of intensive training or advanced education in history, theory, and criticism.

Professional training programs are offered by a number of universities. Such programs are also provided by conservatories and studios not connected with universities and by professional theater companies. Professional training programs normally allow students to spend most of their time on theater courses. Some schools give certificates for the completion of a prescribed program. Some programs offer advanced academic degrees. Other programs offer neither a certificate nor a degree. A student may simply enroll in any class for as long as he or she wishes.

Most professional training schools are in or near cities with professional theaters. Some of the best-known programs are operated by the American Conservatory Theater, the University of California at San Diego, New York University, the Juilliard School, the American Repertory Theatre, and the Yale School of Drama. For almost all the better training programs, auditions are necessary for acting students.

Professional training programs give performers intensive training but do not guarantee employment. Most beginning performers seek work in resident or alternative theater companies. It is often necessary to go to New York City to get started since many companies hire performers there. Many young performers move to Hollywood to try to find employment in motion pictures or television. The supply of performers always greatly exceeds the demand, and most find it difficult to establish a successful career in the theater. Don B. Wilmeth

Related articles. See **Drama** with its list of *Related articles.* See also the following:

American actors and actresses

Aldridge, Ira
Barrymore (family)
Booth, Edwin T.
Booth, John W.
Booth, Junius B.
Brando, Marlon
Brice, Fanny
Cohan, George M.
Fiske, Minnie Maddern
Fonda, Henry
Fonda, Jane
Fontanne, Lynn
Forrest, Edwin
Gillette, William
Gish, Dorothy
Gish, Lillian
Hayes, Helen
Hoffman, Dustin
Jefferson, Joseph
Laughton, Charles
Lindsay, Howard
Lunt, Alfred
Mansfield, Richard
Robeson, Paul
Rogers, Will
Russell, Lillian
Waters, Ethel
Welles, Orson

British actors and actresses

Anderson, Judith
Campbell, Mrs. Patrick
Coward, Noël
Dench, Judi
Garrick, David
Gielgud, John
Guinness, Alec
Gwyn, Nell
Kean, Edmund
Kemble, Fanny
Langtry, Lillie
Lillie, Beatrice
Macready, William C.
Olivier, Laurence
Redgrave, Michael
Siddons, Sarah K.
Terry, Ellen
Ustinov, Peter
Williams, Emlyn

Other actors and actresses

Barrault, Jean-Louis
Bernhardt, Sarah
Boucicault, Dion
Dietrich, Marlene
Duse, Eleonora
Roscius, Quintus
Thespis

Directors, producers, and designers

Belasco, David
Bergman, Ingmar
D'Oyly Carte, Richard
Granville-Barker, Harley
Guthrie, Tyrone
Hammerstein, Oscar, II
Kaufman, George S.
Kazan, Elia
Nichols, Mike
Reinhardt, Max
Stanislavski, Konstantin
Ziegfeld, Florenz

Other related articles

Burlesque
Dance
Europe (picture: Ancient Greek drama)
Globe Theatre
Method acting
Minstrel show
Moscow Art Theater
Motion picture
Musical comedy
Ontario (Annual events)
Opera
Operetta
Pantomime
Puppet
Shakespeare, William (The Elizabethan theater)
Vaudeville

Outline

I. Modern theater architecture
A. The auditorium
B. The stage
C. The behind-the-scenes spaces

II. The producer
A. Acquiring a script
B. Raising money
C. Obtaining a theater
D. Assembling a creative team
E. Keeping financial records

III. The director
A. Interpreting the script
B. Working with the designers
C. Casting
D. Rehearsing
E. The director's assistants

IV. The performers
A. Body and voice
B. Observation and imagination
C. Concentration
D. Systems of acting
E. Creating a role

V. Scene design
A. The scene designer
B. Kinds of scenery
C. Changing scenery
D. Properties and set dressing

VI. Lighting and sound
A. Lighting methods
B. Sound production

VII. Costumes and makeup
A. Costume design
B. Makeup techniques

VIII. Theater in the United States
A. Professional theater
B. Nonprofessional theater groups

IX. Theater in other countries
A. Canada
B. Britain
C. France
D. Germany
E. Italy
F. Scandinavia
G. Russia

X. Training for the theater
A. Colleges and universities
B. Professional training programs

Questions

What is a drop? a scrim? a cyclorama?
What is the difference between a proscenium stage and a theater-in-the-round?
What are the two chief systems of acting?
How can costumes help an audience understand a play?
What kinds of sound can be used in a play?
What is the difference between Broadway, off-Broadway, and off-off-Broadway?
What does the director need to know about a play?
What is the difference between *theater* and *drama?*
What is the oldest state theater in the world still operating?
What is a stage picture?

Additional resources

Banham, Martin, ed. *The Cambridge Guide to Theatre.* 2nd ed. Cambridge, 1995.
Bentley, Nancy, and Guthrie, Donna. *Putting on a Play.* Millbrook, 1996. Younger readers.
Brockett, Oscar G., and Hildy, F. J. *History of the Theatre.* 9th ed. Allyn & Bacon, 2002.
Field, Shelly. *Career Opportunities in Theater and the Performing Arts.* 2nd ed. Facts on File, 1999.
Kuritz, Paul. *Fundamental Acting.* Applause Theatre, 1998.
Lee, Robert L. *Everything About Theatre!* Meriwether, 1996.

Wilmeth, Don B., and Bigsby, Christopher, eds. *The Cambridge History of American Theatre.* 3 vols. Cambridge, 1998-2000.
Wilmeth, Don B., and Miller, T. L., eds. *Cambridge Guide to American Theatre.* 2nd ed. Cambridge, 1996.

Thebes, *theebz,* was a major religious center and the birthplace of many kings of ancient Egypt. The city was located along the Nile River at the site of what is now the city of Luxor. For location, see **Egypt, Ancient** (map).

Thebes was a village of little importance until a Theban prince of Dynasty XI became king of Egypt in 2052 B.C. A *dynasty* is a series of rulers in the same family. Theban kings expanded Egypt's empire to its greatest extent during Dynasty XVIII, from 1554 to 1304 B.C. The Theban god Amun-Re became the most important god in Egypt. Later, kings of Dynasties XIX and XX, who were not from Thebes, built tombs and temples in and near the city. The Romans destroyed Thebes in 29 B.C.

Theban temples still stand at Luxor and nearby Karnak. The ruins of funeral temples of Egyptian rulers lie across the Nile from Luxor. Many tombs of kings lie nearby in the so-called Valley of the Kings (see **Valley of the Kings**). Leonard H. Lesko

Thebes, *theebz,* was an ancient city in Boeotia, a region in central Greece. At one time, it was the most powerful city-state in all Greece, and the head of a confederacy of cities known as the Boeotian League. The city lay in the southeastern part of Boeotia, about 30 miles (48 kilometers) northwest of Athens (see **Greece, Ancient** [map]). According to ancient legends, Cadmus, a prince of Phoenicia, founded Thebes. The city appears in the Oedipus legends (see **Oedipus**).

The historical record of Thebes begins about 500 B.C., when the people of Thebes and of Plataea, another ancient Greek city, began to quarrel. Later, Thebes helped the Persians in their invasion of Greece in 480 B.C. As a result, Thebes became the most hated city in Greece. Thebes fought frequent wars with Athens. The most important of these was the Peloponnesian War, which began in 431 B.C., when a Theban force attacked Plataea. After this war, the Boeotian League fell to pieces under the tyrannical rule of Sparta. The league became important again between 379 and 374 B.C. through the patriotic efforts of Pelopidas. In 371 B.C., the Thebans, led by Epaminondas and Pelopidas, defeated the Spartans at Leuctra, and thus gained control over Greece.

When Epaminondas died in 362 B.C., Theban control of Greece ended. Macedonia, a country north of Greece, defeated Thebes and Athens at Chaeronea in 338 B.C. After this defeat, the exhausted Greek states came under the rule of Philip of Macedon and his son, Alexander the Great. The Thebans revolted against Alexander, and he punished them by destroying their city. Thebes was rebuilt in 316 B.C. and was important under the later Roman Empire. It thrived as a center of the silk trade during the A.D. 1000's and 1100's. Thebes began to decline when the Turks gained control of the city. The town of Thivai now stands on the site of Thebes. Linda J. Piper

See also **Boeotia; Cadmus; Pelopidas; Pindar.**

Theism, *THEE ihz uhm,* is belief in a god or gods. The term comes from the Greek word *theos,* meaning *god.* Theism plays an important role in most religions, but various faiths differ in their teachings about a god or gods. The followers of ancient Greek and Roman religions were *polytheistic*—that is, they worshiped more than one god. Today, the followers of most major religions are *monotheistic.* They accept only one god.

The words *theism* and *theistic* are used mainly in discussing religions that have one god. Such religions include Christianity, Islam, Judaism, and forms of Hinduism. These faiths stress the existence of an all-knowing and all-powerful god. This god may provide ways of life for people to follow and may offer people salvation.

Theism is also a type of philosophical belief. It supports the existence of a god, as opposed to *atheism,* which argues that no god exists. Theism also states that a god exists apart from the world. This concept differs from *pantheism,* the belief that a god exists in all forces of nature and the universe. Nancy E. Auer Falk

See also **Atheism; Deism; God; Polytheism; Religion** (Belief in a deity).

Themistocles, *thuh MIHS tuh KLEEZ* (514?-449? B.C.), was an Athenian statesman and soldier in the Persian wars. He saved Greece by his statesmanship and laid the base for Athens's greatness with his naval policy.

Little is known of Themistocles's early life. He began his political career in 490 B.C. after the Battle of Marathon and the retreat of the Persians. He opposed Aristides, who was then the leader of Athens. About 483 B.C., Themistocles defeated Aristides in a dispute over what was to be done with the silver from the mines at Laurium. Themistocles had always favored naval expansion and proposed that Athens use the silver to increase its fleet. Aristides was banished for opposing this plan, and Themistocles became the political leader of Athens.

Themistocles was certain that the Persians would attack again, but that this time the battle would be decided on the sea. Two years later, the Persians returned. At Thermopylae, they overwhelmed a Greek army led by Spartans under Leonidas. Themistocles then moved the Athenians to Salamis, where he engaged the Persians in battle. He destroyed the Persian fleet and forced the Persians to leave Athens. The following year, the allied Greeks completely defeated the Persians at Plataea.

Themistocles was ambitious and enjoyed taking chances. But many Athenians thought he was arrogant. Eventually, they became convinced that he was involved in disloyal dealings with foreign states. His enemies persuaded the people of Athens to exile him about 471 B.C. Themistocles spent his last years in Persia, where the Persian king gave him an estate. Jennifer Tolbert Roberts

See also **Aristides; Greece, Ancient** (The Persian Wars); **Salamis.**

Theocracy, *thee AHK ruh see,* is a form of government in which God, or a god, is recognized as the supreme ruler. The state may be ruled by priests or other religious leaders acting as God's representatives; by a king thought to have divine power; or by authorities governing according to religious laws. The word *theocracy* comes from two Greek words, *theos,* which means *God,* and *kratein,* which means *to rule.*

Many ancient peoples believed that their god or gods had handed down laws for their government. The famous Code of Hammurabi was supposed to have been divinely revealed. The most famous theocracy was that of the Israelites, who believed God gave them laws and rules—the Ten Commandments—through Moses.

The Puritan government of Massachusetts in the 1600's and 1700's has been called a theocracy. It was conducted for many years on the principle of obedience to divine law, as interpreted by the clergy, although the clergy did not actually control the government.

A few theocracies have existed in the modern world. For example, Iran has been a theocracy since 1979, when Ayatollah Ruhollah Khomeini, an Islamic religious leader, seized power. Today, members of the Islamic clergy hold key positions throughout the Iranian government. From the mid-1990's to 2001, an extremist group called the Taliban ruled Afghanistan according to their strict interpretations of Islam. Tom Mockaitis

Theocritus, *thee AHK rih tuhs* (200's B.C.), was a Greek poet who established the character of Greek pastoral poetry. Pastoral poetry deals with rural themes. Theocritus set the standard for pastoral poetry with his choice of themes, their lively presentation, and their emotional impact.

Thirty complete short poems attributed to Theocritus exist today. Many of them, called *idyls,* re-create conversations or singing contests among herders about such subjects as unreturned love, magic, and epic heroes. Theocritus presented these poems as dialogues, hymns, and short narratives (see **Idyl**). His influence can be seen especially in the *Eclogues* by the Roman poet Virgil.

Theocritus was probably born in Sicily. His search for a patron took him to Alexandria, Egypt. The library there made the city a center of literary activity. Theocritus perfected his writing under the influence of the Alexandrian librarian and poet Callimachus, an advocate of the short, highly polished poem. Joseph R. Tebben

See also **Greek literature** (The Hellenistic Age).

Theodora, *THEE uh DOHR uh* (A.D. 502?-548), was the wife of Justinian I, Byzantine (East Roman) emperor from 527 to 565. A beautiful and strong-willed woman, she tried to influence Justinian's policies and to use her position to advance her friends and ruin her enemies. In 532, a rebellion in the capital city of Constantinople threatened to overthrow the empire. Theodora persuaded Justinian to stay and defend the city rather than to flee. He crushed the rebels, thus securing his absolute power.

Theodora was probably born on Cyprus, to a poor family. She became an actress before marrying Justinian in 522, and was accused of numerous scandals, but many of them have been disproved. She founded homes for the care of poor girls. William G. Sinnigen

See also **Justinian I**.

Theodore Roosevelt National Park is in western North Dakota. The park's outstanding feature is a scenic badlands area along the Little Missouri River. In this area, water and wind erosion have carved deep gullies and steep hills into the landscape. The park includes a cattle ranch that President Theodore Roosevelt operated as a young man. A restored cabin where he once lived is a popular attraction. The area was established as a national memorial park in 1947 and became a national park in 1978. For the park's area, see **National Park System** (table: National parks). For its location, see **North Dakota** (political map). Critically reviewed by the National Park Service

Theodoric, *thee AHD uh rihk* (A.D. 455?-526), was an *Ostrogoth* (East Goth) king who governed Italy from A.D. 493 until his death. He won control of Italy from the barbarians who had taken it from the Romans 17 years earlier. Although a barbarian himself, Theodoric maintained a Roman form of government and Roman law in Italy. His rule was enlightened, peaceful, and just, and he won the praise of both barbarians and Romans. Theodoric let Romans hold high public office, and respected the senatorial class. He employed such prominent Romans as Boethius and Cassiodorus as his advisers and ministers of state. He believed in the Arian heresy, which denied the divinity of Christ. But he permitted his subjects to practice orthodox Christianity.

Theodoric was born in Pannonia, which included parts of what are now Austria, Hungary, and Slovenia. He spent several years in Constantinople (now Istanbul, Turkey). Constantinople was the capital of the Byzantine (East Roman) Empire. When his father, Ostrogoth king Theodemir, died in 471, Theodoric became king.

Theodoric alternately found himself an ally, then an enemy of the Byzantine emperors. He was a victim of a Byzantine plan to weaken barbarians by encouraging rivalries between them and then shifting support from one side to the other. In 488, Byzantine emperor Zeno commissioned Theodoric to attack Odoacer, the barbarian king of Italy. Theodoric invaded Italy in 489. Theodoric defeated Odoacer in 493, then murdered him. Germanic peoples remembered Theodoric in their legends as the heroic Dietrich of Bern. William G. Sinnigen

Theodosius I, *THEE uh DOH shee uhs* (A.D. 346-395), was a Roman emperor and military leader. He was born on Jan. 11, 346, in Spain. His father, a Roman general, was executed on unknown charges in 375, and Theodosius returned to Spain.

In 378, Emperor Gratian recalled Theodosius and asked him to help subdue the Visigoths, who were rebelling in the east. After he achieved some early victories, Gratian made Theodosius co-emperor, responsible for the eastern provinces of the Roman empire. The Visigoths proved difficult to conquer, and in 382 Theodosius signed a peace treaty with them.

When Gratian died in 383, Gratian's brother, Valentinian II, became emperor of the western provinces. Valentinian died in 392, and Eugenius, a civil servant, claimed control of the western provinces. Theodosius defeated Eugenius in 394 and became the last emperor to rule the entire empire. When Theodosius died on Jan. 17, 395, rule of the empire was split between his sons, Honorius and Arcadius.

In 391, Theodosius prohibited all *pagan* (non-Christian) practices in the Roman Empire. For this, later Christian writers referred to him as *The Great.* Robert Gurval

Theology, *thee AHL uh jee,* is the study and description of God. It may also be the expression of religious belief. The word *theology* comes from two Greek words meaning *god* and *discussion.* Theology explores a wide range of questions, such as: "Does God exist? What is the nature of God? What is God's relation to the world and to its inhabitants? and How do human beings know or experience God?" Some branches of theology deal with the history of religion or the study of sacred writings. Other branches deal with the defense of religious doctrines against opposing views or the application of doctrine to daily life.

Approaches to theology vary from one religion to another. They also vary within a religious tradition. For example, some Christian theologians base their understanding of God on such authoritative sources as the Bible and the decrees of church councils. Others explain their understanding of God in terms of philosophy, psychology, or science. In most cases, a theologian's own religious experience plays an important part in his or her theological system. Jerry A. Irish

See also **God; Religion.**

Theosophy, *thee AHS uh fee,* is a system of philosophic and religious thought. It is based on claims of a mystic insight into the nature of God and the laws of the universe. Theosophy holds that the truest knowledge comes not through reason or the senses, but through a direct communion of the soul with divine reality.

The term theosophy has been applied specifically to the beliefs and teachings of the Theosophical Society. This society was founded in the United States in 1875 by Madame Elena Petrovna Blavatsky and others. Hindu and Buddhist thought and doctrines have become prominent in theosophy. A characteristic feature is the belief in reincarnation, in accordance with the Hindu doctrines of Karma and Samsara. The spirit advances to its goal through a succession of earthly lives. These doctrines also state that the consequences of a person's actions in the present life are reaped by his or her successor on earth in a fresh incarnation. Charles H. Lippy

See also **Besant, Annie W.; Karma; Steiner, Rudolf.**

Theotokopoulos, Domenikos. See **Greco, El.**

Theremin, *THEHR uh mihn,* is one of the earliest electronic musical instruments. It is the only instrument that a musician can play without touching it.

The original theremin design resembles a large box or small desk. A rodlike antenna sticks out from the top on one side of the box, and a loop antenna projects from one side. The musician controls the theremin by moving his or her hands in electromagnetic fields around the antennas. The vertical antenna controls the pitch, and the horizontal antenna controls the volume.

The Russian scientist and inventor Leon Theremin (the Russian form of whose name was Lev Sergeyevich Termen) invented the theremin in Russia in the 1920's. One of the most widely known uses of the theremin was in the soundtrack for the 1945 motion picture *Spellbound.* Classical, rock, and pop musicians and composers have used the instrument. Sound effects artists employ the theremin in movies, television, and radio. Leon Theremin also used theremin circuitry in other inventions, including motion detectors that opened doors, turned on lights, and set off alarms. Lew Stedman

Theresa, Saint. See **Teresa, Saint.**

Thermal pollution occurs when hot wastewater is discharged into rivers, lakes, oceans, or other bodies of water. The wastewater raises the temperature of the body of water above its normal level and can harm animals and plants living in the water. For example, warmer water may interfere with fish growth, reproduction, and food supply. In some cases, fish may be killed due to the sudden and rapid rise in temperature.

The major sources of thermal pollution are factories and power plants that use water to cool equipment or heat it to produce steam. In the United States, the Environmental Protection Agency (EPA) has issued regulations controlling the wastewater discharged by these facilities. Many factories and power stations attempt to reduce thermal pollution by cooling wastewater in cooling towers before releasing it, thereby allowing heat to escape into the air. Industries can also reduce thermal pollution by releasing hot water in scattered areas in order to prevent a dangerous temperature rise in any one place. Richard N. L. Andrews

See also **Water pollution** (Industrial wastes).

Thermal springs. See **Hot springs.**

Thermocouple, *THUR moh KUHP uhl,* is an electric device that changes heat into electricity or electricity into heat. It is made by joining the ends of two different kinds of wire, such as iron and copper, to form a *junction.* The opposite ends are also joined to form another junction. If one junction is heated, an ammeter connected to one of the wires between the junctions will show a *thermoelectric* (heat-generated) current flowing. The German physicist T. J. Seebeck discovered this effect in 1821. If a battery instead of an ammeter is connected to the thermocouple, one junction will become hot and the other will become cool. This effect was first noticed by the French physicist J. C. A. Peltier in 1834.

Thermocouples are used as thermometers and to generate electricity. Some refrigeration devices use them. In a thermocouple used as a thermometer, one junction senses the temperature being measured, and the other provides the reference temperature. A voltmeter measures the voltage between the junctions and shows the temperature. Raymond D. Findlay

Thermodynamics, *THUR moh dy NAM ihks,* is the study of various forms of energy, such as heat and work, and of the conversion of energy from one form into another. Engineers, chemists, and physicists use the principles of thermodynamics in understanding events in nature and in such activities as designing machines and calculating energy loss or gain in chemical reactions.

Thermodynamics is based chiefly on two *laws* (principles). The first law states that energy in a *system,* which may be anything from a simple object to a complex machine, cannot be created or destroyed. Instead, energy is either converted from one form into another or transferred from one system to another. For example, a *heat engine,* such as a gas turbine or a nuclear reactor, changes energy from fuel into heat energy. It then converts the heat energy into mechanical energy that can be used to do work. The total amount of energy always remains the same. In addition, all systems have internal energy that undergoes certain changes but is never created or destroyed. Scientists study changes in this internal energy by measuring the differences in such properties as the volume, temperature, and pressure of the system.

The second law of thermodynamics deals with the natural direction of energy processes. For example, according to this law, heat will, of its own accord, flow only from a hotter object to a colder object. The second law accounts for the fact that a heat engine can never be completely efficient—that is, it cannot convert all the heat energy from its fuel into mechanical energy. Instead, the engine transfers some of its heat energy to colder objects in the surroundings. Robert F. Boehm

See also **Entropy; Heat** (Thermodynamics); **Clausius, Rudolf J. E.; Joule, James P.; Mayer, Julius R. von.**

Thermography, *thur MAHG ruh fee,* is a detection technique that converts invisible heat energy into a visible picture. A device called a *thermograph* is used to produce a *thermogram* (heat picture). Thermography is used in industry, medicine, and many other fields.

A thermograph looks like a TV camera connected to a

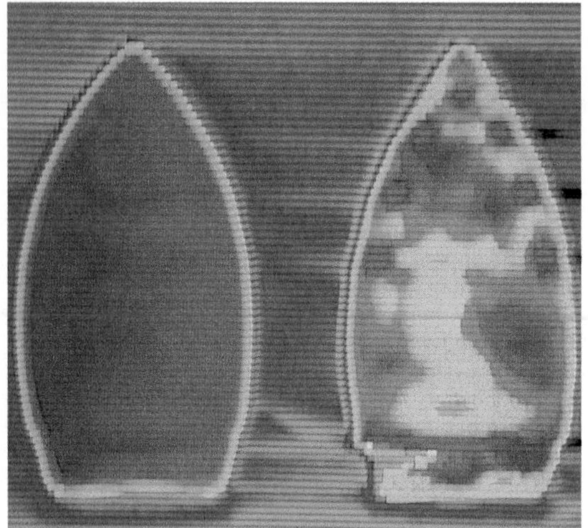

© Howard Sochurek

A thermogram of two irons shows the distribution of heat on their surfaces. The iron on the left has an even temperature. The iron on the right has hotter areas, which appear on the thermogram as light-orange, yellow, and purple.

TV screen. It "sees" temperature by sensing heat energy, called *infrared energy.* Infrared energy is radiated naturally by all objects, and hotter objects radiate more than cooler ones. Inside a thermograph, a solid-state detector converts infrared energy into electrical signals. The TV-like screen displays the signals as pictures. The pictures show different temperature ranges by variations of color or brightness. Scientists can analyze these variations.

Industrial uses of thermography include detecting overheated parts in electrical distribution systems and energy losses in manufacturing processes. The technique also is used to find leaks in the insulation of homes and other buildings. In addition, thermography provides a means of inspecting blast furnaces. A weak spot in a furnace wall is hotter than the surrounding areas, and so it appears lighter on a thermogram.

In medicine, thermography can reveal arthritis, nerve damage, and blood circulation problems. Physicians also use thermography, along with other tests, to confirm the presence of breast tumors.

Military and police forces and fire fighters use thermography to see in the dark and through smoke. Pollution control experts sometimes use the technique to determine the distribution of *thermal* (heat) pollution in bodies of water. Cliff Warren

See also **Energy supply** (picture: Reducing heat loss).

Thermometer is an instrument that measures the temperature of gases, liquids, and solids. As the temperature of a substance changes, some of its chemical and physical properties also change. For example, substances may change in color, shape, or volume. A thermometer measures one of these changes and usually displays the size of the change as a number. This number can be converted to a temperature value by using a suitable temperature scale. Such scales include the *Fahrenheit, Celsius,* and *Kelvin* scales.

This article divides thermometers into five principal types. These types are (1) thermal expansion thermometers, (2) thermocouple thermometers, (3) resistance thermometers, (4) radiation thermometers, and (5) liquid crystal thermometers.

Thermal expansion thermometers are the simplest and best-known thermometers. They measure changes in the volume of a substance as its temperature changes. The *air thermometer* was the oldest such thermometer. It was first used by European scientists in the 1500's and early 1600's. Air thermometers worked by measuring the length of a column of air in a glass tube open at one end. The open end of the tube was placed in a dish filled with water. As the temperature changed, air in the tube would expand or contract and move the water up or down the tube. A person could then estimate a temperature value based on the length of the air column.

By the mid-1600's, air thermometers were replaced by more accurate instruments called *liquid-in-glass thermometers.* These instruments are still widely used for cooking, taking body temperature, and many other functions. They contain a very thin, sealed glass tube partially filled with liquid. When the temperature of the liquid increases, it expands and rises up the narrow tube. A scale attached to the tube expresses the height of the liquid column as a temperature value. Mercury has been the most frequently used liquid in these thermometers. Alcohol is also commonly used. Because mercury is poisonous, many people prefer mercury-free thermometers.

Two other thermal expansion thermometers are *bimetallic thermometers* and *filled-system thermometers.* Bimetallic thermometers consist of a band made from strips of two different metals. The metals are bonded together and coiled. As the temperature of the bimetallic band rises, each metal strip expands at a different rate. This alters the curve of the band. Filled-system thermometers contain a curved, flexible metal tube filled with gas or liquid. A rise in temperature makes the filling expand. The curve of the tube then changes to make room for the increased volume of gas or liquid. In both bimetallic and filled-system thermometers, the motion of one end of the instrument moves an indicating device along an attached scale to show the temperature. Manufacturing industries commonly use both thermometers.

Thermocouple thermometers contain two wires of different metals. The wires are joined at both ends to form junctions, with one wire attached to an instrument called a *voltmeter.* When the two junctions are at different temperatures, a voltage develops between the wires. The voltage rises as the temperature difference between the junctions grows. The voltmeter then measures and displays the voltage, which can be converted to a temperature reading. Many in-

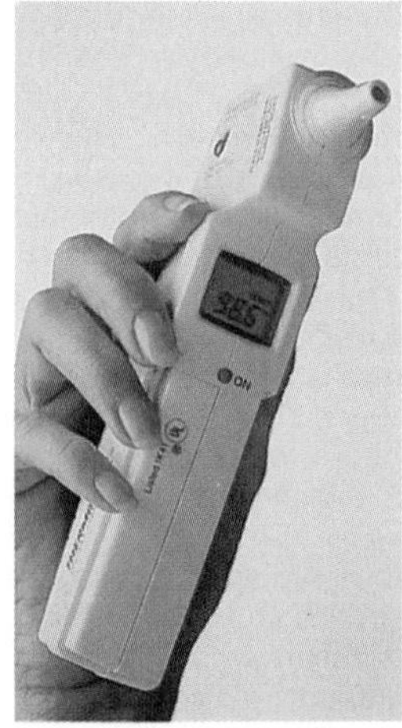

Thermoscan Inc.

An IR thermometer, or *infrared radiation thermometer,* can detect body temperature by measuring *infrared* (heat) rays from a person's eardrum. It displays the temperature value digitally.

dustries use thermocouple thermometers. These instruments can measure a much greater range of temperatures than other thermometers can.

Resistance thermometers indicate temperature by measuring a material's electrical *resistance*—that is, its opposition to the flow of electric current. Temperature changes cause variations in the amount of a material's resistance. Generally, the greater the temperature change, the greater the change in resistance. Resistance thermometers measure the resistance of *conductors* and *semiconductors,* substances through which electric currents flow easily. Examples of these materials include copper, platinum, silicon, and various metal compounds. The thermometers then convert the resistance measurement to a temperature value. Resistance thermometers are also used extensively in industry.

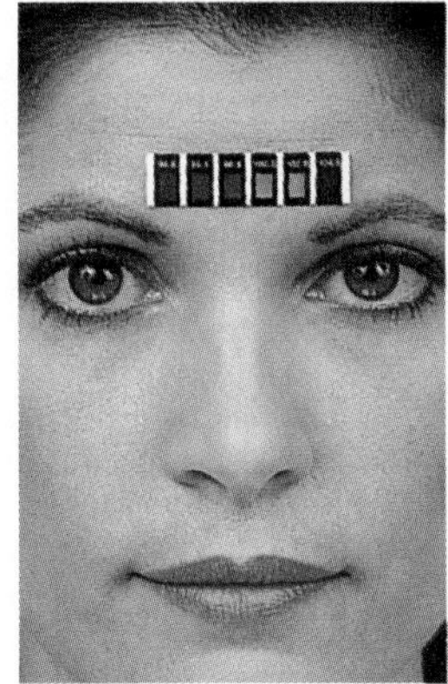

Hallcrest Products, Inc.

Liquid crystals are compounds that can indicate temperature by changing color. The thermometer above consists of liquid crystals applied to tape. The woman's temperature is shown over the box of crystals that turned green.

A common resistance thermometer is the *thermistor,* or *thermally sensitive resistor.* Thermistors often consist of a tiny beadlike semiconductor attached to wire connectors. Thermistors can be used in battery-powered digital thermometers, where they are attached to the end of a slender metal device called a *probe.* Digital thermometers electronically display temperature readings on a digital screen.

Radiation thermometers, also known as *pyrometers,* indicate temperature by detecting *electromagnetic radiation* (electric and magnetic energy). Every substance emits radiation in relation to its temperature. Radiation thermometers measure the radiation and convert the measurement to a temperature value.

A wide range of radiation thermometers exists. One of the most popular varieties is the *IR thermometer,* or *infrared radiation thermometer.* IR thermometers use electronic sensors to detect radiation from *infrared* (heat) rays. The thermometer then converts the measurement to a temperature reading. People use one type to take body temperature. This instrument measures temperature by detecting infrared rays from the eardrum.

Liquid crystal thermometers measure temperature by using *liquid crystals,* compounds that have properties of both liquids and solids. Some liquid crystals change color as the temperature changes. These color changes can be related to a temperature scale. Liquid crystal thermometers come in different forms. In many examples, the crystals are applied to strips of tape. Liquid crystal thermometers are often used in aquariums to check water temperature. Some people use them to measure body temperature. Melvyn C. Usselman

See also **Bolometer; Temperature; Thermocouple; Thermostat.**

Thermonuclear reaction. See Fusion.

Thermopylae, *thuhr MAHP uh lee,* was a mountain pass on the east coast of ancient Greece. It was the site of a famous battle between the Greek and Persian armies in 480 B.C. The Greek word *Thermopylae* means *Hot Gates* and refers to hot springs near the pass. Today, the area has eroded to a wide, marshy plain. But 2,500 years ago, the pass was only about 50 feet (15 meters) wide at its narrowest point and was the best place for travelers to pass into central Greece from the north.

In 480 B.C., King Xerxes I of Persia invaded Greece with a huge army and navy. Xerxes's army traveled along

Other types of thermometers

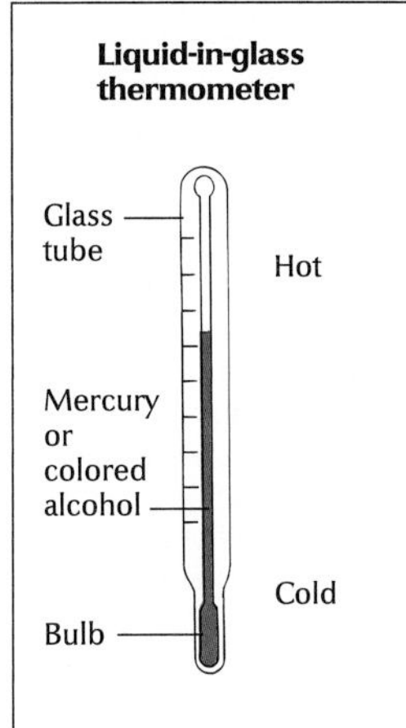

A column of liquid shows the temperature in a liquid-in-glass thermometer. The liquid in most such thermometers is mercury or colored alcohol.

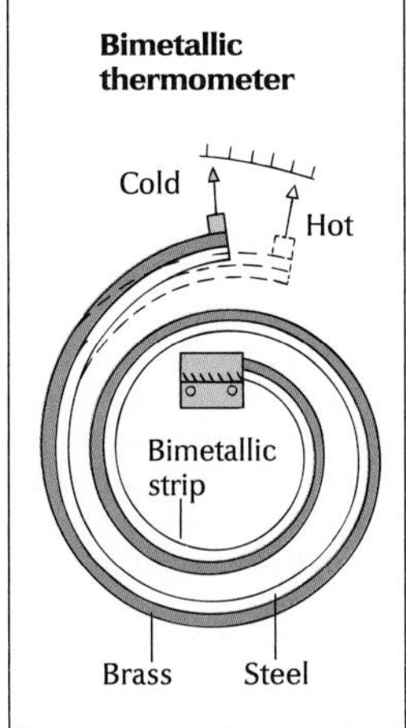

A bimetallic strip, consisting of two metals, can show temperature. As the temperature changes, the strip bends, indicating the temperature.

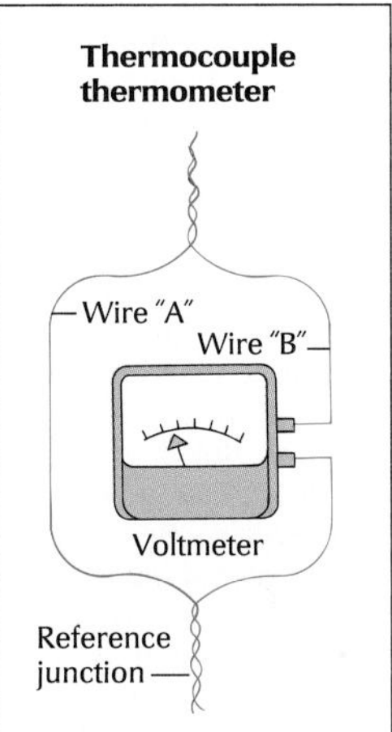

An electric voltage from a device called a *thermocouple* can be measured to show the temperature. A voltmeter measures the voltage.

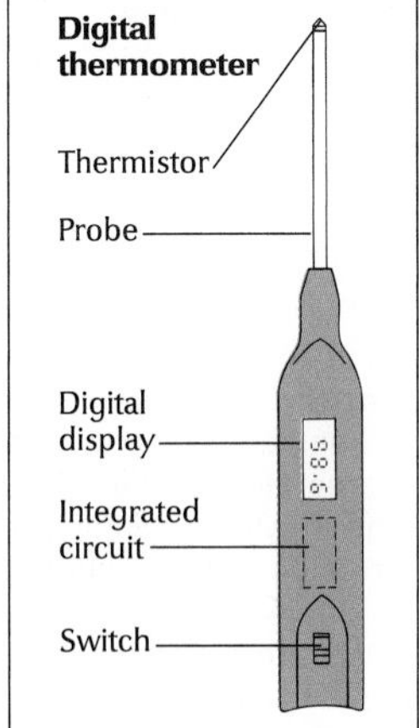

WORLD BOOK diagrams by Arthur Grebetz

This digital thermometer uses a thermistor to detect temperature electronically. The temperature value appears on the digital display window.

the coast intending to march through Thermopylae and into central Greece. The defending Greek army of as many as 10,000 men, including both soldiers and their servants, was much smaller than the Persian army. But the Greeks knew that a small army could successfully defend the narrow mountain pass. They hoped the Greek army, under the command of King Leonidas I of Sparta, would halt the advance of the Persians there.

Xerxes's soldiers attacked Thermopylae for two days, but the Greek army held them off. In the end, the Persians found a second mountain pass and attacked the Greeks from the rear. Before the Greeks were completely surrounded, Leonidas sent most of his troops inland to safety. But Leonidas, 300 other Spartans, and hundreds of other Greeks were killed defending Thermopylae. The two-day standoff at Thermopylae delayed the Persian army long enough for Greece to prepare for battle at the island of Salamis. The bravery of Leonidas and his soldiers inspired Greece to fight on to final victory against the Persians. Ronald P. Legon

See also **Greece, Ancient** (The Persian wars); **Leonidas I; Salamis; Xerxes I.**

Thermos bottle. See **Vacuum bottle.**

Thermosphere, *THUR muh sfihr,* is the uppermost temperature region of Earth's atmosphere. Scientists divide the atmosphere into four regions according to temperature: (1) the troposphere, (2) the stratosphere, (3) the mesosphere, and (4) the thermosphere. The thermosphere begins at the *mesopause* (the upper boundary of the mesosphere) at an average altitude of about 50 miles (80 kilometers). The thermosphere extends into space.

The air in the thermosphere is extremely thin. Molecules of nitrogen and molecules and atoms of oxygen make up most of the lower parts. At about 125 miles (200 kilometers), oxygen atoms begin to outnumber nitrogen molecules. Above about 620 miles (1000 kilometers), the thermosphere contains mainly hydrogen and helium.

Air temperatures in the thermosphere steadily rise with altitude because its upper parts absorb more radiation from the sun than its lower parts do. The temperature rises from about −130 °F (−90 °C) at an altitude of 50 miles (80 kilometers) to more than 2200 °F (1200 °C) at about 220 miles (350 kilometers). Daily and seasonal changes in solar activity cause the temperatures in the thermosphere to vary more than those in any other part of the atmosphere. The high temperatures in the upper thermosphere result from the rapid movement of atoms and molecules there. However, satellites and other spacecraft operate in the thermosphere without becoming hot. They stay cool because the air in the thermosphere is too thin to transfer much heat to objects.

Solar radiation and cosmic rays *ionize* (electrically charge) atoms in the upper atmosphere. The region of ionized particles, known as the *ionosphere,* extends through parts of the upper mesosphere and lower thermosphere. Atoms in the outermost region of the thermosphere, called the *exosphere,* can gain enough speed to escape the atmosphere. Joseph M. Moran

See also **Air** (The thermosphere); **Ionosphere.**

Thermostat, *THUR muh stat,* is a device that helps control the temperature of an indoor area or of an appliance. Thermostats are used in many kinds of equipment, including air conditioners, heaters, electric blankets, ovens, and refrigerators.

A thermostat is set to keep an area or an appliance at a certain temperature. It reacts to temperature changes and automatically controls the heating or cooling unit of the equipment being used. For example, the thermostat in a home heating system turns on the furnace if the temperature drops below the desired level. It shuts off the furnace when the temperature reaches that level.

How thermostats work. Most metals, liquids, and gases expand when their temperature increases. They contract when their temperature decreases. Some thermostats use such expansion and contraction to measure and control temperature.

Most thermostats used in home heaters and air conditioners have a *bimetallic strip* that "senses" changes in temperature. This strip consists of two dissimilar metals fastened together. When the temperature rises, each metal expands at a different rate, causing the strip to bend. The metals contract unequally when the temperature drops. These actions cause the strip to bend in the opposite direction. This action opens or closes the electric circuit that controls heating or cooling equipment.

Some thermostats use the expansion or contraction of a gas or a liquid to open or close a circuit. Other types use electronic detecting devices or infrared detectors that sense temperature changes.

Most thermostats turn heating or cooling equipment completely on or completely off. But some use a method called *proportional control.* These thermostats measure the difference between the actual temperature and the desired temperature. They change the amount of heating or cooling in proportion to this temperature difference. Proportional control thermostats can provide a nearly even temperature. They are used in industry and scientific research to control the temperature so that certain chemical processes can take place. The greatest precision can be achieved using proportional control along with other advanced controls that track the trend of temperature changes.

Uses. Thermostats control air-conditioning and heating systems in buildings to help keep people comfortable. Thermostats keep refrigerators and freezers at the necessary temperature to prevent food from spoiling. They also control the temperature of household ovens, irons, hot water heaters, and heaters for fish tanks.

Industries use thermostats to control the temperature needed for manufacturing certain products, such as plastics and frozen foods. Thermostats control the industrial furnaces used in making such products as bricks and steel. Thermostats also provide the precise temperature needed for many scientific experiments.

Thermostats also control the flow of water in automobile cooling systems. The thermostat operates a valve that opens when the water reaches a certain temperature. The open valve allows water to circulate through the radiator and through the water jacket that surrounds the engine. Qingyan Chen

Theropod. See **Dinosaur** (Saurischians).

Theroux, *thuh ROO,* **Paul** (1941-), an American author, became known for his novels and travel books. Much of Theroux's fiction and nonfiction explores Third World settings, such as Africa and Central America. His books often examine the impact of Third World societies on American or English characters.

Paul Edward Theroux was born on April 10, 1941, in

Medford, Massachusetts. From 1963 to 1965, he taught English in Malawi as a Peace Corps volunteer. Theroux then taught in Uganda from 1965 to 1968. Three of his early novels are set in Africa, *Fong and the Indians* (1968), *Girls at Play* (1969), and *Jungle Lovers* (1971). His novel *Saint Jack* (1973) is about an American in Singapore, where Theroux taught from 1968 to 1971. His other novels include *The Family Arsenal* (1976), *Picture Palace* (1978), *The Mosquito Coast* (1982), *Half Moon Street* (1984), *O-Zone* (1986), *My Secret History* (1989), *Chicago Loop* (1990), *Millroy the Magician* (1993), *My Other Life* (1996), *Kowloon Tong* (1997), and *Hotel Honolulu* (2001).

Theroux's first travel book, *The Great Railway Bazaar* (1975), describes a four-month railway journey the author took through Asia. Several of his other travel books also describe trips by railway, among other forms of transportation. These books include *Dark Star Safari* (2003), which is about a trip through Africa.

A collection of Theroux's essays was published as *Sunrise with Seamonsters: Travels and Discoveries, 1964-1984* (1985). Theroux's short stories have been published in *The Collected Stories* (1997) and *The Stranger at the Palazzo d'Oro* (2004). Arthur M. Saltzman

Theseus, *THEE see uhs* or *THEE soos,* was a great king of early Athens in Greek mythology. He was the son of King Aegeus and Aethra, a princess of Troezen. Aegeus left Aethra in Troezen and went back to Athens before Theseus was born. The king put his sword and sandals under a large rock and told Aethra that when their son could lift the rock, he should take the sword and sandals and come to him in Athens.

When Theseus was old enough to lift the rock, he set out for Athens. After he reached Athens, the sorceress Medea, now Aegeus's wife, tried to poison him. But Aegeus recognized Theseus's sword and saved his life.

According to the legend, Athens had to send seven youths and seven maidens to Crete every year in those days to be eaten by the Minotaur (see **Minotaur**). Theseus decided to go as one of the youths and try to kill the Minotaur. With the help of Ariadne, the daughter of King Minos of Crete, he succeeded, and so he saved his companions. Ariadne left Crete with him, but Theseus deserted her on the way back to Athens.

He had agreed with Aegeus that his ship would fly white sails if he should come back alive. Otherwise, the black sails with which the ship left Athens would not be changed. In his hurry, Theseus forgot to fly white sails. When Aegeus saw black sails on the returning ship, he killed himself, thinking Theseus had perished. Theseus then became the king of Athens. William F. Hansen

Thespis, *THEHS pihs,* a Greek actor and dramatist of the 500's B.C., helped to create drama as we know it. An actor is sometimes called a *Thespian,* after his name.

Thespis was a real person. But the ancient Greeks made him a legend and assigned several "firsts" to him. They said he was the first to use a speaker performing a role in dialogue with a choral group. Tragedy seems to have developed from this character-chorus dialogue, so the Greeks concluded that Thespis invented tragedy. The Greeks also credited Thespis with introducing makeup in the form of white lead paint and, later, masks to be worn by performers. However, it is more likely that he improved on the elements that already existed.

The "Parian Marble" inscription records that, in about 534 B.C. in Athens, Thespis won the prize at the first production of tragedies at the festival honoring the god Dionysus. Competitions in playwriting were held regularly at the festival after this time. Cynthia W. Shelmerdine

Thessalonians, *THEHS uh LOH nee uhnz,* **Epistles to the,** are the 13th and 14th books of the New Testament. They are both letters from the apostle Paul to Christians in Thessaloniki, Greece. Paul wrote the first letter from Corinth about A.D. 50. He wrote to encourage the Thessalonians in their struggles and to explain why he had not returned to visit them. Paul also explained that Christians who had died before the Second Coming of Jesus Christ would rise from the dead and be united with Jesus on the Coming. This letter is the earliest surviving letter of Paul and the earliest known Christian writing.

Some scholars doubt that Paul wrote the second letter. They believe it was written in his name by one of his followers. If Paul was the author, he wrote it shortly after writing the first letter. Its main purpose was to convince the Thessalonians that the Second Coming of Christ was not as near as they believed. Terrance D. Callan

See also **Bible** (The New Testament); **Paul, Saint**.

Thessaloniki, *THEHS ah law NEE kee* (pop. 385,406; met. area pop. 800,764), is Greece's second largest city, after Athens, and the capital of the country's Macedonia region. The city, also called Salonika, is a port on the Gulf of Thermai (see **Greece** [political map]).

Thessaloniki is a leading industrial center and has a modern business section. Its industries include chemical and steel plants, flour mills, foundries, shipyards, and textile mills that manufacture cotton, woolen, and silken goods. The city also produces tobacco, soap, and leather products. The port of Thessaloniki, opened in 1901, is a major Balkan outlet to the Aegean Sea. Chief exports are chemicals, cotton, fruits and vegetables, manganese and chromium ores, and tobacco. A univer-

© Yann Arthus-Bertrand, Corbis

Thessaloniki is the second largest city in Greece. Only Athens is larger. Thessaloniki lies on the Gulf of Thermai, in northern Greece. The city serves as a major port for the Balkan region.

sity and several research institutes are located in Thessaloniki.

Cassander, king of Macedonia, founded Thessaloniki in 316 or 315 B.C. by uniting the town of Therma with a number of nearby villages. He named the city after his wife. Thessaloniki has been ruled by almost every neighboring country. The Muslims invaded in A.D. 904 and sold 22,000 people into slavery. From 1430 until 1912, the city belonged to the Ottoman (Turkish) Empire. It fell to Greece in 1912 in the First Balkan War.

During World War I (1914-1918), the Allies used Thessaloniki as a base for campaigns. A fire destroyed the business section in 1917, but the area was rebuilt. The Germans occupied Thessaloniki from 1941 to 1944 during World War II, and it suffered considerable damage. Greek patriots freed the city in October 1944. The city's industries have expanded since the war, and new factories have been built. John J. Baxevanis

Thessaly, *THEHS uh lee,* is a region located in north-central Greece. It has an area of 5,368 square miles (13,903 square kilometers) and a population of about 734,000 people. Volos and Larisa are the largest cities in Thessaly. Three mountains that border the region—Olympus, Pelion, and Ossa—are important in Greek history and legend (see **Mount Olympus**). Thessaly is an important agricultural region of Greece. Its most important crops include cotton, olives, sugar beets, tobacco, vegetables, and wheat.

In legend, Thessaly was the home of the Greek warrior Achilles, and of Jason, who led the Argonauts in search of the golden fleece. The ancient Thessalians never banded together and so were weak militarily. In 344 B.C., Philip of Macedon conquered Thessaly. Later, the Romans took the area and added it to Macedonia in 146 B.C. Venice and the Ottoman Empire controlled Thessaly for hundreds of years. In 1881, Greece acquired Thessaly from the Ottomans. John J. Baxevanis

See also **Greece** (Thessaly).

WORLD BOOK map

Thessaly is a region in north-central Greece.

Thibault, Jacques A. F. See France, Anatole.

Thiers, *tyair,* **Louis Adolphe,** *lwee a DAWLF* (1797-1877), was the first president of the Third Republic of France. His 10-volume *History of the French Revolution* (1823-1827) made him famous. He helped place Louis Philippe on the throne of France.

Thiers's political life included terms as foreign minister and president of the council. He also wrote a *History of the Consulate and the Empire* (1845-1862). Emerging from retirement in 1870 during the Franco-Prussian War, he negotiated the peace treaty with Otto von Bismarck, Germany's chancellor. Thiers then put down the revolt of the Paris Commune and led the new republic until he resigned in 1873. He was born on April 18, 1797, in Marseille. William M. Reddy

See also **Franco-Prussian War.**

Thimphu, *THIHM poo,* also spelled *Thimbu* (pop. 40,000), is the capital of Bhutan. Thimphu lies on the Wong Chu, a river in western Bhutan. The city is 7,950 feet (2,423 meters) above sea level, but it is close enough to the equator to have mild temperatures. For the location of Thimphu, see **Bhutan** (map).

A remodeled monastery called Tashichhodzong, built in the 1200's, houses most government offices. It is also the residence of a group of Buddhist monks. The king lives in Dechenchholing Palace, north of the city. By law, buildings must fit in with traditional styles.

Shops sell Bhutanese textiles, jewelry, and other handicrafts. The central post office displays books of *commemorative stamps* (postage stamps honoring special people, places, and events), a principal export of Bhutan. Thimphu is also a trading center for lumber, rice, corn, and wheat. A highway connects Thimphu to India and to an airport in nearby Paro. James F. Fisher

Thiopental, *THY oh PEHN tal,* is a barbiturate used to produce sleep for surgery. It is a *general anesthetic*—that is, a drug that causes unconsciousness and loss of feeling in the entire body. The trade name of thiopental is Pentothal or Sodium Pentothal.

The use of thiopental as an anesthetic was first publicly demonstrated in 1934 by John S. Lundy at the Mayo Clinic. Thiopental anesthesia soon came into wide use. Today, thiopental is used to bring about anesthesia for surgery throughout the world.

Thiopental is usually administered by injection into a vein. Because receiving an injection is more pleasant for most patients than breathing the vapors of an inhaled anesthetic, physicians use thiopental to begin anesthesia for surgery. After the patient is asleep, physicians usually maintain anesthesia with nitrous oxide, halothane, or other inhaled anesthetics.

Psychiatrists sometimes give patients small doses of thiopental. The drug helps patients discuss their thoughts and emotions more freely. For this reason, thiopental is sometimes called a "truth serum."

Edwin S. Munson

Third Reich. See **Germany** (History); **Reich.**

Third World is a name sometimes given to economically developing countries, particularly those in Asia, Africa, and Latin America. The term *Third World* has also been used for politically neutral countries. Such countries have been called *neutral nations* or *nonaligned nations* because they did not regularly support either the First World or the Second World during the *Cold War.* The Cold War was a period of tension between non-Communist and Communist nations that began after World War II (1939-1945). The term *First World* referred to several non-Communist countries, including the United States, other Western industrial nations, and Japan. The term *Second World* referred to the Soviet Union and a number of other nations—especially in Eastern Europe—that had Communist governments during the Cold War. Some political experts considered China a Third World country, but others disagreed. The references to First World, Second World, and Third World began to lose their political meaning when Cold War tensions began to decrease sharply in the late 1980's.

The Third World consists of about 120 countries, which have more than half the world's population—even if China is not counted as a Third World nation. Most

Third World countries are former colonies of Western European nations and have gained their independence since 1960. Almost all have economies based on agriculture, and few have developed a significant base for modern industry. Many Third World countries export raw materials to industrial nations in exchange for manufactured goods. In addition, most Third World countries are poor. About 60 percent of the people in the Third World live in extreme poverty.

During the 1960's, Third World countries began to use the United Nations (UN) to promote their interests. Today, the Third World has a majority of the votes in the General Assembly of the United Nations.

Since the mid-1970's, Third World countries increasingly have emphasized their economic problems. They demand financial aid and favorable trade agreements from the industrial countries to redistribute the earth's wealth. They consider the economic differences between developed and developing countries more important than political differences. For this reason, they prefer the terms *North* for the wealthy nations and *South* for themselves, rather than First, Second, or Third World. Most Third World nations are south of most industrial nations.

Since the end of the Cold War, support of Third World countries has become less important to the First World and Second World than it had been before. Partly as a result, richer nations have increasingly rejected demands by Third World countries for aid. Furthermore, the Eastern European nations and the republics of the former Soviet Union have begun to compete with Third World countries for aid from the First World. The World Bank and other international organizations provide funds for development in the Third World. However, progress has been slow because Third World countries continue to suffer from rapid population growth and high rates of disease and illiteracy. W. Scott Thompson

See also **Developing country.**

Thirst is a perception associated with the body's need for water. The body's *internal environment* (the organs and tissues) requires certain amounts of water and mineral salts to function properly. Too much or too little water or salt can damage or destroy cells. Therefore, people and animals must control the balance of water and salt within their bodies. This balance is maintained mainly through the kidneys, which remove water and salts as urine, and the behaviors associated with seeking out and consuming water and other liquids.

People often describe thirst as a dry feeling in the throat. A lack of sufficient saliva can produce this kind of thirst, even when the internal environment has no need for water. In a similar way, the thirst sensation created by the internal environment's need will disappear briefly if water is drunk and wets the throat. But unless the water reaches the internal environment, thirst will recur after a short time.

Sensory nerves in the internal organs and *receptors* (sensors) in the brain are affected by the volume of fluid both inside and outside of the body's cells. These internal sensors detect the amount of water and salt present in different parts of the body (see **Senses**). The information is conveyed to the brain through chemical and nerve signals. Such information affects a region of the brain stem called the *hypothalamus.* The hypothalamus is important in maintaining the internal environment. Nerve activity in portions of the hypothalamus and other parts of the brain is associated with motivation to seek out and consume water. This motivational state is referred to as thirst. Alan Kim Johnson

Thirteen Colonies. See **Colonial life in America; United States, History of the.**

Thirty-Nine Articles were a statement of doctrine issued in England in 1563 and approved by Parliament in 1571. The Articles were created to settle religious disputes caused by the Protestant Reformation. The Articles set forth religious positions that all English people were expected to accept. They remain the doctrine of the churches of the Anglican Communion.

The Articles set the Church of England on a middle ground between the Roman Catholic Church and radical Protestant groups. They condemned several Roman Catholic beliefs and practices, including purgatory, transubstantiation, reverence for saints and relics, indulgences, and the power of the pope. The Articles affirmed the doctrine of predestination—that people are saved solely by God's grace and cannot earn salvation by good deeds. The doctrine of free will was rejected. Contrary to the beliefs of the radicals, the Articles declared that Christians must obey *secular* (nonreligious) governments and could bear arms for the state. They also affirmed infant baptism, rather than the adult baptism practiced by the Anabaptists (see **Anabaptists**).

Some Christians in England who later were called Puritans did not think that the Thirty-Nine Articles went far enough in opposing Roman Catholic doctrine. However, most of the English people accepted the Articles, and the clergy of the Church of England still endorse them.
M. U. Edwards

Thirty Tyrants were 30 Athenians elected to replace the democratic government of Athens after the city surrendered to Sparta in 404 B.C. The politician Critias was their leader. They took steps to make Athens more like Sparta, such as limiting citizenship to 3,000 men. When they were slow to produce a promised new constitution, open resistance to their rule began. They responded by bringing in Spartan soldiers to crush uprisings and by taking weapons away from Athenians. But resistance continued until the Spartan king Pausanias forced a settlement. In 403 B.C., the reign of the Thirty ended, and the new leader declared an *amnesty* (pardon) for all citizens except the Thirty and a few others. These events made Critias's nephew Plato decide against a political career and devote his life to philosophy. Peter Krentz

Thirty Years' War (1618-1648) was a series of religious and political wars that eventually involved most European nations. The conflict began as a civil war between Protestants and Roman Catholics in the Holy Roman Empire and other territories under the administration of the Habsburgs, the royal family of Austria. But before the war ended, it had become a general struggle for territory and political power.

Causes of the war. The underlying cause of the war was the old deep-seated hostility between Protestants and Catholics in central Europe and in the Holy Roman Empire, a German-based empire that included what are now Germany, Austria, and parts of Italy and the Czech Republic. The Protestants and Catholics disagreed in their interpretation of the Peace of Augsburg (1555), which had been intended as a settlement of the religious question in the Holy Roman Empire. Both groups had violated the peace. In addition, the Peace of Augsburg had recognized only Catholics and Lutherans. There were many Calvinists and other Protestants in southern and central Germany, and they also demanded recognition.

The Bohemian period (1618-1624). A conflict over constitutional liberties between Protestants in Bohemia (now the western part of the Czech Republic) and their Roman Catholic rulers led to the war. But the spark that ignited the fighting came when the archbishop of Prague, the capital of Bohemia, ordered a Protestant church destroyed. In anger, the people appealed to Holy Roman Emperor Matthias, who ignored their protests. The Protestants revolted in May 1618 to defend their constitutional privileges. The rebels threw two of the emperor's officials out a window in what became known as the Defenestration of Prague. Protestants in central Europe sided with the Bohemian rebels.

The Bohemian Protestants removed the Catholic king of Bohemia, Ferdinand, from the throne, and chose the Protestant Frederick, *elector* (prince) of the Palatinate, an area in Germany, in Ferdinand's place. But in 1619, Ferdinand was chosen Holy Roman emperor. Ferdinand—who took the title Ferdinand II—had great power in this position. In 1620, his general, Johan Tserclaes, Count of Tilly, decisively defeated the Bohemians in the Battle of the White Mountain. This defeat cost the Bohemians their independence, and Catholicism again became the state religion.

The Danish period (1625-1629). After Bohemia was defeated, the other Protestant countries began to realize their danger. The Protestant king of Denmark, Christian IV, aided by several other countries, opposed Ferdinand's forces in Saxony (now northern Germany). But the emperor had received unexpected help from the famous General Albrecht von Wallenstein, who had a large army of hired soldiers and adventurers.

Wallenstein's army, aided by forces of the Holy League, a military alliance of German Catholic states under the leadership of General Tilly, defeated the Danish king again and again. Christian IV signed the Treaty of Lübeck (1629) and withdrew from Saxony. Meanwhile, the emperor had issued the Edict of Restitution. It provided that all church possessions that the Protestants had acquired be returned to the Catholics. The Edict of Restitution marked the height of the emperor's power. But it forced other leaders in the empire to oppose him because he had issued the edict without consulting them.

The Swedish period (1630-1634). The Swedish king, Gustavus Adolphus, was devoted to the cause of Protestantism. He was also ambitious for Sweden, which would be in danger if Ferdinand became too powerful. So, for the first time, a major political issue entered the war. In 1630, Gustavus Adolphus set sail from Sweden with 13,000 men to relieve the city of Magdeburg, Germany, which Tilly was besieging. The Swedish king had the best-trained and best-disciplined army in Europe, but he arrived too late to prevent the capture, looting, and destruction of the city. In 1631, the Swedish army defeated Tilly in the Battle of Breitenfeld. Afterward, the Swedish forces won another important battle, and Tilly was killed in the fighting.

Emperor Ferdinand now called back Wallenstein, whom he had dismissed. Another army of recruits was gathered from many parts of Europe and placed under Wallenstein's leadership. In addition, Ferdinand made an alliance with Philip IV of Spain. Wallenstein's army met the Swedish forces in the Battle of Lützen (1632). The Swedes won, but Gustavus Adolphus was killed in the battle.

The Swedes continued the struggle until 1634, when their army was destroyed in the Battle of Nördlingen. The emperor suspected that Wallenstein was negotiating with the Protestants and ordered his arrest. Wallenstein tried to escape but was assassinated.

The Swedish-French period (1635-1648). The war now lost most of its religious character and became largely political. Cardinal Richelieu, who ruled France through King Louis XIII, determined to block the growth of Habsburg power by interfering on the side of the Protestants. The war became a struggle between the royal Bourbon family of France and the Austrian Habsburgs. In 1635, Richelieu sent a French army into Germany, where it joined a Swedish army. The combined armies won a long series of battles, giving new hope to the Protestants in Germany.

The Peace of Westphalia (1648). For years the people of the Holy Roman Empire had suffered misery and hardship because of the Thirty Years' War. In 1644, the European countries sent representatives to a peace conference. The Catholic and Protestant delegates met separately in two different cities of Westphalia (now western Germany). The negotiations dragged on for four years, until the Peace of Westphalia was signed in 1648. By this treaty, France acquired Alsace and Lorraine; and Sweden got control of the mouths of the Oder, Elbe, and Weser rivers. Also as a result of the treaty, Calvinism was put on an equal footing with Catholicism and Lutheranism.

Results of the war. The empire was in a pitiable condition by the time the war ended. Many people had been killed. Whole cities, villages, and farms had disappeared, and much property had been destroyed. Art, science, trade, and industry declined. It took almost 200 years for the German territories to recover from the effects of the war. Phillip N. Bebb

See also **Gustavus Adolphus; Richelieu, Cardinal; Wallenstein, Albrecht W. E. von; Tilly, Count of.**

Thisbe. See **Pyramus and Thisbe.**

Thistle is the name given to a group of plants that have sharp spines or prickles. Thistles are often troublesome weeds. They grow in many places throughout the world. The most common thistles are the *Canada thistle,* the *bull thistle,* the *tall thistle,* and the *pasture thistle.* The first two come from Europe, and the last two are native to North America. They grow in pastures and grain and hay fields, and along roads, where the soil is rich. The most troublesome, the Canada thistle, is a perennial. The other three species are biennial.

Thistles have tough, fibrous stems, prickly leaves with many lobes, and soft, silky flowers, usually purple or pinkish-purple in color. The flowers usually grow in round heads that form large, downy seed balls after the blossoms wither. The wind scatters the seeds, and this helps the thistles multiply rapidly. Some kinds have strong roots and are hard to uproot. Root pieces left in the soil may produce new plants. Thistles are very hard to remove from grainfields. Biennial species must be cut down before the flowers bloom. Chemicals that kill thistles but do not harm crops also can be used.

A number of plants similar to thistles are sometimes called thistles. Included among these is the *Russian thistle* or *tumbleweed.* This plant has become a serious pest in large areas of North America. Anton A. Reznicek

Scientific classification. Thistles belong to the composite family, Compositae. The most important genera of thistles include *Carduus, Cirsium,* and *Onopordum.* The Canada thistle is *Cirsium arvense;* the bull, or common, thistle, *C. vulgare;* the tall thistle, *C. altissimum;* and the pasture thistle, *C. pumilum.*

See also **Canada thistle; Composite family; Sowthistle; Tumbleweed.**

Thomas, Clarence (1948-), became an associate justice of the Supreme Court of the United States in 1991. He was the second African American to serve on the court. Thurgood Marshall had been the first. President George H. W. Bush nominated Thomas to fill the vacancy created by Marshall's retirement.

As a Supreme Court justice, Thomas's judgments on key issues, including civil rights matters, have been conservative. His views contrast sharply with those of Marshall, who was considered a liberal.

Thomas was born on June 23, 1948, in Pin Point, Georgia. He graduated from the College of the Holy Cross in 1971 and received a law degree from Yale Law School in 1974. He served as an assistant attorney general for the state of Missouri from 1974 to 1977. He then held a series of other government and legal positions, including that of secretary for civil rights in the United States Department of Education in 1981 and 1982.

In May 1982, Thomas became chairman of the United States Equal Employment Opportunity Commission (EEOC). As chairman of the EEOC, Thomas generated controversy by his outspoken opposition to *affirmative-action programs,* which are designed to remedy the effects of past discrimination against such groups as women and minorities. In 1990, Bush appointed Thomas to the United States Court of Appeals for the District of Columbia.

In 1991, during U.S. Senate hearings to confirm Thomas's nomination to the Supreme Court, many senators accused Thomas of trying to downplay his conservative views. The confirmation process became one of the bitterest in history after Anita F. Hill, a law professor at the University of Oklahoma, accused Thomas of having sexually harassed her when he was her supervisor at the Department of Education and at the EEOC. Thomas denied the charges. Following days of televised hearings, the Senate voted to confirm Thomas by the narrow margin of 52 to 48. Dennis J. Hutchinson

See also **Supreme Court of the United States** (picture).

Thomas, Dylan, *DIHL uhn* (1914-1953), was a Welsh poet who wrote some of the most stirring, passionate, and eloquent verse in modern literature. From the publication of his first book, *Eighteen Poems* (1934), critics recognized him as a brilliant and original poet. The volume bewildered and fascinated readers with its extraordinary verbal and musical energy and with its exploration of emotional extremes. These extremes, alternately ecstatic and morbid, revealed Thomas's obsessions with love, death, religion, and the sound of words. His later verse was collected in *Deaths and Entrances* (1946), which included his well-known poem "Fern Hill."

Thomas's love of life and exuberant sense of humor are revealed in his prose fiction and drama as well as in his verse. *Portrait of the Artist as a Young Dog* (1940) is a collection of stories about Thomas's youth in Wales. A group of his symbolic stories was published as *Adventures in the Skin Trade* in 1955, after his death. *The Collected Stories of Dylan Thomas* was published in 1984. Just before his death, Thomas completed a radio play, *Under Milk Wood.* In this play, he tenderly describes a day in the life of eccentric residents of a Welsh village.

Thomas was born on Oct. 27, 1914, in Swansea. He gained great popularity through public readings of his works in the United Kingdom and the United States. Thomas died of pneumonia aggravated by acute alcoholism while he was on a tour of the United States.

William Harmon

Additional resources

Bold, Alan, ed. *Dylan Thomas.* St. Martin's, 1990.
Davies, James A. *A Reference Companion to Dylan Thomas.* Greenwood, 1998.
Ferris, Paul. *Dylan Thomas.* Rev. ed. Counterpoint Pr., 1999.
Sinclair, Andrew. *Dylan the Bard: A Life of Dylan Thomas.* Thomas Dunne, 2000.

Thomas, Isaiah, *eye ZAY uh* (1749-1831), was the leading printer and publisher in colonial America. His Boston newspaper, the *Massachusetts Spy,* printed strong attacks on the British government.

Thomas was born on Jan. 19, 1749, in Boston and became a printer's apprentice there. He began to publish the *Spy* in 1770. In 1775, he aided Paul Revere in his famous midnight ride and fought at Lexington and Concord in the opening battles of the Revolutionary War in America (1775-1783). Thomas later printed books and magazines, as well as his newspaper. He wrote a book, *The History of Printing in America* (1810), which still ranks as an important work. William Morgan Fowler, Jr.

Thomas, Martha Carey (1857-1935), was an American educator and activist who fought for educational opportunities and voting rights for women. In 1885, Carey Thomas, as she preferred to be known, became dean and English professor at Bryn Mawr College, a women's school in Bryn Mawr, Pennsylvania. Thomas served as president of the college from 1894 to 1922. She worked to make Bryn Mawr as good as the best men's colleges. She set high entrance requirements, hired outstanding teachers, and established a demanding course of study.

Thomas was born on Jan. 2, 1857, in Baltimore and graduated from Cornell University in 1877. She went to Europe for further study because few United States graduate schools would admit women. In 1882, she earned a Ph.D. at the University of Zurich. In 1893, Thomas helped bring about the admission of women to the medical school at Johns Hopkins University. She was also president of the National College Equal Suffrage League from 1908 to 1917. Michele S. Moses

Thomas, Norman Mattoon, *muh TOON* (1884-1968), was an American pacifist and Socialist leader. He ran six times as the Socialist Party candidate for the presidency of the United States. Thomas founded the periodical *World Tomorrow* in 1918. He also helped establish the American Civil Liberties Union.

Thomas was born in Marion, Ohio, on Nov. 20, 1884. He studied at Princeton University and at the Union Theological Seminary. During the 1920's, he ran for mayor of New York City and for governor of New York. He first ran for president in 1928. Thomas was at first somewhat sympathetic to Soviet Communism, but by the mid-1930's he opposed both Soviet Communism and Marxism. He opposed U.S. involvement in World War I (1914-1918), and he later tried to keep the United States out of World War II (1939-1945). But after the Japanese attack on Pearl Harbor in 1941, he supported the war effort. Thomas also wrote several books, including *As I See It* (1932) and *A Socialist Faith* (1951). Stephen Schneck

Thomas, Saint, was one of the 12 apostles of Jesus Christ. He is mentioned often in the Gospel of John, where he is also called *Didymus,* which means *the Twin* in Greek. Thomas encouraged the apostles to go with Jesus into Judea, despite the danger of persecution (John 11:16). When Jesus spoke of His death and Resurrection at the Last Supper, Thomas wanted to know how he and the other apostles could follow Him (John 14:5). Thomas is also known as "Doubting Thomas" because he refused to believe the report of Jesus's Resurrection unless he could touch His wounds (John 20:24, 25). When Jesus allowed him to feel His hands and His side, Thomas became a believer, saying, "My Lord and my God" (John 20:26-29).

According to tradition, Thomas preached in Parthia or India. He was reportedly martyred in India. His feast day in the Roman Catholic Church is July 3. The Eastern Orthodox Churches celebrate his feast on the first Sunday after their Easter celebration. Richard A. Edwards

See also **Apostles.**

Thomas à Becket. See **Becket, Saint Thomas.**

Thomas à Kempis (1380?-1471) was a late medieval Christian spiritual writer. He is considered the author of the *Imitation of Christ,* one of the most widely read works of Christian literature after the Bible. The work first appeared in manuscript form about 1424.

The author wrote the *Imitation* in four parts. The first discusses what is necessary for a spiritual life. The second deals with the role of suffering in Christian life. The third discusses the consolation of being centered in Christ. The final part urges devotion to the Eucharist.

According to the *Imitation,* friendship with God can be obtained only by following the spirit and actions of Jesus Christ. Grace, it teaches, comes through prayer, contemplation, the sacraments, and detachment from worldly goods. The work stresses the importance of humility, penitence, and personal discipline for progress in the spiritual life. Sources for the *Imitation* include the Bible and early Christian authors.

Thomas was born in Kempen, near Düsseldorf, Germany. He was ordained a priest in 1413. As a scholar, Thomas copied countless manuscripts, including the Bible. His devotional works include lives of saints and books of sermons. He died on Aug. 8, 1471. Neil J. Roy

Thomas Aquinas, Saint. See **Aquinas, Saint Thomas.**

Thompson, Manitoba (pop. 13,256), is one of the world's leading centers of nickel production. It lies on the Burntwood River, in north-central Manitoba (see **Manitoba** [political map]). Thompson is the province's third largest city, after Winnipeg and Brandon.

Thompson was founded in 1956, following the discovery of a huge deposit of nickel ore in the area by Inco Limited (then called the International Nickel Company of Canada, Limited). The city was named after John F. Thompson, chairman of the company at that time. The first permanent residents arrived in 1958.

Inco Limited built a huge nickel-producing complex in Thompson. This facility was the first in the world to handle all the processes of nickel production, from mining through refining. Production began in 1961. Inco Limited is Thompson's largest employer.

Thompson is also a government and transportation center for northern Manitoba. Airlines and freight and passenger trains serve the city. Thompson has a mayor-council form of government. Grant Wright

Thompson, Benjamin (1753-1814), was an American-born British scientist and soldier. He conducted experiments showing that heat is not a material substance, disproving what was a common belief at the time. As military commander in Bavaria, now part of Germany, Thompson worked to improve the living conditions of the poor in the city of Munich. This effort gained him the title of Count Rumford in 1791. In 1799, he founded the Royal Institution of Great Britain, an organization that sponsors science lectures and discussions. Thompson was born on March 26, 1753, in Woburn, Massachusetts. Richard G. Olson

Thompson, David (1770-1857), was a Canadian explorer, cartographer, and fur trader. He was the first white person to travel the Columbia River from its source to its mouth. He explored extensive areas of Canada, including the Saskatchewan River system and the western plains, and surveyed the northernmost source of the Mississippi River. From 1816 to 1826, he was a surveyor on the boundary between the United States and Canada. He made an important early map of northwestern North America. He described his explorations in *David Thompson's Narrative.*

Thompson was born on April 30, 1770, in Westminster, England, and was apprenticed to the Hudson's Bay Company when he was 14 years old. He worked for the North West Company from 1797 to 1812. He died on Feb. 10, 1857. Barry M. Gough

Thompson, Francis (1859-1907), was an English poet whose emotional poems reflect his intense Roman Catholic faith. His most famous work is "The Hound of Heaven" (1893). This poem represents Jesus Christ as a kind hunter who pursues and finally captures the fleeing soul of the poet. Thompson's intensity and bold imagery are closer to the poets of the 1600's than to those of his own time. Thompson also became noted for his prose writings, especially his literary criticism.

Francis Joseph Thompson was born on Dec. 18, 1859, in Preston. At the age of 11, he began studying to become a priest but stopped his training six years later. His parents then expected him to become a doctor like his father, but Thompson disliked medical school and gave up medicine for poetry. He cut himself off from his family and settled in London in 1885. There he suffered from illness and extreme poverty and eventually became addicted to opium. He was befriended by the writers Alice and Wilfred Meynell, who helped him overcome his addiction. Jerome Bump

Sir John Sparrow David Thompson

Prime minister of Canada
1892-1894

Abbott
1891-1892

Thompson
1892-1894

Bowell
1894-1896

Detail of a portrait by J. W. L. Forster; Parliament Buildings, Ottawa (John Evans)

Thompson, Sir John Sparrow David (1844-1894), served as the fourth prime minister of Canada from 1892 until his death two years later. He was the first Nova Scotian to hold that office. Thompson, a Conservative, became prime minister during a period of difficulty for his party following the death of Sir John A. Macdonald. Macdonald, the first prime minister of the Dominion of Canada, had led the Conservative Party from 1867 until he died in 1891.

Thompson practiced law for several years before he entered politics in 1872. In 1882, he accepted Macdonald's offer of an appointment to the Nova Scotia Supreme Court. Three years later, after some persuasion, Thompson joined Macdonald's Cabinet as minister of justice.

Thompson's honesty and his ability to combine the roles of lawyer and statesman earned wide respect. He gained fame as a skillful diplomat and helped negotiate several international treaties. He also became known for a sarcastic sense of humor that sometimes offended people.

Early life. John Sparrow David Thompson was born on Nov. 10, 1844, in Halifax, Nova Scotia. His father, John Sparrow Thompson, had emigrated from Ireland in 1828. He had settled in Halifax and worked in the Nova Scotia post office. In 1829, he married Charlotte Pottinger, a Nova Scotian of Scottish descent.

John, the youngest of five children, went to school in Halifax. He then studied law as a clerk in a legal firm. Thompson was admitted to the Nova Scotia bar in 1865. In 1870, he married Annie Affleck of Halifax. She was a Roman Catholic, and Thompson, a Methodist, converted to Catholicism about a year after their marriage.

Early political career. Thompson entered politics in 1872, when Halifax voters elected him as a city alderman. He was elected to the Halifax board of school commissioners in 1874 and later served as board chairman. In 1877, the United States government asked Thompson to advise its delegation to the Halifax Fisheries Commission, which met to regulate international fishing rights off the Atlantic Coast. That same year, Conservative Party leaders urged Thompson to run for the Nova Scotia Legislative Assembly from Antigonish. He won the election and soon gained a reputation as a competent legislator. In 1878, Thompson became attorney general of Nova Scotia.

Thompson and other members of the legislature had supported an attempt to reform municipal government in Nova Scotia. This attempt failed and many of the reform legislators were defeated in the election of June 1882. Thompson, who had served as premier of Nova Scotia for less than a month before the election, retained his seat in the legislature. However, he had become tired of politics. In July, Thompson accepted an appointment by Macdonald to the Supreme Court of Nova Scotia.

Minister of justice. In the fall of 1885, Macdonald offered Thompson the office of minister of justice in his Cabinet. Thompson did not want to leave the provincial supreme court, but his wife persuaded him to do so. He became minister of justice in September and the next month was elected to the House of Commons from Antigonish, Nova Scotia.

Thompson's honesty and legal skill made him one of the most respected members of the government and of the Conservative Party. Macdonald declared that "the best thing I ever invented was Thompson." As minister of justice, Thompson defended some unpopular actions of the Macdonald administration. One such action involved the execution of Louis Riel, who had led an uprising of Canadian *Métis* (people of mixed white and Indian ancestry). Many French Canadians had protested Riel's execution. See **Riel, Louis.**

In 1887 and 1888, Thompson helped draft a U.S.-Canadian treaty on fishing rights. Queen Victoria knighted him in 1888 for this service. Thompson also directed a revision of the Canadian Criminal Code, which clarified the nation's criminal laws.

Prime minister. Macdonald died in 1891, and the Conservatives asked Thompson to take over as party leader and as prime minister. Thompson refused because he feared that Protestant Canadians would not accept a Roman Catholic, particularly one who had converted from a Protestant faith. John J. C. Abbott succeeded Macdonald, and Thompson continued as minister of justice.

In 1892, Abbott became ill and resigned as prime minister. The Conservatives again offered Thompson the positions of party leader and prime minister, and this time he accepted. He was sworn in on Dec. 5, 1892.

Thompson prevented a controversy involving Roman Catholic schools in Manitoba from becoming a major political issue during his term as prime minister. The controversy arose in 1890, when Manitoba's legislature passed a bill that abolished tax support for the province's Catholic schools. The legislature wanted to make all schools in the province part of the public school system. Catholics in Manitoba demanded that the federal government use its authority to *disallow* (reject) the legislation. Thompson tried to let the courts settle the matter. But the dispute did not end until 1896, when Prime Minister Wilfrid Laurier helped work out a compromise.

Thompson also hoped to bring Newfoundland into the Canadian Dominion. He had almost succeeded at the time of his death. Newfoundland did not join the dominion until 1949.

As prime minister, Thompson continued to use his skill as a diplomat. In 1893, he represented the United Kingdom at the Bering Sea Convention in Paris. Partly as a result of his arguments, this conference ruled that the United States had to grant the United Kingdom fishing rights in the Bering Sea. See **Bering Sea controversy.**

In 1894, Thompson met in London with other British statesmen. They discussed publishing laws, commercial shipping regulations, and other issues involving members of the British Empire. At Windsor Castle, on December 12, Thompson was sworn in as a member of the Imperial Privy Council. This council consisted of leading statesmen of the empire. Immediately after the ceremony and in the presence of Queen Victoria, Thompson suffered a heart attack and died within minutes. He was buried in Halifax. Michael Bliss

Thompson, William Hale (1867-1944), a controversial American political leader, was mayor of Chicago from 1915 to 1923 and from 1927 to 1931. He was nicknamed "Big Bill" because of his athletic build. Thompson became nationally known for his stands on issues. He at first opposed U.S. entry into World War I (1914-1918). In his second mayoral race, he supported the cause of Irish independence. During his 1927 campaign, he charged that British propaganda had spread into American textbooks on the Revolutionary War in America (1775-1783). In 1931, he lost his bid for a fourth term when he tried to stir anti-immigrant feeling against his opponent, Bohemian-born Anton J. Cermak. Thompson was born on May 16, 1867, in Boston, but he grew up in Chicago. He died on March 18, 1944. Douglas Bukowski

Thomson, Charles (1729-1824), served as secretary of the Continental Congress from 1774 to 1781 and secretary of the Congress of the Confederation from 1781 to 1789. As secretary of the Continental Congress, Thomson signed the copy of the Declaration of Independence that the Congress adopted and sent for printing on July 4, 1776. John Hancock, president of Congress, was the copy's only other signer. Born in County Derry, Ireland, Thomson came to America at the age of 10 as an orphan. He became a schoolmaster and then a successful merchant. Gary D. Hermalyn

Thomson, Charles Edward Poulett. See **Sydenham, Baron.**

Thomson, James (1700-1748), was the most celebrated Scottish poet of the 1700's before Robert Burns. In 1725, he traveled from Scotland to London where he published his masterpiece, *The Seasons* (1726-1730, revised 1744-1746). Thomson broke with the imitative poetic style of his day. He turned to nature for his subject matter and wrote fresh, vivid descriptions of natural scenes that capture a quality of *sublimity* (nobility and majesty). This style led to the romantic movement of the 1800's.

Thomson was born on Sept. 11, 1700, in Ednam in the Scottish lowlands. He wrote tragedies, the poem *Liberty* (1735-1736), and an imitation of the poetry of Edmund Spenser, *The Castle of Indolence* (1748). Gary A. Stringer

Thomson, Sir Joseph John (1856-1940), a British physicist, received the 1906 Nobel Prize in physics for his discovery of the electron. In 1937, his son and pupil, Sir George Paget Thomson, shared the Nobel Prize in physics with Clinton Davisson, an American physicist.

Thomson began in 1895 to investigate the mysterious rays that occurred when electricity was passed through a vacuum in a glass tube. Because the rays seemed to come from the *cathode* (negative electrical pole in the tube), they were called *cathode rays.* No one had succeeded in deflecting them by an electric force. Some scientists therefore assumed that cathode rays were like light waves. Thomson believed that they were really tiny particles of matter.

He built a special cathode-ray tube in which the rays passed through electric and magnetic fields that were perpendicular to each other. The rays became visible as a dot on the opposite end of the tube. By measuring the deflections of the dot as he changed the strength of the electric and magnetic fields, Thomson determined the ratio of the charge to the mass of the particle (symbolized as e/m). From the direction of their deflection, he decided that the particles were negatively charged. Because their e/m was always the same, he felt sure that they were a fundamental part of all atoms. These particles were later called *electrons* (see **Atom** [diagram: Models of the atom]; **Electron**).

Thomson was also the first to separate isotopes of the chemical elements. This accomplishment spurred the invention of the mass spectrograph by his assistant,

Francis W. Aston (see **Mass spectrometry**).

Thomson was born near Manchester on Dec. 18, 1856, and was educated at Manchester and Cambridge. Thomson's experimental work was invaluable to physics. His theoretical model of the atom, however, became obsolete after new models were proposed by Ernest Rutherford in 1911 and Niels Bohr in 1913. Roger H. Stuewer

See also **Electronics** (picture: The electron).

Thomson, Tom (1877-1917), was a Canadian landscape painter. He was associated with Lawren Harris, Alexander Y. Jackson, J. E. H. MacDonald, and the other Canadian artists who formed the "Group of Seven" after 1920.

From 1914 to 1917, Thomson spent much of each year in Algonquin Park, Ontario, where he sketched the landscape while working as a fire ranger and guide. During the winters, Thomson lived in Toronto and painted major canvases from his sketches. His paintings are brilliant expressions of the unspoiled beauty of the Canadian wilderness. Thomson's paintings *The West Wind* (now in the Art Gallery of Ontario) and *The Jack Pine* (now in the National Gallery of Canada) have become treasured works of Canadian art.

Thomas John Thomson was born on Aug. 4, 1877, near Owen Sound, Ontario. He drowned at Canoe Lake in Algonquin Park. David Burnett

See also **Canada** (The arts [picture]); **Group of Seven** (picture).

Thomson, Virgil (1896-1989), was an American composer and music critic. He gained international fame with his first opera, *Four Saints in Three Acts* (1934). Thomson also became famous for his simple, almost hymnlike style and subtle humor in music.

Thomson was born in Kansas City, Missouri, on Nov. 25, 1896. From 1925 to 1940, he lived in Paris. There, he was influenced by Erik Satie and other modern French composers. Thomson's *Missa Pro Defunctis* (1960), a religious composition for chorus, shows Satie's influence. In Paris, Thomson and American writer Gertrude Stein became friends. They collaborated on two operas, *Four Saints in Three Acts* and *The Mother of Us All* (1947). In New York, he composed the opera *Lord Byron* (1972) with Jack Larsen.

Thomson was a pioneer among concert composers in writing music for motion pictures. He composed the music for two famous documentary films, *The Plow That Broke the Plains* (1936) and *The River* (1937). Thomson won the 1949 Pulitzer Prize for his film score for the documentary *Louisiana Story* (1948). His other works include many compositions, which he called portraits, such as *The Mayor La Guardia Waltzes* (1942), and such descriptive pieces as *The Seine at Night* (1947). He also composed three symphonies (1928, 1931, 1972).

From 1940 to 1954, Thomson served as music critic of the *New York Herald Tribune*. His literary style and insight into modern music made him one of the most respected critics of his time. His reviews were published in such collections as *The Musical Scene* (1945), *The Art of Judging Music* (1948), and *Music Right and Left* (1951). He also wrote *The State of Music* (1939) and an autobiography, *Virgil Thomson* (1966). Richard Jackson

Thomson, William. See **Kelvin, Lord.**

Thor was the god of thunder and lightning in Norse mythology. He was the oldest and most powerful son of Odin, the king of the gods and goddesses. Thor had great strength and was a skilled fighter. His main weapon was a hammer named Mjollnir (also spelled *Mjolnir*). He threw it at his enemies. Mjollnir never missed its mark and always returned to Thor after hitting a target. Thor created lightning when he threw Mjollnir, and thunder was the rumbling of his chariot as it moved across the sky. The day Thursday was named for Thor.

Oil painting on canvas (1917); National Gallery of Canada

Tom Thomson's ***The Jack Pine,*** one of his brilliant landscapes, portrays the beauty of Canada's wilderness.

Of all the Norse gods, Thor best represented the values of the warrior class of medieval Scandinavia. For example, the Vikings held great feasts and glorified combat. Several myths describe Thor's huge appetite. He once ate an ox and eight salmon and drank three barrels of an alcoholic beverage called mead. Another myth tells of a drinking contest in which Thor tried to drink the sea dry. He failed, but he lowered the level of the sea slightly and thus created the first tides. The gods had several huge drinking horns, and only Thor could consume their entire contents.

Thor's most important work was to protect the gods and goddesses from giants. One story describes his battle with Hrungnir, a giant, who hurled a huge stone at him. Thor threw his hammer, and it shattered the stone in the air and killed Hrungnir.

Someday, according to Norse mythology, the gods and goddesses will fight the giants in a great battle called *Ragnarok,* and the world will be destroyed. Thor and the Midgard Serpent, a vicious snake coiled around the world under the sea, will kill each other during the battle. Carl Lindahl

See also **Mythology** (Teutonic mythology).

Thoreau, *THOHR oh,* **Henry David** (1817-1862), was an American writer noted for his attacks on the social institutions he considered immoral and for his faith in the religious significance of nature. The essay "Civil Disobedience" is his most famous social protest. *Walden,* a study of Thoreau's experiment in living close to nature, is chiefly responsible for his literary reputation.

His life. Thoreau was born in Concord, Massachusetts, on July 12, 1817. He was christened David Henry Thoreau but changed his name to Henry David after graduating from college. Unlike most leading writers of his time, Thoreau came from a family that was neither wealthy nor distinguished. His father made pencils in a small shop. His mother took in boarders.

Thoreau graduated from Harvard College in 1837. The writer Ralph Waldo Emerson encouraged him to write, gave him useful criticism, and later employed him as a handyman. Emerson also taught Thoreau the philosophy of Transcendentalism, with its emphasis on mysticism and individualism (see **Transcendentalism**).

Thoreau published only two books in his lifetime, *A Week on the Concord and Merrimack Rivers* (1849) and *Walden.* Many of the books published after his death were based on trips he had taken. These books include *Excursions* (1863), *The Maine Woods* (1864), *Cape Cod* (1865), and *A Yankee in Canada* (1866). The books are organized in a loose chronological form.

His beliefs and works. Thoreau believed that people must be free to act according to their own idea of right and wrong, without government interference. In "Civil Disobedience" (1849), he said that people should refuse to obey any law they believe is unjust. Thoreau practiced this doctrine of *passive resistance* when, in 1846, he refused to pay poll taxes. He did so to express his opposition to slavery as it became an issue in the Mexican War (1846-1848). He spent a night in jail for his refusal.

Thoreau summed up his idea of the role of government in "Civil Disobedience." He wrote, "There will never be a really free and enlightened State until the State comes to recognize the individual as a higher and independent power, from which all its own power and authority are derived, and treats him accordingly." The essay influenced such reformers as Leo Tolstoy of Russia, Mohandas Gandhi of India, and Martin Luther King, Jr., and other leaders of the U.S. civil rights movement.

Thoreau called for an end to slavery. He attacked it in the essay "Slavery in Massachusetts" (1854), and defended abolitionist John Brown's raid at Harpers Ferry in "A Plea for Captain John Brown" (1859).

In 1845, Thoreau moved to the shore of Walden Pond near Concord, Massachusetts. He lived there alone from July 4, 1845, to Sept. 6, 1847. *Walden* (1854) records Thoreau's observations of nature there, and tells how he built his house, paid his bills, and spent his time. It also tells about his visitors and reports what he read and thought. On a deeper level, the book is a celebration of people living in harmony with nature.

Marmel Studios from FPG

Walden Pond, near Concord, Massachusetts, inspired Thoreau's most famous book. He built a cabin near the pond.

Thoreau insisted that his trip to Walden Pond was an experiment in simple living, not an idle withdrawal from society. He wrote, "The mass of men lead lives of quiet desperation." He appealed to people to economize, to simplify their lives, and thus to save the time and energy that will allow them "to live deep and suck out all the marrow of life. ..." John Clendenning

See also **Civil disobedience** (History of civil disobedience).

Additional resources

McGregor, Robert K. *A Wider View of the Universe: Henry Thoreau's Study of Nature.* Univ. of Ill. Pr., 1997.

Myerson, Joel, ed. *The Cambridge Companion to Henry David Thoreau.* Cambridge, 1995.

Richardson, Robert D., Jr. *Henry David Thoreau.* Univ. of Calif. Pr., 1986.

Thorium is a radioactive chemical element used to make fuel for nuclear reactors. It is a soft, silvery metal. Tiny amounts of thorium appear naturally in nearly all rocks, soils, water, plants, and animals. Larger amounts appear in the minerals monazite and thorite. Those minerals are mined chiefly in Brazil, India, and South Africa.

Scientists can convert thorium into uranium 233, a nuclear fuel, by bombarding it with neutrons. Engineers mix thorium with other metals to make strong *alloys* (combinations of two or more metals). Manufacturers use thorium in devices called *photoelectric cells* that measure ultraviolet light. Some camping lanterns use *mantles* (light-producing screens) made of thorium because it gives off a bright white light when heated.

Thorium has 12 *isotopes.* The isotopes of an element have the same number of protons but different numbers of neutrons. Thorium's most stable isotope has an *atomic mass number* (total number of protons and neutrons) of 232. Thorium 232 has a *half-life* of 14 billion years—that is, due to radioactive decay, only half the atoms in a sample of thorium 232 would still be atoms of that isotope after 14 billion years.

Thorium's chemical symbol is Th. Its *atomic number* (number of protons in its nucleus) is 90. Its *relative atomic mass* is 232.0381. An element's relative atomic mass equals its *mass* (amount of matter) divided by $\frac{1}{12}$ of the mass of carbon 12, the most stable isotope of carbon. Thorium melts at 1750 °C and boils at about 4790 °C.

The Swedish chemist Jöns Jakob Berzelius discovered thorium in 1828. The element is named for Thor, the god of thunder in Norse mythology. Richard L. Hahn

See also **Monazite; Radiation** (Naturally radioactive substances).

Thorn is a short, sharp modified stem that grows out of the woody stems of many kinds of trees and shrubs. The honey locust, pyracantha shrub, and hawthorn are examples of plants that bear thorns. Thorns have a short growth period that ends with the formation of a sharp, hardened tip. The thorns protect the plant from damage by grazing animals. Plants with thorns are common in dry, warm areas, such as deserts and savannas.

Thorns are often confused with similar structures that grow from the stems of certain plants. The "thorns" of rose plants are better called prickles because they are simple outgrowths of the surface of the stem. The thorn-like structures on such plants as black locust and barberry are actually modified leaves and should be called spines. Richard C. Keating

Thorn apple. See **Hawthorn; Datura; Jimson weed.**

Thorndike, Edward Lee (1874-1949), an American educational psychologist, made many contributions to the study of learning, teaching, and mental testing. He invented the puzzle-box to investigate how such animals as cats and dogs solve problems. He found that they tend to repeat only those movements that are successful. This leads them to a final quick solution.

Thorndike also studied learning in human beings. He found that being right helped the student to retain a correct response, but that being wrong did not seem to eliminate errors. He conducted large-scale statistical studies to show how the study of Latin, mathematics, and other subjects affects the later school performance of students. He was one of the first to devise tests to measure learning and aptitudes.

Thorndike was born in Williamsburg, Massachusetts, on Aug. 31, 1874. He received a Ph.D. degree from Columbia University, and taught at Teachers College, Columbia University, for 41 years. He developed a method to determine which words are used most often. His data were used as a basis for the Thorndike-Century and the Thorndike-Barnhart school dictionaries. His *Teacher's Word Book* (1944) lists 30,000 words by their frequency of use. His other works include *Mental and Social Measurement* (1904), *The Measurement of Intelligence* (1926), and *Fundamentals of Learning* (1932). Richard M. Wolf

Thornton, Matthew (1714-1803), was a New Hampshire signer of the Declaration of Independence. He served as president of the first New Hampshire Provincial Congress in 1775 and as speaker of the general assembly in 1776. In 1776 and 1778, he was a delegate to the Continental Congress. Thornton was born in Ireland, and came to America about 1718. He practiced medicine in Londonderry, New Hampshire. Gary D. Hermalyn

Thoroughbred. See **Horse** (Saddle horses).

Thoroughwort. See **Boneset.**

Thorpe, Jim (1887-1953), was one of the greatest all-around athletes in history. He became an outstanding college and professional football player and won fame as an Olympic track and field champion. Thorpe also played major league baseball.

In the 1912 Olympic Games, Thorpe became the first athlete to win both the pentathlon and the decathlon (see **Track and field** [The decathlon, heptathlon, and pentathlon]). But about a month later, Olympic officials took away his medals. Prior to the games, Thorpe had played baseball for a small salary. The Amateur Athletic Union ruled that Thorpe was therefore a professional athlete and ineligible to compete in the Olympic Games. In 1982, the International Olympic Committee restored Thorpe's gold medals and added his name to the list of 1912 Olympic champions.

James Francis Thorpe, an American Indian, was born on May 22, 1887, near Prague, Oklahoma. Thorpe began his athletic career at the Carlisle (Pennsylvania) Indian Industrial School. He led the small school to national fame in football. An outstanding runner, place-kicker, and tackler, he won all-America honors in 1911 and 1912.

From 1913 to 1919, Thorpe played baseball as an outfielder on three major league teams. Thorpe began his professional football career in 1915 and played on seven teams during the next 15 years. Thorpe helped establish professional football as a popular sport. In 1920, Thorpe became the first president of the American Professional Football Association, now known as the National Football League. William F. Reed

United Press Int.

Jim Thorpe was one of the greatest all-around athletes in history. He starred in football, track and field, and baseball.

See **Olympic Games** (picture).

Additional resources

Bernotas, Bob. *Jim Thorpe.* Chelsea Hse., 1992. Younger readers.
Coffey, Wayne. *Jim Thorpe.* Blackbirch Pr., 1993. Younger readers.
Lipsyte, Robert. *Jim Thorpe.* 1993. Reprint. HarperCollins, 1995. Younger readers.

Thorvaldsen, *TOOR VAHL suhn,* **Bertel,** *BAIR tuhl* (1770-1844), was a Danish sculptor. His name is also spelled *Thorwaldsen.* During his lifetime, many people considered him the greatest sculptor in Europe. Thorvaldsen was a leader of the Neoclassical movement. Neoclassical artists based their style and subjects on the classical traditions of ancient Mediterranean civilizations, particularly Greece. Thorvaldsen believed that imitation of ancient classical works of art was the surest way of becoming a great artist.

Thorvaldsen was born on Nov. 19, 1770, in Copenhagen. From 1797 to 1837, he lived in Rome and studied classical art. Thorvaldsen took many of his subjects from ancient literature and mythology. Like the ancient Greek artists, he tried to sculpt human figures with clear contours, smooth surfaces, pleasing proportions, and a feeling of tranquillity. Thorvaldsen created most of his works in white marble. They included relief sculptures, monuments, and portrait busts. Sarah Burns

See also **Sculpture** (Sculpture from 1600 to 1900; picture).

Thoth, *thohth* or *toht,* was an ancient Egyptian moon god. He was a patron of civilization and such intellectual arts as writing, astronomy, mathematics, law, magic, and healing. He is most often shown in art with a human body and the head of an ibis bird. He is also portrayed as a dog-headed baboon.

Thoth's most important role in the underworld was to oversee the scales on which the souls of the dead were weighed to determine innocence or guilt. He was also related to many other gods. He was considered the scribe of the sun god Re and even Re's chief administrative officer. In the creation myth from Memphis, Thoth became the tongue of the creator god Ptah, through whom the world was created. Orval Wintermute

See also **Mythology** (Egyptian mythology).

Thothmes III. See Thutmose III.

Thousand and One Nights. See **Arabian Nights**.

Thousand Islands is a group of more than a thousand islands in the St. Lawrence River. The group includes islands on both sides of the boundary between Canada and the United States. No complete count has ever been made, because some of the islands are only small points of rock above the water. But at least 1,700 islands compose the group. A few of the islands are as much as 5 to 6 miles (8 to 10 kilometers) in length. The islands lie in a 40-mile (64-kilometer) stretch of the St. Lawrence where the river runs from 4 to 7 miles (6 to 11 kilometers) wide as it leaves Lake Ontario. They are formed where the river flows over the low hills of the Canadian Shield, which extends southeast into New York state (see **Canadian Shield**).

These rocky islands are noted for their beautiful scenery and mild summer climate. Many have popular public summer resorts. Several have luxurious summer homes. Seventeen of the islands are included in St. Lawrence Islands National Park. The park has been made into a recreational center and game preserve.

The Thousand Islands International Bridge, completed in 1938, spans some of the islands. It consists of two main suspension structures, three smaller bridges, and roadways across two islands. Its total length is about 6 $\frac{1}{2}$ miles (10.5 kilometers). George B. Priddle

Thrace, *thrays,* was the ancient name for a large region in the Balkan Peninsula. It stretched from Macedonia north to the Danube River, and eastward as far as the Black Sea. The mountains of Thrace contained valuable deposits of gold and silver. Its broad plains were used for farming and for raising horses and cattle.

The people of Thrace were Indo-Europeans who liked warfare and looting. They grew rich from trading with Greeks who lived along the Thracian coast in the 600's B.C. The Persians occupied much of Thrace from 520 to 460 B.C. After that time, Thrace became independent and had much contact with the ancient Greeks. The Thracians adopted the Greek artistic style, and the Greeks adopted Thracian myths and religious beliefs. Later, Thrace belonged to the Athenian state and then to Macedonia. Philip II conquered all of Thrace, and the region was held by his son, Alexander the Great. Thrace became a province of the Roman Empire during the hundred years before Christ's birth.

The most important Greek cities of Thrace were Abdera, Sestos, and Byzantium. Ancient Byzantium was the foundation of the modern city of Istanbul (Constantinople). The fall of Constantinople in 1453 brought all Thrace under the rule of the Ottoman Empire, which was based in what is now Turkey.

After the Russo-Turkish War of 1877-1878, northern Thrace became known as Eastern Rumelia. It was united with Bulgaria in 1885. Greece received western Thrace and most of eastern Thrace in post-World War I treaties, but Greece returned eastern Thrace to Turkey in 1923. German troops overran Greek Thrace in 1941, but it was returned to Greece after World War II. Greek Thrace includes the departments of Evros and Rhodope. Turkish Thrace corresponds to Turkey in Europe. Clive Foss

Thrasher is the name of a group of brownish, long-tailed birds found from southern Canada through South America. There are about 17 species. The best-known species is the *brown thrasher* of eastern North America (see **Brown thrasher**). Most thrashers have a brown head and back, and a pale underside with brown streaks. The largest thrashers grow over 1 foot (30 centimeters) long. Thrashers spend most of their time on the ground searching for food. They eat insects, worms, fruit, and seeds. These birds have a song that is loud and repetitive. They build cup-shaped nests, usually in low bushes and shrubs. Thrashers lay from two to six eggs.

Eight species of thrashers range from western North America to Central America. Most of these thrashers have a long, curved bill. Species that live in arid regions of the Southwest also have longer legs and shorter wings than other thrashers. These species do more running than flying and nest in thorny shrubs or cactuses.

Four species live only in the West Indies. Two of them, the *white-breasted thrasher* and the *trembler,* are in danger of extinction. They are nervous ground-dwellers. The trembler was named for its nervous behavior. The other West Indian species, the *pearly-eyed thrasher* and the *scaly-breasted thrasher,* dwell in trees.

Four by Five

The Thousand Islands occupy a 40-mile (64-kilometer) stretch of the St. Lawrence River as it leaves Lake Ontario. The rocky islands are noted for their beautiful scenery and mild summer climate.

© David G. Allen

A brown thrasher looks after its young, *shown here.* This attractive bird is noted for its lovely song.

The pearly-eyed thrasher is the most common West Indian species. It nests in holes in trees. Donald F. Bruning

Scientific classification. Thrashers belong to the mockingbird family, Mimidae. The brown thrasher is *Toxostoma rufum.*

Thread is a fine cord. It is used chiefly to join two or more pieces of material or to sew an object to a piece of fabric. Thread is made of such fibers as cotton, flax, nylon, polyester, rayon, silk, or other textile material. Thread has numerous uses. These uses include sewing clothing, mending tears, and attaching buttons.

Most thread is made by spinning many fibers into a yarn. Several yarns are twisted tightly together to form thread. Each yarn, called a *ply,* adds strength and thickness to the thread. Some thread consists of a single yarn.

Thread is made from three kinds of fibers: (1) plant, (2) animal, and (3) manufactured. Plant and animal fibers are called *natural fibers.* Almost all natural fibers grow in short lengths known as *staple.* For example, cotton staple measures from $\frac{3}{4}$ inch to $1\frac{1}{2}$ inches (1.9 to 3.8 centimeters) long. Cotton ranks as the most widely used natural fiber for making thread. Manufactured fibers, such as nylon and polyester, are produced in long, continuous strands called *filaments.* Silk is the only natural fiber that begins as filament. Silk fibers average from 1,000 to 1,300 yards (914 to 1,189 meters) long.

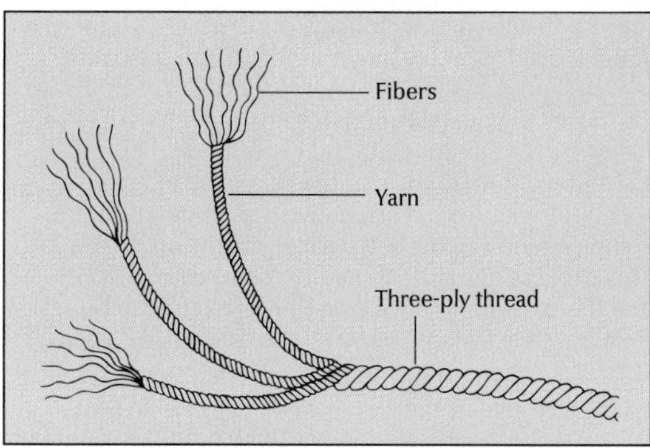

WORLD BOOK diagram by Art Grebetz

Thread consists of many fibers that have been spun into yarns. The yarns are *plied* (twisted together) to form thread.

Most natural and manufactured thread receives some kind of chemical treatment that improves its quality. One such process, called *mercerization,* treats cotton thread in a saltlike solution. This treatment strengthens the thread and gives it a silky finish. Almost all the thread is either bleached or dyed before being packaged.

Making thread from natural fibers. Natural fibers, such as cotton or flax, are first cleaned. Then they are straightened and further cleaned in a process called *carding.* The next step, called *combing,* smooths the staple and removes some of the exceptionally short fibers. The combed fibers pass between sets of powerful rollers that draw many pieces of loosely joined staple into continuous strands of increased strength. The strands are then spun into yarn and wound on bobbins. Several yarns are *plied* (twisted together) to form thread.

Making thread from manufactured fibers involves few steps. Filaments need little preliminary processing because they are specifically produced to be made into thread. A single filament can be used as *monofilament thread,* or many filaments may be twisted together to form *multifilament thread.* Filaments may also be cut into staple lengths, which are drawn into strands and

How thread is made Thread may be made from natural or manufactured fibers. After preliminary processing, the fibers are drawn into strands, spun into yarn, and plied. Most thread is dyed or bleached before packaging.

WORLD BOOK diagrams by Art Grebetz

Natural fibers used in making thread include cotton and flax. The carding and combing processes straighten the fibers and smooth them into a sheet before drawing begins.

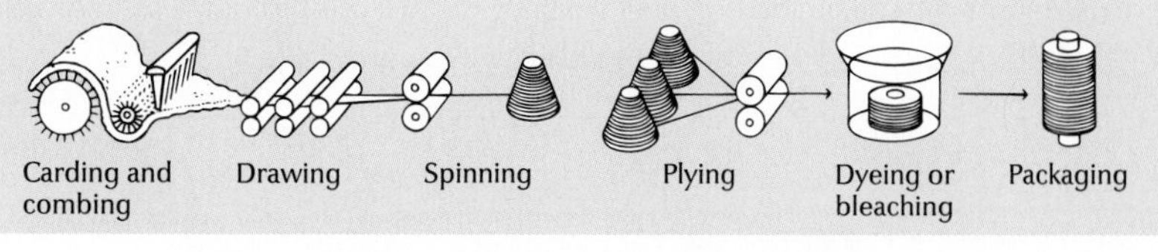

Manufactured fibers, such as nylon and polyester, are made in long continuous strands called *filaments.* To make thread, the filaments are cut into fiber-sized pieces before drawing.

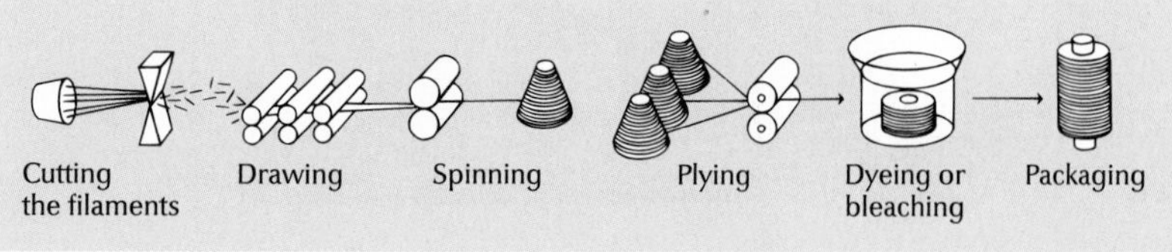

then spun into yarn and plied. This process produces a softer thread than that made directly from filaments.

One type of manufactured thread, called *core thread,* combines the qualities of two kinds of fibers. An example of such a thread is a blend of cotton and polyester. This thread is made by combining a core of multifilament polyester with a protective cotton *wrap.* The resulting strand is plied with two or more similar strands. This process gives the thread the smoothness of cotton and the strength of polyester. Core threads can be sewn on a machine faster than other manufactured thread without heating up and breaking. Core threads are ideal for sewing such textiles as knits, permanent-press fabrics, and fabrics that are made from two or more kinds of fibers. Richard J. DeMasse

See also **Spinning**.

Threadworm. See **Pinworm**.

Threatened species. See **Endangered species.**

Three Gorges Dam, being built on the Yangtze River in China, will be the world's largest dam. It is designed to control flooding and improve navigation on the Yangtze, China's longest river, and generate hydroelectric power. Construction began in 1994. The dam is being built just west of Yichang, in Hubei Province (see **China** [political map]).

According to plans, Three Gorges Dam will be about $1\frac{1}{3}$ miles (2.1 kilometers) long and 610 feet (186 meters) high. A reservoir nearly 400 miles (645 kilometers) long, with a capacity of more than 31 million acre-feet (38 billion cubic meters), will extend upstream. About 150,000 acres (60,700 hectares) of land will be covered with water, including 160 towns and 16 archaeological sites. About $1\frac{1}{3}$ million people will have to be resettled.

The project has stirred much controversy. Supporters say the dam will save lives by preventing floods on the eastern Yangtze and will bring development to the areas along the western Yangtze. They point out that the electric power the project generates will help reduce the use of coal and decrease air pollution. But critics believe the high cost could ruin the Chinese economy. They are concerned about the environmental impact, the loss of cultural relics and historic sites, and the effect of forced relocation on large numbers of people. They charge that China's goal is to build the world's largest dam, without regard for the consequences. Chor-Pang Lo

See also **China** (picture); **Yangtze River.**

Threshing machine is a machine that farmers once used to *thresh* (separate) kernels of grain from stalks. The machine also *winnowed* (blew) the chaff from the kernels. Andrew Meikle of Scotland built the first practical water-powered threshing machine as early as 1788. Before then, farmers had threshed and winnowed by hand—a hard, slow task. Horse-powered threshing machines enabled farmers to process grain much faster than they could by hand. Since the 1930's, combines have replaced most threshing machines (see **Combine**).

Modern threshing machines were based on a type patented in 1837 by two brothers, Hiram and John Pitts of Winthrop, Maine. Horses walking on a treadmill produced power for early threshers. A revolving cylinder knocked the kernels off the stalks, and a fan blew away the chaff. By the 1850's, many farmers used threshing machines. These machines were costly, and so farmers sometimes joined to purchase a thresher and shared it at harvesttime. By the late 1800's, steam engines powered most threshers. Later, farmers used tractors to power their threshers. R. Douglas Hurt

See also **Wheat** (picture: A steam-powered threshing machine).

Thrift institution. See **Bank** (Kinds of banks).

Thrips are short, slender insects with sucking mouthparts. Most species feed on plants and are serious pests. They stunt plant growth and spread disease. A few species prey on other thrips and various small insects. Adult thrips are usually less than 1 millimeter ($\frac{1}{25}$ inch) long. They have two pairs of narrow, fringed wings. Some thrips are wingless.

WORLD BOOK illustration by Oxford Illustrators Limited

Thrips

Most thrips reproduce by laying eggs, but some bear live young. One species, known as *Elaphrothrips tuberculatus,* is the only known animal that can reproduce in both ways. Some females of this species can lay eggs or bear live young. The live young are always males, and the eggs always hatch into females. John R. Meyer

Scientific classification. Thrips make up the order Thysanoptera.

Throat is a term loosely applied to the part of the neck in front of the backbone. The throat contains structures important in breathing and eating. It includes the pharynx, the larynx, part of the esophagus, and part of the trachea. A sore throat results when any of these parts becomes inflamed.

When a person breathes, air enters the nose and travels through a passage called the *pharynx.* From the pharynx, it passes into the *larynx* (voice box), then through

Historical Pictures Service, Chicago

Early threshing machines, like the one shown here, were powered by horses walking on a treadmill. The clean kernels poured out of the machine into a bucket, and a conveyor belt carried the straw away.

the *trachea* (windpipe), and into the lungs. Food, on its way from the mouth to the stomach, passes through the pharynx before it enters the *esophagus,* the tube that leads to the stomach. Thus, part of the pharynx is a common passage for both food and air, and it is possible for food to enter the wrong tube.

Normally, when a person swallows, two actions block off the air passage. The *soft palate* presses against the back of the pharynx, closing the opening to the nose. At the same time, the larynx rises and is covered by the *epiglottis,* a leaf-shaped lid. These actions force the food into its own passage, the esophagus, and muscular waves carry it to the stomach. When a person laughs or talks while swallowing, food may enter the larynx and choke the person until it is removed by coughing.

The largest muscle of the throat region is the *sternocleidomastoid.* It moves the head. This muscle looks like a cord in the side of the neck when the head is turned. It runs diagonally across each side of the neck from the collarbone to the skull behind the ear. Smaller muscles in the throat help in the actions of breathing, speaking, and swallowing.

Large arteries and veins pass through the neck. They carry blood to and away from the face, scalp, and brain. Unconsciousness may result from blockage of the arteries on each side of the trachea. Barry L. Wenig

Related articles. See the Trans-Vision three-dimensional picture with **Human body**. See also:

Esophagus	Larynx	Strep throat	Trachea
Gargle	Pharynx	Tonsil	

Thrombosis. See **Coronary thrombosis**; **Stroke.**

Thrush is the name of a group of songbirds that live in most parts of the world. Many of the thrushes are plain brown birds, with whitish and usually spotted breasts. Robins, wheatears, and bluebirds are all thrushes. These birds are *migratory.* They fly to warmer countries as winter approaches. They live in wooded regions and spend much time on the ground.

The largest and best-known North American type of thrush, except for the American robin, is the *wood thrush.* This bird has bright cinnamon-colored upper parts and spotted white breast and sides. It is noted for its clear, flutelike songs. The wood thrush nests in the eastern United States and southeastern Canada, and winters in Central America. It builds its nest 5 to 20 feet (1.5 to 6 meters) up in a bush or tree. The bird arranges a base of dead leaves and coarse grass, plasters the nest with mud, and lines it with roots or grasses. The female wood thrush lays from three to five greenish-blue eggs.

Other common North American thrushes are the *veery,* the *hermit thrush,* the *varied thrush,* and *Swainson's thrush.* In Europe, the most common thrushes are the *redbreast,* or *robin;* the *song thrush,* or *mavis;* the *mistle thrush;* the *blackbird;* and the *nightingale.*

Donald F. Bruning

Scientific classification. Thrushes make up the family Turdidae. The scientific name of the wood thrush is *Hylocichla mustelina.* The veery is *Catharus fuscescens;* the hermit thrush is *C. guttatus;* and Swainson's thrush is *C. ustulatus.*

Related articles in ***World Book*** include:

Bird (table: State birds; pictures: Birds of inland waters and marshes; Birds' eggs)	Blackbird Nightingale Robin Stonechat

Thucydides, *thoo SIHD ih DEEZ*, a Greek historian of the 400's B.C., is famous for his *History of the Peloponnesian War.* In this work, he describes a war between Athens and Sparta. The war took place from 431 to 404 B.C., but the *History* is unfinished and ends at 411 B.C.

Thucydides thought the war worth recording because, in his opinion, it was the greatest the Greeks had ever fought. He set out to produce an accurate, unbiased account of the war. He visited battlefields and talked to survivors from both sides. He also analyzed the underlying political causes of the war. Thucydides reported political speeches as a way of showing opposing viewpoints and reasons for certain actions. Many historians believe that he invented some of these speeches.

Scholars are not certain exactly when Thucydides was born and when he died. But they do know that Thucydides was a citizen of Athens, born into an aristocratic family. He fought in the Peloponnesian War and became a general. In 424 B.C., he was accused of failing to protect the city of Amphipolis and was banished from Athens. During his exile, he worked on his history. He returned from exile in 404 B.C. Frank L. Vatai

See also **Greek literature** (Historical literature).

Thug is a member of an old criminal society in India, the members of which killed in the name of religion. The term comes from the Hindustani *thag,* meaning a *cheat* or *rascal.* The thugs committed murders and robbed their victims in honor of Kali, the Hindu goddess of destruction and wife of Shiva. The thugs always murdered by strangling. One of their chief principles was not to spill blood. According to legend, the thugs be-

WORLD BOOK illustration by Trevor Boyer, Linden Artists Ltd.

WORLD BOOK illustration by Trevor Boyer, Linden Artists Ltd.

Some members of the thrush family are the European blackbird and the wood thrush. The European blackbird looks like a black robin. The wood thrush has a spotted white breast.

lieved that Kali disposed of the bodies by devouring them. But one member of the society pried into Kali's actions. So the angry goddess condemned them to bury their victims in the future. In 1831, the British began a drive to end *thuggee*—the practice of the thugs. It is almost wiped out. Today, people commonly refer to robbers and other criminals as thugs. Charles S. J. White

Thule, *THOO lee,* was a name given to a remote northern land by the ancient Greeks and Romans. The Greek explorer Pytheas visited Thule before 300 B.C. He described it as north of Britain and near the frozen sea. In Thule, according to Pytheas, the sun did not set in midsummer and did not rise in midwinter. Some scholars believe he was speaking of Norway or Iceland. Others think Thule was one of the Shetland Islands. Some Roman writers called the land Ultima Thule, meaning *most distant Thule.* Today, the term *Ultima Thule* is used to mean any distant place or goal. George E. Pesely

See also **Exploration** (The Greeks); **Pytheas.**

Thulium, *THOO lee uhm,* is one of the rare-earth elements. It occurs with other rare-earth elements in such minerals as gadolinite, euxenite, and xenotime. Portable X-ray units use radioactive thulium. Such units require no electrical equipment, and they need to be recharged with thulium only once every few months. The Swedish scientist Per Cleve discovered thulium in 1879. The element's name comes from *Thule,* the Latin word for the northernmost part of the inhabitable world.

Thulium's chemical symbol is Tm. Its *atomic number* (number of protons in its nucleus) is 69. Its *relative atomic mass* is 168.93421. An element's relative atomic mass equals its *mass* (amount of matter) divided by $\frac{1}{12}$ of the mass of carbon 12, the most abundant form of carbon. Thulium melts at 1545 °C and boils at 1950 °C. It has a density of 9.321 grams per cubic centimeter at 25 °C.

Julia Y. Chan

See also **Element, Chemical** (tables); **Rare earth.**

Thumb. See **Hand.**

Thumb, Tom. See **Stratton, Charles S.**

Thunder is the loud noise that follows a flash of lightning. Many ancient cultures believed that thunder was the sound of the gods roaring in anger when they were displeased. Today, scientists know that thunder is caused by lightning. A stroke of lightning heats a narrow path of air to extraordinarily high temperatures—perhaps higher than 50,000 °F (28,000 °C). The intense heating creates a sharp increase in air pressure. The rising pressure generates a shock wave that moves outward in all directions. As the shock wave travels through the air, it produces the sound waves that we hear as thunder.

Thunder has many sounds. Sound waves from various parts of a lightning stroke reach an observer at different times, resulting in a rumbling noise. A lightning stroke can fork into many branches, which produce a sharp crackling sound. Lightning that strikes nearby produces a sharp clap or crack followed by a loud bang.

The sound of thunder reaches us after we have seen the lightning. The sound lags because light travels 186,282 miles (299,792 kilometers) per second, but sound travels only 0.211 miles (0.340 kilometers) per second. The number of seconds between seeing a lightning flash and hearing the thunder, divided by five, yields the approximate distance of the lightning stroke from the observer in miles. Divided by three, it gives the approximate distance in kilometers. Joseph M. Moran

See also **Lightning; Shock wave.**

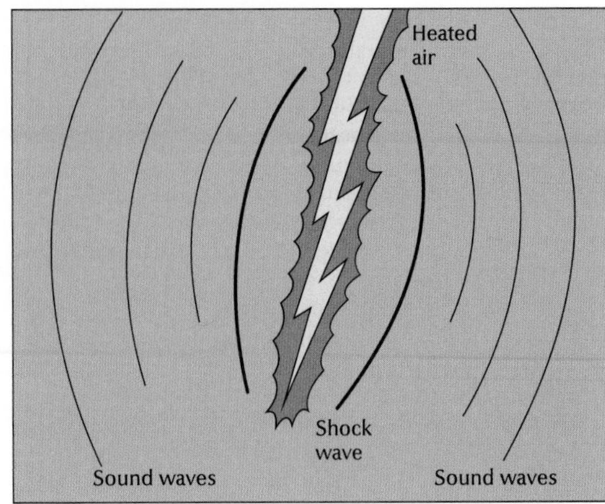

WORLD BOOK illustration by Jay E. Bensen

Thunder is the sound caused by lightning. Lightning heats the air along its path, sharply increasing its pressure. The increase in pressure generates a shock wave. As the shock wave moves through the air, it creates the sound waves we hear as thunder.

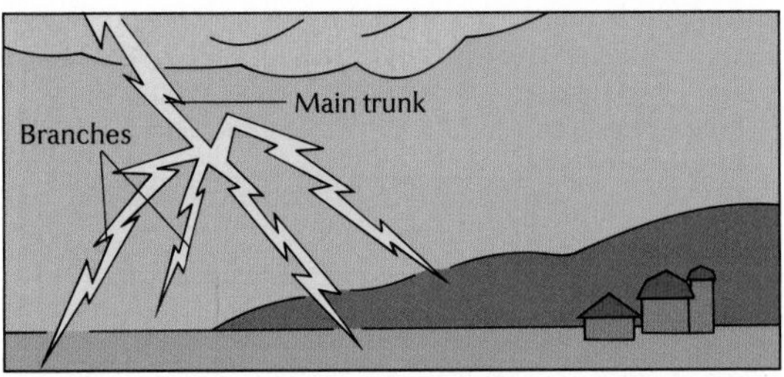

WORLD BOOK illustration by Arthur Grebetz

Different sounds of thunder come from different parts of a bolt of lightning. The main trunk of lightning causes the loudest crash. The branches produce the sharp, crackling sound.

Thunder Bay, Ontario (pop. 109,016; met. area pop. 121,986), is a city on the northwest shore of Lake Superior (see **Ontario** [political map]). Its excellent harbor makes it a shipping center. Thunder Bay was formed in 1970 by the merger of the cities of Fort William and Port Arthur and the townships of McIntyre and Neebing.

Thunder Bay is an international port. It is an important shipping center for the grain produced in western Canada and for potash and coal. Large ships reach Thunder Bay by the St. Lawrence Seaway and the Great Lakes. Thunder Bay has pulp and paper mills, building-board mills, and sawmills. Other industrial activities include railroad car manufacturing, ship repair, and tourism.

Thunder Bay is the home of Lakehead University and Confederation College of Applied Arts and Technology. The city has five public libraries, a museum, and a public art gallery. The Thunder Bay Community Auditorium hosts a variety of entertainment performances. A reconstructed fur trade fort is a major tourist attraction.

In 1679 and 1717, the French built forts at what later became Fort William. After 1805, Fort William served as headquarters for fur traders of the North West Company. Another settlement, Prince Arthur's Landing, grew up alongside Fort William. Fort William was designated a transcontinental rail point in 1875. Prince Arthur's Landing developed as a starting point for the road to western Canada. It was also the center of regional silver-mining activity. Prince Arthur's Landing became the town of Port Arthur in 1882, and Fort William was incorporated as a town in 1884. Both became cities in 1907. The port cities thrived, especially after the St. Lawrence Seaway opened in 1959. Thunder Bay has a mayor-council form of government. Michael D. Grieve

Thunderstorm. See **Cloud** (Storms); **Hail.**

Thurber, James (1894-1961), was a celebrated American humorist. He became famous both for his comic writings and fables and his cartoonlike drawings.

Thurber's works describe the anxieties of the average individual in modern society. He wrote chiefly about oversensitive, dissatisfied men who feel trapped by the complications of the modern world. The men in his stories are frustrated by their domineering wives and rebellious children. They often fear such machines as automobiles and dread the pressures of their jobs. They try to escape from their problems through alcohol or daydreams. Thurber's short story "The Secret Life of Walter Mitty," for example, portrays a man who finds relief from his nagging wife through daydreams. In his daydreams, Mitty always plays the fearless hero.

Many of Thurber's cartoons depict timid men, menacing women, wicked children, and sad dogs. He wrote his first book, *Is Sex Necessary?* (1929), with E. B. White and wrote a play, *The Male Animal* (1940), with Elliott Nugent. Thurber also wrote an autobiography, *My Life and Hard Times* (1933). Much of his work appeared in *The New Yorker* magazine. James Grover Thurber was born on Dec. 8, 1894, in Columbus, Ohio.

Arthur M. Saltzman

Additional resources

Kinney, Harrison. *James Thurber.* 1995. Reprint. Owl Paperback Bks., 1997.

Thurber, James. *Writings and Drawings.* Lib. of Am., 1996.

A Thurber cartoon illustrates one of his favorite subjects, a timid middle-aged man married to a domineering woman.

Thurman, Allen Granberry (1813-1895), was the Democratic candidate for vice president of the United States in 1888. He and President Grover Cleveland lost to Republicans Benjamin Harrison and Levi P. Morton. Thurman served as a U.S. senator from Ohio from 1869 to 1881. He was chief justice of the Ohio Supreme Court from 1854 to 1856 and served in the U.S. House of Representatives from 1845 to 1847. He was born on Nov. 13, 1813, in Lynchburg, Virginia. Edward A. Lukes-Lukaszewski

Thurmond, Strom (1902-2003), served longer in the United States Senate than any other person. Thurmond, a Republican who represented South Carolina, was a senator from 1955 to 2003. He served as *president pro tempore* (temporary president) of the Senate from 1981 to 1987 and from 1995 to 2001.

In the Senate, Thurmond was known for his strong support of states' rights. At one time, he was also known to favor racial segregation. He later modified his views and supported some civil rights legislation.

Thurmond, who began his political career as a Democrat, became a Republican in 1964. But in 1948, he ran for president as the candidate of the States' Rights Democratic (Dixiecrat) Party. The Dixiecrat Party was made up of Southern Democrats who opposed a strong civil rights program (see **Dixiecrat Party**). Thurmond carried four states and received 39 electoral votes.

In 1957, Thurmond launched the longest *filibuster* (delaying speech) in Senate history. He spoke for 24 hours and 18 minutes in an unsuccessful attempt to stop the passage of civil rights legislation.

James Strom Thurmond was born on Dec. 5, 1902, in Edgefield, South Carolina. He graduated from Clemson College. He was governor of South Carolina from 1947 to 1951. Thurmond was first elected to the Senate in 1954 and took office in 1955. He died on June 26, 2003.

Jeremy D. Mayer

Thursday is the fifth day of the week. The ancient Norsemen considered the day sacred to Thor, the Teutonic god of thunder. The name means *Thor's day.* This is probably a translation of the Latin *dies Jovis,* meaning *Jove's day,* for Jove, or Jupiter, the Roman god of thunder. See also **Thor; Week.** Jack Santino

Thurstone, Louis Leon (1887-1955), an American psychologist, played a major role in the development of psychological tests. One of his most significant achievements was the creation of a statistical technique called the *centroid method of factor analysis.* By applying the method to the results of intelligence tests, Thurstone found that intelligence consists of separate abilities, among them being reasoning and numerical aptitude. His findings differed from the common belief of the time that intelligence was a single factor. Thurstone also developed tests to measure attitudes.

Thurstone was born on May 29, 1887, in Chicago. He got a Ph.D. degree in psychology from the University of Chicago and taught psychology there. Richard M. Wolf

Thutmose III, *thoot MOH suh* (reigned about 1490-1436 B.C.), ranks among the greatest of all the kings of ancient Egypt. He is also known as Thothmes III. Thutmose succeeded his father, Thutmose II, but was kept in the background by his stepmother, Queen Hatshepsut. After Hatshepsut died, Thutmose III ordered her name erased from monuments and statues.

Thutmose III became a brilliant general and also a capable administrator. By his well-planned campaigns, mainly in Palestine and Syria, he greatly expanded Egypt's imperial boundaries. The rich booty and many captives taken in his wars provided the means and labor for extensive building operations in Egypt. He greatly enlarged the vast temple at Karnak. Its walls still bear the hieroglyphic records of his wars, long lists of captured cities in Asia and Africa, and pictures of plants and animals collected on his campaigns. Thutmose erected granite *obelisks* (giant stone pillars) in Karnak and Heliopolis. The two he erected at Heliopolis are now known as *Cleopatra's Needles.* One stands in Central Park in New York City, and one on the Thames Embankment in London. Leonard H. Lesko

See also **Egypt, Ancient** (The New Kingdom); **Hatshepsut.**

Thylacine. See **Tasmanian tiger.**

Thyme, *tym,* is the name of a group of fragrant, shrubby mint plants native to the Mediterranean region. The ancient Greeks used thyme as temple incense. Thyme has a bitter flavor that makes it a popular seasoning for chowders, meats, and sauces. Thymol, an antiseptic drug, is prepared from oil extracted from thyme. This drug is used in mouthwashes and cough remedies.

The *common thyme,* also called *garden thyme,* grows to 6 to 8 inches (15 to 20 centimeters) tall. It has hairy, upright stems with many pairs of small elliptical leaves. Clusters of tiny flowers that range in color from whitish to lilac encircle the tips of the branches. Thyme grows well in dry, nutrient-poor soil. Donna M. Eggers Ware

Scientific classification. Thyme belongs to the mint family, Lamiaceae or Labiatae. The scientific name for the common thyme is *Thymus vulgaris.*

Thymus is a flat, pinkish-gray organ that plays an important part in the immune system of the body. It is located high in the chest cavity behind the breastbone and extends into the lower neck below the thyroid gland.

The thymus aids in the development of white blood cells called *lymphocytes,* which help the body fight disease. There are two kinds of lymphocytes, both of which are formed from cells in the bone marrow. Some lymphocytes, called *B cells,* probably mature in the bone marrow itself (see **Immune system** [Parts of the immune system]). The *B* stands for *bone marrow derived.* The other lymphocytes travel to the thymus, where they are changed into *T cells.* The *T* stands for *thymus derived.* The thymus produces a substance called *thymosin,* which scientists believe plays an important part in the change into T cells.

The T cells leave the thymus and inhabit the blood, lymph nodes, and spleen. There, they attack bacteria, cancer cells, fungi, viruses, and other harmful organisms. Killer T cells, also called *cytotoxic T cells,* find and destroy abnormal or infected cells. T cells also attack organs that have been transplanted from one person to another. This is called *transplant rejection.* Powerful drugs are needed to prevent T cells from destroying the transplanted organ.

When a person is born, the thymus weighs about $\frac{1}{2}$ ounce (15 grams). When a person is 12 years old, the thymus is about twice its original size. At that time, the lymph nodes and the spleen take over the task of producing lymphocytes. The thymus then begins to shrink and produces fewer T cells. By adulthood, the organ has shrunk so much that it may be hard to distinguish from the fatty tissue that surrounds it. Babies born without a thymus may fail to develop a normal immune system.

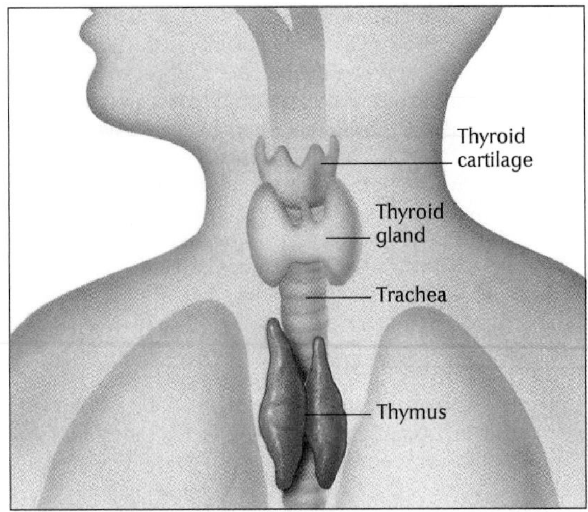

WORLD BOOK diagram by Charles Wellek

The thymus is in the upper chest, behind the breastbone. It aids in the formation of white blood cells called *lymphocytes,* which protect the body from disease.

The thymus may be removed to treat *myasthenia gravis,* a disease characterized by severe muscle weakness. For reasons not completely understood, thymus removal helps many patients with this disease become stronger. Loss of the thymus has no noticeable effect on the immune system. See **Myasthenia gravis.** David D. Oakes

Thyroid gland is a body organ located in the front of the neck. It has two *lobes* (parts), one on each side of the *trachea* (windpipe). The lobes are connected by a thin band of tissue. A network of blood vessels surrounds the gland. The thyroid takes iodine from the blood and uses it to make the active hormones *thyroxine,* also called *tetraiodothyronine,* and *triiodothyronine.* An inactive form of thyroid hormones is stored inside the lobes in small chambers called *follicles.*

Thyroid hormones control the body's *cell metabolism.* When thyroid hormones are released into the bloodstream, cells increase the rate at which they convert oxygen and nutrients into energy and heat for the body's use. During a child's development, thyroid hormones stimulate an increase in growth rate. Release of thyroid hormones also stimulates mental activity and increases the activity of the other hormone-producing glands.

Thyroxine and triiodothyronine are released into the bloodstream in response to such conditions as stress, pregnancy, and low levels of thyroid hormones in the blood. These conditions activate a hormone in the pituitary gland called *thyroid-stimulating hormone* (TSH). TSH regulates the thyroid's production of hormones.

The thyroid gland produces another hormone, *calcitonin,* in response to high levels of calcium in the blood. Calcitonin causes the kidneys to discharge more calcium into the urine, and it raises the amount of calcium stored in the bones.

Underactive thyroid, called *hypothyroidism,* is a defect that results in the low production of thyroid hormones. This deficiency causes an overall decrease in both physical and mental activity. Symptoms appear in

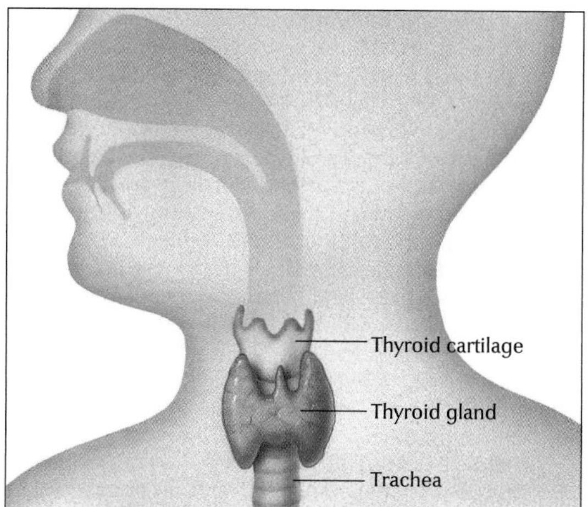

WORLD BOOK diagram by Charles Wellek

The thyroid gland is in the neck. This gland produces and stores a hormone called *thyroxine,* which is essential for mental development and physical growth.

almost every organ system of the body. The skin becomes dry and puffy. Hair thins and becomes brittle. Slow speech, slow reflexes, poor memory, constipation, and fatigue can all result from hypothyroidism. In adults, hypothyroidism is called *myxedema.* If the condition goes untreated in infants, it causes physical and mental retardation (see **Cretinism**). When hypothyroidism is detected in a newborn child, thyroid hormones can be replaced or supplemented by drugs to prevent retardation. A myxedemic adult can also be treated with drugs.

Overactive thyroid, called *hyperthyroidism,* results in an overproduction of thyroid hormones. Excessive thyroid hormones in the blood cause an increase in the rate of most biological reactions. This leads to a higher rate of physical and mental activity. Symptoms of hyperthyroidism may include sweating, excessive nervousness, insomnia, and diarrhea. Hyperthyroidism accompanied by eye problems is called *Graves' disease.*

Treatment of hyperthyroidism may involve surgery to remove a portion of the thyroid gland. Drugs can also be prescribed to lower thyroid production. In some cases, a solution containing radioactive iodine may be administered to destroy the gland. Charlotte H. Greene

See also **Gland; Goiter; Graves' disease; Hormone.**

Tian Shan, *tyehn shahn,* also spelled *Tien Shan,* is a mountain system in central Asia. It runs for more than 1,500 miles (2,410 kilometers) northeast of the Pamirs in Kyrgyzstan and northwestern China (see **Pamirs**). Tian Shan, which means *Heavenly Mountains,* is the highest mountain system north of Tibet. Peak Pobedy, the highest peak, rises 24,406 feet (7,439 meters) above sea level. Rivers flow from Tian Shan into Kyrgyzstan and Kazakstan, and south into China. The system includes some of the world's largest alpine glaciers. For location, see **Asia** (physical map). James A. Hafner

Tiananmen Square. See **China** (Protests).

Tianjin, *tyehn jihn* (pop. 5,804,023), is an important trading center in northern China. Its name was formerly spelled *Tientsin* or *T'ien-chin.* Tianjin lies near the mouth of the Hai River, about 85 miles (137 kilometers) southeast of Beijing. For location, see **China** (political map).

Tianjin and its suburbs form one of China's four municipalities that are ruled directly by the national government. These four metropolitan areas have a political status similar to that of a province. The others are Beijing, Chongqing, and Shanghai. The Tianjin special municipality covers about 4,250 square miles (11,000 square kilometers) and has about 9 million residents.

Railroads connect Tianjin with Beijing, Nanjing, Shanghai, and the cities of the Northeast (sometimes called Manchuria). The city has an airport that offers flights to most other cities in China. Tianjin serves as the chief port for the Beijing area.

Tianjin is one of China's leading manufacturing areas. Goods produced in the region include iron and steel, textiles, processed foods, and industrial products. Offshore oil fields make Tianjin an important center for petrochemical products. Tianjin has a large number of universities and technical schools.

After the Sui dynasty (A.D. 581-618) expanded the Grand Canal north to Tianjin, the city began to serve as an important port for goods traveling between north and south China. In the early 1400's, the Ming dynasty constructed fortified walls around the city.

In 1860, Western nations forced China to open Tianjin and its port to foreign trade. Eight countries established *concessions* in Tianjin. Concessions were tracts of land controlled by the foreign powers. See **China** (Clash with the Western powers).

Fighting between Japan and China in 1937 badly damaged Tianjin. Japan seized the city and held it until the end of World War II in 1945. The last foreign concession in Tianjin returned to Chinese control in 1946.

In 1976, an earthquake struck Tianjin, Tangshan, Beijing, and surrounding areas. About 240,000 people died, mostly in Tangshan. Richard Louis Edmonds

Tiber River, *TY buhr,* is one of the longest rivers in Italy. The Tiber rises in the Apennine Mountains in central Italy, 4,160 feet (1,268 meters) above sea level. The river flows for about 245 miles (394 kilometers), first through the Sabine Mountains, a range of the Apennines, then through Rome and into the Tyrrhenian Sea (see **Italy** [terrain map]). It flows into the sea through branches at Ostia and Fiumicino. The Tiber River has often overflowed its banks. Flood embankments have been built at Rome. David I. Kertzer

Tiberias, Lake. See **Galilee, Sea of.**

Tiberius, *ty BEER ee uhs* (42 B.C.-A.D. 37), was the emperor of Rome during the life of Jesus Christ. His full name was Tiberius Claudius Nero. The second emperor of Rome, Tiberius succeeded the emperor Augustus, who was Tiberius's stepfather and adoptive father.

Tiberius was born on Nov. 16, 42 B.C., on the Italian island of Capri. He became a successful army commander for Augustus. The emperor forced Tiberius to divorce his wife and marry the emperor's daughter, Julia. But Tiberius and Julia were unhappy, and he left her and went to live on the island of Rhodes. By A.D. 4, both of Augustus's grandsons and Tiberius's brother, Drusus Claudius, had died. Augustus then recalled Tiberius to Rome and made Tiberius his heir and successor. When Augustus died in A.D. 14, Tiberius became emperor.

Tiberius was a fine administrator. He carefully supervised tax collections and balanced the budget. He chose efficient governors for the provinces of Rome and maintained friendly relations with the neighboring kingdoms of Parthia and Armenia.

When Germanicus, Tiberius's nephew and possible successor, died, his widow accused Tiberius of causing his death. Because of difficulties with the Senate, Tiberius retired to the island of Capri. He gave great power to Sejanus, the *prefect* (commander) of the Praetorian Guard (see **Praetorian Guard**). Tiberius became unpopular during his last years because of his poor relations with the Senate and because he failed to end widespread prosecutions for treason. But he left a peaceful and prosperous empire to his heir Caligula, a descendant of Augustus (see **Caligula**). F. G. B. Millar

Tibet, *tih BEHT,* is a land in south-central Asia. It is often called the *Roof of the World.* Its snow-covered mountains and windswept plateau are the highest in the world. The world's highest mountain, Mount Everest, rises in southern Tibet. Gar, in western Tibet, is believed to be the highest town in the world. It is more than 15,000 feet (4,570 meters) above sea level. Valley bottoms in Tibet are higher than the mountains of most countries. Lhasa is Tibet's capital.

Tibet has been part of China since the 1950's. However, for much of its history Tibet was an independent or semi-independent state. Although Tibet carried on some trade with other lands, its mountain ranges isolated the country from outside peoples. Tibet was traditionally a religious kingdom. Buddhist monks had a strong voice in the rule of Tibet before China took control.

The land. The Tibet Autonomous Region of China has an area of 471,662 square miles (1,221,600 square kilometers). Prior to the Chinese takeover, Tibet covered about 965,000 square miles (2,500,000 square kilometers). Much of this area now falls in neighboring provinces. The Plateau of Tibet covers much of the land. Along the southern end of the plateau, the Himalaya rises higher than any other mountain chain in the world. Mount Everest (29,035 feet, or 8,850 meters, above sea level) is in the Himalaya. In the north, peaks of the Kunlun range rise more than 20,000 feet (6,000 meters). Tibet has an average elevation of 16,000 feet (4,880 meters).

Large parts of Tibet are wastelands of gravel, rock, and sand that cannot be farmed. But there are also fertile valleys and other areas suitable for farming. In addition, Tibet has grasslands and forests. More than 5,000 different kinds of plants grow in Tibet. Tibet's wild animals include gazelles, tigers, bears, monkeys, pandas, and wild horses. Tibet has hundreds of lakes and streams, but many have barren shores and a high salt content. Some of Asia's great rivers begin in the mountains that border the Plateau of Tibet. These include the Brahmaputra, Indus, Mekong, Salween, and Yangtze rivers.

Climate. Much of Tibet receives less than 10 inches (25 centimeters) of rain annually. The Himalaya shuts out moisture-bearing winds from India. Sudden blizzards and snowstorms are common. Violent winds sweep Tibet in all seasons. January temperatures average 24 °F (−4 °C). July temperatures average 58 °F (14 °C).

The people and their work. The Tibet Autonomous Region has a population of over 2 million. The majority of the people are Tibetans. Most of the rest are Chinese. About 6 million Tibetans live throughout the plateau. Most of the people live in southern Tibet or along the eastern edge of the plateau. Both regions have fertile land for farming and raising livestock. Nomads raise sheep and yaks in the grasslands scattered across the plateau. About 140,000 people live in Lhasa, Tibet's capital and largest city. Some of these people work in jobs in government, light industry, construction, or tourism.

Tibet's main traditional language is Tibetan. Mandarin Chinese is also an official language of Tibet. Both Tibetan and Mandarin Chinese are taught in the schools.

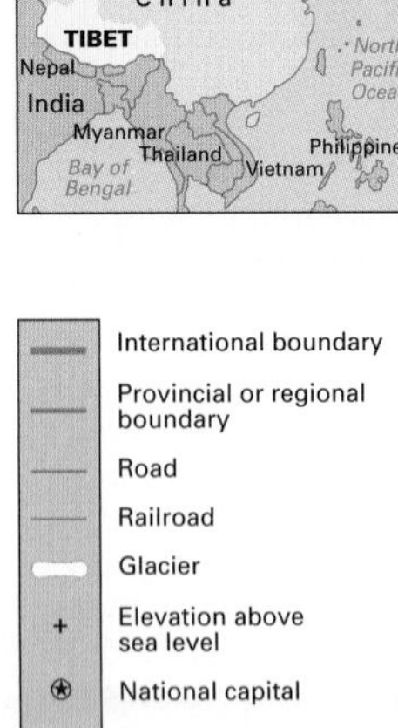

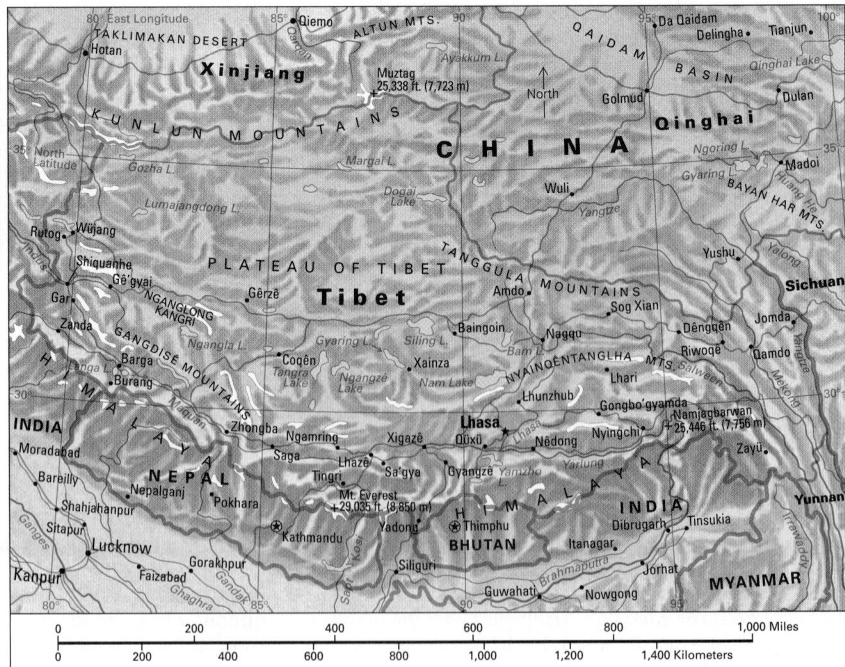

WORLD BOOK map

Before China seized Tibet, the government, the nobility, and the monasteries owned the farmland and governed the country. Most farmers were *bound peasants.* They often were not free to leave the land, and they had to give much of what they produced to the landowners. China, a Communist country, broke up the large estates and distributed them among farmers. Later, China took the land back and created collective farms.

Traditional Tibetan homes have stone or brick walls and flat roofs. Few of these houses have more than two floors. The ground floor is used to house animals. Rural Tibetans still live in traditional houses, but many urban Tibetans live in more modern buildings.

Barley is Tibet's chief crop, and barley flour is the main food. Tibetans mix barley flour with tea and butter. Milk and cheese are also important parts of the diet. Chinese tea is the chief beverage. Tibetans flavor the tea with salt, soda, and yak butter.

The yak, a hairy ox, serves many purposes in Tibet. It provides cloth, meat, milk, and transportation. It is also used as a beast of burden. Its hair is used to make tents, and its hide for shoe leather and boats.

Traditional Tibetan clothing includes a long robe with long sleeves and a high collar. Wool, felt, and sheepskin are used to make cold-weather clothes. Today, many Tibetans wear more modern styles of clothing.

Cloth weaving and carpet making are important household industries in Tibet. Exports include carpets, furs, leather, salt, timber, and wool. Many of these products are exported to other parts of China.

Religion and culture. Tibetans are intensely religious. People turn prayer wheels and recite prayers on the streets. Religious rites are an important part of life. Festivals are religious in character. Long pilgrimages to important temples in Lhasa and elsewhere are popular.

Tibet's religion is a branch of Mahayana Buddhism called *Lamaism.* The Dalai Lama, leader of the Gelugpa school of Tibetan Buddhism, ruled Tibet prior to China's take-over. The word *dalai* is Mongolian for *ocean,* and the title *Dalai Lama* means a spiritual teacher of great depth. Another important Tibetan lama is the Panchen Lama, whom many hold second only to the Dalai Lama. Since 1959, the Dalai Lama has lived in exile in India with a large community of Tibetan refugees.

Tibetans believe that when a lama dies, he is *reincarnated*—he returns to life as another person. They seek a lama's reincarnation among children born after his death. The child thus selected becomes the lama's successor. Tibetans believe the Dalai Lama and many other lamas are previous religious masters or divine figures.

In the past, large numbers of Tibetan men became monks, and a smaller number of women became nuns. Every town and valley had a monastery or convent, and some had several. Before the Chinese take-over, as many as 20 percent of Tibetan males may have been monks. Monks engaged in agriculture and handicrafts. The monasteries were centers of education, art, and public worship. Traditional Tibetan art reflected Chinese and Indian influences, and presented Buddhist themes.

During the 1960's and 1970's, the Chinese Communists closed or destroyed most of the monasteries in Tibet. As a result, the religious emphasis of life in Tibet decreased a great deal. During the 1980's, some monasteries were allowed to reopen and to recruit new monks.

Don Weiss

A public square in Lhasa, Tibet's capital and largest city, is a gathering place for people. Two women from the Kham region of eastern Tibet, *center,* wear traditional clothing.

Today, Tibet has fewer monasteries than it had in the past, but thousands of Tibetans still become monks. However, China continues to tightly control religious activity. China has instituted its own programs of political education in the monasteries to encourage monks to follow Communist principles.

Cities. Lhasa is the political and religious center of Tibet. The Potala Palace is the most impressive landmark in Lhasa. It is a grand, castlelike structure with gold roofs and more than 1,000 rooms. The Potala Palace was formerly a residence of the Dalai Lama and other monks. China preserves it as a museum and tourist attraction. Other cities include Gyangze, Xigaze, and Yadong.

History and government. From the A.D. 600's to the 800's, Tibet ruled a powerful kingdom. Buddhism and writing were introduced from India, and Lhasa was founded. The Dalai Lama became the ruler of Tibet in the 1600's. In the early 1700's, Tibet fell under the control of China.

In 1904, a British mission fought its way into Lhasa against Tibetan resistance. The British and Tibetans signed a treaty, setting up trading posts in Tibet.

Tibet remained in Chinese hands until 1911, when Tibetans forced out the Chinese troops stationed there. Even after 1911, China claimed Tibet as an area within the Chinese domain. In the 1920's, rivalry grew between the Dalai and Panchen lamas over political affairs. The Panchen Lama fled to China with his court. He remained there until his death in 1937. A new Panchen Lama was enthroned in China in 1944, but he was not officially recognized in Tibet until 1949. The Dalai Lama died in 1933. According to custom, a boy was chosen as his successor. The successor, a peasant boy, was officially installed as Dalai Lama in 1940.

Communists gained control of China's government in 1949. In 1950, Chinese forces entered Tibet. In 1951, Tibetan representatives signed an agreement with China in which Tibet surrendered its sovereignty to the Chi-

The Potala Palace in Lhasa, Tibet, was formerly the home of the Dalai Lama and is now a museum. The Potala has 13 floors and more than 1,000 rooms. It was built during the 600's but has been damaged, rebuilt, and enlarged several times since then. Most of the building that stands today was constructed during the 1600's.

Fridmar Damm, Leo de Wys

nese government but kept its right to regional self-government. The agreement promised no immediate change in the political system of Tibet and guaranteed the Tibetans freedom of religious belief.

In 1956, the Preparatory Committee for the Tibetan Autonomous Region was formed with the Dalai Lama as chairman, and a Chinese general and the Panchen Lama as two of the vice chairmen. This committee was set up to establish Tibet as an *autonomous* (self-governing) region. Despite these measures, China's harsh rule of Tibet sparked an uprising in 1959. The uprising failed, and the Dalai Lama fled to India. The Panchen Lama became head of the Preparatory Committee, but he was later imprisoned for over 10 years.

By 1965, when Tibet officially became an autonomous region, the large estates of landlords and monks had been broken up. Peasants were required to grow wheat rather than barley and to sell a fixed amount of grain to the government to feed the Chinese soldiers. Chinese took over a majority of such jobs as local government administrators and teachers. Tibetans faced discrimination by Chinese soldiers and settlers.

In the 1960's and 1970's, China's Cultural Revolution wreaked havoc in Tibet. Religious monuments were destroyed, and thousands of Tibetans died.

In the 1980's, the Chinese government adopted a more liberal policy. Some religious shrines and monasteries were reopened. Farmers were again allowed to decide which crops to grow and to sell them as they chose. But in the late 1980's, Tibetans demonstrated against Chinese rule in the Lhasa area and demanded independence. In 1989, the Panchen Lama died. He had supported some of China's policies in Tibet and favored unity with China, but he had also criticized many Chinese policies.

While living in exile, the Dalai Lama worked to end China's domination of Tibet through nonviolent means. He won the 1989 Nobel Peace Prize for his peaceful campaign. In 1995, the Dalai Lama announced the selection of a new Panchen Lama. But the Chinese government refused to recognize his selection and installed its own candidate. Elliot Sperling

Related articles in *World Book* include:

Buddhism (The Mahayana)
China
Dalai Lama
Lamaism
Lhasa
Mount Everest
Sherpas
Tang dynasty (The middle years)
Yak

Tibetan spaniel is a breed of dog that originated in Tibet hundreds of years ago. Buddhist monks kept these dogs as pets and as watchdogs for monasteries. The dogs were also companions to Tibet's rulers. The breed was first brought to Europe in the 1800's, but it was not officially introduced into the United States until 1967.

Tibetan spaniels are not actually spaniels, despite their name. Although Tibetan spaniels have keen eyesight and a nose for scent, they are not hunters or retrievers. Their alert personalities and intelligence make them useful as watchdogs.

Tibetan Spaniel Club of America, Inc.

A Tibetan spaniel has a thick coat and a curly tail.

The thick, silky coat of a Tibetan spaniel lies flat against the body. The coat may be almost any color or combination of colors. The bushy tail curls over the back, and the shoulders are covered with a *ruff* (frill) slightly longer than the rest of the fur. The dogs stand from $9\frac{1}{2}$ to 11 inches (24 to 28 centimeters) high and normally weigh between 10 and 12 pounds (4.5 and 5.4 kilograms). Critically reviewed by the American Kennel Club

Tibetan terrier is a breed of dog that originated in Tibet, where Buddhist monks raised it in monasteries.

Louise Van der Meid, T.F.H. Publications

The Tibetan terrier has a heavy coat of long hair.

The Tibetans once believed that these dogs were holy, and so monks gave them to important people for good luck.

Tibetan terriers stand from 14 to 17 inches (36 to 44 centimeters) high and resemble miniature Old English sheepdogs. Their thick, shaggy coat may be black, cream, gold, gray, or white, or a combination of those colors. The dog has a fluffy tail that curls over its back.

Critically reviewed by the Tibetan Terrier Club of America

Tic is a term used to describe repetitive, brief, rapid, involuntary movements of various muscle groups. Tics occur at random intervals. Examples of simple tics include shoulder shrugging, eye blinking, facial twitching, head and neck jerking, kicking, and bending movements of the waist. Tics are most commonly seen in the face, head, and neck. See also **Neuralgia; Tourette syndrome.** William J. Weiner

Tick is the name of a small animal which is related to mites, spiders, and scorpions. The tick is oval in shape. It is a parasite, which means that it lives on other animals. Ticks and mites cause various diseases in human beings and in domestic animals. Ticks often carry certain disease germs in their bodies and transfer these germs to the blood of their victims. Sometimes the bites of ticks are poisonous. Cases of paralysis are known to have followed their attacks. However, such effects are not common, and the victim usually recovers rapidly once the tick is removed.

Ticks and mites look much alike in body structure, but ticks are larger. Ticks look somewhat like insects but are not. Most kinds can be seen without a magnifying glass. They live only on animal fluids. But some mites feed on plant juices and tissues, on decaying matter, and on insects and other mites.

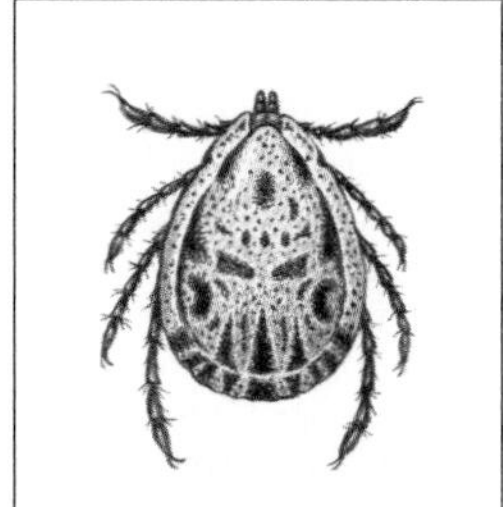

WORLD BOOK illustration by James Teason

Spotted fever tick

The bodies of ticks seem to be all in one piece. But some have a groove behind the head. The head is a movable part at the front end of the body. Ticks draw blood through a beak. Other body parts help ticks cling tightly to their host. Adult ticks have eight legs which stick out on the sides like those of a crab.

R. A. Mendez, Animals Animals

A female tick may lay up to 18,000 eggs at one time. After hatching, the larvae attach themselves to passing animals.

Kim Taylor, Bruce Coleman Ltd.

The sheep tick sucks the blood of animals and people. Its body becomes swollen with blood after it has eaten.

The tick lays eggs in dead leaves or other ground rubbish. The eggs hatch into flat, six-legged larvae. These larvae wait on grass stalks and shrubs for passing animals. Once attached, they gorge on the blood of these animals and swell up. Then, they cease to eat and begin to *molt* (shed their outer covering). After this, they become eight-legged nymphs. The nymphs resume feeding, molt again, and then are adults.

While the various kinds of ticks have special names, such as *chicken, cattle, dog,* or *sheep* tick, few of them are limited to one kind of animal. Many that attack animals also annoy human beings. Eight species are pests on cattle in the United States.

The American dog tick and the Rocky Mountain wood tick transmit *Rocky Mountain spotted fever* to humans. The disease causes a few deaths each year in the United States. Deer ticks transmit *Lyme disease* to humans. If untreated, this disease can lead to chronic arthritis and heart and nerve disorders. The common English sheep tick, which lives in America, infests dogs and cattle.

Wood ticks often trouble people walking and camping in the woods. To remove a wood tick, use fine-tipped tweezers to grasp the tick's mouthparts as close

WORLD BOOK photos by Kevin Shields

Tides rise and fall in a cycle that is regulated mainly by the moon's gravity. From the water's lowest point, *low tide, left,* the water rises gradually for about 6 hours until it reaches *high tide, right.* Then the water falls for about 6 hours until it reaches low tide again, and the cycle repeats itself.

to the skin as possible. Grasping the body may cause the head or mouthparts to break off and cause infection. Apply a firm, steady pull to remove the tick. Do not try to remove a tick by burning it off, or by coating it with nail polish, oil, or petroleum jelly. Avoid handling the tick with bare hands if the hands have cuts or scratches. Wash the hands after removing the tick and apply antiseptic to the wound. Save the tick for identification.

Edwin W. Minch

Scientific classification. Ticks belong to the class of arachnids. Together with mites, they make up the order Acarina. The scientific name for the Rocky Mountain wood tick is *Dermacentor andersoni.* The American dog tick is *D. variabilis.*

See also **Cattle tick; Deer tick; Lyme disease; Mite; Tick fever; Rocky Mountain spotted fever.**

Tick fever is a name for several diseases carried by the bite of ticks. They include Colorado tick fever, relapsing fever, Rocky Mountain spotted fever, and Texas fever. Texas fever is a disease of cattle. These diseases are infections by different microbes, which enter the body through the tick bite. See also **Relapsing fever; Rocky Mountain spotted fever.** Thomas P. Monath

Tickseed. See **Coreopsis.**

Ticonderoga, Battle of. See **Fort Ticonderoga.**

Tidal wave. See **Tsunami.**

Tide is the periodic rise and fall of oceans and other waters of the earth in response to the gravitational forces of the moon and the sun. The forces that produce tides affect all objects on the earth, the atmosphere, and even the solid earth itself. The response to tidal forces is greatest in the oceans. Tides are most noticeable at shorelines where oceans and continents meet.

There are one or two *high tides* and one or two *low tides* each day. The tides occur so regularly that they can be predicted many years in advance.

The regularity of the tides has fascinated people since ancient times. Some Greek and Roman philosophers who lived between the 300's B.C. and the A.D. 300's thought that the earth was a living being whose breathing caused the tides. But other philosophers of ancient China, Greece, and Rome noticed that the times of high and low tides followed the crossing of the moon overhead. However, they did not know how the moon helps produce the tides.

Europeans began to make detailed tables of tides during the Middle Ages. These tables helped ship captains schedule arrival and departure times at ports. The oldest known tables date from 1213. They show the high tides at London Bridge.

Modern thinking about tides began in 1687, when the published works of English scientist Isaac Newton explained the basic laws of motion and gravitation. Newton explained how objects attract one another by means of the gravitational force.

Tidal forces. The basic cause of tides is a difference in the strength of gravitational forces at various points in and on the earth. These forces involve the earth, the moon, and the sun.

The gravitational force between the earth and the moon tends to pull those two bodies together. However, their *inertia* tends to keep them apart. Inertia is a property of all matter. This property tends to make a moving object travel in a straight line at a constant speed unless a force acts upon the object. The combined effect of the gravitational force and inertia keeps the moon in orbit about the earth.

Causes of ocean tides

The main cause of ocean tides is the action of tide-generating forces created by the gravitational attraction between Earth and the sun. These forces are strongest in the area directly below the moon and the area on the opposite side of Earth. As a result, water bulges out as high tides in those areas. As Earth rotates, high tide occurs twice a day.

WORLD BOOK illustrations

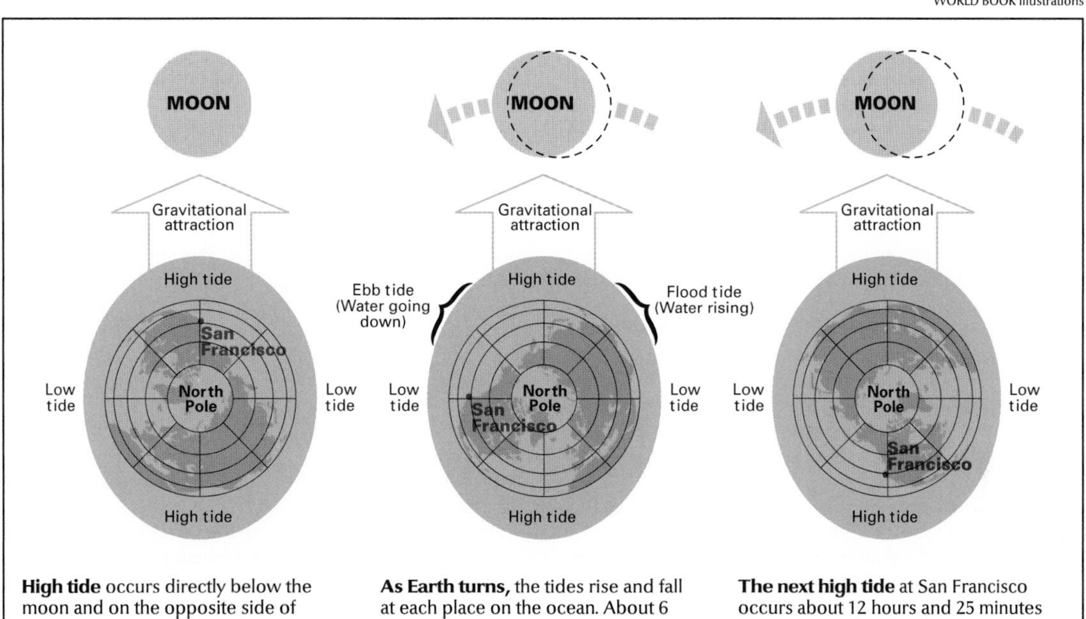

High tide occurs directly below the moon and on the opposite side of Earth. When Earth is in the position above, San Francisco has a high tide.

As Earth turns, the tides rise and fall at each place on the ocean. About 6 hours and 13 minutes after high tide, San Francisco has a low tide, *above.*

The next high tide at San Francisco occurs about 12 hours and 25 minutes after the first. Earth has turned 186° in this time. The moon has moved 6°.

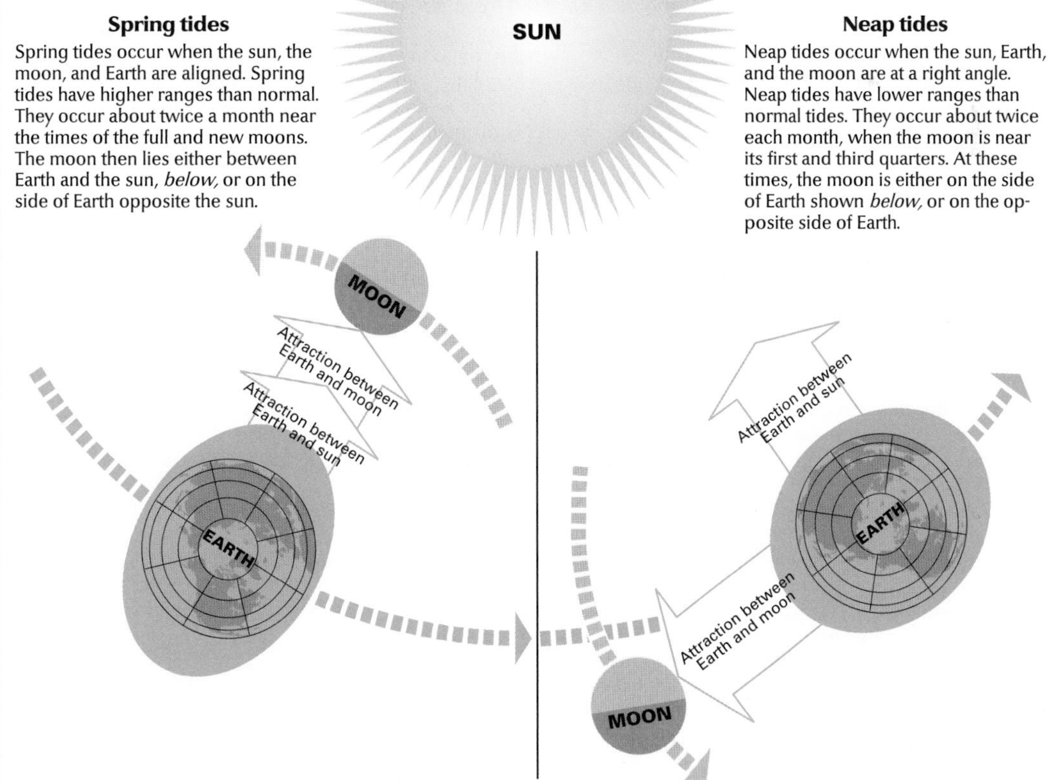

Spring tides

Spring tides occur when the sun, the moon, and Earth are aligned. Spring tides have higher ranges than normal. They occur about twice a month near the times of the full and new moons. The moon then lies either between Earth and the sun, *below,* or on the side of Earth opposite the sun.

Neap tides

Neap tides occur when the sun, Earth, and the moon are at a right angle. Neap tides have lower ranges than normal tides. They occur about twice each month, when the moon is near its first and third quarters. At these times, the moon is either on the side of Earth shown *below,* or on the opposite side of Earth.

At the center of the earth, the gravitational attraction between the earth and the moon exactly balances their inertia. On the surface of the earth, however, the balance is not exact. On the side of the earth closer to the moon, the gravitational attraction is slightly stronger than in the center of the earth. On the opposite side of the earth, the attraction is slightly weaker.

The difference between the gravitational attraction and the inertia can be thought of as a *tide-generating force.* This force produces two large bulges in the waters of the earth. As the earth rotates beneath the bulges, the waters rise and fall relative to the earth.

The tide-generating force produces a bulge on the side of the earth closer to the moon, and another bulge on the opposite side of the earth. The force does not lift the water straight up, however. The force is too weak to do that. Rather, it pulls the water parallel to the earth's surface toward a point directly below the moon and a point directly opposite the first point. The water piles up around these points, forming the bulge.

The earth and the sun also produce a tide-generating force and two bulges. These bulges are smaller than those produced by the earth and the moon, and distort their shape.

The sun's tidal force is only about half as strong as the moon's tidal force, even though the sun is 27 million times more massive than the moon. A calculation based on Newton's discoveries shows how this can be so.

The tide-producing force associated with the sun or moon depends on the *mass* (amount of matter) of that body divided by the *cube* of the body's distance from the earth. The cube of a number is the product obtained when the number is used as a factor three times. For example, the cube of 4 is $4 \times 4 \times 4$, or 64.

The sun has 27 million times the mass of the moon but is about 390 times farther away. Thus, the sun's tide-producing force relative to that of the moon equals 27 million divided by $390 \times 390 \times 390$, or about 0.46—which is roughly one-half.

Tidal patterns. In most parts of the earth, the tide-generating forces due to the moon and the sun produce two high tides and two low tides each day. As the earth rotates beneath the bulges each day, a high tide occurs, then a low tide, then another high tide and another low tide. Because the moon's orbit is tilted, the two high tides each day usually have different heights—as do the two low tides.

The time of high and low tide at any location also changes daily because the moon revolves around the earth more rapidly than the earth rotates about its own axis. The moon revolves around the earth once in about $29\frac{1}{2}$ days in the direction in which the earth rotates. During the 24 hours in which the earth rotates once, the moon moves an additional 12° around the earth. So every day the earth must rotate another 12° to reach the position it had relative to the moon on the previous day. The extra turning takes about 50 minutes. Thus, each succeeding day, the tides occur 50 minutes later.

Ocean tides are affected by the inability of a single tidal bulge to move rapidly enough to stay beneath the moon. The speed of a bulge is limited by the depth of the water, and the continents get in the way of moving bulges. The oceans respond to these restrictions by generating a number of circular systems of moving bulges called *amphidromes.*

The shapes of *ocean basins* (deep, relatively flat areas of sea floors) and ocean coasts also affect the tides. The waters in basins of different shapes respond differently. For example, the east coast of the United States has mainly *semidiurnal* (twice per day) tides. Tides in the Gulf of Mexico are mostly *diurnal* (daily). The west coast has *mixed* tides—semidiurnal tides and diurnal tides occurring together.

Tidal range, the height difference between high tide and low tide, also varies widely throughout the world. Some areas have extremely large ranges. For example, in the Bay of Fundy between the Canadian provinces of New Brunswick and Nova Scotia, the range averages about 39 feet (12 meters). The range is about 33 feet (10 meters) in the Gulf of St.-Malo in France and in the Bristol Channel in the United Kingdom. By contrast, tides on the coasts of the Mediterranean and Caribbean seas and on the shores of Hawaii have ranges of only about 2 feet (0.6 meter).

Tidal cycles. Tidal patterns and ranges also vary over time. The most outstanding variations are the *spring-neap cycle* and the *tropic cycle.* These variations result from changes in the relative positions of the sun, earth, and moon.

Spring tides are semidiurnal tides with unusually high ranges twice per month when the sun, earth, and moon are in line. This alignment occurs at times of full moon and new moon. Spring tide ranges are high because the tide-generating forces associated with the sun and the moon act in a straight line. They can be especially high in the spring and autumn.

Neap tides are semidiurnal tides with unusually low ranges twice per month when an imaginary line from the sun to the earth forms a right angle with an imaginary line from the earth to the moon. This arrangement occurs when the moon is in its first and third quarters. At these times, the tide-generating forces act at a right angle to each other.

Tropic tides are diurnal tides with unusually high ranges twice per month and twice per year. These tides occur when the moon and the sun, respectively, are at the highest or lowest point in their orbits.

Reinhard E. Flick

Related articles in ***World Book*** include:

Bay of Fundy	Estuary	Seashore
Energy supply (Tidal energy)	Ocean (Tides)	Tsunami
	Sea level	

Tie dyeing is a method of dyeing cloth to produce a design. Tie dyeing is one of the oldest methods of printing designs on fabric, and various techniques are found in many cultures.

Typically, parts of a woven material are bunched together in a design and knotted or tied with a cord or string. The fabric is then submerged in dye. The tied sections are protected from absorbing the dye, thus creating the design. The fabric can be retied and submerged into dyes of other colors to create new patterns and color combinations. Patrick H. Ela

Tien Shan. See Tian Shan.

Tientsin. See Tianjin.

Tiepolo, *tee EHP uh LOH,* **Giovanni Battista,** *joh VAH nee baht TEES tah* (1696-1770), sometimes called Giambattista Tiepolo, was the last important painter of the Venetian group. He began as an admirer of Paolo Veronese, but he soon developed a grand, colorful mural style that became popular in Europe during the 1700's. Many of his murals portray historical scenes and fantastic allegories. They show active figures painted in lively pastel colors.

Tiepolo was born on March 5, 1696, in Venice. After 1750, he worked mainly in Germany and Spain. His works include decorations for the archbishop's palace in Würzburg, Germany, and the Royal Palace in Madrid. Some of Tiepolo's small oil sketches for his large murals are displayed in the Metropolitan Museum of Art in New York City. Vernon Hyde Minor

See also **Age of Reason** (picture).

Tierra del Fuego, *tih EH ruh dehl foo AY goh,* is the name of a group of islands lying off the extreme southern tip of South America. The name *Tierra del Fuego* means *Land of Fire.* In 1520, Ferdinand Magellan named the region when he sighted large fires blazing along the shore. He was trying to find a passage to the Pacific. The Indians who lived there usually kept many fires burning to warm themselves.

The islands cover 26,872 square miles (69,598 square kilometers). The Strait of Magellan separates them from the mainland. The largest island, also called Tierra del Fuego, covers 19,280 square miles (49,935 square kilometers). The city of Ushuaia, the world's southernmost seat of government, lies on this island. The islanders are called *Fuegians.* Tierra del Fuego has a population of about 100,000.

Argentina owns the eastern part of Tierra del Fuego island, while Chile controls the western part. In 1948, an Italian settlement was made in the Argentine section. Each country also owns several of the smaller islands. Chile controls the Strait of Magellan, and maintains a naval base on Navarino Island. Cape Horn is at the southern tip of the islands. Jerry R. Williams

Tierra del Fuego is a group of islands at the southern tip of South America. The islands are divided between Argentina and Chile.

WORLD BOOK maps

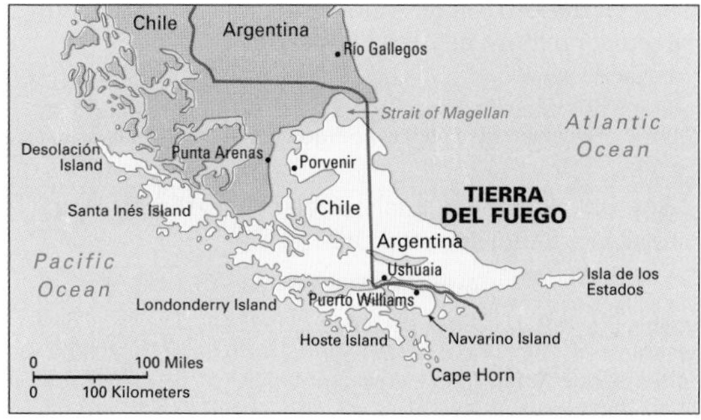

See also **Cape Horn; Clothing** (introduction).

Tiffany, *TIHF uh nee,* **Charles Lewis** (1812-1902), was an American dealer in precious stones. His reputation as a jeweler became so great that his name now stands for the highest quality in jewelry.

Tiffany was born on Feb. 15, 1812, in Killingly, Connecticut. He went to New York City in 1837 and opened a small notions store. Tiffany soon was specializing in jewelry, glassware, and china. Later he imported European crown jewels. He also set up factories to make some of the products he sold. Louis Comfort Tiffany, his son, created the famous Tiffany stained glass (see **Tiffany, Louis Comfort**). John S. Lizzadro

Tiffany, Louis Comfort (1848-1933), was a major stained-glass designer. He was an important American figure in the establishment of an international art style called Art Nouveau. The style flourished from about the 1890's to about 1910 (see **Art Nouveau**).

Tiffany was born on Feb. 18, 1848, in New York City. Charles Lewis Tiffany, his father, founded a famous jewelry business. Tiffany began his career as a painter, but soon developed an interest in the decorative arts, especially stained glass. In 1879, he formed a partnership with several modern artists. The firm specialized in contemporary interior design. In 1880, Tiffany took out a patent for colored glass that was *iridescent*—that is, it changed colors when viewed from different angles. In 1885, he formed his own glass company. In 1894, Tiffany registered the name *Favrile* to describe his handmade works in iridescent glass. John W. Keefe

See also **Glass** (picture: Stained-glass windows).

Tiflis. See **Tbilisi**.

Tiger is the largest member of the cat family. People admire the tiger for its strength and beauty, but they also fear it because it has been known to kill and occasionally eat people. Yet wild tigers prefer to avoid human beings. Tigers that kill and eat people are most often sick or wounded animals that can no longer hunt their natural prey. A hungry tiger may also attack people if prey is extremely scarce.

Wild tigers are found only in Asia. Until the 1800's, many tigers lived throughout much of the southern half of the continent. Now only a few wild tigers remain in most countries, and none of the animals are left in Iran and Pakistan.

Tigers can live in almost any climate. They need only shade, water, and food. Tigers are found in the rain forests of Thailand; the hot, dry thorn woods of India; and the cold, snowy, spruce forests of Siberia. Tigers also live in mangrove swamps, marshes, and tall grasslands. In general, tigers like to be in shade. They seldom go into the open plains as lions do.

The body of a tiger. Most adult male tigers weigh about 420 pounds (190 kilograms) and are 9 feet (2.7 meters) long, including a 3-foot (0.9-meter) tail. Most adult *tigresses* (females) weigh about 300 pounds (140 kilograms) and are 8 feet (2.4 meters) long. The tiger's coat ranges from brownish-yellow to orange-red and is marked by black stripes. Each tiger has a unique stripe pattern, which is as distinctive as a human fingerprint. The fur on the throat, belly, and inner legs is whitish. Many tigers, especially males, have a ruff of hair around the sides of the face. Tigers that live in Siberia, where winters are bitterly cold, have shaggy winter coats.

The tiger's stripes help conceal the animal in its natural surroundings. This female tiger could easily go unseen because her stripes blend with the tall grasses.

Ylla, Photo Researchers

Some tigers have chalk-white fur with chocolate-brown or black stripes. These tigers, called *white tigers,* are also distinctive because they have blue eyes. All other tigers have yellow eyes. White tigers are very rare in the wild. More than 100 white tigers live in the world's zoos. They are all descendants of a white cub caught in India in 1951. A normal-colored tigress can give birth to a litter in which some of the cubs are white.

Tigers and lions look similar except for the color and length of their hair. The two species have even mated in zoos and produced offspring called *ligers* or *tigons.*

How a tiger hunts. Tigers hunt large mammals, such as deer, antelope, wild cattle, and wild pigs. They may even attack young rhinoceroses and elephants. They also catch such small animals as peafowl, monkeys, and frogs. At times, tigers attack porcupines, but the porcupine's quills may stick in the tiger's face and body, causing painful wounds. In many parts of Asia, tigers prey on domestic cattle and water buffalo, especially where hunters have greatly reduced the amount of wildlife.

The tiger usually hunts at night, wandering along animal trails and dry stream beds. A tiger depends chiefly on its sharp vision and keen hearing, but it may also use its sense of smell. After stalking closely or waiting in cover, the tiger rushes at its prey in several bounds. Using its sharp claws, the tiger grasps the victim by the rump or upper body and pulls it down. Its large canine teeth are well suited for holding prey and for killing it.

Tigers are extremely swift for short distances. However, if a tiger fails to catch its prey quickly, it usually will give up because it soon tires. As long as a week may go by without a successful hunt. After a kill, the tiger drags the *carcass* (dead body) to thick cover. The tiger's neck, shoulders, and forelegs are very powerful. A tiger may drag the body of a 500-pound (230-kilogram) water buffalo for $\frac{1}{4}$ mile (0.4 kilometer). The tiger stays near the carcass until it has eaten everything except the large bones and stomach. A tiger may eat at least 50 pounds (23 kilograms) of meat in a night. A tiger often takes a long drink of water and a nap after a meal.

The life of a tiger. Adult tigers usually live alone but are not unfriendly with one another. Two tigers may meet on their nightly rounds, rub heads in greeting, and then part. Several may share in eating a killed prey.

Adult males often claim their own territory and try to keep other males out. In areas with abundant prey, such territories may average about 20 square miles (52 square kilometers). The male tiger marks trees in his territory with his scent and urine. The scent tells other tigers that the territory is occupied. A male's territory overlaps the territories of two or more females. Female territories are smaller than a male's. Each tiger wanders alone, but they communicate with each other. In addition to scent, they communicate with sounds, including a roar that can be heard for up to 2 miles (3.2 kilometers) or more. Some tigers do not have territories and travel widely.

A tigress usually bears her first cubs when she is $3\frac{1}{2}$ to 4 years old. She carries the young within her body for about $3\frac{1}{2}$ months. She then gives birth to from one to six cubs, though usually two or three. Newborn cubs are helpless and weigh about 2 to 3 pounds (0.9 to 1.4 kilograms). Tiger cubs, like kittens, are playful. They are wholly dependent on their mother for food until they are about a year old. Even then, they cannot kill a large animal. Cubs become fully independent at about 2 years old. Female cubs then often settle down in a territory near their mother. Males tend to roam far from their birthplace. Tigers live up to 20 years in the wild.

Tigers are good swimmers. They may swim across rivers or between islands. On hot days, they may cool off in water. Tigers can climb trees but usually do not.

Tigers and people. People have greatly reduced the number of tigers by killing them and by clearing the forests in which they lived. Scientists generally recognize eight varieties of tigers. Of these, three varieties are now extinct and three others—the South China tiger, the Sumatran tiger, and the Amur, or Siberian, tiger—are critically endangered. Several countries, especially India and Nepal, protect tigers in nature reserves. The survival of wild tigers depends on such efforts.

Tigers are easy to breed and raise in zoos. Cubs are popular with zoo visitors. Adult tigers are often trained to perform in circuses. They jump through hoops and are even ridden. Today, enough tigers are born in captivity that no more need to be captured for zoos.

Elizabeth S. Frank

Scientific classification. Tigers belong to the genus *Panthera* in the cat family, Felidae. All tigers are of the same species, *P. tigris.*

See also **Animal** (Animals of the tropical forests [picture]); **Lion; Saber-toothed cat.**

Additional resources

Levine, Stuart P. *The Tiger.* Lucent Bks., 1999.
Matthiessen, Peter. *Tigers in the Snow.* North Point Pr., 2000.
Seidensticker, John. *Tigers.* Voyageur Pr, 1996.

The skeleton of a tiger

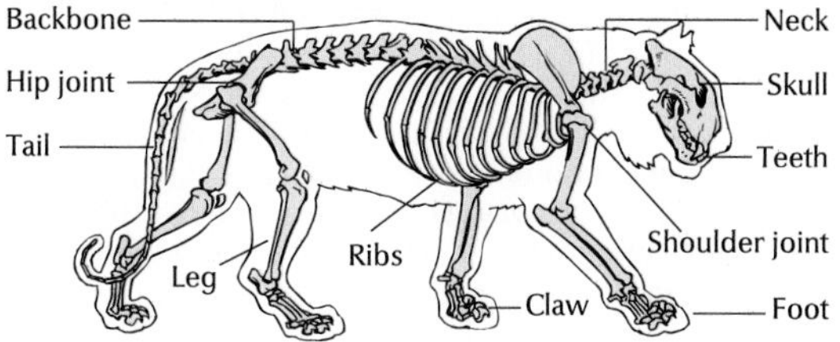

Tiger tracks

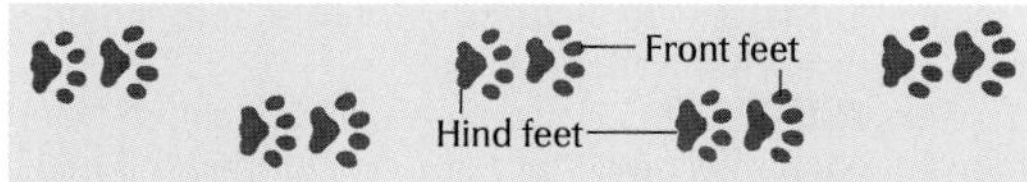

WORLD BOOK diagrams

Where tigers live

The yellow areas in the map show the parts of the world where tigers are found. Most tigers live in southern Asia.

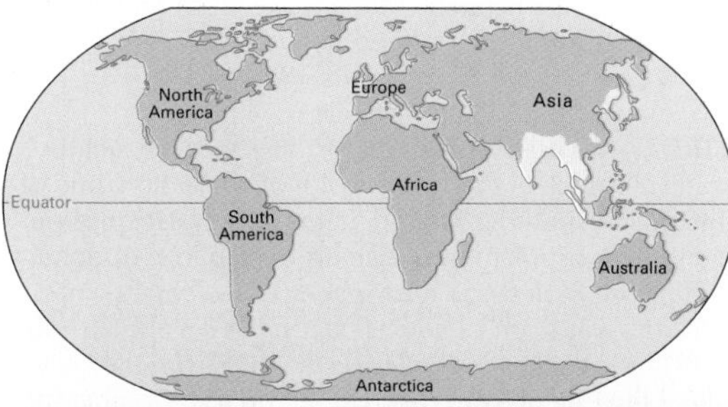

Marc & Evelyne Bernheim, Rapho Guillumette

The male tiger has a heavier ruff of fur around its face than the female. This male is taking a dip on a hot day.

Tiger, Tasmanian. See Tasmanian tiger.

Tiger lily is a tall, hardy garden flower named for its black-spotted, reddish-orange petals, which resemble a tiger's pelt. A few varieties have red, white, or yellow petals. The lily first grew in China, Japan, and Korea but has become a popular garden plant in North America and Europe.

The stems of tiger lilies are greenish-purple or dark brown, and many grow from 4 to 5 feet (1.2 to 1.5 meters) tall. Up to 20 flowers may grow on a stem. The leaves are long and spear-shaped.

WORLD BOOK illustration by Christabel King

Tiger lily flowers have black-spotted orange petals.

Tiger lily plants grow from bulbs. Tiny black *bulbils* (bulblets) develop where the leaves join the stalk. The bulbils eventually drop off, producing new plants. Tiger lilies grow best in bright sunlight and in well-drained, slightly acid soil. Gardeners should cover each bulb with about 4 inches (10 centimeters) of soil. The flowers can withstand cold weather but need some protection in winter. After being planted, tiger lilies flower each August and September with little care.

People in some countries boil tiger lily bulbs and serve them as food. August A. De Hertogh

Scientific classification. The tiger lily belongs to the lily family, Liliaceae. Its scientific name is *Lilium lancifolium or Lilium tigrinum.*

See also Lily.

Tiglath-pileser III, *TIHG lath py LEE zuhr* (?-727 B.C.), was a king of Assyria, a land centered in what is now northern Iraq. He ruled from 744 to 727 B.C.

Tiglath-pileser began the greatest expansion of the Assyrian empire. He defeated the rival kingdom of Urartu, which lay north of Assyria, mainly in what is now Armenia and Turkey. He also extended Assyrian control across the Euphrates River into Syria and Palestine. He conquered the ancient kingdom of Israel and made part of it a province directly under Assyrian control. The remainder of Israel and the kingdom of Judah became *vassal states* of Assyria. Under this arrangement, the kings of Israel and Judah recognized the king of Assyria as their superior and made payments to him. Tiglath-pileser also seized Babylon and, in 729 B.C., was crowned king of Babylonia.

Tiglath-pileser reorganized the Assyrian imperial system. He removed members of the Assyrian nobility from provincial governorships and replaced them with generals and officials from the royal court. These officials were responsible directly to the king. Norman Yoffee

Tigris River, *TY grihs,* is a major river of southwestern Asia. It is about 1,180 miles (1,899 kilometers) long and forms part of the historic Tigris-Euphrates river system. The Tigris rises in mountainous terrain in eastern Turkey, flows southeast to the border between Turkey and Syria, and then enters Iraq. The river winds through Iraq and gradually descends to low flatland. At the town of Al Qurnah, Iraq, it joins the Euphrates River to form the Shatt al Arab. The Shatt al Arab flows into the Persian Gulf. See **Iraq** (map); **Euphrates River** (map).

The area near and between the Tigris and Euphrates rivers has Iraq's most fertile soil, and the rivers provide water for irrigation. Most of Iraq's people live in this area. Baghdad, Iraq's largest city, lies on the Tigris. Dams along the river in Iraq store water used to generate hydroelectric power. Small boats sail on the Tigris, but much of the river is too shallow for large vessels.

The Tigris-Euphrates region was the site of the world's first civilization, which developed in Sumer about 3500 B.C. Assyria and other early civilizations also flourished in the region. The ruins of the Assyrian capital of Nineveh lie along the Tigris River. John Kolars

See also **Mesopotamia; Nineveh; World, History of the** (The Tigris-Euphrates Valley).

Tijuana, *tee WHAN uh* or *tee uh WAH nuh* (pop. 1,212,232), is a city in the Mexican state of Baja California Norte. It lies at Mexico's border with the United States, about 15 miles (26 kilometers) south of downtown San Diego (see **Mexico** [political map]).

Tijuana is a modern city with attractive public buildings and luxury hotels. United States tourists spend millions of dollars in Tijuana each year. The city's attractions include gift shops, fine restaurants, nightclubs, bullfights, and horse races. Tijuana produces electronic products and clothing. It is an export center for grapes, tomatoes, and onions. Many U.S. assembly plants are located in Tijuana. The geographical closeness of Tijuana and San Diego has linked the cities' economies in many ways. More Americans and Mexicans cross the border at Tijuana than at any other location.

Tijuana's name may be derived from an Indian name for the area, or from a huge ranch in the area called the *Tia Juana* (Aunt Jane). In the early 1900's, it was a small village of about 200 people. Since 1940, it has grown rapidly due to its booming tourist trade. Roderic A. Camp

Tikal, *tee KAHL* or *tih KAHL,* was one of the largest cities of the Maya civilization. The city had about 60,000 people in the A.D. 600's and 700's, during the height of its prosperity. Another 30,000 lived in the surrounding area. Tikal's ruins lie in the tropical rain forest of what is now northern Guatemala (see **Guatemala** [map]).

Tikal began as a small agricultural village about 600 B.C. It grew slowly until the 300's B.C., when construction began on a ceremonial center with plazas, palaces, and small pyramids. Eventually, the city's rulers built towering limestone pyramids with temples on top. Separate carved-stone monuments called *stelae* pictured gods as well as rulers and events from Maya history. The ceremonial center was completed about A.D. 800.

By that time, Tikal had become a prosperous center of agriculture, trade, art, and religion. Farmers in the area grew a variety of crops, including corn, beans, and squash. Traders came from as far away as central Mexico to exchange *obsidian* (volcanic glass), salt, feathers, *pigments* (coloring materials), shells, and other goods.

Tikal began to decline in the 800's, probably due to overpopulation, exhaustion of natural resources, and competition with other Maya cities. It was abandoned by 1000. Today, Tikal's ruins form one of Guatemala's national parks. Payson Sheets

See also **Maya** (with pictures); **Monte Albán; National park** (picture: Tikal National Park).

Tilden, Bill (1893-1953), was an American tennis champion known for his powerful serve and forehand. Tilden won the United States National Championships (now the U.S. Open) seven times during the 1920's. He led the U.S. team to Davis Cup victories every year from 1920 to 1926. Tilden was the first American man to win the Wimbledon Championship in England, winning the title in 1920, 1921, and 1930. William Tatem Tilden II was born on Feb. 10, 1893, in Philadelphia. He died on June 5, 1953.

Tony Lance

See also Tennis (picture: Great men players).

Tilden, Samuel Jones (1814-1886), was the Democratic nominee in the 1876 presidential election, one of the most disputed in United States history. Despite winning more popular votes than his Republican opponent, Rutherford B. Hayes, Tilden lost by one electoral vote.

Tilden was born in New Lebanon, New York, on Feb. 8, 1814. He earned a law degree in 1841 from the University of the City of New York. He served as a Democratic member of the New York state Assembly in 1846. He became state party chairman in 1866. In that post, he led the attack on the "Tweed Ring." This group of politicians, led by William M. Tweed, had stolen millions of dollars from New York City through improvement schemes.

In 1874, Tilden won election as governor of New York, running as a reformer. In the 1876 presidential election, he received a majority of the popular votes, but the Democrats and Republicans disagreed over who should receive 20 of the 369 electoral votes. An Electoral Commission created by Congress awarded the disputed electoral votes to Hayes, whom Congress then declared the winner (see **Electoral Commission**). James E. Sefton

Tile is a piece of ceramic, plastic, or other material usually used to cover ceilings, walls, floors, and other surfaces. Squares of tile are used as floor and wall coverings. Tiles for roofing come in various shapes. Sections of tile pipe are cemented together to form sewer pipes. Uncemented tile pipe, laid underground, permits drainage of areas with excess water. Hollow tile blocks used in walls and partitions can support much weight. All of these tiles are commonly made of clay. Thin sheets of clay are pressed or molded into shape and fired in kilns in the same process used in making brick (see **Brick** [Firing bricks]). The tile may be left in its rough state. Or it may be given a smooth, glassy coating called a *glaze.* In addition to clay, floor tiles may be made of rubber, linoleum, stone, cork, asphalt, or plastic. Acoustic ceiling tiles are made of cork granules, wood fiber, and mineral fiber. See also **Clay**. James S. Reed

Tilefish are deep-sea fish that live along the New England coast. The tilefish is the most colorfully decorated ocean fish in northern waters. The body is bluish or olive-green above, fading to pale blue below. The upper sides are thickly dotted with small yellow spots. The tilefish has a yellowish fleshy flap on top of the head. Large tilefish measure about 3 feet (91 centimeters) in length and weigh about 30 pounds (14 kilograms) or more. Tilefish feed chiefly on crabs and other fish. They can be caught on trawl lines and hand lines, with any kind of bait. William J. Richards

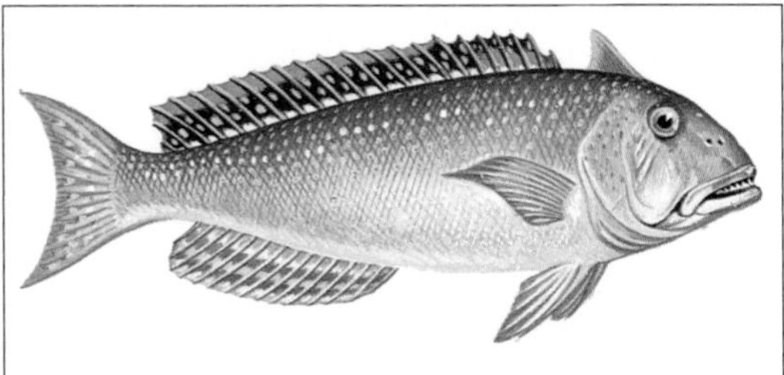

WORLD BOOK illustration by James Teason

The tilefish lives along the coast of New England.

Scientific classification. The tilefish belongs to the tilefish family, Malacanthidae. It is *Lopholatilus chamaeleonticeps.*

Till Eulenspiegel. See **Eulenspiegel, Till.**

Tilley, Sir Samuel Leonard (1818-1896), served as premier of the Canadian colony of New Brunswick from 1861 to 1865, and again in 1866. He represented New Brunswick at three conferences at which the delegates agreed on the terms of a Canadian union. These conferences were the Charlottetown and Quebec conferences of 1864 and the London Conference of 1866. The delegates became known as the Fathers of Confederation.

In the mid-1860's, many New Brunswickers opposed a plan for confederation because they feared they would lose political rights. Tilley helped persuade the people to join the Dominion of Canada by assuring them that the larger provinces would not control the smaller ones.

In 1867, Tilley became minister of customs in the Cabinet of Sir John A. Macdonald, the first prime minister of Canada. Tilley was promoted to minister of finance in 1873 and held that office under Macdonald again from 1878 to 1885. Tilley prepared a program to develop Canadian industries by putting a tariff on many imported products. This program was called the National Policy. Tilley was knighted in 1879. He was born on May 8, 1818, in Gagetown, New Brunswick. C. M. Wallace

Tillich, *TIHL ihk,* **Paul** (1886-1965), was an important German-born theologian. Tillich was a brilliant student of culture. In *Theology of Culture* (1959), he analyzed the forms of culture, showing the religious dimension in all cultural activities. Tillich developed a theory of religious symbols and myths, which he discussed in *Dynamics of Faith* (1957). His masterpiece, the three-volume *Systematic Theology* (1951, 1959, 1963), interprets the meaning of God and Jesus Christ in correlation with philosophical questions of modern life and thought.

Paul Johannes Tillich was born on Aug. 20, 1886, in Starsiedel, near Leipzig. His thought and life were transformed by his experiences as a Lutheran chaplain in World War I (1914-1918). He encountered what he called "the power of nonbeing" in wartime anxieties concerning death, guilt, and loss of meaning. In *The Courage to Be* (1952), he understood God to mean "the power of being itself" in the experience of courageously conquering anxiety.

Tillich left Germany in 1933 after the rise of Nazism. He settled in the United States, teaching at Union Theological Seminary, Harvard University, and the University of Chicago. David E. Klemm

Tilly, Count of (1559-1632), was a leading Roman Catholic general during the Thirty Years' War, a struggle between European Catholics and Protestants. Tilly devoted his life to trying to restore the influence of Roman Catholicism in central Europe.

Tilly was born in February 1559 in Gembloux, Belgium. His given and family name was Johan Tserclaes. When the Thirty Years' War broke out in 1618, Tilly took command of the Catholic League. He won important early victories over both the Bohemians and Danes, and he led the brutal destruction of Magdeburg, Germany, in 1631. However, he was defeated later that year at the decisive Battle of Breitenfeld by King Gustavus Adolphus of Sweden. On April 5, 1632, Tilly was wounded during an unsuccessful attempt to prevent Swedish forces from crossing the Lech River in Germany. He died on April 30 in Ingolstadt, Germany. Derek Croxton

See also **Thirty Years' War.**

Timber. See **Forest products; Forestry.**

Timber line. See **Forest** (Mountain evergreen forests).

Timber wolf. See **Wolf** (with picture).

Timbuktu, *tihm BUHK too* (pop. 20,483), is a trading town in central Mali. Its official name is Tombouctou (pronounced *tawn book TOO*). It lies near the southern edge of the Sahara, about 8 miles (13 kilometers) north of the Niger River (see **Mali** [map]). From the 1300's to the 1600's, it was one of the richest commercial cities of Africa and a center of Islamic learning.

Timbuktu began as a nomad camp in about 1100. It became prominent in the 1300's with the rule of Mansa Musa, emperor of the Mali Empire, who attracted merchants and scholars to Timbuktu from northern Africa. Goods from North Africa were exchanged in Timbuktu for products from the forests and grasslands of West Africa. Camel caravans from North Africa carried cowrie shells that were used as money, as well as salt, cloth, copper, books, dates, figs, and metalwork to Timbuktu. Arab traders also brought slaves, captured or bought in Mediterranean countries. The merchants of Timbuktu traded gold, ivory, kola nuts, and slaves—all from the south. Timbuktu became a center of scholarship in history, law, and the Islamic religion.

Timbuktu's location left it open to attack, and control of the city changed hands many times. From the 1200's through the late 1800's, it was controlled by the Mali Empire, Tuareg nomads, the Songhai Empire, Morocco, the Fulani people, and the Bambara Kingdom. The city was under French rule from the mid-1890's to 1959, the year before Mali became an independent nation. Since the 1600's, Timbuktu has declined in both importance and population. It remains an important historical city that is visited by tourists and scholars. It also continues to serve as a center for trade with the north. Lansiné Kaba

See also **Mansa Musa; World, History of the** (picture: The Sankore Mosque).

Time is one of the world's deepest mysteries. No one can say exactly what it is. Yet, the ability to measure time makes our way of life possible. Most human activities involve groups of people acting together in the same place at the same time. People could not do this if they did not all measure time in the same way.

One way of thinking about time is to imagine a world without time. This timeless world would be at a standstill. But if some kind of change took place, that timeless world would be different "now" than it was "before." The period—no matter how brief—between "before" and "now" indicates that time must have passed. Thus, time and change are related because the passing of time depends on changes taking place. In the real world, changes never stop happening. Some changes seem to happen only once, like the falling of a particular leaf. Other changes happen over and over again, like the breaking of waves against the shore.

Any change that takes place again and again stands out from other changes. The rising and setting of the sun are examples of such change. The first people to keep time probably counted such natural repeating events and used them to keep track of events that did not repeat. Later, people made clocks to imitate the regularity of natural events. When people began to count repeating events, they began to measure time.

Measuring time

Units of time measurement. For early peoples, the only changes that were truly regular—that is, repeated themselves evenly—were the motions of objects in the sky. The most obvious of these changes was the alternate daylight and darkness, caused by the rising and setting of the sun. Each of these cycles of the sun came to be called a *day.* Another regular change in the sky was the change in the visible shape of the moon. Each cycle of the moon's changing shape takes about 29 $\frac{1}{2}$ days, or a *month.*

The cycle of the seasons gave people an even longer unit of time. By watching the stars just before dawn or after sunset, people saw that the sun moved slowly eastward among the stars. The sun made a full circle around the sky in one cycle of the seasons. This cycle takes about 365 $\frac{1}{4}$ days, or a *year.*

For hundreds of years, people tried to fit days and months evenly into a year or a period of several years. But no system worked perfectly. Today, the calendar is based entirely on the year. Although the year is divided into 12 so-called months, the months have no relation to the moon's actual cycle. See **Calendar**.

There is no regular change in the sky that lasts seven days, as does the *week.* The seven-day week came from the Jewish custom of observing a *Sabbath* (day of rest) every seventh day.

The division of a day into 24 *hours,* an hour into 60 *minutes,* and a minute into 60 *seconds* probably came from the ancient Babylonians. The Babylonians divided the imaginary circular path of the sun into 12 equal parts. Then they divided the periods of daylight and darkness into 12 parts each, resulting in a 24-hour day.

The Babylonians also divided the circle into 360 parts called *degrees.* Other ancient astronomers further divided each degree into 60 minutes. Later, clocks became accurate enough to need smaller units than the hour. Clockmakers, following the astronomers' division of the degree, divided the hour into 60 minutes and the minute into 60 seconds. In this way, the face of a clock could easily show hours, minutes, and seconds. A clock face has 12 divisions. Each of these divisions equals one hour for the hour hand, five minutes for the minute hand, and five seconds for the second hand.

Some clock faces are divided into 24 hours. On such a clock, 9 a.m. would be shown as 0900 and 3 p.m. would be 1500. This system avoids confusion between the morning and evening hours.

Measuring time by the sun. Directly above every spot on the earth, an imaginary curved line called the *celestial meridian* passes through the sky. As the earth rotates on its axis, the sun crosses every celestial meridian once each day. When the sun crosses the celestial meridian above a particular place, the time there is noon. Twelve hours later, the time at that place is midnight. The period from one midnight to the next is called a *solar day.* The length of a solar day varies because of the tilt of the earth's axis, the oval shape of its orbit, and its changing speed along the orbit.

To make all solar days the same length, astronomers do not measure solar time with the *apparent* (real) sun. Instead, they use an imaginary *mean* (average) sun that moves at a steady speed around the sky. *Local mean solar noon* occurs when the mean sun crosses the celestial meridian above a particular place. The time between one mean solar noon and the next is always the same. Thus, all *mean solar days* are the same length.

Measuring time by the stars. Astronomers also measure time by the earth's rotation in relation to the stars. This time is called *sidereal time.* Each day, as the earth rotates on its axis, an imaginary point among the stars called the *vernal equinox* crosses the celestial meridian above every place on the earth. The time when this happens is *sidereal noon.* The time between one sidereal noon and the next is one *sidereal day.* A sidereal day is shorter than a mean solar day by 3 minutes 56.555 seconds.

Devices that measure time. The *sundial* was one of the earliest devices for measuring time. But it can work only in uncloudy daylight. Early peoples also used ropes with knots tied at regular intervals or candles marked with regularly spaced lines. When burned, such devices measured time. An *hourglass* or *sandglass* tells time by means of sand trickling through a narrow opening. A *water clock,* or *clepsydra,* measures time by allowing water to drip slowly from one marked container into another. By the 1700's, people had developed clocks and watches that told time to the minute. Modern electronic and atomic clocks can measure time with far greater accuracy. See **Atomic clock.**

Time zones

Local and standard time. Clocks in various parts of the world do not all show the same time. Suppose they all did show the same time—3 p.m., for example. At that time, people in some countries would see the sun rise, and people in other lands would see it high in the sky. In still other countries, the sun could not be seen because 3 p.m. would occur at night. Instead, clocks in all locations show 12 o'clock at midday.

Every place on the earth that is east or west of another place has noon at a different time. The time at any particular place is called the *local time.* At noon local time in one town, the time might be 11 a.m. in another place west of the town or 1 p.m. in a place to the east.

If every community used a different time, travelers would be confused and many other problems would be created. To avoid all such problems, *standard time zones* were established. These zones were set up so there would be a difference of one hour between a place on the eastern edge of a time zone and a place on the western edge if each were on its own local time. But under the time zone system, each of these places is not on its own local time. The local time at the *meridian* (line) of longitude that runs through the center of the zone is used by all places within the zone. Thus, time throughout the zone is the same.

Time zones in the United States and Canada. The United States and Canada each have six standard time zones. Each zone uses a time one hour different from its neighboring zones. The hours are earlier to the west of each zone and later to the east. The Newfoundland Time Zone is not a true standard time zone because it differs from its neighboring zones by only a half hour. The boundaries between the zones are irregular so that neighboring communities can have the same time.

The United States has not always had standard time zones. Every locality once set its own time by the sun. Various railroads tried to make their schedules simpler by establishing *railroad time* along sections of their routes. But in 1883, there were still about 100 different railroad times. That year, all the railroads divided the United States into four standard time zones.

Each zone is centered on a meridian of longitude 15° apart. In the United States and Canada, the Eastern Time Zone is centered on the 75° west meridian, and the Central Time Zone on the 90° west meridian. The Mountain

Standard time zones in the United States and Canada

The United States and Canada each have six standard time zones. This map does not show the Hawaii-Aleutian time zone, which includes Hawaii and the western Aleutian Islands (part of Alaska). The rest of Alaska is in the Alaska time zone. Major zones differ from neighboring zones by one hour. Zone boundaries are irregular so that places near the zone's edge can have the same time.

WORLD BOOK map

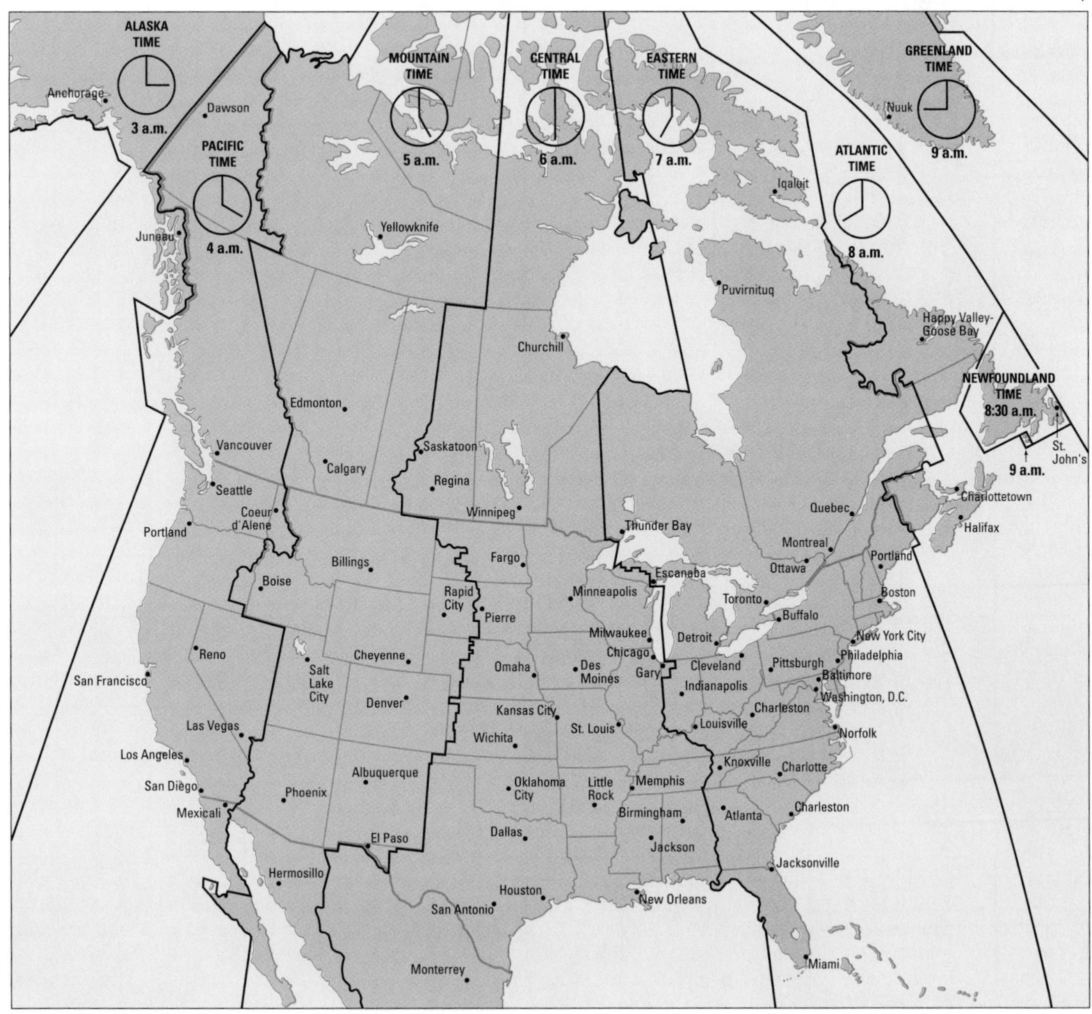

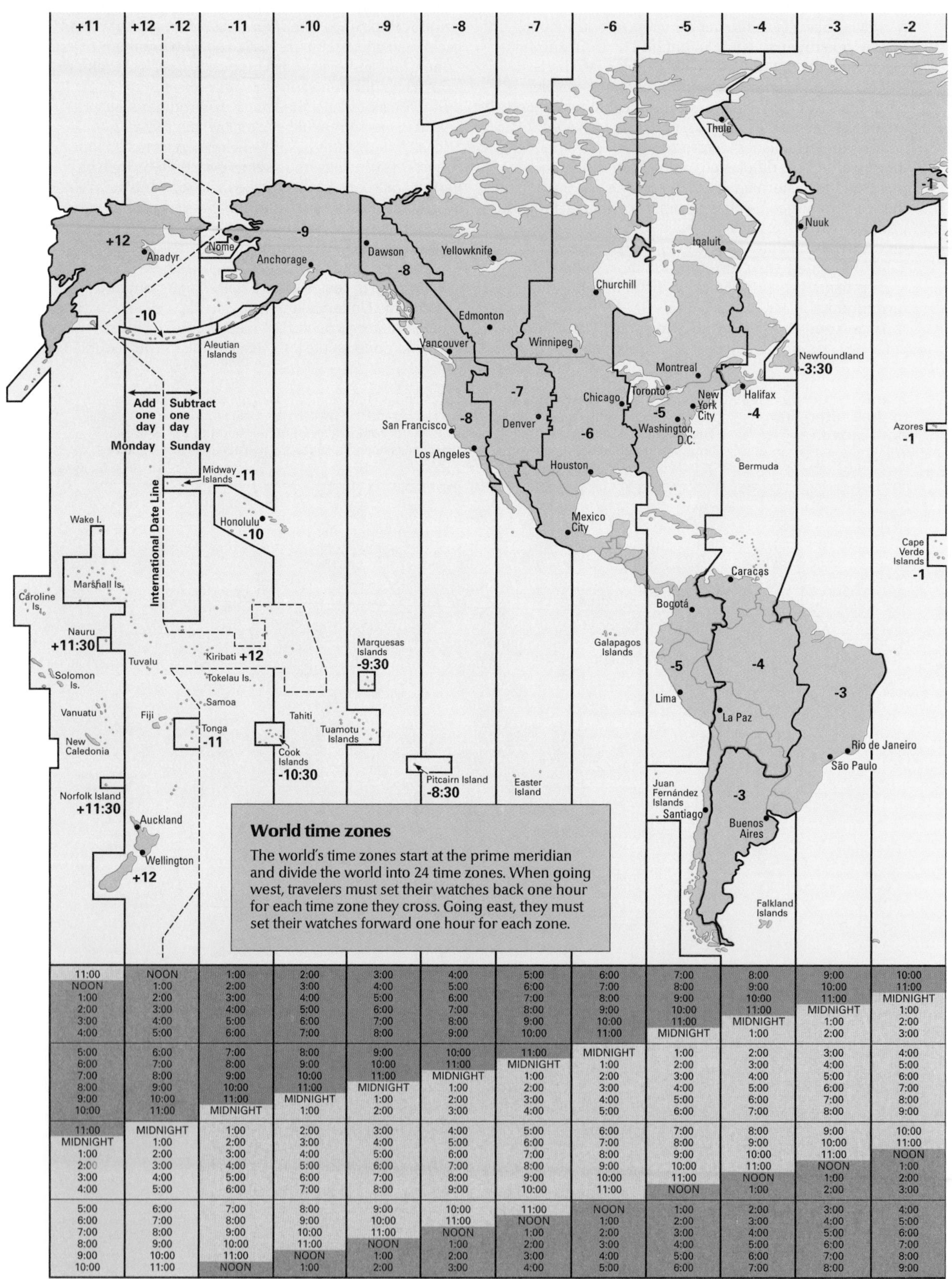

World time zones

The world's time zones start at the prime meridian and divide the world into 24 time zones. When going west, travelers must set their watches back one hour for each time zone they cross. Going east, they must set their watches forward one hour for each zone.

+11	+12 -12	-11	-10	-9	-8	-7	-6	-5	-4	-3	-2
11:00	NOON	1:00	2:00	3:00	4:00	5:00	6:00	7:00	8:00	9:00	10:00
NOON	1:00	2:00	3:00	4:00	5:00	6:00	7:00	8:00	9:00	10:00	11:00
1:00	2:00	3:00	4:00	5:00	6:00	7:00	8:00	9:00	10:00	11:00	MIDNIGHT
2:00	3:00	4:00	5:00	6:00	7:00	8:00	9:00	10:00	11:00	MIDNIGHT	1:00
3:00	4:00	5:00	6:00	7:00	8:00	9:00	10:00	11:00	MIDNIGHT	1:00	2:00
4:00	5:00	6:00	7:00	8:00	9:00	10:00	11:00	MIDNIGHT	1:00	2:00	3:00
5:00	6:00	7:00	8:00	9:00	10:00	11:00	MIDNIGHT	1:00	2:00	3:00	4:00
6:00	7:00	8:00	9:00	10:00	11:00	MIDNIGHT	1:00	2:00	3:00	4:00	5:00
7:00	8:00	9:00	10:00	11:00	MIDNIGHT	1:00	2:00	3:00	4:00	5:00	6:00
8:00	9:00	10:00	11:00	MIDNIGHT	1:00	2:00	3:00	4:00	5:00	6:00	7:00
9:00	10:00	11:00	MIDNIGHT	1:00	2:00	3:00	4:00	5:00	6:00	7:00	8:00
10:00	11:00	MIDNIGHT	1:00	2:00	3:00	4:00	5:00	6:00	7:00	8:00	9:00
11:00	MIDNIGHT	1:00	2:00	3:00	4:00	5:00	6:00	7:00	8:00	9:00	10:00
MIDNIGHT	1:00	2:00	3:00	4:00	5:00	6:00	7:00	8:00	9:00	10:00	11:00
1:00	2:00	3:00	4:00	5:00	6:00	7:00	8:00	9:00	10:00	11:00	NOON
2:00	3:00	4:00	5:00	6:00	7:00	8:00	9:00	10:00	11:00	NOON	1:00
3:00	4:00	5:00	6:00	7:00	8:00	9:00	10:00	11:00	NOON	1:00	2:00
4:00	5:00	6:00	7:00	8:00	9:00	10:00	11:00	NOON	1:00	2:00	3:00
5:00	6:00	7:00	8:00	9:00	10:00	11:00	NOON	1:00	2:00	3:00	4:00
6:00	7:00	8:00	9:00	10:00	11:00	NOON	1:00	2:00	3:00	4:00	5:00
7:00	8:00	9:00	10:00	11:00	NOON	1:00	2:00	3:00	4:00	5:00	6:00
8:00	9:00	10:00	11:00	NOON	1:00	2:00	3:00	4:00	5:00	6:00	7:00
9:00	10:00	11:00	NOON	1:00	2:00	3:00	4:00	5:00	6:00	7:00	8:00
10:00	11:00	NOON	1:00	2:00	3:00	4:00	5:00	6:00	7:00	8:00	9:00

WORLD BOOK map

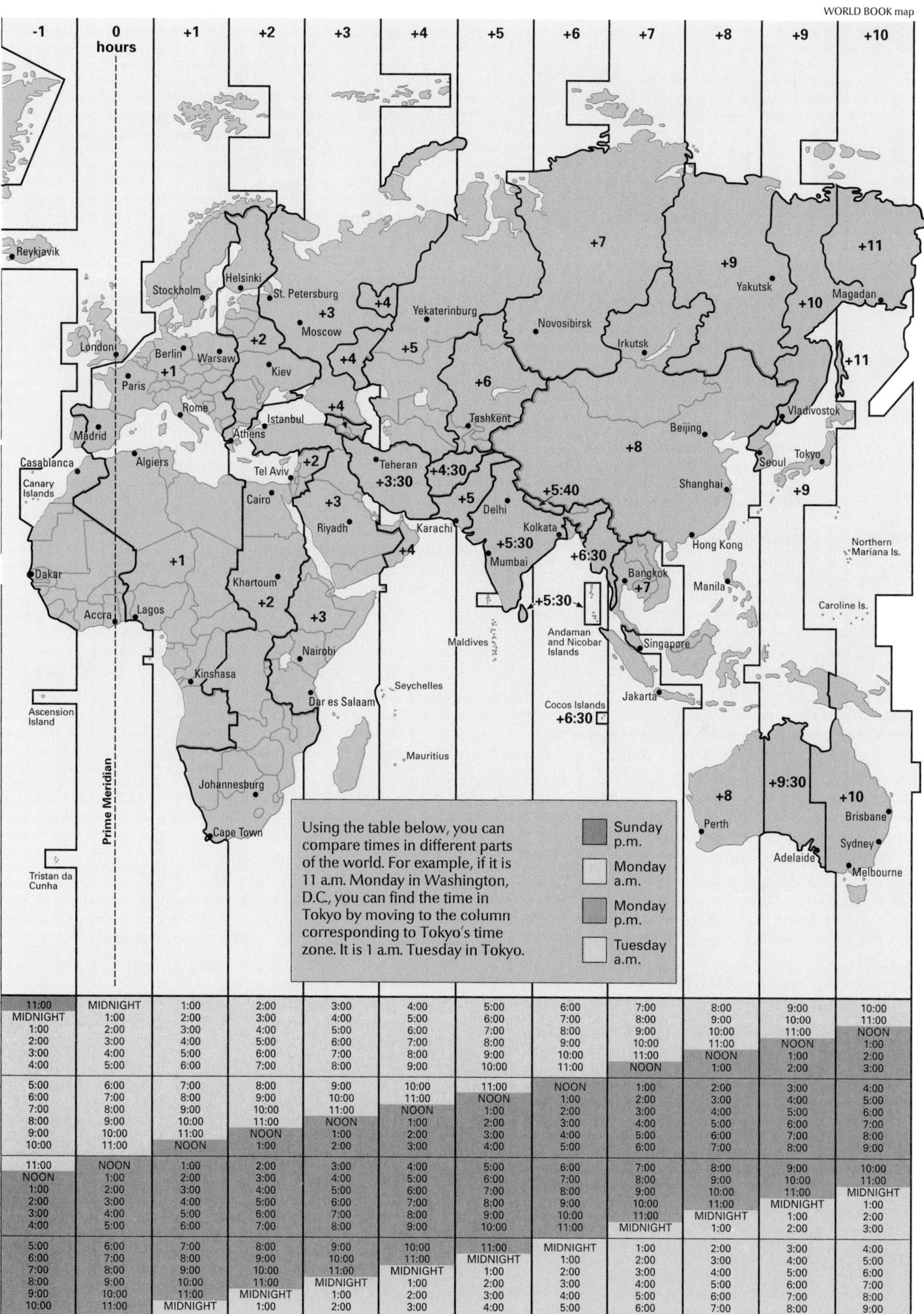

Using the table below, you can compare times in different parts of the world. For example, if it is 11 a.m. Monday in Washington, D.C., you can find the time in Tokyo by moving to the column corresponding to Tokyo's time zone. It is 1 a.m. Tuesday in Tokyo.

-1	0 hours	+1	+2	+3	+4	+5	+6	+7	+8	+9	+10
11:00	MIDNIGHT	1:00	2:00	3:00	4:00	5:00	6:00	7:00	8:00	9:00	10:00
MIDNIGHT	1:00	2:00	3:00	4:00	5:00	6:00	7:00	8:00	9:00	10:00	11:00
1:00	2:00	3:00	4:00	5:00	6:00	7:00	8:00	9:00	10:00	11:00	NOON
2:00	3:00	4:00	5:00	6:00	7:00	8:00	9:00	10:00	11:00	NOON	1:00
3:00	4:00	5:00	6:00	7:00	8:00	9:00	10:00	11:00	NOON	1:00	2:00
4:00	5:00	6:00	7:00	8:00	9:00	10:00	11:00	NOON	1:00	2:00	3:00
5:00	6:00	7:00	8:00	9:00	10:00	11:00	NOON	1:00	2:00	3:00	4:00
6:00	7:00	8:00	9:00	10:00	11:00	NOON	1:00	2:00	3:00	4:00	5:00
7:00	8:00	9:00	10:00	11:00	NOON	1:00	2:00	3:00	4:00	5:00	6:00
8:00	9:00	10:00	11:00	NOON	1:00	2:00	3:00	4:00	5:00	6:00	7:00
9:00	10:00	11:00	NOON	1:00	2:00	3:00	4:00	5:00	6:00	7:00	8:00
10:00	11:00	NOON	1:00	2:00	3:00	4:00	5:00	6:00	7:00	8:00	9:00
11:00	NOON	1:00	2:00	3:00	4:00	5:00	6:00	7:00	8:00	9:00	10:00
NOON	1:00	2:00	3:00	4:00	5:00	6:00	7:00	8:00	9:00	10:00	11:00
1:00	2:00	3:00	4:00	5:00	6:00	7:00	8:00	9:00	10:00	11:00	MIDNIGHT
2:00	3:00	4:00	5:00	6:00	7:00	8:00	9:00	10:00	11:00	MIDNIGHT	1:00
3:00	4:00	5:00	6:00	7:00	8:00	9:00	10:00	11:00	MIDNIGHT	1:00	2:00
4:00	5:00	6:00	7:00	8:00	9:00	10:00	11:00	MIDNIGHT	1:00	2:00	3:00
5:00	6:00	7:00	8:00	9:00	10:00	11:00	MIDNIGHT	1:00	2:00	3:00	4:00
6:00	7:00	8:00	9:00	10:00	11:00	MIDNIGHT	1:00	2:00	3:00	4:00	5:00
7:00	8:00	9:00	10:00	11:00	MIDNIGHT	1:00	2:00	3:00	4:00	5:00	6:00
8:00	9:00	10:00	11:00	MIDNIGHT	1:00	2:00	3:00	4:00	5:00	6:00	7:00
9:00	10:00	11:00	MIDNIGHT	1:00	2:00	3:00	4:00	5:00	6:00	7:00	8:00
10:00	11:00	MIDNIGHT	1:00	2:00	3:00	4:00	5:00	6:00	7:00	8:00	9:00

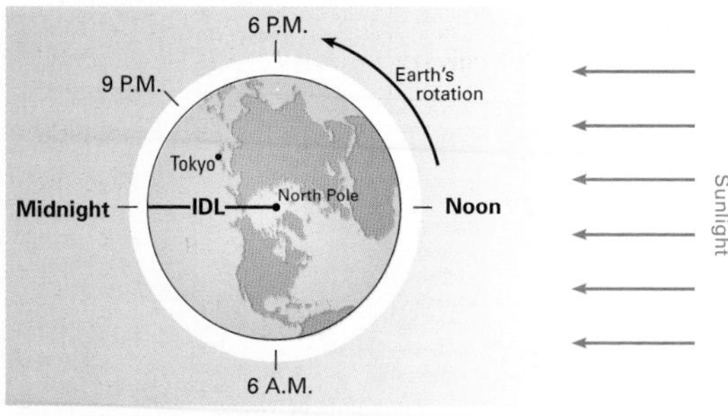

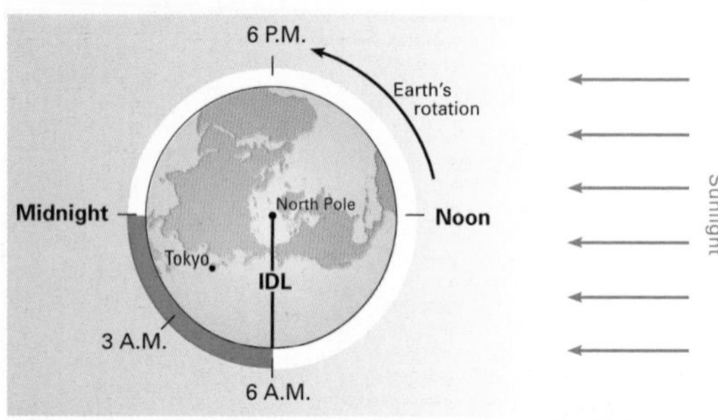

WORLD BOOK diagram

The time and date at any place on the earth change as the earth rotates on its axis in relation to the sun. When the International Date Line (IDL) is on the opposite side of the earth from the sun, *top diagram,* it is midnight there and 9 p.m. in Tokyo. At this instant, every place on the earth has the same date. Six hours later, *bottom diagram,* as the earth continues to rotate, it is 6 a.m. at the IDL. A new day, *shown in red,* has begun in the area between the IDL and midnight. The time in Tokyo is 3 a.m.

Time Zone is centered on the 105° west meridian, and the Pacific Time Zone on the 120° west meridian. The central meridians of the other U.S. and Canadian zones are 60° west for the Atlantic Time Zone, 135° west for the Alaska Time Zone, and 150° west for the Hawaii-Aleutian Time Zone. The Newfoundland Time Zone is a separate zone and has no central meridian.

Worldwide time zones were established in 1884. The meridian of longitude passing through the Greenwich Observatory in England was chosen as the starting point for the world's time zones. The Greenwich meridian is often called the *prime meridian.* The mean solar time at the Greenwich meridian is traditionally known as *Greenwich Mean Time* (GMT) or *Greenwich Civil Time* (GCT).

An international conference in 1884 set up 12 time zones west of Greenwich and 12 to the east. These zones divide the world into 23 full zones and two half zones. The 12th zone east and the 12th zone west are each half a zone wide. They lie next to each other and are separated by an imaginary line called the *International Date Line.* The line is halfway around the world from Greenwich. A traveler crossing this line while headed west, toward China, loses a day. A traveler who crosses the line while traveling eastward gains a day. A few places do not use standard time zones. For example, the polar regions have weeks of constant sunlight or darkness.

In the 1940's, experts began to realize that time based on astronomical measurements was not completely smooth, since the earth slowed down and speeded up in an irregular fashion. As a result, in 1958, the length of the second was redefined in terms of the natural vibration frequency of the cesium atom. However, the length of the year continued to be determined from astronomical observations. This time scale based on both atomic and astronomical measurements is called *Universal Time Coordinated* (UTC).

Scientific ideas about time

Physical time. Scientists think of time as a fundamental quantity that can be measured. Other fundamental quantities include length and mass. The noted physicist Albert Einstein realized that measurements of these quantities are affected by *relative motion* (motion between two objects). Because of his work, time became popularly known as the *fourth dimension.* See **Relativity** (Special relativity); **Fourth dimension.**

Many physicists believe that the apparent nonstop, forward flow of time is not a property of the basic laws of nature. They consider it a result of the fact that the universe is expanding and becoming more disorganized. Some physicists have considered the possibility that, under certain circumstances, time might flow backward. However, experiments have not supported this idea.

Biological time. The activities of many plants and animals are timed to the cycle of day and night. These natural rhythms are called *circadian rhythms.* The most obvious example is the sleep cycle.

Many plants and animals are sensitive to other natural time cycles. Certain plants do not start their next step of growth until daylight each day lasts a certain time. Some sea animals time their activities to the changing tides. These creatures even seem to know such times away from their home waters.

Geological time. Geologists have found clues in the earth's crust that indicate how many billions of years ago it was formed. One of these indicators is the element uranium. Uranium changes slowly into the element lead by means of radioactive decay. By measuring the amount of lead in a sample of uranium ore, scientists can estimate when the rock was formed.

A second clue to geological time is radioactive carbon. This form of carbon is absorbed by every living plant and animal. The rate of the carbon's decay can help a geologist estimate how long ago the plant or animal died. See **Radiocarbon.** James Jespersen

Related articles. See **Calendar** and **Clock** with their lists of *Related articles.* Other related articles include:

Biological clock	Naval Observatory, United States
Day	Radiogeology
Daylight saving time	Ship (Nautical terms [Ship's bell])
Earth (table: Outline of Earth's history)	Sidereal time
Greenwich meridian	Standard time
Hour	Time capsule
International Date Line	

Additional resources

Gardner, Robert. *Experimenting with Time.* Watts, 1995.
Lippincott, Kristen, and others. *The Story of Time.* Merrell Holberton, 1999.
Macey, Samuel L., ed. *Encyclopedia of Time.* Garland, 1994.
Skurzynski, Gloria. *On Time.* National Geographic Soc., 2000. Younger readers.

Time capsule is a container filled with items that represent a particular culture or era. The container is sealed to preserve these items as a historical record for the future. Time capsules vary in their contents, location, and size. Most are intended to be opened after a specified period. Time capsules might include such items as a letter written to oneself to be read in the future; examples of a society's recorded knowledge; or a distinctive article of clothing. The phrase time capsule first described a container buried by the Westinghouse company in 1938 at the New York World's Fair. It was scheduled to be opened in 6939. The phrase may also refer to an object or archaeological site that vividly represents the past.

About 5,000 years ago, Mesopotamians sealed devotional objects in building foundations for later generations to find. The first known time capsule with a fixed retrieval date was the Century Safe, sealed at the Philadelphia Exposition in 1876 and opened in 1976. The 2,000-cubic-foot (57-cubic-meter) Crypt of Civilization in Atlanta, Georgia, holds thousands of items. It includes a small windmill, encyclopedia texts, tools, motion-picture film, toys, and much more. Sealed in 1940, it was scheduled to be opened in 8113. William E. Jarvis

Time zone. See **Time** (Time zones; map).

Timor, *TEE mawr* or *tee MAWR,* is an island in Southeast Asia. It is about 300 miles long and covers about 12,000 square miles (31,000 square kilometers). The Portuguese first visited Timor in the 1500's. In the 1600's, the Netherlands began to compete with Portugal and with local chiefs for control of Timor. In 1859, the two countries divided Timor. The Netherlands took the west, and Portugal took the east. In 1949, West Timor became part of Indonesia. In 1975, Portugal withdrew from East Timor. Indonesia invaded East Timor later that year and occupied it until 1999. In 2002, East Timor became an independent country (see **East Timor**). Geoffrey Robinson

Timothy was one of the friends of Saint Paul. He was probably born in Lystra, in Asia Minor. His father was Greek, and his mother was Jewish but had become a Christian (Acts 16:1). He is thought to have converted to Christianity when Paul made his first missionary journey and talked with him. But Paul never discusses their first meeting, and Timothy is said to be a "disciple" when he meets Paul at Lystra (Acts 16:1-3). Timothy joined Paul on his second journey. References in the New Testament indicate that he was Paul's trusted friend.

The First and Second Epistles to Timothy and the Epistle to Titus are known as the Pastoral Epistles. They have this name because they contain advice to pastors concerning church government, officers, teaching, and Christian faithfulness and endurance. Critics debate whether or not Paul actually wrote these epistles. Some believe that a later author wrote them, using Paul's ideas. This authorship would explain why the epistles give little information about the character and deeds of the original Timothy. The epistles may have been written between A.D. 90 and 110, or even later. Carole R. Fontaine

Timothy is an important grass crop grown primarily for hay. It grows in tufts $1\frac{1}{2}$ to $3\frac{1}{2}$ feet (46 to 107 centimeters) high. The slender, leafy stems bear round spikes of tiny, tightly packed flowers. Timothy is a cool-season plant native to northern Europe and Asia. Timothy is also called *herd's-grass.* The English call it *cat's-tail.*

Timothy is a *perennial*—that is, it grows every year without replanting. But, it does not live long if animals graze on it continually, or it is harvested in an immature stage. Timothy hay's quality improves when it is grown with clover or alfalfa. In the United States and Canada, the first cutting of timothy is often harvested for hay or silage. Later cuttings are left in the pasture for grazing.

Timothy is widely grown in the northern United States and in Canada. New York leads the states in the production of timothy hay, and Ohio leads in the production of commercial timothy seed. Vern L. Marble

Scientific classification. Timothy is a member of the grass family, Poaceae or Gramineae. Its scientific name is *Phleum pratense.*

See also **Grass** (picture: Common grasses).

Timpanogos Cave National Monument, *TIHM puh NOH guhs,* is in northern Utah. It contains limestone caverns with hundreds of stalactites, stalagmites, and helictites in varied colors. Passageways in the caverns lead back into Mount Timpanogos in the Wasatch Range. The monument was established in 1922. For area, see **National Park System** (table: National monuments).

Critically reviewed by the National Park Service

Timur, *tih MOOR* or *TIHM ur* (1336-1405), was an Asian conqueror who created a vast empire that extended from Syria to India. He was also called *Amir Timur* (Lord Timur), Timur the Lame, Tamerlane, or Tamburlaine.

Timur was born near Samarqand in what is now Uzbekistan into a Turkic-speaking Mongol tribe. By 1370, he had defeated rival local leaders and gained control of an extensive kingdom. He made Samarqand his capital. A devout Muslim, he ordered the construction of many mosques and other buildings to make Samarqand one of the most splendid capitals in Asia. From the 1370's to 1390's, his armies struck into Afghanistan, Persia, Asia Minor, Caucasus, and southern Russia. He used terror as a tactic against cities that resisted or rebelled.

Timur invaded India in 1398, sacked Delhi, and massacred most of its people. In 1400 and 1401, he defeated the armies of the Mameluke rulers of Egypt and Syria, taking the Syrian cities Aleppo and Damascus. In 1402, he destroyed an Ottoman army sent against him. He next moved to conquer China but died before he could do so, on Feb. 19, 1405. His empire soon fell apart, though Samarqand flourished as a cultural center until the 1500's under Timur's descendants, the Timurids.

Richard L. Davis

Tin is a white metallic element that people have used since ancient times. The earliest known use of tin occurred sometime after 3500 B.C. in the Zagros Mountains of what is now western Iran. The people of that region made such articles as weapons and tools from bronze, an alloy of tin and copper. Today, tin is used chiefly in the production of *tin plate.* Tin plate consists of steel coated on both sides with an extremely thin film of tin. Most tin plate is made into tin cans.

Tin has the chemical symbol Sn. Its *atomic number* (number of protons in its nucleus) is 50. Its *relative atomic mass* is 118.710. An element's relative atomic mass equals its *mass* (amount of matter) divided by $\frac{1}{12}$ of the mass of carbon 12, the most abundant form of carbon. At 20 °C, tin has a density of 7.2984 grams per cubic centimeter (see **Density**). The difference between its melting point, 231.9 °C, and its boiling point, 2270 °C, is one of the widest of any metal. Tin is also *malleable*—that is, it

How tin is used

Tin's unusual chemical and physical properties enable it to be used in a wide variety of products for the home and industry.

WORLD BOOK illustration by David Cunningham

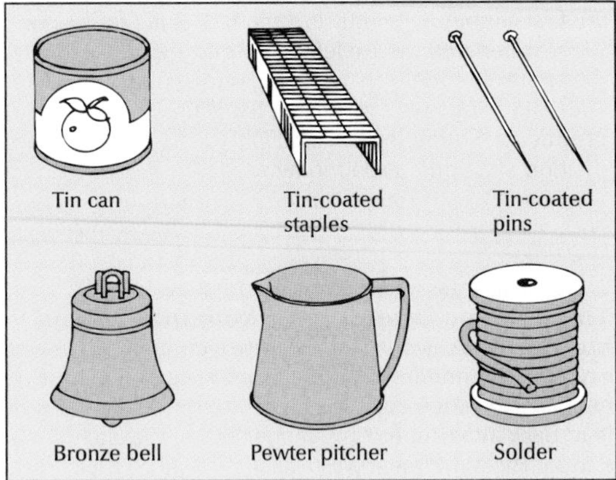

can easily be formed into complex shapes. These and other properties of tin enable it to be used in the manufacture of an extremely wide variety of products.

Uses. The coating on tin cans protects the steel in the cans from rust and provides an attractive appearance. Tin also prevents the weak acids in food from damaging the inside of the cans. See **Tin can**.

Tin coatings also protect many other items. Most paper clips, safety pins, straight pins, and staples are made of steel or brass coated with tin. Many food-preparation containers and utensils have tin coatings.

The second most important use of tin is in *solders* (pronounced *SAHD uhrz)*, which are alloys used to join metal surfaces. Solders made primarily of tin and lead are called *soft solders* and melt at relatively low temperatures. Other important tin alloys include bronze and pewter. See **Solder; Bronze; Pewter**.

The malleability of tin enables manufacturers to make tin into extremely thin foil. One use for such foil is as a moistureproof wrapping. *Terneplate* is iron coated with an alloy of lead and tin. Sheets or strips of terneplate are used for roofing and in making such products as fuel tanks and fire extinguishers.

Manufacturers improve the properties of various metals by adding small amounts of tin. For example, cast iron that contains only 0.1 percent tin is much more durable and easier to work with than ordinary cast iron. Many other products, including bearings, dental fillings, and printing alloys, also contain small amounts of tin, which improves their properties.

Leading tin-mining countries

Tons of tin produced in a year

China	88,200 tons (80,000 metric tons)
Peru	72,100 tons (65,400 metric tons)
Indonesia	59,500 tons (54,000 metric tons)
Bolivia	16,800 tons (15,200 metric tons)
Brazil	14,300 tons (13,000 metric tons)

Figures are for 2002.
Source: U.S. Geological Survey.

Tin combines with other elements to form a great number of useful compounds. Many toothpastes contain *stannous fluoride,* a compound of tin and fluorine that helps prevent tooth decay. Certain compounds that contain tin and carbon are used as pesticides.

Where tin is found. Tin makes up only about 0.001 percent of Earth's crust. As a result, the amount of tin mined annually is small compared with other commonly used metals. Most known deposits of tin are in the Southern Hemisphere. The United States has none large enough to mine.

The principal tin ore is a compound of tin and oxygen called *cassiterite.* The chemical formula of this compound is SnO_2. Some tin ores contain sulfur and small amounts of such other metals as copper, iron, and lead. Tin deposits sometimes occur as narrow veins that run through granite. More than 80 percent of tin ore, however, is found in plains, where flowing water has deposited bits of eroded granite and ore.

China is the world's leading producer of tin. Other important tin-producing countries include Bolivia, Brazil, Indonesia, and Peru.

Refining tin. Tin is produced by heating cassiterite with coal and limestone in a special furnace. After this process, called *smelting,* the tin is refined to a higher purity—usually to a purity of 99.8 percent. For details on refining, see **Metallurgy** (Extractive metallurgy). Most pure tin is cast into *ingots* (bars) that weigh about 100 pounds (45 kilograms). David W. Thompson

See also **Cassiterite.**

Tin can is a container used for packaging, transporting, and marketing hundreds of food and nonfood items for home and industry. Most tin cans are made of steel covered with a thin coat of tin. But millions of cans contain no tin at all, and many are made entirely of aluminum.

The first tin cans were handmade and sealed with solder. Today, manufacturers make and seal them on a series of machines called a *can line* that produce more than 500 a minute. The shape, size, and construction of cans differ to meet the specific need of the product they contain. But cylindrical cans are most commonly used. Many tin cans have enamel on the inside to prevent discoloration of the food. Perishable foods are preserved by heating the sealed can. In 1963, an Ohio man received a patent on a "tab-opening" tin can. The user opens the can by pulling off a strip of aluminum on top. In the 1960's, steel companies began making *thin tin* for tin cans. It is thinner and lighter than the usual tin plate used on tin cans. The United States produces about 30 billion tin cans a year. James A. Clum

Tinamou is any of a group of ground-living birds that live from Mexico to South America. Most tinamous have brownish feathers, dark above and paler below. Their short wings and strong legs make them well suited for life on the ground, and they rarely fly. They grow to between 6 and 20 inches (15 and 50 centimeters) long. Tinamous feed on seeds, berries, and insects. They nest on the ground. A female tinamou may lay 12 or more eggs in the breeding season. Both eggs and young are cared for by the male. James J. Dinsmore

Scientific classification. Tinamous belong to the tinamou family, Tinamidae.

Tinbergen, Jan (1903-1994), a Dutch economist, shared the first Nobel Prize in economic sciences with Ragnar Frisch of Norway in 1969. They received the award for their contributions to the field of *econometrics* (mathematical analysis of economic activity).

Tinbergen was born on April 12, 1903, in The Hague. He graduated from the University of Leiden in 1929. From 1933 to 1973, he was a professor at the Netherlands School of Economics (now part of Erasmus University) in Rotterdam. In the late 1930's, he worked with the League of Nations and developed new methods for measuring economic activity. Tinbergen also served with the Dutch government's Central Bureau of Statistics. He was chairman of the United Nations Committee for Development Planning from 1965 to 1972.

Tinbergen wrote influential books on business cycles, economic policy, and other topics. He died in Amsterdam on June 9, 1994. David B. Sicilia

Tinbergen, Nikolaas (1907-1988), a Dutch-born zoologist, studied how the behavior of animals is adapted to their environment. He also investigated the evolution of animal behavior over time by comparing behavior patterns in various species. Tinbergen shared the 1973 Nobel Prize in physiology or medicine with Austrian naturalists Konrad Lorenz and Karl von Frisch. They received the award for their studies of animal behavior.

Tinbergen worked with birds, butterflies, fish, wasps, and other animals in their natural surroundings. His best-known research concerns the social behavior of gulls. Tinbergen also applied ideas about animal behavior to the behavior of children suffering from a developmental disorder called *autism.*

Tinbergen, the brother of economist Jan Tinbergen, was born on April 15, 1907, in The Hague. He earned a doctorate from Leiden University in 1932. Tinbergen served on the faculty of Oxford University in England from 1949 until his death on Dec. 21, 1988. His books include *The Herring Gull's World* (1953) and *The Animal in Its World* (1972, 1973). He was coauthor of *Autistic Children: New Hope for a Cure* (1983). John A. Wiens

Tinnitus, *tih NY tuhs* or *TIHN ih tuhs,* is the sensation of hearing sounds that seem to come from within the head. Most people with tinnitus hear ringing, buzzing, or hissing noises. Others hear sounds like a cricket's chirping or the ocean's roar. The noise may be continuous or come and go. It may be heard in one or both ears. Tinnitus can be extremely distracting, and in some cases it is loud enough to keep the person awake. It can also cause some hearing loss, ear pain, or dizziness.

Some cases of tinnitus can be traced to a specific condition, such as a blocked ear canal, an ear infection, or the use of certain medicines. Other causes of tinnitus include blood vessel disease, head injury, aging, jaw misalignment, and exposure to loud noises. But in most cases of tinnitus, no cause can be identified. Doctors suspect that such cases are due to abnormal functioning of the inner ear or its nerve connections to the brain.

When physicians can identify the cause of a person's tinnitus, they often can relieve it by treating the underlying condition. In cases with no obvious cause, certain medicines can sometimes reduce the noise and aid sleep. Some people with tinnitus use a device similar to a hearing aid, which masks the noise with more tolerable sounds. For the majority of tinnitus sufferers, however, there is no effective treatment. Frank E. Musiek

Tintoretto, *tihn tuh REHT oh* (1518-1594), was a Venetian painter during the late Italian Renaissance. He became a leading artist of the period for the churches and wealthy families of Venice.

Tintoretto created works noted for their dramatic action. His paintings show the influence of the rich colors that were used by Titian and the vigorous, muscular forms drawn by Michelangelo. Tintoretto achieved a unique style through exaggeration. He sometimes distorted the proportions of his figures for dramatic effect. The figures move energetically through deep space and changing light.

Tintoretto planned his compositions by placing wax or clay figures in a box—like actors on the stage of a theater—and using candles for lighting effects. He studied these arrangements and drew sketches before beginning to paint. The theatrical character of Tintoretto's paintings can be seen in one of his most famous works, *The Last Supper* (1592-1594), which appears in the **Painting** article. The figures bend, gesture, and turn. Tintoretto achieved dramatic contrast by spotlighting some forms with intense color and painting others in softer tones and shadows.

Tintoretto's real name was Jacopo Robusti. He was nicknamed *Il Tintoretto,* which means *the little dyer,* because his father was a dyer. Scholars believe Tintoretto taught himself to paint. He opened his first studio at the age of 21. He died on May 31, 1594. David Summers

Tipi. See **Tepee.**

Tippecanoe, Battle of. See **Indian wars** (Conflicts in the Midwest).

Tipperary, *TIHP uh RAIR ee* (pop. 4,546), is a town in southern Ireland. It lies on the Ara River, in an area called the Golden Vale that has many dairy farms. For location, see **Ireland** (political map). Tipperary serves as a market town and a processing center for dairy products.

Tipperary was founded in the late 1100's. It surrounded a castle built by Prince John (later King John) of England. The name *Tipperary* is well known because of the song "It's a Long, Long Way to Tipperary." This tune was a favorite marching song of Allied troops in World War I (1914-1918). Stephen A. Royle

Tiranë, *tee RAH nuh* (pop. 260,000), is the capital and largest city of Albania. Tiranë, also spelled *Tirana,* lies on a coastal plain about 20 miles (32 kilometers) east of the Adriatic Sea. For location, see **Albania** (map).

Tiranë's central district has wide avenues lined by attractive stone buildings. The city is Albania's educational and cultural center. The State University and several research institutes, museums, and theaters are there. Tiranë is the home of Albania's major publishing and broadcasting companies and of several light industries.

The Ottoman commander Barkinzadeh Suleiman Pasha founded Tiranë in the early 1600's. Tiranë became the capital of Albania in 1920. In the early 1920's, only about 12,000 people lived in the city. In the mid-1900's, the Albanian government expanded Tiranë's boundaries. Since then, many Albanians have moved to the city to work in industries and government. Sabrina P. Ramet

Goodyear

Goodyear

Goodyear

Automobile tires have various tread patterns. A basic tread, *left,* is built for driving in all seasons. A tread designed for wet roads, *middle,* has a central channel and connecting grooves that expel water. A sports car tire, *right,* has large tread areas on its outboard side (the right side as shown) to help maintain road contact when cornering.

Tire is a covering for the outer rim of a wheel. Most tires are made of rubber reinforced with some kind of fabric and are *pneumatic* (filled with compressed air). They are used on airplanes, automobiles, bicycles, buses, earth-moving and mining machinery, motorcycles, recreational vehicles, tractors, trucks, and many other kinds of vehicles. Some rubber tires, such as those used on many wagons and wheelbarrows, are solid rubber.

The main feature of rubber tires is their ability to absorb the shock and strain created by bumps in the road. Tires help provide a comfortable ride and help protect many kinds of cargoes. The air in a rubber tire supports the weight of a vehicle.

Another important feature of rubber tires is their ability to grip the road. The face of a tire, called the *tread,* has many deep grooves. These grooves and many smaller slits called *sipes* make up the *tread pattern.* The tread provides the traction that enables the tires to grip the road in wet weather. The tire body is composed of the rubber *side walls* (sides), which cover and protect the rest of the body and are made of high-strength bundles of wire for holding the tire on the wheel rim. The body also contains layers of rubberized cord fabric. Each layer is called a *ply.*

How tires are made

Preliminary operations. Before a tire can be manufactured, several operations must be performed. They include mixing the rubber with sulfur and other chemicals, coating cord fabric with the rubber, and cutting the rubberized fabric into strips.

A machine called a *Banbury machine* mixes the rubber with the chemicals. The chemicals strengthen the rubber and increase its resistance to wear. The rubber comes from the machine in the form of sheets.

A *calendering machine* coats cord fabric with the rubber sheeting. Cord fabric is made of nylon, polyester, rayon, or steel. The triple rollers of the machine squeeze the cords and the rubber together, producing a rubber-

Parts of a tire The parts of a tire, shown here in cross section, are assembled one by one. Starting with the inner liner, a worker assembles the tire on a turning *drum* (roller). Later, the process of *vulcanization* shapes the tire, seals the parts together, and molds the pattern of grooves and sipes into the tread.

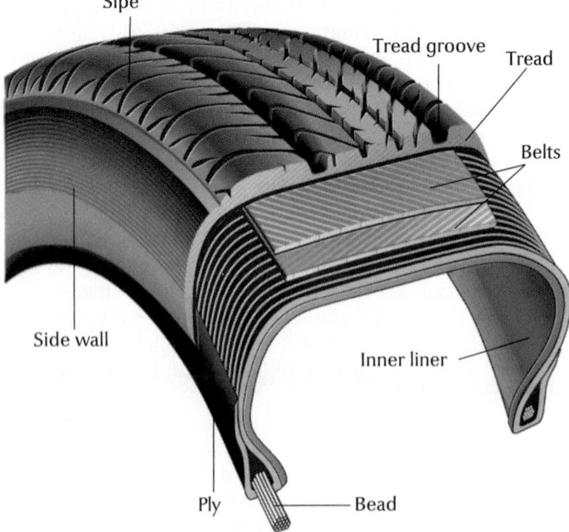

Tire belts improve traction and stability and reduce wear by putting as much tread as possible on the road, as shown in this diagram.

WORLD BOOK diagrams by Paul Perrault

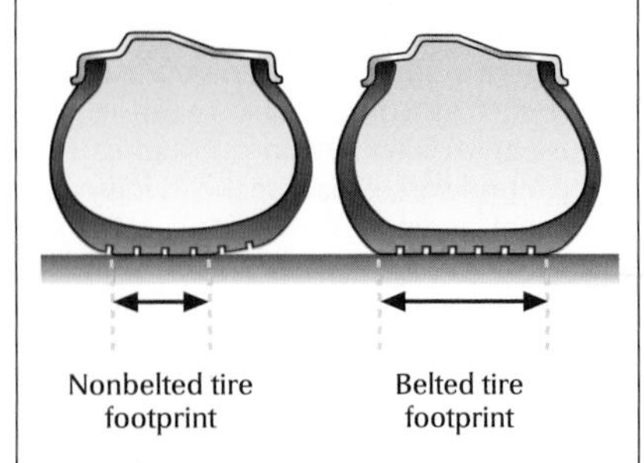

ized fabric. A cutting machine then slices the rubberized cord fabric into strips of the necessary size.

Assembling a tire. A tire is assembled mostly by hand, though some of the steps may be performed by specially designed machinery. The assembly process begins on a slowly rotating roller called a *drum.* The drum has the same diameter as the wheel on which the tire will be used. As the drum turns, a worker called a *tire builder* wraps an *inner liner* around the drum. The inner liner consists of a band of special rubber that makes the tire airtight. The tire builder then wraps the rubberized cord fabric around the drum, ply by ply. Most of today's automobile tires have two *belts* of fabric between the plies and the tread. The belts are made of steel or manufactured fibers that resist stretching. Such fibers include aramid, fiberglass, and rayon.

After putting on the plies, the tire builder adds two *beads.* Each bead consists of several steel wire strands that have been wound together into a hoop and covered with hard rubber. A bead is put on each side of the tire. It is inserted at the point where the tire will come into contact with the rim of the wheel. The two ends of each ply are wrapped around the bead, securing the bead to the tire.

Next, the builder adds the rubber side walls, the belts, and the tread. The various parts of the tire are then pressed together by a set of rollers in a process called *stitching.*

The *green* (uncured) tire is now ready to be *vulcanized.* The vulcanization process combines chemicals with the raw rubber and makes a rubber product strong, hard, and elastic. The tire is taken off the drum and placed in a *curing press.* The press contains a large rubber bag called a *bladder* and a mold that has the sipes and large grooves of the desired tread pattern in it. The press operates like a giant waffle iron. It is closed, heat is applied, and the bladder is filled with steam. The filled bladder presses the tire against the mold. The bladder and the mold squeeze the tire into its final shape, complete with tread pattern. See **Rubber** (Vulcanization).

Retreading tires. After the original tread pattern has worn down, a tire—if it is in good condition—can be *retreaded,* or *recapped.* First, a machine rubs away the old tread. Then a worker applies new tread rubber and puts the tire into a mold. The new tread and tread pattern are then vulcanized to the old tire. Sometimes a new tread with a pattern that has already been vulcanized is cemented to the prepared tire body.

Types of tires and tread patterns

There are three basic kinds of automobile tires: (1) *bias;* (2) *bias belted;* and (3) *radial,* or *radial ply.*

Bias tires are built with the fabric cord running diagonally—that is, on the bias—from one rim to the other. Each ply is added so that its cords run at an angle opposite to the angle of the cords below it.

As a vehicle moves, the plies of its tires rub against each other and against the tread in an action called *flexing and squirming.* This action produces inner heat, one of the major causes of tire wear. Extreme heat can separate the tread or split the plies.

Bias belted tires are made in the same way as bias tires, but cord fabric belts are placed between the plies and the tread. The belts help prevent punctures and fight tread squirm.

Radial tires are built with the body fabric cord running straight across the tire from one rim to the other. All radial tires are belted. The combination of radial ply and belting produces a tire with longer tread life than either bias or bias belted tires. Radial tires give longer wear because they have less flex and squirm than bias ply tires. They also roll more easily and thus save fuel.

Low profile tires are used on many high-performance cars. These tires look pudgier than regular tires. They are wider (from side wall to side wall) than they are high (from tread to wheel rim). They put more tread into contact with the road than standard tires. This additional

Tire size comparison The size of a car's tires depends on the type and weight of the vehicle as well as the size of its wheels. Almost all new automobiles have standard tires. Some cars, including many high-performance cars, use low profile or ultra-low profile tires.

WORLD BOOK diagrams by Paul Perreault

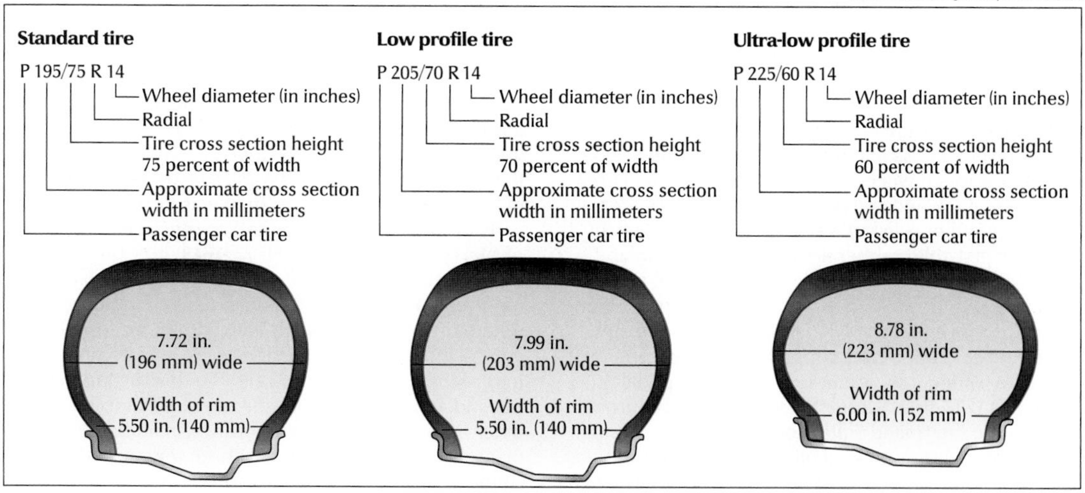

© David Frazier

Tires for earth movers may measure up to 12 feet (3.7 meters) in diameter and weigh as much as 9,500 pounds (4,300 kilograms). These heavy construction vehicles often operate in areas where there are poor roads or no roads at all.

tread creates a wider *footprint* (track), which increases traction. The added stability provided by the tire shape gives a driver more control of a car at high speeds and around curves than standard tires give.

Tire tread patterns are designed for a variety of special purposes. For example, *snow tires* have a tread with extra-deep grooves. This tread bites into snow and mud, providing exceptional traction. Tiny metal spikes called *studs* stick out of *studded snow tires* for added traction on ice. But studded tires have been banned in some areas because they can cause road damage. *All-season,* or *all-weather,* tires provide better traction than regular tires on snow- and rain-covered surfaces. Special tread patterns are made for the tires of racing cars, trucks, and various construction, farming, and military vehicles.

History

The pneumatic tire was invented in 1845 by Robert W. Thomson, a Scottish engineer. At that time, most vehicles had wooden wheels and steel tires. The steel tires preserved the wood and wore well. Thomson's tires gave a smoother ride but were not strong enough. In 1870, the first solid rubber tires appeared in England. They were used on automobiles, bicycles, and buggies.

John B. Dunlop, a Scottish veterinarian, improved on Thomson's invention in 1888. Dunlop developed air-filled rubber tubes for his son's tricycle. These pneumatic tires provided a smoother ride and made pedaling easier than did solid rubber tires. Bike manufacturers in Europe and the United States soon began to use them.

Pneumatic tires appeared on automobiles in 1895. Like bicycle tires, they were single air-filled tubes. But as cars became heavier and were driven faster, the single tube tires could not hold enough air pressure for more than a short time. In the early 1900's, two-part tires were developed. They consisted of a casing and a flexible rubber tube that fit inside the casing and held the air. This *inner tube* held from 55 to 75 pounds per square inch (3.9 to 5.3 kilograms per square centimeter) of air pressure. These tires were called *high-pressure tires.*

Then tire manufacturers learned that less air in the tires would not only support the weight of an automobile but also add comfort to the ride. In 1922, *low-pressure tires,* or *balloon tires,* were introduced. They held from 30 to 32 pounds per square inch (2.1 to 2.2 kilograms per square centimeter) of air pressure.

The tubeless tire was introduced in 1948. Its casing was made airtight by an inner liner. Since 1954, most new cars have been equipped with tubeless tires.

In 1966, the U.S. Congress passed the National Traffic and Motor Vehicle Safety Act. The act called for minimum federal safety standards and a system of grading tires according to heat resistance, traction, and tread wear. These grades aid the consumer in choosing a tire. They are molded into the side wall along with the tire size, brand, maximum inflation pressure, maximum load, cord composition, and the symbol DOT, which shows that the tire meets safety standards.

In the 1970's, manufacturers introduced thin, lightweight, "temporary use" spare tires. They also developed tires that would seal themselves if punctured. All-season tires appeared in the late 1980's. In the 1990's, manufacturers developed a tire that can be driven safely for some distance after being severely punctured. Specially strengthened sidewalls enable this tire to keep its shape even if all of the air escapes from it. Manufacturers also added sensors to some tires that indicate if the tires are properly inflated. Howard A. Colvin

See also **Dunlop, John B.; Firestone, Harvey S.; Goodyear, Charles; Manufacturing** (picture: Steps in manufacturing); **Rubber**.

Tirso de Molina, *TEER soh day moh LEE nah,* was the pen name of Gabriel Téllez (1584-1648), a Spanish playwright. His masterpiece, *The Trickster of Seville* (1630), firmly established the legend of Don Juan in literature (see **Don Juan**).

Tirso probably wrote nearly 400 plays, of which 86 survive. They include historical and religious dramas, light comedies about palace society, and romantic tragedies. Tirso had a good understanding of psychology and showed greater skill in creating characters than any other Spanish playwright of his time. He also wrote light-hearted tales, *The Gardens of Toledo* (1624); and the more serious *Pleasure with Profit* (1635), a collection of stories, plays, and verse. Tirso was born in Madrid early in 1584. He was a friar and an official in the Order of Mercy. He died on March 12, 1648. Harry Sieber

Tishah be-Av, *TIHSH ah buh AHV,* is a Jewish day of mourning observed on the ninth day of the Hebrew month of Av (approximately August). On that day, Jews commemorate the destruction of the First Temple in Jerusalem in 587 or 586 B.C. and the destruction of the Second Temple in A.D. 70. The day also commemorates other tragic events in Jewish history, including Nazi Germany's campaign of mass murder of Jews called the Holocaust. For three weeks before Tishah be-Av, Jews observe partial mourning and hold no weddings or celebrations. Many Jews fast throughout the day.

The Biblical Book of Lamentations is recited in the synagogue the evening that begins the holiday. During the morning service, a collection of poems is added that mourn the destruction of the temples and other tragic occasions. B. Barry Levy

Tisquantum. See Squanto.

Tissue is a group of similar cells that work together with intercellular substances and body fluids to perform a particular function in an organism. Groups of tissues, in turn, form the organs of animals and plants.

Animal tissues are classified into four main types: (1) epithelial tissue, (2) connective tissue, (3) muscle, and (4) nervous tissue.

Epithelial tissue consists of tightly packed cells with little intercellular substance. The two main types of epithelial tissues are membranes and glands. Epithelial membranes form the outer layer of the skin. They also line such internal body surfaces as those of the digestive tract and of the blood vessels. Glands produce secretions, such as hormones and perspiration.

Connective tissue is composed of cells that lie within an abundant intercellular substance. In most connective tissue, the intercellular substance consists of fibers and a clear fluid called *ground substance.* Bone and cartilage are connective tissues that support and protect the body. Blood, which consists of cells suspended in a fluid intercellular substance called *plasma,* is also classified as a connective tissue.

Muscle consists of cells that have the ability to contract. Muscle contractions are responsible for the beating of the heart, the movement of substances through the body, and the wide range of body movements.

Nervous tissue consists of highly specialized cells that conduct nerve impulses throughout the body. Nervous tissue enables the body to coordinate many of its functions and to respond to a wide variety of stimuli.

Plant tissues. Plants have two major types of tissues, *meristematic* and *permanent.* Meristematic tissues consist of immature cells that divide continuously. The growing tips of roots and shoots are composed of meristematic tissue. Permanent tissues consist of mature cells that have special functions. Such tissues include *epidermis, parenchyma, xylem,* and *phloem.* Epidermis forms a plant's protective outer covering. Parenchyma stores food and water in the roots, stems, and leaves of a plant. Xylem conducts water and minerals upward from the roots. Phloem carries sugars and proteins throughout the plant. Charles G. Crispens, Jr.

Related articles in *World Book* include:

Collagen
Connective tissue
Epithelium
Histology
Life (diagram: Structural units)
Membrane
Muscle
Nervous system
Transplant (Tissue transplants)

Titan is the largest satellite of the planet Saturn and the second largest satellite in the solar system. Only Jupiter's moon Ganymede is larger. Titan has a diameter of 3,200 miles (5,150 kilometers), even larger than the planets Mercury and Pluto. The combination of Titan's size and its internal density indicates that it probably has a rocky core covered with a shell of water ice. The temperature of Titan's surface is −290 °F (−179 °C). This is so low that no bodies of liquid water on the surface could persist over long periods of time.

Titan is the only satellite in the solar system with a significant atmosphere. In fact, Titan's atmospheric pressure is about 1.6 times that of Earth. Titan's surface is almost entirely hidden by its atmosphere, a thick red haze that in some ways resembles the smog found on Earth. About 95 percent of Titan's atmosphere is nitrogen. Approximately 3 percent is methane, which is a *hydrocarbon* (a compound of hydrogen and carbon). The remaining 2 percent consists of hydrogen, other hydrocarbons, and argon. Little water vapor exists in the satellite's atmosphere.

Voyager 1 and Voyager 2, two United States space probes, provided information about Titan in 1980 and 1981. The Cassini spacecraft, which began orbiting Saturn in the summer of 2004, carried cloud-penetrating radar and other instruments designed to "see" through Titan's atmosphere. Cassini, which was built by the United States, also carried and released a probe called Huygens, which was built by the European Space Agency.

Huygens parachuted through Titan's hazy atmosphere on Jan. 14, 2005. As it descended, it analyzed chemicals, recorded sounds, and measured wind speeds. At an altitude of about 20 miles (30 kilometers), the haze cleared, enabling the probe's cameras to photograph Titan's surface. The images revealed a landscape marked by features that resemble riverbeds and lakebeds on Earth. On Titan, these features appear to result from erosion caused by rains of liquid methane. Huygens landed in a soft mixture of dirty water ice and hydrocarbon ice. The probe sent pictures and data from Titan's surface for a few hours. Carolyn C. Porco

See also **Cassini.**

Titanic was a British passenger ship that struck an iceberg and sank in the North Atlantic Ocean in 1912. The disaster occurred on the liner's first voyage, from Southampton, England, to New York City. The *Titanic* sideswiped the iceberg at about 11:40 p.m. on April 14. The impact caused a number of small cracks and failed riveted seams in the ship's hull. Seawater flooded through

AP/Wide World

The "unsinkable" *Titanic* was believed to be the safest ship afloat. But in 1912, while crossing the Atlantic on its first voyage, the *Titanic* sank after striking an iceberg. About 1,500 people died in the disaster, and some 700 survived.

the bow of the ship. About 2 ½ hours later, the vessel broke in two and sank.

The *Titanic* carried enough lifeboats for only about half of its approximately 2,200 passengers and crew. The first rescue ship to reach the site, the British liner *Carpathia,* arrived about 4 a.m. and picked up 705 survivors, mostly women and children. A total of 1,517 people died. The *Titanic's* captain, Edward J. Smith, went down with his ship. Also among the dead were many wealthy and famous passengers, including millionaire John Jacob Astor and department store owner Isidor Straus.

The *Titanic* was the largest and most luxurious ocean liner of its time. It *displaced* (moved out of place) over 52,000 long tons (53,000 metric tons) of water and was 882 ½ feet (269 meters) long. Many people believed the ship was unsinkable because its hull was divided into 16 watertight compartments. Even if 2 compartments flooded, the ship could still float. As a result of the collision with the iceberg, 6 compartments initially flooded.

In 1985, a team of French and American scientists led by Robert D. Ballard of the United States and Jean-Louis Michel of France found the Titanic. The ship lay about 400 miles (650 kilometers) southeast of Newfoundland at a depth of about 12,500 feet (3,800 meters).

For years, people thought that the *Titanic* sank because the iceberg cut a huge gash in its hull. But the wreck showed no sign of a gash. A study of steel samples from the ship concluded that the hull was made of a steel that became brittle in the frigid North Atlantic waters and fractured easily during the collision. Inquiries have also shown that the *Titanic* was traveling too fast for an area where there was danger of icebergs. The ship was traveling at about 21 *knots* (nautical miles per hour), nearly its top speed, when lookouts sighted the iceberg. William H. Garzke, Jr.

See also **Ballard, Robert Duane.**

Additional resources

Adams, Simon. *Titanic.* Dorling Kindersley, 1999. Younger readers.

Butler, Daniel A. *"Unsinkable": The Full Story of RMS Titanic.* Stackpole, 1998.

Titanium, *ty TAY nee uhm,* is a strong, lightweight, silver-gray metallic element. Titanium metal has a higher strength-to-weight ratio than steel—that is, objects made of titanium are stronger than steel objects of the same weight. Titanium resists *corrosion* (chemical breakdown) caused by seawater and sea air as well as platinum does and better than stainless steel does. Many highly corrosive acids and bases do not harm titanium. Machine parts made of titanium can withstand operating temperatures up to about 800 °F (430 °C). However, the uses of titanium are limited because it is expensive to produce. Researchers have worked to develop cheaper methods of producing the metal for widespread use.

Titanium's chemical symbol is Ti. Its *atomic number* (number of protons in its nucleus) is 22. Its *relative atomic mass* is 47.867. An element's relative atomic mass equals its *mass* (amount of matter) divided by $\frac{1}{12}$ of the mass of carbon 12, the most stable form of carbon. Titanium has a density of 4.51 grams per cubic centimeter, higher than that of aluminum but lower than that of stainless steel. It melts at 1668 °C and boils at 3287 °C.

Titanium serves as an important element in *alloys* (combinations of two or more metals). Manufacturers use lightweight, heat-resistant titanium alloys in jet and rocket engines and aircraft and spacecraft bodies. Ship and submarine parts made of titanium alloys can operate in saltwater for long periods without corroding. Titanium alloys are also used in artificial knee and hip joints, pacemakers, and other durable, corrosion-resistant devices designed for use inside the body. Also, the metal's alloys are used to make durable, lightweight tools, surgical instruments, armor plating, steam-turbine blades, and golf clubs, bicycles, and other sporting equipment.

Compounds that contain titanium are used in the making of many products. Titanium dioxide (TiO_2) serves as a strong, bright-white pigment in paint. Manufacturers also use titanium dioxide in floor coverings, paper, plastics, porcelain enamels, rubber, sunscreen, and welding rods. Jewelers cut and polish titanium dioxide crystals to make a gemstone called *titania.* Titania shines brighter than diamond but is not as hard. Crystals of barium titanate ($BaTiO_3$) are used in television sets and radar and sonar equipment. Other titanium compounds *catalyze* (stimulate) the chemical reactions that produce the plastic materials polyethylene and polypropylene.

Titanium ranks as the ninth most abundant element in Earth's crust. It never appears naturally in metallic form because it bonds to oxygen readily and strongly. It often occurs in the ores *ilmenite* and *rutile.* Ilmenite is mined mainly in Australia, Canada, India, Malaysia, Norway, South Africa, Ukraine, and the United States. Rutile is mined mainly in Australia and South Africa.

Japan, Kazakhstan, Russia, Ukraine, and the United States produce most of the world's refined titanium metal. China also makes titanium.

William Gregor, an English clergyman and mineralogist, discovered titanium, in the form of titanium dioxide, in 1791. The German chemist Martin H. Klaproth independently discovered the element in 1795 and named it titanium. The New Zealand-born American chemist Matthew A. Hunter made the first pure titanium in 1910. Large amounts of pure titanium were not produced until the 1950's, after the Luxembourg-born inventor Wilhelm J. Kroll developed a way to extract the metal from ilmenite. In the Kroll process, ilmenite is treated with chlorine and carbon to produce a colorless, corrosive liquid called titanium tetrachloride ($TiCl_4$). The liquid reacts with molten magnesium to produce titanium metal. In 1948, companies began using the Kroll process to produce the metal for commercial use. Kenton H. Whitmire

See also **Alloy** (Alloys for strength and lightness); **Ilmenite.**

Titans were the first gods in Greek mythology. Most of them represented, in human form, such natural phenomena as the earth, sky, and sun. Previously, the universe had existed in a state of emptiness called *Chaos.*

The first Titan was Gaea, the earth. She emerged from Chaos and gave birth to Uranus, the sky. She then married him. Gaea and Uranus had many offspring. The youngest and most important was Cronus, who married Rhea, his sister. Cronus castrated Uranus and deposed him, becoming king of the gods.

Rhea bore Cronus many children, but he swallowed them as soon as they were born to prevent one of them from overthrowing him. Rhea was determined to save Zeus, her youngest son. She tricked Cronus into swallowing a stone wrapped in baby clothes instead. Then she hid Zeus on the island of Crete.

After Zeus grew up, he tricked his father into vomiting up all the offspring. Zeus then led his brothers and sisters in a war against Cronus and overthrew him. Zeus banished Cronus and the Titans who had supported him to Tartarus, an underground region. The defeat of Cronus established Zeus as the supreme ruler of the universe and thus played an important role in the religion of the ancient Greeks. C. Scott Littleton

See also **Mythology** (Greek mythology); **Atlas;** Cronus; Prometheus; Tartarus; Uranus; Zeus.

Tithe, *tyth,* is a tax of one-tenth on the profits from the produce of one's land or one's earnings. The word *tithe* comes from an Old English word meaning a *tenth.*

In ancient Israel, the tithe mainly supported the priesthood, but it was also distributed to the poor. Tithing was seen as a way to acknowledge God's authority and to express gratitude for favors. The early Christian church did not require tithing. By the 500's, church law required payment of a tax on income and lands. In the late 700's, Charlemagne made this civil law. Tithing was more common in the West than in the East. Today, members of some Christian churches contribute a tenth of their income to the church, but most churches allow voluntary contribution. Richard L. Schebera

Titi, *tih TEE,* is a type of small South American monkey. Titis live in the tropical rain forests of the Amazon, in the Orinoco River Basin, and in eastern Brazil. Males and females are about the same size. They weigh about $2\frac{1}{4}$ pounds (1 kilogram) and have gray, reddish-brown, or black fur. Titis live in trees and occasionally come to the ground. They feed mainly on fruits but also eat many types of leaves and insects.

Titis live in family groups that consist of an adult male and female pair and their offspring. Titis have one breeding season each year. Both parents care for the newborn. At 2 or 3 years of age, a titi leaves its parents to start its own family. Titi monkeys often demonstrate a curious social behavior called *tail-twining.* Two, three, or four titis sit on a branch and wrap their tails in a spiral.

Michael Dick, Animals Animals

The titi is a small South American monkey. The animal lives in trees in tropical rain forests. The titi feeds mainly on fruits.

Titis exhibit this behavior while resting or sleeping.

People hunt many types of South American monkeys for food. But hunters usually do not kill titi monkeys because of their small size. The greatest enemies of titis are hawks and other predatory birds. Randall L. Susman

Scientific classification. Titis belong to the New World monkey family, Cebidae. They are genus *Callicebus.*

© The Frick Collection, New York City

Titian's *Man in a Red Cap* reflects the subject's personality through his pose and expression. Titian probably completed the portrait in 1516, at the beginning of his mature period.

Titian, *TIHSH uhn* (1487?-1576), was a Venetian painter of the Italian Renaissance. During his long career, which lasted about 70 years, he became one of the most influential and successful painters in the history of art.

Titian's works include portraits and paintings of myths and religious scenes. He developed a style that strongly influenced European painting for more than 200 years. Titian used bright colors, applied his paint in bold brushstrokes, and made one color seem to blend into another. His style is shown in *Crowning with Thorns,* which appears in the **Painting** article. This style of painting influenced many great artists, including El Greco, Rembrandt, and Peter Paul Rubens.

Titian painted portraits of royalty and aristocrats. He portrayed his subjects as elegant but spirited. Titian skillfully showed the human side of his subjects through facial expressions and gestures. The works of many great portrait painters, including Sir Anthony Van Dyck and Diego Velázquez, show his influence.

Titian was born in Pieve di Cadore, near Venice, Italy. His real name was Tiziano Vecellio. Titian moved to Venice as a boy to study painting. He was apprenticed to two artists, Gentile Bellini and then to his brother Giovanni Bellini. Titian's early works show the influence of Giovanni Bellini and of his artist friend Giorgione.

About 1515, Titian began to produce masterpieces.

Titian's success led most of Europe's leading art patrons to buy and pose for his paintings. Titian's clients included Holy Roman emperors Charles V and Ferdinand I, Pope Paul III, King Philip II of Spain, and many of the most important Italian nobles. David Summers

See also **Drawing** (picture: A pen-and-ink drawing); **Painting** (The Renaissance in Venice; picture: *Crowning with Thorns).*

Titicaca, Lake. See Lake Titicaca.

Title is a legal term often used to describe ownership of property. The term began with transfers of land. A history of the ownership of land is called a *chain of title.*

The term *title* can be used to describe the way an owner obtains lawful possession of property. In addition, it often refers to a legal document that describes the interest of the owner. Such documents include deeds to real property, a title to an automobile, the patent for an invention, or the copyright held by an author.

Title to property may be acquired in many ways. If a person buys property from another person, or receives it as a gift or through a will, the title is *derivative.* A title is *original* if the property is not obtained from someone else. For example, trappers may capture wild animals and make them their property. Title by *adverse possession* is a title acquired against the consent of the owner. It is obtained by wrongful entry and continuous possession for a time fixed by state law. Suppose, for example, that Jones farms Smith's land in a particular state for over 10 years without Smith's permission, but Smith does not take legal action against Jones for using the land. If the state's laws require a period of 10 years for adverse possession, Jones has obtained title to the land.

Title to land can also be acquired by *letters patent.* This term refers to a title transferred from the United States government to a private citizen. James L. Winokur

See also **Deed; Torrens system.**

Titmouse is any of a small group of crested North American birds. All titmice have grayish bodies and short, conical bills. The birds measure about 5 to 7 inches (13 to 18 centimeters) long. Titmice become active during the day. They feed mainly on insects but also eat seeds and berries. Enemies of titmice include such birds of prey as hawks and owls.

WORLD BOOK illustration by Trevor Boyer, Linden Artists Ltd.

An oak titmouse has a pointed crest of feathers on its head.

All titmice inhabit wooded areas. The most common type, the *tufted titmouse,* lives in the eastern United States and in Canada. This bird has a gray crest and back, a whitish belly, and brownish flanks. The *bridled titmouse* ranges from Arizona and New Mexico to central Mexico. It has a striking black, white, and gray head. The *juniper titmouse* and *oak titmouse* possess basically plain grayish coloring. Juniper titmice inhabit the southwestern United States. Oak titmice live in western North America from southern Oregon to Baja California in Mexico.

Titmice remain in their territories all year and do not migrate. Titmice pairs stay mated for life. They often nest in old woodpecker holes, lining the nests with fur, feathers, moss, or other soft materials. Most females lay only one brood of five to eight eggs each year. The eggs are whitish with brown spots and blotches. Only the female incubates the eggs, but both parents feed the young.

Sandra L. Vehrencamp

Scientific classification. Titmice belong to the family Paridae. The scientific name of the tufted titmouse is *Baeolophus bicolor.* The bridled titmouse is *B. wollweberi,* the juniper titmouse is *B. ridgwayi,* and the oak titmouse is *B. inornatus.*

See also **Bird** (picture: Birds of forests and woodland); **Chickadee; Verdin.**

Tito, *TEE toh,* **Josip Broz,** *YOH seep brohz* (1892-1980), established a Communist government in Yugoslavia after World War II and then became the country's ruler. He led Yugoslavia in separating from Soviet control. His actions set an example that China and some Eastern European Communist nations later followed. Tito was the first Communist leader to permit his people some economic and social freedom.

Tito was born Josip Broz, the son of a peasant family, on May 7, 1892, in Kumrovec, Croatia. At that time, Croatia was part of Austria-Hungary. Broz became a metalworker. In 1915, during World War I, he was wounded and captured by Russian troops. In 1917, the Communists released him from prison after they had taken power in Russia. Broz joined the Communist Party.

In 1920, Broz returned to his homeland, which had become part of the new Kingdom of the Serbs, Croats, and Slovenes (later renamed Yugoslavia) after World War I ended in 1918. He helped organize the Yugoslav Communist Party. But it was outlawed, and Broz was sent to jail in 1928. He used the name *Tito* to confuse the police after his release in 1934. He later added *Tito* to his real name. He was secretary-general to the Yugoslav Communist Party from 1937 until 1966, when he became party president.

During World War II, Tito organized and led the *Partisans,* guerrillas who fought Germans occupying Yugoslavia. Another resistance group, the anti-Communist *Chetniks,* fought the Partisans, but lost. After the war, Tito had Chetnik leader Draža Mihajlović executed.

Tito set up a Communist government in Yugoslavia in 1945, and it was recognized by Britain, the United States, and the Soviet Union. Tito became prime minister and defense minister. But Soviet efforts to control Yugoslavia led to a split between Tito and Soviet dictator Joseph Stalin. Stalin expelled Yugoslavia from the Soviet bloc in 1948. Tito became the first independent Communist leader. Later, he became a spokesman for nations that refused to take sides in the Cold War.

But Tito kept tight control over the Yugoslav people and tolerated no opposition. In 1963, Tito made himself president for life. Later, he limited the power of the secret police and encouraged some economic and political freedom. In 1968, Tito supported Czechoslovakia's liberalization program, and he criticized the Soviet Union for sending troops into the country to stop the reforms. In 1971, he became head of a presidential council formed to rule Yugoslavia. Stuart D. Goldman

See also **Serbia and Montenegro** (History).

Additional resources

Ridley, Jasper. *Tito.* Constable, 1994.
West, Richard. *Tito.* Carroll & Graf, 1995.

Titus, *TY tuhs* (A.D. 41-81), a Roman emperor, was noted for his generosity and his regard for the people's welfare. He was born on Dec. 30, 41, in Rome, the oldest son of Emperor Vespasian. Titus served as a *military tribune* (military leader) in Germany and Britain. He later helped his father put down a revolt by Jews in Palestine that began in A.D. 66. Titus captured Jerusalem in 70 after a long siege. He played a prominent role during his father's reign and succeeded him in 79. F. G. B. Millar

Titus was an early Christian who was a companion of Saint Paul. Titus was often mentioned in Paul's letters and served as Paul's special representative to the church in Corinth. According to tradition, Titus was the first bishop of Crete. His feast day is January 26.

The Epistle to Titus is a letter to Titus that is the 17th book of the New Testament. The letter is traditionally attributed to Paul, but most modern scholars believe one of Paul's followers wrote it. Richard A. Edwards

Tivoli Gardens. See **Denmark** (Recreation; picture: Tivoli Gardens).

Tlingit Indians, *KLIHN kiht* or *TLIHNG giht,* live mainly along the coast of southeastern Alaska. The tribe once controlled all the land that extends more than 500 miles (800 kilometers) from west of Yakutat Bay to the British Columbia border south of present-day Ketchikan. The Tlingit divided the area into about 15 territories called *quans* (also spelled *kwans*). All Tlingit spoke related dialects of one language.

In their traditional way of life, the Tlingit fished, hunted deer and seals, and gathered berries, bird eggs, and shellfish. To prepare for winter, they smoked, pickled, and dried their foods. In winter, the Tlingit lived in large plank houses, each of which sheltered many related families. Tlingit woodworkers carved masks, totem poles, and other objects.

Tlingit society continues to be strictly ranked. Many personal positions in the tribe are confirmed during feasts called *potlatches,* in which the hosts give gifts to guests. The Tlingit tribe is divided into two groups—the *Ravens* and the *Eagles* or *Wolves.* Each group has many clans. All Tlingit belong to their mother's clan. Members of Raven clans may marry only members of the Eagles, and Eagle members may marry only Ravens.

In the late 1700's, the Russians became the first Europeans to establish relations with the Tlingit. But the Russians left the area in 1867, when the United States bought Alaska from Russia. Some Tlingit belong to the Russian Orthodox Church.

According to the 1990 U.S. census, there are about 14,000 Tlingit. Many work in the logging and fishing industries or have moved to large cities. The tribe got money and land as a result of the Alaska Native Claims Settlement Act of 1971 (see **Alaska** [Land-use issues]).

Robert S. Grumet

TM. See **Transcendental meditation.**

TNT is short for trinitrotoluene, a powerful solid explosive. TNT is made up of the chemical elements nitrogen, hydrogen, carbon, and oxygen. The chemical formula for TNT is $CH_3C_6H_2(NO_2)_3$. The explosive is made by nitrating the chemical compound toluene. The resulting explosive forms in pale yellow crystals that may darken to brown. These crystals of TNT can be handled safely. TNT may even be melted at low heat without igniting, and so can be molded to increase its usefulness. TNT is used alone and in mixtures with other explosives, such as PETN, RDX, and ammonium nitrate. It is chiefly used as the explosive charge for shells and bombs. See also **Explosive.** James E. Kennedy

Toad is a small, tailless animal that closely resembles the frog. Toads and frogs belong to a class of animals called *amphibians* and live part of their life in water and part on land. But toads have broader bodies, drier skin, and shorter, less powerful back legs than do most frogs.

Many toads are dull brown or gray. Others have vivid coloring, such as green stripes or red spots. The skin of most toads is dry, rough, and covered with warts. Despite superstition, a person cannot get warts by touching a toad. But a pair of *parotoid glands* on top of a toad's head produce a poison that can make people ill or cause eye irritation. The poison also has an unpleasant taste that helps protect the toad from enemies.

A toad uses its long, sticky tongue to prey on insects and other small animals. It can flip out its tongue, seize an animal, and swallow it—all in an instant.

Toads and frogs make up a scientific order known as Anura or Salientia. Members of several families in this order are commonly called toads. But zoologists consider only members of the family Bufonidae to be *true toads.* This article describes the true toads. For information on other members of the order Anura, see the section *Kinds of frogs* in the **Frog** article.

The life of a toad. Toads grow up in water but spend most of their adult life on land. They return to water to breed. Temporary pools resulting from spring or sum-

Runk/Schoenberger from Grant Heilman

A fowler's toad flips out its sticky tongue to capture a cricket. A toad's tongue is attached to the front of its lower jaw. Fowler's toads are found in the eastern United States.

Alvin E. Staffan

A male American toad puffs out its throat to utter a loud, flutelike mating call. The soft-voiced females cannot swell their throat. American toads live in the eastern United States.

mer rain are typical breeding sites. In most toads, the male attracts the female with a mating call. A few kinds of toads do not have a mating call.

Almost all female toads lay eggs. Some females lay more than 30,000 eggs at a time. As the female deposits eggs in the water, the male clings to her body and fertilizes them. Toad eggs look like tiny, black spots enclosed in long strings of clear jelly. The jellylike substance helps protect the eggs.

Within a few days, small tadpoles hatch from the eggs. The tadpoles remain in the water as they go through a process called *metamorphosis.* In this process, the tadpoles gradually develop the characteristics of the adult toad. In most toads, metamorphosis takes from three to eight weeks. The young toads then leave the water and begin their life on land. Young toads grow rapidly. Some reach adult size in a year or less.

Toads avoid direct sunlight and heat. They are most active at night or on rainy days. During hot, dry spells, toads dig deep into the ground and remain there. This behavior is called *estivation.* Toads that live in areas with harsh winters hibernate during the cold weather.

Many animals prey on tadpoles and young toads. In North America, a chief enemy of adult toads is the hognose snake. A toad's poison does not affect this snake.

Scientists do not know how long toads live in the wild. Toads in captivity have lived more than 10 years.

Kinds of toads. There are over 300 species of toads. More than a dozen of them live in North America. The *American toad* is common in fields, gardens, and woods of the northeastern United States. It is about the size of a person's fist. The *Southern toad,* slightly smaller, is common in the Southeast. Males of both species have a pleasant, high-pitched call. One of the most widespread North American species is *Woodhouse's toad.* It lives throughout most of the United States and in parts of northern Mexico. The call of the male Woodhouse's toad sounds somewhat like the bleat of a sheep.

The *cane toad,* also called the *giant toad* and *marine toad,* ranks as one of the largest toads. It may grow up to 9 inches (23 centimeters) long. This toad once lived only in southern Texas and tropical regions of North and South America. It is now also found in other regions, including Australia, the Philippines, and Florida. Two of the smallest toads are *Rose's toad* of South Africa and the *oak toad* of the southeastern United States. The adults measure about 1 inch (2.5 centimeters) long. The *African live-bearing toads* are the only toads that do not lay eggs. Females give birth to live young.

J. Whitfield Gibbons

Scientific classification. True toads make up the toad family, Bufonidae. The American toad is *Bufo americanus.* The Southern toad is *B. terrestris* and Woodhouse's toad is *B. woodhousii.*

See also **Cane toad; Midwife toad; Surinam toad; Tadpole.**

Toadfish is the name of a group of large-headed fish that live on the bottom of tropical and temperate seas. There are about 65 species of toadfish. Most measure less than $1\frac{1}{2}$ feet (46 centimeters) long. Some species, such as the *midshipmen,* can produce light called *bioluminescence* (see **Bioluminescence**). Most toadfish make grunting or toadlike noises.

WORLD BOOK illustration by John F. Eggert

The toadfish lives on the bottom of the ocean.

Female toadfish commonly make nests for their eggs. The males guard the nest and can be extremely aggressive if the eggs are threatened. Certain species of toadfish are popular aquarium pets. Leighton R. Taylor, Jr.

Scientific classification. Toadfish make up the toadfish family, Batrachoididae. Species commonly kept in home aquariums belong to either of two genera, *Opsanus* or *Porichthys.*

Toadflax is the name of a group of plants with flowers shaped much like those of snapdragons. Toadflax flowers are tube-shaped and have two lips. Each flower also

WORLD BOOK illustration by Lorraine Epstein

Toadflax has clusters of yellow, tube-shaped flowers.

has a long, spurlike part in which nectar is stored. *Common toadflax,* which is also called *butter and eggs,* grows 1 to 2 $\frac{1}{2}$ feet (30 to 76 centimeters) tall. The plant has showy yellow flowers that grow in a cluster at the top of the stem. The mouth of the flower tube is closed by a thick, orange ridge on the lower lip. The weight of a bee looking for nectar forces the mouth of the tube open.

Common toadflax was introduced to North America from Europe. It is easy to grow in gardens from seed or parts of *rhizomes* (underground stems), but it can become a nuisance because it spreads quickly. *Old field toadflax* is native to North America. It has small blue flowers and is smaller than the common toadflax. Both species grow as weeds in fields and along roads.

Donna M. Eggers Ware

Scientific classification. Toadflax plants are members of the figwort family, Scrophulariaceae. The scientific name for the common toadflax is *Linaria vulgaris.* Old field toadflax is *L. canadensis.*

Toadstool. See Mushroom.

Tobacco is a plant whose leaves are used chiefly in making cigarettes and cigars. Other tobacco products include smoking tobacco for pipes, chewing tobacco, and snuff. Inferior grades of tobacco leaves are used in making insecticides and disinfectants. In addition, tobacco stalks and stems serve as an ingredient for some fertilizers.

Tobacco ranks as an important crop in more than 60 nations. Annual worldwide production totals about 8 $\frac{1}{2}$ million tons (7 $\frac{3}{4}$ million metric tons). China produces the most tobacco, followed by the United States, Brazil, and India.

Farmers in the United States harvest about 820,000 tons (750,000 metric tons) of tobacco annually. Crop sales total about $3 billion. North Carolina and Kentucky are the leading tobacco-growing states. Ontario produces most of Canada's tobacco crop.

WORLD BOOK illustration by James Teason

The tobacco plant lives for only one growing season. It stands from 4 to 6 feet (1.2 to 1.8 meters) high and ranges in color from light green to dark green. The plant has about 20 leaves and grows light pink flowers.

The tobacco industry in the United States produces about 660 billion cigarettes and about 3 billion cigars yearly. About 140 million pounds (65 million kilograms) of tobacco are manufactured annually for smoking tobacco, chewing tobacco, and snuff.

Tobacco products have a *value added by manufacture* of about $25 billion a year. This figure reflects the increase in value of tobacco after it becomes finished goods.

The taxes on tobacco products provide a major source of revenue for the United States government. All of the state governments and some local governments also tax tobacco products. Taxes on tobacco total about three times the amount the growers receive for their crops.

Charles Gupton, Southern Light

Tobacco is *cured* in a special barn before being sent to market. In a modern curing barn, *shown here,* a furnace heats the air, which fans force through the drying leaves.

Tobacco contains small amounts of nicotine, which is a substance that acts as a stimulant on the heart and other organs. Nicotine also stimulates the nervous system, causing many people to become addicted to it. Physicians believe these stimulating effects of nicotine help make smoking pleasurable. But concentrated amounts of the substance are poisonous. The nicotine in cigarettes may contribute to the occurrence of heart attacks and stomach ulcers. Other substances in the smoke aerosol may cause lung cancer. See **Smoking; Drug abuse.**

The tobacco plant

Tobacco is related to such plants as the tomato and the potato. It first grew in the Caribbean countries and in Mexico and South America.

Cultivated tobacco is an *annual* plant—that is, it lives only one growing season. The plant grows 4 to 6 feet (1.2 to 1.8 meters) high. It produces about 20 leaves, which measure from 24 to 30 inches (60 to 75 centimeters) long and 15 to 18 inches (38 to 46 centimeters) wide. The tobacco plant ranges from light green to dark green in color. A vigorous, mature plant can produce a million seeds yearly—enough to plant about 100 acres (40 hectares) of tobacco.

Kinds of tobacco

In the United States, tobacco is classified into four main groups: (1) air-cured tobacco, (2) fire-cured tobacco, (3) flue-cured tobacco, and (4) cigar leaf tobacco. The first three groups are classified according to the method used in *curing* (drying) the leaves. More information on these methods appears in the *Curing tobacco* section. Cigar leaf tobacco is air cured, but it is classified according to its use.

Air-cured tobacco consists of two varieties, light air-cured and dark air-cured. Most cigarettes contain the two major types of light air-cured tobacco, burley and Maryland. Burley tobacco accounts for about 30 percent of the tobacco production in the United States. Dark air-cured tobacco is used primarily for chewing tobacco and snuff.

Fire-cured tobacco has a distinctive smoky aroma and flavor. It is used to make smoking tobacco, chewing tobacco, snuff, and strong-tasting cigars.

Flue-cured tobacco is also called *bright tobacco* because the curing process turns it yellow to reddish-orange. It accounts for more than 60 percent of the tobacco produced in the United States. Most flue-cured tobacco is used in cigarettes.

There are three types of cigar leaf tobacco: (1) cigar filler tobacco, (2) cigar binder tobacco, and (3) cigar wrapper tobacco.

Cigar filler tobacco is used in the body of cigars because it has a sweet flavor and burns evenly. Cigar binder tobacco was once used to hold filler tobacco together, but most cigar manufacturers now use *reconstituted tobacco sheets* instead. These sheets are made from coarse or damaged tobacco leaves. Today, cigar binder is used primarily in making chewing tobacco.

Cigar wrapper tobacco is used for the outside cover of cigars. It must have high-quality leaves that are smooth, thin, and uniform in color. To grow leaves with these characteristics, farmers surround the tobacco with a framework covered by cloth. Producing this tobacco is difficult and expensive, and many manufacturers use reconstituted tobacco sheets to cover their cigars.

Raising and marketing tobacco

Planting and cultivation. The soil and climate conditions that favor tobacco growth vary according to the kind of tobacco being raised. However, most tobacco grows best in a warm climate and in carefully drained and fertilized soil.

Tobacco seeds are planted in seedbeds in late winter or early spring and covered with cloth or plastic. The plants grow 6 to 8 inches (15 to 20 centimeters) tall in 8 to 12 weeks and are then transplanted into the field.

Farmers cultivate the soil several times to keep it loose and to eliminate weeds. The last cultivation occurs after the plants are 18 to 24 inches (45 to 60 centimeters) high. The plant's upper part is *topped* (cut off) when it begins to produce flowers. This allows the remaining leaves to grow larger and heavier.

Harvesting tobacco. Farmers harvest tobacco from 70 to 90 days after it has been transplanted. They use two harvesting methods, *priming* and *stalk-cutting.*

Priming involves picking the individual tobacco leaves as they ripen. The leaves were once picked by hand, but most farmers now use priming machines. The priming method is used to harvest cigar wrapper, flue-cured, and some cigar filler tobaccos.

Stalk-cutting consists of cutting the entire plant with a hatchetlike tool. The stalks are then placed on sticks and left in the field for a day or two to wilt. Growers use the stalk-cutting method to harvest air-cured, fire-cured, and most cigar leaf tobaccos.

Diseases and pests. Diseases that attack tobacco include *black shank* and *black root rot.* Many farmers raise newly developed types of tobacco that resist black shank and various virus diseases. Crop rotation is the most effective way to control black root rot.

Budworms, flea beetles, grasshoppers, and other insects also damage tobacco plants. Farmers use insecticides to control these pests.

Curing tobacco involves drying the sap from newly harvested leaves. This process produces various chemical changes in tobacco that improve its flavor and aroma. There are three methods of curing tobacco: (1) air curing, (2) fire curing, and (3) flue curing. Each type of tobacco responds most favorably to one of these methods. Curing takes place in curing barns that are built specifically for the method used.

Air curing uses natural weather conditions to dry tobacco. Air-curing barns have ventilators that can be opened and closed to control the temperature and humidity. This process takes from four to eight weeks.

Fire curing dries tobacco with low-burning fires. The smoke gives fire-cured tobacco its distinctive taste and aroma. Farmers regulate the heat, humidity, and ventilation in the curing barns in order to avoid scalding the tobacco leaves. Fire curing requires from three days to six weeks.

Flue curing dries tobacco by heat from *flues* (pipes) connected to furnaces. The temperature is gradually

Leading tobacco-growing countries

Tons of tobacco grown in a year

Country	Tons
China	2,689,000 tons (2,439,000 metric tons)
Brazil	660,000 tons (599,000 metric tons)
India	582,000 tons (528,000 metric tons)
United States	489,000 tons (444,000 metric tons)
Zimbabwe	220,000 tons (199,000 metric tons)

Figures are for a three-year average, 2000-2002.
Source: Food and Agriculture Organization of the United Nations.

Leading tobacco-growing states and provinces

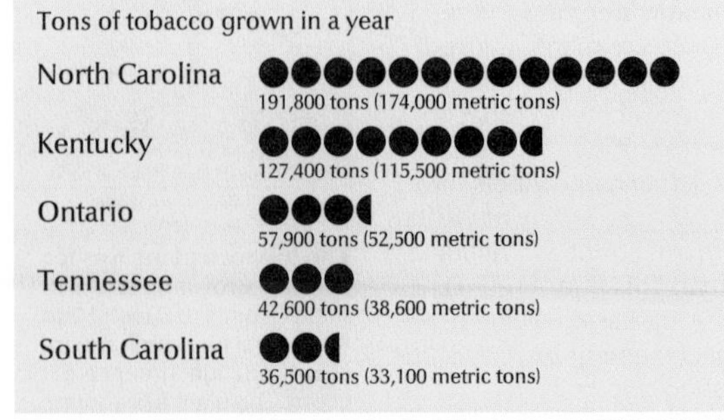

Figures are for a three-year average, 2000-2002.
Sources: U.S. Department of Agriculture; Statistics Canada.

raised from 90 °F (32 °C) to 160 °F (71 °C) until the leaves and stems are completely dry. The flue-curing method takes about a week.

Marketing tobacco. Farmers sell tobacco by two major methods, *loose leaf auctions* and *country sales.*

Loose leaf auctions handle about 95 percent of the tobacco sales in the United States. The term *loose leaf* refers to the practice of displaying and selling tobacco in leaf form rather than packed in containers.

Auction warehouses operate in cities and towns throughout tobacco-growing regions. In the United States, federal inspectors examine tobacco before it is sold and grade it according to government standards.

Buyers from tobacco companies bid on the tobacco, which is usually sold to the highest bidder. The government has *price supports* that guarantee the seller a certain price for tobacco. Government-sponsored organizations known as farmer *cooperatives* buy the tobacco if no bidder offers this amount.

Country sales involve the direct sale of tobacco from farmer to buyer outside the auction system. Most cigar leaf tobacco is sold directly. This system is also called *barn-door marketing* because the buyers usually come to the farm to inspect the crop.

Charles Gupton, Southern Light

A tobacco auction enables buyers to inspect the tobacco and bid on it. Federal inspectors grade most U.S. tobacco.

Manufacturing tobacco products

Freshly cured tobacco has a sharp aroma and bitter taste. Therefore, most tobacco is put into storage and allowed to age before being used in manufacturing tobacco products.

Prior to storage, most tobacco goes through a redrying process, during which it is completely dried and cooled. Manufacturers then restore some water throughout the leaves to ensure uniform moisture content. This practice prevents the leaves from breaking.

Next, tobacco is stored for two or three years in barrellike containers. During storage, it ages and undergoes a chemical change called *fermentation.* Fermentation gives tobacco a sweeter, milder flavor and aroma and reduces its nicotine content. Tobacco also loses moisture and becomes darker during aging.

A somewhat different procedure is used to age cigar leaf tobacco, which does not require redrying. Bales of this tobacco are placed in heated rooms or are simply hung up to ferment before storage.

Cigarettes account for about 85 percent of the tobacco consumed in the United States. The remainder is used in making cigars, smoking tobacco, chewing tobacco, and snuff.

Cigarettes contain blends of burley, Maryland, flue-cured, and imported Turkish tobaccos. Manufacturers add such flavorings as honey, licorice, menthol, and sugar to the blended tobacco. A chemical called *glycerine* is often added to preserve moisture.

Various machines handle the entire process of making and packaging cigarettes. Cigarette-making machines can produce about 4,000 cigarettes each minute.

Cigars consist of about 85 percent cigar filler, 10 percent cigar binder, and 5 percent cigar wrapper tobaccos. Most cigars are made by machines, but the more expensive kinds are hand-rolled.

Most smoking tobacco is used in pipes, but some people smoke it in the form of cigarettes that they roll by hand. For flavor, manufacturers add tonka beans, vanilla leaves, and other substances. Tobacco flavorings are called *saucing compounds.*

Chewing tobacco is made from various types of inferior grade tobacco. Most chewing tobacco is treated with such saucing compounds as honey or licorice.

Snuff consists of coarsely ground tobacco leaves that have been pressed into a fine powder. The powder is strained through cloth and flavored with oils and spices.

History

American Indians smoked tobacco in pipes long before Christopher Columbus sailed to the New World in 1492. Columbus brought some tobacco seeds back to Europe, where farmers began to grow the plant for use as a medicine that helped people relax. In 1560, a French diplomat named Jean Nicot—from whom tobacco receives its botanical name, *Nicotiana*—introduced the use of tobacco in France.

Commercial production of tobacco began in North America in 1612, after an English colonist named John Rolfe successfully cultivated in Virginia a new type of tobacco from the West Indies. The Virginia soil and climate were excellent for tobacco, and it became an important crop there and in other parts of the South.

Most of the tobacco grown in the American Colonies was exported to England until the Revolutionary War began in 1775. Manufacturers in the United States then began to produce smoking tobacco, chewing tobacco, and snuff for domestic use. Cigars were first manufactured in the United States in the early 1800's.

Spaniards and some other Europeans began to smoke hand-rolled cigarettes in the 1600's, but few people in the United States used them until the 1850's. Cigarette smoking became increasingly popular after the first practical cigarette-making machine was invented in the early 1880's.

The use of tobacco products has been a controversial issue for many years. During the 1500's, European physicians declared that tobacco should be used only for medicinal purposes. The Puritans in America considered it a dangerous narcotic. In the 1960's, scientists established that smoking tobacco products—especially cigarettes—could cause lung cancer, heart disease, and other illnesses. Some cigarette manufacturers reacted to the medical findings by reducing the tar and nicotine content of cigarettes. However, doctors state that these measures have not eliminated the dangers of smoking.

Various federal laws have been passed in the United States regarding the sale of tobacco products. Since 1966, manufacturers have been required to include a health warning on all packages and cartons of cigarettes. Another law, which went into effect in 1971, banned radio and television commercials advertising cigarettes. In 1972, manufacturers agreed to include a health warning in all cigarette advertising. Some cities and states prohibit smoking in various public places. In 1996, the Liggett Group became the first tobacco company to agree to pay money for harm to smokers in response to a lawsuit. For more details on settlements made by tobacco companies in response to lawsuits, see **Smoking** (Smoking regulations).

Some other countries also have laws to control the sale of tobacco products. For example, federal laws in Canada also restrict cigarette advertising and require health warnings on cigarette packages. J. H. Smiley

Scientific classification. The tobacco plant belongs to the nightshade family, Solanaceae. The major kind is genus *Nicotiana,* species *N. tabacum.*

Related articles in *World Book* include:

Cigar	Colonial life in America (Farming)	Filter	Pipe
Cigarette	Drug abuse	Kentucky (picture)	Snuff
		Nicotine	Virginia (picture)

Additional resources

Connolly, Sean. *Tobacco.* Heinemann, 2001.
Cordry, Harold V. *Tobacco: A Reference Handbook.* ABC-CLIO, 2001.

Tobago. See **Trinidad and Tobago.**

Tobey, *TOH bee,* **Mark** (1890-1976), was an American artist who painted elaborate linear abstract pictures, often on a small scale. Tobey's delicately colored compositions have dense patterns of lines and small symbols. They have been compared to *calligraphy* (the art of fine handwriting). Tobey described his style as *white writing.* He developed his calligraphic style after a trip to Asia in the 1930's. He maintained that his work reflected his view of a unified universe and its pulsating rhythms. Later he ordered his images into highly complex groupings of tiny forms. Tobey's paintings were admired by Europeans, who saw in them an American blend of Eastern and Western styles. Tobey was born on Dec. 11, 1890, in Centerville, Wisconsin. He died on April 24, 1976. Dore Ashton

Tobogganing, *tuh BAHG uhn ihng,* is the winter sport of coasting on snow or ice by means of toboggans, which are sleds without runners. A toboggan is made of strips of hickory, ash, or maple, with the front ends curved back. The strips are fastened together by crosspieces. The undersurface is highly polished. The sled is usually 6 to 8 feet (1.8 to 2.4 meters) long and $1\frac{1}{2}$ feet (46 centimeters) wide. Four people usually make up a toboggan team. The one at the rear steers the sled. Tobogganists have attained a speed of 900 yards (823 meters) in 30 seconds, or more than 61 mph (98 kph).

Bruce M. Wellman, Stock, Boston

Tobogganing is a popular winter sport. Participants coast down a snowy or icy hill on a sled called a toboggan. A typical toboggan has no runners, and its front end is curved back.

Indian hunters first built toboggans made of bark to carry game over the snow. The Inuit (sometimes called Eskimos) used to make toboggans of whalebone. A bobsled can reach a speed of up to 90 mph (145 kph). Both two-seat and four-seat bobsleds have a standard length of 9 to 12 feet (2.7 to 3.7 meters). Robert M. Hughes

See also **Bobsledding; Sled.**

Tocopherol. See **Vitamin** (Vitamin E).

Tocqueville, *TOHK vihl* or *tawk VEEL,* **Alexis de,** *ah lehk SEE duh* (1805-1859), was a French historian and political philosopher. He became famous for his book *Democracy in America* (1835-1840), a study of political and social institutions in the United States. His other classic work, *The Old Regime and the Revolution* (1856), describes how government policies and conflicts between the upper class and other classes caused the French Revolution (1789-1799).

Unlike many thinkers of his time, Tocqueville believed the spread of some form of democratic government was inevitable. In *Democracy in America,* he analyzed what made free societies work and discussed aspects of social equality. He warned that the "tyranny of the majority" would put great pressure on people to act like everyone else. As a result, democracy would tend to smother individuality and personal freedom. Tocqueville wrote the book after visiting the United States in 1831 and 1832.

Tocqueville was born on July 29, 1805, in Paris into an aristocratic family. He served in the French legislature from 1839 to 1851 and as foreign minister briefly in 1849. He died on April 16, 1859. Seymour Drescher

Todd, Mary. See **Lincoln, Mary Todd.**

Toddler. See **Child** (The toddler stage).

Toe. See **Foot.**

Tofu, *TOH foo,* is a food made of soybean curds pressed into cakes or blocks. Tofu originated in China more than 1,000 years ago. Today, tofu is a major source of protein throughout east Asia. Many people in Europe and North America also eat tofu.

Tofu, formerly known as *bean curd,* resembles custard or a soft white cheese. It is usually prepared by first soaking, grinding, and boiling soybeans. A thickening agent, such as calcium sulfate or magnesium chloride, is then added, causing the protein in the beans to form a custardlike substance called *curd.*

Tofu has little taste of its own, but it picks up the flavors of the foods it is cooked with. Tofu contains no cholesterol. It is rich in calcium and low in calories.

Chunks of tofu can be prepared in many ways and added to many dishes. Tofu may also substitute for a variety of foods in recipes. For example, tofu can take the place of sour cream in dips and dressings, of ground beef in hamburgers, and of ham or cheese in sandwiches. It also may be used in place of cream cheese in cheesecake and cream in ice cream. William Shurtleff

Toga, *TOH guh,* was the outer garment worn by the citizens of ancient Rome. It had a semicircular or oval shape. The toga was wrapped around the body and allowed to fall to the feet in graceful folds. It was usually worn over a loose shirt called a *tunic* that hung to the knees or below. The Romans wore high shoes called *calcei* with the toga. At first, both men and women wore togas. But in time, women began to wear a rectangular cloak called a *palla* instead.

Through the years, the Romans changed the size of the toga and the manner of draping it. The earliest togas were short, like the Etruscan garment on which they were based. Over time, togas became larger, heavier, and more cumbersome, as elaborate ways of draping were developed to hold them more securely in place. Togas eventually became wide enough to wrap around the body two or three times.

The Romans used soft woolen fabrics to make togas. Ordinary citizens usually wore unbleached white togas. Colored borders or fabrics showed rank or station. For example, a candidate for public office wore a bleached, brilliantly white toga called the *toga candida.* Public officials and some priests wore a purple-bordered white toga called the *toga praetexta* at government functions. Boys also wore the fancy *toga praetexta* until they put on the natural white *toga virilis,* or *toga of manhood,* at about the age of 14 to 17. Generals wore a richly decorated purple toga called the *toga purpurea,* or *toga picta,* during celebrations of military victories. From the time of Augustus, who ruled from 27 B.C. to A.D. 14, only the emperor wore the purple toga.

The toga came to stand for the civilian, rather than the military, life. In the 40's B.C., the Roman orator and statesman Cicero wrote in Latin, "Let arms give way before the toga."

Larissa Bonfante

See also **Tunic.**

Marble statue (A.D. 68-96) by an unknown artist; Galleria Borghese, Rome (SCALA/Art Resource)

A Roman toga was worn by Emperor Augustus, *above.*

Togo is a small, narrow country in western Africa. It extends about 343 miles (552 kilometers) inland from the Gulf of Guinea, an arm of the South Atlantic Ocean. Togo is only 31 miles (50 kilometers) wide at the coast and 87 miles (140 kilometers) wide at its widest point. Lomé is the country's capital and only large city. Togo's name in French, the official language, is République Togolaise (Togolese Republic).

Government. The president is Togo's most powerful official. Under the Constitution, the president is elected to a five-year term. The president appoints a prime minister. The lawmaking body, the National Assembly, has 81 members, elected by the people to five-year terms.

People. About two-thirds of the Togolese live in rural areas and work on farms. The Ewe (pronounced *AY vay)* and related peoples make up about 40 percent of the population. The Kabyè *(kah bee YAY)* make up about 13 percent. Togo also has about 35 other ethnic groups. About half the people practice traditional African religions. About one-third of the population are Christians, and about one-sixth are Muslims.

Customs differ throughout Togo, especially between the south and the north. The ancestors of the people in southern Togo came from what are now Benin and Ghana. Many southerners live in groups of dwellings that are sometimes surrounded by a hedge or a fence of braided palms. Most southerners speak the Ewe or

Togo

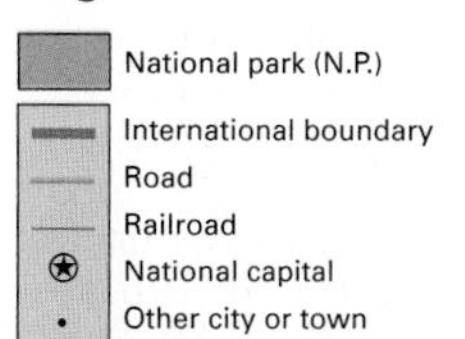

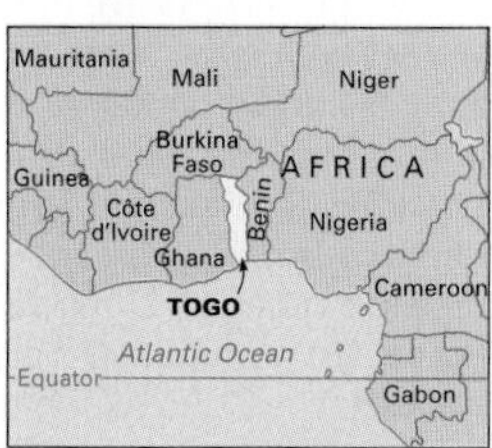

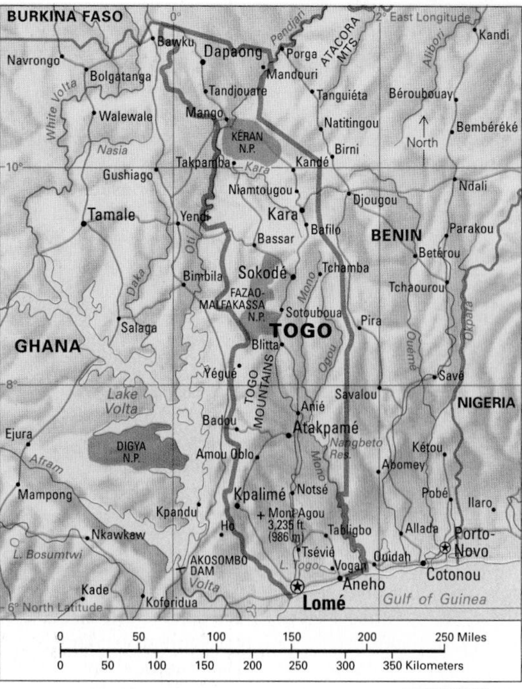

WORLD BOOK maps

Facts in brief

Capital: Lomé.
Official language: French.
Area: 21,925 mi² (56,785 km²). *Greatest distances*—north-south, 343 mi (552 km); east-west, 87 mi (140 km). *Coastline*—31 mi (50 km).
Population: *Estimated 2006 population*—5,243,000; density, 239 per mi² (92 per km²); distribution, 67 percent rural, 33 percent urban. *1981 census*—2,703,250.
Chief products: *Agriculture*—cassava, cocoa, coffee, copra, corn, cotton, millet, palm oil, peanuts, rice, sorghum, yams. *Mining*—limestone, marble, phosphates.
Flag: The flag has five horizontal stripes, three green and two yellow, with a white star on a red square in the upper left corner. Green symbolizes hope and agriculture; yellow, faith; white, purity; and red, charity and fidelity. See **Flag** (picture: Flags of Africa).
Money: *Basic unit*—CFA franc. CFA stands for Communauté Financière Africaine (African Financial Community).

Mina languages. European influence has been greater in the south than in the north. Some southerners work for the government, and others work in business, education, or trade. Most of Togo's Christian population, which is largely Roman Catholic, lives in the south.

Northern Togo was settled by a variety of peoples from what are now Burkina Faso and other countries. Some northerners live in castlelike groups of mud-brick houses with cone-shaped thatched roofs. Many languages, including Kabyè, Kotokoli, and Mina, are spoken in the north. Most of Togo's Muslims live there.

About 70 percent of Togo's children attend primary school. About 20 percent go to secondary school. Togo has a university at Lomé. Many Togolese study abroad, especially in France, Germany, and the United States.

Land. The Togo Mountains stretch from southwest to northeast and cover much of western Togo. Mont Agou (3,235 feet, or 986 meters) is Togo's highest point.

East and south of the Togo Mountains, the land descends across a sloping plateau to a low, sandy coastal plain. Tall grass and clumps of hardwood trees cover the plateau, which is drained by the Mono River. The densely populated coastal plain is dotted with swamps, lagoons, and coconut and oil palm forests.

North of the Togo Mountains, the land descends through rolling grasslands to the border of Burkina Faso. The Oti River drains the region. Few people live there. Thorny trees are scattered across the grasslands.

Togo has a hot climate. Average temperatures at Lomé, on the coast, range from 73 °F (23 °C) to 86 °F (30 °C). At Mango, in the north, average temperatures range from 59 °F (15 °C) to 95 °F (35 °C). Yearly rainfall averages about 40 inches (100 centimeters) in the north, about 70 inches (180 centimeters) in the southwest at Kpalimé, and about 35 inches (89 centimeters) at Lomé.

Economy. Togo is an agricultural country. It can grow sufficient food in years of adequate rainfall. But good land is limited, access to water and fertilizers is often difficult, and income is low.

Most farms in Togo are owned by families producing only enough food to feed themselves. These farms are often 7 acres (3 hectares) or less in size. Family farms throughout Togo raise a variety of food crops. These crops include cassava, corn, millet, rice, sorghum, and yams. Export crops, such as cocoa, coffee, and cotton,

© Penny Tweedie, Corbis

Lomé, the capital of Togo, lies at the southern end of the country. Commercial buildings rise in the background of this photo, and a government building stands in the foreground.

are grown mainly in the south. Togo also exports peanuts, *copra* (dried coconut meat), and the oil from the fruit and seeds of oil palms. Some fishing and livestock raising also contribute to the economy.

Togo has a large phosphate reserve, and phosphate is among Togo's most valuable exports. Limestone and marble also are mined. Oil and gas, discovered in 1998 off Togo's coast, may someday benefit the nation's economy. There is little manufacturing. Togo has about 325 miles (525 kilometers) of railroads and 4,660 miles (7,500 kilometers) of roads. Lomé has an airport and a wharf.

History. Little is known about the early history of what is now Togo. Scholars believe the ancestors of the central mountain peoples were early inhabitants of the region. Near present-day Notsé, archaeologists have found remains of walled cities that may date from about A.D. 1050. Between the 1100's and the 1300's, Ewe-speaking peoples began to move south from the Niger River valley to enter what are now southern Togo and Benin.

European explorers and traders began to visit the Togolese coast in the 1400's. The Portuguese were the first to arrive. Later, Danish, Dutch, British, and French ships all sailed the area. From the 1500's to the 1800's, millions of Africans along the Gulf of Guinea coast were captured and shipped to the Western Hemisphere to work as slaves. The region that is now Togo was sandwiched between two powerful slave-trading kingdoms—the Ashanti kingdom to the west, and the Dahomey kingdom to the east. Many people fled to Togo to avoid the slave trading and wars of these two kingdoms. A small transatlantic slave trade was centered at Aného, on Togo's coast. But most slave trading in the region was conducted at ports in what are now Benin and Ghana.

During the mid-1700's, the Tchokossi people established an Islamic kingdom in northern Togo. In the 1800's, the kola nut trade became the main economic activity in northern Togo. At the same time, trade in oil palm products replaced the slave trade at Aného.

German Protestant missionaries went to southern Togo in the mid-1800's. In 1884, Germany set up a small protectorate on the coast. The Germans used force and treaties to gradually extend the borders of the protectorate northward. Some local peoples resisted the expansion. By 1899, German Togoland included what is now Togo and part of what is now Ghana.

British- and French-directed African troops captured German Togoland in 1914, during World War I (1914-1918). In 1919, the United Kingdom and France divided German Togoland. The western one-third went to the British, and the rest went to the French. In 1922, the League of Nations confirmed *mandates* (authority to govern) for the British and French over Togoland. The United Nations (UN) took over the mandate system and named the Togoland areas *trusteeships* in 1946. When the Gold Coast became independent as Ghana in 1957, it incorporated British Togoland. On April 27, 1960, French Togoland became the independent Republic of Togo.

In Togo's first years of independence, Ewe peoples from the south dominated the government. But the Kabyè and other northern groups dominated the army. Sylvanus Olympio, a southerner who had been prime minister of French Togoland, was the first president of Togo. In 1963, a group of northern army officers assassinated Olympio. The officers installed one of Olympio's political opponents, Nicolas Grunitzky, as president. But the government under Grunitzky remained unstable.

In 1967, army officers led by Étienne Eyadéma, a Kabyè, overthrew Grunitzky in a bloodless coup. Eyadéma took over as president. In 1969, the Rally of the Togolese People, headed by Eyadéma, became Togo's only legal political party. Eyadéma was confirmed as president in a 1972 referendum. He also won presidential elections, unopposed, in 1979 and 1986. He began to be known by his second name, the African name Gnassingbé, in 1974. Under Eyadéma, large numbers of Kabyè and other northerners were given government jobs. In addition, the military was controlled by Eyadéma supporters who used force to help him maintain power.

In the early 1990's, Eyadéma's opponents held protests to demand democratic reforms. Some violence broke out between protesters and Togolese security forces. In 1991, the government legalized political parties and, in 1992, Togo adopted a democratic constitution. But Eyadéma maintained his grip on power. He won presidential elections in 1993, 1998, and 2003, but many people believe the elections were rigged. His government has often been accused of using intimidation and violence against political opponents.

In February 2005, Eyadéma died. The Togolese military immediately installed his son Faure Gnassingbé as president. But under the Constitution, the speaker of the National Assembly was supposed to have assumed power until elections could be held. Leaders of many countries and international groups criticized Faure's appointment, calling it a military coup. Faced with protests in Togo and international pressure, Faure stepped down after only three weeks. But in April 2005, a presidential election was held, and Faure won. Benjamin N. Lawrance

See also **Lomé**.

Toilet. See **Plumbing**.

Tojo, *toh joh,* **Hideki,** *hee deh kee* (1884-1948), was the general who, as prime minister of Japan, led his country into war with the United States in 1941. Tojo had first achieved national influence in the late 1930's as chief of staff of Japan's Kwantung Army.

Tojo was one of a group of political thinkers called *militarists* who believed that military interests should be foremost. The militarists objected to democratic developments within Japan. By provoking "incidents," they tried to commit their government to take decisive steps. They had engineered the Manchurian Incident, an explosion on a Japanese-run railway in Manchuria in 1931. The militarists blamed the Chinese for the explosion and used it as an excuse to occupy Manchuria. The incident was the first in a series of aggressive acts that led to the Sino-Japanese War of 1937-1945.

The United States applied economic pressure to halt Japan's aggression. Tojo and other militarists became convinced that Japan would have to fight the United States to secure access to the raw materials of the European colonies in Southeast Asia. By 1936, military leaders established firm control of Japan's government.

In 1940, Tojo became minister of war. He helped negotiate the Tripartite Pact, a 1940 treaty with Germany and Italy that made Japan a member of the alliance called the Axis. As American embargoes on oil to Japan began to strain the Japanese economy, Tojo insisted that if an agreement with the United States could not be reached, Japan would have to fight. In October 1941, Tojo was appointed prime minister. When talks with the United States failed, Tojo ordered the bombing of the U.S. fleet at Pearl Harbor, Hawaii, on Dec. 7, 1941.

Tojo's popularity in Japan was high after the early victories of World War II, but his influence waned as American victories began to turn the tide. He was forced to resign as prime minister in 1944 after the United States captured the Pacific island of Saipan. He was arrested and convicted as a war criminal after Japan's surrender and was hanged on Dec. 23, 1948.

Tojo was born on Dec. 30, 1884, in Tokyo. His family had a military background. Gary D. Allinson

See also **Japan** (History).

Tokugawa Ieyasu, *TOH koo GAH wah ee yeh YAH soo* (1542-1616), founded the Tokugawa *dynasty* (family of rulers), which governed Japan from 1603 until 1867. He was the *shogun* (military ruler) of Japan from 1603 until 1605, when he turned the title over to his son. However, he continued to hold power until his death.

Ieyasu was born in Okazaki. He was the son of a military lord who governed a small area in central Japan. When Ieyasu was 17, he entered the service of a prominent regional lord. He built up a huge personal domain in central Japan. In the 1590's, he became a high-ranking ally of Toyotomi Hideyoshi, the country's most powerful figure. When Hideyoshi died in 1598, Ieyasu became one of five regents governing for Hideyoshi's heir. In 1600, the regents fought a battle at Sekigahara, and Ieyasu's forces won. Three years later, the emperor gave Ieyasu the title of shogun.

Ieyasu established his government in Edo (now Tokyo). He controlled the country's largest army, about a fourth of its productive land, and its international relations. His *edicts* (public orders) fostered a nationwide system of law and morality. His descendants ruled for 250 years after his death. Ieyasu's splendid mausoleum stands north of Tokyo, in Nikko. Gary D. Allinson

John Callahan, Tony Stone Images

Tokyo at night glows with light. The city is Japan's capital and one of the largest and most crowded cities in the world. The busy Ginza district, *shown here,* in central Tokyo, has many restaurants and shops.

Tokyo

Tokyo is the capital of Japan and one of the largest cities in the world. It is part of a huge urban area that also includes the port city of Yokohama and the manufacturing cities of Chiba and Kawasaki. This area, known as the Tokyo metropolitan region, is the largest urban center in the world. It has an estimated population of more than 26 million people.

Tokyo itself is one of the busiest and most crowded cities in the world. It is the home of the Japanese emperor and the headquarters of the national government. It is Japan's center of business, culture, and education. Its many banks, commercial establishments, and industries help make Japan one of the richest nations in the world.

Tokyo has tall buildings, freeways jammed with traffic, and more neon signs than probably any other city in the world. The people of this Asian city listen to American jazz and rock music, and they eat at restaurants that offer everything from hamburgers to the finest European dishes. Many residents go to baseball games and watch movies and television shows from Western countries.

Gary D. Allinson, the contributor of this article, is Professor of Modern Japanese History at the University of Virginia and the author of Japanese Urbanism *and* Suburban Tokyo.

In spite of such outside influences, however, Japanese tradition remains strong in Tokyo. Large numbers of Tokyo's people take part in dances and parades during the city's many traditional festivals, some of which have been held for hundreds of years. They go to city parks to enjoy the beauty of the cherry trees and lotus blossoms. They visit historic shrines and temples and attend traditional plays and wrestling matches.

Tokyo traces its origin to 1457, when a powerful warrior built a castle there. It became Japan's capital in 1868. It was almost destroyed twice—by a terrible earthquake in 1923 and by air raids in the 1940's during World War II. But the city began growing rapidly after the war.

Facts in brief

Population: *City, or ward area*—8,130,408. *Tokyo Metropolitan Prefecture*—12,064,101. *Tokyo metropolitan region*—33,418,366.

Area: *City, or ward area*—223 mi² (578 km²); *Tokyo Metropolitan Prefecture*—832 mi² (2,156 km²); *Tokyo metropolitan region*—1,089 mi² (2,820 km²).

Altitude: 80 ft (24 m) above sea level.

Climate: *Average temperature*—January, 39 °F (4 °C); July, 76 °F (24 °C). *Average annual precipitation* (rainfall, melted snow, and other forms of moisture)—58 in (147 cm).

Government: *Chief executive*—governor (4-year term). *Legislature*—127-member assembly (4-year terms).

Founded: 1457.

About one-fourth of the people of Japan live in the Tokyo area. Tokyo itself has become extremely crowded, and its housing costs are among the highest in the world. It also faces such problems as pollution and some of the world's heaviest traffic.

The city

Tokyo lies on the southeastern coast of Honshu, Japan's largest island. The city stands in the southern part of a sprawling lowland called the Kanto Plain, a rich agricultural and industrial area. Mount Fuji, Japan's highest and most famous peak, lies about 60 miles (97 kilometers) to the southwest. On clear days, people in Tokyo have a spectacular view of the beautiful mountain, which seems to "float" on the horizon.

The city, or ward area. The city of Tokyo is divided into 23 units called *wards,* and it is often called the *ward area.* It is bordered by the Edo River on the northeast, by an inlet of the Pacific called Tokyo Bay on the east, and by the Tama River on the south. The Sumida River flows into Tokyo Bay in the eastern part of the city.

The Imperial Palace, where the Japanese emperor lives, stands near the center of the city. The town that became Tokyo grew up in this area.

East from the palace to Tokyo Bay, the land is low and flat. Many of Tokyo's chief business, commercial, and industrial districts are in this area. The Marunouchi district, an area of tall office buildings southeast of the palace, is Tokyo's business and financial center.

Part of eastern Tokyo is jammed with office buildings and apartment buildings made of concrete and steel. The oldest and poorest residential sections of Tokyo are also located in the eastern part of the city.

Much of far eastern Tokyo is filled-in land on what had been part of Tokyo Bay. Some of this land lies below sea level. The low-lying areas are always in danger of floods, especially during heavy rains. Dikes have been built along the waterfront and the riverbanks. But the filled-in land sinks lower every year, mainly because of the removal of large amounts of ground water for industrial use. The dikes sink along with the land, making flood control difficult.

West of the Imperial Palace, the land becomes hilly. The chief residential sections of the city are in the west. The residences include large apartment buildings like those in Western cities and simple one- or two-story wooden buildings, the traditional Japanese houses. Many of the wooden houses are small and plain by Western standards. In some sections, rich families and poor families live in the same neighborhood, and their houses are plain and look much alike. But the western part of the city also has luxurious residential sections where the wealthy live.

Tokyo, unlike most other Japanese cities, no longer has large numbers of buildings in the ancient Japanese style that is most familiar to Westerners. This style features low, graceful lines and roofs turned up at the edges. Most of the remaining buildings in this style are religious shrines or temples.

The Tokyo Metropolitan Prefecture is one of 47 prefectures in Japan. Prefectures are the country's main units of regional government. The Tokyo prefecture is called *Tokyo-to* in Japanese. Most prefectures are called *ken.* Tokyo is called a *to* in order to indicate its special status as the nation's capital.

The Tokyo Metropolitan Prefecture is made up of four areas: (1) the city, or ward area, (2) about 25 suburban cities west of the ward area, (3) several towns in a

Tokyo area

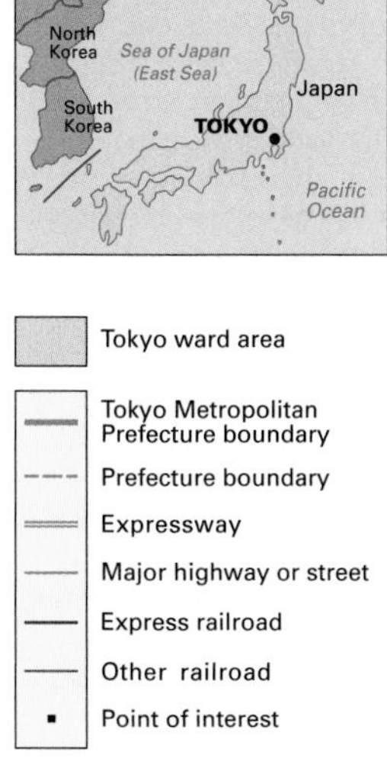

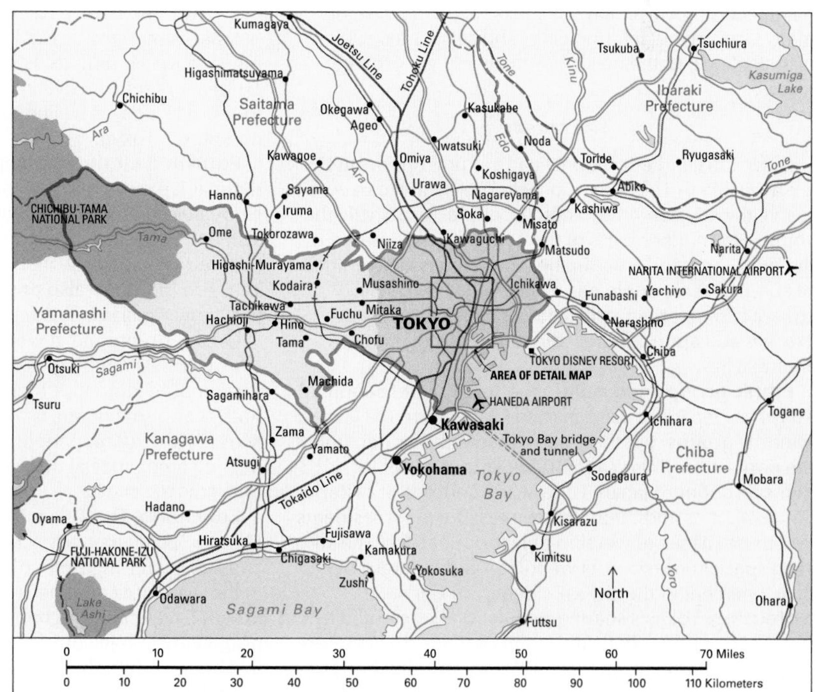

WORLD BOOK maps

A Tokyo family relaxes at home in the evening, *left.* The father and son play a Japanese version of chess, called *shogi.* The food, the furnishings of the home, and the family's clothing reflect a combination of Asian and Western influences that is typical of life in Tokyo.

Paul Chesley, Tony Stone Images

mountainous area on the far western edge of the prefecture, and (4) the Izu Islands and the Bonin Islands, two small island groups in the Pacific Ocean, south of the prefecture. Nearly all of the prefecture's residents live in the ward area or the suburban cities.

The Tokyo metropolitan region is the world's largest urban center. It consists of most of the Tokyo Metropolitan Prefecture and parts of three neighboring prefectures—Kanagawa, Chiba, and Saitama. Kanagawa, to the south, includes the port city of Yokohama and the manufacturing city of Kawasaki. Chiba, on the east, has many large manufacturing cities and residential suburbs. Saitama, to the north, has many rapidly growing towns.

The people

More jobs and educational and cultural opportunities are available in Tokyo than anywhere else in Japan. As a result, the city constantly attracts people—especially the young—from other parts of the country. Tokyo is one of the most crowded cities in the world. It has an average of about 36,000 people per square mile (14,000 per square kilometer)—nearly twice as many as New York City has and approximately three times as many as Mumbai has.

Ethnic groups and religion. Almost all the people of Tokyo are Japanese. Koreans and Chinese are the largest minority groups, but they make up less than 1 percent of the population. Shinto and Buddhism are the chief religions throughout Japan. Tokyo has hundreds of historic Shinto shrines and Buddhist temples. But most residents visit these places of worship only for public festivals or such special occasions as weddings and funerals. Less than 2 percent of the city's residents are Christians.

Housing. Tokyo's soaring population has created a strong demand for housing. In the past, most Tokyo residents lived in small, one- or two-story wooden houses, each with its own yard or garden. As the population grew, many apartment buildings were constructed in the city in an attempt to provide housing for all the people. Even so, a housing shortage continued. The limited amount of housing and land in the city center drove up rents and land prices. Many people—even if they could find housing—could not afford to pay for it. As a result, Tokyo's outlying areas have experienced a building boom since the 1960's.

The Tokyo prefecture has begun financing the construction of low-rent housing projects. One such project, called Tama New Town, houses about 200,000 people. But Tama New Town, like many other Tokyo housing developments, is far from the downtown area. Some workers who live in outlying areas spend up to four hours a day traveling to and from their jobs in downtown Tokyo.

Food and clothing. Many Tokyo residents enjoy traditional Japanese foods. Popular Japanese dishes include *sukiyaki* (beef cooked with vegetables), *tempura* (fish and vegetables fried in batter), and *sushi* (vinegar-flavored rice with raw fish or vegetables). Chinese and Western foods are also popular in Tokyo, and the city has many American fast-food restaurants.

On the streets and at work, most of the people wear Western-style clothing. Some older women still wear a *kimono.* The kimono, a traditional Japanese garment of both men and women, is a long robe tied with a sash. Most Tokyo young people wear a kimono only on holidays or other special occasions. Most students wear uniforms to school.

Education. The Tokyo Metropolitan Prefecture has about 1,500 elementary schools, 900 junior high schools, and 500 senior high schools. Most of these schools are in the ward area and the suburbs. Some parts of Tokyo do not have enough schools for the rapidly growing population. But in some old sections of the city center that are now largely occupied by businesses, many of the schoolhouses stand nearly empty.

The prefecture has about 120 four-year colleges and universities and 80 junior colleges. More than a third of Japan's college students attend these institutions.

Social problems, such as poverty and crime, exist in Tokyo. But they are not as severe as they are in many other large cities. Because of Tokyo's strong economy, most people can find jobs. The local and national governments also provide aid for those who cannot support themselves. Tokyo's crime rate is much lower than the crime rate in most other large cities. Also, since Tokyo has no large minority groups, it has few major problems stemming from racial or other social differences.

Demonstrations are often held in Tokyo to protest such matters as political, educational, and environmental policies. They have sometimes resulted in violence.

Cultural life and recreation

Few cities in the world can match Tokyo as an international center of culture and entertainment. Tokyo's cultural institutions and favorite leisure-time activities reflect the culture of both the East and the West.

The arts. Many of Japan's finest artists and craftworkers live and work in Tokyo. Some still use the styles and methods of their ancestors to create beautiful paintings on paper or silk and colorful wood-block prints. But many Tokyo artists create paintings and sculptures using Western styles and methods.

Tokyo is the center of Japanese drama, music, and other performing arts. Two traditional types of Japanese drama, *no* and *kabuki,* rank as favorite forms of entertainment in Tokyo. For descriptions of these colorful plays, see **Drama** (Japan).

Several professional symphony orchestras that specialize in Western music perform in Tokyo. Other Tokyo musical groups play traditional music, featuring such Japanese instruments as the three-stringed *samisen,* or *shamisen,* and a kind of harp called a *koto.*

Japan's motion-picture industry is also centered in Tokyo. Japanese movies have been praised by audiences throughout the world.

Museums and libraries. Some of Japan's finest museums and libraries are in Tokyo. The Tokyo National Museum, the largest museum in Japan, has a valuable collection of Asian art. The National Museum of Modern Art specializes in works by modern Japanese artists. The National Museum of Western Art houses a large collection of works by Western artists. The National Science Museum focuses on scientific discoveries.

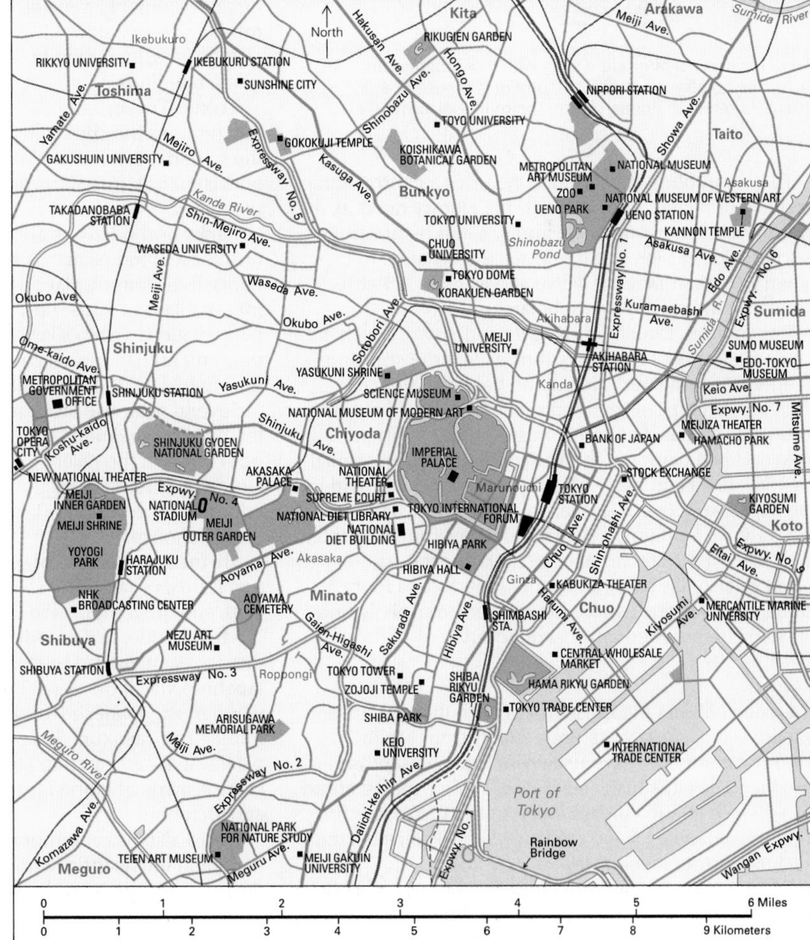

Central Tokyo

The map at the right shows the central part of Tokyo and its major landmarks. The Imperial Palace stands near the center of the city in beautiful parklike grounds. Ueno Park, which lies northeast of the palace, is one of the city's most popular parks. It includes a zoo and several museums and art galleries.

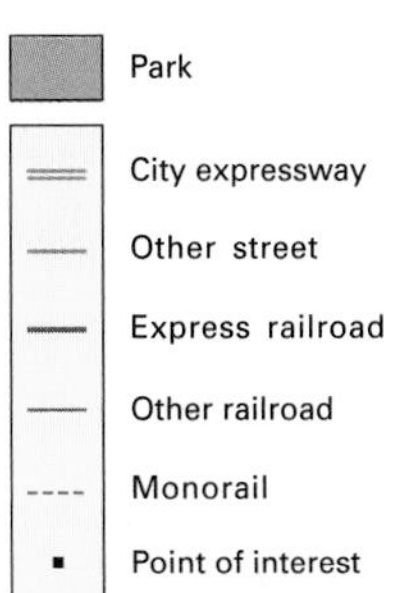

WORLD BOOK map

Superstock

An actor in a *no* play tells a story with movements and gestures. The no play is a traditional form of Japanese drama. Tokyo is Japan's center of drama, music, and other performing arts.

Tokyo's public library system includes a central library and two branches. The National Diet Library ranks as the country's largest library. The library's first responsibility is to provide research and reference assistance to Japan's *Diet* (parliament). It also serves many other needs, including those of scholars.

Recreation. Exhibitions of *judo* and *sumo,* which are Japanese forms of wrestling, rank as favorite sporting events. Western sports, including baseball, bowling, golf, ice skating, soccer, tennis, and track and field, are also popular. Baseball is the most popular sport in Tokyo. Home games of the Yomiuri Giants professional baseball team and many other sports events are held in the 50,000-seat Tokyo Dome. Tokyo's largest stadium, the National Stadium, is the site of many important track and field events. It seats about 72,000 spectators.

Tokyo also has many amusement parks and nightclubs. *Karaoke* bars, where the guests themselves sing on stage to recorded music, are popular.

Visitor's guide

Large numbers of tourists visit Tokyo the year around. In early April, the city's famous cherry trees are in bloom. Autumn in Tokyo usually brings pleasantly mild weather. The city's many festivals are other tourist attractions. These include the exciting parade of Tokyo's firefighters on January 6 and the lively Sanja Festival in the Asakusa district in mid-May.

Tourists can choose from many fine hotels and restaurants in Tokyo. Many of the hotels are built and furnished in Western style. Others are Japanese-style hotels called *ryokan.* They have such traditional features as sliding paper-paneled doors called *shoji,* mats called *tatami* that cover the floors, and heavy quilts called *futon* that serve as beds. Tokyo has thousands of restaurants. Many of these restaurants specialize in Japanese or other Asian dishes, and many others serve Western foods.

This section of the article describes a few of the interesting places to visit in Tokyo. See other sections of the article for discussions of additional places of interest.

The Imperial Palace is the home of Japan's emperor. It stands near the center of the city and consists of several low buildings and beautiful parklike grounds. Stone walls and a series of wide moats separate it from the rest of the city. The palace is open to the public only two days of the year—January 2 and the emperor's birthday. Thousands of Japanese come to pay their respects to the emperor on these two days.

Government buildings. The National Diet Building, a concrete and granite structure with a tall central tower, stands southwest of the Imperial Palace. It is the meeting place of Japan's parliament. The Tokyo Metropolitan Government Office stands in the western part of the city, in an area called the Shinjuku district. This striking concrete building, designed by Japanese architect Kenzo Tange, has twin 48-story towers. It houses the offices of the governor of the Tokyo prefecture and various government agencies. An observation deck at the top is open to visitors. The Shinjuku district has many skyscrapers, including hotels, department stores, and office buildings.

Tokyo Tower, a 1,092-foot (333-meter) steel tower that ranks as the city's tallest structure, stands south of the Imperial Palace. The Tokyo Tower houses radio and television broadcasting studios and has two observation platforms.

Parks and gardens attract many visitors. Ueno Park, northeast of the palace, is one of the city's most popular parks. Its spring displays of cherry blossoms and summer displays of lotus blossoms are outstanding. The park includes Tokyo's largest concert hall, several museums and art galleries, a zoo, a temple and shrine built during the 1600's, and tombs of Japanese rulers.

Several Japanese-style gardens in Tokyo are open to the public. Korakuen Garden and Rikugien Garden—both north of the palace—are two of the oldest and most famous gardens. Many people visit Tokyo's gardens to admire their beautifully landscaped grounds and relax at their teahouses.

Shrines and temples attract millions of worshipers and tourists yearly. The shrines are Shinto places of worship, and the temples are Buddhist.

Meiji Shrine, in a wooded parkland near the Shinjuku district, is one of the best-known shrines in Japan. Many Japanese visit it on New Year's Day, one of the few times when most Japanese women wear traditional dress in public. The Yasukuni Shrine stands northwest of the palace. It is dedicated to Japan's war dead and draws huge crowds of worshipers for special festivals in April and October.

Tokyo also has a number of famous Buddhist temples, including the historic Kannon Temple in the Asakusa district at the city's northeastern outskirts. The temple traces its origins to the 600's, though the present buildings were constructed in the 1950's. Colorful souvenir

Dave Bartruff

Baseball is the most popular sport in Tokyo and a favorite pastime throughout Japan. Tokyo's professional baseball team, the Yomiuri Giants, plays home games at the Tokyo Dome. The Giants, shown here in white uniforms, face the Yokohama Whales.

shops line the approach to the temple. During the Sanja Festival, held in the temple area in mid-May, people parade in traditional Japanese costumes.

Other places of interest. Several well-known districts are near the Imperial Palace. The Ginza district, southeast of the palace, ranks as one of Tokyo's liveliest and most colorful districts. It is famous for its stores and nightclubs. The Kanda district, northeast of the palace, is known for its many bookstores. The Akihabara district, north of Kanda, features hundreds of shops that sell electronics products. The Asakusa district, site of the Kannon Temple, is north of Akihabara. Asakusa is one of Tokyo's oldest entertainment sections. It includes amusement parks, theaters, and restaurants.

The Tokyo Central Wholesale Market, also known as Tsukiji Market, is east of the Ginza. This lively place is the largest fish market in Asia.

A theme park called Tokyo Disney Resort, in the Chiba Prefecture, is a top tourist attraction. The park was built on filled-in land in Tokyo Bay.

Economy

Tokyo is one of the world's most important centers of economic activity. It has long been a center of Japanese manufacturing. Since the 1970's, however, such service industries as finance, trade, and communication have become even more important. Many of Japan's business corporations, including the giant automakers Nissan Motor Company and Honda Motor Company, have their headquarters in Tokyo.

Manufacturing. The manufacture of electronics equipment is one of Tokyo's leading industries. Some of the world's largest electronics firms, including Hitachi Limited and the Toshiba, Sony, and NEC corporations, have their headquarters in Tokyo. These huge companies and many small ones in the city make cassette recorders, compact disc players, computers, fax machines, radios, television sets, video recorders, and other electronics products. Many of these products are exported.

Publishing and printing is also a leading industry in Tokyo. Most of Japan's publishing companies have their headquarters in the city. Much of the material published in Tokyo is also printed there.

Other important products made in Tokyo include chemicals, food, furniture, and paper. Several Tokyo companies rank among the 25 largest manufacturing firms in the world.

Yokohama and Kawasaki also have many manufacturing plants. Products made in the metropolitan region include automobiles, chemicals, iron and steel, machinery, metal products, petroleum products, and ships.

Finance. Tokyo is one of the world's major financial centers. The Tokyo Stock Exchange ranks among the largest stock exchanges in the world. Businesses and industries throughout Japan depend on Tokyo banks for loans. The Bank of Japan, the nation's central bank, has its headquarters in Tokyo. Controlled by the national government, the Bank of Japan regulates the nation's entire banking system. Tokyo also has many commercial banks. The largest commercial banks have branches or offices in many Japanese and foreign cities. Tokyo is also the nation's center for such consumer services as financial planning and credit management.

Trade. Thousands of companies in Tokyo deal in international trade. These firms handle almost half of Japan's export business and over half the nation's import business. The 40-story Tokyo Trade Center displays various types of Japanese goods for international buyers.

AP/Wide World

The Tokyo Stock Exchange is one of the largest stock exchanges in the world. The exchange and Tokyo's many banks help make the city a center of world finance.

The Tokyo International Trade Center sponsors displays of international goods that attract millions of visitors from all over the world each year.

Because Tokyo has a relatively shallow harbor, most large ships that enter Tokyo Bay dock at Yokohama. The Port of Yokohama ranks as Japan's largest port. Railroads, trucks, and barges carry large quantities of freight between the two cities. Chiba and Kawasaki also have port facilities.

Transportation. Motorists in Tokyo drive many more automobiles than the freeways and streets can handle effectively, and severe traffic jams occur frequently. The prefecture government is trying to provide more public transportation as a substitute for automobile travel. The Tokyo Bay bridge and tunnel were built to help relieve traffic congestion.

Tokyo's public transportation system includes railroad, subway, and bus lines. An extensive network of rail lines crisscrosses the Tokyo metropolitan region. High-speed electric trains link Tokyo with Osaka and other cities. These trains, called *Shinkansen* or "bullet trains," carry passengers at speeds of up to 186 miles (300 kilometers) per hour.

Tokyo's commuter trains rank among the fastest and most efficient in the world. Nearly 10 million passengers cram aboard them each day. During rush hours, employees called *oshiya* (pushers) work at the main train stations. Their job involves shoving passengers into crowded trains to make more room (see **City** [picture: Travel in cities]). The Shinjuku commuter station ranks as one of the busiest railway stations in the world. It handles millions of riders a day.

Tokyo has two major airports. Tokyo International Airport, commonly called Haneda Airport, lies in the far southern part of the city. It handles mainly domestic traffic. A *monorail* (single-rail train) operates between central Tokyo and Haneda Airport. Most international flights use the Narita International Airport, which lies about 40 miles (64 kilometers) east of central Tokyo.

Communication. Tokyo's many television and radio stations make the city a broadcasting center. Japanese programs as well as American and European programs with Japanese sound tracks appear on TV. Tokyo's newspaper companies publish more than 25 daily papers.

Government

The governor is the chief official of the Tokyo Metropolitan Prefecture. The people elect the governor to a four-year term. The chief lawmaking body is the Metropolitan Assembly. It has 127 members, whom the voters elect to four-year terms. Each ward, suburb, and other community in the prefecture has at least one representative in the Assembly. The prefecture government also includes a board of education, police and fire departments, and many other agencies.

The wards, suburbs, towns, and villages of the Tokyo Metropolitan Prefecture all have some form of local government. Each elects a council and a mayor or other administrators. However, the prefecture government limits the powers of these local officials. It makes *ordinances* (rules) for all the communities in the prefecture. It also provides police protection and certain other public services for the entire area. But it provides some services, including fire protection and sanitation facilities, for the ward area only.

Local governments must provide services that are not supplied by the prefecture government. They may collect some tax money for these projects, and they receive additional funds from the prefecture and national governments.

History

Early development. The earliest settlement in the Tokyo area for which there is any evidence dates from A.D. 737. Archaeologists uncovered the remains of a Buddhist temple and monastery that had been built there at that time. However, Tokyo marks 1457 as its beginning. In that year, a warrior named Ota Dokan built a castle there. The area had military importance because it overlooked both Tokyo Bay and the Kanto Plain. Ota Dokan worked in the service of a powerful warrior family, one of several who ruled parts of Japan. He built his castle where the Imperial Palace now stands. A town named Edo (now called Tokyo) grew up around the castle.

The development that made the town Japan's chief city began in 1590. In that year, a warrior named Tokugawa Ieyasu made Edo his headquarters. In 1603, Ieyasu became *shogun* (military ruler) of Japan. Edo became the nation's political center. But Kyoto, a city southwest of Edo and the home of the emperor, remained the official capital. By the early 1800's, Edo had grown into a city of over a million people. Ieyasu and his descendants ruled as shogun in Edo until 1867.

Western influence. Beginning in the early 1600's, Japan closed itself off from normal contact with the rest of the world. This policy was known as the *sakoku* (closed country) rule. The government allowed ships from Holland and from China to trade in Japan, but only occasionally and only at the port of Nagasaki. It prohibited Japanese people from traveling to other countries.

In 1853, United States naval officer Commodore Matthew C. Perry arrived at Tokyo Bay on a mission for the U.S. government. His goal was to open diplomatic and trade relations with Japan. Perry sailed into Tokyo Bay with four warships and began talks with Japanese rulers. He returned with more warships the next year and signed a treaty of friendship with the rulers. Partly as a result of Perry's efforts, Japan signed trade treaties with the United States and other Western countries in 1858. The treaties marked the start of modern Western influence in Japan.

Emperor Mutsuhito—who took the title *Meiji,* meaning *enlightened rule*—did much to further Westernization. He took control of Japan from the shogun in 1867. He transferred the capital from Kyoto to Edo in 1868 and moved into the Edo castle. Edo was renamed *Tokyo,* which means *eastern capital.* After 1868, Japan—especially Tokyo—rapidly adopted Western styles and inventions. By the late 1800's, Tokyo began to look like a Western city.

Earthquake and reconstruction. On Sept. 1, 1923, a violent earthquake shook the Tokyo area. Buildings collapsed and fires broke out throughout Tokyo. About 120,000 residents of the city died in the disaster, and most of central Tokyo was destroyed. The city was rebuilt during the next 20 years.

At the time of the earthquake, Tokyo consisted of 15 wards in the vicinity of the Imperial Palace. After the disaster, areas outside the 15 wards began to develop. In 1932, the city took over many of the areas and made them wards, establishing the present city limits.

World War II brought destruction to Tokyo again. American bombers first attacked the city in April 1942. The heaviest raids occurred from March to August of 1945, when Japan announced its intention to surrender. The bombs destroyed about one-third of Tokyo. Hundreds of thousands of people were killed or listed as missing. Thousands fled the city. Tokyo's population dropped from about 7,350,000 in 1940 to about 3,500,000 in 1945. In 1943, Tokyo and communities west of it formed the Tokyo Metropolitan Prefecture.

Rebuilding the city. The people of Tokyo began to rebuild their city after the war, but without much planning. Buildings went up wherever there was room. Tokyo's economy began booming a few years after the war. Population growth accompanied economic growth, and the population of the city nearly tripled between 1945 and 1960. In 1964, Tokyo was host to the Summer Olympic Games. In preparation for the games, the city started a construction program that included new freeways and hotels, and the monorail.

Tokyo's rapid growth made it one of the world's largest cities and gave it a strong economy. But the growth, along with a lack of planning, helped cause such problems as housing shortages, pollution, and traffic jams.

In 1966, the prefecture government started a series of plans to help solve Tokyo's problems. The plans set goals for improving public housing, purifying the polluted air and river water, reducing street noise and traffic jams, and increasing sanitation facilities. Parts of the Tokyo prefecture were set aside for public housing and other community projects. To ease overcrowding, the government has encouraged the development of new suburban towns. A number of such towns are growing rapidly. For example, Tsukuba, which lies about 40 miles (60 kilometers) northeast of Tokyo, was designated in 1963 to become a center for scientific research and teaching. The city now has about 50 research institutes and two universities dedicated to technological studies.

Recent developments. By the 1990's, Tokyo's air was significantly cleaner. The city had also reduced water pollution by building better sewage and waste-disposal plants. Overcrowding and soaring land prices remained serious problems, however. In the early 1990's, both the national and prefecture governments began drafting new land and tax laws in an attempt to make housing more affordable. Because the city's overcrowding had become so severe, some Japanese leaders began to study the possibility of moving the national government out of Tokyo.

Wood-block print (1856); Victoria and Albert Museum, London (Art Resource)

Moonlit Street Scene in Edo is one of many prints of the city created in the 1800's by Japanese artist Hiroshige. Edo was renamed Tokyo in 1868, when it became Japan's capital.

Mike Yamashita

The Imperial Palace is the home of the Japanese emperor. It stands in a beautiful parklike setting near the center of Tokyo. Stone walls and moats separate the palace grounds from the rest of the city. The settlement that became Tokyo was established in this area.

In 1996, the Tokyo International Forum was completed in downtown Tokyo. It houses an exhibition hall; four halls for conventions, concerts, and theatrical performances; and many shops and restaurants. Its most distinctive feature is a giant elliptical glass hall. Gary D. Allinson

Related articles in *World Book* include:

Architecture (picture: The Tokyo Cathedral)
Asia (picture: Two Asian street scenes)
Bonin Islands
Japan (with pictures)
Shogun
World War II (The tide turns; Closing in on Japan)
Yokohama

Outline

I. The city
- A. The city, or ward area
- B. The Tokyo Metropolitan Prefecture
- C. The Tokyo metropolitan region

II. The people
- A. Ethnic groups and religion
- B. Housing
- C. Food and clothing
- D. Education
- E. Social problems

III. Cultural life and recreation
- A. The arts
- B. Museums and libraries
- C. Recreation

IV. Visitor's guide

V. Economy
- A. Manufacturing
- B. Finance
- C. Trade
- D. Transportation
- E. Communication

VI. Government

VII. History

Questions

When was Tokyo made the capital of Japan?
How does the Tokyo metropolitan region rank in size with other urban centers of the world?
What is the most popular sport in Tokyo?
Why do parts of Tokyo face the danger of flooding?
Who was Tokugawa Ieyasu?
What is a disadvantage of many of Tokyo's housing developments?
Where is the Akihabara district?
How many times was Tokyo almost destroyed?
What is a *ryokan?*
What is one of Tokyo's leading industries?

Additional resources

Cybriwsky, Roman A. *Historical Dictionary of Tokyo.* Scarecrow, 1996. *Tokyo.* Wiley, 1998.
Insight Guide: Tokyo. Rev. ed. Langenscheidt Pubs., 2003.
Kallen, Stuart A. *Life in Tokyo.* Lucent Bks., 2001.
Kent, Deborah. *Tokyo.* Children's Pr., 1996. Younger readers.

Tokyo Rose was a name used by United States military personnel to describe women who broadcast in English over Japanese radio during World War II (1939-1945). The name became associated with one broadcaster in particular, Iva Toguri d'Aquino, when she was tried for treason against the United States in 1949.

The Japanese government created radio programs to weaken the morale of U.S. troops in the Pacific during World War II. The programs featured American music and English-speaking announcers. The broadcasts in which d'Aquino took part were called "Zero Hour." They were meant to make U.S. personnel homesick and discouraged. But the broadcasts had little effect on morale.

Many of the broadcasters were women. United States troops called any of these women Tokyo Rose, though none of them actually used that name.

Iva Toguri d'Aquino was a U.S. citizen of Japanese ancestry who had been stranded in Tokyo when the war began. After the war, she was charged with treason for her broadcasts. Some reporters referred to her as Tokyo Rose. She was found guilty, served about six years in prison, and paid a $10,000 fine. However, many came to believe that she was wrongly convicted. In 1977, President Gerald R. Ford granted d'Aquino a full and unconditional pardon. Russell Warren Howe

Toledo, *tuh LEED oh* or *toh LAY thoh* (pop. 68,382), is a city in central Spain. It lies on a high hill 41 miles (66 kilometers) southwest of Madrid (see **Spain** [political map]). The Tagus River flows in a deep ravine around the hill. The city is the capital of Toledo province.

Toledo is a medieval city of narrow, steep, winding streets. It has many historic works of architecture, and the entire city has been declared a Spanish national monument. Its architecture shows a strong Moorish influence. Houses rise straight up, many of them without windows facing the streets. A magnificent Gothic cathedral dominates the city. Its tower rises 300 feet (90 meters). Beautiful chapels inside contain many fine paintings and statues. El Greco lived in Toledo, and his home is now a museum for some of his paintings.

Toledo has little industry, but the city is famous for sabers, firearms, Toledo ware (inlaid steel), and textiles. Its founding date is unknown. Arabs destroyed the city in the 700's. Alfonso VI, king of León and Castile, seized Toledo in 1085 and made it his capital. Philip II made Madrid the capital in 1561. Stanley G. Payne

Toledo, *tuh LEE doh* (pop. 313,619; met. area pop. 618,203), is an industrial and transportation center in northwestern Ohio. It also serves as a major Great Lakes port. Toledo lies on both banks of the Maumee River. At Toledo, the river widens into Maumee Bay at the western end of Lake Erie (see **Ohio** [political map]). For many years, the city was a key glass-manufacturing center and was often called the Glass Capital of the World. However, several of the firms that specialized in glassmaking now make other kinds of products.

The first permanent white settlers in what is now the Toledo area arrived in 1817. The settlers chose the site because of its location on the Maumee River. The city was named for Toledo, Spain, but no one knows why.

Description. Toledo, the county seat of Lucas County, covers 84 square miles (218 square kilometers). Its downtown area lies along the Maumee River. The port is on Maumee Bay.

Institutions of higher education in Toledo include the Medical College of Ohio and the University of Toledo. The Toledo Museum of Art includes one of the largest collections of rare glass objects in the world. Toledo is also the home of the Toledo Symphony Orchestra and the Toledo Opera Association. The Toledo Zoo ranks among the finest zoos in the United States. Promenade Park stretches along the riverfront. Concerts and other events are held in the park during the summer. Several historical monuments are located near the city. They commemorate General Anthony Wayne's victory over Indians in the Battle of Fallen Timbers in 1794 and General William Henry Harrison's defeat of British forces in the War of 1812.

Economy. Most of Toledo's workers are employed in service industries. Many of these people work in hospitals. Others are employed in retail trade. About 15 percent of the city's workers hold jobs in manufacturing. The chief manufactured products are glass products, motor vehicle parts, and motor vehicles. Several large corporations make their home in the metropolitan area.

The port of Toledo handles millions of tons of cargo every year. Coal is the leading product shipped. Other products include iron ore, grain, and petroleum. Toledo is one of the leading U.S. Great Lakes ports in the handling of international cargo. Toledo Express Airport serves Toledo and the surrounding area.

Government. Toledo has a mayor-council form of government. The voters of the city elect a mayor and 12 council members, all to four-year terms. Six districts each elect a council member, and six *members at large* are elected by the city as a whole.

History. Erie Indians lived in the Toledo area before Europeans came there. In 1615, Étienne Brulé, a guide for the French explorer Samuel de Champlain, became the first European to see the area. In 1817, land speculators established a settlement on the site of Fort Industry, a stockade built about 1795. They called this settlement Port Lawrence. Port Lawrence and the nearby village of Vistula united in 1833 to form Toledo. The community received a city charter in 1837.

The city's growth as a transportation center began in 1836, when railroads first reached Toledo. The Wabash and Erie Canal in Indiana and the Miami and Erie Canal in Ohio began operating during the 1840's. They had a joint outlet in Toledo. The city, with its natural lake port, became an important water gateway to the West.

In 1888, Edward Libbey, a glass manufacturer from East Cambridge, Massachusetts, brought skilled workers to the Toledo area and founded the Libbey Glass Company. He was later joined by Michael Owens. The glass industry helped increase the city's population from 3,829 in 1850 to 131,822 in 1900. An automobile plant opened in 1908. By 1930, 290,718 people lived in the city.

In 1950, Toledo had about 303,600 people. The population grew rapidly in the next decade and reached a peak of 379,104 in 1960. The population declined through the rest of the 1900's. In 1987, SeaGate Centre, a convention hall, opened in downtown Toledo. In 2002, a minor league baseball stadium opened in the downtown area's Warehouse District. Mary F. Mackzum

Toleration act is a law allowing people to believe in any religion they choose. One famous toleration act, passed by the colony of Maryland in 1649, gave religious liberty to all Christians. The most famous toleration act was that of 1689, passed by the English Parliament. It granted religious freedom to the Protestant dissenters from the established Anglican Church. This law did not apply to Roman Catholics, Jews, and Unitarians. But the dissenters continued to suffer until the 1800's. Edward C. Papenfuse

Tolkien, *TOHL keen,* **J. R. R.** (1892-1973), an English author and scholar, wrote a popular series of novels about an imaginary people called *hobbits.* Tolkien introduced the short, hairy-footed hobbits in *The Hobbit* (1937). He continued their story in three related novels called *The Lord of the Rings.* These novels are *The Fellowship of the Ring* (1954), *The Two Towers* (1954), and *The Return of the King* (1955).

Hobbits are industrious and good-natured. They live in a world called Middle-earth, along with elves, goblins, wizards, and human beings. In *The Hobbit,* Bilbo Baggins, a hobbit, discovers a ring that conveys the power of invisibility but also corrupts the user. The hero of *The Lord of the Rings* is Frodo Baggins, Bilbo's cousin. After many adventures, Frodo destroys the ring so that Sauron, the evil Dark Lord, cannot use it against Middle-earth's people. Many critics have interpreted *The Lord of the Rings* as a symbolic moral or religious story of the battle between good and evil. But Tolkien insisted he wrote the novels only as fantasies to entertain readers.

In 1917, Tolkien began to write *The Silmarillion,* a history of Middle-earth before the hobbits appeared. He worked on the book occasionally for the rest of his life but died before completing it, and his son Christopher finished the novel. It was published in 1977. A collection of previously unpublished material about Middle-earth and the legendary island of Númenor appeared in 1980 as *Unfinished Tales.*

John Ronald Reuel Tolkien was born Jan. 3, 1892, in Bloemfontein, South Africa, of English parents. From 1925 to 1959, he taught at Oxford University in England. He specialized in medieval languages and literature and wrote many scholarly works in this field. His hobbit stories were influenced by medieval English, German, and Scandinavian languages and literature. The three novels were adapted into three immensely popular motion pictures released in 2001, 2002, and 2003. Garrett Stewart

Additional resources

Carpenter, Humphrey. *Tolkien.* 1977. Reprint. Houghton, 2000.
Tyler, J. E. A. *The Complete Tolkien Companion.* Thomas Dunne, 2004.

Toll road. See Turnpike.

Tollán. See Tula.

Tolman, Edward Chace (1886-1959), was an American psychologist known for his theory of how human beings and other animals learn. Tolman rejected the learning theory of John B. Watson and other behavioral psychologists of the time. These psychologists maintained that learning occurs through a random trial-and-error process. Tolman argued that learning is a systematic process guided by goals and expectations. He believed that learners develop what he called *cognitive maps*—that is, mental images of the probable paths to their goals. He explained his theory in a book called *Purposive Behavior in Animals and Men* (1932). Tolman was born on April 14, 1886, in Newton, Massachusetts. He taught psychology at the University of California at Berkeley from 1918 until his death. Richard M. Wolf

Tolstoy, Alexei (1883-1945), was a Russian novelist and playwright. Tolstoy was an excellent storyteller with a vivid, clear style. His most important novel is the three-part *Road to Calvary* (1921, 1927, 1941). This epic tale describes the tragedies of Russian life during World War I (1914-1918) and deals with the Bolshevik revolution of 1917 and the ensuing Russian civil war (1917-1920). The novel recounts the effects of these events on a group of intellectuals. Tolstoy's other major work is an unfinished historical novel, *Peter the First* (begun in 1929). This monumental work is a rich, though somewhat idealized, portrait of the czar who ruled Russia from 1682 to 1725. Based on extremely thorough historical research, it also presents a broad panorama of Russian life at that time. Tolstoy portrayed Czar Ivan IV in two plays called *Ivan the Terrible* (1942 and 1943).

Alexei Nikolayevich Tolstoy was born on Jan. 10, 1883, in the city of Samara. He was a distant relative of the famous Russian author Leo Tolstoy. He began his literary career as a symbolist poet but soon turned to prose. Anna Lisa Crone

Tolstoy, *TAHL stoy* or *TOHL stoy,* **Leo** (1828-1910), a Russian writer, ranks among the greatest novelists in world literature. Tolstoy was also an important moral and religious thinker and social reformer. His name is sometimes spelled *Tolstoi.*

Early life and works. Leo Nikolaevich Tolstoy was born Sept. 9, 1828, at Yasnaya Polyana, his family's estate near Tula. Both of his parents died when he was young, and he was raised by relatives. He received his elementary education from foreign tutors. He entered the University of Kazan in 1844, but became bored with university instruction and did not earn a degree. He returned to Yasnaya Polyana in 1847 to manage the estate and devote himself to his own study. He wrote three semiautobiographical novels that reflect his formative years—*Childhood* (1852), *Boyhood* (1854), *and Youth* (1857).

As a young man, Tolstoy spent considerable time among the high society of Moscow and St. Petersburg. His diaries reveal that he became restless and dissatisfied with this life, and thus decided to volunteer for the Russian Army.

Tolstoy was a soldier in the Crimean War (1853-1856). He distinguished himself for bravery at the Battle of Sevastopol. He wrote several Sevastopol sketches for magazines in 1855, depicting war as an unglamorous blood bath and attacking romantic ideas of war heroes. Another work based on his travels with the army was the highly praised short novel *The Cossacks* (1863). Olenin, the novel's central character, is a refined aristocrat. He finds much to admire in the wild, free life of the Cossacks of the Caucasus region in southwestern Russia.

Tolstoy retired from military service in 1856. Between 1857 and 1861, he made two trips to western Europe, where he took a keen interest in educational methods. After returning to his estate, he opened a school for peasant children there. Tolstoy was successful as a progressive educator who believed that teaching should be adapted to the needs of each pupil. He published a

AP/Wide World
Leo Tolstoy

journal, called *Yasnaya Polyana,* explaining his educational theories.

His masterpieces. In 1862, Tolstoy married Sonya Behrs. At first they had a happy marriage, but it later became troubled. During this period, Tolstoy wrote *War and Peace* and *Anna Karenina,* his greatest works.

The epic novel *War and Peace* was published in its complete form in 1869. Like many other works of Russian realism, *War and Peace* is a family chronicle. It shows the lives of five families as they go through the universal experiences and stages of life that always concerned Tolstoy—birth, growing up, marriage, sex, childbirth, maturity, old age, and death. *War and Peace* is also a historical novel, describing the political and military events that occurred in Europe between 1805 and 1820. It focuses in particular on Napoleon's invasion of Russia in 1812. In the novel, Tolstoy rejected the "Great Man" theory of history. According to Tolstoy's theory, prominent people or heroes actually have no significant impact on the course of history.

Tolstoy's second masterpiece, *Anna Karenina,* was published in installments from 1875 to 1877. Its plot concerns the open infidelity of a Russian princess, Anna Karenina, to her husband, Karenin. The novel examines Anna's romance with Count Vronsky. Anna and Vronsky show contempt for the disapproving opinions of the members of the high society to which they belong. The difficulties of their relationship eventually lead to Anna's suicide. But *Anna Karenina* is more than a tragic love story. The novel explores broad social, moral, and philosophical issues of Russia and its aristocracy in the 1870's. These issues include the hypocritical attitude of the upper class toward adultery and the role of religious faith in a person's life. Many of these issues are raised through the thoughts and actions of Konstantin Levin, the novel's second most important figure. Through Levin, Tolstoy expresses many of his own views.

His conversion. During the years that Tolstoy was writing *Anna Karenina,* he became obsessed with the questions he had always pondered concerning the meaning and purpose of life. Tolstoy described his agonizing moral self-examination and his quest for life's meaning in the essay "My Confession" (1882).

Tolstoy changed dramatically as a result of his spiritual crisis. Rejecting the authority of the Russian Orthodox Church, he developed his own version of Christianity, which he later detailed in the essay "The Kingdom of God Is Within You" (1894). Tolstoy believed that people are able to know and affirm the good in themselves if they engage in self-examination and willingly reform themselves. Tolstoy also believed that any use of violence or force is harmful, and that force should be opposed nonviolently. He objected to all forms of force, including that represented by organized government and religion, private property, and the bonds of oaths.

Tolstoy produced no fiction between 1878 and 1885, writing instead on his religious beliefs and social themes. In his zeal to live in conformity with his religion, he gave up his property and sex life. He left his estate to his family, and his wife obtained the copyrights to all his works written before 1881. Tolstoy dressed as a peasant and often worked in the fields. He tried to be as self-sufficient as possible. Tolstoy's great fame as a novelist sparked a public interest in his religion that spread quickly. People made pilgrimages from all over the world to visit him. His authority was so great that the Russian Orthodox Church excommunicated him in 1901 in an effort to minimize his influence.

In his essay "What Is Art?" (1898), Tolstoy denounced all of the works he created before his conversion. The essay advances the idea that art should help to morally instruct and improve people. Tolstoy also wrote that art should communicate its ideas to even the simplest people. By these standards, Tolstoy judged most of his earlier works as "aristocratic art" written for vain purposes and not intelligible to the common person.

Later works. Tolstoy returned to writing fiction with the tale "The Death of Ivan Ilyich" (1886). In the story, Ivan Ilyich is the victim of a fatal disease. While he is dying, he sees the emptiness of his life, and he can only accept the inevitability of death. Tolstoy also wrote several plays. His best-known drama, *The Power of Darkness* (1888), is a tragedy about a peasant whose adulterous passion drives him to commit terrible crimes. Tolstoy was interested in the stage for its potential to reach a wide-ranging audience, but his dramas seldom reached the heights of his novels and short stories.

The major novel of Tolstoy's later period is *Resurrection* (1899), the story of the spiritual reformation of a young nobleman. The stories "The Devil" (1889) and "The Kreutzer Sonata" (1891) focus on love, jealousy, and the destructive component of the sex drive. The novel *Hadji Murad,* published after Tolstoy's death, tells the tale of a tribal leader in the Caucasus Mountains. In this story, Tolstoy again shows himself as the masterful psychologist and great literary craftsman of his earlier years.

While important and influential as a moralist, Tolstoy was, first and foremost, a creative writer. Tolstoy's religious and moralistic works are flat when compared to the beauty of his greatest fiction. Anna Lisa Crone

Additional resources

Orwin, Donna T. *Tolstoy's Art and Thought, 1847-1880.* Princeton, 1993.
Rowe, William W. *Leo Tolstoy.* Twayne, 1986.
Wilson, A. N. *Tolstoy.* 1988. Reprint. Norton, 2001.

Toltec Indians, *TOHL tehk,* established an empire in the highlands of central Mexico during the A.D. 900's. They were the dominant people in the region until 1200. The Aztec later honored the Toltec as the founders of urban civilization in the highlands. Aztec legends told about the Toltec and their capital city of Tollán.

In the 900's, the Toltec built a major city whose ruins lie near what is now the town of Tula de Allende, about 45 miles (70 kilometers) north of Mexico City. The site is known as Tula. Some scholars think the ruins are those of the Tollán of the Aztec legends. Toltec buildings included large pyramids topped with temples. Images of Quetzalcóatl (which means Feathered Serpent) appear on several of the pyramids. Quetzalcóatl was a Toltec ruler whom the Toltec came to consider godlike.

The Toltec culture influenced Maya Indians in the Yucatán Peninsula. Some archaeologists even think some Toltec may have migrated to the region. Some of the buildings and artwork at the prehistoric Maya city of Chichén Itzá resemble those at Tula. Images of Quetzalcóatl are displayed on several of the Maya buildings.

During the 1100's, nomads began to cross the northern frontiers of the Toltec empire. As they settled in the Valley of Mexico, Toltec dominance ended. The invading groups included the Aztec, who gradually replaced the Toltec as the most powerful people in the Mexican highlands. William O. Autry

See also **Tula.**

Toluene, *TAHL yu een,* is a colorless liquid related to benzene. Toluene is also called *methylbenzene* (pronounced *MEHTH uhl BEHN zeen*). It belongs to a group of compounds called *aromatic hydrocarbons.* Its chemical formula is $C_6H_5CH_3$. A molecule of toluene has its six carbon atoms arranged in a ring with five hydrogen atoms and a *methyl* (CH_3) group attached.

Manufacturers make toluene by treating petroleum or distilling coal tar. Chemists use toluene as a raw material to produce other chemicals. For example, they sometimes make benzoic acid from it. Benzoic acid is used as a preservative for foods, beverages, and cosmetics. An antiseptic known as chloramine-T is also made from toluene. Makers of explosives use toluene to make trinitrotoluene, commonly called TNT. Paint manufacturers use toluene as a lacquer solvent. Toluene is also used in the manufacture of many dyes and perfumes. Federal regulations require manufacturers to limit the amount of toluene in the air breathed by workers. Excessive exposure to toluene can damage the skin, the eyes, and the central nervous system. James E. Kennedy

See also **Benzene; TNT.**

Tom Thumb. See **Stratton, Charles Sherwood.**

Tom-tom is a musical instrument that belongs to the drum family. Most tom-toms consist of a cylinder with a thin sheet of plastic or calfskin called a *head* stretched across the top, bottom, or both. The tom-tom measures from 6 to 18 inches (15 to 46 centimeters) in diameter and stands from 6 to 20 inches (15 to 51 centimeters) high. It has a dull, hollow sound and may be tuned with a *drum key,* which adjusts the tightness of the heads. Musicians play the tom-tom with felt mallets, drumsticks, or with their hands.

Tom-toms date back to ancient times. The earliest tom-toms consisted of an animal skin stretched across the opening of a hollowed log. Today, tom-toms form part of the drum set used in many jazz and dance bands.

WORLD BOOK photo by Chris Sorensen

The tom-tom is an important rhythm instrument. This drummer is playing three tom-toms. The white drum is called a *floor tom-tom.* The two black drums are known as *concert tom-toms.*

Sets of four one-headed tom-toms are used in concert bands, orchestras, and percussion groups.

John H. Beck

Tomahawk was a small ax that the Indians of North America used as a tool and a weapon. Most tomahawks measured less than 18 inches (45 centimeters) long and were light enough to be used with one hand. Early tomahawks consisted of a *head* (top part) made of stone or bone mounted on a wooden handle. Some tomahawks ended in a ball or knob instead of a flat blade. After Europeans arrived in America, the Indians traded with them for iron tomahawk heads.

The Indians used tomahawks to chop wood, to drive

Some kinds of tomahawks

The Indians of North America used many different types of tomahawks. Some ended in a ball or knob, and some in a flat blade. Early tomahawks had stone or bone heads, and later ones were made of iron. Pipe tomahawks had a pipe bowl on the head and a hollow handle, so that they could be smoked.

National Museum of Natural History, The Smithsonian Institution, Washington, D.C.

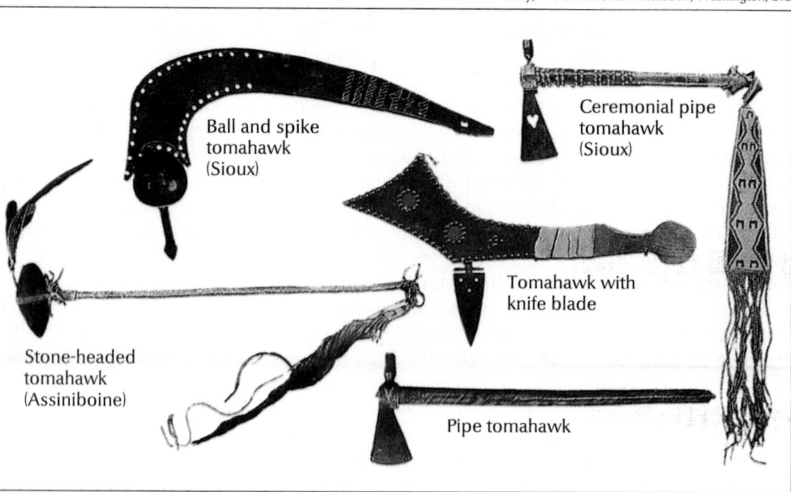

stakes into the ground, and for many other purposes. In battle, warriors used their tomahawks as clubs or threw them at their enemies. Tomahawks also served as hunting weapons.

The Indians used a *pipe tomahawk* in religious ceremonies. This kind of tomahawk had a pipe bowl on the head and a hollow handle, and it could be smoked as a ceremonial pipe. The Indians decorated these tomahawks with feathers or dyed porcupine quills.

Some people think the expression *bury the hatchet* came from an Indian custom of burying a tomahawk to pledge peace. However, many scholars doubt that the Indians ever had such a custom. W. Roger Buffalohead

Tomato, *tuh MAY toh* or *tuh MAH toh,* is a plant grown for its smooth, juicy, usually round fruit. The word *tomato* refers both to the fruit, which people eat, and to the entire plant. The fruit has a slightly acid taste. People cultivate hundreds of varieties of tomatoes.

Botanists classify tomatoes as fruits. Horticulturists, however, classify them as vegetables. Most other people consider tomatoes vegetables because they use fresh tomatoes in much the same way they use lettuce, onions, cauliflower, and many other vegetables. Fresh tomatoes are eaten raw or cooked and are served in salads and other dishes. Manufacturers use much of the commercial tomato crop to make food products. These products include ketchup, canned whole tomatoes, tomato juice, tomato soup, tomato paste, and tomato sauce. Tomatoes provide an important source of vitamins A and C and of certain minerals. They also contain chemicals called *antioxidants,* which scientists believe may help prevent cancer and other diseases.

People grow millions of tons of tomatoes throughout the world each year. Taken together, China and the United States produce almost a third of the world's supply of tomatoes.

Leading tomato-growing countries

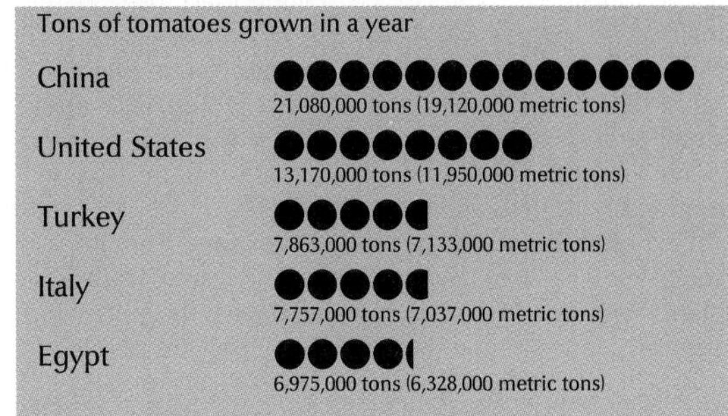

Figures are for a three-year average, 1999-2001.
Source: Food and Agriculture Organization of the United Nations.

The tomato plant has a strong smell and possesses small, hairlike parts on its stems and leaves. It spreads out while growing and produces clusters of small yellow flowers. The flowers develop into ripe tomatoes in 40 to 75 days, depending on the variety. Tomatoes possess green coloring at first, but most turn red as they ripen. Some varieties may turn orange, yellow, pink, or white.

Tomatoes thrive in fertile, warm, well-drained soil. They prefer locations that receive at least six hours of direct sunlight each day. Tomatoes rank as a favorite crop of home gardeners because they will grow in nearly any kind of soil. In addition, a large crop requires relatively little space. Many varieties produce 10 to 15 pounds (4.5 to 7 kilograms) of fruit per plant.

Researchers and growers have bred tomatoes to increase the number of fruits per plant and to improve their quality and other features. For example, leading varieties of tomatoes grown for processing were developed especially for harvesting by machines. Important

WORLD BOOK illustration by Kate Lloyd-Jones, Linden Artists Ltd.

Grant Heilman

Tomatoes are smooth, juicy, usually round fruits that grow in almost any soil. They rank as a favorite crop of home gardeners and commercial growers. In many countries, farmers use machines to harvest most of the tomatoes grown for processing.

fresh tomato types include beefsteak, plum, cherry, and grape tomatoes. Some common home garden varieties include *Ponderosa* and *Better Boy Hybrid.* A variety called *Beefmaster* may produce tomatoes that weigh more than 2 pounds (1 kilogram). *Micro-Tom* is a variety small enough to grow in a flower pot. The variety called *Solar set* produces high-quality tomatoes at unusually high temperatures and humidity levels.

Growing, harvesting, and processing. Tomato seeds require 75 to 85 days to develop into mature plants with ripe fruits. In areas that have a long growing season, seeds are planted outdoors. They are planted indoors in areas where the growing season is too short for outdoor development. Young tomato plants obtained from seeds are transplanted outdoors when the seedlings reach four to six weeks old. Transplanting occurs about two weeks after the last frost of spring, because cold weather can damage the plants.

In gardens and greenhouses, people support most tomato plants with stakes or trellises to keep them from spreading on the ground. Such supports enable growers to place the plants closer together, thus increasing the yield of each unit of land. The supports also help produce a better quality fruit and prevent disease by keeping the fruits off moist ground.

Common tomato diseases include *mosaic virus* and the fungal diseases *early blight, fusarium wilt,* and *verticillium wilt.* Several kinds of insects and worms also attack tomatoes. Plant breeders have developed varieties of the plants that resist some diseases and pests. In addition, many growers use chemicals and biological control methods to fight tomato enemies.

Most tomatoes raised to be eaten fresh are picked by hand. Home gardeners pick tomatoes when they are ripe. Commercial growers pick them before they fully ripen, since unripe tomatoes are less easily damaged during shipping. Workers often use a chemical called *ethylene* to ripen the tomatoes at a packing house. They then ship the ripened produce to warehouses in market areas.

In many industrialized countries, farmers typically use machines to harvest tomatoes grown for processing. Such tomatoes are harvested when ripe. Workers then wash and scald them. Scalding loosens the skins and makes peeling easier. After the tomatoes have been peeled, they undergo different processes, depending on the final product. For example, tomatoes may be cooked or strained. Workers then pack the product into containers, which are heated to destroy harmful bacteria and fungi. Finally, the containers are cooled, labeled, and stored for shipping.

History. Tomatoes originated in South America. The Spanish probably brought them to Europe from Mexico during the mid-1500's. People in Spain and Italy then began to grow tomatoes as food. However, many people considered them poisonous because of their close relationship to several poisonous plants. As a result, tomatoes did not become widely accepted as food until the early 1800's. Tomatoes were sometimes called *love apples,* perhaps because of a superstition that eating them made people fall in love. J. W. Scott

Scientific classification. The tomato belongs to the nightshade family, Solanaceae. Its scientific name is *Lycopersicon esculentum.*

Tomb is any chamber in which the dead are buried. Some tombs are cut out of rocks, and others are built aboveground. Ancient peoples used tombs to keep the bodies of the dead safe. The Egyptians believed the departed person's spirit visited the burial place. They built the Pyramids, the world's greatest tombs, for their kings (see **Pyramids; Valley of the Kings**). Many ancient tombs contained personal possessions. Scholars have learned much about earlier cultures from ancient tombs.

The Jews cut tombs out of rock. Christ was said to have been placed in a new rock tomb belonging to Joseph of Arimathea. Most Greek tombs were simple, but those in the colonies of Asia Minor were elaborate. The most famous of these was the tomb of Mausolus at Halicarnassus in Caria. The word *mausoleum* comes from the name of this tomb. The Romans built stately tombs which lined the roads leading to the city, because burial within the city was not allowed. Ruins of Roman tombs still line the Appian Way. The early Christians built tombs in underground rooms called *catacombs* (see **Catacombs**). Islamic tombs are often large buildings, sometimes with a dome. One of the most famous Islamic tombs is the Taj Mahal in Agra, India (see **Taj Mahal**).

The Tomb of the Unknowns at Arlington National Cemetery in Virginia, Grant's tomb in New York City, and that of George and Martha Washington at Mount Vernon are perhaps the best known in the United States (see picture with **Grant, Ulysses S.**) Richard A. Kalish

See also **Crypt; Funeral customs; Megalithic monuments; Sarcophagus; Sculpture** (Later medieval sculpture).

Tombigbee River, *tahm BIHG bee,* rises in northeastern Mississippi and flows southeastward into western Alabama. In southwestern Alabama, the Tombigbee and Alabama rivers meet and form the Mobile River. The Mobile River flows into Mobile Bay at the deepwater port of Mobile. The bay is an inlet of the Gulf of Mexico (see **Alabama** [physical map]). The Tombigbee is about 400 miles (640 kilometers) long and the Mobile is about 45 miles (72 kilometers) long (see **Mobile River**).

The Black Warrior River is the Tombigbee's chief tributary. It provides a water route from the Tombigbee to the Birmingham area in north-central Alabama.

The Tennessee-Tombigbee Waterway connects the Tombigbee and Tennessee rivers. Construction of the waterway involved building a canal from the east fork of the source of the Tombigbee north to the Tennessee River. It also involved deepening and widening the Tombigbee from its source southward to Demopolis, Alabama, and constructing 10 locks and dams along the rivers. The 234-mile (377-kilometer) Tennessee-Tombigbee Waterway was completed in 1985. Often called the Tenn-Tom Waterway, it ranks among the world's largest navigational projects. Howard A. Clonts, Jr.

Tombouctou. See **Timbuktu.**

Tombstone (pop. 1,504) is a town in southeastern Arizona that was the center of a rich silver-mining district in the late 1800's (see **Arizona** [political map]). Tombstone was named by its founder, prospector Ed Schieffelin. His friends feared he would be killed by Indians, and warned him he would find a tombstone, not a mine. Today, Tombstone attracts many tourists to its museums, historic sites, and mine tours.

Tombstone was founded in 1879. By 1882, its population had grown to an estimated 5,500 because of the silver-mining boom nearby. Lawlessness was widespread in Tombstone, and the famous gunfight at the O.K. Corral took place there in 1881. In 1883, underground water flooded the mine shafts. Mining activities slowed, and practically ended by 1893. The population decreased steadily. But residents promoted tourism and kept Tombstone alive. B. R. Burg

Tomlin, Bradley Walker (1899-1953), was an American Abstract Expressionist painter. His best-known works contain strong lines arranged in a rhythmical order that suggest hieroglyphics. They maintain a balance between carefully structured, overlapping forms and such random elements as curving symbols, letters, and numerals. Tomlin's sense of order and his preference for harmonious colors set him slightly apart from most other Abstract Expressionists. His works are more lyrical and restrained than those of other artists in the movement.

Self-Portrait (1932); collection of the Whitney Museum of American Art, New York City, Gift of Henry Ittleson, Jr.

Bradley Walker Tomlin

Tomlin was born in Syracuse, New York, on Aug. 19, 1899. In 1921, he moved to New York City where he earned a living for a time designing magazine covers. From 1925 to the late 1930's, he painted in a moderate realistic style. From 1939 to about 1944, he concentrated on cubistic blends of still-life elements and abstract forms. This style led to the simplification and abstraction of his later works. He died on May 11, 1953. In 1957, the Whitney Museum of American Art presented a definitive exhibition of his works. Dore Ashton

Tompkins, Daniel D. (1774-1825), was vice president of the United States from 1817 to 1825 under President James Monroe. He was governor of New York from 1807 to 1817. He favored the War of 1812 and defended New York from the British as commander of the state militia.

During the war, poor accounting methods made it difficult for Tompkins to keep track of the funds entrusted to him. For most of the rest of his life, Tompkins fought rumors that he had dishonestly used some of the funds. These false charges affected Tompkins. He became discouraged during his vice presidency, left Washington for long periods, and wasted his energies defending his character against his critics.

Tompkins was born on June 21, 1774, in Fox Meadows (now Scarsdale), New York. He was associate justice of the Supreme Court of New York from 1804 to 1807. He died on June 11, 1825. James C. Curtis

See also **Vice president of the U.S.** (picture).

Ton is the name of three different units used to measure weight and capacity. The units are the *long ton, short ton,* and *metric ton.* The long ton equals 2,240 pounds (1,016.047 kilograms), the short ton equals 2,000 pounds (907.185 kilograms), and the metric ton equals 1,000 kilograms, or 2,204.623 pounds. Most countries use the metric ton. The United States uses the short ton most often. However, the long ton and the metric ton are also used. For instance, coal is weighed and sold at the mines by the long ton, and sold to customers by the short ton. U.S. custom houses use the metric ton in weighing. See also **Metric system; Weights and measures** (table: Weight and mass). Richard S. Davis

Tone, in music, is the sound made by the vibration of a musical instrument or of the human voice. Tones differ in quality, pitch, intensity, and duration. Musicians use the word *tone* to describe the sound of each key on the piano, symbolized by a *note.* They also use it to describe the intervals on a keyboard. An interval between a white key and the nearest white or black key, is a *half,* or *minor, tone.* Two half tones (as from C to D on the keyboard) create the interval of a *whole,* or *major, tone.* Musicians also use the word *tone* to describe sound quality. Thomas W. Tunks

See also **Harmonics; Music** (Tone); **Piano** (The strings); **Sound** (Sound quality).

Tonga, *TAHNG guh,* is a country made up of about 150 islands in the South Pacific Ocean. The islands lie about 1,950 miles (3,140 kilometers) east of Australia. The British explorer Captain James Cook, who first visited the islands in 1773, called them the *Friendly Islands.* In 1789, Captain William Bligh and 18 crewmen of the British ship *Bounty* floated through the islands after being cast adrift by mutineers. Tonga is the only remaining kingdom in Polynesia, one of the three main regions in the

Number 9: In Praise of Gertrude Stein (1950), an oil painting on canvas; Museum of Modern Art, New York City, gift of Mrs. John D. Rockefeller III

A Tomlin painting shows repeated rhythmic lines and muted colors that are typical of his later style. Tomlin became a leading member of the movement in American painting called Abstract Expressionism.

Tonga

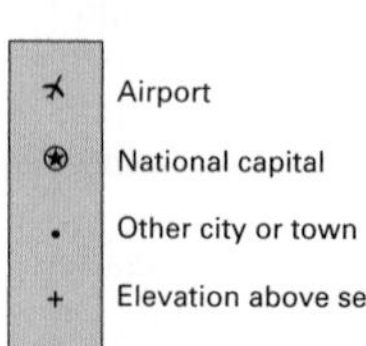

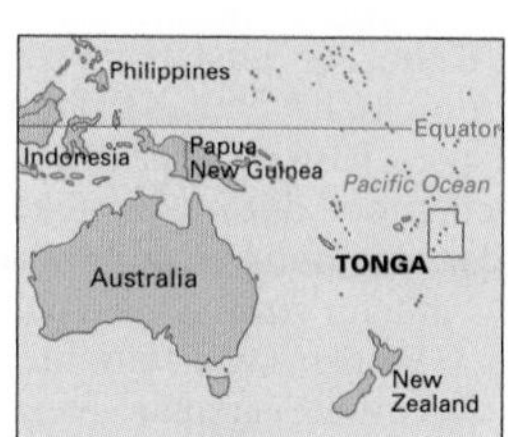

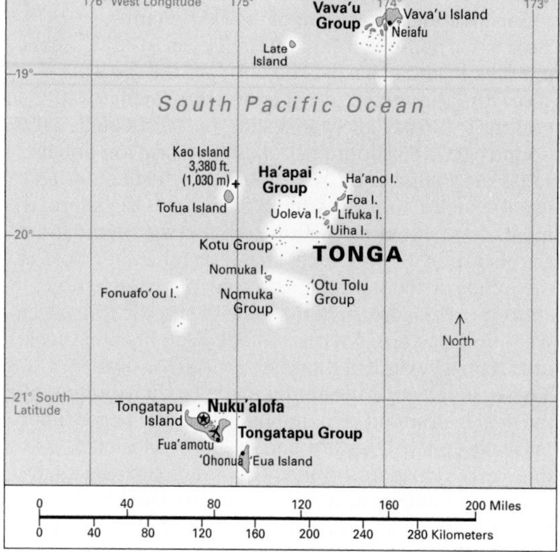

WORLD BOOK maps

Pacific Islands. It became independent in 1970 after being a protectorate of the United Kingdom since 1900. It is a member of the Commonwealth of Nations.

Most Tongans are farmers. About two-thirds of the people live on Tongatapu, the largest island. Nuku'alofa, Tonga's capital, chief port, and commercial center, lies on Tongatapu. Nuku'alofa has about 29,000 people.

Government. Tonga is a constitutional monarchy. The king, a hereditary ruler, appoints a prime minister and a Cabinet to assist him. The Cabinet consists of the prime minister and six other members. The Legislative Assembly is composed of the Cabinet, nine nobles elected by the hereditary nobility, and nine commoners elected by the people. Elections take place every three years. Tongans who are at least 21 years old and can read and write may vote.

The Legislative Assembly meets for two or three months a year. When the assembly is not in session, a privy council has the power to make laws. The privy council, headed by the king, consists of the prime minister, the Cabinet, and the governors of two major island groups—Ha'apai and Vava'u. The assembly may change laws passed by the privy council. The king appoints the governors of Ha'apai and Vava'u.

People. Almost all Tongans are Polynesians and Christians. Tonga's Constitution prohibits work or recreation on Sunday. Most Tongans live in small villages and raise crops. The people also fish for such seafood as shark and tuna. Most of the islands have no running water, and many have no electricity.

The law requires all Tongan children from 6 to 14 years old to go to school. Tonga has about 125 elementary schools and 45 high schools. The government operates about 60 percent of the schools, and the churches direct about 40 percent. The country's official languages are English and Tongan. Schoolchildren enjoy many sports, especially rugby football. A branch of the University of the South Pacific is in Nuku'alofa.

Land. Tonga is made up of three main groups of islands—Ha'apai, Tongatapu, and Vava'u. Most of the islands in these groups are ring-shaped coral reefs called *atolls.* Most of Tonga's people live on these islands. A chain of higher, volcanic islands is located west of the coral islands. Some of the volcanoes are active. Fertile clay soils cover most of Tonga. Strips of sandy soil lie along the coasts. Forests cover about 14 percent of the land.

Tonga has a warm, wet climate with high humidity. Temperatures in Tonga average 78 °F (26 °C). The average annual rainfall varies from 70 inches (180 centimeters) on Tongatapu to 100 inches (250 centimeters) on some northern islands. Most rain falls from December through March. Cyclones sometimes hit Tonga during the rainy season.

Economy. Fertile soils and a warm climate have made agriculture the basis of the Tongan economy. About three-fourths of the workers are farmers. The government owns all the land. Every male who is 16 years old or over is entitled to a plot of land, which he rents from the government. The government has helped establish small-scale manufacturing, especially in Nuku'alofa. Tourism is also becoming important to the economy.

Tonga's crops include bananas, breadfruit, pumpkins, sweet potatoes, tapioca, and yams. The chief exports are fruits, vegetables, and *copra* (dried coconut). Most exports go to New Zealand. However, Japan is the chief buyer of Tonga's pumpkin exports. Australia and New Zealand supply most of the imports, including flour, meat, petroleum, sugar, textiles, and tobacco.

Tonga has over 200 miles (320 kilometers) of roads, mostly on Tongatapu. Shipping services operate among the many islands. Government-owned shipping services connect Tonga with Australia, New Zealand, Hawaii, and other places in the Pacific. Neiafu and Nuku'alofa are Tonga's chief ports. The most important airport operates

Facts in brief

Capital: Nuku'alofa.
Official languages: English and Tongan.
Official name: Kingdom of Tonga.
Area: 289 mi² (748 km²).
Elevation: *Highest*—Kao, an extinct volcano in the Ha'apai Group, 3,380 ft (1,030 m) above sea level. *Lowest*—sea level, along the coasts.
Population: *Estimated 2006 population*—107,000; density, 372 per mi² (143 per km²); distribution, 68 percent rural, 32 percent urban. *1986 census*—94,649.
Chief products: bananas, copra, sweet potatoes, tapioca.
National anthem: "E 'Otua Mafimafi" ("O God Almighty").
Flag: The flag has a red field and a white canton. A red cross in the canton symbolizes the Christian faith of the Tongans. Adopted in 1866. See **Flag** (picture: Flags of Asia and the Pacific).
Money: *Basic unit*—pa'anga. The pa'anga approximately equals the Australian dollar. One hundred seniti equal one pa'anga.

Tongan farmers shell coconuts to obtain copra, one of the nation's chief exports. Copra, the dried meat of the coconut, is used in making soap, margarine, and other products.

C. D'Hotel, Explorer

at Fua'amotu on Tongatapu. Tonga has no railroads. The government publishes a weekly newspaper in both Tongan and English. The government operates the country's one radio station.

History. The first people to settle in Tonga were Polynesians who probably came from the Samoa Islands. Although much of Tonga's early history is based on myths, records of Tongan rulers go back to the A.D. 900's. The early rulers held the hereditary title of *Tu'i Tonga.* The people believed the Tu'i Tonga were sacred representatives of the Tongan gods. About 1470, the ruling Tu'i Tonga gave some governing powers to a nonsacred leader. Through the years, the Tu'i Tonga became only a figurehead. By 1865, after the death of the last Tu'i Tonga, the nonsacred king held all the ruling power.

Two Dutch navigators, Willem Schouten and Jacob Le Maire, became the first Europeans to visit Tonga. They landed on some of the northern islands in 1616. In 1643, Abel Tasman, a Dutch sea captain, visited Tongatapu and other southern islands.

Methodist missionaries from the United Kingdom settled in Tonga during the early 1800's and converted most of the people to Christianity. But civil war spread throughout Tonga. One of the most powerful chiefs, Taufa'ahau, united the islands in 1845. He was crowned King George Tupou I, the first monarch of Tonga. Tupou I developed legal codes that became the basis of the Tongan Constitution, which was adopted in 1875.

After Tupou I died in 1893, his great-grandson, George Tupou II, took the throne. Tonga became a protectorate of the United Kingdom in 1900. Tupou II died in 1918 and was succeeded by his daughter Salote. Queen Salote ruled until her death in 1965. She worked to improve education and health in Tonga. Her son became King Taufa'ahau Toupou IV in 1967.

In 1970, Tonga gained independence from the United Kingdom. Since independence, Tonga—with British aid—has worked to modernize its agriculture and build wharves and airstrips. It has also encouraged foreign investment. Through these efforts, the government hopes to vary the economy and provide more jobs for Tonga's growing population.

Michael R. Ogden

Tongue is the chief organ of taste. It also helps in chewing and swallowing, and plays an important part in forming the sounds of words.

The tongue is made up of many groups of muscles that a person can consciously control. This type of muscle is called *skeletal* muscle. The tongue muscles run in many different directions. They arise from the hyoid bone, and the inner surfaces of the lower jaw and temporal bones. As a result, a person can move the front part of the tongue many different ways. The tongue can move food about, push it between the teeth, and roll it into small masses. It helps clean the mouth by removing

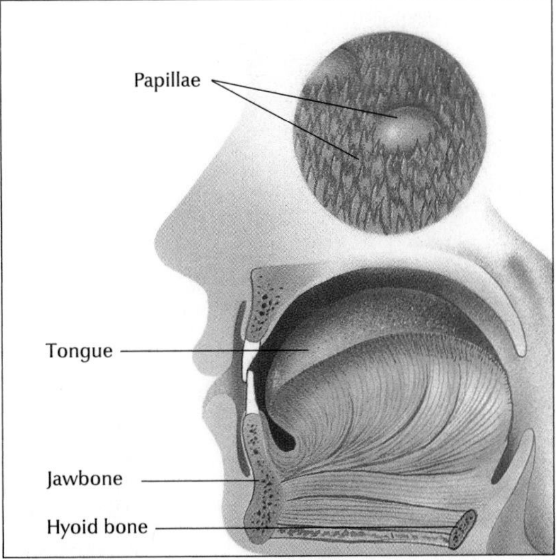

WORLD BOOK illustration by Charles Wellek

The tongue consists of bundles of muscles that run in several directions. It is covered by a mucous membrane, and its upper surface has round and cone-shaped projections called *papillae.*

food from between the cheeks and teeth. In swallowing, the tongue pushes the food back into the *pharynx* (throat). In doing this, the tongue presses against the *palate* (roof of the mouth) and also spreads against the sides of the mouth. This action prevents the food from moving in any direction except back into the pharynx.

The tongue is covered with a mucous membrane. The undersurface of the tongue is smooth. But many *papillae* (small projections) give the tongue a rough surface on the top.

Four types of taste buds, found in the papillae, enable us to distinguish between sweet, sour, salty, and bitter tastes (see **Taste**). The tip of the tongue is more sensitive to touch than any other part of the body (see **Touch**).

The tongue is a highly useful organ to many animals. Frogs and some birds use their tongues to catch insects. Hummingbirds use their long tongues to lap up plant nectar. Dogs, cats, and other animals use their tongues for many purposes, such as to lap up water or milk, to clean their fur, or to express affection. Raymond L. Burich

See also **Chameleon; Snake** (picture); **Toad.**

Tonsil is any of several masses of specialized tissue found in the throat. The term commonly refers to a pair of deep pink, almond-shaped structures, one of which is on each side of the back of the throat. These are the *palatine,* or *faucial,* tonsils. There are two other kinds of tonsils—the *pharyngeal* tonsils and the *lingual* tonsils. Pharyngeal tonsils, commonly called *adenoids,* grow in the back of the throat near the nasal passage. Lingual tonsils are found at the back of the tongue. Together, the three types of tonsils form a continuous ring around the back of the throat.

No one really knows the purpose of tonsils, but many medical scientists believe they aid in protecting the respiratory and digestive systems from infection. Tonsils consist of a type of tissue called *lymphoid tissue.* This tissue produces white blood cells, known as *lymphocytes,* that help fight infection. For example, lymphocytes release antibodies that destroy invading bacteria and viruses or make them harmless (see **Lymphatic system** [Lymphoid tissue]). In addition, the surface of the palatine tonsils has many deep pits, called *crypts.* Bacteria and food particles collect in these crypts. Each lingual tonsil has a crypt, but the pharyngeal tonsils have none.

Sometimes the palatine or pharyngeal tonsils become badly inflamed and must be removed by a surgical operation. As children grow older, their tonsils tend to decrease in size. Barry L. Wenig

See also **Tonsillitis; Adenoids.**

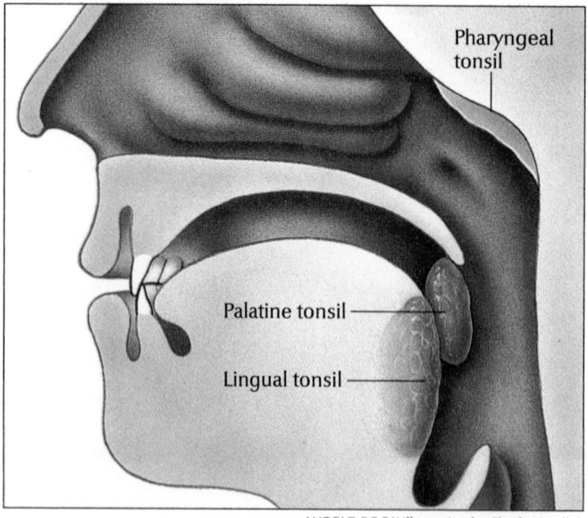

WORLD BOOK illustration by Charles Wellek

Tonsils form a continuous ring around the back of the throat. Medical scientists believe that tonsils help protect the respiratory and digestive systems from infection.

Tonsillitis is a painful disease resulting from inflamed tonsils. It is caused by bacteria or viruses that infect one or both of the palatine tonsils. Most attacks of tonsillitis occur in people between 10 and 40 years old. An attack begins with swelling and pain in the throat and difficulty swallowing. Fever, headache, backache, stiff neck, and nausea occur in severe cases. Sometimes an *abscess* (collection of pus) forms next to the tonsil in the throat.

Physicians generally recommend bed rest, aspirin, and saltwater gargles to relieve the symptoms of tonsillitis. If the infection is bacterial, doctors can cure it with antibiotics. Antibiotics are not effective against viral tonsillitis. Some people suffer from long-lasting or repeated attacks of tonsillitis. Doctors may recommend that the tonsils be removed in such cases. The operation to remove the tonsils is called a *tonsillectomy.*

Barry L. Wenig

Tontons Macoutes. See **Haiti** (History).

Tonty, *TAHN tih,* **Henri de,** *ahn REE duh* (1650-1704), was a French fur trader, explorer, and assistant to the French explorer Sieur de La Salle. Tonty's name is sometimes spelled *Tonti.*

Born in France of Italian parents, Tonty came to Canada in 1678 with La Salle. Tonty supervised the construction of Fort Conti, near Niagara Falls, and of a ship called the *Griffon.* In 1680, Tonty was appointed commandant of Fort Crèvecoeur, near what is now Peoria, Illinois. In 1682, he and La Salle explored the Mississippi River to its mouth in the Gulf of Mexico.

In 1686, Tonty again traveled south, this time to join La Salle, who had planned to found a colony at the mouth of the Mississippi. But Tonty could not locate him. Three years later, he learned La Salle had been murdered. He tried to rescue the survivors of La Salle's expedition but had to turn back in what is now Texas.

Tonty traveled down the Mississippi for the last time in 1699. He spent the remainder of his life working to support the establishment of the French colony of Louisiana. D. Peter MacLeod

See also **La Salle, Sieur de.**

Tool is any instrument that a worker uses to do work. Tools that do their tasks on a machine are called *machine tools* (see **Machine tool**). Small *power-driven* tools are similar to both hand tools and machine tools. The two main kinds of tools are *woodworking tools* and *metalworking tools.*

Woodworking tools. The tools of the carpenter and cabinetmaker include such measuring tools as the *rule* for measuring lengths; the *square* and *protractor* for measuring angles; *compasses* for marking circles and arcs; and *carpenter's levels* and *plumb lines* for ensuring that carpentry work will be straight and true. *Vises* and *clamps* hold material in place while it is being shaped. Shaping tools include *saws, chisels, planes, files,* and *boring bits.* Woodworkers also use *hammers, hatchets, screwdrivers,* and *pliers.* See **Woodworking.**

Metalworking tools. The work of the machinist and toolmaker ordinarily requires much greater precision than that of the woodworker. Thus, measuring tools for metalworking must be very accurate. Many *micrometers* and *calipers* can measure distances as small as $\frac{1}{10,000}$ inch (0.0025 millimeter). The *hacksaw* used for cutting metal is thinner and harder than the woodworking saw. Machinists use *taps* and *dies* to cut threads in machine parts. They also use *wrenches* for repair work and in assembling machinery. Most machining operations on metal parts are done by machine tools, such as lathes, milling machines, shapers, and grinders.

History of tools. Prehistoric people learned that rocks and sticks of certain shapes could help them do things they could not do with their bare hands. They later improved the natural stones they used. They shaped them into knives, hatchets, and hammers, and attached wooden handles to them. Stone Age people developed a drill for drilling soft stone and wood. Bronze Age people developed new tools, such as tongs for holding hot objects. Agricultural civilizations later developed new tools, such as the hoe and the simple plow.

After people learned to work iron and steel, they developed stronger, sharper, and more durable tools. The development of steam engines, gasoline engines, and electric motors made it possible to replace hand tools with machine tools. Today, much work once done by hand is done by small power tools. M. O. M. Osman

Related articles in *World Book* include:

Ax	Indian, American	Pneumatic tool
Die and diemaking	Knife	Prehistoric people (The improvement of tools)
Drill	Level	Saw
Farm and farming	Machine tool	Steam hammer
Forging	Pioneer life in America (Tools)	
Hammer		

Toolmaking chiefly involves the making of precision devices and parts for power-driven machines used to shape metal. Such machines are called *machine tools.* Toolmakers also produce special tools and measuring instruments. Toolmaking is one of the most important and highly skilled crafts in the manufacturing industry.

The main products of toolmaking include *fixtures, jigs,* and *dies* for machine tools. Fixtures hold a *workpiece* (the metal being worked) in place while a manufacturing process, such as boring, cutting, or drilling, is performed on it. Jigs both hold a workpiece in place and guide a machine's cutting tool. Dies are used to mold, punch, bend, and cut out a workpiece. They range in size from huge blocks of steel for shaping automobile bodies to tiny precision devices for making watch gears. See **Die and diemaking**.

Toolmakers must use machine tools in their own work. For example, they use *lathes* to cut metal into round or cylindrical shapes, *milling machines* to cut flat surfaces, and *boring machines* to bore holes in metal. These machine tools are often computer-controlled. Before shaping a new tool, toolmakers may test various tool designs using computer simulations.

Toolmakers are sometimes called *tool-and-die makers.* They typically complete a special training program that lasts at least four years. Glenn S. Daehn

See also **Cast and casting; Machine tool; Tool.**

Toombs, Robert Augustus (1810-1885), was a leading Georgia politician during the American Civil War era. From February to July 1861, he served as secretary of state of the Confederacy. He then became a general in the Confederate Army.

Toombs was born in Wilkes County, Georgia. He was a member of the United States House of Representatives from 1845 to 1853, when he began serving in the U.S. Senate. In February 1861, as Southern States began to *secede* (withdraw) from the Union, he resigned from the Senate. After the war, he refused to swear allegiance to the U.S. government. As a result, Toombs never regained U.S. citizenship and was barred from elective office. Nevertheless, he continued to play an important role in Georgia politics. In 1877, he was a major force at the state's constitutional convention. Michael Perman

Toomer, Jean (1894-1967), was an African American writer. He is best known for *Cane* (1923), a book of poems, short stories, sketches, and a play about black people in the North and the South. African American life in *Cane* is marked by frustration and tragedy but also by a hunger for spiritual integrity and a responsiveness to beauty. The work is noted for its poetic and evocative images of Southern life. *Cane* established Toomer as a leading American writer of the 1920's. The book also inspired authors of the Harlem Renaissance, an important period in black literary history.

Most of Toomer's writings after *Cane* examine philosophical and psychological problems he saw in Americans. He wrote *Essentials* (1931), a collection of short statements called aphorisms on these problems. He also wrote book reviews, essays, poems, stories, and a novelette. Some were collected in *The Wayward and the Seeking,* published in 1980, after his death.

Toomer was born in Washington, D.C. His full name was Nathan Eugene Toomer. William L. Andrews

Tooth. See Teeth.

Toothpaste and toothpowder are substances used with a toothbrush to clean teeth. Both contain a mildly abrasive substance, such as finely powdered chalk (calcium carbonate), and a *detergent* (soaplike material). Some sweetening agent other than sugar, and flavoring oils, are included to make the agent taste good. Glycerol or a similar material is added to these basic ingredients to make toothpaste. Many toothpastes contain *fluoride,* a chemical that helps prevent decay.

Critically reviewed by the American Dental Hygienists' Association

Top is the name for a child's toy. Most tops have cylindrical or pear shapes. They are usually made of wood, metal, or plastic, and often spin on a metal tip.

Kinds of tops. The best-known top receives its motion from a string that has been wrapped around it and suddenly pulled. Pulling the string makes the top spin around and stay erect without being held up. Scientists use this spinning force in a type of gyroscopic top that helps stabilize boats and airplanes (see **Gyroscope**). Other tops spin when a center stem, called a *spindle,* is twirled between the thumb and forefinger. *Mechanical* tops receive power to spin from an inside spring that can be compressed by winding with a key, pinching, or pumping. In *musical* tops, holes, reeds, or whistles inside the top produce sounds when the top spins.

History of tops. No one knows exactly when people first began to use tops. But children in ancient Greece played with them, and tops have been a popular amusement in China and Japan for hundreds of years. In the

© Peter Gonzalez

Tops are popular toys. The small finger tops, *center,* are from India. A Mexican top, *left,* has colorful stripes. An Austrian craftworker made the yellow top, set in motion by pulling its string.

1800's, people in Asia often became professional top spinners. They made tops do many tricks, such as jumping steps and walking up an inclined board. Today, adults in Malaysia compete in top-spinning contests.

Tops became popular in Europe during the 1700's. In a game called *diablo,* the player whipped a top into the air. Sometimes the player tried to see how high the top could be sent. Other times, the top was caught in the hand from various positions. Many types of self-winding tops were used in the 1800's. The *bandilor* top unwinds itself while going up an incline and rewinds as it comes down. The top can be manipulated to wind and unwind itself many times. Tops were among the first toys patented in the United States. The *torpedo* top contained a ball that shot into the air when a paper cap exploded.

R. Wayne Schmittberger

Topaz, *TOH paz,* is a white or light-colored mineral sometimes cut into gems. It is a compound of aluminum, fluorine, silicon, oxygen, and hydrogen. Its chemical formula is $Al_2(SiO_4)(OH,F)_2$. Trace impurities give topaz crystals a wide variety of colors. Topaz is hard. It defines an 8 on the Mohs hardness scale, a ranking of mineral hardness commonly used by geologists. Small amounts of topaz occur in some *igneous rocks,* rocks that form when molten rock cools and solidifies, and *metamorphic rocks,* rocks that have been changed by heat and pressure.

Jewelers cut transparent topaz crystals into gems. The most desirable topaz gems range in color from completely colorless to gold, orange, blue, and pink. Exposing some topaz crystals to heat or radiation can dramatically enhance or even change their color. Jewelers sell blue topaz as a substitute for the gem aquamarine. Citrine, a yellow or brownish variety of quartz, is sometimes sold as a substitute for topaz.

Topaz is found in many parts of the world. Brazil produces most of the world's gem-quality topaz. Many museum collections have large, beautiful topaz crystals that weigh hundreds of pounds or kilograms. Mark Cloos

See also **Gem** (picture).

Topeka, *tuh PEE kuh* (pop. 122,377; met. area pop. 169,871), is the capital and one of the largest cities of Kansas. Topeka is in northeastern Kansas on the Kansas River (see **Kansas** [political map]). The city is an important trade center.

Topeka lies in a region of gently rolling hills. The city has many wide streets lined with tall shade trees. The Capitol towers above Topeka's downtown area. The building, much of which dates from the late 1800's, is topped by a pale-green copper dome.

A large number of Topeka residents work for federal, state, or local government agencies. In addition, hospitals and other medical institutions rank among the city's chief employers. Topeka factories produce electrical wire and cable, greeting cards, cellophane, pet foods, potato chips, steel products, and tires. Other Topeka industries include grain storage, printing and publishing, and the repair of railroad cars. Topeka is the home of Washburn University and the Topeka Zoo. Reinisch Rose Garden, one of the largest in the Midwest, is a landmark.

The Topeka area was once occupied by the Kansa (Kaw) Indians. In 1842, Louis Papan, one of the area's first European settlers, began operating a ferry on the Kansas River. Papan's ferry transported people who were traveling westward to such places as California and Oregon. Topeka was founded in 1854 by a small group of pioneers at the site of Papan's ferry. The pioneers were led

Topeka Chamber

The State Capitol in Topeka stands in a 10-acre (4-hectare) park. Topeka has been the capital of Kansas since 1861.

by Cyrus Holliday, a businessman from Pennsylvania. Holliday later helped found the Atchison, Topeka, and Santa Fe Railroad. In 1878, he helped establish the railroad's headquarters in Topeka. Today, the railroad is part of one of the largest rail networks in the United States, the Burlington Northern and Santa Fe Railway, headquartered in Fort Worth, Texas. Topeka was incorporated in 1857, and it became the state capital in 1861.

Topeka's Sumner Elementary School became the center of national attention in the mid-1900's. It was involved in the 1954 decision of the Supreme Court of the United States that declared racial segregation in public schools unconstitutional (see **Brown v. Board of Education of Topeka**). The city is the seat of Shawnee County and has a mayor-council government. For the monthly weather, see **Kansas** (Climate). Stannie Anderson

See also **Curry, John Steuart; Kansas** (pictures).

Topology, *tuh PAHL uh jee,* is a branch of mathematics that explores certain properties of geometrical figures. The properties are those that do not change when the figures are deformed by bending, stretching, or molding. Topology makes no distinction between a sphere and a cube because these figures can be molded into one another. Topology makes a distinction between a sphere and a *torus* (a doughnut-shaped figure) because a sphere cannot be deformed into a torus without being torn. Topology is called *rubber-sheet geometry* because its figures can be deformed.

Unlike high school geometry, topology ignores straightness, parallelism, and distance because deformation can alter them. Instead, topology studies such problems as the number of intersections made by a curve with itself, whether a surface is closed or has boundaries, and whether or not a surface is connected.

Topology makes up theorems and tries to prove them. The *four-color theorem* applies to maps. It states that four colors are sufficient to color any map so that, in any group of adjacent countries, each country is a different color. The American mathematician Kenneth Appel and the German-born mathematician Wolfgang Haken proved the theorem in 1976. Alan Shuchat

Topsoil is the surface layer of soil. It is usually 4 to 10 inches (10 to 25 centimeters) deep. The structure and consistency of topsoil encourage the growth of plants' root systems. Topsoil is rich in a substance known as *humus,* an important food source for such plants as small grains and grasses (see **Humus**). Topsoil also contains bacteria that are necessary for plant growth. Because fertile topsoil is required for agriculture, landscaping, and gardening, it ranks as one of our most important natural resources. Hundreds of years may be needed for topsoil to develop. For this reason, the preservation of topsoil is one of the chief goals of soil conservation.

Raymond K. Moore

See also **Conservation** (Soil conservation); **Lawn** (Preparing the soil).

Torah, *TAWR uh,* is the Hebrew name for the *Pentateuch* (first five books of the Bible). See **Pentateuch.**

Torch is the term used in the United Kingdom and Commonwealth countries for a flashlight. See **Flashlight.**

Torino. See **Turin.**

Tornado is the most violent of all storms. A tornado, sometimes called a *twister,* consists of a rapidly rotating column of air that forms under a thundercloud or a developing thundercloud. Tornado winds swirl at speeds that may exceed 300 miles (480 kilometers) per hour. A powerful tornado can lift cattle, automobiles, and even mobile homes into the air and destroy almost everything in its path. Fortunately, most tornadoes are relatively weak, and only a few are devastating.

© Howard B. Bluestein

A tornado roars across the Oklahoma plain. A deadly funnel has descended from a dark, heavy *wall cloud* and touched the ground, its violent, rotating winds hurling debris in all directions.

Scientists use the word *cyclone* to refer to all spiral-shaped windstorms that circulate in a counterclockwise direction in the Northern Hemisphere or in a clockwise direction in the Southern Hemisphere. The term *cyclone* comes from the Greek word for *circle.* Cyclones come in many sizes. Among the largest such storms are hurricanes and typhoons, which may reach 250 miles (400 kilometers) across.

Most tornadoes are small, intense cyclones. On rare occasions, the winds whirl in the direction opposite that of a cyclone—for example, clockwise in the Northern Hemisphere.

Most tornadoes have damage paths less than 1,600 feet (500 meters) wide, move at less than 35 miles (55 kilometers) per hour, and last only a few minutes. Extremely destructive twisters may reach 1 mile (1.6 kilometers) in diameter, travel at 60 miles (100 kilometers) per hour, and blow for more than an hour.

The United States has the highest incidence of tornadoes in the world. Most of these storms occur in a belt known as Tornado Alley that stretches across the Midwestern and Southern states, especially Texas, Oklahoma, Kansas, Nebraska, and Iowa. However, tornadoes also strike many other parts of the world. Australia ranks second to the United States in number of twisters, and many damaging tornadoes strike Bangladesh. Tornadoes occur most often during the spring and early summer in the late afternoon and early evening.

A tornado over a body of water is called a *waterspout.* Waterspouts occur frequently in summer over the Florida Keys. Waterspouts also form elsewhere in the Gulf, along the Atlantic and Pacific coasts, over the Great Lakes, and even over the Great Salt Lake in Utah.

The story of a tornado. The majority of tornadoes develop from severe thunderstorms. A hurricane, when it makes landfall, can also generate tornadoes.

The most damaging tornadoes form in large, powerful thunderstorms called *supercells*. For a supercell to form, and perhaps spawn a tornado, several conditions must exist. There must be an adequate supply of moisture to feed the storm. In Tornado Alley, air from the Gulf of Mexico provides the moisture. There must be a layer of warm, moist air near the ground and a layer of much cooler air above. Often, a *front* (the boundary between two air masses at different temperatures) powers an upward flow of warm air. As the warm air rises, it begins to cool, and the moisture it holds condenses into raindrops. The air stops rising at high levels and spreads sideways to form a characteristic anvil-shaped storm cloud.

For a supercell to develop, the winds at higher elevations must differ markedly from those at lower levels in speed, direction, or both. Such a large difference in wind speed or direction is called *wind shear*. Wind shear makes the column of rising air begin to rotate, forming a broad, horizontal tube of swirling air. As the storm continues, this tube turns on its end, producing a rotating column of air called a *mesocyclone*. Studies show that most supercells containing mesocyclones eventually produce tornadoes.

A low, dark, heavy cloud called a *wall cloud* forms underneath the mesocyclone. Tornado funnels develop out of the wall cloud.

The first sign of an approaching tornado may be light rain, followed by heavier rain, then rain mixed with hail. The hailstones may grow to the size of golf balls or even baseballs. After the hail ends, a tornado may strike. In most tornadoes, a funnel-shaped cloud forms and descends from the wall cloud until it touches the ground. However, there might be a tornado even if the funnel does not touch the ground or if the air is too dry for a funnel cloud to form. Sometimes, the first sign of a tornado is dust swirling just above the ground.

A few small tornadoes begin near the ground and build upward with no apparent connection to the storm aloft. Many of these storms occur without mesocyclones and lack a funnel cloud.

Damage by tornadoes. Most tornado damage results from the force of the wind. Each time the wind speed doubles, the force of the wind increases four times. For example, the force of the wind at 220 miles per hour is four times as great as the force at 110 miles per hour. This tremendous strength may knock over buildings and trees. Other damage occurs when the wind picks up objects and hurls them through the air.

Scientists estimate the wind speed of a tornado by the damage it inflicts, using a gauge called the Fujita scale. The scale was developed by the Japanese-born weather scientist T. Theodore Fujita. On the Fujita scale, F0 is the weakest rating and F5 is the strongest. An F5 tornado can remove a house from its foundation.

A tornado sucks up air when passing over a building. For this reason, some people think they should open windows to help equalize the pressure if a tornado threatens. They fear that the air pressure outside the building might drop so suddenly that the structure would explode outward. Safety experts know, however, that air moves in and out of most buildings so quickly that air pressure remains nearly equal inside and out, even during a tornado. Open windows do not reduce damage and may even increase it because wind blowing in may hurl loose objects through the air.

Tornado damage is often localized. A tornado may demolish one house and leave an adjacent house untouched.

Some tornadoes consist of smaller rotating columns of air called *suction spots* or *suction vortices*. The suction spots revolve around the central axis of the tornado and can inflict tremendous damage to small areas.

Forecasting tornadoes. *Meteorologists* (scientists who study weather) can predict possible severe weather 12 to 48 hours in advance. They make such forecasts using data from weather balloons, satellites, and conventional weather radar. Computers help meteorologists analyze the data and recognize when conditions favor the formation of thunderstorms.

Meteorologists use a special type of radar called Doppler radar to look for mesocyclones. This type of

WORLD BOOK illustration by Bruce Kerr

A tornado is a rapidly rotating column of air that can develop under a large, anvil-shaped thundercloud. First, a dark *wall cloud* forms underneath the thundercloud. In most cases, a twisting, funnel-shaped cloud then descends from the wall cloud and touches the ground. Almost all tornadoes in the Northern Hemisphere rotate as shown in the diagram at the left—counterclockwise when viewed from above.

Where tornadoes occur in the United States

Tornadoes most often hit the midwestern and southern United States. This map shows the number of tornadoes that occur yearly in each 10,000 square miles (25,900 square kilometers) of area.

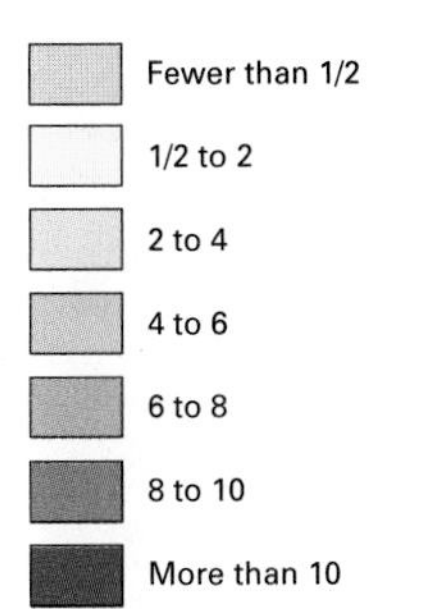

WORLD BOOK map

The Fujita scale

The chart below shows the Fujita scale for estimating the speed, in miles per hour (mph) and kilometers per hour (kph), of tornadoes and other violent winds based on the damage caused.

Scale	Damage	Wind speed: Mph	Kph
F0	Light Tree branches broken, damage to chimneys and large signs.	40-72	64-116
F1	Moderate Trees snapped, surface of roofs peeled off, windows broken.	73-112	117-180
F2	Considerable Large trees uprooted, roofs torn off frame houses, mobile homes demolished.	113-157	181-253
F3	Severe Roof and some walls torn off well-constructed houses, cars overturned.	158-206	254-332
F4	Devastating Well-constructed houses leveled, cars and large objects thrown.	207-260	333-419
F5	Incredible Strong frame houses lifted off foundation and destroyed, car-sized objects thrown more than 300 feet (90 meters).	261-318	420-512

radar works because radar waves change frequency depending on whether the objects they bounce off, such as raindrops or dust particles, are advancing or receding. This change in frequency, called the Doppler effect, can reveal the rotating pattern of a mesocyclone.

In the United States, the National Weather Service issues a *tornado watch* when conditions in the atmosphere promote the formation of tornadoes. If a tornado watch is issued for your area, you should watch for threatening weather and listen to the radio or television for more information.

If Doppler radar detects a mesocyclone in a thunderstorm, the National Weather Service issues a *tornado warning.* The Weather Service also issues a tornado warning if someone actually sees a funnel cloud. If a tornado warning is issued for your location, take cover immediately. The safest place is a basement or other underground shelter. If no underground shelter is available, an interior bathroom or closet is best.

Studying tornadoes. Meteorologists study tornadoes both outdoors and in the laboratory. Tornadoes are difficult to study outdoors because they form and vanish quickly and occupy a small area. Another problem is that scientists do not know exactly what causes tornadoes, so they find it difficult to get to the right place at the right time to gather data.

Many meteorologists form mobile teams of "storm chasers" to study tornadoes outdoors. The storm chasers travel in specially equipped automobiles, vans, trucks, and aircraft, trying to get near tornadoes without coming too close. The researchers drop instruments in or near the paths of tornadoes to measure wind, temperature, and air pressure. They also record flying debris on film or videotape so they can analyze wind patterns. Doppler radar enables storm chasers to map wind speed and direction and to study the changes that take place in a thunderstorm before a tornado forms.

Meteorologists make computer *models* (mathematical representations) of thunderstorms and tornadoes. They also simulate tornadoes using rotating air currents in chambers. Scientists hope to learn why tornadoes form, to know what happens inside a tornado, and to better forecast these destructive storms. Howard B. Bluestein

See also **Cloud; Cyclone; Waterspout.**

Torne River, *TAWR nuh,* also called the Tornio River, rises in Lake Torne in northern Sweden and flows eastward through northern Sweden. Then the river turns southward and forms part of the boundary between Sweden and Finland until it empties into the Gulf of Bothnia. For the location of the Torne River, see **Sweden** (terrain map).

The Finnish people call the part of the river that forms the boundary the Tornio. But in Sweden, the river is called the Torne. The Torne River is more than 250 miles (402 kilometers) long. M. Donald Hancock

© Richard Simpson, Tony Stone Images

Toronto is Canada's largest city and chief center of industry. It is also the capital of the province of Ontario. The CN Tower, a communications and observation tower, dominates the skyline. It stands 1,815 feet (553 meters) tall. To the left of the tower in this photo is the Rogers Centre, a sports stadium.

Toronto

Toronto, *tuh RAHN toh,* is the capital of Ontario and the largest city in Canada. It lies on the northwest shore of Lake Ontario.

Toronto is the chief manufacturing, financial, and communications center of Canada. Plants in the Toronto metropolitan area employ approximately one-fifth of Canada's manufacturing workers. The Toronto Stock Exchange ranks first in the nation in daily trading volume. Toronto has important printing, publishing, and television and motion-picture production industries. It is a leading cultural center, with important libraries and museums.

In 1791, John Graves Simcoe became lieutenant governor of the new British colony of Upper Canada (the southern part of what is now Ontario). Simcoe chose the site of present-day Toronto for a new colonial capital. He established the new capital in 1793 and named it York. In 1834, when it officially became a city, York was renamed *Toronto,* an Indian word that means *meeting place.*

James Lemon, the contributor of this article, is author of Toronto since 1918: an illustrated history *and professor of geography at the University of Toronto.*

The city

Toronto covers 243 square miles (630 square kilometers). More than one-fifth of Ontarians and nearly one-tenth of Canadians live in the city. The official metropolitan area, called the Toronto Census Metropolitan area, occupies 2,279 square miles (5,903 square kilometers).

Layout of Toronto. Three rivers—the Humber, Don, and Rouge—cut through Toronto. They run south into Lake Ontario, through deep ravines that are sites for many winding parks and towering bridges. Yonge Street is the main road that runs north and south. Toronto's main east-west street is Bloor Street/Danforth Avenue.

Major commuter highways ring the outskirts of the city. The Queen Elizabeth Way, the partially elevated Gardiner Expressway, and the Don Valley Parkway carry traffic into the heart of the city along the shore of Lake Ontario.

Landmarks. Near the center of Toronto's downtown business district stands City Hall. This unusual structure consists of two curved office buildings and, between them, the oyster-shaped City Council chambers. The three buildings stand in 12-acre (5-hectare) Nathan Phillips Square, named for Toronto's mayor from 1955 to 1962. Toronto Eaton Centre, a huge office and shopping complex on Yonge Street, includes hundreds of stores and three office buildings.

Downtown Toronto's financial district, centered around Bay Street, has three of the world's 100 tallest buildings. First Canadian Place, a 72-story bank and office tower, rises 951 feet (290 meters). The 68-story Scotia Plaza building is 902 feet (275 meters) tall. Another office building, Canada Trust Tower, has 51 stories and rises 856 feet (261 meters). The CN (Canadian National) Tower, a concrete-and-steel shaft rising 1,815 feet (553 meters), dominates Toronto's skyline. This communications tower includes observation decks and restaurants.

The Rogers Centre, a sports stadium with a retractable roof, stands near the CN Tower. It covers 8 acres (3.2 hectares) and includes a hotel, an entertainment mall, restaurants, meeting rooms, and a health club. The Air Canada Centre contains an indoor sports arena and a theater. The Metro Toronto Convention Center is also downtown.

South of the financial district lies Harbourfront Centre. It has many art galleries, shops, and restaurants, as well as several exhibition areas and a number of theaters that stage plays, music, and dance. Ontario Place is a cultural, recreational, and entertainment complex on the lakefront southwest of downtown. It has an amphitheater, an exhibition area, a marina, a children's water park, a picnic area, and an IMAX theater. Also on the lakefront is Exhibition Place, the site of the Canadian National Exhibition, the world's largest annual fair. Held in late summer, the fair features exhibits and sports events. The restored Old Fort York stands near Exhibition Place. United States forces burned the original fort during the War of 1812.

The Ontario Parliament Buildings stand at the head of University Avenue in Queen's Park, just north of downtown Toronto. The campus of the University of Toronto lies west of the park.

Casa Loma, another Toronto landmark, stands northwest of downtown. Sir Henry Pellatt, a Toronto stockbroker, built this 98-room castle in the early 1900's.

The metropolitan area. Surrounding the City of Toronto is the Greater Toronto Area, which includes the municipalities of Markham, Richmond Hill, and Vaughn to the north; Brampton and Mississauga to the west; and Pickering to the east. The Greater Toronto Area experienced tremendous growth during the 1980's and 1990's. During that time, large amounts of farmland were developed into suburban communities with houses, schools, hospitals, and shopping malls.

People

Ethnic groups. Toronto is one of the most ethnically diverse cities in the world. Overall, the city has more than 150 ethnic groups that speak over 100 languages. The largest ethnic groups in the Toronto area consist of people of English, Irish, and Scottish ancestry. In the mid-1900's, many Europeans immigrated to Toronto, especially Italians and Portuguese. Chinese, Indians, Pakistanis, and Sri Lankans make up other large ethnic groups in the area. Toronto has a growing community of immigrants from the Caribbean Islands and Southeast Asia. This rich mix of cultures has helped make Toronto a lively urban center, with a wide variety of entertainment and foods available throughout the city.

Housing. Toronto is a city of clearly defined neighborhoods. Old red-brick townhouses stand in such neighborhoods as Riverdale and Parkdale. Stately houses can be found in Rosedale, Forest Hill, and Bridle Path. Bungalows sprawl through such communities as Etobicoke and Scarborough. Throughout the suburbs and the surrounding regions, houses are mixed with high-rise apartments and condominiums. Heavy immigration to Toronto from other countries and from other areas of Canada has strained the supply of affordable housing.

Facts in brief

Population: *Toronto*—2,481,494; *Toronto Census Metropolitan Area*—4,682,897.
Area: *Toronto*—243 mi² (630 km²); *Toronto Census Metropolitan Area*—2,279 mi² (5,903 km²).
Altitude: 356 ft (109 m) above sea level.
Climate: *Average temperature*—January, 24 °F (−4 °C); July, 71 °F (22 °C). *Average annual precipitation* (rainfall, melted snow, and other forms of moisture)—32 in (81 cm). For the monthly weather in Toronto, see **Ontario** (Climate).
Government: Mayor-council (3-year terms for the mayor and 44 council members).
Founded: Established as the town of York in 1793; gained a city charter and the name Toronto in 1834.

Largest communities in the Toronto area

Name	Population	Name	Population
Toronto	2,481,494	Oakville	144,738
Mississauga	612,925	Richmond Hill	132,030
Brampton	325,428	Pickering	87,139
Markham	208,615	Ajax	73,753
Vaughan	182,022	Newmarket	65,788

™City of Toronto. Design: Rene deSantis

The flag of Toronto shows the twin towers of City Hall on a blue background. The red maple leaf between the towers represents the City Council chambers.

Toronto lies in southern Ontario. Toronto's location on the northwest shore of Lake Ontario, one of the Great Lakes, has helped make the city an important port.

City of Toronto

The small map shows the City of Toronto and several nearby communities. The large map shows the city and many of its major points of interest.

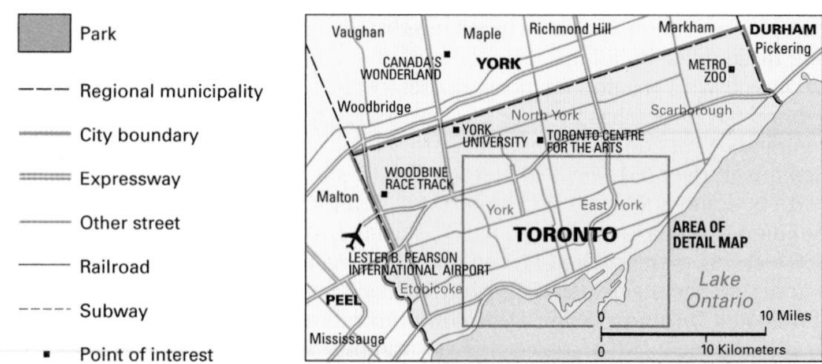

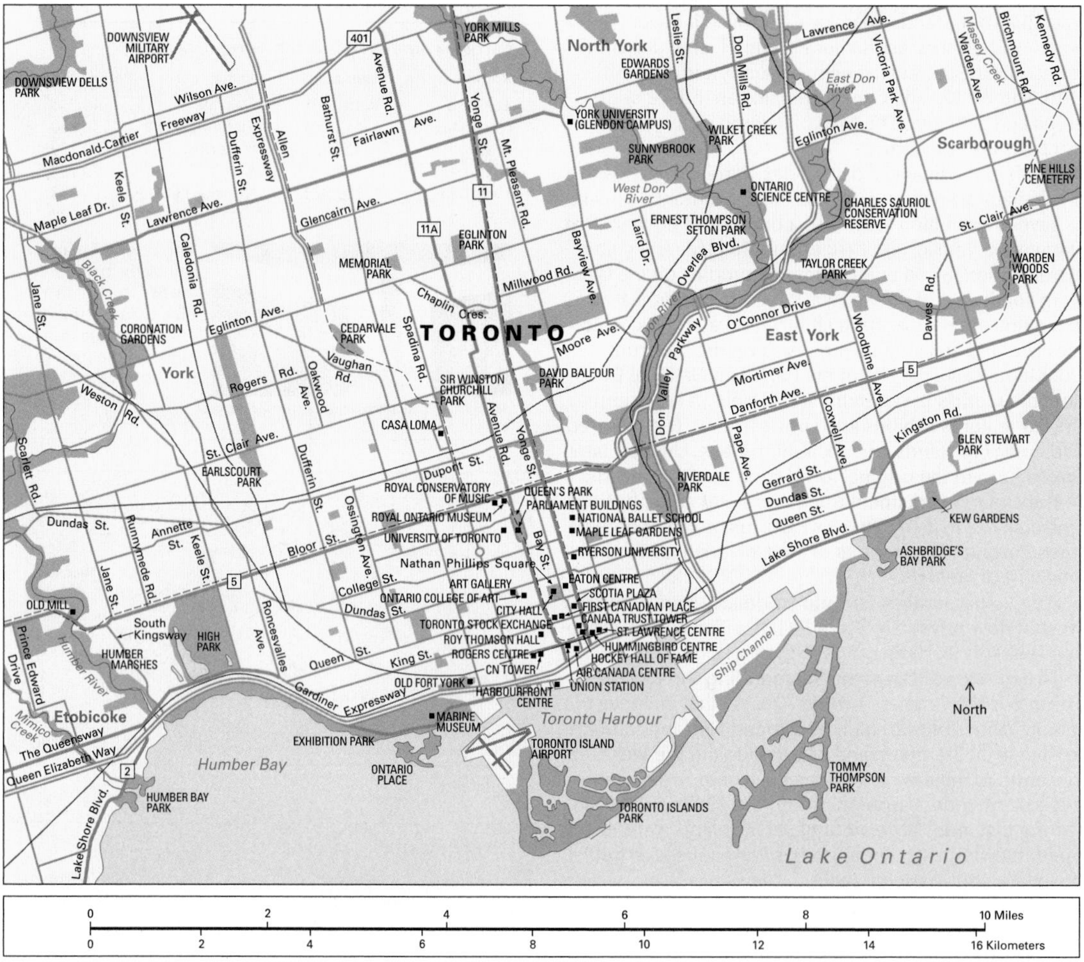

WORLD BOOK maps

Education. About three-fourths of the elementary and high school students in Toronto attend the city's nonreligious public schools. Most of the remaining students are enrolled in Roman Catholic institutions, supervised by a separate and publicly funded Catholic school board. Some privately funded schools operate as well.

Three universities—the University of Toronto, York University, and Ryerson University—are located in Toronto. The University of Toronto, founded in 1827, is the oldest and largest of the three. Other schools in Toronto include the National Ballet School, the Ontario College of Art, the Royal Conservatory of Music, and several community colleges.

Social problems. Toronto prides itself on being "Toronto the good." It has, for example, a relatively low rate of violent crime for a city of its size. Nevertheless, Toronto does have a number of social problems.

In general, Toronto's people have a high standard of living. Like the people of most major urban areas, however, Toronto residents have a wide range of incomes. A shortage of affordable housing has led to increased homelessness among Toronto's poorest residents. Every night, several thousand people sleep in emergency shelters or on the streets of the city. The homeless include the unemployed, the mentally ill, and runaway youths.

Toronto has some environmental problems. Toronto's waterfront, once a popular place for swimming, today attracts few swimmers because of water pollution. The city has spent millions of dollars to upgrade its water-treatment systems in an effort to reduce sewage runoff into the lake during heavy rains. On some hot summer days, the city sits under a yellow haze of smog, caused by car exhaust fumes and industrial smokestack emissions. On the other hand, civic pride and a large crew of city sweepers ensure that the streets stay clean, and the downtown area is almost free of litter.

© Tim Crosby, Liaison Agency

Chinatown is home to many Toronto residents of Chinese and Southeast Asian descent. Toronto's rich mix of cultures has helped make the city a lively urban center.

Cultural life

The arts. The Toronto Symphony Orchestra and the Mendelssohn Choir perform in Roy Thomson Hall. The Hummingbird Centre for the Performing Arts presents programs by the Canadian Opera Company and the National Ballet of Canada. The Toronto Centre for the Arts, in the North York neighborhood, presents live theater. Downtown Toronto also has several theaters. The St. Lawrence Centre for the Arts, St. Lawrence Hall, the Royal Conservatory of Music, and the Canadian Music Centre are also in Toronto. In addition, the city is home to a large motion-picture industry.

The Art Gallery of Ontario is home to the largest public collection of works by the British sculptor Henry Moore. In addition, the gallery owns Canada's second largest collection of paintings by Canadian artists. The National Gallery of Canada in Ottawa has the largest. The Power Plant, at the Harbourfront Centre, and the Art Gallery of York University feature works by contemporary artists. The McMichael Canadian Art Collection houses a large number of paintings by the Canadian landscape artists known as the Group of Seven (see **Group of Seven**).

Museums and libraries. The Royal Ontario Museum is the largest museum in Canada. It offers exhibits of archaeology, ethnology, mineralogy, and paleontology. The museum has one of the world's finest collections of Chinese objects. The Marine Museum of Upper Canada shows the development of shipping on the Great Lakes and the St. Lawrence River. The Ontario Science Centre consists of three buildings that house nine main exhibit halls. The center's exhibits and demonstrations deal with a wide range of scientific and technological subjects.

The Toronto Public Library has branches throughout the city. The library owns the Osborne Collection of early children's books.

Parks. Toronto has an extensive system of parks. Toronto Islands Park, one of the city's largest parks, occupies 570 acres (230 hectares) on an island in Lake Ontario. Other important parks include Centennial Park, which spreads across 525 acres (212 hectares) in the Etobicoke community in the western part of the city, and High Park, which covers a rugged 398 acres (161 hectares) closer to the heart of Toronto. The Metro Toronto Zoo lies in the northeastern part of the city. Tommy Thompson Park, which extends into Lake Ontario, is a wilderness area created on top of a landfill.

Sports. Professional sports teams based in Toronto are the Maple Leafs of the National Hockey League (NHL); the Raptors of the National Basketball Association (NBA); the Argonauts of the Canadian Football League; and the Blue Jays, an American League baseball team. Toronto also has a number of amateur sports leagues. In addition, Toronto is home to the Hockey Hall of Fame.

Economy

Manufacturing. The Toronto metropolitan area is Canada's chief industrial center. Thousands of factories operate in and near the city. About one-sixth of workers in the metropolitan area hold a wide variety of manufacturing jobs. The major industrial activities are food processing and printing and publishing. Other leading products include clothing, electronics and electrical equipment, and paper, rubber, and wood products. Toronto also contributes heavily to Ontario's automobile industry. It has many plants that make automobile parts and assemble motor vehicles.

Finance. Toronto is Canada's leading banking and financial center. More Canadian banks, insurance compa-

E. Ott, Miller Services

Toronto's City Hall is a city landmark. The structure was designed by the Finnish architect Viljo Revell and completed in 1965. It consists of two curved office buildings of unequal height and, between them, the oyster-shaped City Council chambers. The buildings stand in Nathan Phillips Square, a popular gathering place and the site of concerts and other special events.

nies, trust companies, and loan companies have headquarters in Toronto than in any other city in Canada. The Toronto Stock Exchange is one of the largest exchanges in North America in value of shares traded.

Transportation and communication. Toronto is a major transportation center. The region's varied products travel to many parts of the world by air and by ship via the St. Lawrence Seaway. Toronto's port handles about 2 million tons (1.8 million metric tons) of cargo a year.

Leading railways that serve the city include the Canadian National Railway and the Canadian Pacific Railway. VIA Rail passenger trains connect Toronto with other locations in Canada, while Amtrak carries travelers from Toronto to other Canadian and United States cities. A regional rail system known as GO serves commuters. The Toronto subway, which opened in 1954, was Canada's first underground rapid transit railway. The first subway line ran under Yonge Street.

Lester B. Pearson International Airport, about 14 miles (24 kilometers) northwest of downtown Toronto, is Canada's busiest airport. The Toronto Island Airport in Lake Ontario has a seaplane base. A domestic commuter service flies to and from Ottawa, Montreal, and Hamilton.

Toronto has four daily newspapers. They are *The Toronto Star, The Toronto Sun, The Globe and Mail,* and *The National Post.* The Toronto area also has about 175 other local publications, including community papers and magazines. More than 30 radio stations and about 35 cable television stations serve the Toronto area. One of Canada's first two TV stations was CBLT, which started broadcasting from Toronto in 1952.

Government

Toronto has a single level of government. The Toronto City Council, through various agencies, boards, and commissions, is responsible for a wide range of services. They include ambulance service, fire protection, garbage collection, public transportation, roads and traffic control, urban development, and welfare services.

The Toronto City Council consists of a mayor and 44 other members. The voters elect all of these officials to three-year terms. The council is the city's governing and legislative branch. Councilors also sit on committees and serve on local community councils in the area where they were elected.

History

Early settlement. Before Europeans arrived, Algonquin and Iroquois Indians lived in the Toronto area. The site of present-day Toronto lay at the southern end of an Indian *portage* (overland route) between Lakes Huron and Ontario. In 1750, the French began construction on a trading post and fort opposite the peninsula that forms Toronto's harbor. In 1759, the French burned the fort to keep the British from seizing it. In 1763, the Treaty of Paris gave most of Canada to Britain (now the United Kingdom).

In 1787, the Canadian government bought land on the peninsula from the Mississauga Indians. No permanent settlement began until 1793, when John Graves Simcoe chose the site to replace Newark as the capital of the colony of Upper Canada. He named the settlement York after the Duke of York.

The 1800's. During the War of 1812, troops from the United States captured York and burned parts of the town, including Fort York. Among the loot taken by the troops was the *mace* (ceremonial staff) from the legislature. The mace was finally returned in 1934 on the orders of U.S. President Franklin D. Roosevelt.

In 1834, York was renamed Toronto and received its city charter. It had a population of about 10,000. In 1837, William Lyon Mackenzie, a printer who later became Toronto's first mayor, led a revolt against the colony's British government. However, the colonial militia crushed the revolt.

Toronto began to grow as a center of industry and transportation during the late 1800's. Manufacturing expanded rapidly after Canada's federal government adopted policies to protect new Canadian industries from American competition. Also during this period, the federal government opened new areas in the western prairies to grain growing and livestock raising. Toronto became a major banking center and market of the West. The city financed the opening of the rich metal mines in northern Ontario and gained importance as a railroad center.

Growth and federation. The demand for war materials during World War I (1914-1918) and World War II (1939-1945) brought great industrial expansion to the Toronto area. The end of World War II saw a rapid population growth as well. Hundreds of thousands of European immigrants settled in and near Toronto.

Rapid population growth caused numerous problems, including poor transportation, a housing shortage, and, in some communities, a lack of water. The city and the suburbs often failed to work together to solve their problems. Also, some suburban governments could not afford needed improvements. These problems led the Ontario legislature to create the Municipality of Metropolitan Toronto, a federation of Toronto and 12 of its suburbs that came into being on Jan. 1, 1954. The city and the suburbs each had self-government in local matters and sent representatives to a Metropolitan Council.

In 1967, the Ontario provincial legislature merged the 13 units into 6—Toronto, East York, Etobicoke, North York, Scarborough, and York. The federated council brought several rapid improvements. For example, it put into operation the first computer-controlled traffic system in the world. The council built public housing for the elderly and moderate rental housing for poor, younger families. It also doubled the area's water supply.

Urban renewal. The Metropolitan Council expanded Toronto's subway system and built new expressways. In 1968, the council approved the Metropolitan Waterfront Plan, a renewal program for Toronto's waterfront area. The plan included Ontario Place, completed in 1971; the CN Tower, opened in 1976; and a convention center, which opened in 1984. By the early 1980's, hundreds of stores and two office buildings had been completed in Toronto Eaton Centre. Two sports arenas, the SkyDome stadium and the Air Canada Centre, opened in 1989 and 1991, respectively. Urban development slowed markedly after 1990.

Recent developments. In 1997, the Ontario provincial legislature voted to merge the six municipalities that made up Toronto's metropolitan government federation into a single city of Toronto. Many Toronto-area citizens opposed the merger, arguing that it would destroy their distinctive communities and bring a reduction in services, but the provincial government said it would only eliminate duplication of services. The new unified City of Toronto came into being in 1998.

In 2003, construction began downtown on the Four Seasons Centre for the Performing Arts. The center will be home to the Canadian Opera Company.

James Lemon

Casa Loma is a 98-room medieval-style castle built by Sir Henry Pellatt, a Toronto stockbroker, in the early 1900's. The building stands on a hill north of downtown Toronto and overlooks the city. Casa Loma includes two towers, secret passageways, and an underground tunnel that connects the house to stables. The grounds have a colorful flower garden.

Related articles in *World Book* include:

Outline

Questions

Who was the first mayor of Toronto?
Where does the National Ballet of Canada perform?
What is the main north-south street in downtown Toronto?
Who chose the site of present-day Toronto as the capital of the British colony of Upper Canada?
What are some of Toronto's environmental problems?
What is the most common ancestry of people in the Toronto area? What are some of the other ethnic groups in Toronto?
When did the Municipality of Metropolitan Toronto come into being? Why was it created?
What are some of the chief manufactured products in Toronto?
What does the name *Toronto* mean? Why does that name seem especially appropriate today?
What ceremonial item was seized by U.S. troops during the War of 1812 and not returned until 1934?

Toronto, *tuh RAHN toh,* **University of,** is one of Canada's largest universities. It is coeducational and supported chiefly by the province of Ontario. The main campus is in downtown Toronto. The university also operates two colleges of arts and science, one in the town of Erindale and the other in the community of Scarborough, in northeastern Toronto.

The University of Toronto has 11 undergraduate divisions. The school of graduate studies consists of over 75 departments, centers, institutes, and other units. The university operates 50 libraries, with a total of over 7 million volumes. The university also administers an astronomical observatory, more than 35 research centers, and the University of Toronto Press.

The University of Toronto awards arts and science degrees for three other universities—the University of St. Michael's College, the University of Trinity College, and Victoria University. It also grants degrees for the Ontario Institute for Studies in Education. Three theological colleges—Emmanuel, Knox, and Wycliffe—are associated with the university but grant their own degrees. All seven associated institutions are in Toronto.

The university was founded in 1827 as King's College. It received its present name in 1850.

Critically reviewed by the University of Toronto

Torpedo is a self-propelled, underwater weapon used to damage ships and submarines. Modern torpedoes can be launched from submarines, surface vessels, or aircraft. Some are designed for attacking large groups of cargo vessels and fast warships. Other torpedoes are specifically used to combat deep-running submarines.

How a torpedo works. Torpedoes are generally tube-shaped. They vary in size, weight, and mechanical apparatus, depending on their intended purpose. A typical torpedo has four sections. The *nose* section contains acoustic and electronic devices the torpedo uses to hunt and pursue a target. Behind the nose is the *warhead* section, which includes an explosive charge and the *fuzing* mechanism, which causes detonation. The center section houses systems that stabilize the weapon and control its direction. It also contains the torpedo's energy source, which may be compressed air, batteries, or a fuel. The rear section, or *afterbody,* encloses the engine and propellers.

A torpedo is typically launched from a hollow tube pointed toward a target or the target's future position.

U.S. Navy

A torpedo is a self-propelled, underwater weapon. Torpedoes are generally tube-shaped, with four internal sections. The *nose* section contains devices to guide the torpedo to its target. The *warhead* section consists of explosives and the mechanism that causes detonation. The center section includes various controls and the torpedo's energy source. The torpedo's rear section, or *afterbody,* houses the engine and the propeller units. The United States Navy's Mark 48 model is shown here.

WORLD BOOK diagram by Sally Wayland

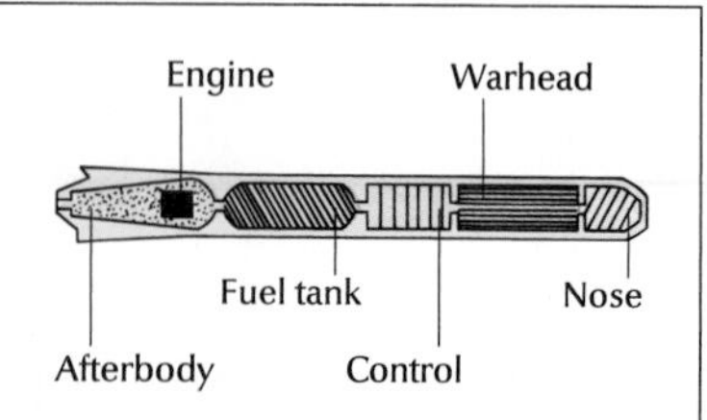

Or an aircraft may drop the torpedo, which is slowed by a parachute before it hits the water. A *starting lever* puts the engine into action when the torpedo enters the water. Power flows from the engine to the propellers, which drive the torpedo forward, and to the tail surfaces that steer the torpedo. Dual propellers *counterrotate* (turn in opposite directions), eliminating *torque* (twisting force) to prevent the torpedo from spinning in the water. As the torpedo hunts for the target, the fuzing mechanism automatically arms the warhead. When acoustic "ears" called *hydrophones* detect noise from the target, the torpedo is within *acquisition range.* It then leaves its hunting course and tracks straight toward the target. The warhead may be set to explode when the torpedo contacts a hull or when magnetic, acoustic, or pressure sensors indicate that it is within range of the target.

A special-purpose torpedo that provides greater accuracy and selectivity can be guided by wire to its target. This torpedo unwinds a reel of wire as it travels to the target area. The attacking ship or submarine sends steering signals over the wire. Another special type of torpedo called a *wake homer* senses the small air bubbles of a ship's wake and follows them until the fuzing mechanism detects the ship.

An *antisubmarine rocket* (ASROC) system uses a warship's sonar equipment to detect a submarine at long ranges. It then computes the target's course and speed. The warship launches a *ballistic* (rocket-propelled) missile containing either an *acoustic-homing* (sound-detecting) torpedo or a depth charge. The rocket and other parts of the missile fall away in the air, and the torpedo, slowed by parachute, falls into the water. The acoustic-homing device then guides the torpedo to its target. A depth charge explodes at a predetermined depth.

History. Until the 1900's, the word *torpedo* was applied to a mine or any other explosive device used against ships. At first, none of these devices had means of propulsion. Surface vessels or submarines rammed a torpedo against an enemy ship or secretly attached the device to its hull. In the early 1800's, the American inventor Robert Fulton experimented with long, narrow, minelike devices he called "torpedoes," but there was little interest in his invention. During the American Civil War (1861-1865), the Union and Confederate navies each sunk an enemy ship with *spar torpedoes.* The torpedoes consisted of charges mounted at the end of a pole sticking out from the attacker's bow. The charges exploded on contact with another vessel.

In 1864, Giovanni Luppis, a captain in the Austrian Navy, took a plan for a torpedo to the famous Scottish engineer Robert Whitehead. By 1868, Whitehead had developed the first real torpedo. Powered by compressed air, the torpedo was completely self-propelled.

Torpedoes used during World War II (1939-1945) were of simple mechanical or electrical design. They were aimed at surface vessels only, and they ran a straight course. They left a telltale wake of air bubbles behind them and made noise as they traveled. A maneuverable ship with an alert crew could evade them.

On the outside, present-day torpedoes resemble earlier ones. On the inside, however, modern torpedoes are vastly more complex. Modern warfare demands versatile, reliable weapons. Today's torpedoes leave no wake behind them and are difficult to detect. They can track ships making evasive maneuvers. Today's torpedo designs involve so many fields of science and are so complicated that the modern torpedo cannot be credited to any one person. Craig M. Payne

See also **Depth charge; Guided missile; PT boat; Submarine.**

Torque, *tawrk,* is the amount of twisting effort that a force or forces exert on an object. The torque around any *axis* (reference line) is calculated by multiplying the force by the distance between the line of force and the axis. The torque increases as the force moves farther from the axis. For this reason, a wheel turns more easily when the force is applied farther from the center. In the inch-pound system of measurement customarily used in the United States, torque is measured in pound-feet. See also **Force; Lever.** James D. Chalupnik

Torquemada, *tawr kay MAH dah,* **Tomás de,** *toh MAHS day* (1420-1498), a Roman Catholic friar, was *inquisitor-general* (chief official) of the Spanish Inquisition for 15 years. During that time, 2,000 people were condemned to death by the Inquisition for *heresy* (beliefs contrary to those of the church) and executed.

Torquemada used the Inquisition for religious and political reasons. He believed punishment of Christian heretics and the exclusion from Spain of non-Christians—chiefly Jews and Muslims—was the only way to achieve political unity in Spain. He was partly responsible for the royal edict of 1492 that expelled 200,000 Jews from Spain. Many people admired him but feared his power. King Ferdinand and Queen Isabella of Spain were among his supporters.

Hulton/Bettmann

Tomás de Torquemada

Torquemada was born in Valladolid. His ancestors included Jews who converted to Christianity. Torquemada became a friar in the Dominican monastery in Valladolid, and later was prior of the monastery of Santa Cruz, at Segovia, for 22 years. He served as confessor to Isabella after she became queen. Torquemada became assistant to the inquisitors in 1482 and the first inquisitor-general for most Spanish lands in 1483. He set rules of procedure and formed branches of the Inquisition in various cities. He retired to a Dominican monastery at Avila in 1496 but continued to direct the Inquisition until his death on Sept. 16, 1498.

Carla Rahn Phillips and William D. Phillips, Jr.

See also **Inquisition.**

Torre, Joe (1940-), gained success both as a player and manager in major league baseball. Torre played for 18 years, from 1960 to 1977, with the Milwaukee (later Atlanta) Braves, St. Louis Cardinals, and New York Mets. He starred as a first baseman, catcher, and third baseman. While playing for St. Louis in 1971, Torre was named the National League Most Valuable Player, leading the league in batting, hits, and runs batted in.

Torre managed the Mets from 1977 to 1981. He then managed the Braves from 1982 to 1984. Torre managed the St. Louis Cardinals from 1990 to 1995 and became manager of the New York Yankees in 1996. The Yankees won the World Series in 1998, 1999, and 2000. The 1998 Yankees set a major league record for regular season victories. Joseph Paul Torre was born on July 18, 1940, in the Brooklyn borough of New York City.

Torrens, Lake. See Lake Torrens.

Torrens River, *TAWR uhnz* or *TAHR uhnz,* lies in South Australia. It rises in the Mount Lofty Ranges and flows for about 50 miles (80 kilometers) to Gulf St. Vincent, passing through Adelaide. The Torrens Valley is noted for its *truck farms*—that is, farms where market vegetables are grown.

Torrens system, *TAWR uhnz* or *TAHR uhnz,* is a system of registering titles to real estate. It is named for Sir Robert Torrens, who introduced it in South Australia in 1858. It has not been widely used in the United States, but nations of the British Commonwealth and Europe have adopted it. Its purpose is to make the transfer of real property as simple and safe as the transfer of other property, and to end repeated examination of titles.

A bureau or court of registration, supervised by a registrar, operates the system. An examiner of titles usually works with the registrar. The system substitutes public registration for *conveyancing* (transferring property by deeds and other written documents).

Under the system, the owner of a piece of land files a petition with the registrar to have the land registered. Searchers make a full inquiry into the title. If they find no flaw, the registrar issues a certificate of title, which a court cannot set aside or overcome. Thereafter, the certificate will always show the state of the title and the person who holds it. Any claim or other legal restriction on the property is listed on the certificate. If someone later has a just claim against the property, an insurance fund pays the person. Registration fees maintain the fund.

In the United States, the first Torrens Act was passed by the legislature of Illinois in 1897. From time to time, other states in the nation have adopted the system. Since each state has its own system of registering titles, the Torrens acts vary. Few states use this system today.

In Canada. In 1861, Vancouver Island adopted a system of land registration based upon the Torrens system. When Vancouver became a part of British Columbia in 1866, the entire province continued the system. The provinces of Alberta, Manitoba, Nova Scotia, Ontario, and Saskatchewan also use the Torrens title system.

Linda Henry Elrod

Torres, *TAWR rays,* **Luis Vaez de,** *loo EES vah AYTH thay* (? -1613?), a Spanish navigator, became the first European to see the strait that lies between Australia and Papua New Guinea. Torres sailed it in 1606, while on an expedition sponsored by King Philip III of Spain. The strait was later named Torres Strait in his honor.

In 1605, the Portuguese navigator Pedro Fernandes de Queirós left Peru in command of an expedition of three ships. The Spanish government charged the expedition with searching for a continent that was rumored to lie in the South Pacific Ocean. The Spanish called this unknown continent *Terra Australis Incognita* (Unknown Southern Land). Torres was the captain and navigator of one of the ships, the *San Pedrico.*

In 1606, the ships reached land, and Queirós named it *Austrialia del Espiritu Santo* (South Land of the Holy Spirit). This land now comprises the country of Vanuatu.

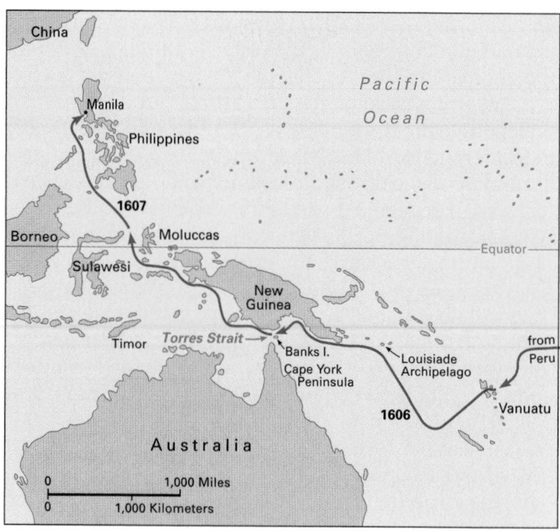

WORLD BOOK map

The voyage of Luis Vaez de Torres to search for a land called *Terra Australis Incognita* (Unknown Southern Land) began in Peru. In 1606, he discovered the strait that now bears his name.

National Library of Australia

Ships commanded by Luis Vaez de Torres reportedly took 34 days to navigate the Torres Strait. During the passage, Torres may have seen Australia's Cape York Peninsula.

Then, suddenly, Queirós left the expedition and sailed for Mexico. Torres continued the voyage with the remaining two vessels.

The ships, following their original instructions, proceeded southwest to search for land at 20° south latitude. Finding no land at this latitude, Torres then turned northwest intending to sail north of New Guinea toward the Philippines. Bad weather prevented him from getting around the eastern end of New Guinea, so he sailed west along the island's south coast. This route took him through the narrow strait between Australia and New Guinea, full of reefs, islands, and treacherous currents. It was a bold move, because mapmakers at that time believed New Guinea was joined to Australia. Torres must have had reasons for thinking they were not joined.

Diego de Prado, an officer on the voyage, wrote that the passage through the strait took 34 days. Torres reported that he saw some big islands to the south during this passage. These islands may, in fact, have been the Cape York Peninsula of Australia. It is also possible that the explorers landed on Banks Island, climbed to higher ground, and saw the Cape York area. No member of the expedition reported a land mass as large as the Australian continent.

After passing through the strait, the ships continued to the Moluccas. They then sailed toward the Philippines and reached Manila on May 6, 1607. There, Torres wrote an account of his discoveries, but his report was soon forgotten. For more than 150 years, cartographers, scholars, and sailors remained uncertain of the existence of a strait in this area. In 1762, an Englishman named Alexander Dalrymple found Torres's report in the Manila archives and named the strait after him.

Little is known of Torres's life. Some historians believe he may have been a Spanish subject who was born in Brittany, in France. I.C. Campbell

Torres Bodet, *TAWR rays baw THEHT,* **Jaime,** *HY may* (1902-1974), was an important Mexican poet, educator, and statesman. Much of his poetry deals with dark themes, such as loneliness, a longing for death, and the author's opposition to what he sees as a hostile, dehumanized modern world. Torres Bodet's first collection of poetry was *Fervor* (1918). His other collections include *Songs* (1922), *The House* (1923), *The Folding Screen* (1925), *Exile* (1930), *Crypt* (1937), *Frontiers* (1954), and *Without Truce* (1957). A bilingual *Selected Poems of Jaime Torres Bodet* was published in 1964. He also wrote six novels from 1927 to 1937, the most praised being *Shadows* (1937).

Torres Bodet was born on April 17, 1902, in Mexico City. He was professor of French literature at the University of Mexico from 1924 to 1929. During the 1930's and early 1940's, he served in Mexican embassies throughout the world. He was Mexico's minister of education from 1943 to 1946, modernizing the country's schools and library system. He was foreign minister of Mexico from 1946 to 1948 and director general of the United Nations Educational, Scientific and Cultural Organization (UNESCO) from 1948 to 1952.

Torres Strait Islands, *TAWR ehs,* are a group of islands in the Torres Strait north of the Australian continent. They include Friday, Hammond, Horn, Prince of Wales, Thursday, Tuesday, and Wednesday islands. The Torres Strait Islands are governed as part of the state of Queensland, Australia.

Torricelli, *TAWR ih CHEHL ee,* **Evangelista,** *eh VAHN jeh LEE stah* (1608-1647), was an Italian physicist and mathematician. Torricelli is best known for his invention of the *mercury barometer* (a device that measures the pressure of the atmosphere). He described this device in 1644. Torricelli also improved the telescope. He studied geometry and motion, and wrote of his research findings in *Opera geometrica* (1644). His work in geometry helped later mathematicians develop *integral calculus,* a system of mathematics.

Torricelli was born on Oct. 15, 1608, in Faenza. He was a friend and disciple of the Italian astronomer and physicist Galileo. A unit of pressure, the *torr,* is named for Torricelli. A. Mark Smith

See also **Barometer; Hydraulics** (Laws of hydrodynamics).

Torrijos Herrera, *tawr REE hohs ehr RAY rah,* **Omar,** *oh MAHR* (1929-1981), was the military dictator of Panama from 1968 until his death. He was best known for his successful negotiations with United States President Jimmy Carter in 1977 over the future of the Panama Canal. The canal is a key waterway linking the Atlantic and Pacific oceans. Torrijos negotiated two treaties that gave Panama control of the canal in stages, with the transfer to be completed on Dec. 31, 1999.

Torrijos also gained popularity as a champion of Panama's lower classes, whom previous governments had often ignored. He instituted important reforms in labor law and land rights to more fairly distribute wealth.

Torrijos was born on Feb. 13, 1929, in Santiago de Veraguas. His parents were both rural schoolteachers. He was educated at El Salvador's military academy and the U.S. School of the Americas, a military training center in Panama. He rose through the ranks of the Panamanian National Guard.

In 1968, he joined other senior officers in deposing the elected civilian government of President Arnulfo Arias Madrid. After a brief power struggle, Torrijos emerged as the nation's strongman. He governed Panama as a military dictator until 1978, when he founded the Democratic Revolutionary Party and formally stepped down as head of the Panamanian government. However, he remained the commander of the National Guard and continued to rule from behind the scenes. Torrijos died in a plane crash on Aug. 1, 1981. J. Mark Ruhl

Torsion balance, *TAWR shuhn,* is a device for measuring small pushing or pulling forces. A torsion balance measures a force by using the force to twist a thin fiber or wire. The balance uses a fine strand of quartz or a fine wire of steel or gold. The wire is mounted on a holding mechanism that can be rotated in a horizontal plane to bring the torsion balance to its zero setting. Suspended from the lower end of the wire is a horizontal pendulum arm. Each end of the arm carries a ball of a heavy substance that resists corrosion, generally gold, lead, or stainless steel.

When the force to be measured is permitted to act on these balls, they swing about, twisting the wire. A tiny mirror mounted at the junction of the wire and the pendulum reflects a beam of light. By noting how much the reflected light moves from zero as the force acts, one measures the amount of force.

Before using the balance, one must calibrate it by twisting the wire with known forces. This test must be repeated often, because molecular changes in the wire may alter its resistance to twisting. James D. Chalupnik

Torsion bar suspension, *TAWR shuhn,* is a method of absorbing the shock, or energy, that results when an automobile travels over uneven road surfaces and bumps. When a car with coil springs strikes a bump, the coils press closer together and absorb the energy. In torsion suspension, a torsion bar replaces the coils in the front end of the car. A torsion bar is actually a coiled spring that has been straightened. Whereas a spring presses together to absorb energy, a torsion bar is subjected to *torsion* (twisting).

A torsion bar consists of a steel rod attached to an arm from the front wheel. When the car strikes a bump,

How torsion bar suspension works

Torsion bars are used in some cars instead of coil springs to help absorb shocks. One end of the torsion bar is attached to an arm connected to the wheel. The other end is attached to the car's frame. When the wheel hits a bump, the bar twists to absorb the jar, *upper right.* It then untwists, *lower right,* to help hold the wheel on the road and keep the car level.

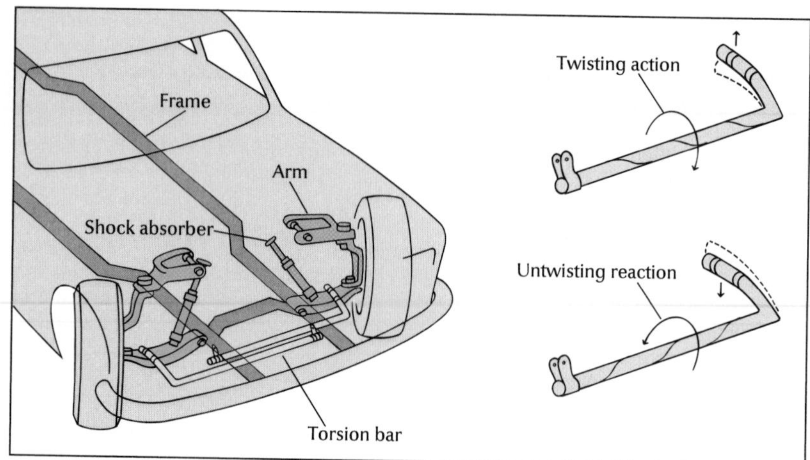

WORLD BOOK illustration by Zorica Dabich

the torsion bar twists to absorb the energy. Torsion bars take up less room than coil springs. William H. Haverdink

See also **Shock absorber; Spring** (hardware).

Tort is a harmful act for which the injured person has the right to collect money for damages. A tort is a violation of *civil law,* which deals with the rights and obligations people have in their relations with one another. The branch of civil law that deals with torts is called *tort law.* Tort law is concerned mainly with injuries to a person's body, property, business, reputation, or privacy. For example, if someone injures you, you may have a right to sue for damages. If a person fails to keep a promise or follow the terms of a contract, another branch of law, called *contract law,* usually determines the right to damages.

Most torts are either *intentional* or *negligent.* An example of an intentional tort is an assault. A negligent tort involves an act of carelessness. For instance, a motorist who accidentally injures a person may be charged with *negligence.*

In many cases, an employer can be held responsible for a tort that is committed by an employee while he or she is working, even though the employer may be free from fault. In such cases, the employee is also personally liable.

A tort may also be a violation of *criminal law.* For example, if someone strikes you, you may be able to recover damages for the torts of assault and battery. But the government may also punish the person for breaking a criminal law that forbids such an act.

Edward J. Kionka

Related articles in *World Book* include:

Assault and battery	Negligence
Damages	Slander
Libel	Trespass

Tortoise is a turtle that lives only on land. Tortoises have stumpy hind legs and feet that look like those of an elephant, quite different from the flippers of sea turtles and the webbed feet of most freshwater turtles. Most tortoises have a high, domed shell. They pull their head, feet, and tail into the shell for protection from predators. Tortoises feed primarily on plants.

There are about 40 species of tortoises. Many occur in hot, dry regions. Three species live in the United States. The *desert tortoise* is found in the deserts of the American Southwest. The *Texas tortoise* inhabits scrublands in southern Texas. The *gopher tortoise* lives in the sandhills of the Southeastern coastal plain. All three of these tortoises rest in burrows that they dig in the ground. Not all tortoises live in dry habitats. For example, the *red-footed tortoise* and the *yellow-footed tortoise* inhabit lowland tropical rain forests in South America.

Tortoises vary widely in size. One of the largest species is the giant *Galapagos tortoise,* which lives on the Galapagos Islands in the Pacific Ocean. It grows up to 4 feet (1.2 meters) long. The *speckled tortoises* of southwestern Africa are among the smallest species. Speckled tortoises are only about 4 inches (10 centimeters) long when fully grown.

Like other turtles, tortoises lay their eggs in holes in the ground. When the eggs hatch, the young dig to the surface to fend for themselves. Most tortoises die in the first 10 years of life. Raccoons, foxes, and other predatory animals feed on tortoise eggs and young tortoises. Tortoises that survive the first several years can live an extremely long time. Some have lived more than 100 years in captivity.

Erwin and Peggy Bauer, Bruce Coleman Ltd.

The tortoise has stumpy, clublike legs and feet. When threatened, this turtle seeks safety inside its high, domed shell.

Tortoise populations are declining quickly because people destroy the animal's habitat and illegally kill tortoises for food. In addition, many tortoises die from diseases introduced by humans. Many countries forbid the capture or killing of tortoises. Laurie J. Vitt

Scientific classification. Tortoises belong to the family Testudinidae in the class Reptilia. The scientific name for the desert tortoise is *Gopherus agassizii;* the Texas tortoise is *G. berlandieri;* and the gopher tortoise is *G. polyphemus.* The Galapagos tortoise is *Geochelone elephantopus.*

See also **Turtle; Animal** (picture).

Tortugas. See **Dry Tortugas National Park.**

Torture is the use of physical or mental pain. It is often used to get information or to punish a person.

Torture began as a legal procedure and was typically used to gain a confession for use as legal proof. Early Greek and Roman law permitted the torture of slaves, foreigners, and people considered dishonorable. In the A.D. 200's and 300's, torture in the Roman Empire spread to other classes of people and became more routine. Its use declined after the empire fell in the late 400's. But in the 1100's, certain Roman legal procedures, including torture, were revived in many parts of Europe. Civil and religious courts legally employed torture to obtain confessions until about 1800. At that time, torture was abolished and widely criticized on moral and legal grounds.

Torture slowly reappeared in the 1800's and 1900's. Military forces, police forces, and other groups with public authority began to use it illegally to punish and control people and to gain information about civil, military, and political matters. Since 1900, torture has especially increased during political revolutions, when leaders have placed political beliefs above human rights.

Forms of torture have long included stretching, burning, and beating the body and suffocating a person with water. Newer and more painful methods involve electricity, pain-causing drugs, or psychological techniques. Human-rights organizations firmly oppose the use of torture. Edward Peters

See also **Brainwashing.**

Tory Island lies 8 $\frac{2}{3}$ miles (14 kilometers) off the coast of County Donegal, Ireland. Interesting features include an ancient fort, the remains of a monastery founded by Saint Columba (also known as Saint Colmcille) in the 500's, and the ruins of a round tower. About 270 people live on the island.

Tory Party was a conservative political party in Britain. The term came from a Gaelic word meaning *pursued* or *pursued man,* and was used in the mid-1600's to mean an Irish outlaw. The word was first used in English politics in 1679 to refer to those who wanted James, Duke of York, to succeed to the throne.

Eventually, the Tory Party became one of the two chief political parties in Britain. The Tories favored maintaining the legal privileges of the Church of England and the powers of the king. Their chief opponents, the Whigs, were in favor of increasing the power of the people in the House of Commons. After 1832, the name *Conservative* began to replace the term *Tory.* During the Revolutionary War in America (1775-1783), those colonists who remained loyal to King George III were referred to as Tories. Today, supporters of Britain's Conservative Party are sometimes referred to as Tories. Chris Cook

See also **Conservative Party; Liberal Democrats.**

Toscanini, *TAHS kuh NEE nee,* **Arturo,** *ahr TOOR oh* (1867-1957), was one of the most influential symphony orchestra and opera conductors of his time. When he began his career, standards of musical performance were set by conductors and musicians of the romantic school. The romantics regarded music as a means for expressing their own emotions, ideas, and performance skills. But Toscanini regarded the performer as the servant of the composer. He insisted that an analytic study of the music should form the basis of a performance. In this way, the composer's intentions could best be understood and would dominate the performance. Toscanini's approach became widely accepted in the 1900's.

As a young conductor, Toscanini emphasized the music of Italian composers of his day. In later years, his performances stressed the established music of the 1700's and 1800's. Toscanini was especially respected as an interpreter of the works of the composers Ludwig van Beethoven and Giuseppe Verdi. He was noted for fast tempos and crisp accents. He could be temperamental on the podium and in rehearsals.

Toscanini was born in Parma, Italy. He attended the local music conservatory, where he studied cello and piano. Toscanini began his conducting career at the age of 19, when he took over a performance of Verdi's opera *Aida* with a traveling Italian opera company in Rio de Janeiro, Brazil. He conducted the premieres of *I Pagliacci* in 1892 and *La Bohème* in 1896. In 1898, he became artistic director of La Scala, Milan, the most important opera house in Italy.

Toscanini's American career began in 1908 when he became a conductor of the Metropolitan Opera. He left that position in 1915. From 1921 to 1929, he again was artistic director at La Scala. Toscanini's hatred of Italy's Fascist government led him to return to the United States. From 1929 to 1936, he was principal conductor of the New York Philharmonic Orchestra. From 1937 to 1954, Toscanini directed the National Broadcasting Company Symphony Orchestra, which NBC formed especially for him. He retired at the age of 87.

Martin Bernheimer

Totalitarianism, *toh TAL uh TAIR ee uh NIHZ uhm,* is a form of government in which the state has absolute control over almost every aspect of people's lives. The individual is considered a servant of the state and is allowed almost no freedom of choice or expression.

A totalitarian government is ruled by one political party headed by, in most cases, a dictator. The party sets certain economic and social goals for the state, and it outlaws any activity that could interfere with the achievement of these goals. Most totalitarian governments prohibit such groups as labor unions and trade associations. Religious practices are forbidden unless they promote the policies of the state.

Under a totalitarian system, the government uses terror tactics to suppress individuals or groups who oppose the state. These tactics are carried out by a secret police force and the armed services. The government also uses censorship to silence anyone who criticizes its policies. The media spread government propaganda, and the schools teach absolute loyalty to the state.

A totalitarian government controls the nation's economy through ownership or management of farmland and industry. Thus, it determines the type and quantity of crops and goods that are produced.

Various totalitarian governments have developed throughout history. In the 1920's and 1930's, however, technological advances in communication and detection systems aided the rise of extreme types of totalitarianism. Totalitarian governments of that period included those of Fascist Italy under Benito Mussolini, Nazi Germany under Adolf Hitler, and the Soviet Union under Joseph Stalin. Today, many governments have some totalitarian policies. These governments are especially common in developing nations that are working to build their economies. Michael Hurst

See also **Communism; Fascism; Government** (Totalitarianism).

Additional resources

Arendt, Hannah. *The Origins of Totalitarianism.* Rev. ed. Harvest Bks., 1973. A classic work.
Gleason, Abbott. *Totalitarianism.* Oxford, 1995.
Halberstam, Michael. *Totalitarianism and the Modern Conception of Politics.* Yale, 1999.

Totem, *TOH tuhm,* is a symbol for a tribe, clan, or family. The Chippewa, or Ojibwa, Indians first used the term for the animals or birds associated with their clans. The clan totem may be a bird, fish, animal, plant, or other natural object. Some groups consider the totem as an ancestor of the clan. A clan may have rules against killing or eating the species to which the totem belongs. Clan members are often known by the name of the clan's totem. Some clans consider the totem holy and pray to it. Totemism, as a form of religion, may have been widespread among American Indians and black Africans.

Many American Indian tribes, particularly those of the Pacific Northwest, carved the family and clan emblems on totem poles. The tribe held a *potlatch,* or feast, when the totem poles were put up.

Totem poles may be seen in Saxman and Ketchikan, Alaska; Vancouver and Victoria, British Columbia; Seattle; in the Field Museum in Chicago; and in the American Museum of Natural History in New York City.

Michael D. Green

See also **British Columbia** (pictures); **Alaska** (picture).

Additional resources

Halpin, Marjorie M. *Totem Poles.* Univ. of Br. Columbia Pr., 1981.
Jensen, Vickie. *Totem Pole Carving.* Douglas & McIntyre, 1999.
Malin, Edward. *Totem Poles of the Pacific Northwest Coast.* 1986. Reprint. Timber, 2002.

Toucan, *TOO kan* or *too KAHN,* is an unusual-looking bird with an enormous bill. In most species, the bill is brilliantly colored. Toucans live in the tropical and subtropical forests of Central and South America.

The bill of a toucan may be black, blue, brown, green, red, white, yellow, or a combination of colors. Toucans probably use their colorful bill to attract their mates. The toucan's huge bill looks heavy, but it actually weighs little because it contains a number of air pockets.

There are about 40 kinds of toucans. The largest species, the *toco toucan,* measures about 25 inches (64 centimeters) long. The smallest toucans, called *aracaris* and

Government of British Columbia

Totem poles, such as the ones pictured here, were wood carvings made by the Indians of the Northwest Coast.

toucanets, grow 13 to 14 inches (33 to 36 centimeters) long. Toucans have a bristly, narrow tongue that resembles a feather. They feed mainly on various small fruits. They sometimes use their bill, which has sawlike edges, to tear off pieces of larger fruits as well.

Most species of toucans live in small flocks that sleep in hollow trees. When toucans sleep, they turn their head around and place their bill down the center of their back. Then they fold their tail over their head.

Most kinds of toucans mate once a year. They build a nest in a hollow tree, and the female lays from two to four white eggs. The male and the female take turns sitting on the eggs. The eggs hatch after about 15 days, and the parents care for the young in the nest for about 8 weeks. James M. Dolan

Scientific classification. Toucans belong to the toucan family, Ramphastidae. The toco toucan is *Ramphastos toco.*

Touch is the sense that gives us notice of contact with an object. It also is called the *tactile sense.* We learn the shape and hardness of objects through this sense. Touching an object can give rise to feelings of warmth, cold, pain, and pressure. Free nerve endings in the tissue give the sense of pain. Touch, warmth, cold, and pain also are called *cutaneous senses.*

There are several kinds of touch organs, called *tactile corpuscles,* in the skin and the mucous membranes. One kind of touch organ is found near hairs, another kind in hairless areas, and still another kind in deeper tissues. The sensation occurs when an object comes in contact with the sense organs and presses them out of shape, or touches a nearby hair. Nerves from the organs then carry nerve impulses to the brain.

Touch is more sensitive in some parts of the body than in others. This difference is because the end organs for touch are not scattered evenly over the body, but are arranged in clusters. The feeling of pressure is keenest where there are the greatest number of end organs. It is most highly developed on the tip of the tongue, and is poorest on the back of the shoulders. The tips of the fingers and the end of the nose are other sensitive areas.

The end organs for warmth, cold, and pain also are distributed unevenly. This can be discovered by running a pointed metal instrument over the skin. The instrument is colder than the skin, but it feels cold only at some points. At other points, the instrument is felt simply as pressure. Daniel S. Barth

Related articles in *World Book* include:

Animal (Adaptations for sensing the environment)
Fish (Touch and the lateral line system)
Insect (Touch)
Mammal (Touch)
Pain
Senses
Spider (Nervous system)

Touch-me-not. See **Impatiens.**

Toulon, *too LAWN* (pop. 166,442; met. area pop. 519,640), is a seaport city on the southeast coast of France. For location, see **France** (political map). Excellent

Emerald toucanet
Aulacorhynchus prasinus
Found from Mexico to Peru
(Body length 14 inches, or 36 centimeters)

Toco toucan
Ramphastos toco
Found in Guianas and Brazil
(Body length 25 inches, or 64 centimeters)

Green aracari
Pteroglossus viridis
Found from Colombia through Brazil
(Body length 13 inches, or 33 centimeters)

WORLD BOOK illustrations by Albert Gilbert

docks along Toulon's coast can accommodate large ships. Toulon is the site of France's second largest naval base, after Brest. Toulon's landmarks include Ste. Marie-Majeure and other old churches; and the Poissonnerie (fish market), which dates from the 1500's. Toulon's main industries include shipbuilding, ship repair, and the production of chemicals and electric machinery.

Roman soldiers established a colony on the site of what is now Toulon in the 100's B.C. In 1942, during World War II, the French Navy destroyed many of its own ships in the Toulon harbor to prevent the ships from being captured by the Germans. Mark Kesselman

Toulouse, *too LOOZ* (pop. 398,423; met. area pop. 761,090), is a city in southwestern France. It is located along the Garonne River (see **France** [political map]). Toulouse has many medieval buildings, including the Romanesque Church of St. Sernin and the Gothic Cathedral of St. Étienne. The University of Toulouse, which was founded in 1229, is the second oldest in France, after the University of Paris. Toulouse is the site of the tomb of the medieval philosopher and theologian Saint Thomas Aquinas.

Toulouse is the center of the French aircraft construction industry. Other industries include electronics, printing, food processing, and the production of chemicals and textiles.

Roman soldiers established a settlement on the site of what is now Toulouse in the 100's B.C. During the Middle Ages, the city served as an artistic and literary center of Europe. Mark Kesselman

Toulouse-Lautrec, *too LOOZ loh TREHK,* **Henri de,** *ahn REE duh* (1864-1901), was a French artist. His favorite subjects were nightclubs, singers, and dancers of Montmartre, the night life district of Paris. Toulouse-Lautrec immortalized many such entertainers, such as Jane Avril, May Belfort, Chocolat, La Goulue, and Yvette Guilbert.

Toulouse-Lautrec was influenced in his style by the French painter Edgar Degas and by Japanese prints. This influence can be seen in the dynamic slant of space, the flat areas of color with no shadows or modeling, and the unusual way he cropped his scenes. These characteristics appear in *At the Moulin Rouge* (1892), which is reproduced on the following page. The painting portrays a crowd at a popular Montmartre dance hall.

Toulouse-Lautrec was a superb draftsman. He was also one of the early masters of the lithographic poster, helping to raise the poster from the level of commercial art to the status of fine art. *Aristide Bruant in His Cabaret* (1893), which is reproduced in the **Poster** article, features bold, flat, outlined forms. But the delicacy of line and hint of shadow in Bruant's profile make it stand out by its animation of expression.

Toulouse-Lautrec was born on Nov. 24, 1864, in Albi to an aristocratic family. In 1878 and 1879, he broke both legs in separate accidents. These injuries compounded a hereditary bone disease, and his legs never grew to their full length. In 1885, he began to exhibit and publish his work. Toulouse-Lautrec participated in several *avant-garde* (experimental) exhibitions, including the Salon des Indépendents in Paris and Les XX in Brussels, Belgium. He died of alcoholism and syphilis at the age of 36.

Ann Friedman

See also **Lithography** (picture); **Postimpressionism.**

Tour de France is a men's bicycle race that ranks among the most popular sporting events in the world. The race varies in length from year to year, but always runs more than 2,000 miles (3,200 kilometers), winding throughout France and sometimes neighboring countries. The Tour is held over a three-week period each year mainly in July, attracting 175 to 200 cyclists.

The Tour de France is one of the most physically demanding of all athletic competitions. It includes exhausting climbs through the Pyrenees and Alps mountains, as well as races on level terrain and time trials. The Tour takes cyclists through many villages and towns. Thousands of spectators line the roads to cheer the racers.

The Tour de France consists of about 20 individual races, called *stages,* that begin and end on the same day. A winner is declared for each daily stage. The champion is the cyclist with the lowest total time after all stages are completed. The overall race leader at the end of each stage puts on an honorary yellow jersey, which he wears during the competition for as long as he maintains the lead. The Tour ends in Paris.

Competitors race in teams, most of which are sponsored by large companies. Teams develop racing strategies that allow one cyclist to race for the championship while his teammates support him. The first Tour de France was held in 1903. Dave Nightingale

See also **Armstrong, Lance; LeMond, Greg.**

Touraco, *TUR uh KOH,* or *turaco,* is any member of a family of African birds that live south of the Sahara. These birds measure from 15 to 30 inches (38 to 76 centimeters) long. Many of them have bright green, red, and violet-blue feathers. Touracos are the only birds that produce a green *pigment* (coloring matter) in their feathers. The green color in other birds results from the reflection of sunlight by the feathers.

Scientists classify touracos into four groups. These groups are (1) crested touracos, (2) go-away birds, (3) great blue touracos, and (4) violet plantain-eaters. Most of the touracos live in pairs or small groups in thick

Anthony Mercieca, NAS

The red-crested touraco and many other forest species of touracos have brightly colored feathers and long tails.

At the Moulin Rouge (1892), an oil painting on canvas; The Art Institute of Chicago

Toulouse-Lautrec's works portray night life in the cafes and music halls of the Paris district called Montmartre. The artist became particularly noted for his skill in capturing the gaiety of the district.

forests, but go-away birds live in dry, open areas.

Touracos are weak fliers. They climb and run along tree branches somewhat as squirrels do. Touracos eat fruits and insects and nest chiefly in trees. The females lay two or three white or greenish eggs. James M. Dolan

Scientific classification. Touracos make up the touraco family, Musophagidae. The family has 4 genera and about 19 species.

Touré, *too RAY,* **Sékou,** *SAY koo* (1922-1984), became Guinea's first president in 1958 and held that position until his death. His government took nearly total control of Guinea's economy. Though Touré worked to build ties among African nations, he often acted with mistrust in his international relations. He remained in power by crushing his political opponents. Touré was born in Faranah on Jan. 9, 1922. He rose in politics as a trade union leader in French Guinea, then a French territory. He led French Guinea to independence in 1958. He died in Cleveland, Ohio, on March 26, 1984. Thomas O'Toole

Tourette syndrome, *tu REHT SIHN drohm,* is an inherited disorder characterized by involuntary utterances and body movements. It affects more men than women. It was named for Georges Gilles de la Tourette, a French doctor who described the symptoms in 1885.

The symptoms of Tourette syndrome begin before the age of 21, usually between 7 and 10 years of age. In most patients, the first symptom is an involuntary eye blink. Most patients soon develop other such *motor tics* (brief, repetitive, purposeless movements of muscles). These tics may include eyebrow raising, nose flaring, mouth opening, head shaking, teeth gnashing, finger cracking, jumping, stamping, or kicking. Some patients also begin to make uncontrollable sounds, called *vocal tics.* These include grunting, barking, belching, speaking unintelligibly, and occasionally *coprolalia.* Coprolalia is the involuntary utterance of vulgar words.

In Tourette syndrome, tics occur multiple times each day and the location of a particular motor tic may vary considerably over time. For example, eye-blinking tics may disappear and shoulder-shrugging tics may appear. Not all children with motor or vocal tics have Tourette syndrome. Before a doctor can make a final diagnosis, the symptoms must be present for at least one year.

Some Tourette syndrome patients have short attentions spans and may also be hyperactive. Although the disorder is not psychological, some patients develop emotional problems trying to deal with it.

Researchers suspect that Tourette syndrome results from an abnormality in the *neurotransmitters,* the chemicals that carry signals between nerve cells. There is no cure, but certain drugs can help control the symptoms. Early diagnosis and treatment can help prevent the development of emotional problems. William J. Weiner

Tourmaline, *TUR muh lihn* or *TUR muh leen,* is any of a group of boron-containing minerals often found in granite. Tourmalines are used as gemstones and for industrial purposes.

Tourmalines have complex chemical compositions. All tourmalines contain boron, silicon, oxygen, and hydrogen. Varieties of tourmaline contain differing amounts of aluminum, calcium, fluorine, iron, magnesium, lithium, and sodium. Tourmalines form long, thin crystals with three, six, or nine sides.

Tourmalines vary greatly in color. The most common tourmalines include *elbaite, dravite,* and *schorl.* Elbaite, which is rich in lithium, can appear pink, blue, green, or yellow. Dravite, a magnesium-rich tourmaline, usually appears brownish. Schorl, rich in iron and manganese, is usually black. The color of some tourmaline crystals varies from the center to the edges. Watermelon tourmaline, for example, appears pink in the center and green at the edges. These changes indicate a change in conditions as the crystal formed.

Tourmaline makes up a minor part of granite and other *igneous* (volcanic) rocks. It also forms scattered grains in metamorphic rock formations. Traces of tourmaline are found in many sandstones. Large tourmalines often develop from boron-rich liquid left over when *magma* (melted rock) cools and begins to harden. Such cooling results in coarse-grained rocks called *pegmatites* that commonly contain clusters of large, radiating tourmaline crystals. Brazil is the world's leading producer of tourmaline.

Tourmaline is *piezoelectric*—that is, its crystals can develop an electric charge when stretched or squeezed. Tourmaline has been used in radio transmitters and pressure sensors. Scientists use slices of tourmaline in the study of *polarized light* (light that vibrates in a single direction). Jewelers commonly cut transparent and flawless tourmaline crystals into gems. Mark Cloos

See also **Gem** (picture); **Polarized light.**

Tourniquet, *TUR nuh keht,* is a tight, twisted cloth wrapped around a limb to control bleeding. The pressure of the tourniquet slows blood supply to the injured area and thus diminishes blood loss. People formerly applied tourniquets as a first aid procedure. But in many cases, improper use of the tourniquet impaired blood circulation in the injured limb and caused *gangrene* (tissue death). Many people have had limbs amputated and have even died because of improperly applied tourniquets. Thus, only doctors and specially trained paramedics should use tourniquets.

Because of the risks associated with them, tourniquets are rarely used today. Instead, medical personnel use special inflated airbags to slow bleeding in emergency situations. The airbags compress the injured limb without impairing blood circulation. David R. Boyd

Tours, *toor* (pop. 137,046. met. area pop. 297,631), is a historic city and important economic center in western France. It lies in the scenic Loire Valley, along the Loire and Cher rivers (see **France** [political map]).

The area around Tours has many old castles. The city's landmarks include the ruins of the Old Basilica of Saint Martin, completed about 470; and the Cathedral of Saint Gatien, which dates from the 1200's. Tours is the capital of the *department* (administrative district) of Indre-et-Loire. The city's industries include banking, insurance, and the production of automobile tires, electric equipment, farm machinery, machine tools, medicines, textiles, and wine.

Roman soldiers founded the town of Caesarodunum on the site of what is now Tours in the 50's B.C. In A.D. 732, the Christian Franks, a European people, defeated invading Muslim armies in a great battle that began near Tours and ended near Poitiers. In World War II (1939-1945), German bombers heavily damaged parts of Tours. These areas were soon rebuilt. Mark Kesselman

Toussaint L'Ouverture, *too SAN loo vair TOOR* (1743-1803), became one of the best-known black revolutionaries of all time. He played a major role in ending slavery in the French colony of Saint Domingue (now Haiti) and in leading a revolution in which Haiti gained its independence from France. Toussaint also served as a general in the French army and as the colonial ruler of Saint Domingue.

Consulate of Haiti

Toussaint L'Ouverture

Toussaint was born into slavery near what is now Cap-Haïtien, Haiti. His full name at birth was François Dominique Toussaint. He later became known as Toussaint L'Ouverture. Toussaint taught himself to read and write and became well educated, even though he was a slave until he was almost 50 years old.

In 1791, a slave revolt erupted in Saint Domingue, and Toussaint became one of its leaders. He led a black army against the French, helping to force France to abolish slavery in the colony in 1793. He then helped France by defeating British and Spanish troops that had invaded Saint Domingue. By April 1796, he ruled the colony with the consent of its French governor.

Saint Domingue prospered under Toussaint. But Napoleon I, France's ruler, wanted to regain full control of the colony. In 1802, he sent a large army to reestablish slavery in Saint Domingue. Toussaint and others resisted and began a revolution to free the colony from French control. Later that year, Toussaint was captured. He was imprisoned in France, where he died in 1803. Jean Jacques Dessalines succeeded Toussaint as leader of the revolution. He declared Saint Domingue the independent country of Haiti in 1804. Patrick Bellegarde-Smith

See also **Dominican Republic** (History).

Additional resources

Myers, Walter D. *Toussaint L'Ouverture.* Simon & Schuster, 1996. Younger readers.

Ros, Martin. *Night of Fire: The Black Napoleon and the Battle for Haiti.* Rev. ed. Perseus Pr., 2001.

Towboat. See **Tugboat.**

Tower is an architectural structure whose height is much greater than its width or its thickness. Towers are generally taller than their surrounding structures. They may stand alone or be attached to walls or buildings. The first towers were for military or religious purposes, but over the centuries towers have assumed other uses.

Towers were rare in ancient times. One of the most famous early towers was the Lighthouse of Alexandria, Egypt, built during the reign of Ptolemy II (283–246 B.C.). During the Middle Ages in Europe, people erected masonry towers along the walls of castles and cities for military defense. The Tower of London is a prominent example of this type of structure. In the late Middle Ages, many European cities built tall slender bell towers on their city halls. They also served as watchtowers.

Towers are important in religious architecture. People who worshiped the sun and stars built towers so that their priests could be closer to the heavens. Buddhists build towers called *pagodas.* A crier calls Muslims to prayer from a tower called a *minaret.* In the 500's, Christians began to build free-standing bell towers beside their churches. These are called *campaniles,* from the Italian word for *bell.* After about 1000, Christians built towers attached to the church itself.

Today, many skyscrapers are called towers. Towns use water towers to create pressure needed to pipe water to homes and businesses. Broadcasting towers support radio or TV antennas. The world's tallest self-supporting structure, the CN (Canadian National) Tower in Toronto, Ontario, is a 1,815-foot (553-meter) broadcasting tower completed in 1976. William J. Hennessey

Related articles in *World Book.* See pictures with the **Architecture** article. See also:

Campanile
Eiffel Tower
Leaning Tower of Pisa
Lighthouse
Minaret
Pagoda
Seven Wonders of the Ancient World (The Lighthouse of Alexandria)
Skyscraper
Tower of Babel
Tower of London

Tower of Babel, *BAY buhl* or *BAB uhl,* was a tower in Babylon, a city in ancient Mesopotamia. It was shaped like a pyramid with terraces—a design known as a *ziggurat.* The tower had seven stories plus a small shrine on top. The Babylonians called the tower *Etemenanki,* which meant *the house of the foundation of heaven and earth. Babel* is the Hebrew name for *Babylon. Babylon* meant *gate of the god* in the Babylonian language.

Scholars know little about the tower. But a story of its construction is told in the Bible, in Genesis 11:1-9. According to the Bible, Noah's descendants settled in southern Mesopotamia after the great Flood. They started to build a great city, including a tower that would reach to heaven. But God did not want the city completed, so He made the builders speak different languages. The builders then could not understand one another, and so they stopped working and scattered over the earth. The ancient Hebrews used this account to explain the origin of languages. John A. Brinkman

See also **Babylon.**

Bettmann Archive

The Tower of Babel was a terraced pyramid, called a *ziggurat,* in the ancient city of Babylon. The Flemish artist Pieter Bruegel the Elder painted this rendition of the tower in 1563.

Tower of London is a group of stone buildings in the East End of London, on the north bank of the River Thames. It has served as a fortress, a prison, and a palace. The oldest of the buildings, a central tower called the White Tower, was built by William I, the Conqueror, and dates from the late 1000's.

The buildings of the Tower of London have great thick walls. A shallow moat and two additional stone walls surround the group of buildings. The Tower of London is so strong that in former days it could have held off a whole army. The British Department of the Environment now uses the buildings chiefly as a showplace and museum. The museum's armor collection was started by Henry VIII in the 1500's.

Many famous people were imprisoned in the damp, dark cells of the Tower of London. The young Edward V and his brother, the Duke of York, were put in the Tower of London when their uncle, Richard III, became king in 1483. The boys were never seen again. In the 1550's, Lady Jane Grey was beheaded in the Tower, following an attempt to make her queen.

The Tower of London also holds the crowns, scepters, and other royal treasures of the English rulers, known as the *regalia.* The tower is guarded by members of the Guards Division and staffed by colorfully outfitted *yeoman warders* (see **Yeoman**). John Gillingham

See also **London** (picture).

Towhee, *TOH hee* or *TOW hee,* is any of several small North American birds related to the sparrows. The *eastern towhee,* the most widespread species, lives from southern Canada to Mexico. This bird is about 8 inches (20 centimeters) long. Its sides are a chestnut color. Its belly is white. The head and back are black in males and brown in females. Eastern towhees that live in western North America have white bars on their wings and white spots on their back.

The eastern towhee makes its home in open woods and bushy fields. It usually builds its nest on the ground, using dead leaves and twigs. There, the female lays two to six whitish eggs with brown speckles. The birds scratch among leaves and grass, searching for insects, spiders, earthworms, berries, and seeds.

Three other species of towhees—*Abert's towhee,* the *brown towhee,* and the *green-tailed towhee*—are found in the Western United States. All these species resemble

WORLD BOOK illustration by Trevor Boyer, Linden Artists Ltd.

The eastern towhee lives mainly on the ground.

the eastern towhee. Sandra L. Vehrencamp

Scientific classification. Towhees belong to the finch family, Fringillidae. The eastern towhee is *Pipilo erythrophthalmus.*

Town is a community of closely clustered dwellings and other buildings in which people live and work. It may be large or small. Most people in the United States and Canada use the word *town* to refer to a municipal unit that is larger than a village and smaller than a city. In New England, the town is the principal unit of local government, combining the roles of both city and county. This unit consists of one or more settlements and the surrounding rural area. Susan H. Ambler

Related articles in *World Book* include:

Boom town	Local government	Township
Borough	Town meeting	Village

Town crier was a person appointed to make public announcements. The town crier was important in Europe, particularly in England, before newspapers were common and was the "walking newspaper" of the American Colonies during the 1600's. The crier sang out the latest news at every corner, and announced the time of town meetings and other events of public interest. The town crier largely disappeared when the printing press, newspaper, and other forms of communication came into general use after the 1750's. Some British communities still have a town crier. Kathryn Kish Sklar

Town meeting is an assembly held once a year in which the adults of a community decide on local issues. In this meeting, the voters elect officials, listen to reports from committees and leaders, pass laws, and vote on the next year's budget. A town meeting is considered one of the purest forms of democracy because the people of the town vote directly on community issues.

Town meetings started in the New England colonies, and many small New England towns still use them. Outside New England, the smallest unit of local government is a division of a county called a *township.* Rural township meetings resemble town meetings.

The term *town meeting* is also applied to other forms of political discussion. Some communities hold such meetings to gather interested people to discuss local issues or hear reports from their legislators. Politicians may hold in-person, televised, or electronic "town meetings" as part of their election campaigns and to learn what voters think about various issues. Robert Agranoff

See also **Township; Vermont** (picture: A town meeting).

Town planning. See **City planning.**

Townsend, *TOWN zuhnd,* **Willard Saxby** (1895-1957), was one of the first black American labor leaders. He improved the wages and working conditions of *redcaps* (railroad baggage porters). He helped redcaps gain a fixed salary, plus retirement and insurance benefits.

Townsend was born on Dec. 4, 1895, in Cincinnati, Ohio, and began working as a redcap there when he was 19 years old. In 1936, he was elected the first president of the Auxiliary of Redcaps, a union that belonged to the American Federation of Labor (AFL). In 1937, he became the first president of an independent union, the International Brotherhood of Redcaps. It became the United Transport Service Employees in 1940 and joined the Congress of Industrial Organizations (CIO) in 1942. Also in 1942, he became the first black member of the CIO executive board. When the AFL and CIO merged in 1955, he was named a vice president of the AFL-CIO.

Townsend was a vice president of the Urban League and an officer of the National Association for the Advancement of Colored People (NAACP). He was coauthor of *What the Negro Wants* (1944). James G. Scoville

Townsend Plan, *TOWN zuhnd,* is an old-age pension plan proposed in 1934 by Francis E. Townsend of Long Beach, California. It provided that all United States citizens over 60 years of age be paid $200 a month. The widespread popularity of the Townsend Plan helped persuade Congress to pass the Social Security Act of 1935. But that act provided retirement benefits for certain workers at age 65, and the pensions were much smaller than those proposed in the Townsend Plan. The funds for the Townsend Plan were to come from a 2 percent tax on the transfer or sale of goods. However, many experts believed that such a tax would not provide nearly enough money to finance the plan. Supporters of the Townsend Plan believed that the plan would stabilize American prosperity, because those receiving pensions would be obligated to spend the money within a month. A modified version of the Townsend Plan was presented to the U.S. House of Representatives on June 1, 1939, but it was voted down. David E. Kyvig

Townshend, *TOWN zehnd,* **Peter** (1945-), an English musician, was the founding guitarist and principal composer for The Who. The Who, an important English rock group, formed in 1964 in London and disbanded in 1982, though the group has reunited occasionally for live performances. Townshend recorded 13 albums with The Who. Both with the group and on his own, he has specialized in rock operas and in *concept albums,* recordings in which all the songs are related. Townshend composed the rock operas *Tommy* (1969) and *Quadrophenia* (1973). His solo concept albums include *White City—A Novel* (1985) and *The Iron Man* and *PsychoDerelict* (both 1993). His best-known songs include "My Generation" (1965), "Pinball Wizard" (1969), and "Let My Love Open the Door" (1980).

Peter Dennis Blandford Townshend was born on May 19, 1945, in London. He wrote *Horse's Neck* (1985), a collection of stories. Townshend was the musical director for the motion-picture version of *Tommy* (1975) and the stage production on Broadway (1993). Don McLeese

See also **Who, The.**

Townshend, *TOWN zuhnd,* **Viscount** (1674-1738), was a British politician and promoter of agricultural reform. In 1730, he retired from a successful political career to his estate in Norfolk, where he experimented with cultivation. Townshend supported a crop-rotation system that used four different crops. His system made farms more productive because fields did not lie fallow (see **Agriculture** [Improved crop-growing methods]). His belief in planting turnips to improve the soil earned him the nickname "Turnip" Townshend. Townshend also urged farmers to use turnips as winter livestock feed, enabling them to raise cattle the year around.

Townshend was born on April 18, 1674, in Norfolk. His given name was Charles Townshend. He became the second Viscount Townshend in 1687. His grandson, also named Charles Townshend, became Britain's chancellor of the exchequer in 1766. R. Douglas Hurt

Townshend Acts. See **Revolutionary War in America** (The Townshend Acts).

Township in the United States is a division of a county that functions as a unit of local government. In most cases it is rural, but it may include cities or towns. Not all states have townships. A township's governing body is usually a board of commissioners, supervisors, or trustees. It can pass ordinances and resolutions that have the force of law. A township's chief duty is construction and maintenance of roads. Today, states are eliminating townships, especially rural ones, and giving their duties to counties. See also **Local government; Town.**

Susan H. Ambler

Toxemia of pregnancy. See **Preeclampsia.**

Toxic shock syndrome, *SIHN drohm,* or *TSS,* is a rare disease that most frequently occurs in young women who are having a menstrual period. It can, however, strike men and women of any age. Symptoms include a high temperature, vomiting, diarrhea, low blood pressure, and a sunburnlike rash.

TSS is caused by a bacterium called *Staphylococcus aureus,* which can produce infection anywhere on or inside the body. Scientists do not understand exactly how these infections cause TSS. They suspect the bacteria release a *toxin* (poison) that spreads through the body, probably by way of the bloodstream, and causes TSS.

Fewer than one-thousandth of 1 percent of all menstruating women are likely to develop TSS each year. Most victims are teen-agers and women in their 20's and 30's who use a *tampon*—a roll of absorbent material inserted into the vagina—during the menstrual period. Physicians do not know why women who wear tampons run a greater risk of developing TSS than those who wear sanitary napkins. Public health doctors have not advised women to stop using tampons, but they do recommend that tampon-users recognize the symptoms of TSS. A woman who develops symptoms should remove the tampon and call a doctor immediately.

Physicians treat TSS with antibiotics and with fluids given through a vein. A female patient not treated with antibiotics may become ill again during her next menstrual period. Most patients recover and have no further problems. But some lose their hair, fingernails, or toenails about three months after developing TSS. About 5 percent of TSS cases are fatal.

Anne Schuchat and Kathryn N. Shands

Toxic wastes. See **Hazardous wastes.**

Toxin, *TAHK suhn,* is a poison produced by a living organism. Toxins may cause many life-threatening diseases and even death. Some toxins remain inside the organism that produces them. They are called *endotoxins.* They cause poisoning only when the organism is broken up and the poison escapes. Other toxins, called *exotoxins* or *ectotoxins,* are secreted into the substance surrounding the organism.

Bacteria that infect the human body may produce toxins that cause diphtheria, tetanus, and scarlet fever. Some bacteria and fungi secrete toxins into the foods in which they grow. Such serious diseases as botulism and ergotism may result if such food is eaten. Some tropical fish produce toxins that can cause illness or death to a person who eats the fish. The venoms of poisonous snakes, spiders, and insects are toxins. Doctors use *antitoxins* to fight toxins (see **Antitoxin**). Frank Welsch

See also **Serum; Disease** (Bacterial diseases).

Toxoplasmosis, *TAHK suh plaz MOH sihs* or *tahk soh plaz MOH sihs,* is a common disease characterized by enlargement of lymph nodes, usually in the neck region. Other symptoms may include fever and fatigue. In rare cases, toxoplasmosis can severely infect the internal organs. It can be fatal if left untreated.

Toxoplasmosis is caused by a *protozoan* (single-celled organism) often found in cats. The scientific name for this protozoan is *Toxoplasma gondii.* People become infected with *T. gondii* by eating food contaminated by cat *feces* (solid body waste) or by eating the uncooked meat of infected animals, such as pigs and sheep.

Symptoms of the disease can last several weeks or months. However, *T. gondii* stays in the body in a dormant state. Usually, it remains dormant for the person's entire life. But if the person's immune system is weakened by cancer or by AIDS or other infections, *T. gondii* may become reactivated. The reactivation infection most commonly occurs in the brain and can be life-threatening. Such cases are treated with an antimalaria drug in combination with sulfa drugs.

If a woman becomes infected with *T. gondii* during her first three months of pregnancy, the infection can spread to her *fetus* (unborn baby). Such infection can cause birth defects or the death of the fetus. It also can cause an eye infection that may lead to blindness later in life. John C. Pottage, Jr.

Toy is an object children can use as a plaything. Children throughout the world play with similar toys, such as balls, dolls, games, and puzzles. Since ancient times, toys have played an important role in children's lives. Some toys enable children to have fun while learning about the world around them. Games can help teach children to get along with others. Toys may also help them learn and develop special skills.

Manufacturers make thousands of different toys. A child plays with toys of increasing sophistication at each stage of his or her development. Toys can be divided into three main groups: (1) toys for infants, (2) toys for early childhood, and (3) toys for late childhood.

Toys for infants. An infant's first toys are often soft musical toys and *mobiles* (colorful, moving structures hung above a crib). These toys begin to stimulate vision and hearing. Later, when babies can hold or grasp toys on their own, they play with rattles, plastic blocks, and stuffed animals. Unbreakable mirrors help infants recognize themselves. As they begin to walk, youngsters like to play with push toys that help them balance. They also push themselves along with their feet on automobiles and other wheeled riding toys. Infants are mentally stimulated by simple puzzles and picture books.

Toys for early childhood. After children learn to walk and run, they become more interested in exploring the world around them. In these years, from ages 2 to 6, children need more physical play to develop the muscles in their arms and legs. Play with large building blocks and wagons helps strengthen these muscles.

Children use their imagination when they play with small, plastic people or farms. Other toys help children develop mentally by encouraging them to count, speak, read, tell time, and work at a table or desk. These toys include plastic letters and numbers, toy telephones, picture storybooks, and pegboards. Puzzles challenge children to take things apart and put them back together. At this time, children often learn about emotions and caring through play with special dolls or stuffed animals.

Toys for late childhood. In late childhood, from ages 6 to 12, toys become part of more elaborate imaginative play. In doll play, children pretend that they are parents and use strollers, doll beds, and feeding equipment. Children also enjoy playing with action figures, such as robots, soldiers, and space aliens. In these years, children may learn to use clay, paints, and pastels as their artistic ability grows. Board and computer games help develop a child's mind. In many of these games, children must plan their own strategies and also guess what their opponents will do.

Near the end of childhood, boys and girls enjoy building model cars and ships and working with hobby kits. Kits, such as woodburning or embroidery, help develop discipline and patience. Children who like science may spend hours with chemistry sets or microscopes. These activities may persist as adult hobbies.

History. Children have played with toys for thousands of years. In ancient Africa, children enjoyed balls, toy animals, and pull toys. Children of ancient Greece and Rome had fun with boats, carts, hoops, and tops. During the Middle Ages in Europe, popular toys included clay marbles, rattles, and puppets.

Before the development of large toy factories, parents or craftworkers made toys. By the 1800's, most children in the United States played with homemade toys or imported toys from Europe. Toy manufacturing became an important U.S. industry in the early 1900's.

In 1969, Congress passed the Child Protection and Toy Safety Act, which enabled the government to recall or prohibit the sale of toys that were shown to be harmful. Such toys may contain poisonous substances, catch fire easily, have loose parts a child can swallow, or have unprotected points or sharp edges.

Doris McNeely Johnson

Related articles in ***World Book.*** See **Game** and its list of Related articles. See also:

Airplane, Model	Hobby	Rocket, Model
Automobile, Model	Kaleidoscope	Ship, Model
Doll	Kite	Skateboarding
Dollhouse	Play	Top
Frisbee	Puppet	Yo-yo
	Railroad, Model	

Additional resources

McClary, Andrew. *Toys with Nine Lives: A Social History of American Toys.* Linnet, 1997. Younger readers.

Pesce, Mark. *The Playful World: How Technology Is Transforming Our Imagination.* Ballantine, 2000.

Wulffson, Don L. *Toys! Amazing Stories Behind Some Great Inventions.* Henry Holt, 2000. Younger readers.

Toy dog is the name of a group of small dogs. Many are relatives of larger dogs. For example, the toy poodle is a tiny poodle. Other toys, such as the Chihuahua, are separate breeds. The recognized toy breeds include the affenpinscher, Brussels griffon, Chihuahua, Chinese crested, English toy spaniel, Italian greyhound, Japanese chin, Maltese, miniature pinscher, papillon, Pekingese, Pomeranian, pug, shih tzu, silky terrier, and Yorkshire terrier. *World Book* has articles on each of the breeds listed here. See also **Dog** (pictures: Toy dogs).

Critically reviewed by the American Kennel Club

Toy fox terrier is a small breed of dog developed in the United States. It grows 8 $\frac{1}{2}$ to 11 $\frac{1}{2}$ inches (21.6 to 29.2 centimeters) high and weighs 4 to 8 pounds (1.8 to 3.6 kilograms). The dog has a muscular body and a smooth, shiny white coat with black, chocolate, or tan markings. Its head is mostly black, chocolate, or tan in color. The head has large, erect, triangular ears and a moderately long muzzle. The short tail also stays erect.

During the early 1900's, breeders in the United States developed this dog by crossing smooth fox terriers with other breeds, including chihuahuas, toy Manchester terriers, and miniature pinschers. Toy fox terriers have loyal, intelligent personalities and can make excellent pets.

Critically reviewed by the American Toy Fox Terrier Club

See also **Dog** (picture: Toy fox terrier).

Toynbee, Arnold (1852-1883), a British social reformer and economist, worked to help the poor. He supported free education, the free operation of trade unions, and the regulation of working conditions in Britain. Toynbee thought religious groups should work for social progress. He taught that imitation of Jesus's service to humanity was true Christianity. His best-known book was *The Industrial Revolution* (1884).

Toynbee was born Aug. 23, 1852, in London. He was educated at the University of Oxford and later taught economics there. He lived in a shabby dwelling in Whitechapel, a London slum district, and his hard work to improve social conditions ruined his health. Shortly after his death, Toynbee Hall, the world's first settlement house, was set up in Whitechapel to help the poor. Toynbee was the uncle of Arnold Joseph Toynbee, a noted historian. Joseph Martin Hernon, Jr.

Toynbee, Arnold Joseph (1889-1975), was a famous British historian. His outline of civilizations, *A Study of History,* was published in 12 volumes from 1934 to 1961. Toynbee divided world history into 26 civilizations and traced their rise, decline, and fall. He explained that the rise and fall of these civilizations resulted from repeating "patterns" in which similar "challenges" were met with similar "responses." See **Civilization** (Why civilizations rise and fall).

Toynbee's original and bold approach to world history had a wide appeal. A two-volume abridgment of his great work sold widely in the United States and Europe. His writings include a number of volumes dealing with social-historical problems, such as *Nationality and the War* (1915), *Civilization on Trial* (1948), and *The World and the West* (1953).

Toynbee was born in London on April 14, 1889. He studied at Oxford University and at the British Archaeological School at Athens, Greece. He became a professor of international history at the University of London in 1925. His uncle Arnold Toynbee was a well-known social reformer and economist. Joseph Martin Hernon, Jr.

Toyota Motor Corporation is the largest automobile manufacturer in Japan and one of the largest automakers in the world. It produces passenger cars, buses, sport utility vehicles, trucks, vans, and automobile parts. In addition, Toyota owns companies that manufacture such products as rubber, steel, and textiles. Toyota also manages real estate and import and export firms.

Toyota has automobile plants in about 25 countries. Well-known Toyota models include the Camry, Celica, Corolla, 4Runner, and Tundra. Toyota also produces a line of luxury automobiles and sport utility vehicles under the trade name Lexus.

Toyota was founded in 1933, when Toyoda Automatic

Loom Works, Ltd. set up a department to make automobiles. During the 1960's, Toyota became Japan's largest automobile manufacturer after it acquired several rival manufacturing firms. Toyota's headquarters are in Toyota City, Japan. For the sales, assets, and number of employees of Toyota, see **Manufacturing** (table: World's leading manufacturers).

Critically reviewed by Toyota Motor Manufacturing North America

Trace elements are minerals needed in small amounts by plants, animals, and human beings. Such major elements as calcium, carbon, chlorine, hydrogen, magnesium, nitrogen, oxygen, phosphorus, potassium, sodium, and sulfur are part of the makeup of all living things. The trace elements are also necessary to life. Scientists know the uses of only a few of the trace elements. But scientists do know that they are necessary for the work of such vital bodily compounds as enzymes and hormones (see **Enzyme; Hormone**).

The trace elements include chromium, copper, fluorine, iodine, iron, manganese, molybdenum, selenium, and zinc. The body needs copper so it can use iron to build hemoglobin, an important part of red blood cells. Iodine is needed to form the hormone *thyroxine.* A lack of iodine in the diet results in *goiter,* a disease characterized by excessive growth of the thyroid gland. Manganese and zinc are required for the normal action of certain enzymes. Without these two minerals, certain reactions in the body cells would stop. Human beings and all animals need the same trace elements, but plants have different requirements. For example, plants do not need iodine or fluorine. Human beings get the required trace elements from their food in a balanced diet.

Mary Frances Picciano

See also **Nutrition** (Minerals).

Tracery, in architecture, originally was the framework of light ornamental stone bars dividing a large window into smaller areas so that the stained glass could be easily placed and supported. Usually tracery took the form of tall, narrow, arched divisions below, with circles, cusps, and other shapes filling the upper part of the window. Later, these shapes were used to decorate wall panels, buttresses, vaulting, and furniture.

Stone tracery in King's College Chapel (completed in the early 1500's); Cambridge, England (Ronald Sheridan Photo Library)

Tracery is the ornamental stone or wooden patternwork that decorates windows and ceilings in medieval Gothic buildings.

Builders first used tracery in the late 1100's, when church windows grew too large to be glazed in one unbroken area. Tracery developed rapidly in delicacy and became a marked feature of nearly all Gothic architecture.

The earliest tracery was known as *plate* tracery, because the upper circles were pierced through a plate of stone in the upper part of the main window arch. *Geometric* tracery, a complete pattern of thin stone bars, later replaced this pierced "plate." In it, all the openings between the bars are simple geometric forms. Still later, *flowing* and *flamboyant* tracery was used, so called because of its flowing and swaying flamelike shapes. During the late 1300's and the 1400's in England, *perpendicular* tracery was the rule. In it, the vertical bars between the lower openings are carried up the whole height of the window, making small vertical panels.

William J. Hennessey

Trachea, *TRAY kee uh,* also called *windpipe,* is the tube that carries air between the lungs and the upper respiratory passages. A human trachea is about 5 inches (13 centimeters) long and just less than 1 inch (2.5 centimeters) in diameter. About half of its length is inside the chest and the rest is in the neck. The trachea is held open by 16 to 20 incomplete rings of cartilage. These C-shaped cartilages form the hard ridges in the neck just below the *Adam's apple.*

The lower end of the trachea divides into two *bronchi* (tubes) that carry air into the lungs. At the top of the trachea is the Adam's apple. This bump in the neck is formed by the *larynx* (voice box). Air that passes over the vocal cords in the larynx causes them to vibrate and to produce the sound used to speak.

Air is breathed into the larynx and trachea through the *pharynx,* the space at the back of the throat where the passages of the nose and mouth meet. The *epiglottis,* a leaf-shaped structure in the pharynx, closes the opening into the larynx during swallowing to prevent food from entering the larynx and trachea. Robert A. Klocke

See the Trans-Vision three-dimensional picture with **Human body.** See also **Larynx; Lung; Pharynx; Throat.**

Trachoma, *truh KOH muh,* is a contagious eye disease caused by a form of *Chlamydia trachomatis* bacteria. Trachoma is relatively rare in the United States because of treatment with antibiotics or sulfonamides. But in Egypt, India, Saudi Arabia, and other developing countries in warm parts of the world, trachoma is still a major cause of blindness. It affects the *conjunctiva* (membrane of the eyeball and lids) and *cornea,* the window of the eye (see **Eye** [Parts of the eye]). Symptoms of conjunctivitis develop and the disease may last for years (see **Conjunctivitis**).

Doctors must report cases of trachoma because the disease spreads easily. People in contagious areas should not use public towels, or rub their eyes with unwashed hands. The disease also is thought to be spread by flies. Severe cases of trachoma may require an operation to repair deformed eyelids or to replace damaged corneal tissue. Ramesh C. Tripathi and Brenda Tripathi

Focus on Sports

A hurdle race is a track event in which competitors run over fencelike obstacles called *hurdles.* The women shown here are competing in an indoor high-hurdle race.

© Steven E. Sutton, Duomo

The steeplechase includes hurdles and water jumps. At a water jump, runners step on the hurdle and then leap into the shallow end of the water pit to soften the landing.

Track and field

Track and field is a sport in which athletes compete in running, walking, jumping, and throwing events. *Track events* consist of running and walking races of various distances. *Field events* are contests in jumping or throwing. Track and field meets can be held indoors or outdoors. Men and women compete separately in a meet. In countries other than the United States, track and field is often called the sport of *athletics.*

Track and field is one of the most popular sports in the world. More than 200 nations belong to the International Amateur Athletic Federation (IAAF), the governing body of track and field. The IAAF recognizes world records in 71 men's and women's events. The organization accepts world records in metric distances only, except for the mile run. The table in this article lists the major men's and women's records.

The track and the field

The track. Outdoor running tracks are oval in shape and usually are laid out in a stadium. IAAF rules specify that an outdoor running track should measure no less than 400 meters around—and most modern outdoor tracks are exactly that length. (One meter equals about $3\frac{1}{4}$ feet.) Older tracks consist of dirt or cinders, but most new tracks are made of a waterproof synthetic material and can be used in rainy weather.

Indoor tracks have a wooden or synthetic surface, and they often have banked turns. According to IAAF rules, the preferred measurement for an indoor track is 200 meters.

Outdoor tracks are divided into eight or nine lanes. Runners must stay in their lanes for all races up to 400 meters and until they pass the first curve of 800-meter races. IAAF rules state that a lane should measure from 1.22 to 1.25 meters (48 to 49 inches) in width.

The field. Most field events take place in an area enclosed by the track. But in some meets, one or more throwing events are held outside the stadium to protect other athletes and spectators who crowd the field area or to avoid damaging the artificial turf that covers many athletic fields. The field includes runways for the jumping events. It also has circular areas of material such as concrete or asphalt for most of the throwing events.

Track events

Track events include a variety of races. Short races, called *sprints,* stress maximum speed, while distance races require more endurance. In such races as the hurdles and steeplechase, runners must go over barriers. Other races, called *relays,* involve teams of runners.

Running races on an outdoor track cover distances from 100 meters to 10,000 meters. Indoors, races may measure from 50 meters to 5,000 meters. *Cross-country races* and *road races* are run outside the stadium. Cross-country competitors run over terrain such as hills and fields. Most U.S. and Canadian schools and colleges compete in cross-country races in the fall. Most road races are open to all runners, and many races award prize money to the winners. The most common distance for road races is 10 kilometers.

Hurdle races are events in which the competitors run over obstacles called *hurdles.* Most of these races have 10 hurdles spaced at equal intervals. There are two types of hurdle races, intermediate and high. Intermediate hurdles are 36 inches (91 centimeters) high for men and 30 inches (76 centimeters) high for women. Men's high hurdles are 42 inches (107 centimeters) high. Women's high hurdles are 33 inches (84 centimeters) high. Intermediate-hurdle races cover 400 meters or 440 yards in men's and women's competition. Most outdoor high-hurdle races are 110 meters or 120 yards for men and 100 meters for women. Runners can knock over hurdles without penalty, but contact with a hurdle normally slows down the runner.

The steeplechase is a race, usually of 3,000 meters, over two kinds of obstacles, hurdles and *water jumps.* Runners must clear 36-inch (91-centimeter) hurdles 28 times. These hurdles are sturdier than the ones used in hurdle races, and runners may put a foot on top of them as they pass over them. Runners must cross water jumps seven times. A water jump consists of a hurdle and a water-filled pit 12 feet (3.66 meters) square. The steeplechaser steps onto the hurdle and leaps across the water. The pit is 27 $\frac{1}{2}$ inches (70 centimeters) deep at the foot of the hurdle and slopes up to the track level. Most steeplechasers come down in the water at the shallow end of the pit to soften their landing.

Walking races are events in which athletes must follow certain rules of walking technique. The front foot must touch the ground before the rear foot leaves the ground. While the foot is touching the ground, the leg must be unbent for at least one moment. Walkers are entitled to one warning for improper form before they are disqualified. Walking races, also called *race walking,* may take place on a track or a road. Most men's walking races cover distances of 20,000 meters or 50,000 meters. Women's world records are recognized for two distances, 5,000 meters and 10,000 meters.

Relays are run by teams of four runners. The first runner carries a baton about 1 foot (30 centimeters) long. After running a certain distance, called a *leg,* the athlete hands the baton to the next team member. This exchange must occur within a zone 20 meters long. If the runners do not exchange the baton within this zone, their team is disqualified.

The most common relays are run at distances of 400 meters or 1,600 meters. The IAAF also keeps world records for relays of 800 meters, 3,200 meters, and—for men only—6,000 meters. In these relays, all four members of a team run an equal distance. Most U.S. relay meets include *medley relays,* in which the athletes run different distances. In the *sprint medley,* two members of the team run 200 meters each, another runs 400 meters, and the final runner covers 800 meters. In the *distance medley,* the members of the team run distances of 400 meters, 800 meters, 1,200 meters, and 1,600 meters.

Field events

Field events take place in specially prepared areas, usually within the oval track. Typical field competition consists of four jumping events and four throwing events. The jumps are the long jump, triple jump, high jump, and pole vault. The throwing events are the discus, hammer, javelin, and shot-put.

Jumping events. In the long jump and triple jump, the athletes jump as far forward as they can. In the high jump and pole vault, they leap over a bar as high as possible.

The long jump, once called the *broad jump,* is completed in a single jump into a pit filled with sand. To begin the long jump, the competitor sprints down a long runway and leaps from a take-off board. If the athlete steps past the board before jumping, the jump is a foul. A jump's length is measured from the front edge of the take-off board to the nearest mark the athlete makes in the sand. When there are many competitors, each one is allowed three jumps, and a certain number of leaders qualify for three more. When fewer athletes compete, each one is allowed six jumps. If two jumpers leap the same distance, the winner is the one with the next-best jump.

The triple jump, originally called the *hop, step, and jump,* consists of three continuous jumps, the first two

John McDonough, Focus on Sports

In the long jump, athletes speed down a runway and leap from a board into a sand pit. A jump is measured from the near edge of the board to the closest mark the jumper makes in the sand.

completed on the runway. On the first jump, the athlete takes off on one foot and lands on the same foot. On the second jump, the athlete lands on the other foot. At the end of the third jump, the athlete lands on both feet in a pit of sand.

High-jumpers and pole-vaulters try to propel themselves over a long thin crossbar held up by two posts called *uprights.* The athletes land on a cushion of foam rubber. If a jumper knocks the crossbar off the uprights, the jump counts as a miss. Three consecutive misses eliminate the jumper. The winner is the one who clears the greatest height. In case of a tie, the winner is the one with the fewest misses at that height. If still tied, the winner is the one with the fewest overall misses.

A high jumper may run toward the bar from any angle. The athlete may use any style of jumping, but he or she must take off from one foot. In the most popular modern style, called the *Fosbury flop,* jumpers go over

© Heinz Kluetmeier, *Sports Illustrated,* Time Inc.

The high jump requires an athlete to leap over a bar that rests on and between two poles. This jumper will kick her legs out and up to complete her headfirst leap.

with their back to the bar and their head clearing first. The style was named for American high-jumper Dick Fosbury, who introduced it in the late 1960's.

Pole vaulters use a long pole usually made of fiberglass. The vaulter begins the event by sprinting down a runway, carrying the pole with both hands. As the vaulter nears the vaulting pit, he or she rams the far end of the pole into a wood or metal box embedded in the ground. The pole bends while the athlete hangs with his or her back to the ground and feet up. As the pole straightens, helping to thrust the vaulter into the air, the athlete pulls himself or herself higher and turns his or her body to face the ground. Before releasing the pole, the vaulter gives a final push with the arms to add to his or her height.

Throwing events require athletes to propel an object as far as they can. Competitors in the discus, hammer, and shot-put all throw from inside a circle. In the discus and hammer events, athletes throw from an enclosure, called a *cage,* to protect spectators from wild throws. In the javelin event, the athlete runs down a runway and throws the javelin before reaching a foul line. In each event, the thrown object must land within a marked area. Ties are decided by the next-best throw.

A discus is a saucer-shaped object made of plastic or wood with a metal rim. The men's discus measures about 22 centimeters (8 $\frac{2}{3}$ inches) in diameter and weighs at least 2 kilograms (4 pounds 6 $\frac{1}{2}$ ounces). The women's discus is about 18 centimeters (7 $\frac{1}{8}$ inches) in diameter and weighs at least 1 kilogram (2 pounds 3 ounces). The athlete grips the discus with one hand, spins around about 1 $\frac{1}{2}$ times, and releases it with a sidearm motion to make it sail through the air.

A hammer consists of a steel wire with a metal ball attached to one end and a handle fastened to the other end. The entire hammer weighs 7.26 kilograms (16 pounds) and measures about 120 centimeters (47 inches) long. Using both hands, the thrower grasps the handle and spins around three or four times before releasing it.

A javelin is a spear made of metal or wood. The men's javelin measures from 2.6 to 2.7 meters (8 feet 6 inches to 8 feet 10 inches) long and weighs at least 800 grams (28 ounces). Women throw a javelin that is 2.2 to 2.3 meters (7 feet 3 inches to 7 feet 7 inches) long and weighs at least 600 grams (21 ounces). The thrower holds the javelin by a cord grip near the center, and then releases it with an overhand throw while running.

A shot is a metal ball. The men's shot measures about 12 centimeters (4 $\frac{3}{4}$ inches) in diameter and weighs at least 7.26 kilograms (16 pounds). The women's shot measures about 10 centimeters (4 inches) in diameter and weighs at least 4 kilograms (8 pounds 13 ounces). Competitors *put* (push) the shot forward. They begin by holding the shot against the neck. There are two styles of shot put. In the *slide,* the athlete starts with a strong shove from one leg and finishes with a powerful push of the arm. In the *rotation* style, the athlete turns 1 $\frac{1}{2}$ times before releasing the shot in a movement similar to throwing the discus.

© Rich Clarkson, *Sports Illustrated,* Time Inc.

The shot-put is a throwing event in which the athletes *put* (push) a metal ball called a *shot.* They hold the heavy shot against their neck and release it with a powerful push.

The decathlon, heptathlon, and pentathlon

The decathlon, heptathlon, and pentathlon are *combined competitions,* in which an athlete competes in several different events over a period of one or two days. The athletes receive a score for their performance in each event, based on IAAF scoring tables. The winner is the athlete who receives the highest total score. Thus, the champion is the best all-around athlete, not necessarily the best competitor in any single event.

The decathlon is a 10-event competition for men. On the first day, the participants compete in the 100-meter run, long jump, shot-put, high jump, and 400-meter run. On the second day, they compete in the high hurdles, discus, pole vault, javelin, and 1,500-meter run.

The heptathlon is a seven-event competition for women. If the competition is conducted over two days, on the first day athletes begin with the high hurdles, followed by the high jump, shot-put, and 200-meter run. On the second day, they compete in the long jump, javelin throw, and the 800-meter run.

The pentathlon, a one-day competition of five events, is rarely held today. The heptathlon replaced the pentathlon for women in 1981. The men's pentathlon events include the long jump, javelin throw, 200-meter run, discus throw, and 1,500-meter run.

Competition

Organizations. The IAAF governs international track and field. It conducts the World Championships and cooperates with the International Olympic Committee in staging the track and field events of the Olympic Games. Other organizations conduct international meets, national championships, and restricted championships, such as college, regional, and high school meets.

In the United States, USA Track and Field (USATF) is the governing body for track and field. The Canadian Track and Field Association (CTFA) governs the sport in Canada. The National Collegiate Athletic Association (NCAA) and the National Association of Intercollegiate Athletics (NAIA) govern U.S. college championships. The National Federation of State High School Associations regulates U.S. high school competition.

Types of competition. The most important international meets are the Olympic Games, which started in 1896, and the World Championships, which began in 1983. The Olympics are held every four years, while the World Championships are held every two years.

Other major international meets include the African Championships, the Commonwealth Games, the European Championships, the Pan American Games, and the World Cup. Many nations compete against each other in annual *dual meets* (competitions between two teams).

In United States and Canadian schools and colleges, local meets may lead to regional, state, or provincial meets and, on the college level, to national meets. Much competition takes place in *open meets,* which any athlete may enter. Some private organizations sponsor *invitational meets.* Only the athletes invited by the organizers may compete in these meets. International *Grand Prix* meets allow athletes to score points for placing high in certain meets. At the end of the season, the athletes with the most points win prize money. Some track and field meets are restricted to a certain age group, such as competitions for children 10 and under and adults 60 and over.

Track and field meets. A typical track meet is like a three-ring circus, with several events taking place at the same time. Officials conduct each event according to its particular rules. A race requires a starter, several judges at the finish line, and sometimes as many as a dozen timers. Electronic equipment is normally used in place of some judges and timers in major meets. In field events, judges measure jumps and throws, and watch for fouls. In some events, judges also check to see that athletes are using the legal form.

Most meets take place in a single day, but the Olympics and the World Championships schedule events over more than a week. Large meets include so many athletes that they cannot all compete at once. In these meets, the athletes must qualify for the finals in *preliminaries.* Eight competitors normally qualify for the finals of track events run in lanes. Most field-event preliminaries reduce the number of finalists to 12.

History

Beginnings. The first footrace probably took place thousands of years ago. A footrace is described in the Greek epic poem the *Iliad,* which was probably composed in the 700's B.C. A footrace was the only event in the first Olympic Games, held in Greece in 776 B.C. Track and field was introduced in England in the 1100's but did not become popular until the 1800's.

Revival in the 1800's. Footraces along the roads became common in England during the 1500's, but races on measured tracks did not begin until well into the 1800's. Modern track and field began in the schools of England. Eton held an interclass meet in 1837. In 1864, Cambridge competed against Oxford in the first intercollegiate track and field meet. The annual English championships began in London in 1866.

The first U.S. amateur meet took place indoors in 1868. The New York Athletic Club sponsored the meet. United States collegiate meets and the first national championships began in 1876. Several other nations held championship meets before 1900. In 1895, the New York Athletic Club met the London Athletic Club in the first notable international meet. In 1896, Athens, Greece, hosted the first modern Olympic Games. Although the track and field performances at Athens were not outstanding, the Olympics stimulated great interest in the sport. Women's competitions, which were not part of the first Olympic Games, also began during the late 1800's.

The early and middle 1900's. In 1912, 16 countries agreed to form the IAAF to govern men's track and field. An international organization for women's competitions was formed in 1917. Separate international women's championships were held until 1928, when women were admitted to Olympic competition.

During the 1920's, long-distance runner Paavo Nurmi of Finland raised track to international popularity. He broke 29 world records and won 9 Olympic gold medals and 3 silver medals. Babe Didrikson of the United States popularized women's track and field. Didrikson won two gold medals and a silver medal in the 1932 Olympic Games. In the 1936 Olympics, Jesse Owens of the United States won four gold medals and retired with world records in seven Olympic events. Early in the 1940's, Cornelius "Dutch" Warmerdam of the United States captured the imagination of the track and field world by pole-vaulting higher than 15 feet a total of 43 times.

During the 1950's, athletes broke all previous world records except Owens's 1935 long-jump mark. Among the greatest athletes in this midcentury surge were long-distance runner Emil Zátopek of Czechoslovakia, and shot-putter Parry O'Brien and discus thrower Al Oerter of the United States. Zátopek won 4 Olympic gold medals in track and held 10 world records at the same time. O'Brien broke the shot-put record 13 times and won 2 firsts, a second, and a fourth in the Olympics. Oerter won the Olympic discus throw four times.

Track and field today. The sport has changed greatly since the mid-1900's. Performances once thought to be impossible are common today. In 1954, the British runner Roger Bannister became the first person to run the mile in less than four minutes. Within the next 20 years, more than 200 men had run the mile in under four minutes. In the early 1990's, the 50 all-time best performances in each event included only a few from before 1980.

There are a number of reasons for this remarkable progress in track and field. They include increased competition internationally as well as improved training methods, equipment, and techniques. Traditionally, track and field has been an amateur sport. However, the rules have been broadened to allow athletes to receive not only prize money but also large sums of money for endorsing athletic shoes or other products and for appearing in invitational meets. The opportunity to earn money has increased the level of competition.

Improved training methods help today's athletes perform well. Training with weights gives athletes greater strength for throwing, jumping, and even running. New equipment has raised performance levels. Synthetic tracks, which have more spring, cut a runner's time by as much as one second per lap. The use of fiberglass vaulting poles instead of wooden ones has reduced Warmerdam's once amazing heights to high-school performance levels. New techniques also help. In the high jump, for example, the use of the Fosbury flop adds about 6 inches (15 centimeters) to most jumps.

Modern track-and-field champions reflect the international popularity of the sport. The biggest names in modern men's track and field have included sprinters

World track and field records

Event	Record	Holder	Country	Date
Men's records				
Running				
100 meters	9.78 s	Tim Montgomery	United States	Sept. 14, 2002
	9.77 s*	Asafa Powell	Jamaica	June 14, 2005
200 meters	19.32 s	Michael Johnson	United States	Aug. 1, 1996
400 meters	43.18 s	Michael Johnson	United States	Aug. 26, 1999
800 meters	1 min 41.11 s	Wilson Kipketer	Denmark	Aug. 24, 1997
1,000 meters	2 min 11.96 s	Noah Ngeny	Kenya	Sept. 5, 1999
1,500 meters	3 min 26.0 s	Hicham El Guerrouj	Morocco	July 14, 1998
1 mile	3 min 43.13 s	Hicham El Guerrouj	Morocco	July 7, 1999
2,000 meters	4 min 44.79 s	Hicham El Guerrouj	Morocco	Sept. 7, 1999
3,000 meters	7 min 20.67 s	Daniel Komen	Kenya	Sept. 1, 1996
5,000 meters	12 min 37.35 s	Kenenisa Bekele	Ethiopia	May 31, 2004
10,000 meters	26 min 20.31 s	Kenenisa Bekele	Ethiopia	June 8, 2004
20,000 meters	56 min 55.6 s	Arturo Barrios	Mexico	March 30, 1991
25,000 meters	1 h 13 min 55.8 s	Toshihiko Seko	Japan	March 22, 1981
30,000 meters	1 h 29 min 18.8 s	Toshihiko Seko	Japan	March 22, 1981
1-hour run	13 miles 194 yards (21,101 meters)	Arturo Barrios	Mexico	March 30, 1991
3,000-meter steeplechase	7 min 53.63 s	Saif Saaeed Shaheen	Qatar	Sept. 3, 2004
Marathon	2 h 4 min 55 s	Paul Tergat	Kenya	Sept. 28, 2003
Hurdles				
110-meter hurdles	12.91 s	Colin Jackson	United Kingdom	Aug. 20, 1993
		Liu Xiang	China	Aug. 27, 2004
400-meter hurdles	46.78 s	Kevin Young	United States	Aug. 6, 1992
Relays				
400-meter relay	37.40 s	U.S. national team (M. Marsh, L. Burrell, D. Mitchell, C. Lewis)	United States	Aug. 8, 1992
		U.S. national team (J. Drummond, L. Burrell, D. Mitchell, A. Cason)	United States	Aug. 21, 1993
800-meter relay	1 min 18.68 s	Santa Monica Track Club (M. Marsh, L. Burrell, F. Heard, C. Lewis)	United States	April 17, 1994
1,600-meter relay	2 min 54.20 s	U.S. national team (J. Young, A. Pettigrew, T. Washington, M. Johnson)	United States	July 22, 1998
3,200-meter relay	7 min 3.89 s	British national team (P. Elliott, G. Cook, S. Cram, S. Coe)	United Kingdom	Aug. 30, 1982
6,000-meter relay	14 min 38.8 s	West German national team (T. Wessinghage, H. Hudak, M. Lederer, K. Fleschen)	West Germany	Aug. 17, 1977
Race walking				
20,000-meter walk	1 h 17 min 25.6 s	Bernardo Segura	Mexico	May 7, 1994
30,000-meter walk	2 h 1 min 44.1 s	Maurizio Damilano	Italy	Oct. 3, 1992
50,000-meter walk	3 h 40 min 57.9 s	Thierry Toutain	France	Sept. 29, 1996
2-hour walk	18 miles 660 yards (29,572 meters)	Maurizio Damilano	Italy	Oct. 3, 1992
Jumping				
High jump	8 ft ½ in 2.45 meters)	Javier Sotomayor	Cuba	July 27, 1993
Pole vault	20 ft 1 ¾ in (6.14 meters)	Sergey Bubka	Ukraine	July 31, 1994
Long jump	29 ft 4 ½ in (8.95 meters)	Mike Powell	United States	Aug. 30, 1991
Triple jump	60 ft ¼ in (18.29 meters)	Jonathan Edwards	United Kingdom	Aug. 7, 1995
Throwing				
Shot-put	75 ft 10 ¼ in (23.12 meters)	Randy Barnes	United States	May 20, 1990
Discus throw	243 ft 0 in (74.08 meters)	Jürgen Schult	East Germany	June 6, 1986
Hammer throw	284 ft 7 in (86.74 meters)	Yuriy Syedikh	Soviet Union	Aug. 30, 1986
Javelin throw	323 ft 1 in (98.48 meters)	Jan Zelezny	Czech Republic	May 25, 1996
Decathlon				
Decathlon	9,026 points	Roman Šebrle	Czech Republic	May 26-27, 2001

*Awaiting ratification.

Event	Record	Holder	Country	Date
Women's records				
Running				
100 meters	10.49 s	Florence Griffith Joyner	United States	July 16, 1988
200 meters	21.34 s	Florence Griffith Joyner	United States	Sept. 29, 1988
400 meters	47.60 s	Marita Koch	East Germany	Oct. 6, 1985
800 meters	1 min 53.28 s	Jarmila Kratochvilova	Czechoslovakia	July 26, 1983
1,000 meters	2 min 28.98 s	Svetlana Masterkova	Russia	Aug. 23, 1996
1,500 meters	3 min 50.46 s	Qu Yunxia	China	Sept. 11, 1993
1 mile	4 min 12.56 s	Svetlana Masterkova	Russia	Aug. 14, 1996
2,000 meters	5 min 25.36 s	Sonia O'Sullivan	Ireland	July 8, 1994
3,000 meters	8 min 6.11 s	Wang Junxia	China	Sept. 13, 1993
5,000 meters	14 min 24.68 s	Elvan Abeylegesse	Turkey	June 11, 2004
10,000 meters	29 min 31.78 s	Wang Junxia	China	Sept. 8, 1993
20,000 meters	1 h 5 min 26.6 s	Tegla Loroupe	Kenya	Sept. 3, 2000
25,000 meters	1 h 27 min 5.9 s	Tegla Loroupe	Kenya	Sept. 21, 2002
30,000 meters	1 h 45 min 50 s	Tegla Loroupe	Kenya	June 6, 2003
1-hour run	11 miles 770 yards (18,340 meters)	Tegla Loroupe	Kenya	Aug. 7, 1998
3,000-meter steeplechase	9 min 1.59 s	Gulnara Samitova	Russia	July 4, 2004
Marathon	2 h 15 min 25 s	Paula Radcliffe	United Kingdom	April 13, 2003
Hurdles				
100-meter hurdles	12.21 s	Yordanka Donkova	Bulgaria	Aug. 20, 1988
400-meter hurdles	52.34 s	Yuliya Pechonkina	Russia	Aug. 8, 2003
Relays				
400-meter relay	41.37 s	East German national team (S. Moller, S. Rieger, I. Auerswald, M. Göhr)	East Germany	Oct. 6, 1985
800-meter relay	1 min 27.46 s	U.S. national team (M. Jones, L. Collander-Richardson, L. Jenkins, N. Perry)	United States	April 29, 2000
1,600-meter relay	3 min 15.17 s	Soviet national team (T. Ledovskaya, O. Nazarova, M. Pinigina, O. Bryzgina)	Soviet Union	Oct. 1, 1988
3,200-meter relay	7 min 50.17 s	Soviet national team (N. Olizarenko, L. Gurina, L. Borisova, T. Podyalovskaya)	Soviet Union	Aug. 5, 1984
Race walking				
5,000-meter walk	20 min 2.60 s	Gillian O'Sullivan	Ireland	July 13, 2002
10,000-meter walk	41 min 56.23 s	Nadezhda Ryashkina	Soviet Union	July 24, 1990
20,000-meter walk	1 h 26 min 52.3 s	Olimpiada Ivanova	Russia	Sept. 6, 2001
	1 h 25 min 41 s*	Olimpiada Ivanova	Russia	Aug. 7, 2005
Jumping				
High jump	6 ft 10 ¼ in (2.09 meters)	Stefka Kostadinova	Bulgaria	Aug. 30, 1987
Pole vault	16 ft 4 ¾ in (5 meters)	Yelena Isinbayeva	Russia	July 22, 2005
	16 ft 5 ¼ in (5.01 meters)*	Yelena Isinbayeva	Russia	Aug. 12, 2005
Long jump	24 ft 8 ¼ in (7.52 meters)	Galina Chistyakova	Soviet Union	June 11, 1988
Triple jump	50 ft 10 ¼ in (15.50 meters)	Inessa Kravets	Ukraine	Aug. 10, 1995
Throwing				
Shot-put	74 ft 3 in (22.63 meters)	Natalya Lisovskaya	Soviet Union	June 7, 1987
Discus throw	252 ft 0 in (76.80 meters)	Gabriele Reinsch	East Germany	July 9, 1988
Hammer throw	249 ft 7 in (76.07 meters)	Mihaela Melinte	Romania	Aug. 29, 1999
	252 ft 10 in (77.06 meters)*	Tatyana Lysenko	Russia	July 15, 2005
Javelin throw	234 ft 8 ½ in (71.54 meters)	Osleidys Menéndez	Cuba	July 1, 2001
	235 ft 3 in (71.70 meters)*	Osleidys Menéndez	Cuba	Aug. 14, 2005
Heptathlon				
Heptathlon	7,291 points	Jackie Joyner-Kersee	United States	Sept. 23-24, 1988

*Awaiting ratification. Source: International Association of Athletics Federations.

Carl Lewis, Maurice Greene, and Michael Johnson, decathlon star Dan O'Brien, and long jumper Mike Powell of the United States; hurdler Colin Jackson of the United Kingdom; pole vaulter Sergey Bubka of Ukraine; high jumper Javier Sotomayor of Cuba; and distance runners Haile Gebrselassie of Ethiopia and Noureddine Morceli of Algeria. Star women athletes have included Jackie Joyner-Kersee of the United States in the heptathlon, long jumper Heike Drechsler of Germany, sprinter Marion Jones of the United States, and distance runner Svetlana Maskerkova of Russia. Michael Takaha

Related articles. See the separate article on **Olympic Games**. See also the following articles:

Events

Cross-country	Hurdling	Pole vault
Decathlon	Javelin	Running
Discus throw	Long jump	Shot-put
Hammer throw	Marathon	Triathlon
Heptathlon	Pentathlon, Modern	Walking
High jump		

Biographies

Bannister, Sir Roger	Owens, Jesse
Joyner-Kersee, Jackie	Rudolph, Wilma
Lewis, Carl	Thorpe, Jim
Nurmi, Paavo	Zaharias, Babe Didrikson

Outline

I. The track and the field
- A. The track
- B. The field

II. Track events
- A. Running races
- B. Hurdle races
- C. The steeplechase
- D. Walking races
- E. Relays

III. Field events
- A. Jumping events
- B. Throwing events

IV. The decathlon, heptathlon, and pentathlon

V. Competition
- A. Organizations
- B. Types of competition
- C. Track and field meets

VI. History
- A. Beginnings
- B. Revival in the 1800's
- C. The early and mid-1900's
- D. Track and field today

Questions

What is one function of a judge in a field event?
Where did modern track and field begin?
Which running races do not take place on a track?
Who was Cornelius Warmerdam?
How is the winner of a combined competition determined?
What is the U.S. governing organization for high school track and field?
How do medley relays differ from other relays?
What are a few causes of the progress in track and field performances since the mid-1900's?
In what way do open meets differ from invitational meets?
What was the triple jump originally called?

Additional resources

Baldwin, David. *Track and Field Record Holders.* McFarland, 1996.
Jackson, Colin. *The Young Track and Field Athlete.* Dorling Kindersley, 1996. Younger readers.
Rogers, Joseph L., and others. *U.S.A. Track and Field Coaching Manual.* Human Kinetics, 2000.

Tractor is a machine that pulls or pushes a tool or a machine over land. Tractors provide the chief source of power on most farms. They are also used for industrial and military purposes, for logging, highway construction, and snow clearance. Tractors have either gasoline or diesel engines (see **Gasoline engine; Diesel engine**).

Parts of a tractor. The modern tractor has several built-in features that enable it to provide power for other farm equipment. These features include the drawbar, a hydraulic system, and a power take-off.

The drawbar is a device for fastening equipment to the tractor for pulling. The drawbar enables a tractor to pull such equipment as plows, wagons, harrows, combines, and hay balers.

The hydraulic system controls the working position of implements hitched to or mounted onto the tractor. An engine-driven hydraulic pump and cylinder provide power to raise and lower these implements. Many rear-wheel-drive tractors have hydraulic systems with a mechanism that shifts weight from the front to the rear wheels of the tractor. The weight shift increases traction for pulling mounted implements.

The power take-off, or *PTO,* provides power for machines that are either mounted on or pulled by the tractor. The coupling device between the PTO and the equipment usually consists of two universal joints, one on each end of a telescoping shaft. The flexible action of the joints and the telescoping action of the shaft allows sharp turning and movement over rough surfaces without harming the power system. The PTO drives the moving parts of mowing machines, harvesters, hay balers, combines, potato diggers, and spray pumps.

Types of tractors. There are two major types of tractors: the wheel tractor and the tracklayer tractor, known as a *crawler.*

Wheel tractors make up the majority of farm tractors in the United States. Many farmers use an *all-purpose* tractor because it does a variety of jobs, such as planting, cultivating, and harvesting. It has high rear wheels. It has either one or two small front wheels placed close together or two front wheels spaced the same as the rear wheels. The spacing of the wheels enables the tractor to be driven between rows of crops. Wheel tractors may have either two-wheel or four-wheel drive. Two-wheel-drive models range in weight from about 3,000

Case IH

A general-purpose tractor performs many jobs on a farm, including plowing, planting, fertilizing, and cultivating.

J I Case

A crawler tractor, also called a *track tractor,* does such work as moving earth for construction jobs.

pounds (1,400 kilograms) to more than 20,000 pounds (9,000 kilograms). Four-wheel-drive tractors may weigh as much as 60,000 pounds (27,000 kilograms). The demand for larger tractors has increased as the average size of farms has increased.

Crawler tractors, also called *track tractors,* are driven on two endless tracks. They are steered by stopping or slowing one of the tracks. Crawler tractors are used for heavy jobs, for land clearing, and for work on soft or rugged land. The smallest crawlers weigh about 3,800 pounds (1,720 kilograms). The largest of these tractors weigh more than 70,000 pounds (32,000 kilograms).

History. Tractors were first used during the 1870's. These tractors, called *traction engines,* were large, four-wheeled machines driven by steam. They provided enough power to pull as many as 40 plows, but they were too awkward to be practical. Smaller machines with internal-combustion engines soon replaced them. But the new machine had only a kerosene engine mounted on a four-wheeled frame. Later, kerosene or gasoline engines were built as part of the tractor frame. The tractors could do almost all the field work but were too low to pull a cultivator through tall crops. Then, in the 1920's, the all-purpose tractor was developed.

Early manufacturing companies usually made only one tractor model or size. But modern companies make a complete line. Modern tractors have both speed and power, and are easy to operate. Most have power steering and power brakes. Many also have enclosed cabs with heating and air-conditioning systems and special structures that protect the operator if the tractor accidentally turns over. Dale E. Farnham

See also **Agriculture** (picture: An early gasoline-powered tractor); **Bulldozer**.

Tracy, Spencer (1900-1967), was an American motion-picture actor, famous for his roles as a strong man of action and conviction in such films as *Bad Day at Black Rock* (1955) and *The Old Man and the Sea* (1958). He also won fame as a sophisticated comedian in several films, such as *Woman of the Year* (1942) and *Father of the Bride* (1950). Tracy won Academy Awards for his performances in *Captains Courageous* (1937) and *Boys Town* (1938), and received seven other Academy Award nominations.

Tracy was born on April 5, 1900, in Milwaukee. He made his stage debut in 1922. A 1930 stage performance led Tracy to a film contract, and he made his movie debut that year in *Up the River. The Power and the Glory* (1933) established him as a star. Tracy made more than 70 films. Among the best known are nine movies he made with his close friend Katharine Hepburn. They are *Woman of the Year* (1942), *Keeper of the Flame* (1942), *Without Love* (1945), *Sea of Grass* (1947), *State of the Union* (1948), *Adam's Rib* (1949), *Pat and Mike* (1952), *Desk Set* (1957), and *Guess Who's Coming to Dinner* (1967). Rachel Gallagher

United Press Int.

Spencer Tracy

Trade is the exchange of goods and services. Trade occurs because people want and need things that they do not have but can get from others. Trade plays an essential role for societies throughout the world.

People need basic things such as food, clothing, and housing. They also want many other things that make life convenient and pleasant, such as cars, computers, and services such as those performed in beauty salons and physicians' offices. Individuals cannot possibly produce all the goods and services they want. Trade occurs naturally when people want to exchange what they have or can produce for what others have or can produce.

Trade occurs within individual countries and across international borders. Trade within a single country is called *domestic trade.* Trade between nations is called *international trade.* Trade has contributed greatly to economic growth and development. It has also exposed people all over the world to new and different cultures. International trade plays a major role in the process of *globalization.* Globalization is the trend toward increased cultural and economic connectedness between people, businesses, and organizations worldwide.

Trade and specialization

The economic systems of most countries have a high degree of *specialization,* or *division of labor.* Specialization means that workers concentrate on producing those goods and services for which they have a *competitive advantage*—that is, they concentrate on the jobs they are best fitted to perform. Firms, in turn, employ workers who enable them to also gain a competitive advantage in the production of goods and services. Countries, regions, and cities also make full use of their competitive advantages by producing certain goods and services. For example, Australia specializes in raising livestock, and Japan in industrial products. Oregon specializes in producing lumber, Detroit in manufacturing automobiles, and Florida in growing oranges.

Specialization makes trade necessary. People cannot produce everything they want, and therefore must obtain products and services from others. Individuals usually sell their labor or products for money, and use the money to buy other goods and services they want.

Trade enables people to enjoy a higher standard of living. People can obtain more goods and services at lower cost through specialization and exchange. If workers specialize, more can be produced than if workers try to do several different tasks at the same time. If firms specialize, they can produce more by using mass production techniques. If countries, regions, and cities specialize, they can use their most plentiful resources. They can establish a group of skilled labor and specialized *capital* (goods used to produce other goods).

Carrying on trade

The use of money. To make trading easier, people have developed *monetary systems.* Large-scale trade is possible only if money is used as a medium of exchange. Without money, people would have to exchange certain goods and services directly for other specific goods and services. Through this system of trade, called *barter,* a computer producer who wanted a car would have to find an automobile producer who wanted some computers. The two traders would then have to agree on how many computers an automobile was worth.

People accept money for things they want to sell because they know it will be accepted by others in exchange for the things they want to buy. The amount of money exchanged for a particular product is the *price* of that product. The price of something is the value placed on it by those who are buying and selling it.

The use of markets. Trade takes place in *markets.* In earlier days, buyers and sellers met in person and bargained with one another at markets. In Europe during the Middle Ages, for example, farmers came to town with their produce on market day. Townspeople shopped in the market and negotiated directly with the sellers. Today, most trade is far more complicated. Often, producers and consumers do not deal directly with one another. Instead, goods are passed on from producers to consumers by people called *middlemen.*

Two kinds of middlemen are *wholesalers* and *retailers.* Wholesalers buy goods from producers and sell them mainly to other business firms. For example, a wholesaler of vegetables buys large amounts of vegetables from the growers and then sells them to grocers. This kind of trade is called *wholesale trade.* The grocers

Carrying on trade Trade takes place because people need or want the things that other people produce or can do. Trade may be carried on in a number of ways. These photographs show trade at local markets, between nations, and at organized markets known as commodity exchanges.

© Marc Bernheim, Woodfin Camp, Inc.

A local market in Morocco

E. R. Degginger

A freight dock in New Jersey

© Robert Frerck, Woodfin Camp, Inc.

A commodity exchange in Chicago

then sell the vegetables to customers who eat them. This kind of trade in which goods are sold to the final consumer is called *retail trade.*

Due to advances in telecommunications technology, buyers and sellers no longer have to meet face-to-face. A large number of goods and services are now bought and sold over the Internet. Often, buyers and sellers do not even need to see the product that is being traded. They can transact their business on the basis of description or sample. For example, a buyer of drapes can examine a small *swatch* (sample) of cloth before making a purchase. Cotton, wheat, and many other farm products are classified by grade. Buyers know exactly what they will get if they specify a particular grade, such as "Number 2 hard ordinary wheat." Agricultural goods are often traded at organized markets called *commodity exchanges.*

The geographic extent of trade. Buyers and sellers exist in all parts of the world. Trade in such basic goods as coffee, sugar, wheat, copper, oil, and rubber is international in scope. For example, the United States is a leading exporter of wheat. It sells large amounts of wheat to India, Pakistan, Japan, Brazil, the Netherlands, and many other countries.

Trade in other products and services may be conducted on a local, regional, national, or international basis. For example, hairstyling is conducted at the local level. Trade in hominy grits is also fairly concentrated, mainly in the southern United States. However, the market for automobiles, cellular phones, clothing, computers, and television sets is usually national and international in scope.

Local trade was once much more important than it is today. This was partly because transportation facilities were limited and goods could not be cheaply transported over great distances. Also, many food items could not be preserved for long, so they had to be consumed near their place of production. But technological advances have reduced these limitations. Trains, trucks, airplanes, and pipelines make it possible to transport large quantities of goods easily and cheaply. Vegetables, meats, and other perishable items are now refrigerated or frozen and shipped all over the world. Airplanes can even fly flowers to distant markets. The Internet makes it possible to provide many services worldwide.

Also in earlier days, people's tastes and preferences varied more widely from one locality to another. Today, however, mass advertising in magazines and newspapers and on radio and television has helped persuade people in different localities to use many of the same products. Millions of people now drink the same kinds of soft drinks, use the same laundry detergents, drive the same cars, and wear the same kinds of clothes. Technological advances have created national and international markets, and widespread trade has taken the place of much purely local trade.

Trade in the United States is carried out mainly by private people and businesses. Governments play a less important role than do private individuals and groups. Sellers range from such giant businesses as the General Motors Corporation, which sells millions of cars and trucks each year, to small neighborhood shops that sell such goods as bakery products or flowers.

Many goods and services are purchased by individual consumers, who buy such things as dresses, computers, and food. Businesses buy raw materials and capital equipment needed for production from other businesses. The various governments in the United States also buy many goods and services. For example, purchases of the federal government include interstate highways, military equipment, and the services of government employees, including members of the armed forces.

The way in which trade is organized and carried on in the United States is often called *capitalism, free enterprise,* or *private enterprise.* Trade is an essential part of a free enterprise economy. In this type of economy, consumers' willingness to pay for what they want determines prices and indicates to producers what ought to be produced. In China and other countries with *centrally planned economies,* government planners make the basic economic decisions about what will be produced and sold at what price.

The development of trade

Early trade. For thousands of years, families produced most of the things they wanted themselves. They grew or hunted their own food, made their own tools and utensils, built their own houses, and made their own clothes. Later, people learned that they could consume more goods and services by specializing and then trading with others. As civilization advanced, exchanges became so common and widespread that some individuals did nothing but conduct trade. This class became known as *merchants.* The most famous early land merchants were the Babylonians and, later, the Arabs. These traders traveled on foot or rode donkeys or camels. The Phoenicians were the chief sea traders of ancient times.

Trade was extremely important during the hundreds of years the Roman Empire ruled much of the world. Roman ships brought tin from Britain, and slaves, cloth, and gems from Asia. For more than 500 years after the fall of the Roman Empire in A.D. 476, little international trade took place.

The expansion of trade began in the 1100's and 1200's, largely because of increased contacts between people. Marco Polo and other European merchants traveled to East Asia to trade for Chinese goods. Italians in Genoa, Pisa, and Venice built great fleets of ships to carry goods from country to country. A great period of overseas exploration began in the 1400's. Trade routes between Europe and Africa, India, and Southeast Asia were established as a result of the explorations. In the 1500's and 1600's, private groups formed companies, usually with governmental approval, to trade in new areas.

Trade between Europe and America was carried on by the chartered companies that established the earliest American colonies. The colonists sent sugar, molasses, furs, rice, rum, potatoes, tobacco, timber, and cocoa to Europe. In return, they received manufactured articles, luxuries, and slaves. Trade also pushed American frontiers westward. Trading posts sprang up in the wilderness. Many of these posts later grew into cities.

Trade today affects the lives of people everywhere. Technological advances and the low cost of transportation have led to trade levels that have never been seen before. As a result, more and better goods and services are being produced and consumed around the world.

James R. Barth and Cindy T. Lee

Related articles in *World Book.* See the trade section of various country articles, such as **Italy** (Trade). See also:

Auction	Customs union	International trade
Balance of payments	E-commerce	Marketing
Bank	European Union	Mass production
Barter	Exploration	Mercantilism
Bazaar	Exports and imports	Money
Bill of exchange	Fair	Price
Business	Fair-trade laws	Reciprocal trade agreement
Capitalism	Federal Trade Commission	Silk Road
Colonial life in America (Trade)	Free trade	Stock exchange
Colonialism	Free trade zone	Tariff
Commodity exchange	Fur trade	Trade association
Common market	Globalization	Trade route
Contraband	Indian, American (Trade)	Trading post
	Industry	World Trade Organization

Additional resources

Hinkelman, Edward G. *Dictionary of International Trade.* 4th ed. World Trade Pr., 2000.

Pomeranz, Kenneth, and Topik, Steven. *The World That Trade Created: Society, Culture, and the World Economy, 1400 to the Present.* M. E. Sharpe, 1999.

Slater, Courtenay M., and Rice, J. B., eds. *Foreign Trade of the United States.* Bernan Pr., 1999.

Trade, Board of. See Commodity exchange.

Trade association is a nonprofit organization that represents a group of business firms. Businesses join their associations voluntarily and manage them cooperatively. The companies work together to accomplish goals that no single firm could reach by itself.

A trade association may have only a few members, as in the ironmaking and steelmaking industry. Or it may have thousands of members, as in an association of retail grocers. The size of the membership has little to do with the effectiveness of the organization. It is more important that the association include most of the companies in the industry.

Trade association activities include promoting business for the industry; encouraging ethical practices in the industry; cooperating with other organizations; and holding conventions. Such associations also work to obtain good relations with the government, the industry's employees, and the general public.

Trade associations sponsor much industrial research work. This research helps improve the quality of goods or services. Setting industry standardization is another important trade association activity. By obtaining agreements among firms, the trade association sets standards of size and quality for articles and services.

A trade association provides information about its industry. It may issue bulletins on business trends and provide statistical information. Some publish magazines. Trade associations date back to the *guilds* formed in Europe during the Middle Ages. R. William Taylor

Related articles in *World Book* include:

Better business bureau	Jaycees
Chamber of commerce	National Association of Manufacturers
Guild	
Iron and Steel Institute, American	

Trade Commission, Federal. See Federal Trade Commission.

Trade deficit. See Balance of payments.

Trade publication is a periodical devoted to a specific professional, business, industrial, or trade field. Trade journals represent about two-thirds of all the periodicals in the United States. Most are weekly or monthly magazines, but there are some newspaper-style weeklies and dailies. These publications carry articles and advertising designed to inform the reader about the particular trade or industry. See also **Advertising** (Magazines); **Magazine.** Richard A. Schwarzlose

Trade route is a route along which goods are transported from one area to another. In early times, trade routes brought the luxuries of Asia and the Middle East into Western Europe. Later, these routes enabled countries to exchange raw materials and manufactured goods. Commerce gave rise to great cities along the routes. Trade routes have also increased contacts between peoples and resulted in an exchange of ideas and ways of doing things. Trade with Muslims of the Middle East brought new goods and knowledge to Europe during the Middle Ages. The travels of the Italian trader Marco Polo revealed China and the Mongol Empire.

Early trade routes existed among primitive peoples. They expanded greatly as people became more civilized. Early Sumerian traders traveled by caravan throughout western Asia to the Mediterranean Sea. The Phoenicians traded by water routes that connected Egypt, Greece, Asia Minor, Italy, and what are now the United Kingdom and Ireland.

Rich commerce flowed from eastern Asia to Europe by three major routes. The northern route, called the Silk Road, cut from China across central Asia either to the east coast of the Mediterranean Sea or to the Black Sea and from there to Byzantium (now Istanbul). But much of the silk commerce traveled by the middle route, which passed through the Persian Gulf and Euphrates Valley and ended either on the Black Sea coast or in such Syrian cities as Damascus. The southern route, by water, led from China around the southern tip of India, up the Red Sea, and overland to the Nile and northern Egypt. Merchants used it to carry spices and pearls from Ceylon (now Sri Lanka); cotton, spices, precious stones, and drugs from India; and cinnamon and incense from Arabia.

Merchants of the Roman Empire carried on a vast amount of trade throughout the then-known world. After the fall of the West Roman Empire, Roman roads were completed and extended. They crossed the Alps and branched out into Spain, France, and Germany. Water transportation also played a large part in European trading. Early traders shipped goods on the Seine, Rhine, and Danube rivers in western Europe and on the Volga and Don in eastern Europe. Through such seaports as Bordeaux and Nantes on the Atlantic Ocean, they exchanged the wine, grain, and honey of France for metals from Britain, and oil and lead from Spain.

Medieval routes. Cities trading with the eastern Mediterranean, such as Venice and Genoa, built powerful commercial empires. Ships brought goods from eastern Asia. Then Italian fleets carried the products to ports in Spain, England, and Flanders (a region in and near what is now Belgium). Other goods crossed overland through Italy and across the Alps to France and to German cities along the Rhine and Danube. Merchants of the Hanseatic League bought these goods in Flanders or Germany and carried them to England, the Baltic countries, Poland, and Russia.

Trade winds are strong winds that occur chiefly in the earth's Tropical Zone. They blow steadily toward the equator from both the northeast and the southeast. Trade winds blow mostly over the oceans because the weather there is more uniform than over the continents.

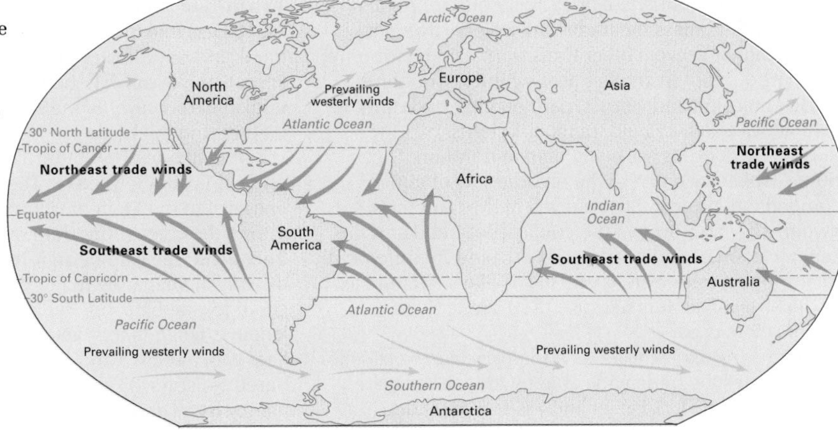

WORLD BOOK map

The search for new routes led to an age of exploration. During the 1400's, European nations began to search for new routes to eastern Asia to avoid the expensive tolls and the many hazards of the long journey from Asia. In addition, Italian city-states had a trade monopoly, which resulted in high prices and low profits to northern European merchants. The voyages of European explorers opened Europeans' eyes to a whole new world. Many new all-water trade routes were established. Nations set up trading companies to govern and control trade. The Portuguese first developed trade between India and the East Indies and Europe. The Spanish, Dutch, French, and English followed. Their commercial empires led to colonial empires.

Today's trade routes are almost numberless and cover the entire world. Highways and networks of railroads cover continents. Airplanes connect distant points on the globe. Ships carry goods on the world's oceans and waterways.

The United States government lists 30 trade routes over which it believes adequate ship service is essential to the national interest. In some cases, the government gives *subsidies* (grants of money) to shippers registered under the U.S. flag for maintaining this service.

Alan W. Cafruny

See also **Colonialism; Exploration; Trade.**

Trade school. See **Vocational education.**

Trade union. See **Labor movement.**

Trade wind is a strong wind that blows toward the equator from the northeast or southeast. In the days of sailing ships, sailors depended greatly on trade winds. The paths of these winds were so regular, especially over the oceans, that early navigators named them *trade winds,* which meant *course,* or *track,* winds. The trade winds are part of a great system of winds that blow over the earth. They blow toward the equator from about the 30th parallels of north and south latitude.

Differences between the temperature in low latitudes and the temperature in the polar regions cause trade winds. The heating of the air in low latitudes makes it expand and become light. Then it rises. This creates an area of low pressure near the surface. Cooler and heavier air from higher latitudes then tends to flow in to fill the area of low pressure. These polar winds do not blow due north or due south because of the eastward whirling of the earth. Instead, these winds blow from the northeast and from the southeast.

The belt of rising air between the trade winds is a region of mild winds and calms. This region is often called the *doldrums* because it is so calm. Sailing ships of early days were often stranded for many weeks in the doldrums. Trade winds have a great deal to do with rainfall on land. When trade winds blow against mountain ranges, they are forced upward. As the warm air rises, it cools. Its moisture condenses and falls as rain on the mountain slopes. James E. Miller

See also **Calms, Regions of; Horse latitudes.**

Trademark is a word or words, a name, a design, a picture, a sound, or any other symbol that distinguishes the products of one company from those of another. A trademark also may consist of any combination of these identifications. Most trademarks appear on the product, on its container, or in advertisements for the product. A *service mark* identifies the source of a service rather than a product. For example, an electric company may use a light bulb as a symbol of the service it offers to its customers.

A *strong trademark* consists of a word that has no recognizable meaning, such as Kodak. Strong trademarks receive broad protection from being used by other companies in a manner that is likely to cause confusion, mistake, or deception.

Weak trademarks consist of a common word, such as Premier, or a word that suggests some characteristic of the product, such as Wet 'n Wash. They receive less protection, unless the public identifies them with a certain manufacturer as a result of wide advertising and long, continuous use.

Trademarks, also known as *brand names,* provide an easy way to determine who makes a certain product. They help consumers identify brands that they liked in the past so they can purchase them again. A trademark represents the manufacturer's reputation, called *good will.*

Most countries have laws that protect the rights of trademark owners. A firm must establish its rights in each country in which it seeks protection.

In the United States, the first company to use a trademark has certain rights to that trademark. The firm may prevent others in the same geographic area from using the same trademark or a similar one for related products. But unless the trademark is very strong, its owner cannot prevent other firms from using it for unrelated products or in another area where it would not cause confusion. Individuals, partnerships, and other legal entities also may hold trademark rights.

Trademark rights are not limited in duration. These rights, which form part of the broader law of unfair competition, protect the good will of the trademark owner. They also protect the public from fraud and deceit. Violation of trademark rights is called *infringement.* An infringing trademark is one that is likely to confuse or deceive consumers because of its similarity to a trademark in use.

A company may register its trademark in each state in which it uses the trademark. Trademarks also may be registered in the U.S. Patent and Trademark Office in Arlington, Virginia. Registration of a trademark serves as notice to everyone of a company's claim of ownership. A trademark owner does not have to register the mark to sue for infringement. But registration gives the owner much stronger rights if a suit is brought.

In other countries, trademark laws differ from those of the United States. Many governments allow a company to register a trademark before using it. Some require registration before any trademark rights can be enforced. David Pressman

See also **Counterfeiting; Intellectual property.**

Trades Union Congress (TUC) is a national organization of British trade unions. It was founded in the 1860's. It is similar to the American Federation of Labor and Congress of Industrial Organizations (AFL-CIO).

Trading post is a type of marketplace where people bring products to sell or to exchange for other goods. In the United States, many posts serve Navajo Indians who live on a large reservation in Arizona, New Mexico, and Utah. At these posts, the Indians sell goods and buy food, clothing, and farm equipment.

In ancient times, trading posts operated in the Near East. Later, Europeans set up trading posts as they explored various parts of the world. At first, before the development of money, traders usually *bartered* with one another—that is, they exchanged items for other items.

The first trading posts in North America were established during the early to mid-1500's in what is now the Canadian province of Newfoundland and Labrador. By the mid-1800's, trading posts had been set up throughout North America. Indians traded furs and hides to white people for such items as cloth, glass beads, guns, gunpowder, liquor, and metal goods.

Private companies and individuals set up many trading posts. The Hudson's Bay Company opened posts along Hudson Bay in Canada after 1670 (see **Hudson's Bay Company**). In 1796, the U.S. government created a system of government trading posts, hoping to keep private traders from cheating the Indians. The government abolished these posts in 1822 because private traders opposed them. Many white traders later opened posts on Indian reservations and charged unfair prices, but the Indians there had nowhere else to buy goods.

Many settlements that grew up around trading posts developed into large U.S. and Canadian cities. These communities included Chicago; Detroit; Kansas City, Missouri; Montreal; and Quebec. Merwyn S. Garbarino

Trafalgar, *truh FAL guhr,* **Battle of,** fought on Oct. 21, 1805, is one of the major naval battles in history. Admiral Horatio Nelson's British fleet defeated a combined French and Spanish fleet. The victory gave England undisputed control of the sea. Nelson was wounded and died during the battle.

The battle was fought off Trafalgar, a low, sandy cape on Spain's southern coast. The cape lies at the western entrance to the Strait of Gibraltar. The battle occurred during the United Kingdom's war against Napoleon Bonaparte (see **Napoleon I**). Napoleon hoped to draw the British fleet away to the West Indies so his armies could invade England. But Napoleon's admiral, Villeneuve, failed in this, and decided to attack the British fleet with a French and Spanish fleet. His fleet outnumbered Nelson's, 33 ships to 27. But Nelson surprised the enemy by having his ships cut through the French battle line. The British fleet did not lose a ship in the battle, but it destroyed or captured over half the French and Spanish ships. Trafalgar Square in London was named in memory of Nelson's victory. Edward Malefakis

See also **London** (picture; map); **Nelson, Horatio.**

Traffic is the movement of people and goods from one place to another. This article deals with traffic on streets and highways. For a discussion of other kinds of traffic, see **Transportation** with its list of *Related articles.*

Traffic problems

The millions of automobiles in the world cause many traffic problems. Automobiles often jam city streets in the morning and evening rush hours. On holidays and weekends, many highways become excessively crowded, causing inconvenience and reducing safety. Through traffic overburdens the main streets of many small towns, making it difficult for local people to get to the stores. It is hard to find a parking place in the business sections of cities and towns.

Communities try to ease traffic problems in many ways. Many have built freeways and expressways to relieve heavy traffic on streets, roads, and highways. Freeways and expressways achieve a smoother traffic flow by controlling where vehicles can enter and leave. Traffic engineers and highway crews constantly maintain and improve these roadways to relieve crowded conditions.

Bypasses take motorists around, rather than through, towns or cities. They ease traffic congestion in towns and the business districts of cities, thus helping local business. In some cities, convenient, comfortable, and inexpensive mass transit systems also help relieve congestion. Better provision for truck loading and unloading at stores, office buildings, and factories eases the problem of truck interference on streets. It also reduces the cost of delivery and distribution of goods.

Many cities and towns prohibit parking at the curb to make additional street space available for traffic. Many places provide parking for large numbers of cars in off-street parking areas.

Traffic engineers achieve more efficient use of existing streets in several ways. These measures include: (1) creating one-way streets; (2) changing traffic lanes to one-way operation during hours of heavy traffic; (3) installing modern coordinated traffic-signal systems, turn controls, and pedestrian controls; and (4) developing through-street systems to move traffic faster.

Traffic control

Every year, traffic accidents kill tens of thousands of people and injure several million. Drivers and pedestrians can reduce the number of traffic accidents, injuries, and deaths by watching and obeying traffic control signs, signals, and pavement markings. Special control devices, such as electric signs that tell when to cross streets and highways, aid pedestrians. These signs operate with vehicle traffic signals.

Signals, signs, and markings. There is no clear record of who invented or first used traffic control devices. Traffic signs date back to the early Roman roads. Railroads used traffic control signals before streets did.

The first electric street signals on record were installed in Cleveland in 1914. It is generally agreed that three-color, four-way traffic lights first appeared in Detroit in the early 1920's. The Wayne County (Michigan) Road Commission developed the use of a white center line for separating driving lanes on highways.

Traffic controls are increasingly necessary for regulating, warning, and guiding motor vehicle and pedestrian traffic. The law requires signs to indicate how certain traffic regulations apply. Adequate use of warning signs, and well-designed and well-located route markings have great value, too, in helping the flow of traffic.

Pavement and curb markings and traffic islands, when properly designed and located, also help guide traffic. Traffic lanes, pedestrian crosswalks, turn markings, and warning signs frequently are painted or otherwise marked.

Modern traffic lights can be set to change when traffic demands it. In most places, the changes are automatic every so many seconds or minutes. Where there are different amounts of traffic on intersecting highways and streets, the light can be set so that it will remain green longer for the highway or street with the most traffic. Some traffic lights also are arranged so that the traffic itself will cause them to change. When vehicles pass over detectors in the roadway, the light changes to let them go through the intersection. Most roadway detectors are electrified wire loops that can sense the presence of metal. Traffic signals can also be set to respond to switches pushed by pedestrians, and to other switches activated by trains or emergency vehicles, such as ambulances and fire trucks.

Sign manufacturers cover many warning and guide signs with luminous paint, or glass or metal beads or buttons, which reflect beams from headlights. The reflections make the signs easier to see at night. Sometimes, various types of reflector buttons or white material are embedded in the surface of the street or highway.

Control devices must be in the right places or they can cause delay and congestion, and lead people to disregard them. Good control devices must be based on sound engineering principles. Studies of types and flow of traffic, accidents, speeds, delays, and physical conditions show the exact nature of a traffic difficulty and indicate the methods of control that are needed.

Traffic regulations are the rules of the road governing the actions of pedestrians and drivers on public roads and streets. Regulations should be uniform, so that drivers everywhere will know exactly what actions to take under like conditions.

Parking meters were first used in Oklahoma City, Oklahoma, in 1935. They were originally located only at the curb. But today, many parking lots also have parking meters. Meters are used to restrict the length of time vehicles can park, or to collect parking fees, or both. The meters may operate mechanically or electronically.

Traffic police enforce traffic-control measures and regulations, and control traffic emergencies. Development of street and highway facilities and traffic-control plans are the responsibilities of highway or traffic engineers. David J. Lovell

Related articles in *World Book* include:

Automobile
Bicycle
Bus
Police
Radar (In controlling automobile speed and traffic)
Road
Safety

Tragedy is a form of drama that deals with serious human actions and issues. Most tragedies show the downfall and death of a great man or a great woman. While the endings of tragedies are sad, they seem just and believable. Tragedy thus faces the fact that not everything in life ends happily. Therefore, tragedy raises deep philosophical questions about morality, the meaning of human existence, and the control human beings have over their fate.

Playwrights have written tragedies throughout the history of drama. The most famous were written during three periods—the 400's B.C. in Greece, the late 1500's and early 1600's in England, and the 1600's in France.

The greatest writers of Greek tragedy were Aeschylus, Euripides, and Sophocles. These writers took most of their plots from Greek mythology. William Shakespeare was the principal tragic dramatist of the English period. His tragedies are noted for their suspenseful plots, insights into human nature, and powerful poetic dialogue. Other leading English playwrights of the period included Christopher Marlowe and John Webster. Jean Racine dominated tragic drama in the French period. His tragic heroes and heroines are victims of violent passions that they cannot control. Pierre Corneille was another important French tragic playwright of the 1600's.

Until the 1700's, almost all tragedies dealt with royalty, famous historical figures, or other notable people. Playwrights did not consider the lives of common men and women important enough to provide material for tragedies. After 1700, a number of dramatists wrote *domestic tragedies,* plays with middle-class people as heroes and heroines. Perhaps the most important of these playwrights was Gotthold Ephraim Lessing of Germany.

Notable tragedies of the late 1700's and early 1800's were written by Friedrich Schiller of Germany and Victor Hugo of France. Most of their works dealt with famous or powerful characters.

Critics disagree about whether any true tragedies have been written since the late 1800's. Some argue that modern serious plays lack the moral, philosophical, or religious significance required for genuine tragedy. Other critics believe several playwrights have created works that can be considered tragedies. These playwrights include Georg Büchner of Germany, Henrik Ibsen of Norway, and Arthur Miller and Eugene O'Neill of the United States. Gerald M. Berkowitz

Each playwright discussed in this article has a separate biography in *World Book.* See also **Aristotle** (Literary criticism); **Drama; Greek literature** (Drama).

Tragopan, *TRAG uh pan,* is the name of five species of quaillike birds. Tragopans live in forests high on mountain slopes of southern and central Asia. Males have a bright-colored *lappet* (loose-hanging skin) on the throat, and a pair of blue, fleshy, erectile horns on each side of the head. Both lappet and horns become enlarged and brilliant during the mating season.

Tragopans eat insects, leaves, fruits, and seeds. They nest in trees. Most other pheasants nest on the ground. Their white eggs are slightly speckled with dull lilac. Tragopans are shy. Hunters usually snare them by driving them slowly toward nooses. David M. Niles

Scientific classification. Tragopans belong to the family Phasianidae and make up the genus *Tragopan.* The best known is *T. satyra,* the satyr tragopan.

WORLD BOOK illustration by Trevor Boyer, Linden Artists Ltd.

A tragopan has colorful, handsome markings. Tragopans live in mountain forests of southern and central Asia.

Trail of Tears was the forced removal of Cherokee Indians from their homelands in northwestern Georgia. The name comes from the Cherokee phrase *nunna-da-ul-tsun-yi,* which means *the trail where they cried.*

In 1829, white settlers discovered gold on Cherokee land. The settlers wanted the land for themselves and asked for the removal of the Cherokee. Supporters of President Andrew Jackson, who had been a famed Indian fighter, helped pass the Indian Removal Act of 1830 in Congress. The act called for the removal of all Indians in the southeastern United States to a territory west of the Mississippi River. Their new land, in what is now Oklahoma, became known as the Indian Territory.

The Cherokee divided over the removal. In 1835, some agreed to move and signed a treaty with the government. But most of the Indians, led by Cherokee leader John Ross, wanted to stay.

Beginning in May 1838, the U.S. Army forced the Cherokee into stockades to prepare for removal. The Army sent off the first group to Indian Territory on June 6, 1838, and the last party arrived on March 24, 1839. They traveled nearly 1,000 miles (1,600 kilometers) in rain and other bad weather. Some groups walked or rode horseback through Tennessee, Kentucky, the southern tip of Illinois, Missouri, Arkansas, and finally into Indian Territory. Others traveled by boat over the Tennessee and Ohio rivers, down the Mississippi River, and then up the Arkansas River to the western land. Many Cherokee became ill during the journey, and thousands died. Donald L. Fixico

See also **Cherokee Indians** (with picture); **Ross, John; United States, History of the** (picture: Eastern Indians).

Trailer is a wheeled vehicle that is pulled by an automobile, truck, or tractor. Trailers are used chiefly (1) as temporary living quarters for either recreational travel or camping, or (2) for cargo hauling. *Mobile homes,* on the other hand, are designed to be used for permanent, year-round living (see **Mobile home**).

Recreational trailers include *travel trailers, folding camping trailers,* and *fifth-wheel trailers.* Any of these vehicles may be connected to electric and water lines. A recreational trailer may have such conveniences as lights, heaters, toilets, air conditioners, refrigerators, ranges, microwave ovens, and television sets.

Travel trailers vary in size from 12 to 35 feet (3.7 to 10.7 meters) long and from 6 to 8 feet (1.8 to 2.4 meters) wide. Some have kitchens, bathrooms, and dining and sleeping quarters for up to eight people.

Folding camping trailers range from 10 to 25 feet (3 to 7.6 meters) long and are about 6 $\frac{1}{2}$ feet (2 meters) wide. They unfold into a tentlike enclosure that can accommodate up to eight people.

Fifth-wheel trailers range from 21 to 40 feet (6.4 to 12.2 meters) long and from 8 to 8 $\frac{1}{2}$ feet (2.4 to 2.6 meters) wide. Most have at least one *slideout,* a section that extends beyond the normal outside walls of the vehicle to enlarge an inside area while the vehicle is parked.

Utility trailers range from 6 to 14 feet (1.8 to 4.3 meters) long, or longer. They are used to carry loads that may be too large to fit in an automobile trunk and to transport farm animals. Most varieties of utility trailers look like boxes without tops.

Critically reviewed by the Recreation Vehicle Industry Association

See also **Recreational vehicle.**

Train. See **Electric railroad; Locomotive; Railroad.**

Training, Military. See **Military training.**

Trajan, *TRAY juhn* (A.D. 53?-117), was a Roman emperor and an important military leader. He expanded the empire by conquest and carried out extensive building programs.

Trajan conquered Dacia (now parts of Romania and Hungary) and made Nabataea part of the Roman Empire. Nabataea was a kingdom in what are now southern Jordan and northwestern Saudi Arabia. Trajan also won victories on the western frontier of Parthia, in present-day Iraq. He founded new cities, including Thamugadi (now Timgad, Algeria), and built bridges and harbors. These included bridges across the Danube River in Dacia and a harbor at the port of Rome. Trajan also introduced a program for the support of children in Italian cities.

Trajan was born Marcus Ulpius Traianus in Italica, Spain, of Roman parents. His father was a senator who became governor of Syria, which was an important province. Trajan became a senator and served in military posts in Spain, Syria, and Germany. In A.D. 97, Emperor Nerva adopted Trajan as his heir and successor. When Nerva died in A.D. 98, Trajan was declared emperor.

Trajan's Column is a monument built in the emperor's honor after he conquered Dacia. It was dedicated in

A.D. 113. The well-preserved column, 100 feet (30 meters) high, stands in Trajan's Forum in Rome. A spiral staircase inside the column leads to the top. The column and its pedestal are covered with carvings portraying events of the Dacian wars. Trajan died in early August in 117. The ashes of Trajan are said to have been placed in the column, but no trace of them has ever been found.

F. G. B. Millar

See also **Library** (Ancient libraries of papyrus); **Rome** (picture: Trajan's Column); **Sculpture** (picture: Trajan's Column [detail]).

Tram is the term used in the United Kingdom and other Commonwealth countries for a streetcar. See **Streetcar**.

Trampoline is a device that a person bounces or jumps on to perform aerial tumbling exercises. A trampoline may be used for recreation or for organized competition.

Trampolines may be circular or rectangular. They consist of a bed of solid or woven material that is suspended from a steel frame by rubber cords or padded steel springs. Trampolines are supported by legs nearly 4 feet (1.2 meters) high. Trampolines that are used in national and international competition are rectangular and have frames approximately 17 feet (5.1 meters) long and 9 $\frac{1}{2}$ feet (2.9 meters) wide. Trampolines used in competition must also have large thick pads, called *safety platforms,* attached to the two short sides. These platforms measure 10 feet (3 meters) long and 7 feet (2.0 meters) wide.

A number of safety rules should be followed to avoid injury while using a trampoline. At least one qualified supervisor should be present. Only one person should perform at a time. One or more *spotters* should stand along any side without a safety platform to protect the athlete if he or she bounces off the trampoline. Somersaults should be prohibited except in competitive programs with qualified instructors.

During competitive training, *spotting belts* are often used when practicing such difficult skills as somersaults.

Freedom Sports, Ltd.

The trampoline is a device used as a springboard to perform tumbling exercises. A trampoline consists of a sheet of strong fabric attached to springs on a circular or rectangular frame.

The belt is attached to an overhead rig and fastened around the athlete's waist. A rope-and-pulley system attached to the rig enables the instructor to control the athlete's movements. For example, the instructor might suspend the athlete in mid-air to prevent an unsafe landing. Some trampolines are placed in a "pit" so that the frame and bed are at floor level. Trampolines should be inspected often for damage. They should also be kept in a locked room when not in use. Bonnie J. Davidson

Trance is a term that is generally used to describe any kind of unnatural sleep or partly conscious state. The term may be used to describe the condition of hypnotized people, spiritualist mediums, and some people with mental disorders. In some cases, trances continue for long periods. But they usually last for only brief periods. The word *trance* was first used to describe conditions in which the soul was believed to have withdrawn from a person's body for a period of time.

There are no physical signs that always indicate a trance. But in many cases, the pulse and breathing rate slow down. A person in a trance is less responsive to changes in surroundings, and may not know what is happening. The person may appear to be responding to forces not actually present.

The best-known type of trance is probably that of the spiritualist medium who appears to have fallen into a deep sleep, but can still speak and write. Such a trance may be similar to a deep hypnosis, and it may involve hallucinations. James E. Alcock

See also **Hypnotism**.

Tranquilizer is a drug that calms a person by acting on the nervous system. Tranquilizers belong to a group of drugs called *antianxiety and hypnotic drugs.* Such drugs formerly were referred to as *depressants.*

There are two types of tranquilizers—*antipsychotic drugs* and *antianxiety drugs.* Antipsychotic drugs are used to treat patients with *psychoses* (severe mental illnesses). Antianxiety drugs are used to treat various emotional problems, particularly anxiety.

Antipsychotic drugs include chlorpromazine (commonly known by the trade name Thorazine), fluphenazine, and trifluoperazine. Doctors prescribe these drugs to treat *schizophrenia,* a mental illness characterized by illogical, unpredictable thinking. The drugs reduce the confusion and excitement experienced by the patient.

Antianxiety drugs include alprazolam, diazepam, and lorazepam, which are commonly known by the trade names Xanax, Valium, and Ativan, respectively. They relax the muscles and reduce tension. Physicians also use antianxiety drugs to calm children who must undergo surgery. In addition, these drugs are used to treat severe anxiety, shakiness, and other symptoms that occur during withdrawal from the effects of alcohol.

Some tranquilizers have undesirable side effects. For example, meprobamate (known by such trade names as Equanil and Miltown) may cause muscle weakness and general fatigue. Some people become addicted to tranquilizers. In addition, tranquilizers may cause drowsiness, especially if a person drinks alcoholic beverages before or after taking the drugs. A person should not drive a motor vehicle for several hours after taking a tranquilizer. N. E. Sladek

See also **Benzodiazepine; Depressant; Drug** (Antianxiety and hypnotic drugs).

Trans fats, also called *trans fatty acids,* are forms of fat found in solid fats, such as stick margarine and vegetable shortening, and in certain processed foods. Scientists have found that people who eat a diet high in trans fats have an increased risk of heart disease.

Foods made with or cooked in partially *hydrogenated* (processed with hydrogen) oil contain trans fats. Trans fats are used to improve flavor, texture, and freshness of many foods. Such foods include cookies, crackers, doughnuts, potato chips, and some salad dressings.

Trans fats in the diet raise the amount of a substance called *LDL cholesterol* in the blood, which increases the risk of heart disease. Nutrition experts recommend that people limit trans fats in their diet as much as possible while still eating a healthy diet. The United States Food and Drug Administration (FDA) requires that food labels list the amount of trans fats contained.

All fats contain fatty acids, which consist of chains of carbon atoms with hydrogen atoms attached. Fatty acids occur in two forms called *saturated* and *unsaturated.* A saturated fatty acid has a chemical structure in which as many hydrogen atoms as possible are linked to its carbon chain. An unsaturated fatty acid contains at least two fewer hydrogen atoms than a saturated fatty acid with the same number of carbon atoms. Trans fats are produced by hydrogenating unsaturated oils at high temperature. This process adds hydrogen atoms and causes the fatty acid chains to straighten out. The straighter chains can stack closer together, forming more solid fats. Ernst J. Schaefer

See also **Cholesterol; Fat** (Structure); **Nutrition** (Fats).

Transatlantic cable. See Cable.

Trans-Canada Highway is a road that runs across Canada from coast to coast, between Victoria in British Columbia and St. John's on the island of Newfoundland. It connects all 10 Canadian provinces. The main route stretches almost 4,900 miles (7,900 kilometers). The road varies from a two-lane highway to a multilane expressway. Ferry boats provide connections at both coasts.

The Trans-Canada Highway has been called the "Main Street of Canada" because it links nearly all major Canadian cities. It also provides access to many of the country's national parks, including Glacier, Mount Revelstoke, and Yoho in British Columbia; Banff in Alberta; and Terra Nova on the island of Newfoundland.

Construction of the highway began in 1950. The Trans-Canada Highway was formally dedicated in 1962. Through the years, additional routes have reached more of the country. A northern prairie route stretches between the main highway west of Winnipeg, Manitoba, and Prince Rupert, British Columbia. Extensions in Ontario and Quebec carry travelers north and south of the main route. Bruce E. Seely

Transcendental Meditation (TM) is a method of relaxing the body that became popular in many countries during the 1970's. It was developed in the 1950's by the Maharishi Mahesh Yogi, a Hindu monk from India. He used the word *transcendental* to describe the process of reaching a state of *pure consciousness,* where the mind is not aware of anything in particular. He declared that people who used this technique became happier and more relaxed and creative. Centers that teach TM operate in many countries, including the United States and Canada. Followers of the Maharishi call TM the Science of Creative Intelligence.

People practice TM by sitting quietly in a comfortable position. They close their eyes and silently repeat their *mantra,* a pleasant-sounding word from the Hindu scriptures. Teachers of TM select a personal, secret mantra for each student. A person who practices TM meditates for 15 to 20 minutes in the morning and evening, before meals.

Scientific studies show that certain bodily changes occur during meditation. For example, the rate of breathing and the amount of oxygen taken in by the body decrease while a person meditates. The blood pressure and the rate of heartbeat also decrease.

In addition, scientists found that *alpha waves* (brain waves that become prominent when a person is relaxed) increase in intensity during meditation. Psychologists report that many people who practice TM feel less anxious and aggressive than before and can handle stress more easily.

The Maharishi claimed that people cannot meditate effectively without training from a TM teacher and the use of a mantra. However, many scientists declare that other forms of meditation and relaxation can produce the same results as TM. Gary E. Schwartz

Trans-Canada Highway The Trans-Canada Highway, shown as a red line, runs from Victoria in British Columbia to St. John's on the island of Newfoundland. It provides a direct route across all 10 provinces.

WORLD BOOK map

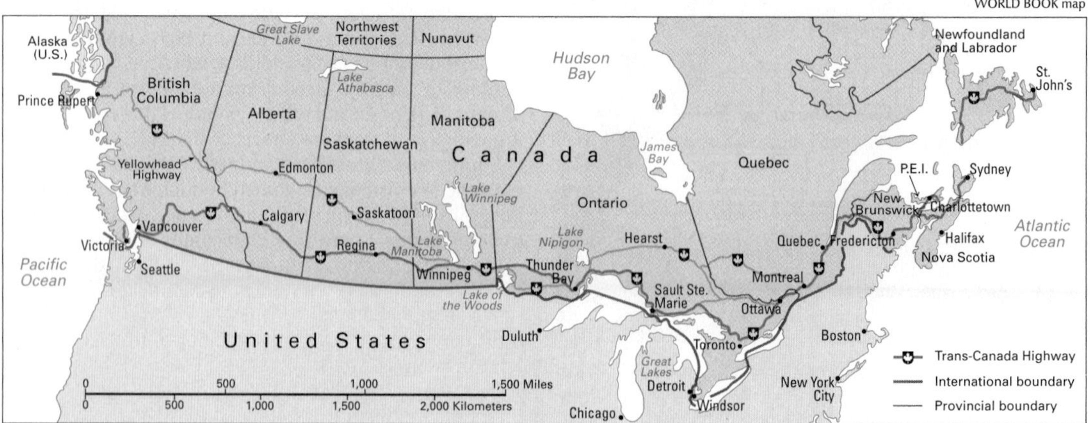

Transcendentalism was a philosophy that became influential during the late 1700's and 1800's. It was based on the belief that knowledge is not limited to and solely derived from experience and observation. It thus opposed the philosophy of Empiricism—that knowledge comes from experience. Transcendentalism also stated that the solution to human problems lies in the free development of individual emotions.

According to Transcendentalism, reality exists only in the world of the spirit. What a person observes in the physical world are only appearances, or impermanent reflections of the world of the spirit. People learn about the physical world through their senses and understanding. They learn about the world of the spirit through another power, known as *reason.* The Transcendentalists defined reason as the personal, independent, and intuitive capacity to know what is absolutely true.

Elements of Transcendentalism can be found in the Neoplatonic philosophy of ancient Greece (see **Neoplatonism**). But the chief source of Transcendentalist ideas was the *Critique of Pure Reason* (1781) by the German philosopher Immanuel Kant.

In the United States, Transcendentalism became both a philosophy and a literary, religious, and social movement. It began among Unitarians in New England and reached its peak during the 1840's. Ralph Waldo Emerson was the leading American Transcendentalist. He taught that the physical world is secondary to the spiritual world. But, said Emerson, the physical world serves humanity by providing beauty, language, discipline, and what he called "commodity," which he defined as "all those advantages which our senses owe to nature." Emerson believed that people should learn as much as possible through observation and science. But he insisted that they should adjust their lives primarily to the truths seen through reason.

Emerson and his followers believed that human beings find truth within themselves, and so they emphasized self-reliance and individuality. They believed that society needs to be reformed. They argued that in order to learn what is right, a person must resist custom and social codes and rely on reason. The Transcendentalists believed that the doctrines and organized churches of orthodox Christianity interfered with the personal relationship between a person and God. The Transcendentalists said that individuals should reject the authority of Christianity and gain knowledge of God by means of reason.

The American Transcendentalists never became numerous, but their writings greatly influenced American intellectual history and literature. Besides Emerson, the leading American Transcendentalists included Bronson Alcott, Margaret Fuller, Theodore Parker, and Henry David Thoreau. John Clendenning

Each person discussed in this article has a biography in *World Book.* See also **New Thought.**

Additional resources

Francis, Richard. *Transcendental Utopias: Individual and Community at Brook Farm, Fruitlands, and Walden.* Cornell Univ. Pr., 1997.

Hansen, Ellen, ed. *The New England Transcendentalists.* Discovery Enterprises, 1993. Younger readers.

Mott, Wesley T., ed. *Encyclopedia of Transcendentalism.* 1996.

Transcontinental railroad. See **Railroad** (The first transcontinental rail lines).

Transducer is a device that converts one form of energy into another. Many transducers convert electric waves into mechanical vibrations—or vice versa. Loudspeakers and microphones are examples of transducers. *Sonar transducers* send and receive sound waves in water. *Ultrasonic transducers* generate and detect vibrations above the frequency range of human hearing. They are used to cut hard materials, to clean delicate instruments, to drill oil wells, and to measure the level of liquids in the fuel tanks of space vehicles.

Transducers work in various ways. Some microphones use *piezoelectric* materials, which produce a voltage when pressure is applied. Loudspeakers use moving coils that vibrate when current moves through them. The vibrations result from an interaction between the coils and powerful permanent magnets. Some ultrasonic transducers use *magnetostrictive* materials, which contract in a magnetic field. Douglas M. Lapp

See also **Sonar; Ultrasound** (Ultrasound devices).

Transfiguration was the change in physical appearance that came over Jesus Christ on one occasion during His ministry. It is described in the Gospels of Matthew, Mark, and Luke. According to these Gospels, Jesus took Peter, James, and John up on a mountain and permitted them to see Him in splendor, with His face shining like the sun and His garments bright with light. Then the Old Testament figures of Moses and Elijah came to talk with Christ. Many artists have portrayed the Transfiguration. One of the greatest paintings on the subject is the altarpiece *The Transfiguration* by the Italian artist Raphael. Stanley K. Stowers

Transformer is a device that increases or decreases the voltage of alternating current. Alternating current is electric current that regularly reverses its direction. Transformers provide a simple, inexpensive way to change such voltage. They enable electric power companies to transmit alternating current easily and efficiently. Transformers also ensure the proper voltage for the circuits of home appliances, lights, industrial machinery, and other electric equipment.

Most transformers consist of two coils of insulated wire. One coil, called the *primary winding,* is connected to the source of the voltage that is to be changed. This voltage is the *input voltage* of the transformer. The other coil, called the *secondary winding,* supplies the *output voltage* to the desired circuit. In most transformers, both coils are wound around a hollow core made of thin iron or steel sheets. Most cores have the shape of a ring or a square. The two coils are not connected to each other.

Transformers work by means of *electromagnetic induction* (see **Electromagnetism**). When the input voltage is applied to the primary winding, it generates alternating current in the coil. As the current flows, it sets up a changing magnetic field in the core of the transformer. When this changing magnetic field passes through the secondary winding, it produces alternating voltage in the coil. If the secondary winding is connected to a circuit, the output voltage causes alternating current to flow through the circuit.

The ratio between a transformer's output voltage and input voltage equals the ratio of the number of turns in the secondary winding to the number in the primary winding. If V represents the voltage and N stands for the

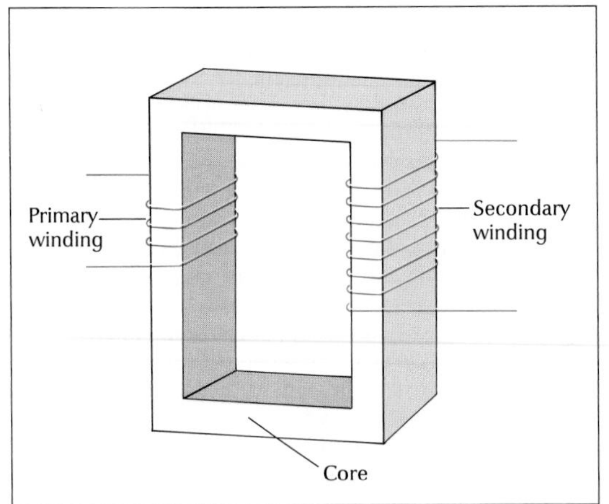

WORLD BOOK diagram by Linda Kinnaman

A typical transformer consists of two coils of wire wound around the sides of a core of thin iron sheets. The ends of the primary winding are connected to the source of the voltage that is to be changed. The ends of the secondary winding are connected to the circuit to which the electricity is to be transferred.

number of turns, then $\frac{V\text{output}}{V\text{input}} = \frac{N\text{secondary}}{N\text{primary}}$. The output voltage will be greater than the input voltage in a transformer whose secondary winding has more turns than the primary winding. Such a transformer is called a *step-up transformer.* If the secondary coil has fewer turns than the primary, the output voltage will be less than the input voltage. This type of transformer is called a *step-down transformer.*

In power plants, step-up transformers increase the voltage of the alternating current produced by generators. High voltages make it possible to transmit the current over long distances with only a small loss in power. When the current reaches the area where it will be used, step-down transformers lower the voltage to the level needed by local consumers (see **Electric power** [Transmitting and distributing electric power]).

Some transformers have special uses. For example, *air-core transformers* and *powdered iron-core transformers* are designed to handle high-frequency alternating currents. *Instrument transformers* are used in measuring extremely large alternating voltages and currents. *Variable transformers* vary the amount of output voltage delivered to a circuit. Douglas M. Lapp

See also **Induction coil.**

Transfusion, Blood. See **Blood transfusion.**

Transistor is a tiny device that controls the flow of electric current in radios, television sets, computers, and almost every other kind of electronic equipment. Transistors vary in size from about 1/10,000 of a millimeter—approximately 1/500 the diameter of a human hair—to a few centimeters across.

Three American physicists—John Bardeen, Walter H. Brattain, and William Shockley—invented the transistor in 1947. By the late 1960's, transistors had replaced electronic components called *vacuum tubes* almost completely. Transistors offered a number of advantages over vacuum tubes. For example, they were smaller, lighter, cheaper to operate, and more reliable than vacuum tubes. Over time, transistors also became cheap to produce. See **Vacuum tube.**

Transistors are the main components built into *computer chips,* devices that carry out computer programs and store data. Some chips no larger than a fingernail contain many millions of transistors. Large, individual transistors are called *discrete transistors.* Because of their size, these units can handle many times the power of transistors in chips. Uses of discrete transistors include providing the power for the speakers of high-fidelity sound systems and the motors of small appliances; turning lights on and off; and controlling electric relays and switches.

What transistors do

A transistor has two basic functions: (1) to switch electric current on and off and (2) to *amplify* (strengthen) electric current. A small voltage called the *input signal* controls both switching and amplification.

Transistors in computers perform rapid switching operations to manipulate electric charges that represent information as the 0's and 1's of the binary numeration system. As the transistors move the charges about, electronic circuits carry out calculations, solve problems in logic, form words and pictures on monitors, control printers, and perform other computer operations. See **Computer** (Parts of computers).

The ability of transistors to amplify signals makes them essential parts of radios and television sets. The broadcast waves that travel through the air generate weak currents in a radio or TV antenna. Transistors detect and amplify these signals. Other components—including additional transistors—use the resulting strong currents to produce sounds and pictures.

Transistor materials

Transistors are made from materials called *semiconductors.* A semiconductor *conducts* (carries) electric current better than an insulator, such as glass, but not as well as a conductor, such as silver or copper. Silicon is the most common semiconductor used for transistors.

A certain minimum voltage must be applied across a semiconductor before any current will flow. In a conductor, any voltage—no matter how small—will cause current to flow. In an insulator, the voltage required to start a current is so strong that starting current flow would destroy the material.

Electric current is a flow of electric charges. In a regular conductor, current is a flow of *free electrons.* In a semiconductor, current can be a flow of free electrons or of *holes.* A free electron is an electron that is not tightly bound to an atom. A hole is a positively charged, "empty" region near an atom that would normally be occupied by an electron.

In an atom, one or more negatively charged electrons orbit a positively charged nucleus. The electrons are arranged in groups called *shells* (see **Atom** [Parts of an atom]). A silicon atom normally has four electrons in its outermost shell. In a pure crystal of silicon, however, there are always a small number of free electrons and holes. This is so because a small percentage of electrons absorb enough heat energy to leave their shells, becoming free electrons—and leaving holes behind. These electrons quickly occupy holes—but in the meantime other electrons leave their shells.

Doping a semiconductor crystal—replacing some of its atoms with atoms of another chemical element—changes the way in which it conducts current. In an *n-type* silicon crystal, a small number of silicon atoms are replaced by phosphorus atoms, which have five electrons in their outermost shells. One of these electrons is not tightly bound to the phosphorus nucleus, so the n-type crystal has extra free electrons. In a *p-type* silicon crystal, a small number of silicon atoms are replaced by boron atoms, which have three electrons in their outermost shells. Thus, a p-type crystal has extra holes. An n-type crystal thus conducts electric current with electrons, while p-type silicon conducts electric current with holes. See **Electronics** (Transistors); **Semiconductor**.

How transistors work

There are two main kinds of transistors: (1) *bipolar transistors* and (2) *metal oxide semiconductor field effect transistors* (MOSFET's). Bipolar transistors are able to work with large currents, but they consume energy when turned on or off. Most discrete transistors are bipolar. MOSFET's are smaller than bipolar transistors, and turning them on and off consumes little energy. Almost all of the chips in computers and other *digital* (numeric) switching circuits use MOSFET's.

Bipolar transistors. A simple bipolar transistor has a thin region of one type of semiconductor material sandwiched between two thicker regions of the opposite type. If the middle region is p-type material, the outside regions are n-type. This design is known as *NPN.* A *PNP* transistor has an n-type inside region and p-type outside regions. In both designs, one outside region is called the *emitter,* and the other is known as the *collector.* The middle region is the *base.*

Connected to each region is an electric terminal. In a discrete transistor, the terminal is one end of a small wire. In a transistor on a chip, it is a thin layer of metal connected to other electronic components on the chip.

The input signal is applied at the base terminal. The current that is amplified or switched off and on flows from the emitter to the collector.

Applied voltages. Before a transistor can operate, its terminals must receive certain voltages. To operate an NPN transistor in the normal way, a positive voltage is applied to the collector, and the emitter receives a voltage of zero. If the base's voltage is also zero, the transistor is off. Applying a small current to the base turns the transistor on.

When the needed voltages are applied, many free electrons and holes move to new positions throughout the transistor. These movements occur because positive voltages attract electrons and negative voltages push away electrons and attract holes.

Charge movement in the collector and base. An *electric field* is a region in which voltage acts on a charged object, such as an electron. Transistors work by varying the voltages in the emitter, collector, and base regions. In an NPN transistor in a nonconducting, or "off," state, the collector terminal is more positive than the base terminal. Thus, the voltage applied to the collector pulls free electrons near the collector-base junction away from the junction and toward the collector terminal. Because the base has a lower positive voltage than the collector, holes near the collector-base junction are pulled away from this junction toward the base terminal. Thus, there are no free electrons or holes at the collector-base junction to flow as electric current.

Charge movement in the emitter. When the base is positive relative to the emitter, free electrons in the emitter are drawn toward the base-emitter junction. But in a typical transistor in which the emitter voltage is zero, there is no significant flow of electrons across the junction until the base voltage reaches about 0.4 volt.

The bipolar transistor as a switch. When the base voltage is low—from 0 to 0.3 volt in a typical silicon transistor—essentially no current flows from the emitter through the base to the collector. The base voltage is too low to pull electrons from the emitter across the base-emitter junction. Thus, the transistor is off.

Increasing the base voltage to about 0.6 volt causes large numbers of electrons to flow from the emitter into the base. Because the base is extremely thin, an electron that enters the base is already close to the collector-base junction. As the concentration of electrons in the base increases, some electrons penetrate all the way through the negative electric field at the collector-base junction, even though this field opposes a flow of electrons. Once the electrons are on the collector side of the junction, they pass easily to the collector terminal, leaving the transistor. Thus, current flows from the emitter terminal through the base and leaves the transistor through the collector terminal. The maximum flow of electrons occurs when the base voltage is about 0.7 volt.

The bipolar transistor as an amplifier. A transistor that functions as an amplifier remains in a conducting state, but the strength of the signal is varied. Increasing the strength of the input signal at the base causes more free electrons in the emitter to flow into the base. More electrons therefore reach the collector. Thus, the current flowing from the emitter to the collector increases in proportion to the increased strength of the input signal.

Decreasing the strength of the input signal decreases the flow of electrons across the base and into the collector. The current from the emitter to the collector decreases in proportion to the decrease in signal strength.

The current flowing across the transistor from the emitter to the collector is therefore a stronger copy of the weak input signal. The ratio of the strength of this output current to that of the input current is called *gain.* In a typical amplifying transistor, the gain may be 100.

A PNP transistor works on the same principles as an NPN transistor. However, the voltages in a PNP transistor are the reverse of those in an NPN transistor.

Metal oxide semiconductor field effect transistors (MOSFET's). The MOSFET's that are used in computer chips are the most common type of *field effect transistors* (FET's). A FET operates by creating an electric field that changes how one of the transistor's semiconductor regions, the *gate region,* conducts electric current. Current flows when enough charge carriers—either electrons or holes—are attracted to the gate region. A FET has three semiconductor regions—the *source*, the *gate region,* and the *drain.* In a MOSFET, the source and drain are made of the same type of semiconductor material—either n-type or p-type. The gate region, which lies between the source and the drain, is made of the opposite type of material. The gate region typically extends into the *substrate,* the underlying chip material.

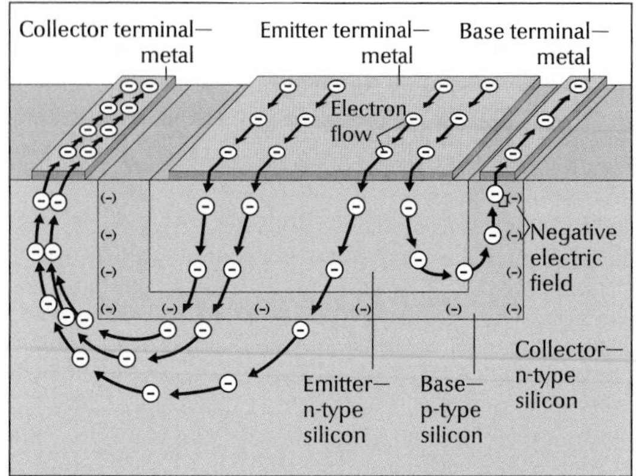

WORLD BOOK diagram by Mark Swindle

An NPN bipolar transistor conducts a large electric current as a flow of electrons from an *emitter* region to a *collector* region of *doped* (altered) silicon. A small current flows to the terminal of a very thin *base.* The emitter normally receives a voltage of zero, the collector a high positive voltage, and the base a low positive voltage. Electrons, which are negatively charged, flow into the positive base. There, some of the electrons crowd others past a negative electric field and into the collector.

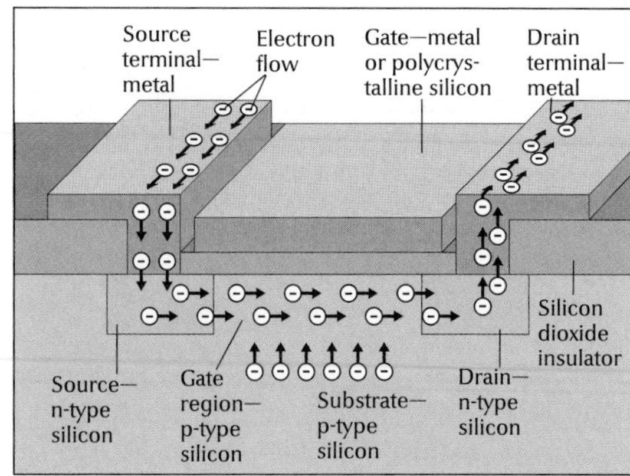

WORLD BOOK diagram by Mark Swindle

An n-channel metal oxide semiconductor field effect transistor (MOSFET) conducts electric current as a flow of electrons between *doped* (altered) regions of silicon—the *source* and the *drain.* The drain receives a voltage that is more positive than the voltage applied to the drain. But for current to flow, the terminal of the *gate* must also receive a positive voltage. This voltage pulls electrons from a *substrate* into a *gate region,* establishing an electron-rich channel for the current.

The source and drain are embedded in the substrate.

Electric terminals are connected to the source and the drain. Above the gate region is a thin layer of silicon dioxide, an insulating material. Above the insulating material is a layer called the *gate,* connected to a third terminal. Gates in early MOSFET's were made of aluminum, but today they are often made of polycrystalline silicon.

A small input voltage signal is applied at the gate terminal. The current that is switched off and on flows from the source terminal to the drain terminal.

In normal operation, the drain is more positive than the source. Thus, current tends to flow from the source to the drain. Whether current actually flows depends upon the type of MOSFET, and whether the voltage to the gate is negative or positive. An *n-channel* MOSFET has a source and drain of n-type silicon on a p-type silicon substrate. A *p-channel* MOSFET has a p-type silicon source and drain on a substrate of n-type silicon. A negative voltage to the gate permits current to flow in an n-channel MOSFET, and a positive voltage has the same effect in a p-channel MOSFET. The voltage to the gate creates an electric field in the gate region. The field increases or reduces the number of charge carriers in that region, thus controlling current flow.

If the gate of an n-channel MOSFET is given a negative voltage, the free electrons in the gate region will be repelled into the substrate. Thus, these electrons will not be available to flow as current from the source to the drain. The MOSFET will be off. If the gate receives a positive voltage, free electrons will be attracted into the gate region. Thus, there will be a continuous band, or *channel,* of material with extra free electrons between the source and the drain. If the gate voltage is sufficiently high, current will flow. The MOSFET will be on. In p-channel MOSFET's, opposite voltages are applied to produce the same effects. Thomas J. Misa

Transit, in astronomy, is the movement of one body in the sky in front of another body that appears larger. As seen from Earth, the planets Mercury and Venus occasionally transit the sun. During a transit, the planet appears as a dark dot moving across the sun's disk. Transits of Mercury occur about 13 times in each century. Venus transits occur in pairs in which one transit happens 8 years after the other. These pairs are separated by alternating intervals of 105 ½ and 121 ½ years.

In 1639, the English astronomers Jeremiah Horrocks and William Crabtree recorded the first observations of a transit of Venus. Edmond Halley, another English astronomer, later proposed timing transit events from various locations to calculate the distance from Earth to the sun. The average such distance is called the *astronomical unit* (AU). Astronomers refined their measurements of the AU during the Venus transits of 1761, 1769, 1874, and 1882. In 2004, the first of a pair of Venus transits occurred. The next transit was expected in 2012.

In the late 1990's, astronomers began to use observations of transits to help discover distant planets. Although the planets are too far away to be seen, astronomers can detect the slight dimming they cause when they pass in front of the star they are orbiting. The United States planned to launch the Kepler spacecraft, designed to look for distant transits in the hope of discovering Earthlike planets, in 2008.

The word *transit* can also mean the instant when a body passes directly over an observer's *meridian.* The meridian is an imaginary north-south line passing through the observer's position. Glenn Schneider

Transit is a service that carries large numbers of people from place to place within cities or between cities and their suburbs. Most large urban areas provide some such service, also called *public transportation.*

Buses are the most common transit vehicles. They usually follow a schedule, and pick up and drop off passengers at designated stops. A typical city bus can carry up to about 70 people. Other common transit systems include three types of rail transportation: (1) light rail, (2) subways and elevated systems, and (3) commuter rail.

Light rail trains have one to six electrically powered

cars. Each car can carry up to about 100 people. In the city center, the tracks are usually in the middle of the street. In less crowded urban areas, and in the suburbs, the tracks are usually next to the street or on a separate *right of way* (strip of land reserved for a particular use).

Subways and elevated systems operate electrically powered trains that usually have from 1 to 10 cars. Each car can carry up to about 100 passengers. The trains run underground, on elevated tracks, or both.

Commuter rail systems operate trains over exclusive rights of way between cities and their suburbs. The trains carry a majority of their passengers during morning and evening rush hours. Many commuter trains use diesel-powered locomotives. Robert E. Paaswell

Related articles in *World Book* include:

Bus
Cable car
Electric railroad
Elevated railroad
Monorail
Streetcar
Subway
Transportation (Passenger transportation)

Transjordan. See Jordan.

Transmission is a device that transmits power from the engine of a vehicle to other parts, from which it is eventually delivered to the wheels. The transmission, also known as the *gearbox,* is a major part of a system called the *drive train,* a series of devices that sends engine power to the wheels.

The drive power of a motor vehicle is a combination of rotational speed and *torque* (twisting effort). The transmission sets an engine speed that provides the wheel speed and other performance characteristics desired by the driver. The transmission can also reverse torque so the vehicle can back up. In addition, when the transmission is set in *neutral,* it delivers no power—even when the engine is running.

Automobiles, trucks, buses, bulldozers, and other types of motor vehicles have transmissions. This article discusses the most common automobile transmissions.

Why automobiles have transmissions

A transmission adjusts an automobile engine's speed to provide such desirable characteristics as engine efficiency and smooth, swift acceleration. An engine can vary its speed and produce a certain range of torque. However, engine efficiency varies greatly under different combinations of speed and torque. If a car did not have a transmission, the engine alone would have to produce all the combinations of speed and torque required in the normal operation of the car. The engine would therefore accelerate the vehicle poorly and would operate inefficiently most of the time.

A car requires a large amount of torque to start moving after it has stopped. At this time, both torque and speed increase. When a car that has been traveling along a level road starts up a hill, it needs more torque merely to maintain its speed.

Transmissions and drives

An automobile's transmission is connected to the engine so that the transmission can receive power directly from the engine. The arrangement of the engine and transmission depends upon the kind of *drive* the car has. Most cars have *front-wheel drive.* This means that the front pair of wheels moves the car. Other automobiles have *rear-wheel drive.* In a *four-wheel drive* vehicle, the drive train can be adjusted to send power to the front two wheels, for ordinary driving, or to all four wheels, for driving on rough terrain or providing extra traction. In an *all-wheel drive* car, power is always provided to all four wheels.

In the most common arrangement in a front-wheel drive vehicle, the engine and transmission are mounted *transversely* (across the car) between the front wheels. In this arrangement, the transmission is a part of a unit called a *transaxle.* This unit also includes a *final drive and differential,* a device that adjusts speed and torque. The transaxle drives the front wheels.

In most rear-wheel drive cars, the engine and transmission are mounted in front. A rotating cylindrical tube called a *drive shaft* delivers power from the transmission to a final drive and differential in the rear of the car.

What a transmission does

A transmission receives a speed and torque input from the engine and delivers a different speed and torque to the final drive and differential. The engine delivers its power to the transmission by means of a rotating *crankshaft.* The transmission receives this power at its *flywheel,* a heavy disk connected to the crankshaft. The flywheel turns whenever the engine is running. The transmission delivers its output power by means of a rotating shaft. Most transmissions adjust speed and torque by means of rotating gears.

Power. A transmission can deliver almost the same quantity of power it receives. All transmissions lose a small amount of power due to friction between metal parts. Transmissions that use a liquid to transmit torque also lose power due to inefficiencies in devices that pump the fluid.

Power is the rate at which work is done. In the case of a rotating part, such as a shaft or a gear, power equals rotational speed times torque. In the inch-pound system of units customarily used in the United States, power is measured in horsepower. In the metric system, power is measured in watts. One horsepower equals 746 watts.

If the transmission receives a constant amount of power from the engine, the transmission cannot adjust its own output torque without also adjusting its output speed. This is so because power must always equal speed times torque. For example, if a transmission doubles the torque that it delivers, it must also decrease the speed of its output shaft by half.

Gears. A pair of rotating gears whose teeth *mesh* (fit together) adjusts speed and torque in proportion to the numbers of teeth in the gears. One gear *drives* (applies torque to) the other. The relationship between the speed of the driver gear and the speed of the driven gear is called a *reduction.* Reduction is expressed numerically by a *gear ratio.* The gear ratio of a pair of gears is equal to the number of teeth in the driven gear divided by the number of teeth in the driver gear. For example, if a gear with 9 teeth drives a gear with 27 teeth, the gear ratio is 3 to 1. This means that, for every three revolutions of the driver gear, the driven gear rotates once. In other words, the driven gear rotates at one-third the speed of the driver gear. The relationship between the torques of the two gears is numerically the same as the gear ratio—with the first number representing the torque of the driven gear. In the example above, the driven gear rotates with three times the torque of the driver gear.

Most transmissions use different sizes of gears to produce various gear ratios and thus various proportions of speed and torque. Gear ratios are often called simply *gears* or *speeds.*

Most transmissions have three to six forward gears, one reverse gear, and a neutral setting. In a typical three-speed transmission, first gear has a ratio of about 3 to 1; second gear, about 2 to 1; and third gear, about 1 to 1. Most transmissions with more than three forward gears have a high gear called *overdrive.* The gear ratio of overdrive is less than 1 to 1—in other words, the speed of the transmission's output shaft is higher than the speed of the crankshaft.

There are two types of transmissions that differ in how they *shift gears* (change from one gear ratio to another). An *automatic transmission* has special devices that automatically shift gears as needed. In a car with a *manual transmission,* the driver uses a hand-operated lever called a *gearshift.*

How an automatic transmission works

An automatic transmission provides various gear ratios as they are needed. Cars with automatic transmissions have a lever called a *selector.* The driver can move the selector to positions for *park, neutral, drive, low,* and *reverse.* The engine can start only when the selector is in park or neutral.

To put a car into forward motion, the driver moves the selector to the drive position. Initially, the transmission will be in first, or low, gear. This gear provides the highest torque and the lowest speed. As the car picks up speed, the transmission will automatically shift into higher gears. In higher gears, speed is higher and torque is lower.

The driver may move the selector to low when going up or down hills or driving through snow or mud. With the selector in low, the transmission will remain in low gear, rather than shift automatically into higher gears. Some cars with automatic transmissions have one or more selector positions between low and drive. These positions prevent shifting above the selected gear.

The major parts of an automatic transmission are a *torque converter,* one or more sets of *planetary gears,* three kinds of *clutches,* and a *controller.*

A torque converter transmits power from the engine to the gears. It also increases torque. It resembles a large doughnut sliced in half. One half, called the *pump* or *impeller,* is bolted to the flywheel. The other half, the *turbine,* is connected to the *input shaft,* which transmits power to the gears. The pump and turbine face each other in a case filled with a liquid known as *transmission fluid.* Both are lined with blades called *vanes.* A bladed wheel called a *stator* lies between them.

The engine causes the pump to rotate and throw transmission fluid against the vanes of the turbine. The moving fluid applies torque to the turbine. After hitting the turbine, the fluid passes into the stator and returns

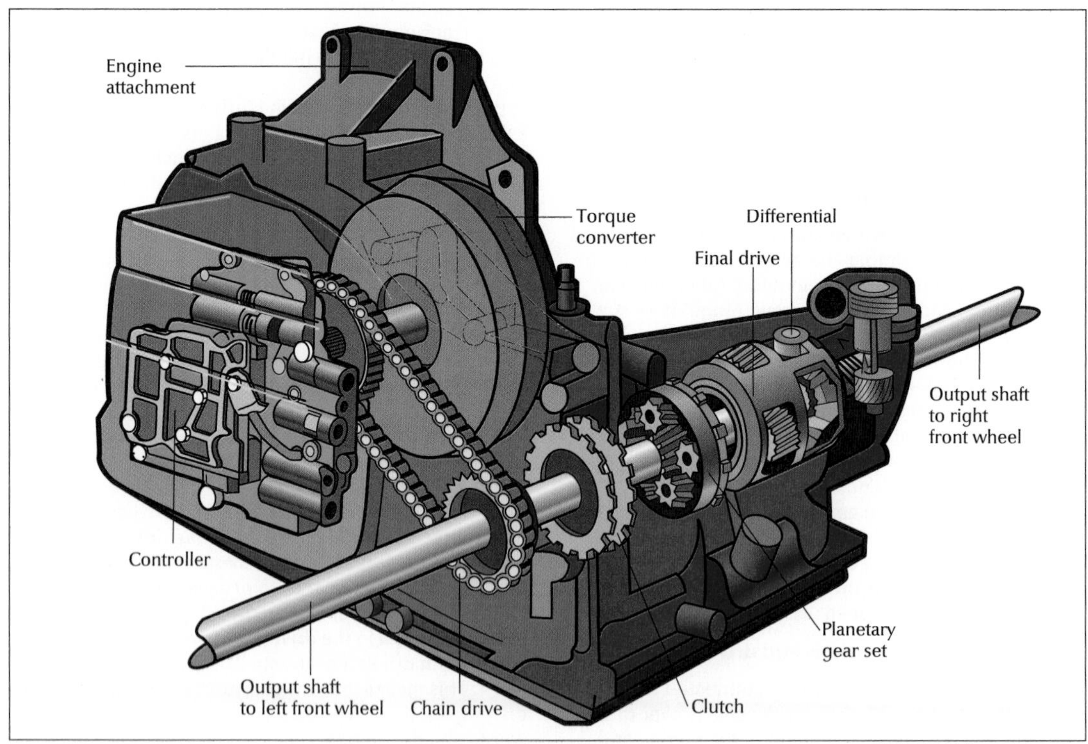

WORLD BOOK diagram by Bruce Kerr

A transaxle delivers engine power to shafts that turn the wheels of an automobile. Engine power flows through a device called a *torque converter* and a chain drive. A hydraulic *controller* regulates several clutches—one of which is shown here—to operate one or two sets of planetary gears. A *differential* gear drive divides twisting effort evenly between the shafts.

to the pump. The energy in the returning fluid helps the engine turn the pump. The addition of this energy makes the torque applied to the turbine higher than it would be if there were no stator.

When the engine is running slowly, the transmission fluid may not transmit enough torque to rotate the turbine. But when the driver presses the accelerator pedal, the engine runs faster and so does the pump. The torque gradually becomes high enough to rotate the turbine, and thus move the car.

As the automobile gains speed, the speed and torque of the turbine gradually approach the speed and torque of the pump. Eventually, when the automobile is cruising in third gear or overdrive, the torques become equal. However, the turbine always tends to run more slowly than the pump. The difference in speed is due to an unavoidable inefficiency in the torque converter. To overcome this inefficiency, many transmissions have a *lock-up clutch.* When the vehicle begins to cruise in a higher gear, the clutch locks the pump and turbine together. The pump and turbine then rotate as if they were a solid unit.

The torque converter transmits power to an assembly of planetary gears and clutches. The arrangement of the torque converter and this assembly depends on the location of the engine and transmission and the type of drive.

In a car with front-wheel drive and a transversely mounted engine and transmission, the torque converter and the assembly are offset from each other. The torque converter delivers power indirectly. A shaft leading from the torque converter drives one sprocket of a chain drive. The other sprocket drives a shaft that leads to the assembly.

In a car with a rear-wheel drive and a front-mounted engine, the assembly is lined up with the torque converter. The torque converter transmits the power directly, by means of a shaft leading to the assembly.

Planetary gears. Most automatic transmissions have two sets of planetary gears arranged in a row. The transmission controls the parts, or *elements,* of these gear sets to produce various gear ratios and reverse.

Each planetary gear set consists of three elements. The first element, the *sun gear,* is mounted at the center of the set. The second element, the *carrier,* surrounds the sun gear. The carrier holds two, three, or four smaller *planet gears.* The planet gears are equally spaced around the sun gear and mesh with it. The third element, the *internal gear,* is a ring with teeth inside it. The internal gear surrounds, and meshes with, the planet gears.

Clutches. Any element of a gear set can be held stationary or locked to one of the other elements to produce different gear ratios. In an automatic transmission, clutches perform these tasks.

A clutch is a device that can connect or disconnect two *components* (parts) of a transmission, one or both of which are rotating. An automatic transmission has three kinds of clutches: (1) plate clutches, (2) band clutches, and (3) one-way clutches.

A plate clutch has a number of washer-shaped plates stacked next to one another. Alternating plates are permanently attached to the two components. With the clutch *disengaged,* the plates are separated so that neither component can drive or hold the other. When the clutch is *engaged,* the plates are pushed together. One component can now drive or hold the other.

A band clutch can stop and hold one element of a planetary gear set. This clutch has a band mounted around the outside of a drum. The drum, in turn, is attached to the planetary element. With the clutch disengaged, the drum is free to rotate. When the clutch is engaged, the band tightens around the drum, stopping and holding the drum.

A one-way clutch drives a component in one direction only. The clutch also enables another part of the transmission to rotate the component more rapidly in the same direction.

The controller is an assembly of valves and passages through which a liquid called *hydraulic oil* flows. The controller is part of the transmission's hydraulic system, which engages and disengages the plate and band clutches. A one-way clutch operates automatically and does not require hydraulic oil to work.

Other parts of the hydraulic system include a pump and various passages leading from the controller to pistons that control the clutches. The pump pushes oil into the controller. The valves shift to direct oil into the appropriate passages. The valves shift automatically, in response to the selector setting, the driver's pressure on the accelerator pedal, and other factors.

How a manual transmission works

The driver shifts the gears of a manual transmission

How planetary gears work

The parts of a planetary gear set can be held from turning or locked together to achieve a variety of gear ratios. The illustrations at the right show a few possible combinations. In all three cases, the internal gear is driving the other parts of the gear set. The effects can be multiplied by two gear sets arranged in line.

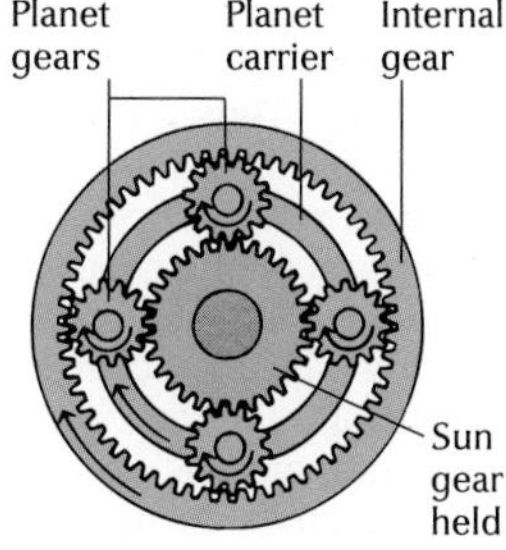

Reduction. Sun gear held. Planet gears "walk" around sun gear, causing planet carrier to rotate more slowly than internal gear.

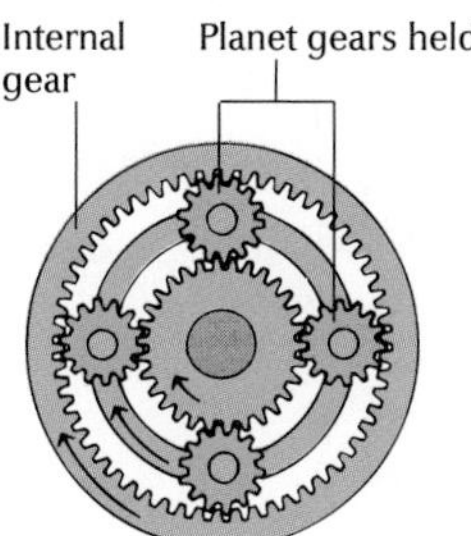

Direct drive. Internal gear and planet carrier locked together. Planet gears cannot turn. Entire gear set rotates as a unit.

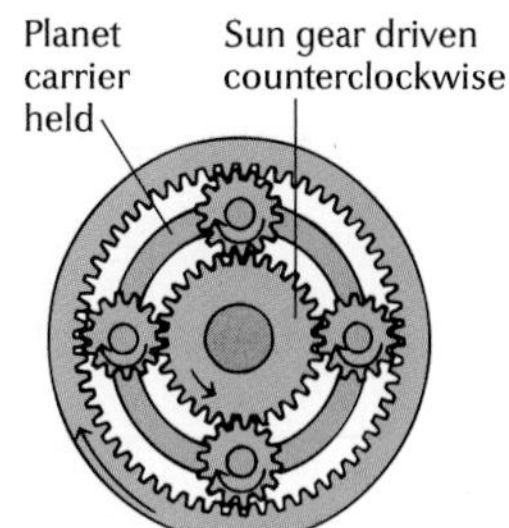

WORLD BOOK diagrams by Richard Fickle

Reverse. Planet carrier held. Internal gear rotates clockwise. Planet gears turn and act as idlers. Sun gear driven counterclockwise.

by means of a gearshift. The driver puts the transmission into the neutral position when starting the engine or when stopping the car with the engine running.

To put a car into forward motion, the driver shifts into first, or low, gear. As the car picks up speed, the driver shifts into second gear, then into third gear, and so on, until the transmission is in the highest gear desired. If extra torque is needed, the driver may *downshift* from a higher gear to a lower one. Such a situation might occur when the car goes up a steep hill.

A clutch connects the engine to the transmission. The driver controls the clutch by pressing and releasing a pedal. The driver must operate the clutch along with the gearshift. When the driver presses the pedal, the clutch is disengaged, and no power is sent to the transmission. When the driver releases the pedal, the clutch is engaged, sending power to the transmission. The driver must disengage the clutch when shifting gears.

The clutch. The main parts of the clutch are three disks: the *flywheel,* the *clutch plate,* and the *pressure plate.* The flywheel and pressure plate are connected to the crankshaft. They therefore turn whenever the engine is running. The clutch plate is mounted between the flywheel and the pressure plate, and is connected to the input shaft of the transmission.

When the clutch is engaged, springs in the pressure plate press the clutch plate against the flywheel. The three disks therefore turn at the same speed. When the clutch is disengaged, the springs are released, so the disks separate.

The gears. Power travels from the clutch plate to the transmission's input shaft. A gear at the end of the input shaft drives a gear on another shaft called the *countershaft.* The countershaft holds several gears of different sizes. These gears drive other gears on a third shaft, the *output shaft.* The output shaft leads to the drive shaft.

The transmission produces various gear ratios by engaging different combinations of gears. For reverse, an extra gear called an *idler* operates between the countershaft and the output shaft. This gear turns the output shaft in the opposite direction of the input shaft, thus making the car go backward.

The final drive and differential

An automatic or manual transmission transmits power by means of a rotating shaft to a final drive and differential unit. This unit, in turn, delivers power by means of two output shafts—one leading to each drive wheel.

The final drive provides an additional reduction. In a transaxle, the final drive is usually a set of planetary gears. In a car with rear-wheel drive and a front-mounted engine and transmission, the final drive is a set of *bevel gears.* The bevel gears mesh at a right angle. One gear is connected to the drive shaft; the other, to the differential. See **Gear.**

The differential is a complex gear set that divides torque evenly between the two drive wheels. The differential also enables one wheel to rotate faster than the other. For example, when a car goes around a corner, the outside wheel must travel farther than the inside one. The differential enables the outside wheel to rotate faster than the inside wheel to cover the longer distance in the same time.

How a continuously variable transmission works

Unlike automatic and manual transmissions, which have set gear ratios between the input and output shafts, *continuously variable transmissions* (CVT's) provide an infinite number of gear ratios between an upper and lower limit. A CVT achieves this using wheels, pulleys, cones, or some combination of these three components. There are many types of CVT's.

A relatively simple example of a CVT is the *disk and wheel.* In this design, a disk is mounted on a shaft driven by the engine. The disk is in contact with a wheel that can slide on an axle mounted at a right angle to the shaft being driven by the engine. The wheel and axle rotate faster when the wheel meets the disk near its edge, and more slowly when the contact point is nearer the disk's center. The gear ratio changes continuously as the wheel moves along the axle.

Other CVT designs have some other device between the driving shaft and the driven shaft. For example, in a variable diameter pulley CVT, two cones face each other with a belt riding between them. The belt is V-shaped so that it rides the "V" formed between the cones. If the cones of the pulley move closer together, the belt rides farther from the axis of the pulley. As the cones move farther apart, the belt comes closer to the axis. Both the driving shaft and the driven shaft have this pulley configuration. Constant tension on the belt is maintained by reducing the distance between the pulley cones on one shaft while increasing the distance between the cones on the other shaft. David E. Foster

See also **Automobile** (The power train; diagram).

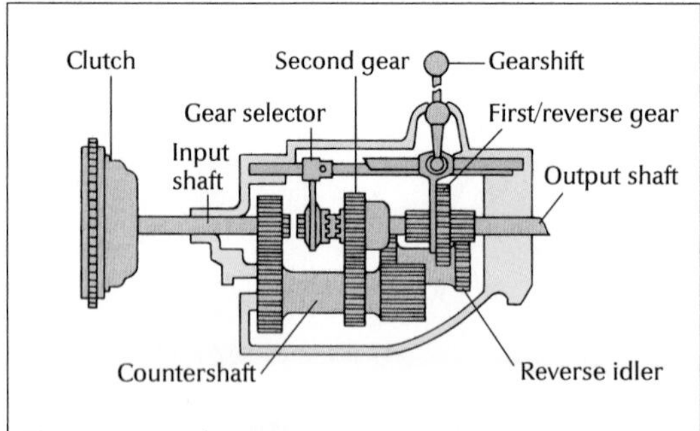

WORLD BOOK diagram by Richard Fickle

A manual transmission contains a system of gears controlled by a gearshift. A clutch connects it to the engine. When the transmission is in neutral, *above,* no power is transmitted.

Transmitter. See **Radio** (How radio programs are broadcast); **Telephone** (How a telephone works); **Television** (Transmitting television signals).

Transmutation of elements is the transformation of an atom of one chemical element into an atom of another element. An atom's nucleus contains one or more *protons* (positively charged particles). All atoms of an element have the same number of protons in their nuclei. This number is called the element's *atomic number.* Transmutation occurs when the number of protons in an atom's nucleus changes.

Transmutation commonly occurs in nature when a radioactive atom *emits* (gives off) a particle. This process is called *radioactive decay.* The most common forms of radioactive decay are *alpha decay* and *beta decay.* In alpha decay, the nucleus emits an *alpha particle* made up of two protons and two neutrons. The atom, with two fewer protons, becomes an atom of the element whose atomic number is two lower. For example, an atom of radium (atomic number 88) has 88 protons in its nucleus. After alpha decay, the atom has 86 protons, making it an atom of radon (atomic number 86).

In beta decay, a neutron changes into a proton or a proton changes into a neutron. The first process emits an electron or *beta particle.* The atom has one more proton in its nucleus than before, changing it into an atom of the element whose atomic number is one higher. The second process emits a positively charged particle called a *positron.* The atom has one fewer protons in its nucleus, changing it into an atom of the element whose atomic number is one lower.

Transmutation can take place artificially when a device called a *particle accelerator* slams a charged particle into a nucleus. If the particle is an alpha particle, for example, the nucleus first absorbs it and then emits a proton. The atom is left with one more proton in its nucleus, making it an atom of the element whose atomic number is one higher. Artificial transmutation can also occur in a device called a *nuclear reactor.* Inside the reactor, neutrons can bombard the nucleus, causing it to *fission* (split) into two nuclei of different elements. In a *fusion* reactor, two nuclei *fuse* (merge) to form a nucleus of a different element. Douglas John Crawford-Brown

Related articles in *World Book* include:

Alpha particle
Atom (Radioactivity)
Beta particle
Fission
Fusion
Radiation

Trans-Neptunian belt. See Kuiper belt.

Transpiration. See Leaf (Transpiration).

Transplant, in medicine, is surgery that transfers any type of tissue or organ from one person to another. Transplanted tissues and organs replace diseased, damaged, or destroyed body parts. Transplants can help restore the health of people who might otherwise die or be seriously disabled. Transfers of such tissues as skin or hair from one part of a person's own body to another part are also called transplants. This article focuses on person-to-person transplants.

There are two major types of transplants—tissue transplants and organ transplants. A *tissue* is a group of similar cells that work together—bone and skin are examples. *Organs* are more complex than tissues. Each organ is made up of at least two kinds of tissue and performs a particular job for the body. For example, the heart—one of the most important organs—pumps blood. Some organs, such as the heart and lungs, cannot survive outside the body for more than a few hours. As a result, doctors must transplant these organs quickly.

Some tissues that are commonly transplanted—including bone, corneas, and skin—can be held for longer periods. Many tissues can be stored for future use in refrigerators or freezers at facilities called *tissue banks.*

Transplanted tissues and organs differ in the way that the body's disease-fighting immune system responds to them. The immune system recognizes that many transplanted organs come from outside the body. It then attacks them as if they were disease-causing invaders. Doctors use special methods and drugs to protect new organs from such attack. Most tissues do not require such protection because the immune system responds less strongly to them.

Tissue transplants

The most commonly transplanted tissues include corneas, skin, and bone marrow. The *cornea* is a piece of clear tissue that lies over the colored part of the eye and enables light to enter. Cornea transplants improve vision for patients whose corneas have been scarred by injury or clouded over by infection.

Skin transplants are used to temporarily cover areas of the body that have been badly burned and thus reduce the risk of infection. These transplants can last for several weeks until skin from another part of a patient's own body can be used for a permanent transplant.

Bone marrow transplants replace the blood-forming tissue inside bones. These procedures are used to treat certain kinds of cancer and serious blood disorders. See **Bone marrow transplant.** The hard outer tissue of bones can also be processed and transplanted to replace bones damaged by cancer or other diseases.

Organ transplants

In most developed countries, organ transplants have become an established form of treatment for a variety of diseases and injuries. Commonly transplanted organs include the heart, lungs, kidney, and liver. Most transplant operations last several hours, and most patients survive the operation. Patients usually remain in the hospital for one to four weeks, depending on the organ transplanted.

Qualifying for a transplant waiting list. The first step in qualifying for a transplant is a thorough medical evaluation. In most hospitals that perform transplants, these evaluations are done by a team of doctors and nurses with broad experience in transplant medicine.

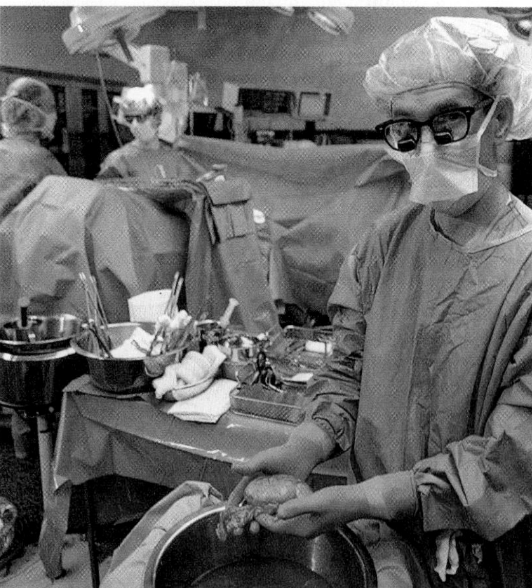

© Eric Sander, Gamma/Liaison

A kidney transplant is one of the most successful types of transplant surgery. In 90 percent or more of all cases, the transplanted kidney is still functioning after one year.

Commonly transplanted body parts

Transplants can be divided into two chief types: organ transplants and tissue transplants. The most commonly transplanted organs include the heart, kidney, liver, and lung. Corneas and bones are frequently transplanted tissues.

WORLD BOOK illustration by Barbara Cousins

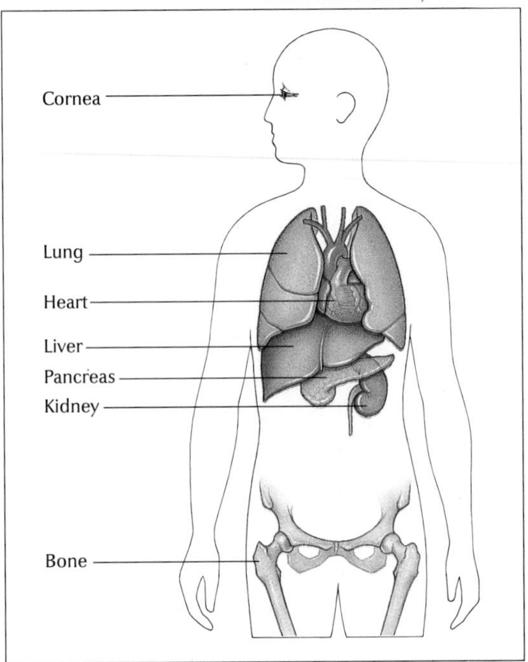

Patients must have badly damaged organs that do not respond to other forms of treatment. The damage must be severe enough to greatly reduce quality of life or significantly shorten life expectancy.

Most transplant teams also include social workers, psychologists, or members of the clergy. These participants help determine that patients can tolerate the emotional and psychological demands of transplant surgery. After patients are accepted as transplant candidates, they must wait until suitable donor organs can be found. In the United States, the United Network for Organ Sharing (UNOS), in Richmond, Virginia, maintains lists of all U.S. patients who are waiting for an organ transplant.

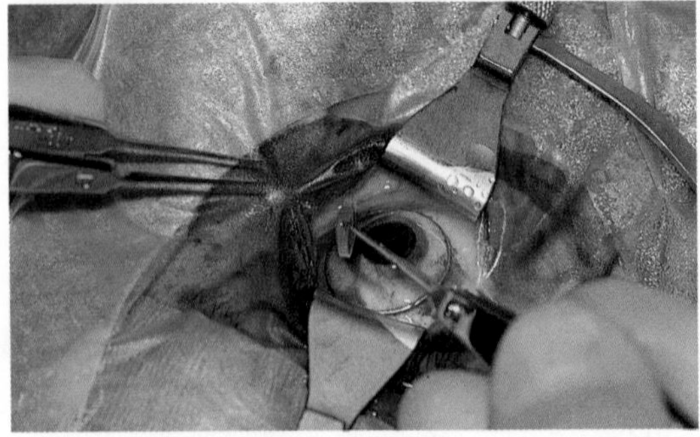

Medical College of Georgia

A transplant of the cornea, the clear tissue covering the eye, can restore sight lost because of injury or illness. Doctors have transplanted more corneas than any other body part.

Sources of donor organs. Other people are the main source of donor organs. Living people can donate organs that they can survive without. For example, a person can donate one kidney and remain healthy. Sometimes people can donate part of an organ without suffering harm. If someone donates part of the liver, the organ will regrow the donated part. But most donor organs come from *cadavers*—bodies of people who have died.

Cadaver organs are usually taken from someone who accidentally received a fatal head injury. After such an accident, the brain dies, but the rest of the body can be kept alive with a respirator or other artificial means. Once all brain activity stops, hospital staff or a representative of a local Organ Procurement Organization (OPO) may ask the family about organ donation. If the family agrees, the OPO begins a search for suitable recipients. After a recipient has been chosen, organs are removed from the donor and taken to recipients' hospitals. Meanwhile, the recipient is prepared for surgery.

Many patients die while awaiting organ transplants because the number of donors falls far short of the number needed. To save lives, health care professionals encourage more people to consider organ donation. Attitudes about organ donation vary among individuals and in different nations. The United States and the United Kingdom, for example, rely on a policy called *informed consent.* In this approach, patients or their closest relatives must directly give permission for organs to be used for transplants. People can express their desire to donate organs by carrying a signed donor card or by marking a space provided on their driver's license.

Other countries—including Austria and Belgium—approach organ transplantation with a policy of *presumed consent.* In this approach, medical professionals assume that organs can be used for transplantation after death.

Nonhuman sources of organs. Because of the shortage of human organs, researchers are actively investigating the possibility of obtaining donor organs from animals. Transplanting organs from one species to another is called *xenotransplantation* (ZEHN *uh* TRANS *plan* TAY *shuhn*). Use of pigs as organ donors is an especially active area of research. Pigs are already widely raised for food and leather, and their organs are about the same size as adult human organs.

A major challenge is preventing the recipient's immune system from destroying a donor organ from another species. The human immune system reacts especially vigorously to nonhuman organs. This reaction is called *rejection.*

Preventing rejection. Rejection occurs when the body's immune system attacks a transplanted organ. The immune system fights disease by finding and destroying bacteria, viruses, and other foreign materials in the body. If the immune system recognizes that a transplanted organ came from outside the body, the system attacks the organ as a dangerous invader. Doctors try to prevent rejection by choosing the best donor and prescribing special medication to protect the transplant.

Matching donors and recipients. To reduce the risk of rejection, doctors must find a donor who has the same blood type as the patient. For some organs—such as the lung, heart, and liver—it is also important that the donor organ be relatively similar in size to the one it replaces.

In addition to matching blood type, physicians also try

to match certain inherited proteins of the donor and the patient. These proteins, called *HLA antigens,* occur on the surface of cells. Each person has a unique combination of HLA antigens, which are determined by *genes* (hereditary instructions in cells). A transplant is more likely to succeed if the donor's and recipient's HLA antigens match. Doctors try to match six different HLA antigens from the donor and recipient. HLA matching is used mainly in kidney and bone marrow transplantation.

The best possible organ donor would be a patient's identical twin. Because identical twins have all the same genes, all antigens would match perfectly and the patient's immune system would not react to the transplant. As a result, rejection would not occur. Other relatives of the patient are the next best organ donors because they are next most likely to have similar HLA antigens.

Using immunosuppressive drugs. Because transplants usually come from unrelated individuals, most patients must take *immunosuppressive (ih MYOO noh suh PREHS ihv) drugs.* These drugs prevent rejection by reducing the activity of the immune system. Unfortunately, the reduced immune activity also hampers the body from defending itself against infections. As a result, patients who take immunosuppressive drugs have an increased risk of infection.

Immunosuppressive drugs commonly used to prevent rejection include *azathioprine (AZ uh THY uh preen), cyclosporine (SY kloh SPAWR een),* and *prednisone (PREHD nuh sohn).* These drugs interfere with the action of cells of the immune system that are directly responsible for the rejection of the organ. Cyclosporine is especially useful because it interferes less than other immunosuppressive drugs with the immune system's ability to fight infection. Most transplant patients require a combination of cyclosporine and other immunosuppressives.

Survival rates. Kidney transplants are the most successful type of organ transplant. Ninety percent or more of these transplants are still functioning after one year. About 80 percent of heart transplant patients and about 75 percent of liver transplant patients survive for at least one year, and about 70 percent of these patients live for three years or longer. But survival requires continued medical care, including close supervision, and patients must take immunosuppressive drugs for the rest of their lives. William A. Baumgartner

Related articles in *World Book* include:

Bone bank	Eye bank	Organ donation
Bone marrow transplant	Heart (Heart failure)	Skin grafting
		Stem cell
Cyclosporine	Liver	Xenotransplant

Transplanting, in gardening, is the process of removing a plant from one place and planting it in another. Many plants are started from seeds in protected areas, such as greenhouses and hotbeds, where growing conditions are ideal. They are often grown by planting seeds in shallow wooden boxes called *flats.* Seeds grown this way are more likely to sprout and will sprout more quickly than those planted outdoors. When the seeds have grown into seedlings, the seedlings are transplanted to a garden. Transplanting enables gardeners to space seedlings properly. Plants also may be transplanted from one place in a garden to another. House plants are transplanted by *repotting* (see **Gardening** [Repotting]).

Transplanting seedlings from an indoor protected area to an outdoor garden is a shock to the system of the plants. To decrease this shock, gardeners place the seedling flat outdoors in a warm, sheltered area, such as a cold frame or a porch, for several days before transplanting the seedlings. William H. Carlson

See also **Cold frame; Gardening; Hotbed; Nursery; Tree** (Planting the tree).

Transport is the term used in Britain and other Commonwealth countries for transportation. See **Transportation.**

Steps in transplanting seedlings

Transplanting involves removing a plant from one place and planting it in another. Many plants are started indoors and then transplanted to a garden after the seeds have grown into seedlings. When transplanting the seedlings, gardeners follow several steps to prevent injury to the plants.

Growing the seedlings indoors protects them from harsh outside conditions. Seedlings are often grown in boxes called *flats.* Flats are placed in sunny areas only after the seeds have sprouted.

Removing the plants from a flat involves carefully digging around the roots and lifting out the seedling. The seedlings should be watered several hours before they are removed from the flat.

WORLD BOOK illustrations by Leon Bishop

Replanting the seedlings is a fast and delicate process. The seedlings must be replanted quickly so the roots do not dry out, and they must be handled gently so they are not damaged.

American Airlines, Inc.

Air transportation provides the fastest practical means of moving passengers and freight long distances. Large jet aircraft, such as this Boeing 777, can carry hundreds of passengers.

Transportation

Transportation is the act of moving people or goods from one place to another. Transportation takes people where they need or want to go, and it brings them the goods they need or desire. Without transportation, there could be no trade. Without trade, there could be no towns and cities. Towns and cities are traditionally the centers of civilization. Therefore, transportation helps make civilization possible.

Throughout most of history, transportation was extremely slow and difficult. In prehistoric times, people traveled mainly on foot. They transported goods on their backs or heads or by dragging them along the ground. About 5000 B.C., people began to use animals to haul loads. By 3000 B.C., wagons and sailing vessels had been invented. The use of animals, wagons, and sailing vessels enabled people to transport loads farther and more easily than before. But the speed of transportation improved only slightly over the centuries.

Inventors produced the first engine-powered vehicles during the late 1700's and the early 1800's. This development marked the beginning of a revolution in transportation that has continued to the present. Today, jet airliners carry travelers nearly as fast as, or faster than, the speed of sound. Freight trains, trucks, and giant cargo ships haul goods to buyers in almost all parts of the world. Automobiles, buses, and passenger trains provide convenient transportation for millions of people.

In some countries, governments own and operate transportation services, such as airlines and railroads. In other countries, almost all transportation is privately owned, and national and local governments only build and maintain public roads and related facilities.

Although engine-powered transportation has benefited people in many ways, it has also created several difficult challenges. For example, the engines use great quantities of fuel and so strain the world's energy supplies. Automobiles jam many streets and highways, making travel slow. In addition, their exhaust fumes pollute the air. Manufacturers, governments, and independent organizations are seeking ways to solve such problems.

This article discusses the kinds of transportation, the history of their development, and modern systems of engine-powered transportation. The article also discusses the transportation industry and current developments in transportation. Vehicles are also used for recreation, warfare, and space exploration. These uses are described in such articles as **Air force; Balloon; Boating; Navy;** and **Space exploration.**

Kinds of transportation

There are three main kinds of transportation: (1) land, (2) water, and (3) air. Land transportation depends mainly on wheeled vehicles, especially automobiles, buses, trains, and trucks. Ships and boats are the most important water vehicles. Air transportation depends almost entirely on airplanes.

Each kind of transportation can be further classified according to whether the vehicles are engine powered or engineless. Most engine-powered vehicles have gasoline, diesel, or jet engines. The majority of engineless vehicles are powered by the muscles of human beings or animals or by natural forces, such as the wind or flowing water.

Engine-powered transportation has many advantages over engineless transportation. It is usually faster and

---

Chris Hendrickson, the contributor of this article, is the Duquesne Light Company Professor of Engineering and Head of the Department of Civil and Environmental Engineering at Carnegie Mellon University.

© Brand X Pictures/Matton Images

Land transportation is the most common kind of transportation. Extensive support systems that include roads, bridges, ramps, and other structures make travel convenient for cars and other engine-powered vehicles.

WORLD BOOK photo by Terry K. McClellan

Water transportation is used mainly to haul cargo. The Panama Canal, *shown here,* enables ships to pass between the Atlantic and Pacific oceans.

more dependable, and it can carry greater loads. However, such transportation is costly. Engine-powered vehicles are expensive to build and to maintain. In most cases, each type of vehicle also requires certain *infrastructure* (supporting facilities). Automobiles need roads. Trains must have tracks. Airplanes require airports. Ships need docks and ports. All these facilities are expensive to build and maintain. Every form of engine-powered transportation also requires a source of energy. The combined cost of the vehicles, supporting facilities, and energy makes engine-powered transportation extremely expensive.

Engine-powered vehicles are the chief means of transportation in industrially developed countries. Engine-powered vehicles also provide transportation in the urban areas of most developing countries, including many African, Asian, and Latin American nations. However, many people who live in rural areas of these countries still rely on the kinds of engineless transportation their ancestors used hundreds or thousands of years ago.

Land transportation is the most common kind of transportation by far. In many cases, it is the only suitable or available transportation.

Engine-powered land transportation. Automobiles, buses, motorcycles, snowmobiles, trains, and trucks are the chief engine-powered land vehicles. All these vehicles, except snowmobiles, ride on wheels. Pipelines are another important form of engine-powered land transportation.

Automobiles, buses, and trucks are the main engine-powered road vehicles. In areas well served by roads, they can provide a variety of transportation services. Automobiles enable people to travel whenever and by whatever route they choose. Buses carry passengers along fixed routes between and within cities. Trucks can provide door-to-door freight service.

Motorcycles are used for transportation on the same road surfaces as automobiles, buses, and trucks. People also ride motorcycles *off-road*—that is, on country trails and other rough, unpaved surfaces.

Unlike road vehicles, trains ride on tracks. As a result, trains usually cannot provide door-to-door freight service, as can trucks, or convenient connecting services, as can buses. But trains can haul far heavier loads than trucks can. They can also carry many more passengers than buses can.

A variety of off-highway trucks carry loads at construction sites, lumber camps, mines, oil fields, and quarries. At certain road-construction sites, for example, huge *earth movers* cut into hills, carry the rocks and dirt along, and drop them into valleys to make a roadbed with gentle *grades* (slopes).

Snowmobiles skim across ice or snow. The vehicles have two skis at the front and a moving track at the rear. An engine powers the track, which propels the vehicle.

Pipelines provide transportation, but the pipes themselves do not move. Most pipelines are built across land, but some span rivers or other bodies of water. Pipelines transport chiefly liquids and gases, especially petroleum and natural gas. Engine-powered pumps force the liquid or gas through the pipes.

Engineless land transportation. Walking is the most basic means of transportation. Carrying a load on one's back or head or using animals to carry loads is also basic. Animals used for this purpose are called *pack animals* or *beasts of burden.* They include camels, donkeys, elephants, horses, llamas, mules, and oxen. People use pack animals mainly in regions that lack modern roads.

© Howard G. Buffett

Carrying a burden on foot is one of the oldest means of moving goods from one place to another. These people in Central America are transporting firewood on their backs.

Such regions include deserts, mountainous areas, and jungles.

People use their muscle power to move such wheeled vehicles as carts, bicycles, and pedicabs. A cart is a small box-shaped vehicle with two or four wheels and an open top. A person may either push or pull a cart. Bicycles are two-wheeled vehicles that the rider powers by means of two pedals. Many people use bicycles to travel to and from work or merely for recreation. A pedicab resembles a bicycle but has two rear wheels instead of one. It also has a passenger carriage at the front or rear. Pedicabs are used as taxicabs in some cities.

Animal-drawn carts and wagons are a major means of transportation in rural areas of developing countries. Carts are usually pulled by donkeys, horses, or oxen. Wagons are large four-wheeled carts that can carry heavy loads. They are pulled by exceptionally strong animals, such as oxen or draft horses.

Water transportation depends mainly on boats, ships, and rafts. Any small watercraft is classed as a boat. People use boats chiefly on rivers, canals, and lakes. A ship is a larger vessel sturdy enough for ocean travel. A raft is a floating platform constructed of such materials as logs or barrels.

Engine-powered water transportation. Engines power nearly all ships and many boats. Most ships specialize in hauling cargo. Cargo ships travel mainly on ocean waters and on bodies of water linked to the ocean, such as the Mediterranean and the Baltic seas. Some cargo ships operate on large inland waterways, such as the Great Lakes.

Some engine-powered boats, especially tugboats, are used in hauling freight. Tugboats have powerful engines that enable them to tow heavily loaded barges. Barges are actually large rafts. Most barges must be pushed or towed. Others have engines and so move under their own power. Barges are used mainly to haul freight along inland waterways.

In general, ships and boats are the slowest engine-powered vehicles. But engineers have developed some fast water vehicles, including *hydrofoils* and *hovercraft.*

Hydrofoils skim across the water on skids or runners. Hovercraft, or *air cushion vehicles,* ride above the water on a cushion of air. One or more powerful fans inside the vehicle create the air cushion. Because hydrofoils and hovercraft ride out of the water, they can travel faster than other watercraft of equal power. Most hydrofoils and hovercraft are too small for ocean travel. They are used mainly to carry passengers locally. Some larger hydrofoils and hovercraft are used to haul cargo along inland and coastal waters.

Except for cruise ships and ferries, few ships specialize in transporting passengers. However, various types of motorboats carry passengers locally.

Engineless water transportation. Engineless water vehicles include dugouts, canoes, rowboats, sailboats, and rafts. People use paddles or oars to propel dugouts, canoes, and rowboats. Sailboats are powered by the wind. Rafts may be propelled by paddles, poles, sails, or water currents.

Broad-bottomed sailboats and rowboats are widely used to haul freight in the Far East. The sailboats are called *junks,* and the rowboats are known as *sampans.* Large junks have as many as five sails and can carry more than 100 tons (90 metric tons). Most sampans haul light cargo. However, many larger sampans have a sail, which enables them to haul heavier loads. In the tropical rain forests of Africa, Asia, and South America, many villagers use dugouts or rafts for transportation along the rivers. Many people of the Pacific Islands use dugouts for travel between islands. Some of the dugouts are equipped with outriggers and sails.

Air transportation depends almost entirely on engine-powered craft, especially airplanes. Engineless vehicles, such as gliders and hot-air balloons, are used mainly for recreation or advertising.

Airplanes provide the world's fastest practical means

of transporting both passengers and freight. Only rocket-powered spacecraft travel faster. Big airliners routinely fly 500 to 600 miles per hour (mph), or 800 to 970 kilometers per hour (kph). Most private planes and some older airliners are powered by gasoline engines and driven by propellers. Nearly all newer airliners and some private planes have jet engines. Supersonic jets fly faster than the speed of sound. The speed of sound is about 760 mph (1,225 kph) at sea level, but it declines as altitude increases. Supersonic jets travel at about 1,500 mph (2,400 kph).

Most airliners chiefly carry passengers. Even the biggest planes can carry only a fraction of the weight that a ship or train can haul. Air freight rates are high as a result. The high cost limits the shipment of goods by air to expensive, lightweight, or perishable cargo.

Helicopters, like airplanes, are powered by engines. But helicopters are smaller than most airplanes and cannot fly as fast or as far. Nor can they carry as many passengers as airplanes. Helicopters therefore play a secondary role in air transportation. However, they are much more maneuverable and have certain special uses. For example, helicopters are used in rescue work and in fighting forest fires.

History

Prehistoric times. Transportation developed slowly until about 3000 B.C. Throughout most of the prehistoric period, people lived by hunting, fishing, and gathering wild plants. They had no beasts of burden, wheeled vehicles, or roads. People traveled on foot and carried their infants and belongings strapped to their backs. Some carried belongings on their heads. Loads too heavy for one person to carry were strapped to a pole and carried by two people.

In time, people learned that they could drag loads along the ground on *sledges* (heavy sleds). They made sledges from logs, poles, or anything else that could hold a load and that one person or more could drag. During late prehistoric times, people began to build sledges with runners. These vehicles slid along the ground more easily than runnerless sledges. In far northern regions, people built lightweight sledges with runners for use on snow and ice. These vehicles became the first sleds.

By about 8000 B.C., various Middle Eastern peoples had developed agriculture and begun to establish permanent settlements. Trade between settlements then began to develop, thus creating a need for better means of transportation. The donkey and the ox, which had been *domesticated* (tamed) to serve as work animals, helped meet this need. Between about 5000 and 3500 B.C., people began to use donkeys and oxen as pack animals. Next, they invented harnesses so that the animals could be used to pull plows and, later, sledges. The use of donkeys and oxen as beasts of burden enabled people to transport heavier loads than they could before.

People also began to develop water transportation during prehistoric times. They built rafts of such materials as logs or reeds. Later, people learned how to make dugouts and canoes. People paddled these early craft with their hands or propelled them with paddles or poles.

These early vessels were fragile, and they were used mainly on rivers and lakes. But archaeological evidence shows that some people used such craft on the open sea. For example, between about 10000 B.C. and 8000 B.C., traders traveled between the Greek mainland and the island of Milos in the Mediterranean Sea.

© Scott T. Smith, Corbis

Pack animals are used to transport goods in many mountainous regions, deserts, and other areas that lack modern roads. This hiker in Oregon is using llamas as beasts of burden.

The wheel was invented about 3500 B.C. The invention probably took place in Mesopotamia, a region of the Middle East. The Egyptians invented sailboats about 3200 B.C. During the following centuries, wheeled vehicles and sailing vessels revolutionized transportation.

The first great civilizations arose in Mesopotamia and Egypt between 3500 and 3000 B.C. From these two centers, civilization gradually spread westward along the shores of the Mediterranean Sea. Sailing vessels played a vital role in the spread of civilization. Sea voyagers transmitted ideas and inventions as they sailed the Mediterranean. Trade goods carried by vessels included weapons, seeds, and food.

The early Mediterranean civilizations flourished from about 3000 B.C. to A.D. 500. During this period, improvements in sailing vessels and wheeled vehicles accounted for the chief advances in transportation.

Early development of sailing vessels. By 3000 B.C., the Egyptians had learned to build sailing vessels sturdy enough to put out to sea. Some of these ships ventured onto the Mediterranean and Red seas on short trading journeys. Between 2000 and 1000 B.C., the Minoans and other Mediterranean peoples developed larger and sturdier vessels. By 1000 B.C., the Phoenicians, who lived along the eastern shores of the Mediterranean Sea, had built a large fleet of merchant ships. The Phoenicians sailed the length of the Mediterranean, from their home waters to Spain. They traded such goods as wine, oil, and laurel and cedar wood, as well as textiles, pottery, and other manufactured goods.

Sea travel remained slow and difficult throughout ancient times. Sailors lacked navigation instruments. As a result, they usually stayed within sight of land. The ships were hard to steer because they had no rudder. Sailors steered them by means of one or two oars at the stern.

In addition, the ships could not depend entirely on the wind for power. The earliest ships had a single sail, which worked well only when the wind blew from behind. For times when there was no wind, many ships had teams of rowers.

Early development of wheeled vehicles. The first known wheeled vehicles were built about 3500 B.C. Many scientists believe that wheeled vehicles were first made in Mesopotamia. The technique spread quickly throughout much of Europe and Central Asia. It reached China and India about the mid-2000's B.C.

The first wheeled vehicles were two- and four-wheeled carts that were pulled by oxen. After about 3000 B.C., donkeys were also used to pull carts. Some early wheels were made from a single plank of wood. But usually each wheel on a cart was a wooden disk made from three rectangular boards.

To construct a wheel, a wheel maker fastened the boards together on edge with wooden braces to make a square. The square was then rounded at the corners to form the disk. These wheels were heavy. The early carts bumped along slowly and probably had to stop frequently for repairs.

The wheelbarrow was invented much later. The Chinese invented the wheelbarrow by about A.D. 100. But Europeans did not develop it until the Middle Ages, which began about the A.D. 400's.

In ancient times, carts were buried with important people as a sign of honor. After 3000 B.C., carts drawn by donkeys carried Mesopotamian troops into battle. Carts were also used to carry passengers and to haul grain, sand, and other goods that were difficult to load onto sledges or pack animals.

Wheels continued to be made of three solid pieces of wood until about 2000 B.C. Between 2000 and 1500 B.C., the first spoked wheels appeared. These wheels consisted of a rim, a hub, and spokes. The wheel maker constructed these parts separately. Spoked wheels provided smoother riding than solid wooden wheels, and they were lighter and faster. The first spoked wheels were probably made for chariots.

Chariots with spoked wheels were light enough for horses to pull. Horses had been tamed for riding by about 3000 B.C. But they could not be used to pull heavy loads because a suitable harness had not yet been invented. The harnesses then in use pressed against a horse's windpipe. If a load was too heavy, the harness hindered the animal's breathing. However, two or more horses could pull a chariot easily. Horse-drawn chariots, used chiefly by rulers and warriors, became the swiftest vehicles of ancient times.

Ancient Greece. During the 400's B.C., Greece became the chief power in the Mediterranean area. The Greeks expanded the sea trade begun by the Phoenicians. They also pioneered in the building of two-masted vessels and increased the number of sails from one to four.

Transportation in prehistoric times Nearly all the methods of transporting goods or people during prehistoric times depended on the muscles of either human beings or animals. Some of these methods are pictured here. Similar methods are still used in many parts of the world.

WORLD BOOK illustrations for the History section, unless otherwise credited, by Robert Addison

Greek cargo ships sailed from home with huge jars of olive oil and wine. Greek traders exchanged these products for wheat and other grains at ports on the Mediterranean and Black seas. The grain trade was extremely important to the Greeks. Wheat was the principal food during ancient times, and the Greeks had to import most of their supply.

The ancient Greeks developed a highly advanced civilization. Greek merchant ships helped spread Greek civilization westward. As civilization spread, trade and shipping increased. By 400 B.C., about 300 ports operated on the Mediterranean and several thousand trading ships of various countries crisscrossed the sea.

Ancient Rome. From the 100's B.C. to the A.D. 400's, Rome ruled the mightiest empire of ancient times. At its peak, the Roman Empire included all the lands bordering the Mediterranean. It also extended as far north as Scotland and as far east as the Persian Gulf. To help hold their vast empire together, the Romans built a highly advanced system of roads.

People had built roads long before Roman times. By about 1000 B.C., the Chinese had begun to construct roadways between their major cities. The Persians built a similar road network during the 500's B.C. But most of the early intercity roads were little more than dirt tracks. The Romans constructed the first extensive system of paved roads. The best Roman roads were 16 to 20 feet (5 to 6 meters) wide and 3 to 6 feet (0.9 to 1.8 meters) thick. They had a base that consisted of several layers of crushed stone and gravel. The roads were paved with stone blocks.

The Romans used their roads chiefly to transport troops and military supplies. But the roads also served as an important communications link between Rome and its provinces. Messengers in horse-drawn carts used the roads to carry government communications. By the A.D. 200's, more than 50,000 miles (80,000 kilometers) of paved roads connected Rome with almost every part of its empire.

During the 400's, Germanic tribes conquered most of the Roman territories in western Europe. The majority of Roman roads fell into ruin during the following centuries. However, a few are still used.

The Romans also built the largest fleet of cargo ships in ancient times. Like the Greeks, the Romans could not survive without sea trade. Roman cargo ships supplied the city of Rome with most of its grain.

The triangular *lateen* sail, which probably originated on Arab vessels called *dhows,* was in use in the Mediterranean Sea by around A.D. 200. Unlike square sails, which were widely used at the time, lateen sails could be positioned to work even when ships sailed into the wind.

The Middle Ages, which lasted from about the A.D. 400's through the 1400's, brought great improvements in land and water transportation. These improvements resulted largely from three remarkable inventions—the rigid horse collar, the iron horseshoe, and the whiffletree. Scholars do not know exactly when or where these devices were invented. But all three had appeared in Europe by the end of the 1000's.

The rigid horse collar appeared about 800. Before this invention came into common use, horses wore a harness that fit across the neck. The harness choked a horse if it pulled a heavy load. The rigid horse collar shifted the weight of a load to a horse's shoulders. Horses collared in this way could pull four or five times as much weight as before.

Vehicles of ancient times Wheeled vehicles and sailing vessels were invented during the 3000's B.C. They became the most widely used means of transportation during ancient times. But many people also continued to use earlier forms of transportation, such as pack animals.

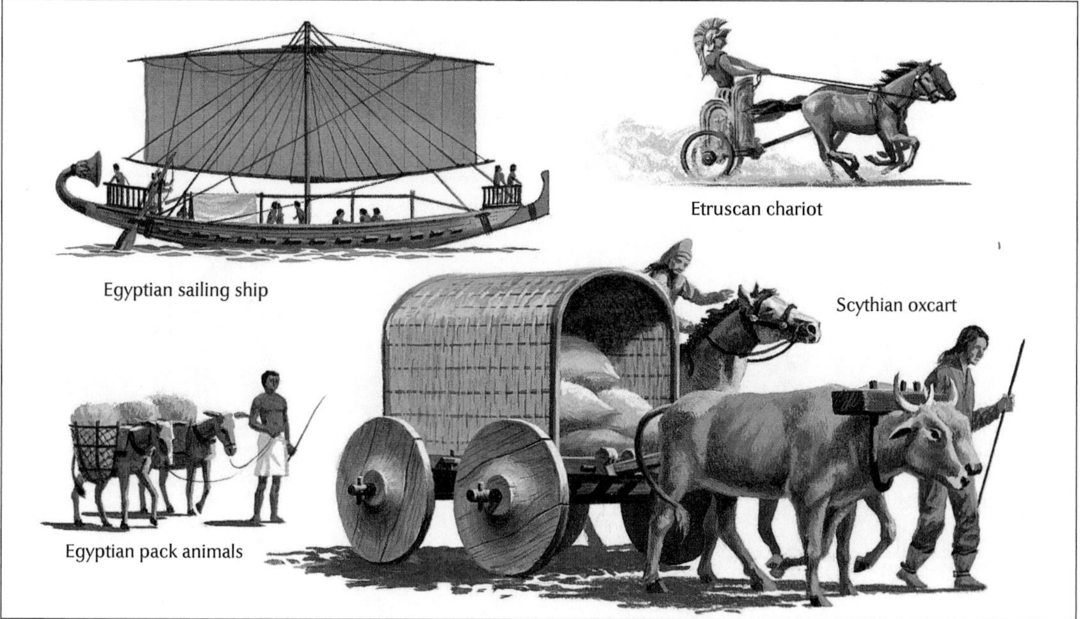

The iron horseshoe appeared in Europe about 900. Horses without shoes often suffered from damaged hoofs if they traveled long distances. Iron shoes protected a horse's hoofs from damage and so enabled the animal to travel farther and faster than it could without them.

The *whiffletree,* which appeared during the 1000's, made it possible for teams of horses to pull wagons. A whiffletree is a pivoted crossbar at the front of a wagon to which a team's harnesses are fastened. It equalizes the pull of the horses. Without such a device, a wagon may be thrown off balance and may even be overturned.

The invention of the rigid horse collar, iron horseshoe, and whiffletree stimulated overland trade. These inventions made it possible for horses to pull as much weight as oxen—and for longer distances and at twice the speed.

The increased speeds of horse-drawn vehicles also encouraged greater use of wagons for passenger transportation. But wagon rides were extremely bumpy. Wagon makers tried to correct this problem by building vehicles with *suspension systems,* which provided a certain amount of cushioning against bumps. However, only rich people could afford such vehicles. Most of the people of the Middle Ages traveled on foot or on horseback, just as people had done in the past.

The design and construction of ships improved greatly during the Middle Ages. The first ships with a rudder rather than steering oars at the stern appeared in Europe about 1300. Rudders could be used to steer much bigger ships than could be steered with oars. During the 1400's, shipbuilders began to produce ships four times as large as any built before. All these ships had a rudder, and most had three masts and at least three sails.

Several important navigation instruments were also developed during the Middle Ages. One such instrument, called a *mariner's compass,* allowed voyagers to navigate their ships even when the sky was overcast and they could not use the positions of the moon, stars, and planets for navigation. By the late 1400's, the advances in ship construction and navigation aids helped make long ocean voyages possible.

The age of overseas expansion. During the late 1400's and the early 1500's, such European explorers as Christopher Columbus, Vasco da Gama, and Ferdinand Magellan made great ocean voyages. As a result of these and other voyages, European civilization spread to North and South America, India and the Far East, and later to Australia and New Zealand. However, this expansion of European culture took several hundred years. Despite the improvements in ship construction, ocean travel remained extremely slow.

Overseas trade began to increase rapidly during the 1600's. Shipbuilders launched bigger and bigger cargo vessels to handle the growing trade. The larger ships had to have more sails, and the added sails helped increase speeds. By the mid-1800's, the fastest merchant ships had as many as 35 sails and traveled at speeds up to 20 *knots* (nautical miles per hour). These vessels, called *clipper ships,* could sail from New York City, around South America, to San Francisco in three to four months. The overland journey from New York to California took twice as long as the voyage by clipper ship.

Development of inland transport. By the 1600's, most people used horse-drawn wagons to haul goods

Transportation in early modern times Beginning in the 1400's, Europeans built ships capable of making long ocean voyages. Stagecoaches became widely used in Europe during the late 1600's and early 1700's. In other parts of the world, such as China, people continued to use older forms of transportation.

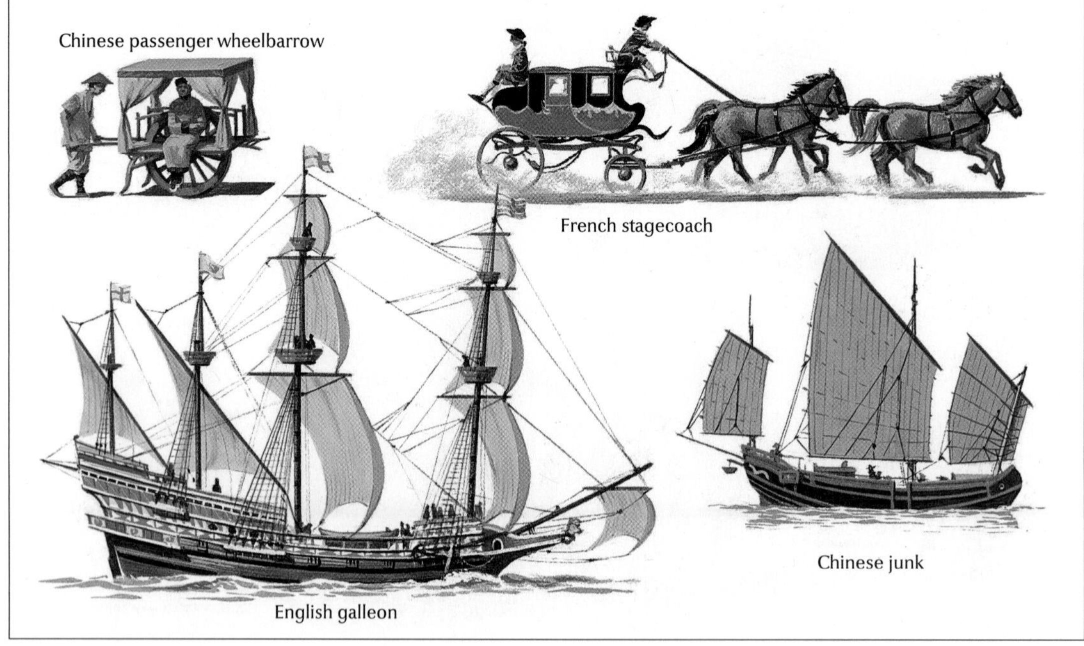

locally. But they seldom used wagons for long hauls because of the poor condition of the roads. Until the mid-1800's, horse-drawn boats and barges were the chief means of long-distance inland transport. The animals trudged along the banks of rivers and canals and pulled the vessels with ropes.

Canal builders in Europe dug hundreds of canals from the late Middle Ages through the early 1800's. The first canals in Britain (now the United Kingdom) were built to carry coal cheaply from mines to industrial towns. Canals also served as routes for transporting raw materials and finished goods. In this way, the canals contributed to the Industrial Revolution, a period of rapid industrialization that began in Britain in the 1700's. The first major American canal, the Erie Canal, opened in New York in 1825. It connected Albany and Buffalo and provided a vital link in an all-water route between New York City and Great Lakes ports. Before the Erie Canal opened, the overland journey between Albany and Buffalo took about 20 days. The canal enabled horse-drawn barges to make the trip in 8 days. The success of the Erie Canal led to a great burst of canal building in the United States. By 1850, the United States had about 4,500 miles (7,200 kilometers) of canals. Canals, rivers, and other waterways carried most of the nation's intercity freight.

During the 1700's, France and Britain constructed the first well-built paved roads since Roman times. By the mid-1800's, the first major United States highway, the National Road, had been completed. The highway connected Cumberland, Maryland, and Vandalia, Illinois. It was a gravel road and inferior to the best French and British roads of the time. American pioneers traveling west from the Mississippi River crossed a wilderness without roads. They drove their covered wagons along well-traveled dirt paths, such as the Santa Fe Trail and the Oregon Trail.

The basic design of wagons and coaches changed little from the late Middle Ages through the 1800's. The first city coach line started in Paris during the 1660's. It was the ancestor of today's public transportation systems. The first long intercity coach line began service between England and Scotland about 1670. The line operated between the cities of London and Edinburgh, a distance of 392 miles (631 kilometers). The coaches were called *stagecoaches* because they traveled in stages, stopping at scheduled places on a route for changes of horses. The first stagecoach lines in the American Colonies began service during the 1730's.

The steam age. The invention of the steam engine marked the beginning of the greatest revolution in transportation since the invention of the wheel and the sailboat. British inventors developed the steam engine during the 1700's. Nicolas-Joseph Cugnot, a French military engineer, built the first self-propelled road vehicle, which was powered by a steam engine, in 1769. In 1807, the first commercially successful steamboat service started in the United States. By the late 1800's, ships powered by steam engines were rapidly taking the place of sailing ships on the world's shipping lanes.

The world's first successful steam railroad went into service in the United Kingdom in 1825. Steam-powered trains played the leading role in the transportation revolution. By the 1840's, the spread of railroads caused canal traffic to decline. Rail service provided faster transportation of goods and a greater number of routes than

Transportation in the 1800's

The steam engine provided a completely new source of power for transportation during the 1800's. It was used to propel locomotives, and paddle wheel boats and ships. However, people also continued to use older sources of power, such as animals, their own muscle power, and the wind.

WORLD BOOK illustrations by Robert Addison and Precision Graphics

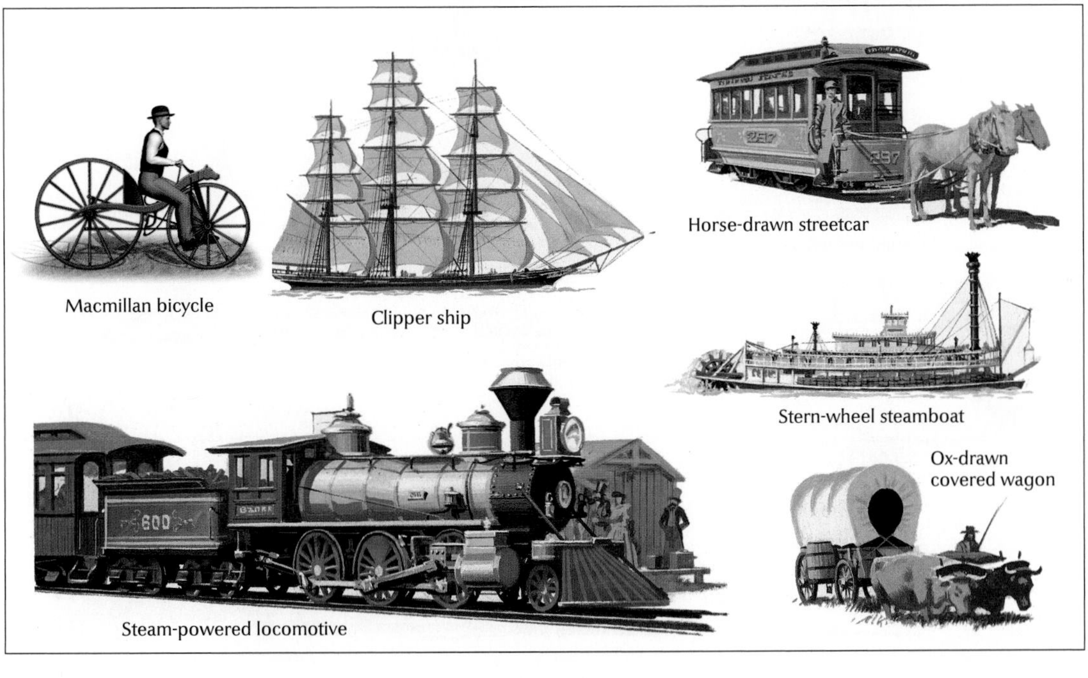

Macmillan bicycle

Clipper ship

Horse-drawn streetcar

Stern-wheel steamboat

Ox-drawn covered wagon

Steam-powered locomotive

canals. By the late 1800's, some steam locomotives traveled at speeds of more than 60 mph (100 kph). They could haul loads hundreds of times heavier than a team of horses could pull. By 1900, rail lines had been built throughout Europe and North America and in many parts of Africa, Asia, Australia, and South America. The overland journey by train from New York City to San Francisco took less than a week. In comparison, the trip took weeks or months by stagecoach or by covered wagon.

As more and more steamships and steam-powered trains went into service, passenger fares and freight rates dropped. The lower costs encouraged travel, trade, and the growth of cities. In addition, many people became accustomed to fast movement and rapid change. The quickening pace of life created a demand for still faster transportation.

The beginnings of modern transportation. In 1839, Kirkpatrick Macmillan, a Scottish blacksmith, added pedals to a scooterlike vehicle called a *draisine* to produce the first bicycle. The first electric trains and streetcars appeared in Europe and the United States during the 1880's. In the 1890's, the German engineer Rudolf Diesel invented the engine that was later named after him. In time, diesel engines replaced steam engines on many ships and on most trains. But of all the inventions of the 1800's, the gasoline engine was the one that brought about the most far-reaching changes in transportation.

German inventors built the first successful four-stroke gasoline engines during the 1880's and used them to power bicycles, boats, and carriages. During the 1890's, French engineers built the first gasoline-powered vehicles with automobile bodies. The first gasoline-powered buses and trucks were built in Germany during the 1890's. In 1903, two American bicycle makers, Orville and Wilbur Wright, used a gasoline engine to power a small airplane that they had built. The Wright brothers' plane became the first one to lift a person into the air and fly successfully.

Automobiles became the chief means of passenger transportation in many industrialized countries during the 1920's. As the number of automobile owners increased, so did the demand for more and better roads.

Transportation from 1900 to 1950

By the early 1900's, oceangoing steamships, giant airships, electric streetcars, powerful steam trains, and the first mass-produced automobiles were carrying people farther and faster than they had ever traveled before. By 1950, modern forms of public transportation had emerged. Buses, diesel trains, and commercial airlines became popular means of intercity public transportation.

Important dates in transportation

c. 5000 B.C. People began to use donkeys and oxen as pack animals.

c. 3500 B.C. The Mesopotamians probably built the first wheeled vehicles.

c. 3200 B.C. The Egyptians invented sails and produced the first sailboats.

300's B.C.-A.D. 200's The Romans built the first extensive system of paved roads.

c. 800 The rigid horse collar appeared in Europe.

1100's Wagon makers in Europe built the first traveling carriages. Carriages with spring suspension systems became known as coaches during the 1400's.

1490's Improvements in ship construction helped make long ocean voyages possible.

1660's The first city coach line opened in Paris.

1700's British inventors developed the steam engine.

1807 The first commercially successful steamboat service began in the United States.

1825 The first successful steam railroad began operations in England.

1880's German inventors built the first successful four-stroke engines and used them to power bicycles, boats, and carriages.

1890's French engineers built the first gasoline-powered vehicles with automobile bodies.

1903 An airplane built by Orville and Wilbur Wright of the United States became the first to lift a person into the air and fly successfully.

1920's Automobiles became the chief means of passenger transportation in the United States.

1950's The first commercial jet airliners began service.

1970's Declining petroleum reserves throughout the world led to shortages of transportation fuel in the United States and other developed countries.

1976-2003 The first supersonic airliner, the Concorde, provided service between Europe and the United States.

1997 The Toyota Prius, the first mass-produced hybrid automobile, went on sale in Japan.

2004 The first commercial maglev rail system began operations in Shanghai, China.

Transportation since 1950

After 1950, even faster and more powerful engine-powered vehicles were developed. The first commercial jet airplane entered service. Air cushion vehicles (ACV's), emergency transport helicopters, supertankers, and other specialized vehicles also came into wide use. Manufacturers began to focus automobile design on the safety, comfort, and convenience of drivers and passengers.

WORLD BOOK illustrations by Robert Addison, Tom Morgan and Precision Graphics

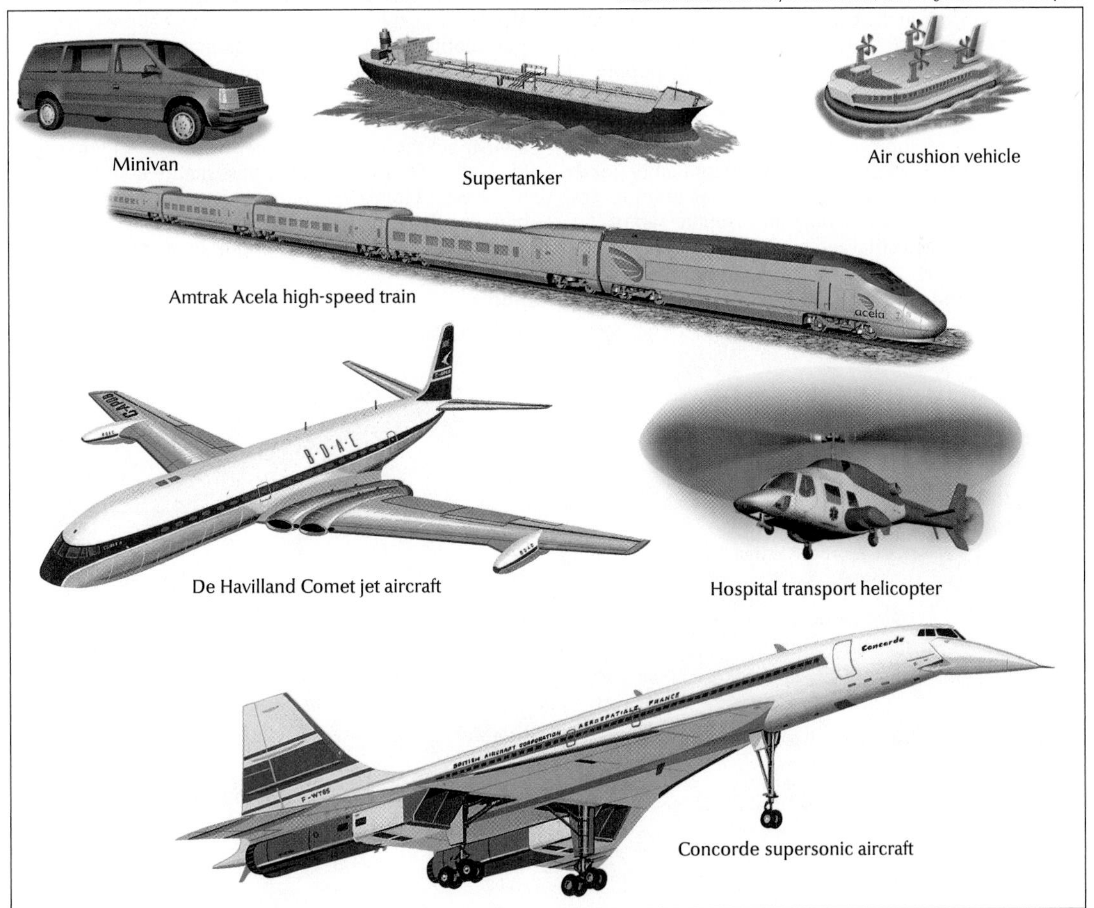

Minivan

Supertanker

Air cushion vehicle

Amtrak Acela high-speed train

De Havilland Comet jet aircraft

Hospital transport helicopter

Concorde supersonic aircraft

The industrialized countries built many new roads between 1900 and 1930. In the United States, for example, about 700,000 miles (1,100,000 kilometers) of surfaced streets and highways were built during this period.

The first commercial airlines began service in Europe in 1919. Airlines began operations in many other parts of the world during the 1920's. By the late 1930's, the world's airlines carried 3 ½ million passengers annually. All airplanes had propellers and gasoline engines. During the late 1930's, German engineers built the first planes with jet engines. All the early jet aircraft were warplanes. The first commercial jet airliners began service during the 1950's.

From 1976 to 2003, the Concorde, the first supersonic passenger aircraft, provided service between Europe and the United States. The plane's routes carried it about 3,500 miles (5,600 kilometers)—in 3 ½ to 4 hours. Service was discontinued because of low profitability.

The great advances in transportation during the 1900's brought about enormous changes in people's lives. The development of commercial air travel made long journeys routine. As a result of improvements in ocean shipping and in refrigeration, goods that were once available only in certain regions began to be distributed worldwide. The development of the automobile led to the growth of suburbs around big cities. Most suburbanites depend on their automobiles for shopping and other personal business. Many also use their cars to get to and from work in the central cities. Without this convenient means of private transportation, suburban living would be impractical or impossible for many people.

Transportation today

Before the development of engine-powered vehicles, nearly all transportation involved the shipment of goods. Passenger transportation was relatively uncommon. Today, passenger transportation is an essential part of everyday life in industrialized countries. Workers in these countries live much farther from their places of employment than workers did in the past. They require quick, dependable transportation each workday. Many children need transportation to and from school. Families depend on transportation for shopping and other errands. Many people travel long distances on vacations. In some industrialized countries, more money is spent on passenger transportation than on the shipment of freight.

This section deals mainly with engine-powered passenger and freight transportation in industrialized countries. In rural areas of developing countries, many people still rely on age-old transportation methods.

Passenger transportation includes both private and public transportation. People who use private transportation operate their own vehicles. Those who use public transportation pay to ride on vehicles owned and operated by private companies or by the government. The three main types of public transportation service are urban, intercity, and overseas.

Private transportation in industrial countries is provided mainly by automobiles, bicycles, motorcycles, and private airplanes. Automobiles are by far the most important means of private transportation.

In large industrialized countries, such as Canada, Australia, and the United States, most people travel chiefly by automobile. People in such countries use their cars largely for local transportation. However, automobiles also serve as the leading means of travel between cities. Automobiles are also the chief means of passenger transportation in smaller industrialized countries, such as Japan, New Zealand, and most of the nations of Western Europe. People in these automobile-using countries own about three-fourths of the world's cars. People in the United States own the largest share—about a fourth of the world total. The countries with the most automobiles also have the best road systems.

Highway travel is far less important in developing

Average speeds of some kinds of passenger transportation

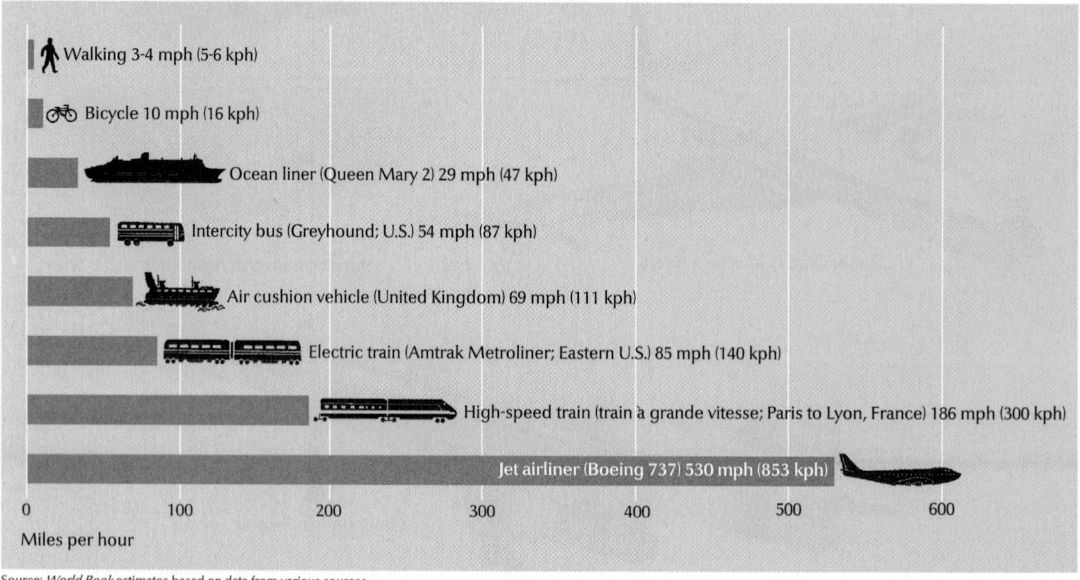

Source: *World Book* estimates based on data from various sources.

© Julio Etchart from Peter Arnold

Bicycles and mopeds are among the most important forms of private transportation in many countries. Many workers, such as these people in Shanghai, China, use these vehicles to commute to and from their jobs. Bicycles and mopeds are less expensive to own and operate than automobiles.

countries than in developed ones. However, the number of city dwellers in developing countries who own a car continues to grow. The biggest cities have had to build more expressways to handle the ever-increasing flow of automobile traffic.

Urban public transportation. Most large urban areas provide some means of public transportation for people who do not own a car or who prefer to avoid city driving whenever possible. Public transportation in urban areas is called *mass transit.* Mass transit between cities and suburbs is often called *commuter service.* Commuter trains are the chief means of public transportation between big cities and their suburbs.

Buses are the chief means of transportation in most of the world's cities. Most cities with mass transit systems offer only bus service. But a majority of the world's largest cities also offer rail service. Many major cities have both subway and surface rail lines. Some also have elevated trains, which run on tracks above the streets.

A growing number of large cities have *light rail vehicles.* A light rail vehicle is an electrically powered railway car that gets its power from an overhead trolley wire or an electrified third rail.

Streetcars, called *trams* in some regions, are a type of light rail vehicle. During the late 1800's and early 1900's, streetcars were an important part of the mass transit systems of many cities. Most streetcar tracks ran down the middle of the street, and increasing automobile traffic began to interfere with the operation of the streetcars. During the mid-1900's, buses replaced streetcars in many cities.

Today's light rail vehicles can run underground, on elevated tracks, or on tracks built alongside city streets. The cars can travel individually, or they may be linked together to form a train. The wheels of many light rail vehicles have metal wheels built over a rubber core, which enable these vehicles to run more smoothly and quietly than other trains.

Another type of mass transit facility is the *people mover.* People movers carry passengers along specially constructed guideways in driverless, electrically powered cars. Most people movers operate over short distances in such places as parks and airports, but a few serve the downtown areas of cities.

Most cities today cannot afford to build extensive new mass transit facilities. But many are trying to improve existing facilities. For example, a number of cities have speeded up bus service by reserving certain traffic lanes for buses only. Some experts believe that light rail systems can help improve mass transit in many cities. Such systems cost less to build than subways, and they run more quietly and smoothly. Unlike buses, they produce no exhaust fumes.

Intercity public transportation is provided mainly by airplanes, buses, and trains. Riverboats and ferryboats carry an extremely small share of intercity passengers.

In some industrialized countries, such as Australia and the United States, airlines handle a large proportion

Chicago Transit Authority

Buses are a chief means of transportation in most major cities. Because they carry many passengers, buses help reduce traffic on city streets. These people are boarding a city bus in Chicago.

AP/Wide World

A water taxi may serve a city built along a waterway. This craft follows a scheduled route to pick up and drop off passengers in New York City. Some water taxis may be hired for private use.

© Corbis

An electric railroad is part of the mass transit system of many of the world's cities. Electric railroads can run underground, at ground level, or on elevated tracks, like these in Taipei, Taiwan.

of intercity passengers on long trips. But automobiles, buses, and trains are the preferred means of transportation for many people, particularly for short trips. In China and India, and most of Africa, railways and buses carry more passengers than automobiles or airplanes. Railroads and buses are the chief modern means of intercity travel in most developing nations. Many countries have high-speed passenger trains. Short-range airliners play an important part in intercity transportation in Europe.

Most industrialized countries seek to improve passenger service on major intercity rail routes. High-speed electric trains provide swift intercity service in Japan, South Korea, the United States, and several European countries, including France, Italy, and the United Kingdom. Japan's "bullet train" links cities on the islands of Honshu and Kyushu. The French TGV *(train à grande vitesse,* or high-speed train) connects Paris with several other French cities and with cities in Belgium. Both the French and the Japanese trains operate at a top speed of 186 mph (300 kph).

High-speed trains can compete with airliners for passengers on journeys of up to about 500 miles (800 kilometers). Most big airports are on the outskirts of large cities. For short- and medium-length flights, the trip to and from the airport may take longer than the flight itself. Trains, on the other hand, usually take passengers all the way to stations in the centers of cities. Passengers on a high-speed train may thus complete their entire journey in less time than it would take by air.

Engineers are developing a type of high-speed passenger train called a *magnetic levitation train* or *maglev train.* The track for maglev trains consists of a single guideway, which the vehicle straddles but does not touch when in motion. Magnets on both the guideway and the underside of the train produce magnetic forces that lift the train above the guideway and push the train forward. There are few commercial maglev systems in the world. A maglev system operating near Papenburg, Germany, carries passengers around a demonstration track at about 280 mph (450 kph). A maglev system in

Growth of intercity passenger traffic in the United States

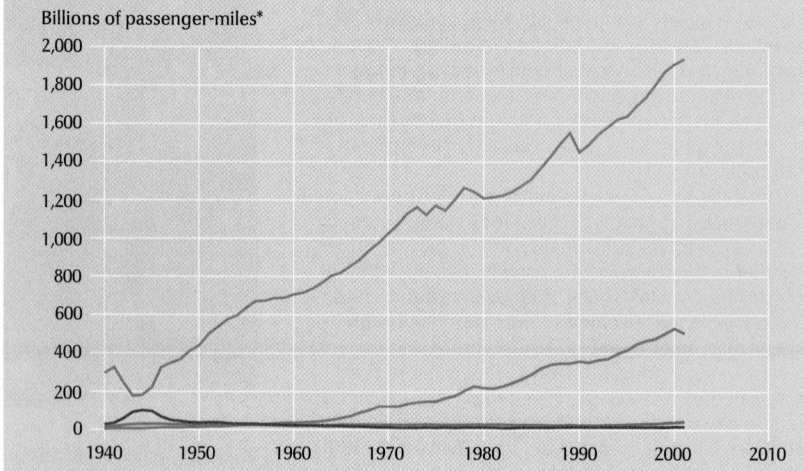

*A passenger-mile is one passenger carried 1 mile (1.6 kilometers).
Source: Eno Transportation Foundation.

Shanghai carries passengers between the city center and Pudong International Airport at speeds up to 310 mph (500 kph). Maglev train systems are in development in many other parts of the world. See **Magnetic levitation train.**

Overseas public transportation. The first overseas airlines began operations during the 1930's. But the planes had to stop frequently during a flight for refueling. Most overseas travelers continued to go by ship until the late 1950's, even though it took much longer to sail than to fly. The voyage across the Atlantic Ocean, for example, took four days or more. The first nonstop transoceanic airliners appeared during the late 1940's. These propeller-driven planes could carry passengers across the Atlantic in hours rather than days. As these planes became more common, overseas travel increased. The first transoceanic jet airliners began service during the 1950's, leading to a tremendous increase in overseas travel.

Today, almost all overseas travelers go by plane. Only one ocean liner, the *Queen Mary 2,* provides regular transatlantic passenger service. Most ocean liners today operate as cruise ships. They specialize in taking vacation travelers to such popular destinations as Alaska, the Caribbean, and the Mediterranean.

Freight transportation. Pipelines provide the cheapest means of transporting petroleum and natural gas. The cheapest way to move general cargo is by water. Rail transportation costs about 3 times as much as water transportation, and truck transportation costs about 10 times as much. Air transportation costs nearly 40 times as much as water transportation. Because air transportation is so costly, cargo planes usually carry only expensive, lightweight, or perishable merchandise.

The various means of moving cargo are used for both (1) domestic freight and (2) international freight.

Domestic freight. Most domestic freight traffic involves the transport of cargo between cities within a country. Airplanes, barges, pipelines, railroads, ships, and trucks carry the cargo. Freight shipments within cities consist mainly of pickups and deliveries. Trucks carry nearly all such local freight.

© Jeremy Hoare, Getty Images

Barge transportation is one of the cheapest ways to haul bulky cargo, such as coal, grain, and gravel. This barge is being pulled by a tugboat. Some barges, however, have built-in engines.

In industrialized countries, rail shipments account for about half of the freight hauled. Shipments by truck account for about one-quarter. Petroleum pipelines and barges and ships carry smaller fractions of the freight, and airplanes, only a tiny amount. Railroads carry a greater share of the intercity traffic in European countries than in the United States. Canal traffic is also greater in Europe.

In many cases, a particular freight shipment must be switched from one type of carrier to one or more other types to reach its destination. For example, many coal shipments travel by train, barge, and truck on their way to the buyer. The movement of freight by more than one method is called *intermodal transport.*

One common type of intermodal transport is known as *containerization.* Freight is packed into large crates called *containers.* The containers are designed to ride on truck trailers and railroad flatcars. They can easily be transferred between the two types of carriers and to specially designed *container ships.*

Growth of intercity freight traffic in the United States

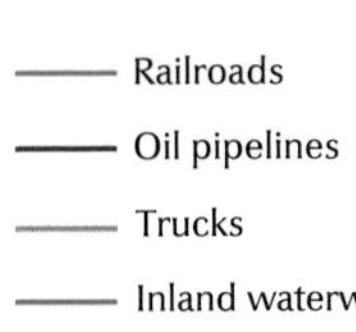

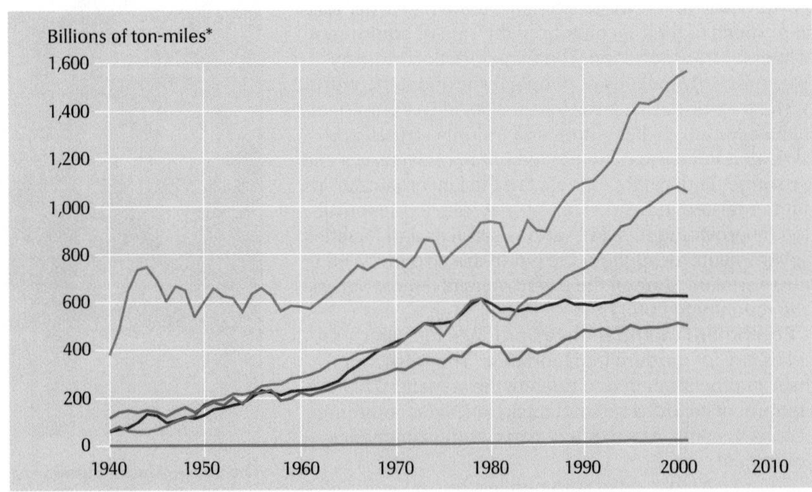

*A ton-mile is 1 ton (0.9 metric ton) carried 1 mile (1.6 kilometers).
Source: Eno Transportation Foundation.

© Corbis

A flatbed truck can be used to haul a heavy load along paved roads and highways. Many highway trucks consist of a trailer unit pulled by a *tractor,* which contains the engine and the *cab,* the section in which the driver sits.

Containerization is used mainly to transport such goods as machinery and household appliances. The method reduces shipping costs, speeds deliveries, and cuts losses due to breakage. Some domestic freight is containerized. But containerization is used mainly in international trade.

International freight is transported mainly by ships. Many of today's merchant ships are designed to carry containers or a particular kind of cargo, such as petroleum, grain, or iron ore. In many cases, the ships require specialized port facilities. Most large ports have been equipped to handle containers. Giant cranes and other lifting devices transfer the containers between container ships and truck trailers or railroad flatcars. Some of the world's busiest seaports specialize in handling oil tanker traffic. These ports have exceptionally deep harbors to accommodate giant tankers. They also have pumping systems and pipelines for loading and unloading the oil.

Some international freight moves by highway, rail, pipeline, inland waterway, or airplane. The countries of Europe, especially, depend on these methods in their trade with one another.

© Stephen Beer, Getty Images

Intermodal transport is the movement of freight by more than one method. For example, containers loaded with freight can be transferred from a ship to trucks for overland delivery.

The transportation industry

Transportation is one of the leading industries in the world. Many of the world's biggest industrial firms earn all or much of their income from the sale of equipment or fuel for transportation. The transportation industry employs many millions of people throughout the world.

The transportation industry consists of (1) equipment manufacturers, (2) passenger and freight carriers, and (3) related industries. The equipment manufacturers and passenger and freight carriers are the key organizations. But the related industries play a vital role in transportation by providing fuel and various services and facilities. Governments throughout the world are also involved in transportation, though the extent of involvement varies from country to country.

Equipment manufacturers produce the vehicles necessary for modern transportation. They also supply the equipment needed to operate the vehicles. This equipment includes railroad tracks, airplane communications systems, replacement parts, and maintenance equipment.

Companies that make automobiles, buses, and trucks are by far the largest producers of transportation equip-

© Steve McCutcheon

The Trans-Alaska Pipeline is part of a vast network of oil pipelines that crisscross the United States. Pipelines are used to transport gas and other products as well as petroleum.

ment. Leading motor vehicle manufacturers include Honda Motor, Nissan Motor, and Toyota Motor of Japan; DaimlerChrysler and Volkswagen of Germany; Fiat of Italy; and General Motors and Ford Motor of the United States.

Passenger and freight carriers include airlines, intercity bus lines, mass transit companies, pipeline companies, railroads, shipping lines, and trucking firms. In most countries, the central government owns and operates the airlines and railroads and some or all of the intercity bus lines. The United States and Canada are chief exceptions. Private companies own and operate all the airlines and intercity bus lines, and nearly all the railroads in the United States and Canada.

In some countries, the central government owns the intercity bus lines, pipelines, and shipping and trucking lines. In other countries, these services are provided by privately owned firms, subject to various forms of government regulation. In nearly every country, local governments control all or most mass transit services.

Related industries include glass, petroleum, steel, and tire production; road construction; the selling of new and used cars; and the servicing of automobiles and other vehicles. Petroleum production is the leading transportation-related industry in terms of value. Several of the world's largest manufacturing companies are oil companies.

Government and transportation. Governments are most deeply involved in transportation in those countries where all or much of the industry is publicly owned. But even in countries in which nearly all transportation companies are privately owned, government plays a major role in the transportation industry. This role consists primarily of (1) providing funds for transportation facilities and (2) regulating transportation.

Government funding. Four kinds of transportation facilities depend almost entirely on public funds. They are (1) air traffic control centers, (2) airports, (3) public roads, and (4) river and harbor facilities. Far more money is spent on the building and upkeep of roads than is spent on the other three facilities put together. Funding for large airports, roads, and river and harbor facilities can come from local, regional, or national governments. Funds for projects in developing countries usually come from international lending bodies, such as the World Bank, or from foreign governments. National governments usually finance air traffic control operations.

© Joseph Sohm, Photo Researchers

Traffic jams occur in many major cities at the *rush hours,* the times when the most people are traveling to or from work. Cars pack this Los Angeles freeway during the evening rush hour.

Mass transit systems in most countries depend heavily on government financial support. Few systems earn enough from passenger fares to pay all their expenses.

Government regulation deals chiefly with transportation safety, the emission of pollutants by vehicle engines, fuel economy, and the business practices of transportation companies. Governments throughout the world establish safety rules for the various methods of transportation. Governments also set and enforce standards for vehicle emissions and regulate the business practices of transportation companies.

Challenges of modern transportation

Modern transportation poses many challenges, including (1) traffic safety, (2) overcrowding of streets and highways, (3) declining fuel reserves, (4) environmental problems, (5) inadequate public transportation facilities, and (6) transportation security. These challenges are most severe in countries that depend heavily on automobile transportation.

Traffic safety. The use of most types of high-speed, engine-powered transportation involves traffic safety problems. In some countries, including the United States, more people are killed in automobile accidents every year than in all other transportation accidents combined. Most automobile accidents could be prevented if every driver obeyed all traffic laws and all the rules for safe driving.

Airlines have one of the best safety records in the field of transportation. But heavy air traffic at major airports has increased the hazards of commercial flying. When many airliners await clearance to land or take off, airport approaches and runways can become dangerously overcrowded. In addition, large airports have an ever-increasing amount of private plane traffic, which makes traffic control even more difficult.

Railroads are generally a safe means of transportation. Train collisions and derailments are rare, but they may occur on busy lines when signaling equipment fails or when track is worn or damaged. Railroad companies have track replacement programs, and they routinely check signaling equipment.

Overcrowding of streets and highways. Traffic *congestion* (overcrowding) on streets and highways increases transportation times and can also make driving more dangerous. Scientists and engineers are developing *intelligent transportation systems* to deal with congestion. One development, an *electronic toll system,* automatically identifies vehicles and charges their owners or drivers for the use of roadways and bridges. Electronic toll systems eliminate waiting at toll booths and reduce the cost of collecting tolls. In Hong Kong, China, tolls are charged electronically on vehicles using congested city streets. Other applications of intelligent transportation systems include automatic tracking of vehicles and rapid identification of accidents.

Declining fuel reserves. Gasoline and other fuels made from petroleum supply nearly all the energy for engine-powered transportation. Energy experts warn that the world's supply of petroleum is being used up rapidly.

Industrialized nations must ensure that all their major transportation systems have enough fuel to function normally. But they must also do all they can to conserve

AP/Wide World

A magnetic levitation train uses magnetic forces to float above a track without touching it. Maglev trains eliminate the friction of wheels on the track and thus can travel at much higher speeds than ordinary trains do. This train is part of the world's first commercial maglev rail system, which began operations in Shanghai, China, in 2004.

fuel. Fuel conservation is necessary not only because of the threat of a serious fuel shortage but also because of the high price of petroleum and the environmental damage caused by the burning of many transportation fuels. Higher petroleum prices result in higher transportation costs, which drive up the prices of transported goods.

Automobiles consume more than half the energy used for transportation in industrialized countries. They therefore contribute heavily to energy supply problems. To help reduce automobile fuel consumption, governments set fuel consumption standards for new cars. These standards encourage automakers to produce smaller, lighter cars, which travel farther per gallon or liter of gasoline than larger models.

In the early 2000's, automobile manufacturers first made *hybrids* available to consumers. Hybrids have all the components of electric cars plus another power source, usually a gasoline engine. They provide better fuel economy than comparably sized vehicles with gasoline engines.

Eventually, however, the transportation industry almost certainly will need substitutes for low-cost petroleum fuels. Energy companies are already producing synthetic liquid fuels from coal, natural gas, biomass, *oil shale* (a rock containing *kerogen,* a substance that yields oil when heated), and *bituminous sands* (sands containing bitumen, a substance from which oil can be obtained). A company in South Africa, for example, makes gasoline from coal. Companies in Brazil make ethanol, also called ethyl alcohol, from sugar cane pulp, and U.S. companies produce the fuel from corn. Another alternative is to increase the use of electric motors to power vehicles.

Environmental problems. The production, delivery, and use of transportation fuels all affect the environment. The drilling of offshore oil fields and the shipment of petroleum by tankers sometimes result in oil spills that pollute the ocean and kill wildlife. Motor-vehicle exhausts rank as a leading source of air pollution. Major pollutants produced by motor vehicles include carbon monoxide, *hydrocarbons* (compounds of carbon and hydrogen), and *nitrogen oxides* (compounds of nitrogen and oxygen). Nitrogen oxides can react with hydrocarbons in the presence of sunlight to produce a form of oxygen called *ozone.* Ozone is the chief component of photochemical smog, a common form of air pollution.

Even the cleanest fuels produce carbon dioxide when they burn. This gas slows the escape of heat released by Earth into space. Thus, an increase in atmospheric carbon dioxide may cause global warming.

Automobiles are the chief cause of traffic congestion in urban areas, and their exhaust fumes contribute heavily to urban air pollution. Many cities plagued by traffic jams and air pollution have taken steps to reduce automobile traffic in their busiest areas. Governments have established ever stricter pollution-control standards for new cars. These standards require automakers to manufacture cars that give off cleaner exhausts than earlier models.

Inadequate public transportation facilities. Greater use of public transportation in many countries would help ease problems caused by heavy dependence on automobiles. But public transportation in many areas must be improved before more automobile drivers can be persuaded to use it.

Transportation security is a continuing concern. A bomb detonated aboard a vehicle can cause great damage not only to the vehicle and its passengers but also to vehicles, structures, and people in the surrounding area. Hijackers may also seek to seize control of a vehicle and cause a collision. Such a collision, especially if it involves a heavy vehicle traveling at high speed, can cause considerable damage. In addition, spilled fuel provides significant fire risk after such a collision.

On Sept. 11, 2001, terrorists crashed hijacked airliners into the World Trade Center in New York City and the

American Honda Motor Company, Inc.

A hybrid car has all of the components of an electric car, plus another power source, usually a gasoline engine. The Honda Insight, *shown here,* was the first hybrid car sold to consumers.

Pentagon Building near Washington, D.C. Soon afterward, the U.S. government formed the Transportation Security Administration. This agency works to prevent criminal acts involving aircraft, airports, bridges, highways, pipelines, ports, and railroads in the United States. Security personnel at airports search travelers, baggage, and freight for bombs or hand weapons. Other transportation systems take similar precautions. For example, some railroads employ specially trained dogs that sniff checked baggage for hidden explosives.

Chris Hendrickson

Related articles in *World Book.* See the *Transportation* section of the country, state, and province articles. See also:

Land transportation

Ambulance
Amtrak
Aqueduct
Automobile
Bicycle
Bridge
Bus
Caravan
Carriage
Chariot
Conveyor belt
Electric car
Electric railroad
Elevated railroad
Elevator
Escalator
Fire department (Fire trucks)
Freight
Hybrid car
Jinrikisha
Locomotive
Magnetic levitation train
Monorail
Motorcycle
Pedicab
Petroleum (Transporting petroleum)
Pipeline
Railroad
Recreational vehicle
Road
Snowmobiling
Streetcar
Subway
Tractor
Transit
Travois
Truck
Tunnel
Viaduct
Wagon
Wheelbarrow

Water transportation

Air cushion vehicle
Barge
Canal
Cruise ship
Harbor
Lighthouse
Merchant marine
Port
Raft
Ship
Submarine
Tanker

Air transportation

Airmail
Airplane
Airport
Airship
Aviation
Balloon
Helicopter

Other related articles

Careers (Transportation)
Colonial life in America (Transportation and communication)
Common carrier
Communication
Containerization
Exploration
Industrial Revolution
Interstate Commerce Commission
Navigation
Rocket
Space exploration
Steam engine
Transportation, Department of
Transportation Security Administration

Outline

I. Kinds of transportation
A. Land transportation
B. Water transportation
C. Air transportation
II. History
III. Transportation today
A. Passenger transportation
B. Freight transportation
IV. The transportation industry
A. Equipment manufacturers
B. Passenger and freight carriers
C. Related industries
D. Government and transportation
V. Challenges of modern transportation
A. Traffic safety
B. Overcrowding of streets and highways
C. Declining fuel reserves
D. Environmental problems
E. Inadequate public transportation facilities
F. Transportation security

Questions

What form of transportation made suburban living possible?
Why is engine-powered transportation expensive?
Which kinds of transportation facilities are commonly owned and operated by national governments?
Which people first built an extensive system of paved roads?
What are the chief mass transit vehicles?
What are some vehicles that are moved by muscle power?
What are some of the challenges posed by modern transportation?
Why is the shipment of goods by air limited to expensive, lightweight, or perishable cargo?
Why are most developed countries trying to improve their intercity passenger train service?
What two inventions of late prehistoric times revolutionized transportation during the following centuries?

Additional resources

Level I

Francis, Dorothy B. *Our Transportation Systems.* Millbrook, 2002.
Maynard, Christopher. *Extreme Machines.* DK Pub., 2000. Describes various transportation vehicles.
Whitman, Sylvia. *Get Up and Go! The History of American Road Travel.* Lerner, 1996.
Wilkinson, Philip, and Pollard, Michael. *Transportation.* Chelsea Hse., 1995.
Woods, Michael and Mary B. *Ancient Transportation.* Runestone Pr., 2000.

Level II

Garrison, William L., and Ward, J. D. *Tomorrow's Transportation.* Artech Hse., 2000.
Kaszynski, William. *The American Highway: The History and Culture of Roads in the United States.* McFarland, 2000.
Macmillan Encyclopedia of Transportation. 6 vols. Macmillan Reference, 1999.
Richter, William L. *The ABC-Clio Companion to Transportation in America.* ABC-Clio, 1995.
Vuchic, Vukan R. *Transportation for Livable Cities.* Ctr. for Urban Policy Research, Rutgers Univ., 1999.

Transportation, Department of, is an executive department of the United States government. The department works to guarantee the availability of safe, economical, and efficient transportation in the United States. The department is sometimes called the DOT.

The secretary of transportation, a member of the president's Cabinet, heads the department. The secretary is appointed by the president with U.S. Senate approval. The secretary serves as the president's chief adviser on transportation matters.

Functions. The Transportation Department promotes safety in all forms of transportation. It sets and enforces safety standards for the design and manufacture of transportation equipment and for the operation of airplanes, trains, and trucks. The department also enforces safety standards for the transportation of chemicals and other hazardous materials.

The Department of Transportation grants money to cities to help provide and improve mass transit facilities. It establishes programs to help reduce the number of highway deaths and injuries. It also helps finance Amtrak, the nation's passenger rail system. The department also grants licenses for the launching of nongovernment satellites and for commercial launch facilities.

The Transportation Department conducts studies to

solve transportation problems and to ensure that U.S. transportation systems comply with the nation's environmental protection laws. The department carries out research and development programs in cooperation with private industry and universities. The department's Web site at www.dot.gov presents additional information on its activities.

The seal of the Department of Transportation

Agencies of the Department of Transportation include the Federal Aviation Administration, the Federal Highway Administration, and the Maritime Administration.

The Federal Aviation Administration operates air traffic control and navigation systems. It certifies civilian pilots, aircraft, airports, and aviation schools. The agency also directs a program of federal aid to airports.

The Federal Highway Administration provides financial assistance to states for the design and construction of highways and bridges. It also works to guarantee the safety of trucks and buses.

The Maritime Administration promotes a strong and efficient U.S. *merchant marine.* The merchant marine consists of the nation's commercial ships—including both cargo and passenger ships—and those who operate them. The Maritime Administration runs the U.S. Merchant Marine Academy at Kings Point, New York, and supports U.S. armed forces in national emergencies.

History. Before the Department of Transportation existed, many agencies, bureaus, and divisions administered federal transportation programs. Congress created the Department of Transportation in 1966, and it began operating in 1967. It took over several agencies and duties from other executive departments.

Some agencies that regulate the affairs of transportation companies operate outside the department as independent agencies. These include the Federal Maritime Commission and the Surface Transportation Board.

Some agencies that deal with transportation issues were transferred from the Department of Transportation to the newly created Department of Homeland Security in 2003. The move was part of a government effort to better protect the nation against terrorism. The moved agencies included the Transportation Security Administration and the U.S. Coast Guard. The Transportation Security Administration enforces security regulations, including those for air, rail, highway, and waterway transportation. The Coast Guard protects life and property at sea and enforces U.S. maritime laws.

Critically reviewed by the Department of Transportation

Secretaries of transportation

Name	Took office	Under president
Alan S. Boyd	1967	Johnson
John A. Volpe	1969	Nixon
Claude S. Brinegar	1973	Nixon, Ford
*William T. Coleman, Jr.	1975	Ford
Brock Adams	1977	Carter
Neil E. Goldschmidt	1979	Carter
Andrew L. Lewis, Jr.	1981	Reagan
*Elizabeth H. Dole	1983	Reagan
James H. Burnley	1987	Reagan
Samuel K. Skinner	1989	G. H. W. Bush
Andrew H. Card, Jr.	1992	G. H. W. Bush
*Federico F. Peña	1993	Clinton
Rodney E. Slater	1997	Clinton
*Norman Y. Mineta	2001	G. W. Bush

*Has a separate biography in *World Book.*

Related articles in *World Book* include:

Amtrak
Federal Aviation Administration
Federal Highway Administration
Flag (picture: Flags of the U.S. Government)
Maritime Administration
Merchant Marine
Saint Lawrence Seaway Development Corporation
United States Merchant Marine Academy

Transportation of convicts was the system of deporting convicted criminals from Britain (later the United Kingdom) to the British colonies from 1615 until 1868. Britain began transporting convicts to its colonies in North America in 1615. Private shippers paid most of the costs of transporting the convicts. They then sold the convicts as *indentured servants* (people who worked in exchange for the price of their voyage and food, clothing, and shelter).

The British also sent convicts to the West Indies, especially Barbados and Jamaica. Transportees included people suspected of plotting against the government; Irish and Scottish soldiers defeated in battle; and common criminals, mostly convicted of theft.

After the start of the Revolutionary War in America (1775-1783), the Americans no longer accepted British convicts. The British government then set up a *penal* (prison) colony in Australia. The first convicts arrived in Australia in January 1788. The convicts worked for the government and, eventually, as laborers or servants for free colonists.

Opposition to transportation became widespread in the 1830's. Reformers questioned its worth as a way to stop crime, and free immigrants in Australia objected to living in a prison colony. The British government ended transportation to Australia in 1868. By then, the British had transported more than 200,000 convicts. At least 162,000 of them were sent to Australia. John S. Morrill

Transportation Security Administration is a United States government agency responsible for protecting the nation's transportation systems. It aims to ensure the continued freedom of movement for people and commerce in the United States. The agency, sometimes called the TSA, works to prevent criminal acts involving aircraft, airports, bridges, highways, pipelines, ports, and railroads. The TSA is part of the U.S. Department of Homeland Security.

On Sept. 11, 2001, terrorists hijacked four commercial airplanes and deliberately crashed two into the World Trade Center in New York City and one into the Pentagon Building near Washington, D.C. The fourth hijacked plane crashed in a field in Pennsylvania. About 3,000 people died in the attacks. In November 2001, Congress passed the Aviation and Transportation Security Act (ATSA). The act established the TSA as part of the U.S. Department of Transportation. The agency was transferred to the Department of Homeland Security in 2003.

Critically reviewed by the Transportation Security Administration

See also **Homeland Security, Department of.**

Transsexualism is a condition in which a person experiences persistent discomfort about his or her sexual designation. Such individuals, called *transsexuals,* want to remove their body's sexual characteristics and obtain the characteristics of the opposite sex. Transsexuals feel a need to act like and be treated as a member of the opposite sex. Transsexualism occurs more in males than in females. Transsexualism's cause is unknown. Some behavioral scientists think it results from an early disturbance in the mother-infant relationship and a lack of proper identification with the same-sex parent. There is no evidence of hormonal abnormalities in transsexuals.

Transsexuals sometimes seek *sexual reassignment surgery* to permanently change their external anatomy to that of the opposite sex. Patients should receive careful psychiatric evaluation before the surgery because various psychiatric disorders can lead to unhappiness with one's sex type. In addition, psychotherapy is needed to explore the motivation for the operation.

People considering sexual reassignment surgery are advised to live and dress as a member of the opposite sex for up to two years. By doing so, they can demonstrate their ability to function as members of the opposite sex. During this time, they can take hormones of the opposite sex to obtain secondary sexual characteristics of that sex. For example, a woman taking male hormones will grow facial hair, and a man taking female hormones will develop breasts. Thomas N. Wise

Trans-Siberian Railroad is the longest railroad in the world, extending over 5,600 miles (9,000 kilometers). It stretches across the width of Russia, from Moscow in the west to Vladivostok at the far southeastern tip of the country. See **Russia** (political map). The trip from one end to the other takes about seven days. Most of the railroad crosses Siberia, the vast, icy region that makes up most of the Asian part of Russia.

The Trans-Siberian Railroad brought an era of development to Siberia. Industries, trade, and mineral exploration developed along the train route. New cities and settlements grew in the railroad's path. During World War I (1914-1918) and World War II (1939-1945), the Trans-Siberian Railroad was used to transport troops and supplies across the vast territory.

Originally called the Great Siberian Way, it was the first railroad built across Siberia. The railroad was built in several sections from 1891 to 1916. The section in eastern Siberia, between Vladivostok and Khabarovsk, was completed about 1897. From 1892 to 1912, other sections were built across western and central Siberia.

Between 1897 and 1903, Russia built the Chinese Eastern Railway across northeastern China, then known as Manchuria. This railroad connected Vladivostok with the sections of the Trans-Siberian in western and central Siberia. By 1904, a continuous railroad stretched from Vladivostok across China and Siberia to the Ural Mountains.

The Russians wanted a railroad route that did not cross China. They built a line north of China from Khabarovsk to Kuenga. Completed in 1916, it was the last link in a continuous railroad on Russian soil between Vladivostok and Moscow.

Since the 1920's, the Trans-Siberian has been joined to other railroads. Beginning in 1929, parts of the railroad were electrified, so that electric trains could use the tracks. The project to electrify the entire Trans-Siberian Railroad was completed in 2002. Craig ZumBrunnen

See also **Irkutsk; Omsk; Russia** (Economy [picture: Railroads]); **Siberia.**

Transubstantiation, *TRAN suhb STAN shee AY shuhn,* is a doctrine of the Roman Catholic Church. It explains the belief that bread and wine are changed into the body and blood of Jesus Christ during the sacrament of the Eucharist, or Mass. Transubstantiation indicates that Jesus is present in a real way under the appearance of bread and wine. The word was first adopted by the church at the Fourth Lateran Council in 1215 and reaffirmed by the Council of Trent in 1551. The term had been in widespread use since the 1100's. Some Eastern Orthodox Christians accept transubstantiation as one of several explanations for the transformation of bread and wine. Some Protestant churches have similar doctrines concerning real presence. Richard L. Schebera

See also **Communion; Mass; Roman Catholic Church** (The Eucharist, or Mass).

Transuranium element, *TRANS yu RAY nee uhm,* is any chemical element heavier than uranium. There are 19 officially recognized transuranium elements. They have *atomic numbers* (numbers of protons) from 93 to 111. In addition, researchers claim to have discovered elements with atomic numbers of 112 through 116. The International Union of Pure and Applied Chemistry (IUPAC) is the recognized authority in crediting the discovery of elements and assigning names to them.

The recognized transuranium elements have official names. Their atomic numbers, names, and chemical symbols are: 93, neptunium, Np; 94, plutonium, Pu; 95, americium, Am; 96, curium, Cm; 97, berkelium, Bk; 98, californium, Cf; 99, einsteinium, Es; 100, fermium, Fm; 101, mendelevium, Md; 102, nobelium, No; 103, lawrencium, Lr; 104, rutherfordium, Rf; 105, dubnium, Db; 106, seaborgium, Sg; 107, bohrium, Bh; 108, hassium, Hs; 109, meitnerium, Mt; 110, darmstadtium, Ds; and 111, roentgenium, Rg.

All transuranium elements are radioactive, and many last only a fraction of a second. They are seldom found in nature because they rapidly change into other elements through a process called *radioactive decay,* also known as *transmutation.*

Scientists produce transuranium elements using devices called *particle accelerators.* The scientists bombard a target nucleus with a beam of *ions* (electrically charged atoms) that have been boosted to tremendous speeds by the accelerator. Some of the nuclei collide and join, forming a new, heavier nucleus. Transuranium elements also are produced in nuclear reactors and in the debris of nuclear explosions.

Scientists have used accelerators to produce evidence of the discovery of transuranium elements that have not yet been named. In 1996, an international team of researchers at the Heavy Ion Research Center in Darmstadt, Germany, announced the creation of element 112. In 1999, Russian and American physicists and chemists working at the Joint Institute for Nuclear Research (JINR) in Dubna, near Moscow, announced that they had created element 114 in experiments ending in December 1998. In addition, in 1999, researchers at Lawrence Berkeley National Laboratory in California announced that they had created elements 116 and

118. However, the Berkeley group withdrew its claim in 2001.

In 2000, the team at JINR announced the discovery of element 116. In 2004, scientists at JINR and Lawrence Livermore National Laboratory in California announced the discovery of elements 113 and 115. Richard L. Hahn

Related articles in *World Book* include:

Americium	Darmstadtium	Lawrencium	Plutonium
Berkelium	Dubnium	Meitnerium	Roentgenium
Bohrium	Einsteinium	Mendelevium	Rutherfordium
Californium	Fermium	Neptunium	Seaborgium
Curium	Hassium	Nobelium	

Transvaal, *trans VAHL,* is a historic region in the northern part of South Africa. From 1910 to 1994, the Transvaal was one of South Africa's four provinces. In 1994, the Transvaal was split into three new separate provinces. The provinces are Gauteng, Mpumalanga, and Limpopo. A northwestern section of the historic region also became part of South Africa's North West Province (see **South Africa** [political map]).

The name *Transvaal* means *beyond the Vaal.* The Boers (settlers of Dutch, German, and French ancestry) gave this name to the region in the early 1800's because it lay beyond the Vaal River. The area that was the Transvaal covers 109,621 square miles (283,917 square kilometers). A large majority of the people are black Africans, mostly of the Sotho and Tswana groups. About 30 percent of the people are white. The Transvaal region contains South Africa's major industrial area, the Witwatersrand (White Waters Ridge). This area, in the southern part of old Transvaal, has many factories and the world's richest gold mines. Johannesburg is the largest city in the Transvaal region. Bruce S. Fetter

See also **Anglo-Boer Wars; Johannesburg; Pretoria; South Africa** (History).

Transylvania, *TRAN sihl VAY nee uh* or *TRAN sihl VAYN yuh,* is a region that covers most of central and northwest Romania. It has an area of about 39,000 square miles (101,000 square kilometers). The Carpathian Mountain System separates Transylvania from the rest of Romania. See **Romania** (map).

The majority of the region's people are Romanians. But about a quarter of the population are Magyars, the national ethnic group of Hungary. Transylvania also has a sizable *Romani* (Gypsy) minority. The region's largest city is Cluj-Napoca.

Transylvania has rich deposits of iron, lead, lignite, manganese, natural gas, and sulfur. The surrounding mountains are covered with beech and oak trees. Transylvania's high plains make good grazing grounds for cattle and sheep. Its valleys produce large bean, corn, potato, tobacco, rice, and wheat crops.

For years, Romanians and Hungarians quarreled over Transylvania. Magyars conquered the region in the 900's. From 1526 to 1699, Transylvania was part of the Ottoman Empire. Hungary controlled the region from 1699 to 1867, when it once again became part of Hungary.

During World War I (1914-1918), Romania joined the Allies after being promised Transylvania. After the war, the region became part of Romania. In August 1940, Germany and Italy forced Romania to give northern Transylvania to Hungary. After World War II (1939-1945), Transylvania was returned to Romania.

Transylvania is the main site of the legend about the vampire Dracula. The character of Dracula is based on Vlad Tepes, a cruel prince of the 1400's who lived in Walachia, a region south of Transylvania. Vlad executed many of his enemies by driving a stake through their bodies. A belief in vampires once held by many Romanian peasants added details to the legend. *Dracula* (1897), a novel by the British author Bram Stoker, made the legend famous. Sharon L. Wolchik

See also **Dracula; Romania** (Land regions).

Trap-door spider digs a burrow in the ground and covers the entrance with a lid, or trap door. It lives in warm climates, including the southern and western United States. It is harmless to human beings. Some grow over 1 inch (2.5 centimeters) long.

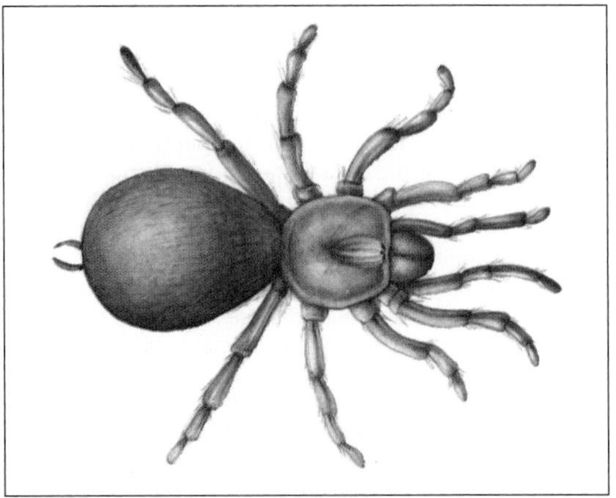

WORLD BOOK illustration by Oxford Illustrators Limited.

The trap-door spider is harmless to human beings.

Trap-door spiders use their burrows for protection and as nests in which to raise young. The burrows are lined with silk. Some burrows are more than 10 inches (25 centimeters) deep and over 1 inch (2.5 centimeters) wide. Some trap-door spiders dig simple, tubelike burrows. Others dig burrows that have a branch tunnel. The branch tunnel, sometimes hidden by a second trap door, serves as an extra hiding place.

The trap doors are made of silk and mud, and are attached to the lining of the burrows by silk hinges. Some trap-door spiders build thin, waferlike doors that cover the burrow entrance loosely. Others construct thick doors, like corks, that fit so snugly into the tunnel entrance they are watertight. Still others build circular folding doors that open in the middle.

Trap-door spiders eat insects, including many kinds that damage valuable plants. The spider waits behind its door until its prey walks by. Then it quickly opens the door, seizes and poisons its victim, and drags it into the burrow. Trap-door spiders are timid, and the females seldom leave their nests. These spiders are a type of *tarantula* (see **Tarantula**). James E. Carico

Scientific classification. Trap-door spiders make up the trap-door spider family, Ctenizidae. The most common trap-door spiders in the United States are genus *Ummidia.*

Trapping is the capture or killing of wild animals in traps. Trapping was one of the first ways that people obtained animals for food and clothing. Later, people began to trap for profit. In North America, many pioneers

Detail of a water color (1858) by Alfred Jacob Miller; Walters Art Gallery, Baltimore

Beaver trapping was a profitable occupation for many pioneers during the 1700's and 1800's in North America. They used steel traps held in place by a chain and stake. The trappers sold the pelts or traded them for food and other supplies. Most beaver pelts were made into hats and sold in Europe.

of the 1700's and 1800's became wealthy by trapping fur-bearing animals. They sold the pelts for use in making fashionable fur garments.

Today, much of the fur supply comes from the manufacture of artificial furs and from farms that raise fur-bearing animals. But many people trap for sport and profit. Popular fur-bearing animals of the United States and Canada include beavers, martens, minks, muskrats, opossums, otters, raccoons, and skunks. Methods of trapping may be found in books at many libraries and in pamphlets published by state agencies.

In some parts of the world, people still trap animals for food and clothing. Some African groups, for example, trap antelope and monkeys for food. People also trap for other reasons. For example, scientists trap wild animals unharmed to study their habits. Farmers and ranchers use traps to catch such animals as coyotes and foxes, which kill chickens and sheep. These animals that prey on other animals are called *predators.* Many homeowners trap mice, moles, and other pests that ruin lawns or invade cupboards looking for food.

Kinds of traps. There are three main types of traps: (1) arresting traps, (2) enclosing traps, and (3) exterminating traps. Bait can be used in any trap but may not be needed.

Arresting traps grip animals but do not kill them. The most common arresting trap is the *steel trap.* Manufacturers make steel traps of various sizes and shapes to catch such animals as raccoons and skunks. Steel traps have jaws that operate with a steel spring and grip an animal by the foot or leg. Some have teeth that can hurt an animal badly if it struggles to get free. The United Kingdom considers steel traps inhumane and bans them. Some U.S. states forbid steel traps with teeth.

Enclosing traps hold animals unharmed. A common type is the *box* or *cage* trap. The trapper uses bait to lure an animal into a box trap, and a door then closes and imprisons the animal. Animal collectors and scientists often use box traps to catch animals for zoos or research. Scientists may trap an animal and tag it so they can follow the creature's movements after freeing it from the trap. Many people use box traps to catch raccoons, squirrels, or other animals in their gardens or homes. They then release the animals in an unpopulated area.

Exterminating traps grip animals and kill them. They include the *mousetrap* used in a large number of homes and barns. A mousetrap has metal rods that snap shut by means of a coiled spring and break the victim's neck. Another exterminating trap, used for catching beavers and muskrats, is the *Conibear.* This type of trap is designed to stun and kill the animal almost instantly in its scissorlike grip.

Trapping and wildlife conservation. Wildlife conservation groups often criticize any trapping that involves killing animals. They fear that certain animals may become extinct if people continue to hunt them.

Some people believe that trapping predators upsets the balance of nature (see **Balance of nature**). They feel that killing predators will in time result in an oversupply of rodents and other animals that predators eat. But others point out that when some animal species become too numerous, the population of predators increases because the predators have a larger food supply.

In the United States, many states have tried to preserve wildlife with various laws, including total bans on the trapping of certain animals. Some states, for example, forbid bear trapping. Trapping laws vary from state to state. Each state issues trapping licenses and determines where and when animals may be trapped. State agencies also decide what species may be trapped and what number of animals may be trapped at one time.

The federal Endangered Species Act of 1973 forbids the hunting and trapping of any endangered species in the United States. It also prohibits the importation of any

Kinds of traps The type of trap a person uses depends on the kind of animal being trapped and on whether the animal is to be unharmed or killed. Bait can be used in any trap, but it may not be necessary. For example, trapping minks and muskrats seldom requires bait. The trapper simply conceals the traps in areas where the animals live and waits for them to trap themselves.

Enclosing traps

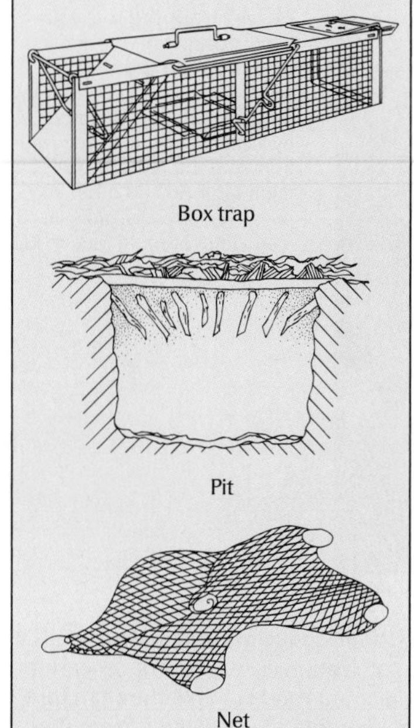

Arresting traps

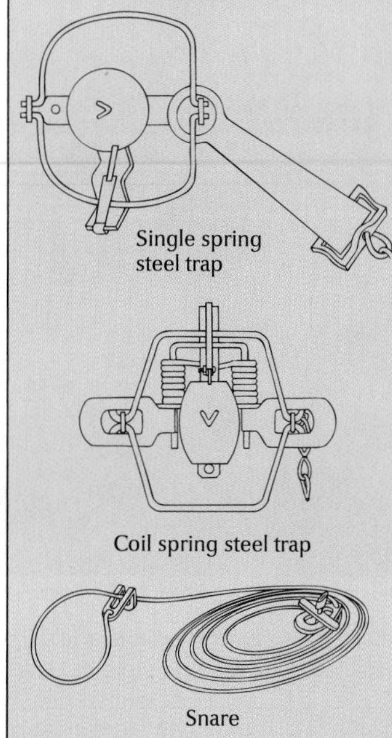

Exterminating traps

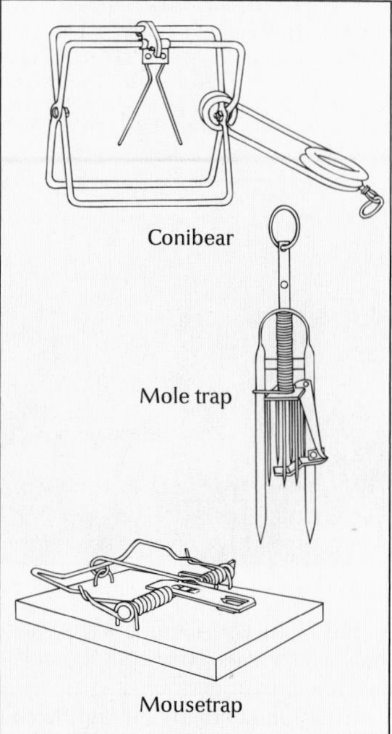

endangered species or of products made from them. Supporters of this law believe fewer of these animals will be trapped and hunted in other countries if there is no U.S. market for them. Special permits may be issued to exclude animals used for research. John W. Peterson

See also **Endangered species; Fur.**

Additional resources

Bateman, James A. *Animal Traps and Trapping.* Rev. ed. Stackpole, 1988.

Geary, Steven M. *Fur Trapping in North America.* Rev. ed. Winchester, 1984.

Trappists are Roman Catholic monks who belong to the Order of Cistercians of the Strict Observance. This branch of the Cistercians dates from a reform begun in 1664 at La Trappe Abbey in Normandy, France, by the abbot Armand-Jean le Bouthillier de Rancé. He restored rules of the original Cistercian abbey that no longer were followed, including almost complete silence, four to six hours of manual labor a day, and seclusion. He added other rules, such as abstaining from meat, except for the infirm. Orders of Cistercian Nuns of the Strict Observance, called Trappistines, were founded in 1794 by the monk Dom Augustin de Lestrange. Their first convent was La Sainte Volonté de Dieu, near Fribourg, in Switzerland. See **Cistercians.** David G. Schultenover

Trapshooting is a sport in which a person shoots at clay disks that are thrown into the air by a machine. Trapshooters use a 12-gauge shotgun that fires shells holding about 500 lead pellets. The disks measure no more than $4\frac{5}{16}$ inches (11 centimeters) in diameter. A machine called a *trap* hurls the disks into the air at speeds of almost 60 miles (97 kilometers) an hour. The trap is housed in a structure called a *traphouse,* which is partially beneath the ground.

A trapshooter stands behind the traphouse in one of five lanes, called *stations.* When the shooter calls out "pull," a disk is launched, and the shooter fires at it once. A disk is called "dead" if a visible piece falls from it. If the shooter misses, the disk is called "lost." Most competitions consist of 100 disks shot in groups of 25. The shooter fires five times from each of the five stations.

Trapshooters compete in *singles, doubles,* and *handicap* events. In singles, one disk at a time is launched. In doubles, competitors shoot at two disks launched simultaneously. In both singles and doubles, shooters stand 16 yards (15 meters) behind the traphouse. In a handicap event, the greater the shooters' ability, the farther they must stand behind the traphouse. The distance varies from 18 to 27 yards (16 to 25 meters).

A related sport called *skeet shooting* has eight stations and two traphouses aboveground. Bonnie Nash

Trauma, *TRAW muh,* in psychiatry, is an unpleasant emotional experience of such intensity that it leaves a lasting impression on the mind. Psychoanalysts believe that childhood traumatic experiences sometimes lead to later emotional symptoms. The study of such traumas plays an important part in the psychotherapeutic treatment given to the emotionally ill (see **Psychotherapy**).

Traumas that occur during adulthood also may have effects that require psychiatric treatment. Such traumas may be physical—such as a serious injury or illness—or psychological. In some cases, an unusually severe trauma may result in a type of mental disorder called a *post-traumatic stress disorder.* Nancy C. Andreasen

See also **Post-traumatic stress disorder.**

Trauma center, *TRAW muh,* is an area of a hospital provided with special staff and equipment to treat the most seriously injured patients. Trauma is life-threatening injury caused by the effects of physical forces on the body. Most trauma results from vehicle accidents, gunshot wounds, falls from high places, or serious burns.

Trauma centers have specialized equipment and permanent staffs of physicians, nurses, and paramedics who are skilled in emergency lifesaving techniques. Staff members provide first aid at the accident site and rapid transportation by ambulance or helicopter to the center itself. Trauma centers developed from military hospitals that provided such service during the Korean War (1950-1953) and the Vietnam War (1957-1975). Today, many trauma centers are part of an Emergency Medical Services system (see **Emergency Medical Services**).

In the United States, pioneer civilian trauma care systems were established by the states of Maryland and Illinois. In 1969, Maryland opened a statewide trauma hospital in Baltimore called the Maryland Institute for Emergency Medical Services. Helicopters pick up accident victims and fly them directly to the institute.

One of the most extensive trauma care systems was established in Illinois in 1971. This statewide system has four kinds of trauma centers: (1) local, (2) areawide, (3) regional, and (4) specialized. Local centers serve rural areas. After receiving basic treatment in a local trauma unit, the most seriously injured accident victims may be transferred to an areawide, regional, or specialized center. Areawide centers have such facilities as blood banks, intensive care units, laboratory services, operating rooms, and specialized X-ray units. Regional centers are located within university medical centers. They have highly trained staffs and can provide sophisticated treatment for seriously injured patients. Specialized trauma centers treat such problems as spinal cord injuries and children's trauma. David R. Boyd

Travel agency is a business that helps people arrange trips by handling travel arrangements. It makes reservations for hotel rooms and transportation and arranges sightseeing tours. It offers customers guidance in obtaining passports and visas, which travelers need for foreign travel. A travel agency also provides information on travel regulations of various governments. Travel agencies arrange tours for individuals and for groups.

A travel agency earns much of its income from commissions paid by businesses in the travel industry. These businesses pay a commission on each reservation an agency makes or on each ticket it sells. A travel agency also earns income through service fees it charges its customers. Travel agencies operate in most countries. Many agencies provide services through the Internet.

Critically reviewed by the American Society of Travel Agents

Travelers Aid International is a network of agencies that provides services for individuals and families who have experienced difficulties related to homelessness, traveling, or moving their place of residence. Such people include people with disabilities, the homeless, immigrants, jobseekers, runaway children, and stranded travelers.

Travelers Aid agencies are located throughout the United States, Canada, and Puerto Rico. They offer such services as financial aid, professional counseling, and employment information, as well as food, clothing, and shelter. The first Travelers Aid organization was founded in St. Louis, Missouri, in 1851. The Travelers Aid Association of America was established in 1917. It was replaced in 1984 by the National Organization of Travelers Aid Societies. In 2000, the National Organization of Travelers Aid Societies changed its name to Travelers Aid International to reflect its activity outside the United States. Travelers Aid headquarters are in Washington, D.C.

Critically reviewed by Travelers Aid International

Traveler's check is a check that can be used as money or as a letter of credit. Banks and travel agencies issue traveler's checks. The purpose of traveler's checks is to protect the money carried by travelers. People sign the checks when they buy them and again when they spend them. Marcellus F. Berry, general agent of the American Express Company, originated the system of traveler's checks in 1891.

In the United States, such checks are issued in denominations of $10, $20, $50, and $100. Almost any bank, or any travel or express agency, sells them and adds a small fee. People can redeem them in foreign currencies abroad at the rate of exchange when converted. Thus, travelers bear the risk of exchange fluctuation. If travelers plan to be chiefly in one country, such as the United Kingdom or Switzerland, they may buy checks denominated in pounds sterling or Swiss francs to avoid this risk. Traveler's checks are accepted the world over in payment for accommodations or merchandise, or in exchange for currency. Joanna H. Frodin

Traveler's-tree is a tropical evergreen that resembles a giant fan. These trees grow more than 40 feet (12 meters) tall and have huge, oblong leaves up to 10 feet (3 meters) long. The leaves spread out in a single row from an unbranched trunk. A deep trough at the base of each leaf collects up to 1 quart (0.95 liter) of rain water. Travelers can drink this water in an emergency.

The traveler's-tree grows wild in Madagascar, an African island country. People use the trunk for wood and the leaves as roofing material. Michael J. Tanabe

Scientific classification. The traveler's-tree belongs to the family Strelitziaceae. It is *Ravenala madagascariensis.*

Patti Murray, Earth Scenes

The traveler's-tree has leaves that fan out from its trunk. Each leaf collects up to 1 quart (0.95 liter) of water.

Travers, P. L. (1899-1996), an Australian-born author, became known for her children's stories about Mary Poppins, an English *nanny* (nursemaid) who has magical powers. Travers introduced the character in *Mary Poppins* (1934). She continued the series with *Mary Poppins Comes Back* (1935), *Mary Poppins Opens the Door* (1943), *Mary Poppins in the Park* (1952), *Mary Poppins from A to Z* (1962), *Mary Poppins in the Kitchen* (1975), and *Mary Poppins in Cherry Tree Lane* (1982). She also wrote several other children's books.

Pamela Lyndon Travers was born on Aug. 9, 1899, in Queensland and settled in England in her early 20's. Her original name was Helen Lyndon Goff. She died on April 23, 1996. Virginia L. Wolf

Travertine, *TRAV uhr tihn* or *TRAV uhr teen,* is a light-colored rock used in building. It is a *limestone,* a rock made up mainly of calcium carbonate ($CaCO_3$). The word *travertine* comes from an old Roman name for Tivoli, a town in Italy where large deposits of the mineral occur.

Much travertine is white, tan, or yellow. Other common shades include orange, red, and brown. Most travertine has bands of different textures that range from dense, solid strips to loose layers of fine, threadlike fibers. *Tufa* is a type of spongy, less compact travertine.

Travertine forms when cooling or evaporating water deposits dissolved calcium carbonate. It appears around the world in limestone caves, where it makes up such formations as *stalagmites,* which rise from the floor, and *stalactites,* which hang from the ceiling. Travertine can also form in cracks near *faults* (breaks in Earth's crust) and around the mouths of warm or hot springs, such as those in Yellowstone National Park in the United States.

Travertine is commonly used as decorative building stone and floor tile. It is easy to cut and polish and has interesting structures and color patterns. Mark Cloos

See also **Limestone; Stalactite; Stalagmite.**

Travis, *TRAV ihs,* **William Barret** (1809-1836), fought in the Battle of the Alamo in 1836, in the war for Texas's independence from Mexico. He commanded the Texans who died defending the Alamo and died with them there on March 6, 1836. Travis was born on Aug. 1, 1809, near Red Bank, South Carolina. He taught school and practiced law in Alabama before he moved to Texas in 1831. Before the Alamo, he led troops at Anahuac and San Antonio. See also **Alamo.** Joseph A. Stout, Jr.

Travois, *truh VOY,* is a device American Indians and other peoples used for carrying loads. It consists of two poles, a net or platform lashed between the poles, and a harness for hitching it to a horse or dog. A travois has no wheels. The ends of the poles drag on the ground as the animal pulls the load. See also **Transportation** (picture: Transportation in prehistoric times). Robert C. Post

Travolta, John (1954-), is an American motion-picture star famous for his versatility. He is also known for his likable screen presence, even playing villains.

Travolta was born on Feb. 18, 1954, in Englewood, New Jersey. He dropped out of school at the age of 16 to enter show business. He took small stage and film roles and eventually appeared in the touring and Broadway productions of the musical *Grease.* Travolta's big break came with his role as Vinnie Barbarino in the popular television series "Welcome Back, Kotter" (1975-1979).

Travolta appeared as a teen-aged villain in the horror movie *Carrie* (1976). He gained movie success for his sexy disco dancing in the musical *Saturday Night Fever* (1977). He danced and sang the leading role in the film version of *Grease* (1978). He also starred in the modern Western *Urban Cowboy* (1980).

© Yoram Kahama, Shooting Star
John Travolta

His career sagged in the mid-1980's before he regained some popularity in the comedies *Look Who's Talking* (1989) and *Look Who's Talking Too* (1990). He returned to stardom as a weirdly funny gangster in *Pulp Fiction* (1994). Travolta then starred in a string of popular movies, including *Get Shorty* (1995), *Broken Arrow* (1996), *Phenomenon* (1996), *Michael* (1996), *Face/Off* (1997), *Primary Colors* (1998), and *A Civil Action* (1998). His other films include *The General's Daughter* (1999), *Lucky Numbers* (2000), and *The Punisher* (2004). Louis Giannetti

Treadmill, *TREHD mihl,* is a wheeled mechanism rotated by people or animals walking on or inside the wheel. A treadmill with an axle is called a *wheel and axle* (see **Wheel and axle**). The movement of the wheel turns the axle and any mechanical device attached to it.

The ancient Romans used treadmills for such tasks as grinding grain, lifting water out of mines, and powering cranes that hoisted construction materials. People and such animals as cows and horses provided the power for treadmills. They were used for heavy work until the 1700's and 1800's, when they were replaced by steam and hydraulic engines. Today, many people exercise indoors by walking or jogging on powered devices called treadmills. Tiny treadwheels provide exercise for hamsters and other small pets in cages. Melvin Kranzberg

Treason, *TREE zuhn,* once meant disloyalty to a sovereign ruler, such as a king. People who criticized the ruler's policies and actions might find themselves convicted of treason. But today, the meaning of treason has changed. The people in the United States or other democratic countries can criticize the government and work as freely as they like for the election of a new government. The U.S. Constitution defines treason as:

"Treason against the United States shall consist only in levying war against them or in adhering to their enemies, giving them aid and comfort." See **Constitution of the United States** (Article III [Section 3]).

This definition protects the right of citizens to oppose the actions of their government in all reasonable ways. Congress determines the penalties for treason against the United States. Many states have laws against treason. Death or life imprisonment is the usual penalty. A person convicted of treason is usually called a *traitor.*

A famous case of treason involved John Brown, an abolitionist who led a raid against the U.S. arsenal at Harpers Ferry in western Virginia (now West Virginia). The raid occurred in October 1859, and Brown was captured soon afterward. He was convicted of charges of treason and hanged. Douglas L. Wheeler

Related articles in ***World Book*** include:

Arnold, Benedict	Burr, Aaron	Quisling, Vidkun
Brown, John	Dreyfus affair	Sedition

Treasury, Department of the, is an executive department of the United States government that handles a variety of economic, financial, and monetary responsibilities. The secretary of the treasury, a member of the president's Cabinet, heads the department. The secretary is appointed by the president with the approval of the United States Senate. The secretary advises the president on financial policies, reports to Congress on the nation's finances, and is the government's chief financial officer.

The seal of the Department of the Treasury

Department functions. The Department of the Treasury collects federal taxes and customs duties. It receives all money paid to the government, serves as custodian of the government's revenues, pays the federal government's expenses, and maintains records of its income and spending. The department manages the national debt and borrows money for the government when Congress authorizes it to do so. It also supervises the operation of national banks, savings banks, and savings and loan associations. In addition, it develops U.S. policies in the fields of international economics and finance.

The Treasury Department manufactures all of the nation's paper money and coins and prints most U.S.

Some important agencies of the Department of the Treasury

Bureau of Alcohol, Tobacco, and Firearms
Regulates the alcohol and tobacco industries and collects taxes from them; enforces federal firearms and explosives laws.

Bureau of Engraving and Printing
Designs and prints paper money, postage stamps, and government securities.

Internal Revenue Service
Administers tax laws and collects taxes imposed by federal law.

United States Mint
Mints (manufactures) coins.

Secretaries of the treasury

Name	Took office	Under president
*Alexander Hamilton	1789	Washington
Oliver Wolcott, Jr.	1795	Washington, Adams
Samuel Dexter	1801	Adams, Jefferson
*Albert Gallatin	1801	Jefferson, Madison
George W. Campbell	1814	Madison
Alexander J. Dallas	1814	Madison
*William H. Crawford	1816	Madison, Monroe
Richard Rush	1825	J. Q. Adams
Samuel D. Ingham	1829	Jackson
Louis McLane	1831	Jackson
William J. Duane	1833	Jackson
*Roger B. Taney	1833	Jackson
Levi Woodbury	1834	Jackson, Van Buren
Thomas Ewing	1841	W. H. Harrison, Tyler
Walter Forward	1841	Tyler
John C. Spencer	1843	Tyler
George M. Bibb	1844	Tyler
Robert J. Walker	1845	Polk
William M. Meredith	1849	Taylor
Thomas Corwin	1850	Fillmore
James Guthrie	1853	Pierce
Howell Cobb	1857	Buchanan
Philip F. Thomas	1860	Buchanan
John A. Dix	1861	Buchanan
*Salmon P. Chase	1861	Lincoln
*William P. Fessenden	1864	Lincoln
Hugh McCulloch	1865	Lincoln, A. Johnson
George S. Boutwell	1869	Grant
William A. Richardson	1873	Grant
Benjamin H. Bristow	1874	Grant
Lot M. Morrill	1876	Grant
*John Sherman	1877	Hayes
William Windom	1881	Garfield, Arthur
Charles J. Folger	1881	Arthur
Walter Q. Gresham	1884	Arthur
Hugh McCulloch	1884	Arthur
Daniel Manning	1885	Cleveland
Charles S. Fairchild	1887	Cleveland
William Windom	1889	B. Harrison
Charles Foster	1891	B. Harrison
John G. Carlisle	1893	Cleveland
Lyman J. Gage	1897	McKinley, T. Roosevelt
Leslie M. Shaw	1902	T. Roosevelt
George B. Cortelyou	1907	T. Roosevelt
Franklin MacVeagh	1909	Taft
William G. McAdoo	1913	Wilson
*Carter Glass	1918	Wilson
David F. Houston	1920	Wilson
*Andrew W. Mellon	1921	Harding, Coolidge, Hoover
Ogden L. Mills	1932	Hoover
William H. Woodin	1933	F. D. Roosevelt
*Henry Morgenthau, Jr.	1934	F. D. Roosevelt, Truman
*Frederick M. Vinson	1945	Truman
John W. Snyder	1946	Truman
George M. Humphrey	1953	Eisenhower
Robert B. Anderson	1957	Eisenhower
Douglas Dillon	1961	Kennedy, L. B. Johnson
Henry H. Fowler	1965	L. B. Johnson
Joseph W. Barr	1968	L. B. Johnson
David M. Kennedy	1969	Nixon
*John B. Connally	1971	Nixon
*George P. Shultz	1972	Nixon
*William E. Simon	1974	Nixon, Ford
W. Michael Blumenthal	1977	Carter
G. William Miller	1979	Carter
Donald T. Regan	1981	Reagan
*James A. Baker III	1985	Reagan
*Nicholas F. Brady	1988	Reagan, G. H. W. Bush
*Lloyd M. Bentsen, Jr.	1993	Clinton
*Robert E. Rubin	1995	Clinton
Lawrence H. Summers	1999	Clinton
Paul H. O'Neill	2001	G. W. Bush
John W. Snow	2003	G. W. Bush

*Has a separate biography in *World Book*.

postage stamps. A department official known as the treasurer of the United States oversees these operations.

The Department of the Treasury enforces antismuggling laws and works to prevent counterfeiting. It also guards and protects the president and vice president, their immediate families, and certain other individuals.

History. The Department of the Treasury, established in 1789, was the second executive department created by the United States Congress. The first was the Department of Foreign Affairs, which Congress had established earlier that year and soon renamed the Department of State. Alexander Hamilton, one of the nation's Founding Fathers, was the first secretary of the treasury.

In 2002, Congress reorganized the federal government to help increase focus on the prevention of terrorism. As part of the plan, the U.S. Customs Service and the U.S. Secret Service, agencies formerly run by the Department of the Treasury, were transferred to the newly created Department of Homeland Security.

Critically reviewed by the Department of the Treasury

Related articles in *World Book* include:

Alcohol, Tobacco, and Firearms, Bureau of
Bank (Regulation of U.S. banks)
Customs Service, United States
Engraving and Printing, Bureau of
Flag (picture: Flags of the United States government)
Internal Revenue Service
Mint
Money
Savings bond
Secret Service, United States

Treaty is a formal agreement between two or more independent governments. It is usually a written document, but it may be a verbal statement agreed to by representatives of the countries. The history of treaty making goes back hundreds of years. As early as 3000 B.C., rulers of ancient countries signed treaties with neighboring kingdoms. Treaties served various purposes. Some treaties ended wars, and other treaties settled boundary disputes. But throughout world history, treaties have played an important part in relations between countries.

Today, only sovereign states are able to make treaties. A sovereign state is one that is free from outside control. For example, Britain is a sovereign state because its government is free to make its own decisions. But the British colony of Gibraltar is not free to make its own decisions. It is therefore not a sovereign state, and cannot make its own treaties.

A treaty is much like a contract between private individuals. In both cases, the signing parties promise to do or not do some act. However, there are important differences between treaties and contracts. A contract is not binding if one of the parties has forced the other party into agreement. But the use of force does not make a treaty void unless the force is used against the government representative who is working out the treaty terms. Unlike a private contract, a treaty does not go into effect until it is *ratified.* For example, a treaty between the United States and the United Kingdom is not official until both the United States Senate and the British Crown approve it.

There are several kinds of international agreements that have the force of treaties. One of these is called a *convention.* This is usually an agreement between states relating to a single topic, such as extradition. A *concordat* is an agreement between the pope and a sovereign state. An agreement between two monarchs on a private matter is not a treaty.

Kinds of treaties. Treaties may be divided into several classes according to their purposes, although inter-

Detail of a lithograph (mid-1800's) by Nathaniel Currier (Granger Collection)

A treaty signed by William Penn established friendship between colonists and Indians in Pennsylvania. Penn agreed to pay the Indians for most of the land he claimed in their territory.

national law recognizes no formal distinctions among treaties. A single treaty may include clauses under several classes. Some of the classes are described below.

Political. A peace treaty is one kind of political treaty. For example, the Treaty of Paris of 1783 ended the Revolutionary War in America. Others deal with alliances between countries and settle disputes. The Clayton-Bulwer Treaty in 1850 gave the United States and the United Kingdom equal protection rights in a future canal through Central America.

Commercial. These treaties include agreements on tariffs, navigation, fisheries, and consular services.

Confederation. Confederation treaties set up such international organizations as the Universal Postal Union.

Extradition. These treaties deal with escaped criminals. For example, let us suppose that two countries have signed an extradition treaty. If a criminal from one country flees to the other for safety, the criminal must be returned, or *extradited,* to stand trial for the crime.

Civil justice. These treaties protect a country's trademarks, copyrights, and patents in foreign countries. Some civil-justice treaties deal with the rights of aliens.

Negotiation. In monarchies, the king or queen and his or her legal agents have the power to make treaties and are represented at negotiations by a diplomatic agent, or *envoy.* For example, in the United Kingdom neither house of Parliament has any power over treaties. That power is reserved for the British Crown or Cabinet.

In republics, the chief executive usually has treaty-making power. This power is often subject to restrictions. In the United States, the president may enter into a treaty with "the advice and consent" of the Senate. Two-thirds of the senators present must agree to the treaty terms. Separate U.S. states may not make treaty agreements. The Department of State carries on treaty negotiations. Sometimes the president enters into an *executive agreement* with a foreign country. This kind of agreement has the force of a treaty in international law, but it does not require Senate approval.

Language used. Until the 1700's, all treaties were written in Latin. Then French became the official language. Today, most treaties are written in the various languages of the treaty-making nations.

Enforcement of treaties. In ancient times, a country had to "back up," or guarantee, its treaty promises. One way of doing this was to exchange hostages. Each country that signed the treaty would send one or more important people to the other countries that had agreed to the treaty. Hostages were held as prisoners. They could be killed if the terms of the treaty were not carried out.

The hostage system has not been used for many years. Today, most countries rely on the good faith of other countries, and on international public opinion. In many countries, including the United States, treaties have the force of law. As a result, treaty provisions become legal requirements for officials. At the same time, however, nations may repeal or abolish these treaties, as they do their own laws. But such actions are generally subject to certain international consequences.

Termination. Treaties may be ended in many ways. They may end upon the agreement of all parties concerned. Sometimes a treaty clause permits either party to cancel the agreement after due notice. The failure of one country to carry out its part of the agreement may cause the other country or countries to refuse to observe the treaty terms. A treaty becomes void when the physical conditions of the agreement become impossible to fulfill. War nullifies many treaties.

Ecclesiastical treaties deal with the religious rights of people who are living in a foreign country. Among Western nations, people may worship as freely in foreign lands as in their homelands. In several non-Christian parts of the world, Christian missionaries are permitted by treaty to teach the beliefs of Christianity. In some countries, ecclesiastical treaties permit foreign residents to practice their own religions but forbid them to try to convert others. Robert J. Pranger

Related articles. Treaties are listed in *World Book* under their respective titles, such as **Clayton-Bulwer Treaty; Ghent, Treaty of.** See also:

Arbitration	International law	Protocol
Extradition	International relations	

Treaty port is the name given to Chinese seaports that were open to trade with certain foreign countries beginning in the mid-1800's. The cities were called treaty ports because the foreign trade there was carried on under treaty agreements. Such agreements were a way of gaining trading rights in China.

In 1842, China entered into a treaty-port agreement with Britain, opening five Chinese ports to British trade. The ports were Guangzhou (Canton), Xiamen (Amoy), Fuzhou (Fu-chou), Ningbo (Ningpo), and Shanghai. Later, China signed treaty-port agreements with the United States and many other countries. By 1894, there were over 60 treaty ports in China. Most of the agreements were forced on China by foreign pressure or wars.

In 1912, China began to object to treaty-port agreements. Britain and the United States gave up their special rights in China in 1943. Today, China no longer has treaty ports. Robert M. Stern

See also **Fuzhou; Guangzhou; Xiamen.**

Treble, *TREHB uhl,* is the upper, or highest, part in choral music of two or more parts. It is often called the *soprano* part, and is sung by women or boys. The treble part in instrumental music is played by such instruments as the violin, flute, clarinet, and oboe. It is also played on the higher keys of the piano or organ, roughly above middle C. *Treble clef* or *G clef* (𝄞) is the sign used to mark the five-line staff from which treble voices or instruments read. Thomas W. Tunks

Treblinka, *truh BLIHNG kuh,* was a death camp near Warsaw in German-occupied Poland during World War II. Treblinka consisted of two facilities. The Nazis opened Treblinka I in April 1941 as a penal facility for Jews and Polish political prisoners, who were forced to work in a nearby quarry. Treblinka II, built a year later, was used to murder Jews. From July 1942 to August 1943, about 840,000 people died in gas chambers there. In August 1943, the forced laborers revolted. They set fire to Treblinka II and tried to escape into the surrounding forest. Most were killed during the attempt. The Nazis tore down the remaining buildings to erase all evidence of the camp. They planted crops over mass graves and turned the area into a farm. Investigators later reconstructed the history of Treblinka from documents, accounts of survivors, and the postwar-trial testimony of camp officials. Charles W. Sydnor, Jr.

David Muench

The magnificent giant sequoias of California rank among the world's oldest and largest living things. Some of these trees are thousands of years old and over 200 feet (61 meters) tall.

Tree

Tree is the largest of all plants. The tallest trees grow higher than 30-story buildings. Many trees also live longer than other plants. Some trees live for thousands of years. They rank as the oldest known living things in the world.

People do not think of trees the way they think of other plants, most of which grow only a short time and then die. People think of trees as permanent parts of the landscape. Year after year, large, old trees shade houses and streets from the sun. Their buds and flowers are a sign of spring each year, and their colorful leaves brighten in autumn in many areas.

Trees continue to grow as long as they live. A tree's leaves make food that keeps the tree alive and helps it grow. Where winters are cold, many trees lose their leaves in autumn. Other trees keep their leaves during the winter and so stay green all year long. Trees that shed their leaves in autumn rest during the winter. In spring, they grow new leaves and flowers. The flowers grow into fruits, which contain seeds for making new trees. Some tree fruits, such as apples and oranges, taste good. Fruit growers raise large amounts of these fruits

Norman L. Christensen, Jr., the contributor of this article, is Professor of Ecology at Duke University.

Theodore F. Welch, Van Cleve Photography

Dwarf trees never reach full size. Some, such as this miniature cypress tree, are deliberately kept small by a special pruning process. But many dwarf trees grow naturally in arctic regions.

WORLD BOOK illustration by James Teason

The coconut palm provides wood and other building materials. The tree's nuts yield sweet-tasting milk and meat. Oil from dried coconut meat is used in making such products as margarine and soap.

Interesting facts about trees

One of the world's largest living things is the General Sherman Tree, a giant sequoia in Sequoia National Park in California. It towers 274 feet (83.5 meters) high and has a trunk about 37 feet (11 meters) wide. It probably dates from before 200 B.C.

The traveler's-tree, which grows in Madagascar, collects up to 1 quart (0.95 liter) of rain water in troughs at the base of each of its long leaf stalks. The tree received its name because thirsty travelers can drink the water in an emergency.

The tallest trees are California's redwoods, which may tower more than 360 feet (110 meters). Australia's eucalyptuses may grow more than 300 feet (91 meters) tall.

The thickest tree trunk is that of a Montezuma baldcypress near Oaxaca, Mexico. Its diameter exceeds 40 feet (12 meters).

The baobab tree of Africa is one of the most useful trees. It has a huge trunk, which people hollow out to store water in or to live in. They eat the tree's leaves, fruit, seeds, and roots and use its parts in many other ways.

The oldest trees are California's bristlecone pines and giant sequoias. Some bristlecone pines have lived between 4,000 and 5,000 years. The oldest sequoias are about 3,500 years old.

The banyan tree of India spreads by growing trunklike roots from its branches. In time, a banyan may cover acres of ground.

The ombú tree of Argentina is one of the hardiest trees. It can live with little water and can survive insect attacks, violent storms, and intense heat. The tree's wood is so moist that it will not burn, enabling it to survive grass fires that are common in its habitat.

The largest seeds are the nuts of the coco-de-mer, or double coconut palm, of the Seychelles, an island group in the Indian Ocean. A nut may weigh up to 50 pounds (23 kilograms).

for sale. Trees also make new wood each year when the weather turns warmer. Wood ranks as one of the most valuable parts of a tree. Mills and factories use wood to manufacture lumber, paper, and many other products.

A tree differs from other plants in four main ways. (1) Most trees grow at least 15 to 20 feet (4.6 to 6.1 meters) tall. (2) They have one woody stem, which is called a *trunk.* (3) The stem grows at least 3 to 4 inches (8 to 10 centimeters) thick. (4) A tree's stem can stand by itself. All other plants differ from trees in at least one of these ways. For example, no plant with a soft, juicy stem is a tree. Most of these plants, called *herbs,* are much shorter than most trees. *Shrubs,* like trees, have woody stems. But most shrubs have more than one stem, and none of the stems grows so thick or so tall as a tree trunk. Some jungle *vines* grow more than 200 feet (61 meters) long and have a woody stem. But the stems of most vines cannot support themselves.

There are thousands of kinds of trees. But most trees belong to one of two main groups—the broadleaf trees and the needleleaf trees. These two types of trees grow in Europe, North America, and many other parts of the world. Most other types of trees, such as palms and tree ferns, grow mainly in warm regions.

The importance of trees

E. R. Degginger

Wood is one of the most useful tree products. In this picture, a circular saw strips bark from a log at a sawmill. The stripped log will be cut into boards and other lumber.

David R. Frazier Photolibrary

A forester checks young trees that were planted as part of a forest conservation project. These trees will replace trees that were cut down for timber.

For thousands of years, trees have provided people with foods, fibers, and medicines. Above all, they have provided people with wood. Prehistoric people used wood to make the first spears, the first boats, and the first wheels. Throughout history, people have used wood to make tools, construct buildings, and create works of art. They have also relied on wood for fuel. Living trees prove as valuable to humankind as do tree products because they help to conserve natural resources.

Wood products. Each year, loggers cut down millions of trees in the world's forests. Logs from these trees are shipped to sawmills and pulp mills. Sawmills cut the logs into lumber, which the building industry uses for many types of construction work. Manufacturers use lumber to make everything from furniture to baseball bats. Pulp mills break down the logs into wood pulp, the main raw material for making paper. The chemical industry uses wood pulp to make alcohol, plastics, and other products. See **Forest products; Lumber**.

Food products. People throughout the world eat fruits, nuts, and other tree products. The greatest variety of fruit trees grow in tropical and subtropical regions. These trees produce such fruits as avocados, grapefruits, mangoes, and oranges. A number of these fruits serve as basic foods in some tropical lands. Cooler, temperate regions—such as most of the United States and Europe—have fewer kinds of fruit trees. But several kinds are widely grown. For example, orchards in the United States produce vast amounts of apples, cherries, and peaches. The most important nut tree from warm regions is the coconut palm, which produces coconuts. Nut trees of temperate regions include almonds, pecans, and walnuts. Trees also supply chocolate, coffee, maple syrup, olives, and such spices as cinnamon and cloves. See **Fruit; Nut**.

Other tree products are used by people in a variety of ways. The rubber tree produces *latex,* a milky fluid used to make natural rubber. Pine trees yield a sticky *resin,* used in making turpentine. The bark of oak and some other trees contains a compound called *tannic acid.* The tanning industry uses this compound to change animal hides into leather. The spongy bark of a type of oak that grows in Mediterranean countries provides cork. Some trees produce substances used as medicines. For example, the bark of the cinchona tree contains *quinine,* which doctors use to treat malaria and other diseases.

Trees in conservation. Trees help conserve soil and water. In open country, trees act as windbreaks and keep the wind from blowing away the topsoil. Their roots prevent soil from being washed away by heavy rains. Tree roots also help store water in the ground. In mountain regions, forests prevent sliding snow from causing avalanches. Forests also provide shelter for wildlife and recreation areas for vacationists. See **Conservation**.

Trees help preserve the balance of gases in the atmosphere. A tree's leaves absorb carbon dioxide from the air. They also produce oxygen and release it into the atmosphere. These two processes are necessary for people to live. People could not survive if the air had too much carbon dioxide or too little oxygen.

Kinds of trees

There are about 20,000 kinds of trees. More than 1,000 kinds grow in the United States. They range from mighty forest trees to fragile ornamentals. The greatest variety of trees grow in wet, tropical regions.

Scientists who study plants divide plants with similar characteristics into various groups (see **Plant** [Kinds of plants]). These scientists, called *botanists,* do not put trees in a separate group of plants. Instead, each kind of tree is grouped with other plants that have certain features in common with it. Therefore, a group of plants may include certain trees, certain shrubs or vines, and certain herbs. For example, locust trees, broom plants, and clover all belong to the same *family.* These plants are grouped together because they reproduce in the same way and have similar flowers. On the other hand, some trees that look much alike, such as tree ferns and palms, belong to different groups of plants.

Trees also can be divided into six groups according to various features they have in common. These six groups are: (1) broadleaf trees; (2) needleleaf trees; (3) palms,

The six main groups of trees Trees can be divided into the six main groups illustrated here. All the trees in each group are similar in appearance and have other features in common.

Broadleaf trees are known for their autumn colors, bare winter branches, and spring flowers, which develop into fruits.

Needleleaf trees have needlelike or scalelike leaves and bear their seeds in cones. Most are evergreen.

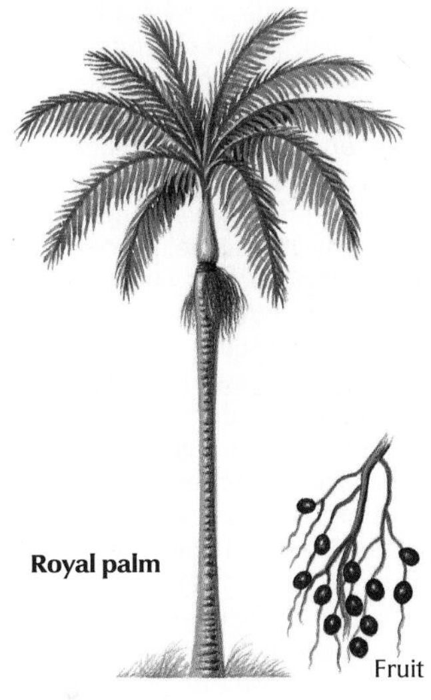

Palms and pandanus and lily trees form a group of mainly tropical trees. Most palms have huge leaves and no branches.

Cycad trees live only in warm, moist regions. They bear heavy cones that may grow 3 feet (91 centimeters) long.

Tree ferns are the only trees that have no flowers, fruits, or seeds. They reproduce by means of *spores.*

WORLD BOOK illustrations by James Teason

Ginkgo trees are a single species. They bear seeds but not fruits or cones. The seeds have an unpleasant odor.

pandanus, and lily trees; (4) cycad trees; (5) tree ferns; and (6) ginkgo trees.

Broadleaf trees are the most numerous and varied of the world's trees. They include ashes, elms, maples, oaks, walnuts, willows, and many other familiar trees of the United States and Canada. They also include most trees of the tropics, such as mahogany trees and mangrove trees.

In addition to their broad, flat leaves, broadleaf trees have other features in common. Almost all broadleaf trees of temperate regions are *deciduous*—that is, they lose their leaves each autumn. A few kinds of broadleaf trees in temperate regions do not lose their leaves in the fall. These broadleaf *evergreens* include the holly trees and live oaks of the southeastern United States. Some tropical broadleaf trees are deciduous, but most are evergreen. See **Deciduous tree; Evergreen.**

Foresters call broadleaf trees *hardwoods* because many of these trees, such as beeches, maples, and oaks, have tough, hard wood. Such wood makes excellent furniture. Some broadleaf trees, including basswoods and cottonwoods, have soft, lightweight wood.

Broadleaf trees belong to a large group of plants called *angiosperms.* These plants have flowers which develop into *fruits* that completely surround the seeds. Fruits are the seed or seeds of a plant together with the parts in which they are enclosed.

Botanists divide angiosperms into two classes—Monocotyledonae (monocotyledons) and Dicotyledonae (dicotyledons). Monocotyledons produce seeds that have one leafy structure called a *cotyledon.* These plants include palm, pandanus, and lily trees. Dicotyledons produce seeds that have two cotyledons. These plants include broadleaf trees. A few kinds of trees that do not have broad, flat leaves belong to the dicotyledon group. An example is the saguaro cactus of the southwestern United States, which has prickly spines. See **Angiosperm; Cotyledon.**

Needleleaf trees include such familiar trees as firs, hemlocks, pines, redwoods, and spruces. There are about 500 species of needleleaf trees. Most of these trees have narrow, pointed, needlelike leaves. But a few types, such as cedars and junipers, have narrow, scalelike leaves.

Most needleleaf trees are evergreen, though they produce new needles each year. The oldest needles turn yellow or brown and drop, but the youngest needles remain green and do not fall.

A few species of needleleaf trees are deciduous. One kind is the larch, which grows in northern forests throughout the world. Another deciduous needleleaf tree is the baldcypress that grows in swamps of the southeastern United States.

Foresters call needleleaf trees *softwoods* because most of them have softer wood than broadleaf trees have. But the wood of Douglas-firs, yews, and some other needleleaf trees is hard.

Needleleaf trees belong to a group of plants called *gymnosperms.* Gymnosperms do not have flowers and their seeds are not enclosed to form fruits. Most gymnosperm trees bear their seeds in cones composed of hard scales. The seeds lie open on the surface of the scales. Botanists call such trees *conifers.* See **Conifer; Gymnosperm.**

Most conifers grow north of the equator. The conifers belong to four families—the pine, yew, cypress, and taxodium families. The *pine family* is by far the largest. It includes not only pines, but also such trees as firs, hemlocks, larches, and spruces. Pine trees make up a large *genus* (group of species) within the pine family. Loblolly pines, ponderosa pines, and white pines are a few North American members of this genus. The *yew family* includes such well-known ornamental trees as English yews and Japanese yews. Although yews are classified as conifers, they do not produce cones but cup-shaped "berries." Many members of the *cypress family,* such as

Trees of the states

Baldcypress
Louisiana

Birch
New Hampshire (White birch)

Cottonwood
Kansas
Nebraska
Wyoming (Plains)

Dogwood
Missouri (Flowering)
Virginia (American)

Douglas-fir
Oregon

Elm (American)
Massachusetts
North Dakota

Hemlock
Pennsylvania
Washington (Western hemlock)

Holly (American)
Delaware

Horsechestnut
Ohio (Buckeye)

Kukui
Hawaii

Magnolia
Mississippi

Maple
New York (Sugar maple)
Rhode Island (Red maple)
Vermont (Sugar maple)
West Virginia (Sugar maple)
Wisconsin (Sugar maple)

Oak
Connecticut (Charter oak)
Georgia (Live oak)
Illinois (White oak)
Iowa
Maryland (White oak)
New Jersey (Red oak)

Palm (Sabal)
Florida

Palmetto (Sabal)
South Carolina

Paloverde
Arizona

Pecan
Texas

Pine
Alabama (Southern longleaf pine)
Arkansas
Idaho (Western white pine)
Maine (White pine)
Michigan (White pine)
Minnesota (Norway, or red, pine)
Montana (Ponderosa pine)
Nevada (Bristlecone pine)
North Carolina

Piñon (Nut pine)
Nevada (Single-leaf piñon)
New Mexico

Redbud
Oklahoma

Redwood
California (California redwood)

Spruce
Alaska (Sitka spruce)
Colorado (Colorado blue spruce)
South Dakota (Black Hills spruce)
Utah (Blue spruce)

Yellow-poplar
Indiana (Tulip-poplar)
Kentucky (Tulip-poplar)
Tennessee (Tulip-poplar)

All state trees are shown in color in the state articles.

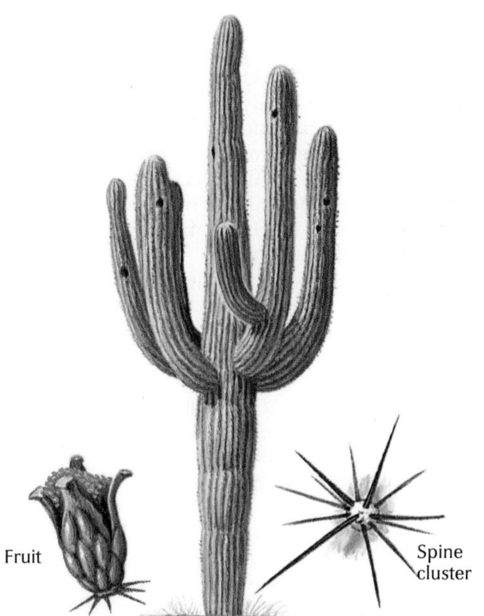

WORLD BOOK illustration by James Teason

The saguaro, or giant cactus, is a tree that has spines instead of leaves. It grows 25 to 50 feet (8 to 15 meters) tall. The saguaro has a thick, woody stem and bears sweet fruit.

Josef Muench

A prehistoric log in the Petrified Forest National Park of Arizona turned to stone millions of years ago. Scientists study such *petrified* logs to learn about the ancestors of today's trees.

arborvitae and junipers, have scalelike leaves and give off a spicy fragrance. The *taxodium family* includes baldcypresses and the largest of all living trees—the redwoods and giant sequoias.

Two conifer families—the *podocarpus family* and the *araucaria family*—grow mainly south of the equator. Podocarpus trees are tall evergreens with broader leaves than those of most needleleaf trees. The araucaria family includes the Chile pine. This strange-looking tree has snakelike branches covered with sharp, scaly leaves. It is sometimes called the monkey puzzle tree because its sharp leaves make it difficult to climb.

Palm, pandanus, and lily trees belong to the large group of flowering plants called monocotyledons. These trees grow mainly in warm climates. Of the three types of trees in this group, palms are the most important.

There are about 2,500 kinds of palm trees. They range from the coconut palms of tropical islands to the date palms of desert oases. Most palm trees have no branches. The trunk has a crown of enormous leaves. The leaves are either feather-shaped or fan-shaped. See **Palm**.

Unlike most palms, pandanus and lily trees have branches. Each branch has a crown of sword-shaped leaves. Most pandanus trees have tall *stilt roots* that extend into the ground from high on the trunk or branches. Lily trees are closely related to the garden flowers called lilies, and many of the trees have attractive, fragrant flowers. The yucca trees of Mexico and the far southern United States are lily trees. The best-known yucca is the colorful Joshua tree found in the deserts of the southwestern United States.

Cycad trees look much like palm trees. They have a trunk without branches and a crown of long, feathery leaves. But cycads are more closely related to pine trees than to palms. They produce seeds in cones that look like large pine cones. Millions of years ago, cycads grew in nearly every part of the world. Today, they grow mainly in a few warm, moist sections of Africa, Asia, and Central America. See **Cycad**.

Tree ferns. Ferns are best known as rather short plants with feathery, green *fronds* (leaves). But in the tropics and some areas with mild climates, many relatives of these plants are trees. Tree ferns look much like palm trees, but they belong to a different group of plants. Tree ferns do not have flowers or cones and so do not reproduce by seeds. They reproduce by means of tiny bodies called *spores,* which develop on the undersides of their fronds. See **Fern**.

Ginkgo trees rank among the oldest of all trees. Millions of years ago, various kinds of ginkgoes existed. Only one species survives today. The ginkgo, like needleleaf trees, is a gymnosperm. But unlike other gymnosperm trees, the ginkgo has fan-shaped leaves. These leaves look like the fronds of a fern called the *maidenhair.* Ginkgoes are sometimes called *maidenhair trees.* They are natives of Asia, but many are grown in the United States and Europe.

Fossil trees. About 300 million years ago, there were whole forests of trees unlike most of the trees that grow today. Huge club-moss trees and horsetail trees grew along with tree ferns in steaming hot swamps. Over millions of years, the trees and other plant life in the swamps died, became buried, and turned into coal. In other places, buried forests became *petrified* (turned into stone). Coal deposits and petrified forests contain fossils of many trees that died out more than 100 million years ago (see **Fossil**). Two of these extinct trees are the club moss tree and horsetail tree of the coal-forming swamps. The club mosses and horsetails living today are herbs.

The parts of a tree

A tree has three main parts: (1) the trunk and branches; (2) the leaves; and (3) the roots. The branches and leaves together are called the *crown.* The trunk supports the crown and holds it up to the sunlight. Tree ferns, cycads, and most palms have no branches. Their crowns consist only of leaves. The roots of most trees are hidden in the ground, but they may take up as much space as the trunk and crown do above the ground. Other important parts of a tree include the seeds and the seed-forming structures.

Trunk and branches give a tree its shape. The trunks of most needleleaf trees grow straight up to the top of the tree. The branches grow out from the trunk. On most needleleaf trees, the branches near the top are shorter than those farther down, which gives the crown a spirelike shape. The trunks of most broadleaf trees do not reach to the top of the tree. Instead, the trunk divides into spreading branches near the base of the crown, giving the crown a rounded shape. The trunks of a few broadleaf trees, such as black willows and white poplars, sometimes divide so close to the ground that the trees seem to have more than one trunk.

The trunks, branches, and roots of broadleaf and needleleaf trees consist of four layers of plant tissue wrapped around one another. These layers, from innermost to outermost, are: (1) the *xylem,* (2) the *cambium,* (3) the *phloem,* and (4) the *cork.*

The xylem is the woody, central part of the trunk. It has tiny pipelines that carry water with a small amount of dissolved minerals from the roots to the leaves. This water is called *sap.* The cambium, which surrounds the xylem, is a thin layer of growing tissue. Its job is to make the trunk, branches, and roots grow thicker. The phloem, also called the *inner bark,* is a layer of soft tissue surrounding the cambium. Like the xylem, the phloem has tiny pipelines. The food made by the leaves moves

Parts of a tree These diagrams show the three main parts of a tree: (1) the leaves, (2) the trunk and branches, and (3) the roots. The branches and leaves together make up a tree's *crown.* The diagrams also show the main types of tissue that compose most trees.

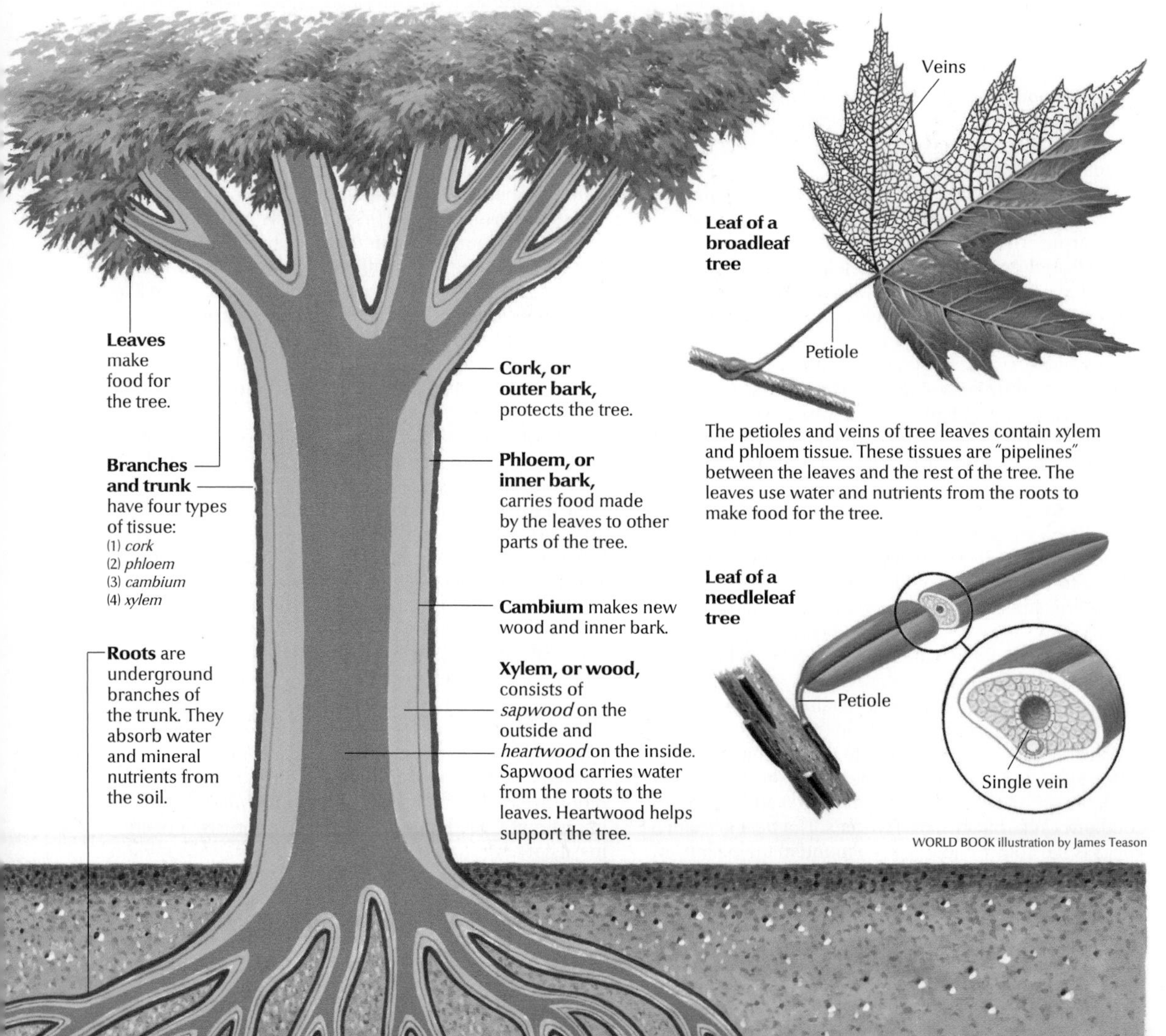

The petioles and veins of tree leaves contain xylem and phloem tissue. These tissues are "pipelines" between the leaves and the rest of the tree. The leaves use water and nutrients from the roots to make food for the tree.

WORLD BOOK illustration by James Teason

Seeds of broadleaf and needleleaf trees

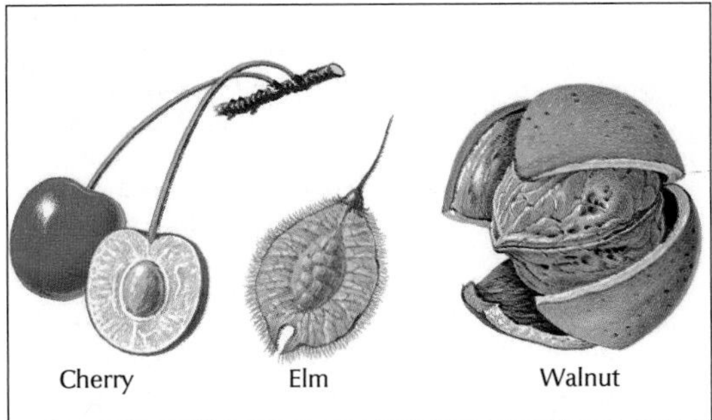

WORLD BOOK illustration by James Teason

Seeds of broadleaf trees, or *angiosperm seeds,* have protective coverings. The seed and covering together are called a fruit. Cherry and walnut seeds are enclosed in a pit or shell with a fleshy outer covering. Elm seeds have thin, winged coverings.

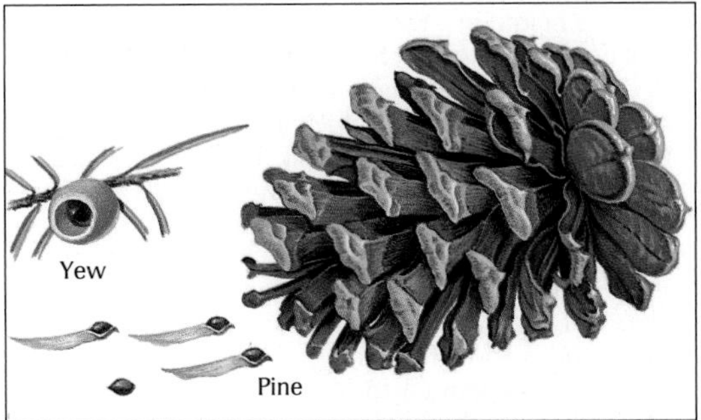

WORLD BOOK illustration by James Teason

Seeds of needleleaf trees, or *gymnosperm seeds,* do not have protective coverings. The seeds of most needleleaf trees lie in cones and are released after the cones ripen. The yew and a few other coneless needleleaf trees have berrylike seeds.

through the phloem to the other parts of a tree. In palms and tree ferns, the xylem and phloem are not separate layers. Instead, bits of xylem and phloem are connected and form small double pipelines scattered throughout the trunk.

The cork layer is the *outer bark* of a tree. It forms a "skin" of hard, dead tissue that protects the living inner parts from injury. The bark stretches to let the trunk and branches grow thicker. The bark of some trees, such as beeches and birches, is smooth because it stretches easily. But the bark of most other trees does not stretch so well. As the trunk and branches grow thicker, they push against the bark. It finally cracks and dries and so becomes grooved and rough. Most trees replace old bark from time to time with a new layer.

Leaves of various species of trees differ greatly in size and shape. Palms have leaves over 20 feet (6 meters) long. The leaves of some needleleaf trees are less than $\frac{1}{2}$ inch (13 millimeters) long. Some broadleaf trees have *compound leaves* made up of small leaflets.

The main job of the leaves is to make food for the tree. Every leaf has one or more *veins,* which consist of xylem and phloem tissue. The tissue that surrounds the veins contains tiny green bodies called *chloroplasts.* Water from the roots passes through the xylem of the trunk, branches, and leaves to the chloroplasts, which use the water to make food sugar. Only a small amount of the water carried to the leaves is used to make sugar. The leaves lose most of the water to the atmosphere through *transpiration* (evaporation). Like the water and dissolved minerals carried from the roots, the food made by the leaves is also called *sap.* It travels through the phloem of the leaves, branches, and trunk to parts of the tree where it is needed. See **Sap**.

Almost all leaves are green in the spring and summer. Their color comes from chlorophyll, a green substance in the chloroplasts. Most trees also have reds and yellows in their leaves. But the green conceals these colors. In late summer and early autumn, the chlorophyll in the leaves of many broadleaf trees breaks down. The leaves then die. But before the leaves fall, they reveal their hidden reds and yellows. After the chlorophyll breaks down, the leaves of many trees also develop scarlets and purples. See **Leaf** (The leaf changes color).

Roots are long, underground branches of the trunk. They have the same layers of tissue as the trunk. The roots anchor a tree in the ground and absorb water with dissolved minerals from the soil. The main roots branch out into small roots, which, in turn, branch out into still smaller roots. The main roots of most trees begin to branch out 1 or 2 feet (30 or 61 centimeters) under the ground. Some trees have one main root larger than the others. This root, called a *taproot,* extends straight down 15 feet (5 meters) or more.

A tree develops millions of small roots. Each root grows longer at its tip, which is as small as a thread. As a root tip grows, it pushes through particles of soil. Thousands of fine, white *root hairs* grow just back of the root tip. When the tip comes in contact with drops of water in the soil, the hairs soak up the water and dissolved minerals. The xylem layer of the roots, trunk, and branches carries this sap to the leaves.

Fungi grow on the roots of most trees in a helpful relationship called *mycorrhiza.* The fungi aid the roots in absorbing water and mineral nutrients. They also protect the roots from some diseases.

Seeds are the means by which all trees except tree ferns reproduce. Tree ferns reproduce by spores.

Angiosperms—broadleaf trees and palm, pandanus, and lily trees—produce seeds by means of flowers. Some broadleaf trees, such as horsechestnuts and magnolias, produce large, showy flowers. Many others have small, plain-looking flowers. Most palm, pandanus, and lily trees have small flowers that grow in bunches. Sometimes these are brightly colored and fragrant.

The seeds of angiosperms are enclosed to form a fruit. The fruits of some broadleaf trees, such as apples and cherries, have a fleshy outer covering. The fruits of other broadleaf trees, including acorns and beechnuts, are hard nuts. Ashes, elms, and maples have thin, winged fruits. Palm, pandanus, and lily trees have a variety of fruits, ranging from nuts to berries.

Gymnosperms—needleleaf trees, cycads, and ginkgoes—do not have flowers or fruits. Their seeds are produced in cones or similar structures. The seeds of needleleaf trees and cycads have no protective coverings. Ginkgo seeds have a fleshy outer covering, but the covering is not a true fruit.

How a tree grows

Most trees begin life as a seed. The young tree that develops from this seed is called a *seedling.* After a tree reaches a height of 6 feet (1.8 meters) or more and its trunk becomes 1 to 2 inches (2.5 to 5 centimeters) thick, it is called a *sapling.* Many trees reach a height of more than 100 feet (30 meters). Some old trees have trunks more than 10 feet (3 meters) in diameter.

Trees need great amounts of water. A large apple tree in full leaf may absorb 95 gallons (360 liters) from the soil daily. Most of the water goes to the leaves. On a sunny summer day, some trees move water up through their trunks at the rate of 3 feet (91 centimeters) per minute. A tree's wood is about half water.

How seeds sprout into trees. A seed contains parts that develop into the trunk and roots of a tree. It also has one or more cotyledons and a supply of plant food. After a seed has left the parent tree, it rests for a while on the ground. Water, air, and sunshine help the seed *germinate* (begin to grow). The part of the seed that develops into the trunk points upward toward the sunlight. As the seed absorbs water, the root part swells and bursts through the seed's shell. As the root grows, it pushes down into the soil. The food stored in the seed nourishes the tree. As the root begins to soak up water from the soil, the trunk begins to develop leaves.

How leaves make plant food. As a leaf develops, it gets sap from the roots. It also absorbs carbon dioxide from the air. The leaf uses the energy of sunlight to change the sap and carbon dioxide into sugar, a process called *photosynthesis.* The sugar provides food for the trunk, branches, and roots. During photosynthesis, the leaves also produce oxygen and release it into the atmosphere. See **Leaf** (How a leaf makes food).

How trees grow taller. Trees grow taller only at the tips of their trunk and branches. Each year, the tips of the trunk and of each branch develop a *bud.* The bud contains a tiny, leafy green stem called a *shoot.* The bud is wrapped in a protective covering of *bud scales.* After a period of rest, the buds swell and open. The shoots that were inside the buds begin to grow and so make the trunk and branches taller. Another type of bud grows on the sides of the trunk and branches. These buds contain a shoot that develops into a leaf-bearing *twig* after the bud opens. As a twig grows larger, it becomes another branch of the tree. Some tree buds develop into flowers. Still others develop into twigs that bear both leaves and flowers. In warm climates, trees produce buds frequently during the year or continue to grow without forming buds. In colder climates, trees produce buds only in the summer. These buds rest during the winter and open after warm weather arrives in spring.

Trees without branches—cycads, most palms, and tree ferns—grow somewhat differently. For example, a young palm tree does not grow taller for a number of years. Its short trunk thickens and produces more and larger leaves each year. After the trunk and crown reach adult size, the tree begins to grow taller. The trunk stays about the same thickness for the rest of the tree's life.

How trunks and branches grow thicker. The trunk and branches of a broadleaf or needleleaf tree grow thicker as long as the tree lives. The cambium tissue just underneath the inner bark causes this thickening. It uses the sugar produced by the leaves to make new plant tissue. On its outside, the cambium makes new phloem, or inner bark, and on its inside, new xylem, or wood.

Wood consists largely of *cellulose,* a tough substance made from sugar. The xylem has two kinds of wood—*sapwood* and *heartwood.* The wood nearest the cambium is the sapwood. It is living wood and contains the tiny pipelines that carry sap. In tropical climates, the sapwood thickens all year. In cooler climates, a new layer of

How a tree reveals its history

Most trees in temperate regions grow a layer of wood each year. After such a tree has been cut down, the layers can be seen as rings in the trunk. These *annual rings* reveal the tree's life story. The pine log in this drawing has 72 annual rings, showing that the tree lived for 72 years.

Narrow center rings indicate that other trees shaded the young tree, depriving it of moisture and sunlight.

Wider rings on the log's lower side after the 30th year show that the tree was slightly bent in this direction. The tree then began to grow more wood on this side than on the other to keep from falling. Most rings after the 38th year are wider than the center rings. This indicates that many surrounding trees had been removed, giving the tree more moisture and sunlight. Differences in the width of rings after the 38th ring were caused mainly by varying amounts of rainfall from year to year.

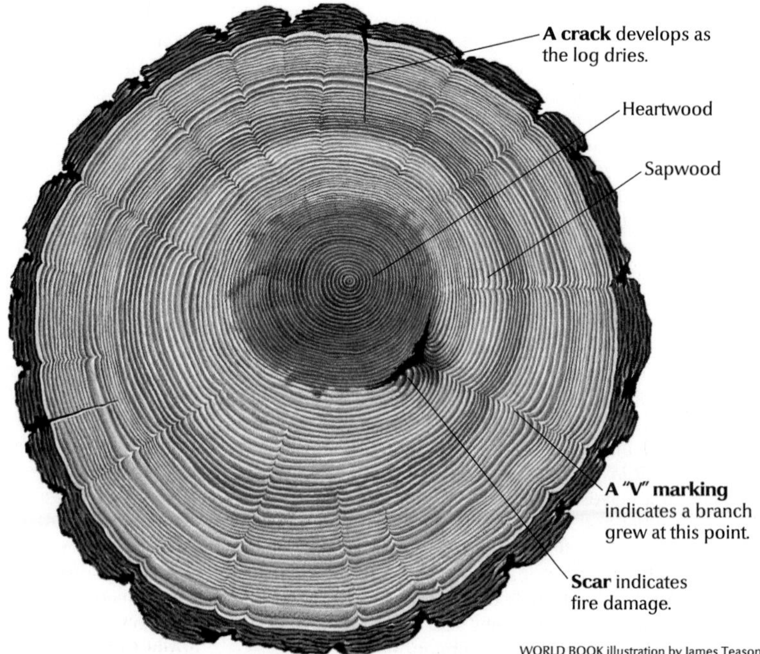

WORLD BOOK illustration by James Teason

How most trees reproduce

Most trees reproduce by means of sex organs in their flowers or cones. Pollen from male organs produces sperm, which *fertilize* (unite with) eggs in female organs. This union produces seeds.

Fruit-bearing trees, or *angiosperms,* have flowers with an *ovary,* which becomes the outer part of the fruit.

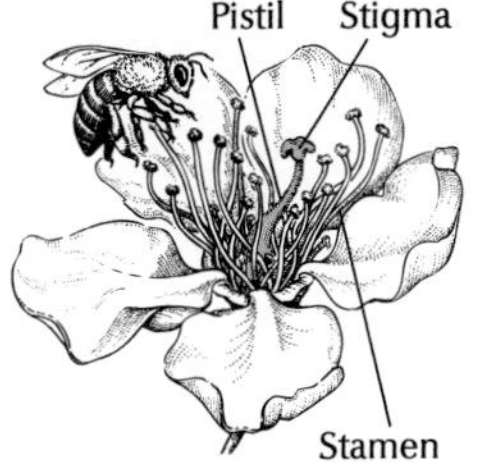

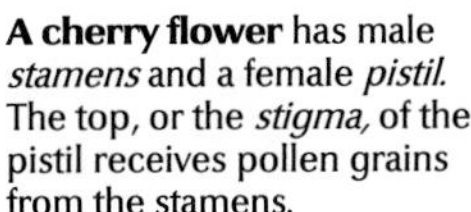

A cherry flower has male *stamens* and a female *pistil.* The top, or the *stigma,* of the pistil receives pollen grains from the stamens.

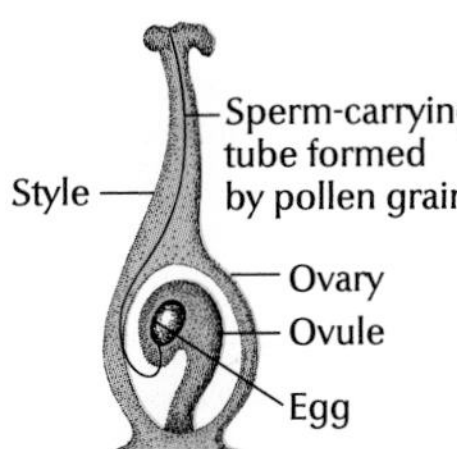

The pistil has an immature seed, or *ovule,* in an *ovary.* A sperm from a pollen grain moves down the *style* and fertilizes the egg.

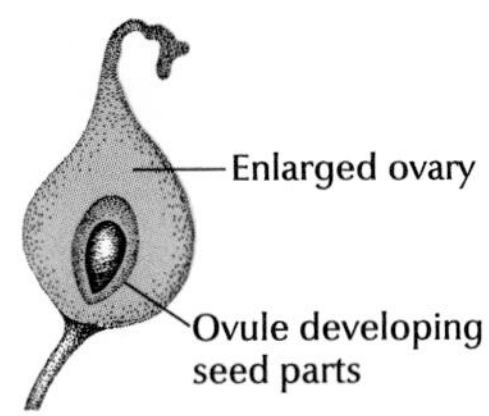

After fertilization, the ovule develops into a seed, and the ovary grows larger. The other parts of the pistil and flower wither and die.

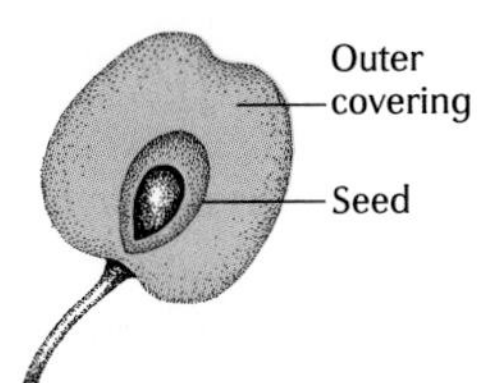

The fruit has an outer covering formed from the ovary. The seed or seeds are inside. A seed will develop into a new tree.

Cone-bearing trees, or *gymnosperms,* have cones without an ovary.

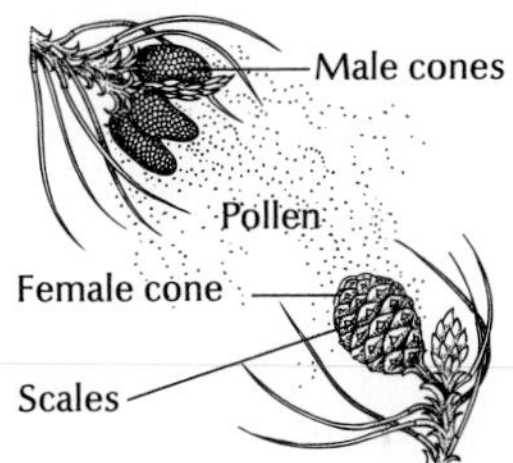

Pine cones are male or female. The wind carries pollen from male cones to the *scales* of a female cone.

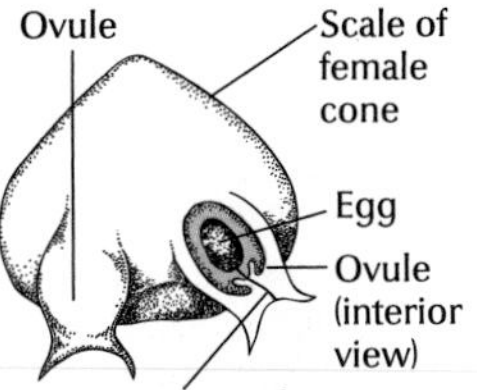

A scale has two ovules, which are not enclosed in ovaries. Pollen enters the ovules and produces sperm.

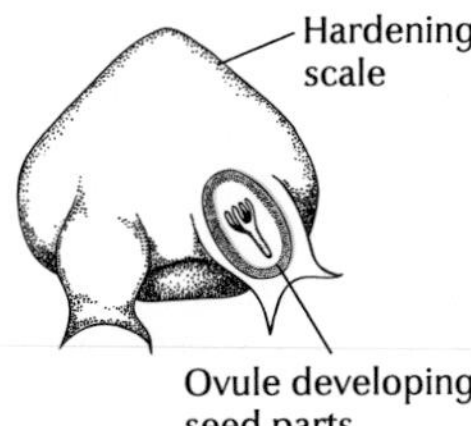

After pollination, the scales harden. Fertilization occurs as a sperm in each ovule unites with the egg.

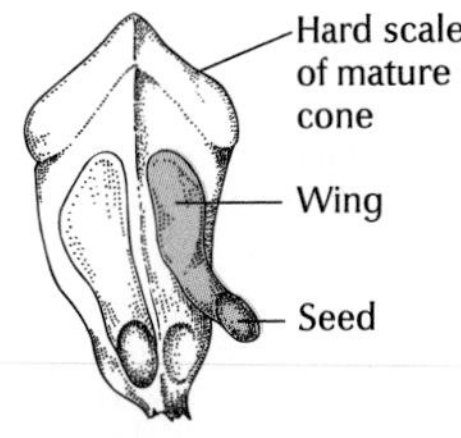

The seed produced from each fertilized ovule has the parts for a new tree. The seeds develop long wings.

WORLD BOOK illustrations by Mary Ann Olson

sapwood usually forms only in early summer. As a tree ages, the wood nearest the center dies. This dead wood is the heartwood. It helps support the tree.

In regions where trees make a new layer of wood once a year, the layers form a series of *annual rings.* Each ring represents one year's growth. After such a tree has been cut down, a person can count the rings to determine the tree's age. Scientists have also found that slight changes in the thickness of these rings reveal the kind of weather that a tree experienced during each year.

How trees reproduce. Most trees reproduce sexually. That is, seeds are produced only after sperm unite with eggs. Sperm are produced by pollen, which forms in the tree's male reproductive parts—either the male part of the flower or the male cone. Eggs form in the female part of the flower or in the female cone. Among many angiosperm species, the flowers have both male and female parts. The pollen from the male part can simply drop onto the female part. Other angiosperms and all gymnosperms have separate male and female flowers or cones, which may grow on the same tree or on separate trees. The pollen of these species is carried to the female flower or cone by insects, the wind, or other means. After contacting the female flower or cone, pollen produces sperm. The sperm then unite with eggs, and one or more seeds develop within a fruit or cone.

When the fruit or cone has ripened, the seeds are ready to leave the tree. The wind scatters the seeds of needleleaf trees and the winglike seeds or fruits of such broadleaf trees as ashes, maples, poplars, and willows. Birds, squirrels, and other animals scatter seeds contained in nuts or fleshy fruits. Ocean currents sometimes carry the seeds of coconut palms and mangroves.

Trees can also reproduce by a process called *vegetative reproduction.* After a tree has been cut or blown down, the stump may develop green sprouts. In time, one or several of these sprouts can grow into trees. A clump of birches or yellow-poplars may be produced in this way. The roots of apple trees, aspens, and some other trees sometimes develop shoots called *suckers* that may also grow into trees. Some spruces found in bogs grow roots from their branches. This method of reproduction is called *layering.* In addition, nursery workers often grow trees from *cuttings*—that is, twigs cut from older trees. The twigs are planted and develop roots.

Broadleaf and needleleaf trees

This section illustrates some of the chief characteristics of various broadleaf and needleleaf trees around the world. The drawings show the summer and winter appearance of each species. They also illustrate the leaf; the fruit or other seed-bearing structure; and, in most cases, the bark. For some species, the flower is shown. Each set of illustrations includes information about the tree's native geographic range—that is, the part of the world where the tree is most likely to be found. But a number of the species shown have spread or have been planted outside their native range. The average height of adult trees of each species is given in feet and in meters alongside the illustration of the tree's shape.

The drawings and other information in this section can help in identifying trees. For example, if the leaf and bark of a tree match the leaf and bark of one of the trees shown here, the tree should be fairly easy to identify. Tree guidebooks can provide additional help in identifying trees. Several guidebooks are listed in the *Study aids* at the end of this article.

Broadleaf trees of North America

WORLD BOOK illustrations by Donald Moss

Broadleaf trees of North America

Broadleaf trees of North America

Broadleaf trees of North America

Broadleaf trees of North America

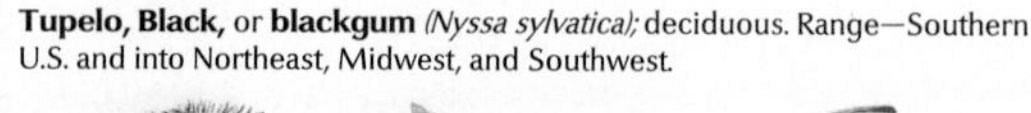

Tupelo, Black, or **blackgum** *(Nyssa sylvatica);* deciduous. Range—Southern U.S. and into Northeast, Midwest, and Southwest.

Walnut, Black *(Juglans nigra);* deciduous. Range—Eastern half of U.S., except far North and far South; southern Ontario.

Willow, Black *(Salix nigra);* deciduous. Range—Most of eastern half of U.S.; southeastern Canada; parts of Mexico.

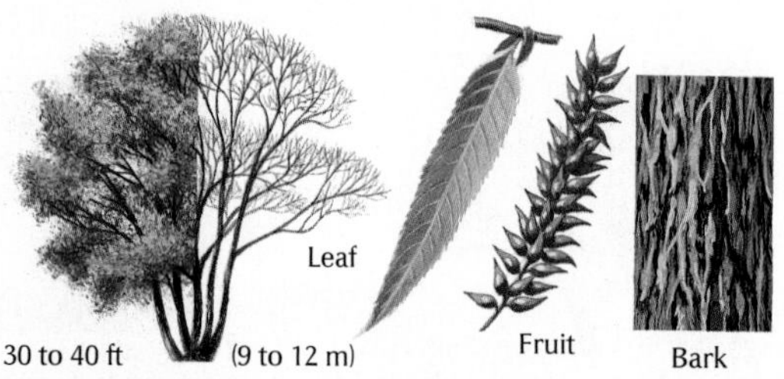

Willow, Weeping *(Salix babylonica);* deciduous. Range—Widely planted in Eastern U.S. and southeastern Canada; native to China.

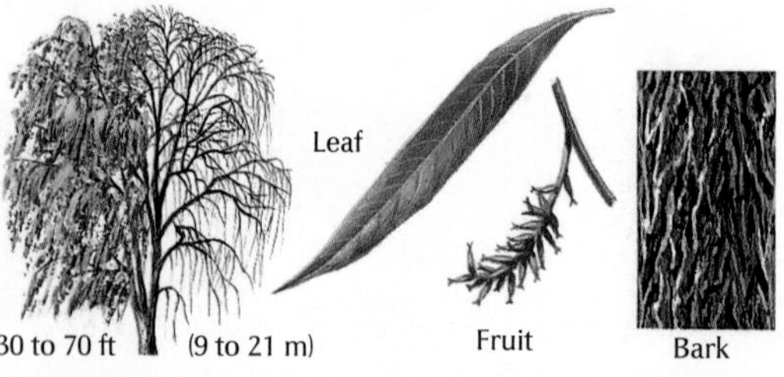

Yellow-poplar, or **tuliptree** *(Liriodendron tulipifera);* deciduous. Range—Southern U.S. and into Northeast and Midwest; southern Ontario.

Needleleaf trees of North America

Arborvitae, American, or **northern white-cedar** *(Thuja occidentalis);* evergreen. Range—Southeastern Canada and into Eastern U.S.

Baldcypress *(Taxodium distichum);* deciduous. Range—Atlantic and Gulf coastal plains and lower Mississippi Valley.

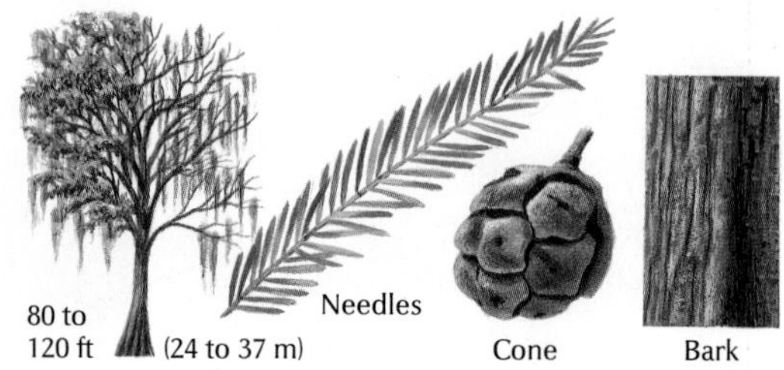

Cypress, Monterey *(Cupressus macrocarpa);* evergreen. Range—Monterey County, California.

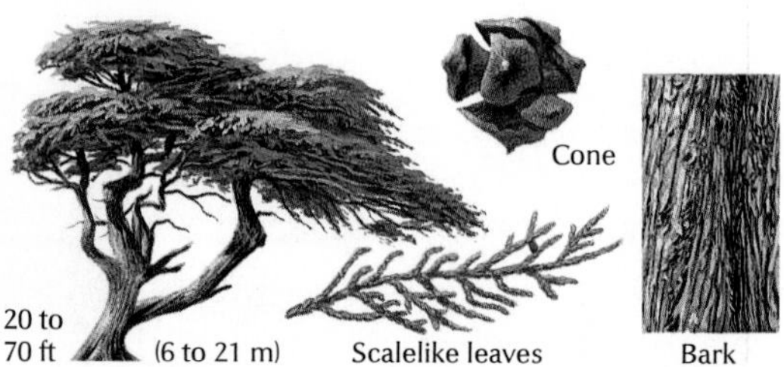

Douglas-fir *(Pseudotsuga menziesii);* evergreen. Range—Chiefly Pacific coast and Rocky Mountain regions of U.S. and Canada.

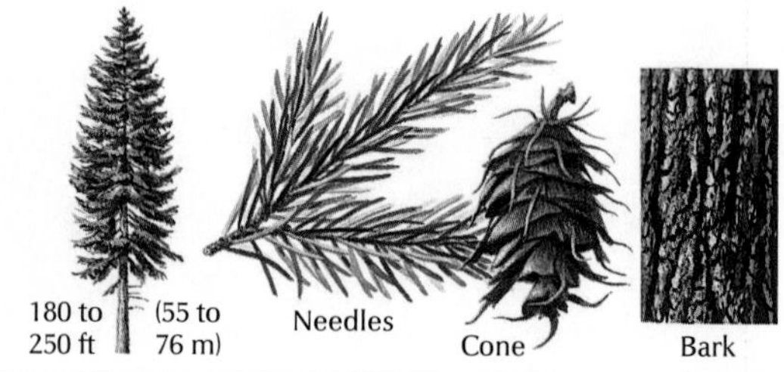

Fir, Balsam *(Abies balsamea);* evergreen. Range—Most of eastern Canada and northwestward into Alberta and southward into Eastern U.S.

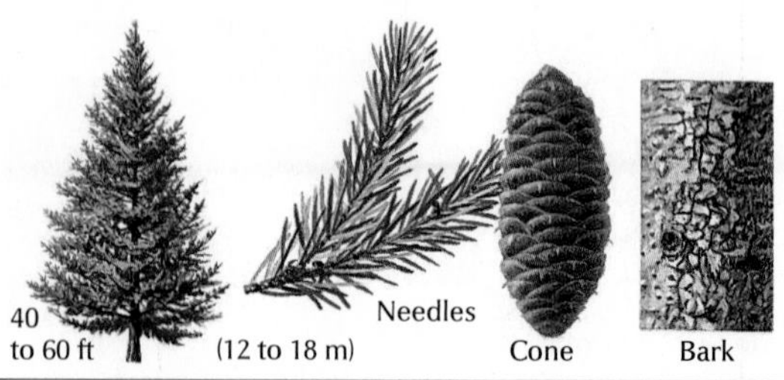

Needleleaf trees of North America

Trees from other parts of the world

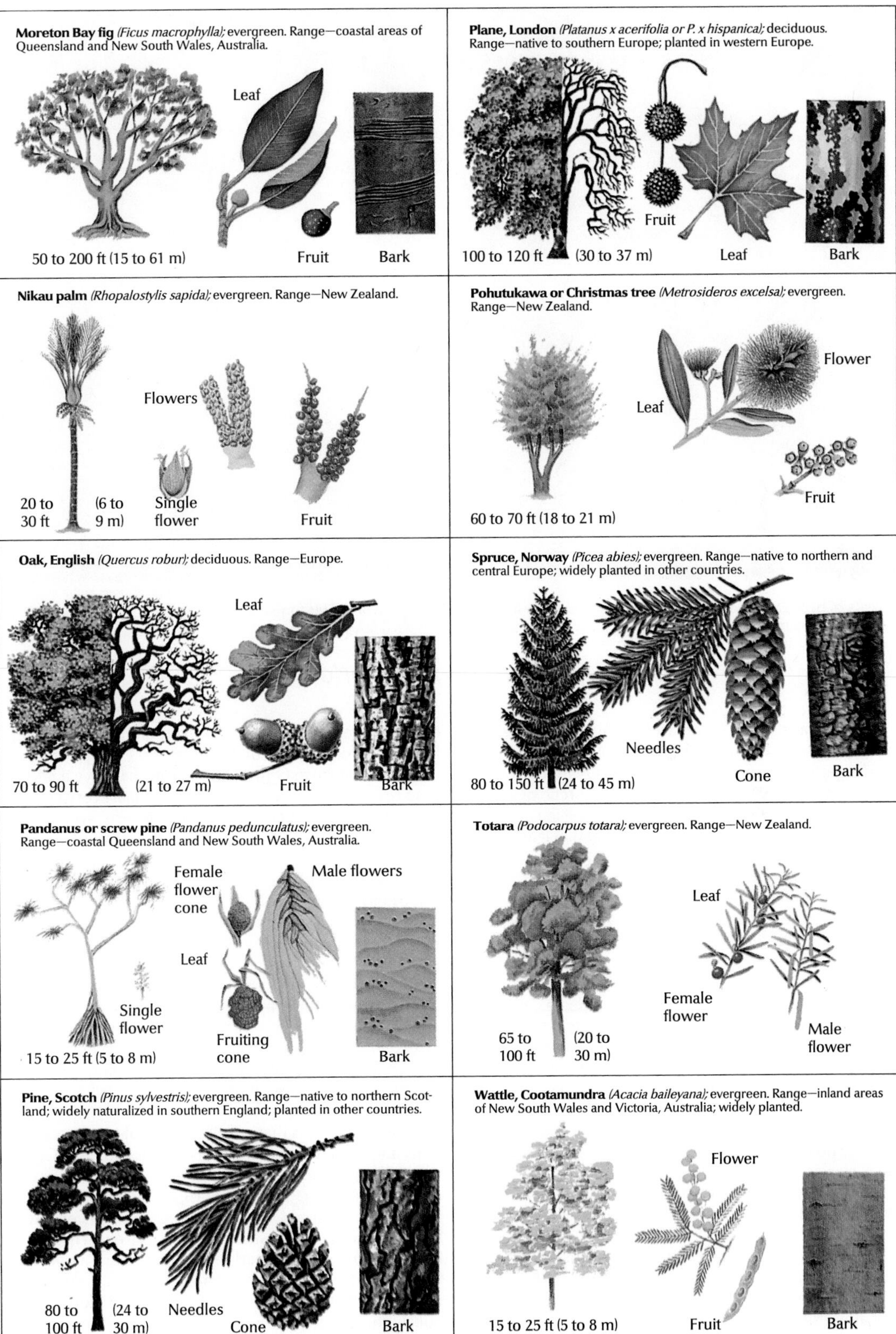
Moreton Bay fig *(Ficus macrophylla);* evergreen. Range—coastal areas of Queensland and New South Wales, Australia.
Leaf
50 to 200 ft (15 to 61 m)
Fruit
Bark
Plane, London *(Platanus x acerifolia or P. x hispanica);* deciduous. Range—native to southern Europe; planted in western Europe.
Fruit
100 to 120 ft
(30 to 37 m)
Leaf
Bark
Nikau palm *(Rhopalostylis sapida);* evergreen. Range—New Zealand.
Flowers
20 to 30 ft
(6 to 9 m)
Single flower
Fruit
Pohutukawa or Christmas tree *(Metrosideros excelsa);* evergreen. Range—New Zealand.
Flower
Leaf
Fruit
60 to 70 ft (18 to 21 m)
Oak, English *(Quercus robur);* deciduous. Range—Europe.
Leaf
70 to 90 ft
(21 to 27 m)
Fruit
Bark
Spruce, Norway *(Picea abies);* evergreen. Range—native to northern and central Europe; widely planted in other countries.
Needles
80 to 150 ft
(24 to 45 m)
Cone
Bark
Pandanus or screw pine *(Pandanus pedunculatus);* evergreen. Range—coastal Queensland and New South Wales, Australia.
Female flower cone
Male flowers
Leaf
Single flower
15 to 25 ft (5 to 8 m)
Fruiting cone
Bark
Totara *(Podocarpus totara);* evergreen. Range—New Zealand.
Leaf
Female flower
65 to 100 ft
(20 to 30 m)
Male flower
Pine, Scotch *(Pinus sylvestris);* evergreen. Range—native to northern Scotland; widely naturalized in southern England; planted in other countries.
80 to 100 ft
(24 to 30 m)
Needles
Cone
Bark
Wattle, Cootamundra *(Acacia baileyana);* evergreen. Range—inland areas of New South Wales and Victoria, Australia; widely planted.
Flower
15 to 25 ft (5 to 8 m)
Fruit
Bark

Toni Schneiders, Bruce Coleman, Ltd.

Forests of broadleaf trees, or *hardwood forests,* grow in many parts of the world. This forest is in Germany. In temperate regions, most broadleaf trees lose their leaves each fall.

Trees around the world

In some parts of the world, trees grow in thick forests. In other regions, they do not grow at all. To grow, trees need a period of more than two months without frost each year. The few trees that grow in the Arctic never reach full tree size. No trees can grow in the ice and bitter cold of Antarctica. Most trees also need at least 15 to 20 inches (38 to 51 centimeters) of rainfall a year. Only a few trees, such as the Joshua tree and some types of palms, can survive in deserts.

Most broadleaf trees grow best in regions that are warm and moist at least three or four months of the year. Colder, dryer climates are better suited to most needleleaf trees. But some broadleaf trees, such as birches and willows, grow well in cool climates. Some needleleaf trees, including baldcypresses and various types of pines, need fairly warm climates. Palm trees grow in warm areas throughout the world, especially the wet and the dry tropics. Pandanus trees, cycads, and tree ferns grow mainly in the wet tropics and other warm, moist regions. Lily trees also thrive in warm areas, but they do not need so much moisture as do pandanus trees, cycads, and tree ferns.

Different kinds of trees also require different soils. Many needleleaf trees grow well in poor, sandy soil. But most broadleaf trees need more fertile soil.

Some trees grow alone or in small groups. Where moisture is scarce, trees may grow only along riverbanks. Tree seeds carried by ocean currents may take root along shorelines. People plant individual trees in such places as parks and gardens. But most trees by far grow in forests. The world's forest regions consist chiefly of broadleaf and needleleaf trees.

Broadleaf forests grow in regions that have a fairly long growing season and plentiful rainfall. Every continent except Antarctica has broadleaf forests, which are also called *hardwood forests.* In areas with cold, snowy winters, almost all the trees in broadleaf forests lose their leaves each autumn. In tropical areas, most broadleaf trees are evergreen.

Before the 1800's, broadleaf forests covered much of the Eastern United States. They included such trees as ashes, birches, maples, and oaks. During the 1800's, most of the trees in these forests were cut down to provide lumber and fuel and to make room for farms and cities. Today, only a few parts of the Eastern United States have large broadleaf forests. Western Europe also had great forests of broadleaf trees, including ashes, beeches, and oaks. But most of these forests have been cut down.

Broadleaf forests that consist largely of quaking aspens and balsam poplars cover parts of southern Canada and large areas of southern Siberia. Forests of birches and oaks grow in eastern Europe and along the Yellow Sea coast of China and Korea. Southeastern Australia has valuable forests of eucalyptus trees. These broadleaf trees grow nearly as tall as California's needleleaf giants, the redwoods. Some eucalyptus trees stand more than 300 feet (91 meters) tall. About 600 kinds of eucalyptus trees grow in Australia. Almost all of these trees are evergreen.

Toni Schneiders, Bruce Coleman, Ltd.

Forests of needleleaf trees, or *softwood forests,* cover huge areas in the far north as well as the slopes of such mountain ranges as the Italian Alps, *shown here.* Most of the trees are evergreen.

In many areas, *mixed forests* of broadleaf and needleleaf trees grow alongside broadleaf or needleleaf forests. Central Canada, the eastern United States, central and southern Europe, and eastern Asia all have large mixed forests.

Remarkable broadleaf forests grow in tropical regions where the weather is always hot and rain falls regularly every month of the year. In these *tropical rain forests,* many of the trees look alike. They are tall, and many tower more than 150 feet (46 meters) high. The trees have leathery, dark-green leaves. Because the trees receive plenty of moisture throughout the year, most of them are evergreen. The trees may thus look alike, but they belong to many species. Many palms grow among the broadleaf trees in the tropical rain forests. The largest rain forests are in South and Central America, central Africa, and Southeast Asia.

Needleleaf forests grow mainly in regions that have long, cold winters. These forests, which are also called *softwood forests,* stretch across Canada, northern Europe, and Siberia. Many firs, larches, and spruces grow in these northern forests, along with a few broadleaf trees, such as birches and willows. Some willows grow even farther north than needleleaf trees do. But they seldom reach more than shrub size. Needleleaf forests also blanket slopes in such mountain ranges as the Alps and the Rocky Mountains.

The Canadian needleleaf forests extend southward into the western United States, where they include many of the world's largest trees. Many California redwoods tower over 300 feet (91 meters) tall. Tall Douglas-firs also grow in the western United States.

A few needleleaf forests grow in warmer regions. For example, the southeast United States has large forests of pines, such as loblolly pines and longleaf pines. These forests provide great quantities of wood for lumber and wood pulp.

How forests spread. Many forests did not always grow where they are growing now. These forests have spread from other areas. For example, broadleaf forests grow today in parts of the northeast United States where only needleleaf forests grew several thousand years ago. The spread of forests from one area to another is called *migration.* The wind helps trees migrate by carrying their seeds beyond the forests. Animals also help spread the seeds. Trees that grow from these seeds produce their own seeds, which may be spread in the same ways. Over hundreds or thousands of years, a particular kind of tree may thus spread to surrounding areas if the climate and soil are suitable.

From about 1.8 million to 11,500 years ago, glaciers advanced and retreated several times across much of North America and Europe. When advancing, these glaciers caused forests of needleleaf and broadleaf trees to migrate south. When the glaciers began melting and retreating, forests of needleleaf trees grew up again on the land the glaciers had covered. As the glacial retreating continued, the climate became warm enough for broadleaf trees. Broadleaf trees usually crowd out needleleaf trees in areas where both are able to grow. As a result, broadleaf forests would often replace needleleaf forests. See **Ice age.**

Forests can migrate over fairly level land but not across oceans or mountain ranges. Yet similar types of forest trees grow in areas separated by oceans or mountains. For example, the United States has oak trees much like those that grow in Europe. Most scientists believe that many millions of years ago, all the continents were connected. Needleleaf trees developed and spread across much of the earth. Broadleaf trees developed next and also spread. Over millions of years, the continents became separated—along with their trees and other forms of life—by the oceans. Mountain ranges rose up on the continents and separated the trees on each side of the mountains. In time, many of the trees on each continent and on each side of the mountain ranges developed into different species.

How people help trees spread. People have transplanted many species of trees across oceans and mountain ranges. Transplanted trees may grow well in a new region with a climate like that of their native lands. In time, these *introduced species* may spread and become native trees in their new surroundings. A kind of rubber tree that once grew only in Brazil was introduced into the Far East during the late 1800's. Today, whole forests of these trees grow in the Far East. About 100 years ago, Australian eucalyptus trees were planted in California. Today, many thousands of eucalyptuses shade streets and parks in several Western states. Monterey pines originally grew only in a small area of California. They now cover large areas in Australia and other countries south of the equator.

Alan Pitcairn, Grant Heilman

Joshua trees, such as this one at California's Joshua Tree National Park, are among the few kinds of trees that grow in deserts. Most trees need more water than deserts provide.

Norman Meyers, Bruce Coleman Inc.

Tropical rain forests grow in Uganda, *shown here,* and in other hot, wet areas. Most of the trees are broadleaf and evergreen. Although they look alike, they belong to many different species.

Homeowners plant various kinds of trees on their property. They plant shade trees for protection from the sun and ornamental trees for beauty. They may also plant trees as windbreaks. Many people enjoy having fruit trees in their yard or garden to provide shade and beauty as well as fruit.

Selecting the right tree. To grow well, a tree must be suited to the region where it is planted. Trees from faraway places should be planted only in regions with similar climates. A tree's special characteristics must also be considered. For example, trees with wide-reaching roots should not be planted near houses because the roots may damage drains and foundations, or plug sewage pipes.

Trees with full, leafy crowns make the best shade trees. The most popular of these trees include ashes, basswoods, maples, and oaks. Trees with showy flowers, such as the catalpa and the crab apple, rank among the most commonly planted ornamental trees. In fairly warm areas around the world, such trees as acacias and pepper trees are planted as both shade and ornamental trees. Needleleaf trees are grown as ornamentals in many regions. They also make good windbreaks. Various broadleaf trees, including cottonwoods and Lombardy poplars, are also planted as windbreaks. Apple and cherry trees are popular fruit trees in temperate climates. In warm climates, many people prefer to grow citrus trees.

Planting the tree. A tree should be planted where it will have enough room when fully grown. The soil should be fertile and should drain well so that water does not collect and drown the roots.

The effort to grow a tree from seed takes much time. Most people prefer to buy their trees from a nursery. If a nursery tree measures more than 15 feet (4.6 meters) tall or if its trunk measures more than 3 inches (8 centimeters) thick, the grower may need special transplanting equipment.

The best time to transplant a tree is when it is resting —that is, in the fall, winter, or early spring. The roots of a deciduous tree can be dug up without a covering of soil. But a grower must keep the roots moist while they remain out of the ground. The roots of an evergreen should be dug up with a ball of soil around them. The hole for any new tree should provide room for all the roots below ground level. A small tree may need to be supported by stakes to keep the wind from blowing it over.

Caring for the tree. A young tree should be kept moderately watered until it is well rooted in the ground. It usually takes about a year for a tree to become firmly rooted.

Pruning improves the shape of trees. Cutting off some of a young shade tree's lower buds will keep it from developing many low branches. But enough buds should be left so that the tree has a full, leafy crown. As the tree develops upper branches, more lower branches may be removed. See **Pruning**.

Insects and diseases may attack a tree. With normal care, it can overcome most minor attacks. But if a tree fails to develop as many leaves as usual or if the leaves look pale, the tree may require the professional care of a tree surgeon. In some areas, air pollution threatens the health of trees. Norman L. Christensen, Jr.

How to plant a tree

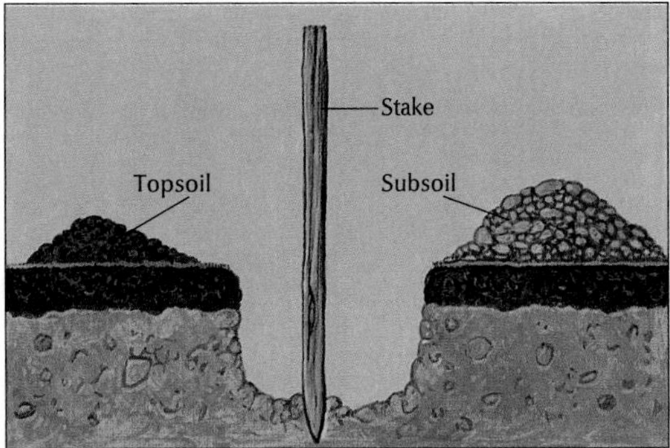

Digging the hole. Dig the hole big enough so all the roots can be spread out. Pile the topsoil and subsoil separately. A supporting stake, if needed, can be inserted at this time.

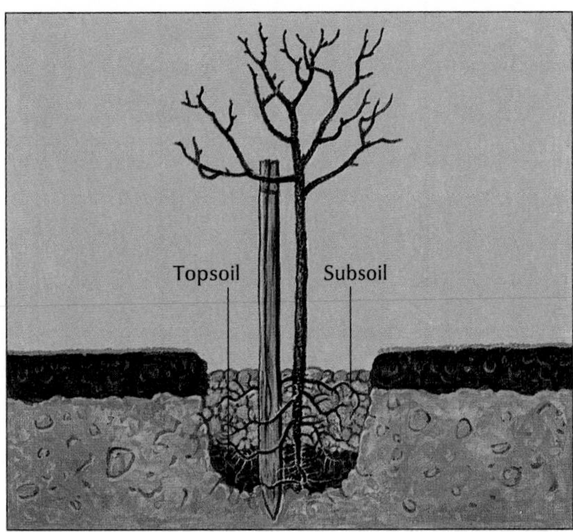

Planting the tree. Carefully spread out the roots in the hole and cover them with topsoil. Use the subsoil, which is less fertile, to fill the top part of the hole.

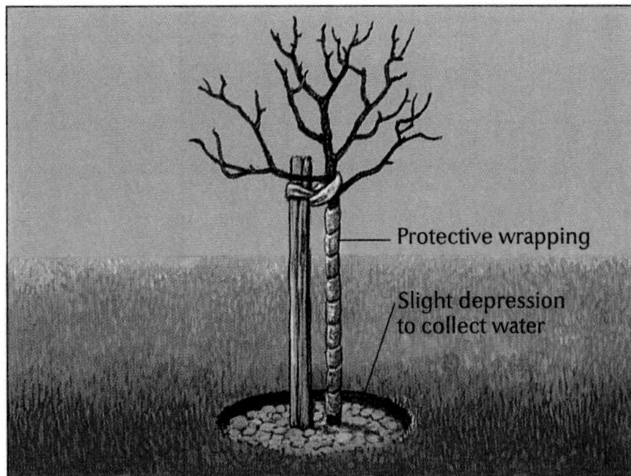

WORLD BOOK illustrations by John D. Dawson

Caring for the tree. Water the tree moderately during the first year. The trunk may be wrapped in burlap or heavy paper for the first two years to protect it from sunburn and insects.

Scientific classification of trees

Trees belong to three *classes* (groups) within the plant kingdom. Botanists further classify the plants in each class into subclasses, orders, and families. Plants are grouped according to the various characteristics they have in common. A few plant families consist largely of trees or shrubs, but some families have no trees at all. This table lists the families with the most species of trees or with one or more outstanding species. The families are arranged in the probable order of evolutionary development.

Ferns

Class Pteridopsida

Family Cyatheaceae—tree ferns
Family Dicksoniaceae—tree ferns

Gymnosperms (cone-bearing and related plants)

Class Gymnospermopsida

Order Cycadales

Family Cycadaceae—cycads

Order Ginkgoales

Family Ginkgoaceae—ginkgo

Order Coniferales

Family Taxaceae—torreyas, yews
Family Podocarpaceae—podocarpuses
Family Pinaceae—deodar cedar, Douglas-firs, firs, hemlocks, larches, pines, piñons, spruces
Family Taxodiaceae—baldcypresses, giant sequoia, redwood
Family Cupressaceae—cypresses, junipers, western redcedar
Family Araucariaceae—Chile pine, kauri pine, paraná pine

Angiosperms (flowering, or fruit-bearing, plants)

Class Anthopsida

Subclass Dicotyledonae

Family Casuarinaceae—beefwoods, or Australian pines
Family Salicaceae—aspens, cottonwoods, poplars, willows
Family Myricaceae—wax myrtles, or bayberries
Family Juglandaceae—butternut, hickories, pecan, walnuts
Family Betulaceae—alders, birches, hazels, hornbeams
Family Fagaceae—beeches, chestnuts, chinquapins, oaks
Family Ulmaceae—elms, hackberry, planer tree, sugarberry
Family Moraceae—banyan, figs, mulberries, Osage orange
Family Proteaceae—macadamias, silky oak, silver tree
Family Santalaceae—sandalwoods
Family Phytolaccaceae—ombú
Family Magnoliaceae—magnolias, sweet bay, tuliptree
Family Annonaceae—cherimoya, pawpaw, ylang-ylang
Family Myristicaceae—nutmegs
Family Lauraceae—avocado, cinnamon, laurels, sassafras
Family Moringaceae—horseradish tree
Family Pittosporaceae—lemonwood, Victoria box
Family Hamamelidaceae—sweet gums, witch hazels
Family Platanaceae—sycamores, or plane trees
Family Rosaceae—almonds, apples, apricots, cherries, crab apples, hawthorns, loquat, medlar, mountain ashes, nectarine, peaches, pears, plums, quinces, serviceberries
Family Fabaceae or Leguminosae—acacias, brazilwoods, carob, honey locusts, locusts, logwood, mesquite, mimosa, paloverdes, poincianas, rain tree, tamarind
Family Zygophyllaceae—lignum-vitae
Family Rutaceae—citruses, hop trees, prickly ashes
Family Simaroubaceae—ailanthus, bitter ashes, bitterbushes
Family Burseraceae—gumbo limbo, Java almond
Family Meliaceae—cedrelas, chinaberry, mahoganies
Family Euphorbiaceae—kukui, manchineel, rubber tree
Family Anacardiaceae—cashew, mango, pistachio, sumacs
Family Aquifoliaceae—hollies, mountain winterberry
Family Celastraceae—canotia, eastern wahoo, maytens
Family Aceraceae—boxelder, maples
Family Hippocastanaceae—buckeyes, horsechestnut
Family Sapindaceae—butterbough, litchi, soapberries
Family Rhamnaceae—buckthorns, jujubes, raisin tree
Family Tiliaceae—basswoods, or lindens
Family Bombacaceae—balsa, baobabs, kapok
Family Sterculiaceae—bottle tree, cacao, kola
Family Theaceae—loblolly bay, mountain stewartia, wild tea
Family Clusiaceae or Guttiferae—copey, mangosteens
Family Tamaricaceae—tamarisks
Family Caricaceae—papayas
Family Cactaceae—prickly pears, saguaro
Family Lythraceae—crape myrtles
Family Lecythidaceae—Brazil-nut, cannon-ball tree
Family Rhizophoraceae—dove tree, mangroves
Family Nyssaceae—tupelos
Family Combretaceae—Indian almond, oxhorn bucida
Family Myrtaceae—bay rum tree, bottlebrushes, clove tree, eucalyptuses, guavas, pimento, turpentine tree
Family Araliaceae—devil's walkingstick, lancewood
Family Cornaceae—cornelian cherry, dogwoods
Family Ericaceae—madroñas, mountain laurel, sorrel tree
Family Sapotaceae—bumelias, gutta-percha tree, sapodilla
Family Ebenaceae—ebonies, persimmons
Family Styracaceae—epaulette tree, silverbells, snowbells
Family Oleaceae—ashes, devilwood, fringetree, olives
Family Loganiaceae—strychnine trees
Family Apocynaceae—devil tree, frangipani, yellow oleander
Family Boraginaceae—anaqua, geiger tree, strongbarks
Family Verbenaceae—Florida fiddlewood, teak
Family Bignoniaceae—calabash tree, catalpas, desert willow, jacaranda, royal paulownia, sausage tree
Family Rubiaceae—buttonbush, cinchonas, coffee trees
Family Caprifoliaceae—black haw, elders, viburnums

Subclass Monocotyledonae

Family Pandanaceae—pandanuses, or screw pines
Family Arecaceae or Palmae—palmettos, palms
Family Liliaceae—aloes
Family Agavaceae—dragon tree, Joshua tree, Spanish bayonet
Family Strelitziaceae—traveler's-tree

Study aids

Related articles in *World Book* include:

Common broadleaf trees

Alder
Ash
Aspen
Beech
Birch
Bitternut hickory
Boxelder
Catalpa
Chestnut
Cottonwood
Elm
Eucalyptus
Gum tree
Hackberry
Honey locust
Horsechestnut
Ironwood
Kentucky coffeetree
Laurel
Linden
Live oak
Locust
Madroña
Maple
Myrtle
Oak
Osage orange
Poplar
Prickly-ash
Sourwood
Sweet gum
Sycamore
Willow
Yellow-poplar

Common needleleaf trees

Bristlecone pine
Cedar
Cypress
Douglas-fir
Fir
Hemlock
Juniper
Larch
Pine
Redwood
Sequoia
Spruce
Yew

Fruit trees

Apple	Date palm	Loquat	Pawpaw
Apricot	Fig	Mango	Peach
Avocado	Grapefruit	Mangosteen	Pear
Breadfruit	Guava	Mulberry	Persimmon
Cherimoya	Kumquat	Nectarine	Plum
Cherry	Lemon	Olive	Pomegranate
Citron	Lime	Orange	Quince
Crab apple	Litchi	Papaya	

Edible-nut trees

Almond	Cashew	Hickory	Pistachio nut
Brazil nut	Coconut palm	Pecan	Walnut
Butternut	Hazel	Piñon	

Trees that yield special products

Balsa	Carob	Kapok	Palm
Bayberry	Cinchona	Kola nut	Rubber
Betel	Cinnamon	Lignum-vitae	Sapodilla
Brazilwood	Clove	Mesquite	Sassafras
Cacao	Coffee	Neem tree	Tallowtree
Calabash	Cork	Nutmeg	Witch hazel
Camphor			

Ornamental trees

Acacia	Magnolia	Poinciana
Box	Mimosa	Redbud
Coral tree	Myrtle	Rhododendron
Holly	Peppertree	Silverbell
Laburnum		

Tropical trees

Baobab	Mangrove	Rain tree	Tamarind
Jacaranda	Protea	Silky oak	Teak
Mahogany			

Unusual trees

Banyan tree	Cycad	Traveler's-tree
Beefwood	Ginkgo	Upas
Bottle tree	Monkey puzzle tree	
Cannon-ball tree		

Parts of trees

Bark	Flower	Root	Stem
Bud	Fruit	Sap	Wood
Cell	Leaf	Seed	

Maps

See the plant life maps with the following articles:

Africa	Australia	North America
Asia	Europe	South America

Other related articles

Bonsai	Ecology	Grafting
Boxelder bug	Environmental pollution	Lumber
Cellulose	Evergreen	Nursery
Chlorophyll	Forest	Plant
Conifer	Forest products	Pruning
Conservation		Tree surgery
Cotyledon		

Outline

I. The importance of trees
- A. Wood products
- B. Food products
- C. Other tree products
- D. Trees in conservation

II. Kinds of trees
- A. Broadleaf trees
- B. Needleleaf trees
- C. Palm, pandanus, and lily trees
- D. Cycad trees
- E. Tree ferns
- F. Ginkgo trees
- G. Fossil trees

III. The parts of a tree
- A. Trunk and branches
- B. Leaves
- C. Roots
- D. Seeds

IV. How a tree grows
- A. How seeds sprout into trees
- B. How leaves make plant food
- C. How trees grow taller
- D. How trunks and branches grow thicker
- E. How trees reproduce

V. Familiar broadleaf and needleleaf trees of North America

VI. Trees around the world
- A. Broadleaf forests
- B. Needleleaf forests
- C. How forests spread
- D. How people help trees spread

VII. Planting and caring for trees
- A. Selecting the right tree
- B. Planting the tree
- C. Caring for the tree

VIII. Scientific classification of trees

Questions

What is *sapwood? Heartwood?*
What is the main job of a tree's leaves?
In what climate do most needleleaf forests grow?
What do root hairs do?
How do forests spread?
How do *deciduous* trees differ from *evergreen* trees?
When is the best time of year to transplant a tree?
How do trees help conserve soil and water?
In what four ways are trees different from all other plants?
How do trees grow taller?

Additional resources

Level I

Burns, Diane L. *Trees, Leaves, and Bark.* Gareth Stevens, 1998.
Cassie, Brian. *National Audubon Society First Field Guide: Trees.* Scholastic, 1999.
Gardner, Robert. *Science Project Ideas About Trees.* Enslow, 1997.
Hickman, Pamela. *Starting with Nature Tree Book.* Kids Can Pr., 1999.
Staub, Frank J. *America's Forests.* Carolrhoda, 1999.

Level II

Benvie, Sam. *The Encyclopedia of North American Trees.* Firefly Bks., 2000.
Dirr, Michael A. *Dirr's Hardy Trees and Shrubs.* Timber, 1997.
Lewington, Anna, and Parker, Edward. *Ancient Trees.* Collins & Brown, 1999.
Thomas, Peter. *Trees: Their Natural History.* Cambridge, 2000.

Tree farming is the growing of trees for profit. Tree farms generally range in size from 10 acres (4 hectares) to nearly 1 million acres (400,000 hectares). Most are on private land. Farmers raise trees primarily for the forest products industry, but some trees are grown for sale by nurseries or for use as Christmas trees.

In some countries, national or local forestry agencies or organizations certify land for tree farming. Farmers generally commit to *sustainable production*—that is, to producing timber using environmentally sound practices that protect soil and water resources and wildlife.

The American Tree Farm System is the world's oldest sustainable forestry and certification program. It began in 1941 with the establishment of the first certified tree farm by the Weyerhaeuser Company on 200,000 acres (80,000 hectares) of land in Montesano, Washington. By 2000, the United States had over 64,000 tree farms covering more than 80 million acres (32 million hectares) in 50 states. Other countries with large certified tree farm systems include Canada and Sweden. Douglass F. Jacobs

See also **Forestry; Washington** (Natural resources).

Tree fern. See **Tree** (Tree ferns; picture: Tree ferns).

Tree frog, also called *tree toad,* spends much of its life in trees. There are several hundred kinds of tree frogs. Most have sticky pads called *adhesive disks* on their feet, and can climb trees and leap through the treetops. Tree frogs are from less than 1 inch (2.5 centimeters) to about 5 inches (13 centimeters) long. They eat insects and other small animals. Most tree frogs can change color.

Tree frogs are common in North and South America. Probably more people hear them than ever see them. In the early spring and sometimes on mild winter days, types of tree frogs called *peepers* may be heard near waterways or marshes throughout the eastern half of North America. The males produce a high-pitched peep to attract females. Male peepers sometimes form a large, noisy group known as a *chorus.*

Other kinds of tree frogs give their call through much of the summer. They may be heard evenings or before rains in woodlands. Male tree frogs do all the calling. When a male calls, its throat swells until it looks like a bubble about to burst. Then it makes the call that is characteristic of its species. This sound is hard to locate, even though it may be nearby.

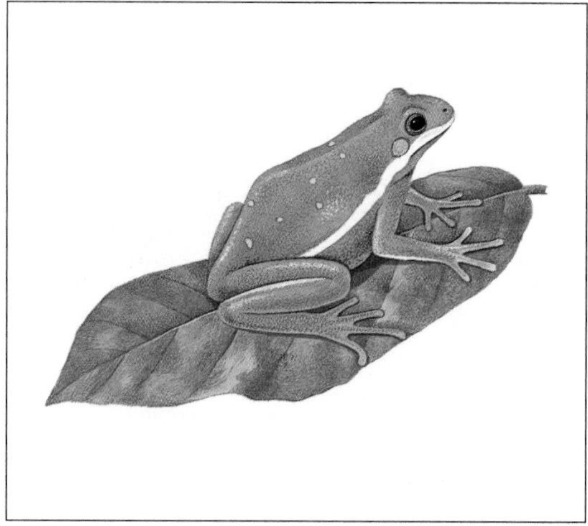

WORLD BOOK illustration by Richard Lewington, The Garden Studio

The tree frog uses its sticky foot pads to climb trees. Most tree frogs can change color to blend with their surroundings.

Tree frogs may be kept in aquariums or terrariums, and fed chopped earthworms and insects. In this way, they will be active through the winter and will not hibernate, as do the frogs that live outdoors. Don C. Forester

Scientific classification. Tree frogs belong to the tree toad family, Hylidae. American tree frogs make up the genera *Acris, Pseudacris,* and *Hyla.*

See also Frog.

Tree of heaven. See Ailanthus.

Tree of life. See Eden.

Tree shrew is the name of a group of small, swift-moving mammals that live in the forests of India, Southeast Asia, and southern China. Tree shrews look and act like small squirrels with long noses. They grow less than 8 inches (20 centimeters) long, not including their tails, and weigh less than 1 pound (0.5 kilogram). A few species of tree shrews live primarily in trees and bushes. But most species spend more time on the ground. Tree shrews feed mainly on fruits, insects, and worms.

© Tom McHugh, Photo Researchers

The tree shrew is a mammal that resembles a small squirrel with a long nose. It lives in trees and bushes and on the ground.

Tree shrews are primitive animals—that is, they represent an early stage of evolution. In the past, many zoologists classified tree shrews among the *primates,* the order of mammals that includes monkeys and apes. Tree shrews, like primates, have relatively large brains and eyes. Other zoologists classified tree shrews with the *insectivores,* the order that includes shrews and moles. Like insectivores, tree shrews have claws on all their fingers and toes. Today, most zoologists place tree shrews in their own order and believe that these animals may resemble the common ancestor of both primates and insectivores. Bruce A. Brewer

Scientific classification. Tree shrews make up the order Scandentia and the family Tupaiidae.

Tree surgery is the care of trees, chiefly by pruning, bracing, and removing dead or dying branches. Professional tree surgeons are known as *arborists.* Arborists not only work with branches, but they also apply pesticides to protect trees from insects and diseases. In addition, they may recommend or apply fertilizer to improve the trees' overall health. Many communities employ arborists to care for trees in parks and recreation areas.

Pruning helps individual trees develop and maintain a strong structure. Proper pruning begins on a young tree and continues every few years throughout the tree's life. To properly prune a branch, an arborist or gardener must first locate the *branch collar,* a swelling at the point where the branch is attached to the trunk. All pruning cuts should be made on the outside of the branch collar. Such cuts will soon heal properly without any *wound dressing,* such as grafting wax or pruning paint.

For large branches, arborists and gardeners use the three-cut method of pruning. They first make a cut on the underside of the branch, 6 to 18 inches (15 to 46 centimeters) from the trunk. The undercut should penetrate at least one-third of the branch's diameter. Pruners make the second cut on the top side of the branch, slightly farther from the trunk than they made the first cut. The branch will then snap off and a stub will remain. The third cut, made at the branch collar, removes the stub. Pruners should hold the stub while cutting it off, and they should make sure this final cut does not tear the bark from the trunk.

Narrow-angled *crotches,* where the tree divides into two branches, may cause trouble because they have a tendency to split. Arborists use a procedure called bracing to prevent splitting. They insert a metal rod through the branches that form the narrow-angled crotch. The rod does not injure the tree because it passes through only a small section of the *cambium,* a layer of living tissue between the wood and bark. Arborists bolt each end of the rod to prevent the branches from shifting.

Gardeners should completely remove diseased or dead branches as soon as possible after detecting them. However, do not attempt to remove decay in the tree's cavities. Attempts to chisel away rotten wood often spread the decay. William H. Carlson

See also **Pruning; Tree** (Caring for the tree).

Tree toad. See **Tree frog.**

Trefoil, *TREE foyl,* meaning *three-leaved,* is the name generally applied to various plants having compound leaves with three leaflets, like the clover. It is specifically applied to the lotus group, which is in the pea family. Several members of this group are found in the temperate parts of the Northern Hemisphere. *Bird's-foot trefoil* is so called because it bears clusters of pods somewhat resembling a crow's foot. Other *species* (kinds) of trefoil include *marsh bird's-foot,* common in damp meadowland, and *coralgem deervetch,* often planted in California. See also **Bird's-foot trefoil.** Daniel F. Austin

Scientific classification. The trefoils belong to the pea family, Fabaceae or Leguminosae. The bird's-foot trefoil is *Lotus corniculatus.* The marsh bird's-foot is *L. uliginosus,* and the coralgem deervetch is *L. bertholeti.*

Trench foot. See **Immersion foot.**

Trench mouth is an infection that affects the mouth and throat. The condition is also known by the terms *Vincent's infection* and *necrotizing ulcerative gingivitis.* It was given the name trench mouth during World War I (1914-1918), when thousands of soldiers got it while fighting in trenches. The infection is caused by bacteria that are normally present in small numbers in everyone's mouth. Most cases of trench mouth occur when such factors as stress, poor nutrition, or smoking disrupt the mouth's environment and these bacteria multiply.

The first symptoms of trench mouth are often mouth pains and bad breath. The infection most commonly affects the gums, which develop swelling, bleeding, and sores. In some cases, trench mouth affects the tonsils, lymph nodes, and other areas of the mouth and throat. Doctors treat the infection with antibiotics and by removing any damaged tissue. Raymond L. Burich

Trent, Council of, was a series of conferences held by the Roman Catholic Church in Trent, Italy, from 1545 to 1563. The council defined doctrines and adopted policies that have influenced the church into the 2000's.

The council was held in response to the Reformation, a religious movement that led to the birth of Protestantism. The council aimed to clarify Catholic teaching and to address matters of discipline within the church. Its work became a major force in the Counter Reformation, a movement that led to a renewal within Catholicism in the 1500's and 1600's. See **Counter Reformation.**

Pope Paul III summoned the council in 1542, but it did not open until Dec. 13, 1545. The council, interrupted by wars and religious disputes, met for a total of 25 sessions over three distinct periods.

During the first period, from 1545 to 1547, the council established that divine revelation is transmitted through both Scripture and *tradition.* Tradition includes the writings of the apostles, the decrees of popes and councils, and the customs practiced by Catholics throughout church history. The council decreed that the church, rather than the individual, has the sole right to interpret Scripture authoritatively. The council also rejected Protestant views on grace, sin, and salvation.

During the second period, from 1551 to 1552, the council dealt with the seven sacraments. The council reaffirmed the doctrine of *transubstantiation,* in which bread and wine are changed into the body and blood of Jesus Christ during the Eucharistic prayer of the Mass.

During the final period, from 1561 to 1563, the council upheld the granting of *indulgences,* a means of releasing sinners from part of the penalty for their sins (see **Indulgence**). It also defended the sacrificial nature of the Mass and the practice of *venerating* (honoring) saints.

The council passed several reforms affecting church discipline. They included establishing seminaries to educate priests and requiring that each bishop reside in his own diocese. Pope Pius IV confirmed all the council's decrees on Jan. 26, 1564. Neil J. Roy

See also **Roman Catholic Church** (picture: The Council of Trent).

Trent Affair was a naval incident in the first year of the American Civil War (1861-1865). It almost brought the United Kingdom into the war on the side of the South. In the fall of 1861, two men representing the Confederacy, James M. Mason and John Slidell, sailed to Europe. Their mission was to enlist the aid of neutral France and the United Kingdom to the Southern cause. Because Northern ships were blockading Southern ports, they boarded a British ship, the *Trent,* in Havana, Cuba. Charles Wilkes, commander of the U.S.S. *San Jacinto,* stopped the British ship without orders to do so. He took Mason and Slidell prisoner and brought them to Boston. This act violated the principle of freedom of the seas, because the United Kingdom was a neutral nation.

The British government demanded an apology and the release of Mason and Slidell. To back up these demands, it ordered 8,000 troops to Canada. President Abraham Lincoln and Secretary of State William Seward realized Wilkes was wrong. The government ordered the prisoners released. Mason and Slidell went on to Europe, but their mission failed. Thomas L. Connelly

See also **Mason, James Murray; Slidell, John; Wilkes, Charles.**

Trenton (pop. 85,403; met. area pop. 350,761) is the capital of New Jersey. The city lies in the west-central part of the state, where the Assunpink Creek flows into the Delaware River (see **New Jersey** [political map]).

In 1679, Quaker farmers led by Mahlon Stacy established the first permanent white settlement in what is now the Trenton area. In 1714, Mahlon Stacy, Jr., sold part of his father's property to William Trent, a merchant who later became chief justice of the New Jersey colony. The community was named *Trent's Town* in 1719, and its name later became *Trenton.*

Description. Trenton, the county seat of Mercer County, covers about 8 square miles (21 square kilometers). The golden dome of the State Capitol rises above the downtown area (see **New Jersey** [picture: The State Capitol]). The New Jersey Cultural Center, near the Capitol, consists of the State Library and Museum and a planetarium. The Battle Monument, 148 feet (45 meters) high, marks the site of a famous Revolutionary War battle (see **Revolutionary War in America** [Trenton and Princeton]). Other landmarks include the 1719 home of William Trent and the Old Barracks, built in 1758 to house British troops. Thomas Edison State College is in Trenton. The College of New Jersey, Princeton University, and Rider University are near the city. McGuire Air Force Base and Fort Dix, a U.S. Army installation, are also nearby (see **Fort Dix**).

Economy. Trenton's chief manufactured products are electrical goods, fabricated metal products, machinery, and rubber products. Printing, publishing, and health care are important industries. State government employs many people.

Government and history. Trenton has a mayor-council form of government. The voters elect the mayor and the seven city council members to four-year terms.

Delaware Indians lived in what is now the Trenton area before the British occupied New Jersey in the 1660's. During colonial times, Trenton became a major stopping place on the stage line between New York City and Philadelphia. In December 1776, during the Revolutionary War, George Washington made his famous crossing of the Delaware River near Trenton. In the battle that followed, Washington's troops defeated the Hessians, professional German soldiers hired by the British.

Trenton served as the nation's capital in November and December 1784. It became the capital of New Jersey in 1790 and received a city charter in 1792. In the 1800's, Trenton developed into an industrial and trade center. An increase in river traffic, combined with the construction of railroads, brought the city great industrial growth. Thousands of factory workers moved to Trenton, and the population rose by about 90,000 from 1880 to 1920. By 1920, Trenton was the leading U.S. pottery producer, with more than 50 potteries in the city. It also ranked high in the production of rubber goods, steel, and wire cable. But after 1920, many of the residents and largest businesses began to move to the suburbs. The population declined through the last half of the 1900's.

In the 1970's and early 1980's, the state built a number of office buildings in Trenton, including the Richard J. Hughes Justice Complex. City projects in the 1990's included building a baseball stadium and a sports arena, refurbishing the State Capitol, and renovating the 1932 War Memorial and its theater. In the beginning of the 2000's, the public school system began a massive building program, funded under a state Supreme Court decision that called for additional state spending in 30 of the state's poorest school districts. Joel J. Bewley

Trenton, Battle of. See **Revolutionary War in America** (Trenton and Princeton).

Trepang, *trih PANG,* is the commercial name of the dried bodies of certain species of wormlike marine animals called *sea cucumbers* (see **Sea cucumber**). Trepang is also called *bêche-de-mer* (pronounced *BEHSH duh MAIR*). Trepang is used as food primarily in the Far East. In preparing trepang, the sea cucumber's inner parts are removed and the body is boiled in salt water. After boiling, the body is either smoked, sun dried, or roasted for five days, and then dried further. This process turns the body into the rubberlike trepang, which is used to thicken and flavor soups. The highest quality trepang is unskinned and is blackish-brown.

The chief center of the trepang industry is Makassar, a seaport of Sulawesi, in Indonesia. California also has a trepang industry. George J. Flick, Jr.

Trephining, *trih FYN ihng,* is a surgical operation that involves cutting out a small, button-shaped piece of the skull. The operation is done with an instrument called a *trephine.* Trephining is used in the treatment of certain head injuries. It relieves pressure on the brain caused by bleeding between the skull and the brain. Trephining is also used to remove blood clots and to gain entry to the brain for certain surgical procedures.

Trephining is the earliest-known surgical treatment. Evidence of trephining has been found in human skulls that date to prehistoric times. Anthropologists have found trephined skulls throughout much of the world. Ancient peoples probably used trephining to release spirits that were believed responsible for headaches, mental disorders, and epilepsy. Some ancient warriors trephined the skulls of people they killed in battle. The warriors wore the piece of bone as a trophy or to ward off evil spirits. The Inca and other Indians of South America practiced trephining. James A. Hill

See also **Medicine** (History; picture: Trephining).

Trespass, in law, is most commonly known as the unlawful entrance upon the property of another. The term also means injury to the person of another. "No trespassing" signs are seen commonly where owners of groves, private estates, and club grounds desire to protect their property from intrusion. Failure to regard such notices is an unlawful act. False imprisonment and assault and battery are examples of trespass to the person. Trespass makes a person liable to a civil suit for damages. See also **Assault and battery; False imprisonment; Tort.**

George T. Felkenes

Trevelyan, *trih VEHL yuhn,* **George Macaulay** (1876-1962), was a famous British historian. His two best-known books are *History of England* (1926) and *English Social History* (1942). Trevelyan's vivid descriptions of social life and his dramatic and imaginative writing style appealed to the general public. In his writings, he promoted the views of the Whig Party, which was important in British politics from the 1600's to the mid-1800's, and of its successor, the Liberal Party. Whigs and Liberals believed the common people had a more positive effect on history than did royalty and that democratic government would bring about steady social progress.

Trevelyan was born on Feb. 16, 1876, near Stratford-upon-Avon. His father was Sir George Otto Trevelyan, a politician and historian. The younger Trevelyan first won wide praise for a three-volume biography of the Italian military hero Giuseppe Garibaldi, published between 1907 and 1911. Trevelyan taught modern history at Cambridge University from 1927 until 1940, when he became master of Trinity College. He also wrote *England Under Queen Anne* (1930 to 1934) and *The English Revolution, 1688-1689* (1938). Joseph Martin Hernon, Jr.

Trevino, *truh VEE noh,* **Lee** (1939-), is an American golfer. Few people had heard of Trevino before he won the U.S. Open in 1968. But he soon gained fame as one of the most colorful and popular figures in sports. During tournaments, Trevino often joked with his many followers, who became known as "Lee's Fleas."

In 1971, Trevino accomplished one of the most remarkable winning streaks in golf history. Within 16 weeks that year, he won five tournaments and finished among the top five money winners in four other tourneys. Trevino also won the U.S. Open in 1971, the British Open in 1971 and 1972, and the Professional Golfers' Association (PGA) Championship in 1974 and 1984. Lee Buck Trevino was born on Dec. 1, 1939, in Dallas. He joined the Senior PGA Tour in 1989. Marino A. Parascenzo

Trevithick, *TREHV uh thihk,* **Richard** (1771-1833), was a British inventor and engineer. He contributed to the development of the steam locomotive.

Trevithick was born on April 13, 1771, in England in the county of Cornwall, a tin-mining region of Britain. As he grew up, he became interested in the steam engines that pumped water from the mines. By the early 1800's, he had developed a new engine that was soon used in most of the local mines. This high-pressure engine was the model for most later steam engines.

In 1801, Trevithick designed and built a steam-powered carriage that ran on the road. In 1804, he built the first steam locomotive to run on rails. It pulled a load of iron along a railway for horse-drawn cars. In 1808, he exhibited a large locomotive in London. None of his locomotives were financially successful, because they were too heavy for the roads and railways of his time. But Trevithick did prove that steam-powered locomotives could be built. Michael M. Sokal

See also **Railroad** (History).

Trial is a method of settling disputes verbally in a court of law. In most cases, the people on each side of the dispute use a lawyer to represent their views, present evidence, and question witnesses. About half the trials held in the United States are jury trials. In the other trials, the defendant chooses to be tried by a judge or a panel of judges instead of a jury.

There are two types of trials, *civil trials* and *criminal trials.* Civil trials settle noncriminal matters, such as contracts, ownership of property, and payment for personal injury. The jury decides who is at fault and how much money must be paid in damages. In a criminal trial, the jury decides the legal guilt or innocence of a person accused of a crime.

A jury trial begins with the selection of the jurors. Then the *prosecutor,* who argues the state's case against the defendant in a criminal trial, and the *defense attorney* make their opening statements to the jury. In a civil trial, one side is represented by the attorney for the *plaintiff* (person who began the lawsuit). The other side is represented by the defense attorney. In their opening statements, the lawyers for both sides declare what they intend to prove during the trial.

Presenting evidence. Each lawyer presents evidence to support his or her side of the case. The evidence may include documents, such as letters or receipts; or objects, such as weapons or clothing. In most cases, the evidence consists of testimony given by witnesses who are sworn to tell the truth. Witnesses generally give their testimony in response to questions asked by an attorney. Then the opposing attorney cross-examines the witnesses and attempts to find mistakes in their testimony. A witness who is suspected of deliberately lying may be accused of *perjury.*

The admission of evidence in a trial is governed by certain rules. In general, information is admitted as evidence only if it is relevant and firsthand. Relevant information is related to a significant question in the case and helps answer the question. Firsthand information comes from personal knowledge, not from hearsay.

Following the testimony and cross-examination, the lawyers for each side summarize the case. Then, in a *charge to the jury,* the judge gives instructions concerning the laws that apply to the case.

The judge in each trial decides what evidence will be admitted. He or she may declare a *mistrial* if improper evidence is heard by a jury or if the fairness of a trial is jeopardized in some other way. A mistrial results in a new trial with new jurors. The judge may also hold in *contempt of court* any person who shows disrespect for the court by disrupting a trial. Such a person may be fined or imprisoned, or both.

Reaching a verdict. The jury is taken to a private room to discuss the case, think about it carefully, and reach a verdict. In cases that have received much publicity, the jurors may be *sequestered* (isolated) from other people, including their families, throughout the trial. Sequestered jurors may read newspapers and magazines only if articles about the trial have been cut out. In some cases, the judge orders that the jurors not be allowed to watch television. These restrictions prevent jurors from reading or hearing anything that could influence their opinions about the trial.

In a criminal trial, the prosecutor tries to prove the defendant's guilt "beyond a reasonable doubt," which is the standard required by law. If the jurors do not feel the prosecutor has done so, they must *acquit* the defendant—that is, find him or her not guilty. If the jury finds the defendant guilty, the judge sets a date for sentencing. In a civil trial, the attorney for the plaintiff must prove the plaintiff's claim by a "fair *preponderance* (greater weight) of the evidence."

A *hung jury* is one in which the required number of jurors cannot agree on a verdict. A new trial—with new jurors—is then held.

In some trials, the evidence points without question to a particular verdict. In such cases, the judge may order the jury to return that verdict. A verdict so returned is called a *directed verdict.* The jury does not discuss a directed verdict. A judge cannot order a guilty verdict.

The criminal defendant's rights. The Constitution of the United States guarantees accused people many rights concerning a fair trial. For example, it specifies the right to a jury trial. Other guarantees are included in the Bill of Rights, the first 10 amendments to the Constitution. The first guarantee is in the Fifth Amendment. It ensures by the right of *due process* that each trial will be conducted according to the law.

The Sixth Amendment sets forth the most important rights of a defendant in a criminal trial. These include the right to "a speedy and public trial." The right to a speedy trial means that a person must be tried as soon as possible after being accused. But the large number of cases awaiting trial may prevent the courts from trying every defendant promptly. The right to a public trial means a defendant cannot be tried in secret. Each trial must be open to public observation.

The Constitution states that a criminal trial must be held in the community in which the crime occurred. The Sixth Amendment requires that the jurors be chosen from that community. In some situations, many local residents have formed an opinion about a case, and so the defendant cannot receive a fair trial there. The defense may then request a *change of venue*—that is, a change in the locality of the trial.

The Supreme Court of the United States has issued many decisions that provide additional rights for the accused. In 1963, for example, the court guaranteed the right to free legal counsel in all felony cases. In 1972, the court extended that right to people accused of any offense involving a jail sentence.

A defendant who has been tried, convicted, and sentenced can use his or her right to *appeal.* In an appeal, the defendant asks that the case be reviewed by a higher court called an *appellate court.* Some cases have an automatic right of appeal. In others, the defendant must show some reason for retrying the case, such as the discovery of new evidence. In most cases, the appellate court will reverse the decision of a lower court only if the appellate court feels there has been a violation of law or of the defendant's constitutional rights. An appellate court does not use a jury. Lawyers present the appeal by written arguments called *briefs* and by oral arguments.

The U.S. legal system is based on the belief that a person should be considered innocent until proven guilty. But only a small percentage of the legal disputes in the United States are settled by a trial. The defendant pleads guilty in most cases, and so no trial is needed.

Many cases are settled by *plea bargaining.* In this procedure, the prosecuting attorney agrees to dismiss certain charges, substitute a less serious charge, or recommend a shorter sentence if the defendant pleads guilty. The state saves time and money by plea bargaining rather than putting a defendant on trial. Critics of plea bargaining feel that it weakens the nation's system of justice. They point out that the defendant's guilt is assumed instead of proven, as it would be in a trial.

History. The Saxons, who lived in England during the Middle Ages, gave accused people a *trial by ordeal* rather than by jury. The defendant was perhaps required to hold a piece of red-hot iron or was deliberately injured in some other way. The Saxons believed that God would heal the accused person's wounds within three days if he or she was innocent. After the Norman Conquest in 1066, two people fought if they disagreed about a matter. They believed that God would grant victory to the one who was right.

The present trial system in the United States and Canada developed from English *common law* and *equity.* Common law is a group of rulings made by judges on the basis of community customs and previous court decisions. Equity is a set of standards based on broad principles of justice. English colonists brought their legal system with them to North America. Jack M. Kress

Related articles in *World Book* include:

Appeal
Constitution of the United States
Contempt
Court
Criminal justice system
Due process of law
Evidence
Judge
Jury
Law
Perjury
Plea bargaining
Sentence
Witness

Triangle, in plane geometry, is an enclosed figure that has three line segments for sides. The sides meet at three points called *vertices,* and each vertex forms an *angle* with two of the sides. The sum of the three angles of a triangle is always 180°. A triangle is a type of polygon (see **Polygon**).

Kinds of triangles. Triangles can be classified according to the relationships of their sides. A *scalene* triangle is a figure with three unequal sides. An *isosceles* triangle has at least two equal sides. A triangle with all three sides of equal length is called an *equilateral* triangle. Therefore, every equilateral triangle is also an isosceles triangle, but not every isosceles triangle is an equilateral triangle.

Triangles are also classified by their angles. A triangle in which every angle is smaller than 90° is an *acute* triangle. An *obtuse* triangle has one angle larger than 90°. A *right* triangle has one right—that is, 90°—angle. No triangle can have more than one obtuse angle or one right angle.

Properties and relationships of triangles. The parts of a triangle have many interesting characteristics and relationships. Sometimes a useful relationship between two or more triangles can also be established. Some of the most notable of these properties and relationships are discussed below.

Perimeter and area. The *perimeter* of a triangle is the sum of the lengths of its sides. To find the *area* of a triangle, we must know the *altitude,* or *height,* which is the perpendicular distance from a vertex to the opposite side, or *base.* The area is calculated by multiplying the base by the altitude and then dividing by 2. Even if the perimeters of several triangles are the same, the areas of those triangles may differ.

Right triangles and the Pythagorean theorem. The sides of a right triangle have a special relationship to each other. This relationship is expressed in a mathematical statement called the *Pythagorean theorem* (see **Pythagorean theorem**). This theorem was known in ancient civilizations, but it is credited to Pythagoras, a Greek philosopher and mathematician. According to the Pythagorean theorem, a triangle is a right triangle if and only if the sum of the squares of the two shorter sides equals the square of the longest side, called the *hypotenuse.* This statement can be written as a formula: $a^2 + b^2 = c^2$. For example, if the sides of a triangle are 6, 8, and 10, it is a right triangle because $36 + 64 = 100$. The formula enables us to find the length of any side of a right triangle if we know the lengths of the other two sides.

The parts of a triangle

A triangle is a plane figure that has three sides and three angles. The line segments that form the sides meet at three points called *vertices.* Each vertex forms an angle with two of the sides.

WORLD BOOK illustration

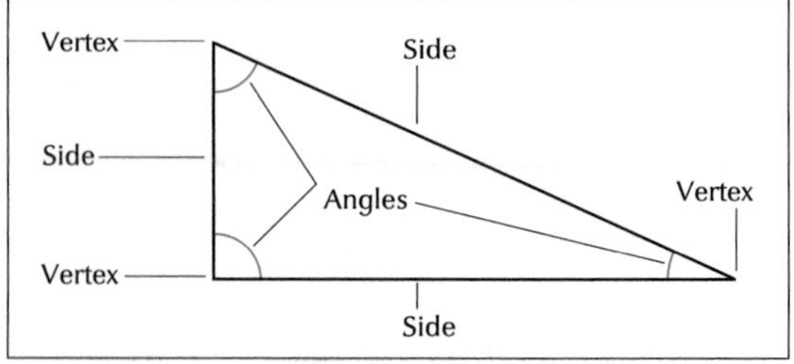

Kinds of triangles

Triangles can be classified by their angles or by the relationships of their sides. In the diagrams below, the blue lines indicate equal sides of a triangle. The red symbols mark equal angles. The gray box marks a *right angle*—that is, an angle of 90°.

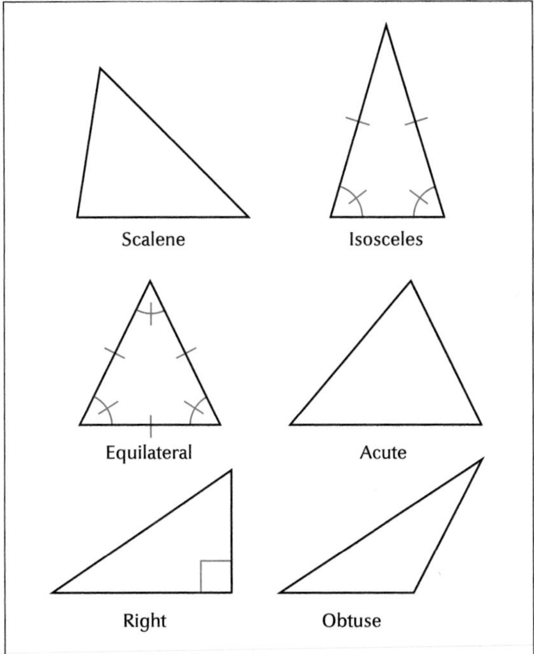

WORLD BOOK illustration

Congruence. Two triangles are *congruent*—that is, they have exactly the same size and shape—if all their corresponding sides and angles are equal. Mathematicians have formulated specific sets of conditions for determining congruence. For example, two triangles are congruent if the sides of one equal the corresponding sides of the other. Using *S* to represent *side,* this statement can be abbreviated as *SSS=SSS.* Other sets of conditions for congruency involve angles as well as sides, with *A* standing for *angle.* These sets are *AAS=AAS, SAS=SAS,* and *ASA=ASA.*

Similarity. Triangles that are *similar* have equal corresponding angles and proportional corresponding sides. Similar triangles have the same shape but not necessarily the same size. For example, if the sides of one triangle are 3, 4, and 5, and those of another are 6, 8, and 10, the sides are proportional.

The similarity of two triangles, like the congruence of two triangles, can be established without knowing all the sides and angles. If two sets of corresponding angles are equal, for example, the triangles are similar. If all three corresponding sides of the triangles are proportional, the triangles are also similar. In a right triangle, the altitude from the right angle divides the triangle into two triangles that are similar to each other and to the parent triangle. Arthur F. Coxford, Jr.

Triangle is a percussion instrument that consists of a steel bar bent in a triangular shape with one open corner. The player strikes the instrument with a short rod called a *beater* to produce a high sound with indefinite pitch. The quality of the tone can be varied by using metal beaters of different thicknesses or by using a wooden, rather than a metal, beater. A musician usually holds the triangle in one hand by a clip at the top and grasps the beater in the other hand. But the triangle can also be clipped to a stand and played with two beaters, one in each hand.

John H. Beck

Northwestern University (WORLD BOOK photo by Ted Nielsen)

A triangle is a steel percussion instrument shaped like a triangle and open at one corner. A player hits it with a rod.

Triangular trade. See **African Americans** (Beginning of the slave trade).

Trianon, *TREE uh nahn* or *tree ah NAWN,* **Treaty of,** was signed by Hungary and the Western Allies after World War I (1914-1918). It was signed in the gallery of the Grand Trianon, a palace at Versailles, France, on June 4, 1920. The treaty punished Hungary severely for its role in the war as part of Austria-Hungary, even though a new Hungarian government had declared Hungary independent of Austria in 1918. The United States, which signed the treaty but never ratified it, made a separate peace with Hungary in 1921.

The Trianon treaty stripped Hungary of more than two-thirds of its territory. The country's population dropped from about 21 million to approximately 8 million, and the nation was left with no seaports. Hungary's complaints against the treaty brought few results.

The treaty forced Hungary to recognize the new boundaries of Austria, Czechoslovakia, Romania, and what became Yugoslavia. Hungary had to give up its claims to the port of Fiume and was allowed to keep an army of only 35,000 men. All Hungarian merchant ships had to be surrendered to the Allies. Hungary lost Slovakia, Transylvania, and Croatia to neighboring countries. About 3 million Magyars were separated from their fellow Hungarians. Diane Shaver Clemens

Triassic Period was a time in Earth's history that lasted from about 248 million to 213 million years ago. The period's name comes from the *Trias,* a formation of three distinct rock layers found in Germany. Geologists first identified rocks from the Triassic Period in the Trias. The Triassic was the first of the three periods that make up the Mesozoic Era, during which the dinosaurs lived.

The Triassic Period followed the *Permian extinction,* the largest extinction in Earth's history. During the Permian extinction, nearly 90 percent of all species of living things died off. Scientists do not know what caused the extinction, but it changed life on Earth so dramatically that it marked the end of the Paleozoic Era, the earliest era of life on Earth.

During the Triassic Period, the plants and animals that survived the Permian extinction spread and developed into many new forms. Reptiles became the dominant animals on land and in the sea. Reptiles of the Triassic Period included the first dinosaurs and early large marine reptiles. Both of these groups would flourish throughout the Mesozoic Era. Also during the Triassic Period, the early ancestors of modern mammals appeared. Plant life during the period included some of the earliest *conifers* (cone-bearing plants). These plants were primitive ancestors of modern pine and spruce trees. Some large amphibians survived the Permian extinction but died off before the end of the Triassic.

During the Triassic Period, most of Earth's land came together to form a giant continent called Pangaea. This arrangement kept much of the land far from the ocean, resulting in a hot, dry inland climate. Global sea levels remained low during the Triassic, and most Triassic Period rocks formed on land. The oceans did flood parts of what is now western and southern Europe, leaving marine fossils in Triassic rocks found there. Toward the end of the Triassic, a series of valleys formed along *faults* (breaks in the rock layers) between what are now eastern North America and western Africa. This faulting was the beginning of the breakup of Pangaea.

Like many geological time periods, the Triassic ended with a widespread extinction. Although it was smaller than the Permian extinction, it still ranks among the largest extinctions in Earth's history. No major groups of living things disappeared, but many species died off and were replaced by others. Steven I. Dutch

See also **Dinosaur; Mammal** (The first mammals); **Pangaea; Prehistoric animal** (The Age of Reptiles).

Triathlon is one of the most challenging endurance competitions in sports. The triathlon consists of three segments, normally conducted without a break. The segments of a typical triathlon, in order, are a 1.5-kilometer (0.9-mile) swim, a 40-kilometer (25-mile) bicycle race, and a 10-kilometer (6.2-mile) run.

As an organized sport, the triathlon began in the mid-1970's in San Diego. Members of the San Diego Track Club began adding swimming and cycling to their workouts to supplement their training runs. Soon, organized swim-bike-run events were being held at Mission Bay in San Diego. In 1978, a group of United States servicemen stationed in Hawaii created the Ironman, the forerunner of the triathlon. It consisted of an ocean swim, followed by a long bike race and run. The present distances for the triathlon segments were established in 1981.

Timothy Downs

Tribe is a term used to describe certain human social groups. Some scholars dislike the term because it lacks a precise meaning and has been applied to many widely different groups. In addition, many of the peoples called tribes consider the term offensive or inaccurate. Most prefer such terms as *ethnic group, nation,* or *people.*

The first use of the word *tribe* in English referred to the Hebrews. Until about 1000 B.C., the Hebrews were loosely organized into 12 groups, each of which traced its descent to one of the 12 sons of Jacob. These groups were called the 12 Tribes of Israel. The term *tribe* was soon extended to mean any group of families who traced themselves to a common ancestor.

Beginning in the 1400's, many European nations established colonies in Africa, Asia, and North and South America. The Europeans often described the peoples of those areas as tribes, though the groups varied greatly in their economic, political, and social organization. Some of the so-called tribes consisted of unrelated groups. Others were more accurately called nations. Most Europeans regarded the colonized peoples, whose technology was less advanced than theirs, as primitive. In time, the word *tribe* acquired the broad meaning of "primitive group."

Anthropologists have added other characteristics to the definition of tribe, though different scholars emphasize different features. Many define a tribe as a group with a sense of shared identity and ties of ancestry, customs, language, and territory. Others believe a tribe also must have some form of political organization, such as a means of making decisions for the group and of settling disputes between its members. Some scientists regard only groups without a written language as tribes. Others define a tribal economy as one that operates to produce only enough food and other necessities for members of the group, with little or no surplus. Almost no groups have all these characteristics, though the Tiv of Nigeria and the Zuñi Indians of the United States come close.

Today, many black Africans and other peoples consider the word *tribe* insulting because they believe it implies that they are primitive. Other so-called tribes consider the term inaccurate because they regard themselves as separate groups. For example, the Yoruba, Nigeria's largest ethnic group, are sometimes called a tribe. But they include the Egba, the Ife, the Oyo, and other peoples, each with their own culture and political organization.

On the other hand, several American Indian groups have struggled since the mid-1900's to gain or regain legal status as tribes. These Indians declare that they need tribal status to get the protection and benefits that have been promised them by treaties.

Some scholars also use the term *tribe* to refer to an early stage in the development of political systems, about 10,000 years ago. The tribe came after the family or band and before the appearance of more centralized and specialized governmental systems, such as chiefdoms and kingdoms. Jennie Keith

See also **Clan; Ethnic group; Nation.**

Tribune, *TRIHB yoon,* was an official in ancient Rome. There were two kinds of tribunes, *military tribunes* and *tribunes of the people.*

The first military tribunes were leaders of the soldiers that the various Roman tribes furnished to serve in the army of the republic. There were six tribunes to each *legion* (group of soldiers). They ranked next after the commander in chief. The early tribunes were appointed by *consuls* (chief government officials). Later, the people elected them. During the Roman Empire period, military tribunes lost much of their importance.

Tribunes of the people were officials elected to protect the rights of *plebeians* (commoners). According to one account, the plebeians left Rome in 494 B.C. and refused to return until they were allowed to elect their own defenders. Historians believe that at first there were only two tribunes. Later, there were four or five and then 10. They held office for a term of one year but could be reelected. The tribunes could defend citizens against unfair acts by officials. In the Senate, they could veto bills. In their own assembly, they could introduce *plebiscites* (resolutions made by the plebeians).

The tribunes were considered sacred and could not be imprisoned. They became the most powerful civil officers in the state, though their powers did not extend beyond the city limits of Rome. Largely because of the work of the tribunes, the plebeians gradually took over many of the political rights which had once belonged only to *patricians* (aristocrats). In 23 B.C., Emperor Augustus received the powers of a tribune. These powers enabled Roman emperors to add civil authority to their military power.

In the A.D. 1300's, an Italian patriot named Cola di Rienzo took the title of tribune when he led the common people in their fight for freedom from the nobles. Those who defend the common people are often called tribunes. See **Cola di Rienzo.** D. Brendan Nagle

See also **Legion; Rome, Ancient** (Government).

Tributary. See **River** (Tributaries).

Triceps. See **Arm; Muscle** (Skeletal muscles).

Triceratops, *try SEHR uh tahps,* was a large, horned, plant-eating dinosaur that lived about 65 million years ago in what is now western North America. The name *Triceratops* means *three-horned face.* The dinosaur had two horns over its eyes and one horn on its nose. *Triceratops* was about 25 feet (7.6 meters) long, stood about 9 ½ feet (2.9 meters) tall at the hips, and weighed about 8 tons (7.3 metric tons).

Triceratops had an enormous head that could grow as long as 7 feet (2.1 meters). At the front was a powerful, turtlelike beak that *Triceratops* used to pull and clip tough plants. The horn on top of the nose was short and thick. The two horns over the eyes were sharp, and they could grow up to 3 feet (0.9 meter) long. A *frill* (bony shield) extended from the back of the skull and protected the neck. Unlike the frill of most horned dinosaurs, the frill of *Triceratops* was a solid sheet of bone, with no openings to lighten it.

Thick, strong legs supported the dinosaur's heavy body. *Triceratops* had a short, heavy tail, which it may have held straight out or dragged on the ground.

With its long horns, bony frill, and large size, *Triceratops* could protect itself well against meat-eating dinosaurs, such as *Tyrannosaurus.* The ability to defend itself and to eat a variety of tough plants made *Triceratops* one of the most common plant-eating dinosaurs. These huge reptiles may have roamed in great herds across western North America. Peter Dodson

See also **Dinosaur** (picture: Dinosaurs of the Cretaceous Period).

Trichina, *trih KY nuh,* is a small roundworm that causes the disease *trichinosis,* also known as *trichinellosis.* The worm is a *parasite.* That is, it lives in and feeds on other animals.

The trichina infects human beings and other animals, especially rats, hogs, and bears. Most infections of trichinosis in the United States and Canada result from eating infected pork that has not been cooked enough. Trichinosis in rats, hogs, and bears usually results from eating garbage that contains infected meat.

The *larvae* (early form of the worms) live in microscopic *cysts* (sacs) in the muscles of the animals that they infect. They usually live in the animal's chest and neck muscles.

If an animal infected by the larvae is allowed to live, the cysts eventually harden, and the larvae die. But sometimes infected animals are killed for meat. In such cases, the larvae can be killed by thoroughly cooking or freezing the meat. However, if the larvae are not killed and the meat is eaten, the larvae are freed from the cysts during digestion. The larvae attach themselves to the intestine of the individual who eats the meat. They become adult worms in about 3 or 4 days. The largest are only about ¼ inch (6 millimeters) long.

The adult females burrow into the wall of the intestine, where they produce large numbers of larvae. The larvae enter the blood and are carried to many parts of the body. They eventually leave the blood and form new cysts in the muscles.

Some people carry trichina worms in their bodies for many years and never have severe symptoms. But in other people, the worms irritate the intestine and cause diarrhea, nausea, and vomiting. When they pass through the blood, fever, headache, and muscular pain occur. After they reach the muscles, they cause swelling of the face and other parts and bleeding under the skin. The worms may form their cysts in the *diaphragm* (chief muscle used for breathing) and make breathing painful. The disease occasionally is fatal.

The prevention of trichinosis involves several steps. Garbage containing meat scraps may carry trichina worms, so it should be cooked before it is fed to hogs. Meat packers should freeze pork to kill any worms the pork may carry. Finally, cooks should be sure the central section of pork is held at a temperature of at least 137 °F (58 °C) for 5 minutes or more. David F. Oetinger

Scientific classification. The trichina is in the trichina family, Trichinellidae. Its scientific name is *Trichinella spiralis.*

Trichoptera. See **Insect** (table).

Trier, *treer* (pop. 100,234), is the oldest city in Germany. It lies on the Moselle River in the state of Rhineland-Palatinate, near Germany's border with Luxembourg. For the location of Trier, see **Germany** (political map).

Trier is the center and market area of the Moselle wine district. The city makes leather goods, steel products, and textiles. Trier is also an important railroad junction. The University of Trier is chief among several institutes of higher education in the city.

Trier was founded by the Romans, probably around 15 B.C. It was named for the Treveri, a Celtic people of ancient Gaul. A number of Roman monuments, including an amphitheater, baths, and the celebrated *Porta Nigra* (fortified north gate), stand in the city. A large building known as the Basilica also dates from Roman times.

The city has been an important center of Roman Catholic tradition since the Middle Ages. It has a number of beautiful examples of church architecture, including the gothic Church of Our Lady and the baroque St. Paulin church.

Trier came under French control in 1794. It was awarded to Prussia by the Congress of Vienna in 1814-1815. In World War I (1914-1918) and World War II (1939-1945), bombs damaged much of the city. Trier's historic buildings have since been restored. John W. Boyer

Trieste, *tree EHST* or *tree EHS tee* (pop. 211,184), is a city in northeastern Italy. It lies on the Gulf of Venice at the northern end of the Adriatic Sea. For the location of Trieste, see **Italy** (political map).

Trieste's free port, which does not tax imported cargo, handles trade between the Mediterranean and central Europe. Products made in the Trieste area include clothing, iron and steel, machinery, and paint. Tourists visit the city's castles and other historic buildings.

Trieste was a Roman colony from the 100's B.C. to about A.D. 500. Austria gained control of the area in the late 1300's. Treaties following World War I (1914-1918) gave Trieste to Italy.

When World War II ended in 1945, both Italy and Yugoslavia claimed Trieste and the surrounding region. The United Nations divided the area into two zones. United States and British troops occupied Zone A, which included the city of Trieste and an area to the north. Yugoslav forces occupied Zone B, an area south of the city. An agreement in 1954 gave Italy control of the city and most of Zone A and Yugoslavia control of Zone B. In 1975, Italy and Yugoslavia signed a treaty that made this arrangement permanent. Pamela Ballinger

Triggerfish is a type of colorful fish that lives in coastal waters of warm and tropical seas. Most triggerfish are less than 1 $\frac{1}{2}$ feet (46 centimeters) long and have a roundish body with flattened sides.

The first three spines of a triggerfish's dorsal fin are specialized. The fish uses these spines to enlarge its body when threatened. The first spine is long and strong. It can be locked in place by the second, smaller spine, which lifts up and acts as a "trigger." When frightened, the fish hides in a crack or crevice and locks its spine. The fish then cannot be removed by predators. It returns to its normal size by releasing its second spine.

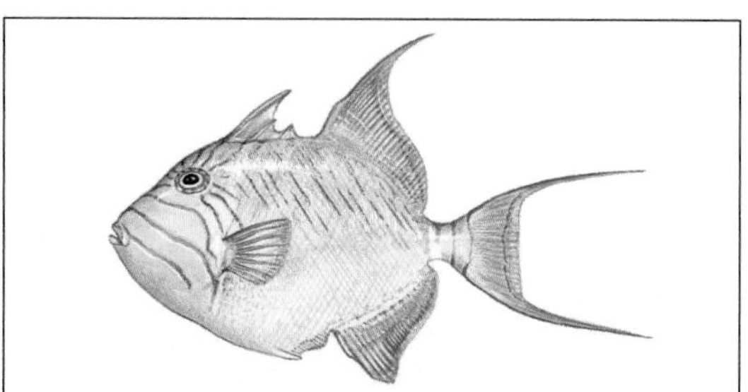

WORLD BOOK illustration by John F. Eggert

The triggerfish lives in warm coastal waters. It is a colorful fish with a roundish body and flattened sides.

Triggerfish are closely related to filefish. There are approximately 120 species of triggerfish and filefish. Sixteen species of triggerfish and filefish live along the Atlantic Coast of the United States. Three species of triggerfish live along the mainland Pacific Coast. The state fish of Hawaii, the Humuhumu-nukunuku-a-pua'a, is a triggerfish. John E. McCosker

Scientific classification. Triggerfish and filefish belong to the family Balistidae.

See also **Fish** (picture: Fish of coral reefs).

Triglyceride is one of the major fatty substances in the blood. Another is cholesterol. High blood levels of triglycerides are often associated with high cholesterol levels, a primary cause of heart disease. An extremely high level of triglycerides in the blood also increases the risk of *pancreatitis* (inflammation of the pancreas).

Each triglyceride molecule consists of one molecule of glycerol combined with three molecules of fatty acids. Triglycerides are consumed in food. During digestion, they break down into separate molecules of fatty acids and glycerol. These molecules may be used by cells for energy, or they may be recombined into triglycerides and stored as fat for later use.

In adults, a triglyceride level of less than 200 milligrams per deciliter of blood is considered desirable. Higher triglyceride levels are often associated with an increased risk of heart disease. People who have triglyceride levels of more than 1,000 milligrams per deciliter are at high risk of pancreatitis.

Several factors lead to elevated triglyceride levels. They include alcohol, stress, weight gain, certain medications, and a diet high in carbohydrates. People can lower their triglyceride levels by reducing the amount of calories and fat in their diet and by exercising regularly. Neil J. Stone

See also **C-reactive protein; Cholesterol; Fat.**

Trigonometry, *TRIHG uh NAHM uh tree,* is a branch of mathematics that deals with the relationships between the sides and angles of triangles. Trigonometry also provides methods of measuring these sides and angles. It has applications in such theoretical sciences as physics and astronomy, and in such practical fields as surveying and navigation. The word *trigonometry* comes from two Greek words meaning *triangle* and *measure.*

There are two kinds of trigonometry—*plane trigonometry* and *spherical trigonometry.* Plane trigonometry is used to determine the unknown sides and angles of triangles that lie in a plane. Spherical trigonometry can be used to find the unknown sides and angles of triangles that lie on a spherical surface.

Both types of trigonometry are based on relationships between the six parts—three sides and three angles—of any triangle. Because of these relationships, in almost all cases any three parts whose measures are known can be used to find the measures of the other three parts, if at least one of the known parts is a side. It is necessary to know the length of at least one side because the corresponding sides of two triangles may be unequal even though all their corresponding angles are equal.

Trigonometry is based on a type of geometry called *Euclidean geometry.* Euclidean geometry was developed from a set of assumptions spelled out about 300 B.C. by the Greek mathematician Euclid (see **Geometry** [Types of geometry]). Spherical trigonometry was first described about A.D. 150 in a work by Ptolemy of Alexandria called the *Almagest.* Plane trigonometry was developed in the 1400's by German mathematician Johann Müller, who was also known as Regiomontanus.

Plane trigonometry

To understand trigonometry, it is necessary first to study the properties of *similar triangles.* Two triangles are said to be similar when all the corresponding angles of the triangles are equal. For example, the triangles *GHI* and *JKL* shown below are similar if angle G = angle J, angle H = angle K, and angle I = angle L. The corresponding sides of similar triangles need not be equal. However, they are in proportion. Therefore, if triangles

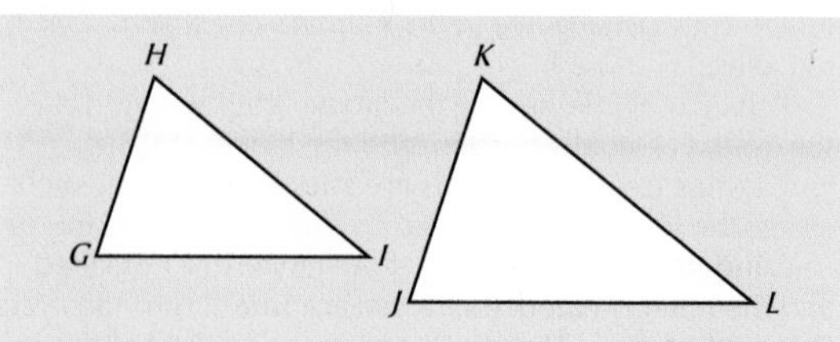

GHI and *JKL* are similar, the ratio *GH:GI* will equal the ratio *JK:JL*. Suppose that $GH = 3$ units, $GI = 5$ units, and $JK = 9$ units. Then $JL = 15$ units, because $\frac{3}{5} = \frac{9}{15}$.

Right triangles. Trigonometry is largely derived from the study of similar *right triangles.* A right triangle is any triangle in which one of the angles equals 90°. The three angles in any triangle total 180°. Therefore, every right triangle has two acute angles that total 90°. If we know one of the acute angles, we can find the other one by subtracting the known angle from 90°. In addition, if an acute angle of one right triangle equals an acute angle of a second right triangle, then the two triangles are similar. In the right triangles *ABC* and *DEF* below, for example, angle *C* and angle *F* are right angles and angle *A* equals angle *D*. Therefore, the two triangles are similar. And because they are similar, their sides must be in proportion, so that $\frac{a}{c} = \frac{d}{f}$, $\frac{b}{c} = \frac{e}{f}$, and $\frac{a}{b} = \frac{d}{e}$.

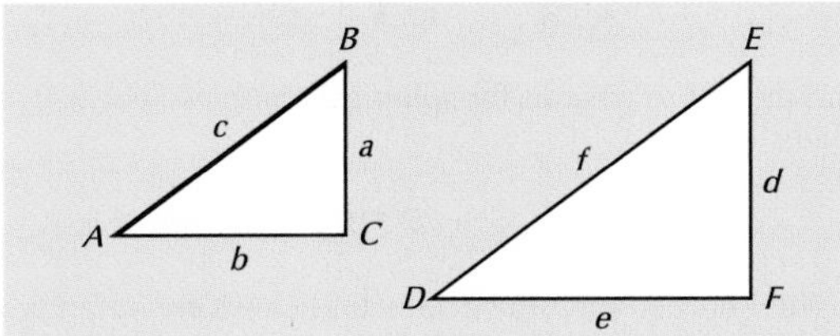

The ratios that make up these proportions will equal the ratios for the corresponding sides of any right triangle that has an acute angle equal to angle *A*. Each of the possible ratios between the sides of a right triangle has been given a special name. In the illustration above, for example, the ratio $\frac{a}{c}$ is called the *sine* of angle *A*, and is written sin *A*. The ratio $\frac{b}{c}$ is called the *cosine* of angle *A*. It is written cos *A*. The ratio $\frac{a}{b}$ is called the *tangent* of angle *A*, and is written tan *A*. Mathematicians have compiled tables that contain the values of these three ratios for all the possible angles of a right triangle. Such tables are programmed into scientific calculators.

Trigonometric tables also include three rarely used ratios called the *secant, cosecant,* and *cotangent.* The secant of angle *A*, written sec *A*, is $\frac{c}{b}$. The cosecant of angle *A*, written csc *A*, is $\frac{c}{a}$. The angle's cotangent, written cot *A*, is $\frac{b}{a}$.

Following are formal definitions of the six trigonometric ratios:

sine	=	$\frac{\text{side opposite the angle}}{\text{hypotenuse}}$
cosine	=	$\frac{\text{side adjacent to the angle}}{\text{hypotenuse}}$
tangent	=	$\frac{\text{side opposite the angle}}{\text{side adjacent to the angle}}$
secant	=	$\frac{\text{hypotenuse}}{\text{side adjacent to the angle}}$
cosecant	=	$\frac{\text{hypotenuse}}{\text{side opposite the angle}}$
cotangent	=	$\frac{\text{side adjacent to the angle}}{\text{side opposite the angle}}$

The trigonometric ratios make it possible to find all three sides of the right triangle *ABC* if we know the measure of one of the acute angles and the length of any side. For instance, if angle *A* is 30°, then we can use a table or calculator to determine that $\sin A = \frac{1}{2}$. And if $\sin A = \frac{1}{2}$, then $\frac{a}{c} = \frac{1}{2}$. Thus, if side *c* is 9 units long, then side *a* must be $4\frac{1}{2}$ units long.

This method has many applications. For example, suppose you are standing at point *O* on the bank of a river and looking at a tree at point *N* on the opposite shore (see the figure below). You can use this method to find the distance from *O* to *N* without crossing the river. First, place a marker at point *O*. Then, walk along a line at right angles to the line *NO* until you come to a convenient point *M*, thus forming the right triangle *MNO*. Next, measure the length of the line *MO*. If *MO* is, say, 75 units long, and angle *M* measures 40°, you can use a calculator or table to determine that tan 40° = 0.8391. Because $\tan M = NO/MO$, $NO = (MO)(\tan 40°) = (75 \text{ units})(0.8391) = 62.93$ units.

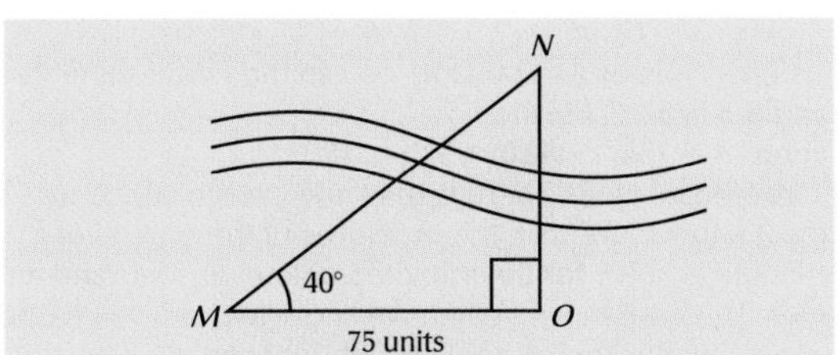

The law of sines. For some applications, you must determine the unknown parts of a triangle that is not a right triangle. If you know two angles and one side of such a triangle, you can find the other two sides and the other angle by using the *law of sines.* This law says:

If we know angle *A* and angle *B*, we can determine an-

For a triangle *ABC* with sides *a, b,* and *c* (see figure below),

$$\frac{a}{\sin A} = \frac{b}{\sin B} = \frac{c}{\sin C}$$

gle *C*, because angle $C = 180° - (\text{angle } A + \text{angle } B)$. If we know side *c*, we can then find sides *a* and *b*, because from the law of sines we know that

$$b = \frac{c(\sin B)}{\sin C} \quad \text{and } a = \frac{c(\sin A)}{\sin C}$$

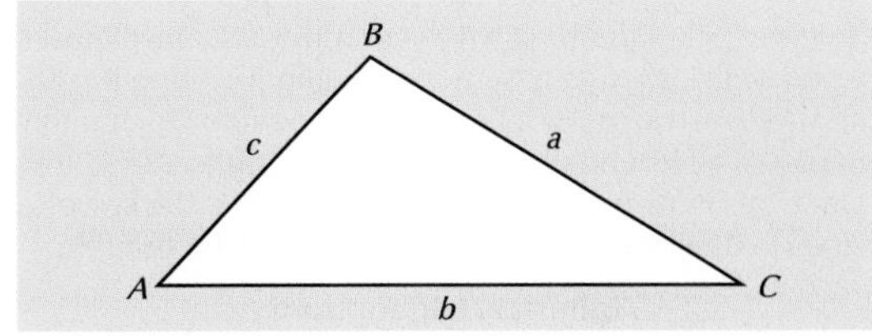

The law of cosines. If we know two sides of a triangle that is not a right triangle, and the angle between them, the remaining parts of the triangle can be found by using the *law of cosines.* The law of cosines states:

For a triangle *ABC* with sides *a, b,* and *c,*

$$c^2 = a^2 + b^2 - 2ab(\cos C).$$

For example, if we know sides *a* and *b* and angle *C*, we can find side *c* by the law of cosines. We can then use the law of sines to find the other two angles. Thus, if side $a = 5$ units, side $b = 7$ units, and angle $C = 52°$, we can solve for the unknown side and angles of the triangle. Using a table or a calculator, we can determine that $\cos 52° = 0.6157$. We can then use the law of cosines to solve for c^2:

$$c^2 = [(25 + 49) - (70 \times 0.6157)] \\ = 30.90$$

Then, we calculate that $c = \sqrt{30.901} = 5.56$ units. Next, because we know from the law of sines that

$\frac{b}{\sin B} = \frac{c}{\sin C}$, we find that $(\sin B)\,c = b(\sin C)$.

Therefore,

$$\sin B = \frac{b(\sin C)}{c} = \frac{7(\sin 52°)}{5.56} = 0.9922.$$

Using a table or a calculator, we can then determine that angle $B = 82.8°$. Finally,
angle $A = 180° - (82.8° + 52°) = 45.2°$.

A special case. There is only one case in which we must know more than the measures of three parts of a triangle to solve for the triangle's unknown sides and angles. This case occurs when we know two sides and one angle, but the known angle is not between the two known sides. In such a case, the triangle could take two possible forms. In the figure below, for example, if we know only angle *G* and sides *g* and *i*, then the triangle may be either triangle *GHI* or triangle *GHI′*.

The two possibilities for the angle opposite side *i* are *GIH* and *GI′H*. These angles are *supplementary*—that is, they total 180°. Sines of supplementary angles are equal,

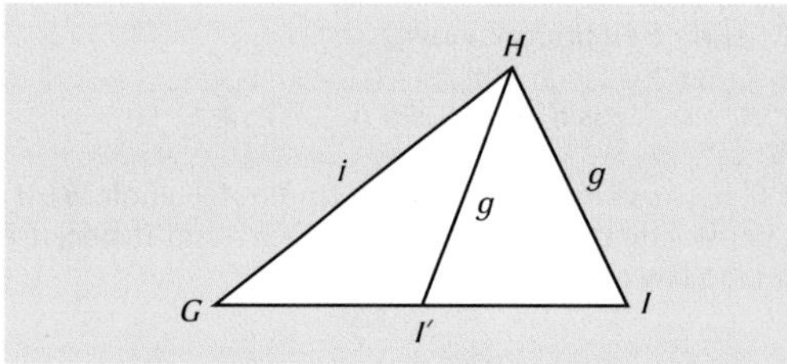

so sin angle *GIH* = sin angle *GI′H*. Thus, we cannot use the law of sines to determine which angle is part of the unknown triangle. To solve the triangle, we must know whether the triangle has an obtuse angle or whether all its angles are acute. If it has an obtuse angle, the triangle is *GHI′*. If all its angles are acute, the triangle is *GHI*. Once this information is known, we can use the law of sines to determine the remaining parts of the triangle.

Spherical trigonometry

On the surface of a sphere, the shortest path between two points is an arc of the circle that contains those two points and whose center is the center of the sphere. Such a circle is called a *great circle*. On a globe, the circles of longitude, which pass through the North Pole and the South Pole, are great circles. Arcs of circles are measured in degrees. A complete circle measures 360 degrees. The circumference of a great circle on Earth is about 24,860 miles (40,008 kilometers). Thus, each degree of arc of a great circle on Earth extends about 69.06 miles (111.13 kilometers). The angle between two great circles is the angle between their *tangents* at the point of intersection. A tangent is a line that touches an arc at one point only, without intersecting it. A *spherical triangle* is formed by the intersections of three great circles.

Because both the angles and the sides of a spherical triangle are measured in degrees, the formulas of spherical trigonometry differ somewhat from the formulas of plane trigonometry. Also, spherical triangles differ from plane triangles in that the angles of a spherical triangle always total more than 180°. But spherical trigonometry uses the same tables that plane trigonometry uses.

The basic formulas in spherical trigonometry are the law of sines for spherical triangles, which reads:

$$\frac{\sin a}{\sin A} = \frac{\sin b}{\sin B} = \frac{\sin c}{\sin C}$$

and the law of cosines for spherical triangles, which reads:

$$\cos c = (\cos a)(\cos b) + (\sin a)(\sin b)(\cos C).$$

The figure below shows how these laws are applied. The distance from New York City to Paris is calculated

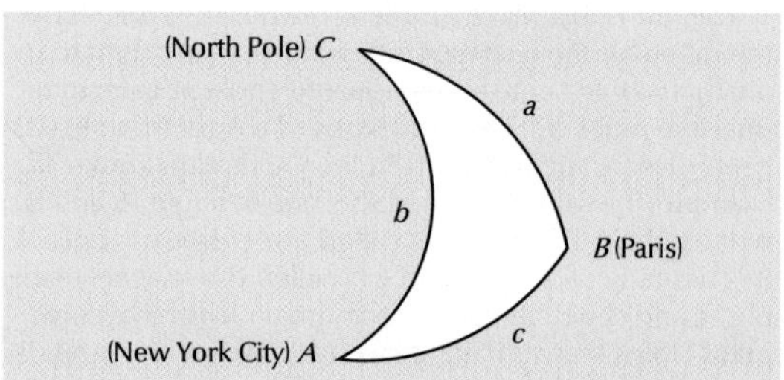

by drawing a spherical triangle whose vertices are New York City, Paris, and the North Pole. Because the longitude of Paris is 2.20° east and the longitude of New York City is 73.58° west, angle *C* is 2.20° + 73.58°, or 75.78°. Because the latitude of Paris is 48.51° north, arc *a* is 90° − 48.51°, or 41.49°. Because the latitude of New York City is 40.40° north, arc *b* is 90° − 40.40°, or 49.60°. By the law of cosines for spherical triangles, the measure of arc *c* can be found by using the equation:

$$\begin{aligned} \cos c &= (\cos 41.49)(\cos 49.60) + \\ &\quad (\sin 41.49)(\sin 49.60)(\cos 75.78) \\ &= (.74907)(.64812) + (.66249)(.76154)(.24565) \\ &= .60942 \end{aligned}$$

We can use a calculator to determine that .60942 is the cosine of a 52.45° arc. Thus, arc *c* is 52.45°, and the distance from New York City to Paris is 69.06 miles (111.13 kilometers) × 52.45, or 3,622 miles (5,829 kilometers).

To find the direction in which Paris lies in relation to New York City, we find the measure of angle *A* by using the law of sines for spherical triangles:

$$\frac{\sin a}{\sin A} = \frac{\sin c}{\sin C}$$
$$(\sin A)(\sin c) = (\sin a)(\sin C)$$
$$\sin A = \frac{(\sin a)(\sin C)}{\sin c}$$
$$= \frac{(.66249)(.96936)}{.79282}$$
$$= .81000.$$

We can use a calculator to determine that angle *A* is 54.1°. From New York City, therefore, the direction to Paris is 54.1° east of north. But the angle between the direction to Paris and the direction to the North Pole changes as a person travels along the great circle from New York City to Paris. Thus, a person cannot reach Paris by traveling continuously in a direction 54.1° east of north. Roger Cooke

Related articles in *World Book* include:

Algebra	Geometry	Navigation	Triangle
Angle	Mathematics	Surveying	

Trillion is a million million. One trillion is written 1,000,000,000,000. It has 12 zeros. This definition is standard in the United States and is used throughout *World Book*. In some European countries and elsewhere, 1 trillion can mean 1 million times 1 million times 1 million, or 1,000,000,000,000,000,000. That number is equivalent to 1 quintillion in the United States. See also **Decimal system** (The decimal system and number words).

Trillium, *TRIHL ee uhm,* is a wildflower that grows in damp, wooded places in North America and Asia. There are about 40 kinds. The flowers have three sepals, three petals, and six stamens. Each stem bears one flower and three leaves. Trilliums are often called *wake-robins* because some kinds bloom when the robins return north. The well-known *white trillium* grows from New England to the Carolinas and west to Minnesota. The *painted trillium* is the most colorful. Its white flowers have deep pink or purple stripes. It grows in much of eastern North America. See also **Flower** (picture: Flowers of woodlands and forests). Anton A. Reznicek

Scientific classification. Trilliums belong to the lily family, Liliaceae. The white trillium is *Trillium grandiflorum;* the painted trillium is *T. undulatum.*

Trilobite, *TRY luh byt,* was a prehistoric sea animal. It lived throughout the *Paleozoic Era,* which lasted from about 544 million years ago to about 248 million years ago. Trilobites lived in all parts of the world, and scientists have identified over 10,000 species from fossils. A soft shell covered much of the animal's body. Most trilobites were under 4 inches (10 centimeters) long. Two grooves divided the animal's shell lengthwise into three *lobes* (sections). The name *trilobite* means *three lobes.* The body had three main parts: the head, the thorax, and the tail. The thorax had many segments, each bearing legs. The trilobite breathed through gills on the legs. See also **Fossil** (pictures). Keith Stewart Thomson

Scientific classification. Trilobites belong to the phylum Arthropoda.

Trimble, David (1944-), became first minister of the government of Northern Ireland in 1998. The first minister and deputy first minister, who have equal power, lead Northern Ireland's 108-member legislative assembly. From 1995 to 2005, Trimble served as the leader of the Ulster Unionist Party (UUP), which favors Northern Ireland's continued union with the United Kingdom.

In 2001, Trimble resigned as first minister to protest a refusal by the Irish Republican Army (IRA) to disarm. For many years, the IRA had used violence in an effort to unite Northern Ireland with the Republic of Ireland. After the IRA began disarming later in 2001, Trimble was reelected to the post. In 2002, the United Kingdom suspended Northern Ireland's government.

Trimble shared the 1998 Nobel Peace Prize with John Hume, the leader of the Social Democratic and Labour Party (SDLP). The SDLP favors Northern Ireland's union with the Republic of Ireland achieved through a democratic process of consent. The two men won the prize for their efforts to bring peace to Northern Ireland. They participated with other political leaders from the United Kingdom and Ireland in talks that concluded with the signing of a peace agreement in April 1998. The agreement established a legislative assembly for Northern Ireland that would control many local affairs. Trimble was elected to the new assembly and became its leader.

William David Trimble was born on Oct. 15, 1944, in Bangor, Northern Ireland. He received a law degree from Queen's University, Belfast, and taught law there from 1968 to 1990. Trimble served in the British House of Commons from 1990 to 2005. Paul E. Gallis

See also **Northern Ireland** (Government; Recent developments); **Ulster Unionist Party.**

Trinidad and Tobago, *TRIHN ih dad* and *tuh BAY goh,* is a country that consists of two islands in the West Indies. It lies in the Caribbean Sea, near the northeast coast of South America. Trinidad, the larger island, is 7 miles (11 kilometers) east of Venezuela. Tobago is about 20 miles (32 kilometers) northeast of Trinidad.

Trinidad contains about 95 percent of the land area of Trinidad and Tobago, and approximately 95 percent of the country's people live there. Port-of-Spain, on Trinidad, is the nation's capital, largest city, and chief port.

Government. Trinidad and Tobago is a republic. A prime minister, who is usually the leader of the majority party in Parliament, serves as the head of the government. The prime minister appoints a Cabinet of any number of members for assistance. A president, elected by the Parliament, serves as head of state. The Parliament consists of a 31-member Senate and a 36-member House of Representatives. Leading government officials appoint the senators. The people elect the members of the House of Representatives. The major political parties are the National Alliance for Reconstruction (NAR), the

Facts in brief

Capital: Port-of-Spain.
Official language: English.
Area: 1,981 mi^2 (5,130 km^2). *Coastline*—292 mi (470 km).
Elevation: *Highest*—Mount Aripo, 3,085 ft (940 m). *Lowest*—sea level.
Population: *Estimated 2006 population*—1,315,000; density, 664 per mi^2 (256 per km^2); distribution, 74 percent urban, 26 percent rural. *2000 census*—1,262,366.
Chief products: Asphalt, oil, sugar.
National anthem: "Forged from the Love of Liberty."
Flag: A black stripe, bordered by white stripes, runs across a red field from the upper left to the lower right corner. See **Flag** (picture: Flags of the Americas).
Money: *Basic unit*—Trinidad and Tobago dollar. One hundred cents equal one dollar.

People's National Movement (PNM), and the United National Congress (UNC).

People. Over 40 percent of the country's people have black African ancestry. About 40 percent are descendants of people from India. People of mixed European and black African ancestry, plus groups of Europeans and Chinese, form the rest of the population.

English is the country's official language, but French, Spanish, and Hindi are also spoken. Many people speak *Trinidad English,* a form of English with French and Spanish influences. Almost all of the adults can read and write. For the literacy rate, see **Literacy** (table: Literacy rates). The law requires all children to go to school for six years. Roman Catholics form the largest religious group, followed by Hindus and Anglicans.

Many people in the country play native musical instruments called *pans,* which are made from empty oil drums. Trinidad is the home of a form of folk music called *calypso* and of the *limbo* dance (see **Calypso**).

Land and climate. Tropical forests and fertile flatlands cover much of Trinidad. A mountain range extends east and west across the northern area, and hills rise in the central and southern sections. Tobago has a central mountain ridge and scenic beaches.

Trinidad and Tobago has a hot, humid climate. Temperatures range from 64 °F (18 °C) to 92 °F (33 °C). The average annual temperature is 78 °F (26 °C) on Trinidad and slightly lower on Tobago. Annual rainfall ranges from about 50 inches (127 centimeters) on southwestern Trinidad to more than 100 inches (254 centimeters) in the mountains of Tobago.

Trinidad and Tobago

- International boundary
- Road
- Railroad
- Swamp
- National capital
- Other city or town
- Elevation above sea level

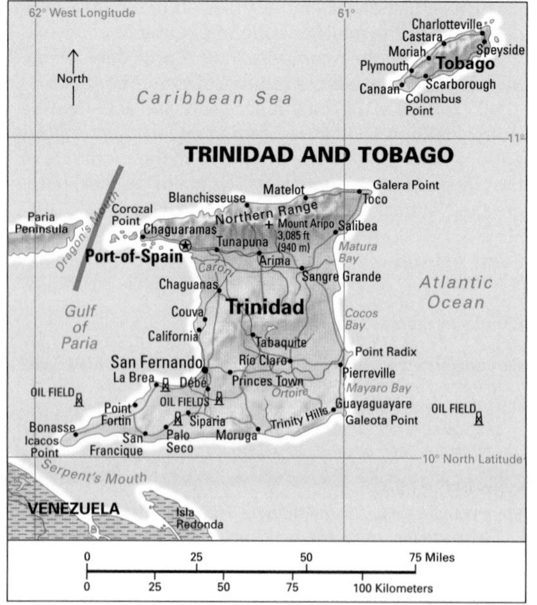

WORLD BOOK maps

Economy of Trinidad and Tobago is based mainly on the production of natural gas and oil and on oil refining. Natural gas is the country's most valuable mined product. The nation produces about 50 million barrels of crude oil annually and imports yet more for refining. Gas and refined petroleum account for about two-thirds of the country's export income. Pitch Lake, on Trinidad, is the world's chief source of natural *asphalt* (a tarlike substance that is used to make paving materials).

Other major industries of Trinidad and Tobago include tourism and agriculture. Sugar, the chief export crop, is also used to produce molasses and rum.

Trinidad and Tobago has about 4,000 miles (6,400 kilometers) of roads, and an airport operates on each island. The country has two daily newspapers, a television station, and two major radio stations.

History. Arawak and Carib Indians lived on Trinidad and Tobago before Europeans arrived. Christopher Columbus claimed Trinidad for Spain in 1498, during his third voyage to the New World. Spain set up a permanent settlement on Trinidad in 1592, but the population did not begin to grow rapidly until 1783. That year, Spain offered land grants on Trinidad to Roman Catholic settlers willing to develop the island's economy. Many planters of French ancestry arrived from Haiti and other nearby islands to claim land. They set up thriving sugar cane plantations, and the island prospered. The British captured Trinidad in 1797 and ruled it for over 150 years.

In 1632, the Dutch settled on Tobago. Britain, France, and the Netherlands fought for possession of the island until 1814, when the British took control of it. Over the years, thousands of black slaves had been brought from Africa to work on the islands' plantations. Labor shortages occurred after the British abolished slavery in 1833, and many workers came to the islands from India.

In 1889, Trinidad and Tobago became one colony under British rule. During the Great Depression of the 1930's, the colony suffered severe economic setbacks. The people began to demand a greater voice in their government. The British allowed a gradual increase in self-government during the 1940's and 1950's, and the colony became an independent nation in 1962.

In the early 1970's, black-power supporters protested against widespread unemployment and what they considered social and economic inequality in Trinidad and Tobago. Violent demonstrations broke out, and the government twice declared a state of emergency. Racial tensions eased in the mid-1970's, but unemployment continued to be a major problem in the country.

In the early 1970's, there was a political movement on Tobago to make the island independent from the rest of the country. In 1980, the national government allowed a local governing council to be established on Tobago. The council has some control of local affairs.

After Trinidad and Tobago became independent in 1962, Eric Williams, founder and leader of the PNM, became the nation's first prime minister. The PNM controlled the government until 1986, when the NAR gained power. In 1991, the voters returned control of the government to the PNM. Following elections in 1995, Basdeo Panday, head of the UNC, became the first person of Indian descent to serve as prime minister of Trinidad

Hutchison Library

Port-of-Spain is the chief port of Trinidad and Tobago. Inter-island vessels and oceangoing ships dock at its busy harbor.

and Tobago. In a 2001 election, the PNM and UNC each won an equal number of seats in the House of Representatives. The country's president appointed PNM leader Patrick Manning as prime minister, but the UNC called for a new election. In 2002, an election was held in which the PNM gained control of the House, and Manning remained prime minister. Kathryn R. Dungy

See also **Port-of-Spain; Naipaul, V. S.**

Trinity, *TRIHN uh tee,* is a term used to express the belief that in the one God there are three Divine Persons—the Father, the Son, and the Holy Spirit (or Holy Ghost). The idea is based on various passages in the New Testament. Belief in Father, Son, and Holy Spirit was defined by early general councils of the Christian church. The Council of Nicaea in 325 and the Council of Constantinople in 381 declared that the Son is of the same essence as the Father, and that the three Persons are one God. The East and West branches of the church later disagreed as to how the Holy Spirit proceeds from the other Divine Persons. The Eastern Church held that the Son comes from the Father, and that the Spirit comes from the Father through the Son. The Western Church held that the Spirit comes from Father and Son together. A special activity has been ascribed to each of the Persons. The Father creates, the Son became human, and the Spirit makes holy. Joseph M. Hallman

See also **Nicene councils; Arianism.**

Tripe is a meat that comes from the stomach walls of cattle. Such animals have stomachs that consist of four compartments. Tripe is produced from the first two compartments. Most tripe is white, and the meat has little taste. Tripe is sold canned, fresh, frozen, or pickled. People bake, broil, or fry tripe, or cook it in water. It is sometimes used to make sausage. Donald H. Beermann

Triple Alliance. See **Bismarck, Otto von** (Bismarck's diplomacy); **World War I** (A system of military alliances).

Triple Entente. See **World War I** (A system of military alliances).

Triple jump is a track and field event in which an athlete leaps as far as he or she can in three continuous jumps. The event, once called the *hop, step, and jump,* requires a blend of speed, strength, and technique.

In the triple jump, the athlete sprints down a runway to a take-off point, usually a wooden board 8 inches (20 centimeters) wide. The athlete then jumps forward on one foot, lands on the same foot, jumps forward again, lands on the other foot, and then leaps into a sand-filled landing pit. The jump is measured from the front edge of the take-off point to the mark in the sand nearest that point. If the jumper's foot crosses the front edge of the take-off point as he or she jumps, the attempt is a foul. Each jumper usually gets six attempts. The winner is determined by the longest fair jump. Michael Takaha

See also **Track and field** (Jumping events; table); **Olympic Games** (table: Track and field).

Triplets. See **Multiple birth.**

Tripod fish is a deep-sea animal named for its unusual posture. The fish has elongated *pectoral fins* (fins behind the gill openings). It uses those two fins and its tail fin to rest on the muddy ocean floor. In this position, the fish resembles a tripod or three-legged stool. Some tripod fish are called *spider fish* because their fins are even longer and float above their heads like spider legs.

Tripod fish live in all oceans, beneath both tropical and cool seas, at depths of 820 to 18,400 feet (250 to 5,600 meters). Like most other creatures that live in the dark depths of the sea, tripod fish have extremely small eyes that are directed upward. They also have flattened heads, a small mouth, and a body covered with smooth scales. Adults grow to be 5 to 14 inches (13 to 36 centimeters) in length. Tripod fish are *hermaphrodites* (pronounced *hur MAF ruh dyts*)—that is, animals with both male and female reproductive organs. They feed mainly on *plankton* (small water organisms). John E. McCosker

Scientific classification. The tripod fish belongs to the family Ipnopidae. They make up the genus *Bathypterois.*

See also **Deep sea; Fish** (picture: Fish of the deep ocean).

Tripoli, *TRIHP uh lee* (pop. 175,000), is the second largest city in Lebanon. Only Beirut has more people. Tripoli's name in Arabic is *Tarabulus.* A seaport and industrial center, Tripoli lies on Lebanon's northwest coast, at the eastern end of the Mediterranean Sea (see **Lebanon** [map]). The city's chief industries include trade; tourism and other services; petroleum refining; the manufacture of furniture, soap, and textiles; and sponge fishing. Citrus fruits are grown in and around Tripoli.

The Castle of St. Gilles, built by crusaders before A.D. 1200, overlooks the city. The Teylan Mosque, a Tripoli landmark built in the traditional Arab style, dates from 1336. Tripoli's name, which means *Three Cities,* is related to its founding. Colonists from three Phoenician cities—Aradus, Sidon, and Tyre—founded the city in the 300's B.C. Elsa Marston Harik and Iliya Harik

Tripoli, *TRIHP uh lee* (pop. 990,697), is Libya's capital and largest city. Its Arabic name is *Tarabulus.* Tripoli is in northern Libya, along the Mediterranean Sea (see **Libya** [map]). The city has a fine harbor and is a shipping center. It is also a trading center for a farming region. Tripoli's industries include oil refining, food processing, and the production of such handicrafts as woven carpets and leather goods. The old city center of Tripoli is surrounded by stone walls. It features a Roman arch that dates from the A.D. 100's and a palace and garden built during the 1500's. Since the 1970's, many modern high-rise buildings have been constructed in the city.

Tripoli was founded by Phoenicians, probably in the 600's B.C. It was originally called Oea. It was later renamed *Tripoli,* meaning *Three Cities.* The name refers to the ancient district of Tripoli, which included three cities—Oea, Leptis Magna (now Lebda), and Sabratha. From the mid-1500's to 1911, Tripoli was part of the Ottoman Empire—which was centered in what is now Turkey—and the capital of the surrounding province of Tripolitania. But the local rulers in Tripoli had almost complete freedom during much of the period. Attacks by Barbary *corsairs* (sea raiders) of North Africa on U.S. shipping led to a war between the United States and Tripoli in 1801. Italy conquered Tripoli in 1911 and ruled it until World War II (1939-1945). Kenneth J. Perkins

See also **Barbary States; Jefferson, Thomas** (War with Tripoli).

Tristan, or Tristram, was a legendary medieval knight whose love affair with Princess Isolt (Isolde) became one of the most famous love stories ever. Accounts of Tristan's love usually include several key episodes. He defeats the giant Morholt (Morold) but suffers a serious wound, which is healed by the queen of Ireland and her daughter Isolt. He accidentally drinks a love potion that makes him love Isolt, the intended bride of his uncle, King Mark of Cornwall. Tristan and Isolt, enchanted by the potion, deceive Mark and live together in the forest.

The story of Tristan originated in ancient Celtic lore. It eventually merged into the legend of King Arthur, with Tristan as a knight of the Round Table. By the 1100's, the tale was popular in French and German poetry. Gottfried von Strassburg's poem *Tristan und Isolde* (about 1210) became the basis of Richard Wagner's opera *Tristan und Isolde* (1865). Edmund Reiss

Triticale, *TRIHT uh KAY lee,* is a grain produced by crossbreeding wheat and rye. It has a high nutritional content because it contains more usable protein than either wheat or rye. The plant stands from 18 to 41 inches (45 to 105 centimeters) tall and has 6 to 10 long, narrow leaves. The head consists of many spikelets, each of which holds three to five kernels of grain.

Botanists first crossbred wheat and rye in 1876. This process yielded a hybrid plant that could not produce seeds. In 1937, scientists discovered that treating seedlings of wheat-rye crosses with a chemical called *colchicine* made the plants fertile. By the 1950's, many countries had triticale breeding programs.

Triticale may become an important food in countries not suited for wheat production. Some varieties can grow in cold climates and in sandy or acid soils. Others resist disease-causing rust fungi better than wheat.

Robert D. Wych

Scientific classification. Triticale is in the grass family, Poaceae or Gramineae. It forms the genus *Triticosecale.*

Tritium, *TRIHT ee uhm,* is a hydrogen isotope used in the release of nuclear energy through fusion, as in the hydrogen bomb. It is three times as heavy as ordinary hydrogen. The name *tritium* comes from the Latin *tri,* meaning *three.* Tritium decays to form helium; half decays in about 12 years. See also **Hydrogen; Nuclear weapon** (Thermonuclear weapons). Clark L. Fields

Triton is the largest moon of Neptune. It is 1,682 miles (2,707 kilometers) in diameter, almost exactly $\frac{7}{9}$ as wide as Earth's moon. Triton is unusual in two ways: (1) it orbits Neptune in the direction opposite that of the planet's rotation, and (2) it is one of only two satellites in the solar system known to have an atmosphere that is dense enough to have weather. Saturn's moon Titan is the other one. Triton was discovered in 1846, only three weeks after the discovery of Neptune.

Triton's orbital direction, known since the discovery of the satellite, indicates that Triton did not form at or near its present location. That is, it did not condense from the dust and gas left over from the formation of Neptune. If it had done so, it would be orbiting the planet in the same direction in which Neptune rotates. Rather, Triton formed in a disk of small bodies outside the orbit of Neptune known as the Kuiper Belt. Triton originally orbited the sun as an independent body, and Neptune's gravity eventually "captured" it.

In 1984, astronomers discovered nitrogen ice on Triton. The satellite also has a thin nitrogen atmosphere with tiny amounts of methane, carbon monoxide, and carbon dioxide. In 1989, the space probe Voyager 2 flew by Triton and transmitted to Earth images of an icy surface with only a few craters. Dust streaks on the surface indicated the presence of strong winds. The images also showed clouds, hazes, and thin plumes rising to an altitude of about 5 miles (8 kilometers). James L. Elliot

See also **Neptune; Satellite; Solar system.**

Triumph, Arch of. See **Arc de Triomphe.**

Triumvirate, *try UHM vuhr iht,* in the history of ancient Rome, was a group of three men who attempted to seize control of the government. Rome had two triumvirates. The first, formed in 60 B.C., was made up of Julius Caesar, Pompey the Great, and Marcus Licinius Crassus. The second was formed in 43 B.C., after Brutus and Cassius had murdered Caesar. Its members were Octavian (Augustus), Marcus Lepidus, and Mark Antony.

The Roman republican form of government suffered severely under the first triumvirate and was destroyed by the second. Both triumvirates ended in civil war to decide the supremacy of one member of the group. In the first war, Caesar defeated Pompey. In the second, Octavian overcame Mark Antony. Arthur M. Eckstein

See also **Antony, Mark; Augustus; Caesar, Julius; Crassus, Marcus Licinius; Pompey the Great.**

Trogon, *TROH gahn,* is a family of birds. Trogons live in warm regions of both the Eastern and the Western hemispheres. The head and back of adult males are metallic green, blue, or violet. The underparts are red, orange, or yellow. Females resemble males but have duller colors on the head and back. A trogon has a short, strong bill. Two of its toes point forward and two backward. Its feet are small and weak. The female lays two to four white, pale blue, or pale green eggs. The nestlings are naked when hatched. African and Asian trogons feed mostly on insects. American trogons eat fruits and insects. See also **Quetzal.** Stuart D. Strahl

Scientific classification. Trogons make up the trogon family, Trogonidae.

Troika, *TROY kuh,* is a Russian word that means *a group of three.* A light, Russian sleigh that is pulled by three horses is called a troika. The term *troika* was applied to a 1960 plan by the Soviet Union to have the United Nations headed by three secretaries-general instead of one. See also **Cold War** (The troika proposal).

Jonathan Grant

Trojan horse. See **Trojan War; Mythology** (picture).

Trojan War was a conflict in which ancient Greece defeated the city of Troy. The legend of the war inspired many leading works of classical literature. Some of the events that occurred during and after the Trojan War became the subject of three great epic poems—the *Iliad* and the *Odyssey,* attributed to the Greek poet Homer, and the *Aeneid* by the Roman poet Virgil. The heroes and victims of the war were portrayed in such Greek tragedies as *Agamemnon* by Aeschylus, *Ajax* by Sophocles, and *The Trojan Women* by Euripides.

Scholars do not agree about the truth behind the legend of the Trojan War. Some of them believe it distorts and exaggerates small conflicts involving the Greeks from about 1500 to 1200 B.C. Others think the legend is based on one great war, which most say probably took place during the mid-1200's B.C. The Homeric epics combine historical material of different times with fictional material. As a result, the works are not reliable historical documents. But archaeologists have found historical evidence in the ruins of Troy and other places that confirms certain events described in the epics.

The beginning of the war. According to ancient Greek myths, the Trojan War resulted from an incident at the wedding feast of Peleus, the king of Phthia, and Thetis, a sea goddess. All the gods and goddesses had been invited except Eris, the goddess of discord. Eris was offended and tried to stir up trouble. She sent a golden apple inscribed "For the most beautiful." Three goddesses—Hera, Athena, and Aphrodite—each claimed the apple, and a quarrel began. Paris, the son of King Priam of Troy, judged the dispute. He awarded the apple to Aphrodite because she promised him Helen, the most beautiful woman in the world.

Helen was already married to King Menelaus of Sparta. But when Paris visited her, she fled with him to Troy. Menelaus and his brother, Agamemnon, organized a large Greek expedition against Troy to win Helen back. The Greek army included such heroes as Achilles, Ajax the Greater, Nestor, and Odysseus (Ulysses in Latin).

The siege of Troy. The Greek army laid siege to Troy for 10 years but could not conquer the city. The *Iliad* describes some of the events that occurred during the last year of the struggle. The war began to go badly for the Greeks after Achilles, their bravest warrior, left the battlefield. Achilles refused to fight because Agamemnon, the Greek commander, had insulted him. The Trojans, led by Hector, drove the Greeks back to their ships. Achilles finally returned to combat after his best friend, Patroclus, had been slain by Hector. Achilles killed Hector to avenge Patroclus's death.

The *Iliad* ends with Hector's funeral, and Greek legends relate events that followed. The Trojans received help from their allies, the Ethiopians and an army of women warriors called Amazons. But Achilles enabled the Greeks to defeat their enemies by killing Penthesilea, the queen of the Amazons, and Memnon, the king of the Ethiopians. Paris, aided by the god Apollo, later shot Achilles in the heel with an arrow and killed him.

The fall of Troy is described in the *Aeneid.* The Greeks built a huge wooden horse, which has become known as the *Trojan horse,* and placed it outside the walls of Troy. Odysseus and other warriors hid inside the horse while the rest of the Greek army sailed away.

The prophetess Cassandra and the priest Laocoön warned the Trojans against taking the horse into their city. But Sinon, a Greek prisoner, persuaded them that the horse was sacred and would bring the protection of the gods. The Trojans then pulled the horse into Troy. That night they fell asleep after celebrating their apparent victory. Odysseus and his companions then crept out of the horse and opened the city gates for the rest of their warriors, who had returned from a nearby island.

The Greeks took back Helen, killed almost all the Trojans, and burned Troy. According to the *Aeneid,* the few Trojan survivors included the warrior Aeneas, whose descendants founded Rome. Cynthia W. Shelmerdine

Related articles in *World Book* include:

Achilles	Ajax the Greater	Helen of Troy	Paris
Aeneas	Ajax the Lesser	Iliad	Priam
Aeneid	Cassandra	Laocoön	Troy
Agamemnon	Hector	Menelaus	Ulysses
		Odyssey	

Additional resources

Caselli, Giovanni. *In Search of Troy.* NTC/ Contemporary Pub. Co., 1999. Younger readers.

Wood, Michael. *In Search of the Trojan War.* Facts on File, 1985.

Troll. See Fairy.

Trolley. See **Electric railroad; Streetcar.**

Trollope, Anthony (1815-1882), was a popular English novelist of the 1800's. He was over 30 years old when his first book was published. But after he started, he wrote with such regularity that his novels and tales fill more than 50 volumes.

Trollope's most famous books are the "Barsetshire Novels." These six stories about life in the imaginary county of Barsetshire, and especially the cathedral city of Barchester, are mildly satirical. But their tone shows Trollope's affectionate tolerance for the weaknesses of his basically generous and well-meaning characters.

The Barsetshire novels are *The Warden* (1855), *Barchester Towers* (1857), *Doctor Thorne* (1858), *Framley Parsonage* (1861), *The Small House at Allington* (1864), and *The Last Chronicle of Barset* (1867). Trollope's other works include social satire novels, such as *The Bertrams* (1859) and *The Way We Live Now* (1875); political novels, such as *The Eustace Diamonds* (1873); and novels of psychological analysis, such as *Cousin Henry* (1879).

Trollope was born on April 24, 1815, in London. In his autobiography, he described his unhappy childhood. His family was poor. Frances Trollope, Anthony's mother, was also a famous writer. She wrote *Domestic Manners of the Americans* (1832) after a visit to the United States. The book sold well but did not provide enough money to pay the family bills. All his life, Trollope remembered the humiliation of those early years.

Before he became a writer, Trollope worked for many years as a postal clerk. He designed the red mailboxes that are still used in England. K. K. Collins

Additional resources

Glendinning, Victoria. *Anthony Trollope.* Knopf, 1993.

Terry, R. C., ed. *Oxford Reader's Companion to Trollope.* Oxford, 1999.

Trombone is a brass instrument that consists chiefly of an oblong tube expanded into a bell at one end. It is played by blowing into a mouthpiece and vibrating the lips. The player changes pitch by tightening the lips and moving a slide attached to the tube back and forth. The trombone is the only brass instrument that can easily play all possible pitches. A *valve trombone,* used mainly in jazz groups, has three valves with an immovable slide. The player presses the valves to change the pitch. The

Northwestern University (WORLD BOOK photo by Ted Nielsen)

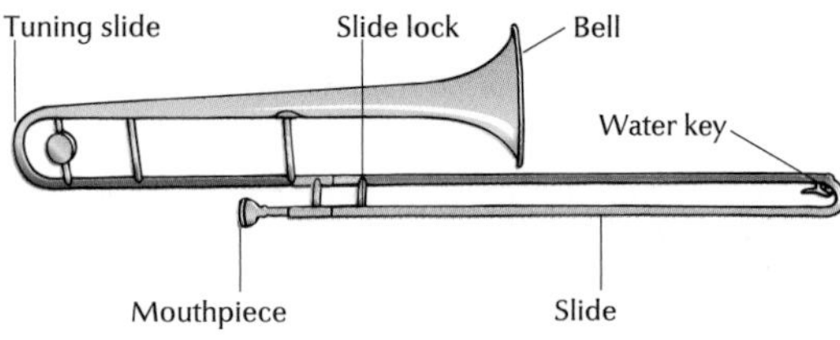

WORLD BOOK illustration by Bensen Studios

The trombone is an important brass instrument in both popular and classical music. It has a long slide attached to a tube. A musician plays different notes by moving the slide.

tenor trombone is the most popular trombone. Many professionals use a tenor trombone with a thumb valve, which enables them to play lower pitches and use more alternate slide positions. The *bass trombone* includes two rotary valves for extending the range downward.

A primitive type of trombone was used as early as 1495 in England. Today, the instrument is popular in concert, marching, and military bands, and in popular music and jazz. Stewart L. Ross

Trona, *TROH nuh,* is a gray, white, or yellowish-white mineral that contains sodium carbonate, sodium bicarbonate, and water. Trona has the chemical formula $Na_2(CO_3)\cdot Na(HCO_3)\cdot 2H_2O$. It forms from ground water that dissolves sodium in rocks. Some of the sodium-rich water pools underground or on Earth's surface. As the water evaporates, trona crystals form. The crystals appear as *fibrous* (threadlike) or *columnar* (columnlike) structures in rock layers or in thick beds deposited by modern or ancient saltwater lakes. Deposits near the surface occur only in dry areas because rainwater rapidly dissolves trona.

Trona is a major source of sodium carbonate or *soda ash,* a chemical used in the making of glass, paper, soap, and water softeners. Trona can be mined or produced artificially by evaporating seawater. The world's largest pure deposit of trona lies underground near Green River, Wyoming. Major trona deposits also occur in Botswana, Mexico, and Turkey. Mark Cloos

See also **Soda; Wyoming** (The mid-1900's).

Trondheim, *TRAWN haym* (pop. 151,408), is the third largest city in Norway. Only Oslo and Bergen have more people. Trondheim lies on the southern shore of Trondheims Fiord, where the Nid River empties into the fiord (see **Norway** [map]). Trondheim is an important export center for copper and iron ores, pyrites, wood pulp, timber, and fish. The city was founded in A.D. 998 by King Olav I Tryggvason. The Nidaros Cathedral, one of the finest Norman Gothic buildings in the world, dates back to the mid-1100's. The modern Technical University of Norway is also in Trondheim. M. Donald Hancock

Troodon, *TROH uh dahn,* was a small, two-legged dinosaur that lived about 76 million to 65 million years ago, during the Late Cretaceous Period. Troodon had an unusually large brain for a dinosaur of its size. It may have ranked among the smartest of all dinosaurs.

Troodon grew about 6 feet (1.8 meters) in length and weighed 50 to 100 pounds (23 to 45 kilograms). Its light, agile body had an elongated head; two arms with long, clawed hands; and long legs. *Troodon* could run fast, using its large tail for balance and for aid in quick turns.

Troodon was a meat eater and an excellent hunter. Its diet probably included such animals as dinosaur hatchlings, lizards, small mammals, and snakes. Scientists believe *Troodon* hunted at night. The dinosaur's large, forward-facing eyes suggest it could see well in the dark and had good depth perception. One toe on each foot ended in a large, hooked claw. The animal probably used these claws to kill prey. *Troodon's* long, slim jaws held about 120 *serrated* (saw-edged) teeth for tearing flesh. The name *Troodon* comes from Greek words meaning *wounding tooth. Troodon* lived in what is now North America. Scientists have discovered its fossils, including some eggs, in western areas of the United States and Canada. Kenneth Carpenter

Tropic bird. See **Tropicbird.**

Tropic of Cancer is an imaginary line that traces the northern boundary of the earth's Tropical Zone. It marks the farthest limit north of the equator where the sun can appear directly overhead. The line lies 23° 27′ north of the equator. The vertical rays of the sun shine down on the Tropic of Cancer at noon on the day of the summer solstice, which is June 20, 21, or 22.

The word *Cancer* means *crab* in Latin, and refers to a constellation of the zodiac. The position of the Tropic of Cancer on the map was first marked by its location directly beneath the constellation of Cancer. The inclination of the earth to the plane of its orbit determines the constellation's position. To an observer on the Tropic of Cancer, the North Star appears at an angle of 23° 27′ above the horizon. Stephen S. Birdsall

See also **Tropics; World** (map).

Tropic of Capricorn is an imaginary line that traces the southern boundary of the earth's Tropical Zone. It marks the farthest limit south of the equator where the sun can appear directly overhead. The Tropic of Capricorn lies 23° 27′ south of the equator. The vertical rays of the sun shine on the Tropic of Capricorn at noon on the day of the winter solstice, which is December 21 or 22.

The Tropic of Capricorn crosses Chile, Argentina, Paraguay, and Brazil in South America. In Africa, it crosses Namibia, Botswana, South Africa, Mozambique, and Madagascar. It also passes through Australia (see **World** [map]). The word *Capricorn* comes from the Latin *caper,* meaning *goat,* and *cornu,* meaning *horn.* It refers to a group of stars representing the sign of the zodiac known as Capricorn. The Tropic of Capricorn used to lie directly below this constellation. Stephen S. Birdsall

See also **Tropics.**

Tropical fish. Many kinds of fish live in the freshwater and saltwater habitats of the tropics. But the term *tropi-*

cal fish is applied particularly to small, brightly colored varieties that breed very rapidly and are popular for home aquariums. Tropical fish, which are often a little smaller than goldfish, usually range in size from 1 to 12 inches (2.5 to 30 centimeters).

Most tropical fish will eat food made from grains, dried shrimp, fish, insects, and aquatic plants. Such food can be bought in a pet shop. Small pieces of shrimp, oyster, crab, canned fish, boiled fish, and other kinds of fish may also be given. Many tropical fish are *carnivores* (meat-eaters), but sometimes plant-eating fish can be trained to eat such food. Some "hard-to-keep" saltwater fishes need special food, such as sponges and live coral, but many species eat a variety of foods. Some people raise worms to feed their fish. A good rule is to feed only the amount that the fish will clean up promptly because uneaten food drops to the bottom and decays. This fouls the water and may kill the fish.

A tropical fish aquarium should be covered with a flat pane of glass to control the temperature. This also keeps the fish from leaping out of the aquarium. Water plants should be grown because they keep the water in better condition and produce oxygen for the fish to breathe.

The most common and best-known tropical fish is the *guppy*. It comes from fresh waters of the West Indies and South America. The female guppy is about 1 ½ inches (3.8 centimeters) long, and the male is even smaller. The female is gray, but the male is brilliantly rainbow-hued. Guppies breed when they are about 3 months old and bear their young alive. Each female guppy produces from 20 to 50 young. See **Guppy**.

Other freshwater tropical fish that bear live young are the *swordtail*, the *platyfish*, and the *black molly*. Some tropical fish that bear their young in eggs are the *barbs*, *rasboras*, *characins*, and *cichlids*. The various *labyrinth fishes* are so named because they have a cavity with many branches in their head, usually above the gills. They store air in this cavity and use it as an accessory breathing organ. Some saltwater fish, such as *clownfish* and some *damsels*, have been successfully bred and raised in home aquariums. Leighton R. Taylor, Jr.

Scientific classification. Most live-bearing, freshwater tropical fish belong to the live-bearer family, Poeciliidae. The guppy is *Poeciliidae reticulata*.

See also **Angelfish; Aquarium, Home; Fightingfish; Fish** (pictures: Fish of coral reefs; Fish of tropical fresh waters); **Goby; Molly.**

Additional resources

Sandford, Gina. *Understanding Tropical Fish.* Howell Bk. Hse., 2000.

Williams, Sarah. *101 Facts About Tropical Fish.* Gareth Stevens, 2001. Younger readers.

Tropical rain forest. See **Rain forest.**

Tropicbird is any of three species of sea birds found in tropical regions. Tropicbirds are also called *boatswains.* They eat fish and squid, which they catch by diving straight down into the water from the air.

Tropicbirds' feathers are mainly white. They have two extremely long, slender middle tail feathers. The *red-billed tropicbird* lives in tropical parts of the Atlantic, Indian, and Pacific oceans. It has a coral-red bill, black wing tips, and many black bars across its back. The bird is nearly 40 inches (100 centimeters) long, including its middle tail feathers, which measure about 20 inches (50 centimeters). Other kinds of tropicbirds are the *white-tailed* and the *red-tailed.*

Tropicbirds nest in holes, in cracks in rocks, or on sand. On land, a tropicbird shuffles along on its breast with outstretched wings because it cannot stand.

James J. Dinsmore

Scientific classification. Tropicbirds make up the family Phaethontidae. The red-billed tropicbird is *Phaethon aethereus.* The white-tailed is *P. lepturus,* and the red-tailed is *P. rubricauda.*

See also **Bird** (picture: Birds of the ocean and the Antarctic).

Tropics are the regions of the earth that lie within about 1,600 miles (2,570 kilometers) north and 1,600 miles south of the equator. Two imaginary lines, the Tropic of Cancer and the Tropic of Capricorn, form the boundaries of the tropics. The Tropic of Cancer is 23° 27′ north of the equator, and the Tropic of Capricorn is 23° 27′ south of the equator. These lines mark the northernmost and southernmost places on the earth where the sun ever shines directly overhead.

Most places in the tropics have warm to hot temperatures the year around. Tropical places near sea level are hot because every day the sun's rays shine almost straight down at noon. Such direct rays produce higher temperatures than do slanted rays.

The temperature does not change much in the tropics because the amount of daylight differs little from season to season. At the equator, the sun shines about 12 hours a day. At the edges of the tropics, daylight varies from about 10 ½ hours a day in winter to about 13 ½ hours a

WORLD BOOK map

The tropics

The tropics, *shown on this map,* lie on both sides of the equator. They are bounded by two imaginary lines called the Tropic of Cancer and the Tropic of Capricorn. Most tropical places are warm to hot the year around.

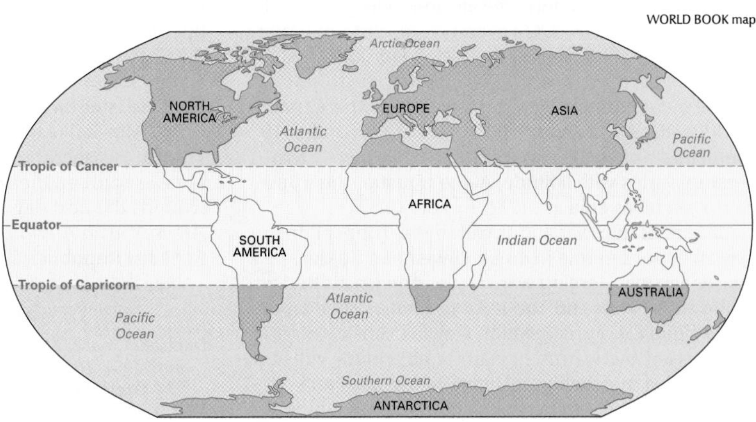

day in summer. Places at the edges of the tropics have cool periods in winter. Tropical places that are in high altitudes are cool because the temperature drops about 3 ½ °F per 1,000 feet (2 °C per 300 meters) of elevation.

Many tropical areas have definite rainy and dry seasons. Most places near the equator get much rain all year and are covered by tropical rain forests (see **Rain forest**). Farther to the north and south, one or two short dry seasons occur yearly. Such areas have forests of trees that lose their leaves during these seasons. Areas even farther from the equator have one long dry season each year. They are covered by *savannas* (grasslands with scattered trees and shrubs). Stephen S. Birdsall

For information on how people live in the tropics, see **Africa** (Ways of life in sub-Saharan Africa); **Asia** (Way of life in Southeast Asia); **Indian, American** (Indians of the Tropical Forest); **Latin America** (Way of life). See also **Fish** (pictures); **Jungle; Savanna; Tropic of Cancer; Tropic of Capricorn.**

Tropism, *TROH pihz uhm,* is a bending movement in living things caused by an outside *stimulus* (signal). For example, sunlight causes plant leaves and stems to bend toward it. A tropism results from differences in the growth rate of various parts of an *organ* (a body structure) when the stimulus is present. The bending usually is slow. Some tropisms in plants take from one hour to several days. They occur only in young tissues.

Tropisms are named for the stimulus that causes them. For example, *gravitropism,* also called *geotropism,* is bending caused by gravity, and *phototropism* is bending caused by light. *Thigmotropism* is bending in response to touch. Tropisms may be *positive* (bending toward the stimulus) or *negative* (bending away from the stimulus). Studies of tropisms led to the discovery of *auxins,* the plant hormones that control growth (see **Auxin**). George B. Johnson

Troposphere, *TROH puh sfihr,* is the layer of the atmosphere closest to Earth's surface. People live in the troposphere, and nearly all of Earth's weather—including most clouds, rain, and snow—occurs there. The troposphere contains about 80 percent of the atmosphere's mass and about 99 percent of its water. Its upper boundary, called the *tropopause,* separates it from the *stratosphere,* the next layer of Earth's atmosphere. The tropopause varies in altitude, lying an average of about 12 miles (19 kilometers) above the equator and about 6 miles (10 kilometers) above the North and South poles.

Within the troposphere, the air generally grows colder as altitude increases. On average, the air temperature drops about 3 ½ Fahrenheit degrees every 1,000 feet (6 ½ Celsius degrees every 1,000 meters). The troposphere's temperature averages about 59 °F (15 °C) near Earth's surface and about −60 °F (−51 °C) at 6 miles (10 kilometers) above the surface. The troposphere's temperature varies with latitude. At the equator, the tropopause can be as cold as −112 °F (−80 °C).

Air temperature variations within the troposphere play an important role in creating weather. Colder, denser air sinks, forcing warmer, less dense air to rise. Rising air expands and cools. As air cools, water vapor forms clouds and precipitation may fall. Sinking air is compressed and warms. In warmer air, clouds either vaporize or fail to develop, resulting in fair weather.

The troposphere helps maintain moderate temperatures at Earth's surface. It allows most sunlight to pass through it and heat the surface. The surface and the atmosphere radiate heat, which eventually escapes into space. Some of the heat, however, is absorbed by certain atmospheric gases—mainly water vapor and carbon dioxide—and radiated back to Earth's surface. This warming, called the *greenhouse effect,* raises Earth's average surface temperature by 59 Fahrenheit degrees (33 Celsius degrees). Joseph M. Moran

See also **Air** (Structure of the atmosphere); **Greenhouse effect; Jet stream; Stratosphere; Weather** (What causes weather).

Trotsky, *TRAHT skee,* **Leon** (1879-1940), also spelled *Trotzky,* was a leader of the Bolshevik revolution in Russia (see **Bolsheviks**). While Lenin lived, Trotsky was the second most powerful man in Russia. After Lenin's death, Trotsky lost the leadership to Joseph Stalin. Trotsky was later exiled. Until his assassination in Mexico City, Trotsky waged a bitter fight against Stalin from abroad. See **Lenin, V. I.; Stalin, Joseph.**

Trotsky was born Lev Davidovich Bronstein on Nov. 7, 1879, in Ukraine. After two years of revolutionary activity as a Social Democrat, he was arrested in 1898. He escaped from Siberian exile in 1902 and went to London, where he met Lenin. He returned to Russia to take an active part in the revolution in 1905.

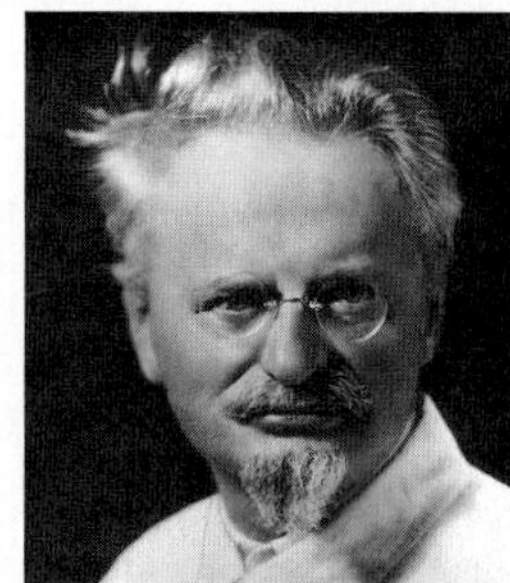
United Press Int.
Leon Trotsky

Trotsky was jailed for his leadership in the St. Petersburg Soviet of 1905. But he escaped in 1907. For 10 years he was a revolutionary writer and editor in western Europe. During World War I, he was expelled from France and Spain and went to New York, where he heard of the czar's downfall in 1917. He returned to Russia. With Lenin, he plotted the seizure of power that brought about a Bolshevik government in November 1917 (October on the old Russian calendar). Trotsky became the first Soviet commissar of foreign affairs and was soon the commissar of war.

In the civil war of 1918-1920, Trotsky efficiently organized the triumphant Red Army. After Lenin's death, many believed that Trotsky would lead the Soviet government. But Stalin outsmarted him. Trotsky was expelled from the Communist Party in 1927, and the next year was exiled to Soviet Central Asia. He was deported to Turkey in 1929. He later moved to Norway and then to Mexico.

By 1940, Stalin apparently regretted his "leniency" with Trotsky. His secret police sent an agent to Mexico. Trotsky was stabbed there on Aug. 20, 1940, and died of his wounds the next day. In 1930, Trotsky wrote *My Life: An Attempt at an Autobiography.* See also **Union of Soviet Socialist Republics** (The October Revolution).

Albert Marrin

Additional resources

Deutscher, Isaac. *The Prophet Armed: Trotsky, 1879-1921.* Oxford, 1954. *The Prophet Unarmed: Trotsky, 1921-1929.* 1959. *The Prophet Outcast: Trotsky, 1929-1940.* 1963.
Volkogonov, Dmitri. *Trotsky.* Free Pr., 1996.

Troubadour, *TROO buh dawr,* was one of a large group of poet-musicians who flourished in southern France during the 1100's and the 1200's. The word comes from the Latin *tropare* (to compose). Many scholars believe the troubadours may have modeled their lyric verse on the works of Spanish Arab poets and classical Roman poets such as Ovid. In turn, non-Arab poets in Spain and elsewhere in Europe imitated the troubadours.

Troubadours composed poetry in a Romance language called Provençal, or *langue d'oc.* The *canso d'amor* (love song) was one of the rich and varied poetic forms used by troubadours. In the *canso,* the poet imagines the lady of his desires as the model of virtue, and dedicates his talents to singing her praises. The troubadours' praise of physical love stood in direct contrast to traditional Christian morality. Their ideal of love and their praise of women influenced many writers, including Dante and Petrarch. Paul B. Diehl

See also **Knights and knighthood** (Knighthood in literature); **Minnesinger; Storytelling** (The Middle Ages); **Trouvère.**

Trout is a fish closely related to salmon, whitefish, and chars. Trout are native to cool waters of the Northern Hemisphere and have been introduced to cool waters throughout the world. Most species of trout spend their entire lives in freshwater streams and lakes. Some species migrate to the ocean to feed and grow and return to fresh water to *spawn* (lay eggs). Trout are prized both as sport fish and as food fish.

Kinds of trout

About 10 species of fish in North America are commonly called trout. All trout have strong teeth and streamlined bodies with small scales. A small, fleshy fin called an *adipose fin* grows on the back near the tail fin. Trout belong to the family Salmonidae. Atlantic trout belong to the fish *genus* (group) *Salmo,* which also includes Atlantic salmon. Pacific trout belong to the genus *Oncorhynchus,* which also includes Pacific salmon. The trout in these two genera are considered true trout. Other trout belong to the genus *Salvelinus,* which also includes chars.

True trout have dark spots on their bodies. The best-known species is the *rainbow trout.* This fish is native to western North America and has been introduced to many other areas. It has black spots on the upper body and the tail and a brilliant reddish band along each side. Some rainbow trout, called *steelhead,* live in the ocean or large freshwater lakes. They return to inland streams to spawn. These fish are a steely blue color.

Several species of true trout live only in waters of

Some kinds of trout

True trout

All true trout, also known as black-spotted trout, have dark markings on a light background. The rainbow trout, *below,* like every true trout of North America, originally lived only in the waters of the western half of the continent.

Bill Noel Kleeman, Tom Stack & Assoc.

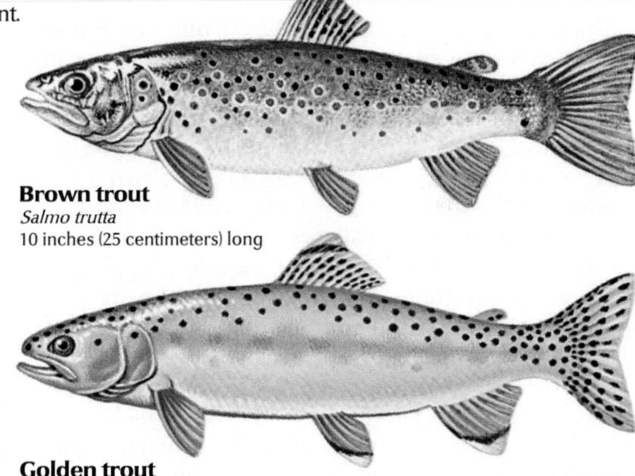

Brown trout
Salmo trutta
10 inches (25 centimeters) long

Golden trout
Oncorhynchus aguabonita
10 inches (25 centimeters) long

Other trout

Other trout are distinguished from true trout by their light red, pink, or cream-colored spots. These fish include the lake trout and the bull trout.

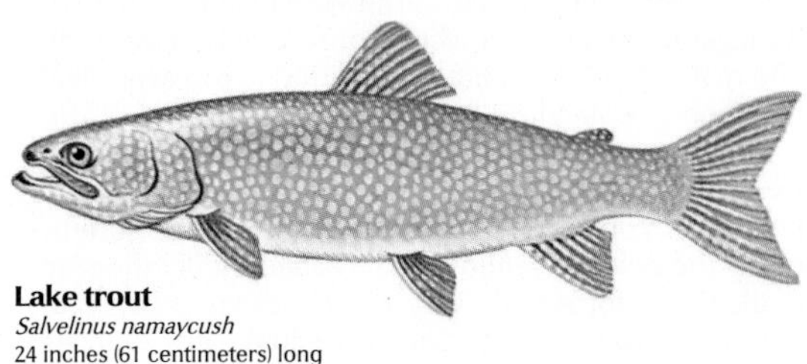

Lake trout
Salvelinus namaycush
24 inches (61 centimeters) long

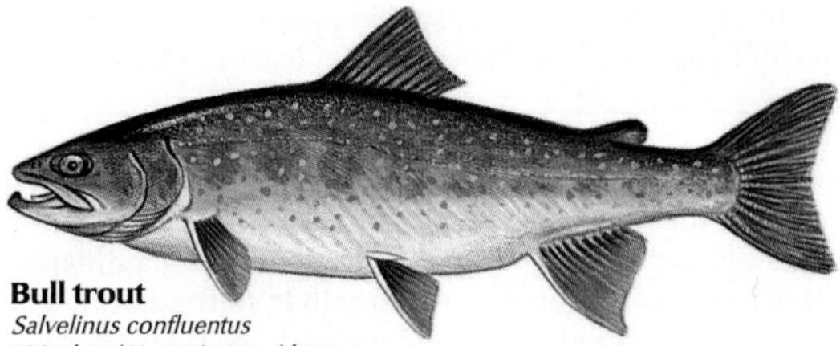

Bull trout
Salvelinus confluentus
16 inches (41 centimeters) long

WORLD BOOK illustrations by James Teason and John F. Eggert

western North America. The *cutthroat trout* ranges from southern Alaska to northern California and in the Rocky Mountains region from Canada to New Mexico. It gets its name from a red-orange slash on each side of the lower jaw. Other Western species include the *golden trout* of the California mountains, the *Apache trout* of Arizona, and the *Gila trout* of Arizona and New Mexico.

The *brown trout* has been introduced throughout North America. It is native to Europe and western Asia. Its body has dark brown or black spots, many of which are surrounded by pale halos. The tail is only slightly forked. This trout may have red or orange spots, surrounded by pale halos, along the sides of the body.

Other trout include the *brook trout,* the *bull trout,* and the *lake trout.* These fish generally have light red, pink, or cream-colored spots. The front edge of the lower fins is white. The brook trout has dark, wavy lines or blotches on the upper fins and tail. It originally was found only in streams in eastern North America. The bull trout lives in waters of the Pacific Northwest. The lake trout inhabits deep lakes and rivers in northern North America. It generally has a gray-green body and a deeply forked tail. Lake trout are the largest species of trout. A lake trout measuring 4 feet 2 inches (1.27 meters) long and weighing 102 pounds (46.3 kilograms) was taken from Lake Athabasca in Saskatchewan, Canada. It is the largest trout ever caught.

The life of a trout

Most trout spawn in streams or rivers, but some spawn in lakes with gravel bottoms and good water flow. Trout spawn in spring or autumn.

The spawning behavior of rainbow trout is typical of that of other trout species. In early spring, rainbow trout move upstream to a spawning area. The female chooses a suitable site, usually a shallow, gravel area at the beginning of a stretch of choppy water. There, the female turns on her side and beats her tail up and down, scooping out a shallow nest called a *redd.* After the redd is prepared, the female positions herself over it. The male courts her by swimming closely alongside her and quivering his body. When the female is ready to spawn, she moves to the bottom of the redd and presses her belly against the gravel. The male positions himself close to her. As the female releases eggs, the male releases sperm that fertilize the eggs.

After the eggs have been fertilized, the female covers them with gravel. The eggs usually hatch in about 2 months. After the young hatch, they move up through the gravel into the water.

Young trout eat mainly *invertebrates* (animals without backbones), including insects. Mature trout also feed on other fish and on crayfish. They occasionally eat young birds, lizards, or other animals that fall into the water. The life span varies among species. Rainbow trout live up to 11 years and lake trout up to at least 25 years.

Trout fishing

All trout species are valued as sport fish. The rainbow trout and the cutthroat trout are especially prized because of their fighting ability and their spectacular leaps when hooked. The brook trout, another spirited fighter, also is a favorite among fishing enthusiasts. Lake trout are usually taken by *trolling* (trailing a line behind a boat) or by dropping a line through the ice in winter.

Some species are important commercially as food. Each year, commercial fishing crews catch great numbers of lake trout and steelhead. Rainbow trout and brook trout are raised in hatcheries and sold for food.

David W. Greenfield

Scientific classification. Trout belong to the trout family, Salmonidae. Atlantic trout are in the genus *Salmo.* Pacific trout are in the genus *Oncorhynchus.* Other trout belong to the genus *Salvelinus.* The scientific name for the rainbow trout is *O. mykiss.* The brook trout is *Salvelinus fontinalis.*

See also **Fish** (Pictures: A leaping trout; Fish of temperate fresh waters; How a fish develops; How fish reproduce).

Trout lily. See **Dogtooth violet**.

Trouvère, *troo VAIR* or *troo VEHR,* was one of a group of poet-musicians who flourished in northern France in the 1100's and 1200's. The word comes from an Old French word meaning *to compose.* The Trouvères composed their poems in an Old French dialect, called *langue d'oïl.* They were strongly influenced by the style and subject matter of the troubadours of southern France. Like the troubadours, the trouvères wrote *chansons d'amor* (love songs). Paul B. Diehl

See also **Troubadour**.

Trovatore, Il. See **Opera** (*Trovatore, Il*); **Verdi, Giuseppe**.

Troy, also called Ilium, was an ancient city in Asia Minor (now part of Turkey) that was made famous in the legends of early Greece. The *Iliad* and the *Odyssey,* epics attributed to the Greek poet Homer, and the *Aeneid,* an epic written by the Roman poet Virgil, tell a story about Troy that is probably only partly true. The city's two names come from Ilus, its legendary founder, and Tros, the father of Ilus.

The legendary Troy was a mighty city ruled by King Priam. The king's son Paris judged a beauty contest between the goddesses Hera, Athena, and Aphrodite. He chose Aphrodite as the winner because she promised to give him the most beautiful woman in the world as his wife. Soon after the contest, Paris visited Menelaus, the king of Sparta. Paris fell in love with Menelaus's wife, Helen, who was known as the most beautiful woman in the world. Paris took Helen to Troy, and thereby angered Menelaus.

The people of the mainland of Greece, called Achaeans by Homer, swore revenge on Paris and the people of Troy. The Greeks sent a great naval expedition to Troy. The expedition was led by Agamemnon, Menelaus's brother, and included Achilles, Odysseus (Ulysses in Latin), and many other Greek heroes.

The Greeks besieged Troy for 10 years. But they could not capture the city, which was protected by high stone walls. Finally, Odysseus ordered workers to build a huge wooden horse, in which some Greek soldiers hid. The rest of the Greeks then pretended to sail away, leaving the horse standing outside the city walls.

The curious Trojans dragged the wooden horse inside the city, though Laocoön, a Trojan priest, warned them not to do so. That night, the Greek soldiers crept out of the horse, opened the city gates, and let the rest of the Greek forces into Troy. The Greeks massacred the people of Troy and looted and burned the city. Only Aeneas, the hero of Virgil's *Aeneid,* and a few other Trojans escaped. Paris was killed in the war, and Helen returned to Menelaus.

The real Troy. Archaeologists have learned that Troy was founded in the early Bronze Age, which began about 3000 B.C. in Asia Minor. The city stood on a high point of a fertile plain in what is now northwestern Turkey. It was near the southern end of the Hellespont, a strait now called the Dardanelles. Archaeologists have discovered that nine cities were built on the site of Troy. Each successive city was built on the ruins of the one before it.

The second Troy and the sixth one were especially wealthy cities. The Trojans farmed, bred and raised horses, herded sheep, and produced woolen goods. They traded with the Mycenaeans, who lived in Greece, and with other people who lived along the Aegean coast of Asia Minor.

Scholars know little about the actual Trojan War. Archaeologists have found evidence that the Greeks may have attacked and destroyed Troy in a great expedition similar to the one described in the *Iliad.* However, no one knows the cause of the war. Ancient Greek scholars believed that Troy fell about 1184 B.C. Many archaeologists think that the seventh city on the site of Troy was the one written about in ancient Greek literature. These scholars believe that the city was destroyed about 1200 B.C.

The archaeological Troy. The first archaeologist to conduct a major study of Troy was a German named Heinrich Schliemann. Other persons had noted that a small mound about 4 miles (6 kilometers) from the Dardanelles seemed to fit the geographical location of Troy described in the *Iliad.* The mound was called *Hissarlik.* Schliemann began digging there in 1870. He found evidence that several cities had been built on the site over a long period. Near the bottom of the excavation, he discovered the ruins of an ancient city with massive walls, well-built houses, and hidden treasures of gold and silver. Schliemann mistakenly believed this city, which he called Troy II, was the Troy described by Homer.

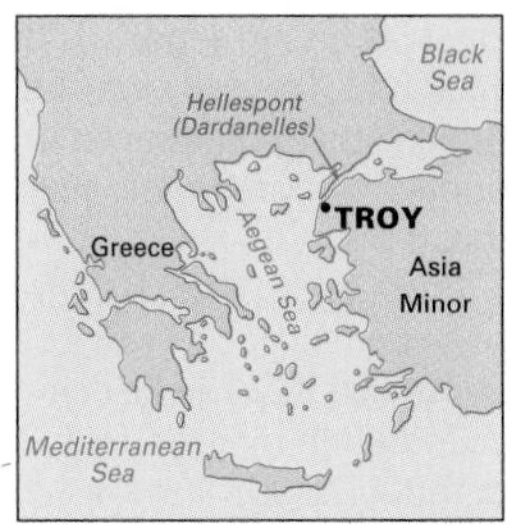

WORLD BOOK map

Troy was an ancient city in Asia Minor. Ruins of Troy have yielded historical relics that are about 5,000 years old.

The German archaeologist Wilhelm Dörpfeld, who had assisted Schliemann, conducted further excavations at Troy in the 1890's. He was the first researcher to recognize that nine cities had stood on the site. Dörpfeld believed the sixth was the city of Homer's *Iliad.* This city, called Troy VI, was larger than the earlier ones and was protected by high walls. The houses were large and rectangular and contained much pottery imported from Greece.

In 1932, Carl Blegen, an American scholar from the University of Cincinnati, began a new research expedition at Troy. His study lasted seven years and confirmed the findings of Dörpfeld, except that Blegen believed the seventh city was the legendary Troy. According to Blegen, Troy VI represented a major stage in the development of the city, even though it was not the Troy of Greek legends. This stage was marked by the arrival of immigrants who shared many cultural characteristics with the Mycenaeans in Greece. Blegen believed that Troy VI was destroyed by an earthquake about 1270 B.C. The next city, which archaeologists called Troy VIIa, had small, crude houses that were crowded together. The

Detail of *The Burning of Troy* (early 1600's), an oil painting on canvas by an unknown French artist; Blois Museum, France (Lauros, Giraudon)

The fall of Troy was made famous in legends. Greek soldiers hid in a huge wooden horse, and curious Trojans dragged it into the city. The Greeks later crept out and attacked Troy.

Peter Loud, Robert Harding Picture Library

The site of Troy has the remains of nine successive cities. The stone walls above are from Troy VI, destroyed by an earthquake about 1270 B.C. It was probably not the Troy of legend.

city was less prosperous than the earlier Troys. Around 1200 B.C., Troy VIIa was burned with great violence. Although Blegen believed that Troy VIIa was the legendary city, archaeologists have not been able to prove that it was.

From about 1100 B.C. to 700 B.C., only small numbers of people lived at Troy. There was a small village there about 700 B.C. The last city on the site, Troy IX, was called Ilium by the Greeks and Romans. Ilium declined in the A.D. 600's and was abandoned about A.D. 1500. It then remained undisturbed until Schliemann discovered it. Jack L. Davis

See also **Trojan War** and its list of *Related articles;* **Homer; Schliemann, Heinrich.**

Additional resources

Allen, Susan H. *Finding the Walls of Troy.* Univ. of Calif. Pr., 1999.
Caselli, Giovanni. *In Search of Troy.* Peter Bedrick, 1999. Younger readers.
Erskine, Andrew. *Troy Between Greece and Rome: Local Tradition and Imperial Power.* Oxford, 2001.

Troy weight is a standard system used in weighing gold, silver, platinum, and coins. It is also used to weigh jewels, except pearls and diamonds, which are weighed in carats. The name *Troy* may come from *Troyes,* a French town. In the 1300's, Troyes had its own system of weights and measures. In the system of troy weight, the pound contains 12 ounces. The ounce equals 20 pennyweights, and the pennyweight equals 24 grains. The troy pound and the apothecaries' pound both contain 5,760 grains. The pound avoirdupois equals 7,000 grains. The grains in all three systems are equal. The troy pound equals 0.373 kilogram. Richard S. Davis

See also **Pennyweight; Weights and measures; Apothecaries' weight; Avoirdupois.**

Truce is a short suspension of hostilities between opposing sides in a war. A truce may be called to allow each side to remove wounded from the battlefield, bury the dead, exchange prisoners, or observe a religious holiday. A truce may also be used for brief negotiations. In such cases, the negotiations are usually conducted under a white *flag of truce,* which indicates the peaceful intentions of the participants.

During the early 1000's, Christian clergy of France instituted a custom called the Truce of God. This custom prohibited warfare on weekends and during certain religious observances. Opponents often ignored the truce.

A truce is different from an *armistice.* An armistice is an agreement to stop fighting that covers a longer period of time than a truce. It may even bring a permanent end of the fighting. Often, an armistice leads to a peace treaty that provides a political settlement of the war. The fighting in World War I (1914-1918) ended with an armistice followed by peace treaties. In the Korean War, truce talks were held from July 1951 to July 1953, when an armistice was signed and the fighting stopped. However, negotiations following the armistice failed to result in a final political settlement. Thus, the armistice did not lead to a peace treaty. In January 1973, a cease-fire agreement occurred during the Vietnam War. But it failed to lead to a peace treaty, and the war continued until 1975. Richard Rosecrance

See also **Flag of truce; Peace** (The Middle Ages).

Truck is a motor vehicle used to carry freight. Trucks transport a wide variety of cargo. They carry food to grocery stores and gasoline to service stations. Trucks haul manufactured products from factories to stores and, in some cases, to consumers' homes. In fact, trucks help transport nearly everything we eat, wear, and use. Some kinds of trucks are commonly called *vans.* The British word for truck is *lorry.*

Trucking is a major industry in developed countries. In the United States, for example, trucks haul about 75 percent of the industrial products and carry most of the goods moved short distances.

Trucks vary greatly in size and style. The smallest and most common type is the *pickup truck.* Another very common but much larger truck is the *tractor-semitrailer,* often called a *semi* or an *18-wheeler.* The tractor is the front part of the truck. It contains the cab and engine, and it pulls the semitrailer. Some tractor-semitrailers also pull a second trailer and are called *doubles* or *twin trailers. Triples* consist of a tractor pulling three trailers.

Trucks are sturdily built to haul heavy loads. Most have engines that are more powerful than automobile engines. The engines of large trucks produce as much as 600 horsepower (375 kilowatts).

Large trucks typically have 9 to 18 forward gears and 2 or more reverse gears. The gears allow the engine to be used most efficiently so that the truck can reach and maintain desired speeds under varying conditions. Low gears make it possible for a truck to climb steep hills with a heavy load, while high gears allow it to accelerate to highway speeds. Large trucks also have strong brakes, and large tires to handle the heavy loads. Some have many axles. Axles with heavy load capacity usually have two pairs of tires.

Uses of trucks

Trucks have a wide variety of industrial, agricultural, and governmental uses. Some trucks have special uses.

Industrial uses. Trucks serve a vital role for manufacturing industries by providing a quick and flexible means to move goods. Industries use trucks to carry raw materials to their factories and to transport manufactured products to warehouses, distribution centers, stores, or customers. In some cases, trucks carry products between factories. For example, the parts for a car may be produced at several factories and then trucked to a plant where the car is assembled. Trucks then transport the cars to automobile dealerships for sale to the public.

Utility industries use trucks extensively to maintain their systems. Trucks haul the tools and supplies needed to maintain their services and facilities. Many trucks are equipped with aerial cranes that can be raised and lowered to enable workers to maintain equipment mounted on utility poles. Many trucks have a *power take-off,* a mechanism that provides power for other machines, such as winches, cranes, and post-hole diggers. Similar trucks are used by tree-trimming services.

Businesses that own or lease trucks and use them to carry their own goods are known as *private carriers.* Trucking companies that transport freight for others are called *for-hire carriers.*

In the United States, there are three types of for-hire carriers: (1) common, (2) contract, and (3) exempt. Common carriers are required by law to transport the goods of any shipper who can pay for the service. Such carriers charge set rates, haul specific types of freight, and operate only on certain routes (see **Common carrier**). Contract carriers work for a limited number of customers. They agree to deliver only the products of these customers. Exempt carriers transport only certain kinds of goods or use their trucks only for specific purposes. Exempt carriers include firms that haul certain agricultural products or carry newspapers. These carriers are exempt from certain government regulations.

Agricultural uses. In agricultural areas, farmers use trucks to move cargo around farms and to and from markets. They haul fertilizer, livestock feeds, and other items needed to operate a farm. Such farm products as fruits, vegetables, and livestock are trucked from farms to markets. They thus help make it possible for supermarkets to offer a wide variety of foods. Because of the quick delivery made possible by trucks, consumers can enjoy fresh fruits and vegetables grown in distant areas.

Governmental uses. Federal, state, regional, and municipal governments use many trucks. Postal services employ trucks to transport mail between cities and to deliver it directly to homes. The military services use trucks to carry equipment, troops, and weapons. Some military trucks are large enough to haul tanks and missile launchers. State and regional governments use trucks in the construction and maintenance of bridges, roads, and parks. Cities and municipalities use trucks for the maintenance of roads, streets, and parks and to sweep streets, clear away snow, and collect garbage. Fire departments require trucks for fire fighting and emergency services.

Special uses. Many people use trucks to move their furniture, household goods, and personal belongings from one apartment or house to another. Trucks called *bookmobiles* serve as traveling libraries. Television networks send trucks outfitted with video equipment to cover news and sports events. Tow trucks haul damaged or disabled vehicles. Trucks built as ambulances have lifesaving equipment and serve as mobile emergency rooms. *Motor homes* are trucks outfitted with living accommodations for people who are camping or traveling (see **Recreational vehicle**).

Trucks are often used in combination with other modes of transportation. For example, a loaded trailer can be separated from a truck tractor and loaded onto a railroad flatcar. The trailer is then transported to a railroad terminal near its final destination, where it is reconnected to another truck tractor and driven to the destination. Standardized shipping containers are transported by ship or train and then loaded onto tractor-semitrailers for delivery to their final destination. See **Containerization.**

Kinds of trucks

Truck manufacturers offer customers a choice of thousands of designs. Trucks vary in size and weight-carrying capacity. Many are outfitted with specialized equipment geared toward particular tasks. Such equipment includes cranes or ladders.

Trucks are classified as *straight* or *combination* vehicles. Straight trucks, which are also called *rigid trucks* or *single-unit trucks,* combine the cab and the cargo space on a single frame. Combination vehicles consist of a tractor and one or more trailers.

Trucks may also be classified by weight in accordance with their *gross vehicle weight rating* in the case of straight trucks, or *gross combination weight rating* in the case of combination vehicles. The ratings reflect the maximum weight of the truck and load for which the truck is designed.

Although there is no universal standard for classifying trucks by name, a *light truck* is generally considered to be one with a gross weight rating less than 14,001 pounds (6,364 kilograms). *Medium trucks* have gross weight ratings from 14,001 to 26,000 pounds (11,818 kilograms). Trucks with a gross weight rating of over 26,000 pounds are considered *heavy trucks.*

Most light trucks are straight trucks. Pickups are the most common and familiar light truck. A pickup has an enclosed cab and an open-topped cargo compartment. Many pickups have engines and transmissions similar to those in automobiles and can carry a load weighing about $1\frac{1}{2}$ tons (1.4 metric tons). Most light trucks have gasoline engines. But some manufacturers produce light trucks with diesel engines, which convert fuel to energy more efficiently than gasoline engines.

Medium trucks are wider and taller than light trucks. They are commonly used as commercial vehicles, such as parcel delivery trucks and beverage trucks. Parcel delivery trucks are designed so the driver can stand behind the steering wheel and easily step in and out of the cab. Beverage trucks have racks to carry bottled goods. Most medium trucks have diesel engines.

Heavy trucks perform a wide variety of rugged tasks. These vehicles include concrete mixers and dump trucks, as well as tractor-semitrailers. Concrete mixers haul a rotating drum in which concrete is mixed while the truck is in transit. The concrete is then discharged at the job site. Dump trucks have an open bed that tilts toward the rear to discharge the load. The trailer of a tractor-semitrailer is supported partially by wheels and partially by the powerful tractor that pulls it. The trailer connects to the tractor through a coupling known as a *fifth wheel.* This coupling enables a trailer to be removed from a tractor and another to be connected. Almost all heavy trucks have diesel engines. The engines are designed to be very durable since they must operate at high power levels for long periods of time.

Another way of grouping trucks is according to where they are used. Trucks may be classified as *on-highway* or *off-highway* trucks.

On-highway trucks are used on roads. The most common types of on-highway trucks include pickups, tractor-semitrailers, and *panels.* A panel is a small, fully enclosed truck. Other kinds of on-highway trucks include *flatbed trucks* and *tank trucks.* Flatbed trucks have an enclosed cab in front of a flat, open platform for loading cargo. The platform may have brackets along its perimeter so that stakes can be inserted to help restrain the load. Flatbed trucks are also called *platform* or *stake trucks.* They are used to haul large pieces of equipment and other bulky cargo. Tank trucks are outfitted with a large tank for carrying liquids, such as gasoline or milk, or compressed gas. Some are straight trucks, and some are tractor-semitrailers.

Light vans are commonly used for delivering goods locally to stores and homes. Heavier vans transport furniture or bulky goods. Refrigerated vans called *reefers* are used to carry perishable food and other products that require cooling.

Off-highway trucks are designed and built for use on rugged terrain rather than on highways. They are used on construction sites and in lumber camps, mines, oil fields, and quarries. These trucks are much larger and can haul much heavier loads than what are allowed on highways. The largest off-highway trucks used in North America measure 47 $\frac{1}{2}$ feet (14.5 meters) long and 30 feet (9.1 meters) wide. These huge trucks are used at mining sites and can transport loads weighing 380 tons (345 metric tons). Some off-highway trucks are equipped with machinery used for earth-moving, hoisting, or pumping. Small electric-powered trucks that carry loads inside factories are also a kind of off-the-highway truck.

Common features of trucks

Truck cabs come in two styles—*conventional* and *cab-over-engine* (COE). Conventionals are identifiable by a cab set behind the hood covering the engine. COE's have the engine placed under the cab with no visible hood protruding in front of the windshield. The cabs of some tractor-semitrailers are equipped with a bed in which drivers can sleep when they stop during long trips. These cabs are called *sleeper cabs.*

Heavy trucks have large brakes at each wheel. Some also have brakes incorporated into the engine or into the *driveline,* which connects the transmission to the driving axle. These brakes, called *retarders,* reduce wear on the wheel brakes by absorbing energy to slow the truck. Many trucks have *anti-lock* brake systems that prevent the wheels from locking during braking so they stop more safely on slippery surfaces.

Trucks have one front axle used for steering. On some trucks this axle may also function as a driving axle. Some special-use trucks have a second axle at the front of the truck that is also used for steering.

Trucks have various types of suspension systems that use rubber, steel springs, or *air springs* (devices that use compressed air to absorb shock and vibration). The suspension system isolates the truck body from the axles to reduce shocks from bumps in the road.

Many trucks have two rear axles known as *tandem axles.* Tandems share a common suspension system to help equalize the loads on the axles. Tandem axle suspensions with *leaf springs* (springs made of layers of curved metal strips) are known as *four-spring suspensions.* Some include beams between the axles known as *walking beams.*

Regulation of trucks

In most countries, the operation of trucks is strictly controlled by laws. Among other things, these laws define the allowable physical size of the truck in terms of width, height, and length, and the maximum weight permitted. In order to use highways, trucking companies must pay taxes on each truck they operate in accordance with the size of the truck.

Truck drivers must take special tests to obtain a license to drive a truck on public highways. Government regulations limit the number of hours each day a driver may operate a truck and require the driver to maintain a daily log of driving time. In some countries, trucks are equipped with devices that automatically record daily driving activities. Some trucks are also equipped with navigation systems that use a network of satellites called the Global Positioning System to provide continuous information about their location.

Most countries apply very strict safety standards to trucks. Some require annual testing of such critical features as brakes, tires, and steering. Special rules govern the transport of chemicals and other hazardous materials.

History

Nicolas-Joseph Cugnot, a French military engineer, built the first self-powered road vehicles in 1769 and 1770. One was a steam-powered, three-wheel vehicle designed to tow artillery pieces. This vehicle might well be considered the first truck.

By the early 1900's, manufacturers in many countries were building trucks. They had solid rubber tires and crude spring suspension systems, which made traveling over the bumpy roads of the time uncomfortable for the driver and rough on the cargo. Nevertheless, the early trucks were more efficient and less costly than the horse-drawn vehicles they replaced. However, the railroads carried most of the long-distance freight.

Improvements in truck design and development of air-filled, pneumatic tires soon enabled trucks to carry heavier loads at greater speeds. The motorized trucking industry grew rapidly. Trucks proved especially valuable during World War I (1914-1918) by carrying supplies to soldiers at the front lines.

During the 1920's, in the United States, the federal and state governments began building a national system of highways. The improved roads enabled trucks to travel between cities more quickly. Trucks were used extensively during World War II (1939-1945). Following the war, many countries began to improve their road systems. In the United States, a network of high-speed interstate highways was built, allowing bigger and faster trucks to compete effectively with trains as freight carriers.

Careers

The trucking industry employs millions of people around the world. These employees include many kinds of workers besides drivers. Dispatchers direct trucks to the proper destination with the correct cargo. Freight handlers and loading-dock and warehouse workers load and unload trucks. Mechanics repair and maintain trucks. Trucking firms employ such office workers as shipping clerks and computer programmers. Truck manufacturers employ engineers and factory workers. In addition, companies that produce engines, tires, and other parts for trucks offer employment opportunities.

Thomas D. Gillespie

See also **Automobile** with its list of *Related articles;* **Fire department** (Fire trucks); **Freight; Transportation** (picture: A flatbed truck).

Truck farming is raising vegetables or fruit, or both, for market. Truck farmers do not usually need as much land for growing vegetables as they would for grain crops, and truck farms often are simply large gardens. But some truck farms cover large areas.

The terms *truck farm* and *truck garden* mean the same thing. They come from an old use of the word

Some kinds of trucks Thousands of kinds of trucks perform specialized work. They range from small pickup trucks that carry light loads to huge *triples* consisting of a tractor with tremendous hauling power towing three trailers.

WORLD BOOK illustrations by Robert Keys

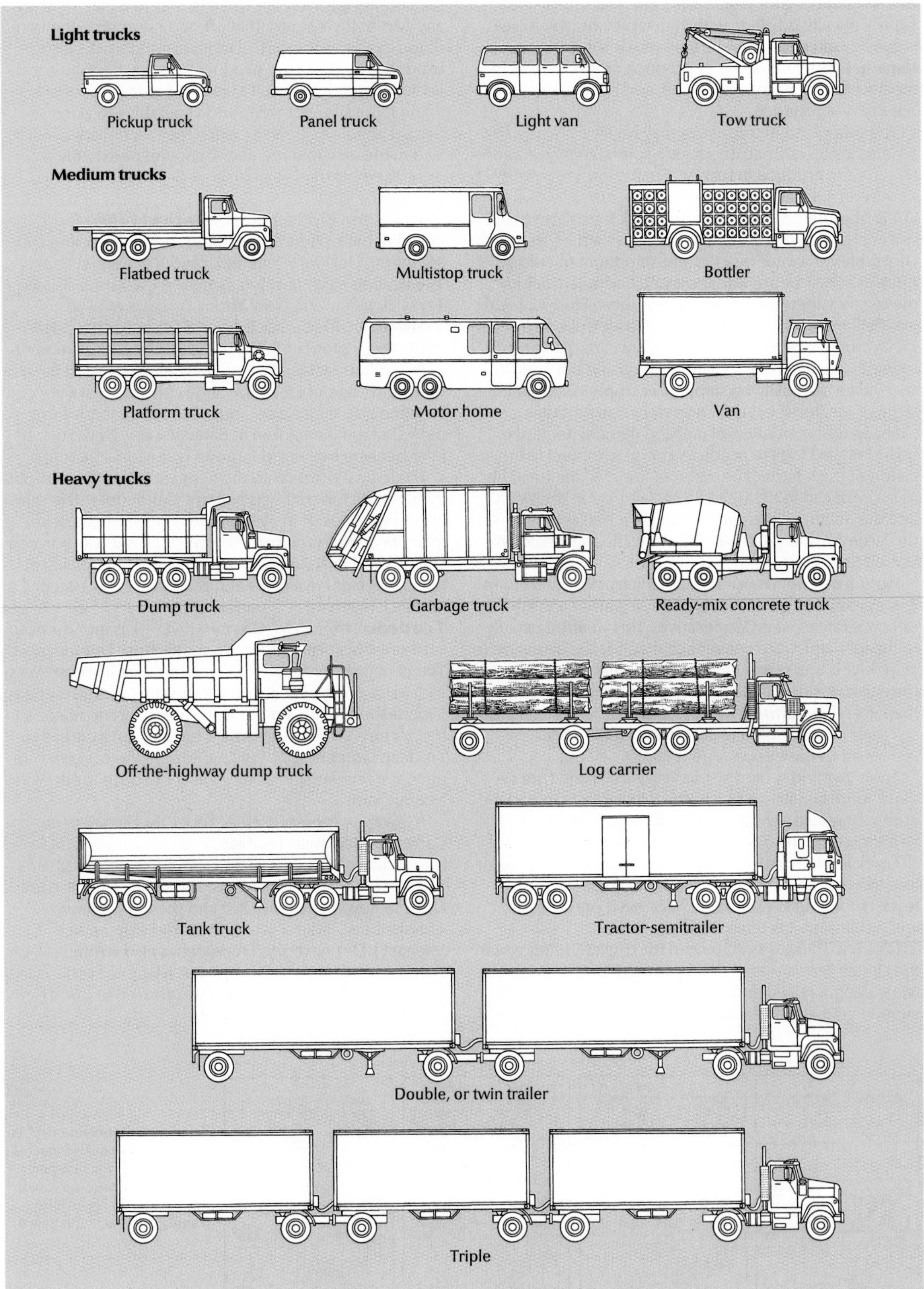

truck, which meant *to exchange or barter goods.* People speak of vegetables raised for sale as *garden truck.*

Kinds of truck farms. In general, there are two kinds of truck farms. Some truck farms are near cities, and supply the city dwellers with vegetables or fruit in season. They often also have greenhouses for growing tomatoes and other kinds of produce out of season. In most cases, such farms are small, and raise many different kinds of produce.

The other kind of truck farm may be far from any city. It depends on railroad, truck, or airplane transportation to carry the produce to market. Such a farm is usually large, and specializes in growing only one or a few kinds of produce. Some of these truck farms are in warm regions where they can produce certain fruits or vegetables in winter months and ship them to cold regions where they are out of season. Examples include the winter vegetable gardens of southern Florida, southern California, Texas, and Arizona. Other truck farms can be far from market because they grow a particular fruit or vegetable that is in demand throughout the country and which can easily be shipped. Examples include the large onion, head lettuce, and celery farms of Idaho and Utah. Special conditions of soil and climate needed to grow certain kinds of produce also may influence the location of truck farms. For example, most of the head lettuce produced in the United States grows in the West and the South, where conditions are most favorable. But the largest market for head lettuce is the northeastern United States.

How truck farms operate. Many truck farmers ship and market their produce through organizations known as cooperatives (see **Cooperative**). This method usually is cheaper and more convenient than for the growers to ship their crops separately. Truck farmers also sell produce at roadside stands and, in urban areas, at outdoor markets called *farmer's markets.* Sometimes, the farmers sell their produce directly to such middlemen as processors, wholesalers, and retailers.

Truck farming is hard work. Vegetables and fruit require more constant and careful cultivation than do field crops. They also are more difficult to harvest. Truck farming produces quick profits, but is risky.

Truck farmers usually rotate their crops every three or four years to keep the soil productive. Most land for truck gardening is expensive, because it must be rich and fertile, and it is often near big cities.

History. There was little need for truck farming when the United States was largely an agricultural country. Most people raised their own vegetables or fruit in the summer and stored them in the winter. But urban growth brought a great need for truck farming. Many city dwellers have no place to grow vegetables or fruit.

The building of railroads and highways throughout the country allowed the truck farmer to locate in nearly any part of the country that offered good growing conditions and good soil. The railroads and trucks also brought out-of-season produce to many people. The invention of refrigeration for railroad cars and trucks made it possible for fruits and vegetables to arrive at market almost as fresh as when they were harvested. It also made possible the distribution of perishable produce in city markets throughout the country during most of the year.

Truck farm products are the second largest food group in the United States in terms of volume and consumption. Only milk and milk products exceed them. The leading truck farming states are California, Florida, Texas, Arizona, and New York. Donald M. Nixon

Trudeau, *TROO doh,* **Edward Livingston** (1848-1915), was a pioneer in the antituberculosis movement in the United States. Trudeau himself contracted the disease at the age of 25. He became convinced of the need for adequate sanitariums and established the Adirondack Cottage Sanitarium at Saranac Lake, New York. It later became the world famous Trudeau Sanitarium.

Trudeau also founded the Saranac Laboratory in 1894, the first U.S. tuberculosis research laboratory. The sanitarium was closed in 1954 because of the great strides made in antituberculosis therapy. Trudeau was born on Oct. 5, 1848, in New York City. He studied medicine at the College of Physicians and Surgeons (now part of Columbia University). Matthew Ramsey

Trudeau, *troo DOH,* **Garry** (1948-), is an American cartoonist best known for his comic strip "Doonesbury." The comic strip has gained fame and stirred controversy with its strong political and social satire. Trudeau draws "Doonesbury" with simple lines to encourage readers to focus more on the strip's message than on its artwork. Trudeau won the 1975 Pulitzer Prize in the cartoon category, the first artist ever to receive the prize for drawing a comic strip.

Trudeau was born in New York City. His full name is Garretson Beekman Trudeau. While a student at Yale University in 1968, he created a comic strip called "Bull Tales" for the *Yale Daily News.* The strip was first syndicated to newspapers in 1970 and the title changed to "Doonesbury," after a character in the strip named Michael J. Doonesbury. Trudeau has also written television scripts and magazine articles. Many collections of "Doonesbury" comic strips have appeared in book form.
Pamela J. Fehl

Trudeau's "Doonesbury" is a satirical comic strip that features a young man named Michael J. Doonesbury, wearing a vest, and his hippie friend, Zonk, with the beard.

Pierre E. Trudeau

Prime minister of Canada
1968-1979
1980-1984

Pearson 1963-1968 | **Trudeau** 1968-1979 | **Clark** 1979-1980

Trudeau 1980-1984 | **Turner** 1984

Trudeau, *troo DOH,* **Pierre Elliott** (1919-2000), served as prime minister of Canada from 1968 to 1979 and from 1980 to 1984. He was the third French-Canadian prime minister. Like the first two—Sir Wilfrid Laurier and Louis S. St. Laurent—he was a Liberal.

The energetic and wealthy Trudeau generated great interest among Canadians, particularly the nation's youth. But during the late 1970's, his popularity and that of his party declined as Canada's economic problems worsened. The Progressive Conservatives defeated the Liberals in May 1979, and the Conservative leader, Joe Clark, succeeded Trudeau as prime minister. However, Clark's government fell from power at the end of the year, and Trudeau led the Liberals to an easy victory in February 1980.

Before his first term as prime minister, Trudeau had worked as a lawyer and law professor and had only three years of experience in public office. His social life had made him famous. He often wore colorful clothes; drove fast cars; and enjoyed skiing, skin diving, and canoeing. Even as prime minister, his personal life generated interest. In 1971, he surprised the nation by marrying Margaret Sinclair, the daughter of a former member of Parliament. Their romance had received no publicity. The Trudeaus had three children, Justin (1971-   ), Alexandre (1973-   ), and Michel (1975-1998). In 1977, Trudeau and his wife separated. Trudeau received custody of the children. The couple divorced in 1984.

As prime minister, Trudeau worked to broaden Canada's contacts with other nations and to ease the long-strained relations between English- and French-speaking Canadians. He achieved a personal goal in 1970, when Canada and China agreed to reestablish diplomatic relations. At home, Trudeau faced such problems as rapid inflation, high unemployment, and a movement to make the province of Quebec a separate nation. Trudeau achieved another major goal in 1982, when the Canadian constitution came under complete Canadian control. Previously, constitutional amendments required the British Parliament's approval.

Early life

Boyhood. Joseph Philippe Pierre Yves Elliott Trudeau was born in Montreal on Oct. 18, 1919. His father's family had gone to Canada from France during the 1600's. His mother's family was descended from British colonists who moved to Canada because of their loyalty to Britain during the Revolutionary War in America (1775-1783). Trudeau, his sister Suzette, and his brother Charles spoke French and English with equal ease. Trudeau's father became wealthy as owner of a chain of service stations.

Education. Trudeau grew up in Montreal, where he attended a Jesuit college, Jean-de-Brébeuf. He received a law degree from the University of Montreal in 1943. While at the University of Montreal, he enlisted in the Canadian Officer Training Corps. He later completed his training with an army reserve unit.

In 1945, Trudeau earned a master's degree in political economy at Harvard University. He then studied at the

Important events during Trudeau's administration

Dennis Brack, Black Star

Prime Minister Trudeau met with Soviet Premier Aleksei N. Kosygin, *left,* in Ottawa in 1971. The two men agreed to broaden contacts between Canada and the Soviet Union.

Bettmann Archive

A crisis broke out in 1970 when French-Canadian separatists kidnapped two government officials. Trudeau is shown leaving an emergency meeting of Parliament.

WORLD BOOK illustration by David Cunningham

The Election Act, passed in 1970, reduced the minimum voting age in national elections from 21 to 18.

École des Sciences Politiques (School of Political Sciences) in Paris and at the London School of Economics and Political Science in Britain.

His travels. In 1948, Trudeau set out to tour Europe and Asia. He traveled by motorbike or hitchhiked with a knapsack on his back. First he visited Germany, Austria, and Hungary. Then he traveled through Eastern Europe. In Jerusalem, the Arabs arrested him as an Israeli spy. But he continued on to Pakistan, Afghanistan, India, Burma (now Myanmar), Thailand, Indochina, and China. He returned to Canada from China in 1949.

Next, Trudeau worked in the Privy Council office in Ottawa as a junior law clerk. He returned to Montreal in 1951 and began to practice law. In 1960, Trudeau and five other Canadians toured China. They were among the first Western tourists admitted since the Communists conquered China in 1949. Trudeau became a law professor at the University of Montreal in 1961.

Entry into public life

During the late 1940's and the 1950's, Trudeau became concerned about the political situation in Quebec. The province was governed by Premier Maurice Duplessis and the Union Nationale Party. Trudeau and a group of youthful liberal friends set out to expose what they saw as dishonesty in the provincial government. They believed this corruption had resulted from political, religious, and business leaders working together to prevent reforms. To express their ideas, they established the magazine *Cité Libre* (Community of the Free).

Trudeau worked in many ways for reform in Quebec. The most publicized event took place in 1949 when miners went on strike in the town of Asbestos. Premier Duplessis ordered the provincial police to aid the company and the nonunion men it tried to hire during the strike. The strikers blockaded the roads into Asbestos and kept the strikebreakers from entering. Trudeau spent more than three weeks rallying the strikers. The police and many ministers called him an "outside agitator."

In 1956, Trudeau helped organize *Le Rassemblement* (The Gathering Together). The group's 600 members worked to explain democracy to the people of Quebec and to persuade them to use it. Trudeau later served as president of the group. In 1960, the Union Nationale Party was voted out of office.

French Canadians demanded more than democratic reform for Quebec. They had always struggled against what they believed was discrimination by Canada's English-speaking majority. Many French Canadians told of being refused jobs in government and industry because they spoke French. They feared that the French language would disappear in Canada if they were required to use English. They also feared that with the loss of their language they would lose their national identity and their culture and customs. Some demanded full equality. Others called for Quebec to become a separate country. During the 1960's, demands for separation from Canada became even stronger.

Trudeau favored preserving the French culture in Canada. But he opposed the creation of any country in

Duncan Cameron, Public Archives of Canada

Trudeau visited China in 1973, three years after Canada and China reestablished diplomatic relations. Chinese Premier Zhou Enlai welcomed the Trudeaus to Beijing.

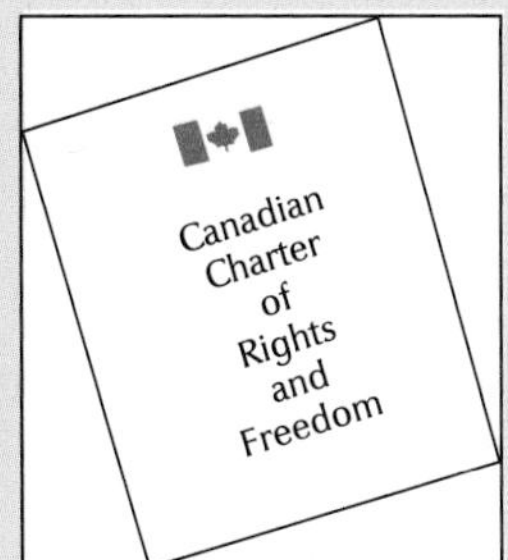

Canada's bill of rights is called the Canadian Charter of Rights and Freedoms. It was adopted as part of the Constitution Act of 1982.

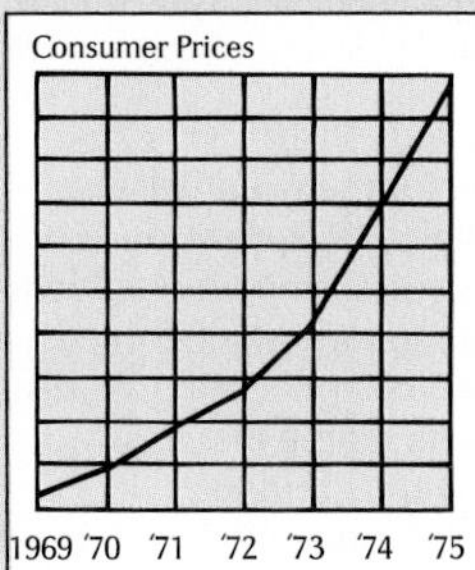

Rapid inflation became one of Canada's chief problems in 1969. To combat inflation, the Trudeau administration set limits on price and wage increases from 1975 to 1978.

Canapress

The Constitution Act was signed by Trudeau and Queen Elizabeth II on April 17, 1982. The act ended the need for British approval of amendments to Canada's constitution.

which nationality was the only major common bond.

Member of Parliament. In 1965, Trudeau decided to enter national politics and run for a seat in the House of Commons as a member of the Liberal Party. In November 1965, he was elected to Parliament from Mont-Royal, a Montreal suburb.

Parliamentary secretary. In January 1966, Prime Minister Pearson appointed Trudeau as his parliamentary secretary. Trudeau used this position to influence the government's policy on constitutional issues. He wanted the constitution changed to provide a stronger federal government and to promote more cooperation among the provinces. For example, Trudeau believed the wealthy provinces should help support the poorer ones. He favored a tax program that would divide tax money more fairly among the provinces. In March 1966, the government adopted this kind of plan.

Minister of justice. In April 1967, Pearson named Trudeau to the Cabinet as minister of justice and attorney general. In this post, Trudeau introduced legislation to strengthen gun-control laws and to reduce restrictions on abortion, divorce, gambling, and homosexuality. He believed that individuals should be free to do whatever they wished if they did not endanger society as a whole. The government sponsored similar legislation after Trudeau became prime minister.

Prime minister

In December 1967, Pearson announced his intention to retire. Trudeau was elected leader of the Liberal Party on April 6, 1968, and he became prime minister on April 20. He called a general election for June 25, and the Canadian voters strongly supported him in that election.

Foreign affairs. Trudeau wanted to strengthen Canada's independence in world affairs. Early in his term, he changed the nation's defense arrangements and expanded its relations with China and the Soviet Union.

New defense policy. Trudeau adopted a defense policy that emphasized the protection of Canadian territory. In 1970, he withdrew about half of the 9,800 Canadian troops serving with forces of the North Atlantic Treaty Organization (NATO) in Europe.

Important dates in Trudeau's life

1919	(Oct. 18) Born in Montreal.
1943	Earned law degree at University of Montreal.
1945	Earned master's degree at Harvard.
1961	Named professor of law at University of Montreal.
1965	Elected to House of Commons.
1966	Named parliamentary secretary to prime minister.
1967	Appointed minister of justice.
1968	Elected leader of Liberal Party and prime minister.
1971	(March 4) Married Margaret Sinclair.
1979	Progressive Conservatives defeated Liberals. Trudeau resigned as prime minister on June 4.
1980	Liberals defeated Progressive Conservatives. Trudeau became prime minister again on March 3.
1984	Trudeau resigned as prime minister on June 30.
2000	(Sept. 28) Died in Montreal.

Foreign relations. In 1970, Canada and China agreed to reestablish diplomatic relations. These ties had ended when the Communists gained control of China in 1949. The agreement had been one of Trudeau's chief goals. Trudeau visited China in 1973. He traveled to the Soviet Union in May 1971, and Premier Aleksei N. Kosygin of the Soviet Union toured Canada five months later. Trade increased with both China and the Soviet Union.

The national scene. Trudeau worked hard to help preserve the French heritage in Canada. For example, he greatly expanded the use of the French language in government services. Trudeau hoped his efforts would strengthen national unity. But relations between English- and French-speaking Canadians remained tense.

Domestic legislation. Parliament passed several far-reaching bills that were supported by Trudeau. In 1969, Parliament approved the Official Languages Act. This law requires courts and other government agencies to provide service in French in districts where at least 10 percent of the people speak French. It also requires service in English in districts where at least 10 percent of the people speak that language. The Election Act, passed in 1970, reduced the minimum voting age in national elections from 21 to 18. In 1971, Parliament extended unemployment insurance benefits to cover nearly all Canadian workers. In 1976, Parliament abolished the death penalty.

The October Crisis. Terrorism by Quebec separatists in October 1970 forced Trudeau to make his most difficult decision as prime minister. Members of the *Front de Libération du Québec* (FLQ), an underground separatist group, kidnapped Pierre Laporte, the labor minister of Quebec, and James R. Cross, the British trade commissioner in Montreal. Trudeau suspended civil liberties and sent federal troops to Quebec. He invoked the War Measures Act, which permits police to search and arrest without warrants and to deny bail.

Laporte was murdered, and four men were later imprisoned for the crime. The government let Cross's kidnappers go to Cuba in return for his release. Trudeau's firm stand received strong popular support.

The economy. Inflation became one of Canada's chief problems in 1969. To halt rising prices, Trudeau reduced government spending and eliminated thousands of civil service jobs. These policies contributed to a sharp increase in unemployment in 1970.

Economic conditions in Canada worsened in August 1971, when the United States placed a 10 percent *surcharge* (extra tax) on many imports. The surcharge affected about a fourth of Canada's exports. In September, unemployment reached 7.1 percent, the highest level since 1961. To encourage spending and help create jobs, Trudeau ordered cuts in individual and corporation income taxes. He also made available several hundred million dollars in loans for construction projects. The U.S. surcharge was ended in December.

The 1972 election. Trudeau called a general election for Oct. 30, 1972. He promised to seek new ways to reduce unemployment if he were returned to office. In the election, the Liberal and Conservative parties each won about 110 seats in the House of Commons. The Liberals failed to win a parliamentary majority, but Trudeau remained prime minister. Canada's economy expanded in 1973. But rapidly rising prices for clothing, food, fuel,

Canapress

Trudeau and his three sons, Michel, *left,* Justin, *top,* and Alexandre, *right,* posed for this photograph in 1982. Trudeau and his wife separated in 1977 and obtained a divorce in 1984.

and shelter caused hardship for many Canadians.

The 1974 election. On May 8, 1974, the House of Commons passed a motion expressing no-confidence in Trudeau's government. This motion, which forced a new general election, came on a vote concerning Trudeau's proposed budget. It was the first time that a Canadian government was defeated over its budget.

In the election of July 1974, Trudeau led the Liberal Party to victory. This time, the party gained a majority in the House of Commons, winning 141 of the 264 seats.

New economic policies. Trudeau's goverment also was concerned about the influence of foreign companies on the Canadian economy. In the mid-1970's, for example, U.S. firms controlled over half of Canada's manufacturing. Trudeau supported establishment of a Federal Investment Review Agency to ensure that foreign investments in Canada serve Canada's best interests. This agency, which was approved by Parliament in 1973, began to operate in 1974.

Inflation continued to soar in 1975. Late that year, the Trudeau administration set limits on price and wage increases. The controls expired in 1978.

The separatist challenge to Canada's national unity became more serious in 1976. The Parti Québécois, a political party that favored the separation of Quebec from Canada, won control of the province's government. Trudeau spoke out strongly against separatism.

The 1979 election. In March 1979, Trudeau called a general election for May 22. During the campaign, the Progressive Conservatives criticized Trudeau and the Liberals for their failure to solve Canada's economic problems. In the election, the Progressive Conservatives won 135 seats in the House of Commons, the Liberals won 115, and 32 seats went to smaller parties. Joe Clark, leader of the Conservatives, replaced Trudeau as prime minister. On November 21, Trudeau announced his intention to resign as party leader.

Return to power. The Liberals planned to select Trudeau's successor in a party convention in March 1980. But on Dec. 13, 1979, the House of Commons passed a motion of no confidence in Clark's government. The vote came during consideration of the government's proposed budget, which called for tax increases.

As a result of his government's defeat, Clark called a general election for Feb. 18, 1980. Trudeau led the Liberals. He climaxed an amazing political comeback when the Liberals won a majority in the House of Commons. Trudeau became prime minister again on March 3.

Soon afterward, the government of Quebec asked Quebecers to vote on whether the provincial government should have authority to negotiate for *sovereignty association* with Canada. Sovereignty association would have given Quebec political independence but maintained its economic ties to Canada. Trudeau campaigned against giving Quebec such authority. Quebec voters rejected the proposal on May 20, 1980.

Trudeau achieved a major goal in 1982, when the British Parliament approved an act giving Canada complete control over its constitution. The Constitution Act of 1982 set up a way to approve constitutional amendments in Canada instead of in Britain. Previously, many amendments required the British Parliament's approval.

A recession struck Canada during the early 1980's. The economy began to recover in 1983. But unemployment remained high, and public support for Trudeau's economic policies steadily declined. On June 30, 1984, Trudeau resigned as prime minister. He had held office for 15 years, longer than almost any other prime minister. W. L. Mackenzie King served for 21 years and Sir John Macdonald for almost 19 years. Trudeau was succeeded by his former finance minister, John N. Turner.

Later years

After he left office, Trudeau continued to play an important role in Canadian politics. He was especially influential as an opponent of Quebec nationalism and of proposals for shifting power from the federal government to the provinces. In the late 1980's and early 1990's, he helped generate opposition to two government plans that were designed to satisfy the demands of Quebec nationalists. These plans, the Meech Lake accord and the Charlottetown accord, called for revising the Canadian constitution to recognize Quebec as a distinct society within Canada. They also called for increasing the powers of Quebec and the other provinces. The plans were proposed by the government of Prime Minister Brian Mulroney. Mulroney, leader of the Progressive Conservatives, had replaced Turner as prime minister in 1984.

Trudeau helped lead opposition to the Meech Lake accord through well-timed speeches and through testimony before Canada's Parliament. The agreement failed in 1990 when the legislatures of Manitoba and Newfoundland rejected it. Trudeau expressed his opposition to the Charlottetown accord in a number of influential speeches and writings. The accord was defeated by a majority of Canadian voters in a referendum in 1992.

Trudeau died on Sept. 28, 2000, after a battle with prostate cancer and Parkinson disease. He was buried next to his parents and grandparents in St.-Rémi-de-Napierville, a town south of Montreal. J. L. Granatstein

See also **Canada, History of; Clark, Joe; Pearson, Lester B.; Prime minister of Canada.**

Additional resources

Butson, Thomas. *Pierre Elliott Trudeau.* Chelsea Hse., 1986.
Christiano, Kevin J. *Pierre Elliott Trudeau.* ECW Pr., 1994.
Clarkson, Stephen, and McCall, Christina. *Trudeau and Our Times.* McClelland, 1990- . Multivolume work.
Trudeau, Pierre E. *Memoirs.* McClelland, 1994.

Truffaut, *troo FOH,* **François,** *frahn SWAH* (1932-1984), was a leading French motion-picture director. He directed several semiautobiographical films, beginning in 1959 with *The 400 Blows.* The character Antoine Doinel reflects Truffaut's delinquent youth. Truffaut continued the story of Doinel's life in *Stolen Kisses* (1968), *Bed and Board* (1971), and *Love on the Run* (1978). Truffaut's *Day for Night* won the 1973 Academy Award as best foreign language film.

Truffaut began his career in the 1950's as a film critic and developed a respect for American suspense and action movies. His *Shoot the Piano Player* (1960) resembles an American gangster film. *The Bride Wore Black* (1967) and *Mississippi Mermaid* (1969) show the influence of American director Alfred Hitchcock. Truffaut's other major films include *Jules and Jim* (1961), *The Wild Child* (1970), and *The Last Metro* (1980).

Truffaut was born on Feb. 6, 1932, in Paris. He wrote an autobiography, *My Life in Film* (1975), and a book-length interview with Alfred Hitchcock, *Hitchcock* (1966, rev. ed. 1984). Gene D. Phillips

Truffle is a type of fungus used as food and as a flavoring. Truffles grow underground on or near the roots of oak, hazel, and other trees. They are round or potato-shaped and range from $\frac{1}{4}$ to 4 inches (0.6 to 10 centimeters) in diameter. Truffles have a firm interior and a smooth to warty exterior. They may be black, brown, white, or other colors. Truffles grow wild throughout the world. The highly prized *Périgord truffle* is grown in France, Spain, and Italy. The *white Piedmont truffle,* from Italy, is also excellent. Truffles produce odors that are easily sensed by animals, so dogs and pigs are used to locate them for harvest. Truffles are among the most expensive edible fungi. Joe F. Ammirati

Scientific classification. Truffles are in the family Tuberaceae. The Périgord truffle is *Tuber melanosporum.* The Piedmont truffle is *T. magnatum.*

Truk Islands, *truhk,* form a large island group in the western Pacific Ocean. Located in the Caroline Island chain, the Truk Islands make up a state of the country of the Federated States of Micronesia. The state is called Chuuk State. For location of the Truk Islands, see **Micronesia, Federated States of** (map). The Truk Islands include 14 volcanic islands that lie inside a barrier coral reef that forms a lagoon 40 miles (64 kilometers) wide. They also include about 50 small islets that lie along the reef. About 38,000 people live on the islands.

French navigator Louis Duperrey first explored the islands in 1825. Spain gained control of them in 1885 and sold them to Germany in 1899. Germany lost them to Japan in World War I (1914-1918). During World War II (1939-1945), the Truk Islands had a key Japanese naval base. Allied bombing raids destroyed the base. The United States took formal control of the islands in 1947 as part of a United Nations trusteeship. In 1978, the Truk Islands and other Carolines formed the Federated States of Micronesia, a political unit that had self-government but remained under U.S. control. In 1986, the Federated States became an independent country in free association with the United States. Robert C. Kiste

33rd president of the United States 1945-1953

F. D. Roosevelt 32nd president 1933-1945 Democrat

Truman 33rd president 1945-1953 Democrat

Eisenhower 34th president 1953-1961 Republican

Alben W. Barkley vice president 1949-1953

Harris & Ewing

Truman, Harry S. (1884-1972), became president at one of the most critical moments in American history. He had been vice president for only 83 days when President Franklin D. Roosevelt died on April 12, 1945. World War II still had to be won. Plans to establish the United Nations organization had just been started.

When Truman became president, he was known mainly for his work as chairman of a wartime Senate investigating committee that had saved millions of dollars in military contracts. The Missouri Democrat met the challenges of his presidency with courage, determination, and imagination. During the first few weeks of his Administration, the Allies won victory in Europe. Truman then made one of the most awesome decisions ever considered by one human being—to use the powerful new atomic bomb against Japan to end World War II.

Truman faced other great problems throughout his years in the White House. The United States had to reorganize its economy from a wartime to a peacetime basis. Many war-torn countries needed large relief programs. Western nations faced Communist subversion and aggression in a Cold War that divided the world. To meet these challenges, Truman's Administration created such far-reaching programs as the Truman Doctrine, the Marshall Plan, the Point Four Program, and the North Atlantic Treaty Organization (NATO).

When Communist forces from North Korea invaded South Korea in 1950, Truman faced another grave decision. If he sent armed forces to intervene without waiting for United Nations action, he risked war with the Soviet Union, a Communist ally of North Korea. But if he delayed, help might be too late. Within two days, the president ordered American armed forces to aid South Korea. His action preserved South Korean independence and demonstrated that the United States would support and defend its allies.

Truman's strong personality and fighting spirit won him loyal friends and bitter enemies. Blunt and outspoken, he often lashed out with strong language at those who opposed him. His opponents said he was too undignified. His friends loved him as a straightforward man of the people.

Early life

Childhood. Harry S. Truman was born in Lamar, Missouri, on May 8, 1884. He was the oldest of the three children of John Anderson Truman and Martha Ellen Young Truman. His parents named him Harry in honor of his uncle, Harrison Young. They chose the middle initial "S." But they gave him no middle name so that both his grandfathers, Solomon Young and Anderson Shippe Truman, could claim that he was named for them.

When Harry was 6 years old, his family moved from a farm near Grandview, Missouri, to Independence, Missouri. Harry went to elementary school and high school in Independence. Severely nearsighted, he began wearing glasses when he was 8. "I was so carefully cautioned by the eye doctor about breaking my glasses and injuring my eyes," he later wrote, "that I was afraid to join in the rough-and-tumble games in the schoolyard and back lot. My time was spent in reading, and by the time I was 13 or 14 years old I had read all the books in the Independence Public Library and our old Bible three times through." During the summers, Harry, his brother Vivian (1886-1965), and his sister Mary Jane (1889-1978) visited their grandparents' farm near Grandview. At the age of 18, Harry joined the Baptist Church.

First jobs. Truman wanted to go to the United States Military Academy at West Point, but his vision was not

War and its aftermath were major concerns. On Aug. 6, 1945, the United States dropped the first atomic bomb used in warfare on the Japanese city of Hiroshima, *left.* World War II ended soon afterward. In 1948 and 1949, the Allies staged a massive airlift, *below,* to deliver food and other necessities to West Berlin, which had been blockaded by the Soviet Union.

The world of President Truman

The first fully electronic digital computer was built by engineers at the University of Pennsylvania in 1946.
"Iron Curtain" was a phrase first used by Winston Churchill in 1946 to describe the barriers against the West set up by Communist governments in Eastern Europe.
Fears of Communist infiltration in postwar America led to congressional hearings, "blacklists" of persons in the entertainment industry, and the controversial spy trials of Alger Hiss and Ethel and Julius Rosenberg.
British India was divided into two independent nations—India and Pakistan—in 1947.
The first supersonic flight took place in 1947. U.S. Air Force Captain Charles Yeager flew a Bell X-1 rocket plane to break the sound barrier.
Jackie Robinson became the first black baseball player in the major leagues when he joined the Brooklyn Dodgers in 1947.
Israel was founded on May 14, 1948. The first Arab-Israeli war began the next day, when Arab countries attacked Israel.
Civil war in Greece ended in 1949 with the defeat of Communist-led rebels.
The Communist People's Republic of China was founded in 1949.
The first nationwide telecast showed President Truman opening the Japanese Peace Treaty Conference in San Francisco in 1951.
Elizabeth II became queen of the United Kingdom in 1952.

Keystone; Walter Sanders, *Life* magazine, © Time Inc.

good enough to meet Army standards. After graduating from high school in 1901, Harry briefly attended business school in Kansas City, Missouri. He also worked for a short time in the mailing room of the *Kansas City Star* and then took a job as a timekeeper for a construction crew of the Atchison, Topeka and Santa Fe Railway Company (now part of the Burlington Northern Santa Fe Corporation). His next employment was as a clerk and later as a bookkeeper in two Kansas City banks. He moved to Grandview in 1906 and, with his father, operated the family farm. He worked on the farm until 1917.

Soldier. Truman was a member of the Missouri National Guard From 1905 to 1911. When the United States entered World War I in 1917, he helped organize a field artillery regiment attached to the 35th Division. He then became a lieutenant. He was sent to France early in 1918. There, as a captain, he led an artillery battery in the Vosges, Meuse-Argonne, and Sommedieu campaigns. Truman was honorably discharged in 1919. He soon joined the Army reserves as a major and later rose to colonel.

Truman's family. Six weeks after he returned home, on June 28, 1919, Truman married his childhood sweetheart, Elizabeth "Bess" Virginia Wallace (1885-1982). They had met at Sunday school when they were children. They had one child, Mary Margaret (1924-), whom they called Margaret. She was a concert soprano, actress, and broadcaster for several years before becoming a best-selling author of detective stories.

Businessman. Before World War I, Truman had lost money in mining and oil investments. In 1919, he and his friend Eddie Jacobson invested their savings in a men's clothing store in Kansas City. They worked hard, keeping the store open from 8 a.m. to 9 p.m., but the business failed during the severe recession that began in 1921. Truman worked about 15 years to pay the store debts.

Political career

Discouraged by the failure of the store, Truman decided to seek a career in politics. He received help from

Important dates in Truman's life

1884	(May 8) Born in Lamar, Missouri.
1917-1919	Served in the U.S. Army during World War I.
1919	(June 28) Married Elizabeth Virginia Wallace.
1922	Elected judge of Jackson County, Missouri.
1934	Elected to the United States Senate.
1944	Elected vice president of the United States.
1945	(April 12) Became president of the United States.
1948	Elected president of the United States.
1972	(Dec. 26) Died in Kansas City, Missoui.

Vincil Warren, Missouri Department of Natural Resources

Truman's birthplace was this house in Lamar, Missouri. The family moved to Independence when Harry was 6 years old.

"Big Tom" Pendergast, the Democratic Party boss of Kansas City. Pendergast's nephew had known and admired Truman in the Army. Pendergast led one of the strongest political machines in the United States. He decided that Truman could win votes because of his farm background, his war record, and his friendly personality.

County judge. Pendergast supported Truman in his campaign for election as county judge of Jackson County. This post in Missouri resembled that of county commissioner in other states. Truman won the election, and served from 1922 to 1924. He lost the 1924 election due to a split in local Democratic forces. Truman attended the Kansas City School of Law in the mid-1920's, but did not obtain a degree. He served as presiding county judge from 1926 to 1934. The Pendergast machine was notoriously dishonest, but Truman won a reputation for honesty and efficiency. He supervised new projects financed by $14 million in tax funds and bond issues.

U.S. senator. Truman was elected to the U.S. Senate in 1934, again with Pendergast's support. As a member of the Senate Interstate Commerce Committee, Truman directed an investigation of railroad finances. His staff found damaging evidence about many of his friends in Missouri, but he ordered the investigation completed. A major result was the Transportation Act of 1940, which regulated railroad financing. Also during this time, a government study of the Pendergast political machine disclosed vote frauds and shady financial dealings. Pendergast pleaded guilty to income tax evasion, and he and many of his followers went to prison. The scandals did not touch Truman, but he refused to disclaim Pendergast. In1940, Truman won reelection to the Senate.

The Truman Committee. In 1940, although the United States was not formally involved in World War II, U.S. defense spending rose to huge sums. Truman realized that the defense effort created many opportunities for waste and corruption. He remembered that many committees had investigated military spending after World War I—when they could not recover wasted funds. Truman urged the Senate to set up a committee to investigate defense spending as it occurred. Early in 1941, the Senate established the Committee to Investigate the National Defense Program. Truman was named chairman. The Truman Committee, as the group became known, uncovered waste and inefficiency. It saved the government about $15 billion and speeded war production.

Harry S. Truman Library

Truman headed a Senate committee that saved the government about $15 billion by finding waste in wartime spending.

Office of War Information courtesy Harry S. Truman Library

Truman took the oath of office as president on April 12, 1945, following the death of Franklin D. Roosevelt. Truman's wife, Bess, witnessed the event, which took place at the White House.

Vice president. In 1944, many Democratic leaders believed that President Roosevelt would not live through a fourth term in the White House. They realized that the man they chose for vice president would probably succeed to the presidency.

The contest for the vice presidential nomination nearly split the party. Many liberals supported Vice President Henry A. Wallace for renomination. Others favored Supreme Court Justice William O. Douglas. Southern conservatives preferred James F. Byrnes, a former court justice. Roosevelt refused to name a preference. But Robert E. Hannegan of St. Louis, Missouri, a Truman supporter and chairman of the party's national committee, backed Truman as a compromise candidate. Truman had a national reputation owing to his committee investigations. He also had a good voting record as a senator, and Roosevelt was willing to accept him. Byrnes withdrew, and the delegates nominated Truman on the second ballot.

Roosevelt and Truman easily defeated their Republican opponents, Governor Thomas E. Dewey of New York and Governor John W. Bricker of Ohio (see **Roosevelt, Franklin D.** [Election of 1944]). As vice president, Truman presided over the Senate. During the 83 days he held this office, he worked hard to obtain Senate approval of Henry A. Wallace as secretary of commerce. He also broke a Senate tie by voting against an amendment prohibiting postwar delivery of goods through the Lend-Lease program (see **Lend-Lease**).

First administration (1945-1949)

On the afternoon of April 12, 1945, Truman was summoned to the White House by telephone. He was taken to Eleanor Roosevelt's study, and she stepped forward to meet him. "Harry," she said quietly, "the president is dead." Truman's first words were: "Is there anything I can do for you?" Mrs. Roosevelt replied: "Is there anything *we* can do for *you?* For you are the one in trouble now."

At 7:09 p.m., Truman took the oath of office as president. The next day, while talking to White House newsmen, he said: "Boys, if you ever pray, pray for me now. I don't know whether you fellows ever had a load of hay fall on you, but when they told me yesterday what had happened, I felt like the moon, the stars, and all the planets had fallen on me."

The end of World War II. When Truman became president, Allied armies were winning the war in Germany, and were preparing to invade Japan. Events moved swiftly. Thirteen days after Truman took office, the first United Nations conference met in San Francisco (see **San Francisco Conference**). Then, on May 7, Germany surrendered. Truman proclaimed May 8 as V-E Day (Victory in Europe Day). It was his 61st birthday.

In July, Truman traveled to Potsdam, Germany, to confer with Prime Minister Winston Churchill of the United Kingdom and Premier Joseph Stalin of the Soviet Union (see **Potsdam Conference**). While in Potsdam, the president received secret word that American scientists had successfully tested an atomic bomb for the first time. On his way home, Truman ordered American fliers to drop an atomic bomb on Japan. The first bomb fell on the city of Hiroshima on August 6. Three days later, a second atomic bomb was dropped on Nagasaki. Truman believed that dropping the atomic bombs would help end the war more quickly, thus saving hundreds of thousands of lives. Japan agreed to end the war on August 14, and formally surrendered on September 2. See **Nuclear weapon** (World War II); **World War II** (The atomic bomb).

Domestic program. Truman wanted to extend Roosevelt's "New Deal" policies. He drew up a program for reconstructing postwar America and presented it to Congress in September 1945. His requests included (1) extensive authority over the economy in the conversion from wartime to peacetime; (2) national health insurance; (3) a permanent Fair Employment Practices Commission (FEPC) to protect minority rights; (4) government aid for scientific research; and (5) public power projects on the Arkansas, Columbia, and Missouri rivers.

Crippling labor disputes and shortages of consumer goods helped the Republicans gain control of Congress in the 1946 elections. The Republicans blocked most of Truman's domestic measures. Congress did approve Truman's plan to unify the armed forces under a single secretary of defense (see **Defense, Department of**). A commission was established to study ways of improving government efficiency, and Truman named former Pres-

Vice president and Cabinet

Vice president	* Alben W. Barkley
Secretary of state	* Edward R. Stettinius, Jr.
	* James F. Byrnes (1945)
	* George C. Marshall (1947)
	* Dean G. Acheson (1949)
Secretary of the treasury	* Henry Morgenthau, Jr.
	* Frederick M. Vinson (1945)
	John W. Snyder (1946)
Secretary of war†	Henry L. Stimson
	Robert P. Patterson (1945)
	Kenneth C. Royall (1947)
Secretary of defense	* James V. Forrestal (1947)
	Louis A. Johnson (1949)
	* George C. Marshall (1950)
	Robert A. Lovett (1951)
Attorney general	Francis Biddle
	* Tom C. Clark (1945)
	J. Howard McGrath (1949)
	James P. McGranery (1952)
Postmaster general	Frank C. Walker
	Robert E. Hannegan (1945)
	Jesse M. Donaldson (1947)
Secretary of the navy†	* James V. Forrestal
Secretary of the interior	* Harold L. Ickes
	Julius A. Krug (1946)
	Oscar L. Chapman (1950)
Secretary of agriculture	Claude R. Wickard
	Clinton P. Anderson (1945)
	Charles F. Brannan (1948)
Secretary of commerce	* Henry A. Wallace
	* Averell Harriman (1946)
	Charles Sawyer (1948)
Secretary of labor	* Frances Perkins
	Lewis B. Schwellenbach (1945)
	Maurice J. Tobin (1948)

*Has a separate biography in *World Book*.
†Reduced to non-Cabinet rank under secretary of defense, 1947.

UPI/Bettmann Newsphotos

At the Potsdam Conference in Germany in July 1945, Truman conferred with Prime Minister Winston Churchill of the United Kingdom and Premier Joseph Stalin of the Soviet Union.

Harry S. Truman Library

The United Nations was established in 1945 at a conference in San Francisco. Truman, *second from left,* watched as U.S. Secretary of State Edward Stettinius signed the UN charter.

Norristown *Times Herald*

On his "whistle-stop" campaign for the presidency in 1948, Truman traveled by train and made more than 350 speeches.

UPI/Bettmann Newsphotos

Truman won an upset victory in 1948. He enjoyed a premature report of a win by Republican Thomas Dewey.

Quotations from Truman

The following quotations come from some of Harry Truman's speeches and writings.

The responsibility of great states is to serve and not to dominate the world.
Message to Congress, April 16, 1945

Sixteen hours ago an American airplane dropped one bomb on Hiroshima ... The force from which the sun draws its power has been loosed upon those who brought war to the Far East.
Address to the nation, August 6, 1945

I believe that it must be the policy of the United States to support free peoples who are resisting attempted subjugation by armed minorities or by outside pressures. I believe that we must assist free peoples to work out their own destinies in their own way.
Speech before Congress, March 12, 1947

We shall not ... achieve the ideals for which this nation was founded so long as any American suffers discrimination ... If we wish to inspire the peoples of the world whose freedom is in jeopardy, if we wish to restore hope to those who have already lost their civil liberties, ... we must correct the remaining imperfections in our practice of democracy.
Message to Congress, Feb. 2, 1948

We must embark on a bold new program for making the benefits of our scientific advances and industrial progress available for the improvement and growth of underdeveloped areas.
Inaugural Address, Jan. 20, 1949

Whenever you have an efficient government you have a dictatorship.
Lecture at Columbia University, April 28, 1959

ident Herbert Hoover to head it (see **Hoover Commission**). In 1947, after a long fight, Congress passed the Labor-Management Relations Act, or Taft-Hartley Act, over the president's veto (see **Taft-Hartley Act**). The act placed numerous restrictions on labor unions.

The Truman Doctrine. Soon after World War II, the Cold War developed between the Soviet Union and its former allies (see **Cold War**). The Communists gained control over one nation after another in Eastern Europe. Truman realized that the United States would have to lead in the fight for freedom, spending as much as necessary to strengthen its war-torn allies. In 1946, Congress approved a $3,750,000,000 loan to the United Kingdom. Then, on March 12, 1947, Truman announced a doctrine of international resistance to Communist aggression. The Truman Doctrine guaranteed American aid to free nations resisting Communist propaganda or sabotage.

The Marshall Plan, outlined by Secretary of State George C. Marshall in 1947, extended the Truman Doctrine. It proposed that the war-damaged nations of Europe join in a program of mutual aid for economic recovery, assisted by grants from the United States. Communist nations rejected the plan, but 18 other countries eventually accepted it. See **Marshall Plan**.

Election of 1948 seemed certain to bring victory to the Republicans. United and confident, they faced a sharply divided Democratic Party. The Democratic National Convention nominated Truman on the first ballot, and picked Senator Alben W. Barkley of Kentucky for Vice President. A group of liberal Democrats had already left the party and formed the Progressive Party. The Progressives nominated former vice president Wallace for president. Another group, made up of Southern Democrats who opposed a strong civil rights program, organized the Dixiecrat Party. They nominated Strom Thurmond, then governor of South Carolina. The Republicans again nominated Dewey for president, and chose Governor Earl Warren of California as his running mate. See **Dixiecrat Party; Progressive Party**.

Every public opinion poll predicted that Dewey would win a landslide victory. But, with an extraordinary show of fighting spirit, Truman made the experts look ridiculous. He traveled 31,000 miles (49,900 kilometers) by train in a "whistle-stop" campaign and made more than 350 speeches. He attacked what he termed the "do nothing" Republican Congress, calling it "the worst in my memory." Truman received a warm response with his simple language, earthy humor, and pluck. He also shrewdly appealed to the groups that had strongly supported Franklin D. Roosevelt—labor, farmers, liberals, minorities, and many middle-class consumers. In one of the biggest upsets in political history, Truman won 28

Truman's election

Place of nominating convention	Philadelphia
Ballot on which nominated	1st
Republican opponent	Thomas E. Dewey
Dixiecrat opponent	Strom Thurmond
Progressive opponent	Henry A. Wallace
Electoral vote	303 (Truman)* to: 189 (Dewey) 39 (Thurmond) 0 (Wallace)
Popular vote	24,105,587 (Truman) to: 21,970,017 (Dewey) 1,169,134 (Thurmond) 1,157,057 (Wallace)
Age at inauguration	64

*For votes by states, see **Electoral college** (table).

states. Dewey won 16 and Thurmond, 4. Truman won with less than 50 percent of the total popular vote.

Life in the White House. Early every day—often as early as 5:30 a.m.—Truman arose and went for a brisk walk, always accompanied by Secret Service agents and members of the media. At the White House, Truman often played the piano for visitors, and particularly enjoyed the music of Chopin and Mozart. The Trumans spent most evenings in a family living room upstairs.

The structural part of the White House had become dangerously weak, and engineers had to make extensive repairs. The work began late in 1948, and the Trumans moved to Blair House, a historic mansion on Pennsylvania Avenue. They lived there until March 1952.

On Nov. 1, 1950, two Puerto Rican nationalists tried to invade Blair House and assassinate the president. They killed one Secret Service guard and wounded another. One of the gunmen was killed and the other captured. Truman commented that "A president has to expect those things." He kept all his appointments that day, and took his usual walk the next morning.

Second administration (1949-1953)

Foreign affairs. In the spring of 1949, the United States, Canada, the United Kingdom, France, and eight other nations signed the North Atlantic Treaty, forming the North Atlantic Treaty Organization (NATO). They agreed that an attack on one member would be considered an attack on all. Other countries later joined NATO and helped group their armed forces to defend Western Europe. General Dwight D. Eisenhower served as the first supreme commander of NATO forces. See **North Atlantic Treaty Organization**.

In his inaugural address, Truman called for "a bold new program for making the benefits of our scientific advances and industrial progress available for the improvement and growth of underdeveloped areas." In 1950, Congress approved $35 million for the first part of this Point Four Program. Late in 1951, Truman asked Congress to set up a new foreign aid program for Communist-threatened countries in Southeast Asia. Congress established the Mutual Security Administration to strengthen military defenses in many countries. Western Europe had recovered economically from the war, so Truman changed the emphasis of foreign aid from economic help to mutual security. He believed that if the nation's allies were strong, America would be strengthened, too. See **Foreign aid**.

The Korean War began on June 25, 1950, when Communist forces from North Korea invaded South Korea. The United Nations demanded that North Korea withdraw. Truman decided to intervene to save South Korea's independence. On June 27, he announced that he had sent U.S. planes and ships to help South Korea. Congress cheered the announcement. That same day, the UN approved sending troops of other nations to join South Korean and American units. Truman ordered ground forces to South Korea on June 30. He later said that sending U.S. troops to South Korea—and thus taking the risk of starting World War III—was the hardest decision of his political career.

General Douglas MacArthur commanded all UN forces in Korea. His troops brought most of Korea under UN control by October 1950. But later that month, Chinese Communist troops joined the North Koreans. Truman recognized the urgency of the situation and put the

UPI/Bettmann Newsphotos

Truman's wife and daughter were known as "the bosses." The president playfully spoke of his wife Bess as "the boss" and of their daughter Margaret as "the one who bosses her." The family is shown here on Truman's 68th birthday.

Detroit News

Truman enjoyed playing the piano. The president often entertained visitors to the White House with a session at the keyboard.

Highlights of Truman's administration

1945	(May 7) Germany surrendered to the Allies.
1945	(July 16) The first atomic bomb was tested.
1945	(Sept. 2) Japan's surrender ended World War II.
1945	(Oct. 24) The United Nations was founded.
1947	(May 15) Congress approved the Truman Doctrine.
1947	(June) Congress passed the Taft-Hartley Act over Truman's veto.
1947	(July) Congress unified the U.S. armed forces.
1948	(April 2) Congress approved the Marshall Plan.
1949	(April 4) The United States and 11 other nations set up the North Atlantic Treaty Organization (NATO).
1950	(June 27) The United States sent forces to defend South Korea against Communist aggression.

United States on a semiwar basis. MacArthur wanted to attack Chinese Communist bases in Manchuria. But Truman believed that the fighting must be confined to Korea, and not be allowed to spread into a possible global war. MacArthur made several public statements criticizing this policy. In April 1951, Truman dismissed MacArthur, creating a nationwide furor. See **Korean War**.

Problems at home. The voters had elected a Democratic Congress in 1948. It soon proved almost as uncooperative in domestic affairs as the preceding Republican Congress had been. Truman waged an extensive reform program, which he called the "Fair Deal." "Every segment of our population and every individual has a right to expect from our government a fair deal," he declared. The program included (1) civil rights legislation; (2) repeal of the Taft-Hartley Act; (3) a new farm program stressing high farm income and low consumer prices; (4) federal aid to education; (5) a federal housing program; and (6) increases in the Social Security program. Southern Democrats joined conservative Republicans to defeat most of the president's domestic proposals. The Democratic Party lost strength in the 1950 congressional elections.

Charges of Communist infiltration into the federal government added to the president's concerns. Truman set up a federal board to investigate the loyalty of government employees, and the Department of Justice prosecuted leaders of the American Communist Party. A House committee investigated charges that Communists worked for the Department of State. The trials of Alger Hiss and Ethel and Julius Rosenberg revealed that spies had stolen secret information and given it to Soviet agents (see **Hiss, Alger; Rosenberg, Julius and Ethel**). Senator Joseph R. McCarthy of Wisconsin also accused the Department of State of employing Communists. Truman strongly rejected McCarthy's charges, and they were never proven.

Campaign of 1952. On March 29, 1952, Truman announced that he would not seek reelection. "I have served my country long, and I think efficiently and honestly," he said. "I do not feel that it is my duty to spend another four years in the White House." Instead, he campaigned for the Democratic candidate, Governor Adlai E. Stevenson of Illinois, who lost to Dwight D. Eisenhower.

Elder statesman

Truman left office on Jan. 20, 1953, and retired to his home in Independence. He published the two volumes of his memoirs, *Year of Decisions* in 1955 and *Years of Trial and Hope* in 1956. Truman also continued his active interest in politics and in the Democratic Party.

After Truman left the White House, his friends collected funds to build the Harry S. Truman Library in Independence. The library holds Truman's papers and souvenirs. It opened in 1957.

Truman became ill late in 1972 and entered the hospital on December 5 with severe lung congestion. He died on December 26. He was buried in Independence in the Truman Library courtyard. Alonzo L. Hamby

Related articles in *World Book* include:

Cold War
Defense, Department of
Dewey, Thomas E.
Dixiecrat Party
Foreign aid
Hoover Commission
Marshall Plan
Nuclear weapon
Pendergast, Thomas Joseph
Potsdam Conference
President of the United States
Roosevelt, Franklin Delano
San Francisco Conference
United Nations
Vice president of the United States
Wallace, Henry Agard
World War II

Outline

I. **Early life**
 A. Childhood
 B. First jobs
 C. Soldier
 D. Truman's family
 E. Businessman
II. **Political career**
 A. County judge
 B. U.S. senator
 C. The Truman Committee
 D. Vice president
III. **First administration (1945-1949)**
 A. The end of World War II
 B. Domestic program
 C. The Truman Doctrine
 D. The Marshall Plan
 E. Election of 1948
 F. Life in the White House
IV. **Second administration (1949-1953)**
 A. Foreign affairs
 B. The Korean War
 C. Problems at home
 D. Campaign of 1952
V. **Elder statesman**

Questions

What reforms did the "Fair Deal" call for?
Where did Truman meet his future wife?
What awesome decision did Truman make to end World War II?
What was the Truman Doctrine?
How did Truman win an upset victory in 1948?
Why did Truman dismiss General MacArthur in Korea?
What did the Truman Committee accomplish?
Why did some Democrats feel that Truman would make a good vice presidential nominee in 1944?
How did Truman fight Communism at home?
Why was the Democratic vice presidential nomination especially important in 1944?

Additional resources

Egendorf, Laura K. *Harry S. Truman.* Greenhaven, 2002.
Ferrell, Robert H. *Harry S. Truman: A Life.* 1994. Reprint. Univ. of Mo. Pr., 1996.
Hamby, Alonzo L. *Man of the People: A Life of Harry S. Truman.* 1995. Reprint. Oxford, 1998.
Lazo, Caroline E. *Harry S. Truman.* Lerner, 2003. Younger readers.
McCullough, David. *Truman.* 1992. Reprint. Simon & Schuster, 1996.

Trumbull, John (1756-1843), an American artist, became known for his paintings of scenes of the Revolutionary War in America (1775-1783). Thomas Jefferson advised him about his historical subjects. From 1789 to 1794, Trumbull made portraits of the individuals he intended to include in the scenes. He later copied the portraits into his compositions.

Trumbull was born on June 6, 1756, into a prominent

family in Lebanon, Connecticut. After graduating from Harvard College in 1773, he enlisted in the Continental Army. During the war, Trumbull served as an aide to George Washington, commander in chief of the colonial army.

After the war, Trumbull resumed the study of painting in London under artist Benjamin West and planned his paintings of the American Revolution. In 1817, Trumbull received a commission to paint four large versions of war subjects in the Rotunda of the U.S. Capitol. The remaining years of his life were disappointing, partly because of his failing eyesight and quarrelsome disposition. Elizabeth Garrity Ellis

For examples of Trumbull's work, see the pictures with the articles **Adams, John; Burgoyne, John; Declaration of Independence; Hamilton, Alexander; Hessians;** and **Revolutionary War in America.**

Trumbull, Jonathan (1710-1785), was governor of Connecticut in the Revolutionary period. He was the only prewar colonial governor who supported the patriots. Trumbull supplied the Continental Army with food, clothing, and munitions. This task kept him in close touch with General George Washington (see **Brother Jonathan**).

Trumbull was born on Oct. 12, 1710, in Lebanon, Connecticut. He built up a business with Britain, which failed just before war began. The experience helped him later in supplying the patriots. He served in the legislature and as deputy governor before holding office as governor from 1769 to 1784. In 1872, his statue was placed in the Capitol in Washington, D.C. John W. Ifkovic

Trumbull, Lyman (1813-1896), was an American political leader. He strongly opposed slavery. As a United States senator, he supported President Abraham Lincoln during the American Civil War (1861-1865) and helped frame Amendment 13 to the U.S. Constitution, which abolished slavery. Trumbull guided Amendment 14, guaranteeing the rights of African Americans, through Congress. He voted against conviction after President Andrew Johnson's impeachment in 1868.

Trumbull was born on Oct. 12, 1813, in Colchester, Connecticut, and moved to Illinois in 1837. He served in public office as a Democrat, a Republican, and a Liberal Republican. Trumbull served on the Illinois Supreme Court from 1849 to 1854 and in the United States Senate from 1855 to 1873. After leaving the Senate, Trumbull was active in Illinois politics as a Democrat and then as a Populist. James M. McPherson

Trumpet is a popular brass instrument in orchestras, bands, and jazz groups. A player produces tones by blowing into a cup-shaped mouthpiece and vibrating the lips. The player changes notes by fingering the instrument's three valves and changing lip tension. The largest part of the trumpet consists of a curved tube. Most trumpets used in bands are pitched in the key of B flat and have a tube 4 ½ feet (1.4 meters) long. Orchestras use those kinds and ones with shorter tubes, pitched in other keys. The small diameter and cylindrical shape of its tube give the trumpet its brilliant, powerful sound.

Trumpets date back to about 1200 B.C. The valve trumpet was developed in 1813. Stewart L. Ross

Related articles in *World Book* include:

Armstrong, Louis	Gillespie, Dizzy	Marsalis, Wynton
Davis, Miles	Jazz (The brass)	Masekela, Hugh

Trunk. See Tree (The parts of a tree).

Trust. See **Antitrust laws**.

Trust estate. See Trust fund.

Trust fund is money or other property managed by one person or group for the benefit of another person or group. Other terms for a trust fund include *corpus, principal,* and *trust estate.* The arrangement under which a trust fund is managed is called a *trust.*

In some cases, the property in a trust fund is taxed less heavily than property owned without such an arrangement. As a result, many people establish trust funds to reduce their taxes. Others create trust funds for the benefit of children or other people who cannot manage property themselves. Some people use trust funds to take advantage of an individual's or institution's special skill in managing property.

How a trust fund works. Most trust funds involve three parties: a *trustor,* a *trustee,* and a *beneficiary.* In some cases, the trustor is also the trustee or the beneficiary. The trustor, also called the *settlor* or *donor,* creates a trust fund by giving property to a trustee. The trustee holds or invests the fund for the good of the beneficiary. The trustee may have charge of the fund for a few years or for more than a lifetime, depending on the terms of the trust. After the trust has *terminated* (ended), the trustee distributes the property as directed in the terms of the trust.

Any sane adult may serve as a trustee. But most trust funds are handled by *trust departments* of banks or by businesses called *trust companies.* In most cases, the fee for the trustee's services is set by an agreement between the trustor and trustee. Trustees must keep accounts of all trust funds they hold, invest, or distribute. In addition, they must follow the trustor's wishes concerning investment of the fund. If the trust does not indicate the trustor's wishes for investment, the trustee must follow guidelines set by state laws. A trustee must make good

WORLD BOOK illustration by Oxford Illustrators Limited

Northwestern University (WORLD BOOK photo by Ted Nielsen)

The trumpet is a popular brass instrument with a brilliant tone. A trumpet player can produce all notes of the scale by pressing the instrument's three piston valves in various combinations.

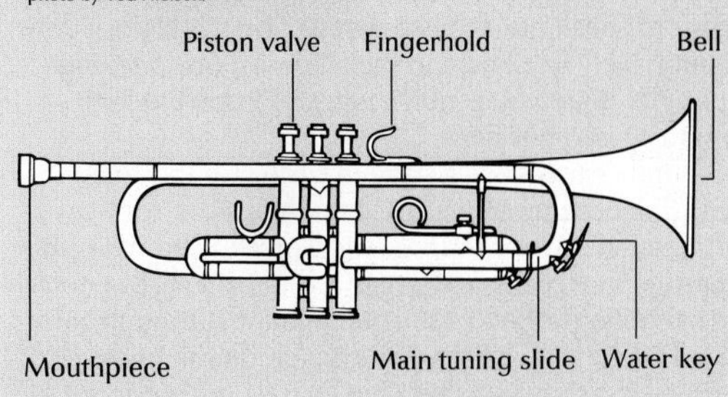

any losses that result from wrongful use of a trust fund.

Beneficiaries receive income from trust funds according to a variety of arrangements. For example, some beneficiaries periodically receive income earned by the trust fund. Other beneficiaries must wait and receive the accumulated income from the fund when they reach a certain age. Some beneficiaries receive payments from the trust fund until they reach a certain age. When they reach that age, the beneficiaries take possession of the fund themselves.

Kinds of trusts. A trust that operates during the trustor's life is called a *living* or *inter vivos trust.* A trust established by a will is called a *testamentary trust.* A *revocable trust* can be changed or abolished by the trustor. A trustor who gives up all rights to the trust fund creates an *irrevocable trust.*

Trusts established for the benefit of churches, colleges, or other nonprofit organizations are *charitable trusts. Life insurance trusts* receive the proceeds of insurance policies on the life of the trustor.

Courts occasionally create *constructive trusts* to protect property. For example, a person who has property that belongs to another may be named *constructive trustee* of that property. Such an arrangement protects the property and ensures that it will be returned to the rightful owner. T. Bryan Underwood, Jr.

See also **Receiver.**

Trust territory refers to an area administered by a country under the supervision of the United Nations (UN) Trusteeship Council. The administering country has complete authority over the government of a trust territory. It administers the territory under an agreement with the UN according to principles set down in the UN Charter.

Eleven trust territories were established after World War II ended in 1945. These territories included the former Italian colony of Somaliland and 10 of the 11 former mandates of the League of Nations (see **Mandated territory**). Of the 11 trust territories, all of them except for the U.S.-administered Trust Territory of the Pacific Islands became independent or voted to become a part of an independent nation between the mid-1950's and the mid-1970's. In 1986, all of the units of the Trust Territory of the Pacific Islands except the Palau Islands gained self-government. The Palau Islands became self-governing in 1994. See **Pacific Islands, Trust Territory of the.** Robert J. Pranger

See also **United Nations** (The Trusteeship Council).

Truth, Sojourner (1797?-1883), was the name used by Isabella Baumfree, one of the best-known American abolitionists of her day. She was the first black woman orator to speak out against slavery. She traveled widely through New England and the Midwest on speaking tours. Her deep voice, quick wit, and inspiring faith helped spread her fame.

Baumfree was born a slave in Ulster County, New York. She became free in 1828 under a New York law that banned slavery. In 1843, she experienced what she regarded as a command from God to preach. She took the name Sojourner Truth and began lecturing in New York. Her early speeches were based on the belief that people best show love for God by love and concern for others. She soon began directing her speeches toward the abolition of slavery.

In 1864, Sojourner Truth visited President Abraham Lincoln in the White House. She stayed in Washington, D.C., and worked to improve living conditions for blacks there. She also helped find jobs and homes for slaves who had escaped from the South to Washington. In the 1870s, she tried to persuade the federal government to set aside undeveloped lands in the West as farms for blacks. But her plan won no government support.

Chicago Historical Society
Sojourner Truth

Otey M. Scruggs

Additional resources

Bernard, Catherine J. *Sojourner Truth.* Enslow, 2001.
Lutz, Norma J. *Sojourner Truth.* Chelsea Hse., 2000. Younger readers.
Painter, Nell I. *Sojourner Truth.* Norton, 1996.
Truth, Sojourner. *Narrative of Sojourner Truth.* 1850, expanded in 1875. Available in many editions.

Truth commission is an investigative body that examines human rights issues relating to a time when a country treated its people unjustly. Truth commissions may be established by governments or international organizations. They provide opportunities for people from all sides of a conflict to speak publicly about violations of human rights. Through this process, truth commissions seek to promote forgiveness and national unity. Truth commissions may grant *amnesty* (pardon) to people accused of human rights abuses if those people confess and provide information about the abuses.

The best-known truth commission is the Truth and Reconciliation Commission (TRC) of South Africa. It began its work in 1996 and issued its final report in 2003. The TRC investigated abuses that occurred between 1948 and 1991 under the country's system of strict racial separation called *apartheid.* Truth commissions have also operated in various countries in Africa, Asia, Europe, and Latin America. Bruce Cronin

See also **Apartheid; South Africa** (History).

Truth in Lending Act. See **Consumerism** (The right to information); **Usury.**

Truth serum. See **Thiopental.**

Truth table is a method of showing logical relationships between statements. Truth tables are used by logicians, computer engineers, and others who reason by symbolic logic.

To understand truth tables, we must first understand some ideas of logic. A basic declarative sentence is a *proposition* if it can be classified as true or false. For example, the following two sentences are propositions: *The door is open. The light is on.*

When propositions are combined using such *logical connectives* as *and, or,* or *if ... then ...*, they form *propositional functions.* For example, the two propositions above may be combined into the propositional function *The door is open, and the light is on.* The truth or falsity of a propositional function depends on the truth or falsity of each of the basic propositions and the way the function relates to them.

The truth table corresponding to the above propositional function would look like this:

Basic propositions		Propositional function
Door open	**Light on**	**Door open and light on**
false	false	false
false	true	false
true	false	false
true	true	true

The table begins with a list of all combinations of true and false values that can be assigned to the basic propositions. The table is completed by indicating the truth or falsity of the propositional function for each combination. Dan Lloyd

Trypanosome, *TRIHP uh nuh sohm* or *trih PAN uh sohm,* is a microscopic one-celled organism. Trypanosomes live as parasites in the blood, spinal fluid, and tissues of human beings and other vertebrates. Some are parasites in plants. Different species cause *African sleeping sickness; South American trypanosomiasis,* also called *Chagas' disease;* and *nagana,* an African disease of animals. A trypanosome is long and thin, with a whiplike extension called a *flagellum* at one end. It also has a thin, waving *undulating membrane* down the length of its body. Many trypanosomes spend part of their life cycle inside certain insects. Felipe Kierszenbaum

Scientific classification. Trypanosomes make up the genus *Trypanosoma* in the kingdom Protista.

See also **Tsetse fly; Sleeping sickness.**

Tschaikowsky, Peter Ilich. See Tchaikovsky, Peter Ilich.

Tserclaes, Johan. See Tilly, Count of.

Tsetse fly, *TSEHT see,* is a two-winged fly of Africa. It carries *trypanosomes,* the animal parasites that cause African sleeping sickness, a potentially fatal human disease, and nagana, a deadly disease of cattle and horses.

There are more than 20 kinds of tsetse flies. Several of them attack people. The flies resemble typical house flies, but they grow larger and fold their wings flat over their backs so that the wings do not stick out at an angle, as they do on house flies. The tsetse fly's long *proboscis* (beak) pierces the body of its host. Most tsetse flies suck blood from mammals, but some kinds take blood from reptiles and birds. As they suck blood, they infect the host. A tsetse fly transmits both nagana and sleeping sickness by biting an infected animal or person, picking up the parasites, and infecting the next host it bites.

The flies usually cannot infect people until the parasites have lived in their bodies several days and have passed through the stomach to their salivary glands. Then the flies can transmit the parasites to anyone they bite. The parasites that infect animals develop in the fly's proboscis or in the stomach and proboscis.

Tsetse flies breed slowly. The female fly produces only one egg at a time. The larva hatches from the egg and is nourished during the growing period inside the body of the parent. When the larva is full-grown, it is deposited on the ground. It then burrows beneath the soil before transforming into a pupa.

All tsetse flies bite during the day. They often live by lakeshores and riverbanks, making parts of Africa uninhabitable. In some regions, insecticide sprays and removal of vegetation control tsetse fly populations. Other control programs use special traps. Drugs that protect cattle from nagana are also used. But political unrest has hampered control efforts in Africa. E. W. Cupp

Scientific classification. Tsetse flies belong to the house fly and blow fly family, Muscidae. The most dangerous tsetse flies are *Glossina palpalis* and *G. morsitans.*

See also **Sleeping sickness; Trypanosome.**

Tsimshian Indians, *TSIHM shee uhn,* once ranked among the wealthiest tribes in North America. Their homeland lies in British Columbia in Canada, chiefly along and between the Nass and Skeena rivers. The Tsimshian became known for their graceful oceangoing canoes and well-crafted totem poles, masks, and carved wooden boxes.

In their traditional way of life, the Tsimshian lived in groups of families related through the women. These groups lived in large plank houses built along rivers and beaches. Family groups placed totem poles in front of their homes and elsewhere to signify the group's social rank and ancestry. A vast supply of timber, plant life, and fish and other game in their homeland helped the Tsimshian become wealthy. Some families owned slaves. Most slaves were enemies captured during wartime or were the descendants of such enemies.

The Tsimshian still hold elaborate feasts called *potlatches* to mark marriages, deaths, or other notable occasions. Potlatches are also used to establish social rank and gain prestige. Hosts achieve these goals by displaying possessions, giving them away, or occasionally destroying them.

Many Tsimshian increased their wealth during the late 1700's and early 1800's, after sea merchants from Europe and the United States began to sail to the northwest coast of North America. The Indians traded furs for metal tools, textiles, and other manufactured goods.

Today, there are about 12,000 Tsimshian. Most live in or near their traditional homeland and work in fishing, mining, and timber industries. Robert S. Grumet

Tsunami, *tsoo NAH mee,* is a series of powerful ocean waves produced by an earthquake, landslide, volcanic eruption, or asteroid impact. Tsunami waves can travel great distances and still retain much of their strength. They differ from common ocean waves, which are caused by wind. The word *tsunami* is a combination of Japanese words meaning *harbor* and *wave.*

Tsunami waves are much longer than common ocean waves. In the open ocean, the water may take from 5 minutes to over 1 hour to reach its highest level and fall back again as a tsunami wave passes. By contrast, a common ocean wave causes the water level to rise and fall in 5 to 20 seconds. Tsunami waves in the open ocean usually raise and lower the water level by 3 feet (1 meter) or less. Because the change happens gradually, tsunamis frequently go undetected by ships.

The deeper the water is, the faster a tsunami wave travels. In the Pacific Ocean basin, where depths average about 13,000 feet (4,000 meters), tsunami waves can travel up to 600 miles (970 kilometers) per hour, as fast as a jet aircraft. As a tsunami wave approaches land, its speed drops to about 20 to 30 miles (30 to 50 kilometers) per hour. As the wave's speed decreases, its height usually grows by at least three times. The resulting flood of

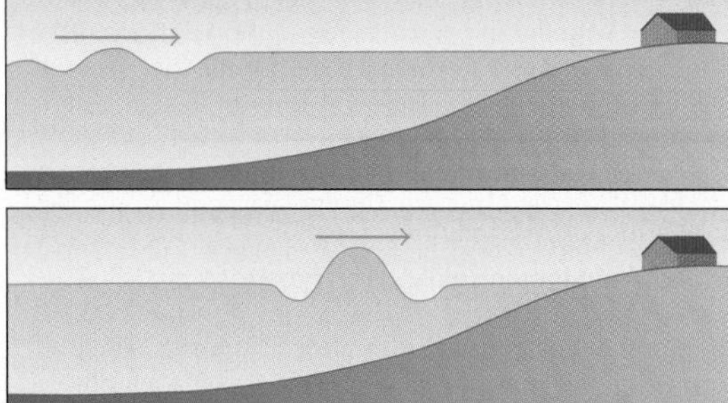

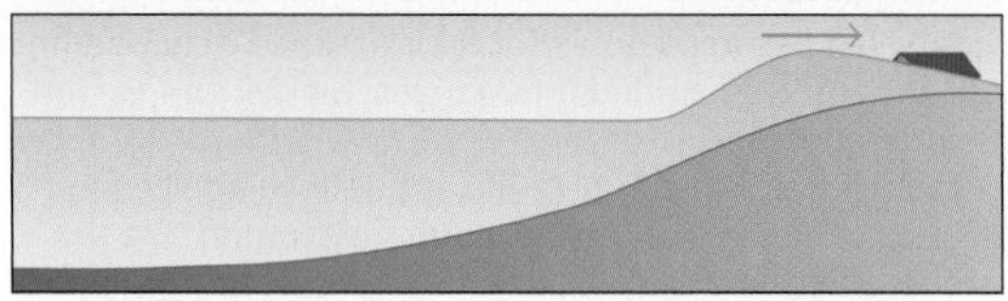

WORLD BOOK illustration

A tsunami wave on the open ocean is long and low, *top*. As the wave enters shallow water, it slows, causing its height to grow dramatically, *middle*. The wave then surges onto land, *bottom*.

water can surge more than ⅝ mile (1 kilometer) inland and pile up in certain places to reach elevations higher than 100 feet (30 meters) above sea level.

Scientists strive to predict tsunamis so that endangered coastal areas can be evacuated. One method uses devices called *seismographs* to measure *seismic waves* (waves of vibration generated by earthquakes). By analyzing seismic waves, scientists can determine when and where an undersea earthquake has occurred and calculate its strength. As a result, they can then estimate the size of a possible tsunami and the time its waves will reach land. Seismic waves travel through the ground much faster than tsunami waves travel through the water. For this reason, scientists can sometimes warn people several hours before tsunami waves strike.

Other forecasting methods use *pressure sensors* placed on the ocean floor. When a sensor detects pressure from a large tsunami, it relays the information to a buoy. The buoy then transmits the data to a warning center. Scientists are also developing methods to detect tsunamis using radar signals from satellites.

In December 2004, an enormous undersea earthquake west of the Indonesian island of Sumatra created a tsunami that pounded low-lying coastlines throughout the Indian Ocean, killing more than 175,000 people and causing billions of dollars in property damage. The greatest number of deaths occurred in Indonesia, Sri Lanka, India, and Thailand. Deaths were reported as far as away as Somalia, about 3,000 miles (4,800 kilometers) from the tsunami's origin. Steven Ward

Tuamotu Islands, *TOO uh MOH too,* are an island group in the South Pacific (see **Pacific Islands** [map]). The group has 76 reef islands and *atolls* (rings of coral islands). It extends across nearly 1,000 miles (1,600 kilometers) of water and has dangerous underwater reefs. The islands cover about 300 square miles (775 square kilometers). Destructive hurricanes sometimes strike the islands, which have a tropical climate. Like other low-elevation atolls, the islands often have shortages of fresh water. This is due to low rainfall and a lack of lakes and rivers. Pearls and copra are the chief sources of income.

In 1606, Pedro Fernandez de Quirós, a Portuguese explorer in Spain's service, became the first European to see the islands. A native king ruled the islands until France annexed them in 1881. France now administers the Tuamotus, as well as the nearby Gambier Islands, as a unit of French Polynesia, an overseas possession of France. The two island groups have a total population of about 16,000. France tested nuclear bombs on Mururoa atoll from 1965 until the early 1990's. Nancy Davis Lewis

Tuareg, *TWAH rehg,* are the largest group of nomads living in the Sahara. More than 300,000 Tuareg live in the desert, chiefly in Algeria, Mali, and Niger. The Tuareg are Muslims. They are related to the Berbers of northern Africa and speak a Berber language (see **Berbers**).

Most Tuareg herd camels, goats, sheep, and cattle and move about in areas of the Sahara where seasonal rainfall provides pasture for their livestock. Families live in tents made of either goatskins or mats woven from palm leaves. Men tend the herds, and women milk the livestock and grind grain to prepare meals. Milk is the most important food in the diet.

The Tuareg are sometimes called the *Blue Men of the Desert.* They often wear indigo-dyed robes, which leave a blue color on their skin. The men wear turbans for protection against sandstorms and the sun. They wrap the turbans around their heads and across their faces to form a veil so that only their eyes can be seen.

Tuareg society has three main social classes. These classes are (1) nobles, (2) vassals, and (3) slaves. The Tuareg are organized into confederations that consist of several noble and vassal tribes. A chief heads each confederation. The vassals choose a noble as chief. Women and men are considered social equals. Husbands and wives own separate property, including livestock.

The Tuareg are believed to be descendants of people who originally lived in Libya more than 2,000 years ago. The Tuareg fought against Turkish, Arab, and European rulers of North Africa. They were fiercely independent until the French defeated them during the late 1800's and early 1900's. Droughts have always threatened the nomadic life of the Tuareg. During a drought that lasted from 1968 to 1974, thousands of Tuareg and entire herds of their cattle died. Candelario Sáenz and Barbara A. Worley

Tuatara, *too uh TAH ruh,* is the name for two kinds of lizardlike reptiles that live only on a few small islands off the coast of New Zealand. Tuataras are the only living members of an ancient group of reptiles that appeared on Earth more than 200 million years ago.

Tuataras have scaly, gray or greenish skin. They have spiny, enlarged scales down the back and tail. Males can grow more than 2 feet (60 centimeters) long. Females are shorter. Tuataras sleep during the day, often in burrows dug by sea birds. They emerge at night to hunt insects, amphibians, snails, birds, and small lizards. They have sharp teeth with which they tear up prey. A tuatara's tail breaks off easily. If an enemy seizes the tail, the tuatara sheds the tail. It then grows a new tail.

The female tuatara lays from 8 to 15 eggs nearly a year after mating. She deposits the eggs in a burrow, where they develop for more than a year before hatching. The eggs of no other reptile take as long to develop.

Tuataras grow slowly and do not mate until they reach about 13 years of age. These animals live a long time. The longest recorded life span for a tuatara is 77 years. Raymond B. Huey

Scientific classification. Tuataras make up the order Sphenodontia in the class Reptilia. The scientific name for the more common species is *Sphenodon punctatus.*

Tuba is the general name for a number of musical instruments in the brass family. Tubas are the largest of the brass instruments and have the lowest pitch, serving as the bass voice in a brass section. A musician plays the tuba by vibrating the lips in a cup-shaped or funnel-shaped mouthpiece. Pitches are determined by the tension of the lips and the fingering of the instrument's valves.

Northwestern University (WORLD BOOK photo by Ted Nielsen)

The upright tuba is used in the brass section of symphony orchestras. The instrument is played in a seated position with the bell pointed upward.

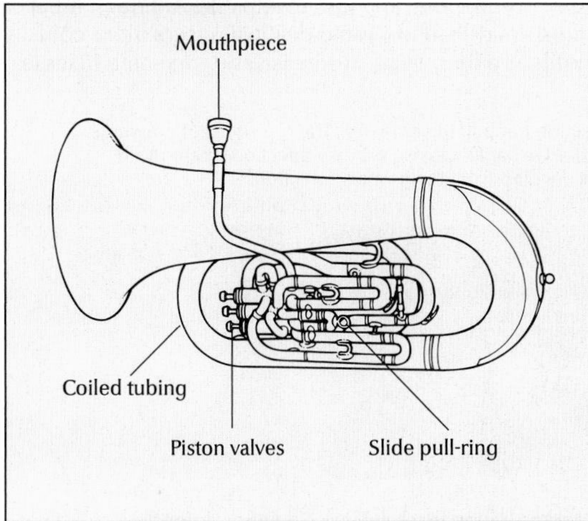

WORLD BOOK illustration by Oxford Illustrators Limited

One popular type of tuba is the *baritone.* It is also called the *euphonium* or the *tenor tuba,* depending on the manufacturer and the diameter of the instrument's tubing. The baritone has three or four valves and is widely used in concert bands and marching bands that play in the same basic range as the trombone. The large *upright tuba* appears in symphony orchestras. It has from three to five valves. The three-valve *sousaphone* wraps around the musician's body and has a large flaring bell. It is the most common tuba in marching bands. The three-valve *marching bugle tuba* is a popular instrument in drum and bugle corps. The tuba is the newest member of the brass family. Stewart L. Ross

Tuber, *TOO buhr,* is a thick, enlarged portion of a stem that usually grows underground. Potatoes, Jerusalem artichokes, and yams are examples of tubers. Tubers bear small scalelike leaves and tiny buds called *eyes.* A tuber can grow into a new plant by a process called *vegetative propagation.* When separated from the parent plant, the eyes may sprout new shoots, obtaining food from the tuber until new leaves and roots form. See also **Jerusalem artichoke; Plant** (Vegetative propagation); **Potato; Yam.** Joseph E. Armstrong

Tuberculosis, *too BUR kyuh LOH sihs,* is an infectious disease that mainly affects the lungs but can also involve other organs. Tuberculosis is often called *TB* and was called *consumption* in the past. This disease once ranked among the most common causes of death in the world. Today, improved methods of prevention, detection, diagnosis, and treatment have greatly reduced both the number of people who get the disease and the number of people who die from it. However, tuberculosis remains a major concern in developing countries where these improved methods are not widely available.

Tuberculosis strikes people of all ages and races. Those at greater risk are homeless or undernourished people, and those with immune systems weakened by diseases, such as cancer or AIDS, or by HIV, the virus that causes AIDS. The disease can also afflict animals, especially such livestock as cattle, hogs, and poultry. The disease is caused by rod-shaped bacteria called *tubercle bacilli.* The German physician Robert Koch discovered tubercle bacilli in 1882 (see **Koch, Robert**). Tubercle bacilli belong to a *genus* (group) of bacteria called *Mycobacterium.* They are *aerobes*—that is, they must have oxygen to live.

How tuberculosis affects the body

In most cases, a person becomes infected with tubercle bacilli by inhaling tiny droplets of moisture that contain *Mycobacterium tuberculosis* bacteria. These droplets form when a person with tuberculosis coughs or sneezes. Infection also can result from eating food contaminated with the bacteria or from drinking milk from cattle infected with *Mycobacterium bovis* bacteria. Such infection rarely occurs in developed countries, where milk is pasteurized and animals are routinely tested for diseases.

The body expels many inhaled tubercle bacilli before they can do harm. Some bacilli settle into the layer of mucus that lines most of the respiratory system, including the nasal passages and the *tracheobronchial tree.* The tracheobronchial tree is the branching system of tubes that brings air to and from tiny air sacs called *alveoli* in the lungs. It consists of the *trachea* (windpipe), two *bronchi,* and hundreds of thousands of smaller airways called *bronchioles.* It is lined with cells that can move the layer of mucus covering them upward. Bacilli trapped in the mucus layer are moved up the airways toward the throat, mouth, and nose. The bacilli may then be sneezed, spat, coughed, or blown out. They also may be swallowed and pass harmlessly through the digestive tract.

Primary infection is likely to result from tubercle bacilli that penetrate beyond airways lined with mucus into the alveolar sacs deep in the lungs. Primary infection is a stage in the development of tuberculosis, but it does not always lead to the disease. Tubercle bacilli that enter an alveolar sac are usually engulfed by large, amebalike cells called *alveolar macrophages.* These cells are usually able to digest bacteria. But tubercle bacilli resist digestion, and most of them actually thrive and multiply inside the macrophages. Some of the macrophages carrying these bacteria may migrate to the mucus layer and be carried out of the body. Others may carry the bacteria to another part of the lungs or even into the blood.

Within several weeks of the initial infection, a small, hard swelling called a *tubercle* forms in the alveolar sac. The tubercle begins to form as macrophages containing tubercle bacilli clump together. These macrophages are joined by *T cells* and possibly other white blood cells. In time, these clumps of cells grow larger and destroy surrounding lung tissue.

As cells inside the tubercle die, they form *caseous* (soft, cheeselike) areas that support the growth of tubercle bacilli. At the same time, tough scar tissue begins to surround the tubercles. This scar tissue prevents further spreading of the bacilli, and it may decrease the amount of oxygen they receive. The bacilli walled off by the scar tissue remain alive but inactive.

In an otherwise normal, healthy adult, primary infection by the bacilli may produce no symptoms and may thus go undetected. In some cases, however, primary infection causes fever, swelling of the glands, and pneumonia.

The disease known as tuberculosis develops if the tubercle bacilli again become active. It may occur immediately after the primary infection, especially in infants, children, and the elderly, and in people who have other illnesses. In most cases, however, tuberculosis develops many years after the primary infection has occurred. What causes this reactivation of the bacilli is not entirely clear. It may occur when the body's defense mechanisms are impaired by another illness or by old age. Reactivation of the bacteria causes the tubercles to rupture and the bacilli to reproduce rapidly. Cells may carry the bacteria to other parts of the lung or into the lymph vessels. The bacteria also may enter blood vessels and be transported to other organs, including the bones, brain, joints, kidneys, and skin.

In tuberculosis of the lungs, called *pulmonary tuberculosis,* alveolar macrophages and white blood cells accumulate at the sites of the reactivated bacteria and form caseous material. The caseous material eventually liquefies and moves up the respiratory tract with the mucus layer. The patient coughs this mucus and caseous material up as *sputum.*

Coughing and sputum production are the most common early symptoms of pulmonary tuberculosis. The cough is not usually severe, and the symptoms are often mistaken for a lingering cold. If blood vessels in the lungs are damaged, there may be blood in the sputum. In advanced stages of TB, patients may cough up large quantities of blood. Other symptoms of advanced tuberculosis include chest pain, fever, sweating at night, fatigue, weight loss, and loss of appetite. Although tuberculosis may lead to a rapid death, it occurs more commonly as a long-term, progressively worsening disease.

How tuberculosis develops

Most cases of tuberculosis begin with an infection deep in the lung, *left.* The top series of drawings below shows how invading bacteria called *tubercle bacilli* cause a primary infection. The bottom drawings illustrate how tuberculosis can later develop from the primary infection.

WORLD BOOK diagram by Robert Demarest

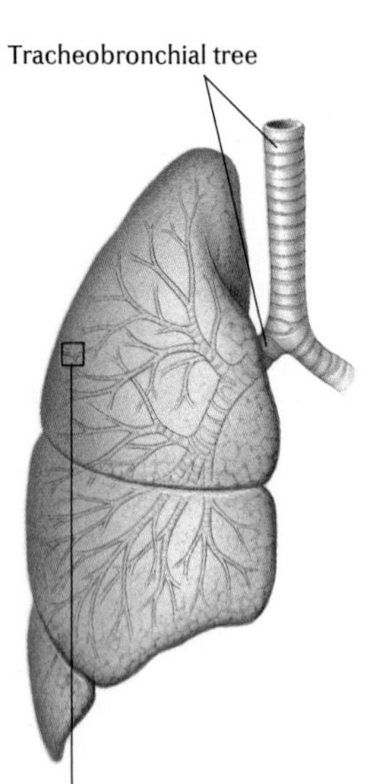

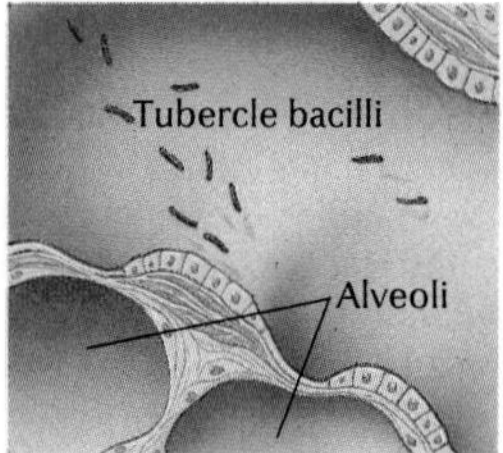

Tubercle bacilli in the air are inhaled deep into the tiniest tubes of the lung at the start of a primary infection.

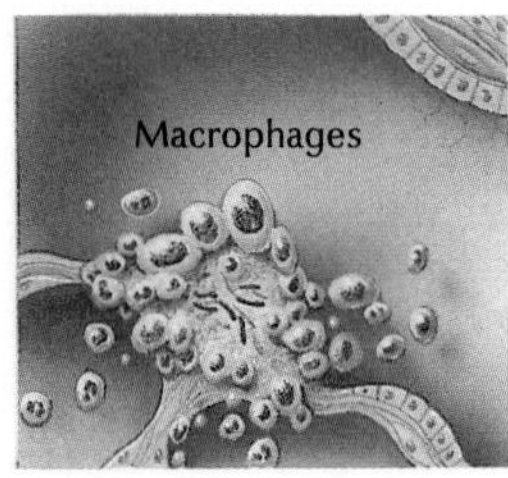

Macrophages attack the invading bacilli. These cells may kill the bacteria or engulf them without killing them.

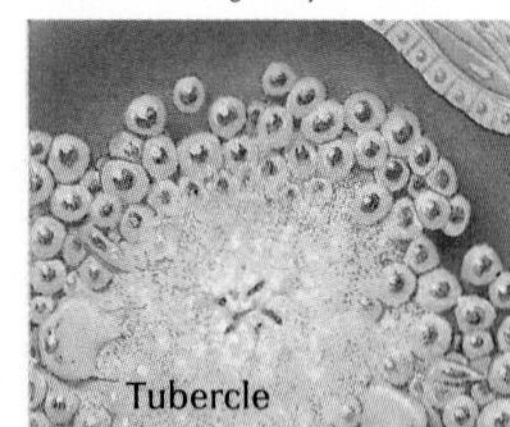

Other defending cells trap the remaining bacilli in hard lumps called *tubercles.* The trapped bacilli are harmless.

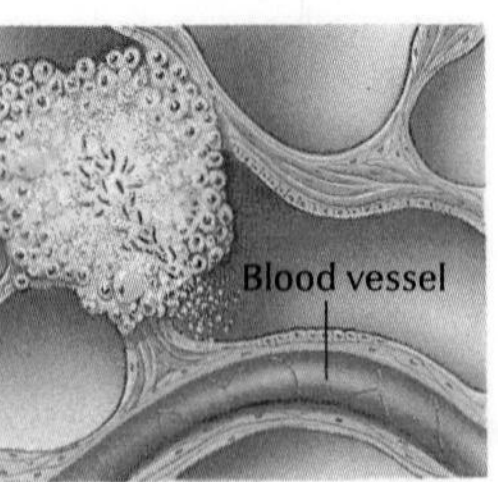

The bacilli break out of the tubercles if the body's defenses weaken. This marks the start of tuberculosis.

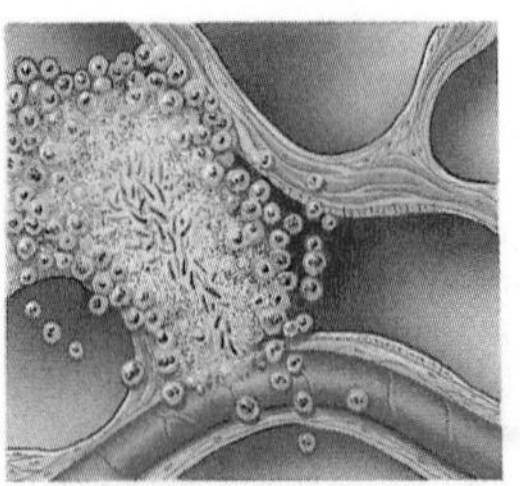

The bacilli multiply and invade surrounding tissue. Macrophages unsuccessfully attack the bacilli.

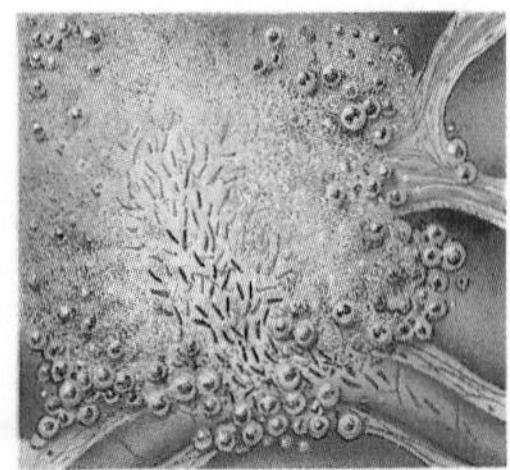

Multiplying bacilli break through the lung tube wall and invade a blood vessel. They may then spread.

Diagnosis of tuberculosis

Physicians use several methods to detect tuberculosis. The chief methods are skin tests, chest X rays, and laboratory tests.

Skin tests can determine if a person has been infected with tubercle bacilli in the past. However, further tests are needed to determine whether the patient has the active disease or an inactive infection. All types of skin tests are based on specific allergic reactions to the tubercle bacilli. The body develops the allergy to the bacilli within a few weeks after the primary infection.

Chest X rays may reveal tubercles or other signs of tuberculosis in the lungs. Chest X rays are usually done after a skin test has indicated a previous infection. However, chest X rays done for other reasons sometimes reveal the presence of tubercles.

Laboratory tests are normally the final step in the diagnosis of tuberculosis. A physician examines the patient's sputum under a microscope to determine if bacilli are present. If bacilli are present, they are *cultured* (grown in laboratory dishes or test tubes). Culturing determines if they are *M. tuberculosis* or other bacilli. It also helps find out which drugs will be most effective against the bacteria.

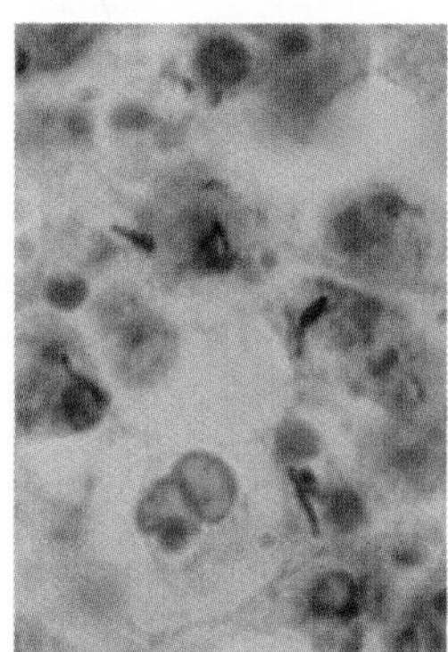

John R. Dainauskas, M.D.

In diseased lung tissue, *shown here,* tubercle bacilli appear as short, red rods.

Treatment of tuberculosis

The first effective treatment for tuberculosis was provided by health resorts called *sanitariums.* Sanitariums were developed during the later 1800's by physicians in Europe and the United States. At a sanitarium patients received bed rest, fresh air, and mild exercise. They also were isolated from the general public and thus kept from infecting other people. Sanitarium treatment helped many tuberculosis patients overcome the disease. However, most of them had to spend months or even years in a sanitarium before they recovered.

Today, almost all tuberculosis patients can be treated successfully with drugs taken for a period of six months. Physicians prescribe combinations of drugs, for example isoniazid (INH) in combination with rifampin, pyrazinamide, ethambutol, or streptomycin. These drugs stop the bacteria from multiplying in the body. Doctors typically prescribe multiple drugs because tubercle bacilli can become resistant to one or more medications. Drug-resistant TB (MDRTB) can also develop if a patient stops taking the prescribed medications before the disease is completely cured. Tuberculosis that is resistant to one or more drugs is difficult to treat and cure. If it spreads, it can be dangerous to other people.

Prevention of tuberculosis

The most effective way to limit the spread of TB is to identify people with the active disease and treat them adequately. A patient with untreated, active TB can infect an estimated 15 people in a year. The drug isoniazid prevents most detected tuberculosis infections from developing into the disease. Doctors often prescribe isoniazid for people who have a positive skin test. In hospitals and other places where patients come into contact with people who do not have the disease, the use of ultraviolet overhead light helps prevent TB from spreading.

A vaccine called BCG *(Bacillus Calmette-Guérin)* has been used in many parts of the world in an effort to prevent tuberculosis. However, the vaccine is not always effective, especially among certain populations.

In the 1980's, outbreaks began to increase in the United States and other developed nations where TB had been declining. The number of TB infections grew dramatically among people weakened by HIV. TB infections also rose among drug abusers and the homeless.

As the number of infections rose, a growing number of TB bacteria began to develop resistance to drugs used to treat the disease. This development led to renewed concern about TB as a worldwide public health problem. In 1998, researchers successfully identified the complete sequence of *genes* (units of heredity) in tuberculosis bacteria. These genes contain chemical instructions that control all the processes in the bacterial cells, including how they infect people and how they resist drugs. Scientists hope that knowledge about the bacterial genes will reveal more effective ways to prevent and treat TB. Michael G. Levitzky

Related articles in *World Book* include:

American Lung Association
Quinolone
Races, Human (Susceptibility to genetic diseases)
Scrofula
Trudeau, Edward L.
Veterinary medicine

Additional resources

Dormandy, Thomas. *The White Death: A History of Tuberculosis.* N.Y. Univ. Pr., 2000.

Ramen, Fred. *Tuberculosis.* Rosen Pub. Group, 2001. Younger readers.

Tuberose, *TOOB rohz,* is a plant of the agave family. It grows wild in tropical America and Asia. The plant is

WORLD BOOK illustration by Lorraine Epstein

The tuberose is named for its tube-shaped rootstock, from which slender stems grow. Tuberose blossoms have a heavy, sweet fragrance. The flowers are used in making perfumes.

also raised for use in perfumes and toilet preparations in central Europe, southern Africa, and in North Carolina and New Jersey. In addition, it is grown in Hawaii for use in making *leis* (wreaths of flowers strung together). The tuberose has a heavy, almost sickening, odor. Its slender stem springs from a tubelike rootstock, and often grows 3 feet (90 centimeters) high. The stem of the tuberose bears waxy-white blossoms and has eight sword-shaped leaves. The tuberose is named for the shape of its rootstock, not for its resemblance to a tube-shaped rose. The tuberose is not a rose. Michael J. Tanabe

Scientific classification. The tuberose belongs to the agave family, Agavaceae. It is *Polianthes tuberosa.*

Tubman, Harriet (1820?-1913), was an African American whose daring rescues helped hundreds of slaves escape to freedom. She became the most famous leader of the *underground railroad,* which aided slaves fleeing to the free states or to Canada (see **Underground railroad**). Blacks called her Moses, after the Biblical figure who led the Jews from Egypt.

Tubman was born a slave in Bucktown, Maryland, near Cambridge. Her name was Araminta Ross, but as a child, she became known by her mother's name, Harriet. Her father taught her a knowledge of the woods that later helped her in her rescue missions. When Harriet was 13, she interfered with a supervisor to save another slave from punishment. The enraged supervisor fractured Harriet's skull with a 2-pound (0.9-kilogram) weight. She recovered but suffered blackouts for the rest of her life. She married John Tubman, a freed slave, in 1844.

Harriet Tubman escaped from slavery in 1849 and went to Philadelphia via the underground railroad, without her husband. She then vowed to return to Maryland and help other slaves escape. Tubman made her first trip back shortly after Congress passed the Fugitive Slave Act of 1850. This law made it a crime to help a runaway slave. Tubman returned 18 more times during the 1850's and helped about 300 slaves escape.

On one rescue mission, she sensed that pursuers were close behind, and so she and the fugitives got on a southbound train to avoid suspicion. On another mission, Tubman had just bought some live chickens in Bucktown when she saw her former master walking toward her. She quickly let the chickens go and chased after them before he could recognize her. In 1857, Tubman led her parents to freedom in Auburn, New York.

Tubman never was caught and never lost a slave on any of her 19 rescue trips. She carried a gun and threatened to kill anyone who tried to turn back. Rewards for her capture once totaled about $40,000.

In the late 1850's, Tubman met with the radical abolitionist John Brown, who told her of his plan to free the slaves (see **Brown, John**). Tubman considered Brown the true liberator of her race. Soon after meeting with Brown, Tubman also became active in the women's rights movement.

Library of Congress

Harriet Tubman

In the American Civil War (1861-1865), Tubman served as a nurse, scout, and spy for the Union Army in South Carolina. During one military campaign, she helped free more than 750 slaves.

After the war, Tubman returned to Auburn, where she helped raise money for black schools. The author Sarah H. Bradford wrote *Scenes in the Life of Harriet Tubman* (1869), which described Tubman's work against slavery. In 1908, Tubman established the Harriet Tubman Home; a home in Auburn for elderly and needy blacks. The people of Auburn erected a plaque in her honor. A U.S. postage stamp bearing her portrait was issued in 1978. She died on March 10, 1913. Otey M. Scruggs

See also **African Americans** (picture).

Additional resources

Bentley, Judith. *Harriet Tubman.* Watts, 1990.
Janney, Rebecca P. *Harriet Tubman.* Bethany Hse., 1999.
Kulling, Monica. *Escape North! The Story of Harriet Tubman.* Random Hse., 2000. Younger readers.
Schraff, Anne E. *Harriet Tubman.* Enslow, 2001. Younger readers.

Tubman, William V. S. (1895-1971), was president of Liberia from 1944 until his death in 1971. Educated in Liberia, he became a lawyer, and later a senator and associate justice of the Liberian Supreme Court. As president, he worked for progress in health, agriculture, and education. Tubman was born on Nov. 29, 1895, in Harper, Liberia. Peter P. Garretson

See also **Liberia** (History).

Tuchman, *TUHK muhn,* **Barbara Wertheim** (1912-1989), was an American historian who won two Pulitzer Prizes for general nonfiction. She received the first in 1963 for *The Guns of August* (1962), which deals with the early phase of World War I (1914-1918). She won the second in 1972 for *Stilwell and the American Experience in China, 1911-1945* (1971), which centers on the career of United States Army General Joseph W. Stilwell.

Tuchman was born on Jan. 30, 1912, in New York City. During 1934 and 1935, she worked as a research assistant for the Institute of Pacific Relations. She then became a reporter for the *Nation* magazine and covered the Spanish Civil War (1936-1939). Her first book, *The Lost British Policy: Britain and Spain Since 1700,* was published in 1938. Her other historical works include *Bible and Sword: England and Palestine from the Bronze Age to Balfour* (1956), *The Zimmermann Telegram* (1958), *The Proud Tower: A Portrait of the World Before the War, 1890-1914* (1966), *Notes from China* (1972), *A Distant Mirror: The Calamitous Fourteenth Century* (1978), *Practicing History: Selected Essays* (1981), and *The March of Folly: From Troy to Vietnam* (1984). Arthur I. Cyr

Tucker, Richard (1913-1975), is generally considered the outstanding American operatic tenor of his day. He gained special recognition for his performances as passionate characters in Italian operas.

Tucker was born on Aug. 28, 1913, in the Brooklyn section of New York City. His given and family name was Reuben Ticker. A devout Orthodox Jew, Tucker also sang as a *cantor* (religious singer) in synagogues. He made his debut at the Metropolitan Opera in New York City in 1945 in Amilcare Ponchielli's *La Gioconda.* His first European appearance came in the same opera in 1947 in Verona, Italy. Tucker starred at the Metropolitan Opera and also sang with other opera companies. In addition, he was a popular concert singer. Tucker's brother-in-law was the famous American tenor Jan Peerce.

Charles H. Webb

Tucson, *TOO sahn* or *too SAHN,* Arizona (pop. 486,699; met. area pop. 843,746), is a commercial and research center of the Southwest. It ranks second to Phoenix among Arizona's largest cities. Tucson's warm, dry, sunny climate makes it a popular health and winter resort area and retirement center. Tucson lies in southern Arizona (see **Arizona** [political map]).

The Tucson Convention Center stands in downtown Tucson. La Placita is also in downtown Tucson. La Placita includes office buildings, restaurants, and shops in a plaza designed to look like a Mexican village.

Tucson is the home of the University of Arizona. Museums in the city include the Tucson Museum of Art, the Arizona Historical Society, and—at the university—the Arizona State Museum, and the university's Museum of Art and its Mineral Museum. The nearby Arizona-Sonora Desert Museum features animals and plants of the Sonora Desert in their natural surroundings. Kitt Peak, southwest of Tucson, is the site of the world's largest solar telescope. A noted landmark in the Tucson area is San Xavier del Bac Mission, called the "White Dove of the Desert."

The University of Arizona and the federal, state, and local governments are the city's major employers. Tucson's industries include tourism, electronics manufacturing, and the production of copper.

Pima Indians and *Tohono O'odham* (Desert People), also known as Papago Indians, lived in what is now the Tucson area before European explorers arrived there. In 1776, Juan Bautista de Anza established Tucson as a military outpost for the part of the Spanish territory in America that was called New Spain. In 1853, the city became part of the United States as a result of the Gadsden Purchase (see **Gadsden Purchase**). From 1867 to 1877, it was the capital of the Arizona Territory.

Tucson's population boomed from 1950 to 1965, increasing from 45,454 to 234,600. A large number of the new residents had been stationed in the area with the armed services during World War II (1939-1945). Tucson has continued to grow rapidly.

Tucson is the seat of Pima County. It has a council-manager government. June Johnson Caldwell Martin

Thomas Kitchen, Tom Stack & Assoc.

Tucson is an important commercial, mining, and research center in southern Arizona. Because of its warm, dry, sunny climate, the city is also a popular resort and retirement center.

Tudor, *TOO duhr,* **House of,** was the family that ruled England from 1485 to 1603. The first Tudor ruler was Henry VII. He won his crown at the battle of Bosworth Field, defeating Richard III and ensuring a victory for his own side in the Wars of the Roses. Henry claimed the throne through his mother, Margaret Beaufort, a descendant of Edward III. He also claimed he had a *divine right* to rule—that is, that his right to govern came from God. Henry restored order to England after 30 years of repeated outbreaks of civil war.

His son Henry VIII continued Henry VII's work of unifying the country. Henry VIII broke all ties between England and the Roman Catholic Church and made the monarch head of the church in England. Henry VIII was succeeded first by his son, Edward VI, and then in turn by his daughters, Mary I and Elizabeth I. The reigns of Edward and Mary were short and unhappy due to civil unrest, foreign wars, severe economic problems, and religious disturbances. But under Elizabeth, England became a major European power. After Elizabeth's death in 1603, the crown passed to King James VI of Scotland, the great-grandson of Henry VII's oldest daughter. He was England's first Stuart king. Richard L. Greaves

See also **England** (History); **Henry VII; Henry VIII.**

Tuesday is the name of the third day of the week. Its name comes from *Tiu,* or *Tiw,* the old Anglo-Saxon form of *Tyr,* name of the Norse god of war. Tyr was the son of Odin, or Woden, for whom Wednesday was named. The French call Tuesday *Mardi,* for Mars, the Roman war god. *Shrove Tuesday,* the day before Lent, was so-called because it was customary to confess and be *shriven* or *shrove* (receive absolution) by a priest. See also **Shrove Tuesday; Week.** Jack Santino

Tugboat, also called *tug,* is a small, powerful boat that maneuvers large vessels. Tugs that are used in harbors can tow large ocean liners or freighters and aid all types of vessels in entering or leaving their anchoring places. They can tow from the front or side, or push from the back. Tugs measure from 65 to more than 250 feet (20 to 76 meters) long. The largest tugboats are the oceangoing tugs, which rescue or assist ships at sea. Tugs used on inland lakes and rivers tow or push long lines of barges loaded with heavy cargoes. Modern tugs can push 40 or more barges at once. See also **Barge** (picture). Octavia N. Cubbins

Tuileries, *TWEE luh reez* or *TWEEL REE,* a famous royal palace, stood on the right bank of the River Seine in Paris. During the French Revolution, mobs forced Louis XVI and his family to live there instead of at Versailles. For a time, the National Convention held its sessions in the Tuileries. Napoleon I made it his home, and it served as the royal residence after the Restoration.

Catherine de Médicis began the building of the palace in 1564, but much of it was built in the 1600's. The original architect was Philibert de l'Orme. The palace was formed by a series of long, narrow buildings with high roofs that created one major and two minor courtyards. At the southeast corner it joined the Louvre. Supporters of the Commune destroyed most of the palace in 1871, but the gardens west of the palace remain.

These gardens, covering about 63 acres (25 hectares), still closely follow a design laid out by landscape architect André Le Nôtre in the 1600's. J. William Rudd

See also **Paris** (map).

Tula is the site of a major Toltec Indian city that flourished in what is now Mexico from the A.D. 900's to about 1200. The site—and the city's ruins—lie near the town of Tula de Allende, about 45 miles (70 kilometers) north of Mexico City. No one knows what the Indians themselves called the Toltec city, but it is usually referred to as Tula.

Numerous archaeologists believe Tula was the capital of the Toltec empire. Some think Tula was in fact Tollán, a Toltec capital described in legends of the Aztec Indians. Others believe the name *Tollán* refers to some other city, possibly Teotihuacán, which thrived northeast of present-day Mexico City until the A.D. 700's.

Tula's economy was based on the manufacture and trade of a variety of goods, but especially of tools made of *obsidian* (volcanic glass). Its people also used irrigation to grow such crops as corn and beans.

Most of Tula's houses were one-story buildings with adobe walls and flat roofs. In addition, the city had ball courts, and pyramids with temples on top.

Tula was just a small village until the A.D. 900's. Some archaeologists think its importance increased when it gained control of nearby obsidian mines. Its population then grew to about 50,000. Tula declined about 1200, and nomads from the north overran the area. The Aztec Indians temporarily revived Tula in the 1400's and early 1500's. Payson Sheets

See also **Mexico** (The Toltec and the Aztec); **Toltec Indians.**

Tulane University is a private university in New Orleans. It includes two liberal arts schools—the College of Arts and Sciences for men and H. Sophie Newcomb College for women. Tulane also has coeducational schools of architecture, business administration, continuing education, engineering, graduate studies, law, medicine, public health and tropical medicine, and social work. The university offers a junior-year program of study abroad and special programs in comparative law, Latin American studies, and political economy.

Tulane was founded in 1834 as the Medical College of Louisiana. In 1884, it was renamed in honor of Paul Tulane, a New Orleans merchant who gave the university its first endowment. Critically reviewed by Tulane University

Tularemia, *TOO luh REE mee uh,* also called rabbit fever, is an infectious disease of many mammals, including human beings. Tularemia is caused by a bacterium, *Francisella tularensis.* It was first reported in Tulare County, California, in 1911. Tularemia is most often transmitted by the bite of a tick or an insect. Human beings also can catch this disease by handling infected animals, such as squirrels, rabbits, and rats. Tularemia causes a fever that comes and goes, and lasts several weeks. The lymph glands become swollen around the bite. If not treated by a physician, tularemia often causes death.

Gary A. Heidt

Tulip is a lovely, graceful garden flower that came from southern Europe and Asia. Although tulips grow in many parts of the world, we generally associate them with the Netherlands.

Tulips bloom in spring. They grow from bulbs, and the leaves, stems, and flowers grow directly out of the bulb. The stems range from 4 inches (10 centimeters) to over 30 inches (76 centimeters) tall. The tulip usually develops one large, bell-shaped flower at the tip of its stem. The flowers may be almost any solid color, and some tulips have flowers with two colors. The flowers of some tulips become streaked with other colors because of virus diseases that affect the plant's color but not its health.

Derek Fell

Tulips are colorful garden flowers that bloom in the spring. Tulip leaves and the flower stem grow directly out of a bulb.

Gardeners plant tulip bulbs in autumn. They require a well-drained, loamy soil of average richness. Usually only professional tulip growers or plant breeders grow the flowers from seed, because tulip seed does not produce a flowering bulb for four to seven years.

Thousands of varieties of tulips have developed from a few *species* (kinds). Almost all the cultivated kinds of tulips were developed from tulips of Asia Minor that were brought to Vienna, Austria, from Constantinople, Turkey (now Istanbul), in the 1500's. The name *tulip* comes from a Turkish word meaning *turban.* The beautiful blossoms of tulips look a little like turbans. Popular garden varieties of tulips include the Darwin hybrids and the Triumphs, Lily-flowered, Fringed, and Parrot tulips.

After the tulip was brought to Europe, it became the most fashionable flower in both England and Holland. Interest in the flower developed into a craze in Holland, called the *tulipomania,* between 1634 and 1637. Individual bulbs sold for huge prices. People invested their money in tulips as American business people might invest in high-technology stocks. Many people lost fortunes in the tulip market, and the government was forced to regulate the trade in bulbs.

Tulip cultivation is an important industry in the Netherlands today. It is also important in the northwestern part of the United States. Billions of tulip bulbs are produced every year. Dutch growers produce nearly 2,000 varieties. August A. De Hertogh

Scientific classification. Tulips belong to the lily family, Liliaceae. The tulip brought to Europe in the 1500's is *Tulipa gesneriana.*

See also **Netherlands** (picture); **Oregon** (picture: A tulip farm).

Tuliptree. See **Yellow-poplar.**

Tull, *tuhl,* **Jethro** (1674-1741), an English farmer, built the first practical farm tool for planting seeds in rows. In Tull's day, farmers sowed seed by hand. This practice wasted seed and produced an uneven yield. European inventors had experimented with a mechanical seeding device, but none achieved Tull's success. About 1700, Tull developed a mechanical seed *drill,* which made rows of small trenches in the soil and dropped seeds in them. His horse-drawn seed drill planted three rows at a time and used less seed than did sowing by hand. This device marked the first step toward the mechanization of British agriculture.

Tull was born in Berkshire. He attended Oxford University and studied law at Gray's Inn in London. He traveled widely in Europe to observe agricultural practices. Tull described and illustrated his seed drill in his book *Horse-Hoeing Husbandry* (1731). R. Douglas Hurt

Tulsa, *TUHL suh* (pop. 393,049; met. area pop. 803,235), is a major center of the United States petroleum industry and the busiest port and chief manufacturing center of Oklahoma. Tulsa is the state's second largest city. Only Oklahoma City has more people. Tulsa lies in northeastern Oklahoma along the Arkansas River. For location, see **Oklahoma** (political map).

During the 1830's, Creek Indians from Tallassee, Alabama, settled in what is now the Tulsa area. They named their village after their former community, but in time the name was changed to Tulsa. Construction of the first railroad to Tulsa in 1882 brought European settlers to the area. But until 1901, Tulsa remained a small village. That year, the discovery of oil in nearby Red Fork attracted many people to the area. The city then grew quickly.

The city. Tulsa, the county seat of Tulsa County, covers about 177 square miles (458 square kilometers), including 5 square miles (13 square kilometers) of inland water. The Arkansas River divides the city into two parts, the larger of which lies east of the river. Tulsa's metropolitan area covers five entire counties—Creek, Osage, Rogers, Tulsa, and Wagoner.

A group of government buildings called the Civic Center forms the heart of downtown Tulsa. These buildings cover eight square blocks and include the city hall, the county courthouse, the main public library, and police headquarters. The Assembly Center, which has exhibit halls and an arena, also stands in this area. A federal office building is nearby.

Economy. Tulsa has more than 1,000 manufacturing plants. The chief industries manufacture fabricated metal products and nonelectric machinery. The city leads the world in the manufacture of industrial heaters and hoisting devices called *winches.* Other Tulsa products include transportation equipment; metals; and clay, glass, and stone articles. The city's largest employers include American Airlines, which has maintenance and engineering centers there, and the energy and communications firm Williams Companies, Inc.

Oklahoma's largest oil refinery is just outside the Tulsa business district. But the city is more important as an administrative center of the United States petroleum industry than as an oil producer. Tulsa serves as a major control center of the industry, with many distributors, manufacturers, producers, and research activities.

About 750 oil or oil-related companies maintain offices in the Tulsa area. More than 250 of these firms have headquarters in the city. Tulsa has large data-processing offices, including the credit card centers of several major oil companies. The city also is the national headquarters of the United States Jaycees.

Tulsa became a major port in 1970, after the McClellan-Kerr Arkansas River Navigation System was extended to Catoosa, 3 miles (5 kilometers) east of the city. This system links Tulsa's port, near Catoosa on the Verdigris River, to the Mississippi River, the Gulf of Mexico, and the Atlantic Ocean. An industrial area is near the port. Many airlines use Tulsa International Airport. Freight trains also serve the city. Tulsa has one daily newspaper, the *Tulsa World.*

Education and cultural life. Tulsa's public school system includes about 95 elementary schools and 10 high schools. The city also has about 12 parochial and private schools. Colleges include the Oklahoma State University College of Osteopathic Medicine, Oklahoma State University-Tulsa, Oral Roberts University, Tulsa Community College, and the University of Tulsa.

The Gilcrease Museum features one of the world's finest collections of Native American art and historical documents. It also exhibits the world's largest collections of works by the American painters Thomas Moran, Frederic Remington, and Charles M. Russell. The Philbrook Museum of Art displays Italian Renaissance paintings and sculpture, Chinese jewelry, and American Indian baskets and pottery. The Tulsa Civic Ballet and the Tulsa Opera Company perform at the Tulsa Performing Arts Center, which has four theaters.

Tulsa's largest park is Mohawk Park, which occupies 2,817 acres (1,140 hectares). It includes a golf course and a zoo. The Tulsa Municipal Rose Garden, in Woodward Park, features thousands of rose plants. The annual Tulsa State Fair begins in late September at the Tulsa State Fairgrounds. The fairgrounds includes the world's largest livestock display barn and show ring and the Tulsa Exposition Center. The center has a $10\frac{1}{2}$-acre (4.2-hectare) continuous-area exhibition hall.

Government. Tulsa has a mayor-council form of government. The voters elect a mayor and nine councilors to two-year terms. Tulsa gets most of its revenue from a sales tax.

History. Several Indian tribes once hunted in the area that is now Tulsa. During the 1830's, Creek Indians from Tallassee, Alabama, settled in the Tulsa area. According to tradition, a Creek named Archie Yahola led tribal councils under a huge tree called the Council Oak in 1836. This tree still stands on Cheyenne Avenue in Tulsa.

In 1848, Lewis Perryman, a Creek, opened a village trading post on the Arkansas River. A post office called Tulsa was established at the ranch of his son, George Perryman, in 1879. The village had fewer than 1,000 people in 1882, when the Atlantic and Pacific Railroad—now part of the Burlington Northern Santa Fe Corporation—was extended from Vinita, Oklahoma, to the Arkansas River near the present site of downtown Tulsa. Tulsa, or Tulsey Town, as it was sometimes called, became a cattle-shipping terminal. Tulsa was incorporated as a town in 1898. In 1900, it had a population of 1,390.

In 1901, the discovery of oil at nearby Red Fork attracted large numbers of people to the area. Tulsa became

© Don Sibley, Tulsa Chamber of Commerce

Tulsa is Oklahoma's chief manufacturing center. The city is also a center for the petroleum industry in the United States. Downtown Tulsa is shown here.

an oil center in 1905, when the large Glenn Pool oil field opened 15 miles (24 kilometers) southwest. When Oklahoma gained statehood in 1907, Tulsa had a population of 7,298. Tulsa received a city charter in 1908. The oil boom increased the city's population to 72,075 by 1920 and to 141,258 by 1930, and Tulsa became known as the *Oil Capital of the World.*

On May 31, 1921, a race riot destroyed much of Tulsa's black business district. Blacks and whites clashed after a white mob gathered to lynch a black man accused of attacking a white woman. During the violence that followed, whites burned and looted more than 1,200 structures. There is documented evidence of at least 40 deaths, but some historians estimate that as many as 300 people were killed.

During World War II (1939-1945), workers flocked to Tulsa from rural areas to take factory jobs. The government built a huge bomber airplane factory in the city. By 1945, this plant employed almost 22,000 people and had become the largest factory in Oklahoma. The increased defense activities helped raise Tulsa's population to 182,740 by 1950.

During the 1960's, Tulsa completed its Civic Center. In 1970, the completion of the McClellan-Kerr Arkansas River Navigation System made Tulsa a major port. The navigation project, which included construction of many dams and locks, cost about $1 \frac{1}{4}$ billion.

Tulsa's tallest building, the 50-story Bank of Oklahoma Tower, was completed in 1977. The 60-story City of Faith Hospital Building at Oral Roberts University has more floors. However, it is slightly lower than the Bank of Oklahoma Tower. The tower forms part of the Williams Center, an office complex covering 11 square blocks in downtown Tulsa. The Williams Center includes the Tulsa Performing Arts Center, which was completed in 1977.

Tulsa's population almost doubled between 1950 and 1980 to 360,919. During the late 1900's, the city's dependence on the oil industry declined, though Tulsa still remained a center of the industry.

In 1997, the Oklahoma Legislature created a commission to study and officially document the 1921 Tulsa race riot. In 2000, the commission recommended to the Legislature that *reparations* (payments for injury) be made to the riot's survivors, their descendants, or the community. The reparations could take the form of a memorial, scholarships, or direct payments. Susan Ellerbach

For the monthly weather in Tulsa, see **Oklahoma** (Climate). See also **Oklahoma** (pictures).

Tumbleweed is the popular name for several plants that grow in the prairie and plains regions of the United States. These plants develop rounded tops, and in autumn they wither and break off at the ground level. The dried plants are then carried or tumbled about by the wind, like great, light balls. As they move, they scatter their seeds about over the plains. These plants are considered great pests by farmers and ranchers. Tumbleweeds often pile up against barbed-wire fences or fill small gullies.

The common tumbleweeds include the *Russian thistle* and an amaranth. All tumbleweeds are *annuals*—that is, they grow from seed to maturity and then die within one year. Anton A. Reznicek

Scientific classification. The Russian thistle is a member of the goosefoot family, Chenopodiaceae. Its scientific name is *Salsola kali.*

Tumboa. See **Welwitschia**.

Tumor is an abnormal growth of tissues in the body. Tumors are also called *neoplasms.* Some tumors are *benign.* They limit themselves to a certain region and do not spread elsewhere in the body. Once benign tumors are removed, they usually do not grow again. *Malignant tumors* (cancers) that are not completely removed can spread throughout the body, often destroying other tissues in the body (see **Cancer** [How damaged genes cause cancer]). When cancer arises from the skin, tissues that line the body cavities, or nonblood-forming organs, it is called *carcinoma.* Cancer that affects bones, cartilages, and soft tissues is called *sarcoma. Leukemia* is cancer of the bone marrow or other blood-forming organs. Only a doctor can determine whether a tumor is benign or malignant.

Tumors may grow from any kind of tissue in the body. They may develop in the skin, in muscles, nerves, blood vessels, bones, or any organ. A well-known tumor is the mastoid tumor, which grows over the mastoid process just behind the ear.

Tumors are often named after the tissue from which they grow. For example, a *lipoma* is a benign tumor made up of *lipid* (fat) tissue. *Gliomas* (nerve-tissue tumors) are made up of *glia,* the branched cells that support the nerves. *Lymphoma* is a malignant tumor of lymphoid tissue. It is one of the best-studied tumors, and it is highly treatable by chemotherapy and radiation therapy. Martin D. Abeloff

Related articles in *World Book* include:

Biopsy
Birthmark
Brain (Tumors)
Cancer
Chemotherapy
Epithelioma
Leukemia
Malignancy
Mole [dermatology]
Monoclonal antibody
Neurofibromatosis
Skin (Tumors)

Tuna, a fruit. See **Prickly pear**.

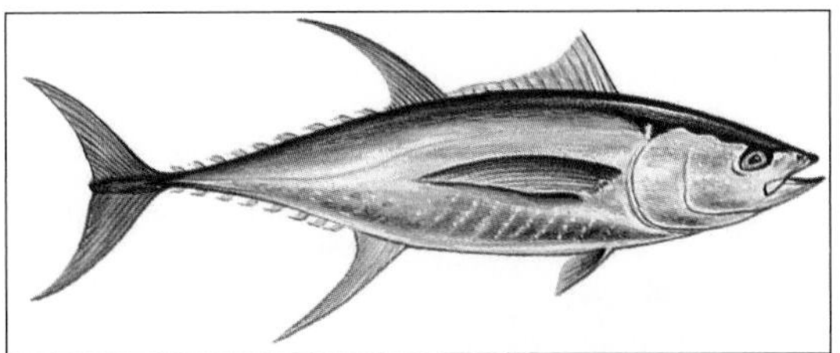

WORLD BOOK illustration by John F. Eggert

The yellowfin tuna provides light meat for canning.

Tuna is any of a group of saltwater fish in the mackerel family. Tuna meat ranks as a popular food in many countries, especially in North America, Europe, and East Asia. The meat is sold canned, fresh, and frozen. Tuna also serves as a leading game fish. Major commercial types include the *albacore, Atlantic bluefin, bigeye, Pacific bluefin, skipjack,* and *yellowfin* tunas. China, Indonesia, and Japan rank as the leading tuna-fishing countries.

The largest tuna, the *Atlantic bluefin,* grows up to 14 feet (4.3 meters) long and weighs up to 1,600 pounds (730 kilograms). The smallest tuna is the *bullet tuna.* It grows up to 20 inches (51 centimeters) long and weighs up to 5 pounds (2.3 kilograms).

Tuna rank among the swiftest fish. The Atlantic bluefin can swim as fast as 45 miles (72 kilometers) per hour. Like other fish, a tuna has gills that take oxygen from the water passing over them. But unlike most fish, a tuna cannot pump water over its gills. Therefore, it must swim continuously in order to breathe.

Tuna live near the surface of temperate and tropical ocean waters. Their diet includes small fish, squid, and such crustaceans as crabs and krill. In summer, tuna in the Northern Hemisphere go as far north as Newfoundland and Norway in the Atlantic Ocean, and British Columbia and northern Japan in the Pacific Ocean. Tuna in the Southern Hemisphere go as far south as the Southern Ocean. Major fisheries operate in the Atlantic, Pacific, and Indian oceans, and in the Mediterranean Sea.

Tuna sometimes migrate long distances and can cross oceans or move from one ocean to another. One individual was tagged and released off Japan and then recaptured near Mexico. This fish had to swim at least 6,700 miles (10,800 kilometers) to reach its destination.

© Animals Animals, Robert Meyer

Tuna may be caught in large nets called *purse seines.* This photograph shows members of a fishing crew with a catch of yellowfin tuna, an important commercial type of tuna.

Tuna are caught in three main ways. In *bait fishing,* crews throw live bait overboard to attract the tuna and then catch them by hooks and lines attached to long poles. In *long-lining,* tuna are caught with a line that is up to 81 miles (130 kilometers) long and has over 3,000 shorter lines with baited hooks. *Purse seining,* the chief method of catching skipjack and yellowfin tuna, encircles the fish in large nets called *purse seines.* Crews sometimes locate yellowfin and slipjack tuna by seeking dolphins that typically swim near the fish. Dolphins often have been trapped in purse seines and accidentally killed. Many countries now require the nets to have openings through which dolphins can escape. In addition, countries have laws restricting the purchase of tuna caught in nets that also kill dolphins. Talbot Murray

Scientific classification. Tuna belong to the mackerel family, Scombridae. The albacore is *Thunnus alalunga.* The bigeye is *T. obesus;* the yellowfin, *T. albacares;* the Atlantic bluefin, *T. thynnus,* and the Pacific bluefin, *T. orientalis.* The skipjack is *Katsuwonus pelamis.* The bullet tuna is *Auxis rochei.*

See also **Fish** (picture: Fish of coastal waters [Bluefin tuna]); **Fishing industry** (Where fish are caught).

Tundra is a term most often used for the cold, dry, treeless lands of the Arctic. These lands have a cover of ice and snow for most of the year. They include northern parts of North America, Europe, and Asia, and much of Greenland. People sometimes use the term tundra for treeless *alpine* (mountainous) regions and for lands in and around Antarctica.

Most tundra areas lie north of the Arctic Circle. They have continuous daylight in midsummer and continuous darkness in midwinter. Tundra regions experience long, often bitterly cold winters. The warmest summer climates average between 32 and 50 °F (0 and 10 °C).

Scientists classify tundra as a *biome*—that is, a plant and animal community that covers a large geographical area. The tundra biome lies north of the *tree line,* meaning forests will not grow there. Small clusters of shrubs, usually birch or willow, sometimes occur within tundra regions. But these appear only in a few areas, including parts of the Labrador coast in Canada. Most tundra regions receive little snow or rain. The low temperature of tundra *air masses* (huge volumes of air) means they contain little water vapor. Many tundra regions are so dry, people often call them *Arctic deserts.*

The land beneath the tundra surface normally remains frozen all year. This frozen soil, called *permafrost,* often extends hundreds of feet or meters down. Permafrost is seldom continuous and contains many unfrozen zones, particularly beneath lakes and ponds. In warmer regions, the tundra surface thaws during summer and enables plants to grow.

Many distinct landforms appear in a tundra. Small conical hills called *pingos* form in numerous low-lying areas, often from the freezing of spring water. The melting of permafrost may create temporary *thaw lakes.* At the highest elevations, the tundra has rocky plateaus. Lower terrains include finer materials and are often patterned. Such patterns usually consist of *polygons* (many sided figures) where the ground is level and stripes where it is sloped. The polygons are separated by

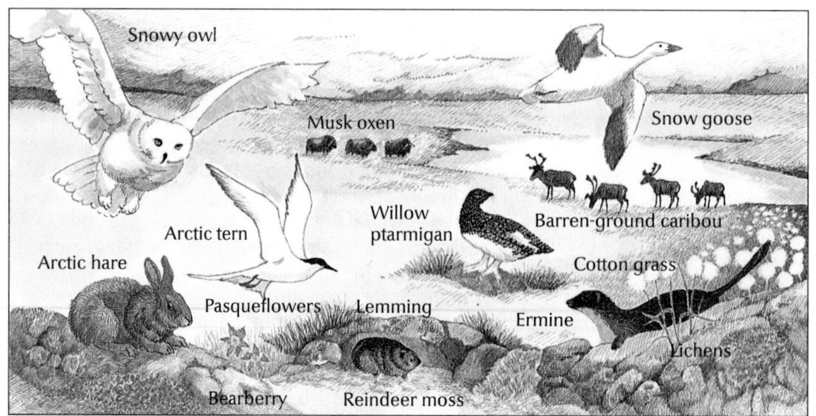

Many living things inhabit the Arctic tundra. Mosses, bright flowers, and plantlike organisms called lichens cover the ground in summer. Each fall, Arctic hares, ermines, willow ptarmigans, and other tundra animals grow white winter coats. These white coats blend with the snow and help protect the animals from such enemies as wolves and foxes.

WORLD BOOK illustration by Jean Helmer

borders of ice wedges, boulders, or other materials.

Tundra soils generally contain partially decayed plant material called *peat.* Peat accumulates because low temperatures inhibit the decay of dead vegetation.

Tundra plant life features such flowering *herbaceous* (nonwoody) plants as grasses and sedges, as well as dwarf shrubs and mosses. The tundra also contains plantlike organisms called lichens. Toward the southern borders of the tundra, lowland regions have a continuous cover of vegetation. Plants become more sparse at higher elevations and in northern areas.

The tundra supports a remarkable variety of animals. Caribou, reindeer, and musk oxen eat tundra plants. So do hares, lemmings, and mice. Foxes, owls, and wolves feed primarily on the smaller animals. Wolves also may eat the young or *carrion* (dead and decaying flesh) of the larger grazing mammals. Numerous birds, including the Canada goose, migrate to tundra regions in summer.

People have traveled through and lived in the tundra for thousands of years. Many permanent tundra residents traditionally survived by hunting and by fishing in nearby Arctic waters. The most widespread of these peoples, the Inuit (sometimes called Eskimos), live in Alaska, Greenland, northern Canada, and the northeastern tip of Russia. Today, however, few Arctic peoples follow their traditional ways of life.

Tundra regions possess large deposits of coal, natural gas, oil, iron ore, lead, and zinc. Since the late 1800's, people have increasingly come to the tundra to mine these resources. Increased human activity threatens the tundra's natural environment, as well as the remaining traditional Arctic cultures. Robert J. Rogerson

See also **Arctic; Biome** (map); **Permafrost.**

Additional resources

Walsh Shepherd, Donna. *Tundra.* Watts, 1996. Younger readers.
Zwinger, Ann H., and Willard, B. E. *Land Above the Trees: A Guide to American Alpine Tundra.* 1972. Reprint. Johnson Bks., 1996.

Tundra wolf. See Wolf.

Tung oil is an oil that comes from the seed kernels of the tung tree. The tung tree originally grew in East Asia, chiefly in China. Tung oil is also called *China-wood oil, Japanese-wood oil,* or simply *wood oil.* The tree has also been successfully grown in the southern United States. Tung oil is one of the most powerful drying agents. The oil resists acids, alkalis, and alcohols.

Tung oil is widely used in paints, lacquers, varnishes, and printing inks. Paints containing tung oil help seal the underwater surfaces of swimming pools, dams, piers, and boats. Varnishes made with it help insulate wire and metallic surfaces. Tung oil is used to waterproof paper and fabrics. It is also used as a finish for wood. Because of its relatively high cost, tung oil is sometimes replaced with epoxy resins and other synthetics. Roger D. Barry

Scientific classification. The tung tree belongs to the spurge family, Euphorbiaceae. It is classified as *Aleurites fordii.*

Tungsten, also called *wolfram,* is a fairly hard, silver-white metallic element. Tungsten remains strong at high temperatures. It melts at about 3422 °C, the highest melting temperature of any metal. Manufacturers often use tungsten to make equipment that must withstand extreme heat. Tungsten's chemical symbol is W.

Manufacturers add tungsten to steel to make the steel stronger and more elastic. Tungsten steel tools last longer than ordinary steel tools. Tungsten and carbon form tungsten carbide (WC), an extremely hard substance used in the tips of mining drills and high-speed cutting tools. Electronics manufacturers use heating filaments made of tungsten in vacuum tubes for television sets and other electronic equipment. Filaments for electric lights and contact points for the ignition systems of automobiles are also made of tungsten.

Tungsten can combine with either calcium or magnesium to form chemical compounds called *phosphors.* Phosphors give off visible light when exposed to certain kinds of energy. Tungsten-containing phosphors con-

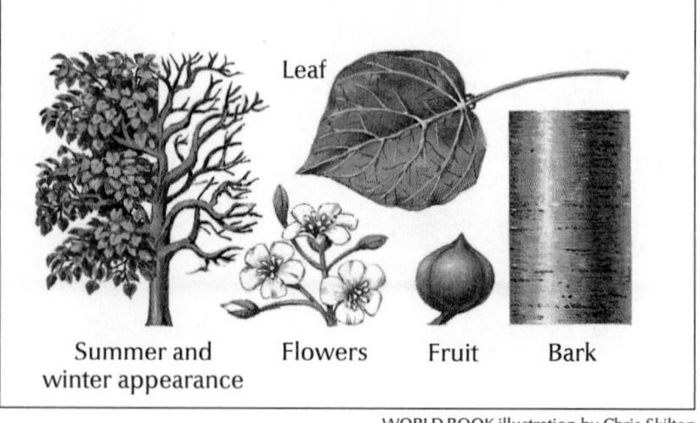

WORLD BOOK illustration by Chris Skilton

The tung tree is the source of tung oil.

vert ultraviolet rays into visible light in some fluorescent lamps.

Tungsten trioxide (WO_3) can mix with elements called *alkali metals* to form a class of compounds known as *tungsten bronzes.* Tungsten bronzes that have nearly equal amounts of alkali ions and tungsten ions are good electrical conductors, while those with fewer alkali ions are semiconductors. Tungsten bronzes are colorful and have been used as pigments in paint.

Tungsten occurs in nature in the minerals *scheelite* ($CaWO_4$) and *wolframite* ($[Fe,Mn]WO_4$). The element's name comes from scheelite, which the Swedish once called *tung sten,* meaning *heavy stone.* Scheelite was later renamed in honor of the German-born Swedish chemist Carl Wilhelm Scheele. In 1781, Scheele became the first person to isolate an oxide of tungsten. He extracted tungsten trioxide from scheelite. In 1783, two brothers, the Spanish chemists Fausto and Juan José de Elhuyar, used wolframite to prepare the first sample of tungsten metal.

Workers use a variety of chemical processes to extract tungsten metal from wolframite and scheelite. Most of these methods produce crystals of a compound called *ammonium paratungstate.* These crystals are then heated to produce tungsten trioxide. Workers usually heat tungsten trioxide with hydrogen at around 850 °C to produce pure tungsten. China produces most of the world's tungsten.

Tungsten's *atomic number* (number of protons in its nucleus) is 74. Its *relative atomic mass* is 183.84. An element's relative atomic mass equals its *mass* (amount of matter) divided by $\frac{1}{12}$ of the mass of carbon 12, the most stable isotope of carbon. Tungsten boils at about 5555 °C. Kenton H. Whitmire

See also **Electric light** (The filament); **Wolframite.**

Tunic, *TOO nihk,* is a loose, short garment that is slipped on over the head and usually belted at the waist. The name comes from the Latin word *tunica.* The tunica was a garment worn by people of ancient Rome. The men covered it with the *toga,* and the women with the *palla.* In ancient Greece, men and women wore a similar garment called the *chiton.* In the Middle Ages, Europeans wore tunics called *surcoats.* Today, tunic-style dresses and shirts are often worn. Tunic, or *tunicle,* also means a robe worn by subdeacons of the Roman Catholic Church and some Episcopal churches. They wear it at Mass. Rachel K. Pannabecker

See also **Clothing** (Ancient times; The Middle Ages; pictures); **Toga.**

Tuning fork is a device used for tuning musical instruments and for finding a standard pitch. It is made of metal and shaped like a U with a handle on the bottom.

A tuning fork produces a tone when struck. The tone is not affected by moisture and most other conditions that affect the pitch and tone of musical instruments. But the tone is slightly affected by variations in temperature. The forks are made for any note of the scale. Those most often used are A, B flat, or the C above middle C. Most forks are stamped with the note name and frequency of vibration, indicating the tuning standard. John Shore, an English trumpeter, is said to have invented the tuning fork in 1711. Today, various electronic devices are also used to tune musical instruments. Thomas W. Tunks

See also **Sound** (pictures).

Tunis, *TOO nihs* (pop. 705,000), is the capital and largest city of Tunisia. Tunis lies on the western shore of the Lake of Tunis, a shallow lagoon linked to the Mediterranean Sea by a narrow channel. For location, see **Tunisia** (map). In addition to serving as the governmental center of Tunisia, Tunis is the headquarters for most of its banks and insurance companies. The Tunis area is Tunisia's chief industrial center. The main industries are food processing and textile manufacturing. Commerce and tourism also play important roles in the economy.

Tunis consists of an old section and a modern section. The old section, called the *medina,* is a crowded area with narrow, winding streets. The modern section has newer buildings and broad, treelined boulevards.

Settlements on the site of present-day Tunis were part of the ancient empire of Carthage. They gradually developed into the city of Tunis. Arab Muslims captured the city in A.D. 698. From the early 1200's to the late 1500's, Tunis was a center for trade between Africa and Europe. From 1881 to 1956, when Tunisia was a protectorate of France, Tunis served as the headquarters of the protectorate. Kenneth J. Perkins

Tunisia extends farther north than any other country in Africa. Its northern tip is only 85 miles (137 kilometers) from Sicily, a part of Europe. Both northern and eastern Tunisia border the Mediterranean Sea.

Almost all Tunisians speak Arabic and follow an Arab way of life. For hundreds of years, trade routes have connected Tunisia to Europe, the Middle East, and Africa south of the Sahara. France controlled Tunisia from 1881 until Tunisia became independent in 1956. Tunisia shows many French influences. Tunis is its capital and largest city.

Government. Tunisia is a republic headed by a president. The people elect the president to a five-year term. The president appoints a Cabinet headed by a prime minister to assist him. Tunisia has a two-house legislature. The Chamber of Deputies has 189 members, elected by the people to five-year terms. The Chamber of Counselors has 126 members. An electoral college of deputies and local officials elects two-thirds of the counselors, and the president appoints the rest. All people who have been citizens for five years and who are 20 or older may vote. The president appoints a governor to head each of Tunisia's 24 local *governorates.* Tunisia has

Facts in brief

Capital: Tunis.

Official language: Arabic.

Area: 63,170 mi² (163,610 km²). *Greatest distances*—north-south, 485 mi (781 km); east-west, 235 mi (378 km). *Coastline*—639 mi (1,028 km).

Population: *Estimated 2006 population*—10,147,000; density, 161 per mi² (62 per km²); distribution, 63 percent urban, 37 percent rural. *1994 census*—8,785,711.

Chief products: *Agriculture*—barley, dates, citrus fruit, olives, wheat. *Manufacturing*—chemicals, construction materials, machinery, mineral processing, paper, processed foods, textiles, wood. *Mining*—aluminum, fluorite, iron, lead, petroleum, phosphates, sea salt, zinc.

Flag: The flag has a large white circle on a red field. Inside the circle are a red crescent and star, emblems of the Muslim religion. See **Flag** (picture: Flags of Africa).

Money: *Basic unit*—Tunisian dinar. One thousand millimes equal one dinar.

Tunisia

	International boundary
	Road
	Railroad
	Oil pipeline
⊛	National capital
•	Other city or town
+	Elevation above sea level

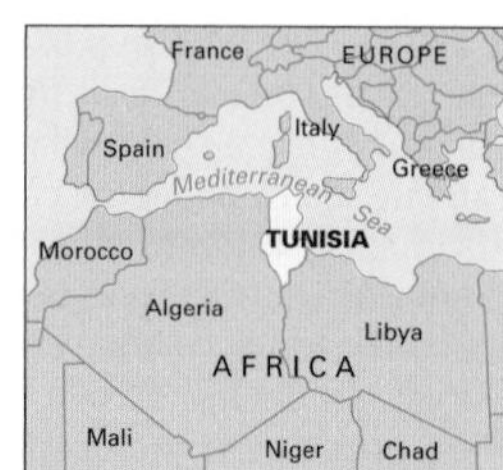

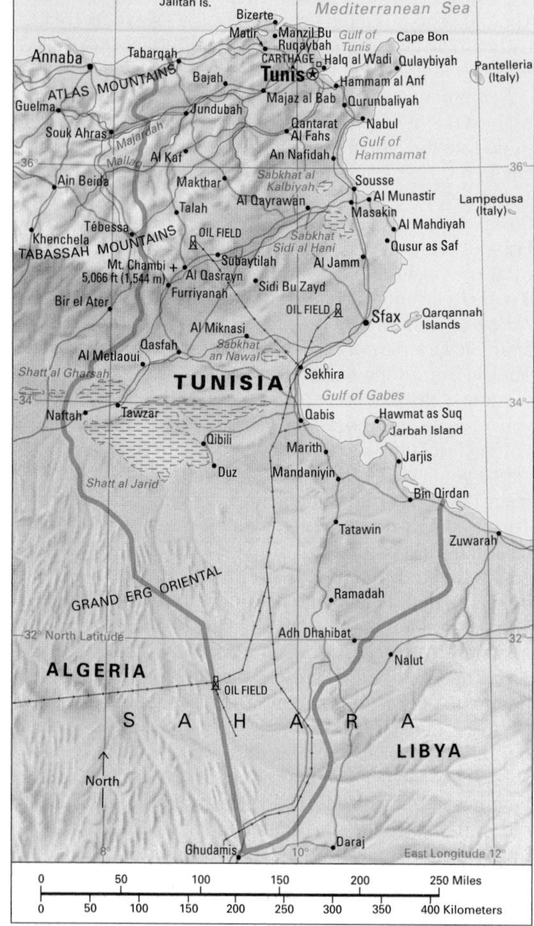

WORLD BOOK maps

several political parties. The Democratic Constitutional Rally is by far the largest. It has controlled the government since Tunisia became independent.

People. Life in Tunisia is more uniform than it is in most other African and Middle Eastern countries. This uniformity is chiefly due to the people's similarity in language and religion, and to the fact that political and cultural life is centered in one city, Tunis.

Small groups of Europeans, Jews, and Berbers live in Tunisia. But almost all Tunisians are Arabs and Muslims. French culture has influenced several features of Tunisian life, including architecture and food. Many Tunisians speak French as a second language.

Most of Tunisia's cities are divided into old and new sections. Narrow streets and covered markets characterize the old sections. Treelined avenues and European-style buildings are typical of the new sections. Many people in the cities wear Western-style clothes.

B. Regent, Hutchison Library

At a Tunisian marketplace, people meet to buy and sell various commodities. In this picture, merchants are weighing quantities of nuts and selling them to shoppers.

In the past, rural dwellings in Tunisia included many mud huts and tents. But today, most rural houses are made of stone or concrete. Many people in the rural areas continue to wear traditional Arab clothing—a turban or skullcap, and a long, loose gown, or a long coat-like garment with long sleeves.

Almost all primary school-age children and about one-third of secondary school-age children attend school. The country's higher education system includes the University of Tunis and professional schools. Most of Tunisia's adults can read and write. For the country's literacy rate, see **Literacy** (table: Literacy rates for selected countries).

Land. The uniformity of Tunisian life is also partly due to the country's geography. Two branches of the Atlas mountain range, which crosses northwestern Africa, extend into Tunisia. In Tunisia, the northern branch is called the Atlas Mountains, and the southern branch, the Tabassah Mountains. But the mountains are low. Few peaks reach more than 2,000 feet (610 meters), and the highest, Mount Chambi, is just 5,066 feet (1,544 meters) above sea level.

Hills and grassland lie between the mountain ranges. Much of Tunisia's wheat is grown in the Majardah River valley in the north. The Majardah is the only river in Tunisia that does not dry up in summer.

From the Tabassah range, the land descends across a plateau to the Sahara in the south and to a coastal plain in the east. Coarse grass covers the plateau. The people raise cattle, sheep, and goats. The southern desert has great salt lakes and date palm oases. The fertile coastal plain extends along the east coast from Sfax to Tunis. Cereals, citrus fruits, and olives are grown there. This re-

Kurt Scholz, Shostal

Tunis, the capital and largest city of Tunisia, is the nation's political and cultural center. The building that houses the nation's Finance Ministry stands in the foreground, overlooking a tree-shaded square.

gion also has Tunisia's largest towns and cities.

Tunisia has hot, dry summers and warm, wet winters. The average coastal temperatures are 79 °F (26 °C) in summer and 52 °F (11 °C) in winter. In the southern desert, temperatures average 89 °F (32 °C) in the summer and 53 °F (12 °C) in the winter. In the north, most rain falls in winter, but it is irregular and droughts occur every three or four years. There is little rain in the south.

Economy. Food processing, textiles, and the manufacture of basic consumer goods account for most of Tunisia's industrial production. The country is a leading producer of phosphates and has petroleum resources that are used for its own needs and for export. Clothing, leather products, and other basic manufactured goods account for slightly more than half the value of Tunisia's exports. Wheat, barley, grapes, olives, olive oil, and dates make up Tunisia's chief farm products. Tourism also contributes to the economy.

Most of Tunisia's major cities, industries, and fertile land are in the north and east. These regions are richer than the dry, less developed south. Although Tunisia is not rich in natural resources, it does have a more balanced economy than many of its neighbors.

The French left Tunisia with a good road and railroad system, and even more improvements have been achieved since independence in the mid-1950's. Tunisia's chief ports are Tunis, Bizerte, Sousse, and Sfax. Oil and gas are shipped from a port located at Sekhira.

History. People and ideas have entered northwest Africa through Tunisia for centuries. According to tradition, the Phoenicians began to colonize the coast of Tunisia about 1100 B.C. and founded the famous city of Carthage near present-day Tunis about 814 B.C. The Romans defeated Carthage in 146 B.C., and ruled Tunisia for the next 600 years. In A.D. 439, the Vandals, a European tribe, invaded Tunisia, defeated the Romans, and captured Carthage. The Byzantines, from Constantinople (now Istanbul), ousted the Vandals in 534.

The Byzantines had loose control over Tunisia when Muslim Arabs from the Middle East invaded in the mid-600's. The Arab invasion was a turning point in Tunisia's history. Tunisia began to slowly become a part of Arab-Muslim civilization. The Ottoman Empire, which was centered in Asia Minor (now part of Turkey), won control of Tunisia in 1574. The Ottoman rulers appointed a *bey* (ruler) to govern Tunisia from Tunis. Tunisia was technically part of the Ottoman Empire until after World War I ended in 1918, but by the 1700's the beys in Tunis had achieved a large measure of independence.

In 1881, France imposed a protectorate over Tunisia. It controlled Tunisia's financial, foreign, and military affairs, leaving the bey only minor authority.

A Tunisian independence movement began before World War I started in 1914, but the most successful movement did not begin until 1934. In that year, Habib Bourguiba founded the Neo-Destour (New Constitution) Party—later called the Socialist Destour Party and now known as the Constitutional Democratic Rally Party. Bourguiba led the independence struggle for more than 20 years. France finally granted Tunisia internal self-government in 1955, and full independence in 1956. However, France kept troops and military bases in Tunisia after independence. During the late 1950's and early 1960's, France, at Tunisia's demand, finally withdrew its troops and gave up its Tunisian bases.

Tunisia became a republic in 1957, and the people elected Bourguiba president. Bourguiba was reelected in 1959, 1964, and 1969. In 1975, he was named president for life. His government introduced many social and economic reforms. It gave voting rights to women and set up a national school system.

Tunisia experienced enormous changes after gaining independence. But some of its successes created new problems. The number of Tunisians who received an education increased greatly, but many of the educated people could not find jobs that required their skills. Tourism provided income and jobs, but some people feared that contact with tourists might cause the country to lose its Arab-Muslim heritage.

Many Tunisians admired the work of President Bourguiba and his party, but a growing number became dissatisfied with Bourguiba's domination of politics. From 1963 to 1981, Bourguiba's party was Tunisia's only legal political party. In 1987, Prime Minister Zine El-Abidine Ben Ali removed Bourguiba from office. Ben Ali, a member of Bourguiba's party, claimed Bourguiba had become incapable of handling the presidency. Ben Ali then became president. In 1989, 1994, 1999, and 2004, he won presidential elections in which he faced little or no opposition. Kenneth J. Perkins

See also **Arab League; Bourguiba, Habib; Carthage; Tunis.**

Tunnel is an underground passageway. Tunnels are dug through hills and mountains, and under cities and waterways. They provide highways, subways, and railroads with convenient routes past natural and artificial obstacles. Miners use tunnels to reach valuable minerals deep within the earth. Tunnels also carry large volumes of water for hydroelectric power plants. Some tunnels provide fresh water for irrigation or drinking, and others transport wastes in sewer systems. In addition, tunnels provide underground space for cold storage.

How tunnels are built

People dig some tunnels through rock or soft earth. Other tunnels, called *submerged tunnels,* lie in trenches dug into the bottoms of rivers or other bodies of water.

Rock tunnels. The construction of most rock tunnels involves blasting. To blast rock, workers first move a scaffold called a *jumbo* next to the tunnel *face* (front). Mounted on the jumbo are several drills, which bore holes into the rock. The holes are usually about 10 feet (3 meters) long, but may be longer or shorter depending on the rock. The holes measure only a few inches or centimeters in diameter. Workers pack explosives into the holes. After these charges are exploded and the fumes sucked out, carts carry away the pieces of rock, called *muck.*

If the tunnel is strong, solid rock, it may not require extra support for its roof and walls. But most rock tunnels are built through rock that is naturally broken into large blocks or contains pockets of fractured rock. To prevent this fragmented rock from falling, workers usually insert long bolts through the rock or spray it with concrete. Sometimes they apply a steel mesh first to help hold broken rock. Workers using an older method erect rings of steel beams or timbers. In most cases, they add a permanent lining of concrete later.

Tunnel-boring machines dig tunnels in soft, but firm rock such as limestone or shale and in hard rock such as granite. A circular plate covered with *disk cutters* is attached to the front of these machines. As the plate rotates slowly, the disk cutters slice into the rock. Scoops on the machine carry the muck to a conveyor that removes it to the rear. To cut weaker rock, such as sandstone, workers use road headers and other machinery.

Earth tunnels include tunnels that are dug through clay, silt, sand, or gravel, or in muddy riverbeds. Tunneling through such soft earth is especially dangerous because of the threat of cave-ins. In most cases, the roof and walls of a section of tunnel dug through these materials are held up by a steel cylinder called a *shield.* Workers leave the shield in place while they remove the earth inside it and install a permanent lining of cast iron or precast concrete. After this work is completed, jacks push the shield into the earth ahead of the tunnel, and the process is repeated. Some tunnel-boring machines have a shield attached to them and are able to position sections of concrete tunnel lining into place as they dig. Such a machine dug part of the London subway system.

If the soil is strong enough to stand by itself for at least a few hours, workers may not use concrete sections. Instead, they would hold the soil in place with bolts, steel ribs, and sprayed concrete.

Tunneling through the earth beneath bodies of water adds the danger of flooding to that of cave-ins. Engineers generally prevent water from entering a tunnel during construction by compressing the air in the end of the tunnel where the work is going on. When the air pressure inside the tunnel exceeds the pressure of the water outside, the water is kept out. This method was used to build the subway tunnels under the East River in New York City and the River Thames in London.

Submerged tunnels are built across the bottoms of rivers, bays, and other bodies of water. Submerged tunnels are generally less expensive to build than those dug by the shield or compressed-air methods. Construction begins by dredging a trench for the tunnel. Closed-ended steel or concrete tunnel sections are then floated over the trench and sunk into place. Next, divers connect the sections and remove the ends, and any water in the tunnel is pumped out. In most cases, the tunnels are then covered with earth. Submerged tunnels include the railroad tunnel under the Detroit River and the rapid transit tunnel under San Francisco Bay.

Kinds of tunnels

There are four main types of tunnels. They are: (1) railroad tunnels, (2) motor-traffic tunnels, (3) water tunnels, and (4) mine tunnels.

Switzerland Tourism

The St. Gotthard Road Tunnel cuts through the central Alps in Switzerland. It is one of the world's longest road tunnels. This photograph shows the tunnel's south entrance, near Airolo.

Notable railroad tunnels

Tunnel	Location	Length In miles	Length In kilometers	Year opened
Seikan	Japan	33.5	53.9	1988
Channel	England-France	31.1	50.0	1994
Iwate Ichinohe	Japan	16.0	25.8	1994
Oshimizu	Japan	13.8	22.2	1982
Simplon I, II	Italy-Switzerland	12.3	19.8	1906, 1922
Verenia	Switzerland	11.9	19.1	1994
Shin Kanmon	Japan	11.6	18.7	1975
Apennine	Italy	11.5	18.5	1934
Rokko	Japan	10.1	16.3	1972
St. Gotthard	Switzerland	9.3	15.0	1882

Notable motor-traffic tunnels

Tunnel	Location	Length In miles	Length In kilometers	Year opened
Lærdal	Norway	15.2	24.5	2000
St. Gotthard Road	Switzerland	10.5	16.9	1980
Arlberg	Austria	8.7	14.0	1978
Fréjus	France-Italy	8.0	12.9	1980
Mt. Blanc	France-Italy	7.3	11.7	1965
Gudvanga	Norway	7.1	11.4	1991
Folgefonn	Norway	7.0	11.2	2001
Gran Sasso	Italy	6.3	10.2	1976
Seelisberg	Switzerland	5.8	9.3	1980
Ena	Japan	5.3	8.5	1976
Rokko II	Japan	4.3	6.9	1974

Railroad tunnels. Among the world's greatest engineering feats was the boring of long railroad tunnels through the rocks of the Alps and the Rocky Mountains. Railroad tunnels reduce traveling time and increase the efficiency of trains. The steeper a locomotive must climb, the less weight it can pull. Tunnels through mountains reduce steep grades, allowing trains to haul more goods and people.

Motor-traffic tunnels provide routes for automobiles, trucks, and other motor vehicles. Such tunnels have special equipment to remove exhaust fumes. For example, the Holland Tunnel, which is situated under the Hudson River and which links New York City and New Jersey, uses electric fans for ventilation. These fans are capable of completely changing the air in the tunnel every 90 seconds. Many motor-traffic tunnels also have signal lights and special monitoring systems to help prevent traffic jams.

Water tunnels. Many tunnels provide water to city waterworks, to hydroelectric power plants, or to farms for irrigation. Others carry storm drainage or sewage. Most water tunnels measure 10 to 20 feet (3 to 6 meters) or more in diameter, and they have smooth linings that help the water flow. Many tunnels carrying water to hydroelectric power plants are lined with steel to withstand extremely high water pressures.

Mine tunnels are made by blasting or by tunneling machines. Mine shafts are not usually lined, but they may have supports.

History

In Africa, there is evidence of mines created tens of thousands of years ago with tools made of deer antlers and horse bones. Prehistoric people in Europe used similar tools to mine flint. The Egyptians may have been the first to fracture rock at a tunnel face by building fires in front of the face and then pouring water on it. The Egyptians built tunnels to mine metals and store water, and as approaches to tombs.

In the A.D. 1600's, people began to use gunpowder to blast through hard rock. The rise of railroads during the 1800's caused a sharp increase in tunnel building and stimulated the invention of tunnel-building devices. In 1825, workers used a tunnel shield to build a railroad tunnel under the River Thames in London. This tunnel, completed in 1843, was the first tunnel built under a

How a tunnel is constructed A tunnel-boring machine digs into rock with attachments called *disk cutters.* The broken rock, called *muck,* then is removed by conveyor and rail car and brought to the surface in an elevator. Meanwhile, concrete sections of the tunnel lining are lowered through a shaft. A shield on the tunnel-boring machine holds up the roof until workers can erect a new section of tunnel lining.

WORLD BOOK illustration by Bill and Judie Anderson

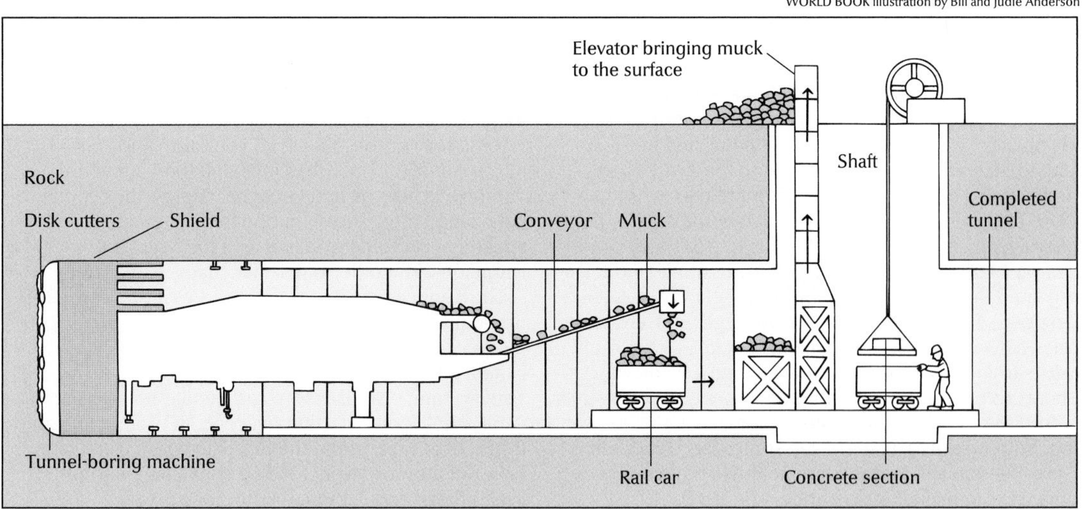

navigable river. The 9 1/3-mile (15-kilometer) St. Gotthard railroad tunnel, dug through the Swiss Alps between 1872 and 1882, was the first major tunnel built using dynamite and a jumbo. In the early 1900's, tunnel building speeded up with the invention of faster and lighter drills, harder drill bits, and mechanical muck loaders.

In 1882, the British used the first tunnel-boring machine to begin to drill a tunnel under the English Channel. This machine dug at a rate of about 50 feet (15 meters) in a day. Today, many boring machines are more than 10 times as fast as that.

The United Kingdom stopped work on the channel tunnel after about 8,000 feet (2,400 meters) of material had been drilled. The British feared that foreign armies could use the "chunnel" to invade the United Kingdom. In 1987, work began once more on a tunnel under the English Channel. Workers used huge boring machines, each longer than two football fields. The tunnel was completed in 1994. It consists of two railway tubes connected to a small tube for service and maintenance vehicles. Three kinds of trains can use the tunnel: (1) freight trains, (2) high-speed passenger trains, and (3) shuttle trains for passengers and their automobiles.

The longest underwater tunnel, Japan's Seikan Tunnel, opened in 1988. This railroad tunnel stretches 33 1/2 miles (53.9 kilometers) under the Tsugaru Strait between Honshu and Hokkaido islands. The longest highway tunnel, Norway's Lærdal Tunnel, opened in 2000. It extends 15.2 miles (24.5 kilometers) under the Jotunheimen mountain range in southern Norway. Peter K. Kaiser

Related articles in World Book include:

Apennine Tunnel
Channel Tunnel
Fréjus Tunnels
Hudson River Tunnels
Moffat Tunnel
Saint Gotthard Tunnels
Simplon Pass and Tunnel
Subway

Tunney, Gene (1897-1978), an American boxer, defeated Jack Dempsey in 1926 to become world heavyweight champion. Tunney defended his title twice—against Dempsey in 1927 and Tom Heeney in 1928—and then retired. The second Tunney-Dempsey bout featured a controversial "long count." Dempsey knocked Tunney down in the seventh round but refused to go immediately to a neutral corner. The referee delayed starting the count over Tunney for several seconds. Tunney rose at the count of nine and went on to win the fight. See **Dempsey, Jack.**

Tunney was born on May 25, 1897, in New York City. He was christened James Joseph but called Gene since that was how his baby sister pronounced Jim. He began his boxing career in 1915. In 1918, he enlisted in the United States Marine Corps and won the American Expeditionary Forces light heavyweight title in Paris in 1919. Tunney defeated Battling Levinsky for the U.S. light heavyweight title in 1922. He lost his title to Harry Greb later in 1922, his only defeat in 77 professional bouts. He regained the title from Greb in 1923. Bert Randolph Sugar

Tupelo, *TOO puh loh,* is the name of several attractive trees native to North America and Southeast Asia. Tupelos bear tiny greenish-white flowers and berrylike fruits. The fruits provide food for migrating birds. Tupelo wood is light-colored and used to make baskets, paneling, pulp, shipping boxes, tool handles, and woodenware. Bees collect nectar from the flowers of certain tupelo trees to make tupelo honey.

The *water tupelo,* also known as *sourgum* or *tupelo-gum,* reaches heights of up to 115 feet (35 meters). It grows in swamps in the southeastern United States. The trunk of the water tupelo is swollen at the base and may be more than 7 feet (2.1 meters) wide. Its large pointed leaves turn scarlet in the fall. The water tupelo bears fleshy reddish-purple fruits.

The *black tupelo,* also called *blackgum* or *pepperidge,* usually grows from 35 to 80 feet (11 to 24 meters) tall. It is found in moist woods or swamps in the eastern, southern, and central United States; in southern Ontario in Canada; and in Mexico. The black tupelo has glossy leaves. In autumn, the leaves turn brilliant scarlet, orange, and yellow, and blue-black fruits appear. The black tupelo is sometimes used as a yard or street tree.

Water tupelo trees grow in swamps in the southeastern United States. These trees grow up to 115 feet (35 meters) tall.

The *Ogeechee tupelo,* also called *Ogeechee-lime,* is a medium-sized tree that grows from 30 to 40 feet (9 to 12 meters) tall. It may also be a large shrub. The Ogeechee tupelo grows only in stream banks and river swamps in the southern tip of South Carolina, in Georgia, and in northern Florida. Its sour, bright red fruits are used to make preserves. Kenneth R. Robertson

Scientific classification. Tupelo trees belong to the tupelo family, Nyssaceae. The scientific name for the water tupelo is *Nyssa aquatica,* the black tupelo is *N. sylvatica,* and the Ogeechee tupelo is *N. ogeche.*

Tupí-Guaraní Indians, *too PEE GWAH rah NEE,* formed many tribes that lived in eastern and central South America. The tribes included the Tupinambá, Tupinikin, Guaraní, and Omagua. These tribes spoke related languages. Today, the Guaraní language is widely spoken in Paraguay and is one of the nation's two official languages. The other official language is Spanish.

The Tupí-Guaraní were farmers. Cassava, a root crop, provided their main food. They also planted yams, corn, peppers, and cotton. In addition, the tribes hunted, fished, and gathered fruits. Most of their villages consisted of one or more large rectangular houses. Each family had its own partitioned section in a house. Some tribes, especially along the Brazilian coast, were cannibals. But they are extinct. A few Tupí-Guaraní tribes still live in Brazil and Paraguay. Roberto DaMatta

Sir Charles Tupper

Prime minister of Canada
1896

Bowell
1894-1896

Tupper
1896

Laurier
1896-1911

Detail of a portrait by V. A. Long; Parliament Buildings, Ottawa (John Evans)

Tupper, Sir Charles (1821-1915), served as prime minister of Canada for about 10 weeks in 1896. He was the oldest person to hold that office. Tupper, whose fellow Canadians called him the Grand Old Man of Canada, was almost 75 years old when he became prime minister.

Tupper accomplished little as his nation's leader because he held office for such a short time. He worked hard, but with little success, to unite the Conservative Party, which had been badly divided since the death of Prime Minister John A. Macdonald in 1891.

Before Tupper became prime minister, he served in the Nova Scotia legislature and as premier of the province. Tupper helped establish the Dominion of Canada in 1867 and was one of the Fathers of Confederation. He also played an important part in bringing Nova Scotia into the Dominion. Tupper won election to the Canadian House of Commons in 1867. He held several Cabinet positions under Macdonald, who was prime minister from 1867 to 1873 and from 1878 to 1891.

Tupper, a master politician, became known for his ability to gain the cooperation of other public officials. He was a shrewd, unyielding debater and a skilled public speaker.

Early life

Family background. Charles Tupper was born on July 2, 1821, in Amherst, Nova Scotia. He was the oldest of the three sons of Charles Tupper, a Baptist minister, and of Miriam Lockhart Lowe Tupper. Charles attended Horton Academy and Acadia College in Wolfville, Nova Scotia. He later studied medicine at the University of Edinburgh in Scotland and earned an M.D. degree in 1843. Tupper then returned to Amherst and entered the practice of medicine. He helped found the Canadian Medical Association in 1867 and served as its first president.

Tupper's family. In 1846, Tupper married Frances Amelia Morse, the daughter of the chief clerk of the court in Amherst. The couple had three sons and three daughters. Their second son, Charles H. Tupper, served in the Canadian Parliament from 1882 to 1904 and held Cabinet positions from 1888 to 1896. Tupper's youngest son, William J. Tupper, served in the Manitoba Legislative Assembly from 1920 to 1922. In addition, he held office as lieutenant governor of Manitoba from 1934 to 1940.

Early public career

Entry into politics. Tupper became well known in Nova Scotia through his successful medical practice. He entered politics in 1855, when he won election to the Nova Scotia legislature as a Conservative representative from Cumberland. He defeated Joseph Howe, the leader of the Liberal Party in Nova Scotia. Howe had been known for his role in persuading the United Kingdom to grant more control over local affairs to its North American colonies.

The leaders of the Nova Scotia Conservative Party quickly recognized Tupper's political and debating skills. In 1857, he became provincial secretary in the Cabinet of Premier J. W. Johnston of Nova Scotia, a Conservative. The Liberals gained a majority in the legislature and returned to power in 1860, but Tupper won reelection from Cumberland. In addition to serving as a member of the legislature in Halifax, he practiced medicine and served as the city's medical officer. He also was editor of the *British Colonist*, a Nova Scotia newspaper that supported the Conservative Party. Tupper campaigned to help the Nova Scotia Conservatives defeat the Liberals in 1863, and Johnston became premier again. In 1864, after Johnston left office to become a federal judge, the Conservatives named Tupper leader of the party and premier of Nova Scotia.

Premier. As premier, Tupper worked for government construction of railroads and for a system of nonreligious public schools. Tupper showed great courage when he introduced the School Act of 1864, which established public schools supported by tax funds. This act was unpopular in Nova Scotia.

Tupper also worked to promote a union of the three small maritime colonies—New Brunswick, Nova Scotia, and Prince Edward Island. He believed such a union would strengthen those colonies politically and economically. Talk of a confederation of all of British North America began before Tupper's idea won public acceptance.

Confederation. Tupper was a delegate from Nova Scotia at the Charlottetown and Quebec conferences of 1864. These conferences led to Confederation. The Quebec Resolutions, prepared at the Quebec Conference, proposed a union of the colonies of British North America. This union became known as the Dominion of Canada.

The Nova Scotia legislature, led by Tupper, approved the plan for the Canadian confederation. Nova Scotia became an original member of the Dominion when the British Parliament approved the resolutions in 1867. However, many people in Nova Scotia opposed the union. They were afraid of losing the increased independence they had gained in 1848, when the United Kingdom granted Nova Scotia more control over local affairs. In the 1867 election, the Liberals, led by Howe, opposed Confederation and won control of the Nova Scotia legislature.

Tupper was elected to the Canadian House of Commons in 1867. He was the only Nova Scotia supporter of Confederation whom the province elected to the House of Commons that year.

In 1868, the Nova Scotia legislature voted to withdraw from Canada. Howe went to London and presented his anti-Confederation views to the colonial office. Tupper also went to the British capital, arguing that Nova Scotia should not leave the Dominion. The British government refused to let Nova Scotia drop out, and so the province remained in the Dominion.

Tupper persuaded Macdonald, the first prime minister of the Dominion, to offer a Cabinet position to Howe. Tupper then persuaded Howe to accept the post. By helping to bring Howe into the Dominion government, Tupper assisted in ending the anti-Confederation movement in Nova Scotia.

National prominence

Federal offices. Tupper held various Cabinet positions under Macdonald. He served as minister of inland revenue in 1872, as minister of finance in 1873 and 1874, and as minister of public works in 1878. Queen Victoria of the United Kingdom knighted Tupper in 1879. From 1879 to 1884, he served as minister of railways and canals, one of the most important government positions. Tupper held that office during most of the construction of the Canadian Pacific Railway, Canada's first transcontinental railroad.

Canadian high commissioner. In 1884, Tupper traveled to London as Canadian high commissioner (ambassador) to the United Kingdom. He returned to Canada in 1887 and again took took over the post of finance minister. In 1888, Tupper returned to London to serve again as high commissioner. In this position, he worked to expand trade between Canada and the United Kingdom and to increase emigration from the United Kingdom to Canada. Tupper also encouraged British investment in Canada.

Prime minister

Macdonald died in 1891, three months after the Conservatives won the election that year. Tupper continued to serve as high commissioner in the Conservative governments of Sir John Abbott, Sir John Thompson, and Sir Mackenzie Bowell. Bowell became prime minister after Thompson died in 1894. In 1896, Bowell called Tupper home from London to serve as secretary of state in his Cabinet.

Bowell's poor handling of a government crisis over Manitoba schools led to the resignation of seven members of the Cabinet. Bowell resigned three months later, in April 1896. The Conservatives called on Tupper to serve as prime minister and lead the party in the June election. Tupper succeeded Bowell as prime minister on April 27, 1896.

Tupper's many years spent in England had weakened his political standing at home. As prime minister, Tupper faced a divided party and many political problems. The Manitoba school dispute continued to cause a crisis in the provincial government. This problem had begun when the Manitoba legislature voted in 1890 to stop

© Albert Lee, Canapress

Sir Charles Tupper's home in Halifax, built in 1865, still stands at the corner of Tupper Grove and Armview Avenue.

supporting the province's French-language Roman Catholic schools. While Tupper was in Bowell's Cabinet, he supported a bill in Parliament to restore the Catholic schools in Manitoba. However, the Liberals did not allow a vote on the bill before the election. The Manitoba school dispute became the major issue of the 1896 campaign.

The Liberals won the June election, and Tupper left office on July 8. Wilfrid Laurier, the French-Canadian leader of the Liberal Party, became prime minister. Tupper took over as leader of the Opposition in the House of Commons.

Later years

Tupper served as Opposition leader until 1900, when he lost the election for his seat in the House. He then retired from public life and moved to Kent, England. Tupper visited Canada a number of times between 1900 and 1908.

Tupper spent much time writing his memoirs and magazine articles on political issues. He died at his home in Kent on Oct. 30, 1915. Tupper was the last surviving Father of Confederation. Michael Bliss

Turaco. See Touraco.

Turban is a headdress worn by men in Muslim and Hindu countries. The name comes from a Persian word that means a long scarf wound around the head or around a small hat. A turban protects the head from the sun's heat. The wearer may wrap a portion of the turban around the lower half of the face to protect the nose and mouth against blowing sand and dirt. The style and decoration on a turban may indicate the social rank of the wearer. Princes of India wore colorful silk and gold turbans.

Turban also means a small hat worn by women that resembles a scarf wrapped around the head. Turbans for women have been in and out of style since the 1400's. Rachel K. Pannabecker

See also **Hat** (picture).

Turbinate bone. See Nose.

Turbine, *TUR bihn* or *TUR byn,* is a device with a rotor turned by a moving fluid, such as water, steam, gas, or wind. A turbine changes *kinetic energy* (energy of movement) into *mechanical energy* (energy in the form of mechanical power). Such energy can be used to run machinery. Mechanical energy is transmitted by a turbine through the spinning motion of the rotor's axle.

Turbines provide power for a variety of machines. Generators driven by turbines produce most of the electric power used to light homes and run factories. Turbines that power water pumps play an important role in irrigation projects throughout the world. Turbines are also used to turn the propellers of ships, and they are an essential part of jet-airplane engines.

The earliest known turbines date back to simple water wheels used by the ancient Greeks approximately 2,000 years ago. Today, turbines vary greatly in size and power, depending on their use. For example, a huge turbine that turns an electric generator can deliver nearly 750 million watts of power. But some turbines used to run shop machinery measure less than 1 inch (2.5 centimeters) in diameter and deliver less than 750 watts. Turbines less than $\frac{1}{5}$ inch (5 millimeters) in diameter may someday power microengines designed to output 20 to 100 watts.

How turbines work

The rotor is the rotating part of a turbine. In a simple turbine, it consists of a disk or wheel mounted on an axle. The wheel has curved blades or buckets around the edges. Nozzles or movable gates called *guide vanes* aim the fluid at the blades or buckets and adjust its speed. In many turbines, a *casing* encloses the rotor. The casing holds the fluid against the rotor so that none of the fluid's energy is lost.

As a fluid passes through a turbine, it hits or pushes against the blades or buckets and causes the wheel to turn. When the wheel rotates, the axle turns along with it. The axle is connected directly or through a series of gears to an electric generator, air compressor, or other machine. Thus, the motion of the spinning rotor drives a machine.

The rotors of some turbines have only one wheel. But the rotors of others have as many as 50 or more. Multiple wheels increase the efficiency of the turbines, because each wheel extracts additional energy from

© Mete, Sipa Press

© Marc & Evelyne Bernheim, Woodfin Camp, Inc.

© George Holton, Photo Researchers

© Craig Aurness, Woodfin Camp, Inc.

Turbans provide protection from the sun in hot countries of Asia and Africa. In addition, some Western women wear turbans as decorative hats. The turbans shown here are worn by, *left to right,* an American woman, and men of Niger, Algeria, and Morocco.

Principles of turbine operation

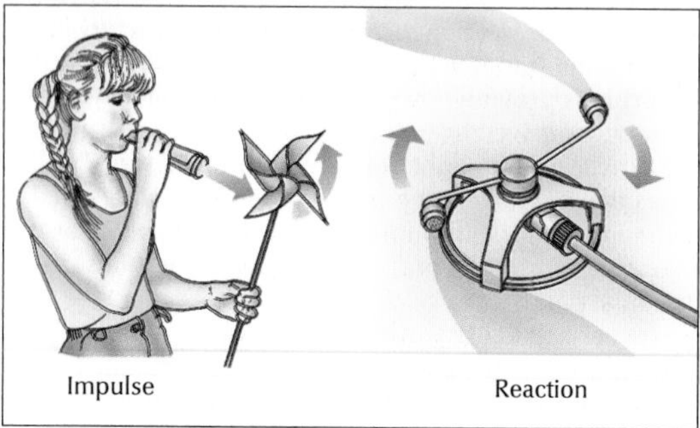

WORLD BOOK illustrations by Oxford Illustrators Limited

Turbine wheels turn by *impulse* or *reaction.* A pinwheel, *left,* is a simple impulse turbine that rotates when you blow air against the blades. A sprinkler, *right,* is a simple reaction turbine. Water squirting out of it under pressure causes the wheel to turn.

the moving fluid. In a turbine with more than one wheel, the wheels are mounted on a common axle, one behind the other. A stationary ring of curved blades is attached to the inside of the casing in front of each wheel. These stationary blades direct the flow of fluid toward the wheels. A wheel and a set of stationary blades is called a *stage. Multistage* turbines have many stages.

Kinds of turbines

Turbines are sometimes classified according to their principle of operation. All turbines operate by *impulse* or *reaction,* or by a combination of these principles. In an impulse turbine, the force of a fast-moving fluid striking the blades makes the rotor spin. In a reaction turbine, the rotor turns primarily as a result of the weight or pressure of a fluid on the blades.

Turbines are more commonly classified by the type of fluid that turns them. According to this method, there are four main kinds of turbines: (1) water turbines, (2) steam turbines, (3) gas turbines, and (4) wind turbines.

Water turbines are also called *hydraulic turbines.* Most water turbines are driven by water from waterfalls or by water that is stored behind dams. The turbines are used primarily to power electric generators at hydroelectric power plants. There are three main kinds of water turbines: (1) the Pelton wheel, (2) the Francis turbine, and (3) the Kaplan turbine. The type of water turbine used at a plant depends on the *head* available. A head is the distance the water falls before it strikes the turbine. Heads range from about 8 feet (2.4 meters) to more than 1,000 feet (300 meters).

The Pelton wheel is an impulse turbine. It is used with heads of more than 1,000 feet (300 meters). A Pelton's rotor consists of a single wheel mounted on a horizontal axle. The wheel has cup-shaped buckets around its perimeter. Water from a lake or reservoir drops toward the turbine through a long pipe called a *penstock.* One to six nozzles at the end of the penstock increase the water's velocity and aim the water toward the buckets. The force of these high-speed jets of water against the buckets turns the wheel.

The Francis turbine is used when the head is between about 100 feet (30 meters) and 1,000 feet (300 meters). A Francis turbine's rotor is enclosed in a casing. Its wheel has as many as 24 curved blades. Its axle is vertical. The wheel operates underwater. It is encircled by a ring of guide vanes, which can be opened or closed to control the amount of water flowing past the wheel. The spaces between the vanes act as nozzles to direct the water toward the wheel's center. The rotor is turned chiefly by the weight or pressure of the flowing water.

The Kaplan turbine is used for heads of less than 100 feet (30 meters). The rotor resembles a ship's propeller. It has from three to eight blades on a vertical axle. It works in a way similar to that of a Francis turbine. The Kaplan and Francis turbines are reaction turbines.

Steam turbines drive the electric generators in most U.S. power plants. They also power ocean liners and

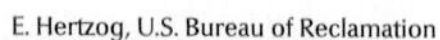

E. Hertzog, U.S. Bureau of Reclamation

A water turbine is driven by water that "falls" from a great height through a pipe or other channel. The Pelton wheel turbine shown in this photograph powers electric generators at Hoover Dam on the Arizona-Nevada border.

large machinery. Multistage steam turbines are among the world's most powerful engines. Some steam turbines produce more than 1 billion watts of power.

Steam turbines are run by steam. In most cases, the steam is produced by water heated in a boiler by burning such fuels as coal, oil, or natural gas. In nuclear power plants, however, heat produced by splitting atoms in a nuclear reactor changes water to steam.

Steam enters a turbine at temperatures as high as 1200 °F. (649 °C) and pressures as high as 3,500 pounds per square inch (24,100 kilopascals).The high-pressure steam rushes through the turbine, causing the turbine wheels to spin rapidly. Steam turbines are designed to use the impulse principle, the reaction principle, or a combination of both.

Many modern steam turbines have 50 or more stages set on a horizontal axle. Each stage of the turbine consists of a wheel and a ring of stationary blades. The curved blades of both the wheels and the stationary rings are shaped so that the spaces between them act as nozzles. The nozzles aim the steam and increase its speed before it goes on to the next stage. The steam follows a zigzag path between the wheel blades of one stage and the stationary blades of the next.

As steam passes through a multistage turbine, it expands to as much as 1,000 times its original volume. Each successive stage of the turbine is therefore larger than the previous one in order to make efficient use of the expanding steam. This arrangement of larger and larger stages gives steam turbines their characteristic conical shape.

Steam turbines may be either *condensing* or *noncondensing,* depending on how the steam leaving the turbine is used. Steam from a condensing turbine goes directly into a condenser. Cold water circulating in pipes in the condenser cools the steam into water. A vacuum is thus created, because the volume of water is much less than that of steam. The vacuum helps force steam through the turbine. The water is pumped back to the boiler to be made into steam again. The exhaust steam from noncondensing turbines is not cooled into water. Instead, it is used to provide heat for buildings and for a variety of industrial processes.

Gas turbine systems burn such fuels as oil and natural gas. Instead of using the heat to produce steam, as in steam turbines, gas turbines use the hot gases directly. Gas turbines are used to power electric generators, ships, and high-speed cars. They are also an important part of the engines in jet aircraft.

Most gas turbine systems have three main parts: (1) an air compressor, (2) a combustion chamber, and (3) a turbine. The combination of the air compressor and combustion chamber is commonly called a *gas generator.* In most gas turbine systems, the air compressor and turbine are mounted at either end of a common horizontal axle, with the combustion chamber between them. Part of the turbine's power runs the air compressor.

The air compressor sucks in air and compresses it, thereby increasing its pressure. In the combustion chamber, the compressed air combines with fuel and the resulting mixture is burned. The greater the pressure of the air, the better the fuel-air mixture burns. The burning gases expand rapidly and rush into the turbine, where they cause the turbine wheels to rotate. Hot gases move through a multistage gas turbine in much the same way that steam moves through a steam turbine. Stationary blades aim the moving gas at the rotor blades and adjust its velocity.

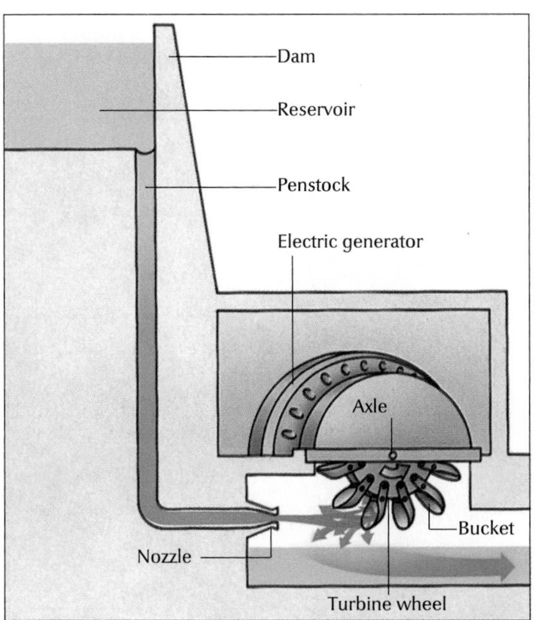

The Pelton wheel is an impulse water turbine. The force of water striking the turbine wheel causes it to spin. Water falls toward the turbine through a pipe called the *penstock* and hits the buckets on the wheel in a high-speed jet.

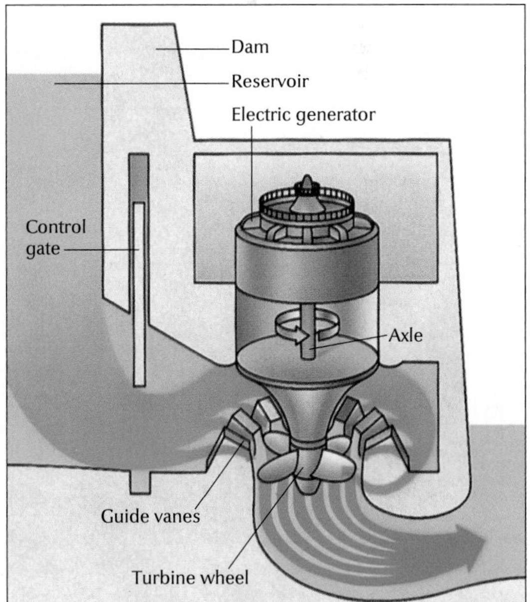

WORLD BOOK illustrations by Oxford Illustrators Limited

The Kaplan turbine is a reaction water turbine. The turbine wheel, which is completely underwater, is turned by the pressure of water against its blades. Guide vanes and a control gate regulate the amount of water reaching the wheel.

Most gas turbine systems make use of the hot exhaust gases from the turbine. In some systems, some of the exhaust gases are circulated to a device called a *regenerator.* There, the gases are used to warm up the high-pressure air from the compressor before it enters the combustion chamber. Such preheating of the air reduces the amount of fuel needed for combustion. In jet engines, much of the gas stream is used to develop thrust (see **Jet propulsion**).

Gas turbines run at even hotter temperatures than steam turbines. The hotter a gas turbine runs, the more efficiently it operates. The temperature in many gas turbines is 2000 °F (1093 °C) or higher.

Wind turbines, which are commonly called *windmills,* are driven by the wind. They were developed about 1,300 years ago and, through the centuries, they have been used chiefly to grind grain and pump water. In the late 1800's, thousands of communities in the United States used windmills to draw water from the ground. During the 1970's, shortages of oil led to increased interest in wind turbines as a potential source of energy for generating electricity.

There are two basic types of wind turbines: (1) horizontal axis wind turbines (HAWT's) and (2) vertical axis wind turbines (VAWT's).

Horizontal axis wind turbines. Traditional HAWT's have rotors with multiple blades or sails. They include *Dutch windmills* and *American windmills* (see **Windmill**). Most modern HAWT's used to generate electricity have two propellerlike blades. The rotor of these HAWT's is mounted on a tower or mast that holds the blades high enough off the ground to catch the wind stream. In order for the turbine to operate efficiently, the blades need to face into the wind, and the axle must lie parallel to the wind stream. As the wind blows, the rotor turns as a result of the impact of the air on the specially shaped blades. HAWT's are designed to adjust to changes in the speed and direction of the wind. The angle of the blades can be changed to keep the turbine operating at a constant rate, no matter what the wind speed is. In addition, these turbines can be rotated around a vertical axis to keep the rotor blades facing into the wind.

Vertical axis wind turbines. The most efficient kind of vertical axis wind turbine was developed in the 1920's by a French inventor named Georges Darrieus. The Darrieus wind turbine looks like a giant eggbeater. It has two or three long curved blades attached at both ends to a vertical shaft. The Darrieus wind turbine can catch the flow of wind from any direction.

History

Water wheels are the oldest known turbines. They were used by the ancient Greeks as long ago as 100 B.C. for grinding grain and squeezing oil from olives. By the A.D. 300's, the Romans had introduced water wheels into many other parts of Europe.

The first windmills were probably built in the A.D. 600's in Iran. These early windmills were used for grinding grain and irrigating crops. By the 1100's, they had spread to Europe. In the 1400's, people in the Netherlands began using windmills to drain marshes and lakes near the sea.

For many centuries, water wheels and windmills were the only useful turbines. The scientist Hero of Alexandria had built a small steam turbine about A.D. 60, but it had not been used to power anything (see **Steam engine** [History]). In 1629, Giovanni Branca, an Italian engineer,

How a steam turbine works

Steam rushes through a steam turbine, turning a series of bladed wheels on a common axle. After the steam leaves the turbine, a condenser changes it into water, *left.* The cutaway view of a steam turbine, *right,* shows how a ring of stationary blades is positioned between each rotating wheel. Both the stationary blades and wheel blades aim the steam and increase its speed.

WORLD BOOK illustrations by Oxford Illustrators Limited

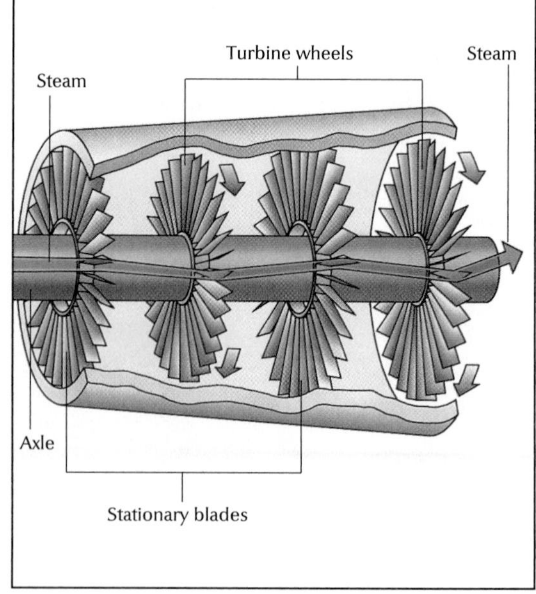

built an impulse steam turbine, but it was impractical.

Early water wheels and windmills were less efficient than modern turbines, because much of the moving fluid escaped around the edges of the rotor blades. During the 1800's, engineers and inventors began developing more efficient, enclosed turbines. In 1824, Claude Burdin, a French engineer, introduced the word *turbine* in a scientific paper. It comes from the term *turbo,* the Latin word for a spinning object. Benoît Fourneyron, a French engineer, built the first successful enclosed water turbine in 1827. After Fourneyron's success, engineers soon overcame most of the problems that were involved in building efficient water turbines.

In 1849, an English-born inventor named James B. Francis built the first Francis turbine. The Pelton wheel, invented by an American mining engineer named Lester A. Pelton, began to be produced during the 1880's. Victor Kaplan, an Austrian inventor, developed the design for the Kaplan turbine during the early 1900's.

In 1884, an English inventor, Charles A. Parsons, developed a reaction steam turbine that became the first successful steam turbine. In 1897, he used steam turbines to power his vessel, the *Turbinia.* In 1895, Charles G. Curtis, an American inventor, patented a multistage steam turbine that worked by both reaction and impulse. This turbine started a revolution in power production, because it was extremely efficient for its size and weight. During the early 1900's, steam turbines replaced steam engines in electrical generating stations.

John Barber, an English inventor, was issued a patent on a simple gas turbine system in 1791. In 1930, an English engineer named Frank Whittle received the first patent on the application of a gas turbine to propel aircraft. The first airplane to be powered by a turbojet engine

The Darrieus wind turbine is a vertical axis wind turbine. Darrieus wind turbines are extremely efficient because they can catch the flow of wind from any direction.

How a gas turbine system works

In a gas turbine system, compressed air is forced into a combustion chamber and mixed with fuel. A spark ignites the mixture and hot gases rush through the turbine, spinning the wheels. Wheel blades and stationary blades direct the gases through the turbine and increase their speed. Part of the turbine's power is used to run the air compressor.

WORLD BOOK illustration by Oxford Illustrators Limited

Air compressor
Combustion chamber
Turbine
Air intake
Fuel
Spark
Turbine wheels
Exhaust
Workload
Axle
Axle
Spark
Fuel
Stationary blades

was built by the Heinkel Company of Germany in 1939.

Brian M. Argrow

Related articles in *World Book* include:

WORLD BOOK illustration by Colin Newman, Linden Artists Ltd.

The flat-bodied turbot of Europe's North Atlantic coastal waters has eyes only on one side of its body. When it swims, the eyeless side is on the underside.

Turbot, *TUR buht,* is a large flatfish that lives along the Atlantic Coast of Europe and in the Mediterranean Sea. From the side it looks almost as round as a plate. It seldom grows over 2 feet (60 centimeters) long and usually weighs from 18 to 30 pounds (8 to 14 kilograms). But fishing crews sometimes catch 55-pound (25-kilogram) turbot that measure more than 30 inches (76 centimeters) long.

The turbot is flat and wide, with a long fin on its top and bottom ridges. Hard, round knobs cover its brown upper side. Both eyes are on the left side. The turbot lays as many as 10 million eggs, which float on the surface of the ocean. The young fish that hatch settle to the bottom and live there.

Turbot are valuable commercially and are exported. Turbot became a favorite fish of the English. The *American spotted turbot* and the *hornyhead turbot* also are flatfishes but belong to a different family.

David W. Greenfield

Scientific classification. The European turbot belongs to the family Bothidae. It is *Scophthalmus maximus.*

See also **Flatfish; Flounder.**

Turbulence, Air. See **Air turbulence.**

Turgenev, *tur GEN nyuhf,* **Ivan** (1818-1883), was one of the greatest Russian novelists. He was the first Russian writer to achieve substantial recognition in the West. Turgenev became noted for his realistic portrayals of the Russian nobility and intellectuals. He examined social and cultural interests in novels that read like a diary of that part of Russian society from the 1840's to the 1870's. These novels are *Rudin* (1856), *A Nest of Gentlefolk* (1859), *On the Eve* (1860), *Fathers and Sons* (1862), *Smoke* (1867), and *Virgin Soil* (1877).

In his novels and in the short story "The Diary of a Superfluous Man" (1850), Turgenev described a type of educated, well-meaning, but disillusioned Russian nobleman. This type of character, known as the "superfluous man," is unable to find an outlet for his talents and energies. This passive and politically ineffective figure was the most common type of male character in Russian literature of Turgenev's time. In contrast, the female characters in Turgenev's novels are more resourceful and strong-willed.

Turgenev's masterpiece, *Fathers and Sons,* is about the young Russian radicals of the 1860's. Bazarov, the main character of the book, is a *nihilist*—that is, a person who opposes all tradition and authority (see **Nihilism**). Bazarov is a powerful and convincing character, but he dies inactive and frustrated.

Ivan Sergeyevich Turgenev was born on Nov. 9, 1818, in Orel, southwest of Moscow. He was raised at his family's estate there. Turgenev first won recognition as a writer in 1852 with his collection titled *A Sportman's Sketches.* This collection contains sympathetic portrayals of the Russian peasants. Turgenev's best-known drama is *A Month in the Country* (1850). Turgenev spent several decades in the West, and he was part of a group of people who believed that the future of Russia depended on its adoption of the best elements of Western culture. Anna Lisa Crone

Turin, *TOO rihn* (pop. 865,263), is a beautiful and historic city in northern Italy. Its Italian name is Torino (pronounced *toh REE noh).* Turin is the capital of the Piedmont region. The city lies at the base of the Alps on the Po River. For location, see **Italy** (political map).

Turin has many examples of Baroque architecture, a highly decorative style that developed in the 1600's and 1700's. These include the Savoy Royal Palace and the Basilica of Superga, the burial place of the Savoy royal family. The Cathedral of St. John the Baptist dates from the 1490's. A chapel added to the cathedral in the 1600's contains the Shroud of Turin, which some people believe was the burial cloth of Jesus Christ. See **Shroud of Turin.**

© Grazia Neri, Corbis

Turin is a beautiful and historic city in northern Italy. It is the capital of Italy's Piedmont region. In this picture, the dome and spire of the Mole Antonelliana rise above downtown Turin.

The dome and spire of a city landmark, the Mole Antonelliana, rise over Turin's skyline. Many beautiful *piazzas* (public squares) provide open space in the city. Parks and botanic gardens stretch along the banks of the Po.

The University of Turin was founded in 1404. The city's Egyptian Museum houses one of the world's leading collections of ancient Egyptian relics. The Automobile Museum traces the history of the automobile.

Turin's important industries include manufacturing, banking, and insurance. Automobiles, fine chocolates, and textiles are among the city's chief products. The Fiat corporation, a leading automobile manufacturer, has its headquarters in Turin.

The city began over 2,300 years ago as the home of the Taurini, a Celtic tribe. In 218 B.C., the Carthaginian general, Hannibal, captured and heavily damaged Turin. Julius Caesar rebuilt the city in 28 B.C. In the 1200's, the Savoy family took control of Turin. From 1861 to 1865, Turin served as the first capital of the Kingdom of Italy. Turin was chosen to host the 2006 Winter Olympic Games. Pamela Ballinger

Turing, Alan Mathison (1912-1954), an English mathematician, made important contributions to the development of electronic digital computers. In 1937, he described a hypothetical computing machine, now called the *Turing machine,* that could, in principle, perform any calculation. The device had a long tape divided into squares on which symbols could be written or read. The tape head of the machine could move to the left or to the right. The machine also had a table to tell it the order in which to carry out operations. The Turing machine became an important tool for determining what could be programmed on a computer.

Turing was born on June 23, 1912, in London. He studied mathematics at Cambridge University and at Princeton University. He helped crack German codes during World War II (1939-1945). After the war, he worked on a project to build the first British electronic digital computer. In 1950, he proposed a test for determining if machines might be said to "think." This test, now called the *Turing test,* is often mentioned in discussions of *artificial intelligence* (see **Artificial intelligence**). Arthur Gittleman

Turkestan, *TUR kih STAN,* also spelled *Turkistan,* is a vast region in Asia. It has no definite boundaries. It stretches from Siberia on the north to Iran, Pakistan, India, and Tibet on the south. The Mongolian Desert lies to the east, and the Caspian Sea to the west. The name *Turkestan* refers to the Turkic-speaking tribes that have lived in this region since as early as the A.D. 500's.

For hundreds of years, Turkestan has linked Europe with eastern Asia. Many ancient trade routes crossed the area, including Marco Polo's Golden Road. During World War II (1939-1945), Turkestan provided a route for transporting arms from the Soviet Union to China.

Western Turkestan, formerly also called Soviet Turkestan, lies between the Caspian Sea and the Tian Shan range. Kazakhstan, Kyrgyzstan, Tajikistan, Turkmenistan, and Uzbekistan make up Western Turkestan. Flat and sandy in the north and west, the land rises to form mountains in the southeast. Rivers from the mountains flow inward, to disappear in the desert sands. Most of the people are Muslims and make their living by farming and raising cattle. Irrigation ditches provide water for wheat, rice, millet, oats, and cotton. Chief cities include Tashkent, Almaty, Qaraghandy, Bishkek, Dushanbe, and Samarqand.

Chinese Turkestan, also called Eastern Turkestan, in the heart of Asia, extends east from Western Turkestan to Tibet and the desert known as the Gobi. The Tian Shan range on the north, and the Kunlun Mountains, rising over 20,000 feet (6,100 meters) on the south, border the region. Chinese Turkestan, which forms part of China's Xinjiang region, has a harsh, dry climate. The people are of Turkish origin and are called *Uygurs.* They make their living by farming, raising domestic animals, and trading. Most of them are Muslims. Major cities include Urumqi, Hami, Karamay, Kashi, and Yining.

Afghan Turkestan is bounded on the north by the Amu Darya (Oxus River), and on the northwest by Western Turkestan. Uzbek chiefs ruled the country for a long time before Afghanistan gained possession of it. This part of southern Turkestan forms the Afghan province of Mazar-i-Sharif. The many mountains found in Afghan Turkestan have rich copper, iron, lead, and gold deposits. The people of this region are chiefly of Persian and Uzbek stock.

History. The known history of Turkestan began about the time of Christ, when much of the region belonged to the Chinese Empire. In the 500's, Turkic-speaking tribes conquered the rich trading cities of Bukhara and Samarqand. During the 600's, Tibet gained control of Eastern Turkestan. Later, however, the Chinese again took the region. In the 900's, the Muslim religion began to spread over Eastern Turkestan. Turkic-speaking nomads from central Asia invaded Turkestan in 1073. Followers of Genghis Khan swept through the land in the 1200's. Bukhara and Samarqand, in Western Turkestan, became centers of Muslim culture during the 1300's and 1400's.

The Muslims in Eastern Turkestan made repeated attempts to set up their own government, especially in the 1800's. Chinese Turkestan almost became an independent state from 1872 to 1876, under the kingship of Yakub Beg. But after he died, China regained control. Chinese Turkestan is now governed as a part of the province of Xinjiang.

Russia began to extend its rule to Western Turkestan soon after the Russian conquest of Siberia during the 1600's. During the 1700's, Kazakh tribes accepted Russian authority. Most of Western Turkestan became Russian during the 1800's. The Russian czar's government created the province of Turkestan and made Tashkent the capital of the province. In 1887, an Anglo-Russian commission established the boundary between Afghanistan and Russian Turkestan.

In the 1920's and 1930's, Western Turkestan was divided into five separate states of the Soviet Union: the Kazakh, Kyrgyz, Tajik, Turkmen, and Uzbek Soviet Socialist Republics. The Soviet government developed the region's resources. It also built schools, extended irrigation systems, and laid additional railroad lines. In 1991, following the collapse of the Soviet Union, each of the five republics became independent. Zvi Gitelman

Related articles in *World Book* include:

Aral Sea	Tajikistan
Genghis Khan	Tashkent
Kazakhstan	Turkmenistan
Kyrgyzstan	Uzbekistan
Samarqand	Xinjiang

Turkey has many towering mountains and barren plains. Mount Ararat, *shown here,* is part of the Anatolian Plateau, an area of dry highlands that stretches across central Turkey. The peak is Turkey's highest point, rising 16,946 feet (5,165 meters) above sea level near Turkey's border with Iran.

Turkey

Turkey is a Middle Eastern country that lies both in Europe and in Asia. About 3 percent of Turkey lies in Thrace, at the eastern edge of southern Europe. To the east, the rest of Turkey covers a large, mountainous peninsula called Anatolia or Asia Minor. Istanbul, Turkey's largest city, lies on both sides of the Bosporus (also spelled Bosphorus), a narrow body of water separating Thrace and Anatolia.

Turkey borders Bulgaria and Greece on the northwest; Georgia, Armenia, Azerbaijan, and Iran on the east; and Iraq and Syria on the southeast. The Black Sea lies to the north, the Aegean Sea to the west, and the Mediterranean Sea to the south.

Three bodies of water—the Bosporus, the Sea of Marmara, and the Dardanelles—separate Anatolia from Thrace. The Bosporus and the Dardanelles, often called the Straits, have played a major role in Turkey's history. By its control of the Straits, Turkey could regulate ship movement between the Mediterranean and Black seas.

Turkey has several large cities, including Istanbul and Ankara, Turkey's capital, and areas of rich farmland. But much of the country is rocky, barren, and mountainous. About two-thirds of Turkey's people live in cities or towns. Most of the rest live in villages. Nearly all the people are Muslims—that is, followers of Islam. Turkey is a developing country, and nearly half of its workers are farmers. However, the economy has become increasingly industrialized since the 1950's. Manufacturing now contributes more to national income than does agriculture.

Various Asian and European peoples have ruled what is now Turkey since ancient times. During the A.D. 1300's, a group of Muslim Turks called the Ottomans be-

Caglar Keyder, the contributor of this article, is Professor of Sociology at the State University of New York at Binghamton and Adjunct Professor of Sociology at Bogazici University in Istanbul, Turkey.

Facts in brief

Capital: Ankara.
Official language: Turkish.
Official name: Türkiye Cumhuriyeti (Republic of Turkey).
Area: 299,158 mi² (774,815 km²). *Greatest distances*—east-west, 1,015 mi (1,633 km); north-south, 465 mi (748 km). *Coastline*—2,211 mi (3,558 km).
Elevation: *Highest*—Mount Ararat, 16,946 ft (5,165 m) above sea level. *Lowest*—sea level along the coast.
Population: *Estimated 2006 population*—74,204,000; population density, 248 per mi² (96 per km²); distribution, 59 percent urban, 41 percent rural. *2000 census*—67,844,903.
Chief products: *Agriculture*—barley, corn, cotton, fruits, potatoes, sugar beets, wheat. *Manufacturing*—fertilizers, iron and steel, machinery, motor vehicles, processed foods and beverages, pulp and paper products, textiles and clothing.
National anthem: "Istiklâl Marsi" ("Independence March").
Money: *Basic unit*—new Turkish lira. One hundred new kurus equal one new lira..

© Pietro Cenini, Panos Pictures

Istanbul, Turkey's largest city, is divided by a waterway called the Golden Horn, *front,* an inlet of the Bosporus. Two of the city's fine *mosques* (Islamic houses of worship) are the New Mosque, *center,* and the Mosque of Süleyman I, *background.*

gan to build a powerful empire that eventually controlled much of the Middle East, southeastern Europe, and northern Africa. The Ottoman Empire ended in 1922. The next year, Turkey became a republic.

Islamic law had strongly influenced Turkish life for nearly 1,000 years. Starting in the 1920's, Turkey's new republican government introduced sweeping cultural and political changes that discouraged or outlawed many traditional Islamic practices. Most people accepted the changes, but others resisted them. Turkey's people continue to debate the role of Islam in Turkish life.

Government

Turkey is a republic. Its current Constitution was adopted in 1982, following two years of military rule. The Constitution provides for a parliamentary form of government that includes a president, a prime minister and cabinet, and a legislature called the Grand National Assembly. The charter protects state institutions against criticism and attack from citizens. It does not provide for full freedom of speech and other basic rights.

National government. Executive power in Turkey is shared by the president and the prime minister. The president is Turkey's head of state and commander in chief of the armed forces. The Grand National Assembly elects the president to a seven-year term.

The prime minister is Turkey's head of government and directs the day-to-day operation of the government. The president selects the prime minister from among the most influential members of the legislature. Generally, the leader of the party with the most legislative seats becomes prime minister. Members of the cabinet, called the Council of Ministers, are nominated by the prime minister and appointed by the president. The ministers supervise the government departments.

The Grand National Assembly makes Turkey's laws, ratifies treaties, and has the power to declare war. The Assembly consists of 550 deputies elected by the voters to five-year terms.

Court system. Courts throughout Turkey handle commercial disputes, family law, criminal trials, and other cases. Appeals courts review the decisions of lower courts. The Constitutional Court determines the legality of laws passed by the legislature.

Local government. Turkey is divided into about 80 provinces. Each province has a governor appointed by the president and a council elected by the province's voters. Provinces are divided into counties, districts, and villages. Settlements with more than 2,000 people are organized as municipalities. The mayor and municipal council are elected by the people of the municipality.

Political parties. Turkey has a number of political parties. Among the largest are the center-right Motherland and True Path parties, the center-left Democratic Left Party, a Turkish nationalist party called the Nationalist Action Party, and a pro-Islamic party called the Justice and Development Party.

Armed forces. About 610,000 men serve in Turkey's army, navy, and air force. At some time between the ages of 20 and 32, all men are drafted for service of up to 18 months. The military has high status in Turkey and can, in effect, overrule certain government decisions.

Turkey's flag was adopted in 1936. The crescent and five-pointed star are traditional symbols of the Islamic faith.

WORLD BOOK map

Turkey is a country in the Middle East. It covers the peninsula of Asia Minor, also called Anatolia. In addition, a small part of Turkey occupies a region called Thrace in southeastern Europe.

Turkey map index

Cities and towns

*Does not appear on map; key shows general location.

Source: 1990 census.

© Adam Woolfitt, Woodfin Camp, Inc.

Ankara became Turkey's capital when the Republic of Turkey was established in 1923. A statue of Kemal Atatürk, the founder of the republic, stands on this Ankara street.

People

Most of Turkey's people live in cities and towns. The number of urban dwellers has increased rapidly since the 1940's. Hundreds of thousands of people have left their farms and villages to seek work in the cities. But the cities do not have enough jobs for all the people. In the 1960's and 1970's, many of Turkey's people went abroad to work. More than 3 million Turkish citizens live in European countries, especially Germany. Other countries where Turkish citizens work include other Middle Eastern countries and Australia.

Ancestry. More than 80 percent of Turkey's people consider themselves descendants of a people called Turks. The Turks began migrating from central Asia to Anatolia during the A.D. 900's. Kurds form Turkey's largest minority group, with about 15 percent of the population. Many Kurds live in mountainous regions in the southeast. Arabs, most of whom are farmers, live near the Syrian border. Caucasians—people whose ancestors came from the Caucasus Mountains region just northeast of Turkey—live in the provinces bordering the Black Sea. Greeks, Armenians, and Jews live mostly in the Istanbul area. During the 1800's and 1900's, many Greeks and Armenians left Turkey, either voluntarily or by force.

Languages. Most people speak Turkish, the country's official language. Many Kurds speak Kurdish. Small groups of people speak Arabic, Armenian, Circassian, Greek, or other minority languages.

The government began to develop the modern Turkish language during the late 1920's. For hundreds of years, the written language was Ottoman Turkish, a complicated language written in Arabic characters and using some Persian and Arabic vocabulary. The Arabic alphabet had no letters to represent many sounds used in spoken Turkish. Ottoman Turkish was so difficult that only scholars and the ruling class learned to read it. In 1928, the government established a new alphabet and eliminated most foreign words from the language.

Way of life

In the 1920's, when the Republic of Turkey was established, the government set out to make Turkey a modern state. Government officials began a program to sweep away the customs and traditions of centuries.

One of the government's major goals has been to change the status of women in Turkish life. Men have dominated Turkish society for hundreds of years. Before the 1920's, women had almost no civil rights. Parents arranged the marriages of their daughters by means of a contract with the groom's family. Women could not vote and had difficulty getting a divorce. During the 1920's, the government outlawed the arrangement of marriages by contract, made it easier for women to get a divorce, and gave women the right to vote. Today, increased educational opportunities are gradually improving the position of Turkish women. Women now make up about 40 percent of all university students in Turkey.

The government also tried to bring the Kurds and other tribal people into the mainstream of Turkish life. Many Kurds lived in tribal groups as nomads or in isolated communities for centuries. During the 1920's, the government began to force these people to abandon their tribal way of life as a means of modernizing Turkish society. The Kurds revolted against these attempts several times in the 1920's and 1930's. Since then, many Kurds have adopted modern Turkish culture. The majority of Kurds now live in large cities. Others are settled in rural villages, where they farm or raise livestock.

City life. The look of most Turkish cities has changed greatly since the mid-1900's. Much new construction has taken place to accommodate the growing population. Most cities are dominated by small factories, retail shops, restaurants, and professional offices. The western part of Turkey has several important industrial cities, such as İzmit and Bursa. Large parts of the cities have many poor people and lack basic services.

© Max Engel, Woodfin Camp, Inc.

Kurds, shown here performing a traditional dance, rank as Turkey's largest minority group. They make up about 15 percent of the population. Many Kurds live in Turkey's mountain areas.

Rural life has changed rapidly since the 1980's. Almost all villages have electric power and telephone connections. Most rural households have a television set and a refrigerator. Villagers in the western regions and on the southern coast are generally well off. Much more poverty exists in the mountainous eastern area and in parts of the northern Black Sea region.

Housing varies throughout Turkey. Peasants who live near the Black Sea build thatch-roofed cottages with timber from nearby forests. Many villagers in central Anatolia live in flat-roofed houses of sun-dried brick. Stone houses are common in southern and western Anatolia. In rural areas of Turkey, many people have replaced their old traditional homes with one-story houses of cinder blocks. New urban construction throughout Turkey is mostly reinforced concrete and brick.

Most wealthy Turks own comfortable private apartments in the city centers, on the outskirts, or in the suburbs. Most middle-class city dwellers live in apartment buildings. The rapid growth of the cities has created neighborhoods of low-quality, makeshift housing. These shantytowns lack good roads and basic services.

Clothing worn in Turkey changed dramatically during the 1920's. The government discouraged or forbade the wearing of certain garments required by Islamic custom. City dwellers and many rural people then adopted Western clothing styles. But some rural people still follow Islamic tradition. A few men wear the traditional loose-fitting cloak and baggy trousers. Some peasant women wear a simple blouse and pantaloons. They cover their head and sometimes the lower part of their face with a scarf as a sign of modesty. A few women, especially in the poorer parts of large cities, wear a long black cloth that covers the head and drapes over their other clothing.

Food and drink. Wheat bread is the chief food of most people in Turkey. Other common foods are rice, vegetables, and lamb. In villages, a meal often consists of *bulgur* (cracked wheat) and yogurt, along with fruit, vegetables, and bread. Turkish cooking is especially famous for *shish kebab,* which consists of pieces of lamb, tomatoes, peppers, and onions cooked together on a skewer. People also enjoy *borek,* a flaky pastry stuffed with meat or cheese. A popular dessert is *baklava,* made of thin layers of pastry, honey, and chopped nuts. Another pastry, *kadayıf,* is made with shredded wheat. Favorite beverages in Turkey include tea, thick coffee, and a liquor called *rakı,* which is flavored with anise.

Recreation. Many men spend their leisure time in coffee houses playing the ancient dice game of backgammon and various card games. One tradition in the cities is the *meyhane,* a kind of restaurant where cold dishes and drinks, usually beer or rakı, are served.

Soccer is extremely popular and a favorite topic of conversation. Everywhere in Turkey, boys and men kick soccer balls around on the street.

Turkish people also enjoy concerts, motion pictures, and stage plays. Large stadium concerts by Turkish and foreign pop music stars draw big crowds.

Religion. More than 98 percent of the Turkish people are Muslims. However, Turkey has no state religion, and the Constitution guarantees religious freedom. Some people are Armenian Apostolic and Eastern Orthodox Christians, Roman and Eastern Catholics, and Jews. The highest spiritual leader of the Eastern Orthodox Churches, known as the patriarch of the Church of Constantinople or the *ecumenical patriarch,* resides in Istanbul.

In the 1920's, the government adopted an official policy of *secularism* (the separation of religion and politics). It declared religion to be a strictly private matter and restricted many traditional religious practices. Many people objected to the restrictions. Today, the dispute continues over what part Islam should play in Turkish life. The army and most citizens prefer a secular state. Some groups, however, dislike the idea of strict separation between government and religion. One dispute concerns regulations that have prohibited women from covering their heads while attending university classes or working in public offices. Many people believe Muslim women should be allowed to cover their heads in public if they wish.

Education. Most of Turkey's people can read and write. For the country's literacy rate, see **Literacy** (table: Literacy rates for selected countries). The government spends about 10 percent of its budget on public education. But rising costs and teacher shortages prevent the nation from providing enough schools and teachers, especially in rural areas.

Turkish law requires all children to attend an eight-year primary school until they graduate or reach the age of 15. But this law is difficult to enforce. After graduation, students may attend high school for three years, enroll in a vocational school, or enter the work force. Many high school graduates go on to college. They must pass through a highly competitive testing process to determine the universities and fields of study for which they qualify. Turkey has about 60 universities. Istanbul University, the oldest and largest university in Turkey, traces its history back to a religious school that was founded in 1453.

© Dave G. Houser

A Turkish weaver creates an Oriental rug on a traditional hand loom. The country's rug makers have long been famous for their beautiful, elaborately designed Turkish carpets.

The Cappadocia region of east-central Turkey features many unusual volcanic rock formations. Many tourists visit the region each year to see its natural wonders. Tourism has become an important economic activity in Turkey.

© Hans Georg Roth, Corbis

The arts. Turkey's most important contribution to the arts is in the field of architecture. In Istanbul stands the great-domed cathedral Hagia Sophia, a classic example of Byzantine architecture. It was built in the A.D. 500's, when the area was part of the Byzantine Empire. Many of Turkey's finest buildings were built during the 1400's and the 1500's, when the Ottoman Empire was at its height. Many were designed by Turkey's greatest architect, Mimar Sinan. *Mimar* means *the architect.* Sinan's Mosque of Süleyman I in Istanbul is one of the world's most beautiful *mosques* (Islamic houses of worship).

For hundreds of years, Turkish craftworkers have made excellent dishes, bowls, and other ceramic objects. Richly colored ceramic tiles decorate many mosques and palaces in Turkey. Especially famous are elegant tiles with designs featuring a distinctive shade of blue that were made in İznik during the 1500's and 1600's. Turkish weavers have long been famous for their elaborately designed rugs. They made many of the first Oriental rugs used in Europe. Turkish villagers still produce these beautiful rugs on traditional hand looms.

Much Turkish literature before the 1920's was written in the complicated Ottoman Turkish language and deals with religious themes and life during Ottoman rule. Modern Turkish literature centers largely on nationalism, social justice, and history. Two of the most famous modern Turkish writers are the novelists Orhan Pamuk and Yaşar Kemal. Istanbul and Ankara have a lively art scene of young painters and graphic artists.

The land

Turkey lies in the northwestern part of the Middle East. Much of Thrace and the coastal areas of Anatolia consist of lowlands and green, rolling plains. A broad expanse of dry highlands called the Anatolian Plateau stretches across central Anatolia. The plateau is bordered by the Pontic Mountains on the north and the Taurus Mountains on the south.

Turkey has several large saltwater lakes and numerous rivers. But most of the rivers dry up during the hot, dry summers. In the spring, many rivers in Turkey become torrents as waters from the melting snows rush down from the mountains and overflow the riverbanks.

Turkey can be divided into eight land regions. They are (1) the Northern Plains, (2) the Western Valleys, (3) the Southern Plains, (4) the Western Plateau, (5) the Eastern Plateau, (6) the Northern Mountains, (7) the Southern Mountains, and (8) the Mesopotamian Lowlands.

The Northern Plains cover Thrace and extend along the Black Sea coast of Anatolia. Thrace's gently rolling grasslands make it an important farming and grazing region. Along the Black Sea coast, farmers raise corn, fruits, nuts, tea, and tobacco.

The Western Valleys are broad, fertile river valleys along the coast of the Aegean Sea. The region produces barley, cotton, olives, tobacco, and wheat. The value of its crop output is the highest of any region in Turkey.

The Southern Plains are a narrow strip of land along the Mediterranean Sea. A great variety of crops, including cereal grains, citrus fruits, cotton, and *pulses* (peas and beans), grow in the region's rich soil. Farmers must irrigate their fields during the hot, dry summer.

The Western Plateau, a region of highlands and scattered river valleys, extends across central Anatolia. The region receives little rainfall. Farmers raise barley and wheat in the river valleys and wherever irrigation water is available. Goats, sheep, and other livestock graze on uncultivated land.

The Eastern Plateau is an area of towering mountains and barren plains. It extends from the Western Plateau to Turkey's eastern border. The Taurus and Pontic mountains meet in the Eastern Plateau. Mount Ararat, Turkey's highest point, rises 16,946 feet (5,165 meters) above sea level near the Iranian border. Most people in the region have small farms and raise sheep and cattle.

The Northern Mountains, or Pontic Mountains, rise between the Northern Plains and the Anatolian Plateau. Only a few roads and railroads cross the mountains to connect the plateau with the Black Sea.

The Southern Mountains consist of the Taurus Mountains and smaller ranges on the southern edge of the Anatolian Plateau. These mountains almost completely cut off the plateau from the Mediterranean Sea.

The Mesopotamian Lowlands in southeastern Anatolia consist of fertile plains and river valleys. Cereal grains and fruits grow well in the region's rich soil. The

Southeast Anatolian Project, consisting of dams and an irrigation network, is under construction in the region. It will use waters of the Tigris and Euphrates rivers to produce electric power and irrigate fields.

Climate

The climate differs greatly from one region of Turkey to another. The south and west coasts of Anatolia have mild, rainy winters and hot, dry summers. Summer temperatures along the Aegean often rise above 90 °F (32 °C). The Black Sea coast has cooler summers, with an average temperature of about 72 °F (22 °C). Yearly rainfall in coastal areas averages from 20 to 30 inches (51 to 76 centimeters) along the Aegean and Mediterranean to more than 100 inches (254 centimeters) near the Black Sea. Northeastern Turkey has mild summers but bitterly cold winters. Temperatures sometimes fall to −40 °F (−40 °C). Southeastern Turkey and the interior of Anatolia have cold winters with heavy snowstorms. Summers are hot, windy, and extremely dry.

Economy

Turkey has a developing and rapidly changing economy. The western and coastal regions of Turkey are wealthier than the interior and the eastern areas. Also, cities are richer than rural areas.

The government has long been heavily involved in many aspects of Turkey's economy. The government has owned much of the country's transportation and communications industries, and it has controlled other industries as well. However, private companies have become increasingly important. During the late 1980's, the government began a program to reduce its control of industries and to allow more private ownership.

Agriculture accounts for only about 15 percent of the value of all goods and services produced in Turkey in a year. About 45 percent of the country's people work in agriculture.

Turkey's most productive farmlands are in the coastal regions, which have fertile soil and a mild climate. The desertlike Anatolian Plateau often has long droughts that cause serious losses of crops.

In most years, Turkey's farmers produce enough food for all the people plus a surplus to sell abroad. About 50 percent of the cropland is used for grains. Wheat is the chief grain, followed by barley and corn. Cotton is grown for both fiber and cottonseed oil. Tobacco, a major export, is grown along the Black and Aegean seas. Turkey is a major producer of fruits, nuts, and vegetables, including apples, eggplants, grapes and raisins, hazelnuts, melons, oranges, potatoes, sugar beets, and tomatoes. Many people raise sheep, goats, and other livestock. Wool is the most valuable livestock product.

Manufacturing. When Turkey's republican government came to power in the 1920's, Turkey was almost entirely an agricultural country. Today, Turkey has thousands of factories. Manufacturing employs only about 20 percent of all workers, but the value of industrial production is about twice that of agricultural output.

Turkey's largest manufacturing industries are food and beverage processing and textile production. Other manufactured products include fertilizers, iron and steel, machinery and metal products, motor vehicles, and pulp and paper products. Most factories and mills lie in and around the large cities of the north and west.

Mining. Turkey is rich in mineral resources, but the

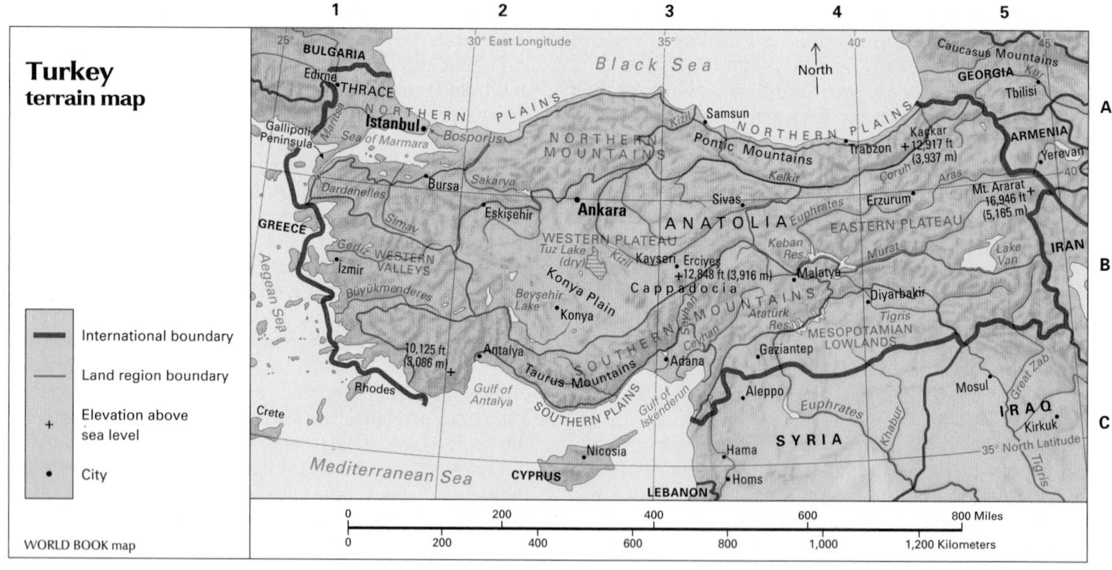

Physical features

Feature		
Aegean Sea	B	1
Anatolia (region)	B	3
Aras River	A	5
Beysehir Lake	B	2
Black Sea	A	3
Bosporus (strait)	A	2
Büyükmenderes River	B	1
Cappadocia	B	3
Ceyhan River	B	3
Çoruh River	A	4
Dardanelles (strait)	A	1
Erciye (mountain)	B	3
Euphrates River	B	4
Gallipoli Peninsula	A	1
Gulf of Antalya	C	2
Kaçkar (mountain)	A	4
Kelkit River	A	4
Kizil River	A	3
Konya Plain	B	2
Lake Van	B	5
Maritsa River	A	1
Mount Ararat	B	5
Murat River	B	4
Pontic Mountains	A	3
Sakarya River	A	2
Sea of Marmara	A	1
Seyhan River	B	3
Simav River	B	1
Taurus Mountains	C	2
Thrace (region)	A	1
Tigris River	B	4
Tuz Lake	B	2

© M & M Hunn, Photo Researchers

Ephesus, near present-day İzmir on Turkey's west coast, was an ancient Greek city. It was founded in the early 1000's B.C. Archaeologists uncovered the ruins of the city in the late A.D. 1800's.

mining industry is largely undeveloped. The country's most abundant mineral is coking coal, which is used in making steel. Turkey is one of the world's largest producers of chromite, the mineral from which chromium is obtained. Turkey is also a major producer of boron. Other minerals produced in Turkey include bauxite, copper, iron ore, and *meerschaum,* a soft, white mineral that is used to make jewelry and tobacco pipes.

Energy. Except for coal and hydroelectric power, almost all of Turkey's energy is imported. Several large refineries process imported oil. Natural gas imports have been growing. Natural gas has been replacing coal in heating urban buildings, helping to reduce air pollution.

International trade. Turkey's chief imports include chemicals, machinery, iron and steel, motor vehicles, and petroleum. The country's major exports include clothing and textiles, iron and steel, and other manufactured goods. Fruits, nuts, and vegetables are also important exports. Turkey's main trading partner is Germany. Other leading partners include France, Italy, Russia, the United Kingdom, and the United States.

Tourism has become a significant activity in Turkey. Millions of tourists visit Turkey every year, most of them from European countries and Russia. The visitors spend beach holidays on the Mediterranean and Aegean coasts. They also visit Turkey's cities; ancient sites, such as Troy and Pergamum in northwestern Turkey, and Ephesus, near present-day İzmir; and the unusual rock formations and other natural wonders of Cappadocia in east-central Turkey and the Eastern Plateau.

Transportation and communication. Turkey's road network varies in quality but reaches almost all the nation's towns. Turkey has about one car for every 15 inhabitants. Most Turks use buses, trains, or taxis. The railroad system links only the largest cities on slow tracks. Cities in Turkey with international airports include Istanbul, Ankara, İzmir, and Antalya. Turkish Airlines serves many cities in Turkey, Europe, and the Middle East. Turkey has many fine natural harbors. Istanbul and İzmir are the primary ports.

Turkey has more than 50 daily newspapers, representing many different political views. Most people, however, get their information from television. There are more than 20 nationwide TV channels. Most households own a color TV set and have a telephone. Many people own cellular phones. Many members of the middle and upper classes own personal computers.

History

Archaeologists have found evidence of an advanced society in what is now Turkey before 6000 B.C. One of the world's earliest known human settlements is at Çatalhöyük (also spelled Çatalhüyük or Çatal Hüyük). It is near Konya and is still being excavated. The first inhabitants of the area to be recorded in history were called the Hittites. About 2000 B.C., they began migrating to central Anatolia from Europe or central Asia. In the next several hundred years, they conquered much of Anatolia and parts of Mesopotamia and Syria. By 1500 B.C., the Hittites had created a powerful empire that made them the leading rulers of the Middle East. See **Hittites.**

From about 1200 to 500 B.C., large areas of Anatolia fell to the Phrygians, the Lydians, and other peoples. Between about 550 and 513 B.C., the Persian Empire seized control of Anatolia and Thrace. The Persians ruled until Alexander the Great of Macedonia crushed their army in 331 B.C. After Alexander's death in 323 B.C., Anatolia became a battleground in the wars among his successors. Small kingdoms rose and fell until 63 B.C., when the Roman general Pompey conquered the region. Anatolia had peace under Roman rule for about 400 years.

In A.D. 330, the Roman emperor Constantine the Great moved the capital from Rome to the ancient town of Byzantium, on the Bosporus. Byzantium was renamed Constantinople, meaning *city of Constantine.* In 395, the Roman Empire split into the West Roman Empire and the East Roman Empire, also called the Byzantine Empire, which included Anatolia and Thrace. Byzantine emperors ruled all of what is now Turkey until the late 1000's. See **Byzantine Empire.**

The Seljuk Turks became one of the first Turkic peoples to rule in what is now Turkey. The Seljuks were Muslims from central Asia east of the Caspian Sea. During the mid-1000's, they conquered Armenia, Palestine, and most of Iran. Then they invaded Anatolia. In 1071, the Seljuks destroyed most of the Byzantine power in Anatolia by defeating the Byzantine army in the Battle of Manzikert. They set up an empire with Iconium (now Konya) as the capital. From this point onward, the Christian religion and the Greek language of the Byzantine Empire were gradually replaced in Anatolia by Islam and the Turkish language.

In 1095, Christians in Western Europe organized the first of a series of military expeditions called the Crusades to drive the Seljuk Turks from the Holy Land (see **Crusades**). During the First Crusade (1096-1099), Christian troops defeated the Seljuks in western Anatolia. As a result, the Byzantine Empire recovered about a third of Anatolia. But the crusaders then left the peninsula to fight in the Holy Land, also called Palestine. The Seljuk Empire thus endured until 1243, when it was invaded by Asian nomads known as Mongols (see **Mongol Empire**).

The rise of the Ottoman Empire. The Mongol Empire was torn by internal struggles and soon fell apart. As a result, the Turks' influence in Anatolia continued to grow. During the 1300's, a group of Turks who became known as the Ottomans began to build a mighty empire. In 1326, they seized the Anatolian city of Bursa, which became their capital. By the late 1300's, the Ottomans had conquered the western two-thirds of Anatolia; most of Thrace; and much of the Balkan Peninsula, including Greece. All that remained of the Byzantine Empire was the area around Constantinople.

In 1453, Ottoman forces led by Mehmet II captured Constantinople, ending the Byzantine Empire. The Ottomans called the city Istanbul and made it their capital. By 1481, their empire extended from the Danube River in Europe to southern Anatolia.

The Ottoman Empire reached its height in the 1500's. During the reign of Sultan Bayezit II, who ruled from 1481 to 1512, the empire became the leading naval power in the Mediterranean region. Ottoman forces conquered Syria in 1516 and Egypt in 1517. Süleyman I, whom Europeans called the Magnificent, ruled from 1520 to 1566. In 1526, his army conquered much of Hungary in the Battle of Mohács. Süleyman expanded the

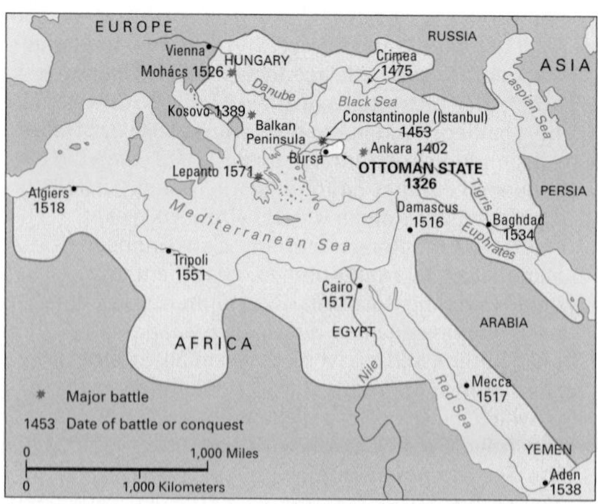

WORLD BOOK map

The Ottoman Empire began during the 1300's as a small state around the city of Bursa. It grew to include much of the Middle East and parts of northern Africa and southeastern Europe.

empire's borders to Yemen on the south, Morocco on the west, and Persia on the east.

The Ottoman decline. After the Battle of Mohács, European powers feared that the Ottomans would overrun Europe. However, European forces successfully defended Vienna, Austria, during an Ottoman attack in 1529. In 1571, European fleets defeated the Ottoman navy in the Battle of Lepanto, near Greece. The Ottomans again failed to capture Vienna in 1683.

During the 1700's, the Ottoman Empire continued to weaken. In 1774, the Ottomans lost a six-year war against Russia and were forced to allow Russian ships to pass through the Straits—the waters linking the Black Sea with the Mediterranean. The Ottoman Empire lost the Crimea, a peninsula in the Black Sea, to Russia in 1783.

The empire lost more territory during the 1800's. In 1821, Greek nationalists revolted against Ottoman rule. France, the United Kingdom, and Russia sided with the Greeks and sent forces to fight the Ottomans (see **Greece** [History]). The Treaty of Adrianople (Edirne) ended the fighting in 1829. This treaty acknowledged the independence of Greece and gave Russia control of the mouth of the Danube River. The Ottomans also lost other Balkan territory in a series of wars with Russia (see **Russo-Turkish wars**). European powers forced Russia to give up much of its gains at the Congress of Berlin in 1878. But the Ottoman Empire continued to decline. The empire had lost Algeria to France in 1830, and France seized Tunisia in 1881. The United Kingdom gained Cyprus in 1878 and began to effectively rule Egypt in 1882, although both areas officially remained part of the Ottoman Empire until 1914.

Ottoman leaders tried to halt the empire's decline through a reform program starting in 1839. They reorganized the military and improved the educational system. In 1876, the empire's first constitution was adopted. It provided for representative government and granted the people various freedoms. But Sultan Abdülhamit II, who came to the throne the same year, set the constitution aside and ruled as a dictator. Government policies became increasingly oppressive, and Abdülhamit ruled by the use of fear. Religious persecution began to spread as members of various religious minorities became revolutionaries. Nationalist feelings were strong among the minorities. Ottoman officials, fearing further collapse of the already declining empire, reacted harshly. Violent attacks took place. Between 1894 and 1918, Christian Armenians in the Ottoman Empire suffered an especially large loss of life (see **Armenia** [History]).

The Young Turks. During the late 1890's, small groups of students and military officers who opposed Abdülhamit's harsh policies banded together secretly. These groups were collectively known as the Young Turks. The most influential group was the Committee of Union and Progress. In 1908, members of this group led a revolt against Abdülhamit and forced him to restore constitutional government. The Young Turks made him give up the throne in 1909. They then ruled the empire through his brother Mehmet V.

The Young Turks wanted to restore the greatness of the Ottoman Empire. However, many people no longer cared about the idea of maintaining an empire. The empire's Christian minorities demanded freedom from Ottoman rule. And so the empire continued to crumble.

Important dates in Turkey

1500 B.C.	The Hittites ruled in Anatolia.
63 B.C.	The Roman general Pompey conquered Anatolia.
A.D. 330	Constantine the Great moved the capital of the Roman Empire to Byzantium and renamed the town Constantinople.
1071	The Seljuk Turks conquered most of Anatolia by defeating the Byzantine forces in the Battle of Manzikert.
1326	The Ottoman Turks captured Bursa, which marked the beginning of the Ottoman Empire.
1453	The Ottomans captured Constantinople, ending the Byzantine Empire.
1783-1914	The Ottoman Empire lost much of its territory in a series of military defeats.
1908	The Young Turks revolted against the government.
1914-1918	In World War I, the Ottoman Empire allied with Germany and lost much of its remaining territory.
1923	Mustafa Kemal (Atatürk) set up the Republic of Turkey and began a program to modernize the nation.
1960	Turkish army units overthrew the government and ruled until free elections were held in 1961.
1974	Turkish forces invaded Cyprus.
1980-1983	Army units again controlled the government.
1999	A powerful earthquake struck northwestern Turkey, killing more than 17,000 people.

Soon after the revolution in 1908, Bulgaria declared its independence, and Austria-Hungary annexed Bosnia-Herzegovina. Italy took Libya in 1912. In 1913, the Ottoman Empire surrendered Crete, part of Macedonia, southern Epirus, and many Aegean islands to Greece. By 1914, the empire had lost all its European territory except eastern Thrace.

In 1914, the Ottoman Empire entered World War I on the side of Germany and Austria-Hungary in an attempt to regain lost territory. In 1915, British, French, and other Allied troops tried to gain control of the Straits so that aid could be shipped to Russia. The Ottomans drove back the invaders at the Gallipoli Peninsula west of the Dardanelles, dealing the Allies a crushing defeat. However, the Allies won the war in 1918.

After World War I, the Allies set out to break up the Ottoman Empire. Allied troops occupied Istanbul and the Straits. In May 1919, Greek troops, protected by Allied fleets, landed at the Ottoman port of İzmir and advanced into the country. Turks deeply resented the Ottoman government's inability to defend their homeland.

A Turkish military hero named Mustafa Kemal (later called Kemal Atatürk) quickly organized a nationalist movement. Under his leadership, a series of nationalist congresses met in Anatolian cities and formed a *provisional* (temporary) government. In April 1920, a new Turkish Grand National Assembly met in Ankara and elected Kemal as Assembly president.

In August 1920, the sultan's government signed the harsh Treaty of Sèvres with the Allies (see **Sèvres, Treaty of**). The treaty granted independence to some parts of the empire and gave other parts to various Allied powers. The empire was reduced to Istanbul and a portion of Anatolia. As a result of the treaty, the sultan's popularity among the Turks declined further, while the power of Kemal and the nationalists grew. In September 1922, the nationalist forces finally drove the Greeks from Turkey. The Allies agreed to draw up a new peace treaty with the nationalists. The Treaty of Lausanne, signed in 1923, set Turkey's borders about where they are today.

The Republic of Turkey. The Grand National Assembly proclaimed Turkey to be a republic on Oct. 29, 1923, and elected Kemal as president. Kemal and other nationalist leaders believed that the new nation could not survive without sweeping social changes.

During the 1920's and 1930's, the government did away with such traditions as Muslim schools, the Islamic legal system, and the wearing of the veil by women and the fez by men. It abolished the religious and civil office of the caliph. It also outlawed *polygyny,* the practice of having more than one wife at the same time. Women received the right to vote and to hold public office. All Turks were required to choose a family name. At the same time, the Grand National Assembly gave Kemal his surname—Atatürk, which means *father of the Turks.*

Atatürk held enormous political power. He controlled the Assembly and could appoint and dismiss the prime minister and cabinet without Assembly approval. Some Turks opposed Atatürk's anti-Islamic policies. The Kurds revolted against the policies in 1925, but the government put down the uprising.

Atatürk served as Turkey's president until he died in 1938. Ismet İnönü then became president. Under İnönü's leadership, Turkey avoided entering World War II (1939-1945) until February 1945.

The 1950's and 1960's. The Republican People's Party, established by Atatürk, had governed Turkey since the establishment of the republic. However, in 1950, the Democrat Party won a majority in the Grand National Assembly. Celâl Bayar became president, and Adnan Menderes became prime minister. Unlike the Republicans, the Democrats encouraged foreign investment and wanted less government control of the economy. But by the late 1950's, a rise in the national debt and restrictions on freedom of speech made the Democrat Party government unpopular.

Turkish military forces believed the Democrats had strayed too far from Atatürk's political principles. In 1960, army units seized control of the government and set up a provisional government. The military placed a large number of former government leaders on trial. Prime Minister Menderes was hanged. President Bayar

© Hulton/Archive

Kemal Atatürk founded the Republic of Turkey in 1923 and was its first president. In an attempt to modernize the nation, he introduced major cultural, political, and economic reforms.

was sentenced to life in prison but was later released.

In 1961, Turkey adopted a new Constitution. The provisional government then held free national elections. No party won a majority in the legislature. İnönü, of the Republican People's Party, was chosen to become prime minister. In 1965, the Justice Party won a majority, and party leader Süleyman Demirel became prime minister.

The Cyprus crisis. In the 1960's, Turkey and Greece nearly went to war over the issue of the Mediterranean island of Cyprus. In 1964 and 1967, fighting broke out on Cyprus between people of Turkish ancestry and people of Greek ancestry. Turkish Cypriots make up a minority of the people, and Greek Cypriots make up the majority. Both Turkey and Greece threatened to intervene before outside peacemakers arranged a settlement. But in 1974, Greek military officers overthrew the president of Cyprus. Turkish troops then invaded the island and captured much territory. Turkish Cypriots later set up a separate government. They declared the captured territory an *autonomous* (self-governing) region in 1975, and an independent republic in 1983. But Greek Cypriots protested against these measures. See **Cyprus** (History).

Political changes. In the late 1960's, radical groups of Turks began staging bombings, kidnappings, and murders to try to overthrow the government. In the 1970's, deep divisions developed between secular and religious groups. No party could form a stable government. In this period, Demirel headed several coalition governments. In 1980, the military seized control of the government and ruled until a return to civilian rule in 1983.

The Motherland Party, led by Turgut Özal, controlled the government from 1983 until the True Path party won the most legislative seats in 1991 elections. Süleyman Demirel, who had become leader of the True Path, again became prime minister. The legislature elected Demirel president in 1993. Tansu Çiller of the True Path then became Turkey's first woman prime minister.

In elections in 1995, the Welfare Party, a strongly pro-Islamic party, won the most legislative seats. In 1996, the Welfare and True Path parties formed a coalition government. Necmettin Erbakan, the Welfare Party leader, became prime minister. He was the first Islamic party leader to head the government since Turkey became a republic. The coalition lost control of parliament in 1997.

In 1998, the Constitutional Court banned the Welfare Party, ruling that its goal of creating an Islamic state was unconstitutional. Some Welfare Party members joined the more moderate pro-Islamic Virtue Party. After elections in 1999, former Prime Minister Bülent Ecevit, the leader of the Democratic Left Party, became head of a coalition government. In 2000, Turkey's legislature elected Ahmet Necdet Sezer president. The Constitutional Court banned the Virtue Party in 2001. Moderate Islamists then formed the Justice and Development Party.

Recent developments. A Kurdish nationalist movement developed in southeastern Turkey in the 1980's. Turkey's government battled Kurdish guerrillas throughout the late 1980's and the 1990's. About 30,000 people died in the fighting. In 1999, Turkish intelligence agents arrested the Kurdish guerrilla leader Abdullah Öcalan. A Turkish court convicted Öcalan of treason and separatism. After Öcalan's capture, most fighting ended.

In August 1999, a powerful earthquake struck northwestern Turkey. More than 17,000 people were killed.

In 1999, the European Union (EU) accepted Turkey as a candidate for membership. In the early 2000's, to meet EU requirements, Turkey passed several political and economic reforms. These reforms included the abolishment of capital punishment, the revision of other criminal penalties, the expansion of civil rights for Kurds and women, and the reduction of the military's role in politics. The EU was scheduled to begin membership talks with Turkey in October 2005.

In 2002, the Justice and Development Party won legislative elections. In 2003, the party's leader, Recep Tayyip Erdogan, became prime minister. Caglar Keyder

Related articles in *World Book* include:

Biographies

Atatürk, Kemal
Barbarossa
Mehmet II
Muhammad Ali
Osman I
Süleyman I

Cities and towns

Ankara
Antioch
Edirne
Istanbul
İzmir
Tarsus

History

Armenia
Asia Minor
Balkans
Byzantine Empire
Crimean War
Cyprus
Greece (History)
Janissaries
Kurds
Ottoman Empire
Russo-Turkish wars
Seljuks
Sèvres, Treaty of
Sultan
Thrace
Turks
World War I

Physical features

Ararat
Bosporus
Dardanelles
Euphrates River
Marmara, Sea of
Mount Ararat

Outline

I. Government
A National government
B Court system
C. Local government
D. Political parties
E. Armed forces

II. People
A. Ancestry
B. Languages

III. Way of life
A. City life
B. Rural life
C. Housing
D. Clothing
E. Food and drink
F. Recreation
G. Religion
H. Education
I. The arts

IV. The land
A. The Northern Plains
B. The Western Valleys
C. The Southern Plains
D. The Western Plateau
E. The Eastern Plateau
F. The Northern Mountains
G. The Southern Mountains
H. The Mesopotamian Lowlands

V. Climate

VI. Economy
A. Agriculture
B. Manufacturing
C. Mining
D. Energy
E. International trade
F. Tourism
G. Transportation and communication

VII. History

Questions

What are Turkey's chief economic activities?
Why was a new Turkish language developed?
What are the Straits?
How has the role of Turkish women changed since 1900?
Who are the Kurds?
Who was Kemal Atatürk?
How did Atatürk's modernization program affect Turkish life?
Who were the Young Turks?
What are the chief foods of most Turks?
What was the Ottoman Empire?

Additional resources

Baralt, Luis A. *Turkey.* Childrens Pr., 1997. Younger readers.
Goodwin, Jason. *Lords of the Horizons: A History of the Ottoman Empire.* 1999. Reprint. Henry Holt, 2000.
Heper, Metin. *Historical Dictionary of Turkey.* Scarecrow, 1994.
Pope, Nicole and Hugh. *Turkey Unveiled.* Overlook, 1998.
Stierlin, Henri. *Turkey.* Taschen, 1998. A survey of Turkey's architecture.
Zurcher, Erik. J. *Turkey.* Rev. ed. I. B. Tauris, 1998.

Turkey is a large North American bird related to chickens, peafowl, and pheasants. American Indians raised turkeys for food as early as A.D. 1000. Today, most traditional Thanksgiving dinners in North America, and many Christmas dinners around the world, include turkeys.

Male turkeys are called *toms,* and female turkeys are known as *hens.* Baby turkeys are called *poults.* Scientists classify two species of wild turkeys: the *ocellated turkey* and the *North American turkey.* The ocellated turkey lives in Guatemala and the Yucatan Peninsula of Mexico. It has brilliant coloring with eyelike spots on its tail. The North American turkey inhabits the United States and other areas in Mexico. This article mostly discusses the North American turkey.

The body of a turkey. Toms have reddish and featherless heads and necks. A long, loose piece of skin called a *wattle* extends from beneath the lower jaw along the neck. At the base of the neck are small, wartlike structures called *caruncles.* A long, beardlike tuft of bristly feathers hangs from the center of the breast. Wild toms have deep bronze-colored plumage. The color of domestic toms depends on the variety. Adult hens have dull coloring and rarely possess a beardlike tuft of feathers.

Adult toms usually have a wingspan of about 4 feet (1.2 meters). Wild toms weigh from 10 to 16 pounds (4.5 to 7.3 kilograms), but domestic toms can weigh as much as 50 pounds (23 kilograms). Hens grow smaller than toms. Wild hens weigh from 6 to 10 pounds (2.7 to 4.5 kilograms), while some domestic hens weigh as much as 16 pounds (7.3 kilograms). Wild turkeys can fly and run quickly. However, domestic turkeys cannot fly because their wings cannot support their considerably greater body weight.

WORLD BOOK illustration by John Rignall, Linden Artists Ltd.

Common turkeys include the Bronze, *shown at top;* the Bourbon Red, *middle;* and the wild North American turkey, *bottom.*

Leading turkey-raising states and provinces

Number of turkeys raised in a year

State/Province	Number of turkeys
Minnesota	44,000,000 turkeys
North Carolina	43,000,000 turkeys
Arkansas	27,000,000 turkeys
Missouri	24,000,000 turkeys
Virginia	24,000,000 turkeys
California	18,700,000 turkeys
Indiana	14,000,000 turkeys
Pennsylvania	9,500,000 turkeys
South Carolina	9,200,000 turkeys
Ontario	8,500,000 turkeys

Figures are for 2001.
Sources: U.S. Department of Agriculture; Ontario Ministry of Agriculture and Food.

How wild turkeys live. Wild turkeys gather in small flocks in the forests. They eat seeds, insects, and small nuts and fruits. At night, wild turkeys rest in trees. They build simple nests of dry leaves on the ground. Turkey eggs have a creamy-tan color, speckled with brown.

Domestic turkeys. Native Americans from what is now the southwestern United States, Mexico, and Central America first domesticated turkeys. In about 1520, Spanish explorers introduced the domesticated Mexican turkey to Spain. This turkey soon spread rapidly across Europe. During the 1600's, settlers brought the domestic turkey from Europe to the American Colonies. They soon crossbred their turkey with wild turkeys that lived around them. Such breeding led to the development of many modern varieties of turkeys.

Today, the major turkey varieties are the Bronze, the White Holland, the Narragansett, the Bourbon Red, the Black, the Slate, the Royal Palm, and the Beltsville Small White. The most popular commercially raised turkey, the Broad-Breasted White, is a hybrid developed from cross-breeding the White Holland with a subvariety of the Bronze called the Broad-Breasted Bronze. Broad-Breasted Whites have all-white plumage.

The Bronze turkey, once the most popular commercial variety, has dull black feathers glossed with red and green on the front and bronze in the rear. Its tail feathers have white tips. The White Holland possesses white feathers. The Narragansett resembles the Bronze but does not have the red and green or bronze colors. The Bourbon Red is brownish-red with white wings. The Black turkey is all black, and the Slate turkey has slate-colored feathers. The Royal Palm is a small, black-and-white turkey. The Beltsville Small White is all white.

Turkeys need much the same care as chickens but require more living space. Turkeys are more delicate than chickens, especially when young. Turkeys are particularly susceptible to cold rains. Young turkeys need more nutrients than young chickens because they grow faster. Toms reach market weight—about 22 pounds (10 kilograms) on average—approximately 17 weeks after they hatch. Hens are marketed at around 14 weeks of age, and weigh about 14 pounds (6.4 kilograms) on average.

Because of their size, turkeys yield a large amount of meat per bird. Large turkeys often provide meat for restaurants. However, they are too large for most families to eat at one meal. As a result, the turkey industry has developed boneless turkey roasts and steaks and ground turkey for sale to consumers. Food companies process turkey meat to make such products as cold cuts and hot dogs. B. M. Hargis

Scientific classification. Turkeys make up the turkey subfamily, Meleagridinae, in the pheasant family Phasianidae. The scientific name for the ocellated turkey is *Agriocharis ocellata.* The North American turkey is *Meleagris gallopavo.*

See also **Farm and farming** (picture: Poultry farming); **Poultry** (Raising poultry).

Turkish bath is a type of bath that involves exposure to dry heat, moist heat, massage, and cold. Bathers wear only bathing clothes, or none at all. They first enter a sweating room that has dry heat of about 160 °F (71 °C). They then move to a room in which wet steam reaches about 128 °F (53 °C). The wet steam causes the bathers to perspire freely. The skin is then washed with warm water and soap or salve, and an attendant massages the muscles. After being scrubbed and rubbed, the bathers dry off with a rough cloth or towel. Sometimes the hard skin of the feet is rubbed off with pumice stone. The bathers next take a cold shower or a swim, and then rest until their body temperature returns to normal.

The Turkish bath is refreshing and relaxing. However, people who have heart trouble or a kidney disease should never take a Turkish bath.

The Turks of medieval times believed in taking hot-air baths to preserve health, and their warriors spread this custom to most of the Middle East and parts of Europe. Many people in the Western world greatly enjoyed taking these baths, and they called them *Turkish baths.* The *Russian bath* is similar to the Turkish bath, except that only steam is used. The Finns have a *sauna,* a system of dry-heat bathing (see **Sauna**). Brian V. Reed

Turkmenistan is a country in west-central Asia. It is in a broad, dry lowland extending east from the Caspian Sea. Most of the country is desert. The capital and largest city of Turkmenistan is Ashgabat. The country's official language is Turkmen, which is a Turkic language.

Turkmenistan became independent in 1991. From 1924 to 1991, it had been one of the republics of the Soviet Union. It was called the Turkmen Soviet Socialist Republic, or Turkmenia.

Government. Turkmenistan is a republic. It has a president as head of state and head of government. According to the constitution, voters elect the president to a five-year term. However, the Turkmenistan legislature granted the office for life to Saparmurad A. Niyazov, who has been president since 1992. The president appoints a Cabinet of Ministers to help carry out government operations. The country also has a 50-member legislature called the Majlis, whose members are elected by the voters to five-year terms.

Turkmenistan is divided into five regions for the purpose of local government. The country's highest court is the Supreme Court. There are also regional courts and local courts.

People. About 70 percent of Turkmenistan's people are ethnic Turkmen, and about 10 percent are Russians. Other ethnic groups include Uzbeks, Kazakhs, Tatars, Ukrainians, and Armenians. Most people live along rivers or in oases.

The Turkmen are Sunni Muslims. Other religious groups in Turkmenistan include Shiite Muslims and Russian Orthodox Christians. Although most Muslims worship in mosques, Turkmen follow a special Muslim practice of worshiping primarily at tombs of holy men.

Most city dwellers live in red brick or limestone apartment buildings. Most rural dwellers live in brick houses. Only a few rural people still live in tentlike *yurts,* constructed of a wooden frame covered with felt.

Tribal organizations play an important role in Turkmen social customs. Turkmen social life is centered around the family. In the countryside, many members of an extended family live together in one household. Such a household might include parents, married children and their offspring, and other relatives.

People in Turkmenistan wear both Western-style and traditional clothing. Traditional dress for men includes a white shirt, dark trousers, and a red robe. Some men also wear a shaggy sheepskin hat. Women typically wear a long, loose dress trimmed with embroidery.

Turkmen dishes include *chorba* (a peppery meat soup), *unash* (noodles and peas in broth), and *pilaf,* a rice dish. Milk products form an important part of the

Facts in brief

Capital: Ashgabat.
Official language: Turkmen.
Area: 188,456 mi² (488,100 km²). *Greatest distances*—east-west, 750 mi (1,205 km); north-south, 525 mi (845 km).
Elevation: *Highest*—Kugitangtau (mountain range), 10,292 ft (3,137 m) above sea level. *Lowest*—Garabogazkol Gulf, 102 ft (31 m) below sea level.
Population: *Estimated 2006 population*—5,092,000; density, 27 per mi² (10 per km²); distribution, 53 percent rural, 47 percent urban. *1995 census*—4,483,251.
Chief products: *Agriculture*—camels, cotton, grains, grapes, horses, potatoes, sheep. *Manufacturing*—cement, chemicals, glass, textiles. *Mining*—bromine, copper, gold, iodine, lead, mercury, natural gas, petroleum, salt, sodium sulfate, zinc.
Flag: The flag has three unequal vertical stripes of green, maroon, and green. On the maroon stripe are five different carpet patterns in black, white, maroon, and orange. To the upper right of the maroon stripe are five white stars and a white crescent. See **Flag** (picture: Flags of Asia and the Pacific).
Money: *Basic unit*—Turkmen manat. One hundred tenge equal one manat.

Raising horses is an important economic activity in Turkmenistan. The farmers shown here herd a special breed of Turkoman horses. Other livestock raised in Turkmenistan include camels and Karakul sheep.

Sovfoto/Eastfoto

Turkmen diet. Turkmen drink green tea after meals.

Turkmen are known for weaving beautiful woolen carpets displaying geometric patterns in reds, yellows, and blues. Other crafts include embroidery, handmade fabrics, leathercraft, and jewelry.

Nearly all adults can read and write. The government requires children to attend school from the ages of 6 to 17. The country has one university and several other schools of higher learning.

Land and climate. The Karakum desert covers over 80 percent of Turkmenistan. This vast desert is largely uninhabited. The Kopet-Dag mountains stretch along the south and southwest of the country. The Amu Darya river flows into Turkmenistan from mountains southeast of the country. It flows through eastern Turkmenistan into Uzbekistan, where it drains into the Aral Sea. Turkmenistan's other rivers include the Murgab and the Tedzhen. The most heavily settled regions of the country are the valleys of the Amu Darya, Murgab, and Tedzhen rivers, and the foothills of the Kopet-Dag mountains.

Summers in Turkmenistan are long, hot, and dry. Winters are cold. Desert temperatures range from about 95 to 122 °F (35 to 50 °C) in summer. Winter temperatures in the desert can drop below 32 °F (0 °C). Turkmenistan receives about 3 to 12 inches (8 to 30 centimeters) of rainfall annually.

Economy. The government largely controls Turkmenistan's economy. It owns many of the country's businesses and factories and much of its farmland.

Agriculture accounts for about one-fourth of the value of Turkmenistan's economic production. Cotton and wheat, the chief crops, occupy about three-fourths of the farmland. Other farm products include fruits, milk, wool, and *Persian lamb* (a fur taken from young lambs). Some Turkmen raise camels, Karakul sheep, and a special breed of Turkoman horses. Pelts from the Karakul sheep are highly prized for fur coats. Some farmers also raise silkworms.

Crops in Turkmenistan can only be grown by irrigation. An extensive system of canals moves water from the major rivers of the region to dry areas. The 750-mile (1,200-kilometer) Karakum Canal transports water across the desert from the Amu Darya, past Ashgabat, to Kizyl-Arvat. Most of the farming regions in Turkmenistan lie along the Amu Darya and the Karakum Canal.

Manufacturing makes up more than a third of the value of production in Turkmenistan. Most of the country's manufacturing income comes from the processing of petroleum and cotton. Other industries produce cement as well as textiles made of wool and silk. Ashgabat, Balkhan, and Chardzhoy are the country's industrial centers.

Turkmenistan's chief natural resources are natural gas and petroleum. Other resources include bromine, copper, gold, iodine, lead, mercury, salt, sodium sulfate,

Turkmenistan

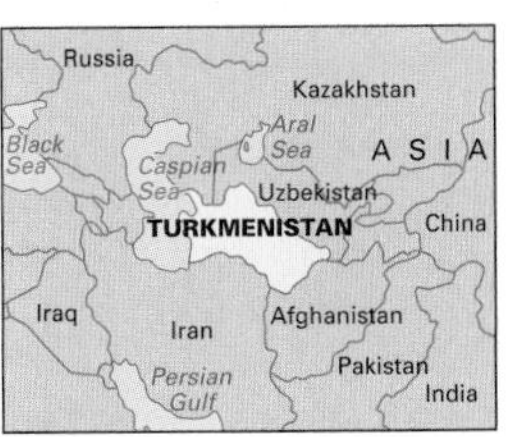

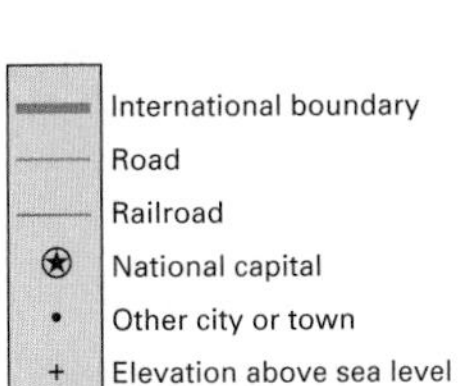

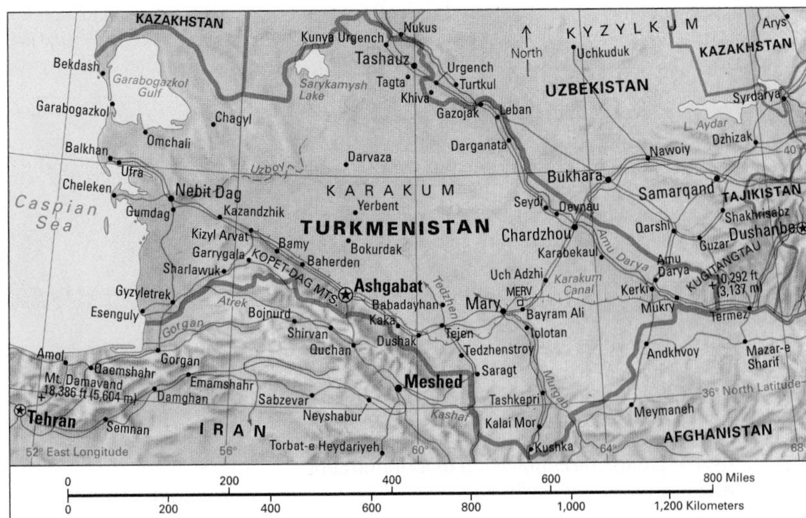

WORLD BOOK maps

zinc, and such building materials as sand and limestone.

Turkmenistan has a limited highway and railroad system, linking only major urban areas. An airport at Ashgabat handles all flights to and from Turkmenistan.

A radio station and a television station broadcast from Ashgabat in Turkmen and Russian. Newspapers and magazines are published in the same two languages.

History. People have lived in the area now known as Turkmenistan for thousands of years. The earliest inhabitants were probably nomads who lived by raising livestock in the desert areas and farmers who lived along rivers and oases.

Persians of the Achaemenid Empire ruled the area from about 500 to 331 B.C., when Alexander the Great gained control of much of their empire. The kingdom of Parthia controlled the region between about 250 B.C. and A.D. 224, followed by Persians of the Sasanian dynasty. In the mid-600's, Muslim Arabs invaded the area.

By the 900's, some Turkic tribes had settled in the area of Turkmenistan. The term *Turkmen* dates from this period. These tribes ruled until the Mongols, led by Genghis Khan, invaded the region in the early 1200's. By the 1300's, Islamic missionaries called *sufis* had established Islam, the Muslim religion, in the region.

During the late 1300's, the Mongol conqueror Timur (also called Tamerlane) made the area part of his vast empire. Between the 1400's and 1600's, the Safavids, a Persian dynasty, controlled the southern part of what is now Turkmenistan. Tribes from whom today's Turkmen are descended began moving into the region around 1600. In the 1800's, an alliance of Turkic tribes called the Tekke Confederation gained control of the area.

Soviet rule. Russia began a conquest of the region in the mid-1870's. By 1885, all Turkmen lands were under Russian control. Revolutionaries known as Bolsheviks (later called Communists) gained control of Russia in 1917. In 1922, the Soviet Union was formed under Russia's leadership. In 1924, in spite of much resistance from local tribes, Turkmenistan became a republic of the Soviet Union. The republic was called the Turkmen Soviet Socialist Republic.

The Soviets made many changes in Turkmenistan. They built roads, schools, housing, hospitals, and communications systems. They *collectivized* agriculture—that is, they ended private farming and transferred control of farms and livestock to the government. The Soviets also tried to discourage religious worship and to suppress much of traditional Turkmen culture.

Independence. The Soviet government maintained strict control of all aspects of life until the late 1980's. In 1990, Turkmenistan declared that its laws overruled those of the Soviet central government. In October 1991, the republic declared its independence. In December, Turkmenistan joined other republics in a loose association called the Commonwealth of Independent States. The Soviet Union was formally dissolved December 25.

In 1992, Saparmurad A. Niyazov, president of the former Turkmen Soviet Socialist Republic, was elected president of independent Turkmenistan. A 1994 referendum extended Niyazov's term to 2002. In 1999, the legislature granted him the office for life. Larry V. Clark

See also **Ashgabat; Commonwealth of Independent States; Karakum; Merv.**

Turks make up an ethnic group descended from nomads of central Asia. They speak Turkish, one of several Turkic languages. Turks are closely related to the Azerbaijanis, Iranians, Kazakhs, Kyrgyz, Turkmen, Uzbeks, and other Turkic-speaking peoples of central Asia. The majority of Turks live in the Republic of Turkey. Ethnic Turks account for about four-fifths of Turkey's population. Sizable Turkish communities also exist in southeastern and western Europe, especially in Germany, and in Australia, Canada, and the United States. Most Turks are Sunni *Muslims* (followers of Islam).

The Turks have had an important history. Their ancestors, who included the Huns, migrated westward from central Asia. The Huns conquered much of Europe during the A.D. 400's. The Seljuk Turks had taken over Persia (now Iran) and most of Asia Minor (now part of Turkey) by the 1100's. The Ottoman Turks rose to prominence in the northwestern corner of Asia Minor in the 1200's. By the 1500's, the Ottomans controlled most of the Middle East, northern Africa, and southeastern Europe, establishing a large and powerful empire. The Ottomans were defeated in World War I (1914-1918). After World War I, Turks waged a successful war of independence against Greek and other occupying forces in Asia Minor. They founded the Turkish Republic in 1923. Ali Eminov

See also **Ottoman Empire; Seljuks; Turkey** (People).

Turks and Caicos Islands are made up of more than 30 low-lying islands in the West Indies, about 90 miles (145 kilometers) north of the Dominican Republic (see **West Indies** [map]). The two island groups form an overseas territory of the United Kingdom in the Commonwealth of Nations. The main islands are Grand Turk and Salt Cay in the Turks Islands, and South Caicos, East Caicos, Grand or Middle Caicos, North Caicos, Providenciales, and West Caicos in the Caicos Islands. The Turks and Caicos Islands have many beautiful beaches and are surrounded by numerous coral reefs.

The islands cover a total land area of 166 square miles (430 square kilometers) and have 23,000 residents. Financial services, fishing, and tourism are important industries. Lobster is the chief export. The capital and largest town is Grand Turk, also called Cockburn Town, on the island of Grand Turk. Europeans discovered the islands in the early 1500's. Settlers from Bermuda arrived in the late 1600's to obtain salt. Gerald R. Showalter

Turmeric, *TUR muhr ihk,* is a plant that grows in southern Asia. Its fleshy roots are the source of a sub-

WORLD BOOK illustration by Lorraine Epstein

The turmeric plant is native to southern Asia. Its dried roots yield a yellowish powder used as a dyestuff and a spice.

stance, also called turmeric, which is used mainly for dyeing. These roots are hard and tough. On the outside, they are brownish- or yellowish-green. When they are broken, they show a resinous interior that varies from orange-brown to deep reddish-brown. The roots are ready for the market after being cleaned, boiled for some hours, and then dried in an oven. The yellowish powder that they yield when ground has a strong, aromatic odor and a strong, pungent taste.

Turmeric has been used for hundreds of years as a dyestuff and as a spice. It is an important ingredient of curry powder and is used to color mustard (see **Curry**). It does not yield a fast color, however, as a dyestuff. It has gone out of use as a medicine, but in India people mix it with milk to form a cooling lotion for the skin and eyes. Turmeric is useful in chemistry in making test papers for alkalis. With the addition of alkali, white paper soaked in a tincture of turmeric turns to reddish-brown and, on drying, to violet. Howard L. Needles

Scientific classification. Turmeric belongs to the ginger family, Zingiberaceae. Its scientific name is *Curcuma longa.*

Turner, Frederick Jackson (1861-1932), an American historian, became famous for a theory he presented in 1893 in his paper "The Significance of the Frontier in American History." He claimed that the nature of American democracy was a product of the frontier, which rewarded resourcefulness and ingenuity, encouraged individualism, and offered land and hope for a better life.

Another of Turner's works, *The Significance of Sections in American History* (1932), won the Pulitzer Prize for history in 1933. Turner's list of publications is relatively short for a historian of such stature, but he had an enormous influence on his students and others. Many outstanding works in Western history were done by people inspired by Turner and stimulated by his ideas. Turner also pioneered in using the materials and methods of the geographer, the economist, the sociologist, and the statistician in history. He was born on Nov. 14, 1861, in Portage, Wisconsin, and taught at the University of Wisconsin and Harvard University. Robert C. Sims

Turner, J. M. W. (1775-1851), was perhaps the greatest landscape painter in the history of British art. In many oil paintings and water colors, Turner departed from traditional ways of dealing with atmosphere, light, and color. Earlier artists had treated such elements realistically. In Turner's works, forms and outlines seem to dissolve into shimmering mist, steam, or smoke, or into the intense light of bright sky or water. An example of this style, *Snowstorm: Steamboat off a Harbour's Mouth,* appears in **Painting** (Romanticism). By changing the way artists represented reality, Turner began a process continued by the Impressionists and many other artists of the late 1800's and the 1900's.

Joseph Mallord William Turner was born on April 23, 1775, in London. He began art training at the Royal Academy of Arts at age 14 and became an accomplished water-colorist. His early style shows the influence of the British artists J. R. Cozens and Thomas Girtin. The young painter was also influenced by the landscapes of the French painters Nicolas Poussin and Claude. Beginning in 1790, Turner exhibited at the Royal Academy. He was elected a member of the academy in 1802.

Turner's early paintings emphasize drama and romance. His oil painting *The Shipwreck* (1805) is an example. Later in his career, Turner stressed atmosphere in his pictures. He traveled widely, producing thousands of water-color sketches. In many of these sketches, he experimented with the brilliance of color. During the 1830's and 1840's, Turner painted a series of water-color views of Venice that rank among his masterpieces. He achieved a colorful, abstract quality in such oil paintings as *Slavers Throwing Overboard the Dead and Dying--Typhoon Coming On* (1840) and *Rain, Steam, and Speed--The Great Western Railway* (1844). Many of his oil paintings show his fascination with the visual effects of fire and water. Turner died on Dec.19, 1851.

Douglas K. S. Hyland

See also **Ruskin, John**.

Procession of Boats with Distant Smoke, Venice (about 1840), an oil painting on canvas; The Tate Gallery, London

A painting by J. M. W. Turner, *shown here,* shows his fascination with the atmospheric effects of the sky, water, and intense light. This painting is one of many shimmering scenes of Venice that Turner painted late in his career.

John N. Turner

Prime Minister of Canada
1984

Trudeau 1980-1984 | **Turner** 1984 | **Mulroney** 1984-1993

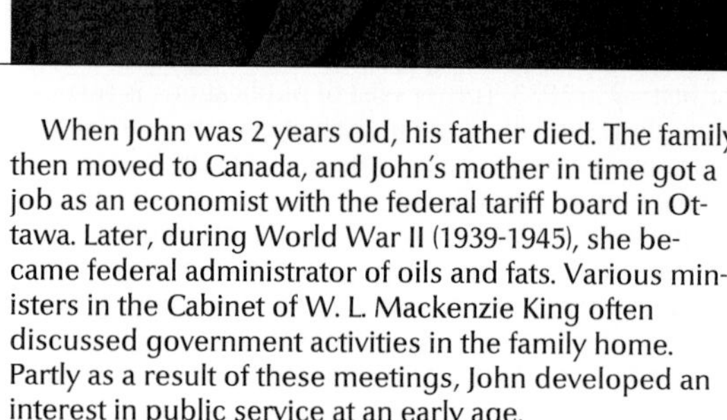

Turner, John Napier (1929-), served as prime minister of Canada for 2 $\frac{1}{2}$ months in 1984. Turner, a Liberal, succeeded Prime Minister Pierre Trudeau, who had resigned. Turner called for a general election soon after he took office. But Brian Mulroney, the leader of the Progressive Conservatives, led his party to a landslide victory and replaced Turner as prime minister.

In 1988, Turner led the Liberal Party in another general election. But the Progressive Conservatives won the election, and Mulroney remained as prime minister.

Turner had been a corporation lawyer before he entered politics. He first held office in 1962, when voters from Montreal elected him to the Canadian House of Commons. Turner later served as registrar general and minister of consumer and corporate affairs in the Cabinet of Prime Minister Lester B. Pearson. Trudeau succeeded Pearson in 1968. Under Trudeau, Turner served as solicitor general and as minister of justice and attorney general before becoming minister of finance.

Turner's silver hair, blue eyes, and athletic build made him an impressive figure. Turner liked to ski, go canoeing, and play squash and tennis. He also enjoyed music, especially opera, and reading biographies.

Early life

Boyhood. John Napier Turner was born on June 7, 1929, in Richmond, England, near London. His father, Leonard Turner, was a British gunsmith. His mother, Phyllis Gregory Turner of Rossland, British Columbia, was an economist. She was studying at the London School of Economics and Political Science when she met her future husband. They were married in England. John had a sister, Brenda, born in 1931.

When John was 2 years old, his father died. The family then moved to Canada, and John's mother in time got a job as an economist with the federal tariff board in Ottawa. Later, during World War II (1939-1945), she became federal administrator of oils and fats. Various ministers in the Cabinet of W. L. Mackenzie King often discussed government activities in the family home. Partly as a result of these meetings, John developed an interest in public service at an early age.

John attended schools in Ottawa. He went to Normal Model Public School, Ashbury College, and St. Patrick's College. He was a bright, popular student, and he was active in sports. In 1945, John's mother married Frank Ross, a Vancouver industrialist.

College years. Turner graduated from St. Patrick's in 1945 and then entered the University of British Columbia. He was an outstanding student and won honors in political science. Turner also became a star sprinter on the track and field team. An injury ruined his chances to qualify for Canada's 1948 Olympic team. Turner received a Bachelor of Arts degree in 1949. He was named the most popular student in his class.

Turner won a Rhodes Scholarship to study at Oxford University in England. He studied law there and earned a bachelor's degree in jurisprudence in 1951 and a bachelor's degree in civil law in 1952. In 1952 and 1953, he took graduate courses in French civil law at the Sorbonne in Paris. He also became fluent in French. In 1954, he joined the Stikeman, Elliott law firm in Montreal.

Early political career

Entry into politics. Turner's government career began in June 1962, when he was elected to the Canadian House of Commons. Turner had run for office as a Liberal from the Montreal riding of St. Lawrence-St. George.

On May 11, 1963, Turner married Geills McCrae Kilgour of Winnipeg, one of his campaign workers. He and his wife had four children, Elizabeth (1964-), Michael (1965-), David (1968-), and James (1971-).

Early Cabinet posts. As a member of Parliament, Turner impressed Prime Minister Pearson. Pearson brought Turner into his Cabinet in 1965 as minister without portfolio. In April 1967, Pearson appointed Turner registrar general. In December 1967, Turner became minister of consumer and corporate affairs.

Pearson resigned as party leader and prime minister in April 1968. Turner campaigned hard to succeed him. But the party chose Pierre Trudeau, a Montreal professor. Turner ran third in the balloting.

In Trudeau's Cabinet. In April 1968, Trudeau gave Turner the additional office of solicitor general. Later in 1968, Trudeau made Turner minister of justice and attorney general. In this position, Turner introduced changes in criminal law that guaranteed legal services and eased bail requirements for the poor. He also established the Law Reform Commission of Canada. Many reforms proposed by this agency have become part of Canada's civil and criminal law.

In 1969, Turner helped push the Official Languages Act through the House of Commons. This act required federal facilities to provide service in both French and English if 10 percent of the people in a particular area speak either language. In 1970, a crisis arose when the *Front de Libération du Québec* (FLQ), a terrorist group, kidnapped two officials. Turner worked to win parliamentary permission to put the War Measures Act into effect. This act allows the government to suspend civil liberties. Trudeau felt the act was necessary to help police deal with the crisis.

In January 1972, Trudeau appointed Turner minister of finance. In 1974, Turner introduced inflation-indexed personal tax exemptions. This system allowed individuals to make income tax deductions that reflected increases in the rate of inflation.

Return to private life. In September 1975, Turner surprised the nation by resigning from his powerful position in the Cabinet. In February 1976, he resigned from the House of Commons. Turner's once promising political career appeared to be finished.

Political comeback

After ending his government service, Turner became a partner in the law firm of McMillan, Binch in Toronto. He greatly increased his personal wealth and was chosen to serve as a director by 10 large companies.

Return to politics. In February 1984, Trudeau announced his desire to resign as party leader and prime minister. Turner declared his candidacy for the leadership in March. During the leadership campaign, he promised programs to strengthen the then stalled Canadian economy. In June, the Liberal Party leadership convention chose Turner on the second ballot. Turner became prime minister on June 30.

The 1984 election. Early in July, Turner called a general election for Sept. 4, 1984. His rival party leaders were Brian Mulroney of the Progressive Conservative Party and Edward Broadbent of the New Democratic Party. In the campaign, Turner said his first major goal as prime minister would be to lower the unemployment rate, which stood at 11 percent. Mulroney and Broadbent charged that the Liberals did not know how to strengthen the economy.

In the election, the Liberals won only 40 of the 282 seats in the House of Commons—their worst defeat. The Conservatives won 211 seats. Mulroney succeeded Turner as prime minister on September 17.

The 1988 election. In 1988, Turner forced Mulroney to call another general election. He did so by asking Liberal Party members of the Canadian Senate to delay Parliament's ratification of a major U.S.-Canadian free-trade pact. Mulroney and U.S. President Ronald Reagan had signed the agreement in January 1988. The pact was to go into effect Jan. 1, 1989, but Turner declared that the Liberal senators would delay ratification until after that date. He promised that the senators would ratify the agreement before January 1 if the Progressive Conservatives won the election.

Mulroney called a general election for Nov. 21, 1988. The Progressive Conservatives won the election, and Mulroney remained as prime minister. After the election, the Canadian Senate approved the U.S.-Canadian free-trade agreement. The pact took effect on schedule.

Resignation as party head. In 1990, Turner joined the law firm of Miller Thomson in Toronto and resigned as leader of the Liberal Party. He was succeeded as Liberal Party leader by Jean Chrétien. Turner retained his seat in the House of Commons. Christina McCall

Important dates in Turner's life

1929 (June 7) Born in Richmond, England.
1949 Graduated from University of British Columbia.
1962 First elected to House of Commons.
1963 (May 11) Married Geills McCrae Kilgour.
1968 Appointed minister of justice and attorney general.
1972 Appointed minister of finance.
1975 Resigned as minister of finance.
1984 (June 30) Became prime minister.
1984 (Sept. 4) Liberals defeated in general election.
1988 (Nov. 21) Liberals lose another general election.

Turner, Nat (1800-1831), a black slave and preacher, led the most famous slave revolt in United States history. In 1831, Turner and about 70 other slaves liberated themselves by killing 60 whites in Virginia, including the family of Joseph Travis, Turner's owner.

More whites died during the rebellion led by Turner than in any other slave revolt in the nation's history. The Virginia militia captured and hanged 20 rebels, including Turner. In addition, whites seeking vengeance murdered about 100 innocent slaves. The rebellion caused the Virginia General Assembly to debate, but ultimately reject, a plan to abolish slavery and establish a West African colony for freed slaves.

Turner was born on Oct. 2, 1800, on Benjamin Turner's plantation in Southampton County, Virginia. His parents and grandmother encouraged him to become educated and fight slavery. In 1825, he began to read the Bible zealously and to experience visions. He related these visions at Sunday services.

After his capture, Turner narrated a lengthy confession before he was hanged on Nov. 11, 1831. Thomas R. Gray, the lawyer assigned to defend him, later published Turner's confession as a pamphlet. Douglas R. Egerton

Additional resources

Bisson, Terry. *Nat Turner.* Chelsea Hse., 1988.
Edwards, Judith. *Nat Turner's Slave Rebellion in American History.* Enslow, 2000.

Turner, Ted (1938-), an American broadcasting executive, is the founder of Cable News Network (CNN). The network transmits news worldwide by satellite.

Robert Edward Turner III was born in Cincinnati, Ohio, on Nov. 19, 1938. In 1976, he became one of the first broadcasters to use a communications satellite to relay programs to local cable television companies. The programs—sports broadcasts and motion-picture reruns—originated at WTCG, now known as WTBS, a television station Turner owned in Atlanta, Georgia.

Turner founded CNN, which began broadcasting in 1980, through his company Turner Broadcasting System, Inc. (TBS). In 1996, he sold TBS to Time Warner Inc. Time Warner took over TBS's holdings, which included several cable television networks and the Atlanta Braves major league baseball team. Turner became vice chairman of Time Warner. In 2001, it merged with America Online Inc. to form AOL Time Warner Inc. The company was renamed Time Warner Inc. in 2003. Turner was vice chairman of AOL Time Warner from 2001 to 2003. He continued to serve on the company's board of directors.

Turner has also been a champion yacht racer. His boat won the America's Cup, the world's most famous sailing competition, in 1977. Turner is a strong supporter of world peace and environmental causes. In 1997, Turner pledged to give as much as $1 billion to United Nations agencies over a period of 10 years. Michael Emery

Turner, Tina (1939-), is an American rhythm and blues and rock singer known for her raspy voice and dynamic stage performances. The biggest success of her career came in 1984, when her *Private Dancer* album and its single "What's Love Got to Do with It" became best-selling records.

Graziano Arici, Sygma

Tina Turner

Turner was born in Brownsville, Tennessee, on Nov. 25, 1939. Her real name was Anna Mae Bullock. Guitarist-bandleader Ike Turner met her in an East St. Louis, Illinois, nightclub in 1956 and later hired her as a singer. They performed together as Ike and Tina Turner and were married. The couple's first hit record was "A Fool in Love" (1960). Their best-selling record was "Proud Mary" (1971). Ike and Tina Turner separated in 1976. They were divorced in 1978. Tina then went on to build her own career in music.

Tina Turner had a major role in the motion picture *Mad Max Beyond Thunderdome* (1985). Her autobiography, *I, Tina* (1986), was made into the motion picture *What's Love Got to Do with It* (1993). Don McLeese

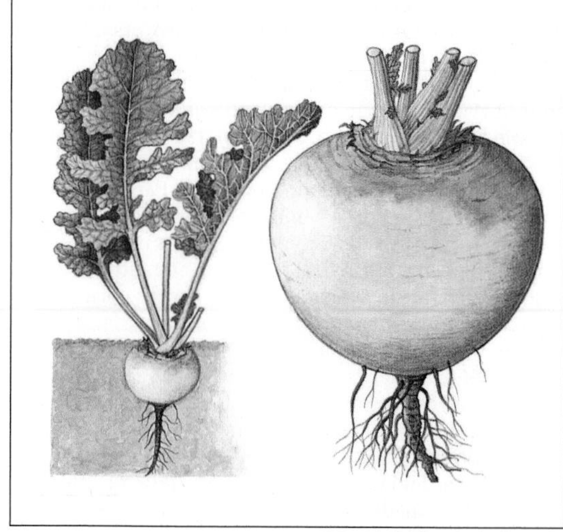

WORLD BOOK illustration by Jill Coombs

Turnips are grown on farms and in home gardens for their edible roots and leaves. The edible part of the root consists of smooth, firm flesh, *right.* The leaves grow on stems, *left.*

Turnip is a vegetable grown mostly for its fleshy root. Turnip roots usually measure from 2 to 3 inches (5 to 8 centimeters) in diameter when harvested and weigh between $\frac{1}{2}$ and 1 pound (225 and 450 grams). Their smooth, firm flesh may be white or light yellow. People also eat turnip leaves. These thin, hairy leaves grow on stems that can reach a height of 18 inches (46 centimeters).

Turnip roots provide a good source of vitamin C, and the leaves are rich in iron and vitamin A. People may eat the roots boiled, mashed, or as fried strips. Young turnip leaves can form part of salads, soups, and stews.

Turnips are grown on farms and in home gardens throughout Europe and in Canada and the United States. Turnips thrive in cool weather, being able to withstand light frost. The plants grow quickly and are usually ready for harvest 45 to 55 days after planting. The seeds are planted in March for a spring harvest and in August or September for a fall harvest. Turnip seeds develop best in moderately dry, loose soil. Turnips require adequate fertilizer, especially those planted in the spring. Aphids, cabbage worms, and various beetle larvae are the chief pests of turnips. Once harvested, however, turnips have a long storage life.

Turnips probably originated in Asia or Europe. Ancient Greeks and Romans grew turnips and may have introduced them into northern Europe. People in England and Ireland once used turnips to make jack-o-lanterns for Halloween, before pumpkins became common for that purpose. The rutabaga, a close relative of the turnip, is sometimes called a Swedish turnip. Albert Liptay

Scientific classification. The turnip plant belongs to the mustard family, Brassicaceae or Cruciferae. It is *Brassica rapa.*

See also **Agriculture** (Improved crop-growing methods); **Cabbage; Rutabaga.**

Turnpike is a road upon which a traveler must pay a fee, or toll, to use the highway. Such roads were named *turnpikes* because in the early days travelers stopped at gates made of logs or spears called *pikes.* The gates were turned open after the payment of a toll. The first record of tolls being collected was on a Persian military road between Babylon and Syria about 2000 B.C.

Investors brought the idea of building turnpikes to the United States from England. They formed turnpike companies to build the roads and operated them for profit. The first U.S. turnpike was built in Virginia in 1785. The nation's first major hard-surfaced road, the Lancaster Turnpike, was built from 1792 to 1794 between Philadelphia and Lancaster, Pennsylvania. It was made of stone covered with gravel. From 1792 to 1810, investors organized 175 companies in New England to build and improve nearly 3,000 miles (4,800 kilometers) of road.

Turnpike companies brought about many improvements in early American roads. They built bridges and surfaced the roads. Stage lines came into wide use as a result of the building of turnpikes. But in spite of the good they did, turnpikes proved to be poor business investments. By 1825, U.S. turnpike stocks had become nearly worthless, because the toll fees seldom paid for more than the cost of the road's upkeep.

State and local governments in the United States took over the task of building and maintaining roads. Interest in toll roads revived during the 1930's, and several major ones were built after World War II. Toll roads remain important today in many areas. J. P. Hartman

See also **Pennsylvania Turnpike; Road.**

Turnsole. See **Heliotrope.**

Turnstone is the name of two species of small shore birds. The name refers to their habit of turning over shells and pebbles with their bills as they look for food. The *ruddy turnstone* nests on *tundras* (treeless plains) in Arctic regions worldwide. In winter, it flies as far south as South America, Africa, and Australia, reaching both coasts of the United States in its travels. It is about 9 inches (23 centimeters) long, with black, white, and reddish-brown feathers in a complex pattern. The pattern helps camouflage the bird when it sits on its nest on the ground.

WORLD BOOK illustration by Malcolm Ellis, Bernard Thornton Artists

Ruddy turnstone

The *black turnstone* is slightly larger than the ruddy turnstone and lacks the reddish color. It nests along the shores of the Bering Sea in Alaska. It winters from southeastern Alaska to Lower California. Peter G. Connors

Scientific classification. Turnstones belong to the family Scolopacidae. The scientific name for the ruddy turnstone is *Arenaria interpres.* The black turnstone is *A. melanocephala.*

Turntable. See **Phonograph.**

Turpentine is a colorless or yellowish liquid that has a strong odor and is highly flammable. It is used chiefly in making such chemical products as disinfectants, insecticides, medicines, and perfumes, and in making synthetic rubber. It can be used as a *solvent* (substance that dissolves another substance) to remove tar, adhesives, and some paint stains. Some turpentine is used in the processing and flavoring of certain foods.

Turpentine is made from *coniferous* (cone-bearing) trees, primarily pines. There are three types of turpentine. They are, in order of importance: (1) sulfate turpentine, (2) gum turpentine, and (3) wood turpentine.

Sulfate turpentine accounts for nearly 70 percent of the turpentine produced in the world. As trees are converted to pulp, a vapor containing sulfate turpentine forms. After condensation occurs, the sulfate turpentine can be separated and collected as a liquid.

Gum turpentine is produced by *wounding* (cutting) the bark of living trees. A solution of sulfuric acid is applied to the wound, which measures about $\frac{1}{2}$ inch (1.3 centimeters) wide and $\frac{1}{2}$ inch deep. The acid causes gum to ooze out for as long as four weeks, until the wound closes. The wound is then reopened, and a sulfuric acid solution is applied again. This procedure is repeated throughout the gathering period, which generally lasts from early spring to mid-fall. The gum is taken to a steam distillery, where the turpentine is separated and collected. Gum turpentine accounts for about 30 percent of world turpentine production.

Wood turpentine is produced from stumps and logs. The wood is gathered and taken to a steam distillation plant. There, it is shredded and mixed with a solvent, which dissolves the turpentine. The resulting solution is then heated to vaporize the turpentine, which is then cooled until it forms a liquid. Wood turpentine makes up only a small percentage of the turpentine made in the world. Jeanine M. Maxwell

Turpin, Dick (1706-1739), was an English robber whose exploits have appeared in English legends and literature. As a youth, he joined a band of thieves who stole farm animals and deer. Later, he worked with Tom King as a highwayman, robbing travelers along the road from London to Oxford. He accidentally killed King while shooting at a constable. Finally, Turpin was arrested in York for stealing horses, was found guilty, and was hanged on April 7, 1739. William Ainswort's novel *Rookwood* (1834) described Turpin's famous ride from London to Yorkshire on his horse, Black Bess. The story of this ride was originally told of an earlier highwayman named "Nicks." Richard Turpin was born in Hempstead, Essex, the son of an innkeeper. James Anthony Sharpe

Turquoise, *TUR koyz* or *TUR kwoyz,* is a mineral widely used as a gemstone. It is prized for its color, which ranges from bright blue to blue-green. Turquoise is relatively soft, and so it is easy to shape and polish. It has a dull, waxy luster and is nearly *opaque* (nontransparent). Turquoise consists chiefly of a *hydrous aluminum phosphate,* a compound in which aluminum and phosphorus are chemically combined with water. It also contains copper, which gives it its bluish color.

Turquoise occurs in arid regions. It is formed when surface rocks that are rich in aluminum undergo a chemical change. In most cases, turquoise results from the weathering of lava. Major deposits of turquoise are found in Iran and Tibet. Large amounts of the mineral also occur in the southwestern United States, especially in Nevada and New Mexico.

People have used turquoise for jewelry and other decorative purposes since ancient times. It is one of the December *birthstones* (see **Birthstone**). The demand for turquoise remains so great that artificial varieties of the stone are produced. Maria Luisa Crawford

See also **Gem** (picture).

E. R. Degginger

William M. Stephens, Tom Stack & Associates

Clem Haagner, Bruce Coleman Inc.

Turtles live in a variety of habitats. The painted turtle, *upper left,* makes its home in fresh water. It uses its webbed feet for both swimming and walking. The green turtle, *lower left,* dwells in the sea. It has long, paddlelike flippers. The leopard tortoise, *above,* lives on land. Its stumpy legs and feet are well suited for walking on dry, rough ground.

Turtle is the only reptile with a shell. Most kinds of turtles can pull their head, legs, and tail into their shell, which serves as a suit of armor. Few other backboned animals have such excellent natural protection.

Turtles, like all reptiles, are cold-blooded—that is, their body temperature stays about the same as the temperature of the surrounding air or water. Turtles cannot be warm and active in cold weather, and so they cannot live in regions that are cold throughout the year. They live almost everywhere else—in deserts, forests, grasslands, lakes, marshes, ponds, rivers, and the sea.

There are more than 250 species of turtles, about 50 of which live in North America north of Mexico. Some turtles live only on land, but others spend almost their entire life in the sea. Most other species dwell mainly in fresh water or live about equally on land and in fresh water. Many turtles live their entire life within a few miles or kilometers of where they were hatched. But large numbers of sea turtles migrate thousands of miles or kilometers from their birthplace.

Turtles vary greatly in size. The largest turtle species, the leatherback turtle, grows from 4 to 8 feet (1.2 to 2.4 meters) long. But the common bog turtle measures only about 4 inches (10 centimeters) in length.

Sea turtles, all of which swim rapidly, rank as the fastest turtles. One of these species, the green turtle, can swim for brief periods at a speed of nearly 20 miles (32 kilometers) per hour. On land, many kinds of turtles are slow, lumbering creatures. But some land turtles can move with surprising speed. For example, the smooth softshell turtle, a freshwater species of North America, often can outrun a human being on level ground.

The first turtles lived more than 185 million years ago. The *Archelon,* a sea turtle of about 70 million years ago, grew about 12 feet (3.7 meters) long. This creature died out, as did many other species. Today, many species of turtles face extinction because people hunt them for food and for their shells and gather their eggs. People also destroy their natural homes to make way for cities and farms.

At one time, pet shops throughout the United States sold thousands of painted turtles and red-eared turtles yearly. But medical researchers discovered that many of these turtles carried bacteria that cause *salmonella poisoning,* a serious illness in human beings. In 1975, the U.S. Food and Drug Administration banned the sale of most pet turtles.

The body of a turtle

Shell. Most species of turtles can pull their head, legs, and tail into their shell for protection. A few kinds of turtles, particularly sea turtles, cannot withdraw into their shell.

A turtle's shell consists of two layers. The inner layer

is made up of bony plates and is actually part of the skeleton. Among most species, the outer layer consists of hard, horny structures called *scutes,* which are formed from skin tissue. Soft-shelled turtles and the leatherback turtle have an outer layer of tough skin rather than scutes. The part of the shell that covers the turtle's back is called the *carapace,* and the part that covers the belly is called the *plastron.* The carapace and the plastron are joined along each side of the body by a bony structure called the *bridge.*

Most turtles that live on land have a high, domed shell. Those that live in water have a flatter, more streamlined shell. Some species of turtles, including Blanding's turtle, box turtles, and mud turtles, have a hinged plastron. These turtles can close the plastron tightly against the carapace after withdrawing into their shell.

The shells of some kinds of turtles are plain black, brown, or dark green. But others have bright green, orange, red, or yellow markings.

Head. The head of most species of turtles is covered by hard scales. Turtles have no teeth, but they have a beak with a hard, sharp edge that they use to cut food. Many turtles have powerful jaws, with which they tear food and capture prey.

Legs and feet. A turtle's legs and feet vary according to the habitat of the species. Land turtles, particularly tortoises, have heavy, short, clublike legs and feet. Most freshwater turtles have longer legs and webbed feet. Sea turtles have legs shaped like long paddles, with flippers instead of feet.

The hip bones and shoulder bones of the turtles, unlike those of any other animal, are inside the ribcage. This unusual feature enables most kinds of turtles to pull their legs inside their shell. The species that are unable to withdraw their legs cannot do so because the shell is too small.

William M. Partington, NAS

Hladik, Jacana

Turtles have a hard beak. Among most species, such as the mud turtle, *left,* the beak is not covered. But a soft-shelled turtle, *right,* has fleshy lips that cover its beak.

Senses. Turtles have a well-developed sense of sight and of touch. Scientific experiments indicate that they also have a good sense of smell, at least for nearby objects. Turtles have a middle ear and inner ear, and a *tympanic membrane* (eardrum) forms their outer ear. A turtle can hear low-pitched sounds about as well as a human being can.

The life of a turtle

Young. Turtles hatch from eggs, which are fertilized within the female's body. One mating can result in the fertilization of all the eggs of a female for several years. Most species lay their eggs between late spring and late autumn, and some lay eggs more than once during this period. A green turtle may lay as many as seven *clutches* (groups) of eggs during one breeding season.

The skeleton of a land turtle

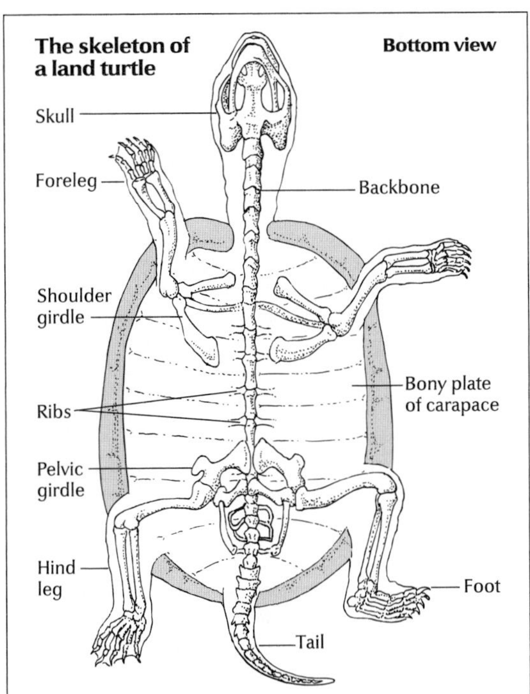

A turtle's shell provides excellent protection. Most turtles retract their head by pulling their long, flexible neck straight back in a U-curve. Scales protect the parts of the body exposed at the shell openings.

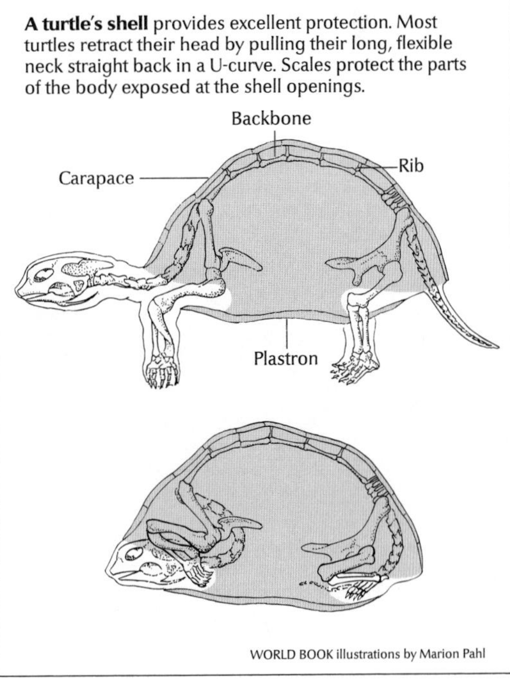

WORLD BOOK illustrations by Marion Pahl

R. R. Pawlowski, Bruce Coleman Inc.

All turtles lay their eggs on land. Among most species, the female digs a hole in the ground, lays her eggs and covers them, and then leaves them. The sun's heat hatches the eggs. The female shown here is one of the side-necked species.

All turtles, including sea and freshwater species, lay their eggs on land. Among most species, the female digs a hole in the ground with her back feet when ready to lay her eggs. She lays the eggs in the hole and covers them with soil, sand, or rotting plant matter. The number of eggs laid varies. An African pancake tortoise lays only one egg per clutch, but a sea turtle may lay 200 eggs at a time.

The female turtle walks away after covering her eggs and does not return. The warmth of the sun hatches the eggs. The temperature at which the eggs are incubated also determines the sex of the hatchlings. Newly hatched turtles must dig their way to the surface of the ground, obtain food, and protect themselves—all on their own.

Many animals prey on turtle eggs and newborn turtles. Various birds and mammals flock to beaches and eat baby sea turtles as they crawl toward the water. Fish attack many others as they enter the sea. Skunks, raccoons, and snakes dig up the nests of freshwater turtles and devour the eggs.

Scientists believe turtles live longer than any other backboned animal. Some box turtles and tortoises have lived more than 100 years. Most of a turtle's growth occurs during the animal's first 5 to 10 years. The turtle continues to grow after reaching this age, but at a much slower rate.

Alan Blank, Bruce Coleman Inc.

A baby desert tortoise hatches from its egg after about 100 days. Young turtles have a horny growth on the tip of their beak. This growth, called a *caruncle,* helps break open the shell.

Food. Most kinds of turtles eat both animals and plants. The organisms eaten by a turtle vary among the species. A few kinds of turtles, including green turtles and tortoises, feed almost entirely on plants. Certain freshwater species, such as map turtles and soft-shelled turtles, eat chiefly animals.

Hibernation. Turtles, like other cold-blooded animals, cannot remain active in cold weather. Species that live in regions with harsh winters must hibernate. Most freshwater turtles hibernate by burrowing into the warm, muddy bottom of a pond, stream, or other body of water. Land turtles bury themselves in soil or under rotting vegetation.

Some species of turtles survive hot, dry periods by going into a state of limited activity called *estivation.* Estivation somewhat resembles hibernation.

Kinds of turtles

There are seven main groups of turtles: (1) mud and musk turtles, (2) pond and marsh turtles, (3) sea turtles, (4) side-necked turtles, (5) snapping turtles, (6) soft-shelled turtles, and (7) tortoises.

Mud and musk turtles make up a family of 22 freshwater species. They live in the Western Hemisphere, particularly in Central America. Mud and musk turtles of the United States include the common mud turtle, common musk turtle, razor-backed musk turtle, and yellow mud turtle.

Few mud and musk turtles grow more than 6 inches (15 centimeters) long. But these turtles have large heads and strong jaws, and they may bite. When disturbed, these turtles give off a foul-smelling substance called *musk* from glands on the bridge in front of their hind legs. The common musk turtle, whose musk has a particularly strong, unpleasant scent, is often called the "stinkpot."

Pond and marsh turtles form the largest family of turtles—about 90 species. Members of this family live in Asia, Europe, North and South America, and northern Africa. Pond and marsh turtles of North America include the box turtle, chicken turtle, diamondback terrapin, map turtle, painted turtle, red-eared turtle, spotted turtle, and wood turtle. Many of these species are brightly colored, with green, red, or yellow markings on their head, legs, and shell. Most pond and marsh turtles found in the United States are small, but some kinds may grow more than a foot (30 centimeters) long. The majority of pond and marsh turtles live in lakes, ponds, rivers, streams, and tidewater areas. A few species, including box turtles and wood turtles, dwell mainly on land.

Sea turtles. There are at least seven species of sea turtles. Six of them—the green turtle, the flatback, the hawksbill, the loggerhead, the Atlantic ridley, and the Pacific ridley—have bony, scute-covered shells. Most zoologists classify these species into one family. The seventh species, the leatherback, forms its own family. Its shell has far fewer bones than that of the other sea turtles and is covered with skin rather than scutes. Most sea turtles live in warm seas throughout the world. The leatherback often ventures into cold Canadian waters.

All except the Australian flatback may be found in the coastal waters of the United States.

Sea turtles rank among the largest species. Even the smallest ones, the ridleys, grow up to 28 inches (70 centimeters) long and weigh nearly 100 pounds (45 kilograms). A leatherback may measure 8 feet (2.4 meters) long and weigh 1,500 pounds (680 kilograms). Sea turtles swim by beating their flippers much as a bird flaps its wings. Other turtles swim with a back-and-forth paddling motion. Sea turtles cannot withdraw into their shell, and so they depend on their size and swimming speed for defense.

Female sea turtles do not normally leave the water except to lay their eggs. Most of the males never return to land after entering the sea as hatchlings. The females often migrate thousands of miles or kilometers to reach their breeding beaches. They drag themselves onto a sandy beach, bury their eggs, and then return to the sea. Female sea turtles are almost completely helpless while they are on land.

Side-necked turtles bend their neck sideways when withdrawing their head, instead of pulling straight back into their shell. There are about 55 species, which are divided into two families. They live in Africa, Australia, and South America, mainly in areas south of the equator.

Snapping turtles make up a family of large, freshwater turtles that live only in North America, Central America, and northern South America. There are two species of snappers. The common snapper, which may be found from Canada to Ecuador, grows as long as 19 inches (47 centimeters). The other species, the alligator snapper, lives in the Central and Southeastern United States. Alligator snappers are the largest turtles of North America, except for sea turtles. An alligator snapper may measure more than 24 inches (60 centimeters) long and weigh over 200 pounds (91 kilograms).

Snapping turtles eat small water animals, such as fish, frogs, insects, snails, and young waterfowl. They also feed on plants and *algae* (simple aquatic organisms). Snappers have a large head and strong jaws. They may bite fiercely if disturbed. A snapper's small shell does not give much protection, and so it depends on its strong, sharp-edged jaws for defense.

Jim Teason

The common snapping turtle has a small shell in relation to the rest of its body. The snapper cannot retreat into its shell for protection, and so it depends on its strong jaws for defense.

Leonard Lee Rue, Bruce Coleman Inc.

A box turtle is well protected by its shell. The *carapace* (upper shell) forms a high dome. The *plastron* (lower shell) is hinged and can be pulled up against the carapace when the turtle is inside the shell. The box turtle shown here has its plastron only partly pulled up.

Soft-shelled turtles make up a family of 21 species. These freshwater turtles have a shell covered by smooth skin. They live in Africa, Asia, and North America. Three species of soft-shelled turtles—the smooth softshell, the spiny softshell, and the Florida softshell—live in the continental United States. Two species of Chinese softshells, both Asian species, are found in Hawaii.

Unlike other turtles, softshells have fleshy lips that cover their beak. Most kinds of softshells also have a long, tube-shaped nose that they push above the surface of the water in order to breathe. Most softshells do not grow much longer than a foot (30 centimeters), but some species measure up to 3 feet (91 centimeters) long. A soft-shelled turtle may bite when disturbed, and it can strike with lightning speed.

Tortoises form a family of about 40 species. These land turtles live in Africa, Asia, Europe, and North and South America, and on certain ocean islands. The tortoises of the Aldabra Islands and the Galapagos Islands are the world's largest land turtles. These huge reptiles may measure up to 4 feet (1.2 meters) long and may weigh up to 600 pounds (270 kilograms).

Three species of tortoises live in the United States. The desert tortoise makes its home in the dry areas of the Southwest. The gopher tortoise lives in sandy-soiled areas of the Southeastern United States. The Texas tortoise is found in scrub forests of southern Texas.

Tortoises live only on land. Most species are slow-moving creatures with a high, domed shell. But the African pancake tortoise has a flat, flexible shell. When in danger, this tortoise runs quickly into a crack in a nearby rock. It then takes a deep breath and inflates its body, wedging itself tightly in the crack.

Turtles and human beings

The activities of human beings are a serious threat to the survival of many turtles, and turtle conservation must improve to prevent certain species from becoming extinct. Wildlife experts classify more than 40 kinds of turtles as endangered. These rare turtles include many types of tortoises and most sea turtles.

Udo Hirsch, Bruce Coleman Ltd.

The Galapagos tortoise ranks as one of the largest land turtles. This huge reptile measures up to 4 feet (1.2 meters) long and may weigh more than 600 pounds (270 kilograms).

People have long used turtle meat and eggs for food and turtle shells as ornaments. The most threatened species of turtles include the most economically valuable ones. For example, the green turtle is a popular food in many parts of the world. The use of its meat and eggs by humans has seriously endangered its survival. The hawksbill turtle also has almost been killed off because *tortoise shell,* a substance that is used in making ornamental objects, comes from its carapace. People further endanger turtles by poisoning their homes with pollution. People also continually replace forests, swamps, and other natural areas with cities and farms. This activity almost ensures the extinction of certain kinds of turtles.

Some governments forbid the capture of rare species of turtles. Turtle preserves have been established in certain areas, and scientists are experimenting with raising valuable species on turtle farms. But zoologists must know more about how turtles live in the wild to save many of the endangered ones. Carl H. Ernst

Scientific classification. Turtles make up the order Testudines (sometimes called Chelonia) in the class Reptilia and the phylum Chordata.

See also **Terrapin; Tortoise.**

Turtle dove is a small dove that breeds in woodland and open country in Europe, western Asia, and northern Africa. They fly swiftly and directly, with a flickering wing action. The turtle dove feeds on seeds of weeds and grains. Its purring coo is a common sound in spring. The turtle dove nests in thickets and orchards. The female generally lays two eggs on a thin platform of twigs and grass. Both parents provide care for the young. The mourning dove of North America is sometimes wrongly called a turtle dove. Dennis Paulson

Scientific classification. The turtle dove belongs to the pigeon and dove family, Columbidae. Its scientific name is *Streptopelia turtur.*

Tuscany, *TUHS kuh nee,* is a political region, or state, in Italy. Its Italian name is Toscana (pronounced *toh SKAHN uh*). Tuscany lies on the west coast of Italy. It is made up of nine provinces. It covers 8,877 square miles (22,991 square kilometers) and has a population of about $3\frac{1}{2}$ million. Tuscany is an important agricultural and industrial center. Its Chianti district is famous for its wine. Straw hats made in Tuscany are known as *Leghorns.* Tuscany includes the famous Italian cities of Florence, Pisa, Siena, and Livorno.

Tuscany has long been an important Italian center of art and learning. In early times, the territory was the home of an ancient people known as *Etruscans.* The Italian poets, Dante and Petrarch, used the language of Tuscany for their poems. Anthony James Joes

See also **Etruscans; Florence.**

Tuscarora Indians. See **Iroquois Indians.**

Tusk. See **Elephant; Hog** (Teeth); **Boar, Wild.**

Tuskegee Airmen were a group of African Americans who served in the Army Air Corps during World War II (1939-1945). The name *Tuskegee Airmen* is used most often to refer to combat aviators, but the group also included bombardiers, navigators, maintenance crews, and support staff. Members of the Tuskegee Airmen were the first African Americans to qualify as military pilots in any branch of the armed forces. Many became decorated war heroes.

At the time of World War II, the United States War Department had a policy of racial segregation. Blacks were trained separately from whites and served in separate units. They were not allowed into elite military units. In 1941, under pressure from African American organizations and Congress, the Army Air Corps began accepting black men and admitting them into flight training. The men were trained at Tuskegee Army Air Base, near Tuskegee Institute (now Tuskegee University), a college for blacks in rural Alabama.

The training program began in 1941. One of the first men to earn the wings of an Army Air Corps pilot was Benjamin O. Davis, Jr., who later became the first black general in the U.S. Air Force. Davis commanded the 99th Pursuit Squadron, the nation's first all-black squadron, which trained at Tuskegee. The 99th operated in North Africa. Davis later commanded the 332nd Fighter Group, which also trained at Tuskegee. The 332nd became known for its success in escorting bomber pilots to strategic bombing missions in Europe. The Tuskegee

WORLD BOOK illustration by Trevor Boyer, Linden Artists Ltd.

The turtle dove is a slender bird known for its soft cooing call. It lives in Europe, western Asia, and northern Africa.

Airmen never lost a pilot that they were assigned to escort.

Training at Tuskegee ended in 1946. A total of 992 pilots had graduated from the program. The success of the Tuskegee aviators helped lead to a decision by the United States government calling for an end to racial discrimination in the military. Well-known graduates of the Tuskegee program include Daniel James, Jr., who was the first black four-star general; and Coleman A. Young, who served as mayor of Detroit from 1973 to 1993. Alton Hornsby, Jr.

See also **Davis, Benjamin Oliver, Jr.; James, Daniel, Jr.**

Tuskegee University is a privately controlled, nonprofit coeducational institution in Tuskegee, Alabama. It has a college of arts and sciences and schools of agriculture and home economics, business, education, engineering and architecture, nursing and allied health, and veterinary medicine. The university offers bachelor's and master's degrees and a doctor's degree in veterinary medicine. Tuskegee University is the home of the George Washington Carver Research Foundation, the Center for Sweet Potato Research, and the General Daniel "Chappie" James Center for Aerospace Science and Health Education.

The school was founded in 1881 by Booker T. Washington as the Tuskegee Normal and Industrial Institute, but it was more commonly known as the Tuskegee Institute. Washington was the most influential black leader and educator of his time in the United States. He served as Tuskegee's principal and instructor for 33 years. He stressed the importance of training in practical trade skills. The scientist George Washington Carver was one of the school's best-known instructors. In 1974, Congress established the Tuskegee Institute National Historic Site, which includes the George Washington Carver Museum. The school became Tuskegee University in 1985. Critically reviewed by Tuskegee University

See also **Carver, George Washington; Tuskegee Airmen; Washington, Booker T.**

Tussaud, *tuh SOH* or *too SOH,* **Marie Gresholtz,** *GREHS hohlts* (1761?-1850), a Swiss modeler in wax, founded Madame Tussaud's Exhibition in London in 1802. Her descendants still maintain this famous museum of wax figures of prominent people. Some of the characters and scenes in the exhibition were modeled from life by Madame Tussaud and members of her family with remarkable accuracy. Additional figures for the museum are made each year.

Marie Gresholtz was born in Bern, Switzerland, and learned to model in her uncle's museum in Paris. In 1794 she married François Tussaud. During the French Revolution, she was suspected of sympathy for the king. She was forced to model heads of the revolutionary leaders, and of victims of the guillotine. She was later imprisoned. When released, she moved to London with one of her two sons. Donald Sutherland

Tussock moth, *TUHS uhk,* makes up a family whose caterpillars have *tussocks* (tufts) of hair along the back. These hair tufts are often brightly colored. The caterpillars may also have distinct stripes on the back. The adult moths develop only dull colors.

About 20 kinds of tussock moths live in the United States. The *gypsy moth* and *browntail moth* were brought to the United States from Europe. Their caterpillars have done much damage to New England trees. The *whitemarked tussock moth* is common in the eastern United States. The female has no wings.

The caterpillars, which are the moth larvae, damage trees by eating the leaves. They often destroy whole orchards and forests. One method of control has been to import beetles that eat the caterpillars. Bernd Heinrich

Scientific classification. Tussock moths make up the family Lymantriidae. The scientific name for gypsy moth is *Lymantria dispar.* The browntail moth is *Euproctis chrysorrhea.*

See also **Browntail moth; Gypsy moth; Moth** (Tussock moths; illustrations).

Tutankhamen, *TOOT ahngk AH muhn,* served as king of Egypt from about 1347 B.C. until his death in 1339 B.C. His name is also spelled *Tutankhamun* or *Tutankhamon.* Today, some sources refer to him informally as *Tut* or *King Tut.* His reign was unimportant. But interest in Tutankhamen began in 1922, when the British archaeologist Howard Carter discovered his tomb. The tomb had not been opened since ancient times and still contained most of its treasures. It is the only tomb of an ancient Egyptian king to be discovered almost completely undamaged. See **Carter, Howard.**

Tutankhamen became king at about the age of 9. He probably received much assistance from Ay, his *vizier* (minister of state). Scholars disagree on who Tutankhamen's relatives were. Some believe the king was a son-in-law of King Akhenaten. Others think Tutankhamen was the son of Akhenaten and the grandson of King Amenhotep III. Still others argue that Tutankhamen and Akhenaten were brothers. Tutankhamen's original name was *Tutankhaten,* meaning *the living image of Aten* or *the life of Aten is pleasing.*

Akhenaten had made Aten the sole god of Egypt. He wanted Egyptians to stop worshiping the chief sun god Amun and other traditional gods. But many Egyptians, including the powerful priests devoted to Amun, rejected the worship of Aten. About four years after becoming king, Tutankhaten took the name Tutankhamen and restored Egypt's old religion. See **Akhenaten.**

Historians believe Tutankhamen died at about the age of 18, but they are unsure about the cause of his death. Ay succeeded Tutankhamen as king and held his funeral in the Valley of the Kings, a burial center at Thebes. Horemheb, a leading general, later succeeded Ay as king. Horemheb and his successors destroyed or removed all monuments built by or in honor of Tutankhamen and others who had accepted Aten as Egypt's chief god. Partly because of these actions, little was known about Tutankhamen until Carter's discovery.

Carter searched for Tutankhamen's tomb for nearly six years. He finally discovered that its entrance had been hidden by debris from digging at the entrance of the nearby tomb of King Ramses VI. Tutankhamen's four-room tomb contained more than 5,000 objects, including many beautiful carved and gold-covered items. A magnificent lifelike gold mask of Tutankhamen covered the head and shoulders of the royal mummy.

Among the items discovered were luxurious chests, thrones, beds, linens, clothing, necklaces, bracelets, rings, and earrings. Carter also found chariots, bows and arrows, swords, daggers, shields, ostrich feather fans, trumpets, statues of Tutankhamen and many Egyptian gods, figures of animals, models of ships, toys,

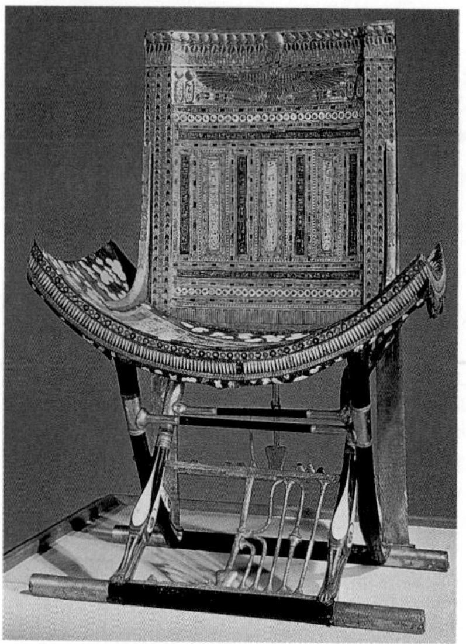
Robert Harding Associates

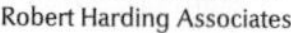

Ronald Sheridan

© Lee Boltin

© Lee Boltin

Beautiful treasures of Tutankhamen were found inside the young king's tomb. The most exquisite items included, *left to right,* a throne, a necklace honoring the sun, a gold death mask, and a small alabaster boat and pedestal.

games, and storage jars containing precious oils. The ancient Egyptians believed in a life after death, called the *afterlife.* They had their favorite possessions and practical objects buried with them for later use in the afterlife. Most of the items found in Tutankhamen's tomb are now displayed in the Egyptian Museum in Cairo.

One of the most informative items in the tomb was a note on the handle of the king's fan. The note indicated that the young Tutankhamen hunted at Heliopolis, near modern Cairo. Wine-jar labels indicated the length of Tutankhamen's reign. Several objects included scenes that show Tutankhamen slaying foreign enemies in battle. But scholars doubt that these scenes pictured actual events. Leonard H. Lesko

Additional resources

Carter, Howard, and Mace, A. C. *The Tomb of Tut-ankh-amen.* 3 vols. 1923-1933. Reprint. Cooper Square, 1963.
Caselli, Giovanni. *In Search of Tutankhamun: The Discovery of a King's Tomb.* Bedrick, 1999. Younger readers.
Green, Robert. *Tutankhamun.* Watts, 1996. Younger readers.
James, T. G. H. *Tutankhamun.* Friedman/Fairfax, 2000.

Tutsi, *TOOT see,* are an African people who live mainly in the central African nations of Burundi and Rwanda. They are sometimes called Batutsi or Watusi. The Tutsi population is about 2 million.

The Tutsi are by tradition a cattle-keeping people. They began to arrive in their present lands in the A.D. 1300's or 1400's, coming from northeastern Africa, probably in search of grazing land for their herds. Hutu people (also called Bahutu) were already living in the area when the Tutsi arrived. The Hutu were an agricultural people and were not as skilled in warfare as the Tutsi. The Tutsi gradually established themselves as the dominant group in the region politically and economically. Over the centuries, the two groups developed a common language and culture. Most Tutsi are Christians. However, many Tutsi also follow traditional African beliefs.

The region came under European control in the late 1800's. The Europeans strengthened Tutsi dominance even though the Tutsi remained a minority in the region. Tensions between the Hutu and Tutsi have resulted in much violence, especially after Burundi and Rwanda became independent countries in 1962. Widespread ethnic fighting killed hundreds of thousands of people in the two countries in the 1990's. John W. Burton

See also **Burundi; Hutu; Ruanda-Urundi; Rwanda.**

Tutu, *TOO too,* **Desmond** (1931-), is a South African civil rights leader and former Anglican archbishop. He worked to end South Africa's strict racial segregation policy, known as *apartheid.* To help end apartheid, Tutu asked foreign nations and businesses to limit trade and investment activities in South Africa. In 1991, the South African government repealed the last of the laws that formed the legal basis of apartheid.

A. Tannenbaum, Sygma

Desmond Tutu

Tutu won the 1984 Nobel Peace Prize for his nonviolent campaign against apartheid. In 1995, South African President Nelson Mandela named Tutu head of a special Truth and Reconciliation Commission. This panel investigated accounts of political crimes committed under apartheid. It began its work in 1996 and issued its final report in 2003.

Tutu was born on Oct. 7, 1931, in Klerksdorp. In 1961, he was ordained an Anglican priest. In the 1960's, he received degrees in divinity and theology from King's College in London. He worked as an educator in the early 1970's. Tutu was named Anglican dean of Johannesburg, South Africa, in 1975. He became bishop of Lesotho in 1976 and bishop of Johannesburg in 1984. In 1986, he became the first black to be elected archbishop of Cape Town. He retired from this post in 1996. Robert I. Rotberg

Tutuila. See **American Samoa.**

Tuva, *TOO vah,* is a republic of Russia. It is located in central Asia, between Siberia and Mongolia. Tuva has an area of 65,830 square miles (170,500 square kilometers) and a population of about 276,000.

About 60 percent of the people are Tuvinians, whose ancestors were Turkic-speaking people. The Tuvinians practice a form of Buddhism called *Lamaism.* Most of them raise cattle, sheep, and other animals. Minerals produced include asbestos and coal. The chief exports are wool and animal hides. Kyzyl is Tuva's capital.

The region was part of Outer Mongolia (now Mongolia) until 1911. It then became independent, but Russia and China had strong influence there. It became a Russian protectorate in 1914. In 1921, it became the independent nation of Tannu Tuva, later known as Tuva. The Soviet Union, which had been formed under Russia's leadership in 1922, annexed Tuva in 1944. Tuva became an autonomous republic within the Soviet republic of Russia. The Soviet Union was dissolved in 1991, but Tuva remained part of Russia. Jaroslaw Bilocerkowycz

Tuvalu, *TOO vuh LOO* or *too VAH loo,* is a small island country in the South Pacific Ocean. It has a population of about 11,000 and a land area of 10 square miles (26 square kilometers). Among the nations of the world, only Vatican City has fewer people, and only Vatican City, Monaco, and Nauru are smaller in area. Tuvalu lies about 2,000 miles (3,200 kilometers) northeast of Australia. It consists of nine islands in a chain that extends about 360 miles (580 kilometers). People live on eight of the islands. Tuvalu means *eight standing together.*

Tuvalu, formerly called the Ellice Islands, was ruled by the United Kingdom from the 1890's to 1978. It became independent in 1978. The capital of Tuvalu is an islet called Funafuti. This islet is part of an *atoll* (ring-shaped coral reef) that is also called Funafuti. The country's national anthem is "Tuvalu mo te Atua" ("Tuvalu for God"). Its unit of money is the Australian dollar. For a picture of Tuvalu's flag, see **Flag** (Flags of Asia and the Pacific).

Government. Tuvalu is a member of the Commonwealth of Nations (see **Commonwealth of Nations**). A prime minister, chosen by a parliament of 12 members elected by the people, heads the government. Local governments include seven island councils and the Town Council at Funafuti. The island councils have six elected members and up to four additional members appointed by various groups. Communities help control the government through gatherings in communal meeting houses called *maneapa.* Island courts handle most trials. The High Court of Tuvalu hears appeals.

People. Most of the Tuvaluans are Polynesians. Most live in villages built around a church and a meeting house. Tuvaluan houses have raised foundations, open sides, and thatched roofs. However, houses made of cement blocks and iron roofing are becoming more common. The main foods of the people are bananas, coconuts, fish, and *taro,* a tropical plant with one or more edible underground stems called *tubers.* In addition, the islanders raise pigs and chickens, which they eat at feasts. They usually wear light, bright-colored cotton clothing.

The people speak the Tuvaluan language, and many also know English. Both languages are used in official government business. Each of the eight inhabited islands has at least one elementary school supported by the government. There are only two secondary schools in Tuvalu. A few Tuvaluans attend the University of the South Pacific in Fiji, an island country to the south.

Tuvalu

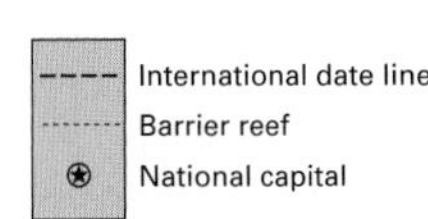

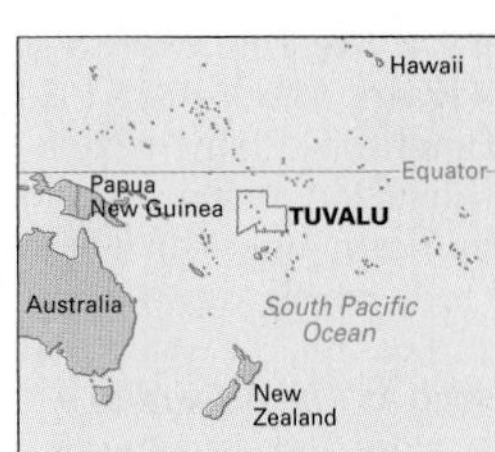

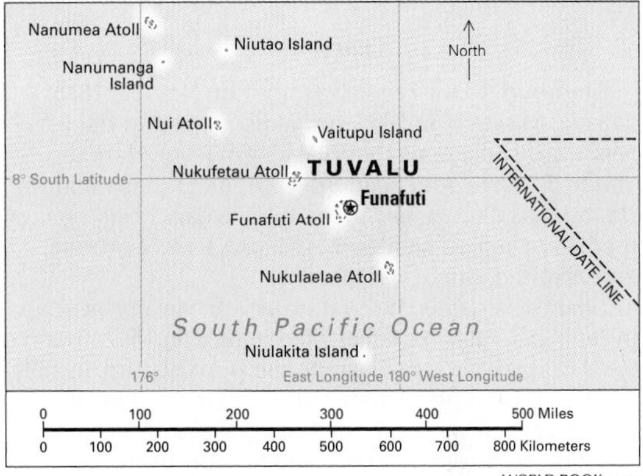

WORLD BOOK maps

Land and climate. The nine islands of Tuvalu are, from north to south, Nanumea, Niutao, Nanumanga, Nui, Vaitupu, Nukufetau, Funafuti, Nukulaelae, and Niulakita. Niulakita is uninhabited. Most of the islands are atolls that surround lagoons. The principal trees of Tuvalu are coconut palms and pandanus palms.

Tuvalu has a tropical climate, with daytime temperatures of about 80 °F (27 °C). The southern islands receive about 140 inches (356 centimeters) of rain a year. The northern islands are drier.

Economy. Tuvalu is one of the least developed countries. It has poor soil, few natural resources, almost no manufacturing, and no mining. Coconut palm trees cover much of the country, and the islanders use the coconuts to produce *copra* (dried coconut meat), their chief export. Fees charged to foreign vessels fishing for tuna in the waters around Tuvalu are becoming another important source of income. Tuvalu women weave baskets, fans, and mats for export. Many young islanders work on ocean ships because of a lack of jobs at home. Countries that provide aid to Tuvalu include Australia, Japan, New Zealand, and the United Kingdom.

History. The first inhabitants of Tuvalu probably came from the Samoa Islands hundreds of years ago. In 1568, Álvaro de Mendaña, a Spanish explorer, became the first European to see part of Tuvalu. But the islands remained largely unknown to Europeans until the early 1800's. Europeans called them the Ellice Islands. The United Kingdom took control of the islands in the 1890's. In 1916, the United Kingdom combined the islands with the Gilbert Islands to the north to form the Gilbert and Ellice Islands Colony. In 1975, the two island groups were separated. The Ellice Islands were renamed Tuvalu. The United Kingdom granted Tuvalu independence on Oct. 1, 1978. Michael R. Ogden

See also **Funafuti.**

TV. See **Television.**

TVA. See Tennessee Valley Authority.

Twain, Mark (1835-1910), was the pen name of Samuel Langhorne Clemens, one of the major authors of American fiction. Twain is also considered the greatest humorist in American literature. Twain's varied works include novels, travel narratives, short stories, sketches, and essays. His writings about the Mississippi River, such as *The Adventures of Tom Sawyer, Life on the Mississippi,* and *Adventures of Huckleberry Finn,* have been especially popular among modern readers.

Early life

Boyhood. Mark Twain was born on Nov. 30, 1835, in Florida, Missouri. In 1839, his family moved to Hannibal, Missouri, a village on the Mississippi River. Here the young Twain experienced the excitement of the colorful steamboats that docked at the town wharf, bringing comedians, singers, gamblers, swindlers, slave dealers, and assorted other river travelers.

Twain also gained his first experience in a print shop in Hannibal. After his father died in debt in 1847, Twain went to work for a newspaper and printing firm. In 1851, he began assisting his older brother Orion in the production of a newspaper, the Hannibal *Journal.* Twain contributed reports, poems, and humorous sketches to the *Journal* for several years. Like many American authors of his day, Twain had little formal education. Instead of attending high school and college, he gained his education in print shops and newspaper offices.

Travels. In 1853, Twain left Hannibal, displaying the yearning for travel that he would experience throughout his life. He stayed briefly in cities such as St. Louis, New York City, Philadelphia, and Cincinnati, working for low wages in print shops. He then traveled to Keokuk, Iowa, to assist his brother with more printing business.

In 1857, Twain made plans to travel to South America, and in April of that year, he started down the Mississippi River toward New Orleans. At this point, he made a decision with important consequences for his life and career. Instead of traveling to South America, he persuaded a riverboat pilot named Horace Bixby to teach him the skills of piloting. By April 1859, Twain had become a licensed riverboat pilot.

Mark Twain Memorial

Mark Twain was a great American humorist. A white linen suit and a cigar became his trademarks in public appearances.

The New York Public Library

A poster advertises a lecture by Mark Twain. The frog was a character in the author's first important short story. Beginning in 1866, Twain traveled widely, delivering humorous lectures.

The profession of riverboat piloting paid well and brought Twain much attention, which he enjoyed. His piloting experiences also allowed him to observe the many kinds of people who traveled aboard the steamboats. He later reported that "in that brief, sharp schooling, I got personally and familiarly acquainted with about all the different types of human nature that are to be found in fiction, biography, or history."

Newspaper work in the West. The beginning of the American Civil War (1861-1865) abruptly closed commercial traffic on the Mississippi River. After serving for two weeks with a Confederate volunteer company, Twain chose not to become involved in the war. He traveled to Carson City, Nevada, in 1861 with his brother Orion. Later, in *Roughing It* (1872), Twain humorously described his unsuccessful attempts at prospecting for gold and silver during this time and his eventual conclusion that he must support himself by newspaper journalism. He joined the staff of the Virginia City, Nevada, *Territorial Enterprise* in the summer of 1862. He first began publishing under his pen name on Feb. 3, 1863, while working for the *Enterprise.* "Mark Twain" comes from a riverboat term meaning *two fathoms* (a depth of 12 feet, or 3.7 meters).

Twain next drifted westward to California, where he wrote for the San Francisco *Morning Call* and a literary journal, the *Californian.* On Nov. 18, 1865, his first popular story—about "The Celebrated Jumping Frog of Calaveras County"—appeared in the New York *Saturday*

Press. In 1866, Twain traveled to the Hawaiian Islands, where he acted as a correspondent for the Sacramento *Union.* Following his return to San Francisco, he began a profitable lecture tour. Twain soon began to sense that his talents were growing beyond the limitations of the West Coast newspapers and magazines of his day.

Success and fame

Return to the East. In 1867, Twain took a voyage to Europe and the Holy Land aboard the steamship *Quaker City.* His travel letters to the San Francisco *Alta California* and the New York *Tribune* were collected in a popular book, *The Innocents Abroad* (1869). In the book, Twain ridiculed the sights and manners of the countries he visited, and the American tourists traveling abroad.

Encouraged by the prospect of future wealth from a literary career, Twain courted a young woman from Elmira, New York, named Olivia L. Langdon, whose brother had sailed with him on the *Quaker City.* The couple were wed on Feb. 2, 1870. Following Twain's brief career as a newspaper editor and columnist in Buffalo, New York, he and his wife moved to Hartford, Connecticut, in 1871. Their infant son, Langdon, died in 1872, but three daughters, Susy, Clara, and Jean, were born between 1872 and 1880.

Productive years in Hartford. In 1874, Twain and his family moved into a luxurious new 19-room house in Hartford. There, Twain entertained many prominent authors. Literary periodicals in Boston and New York City published many of his writings. In his 20 years in Hartford, Twain wrote most of his best works either at home or in his study at Quarry Farm, near Elmira, New York.

The Gilded Age (1873), which followed *Roughing It,* was Twain's first novel. He wrote it with his friend and fellow Hartford writer, Charles Dudley Warner. The title refers to the decades following the Civil War. This book satirizes the selfishness and money-making schemes that were common during that time.

The Adventures of Tom Sawyer (1876) represents Twain's first major use of memories of his childhood. Twain modeled St. Petersburg—the home of an imaginative boy named Tom Sawyer, his friend Huck Finn, and the evil Injun Joe—after his hometown of Hannibal.

A Tramp Abroad (1880) draws on a European tour that Twain took in 1878. The book's narrator describes a walking tour of Germany, Switzerland, and Italy. He mixes stories, jokes, legends, and character sketches, while criticizing European guidebooks and culture.

The Prince and the Pauper (1882), set in England in the 1500's, describes the exchange of identities between the young Prince Edward and a poor boy named Tom Canty. This book pleased a refined circle of New England readers, but disappointed those who preferred the rugged energy of Twain's previous works.

Life on the Mississippi (1883) describes the history, sights, people, and legends of the steamboats and towns of the Mississippi River region. In the most vivid passages, chapters 4 through 17, Twain recalled his own piloting days. These chapters had originally been published in the *Atlantic Monthly* in 1875 as "Old Times on the Mississippi."

Adventures of Huckleberry Finn, generally considered Twain's greatest work, was published in the United Kingdom in 1884 and in the United States in 1885. Twain had begun the book in 1876 as a sequel to *Tom Sawyer.* It describes the adventures of two runaways—the boy Huck Finn and the black slave Jim—and is told from the point of view of Huck himself. Twain used realistic language in the novel, making Huck's speech sound like actual conversation and imitating a variety of dialects to bring the other characters to life. Tom Sawyer also reappears in certain chapters, and his antics provide the familiar humor for which Twain was known.

Twain's story about Huck Finn, the son of a town drunkard, became a controversial book. Huck's casual morals and careless grammar disturbed many readers in Twain's time, and the Concord, Massachusetts, Free Public Library banned the novel in 1885. Some people have continued to dislike the novel because of Huck's unrefined manners and language. In addition, some modern readers object to Huck's simple acceptance of the principles of slavery and his use of racial stereotypes and the insulting term "nigger." However, for his time, Twain was liberal on racial issues. The deeper themes of *Huckleberry Finn* argue for the fundamental equality and universal aspirations of people of all races.

A Connecticut Yankee in King Arthur's Court (1889) introduces another colorful character, a machine shop foreman from Hartford, Connecticut, named Hank Morgan. Morgan finds himself magically transported back to England in the A.D. 500's. He decides to reform that society by introducing the economic, intellectual, and moral benefits of life in the 1800's. Through events in the book, Twain indirectly satirizes the reverent attitude of some British authors toward the legendary Knights of the Round Table. But at the same time, he raises questions about certain values in the American culture of his time.

Later years

Disappointments. In the 1880's, Mark Twain established and operated his own publishing firm. He also became interested in various investments, especially an elaborate typesetting machine. He lost almost $200,000 in investments in the machine between 1881 and 1894. Also, his publishing company declared bankruptcy in April 1894. Thus, in January 1895, Twain found himself publicly humiliated by his inability to pay his debts.

Twain eventually recovered from his financial difficulties, through his continued writing and a successful lecture tour in 1895 and 1896. During this much-publicized tour, Twain lectured in such places as India, South Africa, and Australia. By the time he returned, he had become an international hero. Twain enjoyed this attention, and his habits of smoking cigars or a pipe and wearing unconventional white suits contributed to his showy image. He also made use of his position as a public figure to cynically criticize U.S. foreign policy.

Although he was recovering from his financial problems by 1898, Twain had begun to experience tragedy in his personal life. Susy, his oldest daughter, died of meningitis in 1896, while her parents and sister Clara were abroad. In 1903, Twain sold the beloved house in Hartford, which had become too closely associated with Susy's death. His wife, Olivia, who had developed a heart condition, died on June 5, 1904. His youngest daughter, Jean, died on Dec. 24, 1909.

Later works. Despite his business and personal difficulties, Twain managed to continue writing. His works during his final years included *The American Claimant* (1892), about an impractical character named Colonel Mulberry Sellers. The novel was based on an unsuccessful play he wrote with author-critic William Dean Howells in 1883. *The Tragedy of Pudd'nhead Wilson* (1894) is a detective novel set in the village of Dawson's Landing, another name for Hannibal. In this story, Twain focused on racial prejudice as the most critical issue facing American society. He drew on actual historical sources in *Personal Recollections of Joan of Arc* (1896). In *Following the Equator* (1897), Twain recounted his experiences on his overseas lecture tour of 1895 and 1896. In his story "The Man That Corrupted Hadleyburg" (1899), he described a practical joke that exposed the greed of the smug leaders of a town.

As Twain's career progressed, he seemed to become increasingly removed from the humorous, cocky image of his younger days. More and more of his works came to express the gloomy view that all human motives are ultimately selfish. These works also reflect Twain's lifelong doubts about religion and his belief that all human acts are predetermined and free will is an illusion.

Twain died of heart disease on April 21, 1910. He left behind numerous unpublished manuscripts, including his large but incomplete autobiography. One pessimistic but fascinating tale, *The Mysterious Stranger,* was published in 1916, after Twain's death. This story, which exists in three versions, describes a visit by Satan to an Austrian village during the Middle Ages.

Modern reputation

Since the 1960's, some people have come to view Mark Twain's life and outlook as gloomy and even tragic. His later, more bitter works, such as *The Mysterious Stranger,* were neglected in the years immediately following his death. But they have recently received more attention, resulting in a broader understanding of Twain's personality and works.

Although viewed as having a serious, sometimes pessimistic side, Twain remains best known as a humorist. He effectively used comic exaggeration to attack the false pride and self-satisfaction he saw in humanity. One of his greatest accomplishments was the development of a writing style that was distinctly American, rather than an imitation of the style of English writers. The loose rhythms of the language in his books give the impression of real speech. Twain's realistic prose style has influenced numerous American writers. Ernest Hemingway stated that "all modern American literature comes from ... *Huckleberry Finn.*" Alan Gribben

See also **Connecticut** (Places to visit; picture); **Missouri** (Places to visit).

Additional resources

Budd, Louis J. *Our Mark Twain.* Univ. of Penn. Pr., 1983.
De Koster, Katie, ed. *Readings on Mark Twain.* Greenhaven, 1996.
LeMaster, J. R., and Wilson, J. D., eds. *The Mark Twain Encyclopedia.* Garland, 1993.
Lyttle, Richard B. *Mark Twain.* Atheneum, 1994.
Powers, Ron. *Dangerous Water: A Biography of the Boy Who Became Mark Twain.* Basic Bks., 1999.

Tweed is a rough, heavy, hairy, woolen cloth that may contain synthetic fibers. Tweed is usually woven of fibers in two or more colors. Some tweed has a plain weave. Other tweed has a *twill* weave, with raised diagonal lines. Another tweed has a *herringbone twill* weave, with diagonal raised lines of yarn that meet to form "V's." In Scotland, where tweed was first woven, *twill* is often pronounced *tweel,* and *tweed* may have developed from this. Some people believe the cloth was named for the River Tweed. Genuine Harris Tweeds are made by hand. They are woven on the islands of the Outer Hebrides—chiefly on Lewis with Harris Island.

The yarns are dyed the colors of the heather in the Hebrides. The dyes are made from a type of vegetation called *lichens,* which grow on the rocks of the islands. The lichen has an odor, called *cretal smell,* which never leaves the cloth. Rainy weather brings out this smell in a Harris Tweed suit.

After the yarn is dyed, the longwise, or *warp,* threads are put on the looms. When the cloth is woven, the weavers have a ceremony called *waulking,* which means *shrinking.* The cloth is soaked in soapy water. The weavers stand around a table and pass the cloth while singing *waulking songs.* Each weaver pounds and rubs the cloth. The cloth is then washed and dried and is ready to be made into clothing.

Tweed is a favorite cloth for sports clothing, and men's and women's coats and suits. Some tweeds are made in the United States, but they are usually lighter in weight and softer in texture than the cloth made in Scotland and England. O. Frank Hunter

Tweed, River, is a waterway in the United Kingdom. The Tweed, which is 96 miles (154 kilometers) long, rises in Scotland's Southern Uplands. It flows eastward and forms the border between Scotland and England for about 17 miles (27 kilometers). It then flows through England for a short distance before emptying into the North Sea at Berwick-upon-Tweed (see **United Kingdom** [terrain map]). It is navigable only near its mouth. Salmon and trout fishing are popular sports along the river.

Small towns, including Galashiels, Kelso, Peebles, and Melrose, lie along the banks of the River Tweed. During the 1800's, these towns built mills along the river to provide water power for their cloth and hosiery industries. Tweed cloth may have been named for the river. Abbotsford, the estate of Scottish author Sir Walter Scott, stands on the Tweed near Melrose. Molly Warrington

Tweed, William Marcy (1823-1878), was an American politician who swindled New York City out of millions of dollars. Tweed, known as "Boss" Tweed, entered politics at an early age. By the 1860's, Tweed became head of Tammany Hall, a powerful group of Democratic politicians. He organized his associates into the *Tweed Ring,* which sponsored schemes for city improvements. Millions of dollars went into the pockets of Tweed Ring members. Thomas Nast exposed these corrupt practices in his political cartoons. In 1871, the ring was broken up. Tweed was jailed in 1873 but escaped to Spain in 1876. Later that year, the Spanish government returned him to the United States. Tweed was born on April 3, 1823, in New York City. He died on April 12, 1878.

Edward A. Lukes-Lukaszewski

See also **Nast, Thomas; Tammany, Society of.**

Additional resources

Allen, Oliver E. *The Tiger: The Rise and Fall of Tammany Hall.* Addison-Wesley, 1993. Includes information about Tweed.
Jackson, Kenneth T., ed. *The Encyclopedia of New York City.* Yale, 1995. Includes articles on Tweed and related topics.

Mandelbaum, Seymour J. *Boss Tweed's New York.* 1965. Reprint. Ivan R. Dee, 1990.

Tweedsmuir, Baron. See **Buchan, John.**

Twelfth Night is a Christian holiday celebrated 12 days after Christmas, on January 6. Twelfth Night marks the end of the Christmas season. In addition, Christians observe the Feast of Epiphany on January 6 (see **Epiphany**). In Western Christian churches, this holiday commemorates the coming of the wise men to the Christ child. Among Eastern Christians, Twelfth Night celebrates the baptism of Jesus. In Italy and Spain, children still receive gifts on this day in remembrance of the gifts the wise men brought to the infant Jesus. In the Greek Orthodox Church, the Blessing of the Waters takes place on January 6. In this ceremony, a priest throws a cross into a body of water, then divers retrieve the cross.

Twelfth Night was originally celebrated in the Middle Ages at the end of the 12 days of Christmas. William Shakespeare's comedy *Twelfth Night* was possibly first performed on January 6. Robert J. Myers

Twelve Tables, Laws of the, were the first written laws of the Romans. The laws were inscribed on 12 tables, or tablets, that originally were fastened to the speaker's stand in the Roman Forum, where legal trials occurred. They represented a guarantee of equality before the law for all Roman citizens.

The laws were based on earlier civil, criminal, and religious customs. They formally established legal procedures and the rights of Roman citizens. The laws dealt with a variety of issues, including building codes, marriage, the ownership of property, and murder and other crimes.

The laws were drawn up in 451 and 450 B.C. by *decemvirs* (members of a council of 10 men) to settle class conflicts. Large parts of the laws are preserved in the works of Roman writers who, like other Romans, had learned them by heart. The laws began to be revised in the 200's B.C. C. J. Bannon

12-tone music. See **Music** (Tone); **Schoenberg, Arnold; Berg, Alban.**

Twelve Tribes. See **Jacob; Jews** (Beginnings); **Palestine** (Early history and settlement; map).

Twilight is the period just before sunrise and the period just after sunset when the light in the sky is soft and mellow. Although the sun is below the horizon, light can be seen because the rays are scattered by molecules of the earth's atmosphere. Morning twilight begins when the center of the sun is 18 degrees below the horizon and ends when the sun reaches the horizon. Evening twilight begins when the sun drops below the horizon and ends when its center has sunk to 18 degrees below the horizon.

Twilight lasts for the longest time at the North and South poles and for the shortest time at the equator. During the six sunless months at the North and South poles, dawn and dusk last a month each. But there is a period during Arctic and Antarctic summers when the sun never sinks below the horizon, and twilight does not occur. Just south of the Arctic, the summer sun never reaches 18 degrees below the horizon, and twilight lasts from sunset to sunrise. At the equator, twilight lasts about an hour, with some seasonal variations.

James Jespersen

Twill is a weave that is used in making many kinds of strong, durable cloth. In twill, the lengthwise threads, known as *warp*, meet the crosswise threads, called *weft* or *filling*, in such a way that diagonal lines form on the surface of the finished cloth in the areas where the yarns interlace. These diagonal lines may slant to the left or the right. They may be raised a little or a great deal. Many twill fabrics display an even number of warp and weft yarns on the surface, but some show more of one type than the other. Twill weaves can be varied to produce broken, entwining, figured, or reversing lines. Such materials as *serge, gabardine, denim,* and *cheviot* are twill-weave fabrics. Phyllis Tortora

Twine is a tough cord made of twisted strands of certain fibers. It may contain fibers from such plants as abacá, cotton, henequen, jute, or sisal. The fibers may also be plastic. Twine may consist of a single, tightly spun strand, or several spun strands twisted together. People use twine to tie such items as parcels and bales.

Subhash K. Batra

See also **Abacá; Sisal.**

Twinflower is a shrubby evergreen plant common in rock gardens. The twinflower has roundish leaves and long, woody stems that trail along the ground. Its fragrant, delicate, bell-shaped flowers are either pink or white. The tiny fruits are yellow. The plant grows best in loose, moist soil.

The twinflower is native to northern Europe, to Asia, and to North America. The plant was given the genus name *Linnaea* in honor of Carolus Linnaeus, the Swedish botanist who established the scientific method of naming plants and animals. The twinflower became Linnaeus's favorite plant. Daniel F. Austin

Scientific classification. The twinflower belongs to the honeysuckle family, Caprifoliaceae. Its scientific name is *Linnaea borealis.*

Twins. See **Multiple birth; Conjoined twins.**

Twister. See **Tornado.**

Two Sicilies, Kingdom of the. See **Sicilies, Kingdom of the Two.**

Tyler, Anne (1941-), is an American author whose novels reveal sensitive truths about the contemporary family. Many of Tyler's novels center on a woman character, but that woman is of most interest because of her role within a family unit. Few of Tyler's women determine their own destiny, free from the responsibilities of child rearing or family participation. Tyler's novel *Breathing Lessons* (1988) was awarded the 1989 Pulitzer Prize for fiction.

In 1964 and 1965, Tyler published her first novels, *If Morning Ever Comes* and *The Tin Can Tree.* Her next novels grew in dimension and impact. They were *A Slipping-Down Life* (1970), *The Clock Winder* (1972), *Celestial Navigation* (1974), *Searching for Caleb* (1976), and *Earthly Possessions* (1977). Tyler gained wide critical praise with her novels *Morgan's Passing* (1980), *Dinner at the Homesick Restaurant* (1982), *The Accidental Tourist* (1985), *Saint Maybe* (1991), *Ladder of Years* (1995), *A Patchwork Planet* (1998), *Back When We Were Grownups* (2001), and *The Amateur Marriage* (2004). In addition, Tyler has published many short stories and book reviews.

Tyler was born on Oct. 25, 1941, in Minneapolis. She lives in Baltimore, the setting for much of her fiction.

Linda Wagner-Martin

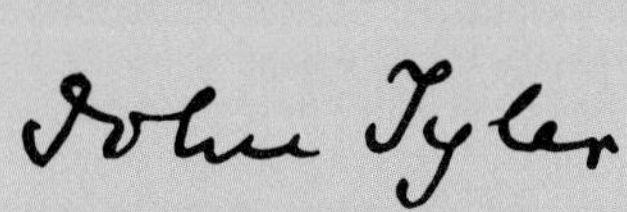

10th president of the United States 1841-1845

W. H. Harrison	**Tyler**	**Polk**
9th president	10th president	11th president
1841	1841-1845	1845-1849
Whig	Whig	Democrat

Oil painting on canvas (1842) by George Peter Alexander Healy; Corcoran Gallery of Art, Washington, D.C.

Tyler, John (1790-1862), was the first vice president to become president upon the death of a chief executive. He succeeded William Henry Harrison, who died a month after taking office. Tyler, a Southern Democrat, had split with his party and had run with Harrison on the Whig Party ticket.

As president, Tyler soon became a man without a party. The Whig program clashed with many of Tyler's lifelong beliefs. He vetoed almost every important bill. Angry Whigs tried to impeach him, the first such move against a president. They failed, but the resulting friction destroyed the Whig program.

For more than 75 years after the courteous, soft-spoken Tyler left office, historians dealt harshly with him. President Theodore Roosevelt summed up this opinion when he said: "Tyler has been called a mediocre man, but this is unwarranted flattery. He was a politician of monumental littleness."

Many historians today take a different view. They regard Tyler as a president of exceptional courage and imagination who displayed great devotion to the principles of Thomas Jefferson. He inherited a political situation he had never expected and could not support. He could not have acted other than the way he did.

Historians also point to Tyler as the man who firmly established the right of the vice president to succeed completely to the presidency. When Harrison died, many Whig leaders suggested that Tyler be called only "Acting president." Tyler, with a patience that irritated his enemies even further, took over the presidency in fact as well as in name.

During Tyler's Administration, many regions began to show signs of their future importance. Pittsburgh, Pennsylvania, was becoming the home of busy ironworks. Cincinnati boasted of its well-paved streets and its schools that required children from 6 to 10 years old to learn algebra. Texas won its long fight to join the Union. Fighting with the Seminole Indians in Florida ended in 1842. Just two days after he signed the bill approving statehood for Texas, Tyler signed a bill making Florida a state. Texas formally became a state after Tyler left office.

Early life

John Tyler was born at Greenway estate in Charles City County, Virginia, on March 29, 1790. He was the second son of John and Mary Armistead Tyler. His father served at various times as governor, as speaker of the Virginia House of Delegates, and as a judge.

John's father sent him to William and Mary College in 1802. The boy studied hard and became especially interested in political subjects. He relaxed from his studies by writing poetry and playing the violin. John graduated at the age of 17. He then studied law under his father and was admitted to the Virginia bar in 1809.

Public and political career

State legislator. At the age of 21, Tyler won election to the Virginia House of Delegates. He became a captain of volunteers in the summer of 1813, during the War of 1812. But he resigned and returned to the legislature after a month because his company had seen no action.

Tyler's family. On March 29, 1813, Tyler married Letitia Christian (Nov. 12, 1790-Sept. 10, 1842), the daughter of a Virginia planter. They had five daughters and three sons. Mrs. Tyler died during her husband's presidency, and Tyler remarried 22 months later.

Congressman. Tyler ran for a vacant seat in the United States House of Representatives in 1816 and won

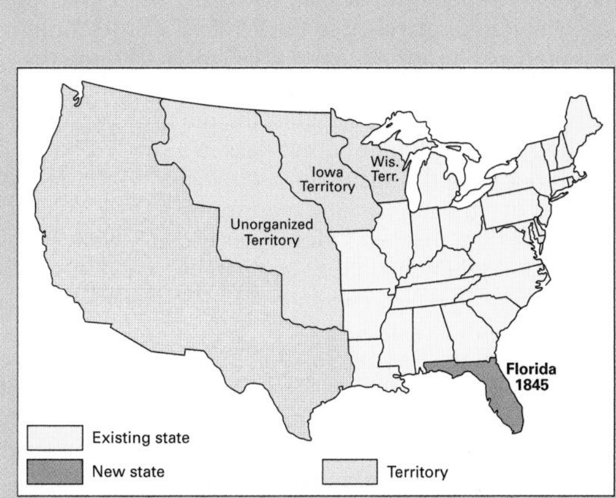

Florida became the 27th state on March 3, 1845, President Tyler's last full day in office. Tyler had brought an end to the Seminole War in Florida in 1842.

The world of President Tyler

Pioneers in covered wagons began to settle the West in the early 1840's. The first large group of settlers arrived in California in 1841. They had traveled in a train of 48 wagons along the Oregon Trail, the Humboldt River, and through the Sierra Nevada.
Newspaper editor Horace Greeley founded the *New York Tribune* in 1841 and remained its editor until his death in 1872. He became an influential spokesman against slavery.
James Fenimore Cooper completed *The Deerslayer* in 1841. It was the last of five novels by Cooper, called *The Leather-Stocking Tales,* that described life in the wilderness.
Experiments in communal living took root in Massachusetts, New York, and other states. One of the most famous communities was Brook Farm, near West Roxbury, Mass. It was founded in 1841 by social reformer George Ripley.
John C. Frémont and Kit Carson explored much of the territory between the Rocky Mountains and the Pacific Ocean in a series of expeditions in the early 1840's.
Ralph Waldo Emerson was a leading philosopher and literary figure of the 1840's. His two volumes entitled *Essays* were published in 1841 and 1844. He edited *The Dial,* a magazine of literature and philosophy, from 1842 to 1844.
The YMCA was founded in 1844 by a London clerk, George Williams.
The first public telegraph message was sent by inventor Samuel F. B. Morse in a demonstration for Congress in 1844. Morse tapped the message "What hath God wrought!" on a telegraph line from Washington, D.C., to Baltimore.

WORLD BOOK map

an easy victory. He then was elected to a full term. In Congress, Tyler fought for a strict interpretation of the U.S. Constitution. He opposed any measure that extended the powers of the federal government. Tyler opposed the American System, an economic plan proposed by Representative Henry Clay of Kentucky. The plan called for increased federal spending on roads and other internal improvements, and high tariffs to aid American manufacturers. Tyler also denounced the Bank of the United States (see **Bank of the United States**). Tyler resigned his seat in the House in January 1821 because of poor health.

Governor and senator. Tyler served briefly as chancellor of William and Mary College, then as governor of Virginia from 1825 to 1827. He was elected to the Senate in 1827, and his convictions on strict interpretation of the Constitution soon put him in an awkward position. He denounced South Carolina's attempt to nullify acts of Congress, but he also believed that President Andrew Jackson's measures against nullification were illegal (see **Nullification**). Tyler became increasingly dissatisfied with Jackson's policies. In 1836, the Virginia legislature instructed Tyler to vote for the removal of a vote that *censured* (condemned) Jackson. Tyler refused and resigned from the Senate.

Tyler becomes a Whig. In 1840, the Whig Party was a loose coalition of groups with no agreed policies or political beliefs. In hope of luring Southern votes, the Whigs chose Tyler as the vice presidential running mate of William Henry Harrison. Tyler accepted, believing that the Whigs had dropped their fight for a national

Important dates in Tyler's life

1790	(March 29) Born in Charles City County, Virginia.
1813	(March 29) Married Letitia Christian.
1816	Elected to the U.S. House of Representatives.
1825	Elected governor of Virginia.
1827	Elected to the United States Senate.
1840	Elected vice president of the United States.
1841	(April 6) Sworn in as president.
1842	Mrs. Letitia Tyler died.
1844	(June 26) Married Julia Gardiner.
1861	Elected to Confederate House of Representatives.
1862	(Jan. 18) Died near Charles City, Virginia.

Virginia Division of Historic Landmarks

John Tyler's birthplace was this house on the family estate, called Greenway, in Charles City County, Virginia. Greenway lies on the James River between Richmond and Williamsburg.

Letitia Christian Tyler, John Tyler's first wife, suffered a stroke in 1839. She remained an invalid in the White House until her death in 1842. The president remarried 22 months later.

bank and protective tariffs. Tyler opposed these measures. The Whigs barnstormed to victory, shouting the slogan "Tippecanoe and Tyler too." Harrison and Tyler defeated President Martin Van Buren by a huge majority. See **Harrison, William Henry.**

Tyler's administration (1841-1845)

Opposition to the Whigs. President Harrison died one month after his inauguration, and Tyler was sworn in as president on April 6, 1841. He kept all the members of Harrison's Cabinet. Henry Clay, by then a senator and the Whig leader in Congress, quickly submitted a legislative program. It called for a new Bank of the United States and for higher tariffs. Congress passed these bills, and Tyler replied with a sharply worded veto. That night, an armed mob marched to the White House. Hoodlums shouted insults at Tyler and hurled rocks through the windows. Tyler calmly issued guns to the White House servants and stood firm against the mob. The rioters melted away. When Congress passed a second bank bill, Tyler vetoed it again. He said it included all the abuses of a private banking monopoly.

Tyler's Cabinet

Secretary of state	* Daniel Webster Abel P. Upshur (1843) * John C. Calhoun (1844)
Secretary of the treasury	Thomas Ewing Walter Forward (1841) John C. Spencer (1843) George M. Bibb (1844)
Secretary of war	*John Bell John C. Spencer (1841) James M. Porter (1843) William Wilkins (1844)
Attorney general	John J. Crittenden Hugh S. Legaré (1841) John Nelson (1843)
Postmaster general	Francis Granger Charles A. Wickliffe (1841)
Secretary of the navy	George Edmund Badger Abel P. Upshur (1841) David Henshaw (1843) Thomas W. Gilmer (1844) John Y. Mason (1844)

*Has a separate biography in World Book.

The Whigs disown Tyler. Tyler's second veto set off more Whig demonstrations against the president. Mobs burned him in effigy. The entire Cabinet resigned, except for Secretary of State Daniel Webster. Clay resigned from the Senate. Soon afterward, the Whigs rushed through a bill to give the states money from public-land sales. Tyler vetoed it. The Whigs came back with another measure linking distribution of this money with a higher tariff. Tyler vetoed that bill, too.

Attempt at impeachment. The fight between Tyler and his own party became increasingly bitter. On Jan. 10, 1843, Whigs introduced impeachment resolutions in the House of Representatives. But the charges were so farfetched that even some Whigs sided with the Democrats to defeat the resolutions by a vote of 127 to 83.

Tyler's accomplishments. In 1841, Tyler approved the Pre-Emption Act, which allowed a settler to claim 160 acres (64.7 hectares) of land by building a cabin on the property. This law sped settlement of Illinois, Wisconsin, Minnesota, and Iowa. Tyler brought an end to the Seminole War in Florida in 1842. That same year, a dispute with the United Kingdom over the boundary between Maine and Canada was settled on terms set up by Webster, who had remained in the Cabinet for this purpose (see **Webster-Ashburton Treaty**). The United States signed a treaty with China in 1844 that opened Asia to American traders for the first time.

The annexation of Texas provided the chief issue during the last half of Tyler's term. The Texans had declared their independence from Mexico in 1836 and had petitioned to join the Union. Tyler favored annexation, but Northern congressmen opposed him because Texas would have been a slave state. Congress did not act until after the election in 1844 of James K. Polk, who supported annexation. With annexation then a certainty, the House and Senate passed a joint resolution admitting Texas. Tyler signed it on March 1, 1845. Two days later, on Tyler's last full day in office, he signed a bill admitting Florida to the Union. Texas formally joined the Union on Dec. 29, 1845, after Tyler had left office.

Life in the White House. Letitia Tyler was suffering from the effects of a paralytic stroke when her husband became president. Her only public appearance in the White House was at the wedding of her daughter Elizabeth on Jan. 31, 1842. Mrs. Tyler died on Sept. 10, 1842. Tyler's daughter-in-law Priscilla Cooper Tyler served as White House hostess until the spring of 1844. Tyler's daughter Letitia Tyler Semple then served as hostess until June of that year.

In 1844, Tyler was cruising on the U.S.S. *Princeton* to watch the firing of a new naval gun. The gun exploded, killing eight people, including David Gardiner, a former New York state senator. Tyler had been courting Gardiner's daughter Julia (1820-1889), who was also among the guests on the ship. The death brought Tyler and

Detail of an oil painting on canvas (1849) by Francisco Anelli; Copyrighted by the White House Historical Association (photograph by the National Geographic Society)

Julia Gardiner Tyler was 24 years old when she married the widowed president in New York City. Their marriage in 1844 made Tyler the first president to marry while in office.

Julia closer. They were married in New York City on June 26, 1844. Tyler was the first president to be married while in office. Julia was first lady for eight months and delighted the capital with her brilliant entertaining. President Tyler and his second wife had seven children.

Later years

Spurned by both Whigs and Democrats, Tyler retired to Sherwood Forest, his estate near Charles City, Virginia. He lived quietly until just before the Civil War. Then, in February 1861, he headed a Southern peace mission to Washington seeking a compromise on the issues that threatened the Union. Congress rejected the Southerners' proposals. In April, at a Virginia secession convention, Tyler voted in favor of Virginia leaving the Union. He won election to the Confederate House of Representatives in November 1861 but died on Jan. 18, 1862, before taking his seat. In 1915, Congress dedicated a monument to Tyler's memory in Hollywood Cemetery, at Richmond, Virginia, where he is buried beside his second wife. John T. Hubbell

Related articles in ***World Book*** include:

Bank of the United States
Clay, Henry
Florida (History)
Harrison, William Henry
President of the U.S.
Texas (History)

Outline

I. Early life
II. Public and political career
A. State legislator
B. Tyler's family
C. Congressman
D. Governor and senator
E. Tyler becomes a Whig
III. Tyler's administration (1841-1845)
A. Opposition to the Whigs
B. The Whigs disown Tyler
C. Attempt at impeachment
D. Tyler's accomplishments
E. The annexation of Texas
F. Life in the White House
IV. Later years

Questions

Why did Tyler resign from the Army?
Why and how did the Whigs desert Tyler?
What were some of Tyler's accomplishments as president?
How did Tyler show independence as a U.S. senator?
Why did Tyler's second marriage arouse interest?
Why did Daniel Webster remain in Tyler's Cabinet after the other members had resigned?
Why did Tyler oppose the Bank of the United States?

Additional resources

Chitwood, Oliver P. *John Tyler.* 1939. Reprint. Am. Political Biography Pr., 1990.
Falkof, Lucille. *John Tyler.* Garrett Educational, 1990.

Tyler, Moses Coit (1835-1900), became the first great authority on early American literature. His chief books were *A History of American Literature During the Colonial Time, 1607-1765* (1878) and *The Literary History of the American Revolution, 1763-1783* (1897). In 1881, at Cornell University, he became the first professor of American history in the United States. He was born on Aug. 2, 1835, in Griswold, Connecticut. Glenn Smith

Tyler, Royall (1757-1826), was an American playwright and lawyer. His satire *The Contrast* (1787) was the second American play and the first American comedy performed by professional actors. The play was inspired by a New York CIty performance of Richard Brinsley Sheridan's English comedy *The School for Scandal* (1777). The "contrast" in Tyler's comedy of manners is between British-inspired vanity and homespun American ingenuity. The latter is represented by Jonathan, the first in a long line of "stage Yankees" in American theater.

Tyler's writing is patriotic and humorous. He wrote five other plays, but only one was performed. Tyler also wrote a novel, *The Algerine Captive* (1797); and a series of satirical letters, *The Yankey in London* (1809).

Tyler was born on July 18, 1757, in Boston. He graduated from Harvard College in 1776. Tyler served as chief justice of the Vermont Supreme Court from 1807 to 1813. Frederick C. Wilkins

Tyler, Wat. See **Wat Tyler's Rebellion.**

Tylor, Sir Edward Burnett (1832-1917), a British anthropologist, is often regarded as the father of anthropology in the English-speaking world. His books stimulated the development of this science. Tylor was born on Oct. 2, 1832, in London. He traveled widely. Although he never studied formally at a university, he was professor of anthropology at Oxford from 1896 to 1909. He wrote *Researches into the Early History of Mankind* (1865) and *Primitive Culture* (1871). See also **Mythology** (How myths began); **Religion** (The origin of religion). David B. Stout

Tyndale, *TIHN duhl,* **William** (1494-1536), was an early English leader of the Reformation. He is best known for translating the Bible from Greek and Hebrew into English. His work later became important as a basis for the King James Version of the Bible.

Tyndale first translated the New Testament in an effort to make the Scriptures more widely available, but he could not get it published in England. After leaving England permanently in 1524, he finally had his translation published in Germany and had copies smuggled into England. See **Bible** (Early English translations).

Tyndale was born in Gloucestershire. He studied at Oxford and Cambridge universities from 1510 to about

1521 and was ordained a priest. He was strongly influenced by the ideas of his friend, the German Reformation leader Martin Luther. Tyndale was executed by Roman Catholic authorities as a Protestant heretic in Belgium. Peter W. Williams

Tyndall, *TIHN duhl,* **John** (1820-1893), was a British physicist and natural philosopher. He is known for his experiments on the scattering of light of different colors by small particles. The bluish appearance of a light beam passing through something like a soap solution is called the *Tyndall effect.* Tyndall also did work in the biological sciences. In 1876—more than 50 years before the discovery of penicillin—he described the action of a *Penicillium* mold in slowing the growth of bacteria. Tyndall was born on Aug. 2, 1820, in Leighlin Bridge, Ireland. He became superintendent of the Royal Institution in 1867. Tyndall often gave public lectures and had a special interest in clarifying concepts of physics for nonscientists. Kenneth R. Manning

Type is a letter, number, or other character used in printing. The words and numbers in all printed materials, including books, magazines, and newspapers, are made from type. There are three kinds of type: (1) metal type, (2) photographic type, and (3) digital type.

Metal type, also called *hot type,* consists of small pieces of metal that have raised letters on top. It is made by machines that force a mixture of molten lead and other metals into *matrices* (molds) of each character.

Photographic type, also called *cold type,* consists of photographic images of letters. It may be produced by several kinds of typesetting devices called *photocomposition machines.* Early photocomposition machines contained a film negative of a *font,* a set of all the characters of one type style. A beam of light projected through a character on the negative produced a positive of that character on film or on photosensitive paper.

Today, a computer stores instructions for forming each character in a font. Linked to the computer is a photocomposition machine that contains a laser. The machine uses the instructions stored in the computer to create images of type characters. Light pulses form the images on photosensitive paper or film, or directly on a printing plate.

Today, the most commonly used type is digital type.

David R. Frazier

Type is used in producing books, magazines, newspapers, and other printed materials. The three chief kinds of type are digital type and metal and photographic type (both shown here).

Modern printers create type as patterns of dots on paper, film, printing plates, or other material. The *resolution* (clarity) of the type is expressed as *dots per inch* (dpi). For example, 1,000 dpi means that on 1 square inch (6.5 square centimeters) of paper there are 1,000 dots across and 1,000 dots down. Each dot is located in a grid called a *bitmap* or *raster* and can be turned on or off.

A special computer language defines the shapes of characters using a set of program instructions. Each character is an individual program, and a font is a collection of these programs. All digital fonts are outlines that can be scaled to any size without distorting their shapes. They are then converted to a bitmap. A *raster image processor* (RIP), which may be either a computer program or a separate machine, processes digital fonts. It produces instructions that allow the characters to be either displayed on a computer monitor or printed. Because a monitor and a printer generally have different resolutions, they require different bitmap patterns. The RIP creates the required bitmap grid for the monitor or printer and forms the characters by turning the dot at each bitmap position on or off.

Classes of type Type is made in thousands of styles. These type styles are grouped into four general classes: roman, sans-serif, script, and italic. A few styles of each class are shown here.

WORLD BOOK diagram

Roman

Give me liberty or give me death.
14-point Baskerville

Give me liberty or give me death.
14-point Garamond

Sans-Serif

Give me liberty or give me death.
14-point Helvetica Medium

Give me liberty or give me death.
14-point Univers Medium

Script

Give me liberty or give me death.
14-point Bank Script

Give me liberty or give me death.
14-point Kaufmann Bold

Italic

Give me liberty or give me death.
14-point Garamond Italic

Give me liberty or give me death.
14-point Futura Medium Italic

Parts of letters

This diagram shows the main parts of lower-case letters. Printers measure the distance from the top of an *ascender* to the bottom of a *descender* to determine the point size of the type.

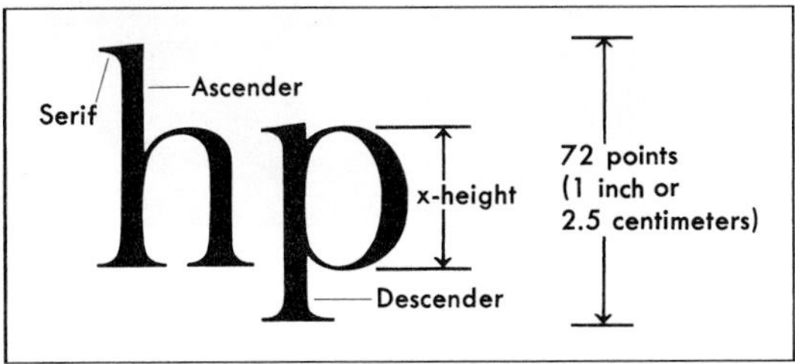

WORLD BOOK diagram

Type is made in many sizes and thousands of styles. Each style, called a *type face,* has its own characteristics. Virtually all type faces are available in digital form.

Classes of type. There are four general classes of type styles. They are (1) roman, (2) sans-serif, (3) script, and (4) italic.

Roman types have small finishing strokes called *serifs* that extend from the main strokes of the letters. These types include most commonly used styles. Printers use roman types for books, magazines, and newspapers. Popular roman styles include Baskerville, Bodoni, Garamond, and Times Roman.

Roman types include a few designs called *black letter* and a few called *uncial.* Black letter designs have highly decorative letters with thick, heavy lines. The first European printing type was black letter. Uncial designs are based on a letter style that was popular from the A.D. 300's to 700's. They were first produced in type in the 1900's. Most uncial letters look like rounded capitals. The first roman-style type similar to the ones used today was perfected about 1470 by a French printer named Nicolas Jenson.

Sans-serif types have no serifs. *Sans* is a French word that means *without.* Sans-serif styles are often used for advertisements, headings, and texts. Popular styles of this class include Futura, Helvetica, and Univers. William Caslon IV, a British printer, made the first sans-serif type about 1816.

Some type sizes

The most common sizes of type range from 6 point to 72 point. A few of the sizes within this range are shown here.

WORLD BOOK diagram

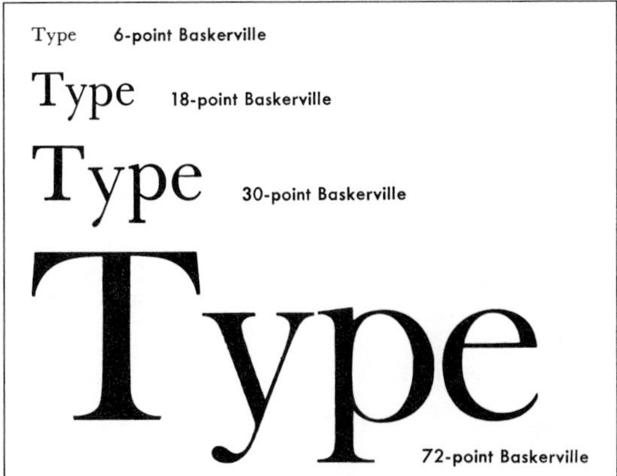

Script types resemble handwriting. The *lower-case* (small) letters of many script styles are joined together. This class is widely used in advertising. Script types include such styles as Bank Script, Brush, and Kaufmann. The first script styles were produced in the mid-1500's.

Italic types have slanted letters that *look like this.* Italics are often used to emphasize a word or group of words. Most italic types are designed to accompany a roman or sans-serif type. The titles of many books, magazines, and newspapers are printed in italics. This class includes such styles as Baskerville Italic and Futura Italic. Aldus Manutius, an Italian printer, developed the first italic type with Francesco Griffo, an Italian metalsmith, in 1500.

Sizes of type. Printers in some countries, including Canada, Mexico, the United Kingdom, and the United States, use a special scale to measure the size of type and the length of lines of type. This scale is called the American Point System. One *point* on the scale equals 0.013837 inch (0.3514598 millimeter). One inch (2.5 centimeters) equals about 72 points. One *pica* equals 12 points. In some European countries, including France, Germany, and Italy, type is measured by the *Didot point.* This point is slightly larger than the American point.

The point size of type refers to the height of the characters. The height of the main part of a small letter is called the *x-height.* Such letters as *a, c, e,* and *x* have only an x-height, but others have strokes that extend above or below the x-height. Letters with *ascenders* include *b, d,* and *f.* Letters with *descenders* include *g, j,* and *p.* The point size of any type is the distance from the top of the ascenders to the bottom of the descenders. It may include a slight space above the ascenders or below the descenders.

Metal type ranges in size from 4 point to 120 point. Most styles are not made in all sizes, however. The most common sizes include those from 6 point to 72 point. You are now reading 8.3-point type.

A majority of photographic type is made in only a few small sizes. A font can be enlarged or reduced to other sizes by lenses in the photographic equipment. In digital composition, instructions for enlarging or reducing type size are stored in the computer.

History. Until the 1400's, most books were produced by people who copied them by hand. About 1440, a German goldsmith named Johannes Gutenberg made the first use in Europe of *movable type.* Movable type consists of a piece of type for each character. It had been invented about 1045 by Bi Sheng (Pi Sheng), who was a Chinese printer, but this invention had not spread to Europe.

For about 400 years, printers *set* (assembled) all type by hand. In the 1880's, Ottmar Mergenthaler, a German instrument maker, invented the Linotype. This machine set type mechanically, eliminating the need for hand setting and increasing the speed of typesetting. It assembled matrices from which whole lines of type were *cast* (molded) as solid slugs. In 1887, an American inventor named Tolbert Lanston developed a machine called the Monotype, which cast individual pieces of type and set them into lines. Modern printers still use Linotype and Monotype machines. See **Linotype; Monotype.**

One of the first commercially practical machines to produce and set photographic type was invented in the 1940's. During the 1950's and 1960's, engineers developed new phototypesetting machines that could set type much faster than earlier kinds. Such machines are linked to powerful computers that can handle many different tasks formerly performed by people. For example, the computers tell the machine how to *justify* lines of type—that is, make them the right length—and how to hyphenate words. In the 1990's, digital type became the most widely used kind of type. Frank J. Romano

Related articles in *World Book.* See the article on **Printing** for an explanation of how type is used in the printing process. See also the following articles:

Baskerville, John
Bodoni, Giambattista
Book (The development of printed books)
Desktop publishing
Goudy, Frederic
Gutenberg, Johannes
Italics
Jenson, Nicolas
Photocomposition
Stereotyping

Type metal. See **Alloy** (Other alloys).

Typesetting. See **Printing** (Typesetting).

Typewriter is a machine that produces printed letters and figures on paper. For more than 100 years, people in homes and offices throughout the world used typewriters to write rapidly and neatly. By the late 1900's, however, personal computers with word-processing programs had replaced typewriters almost entirely. Such machines can perform many useful functions that typewriters cannot perform.

Kinds of typewriters. There are three basic kinds of typewriters: (1) manual, (2) electric, and (3) electronic. A manual typewriter operates entirely by the power supplied by the typist's hands. An electric typewriter has an electric motor to provide power, and so it requires less effort from the typist.

Electronic typewriters resemble electric typewriters but contain a computer chip called a *microprocessor.* This device enables the typewriter to automatically perform such functions as centering a line on the page, starting a new line, underlining, and *justifying* (adjusting space between words so that full lines are of the same length). Many electronic typewriters have a memory that can store names, dates, addresses, and other material that a typist often repeats. When the typist presses the appropriate key, the machine "recalls" the stored material and types it automatically. Some of these machines, called *text-editing typewriters,* enable the typist to delete, add, or move letters, words, lines, and paragraphs without retyping the entire document.

Ted Nielsen

WORLD BOOK photo by Ralph Brunke

A typewriter prints when a typist strikes a key, forcing a character against an inked ribbon onto paper. The characters on some typewriters are on levers, *left.* Others have the characters on the spokes of a *daisy wheel, right.*

How a typewriter works. All three kinds of typewriters have a *keyboard* that consists of buttons called *keys.* A typist can use most keys to produce two different *characters*—letters, numbers, punctuation marks, or other symbols. The typist produces one character by pressing a key alone, and another by pressing the same key in combination with a *shift key.* In manual and some electric typewriters, each key forms one end of a lever that has a bar of metal type at the other end. When the typist strikes a key, the type bar rises and hits an inked ribbon or a thin strip of carbon tape. The ribbon or tape is in front of the paper, on which the type bar prints a character. A hard rubber roll called a *platen* holds the paper in the typewriter. The platen and paper automatically move one space to the left after the typist strikes a key.

Some typewriters do not have type bars. *Single-element typewriters,* for instance, have a ball-shaped *font element* or *typing element* that contains all the characters. When the typist strikes a key, the ball turns so that the correct character hits the paper. The ball moves along the line that is being typed, but the platen does not move. A typist can change the type style or type size

The Bridgeman Art Library, Robert Wyatt Collection

Early typewriters included a Lambert, *left,* made by the Gramophone and Typewriter Company about 1900; a Columbia, *center,* produced in 1886; and a Blickensderfer, *right,* first made in 1893. The earliest successful portable typewriter appeared in the early 1900's.

by replacing the ball. Another printing element is called a *daisy wheel.* Each character is at the end of a long spoke. When the typist strikes a key, the wheel spins to move the correct character into place.

Most typewriters have other features in common. An *audible indicator,* such as a warning bell, alerts typists when they near the end of the margin. A *margin lock* prevents any typing past a margin unless the typist presses the margin-key release. A *tabulator,* or *tab,* helps line up numbers or words in columns.

Typewriter manufacturers produce typewriters with the letters and symbols used in many different languages. Some typewriters produce special symbols, such as those used in mathematical equations. Special typewriters for the blind type in braille.

On many typewriters, each character fills the same amount of space on the paper. But some typewriters feature *proportional spacing,* in which the space taken by each character varies according to its size.

History. During the 1700's and 1800's, many inventors tried to develop a practical typewriter. In 1867, Christopher Latham Sholes, an inventor from Milwaukee, designed the first one with the help of Carlos Glidden and Samuel W. Soulé. They patented this typewriter in 1868. In 1874, E. Remington and Sons, a gun manufacturer, marketed the new machine.

The earliest typewriters used keyboard layouts that had letters arranged alphabetically. These layouts enabled the typist to locate keys easily. However, a problem often occurred. When the typist struck in rapid succession two or more keys whose type bars were next to one another, the bars frequently jammed. To remedy this problem, Sholes helped develop another layout in the 1870's. This layout, known as QWERTY, is still the standard for keyboards in most English-speaking countries. It is called QWERTY because the letters Q, W, E, R, T, and Y appear in succession near the upper left-hand corner of the keyboard. In the QWERTY layout, the bars for the letters that most often appear in combination in the English language are far apart.

The first successful portable typewriter appeared in the early 1900's. Electric typewriters came into use in the 1920's. The first simple word processors, often called *automatic typewriters,* came into the market during the early 1960's. Manufacturers developed the electronic typewriter during the late 1970's. Beginning about 1980, personal computers and printers began to replace typewriters for home and office use. Frank J. Romano

See also **Glidden, Carlos; Keyboard; Sholes, Christopher Latham; Word processing.**

Typhoid fever is a serious bacterial disease that results in fever, weakness, and, in severe cases, death. It was once common in all heavily populated regions. However, as methods of good hygiene and sanitation were developed, typhoid fever occurred less often. Today, it is relatively rare in areas with modern standards of sanitation.

Cause and spread. Typhoid fever is caused by a bacterium called *Salmonella typhi* (abbreviated *S. typhi).* This organism passes indirectly from one person to another, chiefly through contaminated water or food. Victims of typhoid fever shed *S. typhi* in their *feces* (solid body wastes) and urine. Apparently healthy people, called *carriers,* also spread the bacteria. Carriers do not have symptoms of typhoid fever, but they harbor the bacteria in their body and release it in their feces.

Human body wastes that contain *S. typhi* can contaminate food or water in several ways. For example, flies can carry the bacteria from feces to food. Food that has been handled by carriers is another common source of infection. In regions with poor sanitation, the bacteria often spread after water supplies are contaminated by human wastes.

Symptoms of typhoid fever usually develop one to three weeks after a person has consumed contaminated food or water. Most cases last about four weeks after the symptoms begin. During the first week, the person has a rising fever, with headaches and abdominal pain. The fever peaks and remains high during the second week. In many cases, rose-colored spots appear on the chest and abdomen. The person becomes weak and, in severe cases, delirious. By the start of the third week, a greenish, soupy diarrhea develops in most cases. The disease reaches its height at this point. Unless complications occur, the person gradually improves during the end of the third week and during the fourth week.

Serious, sometimes fatal, complications can develop. The bacteria may produce *ulcers* (open sores) in the intestine. If the ulcers become severe, they can make holes in the intestinal wall. In such cases, the contents of the intestines spill into the abdomen, and serious abdominal infections can follow. In other instances, the intestines may bleed severely. Blood transfusions may be necessary to prevent death.

Treatment and prevention. Physicians use antibiotic drugs to treat typhoid fever (see **Antibiotic**). These drugs check the growth of *S. typhi* and speed recovery. The use of antibiotics greatly reduces the risk of dying from typhoid fever.

Good personal hygiene and public sanitation are the best methods of preventing the spread of typhoid fever. Effective control of the disease also requires the identification and treatment of carriers. Such measures have made typhoid fever rare in developed countries.

A vaccine made from killed typhoid fever bacteria provides partial protection for several years. This vaccine is given to people who live in or travel to countries where the disease is widespread.

Paratyphoid fever is a disease that resembles typhoid fever in terms of symptoms, spread, and treatment. It results from infections of *Salmonella* organisms other than *S. typhi.* James L. Franklin

See also **Typhoid Mary.**

Typhoid Mary was a name sometimes used in referring to Mary Mallon (1868?-1938), the first known carrier of typhoid fever in the United States. She had recovered from the disease but, as a carrier, continued to spread typhoid fever germs to others. She infected at least 53 persons with typhoid fever between 1900 and 1915. Three of these people died of the disease.

Little is known about Mary Mallon's early life. She was born in Ireland and went to New York, where she worked as a cook. George Soper, a sanitation engineer, connected her to at least six typhoid fever outbreaks in that state. Mallon refused to quit working as a cook, and so she was confined to a hospital. She remained there for over 20 years until she died on Nov. 11, 1938.

Peter C. English

NASA

Typhoon clouds and winds whirl around the *eye,* a calm area in the center of the storm. This photograph was taken in 1984 from the space shuttle *Discovery, lower right.*

Typhoon is a violent cyclone that occurs in the northwest Pacific Ocean. Typhoons feature heavy rains and winds that maintain speeds equal to or greater than 74 miles (119 kilometers) per hour. Similar storms that occur in other parts of the world are called *tropical cyclones* or *hurricanes.* The word typhoon comes from the Chinese term *tai-fung,* meaning *great wind.*

Typhoons occur most frequently in the late summer. They form over warm seas between about 5 and 20 degrees of latitude from the equator. They tend to move west, northwest, and eventually northeast at speeds of 10 to 20 miles (16 to 32 kilometers) per hour. Inside a typhoon, strong winds blow in a counterclockwise direction around an area of low pressure at the storm's center, which is called the *eye.* The eye usually measures about 10 to 40 miles (16 to 64 kilometers) in diameter. The strongest winds blow inside the *eyewall,* a ring of clouds that surrounds the eye. These winds often reach speeds of more than 110 miles (180 kilometers) per hour.

The heavy rains and strong winds of a typhoon can cause great loss of life and billions of dollars in property damage. As a typhoon approaches lands, its winds produce a rush of seawater called a *storm surge* that can devastate coastal areas. Gary Barnes

Jeffrey Sylvester, FPG

Huge waves pound a coastline as a typhoon moves onto land. This violent onrush of seawater, called a *storm surge,* can demolish buildings and cause floods, sometimes taking many lives.

See also **Cyclone; Hurricane.**

Typhus, *TY fuhs,* is any one of a group of important diseases caused by *rickettsias.* These are tiny organisms that look like small bacteria but often behave like viruses (see **Rickettsia**). In human beings, they damage the lining and walls of blood vessels, causing bleeding and skin rashes. Some types of these germs infect animals as well as people. Scientists often call the infected animals "reservoirs" of the disease. Typhus diseases may be transmitted from person to person or from animals to people by lice, fleas, ticks, or mites. The diseases are named for the way they affect the human population *(epidemic typhus),* for the type of reservoir host *(murine,* or *rat, typhus),* or for the *vector,* or carrier *(tick typhus).* In the United States, tick typhus is called Rocky Mountain spotted fever (see **Rocky Mountain spotted fever**).

Epidemic typhus is a serious type of typhus spread by the human body louse. This typhus has been associated with wars throughout history. Crowding, uncleanliness, and human misery during wartime favor the transfer of infected lice from one person to another. Often, more soldiers die of typhus than in combat. Observers estimated that typhus killed more than 3 million people in Russia in the revolutionary period during and after World War I (1914-1918). Typhus epidemics occurred in North Africa, Yugoslavia, Japan, and Korea during World War II (1939-1945). Typhus was common in many Nazi concentration camps. Scientists estimate that about 25 of every 100 people infected during an epidemic die.

Primary symptoms of all typhus diseases are headache, skin rash, and stupor or delirium. The patient's temperature may rise to more than 104 °F (40 °C), remain high for three or four days, and then drop rapidly. Some people who recover from typhus harbor the live germs in their bodies. Years later, these organisms may cause another attack. This makes it possible for immigrants to the United States to have typhus years after their arrival. When typhus recurs in this way, it is called *Brill-Zinsser disease.* The disease was named for two American physicians who studied it extensively.

Murine typhus, also called *endemic typhus,* is a mild form of the disease. It is transmitted to people by the rat flea. Like epidemic typhus, this disease occurs throughout the world, but it does not spread as easily or rapidly. Improved control of rat populations and rat fleas in urban areas has resulted in a sharp decline in the occurrence of murine typhus.

Treatment. Doctors use antibiotics, particularly the tetracyclines and chloramphenicol, to treat typhus. They also use specially prepared vaccines to prevent the diseases. To control the spread of typhus, particularly during an epidemic, medical personnel frequently use insecticides. They dust people and their clothing with these substances, which kill the insects that carry the disease.

In 1998, scientists completed identification of the entire *genome* (sequence of hereditary material) in louse-borne typhus. Researchers hope that studying the typhus genome will one day reveal why typhus is so deadly and lead to new treatments. Thomas P. Monath

See also **DDT; Virus.**

Tyrannosaurus, *tih RAN uh SAWR uhs* or *ty RAN uh SAWR uhs,* was a large, meat-eating dinosaur that lived about 68 million to 65 million years ago in what is now western North America. The name *Tyrannosaurus* means *tyrant lizard.* A tyrant is a cruel, powerful ruler. *Tyrannosaurus* got its name because scientists thought that such a huge beast must have ruled over all other animals, killing whatever and whenever it chose. The scientific name for this species is *Tyrannosaurus rex.*

Tyrannosaurus was one of the largest meat-eating dinosaurs. It was about 40 feet (12 meters) long, stood about 12 feet (3.7 meters) high at the hips, and weighed about 7 tons (6.3 metric tons). *Tyrannosaurus* could rear up to a height of 18 feet (5.5 meters). But the animal usually walked with its body parallel to the ground, holding its heavy, muscular tail out behind for balance.

Tyrannosaurus had a huge skull that grew as long as $4\frac{1}{2}$ feet (135 centimeters). The strong jaws had sharp teeth that were about 6 inches (15 centimeters) long. The animal's short, flexible neck and powerful body allowed *Tyrannosaurus* to use its monstrous jaws to rip off large chunks of flesh. The dinosaur's other deadly weapons were the sharp claws on its feet. *Tyrannosaurus* could hold an animal in its jaws and slash and tear at the body with its large claws.

Unlike the rest of the dinosaur's body, its arms were tiny, and its hands had only two fingers tipped with little claws. Although the arms were small, they were strong. *Tyrannosaurus* may have used the arms to push itself up after it had been lying down.

Some scientists have suggested that the huge *Tyrannosaurus* would have moved too slowly to hunt live animals and instead fed on dead animals. But most scientists think *Tyrannosaurus* was an active hunter that could run for short distances. *Tyrannosaurus* may have waited in hiding for a plant-eating dinosaur, such as the duck-billed dinosaur, to get close. *Tyrannosaurus* could then make a quick rush and attack the animal with its sharp teeth and strong jaws. Peter Dodson

See also **Dinosaur** (pictures).

Tyranny, *TIHR uh nee,* is a term used throughout history to describe various forms of government by rulers who have unrestricted power. In ancient Greece, for example, *tyranny* simply meant absolute rule by one person. Many Greek tyrants were kind, capable rulers.

Tyranny can also refer to government by an absolute ruler who gained power through military force or political trickery. Such tyrants are not supported by a majority of the people. As a result, they must use force to remain in power.

Another definition of *tyranny* is a government in which a person or a group of persons rules in cruel, oppressive, or unjust ways. In many cases, tyrants use their power primarily for their own benefit. Absolute rulers who intend to promote the welfare of society also may be called tyrants if they suppress the freedom of the people. Today, the word *tyranny* is frequently used to describe a dictatorship. Alexander J. Groth

See also **Absolutism; Dictatorship.**

Tyre, *tyr,* was an ancient Phoenician seaport. It stood on the Mediterranean Sea in what is now southern Lebanon. Part of Tyre stood on the mainland and part on an island across a narrow channel. Tyre was an important shipping port, handling goods from Mesopotamia and Arabia. The people of Tyre were noted as sailors and for their cultural and intellectual activities.

Egypt controlled Tyre before about 1100 B.C. Tyrians carried on trade for the Egyptians with the peoples of Asia Minor and the Aegean Sea. The city enjoyed its greatest prosperity between 1100 and 573 B.C. Part of that time, Tyre was ruled by Assyria and then by Babylonia. Tyre founded several colonies, including Carthage on the Mediterranean coast of North Africa.

Museum of Science, Boston

Tyrannosaurus rex was one of the most fearsome meat-eating dinosaurs. Its huge head contained sharp teeth that grew about 6 inches (15 centimeters) long. *Tyrannosaurus* used these teeth to rip off large chunks of flesh from the plant-eating dinosaurs that it ate.

In 573 B.C., King Nebuchadnezzar II of Babylonia crushed a 13-year Tyrian revolt. Alexander the Great conquered the city in 332 B.C. and built a road from the mainland to the island, creating a peninsula upon which the present town of Tyre—also called Sur—stands (see **Lebanon** [map]). Tyre later became a part of the Roman and then Byzantine (East Roman) Empire. Christian crusaders occupied the city from A.D. 1124 until Muslims captured it in 1291. Louis L. Orlin

Tyrol, *TY rohl* or *tuh ROHL,* also spelled *Tirol,* is a beautiful mountainous region in western Austria and northern Italy. The Alps cover most of the area, and they attract many vacationers to the Tyrol.

The Austrian Tyrol, or the North Tyrol and the East Tyrol, has an area of 4,883 square miles (12,647 square kilometers), and about 631,000 people. It is a province of Austria. The Italian Tyrol, or South Tyrol, is known as Trentino-Alto Adige. It extends south from the border of Austria and is divided into the provinces of Bolzano and Trento. It covers 5,256 square miles (13,613 square kilometers). About 870,000 people live in the area.

The Romans conquered the Tyrol in 15 B.C. Later, the region fell into the hands of various Germanic tribes. In 1363, it became part of Austria. After World War I (1914-1918), the northern part of the Tyrol became a province of the Austrian republic. The southern Tyrol was given to Italy. The Italians promised political and cultural autonomy to the large German-speaking minority in the Italian Tyrol, but the Fascist government of Italy suppressed the use of German language in the area.

After World War II (1939-1945), in spite of Austrian objections, the southern Tyrol was again given to Italy. Italy promised autonomy for German-speaking South Tyroleans. In the late 1950's, these people said they did not have autonomy and began fighting for it. In 1971, the southern Tyrol conflict was settled after Italy granted the region a large amount of autonomy. William J. McGrath

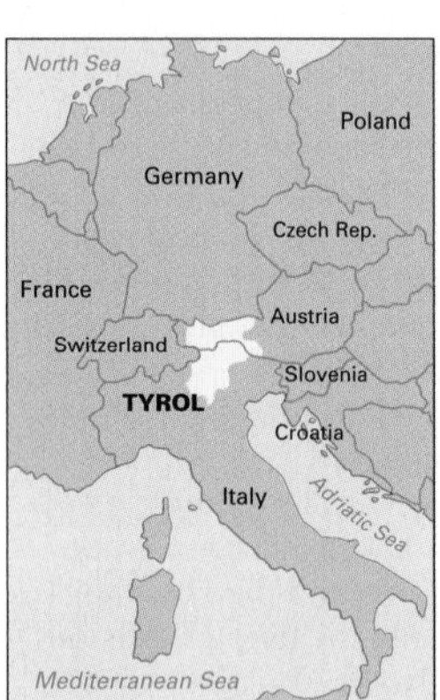

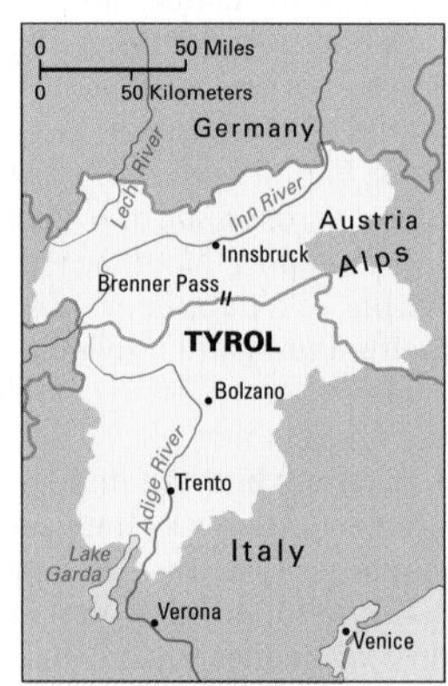

WORLD BOOK maps

The Tyrol is a region in Europe that includes part of western Austria and northern Italy. The map at the left shows its location. A map of the region itself appears at the right.

See also **Austria** (picture: A centuries-old festival).

Tyrrell, *TIHR ehl,* **Joseph Burr** (1858-1957), was a Canadian geologist, historian, and mining engineer. He conducted studies during several expeditions in the northwestern part of Canada that aided in the development of the Canadian mining industry.

Tyrrell was born on Nov. 1, 1858, in Weston, Ontario, near Toronto. A graduate of the University of Toronto, he joined the Geological Survey of Canada in 1881. In 1884, near Drumheller, Alberta, he discovered the first dinosaur bones found in Canada. Soon afterward, he found one of Canada's largest coal deposits nearby.

During 1893 and 1894, Tyrrell traveled from Lake Athabasca across the barren lands of what are now the Northwest Territories and Nunavut to Hudson Bay. During one eight-month period, he covered about 3,200 miles (5,150 kilometers), including about 900 miles (1,448 kilometers) traveled largely on snowshoes. Tyrrell mapped the region and predicted correctly that the minerals there would greatly increase Canada's wealth.

Tyrrell left the Geological Survey of Canada in 1898 and became a mining engineer and manager. He joined the Kirkland Lake Gold Mining Company in 1924 and later became its president. Barry M. Gough

Tyrrhenian Sea, *tih REE nee uhn,* is a part of the Mediterranean Sea. It is enclosed by the western mainland of Italy and the islands of Corsica, Sardinia, and Sicily (see **Italy** [terrain map]). The Tyrrhenian Sea has an area of about 60,000 square miles (155,400 square kilometers). It is sometimes called the Tuscan Sea. The Italian name for it is Mare Tirreno. The Tyrrhenian Sea joins the Ligurian Sea to the north and is linked to the Ionian Sea by the Strait of Messina to the south. Chief ports on its shores include Naples and Palermo. Howell C. Lloyd

Tyson, Mike (1966-), became the youngest heavyweight champion in boxing history when he won the World Boxing Council (WBC) version of the title in 1986. Tyson was 20 years old when he won the championship. He became the undisputed champion in 1987 by also winning the World Boxing Association (WBA) and International Boxing Federation (IBF) versions of the title. Tyson lost the championship in 1990 to Buster Douglas. Tyson had been undefeated in 37 consecutive fights.

Tyson was born on June 30, 1966, in the Brooklyn section of New York City. He became a professional boxer in 1985. He stands 5 feet 11 ½ inches (182 centimeters) tall and weighs about 235 pounds (106 kilograms).

From 1992 to 1995, Tyson served three years of a six-year prison sentence for rape. In 1996, he defeated Frank Bruno to regain the WBC heavyweight title. Later that year, he gave up that title. He regained the WBA title by defeating Bruce Seldon in 1996. Tyson lost the title later that year to Evander Holyfield. In a return match in 1997, Tyson was disqualified for biting Holyfield's ear. He returned to the ring in 1999, winning a fight. But he was sent back to jail for about four months for assaulting two people after an automobile accident.

AP/Wide World

Mike Tyson

After his release, Tyson resumed his career. In 2002, he lost to defending champion Lennox Lewis in a fight for the WBC heavyweight title. Tyson announced his retirement in 2005 after losing to Irish boxer Kevin McBride.

Nigel Collins